Francis J Schulte

Farmer's encyclopedia and business guide

A repository of practical knowledge

Francis J Schulte

Farmer's encyclopedia and business guide
A repository of practical knowledge

ISBN/EAN: 9783742827364

Manufactured in Europe, USA, Canada, Australia, Japa

Cover: Foto ©Andreas Hilbeck / pixelio.de

Manufactured and distributed by brebook publishing software
(www.brebook.com)

Francis J Schulte

Farmer's encyclopedia and business guide

Thomas A. Edison

ARMSTRONG'S
GIANT
CYCLOPEDIA
AND
TREASURY
OF
PRACTICAL
KNOWLEDGE
AUTHOR OF THE LITTLE GIANT CYCLOPEDIA
AND
THE PEOPLES PROBLEMS
ETC.
BY
K. L. ARMSTRONG.
UNION PUBLISHING HOUSE

PREFACE TO FIRST EDITION

NAPOLEON, that man of great ideas, conceived at least one idea which it was not his good fortune to see carried out—that was, to have made for his own personal use a perfect travel library. Each book in this library was to be printed especially for it, in the best possible manner, and to be handsomely and substantially bound, but, by dispensing with wide margins and other non-essentials, and avoiding blank pages, etc., an elegant book was to be compressed into one-quarter of the space usually allotted to it.

Many improvements have been made in the art of book-making since the days of the great Bonaparte, and numberless bulky encyclopedias have been printed. For the use of any one of these, if he could have obtained it in his day, Napoleon would gladly have exchanged a fortune. But among them all there is not one which answers all the practical questions which come up for settlement in ordinary every-day life. The compiler of the present work believed that it was possible to present in one compact volume a reference library such as Napoleon would have prized above a kingdom, one which, although compressed into one volume, would answer more every-day questions than all the other encyclopedias combined. In order to test the practicability of such a project, "THE LITTLE GIANT CYCLOPEDIA" was placed before the public a few years ago. This, although a much smaller work than the present venture, immediately found favor, and when it had reached a sale of over one hundred thousand copies, which it did within less than two years after its first publication, work was at once commenced upon this larger and more comprehensive compilation. In this, as in the smaller work, it has been the aim of the author to compress vast masses of information into compact sentences and paragraphs—as Cotter says, "to effect for bales of manuscript what the hydrostatic screw performs for bales of cotton—condense into a period what before occupied a page." The work has been done faithfully and conscientiously, and the publishers confidently present "THE GIANT CYCLOPEDIA" to the public for criticism and approval. Suggestions as to improvement in future editions will be thankfully received and carefully considered at all times.

A few words more to the seeker after information: In order to condense and simplify the material presented in this volume, much of it has been arranged in the form of tables, charts and diagrams, and the usual alphabetical arrangement of subjects was found impracticable as interfering with the author's design to make the "Giant Cyclopedia" an educational work as well as a work of reference. The information given was, therefore, arranged under various headings in such classification as seemed to the author most desirable. Many items of information could have been appropriately placed under two or more of these headings. Repetition, however, has been carefully avoided. Therefore, if any particular subject is not treated of under the heading in which one would most naturally expect to find it, the reader should carefully consult the alphabetical index, which has been made full and complete.

Summary of Contents

How to Remember

LOISETTE'S SYSTEM OF MEMORY CULTURE

SO MUCH has been said about Loisette's memory system, the art has been so widely advertised, and so carefully guarded from all the profane who do not send five or many dollars to the Professor, that a few pages showing how every man may be his own Loisette may be both interesting and valuable.

In the first place, the system is a good one, and well worth the labor of mastering, and if the directions are implicitly followed there can be no doubt that the memory will be greatly strengthened and improved, and that mnemonic feats otherwise impossible may be easily performed. Loisette, however, is not an inventor, but an introducer. He stands in the same relation to Dr. Pick that the retail dealer holds to the manufacturer: the one produced the article; the other brings it to the public. Even this statement is not quite fair to Loisette, for he has brought much practical common sense to bear upon Pick's system, and, in preparing the new art of mnemonics for the market, in many ways he has made it his own.

If each man would reflect upon the method by which he himself remembers things, he would find his hand upon the key of the whole mystery. For instance, the author was once trying to remember the word *Blythe*. There occurred to my mind the words "bellman," "belle," and then the verse:

"—— the peasant upward climbing
Hears the bells of *Bedose* chiming,"

"Barcarole," "barrack," and so on until finally the word "Blythe" presented itself with a strange insistence, long after I had ceased trying to recall it.

On another occasion, when trying to recall the name "Richardson," I got the words "hay-rick," "Robertson," "Randallstown," and finally "wealthy," from which, naturally, I got "rich" and "Richardson" almost in a breath.

Still another example: trying to recall the name of an old schoolmate, "Grady," I got "Brady," "gravy," "gascon," "gastronomic," "gracious," and I finally abandoned the attempt, simply saying to myself that it began with a "G," and there was an "a" sound after it. The next morning, when thinking of something entirely different, the name "Grady" came up in my mind with as much distinctness as though some one had whispered it in my ear. This remembering was done without any conscious effort on my part, and was evidently the result of the exertion made the day before when the mnemonic processes were put to work. Every reader must have had a similar experience which he can recall, and which will fall in line with the examples given.

It follows, then, that when we endeavor, without the aid of any system, to recall a forgotten fact or name, our memory presents to us words of similar sound or meaning in its journey toward the goal to which we have started it. This goes to show that our ideas are arranged in groups in whatever secret cavity or recess of the brain they occupy, and that the arrangement is one not alphabetical exactly, and not entirely by meaning, but after some fashion partaking of both.

If you are looking for the word "meadow" you may reach "middle" before you come to it, or "Mexico," or many words beginning with the "m" sound, or containing the "dow," as "window" or "dough," or you may get "field" or "farm" — but you are on the right track, and if you do not interfere with your intellectual process you will finally come to the idea which you are seeking.

How often have you heard people say, "I forget his name; it is something like Beadle or Beagle — at any rate it begins with a B." Each and all of those were unconscious Loisettians, and they were practicing blindly, and without proper method or direction, the excellent system which he teaches. The thing, then, to do — and it is the final and simple truth which Loisette teaches — is to travel over this ground in the other direction—to connect the fact you wish to remember to some other fact or word which you know will be brought out by the implied conditions—and thus you will always be able to travel from your given starting-point to the thing which you wish to call to mind.

To illustrate: let the broken line in the annexed diagram represent a train of thought. If we connect the idea "a" with "e" through the steps b, c and d, the tendency of the mind ever afterwards will be to get to e from a that way, or from any of the intermediates that way. It seems as though a channel were cut in our mind-stuff along which the memory flows. How to make it flow this way will be seen later on. Loisette, in common with all the mnemonic teachers, uses the old device of representing numbers by letters—and as this is the first and easiest step in the art, this seems to be the most logical place to introduce the accepted equivalents of the Arabic numerals:

0 is always represented by s, z or c soft.
1 is always represented by t, th or d.
2 is always represented by n.
3 is always represented by m.
4 is always represented by r.
5 is always represented by l.
6 is always represented by sh, j, ch soft or g soft.
7 is always represented by g hard, k, c hard, q or final ng.
8 is always represented by f or v.
9 is always represented by p or b.

All the other letters are used simply to fill up. Double letters in a word count only as one. In fact, the system goes by sound, not by spelling—for instance, "this" or "dizzy" would stand for ten; "cash" or "gush" would stand for 76, and the only difficulty is to make some word or phrase which will contain only the significant letters in the proper order, filled out with non-significants in some guise of meaning or intelligibility.* Suppose you wished to get some phrase or word that would express the number 3,685, you arrange the letters this way:

	3	—	6	—	8	—	5
a e i o u h w x y	m	a e i o u h w x y	sh j ch g	a e i o u h w x y	f v	a e i o u h w x y	l

You can make out "image of law," "my shuffle," "matchville," etc., etc., as far as you like to work it out.

Now, suppose that you wished to memorize the fact that $1,000,000 in gold weighs 3,685 pounds, you go about it in this way, and here is the kernel and crux of Loisette's system:

"How much does $1,000,000 in gold weigh?"
"Weigh—scales."
"Scales—statue of Justice."
"Statue of Justice—*image of law*."

The process is simplicity itself. The thing you wish to recall, and that you fear to forget, is the weight; consequently you cement your chain of suggestion to the idea which is most prominent in your mental question. What do you weigh with? Scales. What does the mental picture of scales suggest? The statue of Justice, blindfolded and weighing out award and punishment to men. Finally, what is the statue of Justice but the image of law? and the words "image of law," translated back from the significant letters m, g soft, f and l, give you 3-6-8-5, the number of pounds in $1,000,000 in gold. You bind together in your mind each separate step in the journey, the one suggests the other; and you will find a year from now that the fact will be as fresh in your memory as it is to-day. You cannot lose it. It is chained to you by an unbreakable mnemonic tie. Mark, that it is not claimed that "weight" will of itself suggest "scales," and "scales" "statue of Justice," etc., but that, having once passed your attention up and down this ladder of ideas, your

* "You can remember the equivalents by noting that s is the first letter of "zero," and c of "cipher," t has but one stroke, n has two, m three. The script f is very like 8, the script p like 9; r is the last letter of four, l is the Roman numeral for fifty, which suggests five. The others may be retained by memorizing these two nonsense lines:

Six shy Jewesses chew George.
Seven great kings came quarreling.

mental tendency will be to take the same route, and get to the same goal again and again. Indeed, beginning with the weight of $1,000,000, "image of law" will turn up in your mind without your consciousness of any intermediate station on the way, after some iteration and reiteration of the original chain.

Again, so as to fasten the process in the reader's mind even more firmly, suppose that it were desired to fix the date of the battle of Hastings (A. D. 1066) in the memory; 1066 may be represented by the words "the wise judge" (*th* = 1, *s* = 0, *j* = 6, *dg* = 6; the others are non-significants); a chain might be made thus:

Battle of Hastings — arbitrament of war.
Arbitrament of war — arbitration.
Arbitration — judgment.
Judgment — the wise judge.

Make mental pictures, connect ideas, repeat words and sounds, go about it any way you please, so that you will form a mental habit of connecting the "battle of Hastings" with the idea of "arbitrament of war," and so on for the other links in the chain, and the work is done.

Loisette makes the beginning of his system unnecessarily difficult, to say nothing of his illogical arrangement in the grammar of the art of memory, which he makes the first of his lessons. He analyzes suggestion into —

1. Inclusion.
2. Exclusion.
3. Concurrence.

All of which looks very scientific and orderly, but is really misleading, and badly named. The truth is that one idea will suggest another:

1. By likeness or opposition of meaning, as "house" suggests "room" or "door," etc.; or, "white" suggests "black;" "cruel," "kind," etc.

2. By likeness of sound, as "harrow" and "barrow"; "Henry" and "Hennepin."

3. By mental juxtaposition, a peculiarity different in each person, and depending upon each one's own experience. Thus, "St. Charles" suggests "railway bridge" to me, because I was vividly impressed by the breaking of the Wabash bridge at that point. "Stable" and "broken leg" come next each other in my experience, so do "cow" and "shot-gun" and "kicking."

Out of these three sorts of suggestion, it is possible to get from any one fact to any other in a chain certain and safe, along which the mind may be depended upon afterwards always to follow.

The chain is, of course, by no means all. Its making and its binding must be accompanied by a vivid, methodically directed attention, which turns all the mental light possible in a focus upon the subject passing across the mind's screen. Before Loisette was thought of this was known. In the old times in England, in order to impress upon the mind of the rising generation the parish boundaries in the rural districts, the boys were taken to each of the landmarks in succession, the position and bearings of each pointed out carefully, and, in order to deepen the impression, the young people were then and there vigorously thrashed, a mechanical method of attracting the attention which was said never to have failed. This system has had its supporters in many of the old-fashioned schools, and there are men who will read these lines who can recall with an itching sense of vivid expression the 144 lickings which were said to go with the multiplication table.

In default of a thrashing, however, the student must cultivate so that he can use an intense fixity of perception upon every fact or word or date that he wishes to make permanently his own. It is easy. It is a matter of habit. If you will you can photograph an idea upon your cerebral gelatine so that neither years nor events will blot it out or overlay it. You must be clearly and distinctly aware of the thing you are putting into your mental treasure-house, and drastically certain of the cord by which you have tied it to some other thing of which you are sure. Unless it is worth your while to do this, you might as well abandon any hope of mnemonic improvement, which will not come without the hardest kind of hard work, although it is work that will grow constantly easier with practice and reiteration.

You need, then:

1. Methodic suggestion.
2. Methodic attention.
3. Methodic reiteration.

And this is all there is to Loisette, and a great deal it is. Two of them will not do without the third. You do not know how many steps there are from your hall-door to your bed-room, although you have attended to and often reiterated the journey. But if there are twenty of them, and you have once bound the word "nice," or "name," or "news," or "hyenas," to the foot of the stairway, you could never forget it.

The Professor makes a point, and very wisely, of the importance of working through some established chain, so that the whole may be carried away in the mind — not alone for the value of the facts so bound together, but for the mental discipline so afforded.

Here, then, is the "President Series," which contains the name and date of inauguration of each president from Washington to Cleveland. The manner in which it is to be mastered is this: Beginning at the top, try to find in your mind some connection between each word and the one following it. See how you can at some future time make one suggest the next, either by suggestion of sound or sense, or by mental juxtaposition. When you have found this dwell on it attentively for a moment or two. Pass it backward and forward before you, and then go on to the next step.

The chain runs thus, the names of the presidents being in small caps, the date words in italics:

President........Chosen as the first word as the one most apt to occur to the mind of any one wishing to repeat the names of the presidents.
Dentist...........President and dentist.
Draw.............What does a dentist do?
To give up.......When something is drawn from one it is given up. This is a date phrase meaning 1789.
Self-sacrifice.....There is an association of thought between giving up and self-sacrifice.
WASHINGTON......Associate the quality of self-sacrifice with Washington's character.
Morning wash....Washington and wash.
Dew.............Early wakers and dew.
Flower beds......Dew and flowers.
Took a bouquet..Flowers and bouquet. Date phrase (1797).
Garden..........Bouquet and garden.
Eden.............The first garden.
Adam.............Juxtaposition of thought.
ADAMS...........Suggestion by sound.
Fall..............Juxtaposition of thought.
Failure...........Fall and failure.
Deficit..........Upon a failure there is usually a deficit. Date word (1801).
Debt.............The consequence of a deficit.
Bonds............Debt and bonds.
Confederate bonds.Suggestion by meaning.
Jefferson Davis...Juxtaposition of thought.
JEFFERSON.

Now follow out the rest for yourself, taking about ten at a time, and binding those you do last to those you have done before, each time, before attacking the next batch.

1	2	3
JEFFERSON	*tough make*	*Theophilus*
Judge Jeffreys	oaken furniture	fill us
bloody assizes	bureau	FILLMORE
bereavement	VAN BUREN	more fuel
too heavy a sob	rent	*the flame*
parental grief	side-splitting	flambeau
sad son	divert	bow
MADISON	funny	arrow
Madeira	harassing	PIERCE
first-rate wine	HARRISON	hurt
frustrating	Old Harry	*feeling*
defeating	the tempter	wound
feet	*the fiend*	soldier
toe the line	puddled clay	cannon
row	baked clay	BUCHANAN
MONROE	tiles	rebuke
row	TYLER	official censure
boat	Wat Tyler	*to officiate*
steamer	poll tax	wedding
the funnel	compulsory	linked
windpipe	*free will*	LINCOLN
throat	free offering	link
quinsy	burnt offering	skull
QUINCY ADAMS	poker	sea shore
quince	POLK	*the heavy shell*
fine fruit	sort of dance	mollusk
the fine boy	termination 'ly'	unfamiliar word
sailor boy	adverb	dictionary
sailor	part of speech	Johnson's
jack tar	part of a man	JOHNSON
JACKSON	TAYLOR	son
stone wall	measurer	bad son
indomitable	theodolite	dishonest boy

thievish boy	hazy	well fed
take	clear	well read
give	weird	author
Gunner	brightly lighted	Arthur
award	camp fire	round table
school premium	war field	tea table
examination	Garfield	tea cup
examining	Guiteau	*half full*
flogging	murderer	divide
laborer	prisoner	share
hay field	prison fare	Cleveland
Hayes	*half fed*	

It will be noted that some of the distinct words, as "free will," only give three figures of the date, 845; but it is to be supposed that if the student knows that many figures in the date of Polk's inauguration he can guess the other one.

The curious thing about this system will now become apparent. If the reader has learned the series so that he can say it down from President to Cleveland, he can with no effort, and without any farther preparation, say it backward from Cleveland up to the commencement! There could be no better proof that this is the natural mnemonic system. It proves itself by its works.

The series should be repeated backwards and forwards every day for a month, and should be supplemented by a series of the reader's own making, and by this one, which gives the numbers from 0 to 100, and which must be chained together before they can be learned:

0—hose

1 wheat	23 name	45 royal	67 jockey	78 coffee	89 fib
2 hen	24 owner	46 arch	68 shave	79 cube	90 pies
3 home	25 nail	47 rock	69 ship	80 vase	91 putty
4 hair	26 hinge	48 wharf	70 eggs	81 foot	92 pawn
5 oil	27 ink	49 rope	71 gate	82 vein	93 bomb
6 shoe	28 knife	50 wheels	72 gun	83 fame	94 beer
7 hook	29 knob	51 lad	73 comb	84 fire	95 bell
8 off	30 mouse	52 lion	74 hacker	85 vial	96 peach
9 bee	31 mayday	53 lamb	75 coal	86 fish	97 book
10 daisy	32 hymen	54 lair	76 cage	87 fig	98 beef
11 tooth	33 mamma	55 lily	77 cake	88 fife	99 pope
12 tin	34 mower	56 lodge			
13 dome	35 mill	57 lake			
14 tower	36 image	58 leaf			
15 doll	37 mug	59 elbow			
16 ditch	38 muff	60 chess			
17 duck	39 mob	61 cheat			
18 dove	40 rice	62 chain			
19 tubby	41 heart	63 shame			
20 hyenas	42 horn	64 chair			
21 hand	43 army	65 jail			
22 nun	44 warrior	66 judge			

100—disease

By the use of this table, which should be committed as thoroughly as the President series, so that it can be repeated backwards and forwards, any date, figure or number can be at once constructed, and bound by the usual chain to the fact which you wish it to accompany.

When the student wishes to go farther and attack larger problems than the simple binding of two facts together, there is little in Loisette's system that is new, although there is much that is good. If it is a book that is to be learned as one would prepare for an examination, each chapter is to be considered separately. Of each a précis is to be written in which the writer must exercise all his ingenuity to reduce the matter in hand to its final skeleton of fact. This he is to commit to memory, both by the use of the chain and the old system of interrogation. Suppose after much labor through a wide space one boils a chapter or an event down to the final irreducible sediment: "Magna Charta was exacted by the barons from King John at Runnymede."

You must now turn this statement this way and that way, asking yourself about it every possible and impossible question, gravely considering the answers, and, if you find any part of it especially difficult to remember, chaining it to the question which will bring it out. Thus, "What was exacted by the barons from King John at Runnymede?" "Magna Charta." "By whom was Magna Charta exacted from King John at Runnymede?" "By the barons." "From whom was," etc., etc.? "King John." "From what king," etc., etc.? "King John." "Where was Magna Charta," etc., etc.? "At Runnymede."

And so on and so on, as long as your ingenuity can suggest questions to ask, or points of view from which to consider the statement. Your mind will be finally saturated with the information, and prepared to spill it out at the first squeeze of the examiner. This, however, is not new. It was taught in the schools hundreds of years before Loisette was born. Old newspaper men will recall in connection with it Horace Greeley's statement that the test of a news item was the clear and satisfactory manner in which a report answered the interrogatories, "What?" "When?" "Where?" "Who?" "Why?"

In the same way Loisette advises the learning of poetry, e. g.,

"The Assyrian came down like a wolf on the fold."

"Who came down?"

"How did the Assyrian come down?"

"Like what animal did?" etc.

And so on and so on, until the verses are exhausted of every scrap of information to be had out of them by the most assiduous cross-examination.

Whatever the reader may think of the availability or value of this part of the system, there are so many easily applicable tests of the worth of much that Loisette has done, that it may be taken with the rest.

Few people, to give an easy example, can remember the value of π — the ratio between the circumference and the diameter of the circle — beyond four places of decimals, or at most six — 3.141592+. Here is the value to 108 decimal places:

3.14159265·3589793238·4626433832·7950288
419·7169399375·1058209749·4459230781·6
406286208·9986280348·2534211706·798214
8086+

By a very simple application of the numerical letter values these 108 decimal places can be carried in the mind and recalled about as fast as you can write them down. All that is to be done is to memorize these nonsense lines:

Mother Day will buy any shawl.
My love pick up my new muff.
A Russian jeer may move a woman.
Cabin enough for Utopia.
Get a cheap ham pie by my cookey.
The slave knows a bigger ape.
I rarely hop on my sick foot.
Cheer a sage in a fashion safe.
A baby fish now views my wharf.
Annually Mary Ann did kiss a jay.
A tabby found a rough savage.

Now translate each significant into its proper value and you have the task accomplished. "Mother Day," m = 3, th = 1, r = 4, d = 1, and so on. Learn the lines one at a time by the method of interrogatories. "Who will buy any shawl?" "Which Mrs. Day will buy a shawl?" "Is Mother Day particular about the sort of shawl she will buy?" "Has she bought a shawl?" etc., etc. Then connect the end of each line to the beginning of the next one, thus, "Shawl" — "warm garment" — "warmth" — "love" — "my love," and go on as before. Stupid as the work may seem to you, you can memorize the figures in fifteen minutes in this way so that you will not forget them in fifteen years. Similarly you can take Haydn's Dictionary of Dates, and turn fact after fact into nonsense lines like these which you cannot lose.

And this ought to be enough to show anybody the whole art. If you look back across the sands of time and find out that it is that ridiculous old "Thirty days hath September" which comes to you when you are trying to think of the length of October — if you can quote your old prosody,

"O datur ambiguis," etc.,

with much more certainty than you can serve up your Horace; if, in fine, jingles and alliterations, wise and otherwise, have stayed with you, while solid and serviceable information has faded away, you may be certain that here is the key to the enigma of memory.

You can apply it yourself in a hundred ways. If you wish to clinch in your mind the fact that Mr. Love lives at 485 Dearborn Street, what is more easy than to turn 485 into the word "rifle" and chain the ideas together, say thus: "Love — happiness — good — time picnic — forest — wood rangers — range — rifle range — rifle — fine weapon — costly weapon — dearly bought — Dearborn."

Or, if you wish to remember Mr. Bowman's name, and you notice he has a mole on his face which is apt to attract your attention when you next see him, connect the ideas thus: "Mole, mark, target, archer, Bowman."

500 Errors Corrected

CONCISE RULES

IN

GRAMMAR, SPELLING AND PRONUNCIATION

THERE are several kinds of errors in speaking. The most objectionable of them all are those in which words are employed that are unsuitable to convey the meaning intended. Thus, a person wishing to express his intention of going to a given place says: "I *propose* going," when, in fact, he *purposes* going. The following affords an amusing illustration of this class of error: A sensible matron was speaking of her son, who, she said, was quite stage-struck. "In fact," remarked the old lady, "he is going to a *premature* performance this evening!" Considering that most *amateur* performances are premature, it cannot be said that this word was altogether misapplied; though, evidently, the maternal intention was to convey quite another meaning.

Other errors arise from the substitution of sounds similar to the words which should be employed; that is, spurious words instead of genuine ones. Thus, some people say "*renumerative*," when they mean "*remunerative*." A nurse, recommending her mistress to have a *perambulator* for her child, advised her to purchase a *preamputator*.

Other errors are occasioned by imperfect knowledge of the English grammar. Thus, many people say "Between you and I," instead of "Between you and me." And there are numerous other departures which will be pointed out hereafter.

MISUSE OF THE ADJECTIVE: "What *beautiful* butter!" "What a *nice* landscape!" They should say "What a *beautiful landscape!*" "What *nice butter!*" Again, errors are frequently occasioned by the following causes:

MISPRONUNCIATION OF WORDS: Many persons say *pronounciation*; others say *pro-nun-ci-a-shun*, instead of *pro-nun-she-a-shun*.

MISDIVISION OF WORDS AND SYLLABLES: This defect makes the words *an ambassador* sound like *a nambassador*, or *an adder* like *a nadder*.

IMPERFECT ENUNCIATION, as when a person says *hebben* for *heaven*, *ebber* for *ever*, *jocholate* for *chocolate*.

To correct these errors by a systematic course of study would involve a closer application than most persons could afford, but the simple and concise rules and hints here given, founded upon usage and the authority of scholars, will be of great assistance to inquirers.

Rules and Hints for Correct Speaking.

Who and *whom* are used in relation to persons, and *which* in relation to things. But it was once common to say "the man *which*." This should now be avoided. It is now usual to say, "Our Father *who* art in heaven," instead of "*which* art in heaven."

Whose is, however, sometimes applied to things as well as to persons. We may therefore say, "The country *whose* inhabitants are free."

Thou is employed in solemn discourse, and *you* in common language. *Ye* (plural) is also used in serious addresses, and *you* in familiar language.

The uses of the word *It* are various, and very perplexing to the uneducated. It is not only used to imply persons, but things, and even ideas, and therefore, in speaking or writing, its assistance is constantly required. The perplexity respecting this word arises from the fact that in using it in the construction of a long sentence sufficient care is not taken to insure that when it is employed it really points out or refers to the object intended. For instance: "It was raining when John set out in his cart to go to market, and he was delayed so long that it was over before he arrived." Now what is to be understood by this sentence? Was the rain over? or the market? Either or both might be inferred from the construction of the sentence, which, therefore, should be written thus: "It was raining when John set out in his cart to go to market, and he was delayed so long that the market was over before he arrived."

Rule. — After writing a sentence always look through it, and see that wherever the word *it* is employed, it refers to or carries the mind back to the object which it is intended to point out.

The general distinction between *this* and *that* may be thus defined: *this* denotes an object present or near, in time or place; *that* something which is absent.

These refers, in the same manner, to present objects, while *those* refers to things that are remote.

Who changes, under certain conditions, into *whose* and *whom*; but *that* and *which* always remain the same, with the exception of the possessive case, as noted above.

That may be applied to nouns or subjects of all sorts; as, the *girl that* went to school, the *dog that* bit me, the *opinion that* he entertains.

The misuse of these pronouns gives rise to more errors in speaking and writing than any other cause.

When you wish to distinguish between two or more persons, say, "*Which* is the happy man?" not *who* — "*Which* of those ladies do you admire?"

Instead of "*Whom* do you think him to be?" say, "*Who* do you think him to be?"

Whom should I see?

To *whom* do you speak?

Who said so?

Who gave it to you?

Of *whom* did you procure them?

Who was he?

Who do men say that I am?

Self should never be added to *his*, *their*, *mine* or *thine*.

Each is used to denote *every* individual of a number.

Every denotes all the individuals of a number.

Either and *or* denote an alternative: "I will take *either* road, at your pleasure." "I will take this or that."

Neither means *not either*; and *nor* means *not the other*.

Either is sometimes used for *each* — "Two thieves were crucified, on *either* side one."

"Let each esteem others as good as themselves," should be, "Let *each* esteem others as good as *himself*."

"There are bodies, each of which *are* so small," should be, "each of which *is* so small."

Do not use double superlatives, such as most *straightest*, most *highest*, most *finest*.

The term *worser* has gone out of use; but *lesser* is still retained.

The use of such words as *chiefest*, *extremest*, etc., has become obsolete, because they do not give any superior force to the meanings of the primary words, *chief*, *extreme*, etc.

Such expressions as *more impossible*, *more indispensable*, *more universal*, *more uncontrollable*, *more unlimited*, etc., are objectionable, as they really enfeeble the meaning which it is the object of the speaker or writer to strengthen. For instance, *impossible* gains no strength by rendering it *more* impossible. This class of errors is common with persons who say, "A *great large* house," "A *great big* animal," "A *little small* foot," "A *tiny little* head."

Here, *there* and *where*, originally denoting place, may now, by common consent, be used to denote other meanings; such as, "*There* I agree with you," "*Where* we differ," "We find pain *where* we expected pleasure," "*Here* you mistake me."

Hence, *whence* and *thence*, denoting departure, etc., may be used without the word *from*. The idea of *from* is included in the word *whence* — therefore it is unnecessary to say, "*From whence*."

Hither, *thither* and *whither*, denoting to a place, have generally been superseded by *here*, *there* and *where*. But there is no good reason why they should not be employed. If, however, they are used, it is unnecessary to add the word *to*, because that is implied — "*Whither* are you going?" "*Where* are you going?" Each of these sentences is complete. To say, "Where are you going *to*?" is redundant.

Two *negatives* destroy each other, and produce an affirmative. "*Nor* did he *not* observe them," conveys the idea that he *did* observe them.

But negative assertions are allowable. "His manners are *not* impolite," which implies that his manners are in some degree marked by politeness.

Instead of "Let you and *I*," say "Let you and me."

Instead of "I am not so tall as *him*," say "I am not so tall as he."

When asked "Who is there?" do not answer "*Me*," but "I."

Instead of "For you and *I*," say "For you and me."

Instead of "*Says I*," say "I said."

Instead of "You are taller than me," say "You are taller than I."

Instead of "I *ain't*," or "I *aren't*," say "I am not."

Instead of "Whether I be present or no," say "Whether I be present or not."

For "Not that I know *on*," say "Not that I know."

Instead of "Was I to do so," say "Were I to do so."

Instead of "I would do the same if I was *him*," say "I would do the same if I were he."

Instead of "I *had as lief* go myself," say "I would as soon go myself," or "I would rather."

It is better to say "Six weeks ago," than "Six weeks back."

It is better to say "Since which time," than "Since when."

It is better to say "I repeated it," than "I said so over again."

Instead of "He was too young to have suffered much," say "He was too young to suffer much."

Instead of "*Less* friends," say "Fewer friends." Less refers to quantity.

Instead of "A *quantity* of people," say "A number of people."

Instead of "*He and they* we know," say "Him and them."

Instead of "*As* far as I can see," say "So far as I can see."

Instead of "A *new pair* of gloves," say "A pair of new gloves."

Instead of "I hope you'll think nothing on it," say "I hope you'll think nothing of it."

Instead of "Restore it *back* to me," say "Restore it to me."

Instead of "I suspect the *veracity* of his story," say "I doubt the truth of his story."

Instead of "I seldom or ever see him," say "I seldom see him."

Instead of "I expected *to have* found him," say "I expected to find him."

Instead of "Who *learns* you music?" say "Who teaches you music?"

Instead of "I *never* sing *whenever* I can help it," say "I never sing when I can help it."

Instead of "Before I do that I must *first* ask leave," say "Before I do that I must ask leave."

Instead of saying "The *observation* of the rule," say "The observance of the rule."

Instead of "A man *of* eighty years of age," say "A man eighty years old."

Instead of "Here *lays* his honored head," say "Here lies his honored head."

Instead of "He died *from* negligence," say "He died through neglect," or "in consequence of neglect."

Instead of "Apples are plenty," say "Apples are plentiful."

Instead of "The *latter end* of the year," say "The end, or the close, of the year."

Instead of "The *then* government," say "The government of that age, or century, or year, or time."

Instead of "A *couple* of chairs," say "Two chairs."

Instead of "They are united *together* in the bonds of matrimony," say "They are united in matrimony," or "They are married."

Instead of "We travel *slow*," say "We travel slowly."

Instead of "He plunged *down* into the river," say "He plunged into the river."

Instead of "He jumped *from off of* the scaffolding," say "He jumped off the scaffolding."

Instead of "He came the last *of all*," say "He came the last."

Instead of "*universal*," with reference to things that have any limit, say "general;" "generally approved," instead of "universally approved;" "generally beloved," instead of "universally beloved."

Instead of "They ruined *one another*," say "They ruined each other."

Instead of "If in case I succeed," say "If I succeed."

Instead of "A *large enough* room," say "A room large enough."

Instead of "I am slight in comparison *to* you," say "I am slight in comparison with you."

Instead of "I went *for* to see him," say "I went to see him."

Instead of "The cake is all *eat up*," say "The cake is all eaten."

Instead of "Handsome is *as* handsome does," say "Handsome is who handsome does."

Instead of "The book fell *on* the floor," say "The book fell to the floor."

Instead of "His opinions are *approved of* by all," say "His opinions are approved by all."

Instead of "I will add *one more* argument," say "I will add one argument more," or "another argument."

Instead of "A sad *scene* is war," say "War is a sad scene."

Instead of "He stands six *foot* high," say "He measures six feet," or "His height is six feet."

Instead of "I go *every now and then*," say "I go sometimes (or often)."

Instead of "Who finds him in clothes," say "Who provides him with clothes."

Say "The first two," and "the last two," instead of "the two *first*," "the two last."

Instead of "His health was *drank with enthusiasm*," say "His health was drunk enthusiastically."

Instead of "*Except* I am prevented," say "Unless I am prevented."

Instead of "In its *primary* sense," say "In its primitive sense."

Instead of "It grieves me to see you," say "I am grieved to see you."

Instead of "Give me *them* papers," say "Give me those papers."

Instead of "*Those* papers I hold in my hand," say "These papers I hold in my hand."

Instead of "I could scarcely imagine *but what*," say "I could scarcely imagine but that."

Instead of "He was a man *notorious* for his benevolence," say "He was noted for his benevolence."

Instead of "She was a woman *celebrated* for her crimes," say "She was notorious on account of her crimes."

Instead of "What may your name be?" say "What is your name?"

Instead of "I lifted it *up*," say "I lifted it."

Instead of "It is *equally of the same* value," say "It is of the same value," or "equal value."

Instead of "I knew it *previous* to your telling me," say "I knew it previously to your telling me."

Instead of "You *was* out when I called," say "You were out when I called."

Instead of "I thought I should *have won* this game," say "I thought I should win this game."

Instead of "*This* much is certain," say "Thus much is certain," or "So much is certain."

Instead of "He went away *as it may be* yesterday week," say "He went away yesterday week."

Instead of "He came *the Saturday as it may be before the Monday*," specify the Monday on which he came.

Instead of "Put your watch *in* your pocket," say "Put your watch into your pocket."

Instead of "He has *got* riches," say "He has riches."

Instead of "Will you *set* down?" say "Will you sit down?"

Instead of "No, *thanks*," say "No, thank you."

Instead of "I cannot do it without *farther* means," say "I cannot do it without further means."

Instead of "No sooner *but*," or "No other *but*," say "than."

Instead of "Nobody *else* but her," say "Nobody but her."

Instead of "He fell *down* from the balloon," say "He fell from the balloon."

Instead of "He rose *up* from the ground," say "He rose from the ground."

Instead of "*These* kind of oranges are not good," say "This kind of oranges is not good."

Instead of "Somehow *or another*," say "Somehow or other."

Instead of "*Will* I give you some more tea?" say "Shall I give you some more tea?"

Instead of "Oh dear, what *will* I do?" say "Oh dear, what shall I do?"

Instead of "I think *indifferent* of it," say "I think indifferently of it."

Instead of "I will send it *conformable* to your orders," say "I will send it conformably to your orders."

Instead of "To be *given away gratis*," say "To be given away."

Instead of "Will you enter in?" say "Will you enter?"

Instead of "*This* three days or more," say "These three days or more."

Instead of "He is a *bad grammarian*," say "He is not a grammarian."

Instead of "We accuse him *for*," say "We accuse him of."

Instead of "We acquit him *from*," say "We acquit him of."

Instead of "I am averse *from* that," say "I am averse to that."

Instead of "I confide *on* you," say "I confide in you."

Instead of "As soon *as ever*," say "As soon as."

Instead of "The *very best*," or "The *very worst*," say "The best," or "The worst."

Avoid such phrases as "No great shakes," "Nothing to boast of," "Down in my boots," "Suffering from the blues." All such sentences indicate vulgarity.

Instead of "No one *hasn't* called," say "No one has called."

Instead of "You have a *right* to pay me," say "It is right that you should pay me."

Instead of "I am going *over* the bridge," say "I am going across the bridge."

Instead of "I *should just* think I could," say "I think I can."

Instead of "There has been a *good deal*," say "There has been much."

Instead of saying "The effort you are making *for* meeting the bill," say "The effort you are making to meet the bill."

To say "Do *not* give him no more of your money," is equivalent to saying "Give him some of your money." Say "Do not give him any of your money."

Instead of saying "They are not what nature designed them," say "They are not what nature designed them to be."

Instead of saying "I had not the pleasure of hearing his sentiments when I wrote that letter," say "I had not the pleasure of having heard," etc.

Instead of "The quality of the apples were good," say "The quality of the apples was good."

Instead of "The want of learning, courage and energy are more visible," say "Is more visible."

Instead of "We die *for* want," say "We die of want."

Instead of "He died *by* fever," say "He died of fever."

Instead of "I *enjoy* bad health," say "My health is not good."

Instead of "*Either* of the three," say "Any one of the three."

Instead of "Better *nor* that," say "Better than that."

Instead of "We often think on you," say "We often think of you."

Instead of "Mine is so good as yours," say "Mine is as good as yours."

Instead of "This town is not as large as we thought," say "This town is not so large as we thought."

Instead of "*Because* why?" say "Why?"

Instead of "That *there* boy," say "That boy."

Instead of "That horse is not much *worth*," say "The horse is not worth much."

Instead of "The *subject-matter* of debate," say "The subject of debate."

Instead of saying "When he was come back," say "When he had come back."

Instead of saying "His health has been *shook*," say "His health has been shaken."

Instead of "It was *spoke* in my presence," say "It was spoken in my presence."

Instead of "*Very right*," or "*Very wrong*," say "Right," or "Wrong."

Instead of "The *mortgageor* paid him the money," say "The mortgagee paid him the money." The mortgagee lends; the mortgageor borrows.

Instead of "I *took you to be* another person," say "I mistook you for another person."

Instead of "On *either* side of the river," say "On each side of the river."

Instead of "*There's* fifty," say "There are fifty."

Instead of "The *best* of the two," say "The better of the two."

Instead of "My clothes have *become too small* for me," say "I have grown too stout for my clothes."

Instead of "Two *spoonsful* of physic," say "Two spoonfuls of physic."

Instead of "She said, says she," say "She said."

Avoid such phrases as "I said, says I," "Thinks I to myself," etc.

Instead of "I *don't think* so," say "I think not."

Instead of "He was in *eminent* danger," say "He was in imminent danger."

Instead of "The weather is *hot*," say "The weather is very warm."

Instead of "I *sweat*," say "I perspire."

Instead of "I *only* want two dollars," say "I want only two dollars."

Instead of "Whatsomever," say "Whatever," or "Whatsoever."

Avoid such exclamations as "God bless me!" "God deliver me!" "By God!" "By Gosh!" "My Lord!" "Upon my soul," etc., which are vulgar on the one hand and savor of impiety on the other, for—"Thou shalt not take the name of the Lord thy God in vain."

Pronunciation.

Accent is a particular stress or force of the voice upon certain syllables or words. This mark ´ in printing denotes the syllable upon which the stress or force of the voice should be placed.

A word may have more than one accent. Take as an instance *aspiration*. In uttering this word we give a marked emphasis of the voice upon the first and third syllables, and therefore these syllables are said to be accented. The first of these accents is less distinguishable than the second, upon which we dwell longer; therefore the second accent in point of order is called the primary or chief accent of the word.

When the full accent falls on a vowel, that vowel should have a long sound, as in *vo´cal*; but when it falls on or after a consonant, the preceding vowel has a short sound, as in *hab´it*.

To obtain a good knowledge of pronunciation, it is advisable for the reader to listen to the examples given by good speakers, and by educated persons. We learn the pronunciation of words, to a great extent, by imitation, just as birds acquire the notes of other birds which may be near them.

But it will be very important to bear in mind that there are many words having a double meaning or application, and that the difference of meaning is indicated by the difference of the accent. Among these words, nouns are distinguished from verbs by this means: nouns are mostly accented on the first syllable, and verbs on the last.

Noun signifies name; nouns are the names of persons and things, as well as of things not material and palpable but of which we have a conception and knowledge, such as *courage*, *firmness*, *goodness*, *strength*; and verbs express *actions*, *movements*, etc. If the word used signifies that anything has been done, or is being done, or is to be done, then that word is a verb.

Thus when we say that anything is "an in´sult," that word is a noun, and is accented on the first syllable; but when we say he did it "to insult´ another person," the word insult´ implies *acting*, and becomes a verb, and should be accented on the last syllable.

A list of nearly all the words that are liable to similar variation is given here. It will be noticed that those in the first column, having the accent on the first syllable, are mostly nouns; and that those in the second column, which have the accent on the second and final syllable, are mostly verbs:

Noun, etc.	*Verb, etc.*
Ab'ject	abject'
Ab'sent	absent'
Ab'stract	abstract'
Ac'cent	accent'
Af'fix	affix'
As'pect	aspect'
At'tribute	attrib'ute
Aug'ment	augment'
Au'gust	august'
Bom'bard	bombard'
Col'league	colleague'
Col'lect	collect'
Com'ment	comment'
Com'pact	compact'
Com'plot	complot'
Com'port	comport'
Com'pound	compound'
Com'press	compress'
Con'cert	concert'
Con'crete	concrete'
Con'duct	conduct'
Con'fine	confine'
Con'flict	conflict'
Con'serve	conserve'
Con'sort	consort'
Con'tent	content'
Con'tract	contract'
Con'trast	contrast'
Con'verse	converse'
Con'vert	convert'
Con'vict	convict'
Con'voy	convoy'
De'crease	decrease'
Des'cant	descant'
Des'ert	desert'
De'tail	detail'
Di'gest	digest'
Dis'count	discount'
Es'cort	escort'
Es'say	essay'

Noun, etc.	*Verb, etc.*
Ex'ile	exile'
Ex'port	export'
Ex'tract	extract'
Fer'ment	ferment'
Fore'cast	forecast'
Fore'taste	foretaste'
Fre'quent	frequent'
Im'part	impart'
Im'port	import'
Im'press	impress'
Im'print	imprint'
In'cense	incense'
In'crease	increase'
In'lay	inlay'
In'sult	insult'
Ob'ject	object'
Out'leap	outleap'
Per'fect	perfect'
Per'fume	perfume'
Per'mit	permit'
Pre'fix	prefix'
Prem'ise	premise'
Pres'age	presage'
Pres'ent	present'
Prod'uce	produce'
Proj'ect	project'
Pro'test	protest'
Reb'el	rebel'
Rec'ord	record'
Ref'use	refuse'
Re'tail	retail'
Sub'ject	subject'
Su'pine	supine'
Sur'vey	survey'
Tor'ment	torment'
Trans'fer	transfer'
Trans'port	transport'
Un'dress	undress'
Up'cast	upcast'
Up'start	upstart'

Cement' is an exception to the above rule, and should always be accented on the last syllable. So also the word consols'.

Rules of Pronunciation.

C before *a*, *o*, and *u*, and in some other situations, is a close articulation, like *k*. Before *e*, *i*, and *y*, *c* is precisely equivalent to *s* in *same*, *this*; as in *cedar*, *civil*, *cypress*.

E final indicates that the preceding vowel is long; as in hate, mete, sire, robe, lyre, abate, recede, invite, remote, intrude.

E final indicates that *c* preceding has the sound of *s*; as in *lace*, *lance*; and that *g* preceding has the sound of *j*, as in *charge*, *page*, *challenge*.

E final, in proper English words, never forms a syllable, and in the most used words, in the terminating unaccented syllable it is silent. Thus, *motive*, *genuine*, *examine*, *granite*, are pronounced *motiv*, *genuin*, *examin*, *granit*.

E final, in a few words of foreign origin, forms a syllable; as *syncope*, *simile*.

E final is silent after *l* in the following terminations: *ble*, *cle*, *dle*, *fle*, *gle*, *kle*, *ple*, *tle*, *zle*; as in *able*, *manacle*, *cradle*, *ruffle*, *mangle*, *wrinkle*, *supple*, *rattle*, *puzzle*, which are pronounced *a'bl*, *man'a kl*, *cra'dl*, *ruf'fl*, *man'gl*, *wrin'kl*, *sup'pl*, *puz'zl*.

E is usually silent in the termination *en*; as in *token*, *broken*; pronounced *tokn*, *brokn*.

OUS, in the termination of adjectives and their derivatives, is pronounced *us*; as in *gracious*, *pious*, *pompously*.

CE, CI, TI, before a vowel, have the sound of *sh*; as in *cetaceous*, *gracious*, *motion*, *partial*, *ingratiate*; pronounced *cetashus*, *grashus*, *moshun*, *parshal*, *ingrashiate*.

SI, after an accented vowel, is pronounced like *zh*; as in *Ephesian*, *confusion*; pronounced *Ephezhan*, *confuzhon*.

GH, both in the middle and at the end of words, is silent; as in *caught*, *bought*, *fright*, *nigh*, *sigh*; pronounced *caut*, *baut*, *frite*, *ni*, *si*. In the following exceptions, however, *gh* is pronounced as *f*: *cough*, *chough*, *clough*, *enough*, *laugh*, *rough*, *slough*, *tough*, *trough*.

When WH begins a word, the aspirate *h* precedes *w* in pronunciation; as in *what*, *whiff*, *whale*; pronounced *hwat*, *hwiff*, *hwale*, *w* having precisely the sound of *oo*, French *ou*. In the following words *w* is silent: *who*, *whom*, *whose*, *whoop*, *whole*.

H after *r* has no sound or use; as in *rheum*, *rhyme*; pronounced *reum*, *ryme*.

H should be sounded in the middle of words; as in forehead, abhor, behold, exhaust, inhabit, unhorse.

H should always be sounded except in the following words: heir, herb, honest, honor, hour, humor and humble, and all their derivatives, such as humorously, derived from humor.

K and G are silent before *n*; as *know*, *gnaw*; pronounced *no*, *naw*.

W before *r* is silent; as in *wring*, *wreath*; pronounced *ring*, *reeth*.

B after *m* is silent; as in *dumb*, *numb*; pronounced *dum*, *num*.

L before *k* is silent; as in *balk*, *walk*, *talk*; pronounced *bauk*, *wauk*, *tauk*.

PH has the sound of *f*; as in *philosophy*; pronounced *filosofy*.

NG has two sounds, one as in *singer*, the other as in *finger*.

N after *m*, and closing a syllable, is silent; as in *hymn*, *condemn*.

P before *s* and *t* is mute; as in *psalm*, *pseudo*, *ptarmigan*; pronounced *salm*, *sudo*, *tarmigan*.

R has two sounds, one strong and vibrating, as at the beginning of words and syllables, such as *robber*, *reckon*, *error*; the other is at the termination of the words, or when succeeded by a consonant, as *farmer*, *morn*.

There are other rules of pronunciation affecting the combination of vowels, etc.; but as they are more difficult to describe, and as they do not relate to errors which are commonly prevalent, it will suffice to give examples of them in the following list of words. When a syllable in any word in this list is printed in italics, accent or stress of voice should be laid on that syllable.

Words Often Mispronounced.

Again, usually pronounced a-gen, not as spelled.

Alien, *ale*-yen, not a-li-en.

Antipodes, an-*tip*-o-dees.

Apostle, as a-*pos'l*, without the t.

Arch, *arch* in compounds of our own language, as in archbishop, archduke; but *ark* in words derived from the Greek, as archaic, ar-*ka*-ik; archaeology, ar-ke-*ol*-o-gy; archangel, ark-*ain*-gel; archetype, *ar*-ke-type; archiepiscopal, ar-ke-e-*pis*-co-pal; archipelago, ar-ke-*pel*-a-go; archives, *ar*-kivz, etc.

Asia, a-shi-a.

Asparagus as spelled, not asparagrass.

Aunt, ant, not aunt.

Awkward, awk-ward, not awk-ard.

Bade, bad.

Because, be-cawz, not be-cos.

Been, bin.

Beloved, as a verb, be-*luvd*; as an adjective, be-*luv*-ed. Blessed, cursed, etc., are subject to the same rule.

Beneath, with the *th* in breath, not with the *th* in breathe.

Biog'raphy, as spelled, not beography.

Caprice, ca-preece.

Catch, as spelled, not ketch.

Chaos, *ka*-os.

Charlatan, *shar*-la-tan.

Chasm, kazm.

Chasten, chasn.

Chivalry, shiv-al-ry.

Chemistry, *kem'*-is-try.

Choir, kwire.

Coquet, *ko*-ket.

Conduit, *kon*-dit or *kun*-dit.

Corps, kor; the plural corps is pronounced korz.

Covetous, cuv-e-tus, not cuv-e-chus.

Courteous, curt-yus.

Courtesy (politeness), cur-te-sy.

Courtesy (a lowering of the body), curt-sey.

Crocus, as spelled, not crocus.

Curiosity, cu-re-os-e-ty, not curosity.

Cushion, coosh-un, not coosh-in.

Daunt, dawnt, not dant or darnt.

Desist has the sound of s, not of z. Design may be pronounced either design or dezign.

Desire should have the sound of z.

Dew, due, not doo.

Diamond, as spelled, not *di*-mond.

Diploma, de-*plo*-ma, not dip-lo-ma.

Diplomacy, de-*plo*-ma-cy, not dip-lo-ma-cy.

Divers (several), *di*-vers; but diverse (different), di-*verse*.

Drought, drowt, not drawth.

Duke as spelled, not dook.

Dynasty, *dy*-nas-ty, not *dyn*-as-ty.

Edict, e-dict, not ed-ict.

E'en and e'er, een and air.

Egotism, e-go-tism, not *eg*-o-tism.

Either, e-ther.

Engine, en-jin, not in-jin.

Epistle, without the *t*.

Epitome, e-*pit*-o-me.

Epoch, ep-ock, not e-pock.

Equinox, e-qui-nox, not eq-kwe-nox.

Europe, *U*-rup, not *U*-rope.

European, Euro-*pe*-an, not Eu-ro-pean.

Every, ev-er-y, not ev-ry.

Executor, egz-ec-utor, not with the sound of x.

Extraordinary, ex-*tror*-di-na-ri, not extra-ordinary, nor extrornary.

February, as spelled, not Febuary.

Finance, fe-*nance*, not *fi*-nance.

Foundling, as spelled, not *fond*-ling.

Garden, gar-dn, not gar-den, nor gard-ing.

Gauntlet, gawnt-let, not *gant*-let.

Geography, as spelled, not jography, or gehography.

Geometry, as spelled, not *jom*-etry.

Haunt, hawnt, not hant.

Height, hite, not highth.

Heinous, *hay*-nus, not *hee*-nus.

Horizon, ho-*ri*-zn, not *hor*-i-zon.

Hymeneal, hy-men-*e*-al, not hy-meneal.

Instead, in-*sted*, not instid.

Isolate, *i*-so-late, not *is*-o-late, nor *iz*-o-late.

Jalap, *jal*-ap, not jolup.

January, as spelled, not Jenuary nor Janewary.

Leave, as spelled, not leaf.

Legend, *le*-jend, not *le*-gend.

Many, men-ny, not man-ny.

Marchioness, *mar*-shun-ess, not as spelled.

Massacre, *mas*-sa-ker.

Mistress, as spelled, not *mis*-tress.

Matron, *ma*-trun, not mat-run.

Medicine, med-e-cin, not *med*-sin.

Minute (sixty seconds), *min*-it.

Minute (small), mi-*nute*.

Mischievous, *mis*-chiv-us, not mis-*chee*-vus.

Ne'er, for never, nare.

New, nu, not noo.

Oblige, as spelled, not obleege.

Oblique, ob-*leek*, not o-*blike*.

Odorous, o-dor-us, not od-or-us.

Of, ov, except when compounded with there, here and where, which should be pronounced here-*of*, there-*of*, and where-*of*.

Oft, as spelled, not awf.

Ostrich, os-trich, not os-tridge.

Pageant, paj-ent, not pa-jant.

Parent, pare-ent, not par-ent.

Partisan, par-ti-zan, not par-ti-san, nor par-ti-zan.

Physiognomy, as fiz-i-og-nomy, not physi-onomy.

Pincers, pin-cers, not pinch-ers.

Plaintiff, as spelled, not plantiff.

Precedent (noun), pres-e-dent; pre-ce-dent (going before in point of time, previous, former) is the pronunciation of the adjective.

Prologue, pro-log, not prol-og.

Radish, as spelled, not red-ish.

Raillery, rail-er-y, or ral-er-y, not as spelled.

Rather, ra-ther, not ray-ther.

Recess, re-cess.

Resource, re-source.

Respite, res-pit, not as spelled.

Rout (a party; and to rout) should be pronounced rowt. Route (a road), root or rowt.

Saunter, sawn-ter, not sarn-ter or san-ter.

Sausage, saw-sage, not sos-sidge, sassage.

Schedule, shed-ule, not sked-ule.

Seamstress is pronounced sem-stress, but sempstress, as the word is sometimes spelled, is pronounced semp-stress.

Shire, as spelled, when uttered as a single word, but shortened into shir in composition.

Shone, shon, not shun.

Soldier, sole-jer.

Solecism, sol-e-cism, not so-le-cism.

Soot, as spelled, not sut.

Sovereign, sov-er-in, or suv-er-in.

Specious, spe-shus, not spesh-us.

Stomacher, stum-a-cher.

Stone (weight), as spelled, not stun.

Synod, sin-od, not sy-nod.

Tenure, ten-ure, not te-nure.

Tenet, ten-et, not te-net.

Than, as spelled, not thun.

Tremor, trem-ur, not tre-mor.

Twelfth should have the th sounded.

Umbrella, as spelled, not um-ber-el-la.

Vase, vaiz or vahz, not vawse.

Was, woz, not wuz.

Weary, wee-ri, not wery.

Were, wer, not ware.

Wrath, rath (a as in far), not rawth; as an adjective it is spelled wrath, and pronounced with the vowel sound shorter, as in wrathful, etc.

Yacht, yot, not yat nor yatch.

Zenith, zen-ith, not ze-nith.

Zodiac, zo-di-ak.

Zoology should have both o's sounded, as zo-ol-o-gy, not zoo-lo-gy.

Note.—The tendency of all good elocutionists is to pronounce as nearly in accordance with the spelling as possible.

Pronounce—

—ace, not iss; as furnace, not furniss.

—age, not idge, as cabbage, courage, postage, village.

—ain, ine, not in, as certain, certains, not certin.

—ate, not it, as moderate, not moderit.

—ect, not ec, as aspect, not aspec; subject, not subjec.

—ed, not id, or ud, as wicked, not wickid, or wickud.

—el, not l, model, not modl; novel, not novl.

—en, not n, as sudden, not suddn.—Harden, heathen, garden, lengthen, seven, strengthen, often, and a few others, have the e silent.

—ence, not unce, as influence, not influ-unce.

—es, not is, as glasses, not glassis.

—ile should be pronounced il, as fertil, not fertile, in all words except chamomile (cam), exile, gentile, infantile, reconcile, and senile, which should be pronounced ile.

—in, not n, as Latin, not Latn.

—nd, not n, as husband, not husban; thousand, not thousan.

—ness, not niss, as carefulness, not carefulniss.

—ng, not n, as singing, not singin; speaking, not speakin.

—ngth, not nth, as strength, not strenth.

—son, the o should be silent; as in treason, tre-zn, not tre-son.

—tal, not tle, as capital, not capitle; metal, not mettle; mortal, not mortle; periodical, not periodicle.

—xt, not x, as next, not nex.

What's in a Name?

An Englishman whose name was Wemyss
Went crazy at last, it seemyss,
Because the people would not
Understand that they ought
To call him not Weemis, but Weems.

Another whose last name was Knollys
Tried vainly to vote at the pollys;
But no ballot he cast,
Because to the last
The clerk couldn't call Knollys Noles.

And then a young bather named Belvoir
Went and murdered a man with a cleavoir
Because the man couldn't,
Or possibly wouldn't,
Pronounce his name properly Beever.

There was an athlete named Strachan
Who had plenty of sinew and brachan,
And he'd knock a man down
With an indignant frown,
If he failed to pronounce his name Strawn.

Short Rules for Spelling.

Words ending in *e* drop that letter on taking a suffix beginning with a vowel. Exceptions—words ending in *ge*, *ce*, or *oe*.

Final *e* of a primitive word is retained on taking a suffix beginning with a consonant. Exceptions—words ending in *dge*, and truly, duly, etc.

Final y of a primitive word, when preceded by a consonant, is generally changed into *i* on the addition of a suffix. Exceptions—retained before *ing* and *ish*, as pitying. Words ending in *ie* and dropping the *e* by Rule 1, change the *i* to *y*, as lying. Final *y* is sometimes changed to *e*, as duteous.

Nouns ending in *y*, preceded by a vowel, form their plural by adding *s*: as money, moneys. *Y* preceded by a consonant is changed to *ies* in the plural, as bounty, bounties.

Final *y* of a primitive word, preceded by a vowel, should not be changed into *i* before a suffix; as joyless.

In words containing *ei* or *ie*, *ei* is used after the sound of *s*; as ceiling, seize, except in singe and a few words ending in *ster*. Inveigle, neither, leisure and weird also have *ei*. In other cases it is used, as in believe, achieve.

Words ending in *cede* or *ceed*, when relating to matter, end in *cede*; all others in *ceed*.

Words of one syllable, ending in a consonant, with a single vowel before it, double the consonants in derivatives; as ship, shipping, etc. But if ending in a consonant with a double vowel before it, they do not double the consonant in derivatives; as troop, trooper, etc.

Words of more than one syllable, ending in a consonant preceded by a single vowel, and accented on the last syllable, double that consonant in derivatives; as commit, committed; but except chagrin, chagrined.

All words of one syllable ending in *l*, with a single vowel before it, have *ll* at the close; as mill, sell.

All words of one syllable ending in *l*, with a double vowel before it, have only one *l* at the close; as mail, sail.

The words foretell, distill, instill and fulfill, retain the double *ll* of their primitives. Derivatives of dull, skill, will and full also retain the double *ll* when the accent falls on these words; as dullness, skillful, willful, fullness.

Punctuation.

A period (.) after every declarative and every imperative sentence; as, It is true. Do right.

A period (.) after every abbreviation; as, Dr., Mr., Capt.

An interrogation point (?) after every question.

The exclamation point (!) after exclamations; as, Alas! Oh, how lovely!

Quotation marks (" ") enclose quoted expressions; as, Socrates said: "I believe the soul is immortal."

A colon (:) is used between parts of a sentence that are subdivided by semicolons.

A colon is used before a quotation, enumeration, or observation, that is introduced by *as follows*, *the following*, or any similar expression; as, Send me the following: 10 doz. Armstrong's Cyclopedia," 25 Schiefer's Manual, etc.

A semicolon (;) between parts that are subdivided by commas.

The semicolon is used also between clauses or members that are disconnected in sense; as, Man grows old; he passes away; all is uncertain. When *as*, *namely*, *that is*, is used to introduce an example or enumeration, a semicolon is used before it and a comma after it; as, The night was cold; that is, for the time of year.

A comma (,) is used to set off co-ordinate clauses, and subordinate clauses not restrictive; as, Good deeds are never lost, though sometimes forgotten.

A comma is used to set off transposed phrases and clauses; as, "When the wicked entice thee, consent thou not."

A comma is used to set off interposed words, phrases and clauses; as, Let us, if we can, make others happy.

A comma is used between similar or repeated words or phrases; as, The sky, the water, the trees, were illumined with sunlight.

A comma is used to mark an ellipsis, or the omission of a verb or other important word.

A comma is used to set off a short quotation informally introduced; as, Who said, "The good die young?"

A comma is used whenever necessary to prevent ambiguity.

The marks of parenthesis () are used to enclose an interpolation where such interpolation is by the writer or speaker of the sentence in which it occurs. Interpolations by an editor or by any one other than the author of the sentence should be inclosed in brackets, [ ].

Dashes (—) may be used to set off a parenthetical expression, also to denote an interruption or a sudden change of thought or a significant pause.

It is in signs and advertisements that faulty punctuation is especially objectionable. Following are some examples of signs, etc., correctly put. Errors occur most frequently in the use of the period (.) and the apostrophe ('). As a rule, a period should follow every complete sentence, even though it be but one word. Modern custom, however, permits the omission of the period or comma at the end of a line, but the period after an abbreviation must never be omitted:

WELLS' LAUNDRY.

U. S. POST-OFFICE.

BOOKS AND STATIONERY.

BROWN & CO.,
DEALERS IN GENTS' FURNISHING GOODS.

ROB'T JOHNSON & CO.
or ROBT. JOHNSON & CO.

In the above, either the apostrophe or period may be used to indicate the abbreviation. The same rule applies to Chas. (or Cha's), Thos. (or Tho's), Saml. (or Sam'l). In all such cases, however, it is in better taste to spell out the name in full.

MEN'S AND BOYS' SHOES.

SMITH-JONES COMPANY,
MANUFACTURERS OF
LADIES AND CHILDREN'S HOSIERY.

In the above the apostrophe is not required after the word ladies, as it is necessary to indicate the possessive case only in the last of two or more of a series.

JOHNSON BROS.' BANK.
(Meaning the Bank of the Johnson Brothers)

JOHNSON & BROS.' BANK.
(Meaning the Bank of Johnson & Brothers.)

JOHNSON & BRO.'S BANK.
(Meaning the Bank of Johnson & Brother.)

SCIENTIFIC PUBLISHING CO.'S PUBLICATIONS,
C. S. WATKINS, GEN'L AG'T.

THE HUBBARD COMPANY
MFRS. OF CHILDREN'S UNDERGARMENTS.

FISK SISTERS,
DEALERS IN CROCKERY, QUEENSWARE, ETC.

THE CUNNINGHAM SONS CO.

CUNNINGHAM'S SONS & CO.

CUNNINGHAM, SONS & CO.

CUNNINGHAM SONS, FISHER & CO.

MCMURDY & DEYOUNG,
ATTORNEYS AT LAW.

The Use of Capitals.

1. Every entire sentence should begin with a capital.

2. Proper names, and adjectives derived from them, should begin with a capital.

3. All appellations of the Deity should begin with a capital.

4. Official and honorary titles begin with a capital.

5. Every line of poetry should begin with a capital.

6. Titles of books and the heads of their chapters and divisions are printed in capitals.

7. The pronoun *I*, and the exclamation *O*, are always capitals.

8. The days of the week, and the months of the year, begin with capitals.

9. Every quotation should begin with a capital letter.

10. Names of religious denominations, of political parties, etc., begin with capitals.

11. In preparing accounts, each item should begin with a capital.

12. Any word of special importance may begin with a capital.

How to Write a Letter.

A business letter should be written clearly, explicitly, and concisely.

Figures should be written out, except dates; sums of money should be both in writing and figures.

Copies should be kept of all business letters.

When you receive a letter containing money, it should be immediately counted and the amount marked on the top margin.

Letters to a stranger about one's own personal affairs, requesting answer, should always inclose a stamp.

Short sentences are preferable to long ones.

Letters requiring an answer should have prompt attention.

Never write a letter while under excitement or when in an unpleasant humor.

Never write an anonymous letter.

Do not fill your letter with repetitions and apologies.

Avoid writing with a pencil. Use black ink. Blue or violet may be used, but black is better.

In acknowledging receipt of a letter always mention date.

Paper. Note, packet or letter size should be used. It is unbusiness-like and very poor taste to use foolscap or mere scraps.

Paging. If single sheets are used, they should be carefully paged. Business letters should be written on but one side of the sheet.

Folding. A letter sheet should be folded from bottom upward. Bring lower edge near the top so as to make the length a trifle shorter than the envelope, then fold twice the other way. The folded sheet should be just slightly smaller than the envelope.

If note sheet, fold twice from bottom upward. If envelope is nearly square, single fold of note sheet is sufficient.

Envelopes, like the paper, should be white, and of corresponding size and quality. It is poor taste to use colored paper, or anything but black ink.

The postage stamp should be placed at the upper right-hand corner.

Address. This should be so plainly written that no possible mistake could be made either in name or address. It is unnecessary to add the letters P. O. after the name of the place. When the letter reaches the town it is not likely to go to the court-house or jail. Letters of introduction should bear upon envelope the name and address of the person to whom sent, also the words in the lower left-hand corner, "Introducing Mr. ——."

Rates of Postage.

Letters.—Prepaid by stamps, 2 cents each ounce or fraction thereof to all parts of the United States and Canada; forwarded to another postoffice without charge on request of the person addressed; if not called for, returned to the writer free, if indorsed with that request. If the stamp is omitted the letter is forwarded to the Dead-Letter Office and returned to the writer. For registering letters the charge is 10 cents additional. Drop letters at letter-carrier offices, 2 cents per ounce or fraction thereof; at other offices, 1 cent per ounce or fraction thereof. On insufficiently prepaid matter mailed in Canada, 3 cents per ½ ounce or fraction thereof. Stamped postal cards, furnished only by government, 1 cent each; if anything except a printed address slip is pasted on a postal card, or anything but the address written on the face, letter postage is charged. Postage on all newspapers and periodicals sent from newspaper offices to any part of the United States, to regular subscribers, must be paid in advance at the office of mailing.

Second-Class Matter.—Periodicals issued at regular intervals, at least four times a year, and having a regular list of subscribers, with supplement, sample copies, 1 cent a pound; periodicals, other than weekly, if delivered by letter-carrier, 1 cent each; if over 2 ounces, 2 cents each. When sent by other than publishers, for 4 ounces or less, 1 cent.

Third-Class Matter (not exceeding four pounds).—Printed matter, books, proof-sheets, corrected or uncorrected, unsealed circulars, inclosed so as to admit of easy inspection without cutting cords or wrappers, 1 cent for each 2 ounces.

Fourth-Class Matter.—Not exceeding four pounds, embracing merchandise and samples, excluding liquids, poisons, greasy, inflammable or explosive articles, live animals, insects, etc., 1 cent an ounce. Postage to Canada and British North American states, 2 cents per ounce; must be prepaid; otherwise, 6 cents.

Postage Rates to Foreign Countries.—To the countries and colonies which, with the United States, comprise the Universal Postal Union, the rates of postage are as follows: Letters, per 15 grams (½ ounce), pre-payment optional, 5 cents; postal cards, each, 2 cents; newspapers and other printed matter, per 2 ounces, 1 cent. Commercial papers—First 10 ounces or fraction thereof, 5 cents; every additional 2 ounces, 1 cent. Samples of merchandise—First 4 ounces, 2 cents; every additional 2 ounces, 1 cent. Registration fee on letters or other articles, 10 cents. All correspondence other than letters must be prepaid at least partially.

Printed matter other than books received in the mails from abroad under the provisions of postal treaties or conventions is free from customs duty.

Dutiable books forwarded to the United States from the Postal Union are delivered to addresses at postoffices of destination upon payment of the duties levied thereon.

Postal Money Orders.—The limit of a single money order is $100, instead of $50, as formerly. The fees charged are as follows: For orders not exceeding $10, 8c.; $10 to 15, 10c.; $15 to $30, 15c.; $30 to $40, 20c.; $40 to $50, 25c.; $50 to $60, 30c.; $60 to $70, 35c; $70 to $80, 40c.; $80 to $100, 45c.

To Switzerland, Germany, Belgium, Portugal, Canada, Newfoundland, Italy, France, Algeria, New South Wales, Victoria, Tasmania, New Zealand, Jamaica: Fees, for not exceeding $10, 15 cents; $10 to $20, 30 cents; $20 to $30, 45 cents; $30 to $40, 60 cents; $40 to $50, 75 cents. To Great Britain and Ireland and adjacent islands: Fees, for not exceeding $10, 25 cents; $10 to $20, 50 cents; $20 to $30, 70 cents; $30 to $40, 85 cents; $40 to $50, $1. To British India: Fees, for sums not exceeding $10, 35 cents; not exceeding $20, 70 cents; not exceeding $30, $1; not exceeding $40, $1.25; not exceeding $50, $1.50.

"They that deny a God destroy a man's nobility; for certainly man is of kin to the beasts by his body, and if he is not kin to God by his spirit he is a base and ignoble creature."—*Bacon.*

"If thou sustain injustice, console thyself: the true unhappiness is in doing it."—*Democritus.*

It never pays to fret and growl
When fortune seems our foe;
The better-bred will push ahead,
And strike the braver blow.
For luck is work,
And those who shirk
Should not lament their doom,
But yield the play,
And clear the way,
That better men have room.

Hints for Writers

That writer does the most who gives his reader the most knowledge and takes from him the least time. Sidney Smith once remarked: "After you have written an article, take your pen and strike out half of the words, and you will be surprised to see how much stronger it is." In literature, our taste will be discovered by that which we give and our judgment by that which we withhold.

There is nothing so fascinating as simplicity and directness. A writer who has an object and goes right on to accomplish it will compel the attention of his readers. Montaigne, the celebrated French essayist, whose clear style, as well as vigor of thought, has been the praise of good critics the world over, made his boast that he never used a word that could not be readily understood by anybody in the Paris markets. Plain words are ever the best.

A man cannot put his thoughts, if he have any, into language too plain. Good writing, like good speaking, consists in simplicity and force of diction, and not in inflated, studiously balanced or elaborately constructed sentences. The best writing is but a degree above the best conversation, and that only because the writer has a little more time to select his words than the speaker has.

Do not assume that because you have something important to communicate, it is necessary to write a long article. A tremendous thought may be packed into a small compass — made as solid as a cannon ball, and, like the projectile, cut down all before it. Short articles are generally more effective, find more readers and are more widely copied than long ones. *Pack your thoughts close together*, and, though your article may be brief, it will be more likely to make an impression.

Remember all the time that facility in composition, as in all other accomplishments, can only be obtained by practice and perseverance —

True grace in writing comes by art, not chance;
As they move easiest who have learned to dance.

It should never be forgotten that the sole use of words and sentences is to convey thought and impressions. Hence words and sentences should not be seen. The highest art in the use of language is to conceal itself. The old maxim is in place: "*Ars est celare artem.*"—"Art is in concealing art." The perfection of a window pane is in concealing itself, so that as you look through it upon the objects beyond you do not see it, are not conscious that it is there.

Many a man's destiny has been made or marred for time and for eternity by the influence which a single sentiment has made on his mind, by its forming his character for life, making it terribly true that moments sometimes fix the coloring of our whole subsequent existence. Hence those who write for the public should do so under a deep sense of responsibility, and endeavor to do it in that healthful and equable state of mind and body which favors a clear, unexaggerated and logical expression of ideas.

Mr. Webster once replied to a gentleman who pressed him to speak on a subject of great importance: "The subject interests me deeply, but I have not time. There, sir," pointing to a huge pile of letters on the table, "is a pile of unanswered letters to which I must reply before the close of this session [which was then three days off]. I have no time to master the subject so as to do it justice." "But, Mr. Webster, a few words from you would do much to awaken public attention to it." "If there is so much weight in my words as you represent, it is because I do not allow myself to speak on any subject until my mind is imbued with it."

The writer who uses weak arguments and strong epithets makes quite as great a mistake as the landlady who furnished her guests with weak tea and strong butter. More people commit suicide with the pen than with the pistol, the dagger and the rope. A pin has as much head as a good many authors, and a great deal more point. Good aims do not always make good books.

Alexander Hamilton once said to an intimate friend: "Men give me some credit for genius. All the genius I have lies just in this: When I have a subject in hand, I study it profoundly. Day and night it is before me. I explore it in all its bearings. My mind becomes pervaded with it. Then the effort which I make the people are pleased to call the fruit of genius. It is the fruit of labor and thought."

Obscurity in writing is commonly an argument of darkness in the mind. The greatest learning is to be seen in the greatest plainness. Obscure writers, like turbid streams, seem deeper than they are. Unintelligible language is a lantern without a light. Some authors write nonsense in a clear style, and others sense in an obscure one; some can reason without being able to persuade, others can persuade without being able to reason.

"As 'tis a greater mystery in the art
Of painting to foreshorten any part
Than draw it out; so 'tis in books the chief
Of all perfections to be plain and brief."

"Therefore, since brevity is the soul of wit,
And tediousness the limbs and outward flourishes —
I will be brief."—*Shakespeare.*

Synonyms and Antonyms

A DICTIONARY OF TWELVE THOUSAND WORDS OF SIMILAR AND CONTRARY MEANING

NO TWO words in the English language have exactly the same significance, but to express the precise meaning which one intends to convey, and also to avoid repetitions, it is often desirable to have at hand a Dictionary of Synonyms. Take President Cleveland's famous phrase, "innocuous desuetude." If he had said simply, "harmless disuse," it would have sounded clumsy, whereas the words he used expressed the exact shade of meaning, besides giving the world a new phrase and the newspapers something to talk about.

The following list of SYNONYMS, while not exhaustive, is quite comprehensive, and by cross-reference will answer most requirements. The appended ANTONYMS, or words of opposite meaning, enclosed in parenthesis, will also be found extremely valuable, for one of the strongest figures of speech is *antithesis*, or contrast:

ABANDON, leave, forsake, desert, renounce, relinquish, quit, forego, let go, waive. (Keep, cherish.) *Abandoned*, deserted, forsaken, wicked, reprobate, dissolute, profligate, flagitious, corrupt, depraved, vicious. (Cared for, virtuous.) *Abandonment*, leaving, desertion, dereliction, renunciation, defection. *Abasement*, degradation, fall, degeneracy, humiliation, abjection, debasement, servility. (Honor.) *Abash*, bewilder, disconcert, discompose, confound, confuse, shame. (Embolden.) *Abbreviate*, shorten, abridge, condense, contract, curtail, reduce. (Extend.) *Abdicate*, give up, resign, renounce, abandon, forsake, relinquish, quit, forego. *Abet*, help, encourage, instigate, incite, stimulate, aid, assist. (Resist.) *Abettor*, assistant, accessory, accomplice, promoter, instigator, particeps criminis, coadjutor, associate, companion, cooperator. (Opponent.) *Abhor*, dislike intensely, view with horror, hate, detest, abominate, loathe, nauseate. (Love.) *Ability*, capability, talent, faculty, capacity, qualification, aptitude, aptness, expertness, skill, efficiency, accomplishment, attainment. (Incompetency.) *Abject*, groveling, low, mean, base, ignoble, worthless, despicable, vile, servile, contemptible. (Noble.) *Abjure*, recant, forswear, disclaim, recall, revoke, retract, renounce. (Maintain.) *Able*, strong, powerful, muscular, stalwart, vigorous, athletic, robust, brawny, skillful, adroit, competent, efficient, capable, clever, self-qualified, telling, fitted. (Weak.) *Abode*, residence, habitation, dwelling, domicile, home, quarters, lodging. *Abolish*, quash, destroy, revoke, abrogate, annul, cancel, annihilate, extinguish, eliminate, invalidate, nullify. (Establish, enforce.) *Abominable*, hateful, detestable, odious, vile, execrable. (Lovable.) *Abortive*, fruitless, ineffectual, idle, inoperative, vain, futile. (Effectual.) *About*, concerning, regarding, relative to, with regard to, as to, respecting, with respect to, referring to, almost, nearly, approximately. *Abscond*, run off, steal away, decamp, bolt. *Absent*, a., inattentive, abstracted; not attending to, listless, dreamy. (Present.) *Absolute*, entire, complete, unconditional, unqualified, unrestricted, despotic, arbitrary, tyrannous, imperative, authoritative, imperious. (Limited.) *Absorb*, engross, swallow up, engulf, imbibe, consume, merge, fuse. *Absurd*, silly, foolish, preposterous; ridiculous, irrational, unreasonable, nonsensical, inconsistent. (Wise, solemn.) *Abuse*, v., asperse, revile, vilify, reproach, calumniate, defame, slander, scandalize, malign, traduce, disparage, depreciate, ill-use. (Praise, protect.) *Abuse*: n., scurrility, ribaldry, contumely, obloquy, opprobrium, foul invective, vituperation, ill-usage. (Praise, protection.) *Accede*, assent to, consent, acquiesce, comply with, agree, coincide, concur, approve. (Protest.) *Accelerate*, hasten, hurry, expedite, forward, quicken, despatch. (Retard.) *Accept*, receive, take, admit. (Refuse.) *Acceptable*, agreeable, pleasing, pleasurable, gratifying, welcome. (Displeasing.) *Accident*, casualty, incident, contingency, adventure, chance. *Accommodate*, serve, oblige, adapt, adjust, fit, suit. (Disoblige, impede.) *Accomplice*, confederate, accessory, abettor, coadjutor, assistant, ally, associate, particeps criminis. (Adversary.) *Accomplish*, do, effect, finish, execute, achieve, complete, perfect, consummate. (Fail.) *Accomplishment*, attainment, qualification, acquirement. (Defect.) *Accord*, grant, allow, admit, concede. (Deny.) *Accost*, salute, address, speak to, stop, greet. *Account*, narrative, description, narration, relation, detail, recital, moneys, reckoning, bill, charge. *Accountable*, punishable, answerable, amenable, responsible, liable. *Accumulate*, bring together, amass, col-ble, gather. (Scatter, dissipate.) *Accumulation*, collection, store, mass, congeries, concentration. *Accurate*, correct, exact, precise, nice, truthful. (Erroneous, careless.) *Achieve*, do, accomplish, effect, fulfill, execute, gain, win. *Achievement*, feat, exploit, accomplishment, attainment, performance, acquirement, gain. (Failure.) *Acknowledge*, admit, confess, own, avow, grant, recognize, allow, concede. (Deny.) *Acquaint*, inform, enlighten, apprise, make aware, make known, notify, communicate. (Deceive.) *Acquaintance*, familiarity, intimacy, cognizance, fellowship, companionship, knowledge. (Unfamiliarity.) *Acquiesce*, agree, accede, assent, comply, consent, give way, coincide with. (Protest.) *Acquit*, pardon, forgive, discharge, set free, clear, absolve. (Condemn, convict.) *Act*, do, operate, make, perform, play, enact. *Action*, deed, achievement, feat, exploit, accomplishment, battle, engagement, agency, instrumentality. *Active*, lively, sprightly, alert, agile, nimble, brisk, quick, supple, prompt, vigilant, laborious, industrious. (Lazy, passive.) *Actual*, real, positive, genuine, certain. (Fictitious.) *Acute*, shrewd, intelligent, penetrating, piercing, keen. (Dull.) *Adapt*, accommodate, suit, fit, conform. *Addicted*, devoted, wedded, attached, given up to, dedicated. *Addition*, increase, accession, augmentation, reinforcement. (Subtraction, separation.) *Address*, speech, discourse, appeal, oration, tact, skill, ability, dexterity, deportment, demeanor. *Adhesion*, adherence, attachment, fidelity, devotion. (Alienation.) *Adjacent*, near to, adjoining, contiguous, conterminous, bordering, neighboring. (Distant.) *Adjourn*, defer, prorogue, postpone, delay. *Adjunct*, appendage, appurtenance, appendancy, dependency. *Adjust*, set right, fit, accommodate, adapt, arrange, settle, regulate, organize. (Confuse.) *Admirable*, striking, surprising, wonderful, astonishing. (Detestable.) *Admit*, allow, permit, suffer, tolerate. (Deny.) *Advantageous*, beneficial. (Hurtful.) *Affection*, love. (Aversion.) *Affectionate*, fond, kind. (Harsh.) *Agreeable*, pleasant, pleasing, charming. (Disagreeable.) *Alternating*, intermittent. (Continual.) *Ambassador*, envoy, plenipotentiary, minister. *Amend*, improve, correct, better, mend. (Impair.) *Anger*, ire, wrath, indignation, resentment. (Good nature.) *Appropriate*, assume, ascribe, arrogate, usurp. *Argue*, debate, dispute, reason upon. *Arise*, flow, emanate, spring, proceed, rise, issue. *Artful*, disingenuous, sly, tricky, insincere. (Candid.) *Artifice*, trick, stratagem, finesse. *Association*, combination, company, partnership, society. *Attack*, assail, assault, encounter. (Defend.) *Audacity*, boldness, effrontery, hardihood. (Meekness.) *Austere*, rigid, rigorous, severe, stern. (Dissolute.) *Avaricious*, niggardly, miserly, parsimonious. (Generous.) *Aversion*, antipathy, dislike, hatred, repugnance. (Affection.) *Awe*, dread, fear, reverence. (Familiarity.) *Awkward*, clumsy. (Graceful.) *Axiom*, adage, aphorism, apothegm, byword, maxim, proverb, saying, saw.

BABBLE, chatter, prattle, prate. *Bad*, wicked, evil. (Good.) *Baffle*, confound, defeat, disconcert. (Aid, abet.) *Base*, vile, mean. (Noble.) *Battle*, action, combat, engagement. *Bear*, carry, convey, transport. *Bear*, endure, suffer, support. *Beastly*, brutal, sensual, bestial. *Beat*, defeat, overpower, overthrow, rout. *Beautiful*, fine, handsome, pretty. (Homely, ugly.) *Becoming*, decent, fit, comely, suitable. (Unbecoming.) *Beg*, beseech, crave, entreat, implore, solicit, supplicate. (Give.) *Behavior*, carriage, conduct, deportment, demeanor. *Belief*, credit, faith, trust. (Doubt.) *Beneficent*, bountiful, generous, liberal, munificent. (Covetous, miserly.) *Benefit*, favor, advantage, kindness, civility. (Injury.) *Benevolence*, beneficence, benignity, humanity, kindness, tenderness. (Malevolence.) *Blame*, censure, condemn, reprove, reproach, upbraid. (Praise.) *Blemish*, flaw, speck, spot, stain. (Ornament.) *Blind*, sightless, heedless. (Far-sighted.) *Blot*, cancel, efface, expunge, erase, obliterate. *Bold*, brave, daring, fearless, intrepid, undaunted. (Timid.) *Border*, brim, brink, edge, margin, rim, verge, boundary, confine, frontier. *Bound*, circumscribe, confine, limit, restrict. *Brave*, dare, defy. *Bravery*, courage, valor. (Cowardice.) *Break*, bruise, crush, pound, squeeze. *Breeze*, blast, gale, gust, hurricane, storm, tempest. *Bright*, clear, radiant, shining. (Dull.) *Brittle*. *Burial*, interment, sepulture. (Resurrection.) *Business*, avocation, employment, engagement, occupation, art, profession, trade. *Bustle*, stir, tumult, fuss. (Quiet.)

CALAMITY, disaster, misfortune, mischance, mishap. (Good fortune.) *Calm*, collected, composed, placid, serene. (Stormy, unsettled.) *Capable*, able, competent. (Incompetent.) *Captious*, fretful, cross, peevish, petulant. (Good-natured.) *Care*, anxiety, concern, solicitude, heed, attention. (Heedlessness, negligence.) *Caress*, kiss, embrace. (Spurn, buffet.) *Carnage*, butchery, massacre, slaughter. *Cause*, motive, reason. (Effect, consequence.) *Cease*, discontinue, leave off, end. (Continue.) *Censure*, animadvert, criticise. (Praise.) *Certain*, secure, sure. (Doubtful.) *Cessation*, intermission, rest, stop. (Continuance.) *Chance*, fate, fortune. (Design.) *Change*, barter, exchange, substitute. *Changeable*, fickle, inconstant, mutable, variable. (Unchangeable.) *Character*, reputation, repute, standing. *Charm*, captivate, enchant, enrapture, fascinate. *Chastity*, purity, continence, virtue. (Lewdness.) *Cheap*, inexpensive, inferior, common. (Dear.) *Cheerful*, gay, merry, sprightly. (Mournful.) *Chief*, chieftain, head, leader. (Subordinate.) *Circumstance*, fact, incident. *Class*, degree, order, rank. *Clear*, bright, lucid, vivid. (Opaque.) *Clever*, adroit, dexterous, expert, skilful. (Stupid.) *Clothed*, clad, dressed. (Naked.) *Coarse*, rude, rough, unpolished. (Fine.) *Coax*, cajole, fawn, wheedle. *Cold*, cool, frigid, wintry, unfeeling, stoical. (Warm.) *Color*, dye, stain, tinge. *Colorable*, ostensible, plausible, specious. *Combination*, cabal, conspiracy, plot. *Command*, injunction, order, precept. *Commodity*, goods, merchandise, wares. *Common*, mean, ordinary, vulgar. (Uncommon, extraordinary.) *Compassion*, sympathy, pity, clemency. (Cruelty, severity.) *Compel*, force, oblige, necessitate. (Coax, lead.) *Compensation*, amends, recompense, remuneration, requital, reward. *Compendium*, compend, abridgment. (Enlargement.) *Complain*, lament, murmur, regret, repine. (Rejoice.) *Comply*, accede, conform, submit, yield. (Refuse.) *Compound*, complex. (Simple.) *Comprehend*, comprise, include, embrace, grasp, understand, perceive. (Exclude, mistake.) *Comprise*, comprehend, contain, embrace, include. *Conceal*, hide, secrete. (Uncover.) *Conceive*, comprehend, understand. *Conclusion*, inference, deduction. *Condemn*, censure, blame, disapprove. (Justify, exonerate.) *Conduct*, direct, guide, lead, govern, regulate, manage. *Confirm*, corroborate, approve, attest. (Contradict.) *Conflict*, combat, contest, contention, struggle. (Peace, quiet.) *Confute*, disprove, refute, oppugn. (Approve.) *Conquer*, overcome, subdue, surmount, vanquish. (Defeat.) *Consequence*, effect, event, issue, result. (Cause.) *Consider*, reflect, ponder, weigh. *Consistent*, constant, compatible. (Inconsistent.) *Console*, comfort, solace. (Harass, worry.) *Constancy*, firmness, stability, steadiness. (Fickleness.) *Contaminate*, corrupt, defile, pollute, taint. *Contemn*, despise, disdain, scorn. (Esteem.) *Contemplate*, meditate, muse. *Contemptible*, despicable, paltry, pitiful, vile, mean. (Noble.) *Contend*, contest, dispute, strive, struggle, combat. *Continual*, constant, continuous, perpetual, incessant. (Intermittent.) *Continuance*, continuation, duration. (Cessation.) *Continue*, persist, persevere, pursue, prosecute. (Cease.) *Contradict*, deny, gainsay, oppose. (Confirm.) *Cool*, cold, frigid. (Hot.) *Correct*, rectify, reform. *Cost*, charge, expense, price. *Covetousness*, avarice, cupidity. (Beneficence.) *Cowardice*, fear, timidity, pusillanimity. (Courage.) *Crime*, sin, vice, misdemeanor. (Virtue.) *Criminal*, convict, culprit, felon, malefactor. *Crooked*, bent, curved, oblique. (Straight.) *Cruel*, barbarous, brutal, inhuman, savage. (Kind.) *Cultivation*, culture, refinement. *Cursory*, desultory, hasty, slight. (Thorough.) *Custom*, fashion, manner, practice.

DANGER, hazard, peril. (Safety.) *Dark*, dismal, opaque, obscure, dim. (Light.) *Deadly*, fatal, destructive, mortal. *Dear*, beloved, precious, costly, expensive. (Despised, cheap.) *Death*, departure, decease, demise. (Life.) *Decay*, decline, consumption. (Growth.) *Deceive*, delude, impose upon, over-reach, gull, dupe, cheat. *Deceit*, cheat, imposition, trick, delusion, guile, beguilement, treachery, sham. (Truthfulness.) *Decide*, determine, settle, adjudicate, terminate, resolve. *Decipher*, read, spell, interpret, solve. *Decision*, determination, conclusion, resolution, firmness. (Vacillation.) *Declamation*, oratory, elocution, harangue, effusion, debate. *Declaration*, avowal, manifestation, statement, profession. *Decrease*, diminish, lessen, wane, decline, retrench, curtail, reduce. (Growth.) *Dedicate*, devote, consecrate, offer, set, apportion. *Deed*, act, action, commission, achievement, instrument, document, muniment. *Deem*, judge, estimate, consider, think, suppose, conceive. *Deep*, profound, subterranean, submerged, designing, abstruse, learned. (Shallow.) *Deface*, mar, spoil, injure, disfigure. (Beautify.) *Default*, lapse, forfeit, omission, absence, want, failure. *Defect*, imperfection, flaw, fault, blemish. (Beauty, improvement.) *Defend*, guard, protect, justify. *Defence*, excuse, plea, vindication, bulwark, rampart. *Defer*, delay, postpone, put off, prorogue, adjourn. (Hasten, expedite.) *Deficient*, short, wanting, inadequate, scanty, incomplete. (Complete, perfect.) *Defile*, v., pollute, corrupt, sully. (Beautify.) *Define*, fix, settle, determine, limit. *Defray*, meet, liquidate, pay, discharge. *Degree*, grade, extent, measure. *Deliberate*, v., consider, meditate, consult, ponder, debate. *Deliberate*, a., purposed, intentional, designed, determined. (Hasty.) *Delicacy*, nicety, dainty, refinement, tact, softness, modesty. (Coarseness, indelicacy.) *Delicate*, tender, fragile, dainty, refined. (Coarse.) *Delicious*, sweet, palatable. (Nauseous.) *Delight*, enjoyment, pleasure, happiness, transport, ecstasy, gladness, rapture, bliss. (Annoyance.) *Deliver*, liberate, free, rescue, pronounce, give, hand over. (Retain.) *Demonstrate*, prove, show, exhibit, illustrate. *Depart*, leave, quit, decamp, retire, withdraw, vanish. (Remain.) *Deprive*, strip, bereave, despoil, rob, divest. *Depute*, appoint, commission, charge, entrust, delegate, authorize, accredit. *Derision*, scorn, contempt, contumely, disrespect. *Derivation*, origin, source, beginning, cause, etymology, root. *Describe*, delineate, portray, explain, illustrate, delineate, picture. *Desecrate*, profane, secularize, misuse, abuse, pollute. (Keep holy.) *Deserve*, merit, earn, justify, win. *Design*, n., delineation, sketch, drawing, cunning, artfulness, contrivance. *Desirable*, expedient, advisable, valuable, acceptable, proper, judicious, beneficial, profitable, good. *Desire*, n., longing, affection, craving. *Desist*, cease, stop, discontinue, drop, abstain, forbear. (Continue, persevere.) *Desolate*, bereaved, forlorn, forsaken, deserted, wild, waste, bare, bleak, lonely. (Pleasant, happy.) *Desperate*, wild, daring, audacious, determined, reckless. *Despised*. *Destiny*, fate, decree, doom, end. *Destructive*, detrimental, hurtful, noxious, injurious, deleterious, baleful, baneful, subversive. (Creative, constructive.) *Desuetude*, disuse, discontinuance. (Maintenance.) *Desultory*, rambling, discursive, loose, unmethodical, superficial, unsettled, erratic, fitful. (Thorough.) *Detail*, n., particular, specification, minutiæ. *Detail*, v., particularize, enumerate, specify. (Generalize.) *Deter*, warn, stop, dissuade, terrify, scare. (Encourage.) *Detriment*, loss, harm, injury, deterioration. (Benefit.) *Develop*, unfold, amplify, expand, enlarge. *Device*, artifice, expedient, contrivance. *Devoid*, void, wanting, destitute, unendowed, unprovided. (Full, replete.) *Devoted*, attached, fond, absorbed, dedicated. *Dictate*, prompt, suggest, enjoin, order, command. *Dictatorial*, imperative, imperious, domineering, arbitrary, tyrannical, overbearing. (Submissive.) *Die*, expire, depart, perish, decline, languish, wane, sink, fade, decay. *Diet*, food, victuals, nourishment, nutriment, sustenance, fare. *Difference*, separation, disagreement, discord, dissent, estrangement, variety. *Different*, various, manifold, diverse, unlike, separate, distinct. (Similar, homogeneous.) *Difficult*, hard, intricate, involved, perplexing, obscure, unmanageable. (Easy.) *Diffuse*, discursive, prolix, diluted, copious. *Dignify*, aggrandize, elevate, invest, exalt, advance, promote, honor. (Degrade.) *Dilate*, stretch, widen, expand, swell, distend, enlarge, descant, expatiate. *Dilatory*, tardy, procrastinating, behindhand, lagging, dawdling. (Prompt.) *Diligence*, care, assiduity, attention, heed, industry. (Negligence.) *Diminish*, lessen, reduce, contract, curtail, retrench. (Increase.) *Disability*, unfitness, incapacity. *Discern*, descry, observe, recognize, see, discriminate, separate, perceive. *Discipline*, order, strictness, training, coercion, punishment, organization. (Confusion, demoralization.) *Discover*, make known, find, invent, contrive, expose, reveal. *Discreditable*, shameful, disgraceful, scandalous, disreputable. (Creditable.) *Discreet*, cautious, prudent, wary, judicious. (Indiscreet.) *Discrepancy*, disagreement, difference, variance. (Agreement.) *Discrimination*, acuteness, discernment, judgment, caution. *Disease*, complaint, malady, disorder, ailment, sickness. *Disgrace*, n., disrepute, reproach, dishonor, shame, odium. (Honor.) *Disgrace*, v., debase, degrade, defame, discredit. (Exalt.) *Disgust*, dislike, distaste, loathing, abomination, abhorrence. (Admiration.) *Dishonest*, unjust, fraudulent, unfair, deceitful, cheating, deceptive, wrongful. (Honest.) *Dismay*, v., terrify, frighten, scare, daunt, appal, dishearten. (Encourage.) *Dismay*, n., terror, dread, fear, fright. (Assurance.) *Dismiss*, send off, discharge, discard, banish. (Retain.) *Dispel*, scatter, drive away, disperse, dissipate. (Collect.) *Display*, show, spread out, exhibit, expose. (Hide.) *Dispose*, arrange, place, order, give, bestow. *Dispute*, v., argue, contest, contend, question, impugn. (Assent.) *Dispute*, n., argument, debate, controversy, quarrel, disagreement. (Harmony.) *Dissent*, disagree, differ, vary. (Assent.) *Distinct*, clear, plain, obvious, different, separate. (Obscure, indistinct.) *Distinguish*, perceive, discern, mark out, divide, discriminate. *Distinguished*, famous, glorious, far-famed, noted, illustrious, eminent, celebrated. (Obscure, unknown; ordinary.) *Distract*, perplex, bewilder. (Calm, concentrate.) *Distribute*, allot, share, dispense, apportion, deal. (Collect.) *Disturb*, derange, discompose, agitate, rouse, interrupt, confuse, annoy, trouble, vex, worry. (Pacify, quiet.) *Disuse*, discontinuance, abolition, desuetude. (Use.) *Divide*, part, separate, distribute, deal out, sever, sunder. *Divine*, godlike, holy, heavenly, sacred, a parson, clergyman, minister. *Do*, effect, make, perform, accomplish, finish, transact. *Docile*, tractable, teachable, compliant, tame. (Stubborn.) *Doctrine*, tenet, article of belief, creed, dogma, teaching. *Doleful*, dolorous, woebegone, rueful, dismal, piteous. (Joyous.) *Doom*, n., sentence, verdict, judgment, fate, lot, destiny. *Doubt*, n., uncertainty, suspense, hesitation, scruple, ambiguity. (Certainty.) *Draw*, pull, haul, drag, attract, inhale, sketch, describe. *Dread*, n., fear, horror, terror, alarm, dismay, awe. (Boldness, assurance.) *Dreadful*, fearful, frightful, shocking, awful, horrible, horrid, terrible. *Dress*, n., clothing, attire, apparel, garments, costume, garb, livery. *Drift*, purpose, meaning, scope, aim, tendency, direction. *Droll*, funny, laughable, comic, whimsical, queer, amusing. (Solemn.) *Drown*, inundate, swamp, submerge, overwhelm, engulf. *Dry*, a., arid, parched, lifeless, dull, tedious, uninteresting, meagre. (Moist, interesting, succulent.) *Due*, owing to, attributable to, just, fair, proper, debt, right. *Dull*, stupid, gloomy, sad, dismal, commonplace. (Bright.) *Dunce*, simpleton, fool, ninny, idiot. (Sage.) *Durable*, lasting, permanent, abiding, continuing. (Ephemeral, perishable.) *Dwell*, stay, stop, abide, sojourn, linger, tarry. *Dwindle*, pine, waste, diminish, decrease, fall off. (Grow.)

EAGER, hot, ardent, impassioned, forward, impatient. (Diffident.) *Earn*, acquire, obtain, win, gain, achieve. *Earnest*, a., ardent, serious, grave, solemn, warm. (Trifling.) *Earnest*, n., pledge, pawn. *Ease*, n., comfort, rest. (Worry.) *Ease*, v., calm, alleviate, allay, mitigate, appease, assuage, pacify, disburden, rid. (Annoy, worry.) *Easy*, light, comfortable, unconstrained. (Difficult, hard.) *Eccentric*, irregular, anomalous, singular, odd, abnormal, wayward, particular, strange. (Regular, ordinary.) *Economical*, sparing, saving, provident, thrifty, frugal, careful, niggardly. (Wasteful.) *Edge*, border, brink, rim, brim, margin, verge. *Efface*, blot out, expunge, obliterate, wipe out, cancel, erase. *Effect*, n., consequence, result, issue, event, execution, operation. *Effect*, v., accomplish, fulfill, realize, achieve, execute, operate, complete. *Effective*, efficient, operative, serviceable. (Vain, ineffectual.) *Efficacy*, efficiency, energy, agency, instrumentality. *Efficient*, effectual, effective, competent, capable, able, fitted. *Eliminate*, drive out, expel, thrust out, eject, cast out, oust, dislodge, banish, proscribe. *Eloquence*, oratory, rhetoric, declamation. *Elucidate*, make plain, explain, clear up, illustrate. *Elude*, evade, escape, avoid, shun. *Embarrass*, perplex, entangle, distress, trouble. (Assist.) *Embellish*, adorn, decorate, bedeck, beautify, deck. (Disfigure.) *Embolden*, inspirit, animate, encourage, cheer, urge, impel, stimulate. (Discourage.) *Eminent*, distinguished, signal, conspicuous, noted, prominent, elevated, renowned, famous, glorious, illustrious. (Obscure, unknown.) *Emit*, give out, throw out, exhale, discharge, vent. *Emotion*, perturbation, agitation, trepidation, tremor, mental conflict. *Employ*, occupy, busy, take up with, engross. *Employment*, business, avocation, engagement, office, function, trade, profession, occupation, calling, vocation. *Encompass*, v., encircle, surround, gird, beset. *Encounter*, attack, conflict, combat, assault, onset, engagement, battle, action. *Encourage*, countenance, sanction, support, foster, cherish, inspirit, embolden, animate, cheer, incite, urge, impel, stimulate. (Deter.) *End*, n., aim, object, purpose, result, conclusion, upshot, close, expiration, termination, extremity, sequel. *Endeavor*, attempt, try, essay, strive, aim. *Endurance*, continuation, duration; fortitude, patience, resignation. *Endure*, v., last, continue, support, bear, sustain, suffer, brook, submit to, undergo. (Perish.) *Enemy*, foe, antagonist, adversary, opponent. (Friend.) *Energetic*, industrious, effectual, efficacious, powerful, binding, stringent, forcible, nervous. (Lazy.) *Engage*, employ, busy, occupy, attract, invite, allure, entertain, engross, take up, enlist. *Engross*, absorb, take up, busy, occupy, engage, monopolize. *Engulf*, swallow up, absorb, imbibe, drown, submerge, bury, entomb, overwhelm. *Enjoin*, order, ordain, appoint, prescribe. *Enjoyment*, pleasure, gratification. (Grief, sorrow, sadness.) *Enlarge*, increase, extend, augment, broaden, swell. (Diminish.) *Enlighten*, illumine, illuminate, instruct, inform. (Befog, becloud.) *Enliven*, cheer, vivify, stir up, animate, inspire, exhilarate. (Sadden, grieve.) *Enmity*, animosity, hostility, ill-will, maliciousness. (Friendship.) *Enormous*, gigantic, colossal, huge, vast, immense, prodigious. (Insignificant.) *Enough*, sufficient, plenty, abundance. (Want.) *Enraged*, infuriated, raging, wrathful. (Pacified.) *Enrapture*, enchant, fascinate, charm, captivate, bewitch. (Repel.) *Enroll*, enlist, list, register, record. *Enterprise*, undertaking, endeavor, venture, energy. *Enthusiasm*, earnest, devotion, zeal, ardor. (Ennui, lukewarmness.) *Enthusiast*, fanatic, visionary. *Equal*, equable, even, like, alike, uniform. (Unequal.) *Eradicate*, root out, extirpate, exterminate. *Erroneous*, incorrect, inaccurate, inexact. (Exact.) *Error*, blunder, mistake. (Truth.) *Especially*, chiefly, particularly, principally. (Generally.) *Essay*, dissertation, tract, treatise. *Establish*, build up, confirm. (Overthrow.) *Esteem*, regard, respect. (Contempt.) *Estimate*, appraise, appreciate, esteem, compute, rate. *Estrangement*, abstraction, alienation. *Eternal*, endless, everlasting. (Finite.) *Evade*, equivocate, prevaricate. *Even*, level, plain, smooth. (Uneven.) *Event*, accident, adventure, incident, occurrence. *Evil*, ill, harm, mischief, misfortune. (Good.) *Exact*, nice, particular, punctual. (Inexact.) *Exalt*, ennoble, dignify, raise. (Humble.) *Examination*, investigation, inquiry, research, search, scrutiny. *Exceed*, excel, outdo, surpass, transcend. (Fall short.) *Exceptional*, uncommon, rare, extraordinary. (Common.) *Excite*, awaken, provoke, rouse, stir up. (Lull.) *Excursion*, jaunt, ramble, tour, trip. *Execute*, fulfill, perform. *Exempt*, free, cleared. (Subject.) *Exercise*, practice. *Exhaustive*, thorough, complete. (Cursory.) *Exigency*, emergency. *Experiment*, proof, trial, test. *Explain*, expound, interpret, illustrate, elucidate. *Express*, declare, signify, utter, tell. *Extend*, reach, stretch. (Abridge.) *Extravagant*, lavish, profuse, prodigal. (Parsimonious.)

FABLE, apologue, novel, romance, tale. *Face*, visage, countenance. *Facetious*, pleasant, jocular, jocose. (Serious.) *Factor*, agent. *Fail*, to fall short, be deficient. (Accomplish.)

Faint, feeble, languid. (Forcible.) *Fair*, clear. (Stormy.) *Fair*, equitable, honest, reasonable. (Unfair.) *Faith*, creed. (Unbelief, infidelity). *Faithful*, true, loyal, constant. (Faithless.) *Faithless*, perfidious, treacherous. (Faithful.) *Fall*, drop, droop, sink, tumble. (Rise.) *Fame*, renown, reputation. *Famous*, celebrated, renowned, illustrious. (Obscure.) *Fanciful*, capricious, fantastical, whimsical. *Fancy*, imagination. *Fast*, rapid, quick, fleet, expeditious. (Slow.) *Fatigue*, weariness, lassitude. (Vigor.) *Fear*, timidity, timorousness. (Bravery.) *Feeling*, sensation, sense. *Feeling*, sensibility, susceptibility. (Insensibility.) *Ferocious*, fierce, savage, wild, barbarous. (Mild.) *Fertile*, fruitful, prolific, plenteous, productive. (Sterile.) *Fiction*, falsehood, fabrication. (Fact.) *Figure*, allegory, emblem, metaphor, symbol, picture, type. *Find*, descry, discover, espy. (Lose, overlook.) *Fine*, a., delicate, nice. (Coarse.) *Fine*, n., forfeit, forfeiture, mulct, penalty. *Fire*, glow, heat, warmth. *Firm*, constant, solid, steadfast, fixed, stable. (Weak.) *First*, foremost, chief, earliest. (Last.) *Fit*, accommodate, adapt, adjust, suit. *Fix*, determine, establish, settle, limit. *Flame*, blaze, flare, flash, glare. *Flat*, level, even. *Flexible*, pliant, pliable, ductile, supple. (Inflexible.) *Flourish*, prosper, thrive. (Decay.) *Fluctuating*, wavering, hesitating, oscillating, vacillating, change. (Firm, steadfast, decided.) *Fluent*, flowing, glib, voluble, unembarrassed, ready. (Hesitating.) *Folks*, persons, people, individuals. *Follow*, succeed, ensue, imitate, copy, pursue. *Follower*, partisan, disciple, adherent, retainer, pursuer, successor. *Folly*, silliness, foolishness, imbecility, weakness. (Wisdom.) *Fond*, enamored, attached, affectionate. (Distant.) *Fondness*, affection, attachment, kindness, love. (Aversion.) *Foolhardy*, venturesome, incautious, hasty, adventurous, rash. (Cautious.) *Foolish*, simple, silly, irrational, brainless, imbecile, crazy, absurd, preposterous, ridiculous, nonsensical. (Wise, discreet.) *Fop*, dandy, dude, beau, coxcomb, popinjay, jackanapes. (Gentleman.) *Forbear*, abstain, refrain, withhold. *Force*, n., strength, vigor, dint, might, energy, power, violence, army, host. *Force*, v., compel. (Persuade.) *Forecast*, forethought, foresight, premeditation, prognostication. *Forego*, quit, relinquish, let go, waive. *Foregoing*, antecedent, anterior, preceding, previous, prior, former. *Forerunner*, herald, harbinger, precursor, omen. *Foresight*, forethought, forecast, premeditation. *Forge*, coin, invent, frame, feign, fabricate, counterfeit. *Forgive*, pardon, remit, absolve, acquit, excuse, except. *Forlorn*, forsaken, abandoned, deserted, desolate, lone, lonesome. *Form*, n., ceremony, solemnity, observance, rite, figure, shape, conformation, fashion, appearance, representation, semblance. *Form*, v., make, create, produce, constitute, arrange, fashion, mould, shape. *Formal*, ceremonious, precise, exact, stiff, methodical, affected. (Informal, natural.) *Former*, antecedent, anterior, previous, prior, preceding, foregoing. *Forsaken*, abandoned, forlorn, deserted, desolate, lone, lonesome. *Forthwith*, immediately, directly, instantly, instantaneously. (Anon.) *Fortitude*, endurance, resolution, fearlessness, dauntlessness. (Weakness.) *Fortunate*, lucky, happy, auspicious, prosperous, successful. (Unfortunate.) *Fortune*, chance, fate, luck, doom, destiny, property, possession, riches. *Foster*, cherish, nurse, tend, harbor, nurture. (Neglect.) *Foul*, impure, nasty, filthy, dirty, unclean, defiled. (Pure, clean.) *Fractious*, cross, captious, petulant, touchy, testy, peevish, fretful, splenetic. (Tractable.) *Fragile*, brittle, frail, delicate, feeble. (Strong.) *Fragments*, pieces, scraps, chips, leavings, remains, remnants. *Frailty*, weakness, failing, foible, imperfection, fault, blemish. (Strength.) *Frame*, v., construct, invent, coin, fabricate, forge, mold, feign, make, compose. *Franchise*, right, exemption, immunity, privilege, freedom, suffrage. *Frank*, artless, candid, sincere, free, easy, familiar, open, ingenuous, plain. (Tricky, insincere.) *Frantic*, distracted, mad, furious, raving, frenzied. (Quiet, subdued.) *Fraud*, deceit, deception, duplicity, guile, cheat, imposition. (Honesty.) *Freak*, fancy, humor, vagary, whim, caprice, crotchet. (Purpose, resolution.) *Free*, a., liberal, generous, bountiful, bounteous, munificent, frank, artless, candid, familiar, open, independent, unconfined, unreserved, unrestricted, exempt, clear, loose, easy, careless. (Slavish, stingy, artful, costly.) *Free*, v., release, set free, deliver, rescue, liberate, enfranchise, affranchise, emancipate, exempt. (Enslave, bind.) *Freedom*, liberty, independence, unrestraint, familiarity, license, franchise, exemption, privilege. (Slavery.) *Frequent*, often, common, usual, general. (Rare.) *Fret*, gall, chafe, agitate, irritate, vex. *Friendly*, amicable, social, sociable. (Distant, reserved, cold.) *Frightful*, fearful, dreadful, dire, direful, terrific, awful, horrible, horrid. *Frivolous*, trifling, trivial, petty. (Serious, earnest.) *Frugal*, provident, economical, saving. (Wasteful, extravagant.) *Fruitful*, fertile, prolific, productive, abundant, plentiful, plenteous. (Barren, sterile.) *Fruitless*, vain, useless, idle, abortive, bootless, unavailing, without avail. *Frustrate*, defeat, foil, balk, disappoint. *Fulfill*, accomplish, effect, complete. *Fully*, completely, abundantly, perfectly. *Fulsome*, coarse, gross, sickening, offensive, rank. (Moderate.) *Furious*, violent, boisterous, vehement, dashing, sweeping, rolling, impetuous, frantic, distracted, stormy, angry, raging; fierce. (Calm.) *Futile*, trifling, trivial, frivolous, useless. (Effective.)

GAIN, n., profit, emolument, advantage, benefit, winnings, earnings. (Loss.) *Gain*, v., get, acquire, obtain, attain, procure, earn, win, achieve, reap, realize, reach. (Lose.) *Gallant*, brave, bold, courageous, gay, fine, showy, intrepid, fearless, heroic. *Galling*, chafing, irritating, vexing. (Soothing.) *Game*, play, pastime, diversion, sport, amusement. *Gang*, band, horde, company, troop, crew. *Gap*, breach, chasm, hollow, cavity, cleft, crevice, rift, chink. *Garnish*, embellish, adorn, beautify, deck, decorate. *Gather*, pick, cull, assemble, muster, infer, collect. (Scatter.) *Gaudy*, showy, flashy, tawdry, gay, glittering, bespangled. (Sombre.) *Gaunt*, emaciated, scraggy, skinny, meagre, lank, attenuated, spare, lean, thin. (Well-fed.) *Gay*, cheerful, merry, lively, jolly, sprightly, blithe. (Solemn.) *Generate*, form, make, beget, produce. *Generation*, formation, race, breed, stock, kind, age, era. *Generous*, beneficent, noble, honorable, bountiful, liberal, free. (Niggardly.) *Genial*, cordial, hearty, festive, joyous. (Distant, cold.) *Genius*, intellect, invention, talent, taste, nature, character, adept. *Genteel*, refined, polished, fashionable, polite, well-bred. (Boorish.) *Gentle*, placid, mild, bland, meek, tame, docile. (Rough, uncouth.) *Genuine*, real, true, unaffected, sincere. (False.) *Gesture*, attitude, action, posture. *Get*, obtain, earn, gain, attain, procure, achieve. *Ghastly*, pallid, wan, hideous, grim, shocking. *Ghost*, spectre, sprite, apparition, shade, phantom. *Gibe*, scoff, sneer, flout, jeer, mock, taunt, deride. *Giddy*, unsteady, flighty, thoughtless. (Steady.) *Gift*, donation, benefaction, grant, alms, gratuity, boon, present, faculty, talent. (Purchase.) *Gigantic*, colossal, huge, enormous, vast, prodigious, immense. (Diminutive.) *Give*, grant, bestow, confer, yield, impart. *Glad*, pleased, cheerful, joyful, gladsome, gratified, cheering. (Sad.) *Gleam*, glimmer, glance, glitter, shine, flash. *Glee*, gayety, merriment, mirth, joviality, joy, hilarity. (Sorrow.) *Glide*, slip, slide, run, roll on. *Glimmer*, v., gleam, flicker, glitter. *Glimpse*, glance, look, glint. *Glitter*, gleam, shine, glisten, glister, radiate. *Gloom*, cloud, darkness, dimness, blackness, dullness, sadness. (Light, brightness, joy.) *Gloomy*, lowering, lurid, dim, dusky, sad, glum. (Bright, clear.) *Glorify*, magnify, celebrate, adore, exalt. *Glorious*, famous, renowned, distinguished, noble, exalted. (Infamous.) *Glory*, honor, fame, renown, splendor, grandeur. (Infamy.) *Glut*, gorge, stuff, cram, cloy, satiate, block up. *Go*, depart, proceed, move, budge, stir. *God*, Creator, Lord, Almighty, Jehovah, Omnipotence, Providence. *Godly*, righteous, devout, holy, pious, religious. *Good*, benefit, weal, advantage, profit, boon. (Evil.) *Good*, a., virtuous, righteous, upright, just, true. (Wicked, bad.) *Gorge*, glut, fill, cram, stuff, satiate. *Gorgeous*, superb, grand, magnificent, splendid. (Plain, simple.) *Govern*, rule, direct, manage, command. *Government*, rule, state, control, sway. *Graceful*, becoming, comely, elegant, beautiful. (Awkward.) *Gracious*, merciful, kindly, beneficent. *Gradual*, slow, progressive. (Sudden.) *Grand*, majestic, stately, dignified, lofty, elevated, exalted, splendid, gorgeous, superb, magnificent, sublime, pompous. (Shabby.) *Grant*, bestow, impart, give, yield, cede, allow, confer, invest. *Grant*, gift, boon, donation. *Graphic*, forcible, telling, picturesque, vivid, pictorial. *Grasp*, catch, seize, gripe, clasp, grapple. *Grateful*, agreeable, pleasing, welcome, thankful. (Harsh.) *Gratification*, enjoyment, pleasure, delight, reward. (Disappointment.) *Grave*, a., serious, sedate, solemn, sober, pressing, heavy. (Giddy.) *Grave*, n., tomb, sepulchre, vault. *Great*, big, huge, large, majestic, vast, grand, noble, august. (Small.) *Greediness*, avidity, eagerness, voracity. (Generosity.) *Grief*, affliction, sorrow, trial, woe, tribulation. (Joy.) *Grieve*, mourn, lament, sorrow, pain, hurt, wound, bewail. (Rejoice.) *Grievous*, painful, afflicting, heavy, baleful, unhappy. *Grind*, crush, oppress, grate, harass, afflict. *Grisly*, terrible, hideous, grim, ghastly, dreadful. (Pleasing.) *Gross*, coarse, outrageous, unseemly, shameful, indelicate. (Delicate.) *Group*, assembly, cluster, collection, clump, order, class. *Grovel*, crawl, cringe, fawn, sneak. *Grow*, increase, vegetate, expand, advance. (Decay, diminution.) *Growl*, grumble, snarl, murmur, complain. *Grudge*, malice, rancor, spite, pique, hatred, aversion. *Gruff*, rough, rugged, blunt, rude, harsh, surly, bearish. (Pleasant.) *Guile*, deceit, fraud. (Candor.) *Guileless*, harmless, innocent. *Guilty*, culpable, sinful, criminal.

HABIT, custom, practice. *Hail*, accost, address, greet, salute, welcome. *Happiness*, beatitude, blessedness, bliss, felicity. (Unhappiness.) *Harbor*, haven, port. *Hard*, firm, solid. (Soft.) *Hard*, arduous, difficult. (Easy.) *Harm*, injury, hurt, wrong, infliction. (Benefit.) *Harmless*, safe, innocuous, innocent. (Hurtful.) *Harsh*, rough, rigorous, severe, gruff, morose. (Gentle.) *Hasten*, accelerate, dispatch, expedite, speed. (Delay.) *Hasty*, hurried, ill-advised. (Deliberate.) *Hateful*, odious, detestable. (Lovable.) *Hatred*, enmity, ill-will, rancor. (Friendship.) *Haughtiness*, arrogance, pride. (Modesty.) *Haughty*, arrogant, disdainful, supercilious, proud. *Hazard*,

sick, virulent. *Healthy*, salubrious, salutary, wholesome. (Unhealthy.) *Heap*, accumulate, amass, pile. *Hearty*, a., cordial, sincere, warm. (Insincere.) *Heavy*, burdensome, ponderous, weighty. (Light.) *Heed*, care, attention. *Heighten*, enhance, exalt, elevate, raise. *Heinous*, atrocious, flagitious, flagrant. (Venial.) *Help*, aid, assist, relieve, succor. (Hinder.) *Heretic*, sectary, sectarian, schismatic, dissenter, non-conformist. *Hesitate*, falter, stammer, stutter. *Hideous*, grim, ghastly, grisly. (Beautiful.) *High*, lofty, tall, elevated. (Deep.) *Hinder*, impede, obstruct, prevent. (Help.) *Hint*, allude, refer, suggest, intimate, insinuate. *Hold*, detain, keep, retain. *Holiness*, sanctity, piety, sacredness. *Holy*, devout, pious, religious. *Homely*, plain, ugly, coarse. (Beautiful.) *Honesty*, integrity, probity, uprightness. (Dishonesty.) *Honor*, v., respect, reverence, esteem. (Dishonor.) *Hope*, confidence, expectation, trust. *Hopeless*, desperate. *Hot*, ardent, burning, fiery. (Cold.) *However*, nevertheless, notwithstanding, yet. *Humble*, modest, submissive, plain, unostentatious, simple. (Haughty.) *Humble*, degrade, humiliate, mortify, abase. (Exalt.) *Humor*, mood, temper. *Hunt*, seek, chase. *Hurtful*, noxious, pernicious. (Beneficial.) *Husbandry*, cultivation, tillage. *Hypocrite*, dissembler, impostor, canter. *Hypothesis*, theory, supposition.

IDEA, thought, imagination. *Ideal*, imaginary, fancied. (Actual.) *Idle*, indolent, lazy. (Industrious.) *Ignominious*, shameful, scandalous, infamous. (Honorable.) *Ignominy*, shame, disgrace, obloquy, infamy, reproach. *Ignorant*, unlearned, illiterate, uninformed, uneducated. (Knowing.) *Ill*, n., evil, wickedness, misfortune, mischief, harm. (Good.) *Ill*, a., sick, indisposed, unwell, diseased. (Well.) *Ill-tempered*, crabbed, sour, surly, acrimonious. (Good-natured.) *Ill-will*, enmity, hatred, antipathy. (Good-will.) *Illegal*, unlawful, illicit, contraband, illegitimate. (Legal.) *Illimitable*, boundless, immeasurable, unlimited, infinite. *Illiterate*, unlettered, unlearned, untaught, uninstructed. (Learned, educated.) *Illusion*, fallacy, deception, phantasm. *Illusory*, imaginary, chimerical, visionary. (Real.) *Illustrate*, explain, elucidate, clear. *Illustrious*, celebrated, noble, eminent, famous, renowned. (Obscure.) *Image*, likeness, picture, representation, effigy. *Imaginary*, ideal, fanciful, illusory. (Real.) *Imagine*, conceive, fancy, apprehend, think, presume. *Imbecility*, silliness, senility, dotage. *Imitate*, copy, ape, mimic, mock, counterfeit. *Immaculate*, unspotted, spotless, unsullied, stainless. (Soiled.) *Immediate*, pressing, instant, next, proximate. *Immediately*, instantly, forthwith, directly, presently. *Immense*, vast, enormous, huge, prodigious, monstrous. *Immunity*, privilege, prerogative, exemption. *Impair*, injure, diminish, decrease. *Impart*, reveal, divulge, disclose, discover, bestow, afford. *Impartial*, just, equitable, unbiased. (Partial.) *Impassioned*, glowing, burning, fiery, vehement, intense. *Impeach*, accuse, charge, arraign, censure. *Impede*, hinder, retard, obstruct, prevent. (Help.) *Impediment*, obstruction, hindrance, obstacle, barrier. (Aid.) *Impel*, animate, induce, incite, instigate, embolden. (Retard.) *Impending*, imminent, threatening. *Imperative*, commanding, authoritative, despotic. *Imperfection*, fault, blemish, defect, vice. *Imperil*, endanger, hazard, jeopardize. *Imperious*, commanding, dictatorial, authoritative, imperative, lordly, overbearing, domineering. *Impertinent*, intrusive, meddling, officious, rude, saucy, impudent, insolent. *Impetuous*, violent, boisterous, furious, vehement. (Calm.) *Impious*, profane, irreligious, godless. (Reverent.) *Implicate*, involve, entangle, embarrass, compromise. *Imply*, involve, comprise, infold, import, denote, signify. *Importance*, signification, significance, avail, consequence, weight, gravity, moment. *Imposing*, impressive, striking, majestic, august, noble, grand. (Insignificant.) *Impotence*, weakness, incapacity, infirmity, frailty, feebleness. (Power.) *Impotent*, weak, feeble, helpless, enfeebled, nerveless, infirm. (Strong.) *Impressive*, stirring, forcible, exciting, affecting, moving. *Imprison*, incarcerate, shut up, immure, confine. (Liberate.) *Imprisonment*, captivity, durance. *Improve*, amend, better, mend, reform, rectify, ameliorate, apply, use, employ. (Deteriorate.) *Improvident*, careless, incautious, imprudent, prodigal, wasteful, reckless, rash. (Thrifty.) *Impudence*, assurance, impertinence, confidence, insolence, rudeness. *Impudent*, saucy, brazen, bold, impertinent, forward, rude, insolent, immodest, shameless. *Impulse*, incentive, incitement, motive, instigation. *Impulsive*, rash, hasty, forcible, violent. (Deliberate.) *Imputation*, blame, censure, reproach, charge, accusation. *Inadvertency*, error, oversight, blunder, inattention, carelessness, negligence. *Incentive*, motive, inducement, impulse. *Incite*, instigate, excite, provoke, stimulate, encourage, urge, impel. *Inclination*, leaning, slope, disposition, tendency, bent, bias, affection, attachment, wish, liking, desire. (Aversion.) *Incline*, v., slope, lean, slant, tend, bend, turn, bias, dispose. *Inclose*, surround, shut in, fence in, cover, wrap. *Include*, comprehend, comprise, contain, embrace, take in. *Incommode*, annoy, plague, molest, disturb, inconvenience, trouble. (Accommodate.) *Incompetent*, incapable, unable, inadequate, insufficient. (Competent.) *In-*

crease, v., extend, enlarge, augment, dilate, expand, amplify, raise, enhance, aggravate, magnify, grow. (Diminish.) *Increase*, n., augmentation, accession, addition, enlargement, extension. (Decrease.) *Incumbent*, obligatory. *Indefinite*, vague, uncertain, unsettled, loose, lax. (Definite.) *Indicate*, point out, show, mark. *Indifference*, apathy, carelessness, listlessness, insensibility. (Application, assiduity.) *Indigence*, want, neediness, penury, poverty, destitution, privation. (Affluence.) *Indignation*, anger, wrath, ire, resentment. *Indignity*, insult, affront, outrage, obloquy, opprobrium, reproach, ignominy. (Honor.) *Indiscriminate*, promiscuous, mixed, indistinct, confused. (Select, chosen.) *Indispensable*, essential, necessary, requisite, expedient. (Unnecessary, supernumerary.) *Indisputable*, undeniable, undoubted, incontestable, indubitable, unquestionable, sure, infallible. *Indorse*, ratify, confirm, superscribe. *Indulge*, foster, cherish, fondle. (Deny.) *Ineffectual*, vain, useless, unavailing, fruitless, abortive, inoperative. (Effective.) *Inequality*, disparity, disproportion, dissimilarity, unevenness. (Equality.) *Inevitable*, unavoidable, not to be avoided, certain. *Infamous*, scandalous, shameful, ignominious, opprobrious, disgraceful. (Honorable.) *Inference*, deduction, corollary, conclusion, consequence. *Infernal*, diabolical, fiendish, devilish, hellish. *Infest*, annoy, plague, harass, disturb. *Infirm*, weak, feeble, enfeebled. (Robust.) *Inflame*, anger, irritate, enrage, chafe, incense, nettle, aggravate, embitter, exasperate. (Allay, soothe.) *Influence*, v., bias, sway, prejudice, prepossess. *Influence*, n., credit, favor, reputation, character, weight, authority, sway, ascendency. *Infringe*, invade, intrude, contravene, break, transgress, violate. *Ingenuous*, artless, candid, generous, open, frank, plain, sincere. (Crafty.) *Inhuman*, cruel, brutal, savage, barbarous, ruthless, merciless, ferocious. (Humane.) *Iniquity*, injustice, wrong, grievance. *Injure*, damage, hurt, deteriorate, wrong, aggrieve, harm, spoil, mar, sully. (Benefit.) *Injurious*, hurtful, baneful, pernicious, deleterious, noxious, prejudicial, wrongful, damaging. (Beneficial.) *Injustice*, wrong, iniquity, grievance. (Right.) *Innocent*, guiltless, sinless, harmless, inoffensive, innocuous. (Guilty.) *Innocuous*, harmless, safe, innocent. (Hurtful.) *Inordinate*, intemperate, irregular, disorderly, excessive, immoderate. (Moderate.) *Inquiry*, investigation, examination, research, scrutiny, disquisition, question, query, interrogation. *Inquisitive*, prying, peeping, curious, peering. *Insane*, mad, deranged, delirious, demented. (Sane.) *Insanity*, madness, mental aberration, lunacy, delirium. (Sanity.) *Insinuate*, hint, intimate, suggest, infuse, introduce, ingratiate.

Insipid, dull, flat, mawkish, tasteless, vapid, inanimate, lifeless. (Bright, sparkling.) *Insolent*, rude, saucy, pert, impertinent, abusive, scurrilous, opprobrious, insulting, offensive. *Inspire*, animate, exhilarate, enliven, cheer, breathe, inhale. *Instability*, mutability, fickleness, mutableness, wavering. (Stability, firmness.) *Instigate*, stir up, persuade, animate, incite, urge, stimulate, encourage. *Instil*, implant, inculcate, infuse, insinuate. *Instruct*, inform, teach, educate, enlighten, initiate. *Instrumental*, conducive, assistant, helping, ministerial. *Insufficiency*, inadequacy, incompetency, incapability, deficiency, lack. *Insult*, affront, outrage, indignity, blasphemy. (Honor.) *Insulting*, insolent, rude, saucy, impertinent, abusive. *Integrity*, uprightness, honesty, probity, entirety, entireness, completeness, rectitude, purity. (Dishonesty.) *Intellect*, understanding, sense, brains, mind, intelligence, ability, talent, genius. (Body.) *Intellectual*, mental, ideal, metaphysical. (Brutal.) *Intelligible*, clear, obvious, plain, distinct. (Abstruse.) *Intemperate*, immoderate, excessive, drunken, nimious, inordinate. (Temperate.) *Intense*, ardent, earnest, glowing, fervid, burning, vehement. *Intent*, design, purpose, intention, drift, view, aim, purport, meaning. *Intercourse*, commerce, connection, intimacy, acquaintance. *Interdict*, forbid, prohibit, inhibit, proscribe, debar, restrain from. (Allow.) *Interfere*, meddle, intermeddle, interpose. *Interminable*, endless, interminate, infinite, unlimited, illimitable, boundless, limitless. (Brief, concise.) *Interpose*, intercede, arbitrate, mediate, interfere, meddle. *Interpret*, explain, expound, elucidate, unfold, decipher. *Intimate*, hint, suggest, insinuate, express, signify, impart, tell. *Intimidate*, dishearten, alarm, frighten, scare, appal, daunt, cow, browbeat. (Encourage.) *Intolerable*, insufferable, unbearable, insupportable, unendurable. *Intrepid*, bold, brave, daring, fearless, dauntless, undaunted, courageous, valorous, valiant, heroic, gallant, chivalrous, doughty. (Cowardly, faint-hearted.) *Intrigue*, plot, cabal, conspiracy, combination, artifice, ruse, amour. *Intrinsic*, real, true, genuine, sterling, native, natural. (Extrinsic.) *Invalidate*, quash, cancel, overthrow, vacate, nullify, annul. *Invasion*, incursion, irruption, assault, aggression, raid, foray. *Invective*, abuse, reproach, railing, censure, sarcasm, satire. *Invent*, devise, contrive, frame, find out, discover, design. *Investigation*, examination, search, inquiry, research, scrutiny. *Inveterate*, confirmed, chronic, malignant. (Inchoate.) *Invidious*, envious, hateful, odious, malignant. *Invigorate*, brace, harden, nerve, strengthen, fortify. (Enervate.) *Invincible*, unconquerable, impregnable, insurmountable. *Invisible*, ness, imperceptible, impalpable, unperceivable. *Invite*, ask, call, bid, request, allure, attract, solicit. *Invoke*, invocate, call upon, appeal, refer, implore, beseech. *Involve*, implicate, entangle, compromise, envelop. *Irksome*, wearisome, tiresome, tedious, annoying. (Pleasant.) *Irony*, sarcasm, satire, ridicule, raillery. *Irrational*, foolish, silly, imbecile, brutish, absurd, ridiculous. (Rational.) *Irregular*, eccentric, anomalous, inordinate, intemperate. (Regular.) *Irreligious*, profane, godless, impious, sacrilegious, desecrating. *Irreproachable*, blameless, spotless, irreprovable. *Irresistible*, resistless, irrepressible. *Irresolute*, wavering, undetermined, undecided, vacillating. (Determined.) *Irritable*, excitable, irascible, susceptible, sensitive. (Calm.) *Irritate*, aggravate, worry, embitter, madden, exasperate. *Issue*, v., emerge, rise, proceed, flow, spring, emanate. *Issue*, n., end, upshot, effect, result, offspring, progeny.

JADE, harass, weary, tire, worry. *Jangle*, wrangle, conflict, disagree. *Jarring*, conflicting, discordant, inconsistent, inconsonant. *Jaunt*, ramble, excursion, trip. *Jealousy*, suspicion, envy. *Jeopard*, hazard, peril, endanger. *Jest*, joke, sport, divert, make game of. *Journey*, travel, tour, passage. *Joy*, gladness, mirth, delight. (Grief.) *Judge*, justice, referee, arbitrator. *Joyful*, glad, rejoicing, exultant. (Mournful.) *Judgment*, discernment, discrimination, understanding. *Justice*, equity, right. Justice is right as established by law; equity according to the circumstances of each particular case. (Injustice.) *Justness*, accuracy, correctness, precision.

KEEP, preserve, save. (Abandon.) *Kill*, assassinate, murder, slay. *Kindred*, affinity, consanguinity, relationship. *Knowledge*, erudition, learning, science. (Ignorance.)

LABOR, toil, work, effort, drudgery. (Idleness.) *Lack*, need, deficiency, scarcity, insufficiency. (Plenty.) *Lament*, mourn, grieve, weep. (Rejoice.) *Language*, dialect, idiom, speech, tongue. *Lascivious*, loose, unchaste, lustful, lewd, lecherous. (Chaste.) *Last*, final, latest, ultimate. (First.) *Laudable*, commendable, praiseworthy. (Blamable.) *Laughable*, comical, droll, ludicrous. (Serious.) *Lawful*, legal, legitimate, licit. (Illegal.) *Lead*, conduct, guide. (Follow.) *Lean*, meager. (Fat.) *Learned*, erudite, scholarly. (Ignorant.) *Leave*, v., quit, relinquish. *Leave*, n., liberty, permission, license. (Prohibition.) *Life*, existence, animation, spirit, vivacity. (Death.) *Lifeless*, dead, inanimate. *Lift*, erect, elevate, exalt, raise. (Lower.) *Light*, clear, bright. (Dark.) *Lightness*, flightiness, giddiness, levity, volatility. (Seriousness.) *Likeness*, resemblance, similarity. (Unlikeness.) *Linger*, lag, loiter, tarry, saunter. (Hasten.) *Little*, diminutive, small. (Great.) *Livelihood*, living, maintenance, subsistence, support. *Lively*, jocund, merry, sportive, sprightly, vivacious. (Slow, languid, sluggish.) *Long*, extended, extensive. (Short.) *Look*, appear, seem. *Lose*, miss, forfeit. (Gain.) *Loss*, detriment, damage, deprivation. (Gain.) *Loud*, clamorous, high-sounding, noisy. (Low, quiet.) *Love*, affection. (Hatred.) *Low*, abject, mean. (Noble.) *Lunacy*, derangement, insanity, mania, madness. (Sanity.) *Luster*, brightness, brilliancy, splendor. *Luxuriant*, exuberant. (Sparse.)

MACHINATION, plot, intrigue, cabal, conspiracy. (Artlessness.) *Mad*, crazy, delirious, insane, rabid, violent, frantic. (Sane, rational, quiet.) *Madness*, insanity, fury, rage, frenzy. *Magisterial*, august, dignified, majestic, pompous, stately. *Make*, form, create, produce. (Destroy.) *Malediction*, anathema, curse, imprecation, execration. *Malevolent*, malicious, virulent, malignant. (Benevolent.) *Malice*, spite, rancor, ill-feeling, grudge, animosity, ill-will. (Benignity.) *Malicious*, see malevolent. *Manacle*, v., shackle, fetter, chain. (Free.) *Manage*, contrive, concert, direct. *Management*, direction, superintendence, care, economy. *Mangle*, tear, lacerate, mutilate, cripple, maim. *Mania*, madness, insanity, lunacy. *Manifest*, v., reveal, prove, evince, exhibit, display, show. *Manifest*, a., clear, plain, evident, open, apparent, visible. (Hidden, occult.) *Manifold*, several, sundry, various, divers, numerous. *Manly*, masculine, vigorous, courageous, brave, heroic. (Effeminate.) *Manner*, habit, custom, way, air, look, appearance. *Manners*, morals, habits, behavior, carriage. *Mar*, spoil, ruin, disfigure. (Improve.) *March*, tramp, tread, walk, step, space. *Margin*, edge, rim, border, brink, verge. *Mark*, n., sign, note, symptom, token, indication, trace, vestige, track, badge, brand. *Mark*, v., impress, print, stamp, engrave, note, designate. *Marriage*, wedding, nuptials, matrimony, wedlock. *Martial*, military, warlike, soldier-like. *Marvel*, wonderful, miracle, prodigy. *Marvelous*, wondrous, wonderful, amazing, miraculous. *Massive*, bulky, heavy, weighty, ponderous, solid, substantial. (Flimsy.) *Mastery*, dominion, rule, sway, ascendancy, supremacy. *Matchless*, unrivaled, unequaled, unparalleled, peerless, incomparable, inimitable, surpassing. (Common, ordinary.) *Material*, a., corporeal, bodily, physical, temporal, momentous, important. (Spiritual, immaterial.) *Maxim*, adage, apothegm, proverb, saying, by-word, saw. *Meager*, poor, lank, emaciated, barren, dry, uninteresting. (Rich.) *Mean*, a., stingy, niggardly, low, abject, vile, ignoble, degraded.

contemptible, vulgar, despicable. (Uncommon.) *Mean*, v., design, purpose, intent, contemplate, signify, denote, indicate. *Meaning*, signification, import, acceptation, sense, purport. *Medium*, organ, channel, instrument, means. *Medley*, mixture, variety, diversity, miscellany. *Meek*, unassuming, mild, gentle. (Proud.) *Melancholy*, low-spirited, dispirited, dreamy, sad. (Jolly, buoyant.) *Mellow*, ripe, mature, soft. (Immature.) *Melodious*, tuneful, musical, silver, dulcet, sweet. (Discordant.) *Memorable*, signal, distinguished, marked. *Memorial*, monument, memento, commemoration. *Memory*, remembrance, recollection. *Menace*, n., threat. *Mend*, repair, amend, correct, better, ameliorate, improve, rectify. *Mention*, tell, name, communicate, impart, divulge, reveal, disclose, inform, acquaint. *Merciful*, compassionate, lenient, clement, tender, gracious, kind. (Cruel.) *Merciless*, hard-hearted, cruel, unmerciful, pitiless, remorseless, unrelenting. (Kind.) *Merriment*, mirth, joviality, jollity, hilarity. (Sorrow.) *Merry*, cheerful, mirthful, joyous, gay, lively, sprightly, hilarious, blithe, blithesome, jovial, sportive, jolly. (Sad.) *Metaphorical*, figurative, allegorical, symbolical. *Method*, way, manner, mode, process, order, rule, regularity, system. *Mien*, air, look, manner, aspect, appearance. *Migratory*, roving, strolling, wandering, vagrant. (Settled, sedate, permanent.) *Mimic*, imitate, ape, mock. *Mindful*, observant, attentive, heedful, thoughtful. (Heedless.) *Miscellaneous*, promiscuous, indiscriminate, mixed. *Mischief*, injury, harm, damage, hurt, evil, ill. (Benefit.) *Miscreant*, caitiff, villain, ruffian. *Miserable*, unhappy, wretched, distressed, afflicted. (Happy.) *Miserly*, stingy, niggardly, avaricious, griping. *Misery*, wretchedness, woe, destitution, penury, privation, beggary. (Happiness.) *Misfortune*, calamity, disaster, mishap, catastrophe. (Good luck.) *Miss*, omit, lose, fail, miscarry. *Mitigate*, alleviate, relieve, abate, diminish. (Aggravate.) *Moderate*, temperate, abstemious, sober, abstinent. (Immoderate.) *Modest*, chaste, virtuous, bashful, reserved. (Immodest.) *Moist*, wet, damp, dank, humid. (Dry.) *Monotonous*, unvaried, dull, tiresome, undiversified. (Varied.) *Monstrous*, shocking, dreadful, horrible, huge, immense. *Monument*, memorial, record, remembrancer, cenotaph. *Mood*, humor, disposition, vein, temper. *Morbid*, sick, ailing, sickly, diseased, corrupted. (Normal, sound.) *Morose*, gloomy, sullen, surly, fretful, crabbed, crusty. (Joyous.) *Mortal*, deadly, fatal, human. *Motion*, proposition, proposal, movement. *Motionless*, still, stationary, torpid, stagnant. (Active, moving.) *Mount*, arise, rise, ascend, soar, tower, climb, scale. *Mournful*, sad, sorrowful, lugubrious, grievous, doleful, heavy. (Happy.) *Move*, actuate, impel, induce, prompt, instigate, persuade, stir, agitate, propel, push. *Multitude*, crowd, throng, host, mob, swarm. *Murder*, v., kill, assassinate, slay, massacre, dispatch. *Muse*, v., meditate, contemplate, think, reflect, cogitate, ponder. *Music*, harmony, melody, symphony. *Musical*, tuneful, melodious, harmonious, dulcet, sweet. *Musty*, stale, sour, fetid. (Fresh, sweet.) *Mute*, dumb, silent, speechless. *Mutilate*, maim, cripple, disable, disfigure. *Mutinous*, insurgent, seditious, tumultuous, turbulent, riotous. (Obedient, orderly.) *Mutual*, reciprocal, interchanged, correlative. (Sole, solitary.) *Mysterious*, dark, obscure, hidden, secret, dim, mystic, enigmatical, unaccountable. (Open, clear.) *Mystify*, confuse, perplex, puzzle. (Clear, explain.)

NAKED, nude, bare, uncovered, unclothed, rough, rude, simple. (Covered, clad.) *Name*, v., denominate, entitle, style, designate, term, call, christen. *Name*, n., appellation, designation, denomination, title, cognomen, reputation, character, fame, credit, repute. *Narrate*, tell, relate, detail, recount, describe, enumerate, rehearse, recite. *Nasty*, filthy, foul, dirty, unclean, impure, indecent, gross, vile. *Nation*, people, community, realm, state. *Native*, indigenous, inborn, vernacular. *Natural*, original, regular, normal, bastard. (Unnatural, forced.) *Near*, nigh, neighboring, close, adjacent, contiguous, intimate. (Distant.) *Necessary*, needful, expedient, essential, requisite, indispensable. (Useless.) *Necessitate*, compel, force, oblige. *Necessity*, need, occasion, exigency, emergency, urgency, requisite. *Need*, n., necessity, distress, poverty, indigence, want, penury. *Need*, v., require, want, lack. *Neglect*, v., disregard, slight, omit, overlook. *Neglect*, n., omission, failure, default, negligence, remissness, carelessness, slight. *Neighborhood*, environs, vicinity, nearness, adjacency, proximity. *Nervous*, timid, timorous, shaky. *New*, fresh, recent, novel. (Old.) *News*, tidings, intelligence, information. *Nice*, exact, accurate, good, particular, precise, fine, delicate. (Careless, coarse, unpleasant.) *Nimble*, active, brisk, lively, alert, quick, agile, prompt. (Awkward.) *Nobility*, aristocracy, greatness, grandeur, peerage. *Noble*, exalted, elevated, illustrious, great, grand, lofty. (Low.) *Noise*, cry, outcry, clamor, row, din, uproar, tumult. (Silence.) *Nonsensical*, irrational, absurd, silly, foolish. (Sensible.) *Notable*, plain, evident, remarkable, signal, striking, rare. (Obscure.) *Note*, n., token, symbol, mark, sign, indication, remark, comment. *Noted*, distinguished, remarkable, eminent, renowned. (Obscure.)

Notice, n., advice, notification, intelligence, information. *Notice*, v., mark, note, observe, attend to, regard, heed. *Notify*, v., publish, acquaint, apprise, inform, declare. *Notion*, conception, idea, belief, opinion, sentiment. *Notorious*, conspicuous, open, obvious, ill-famed. (Unknown.) *Nourish*, nurture, cherish, foster, supply. (Starve, famish.) *Nourishment*, food, diet, sustenance, nutrition. *Novel*, modern, new, fresh, recent, unused, strange, rare. (Old.) *Noxious*, hurtful, deadly, poisonous, deleterious, harmful. (Beneficial.) *Nullify*, annul, vacate, invalidate, quash, cancel, repeal. (Affirm.) *Nutrition*, food, diet, nutriment, nourishment.

OBDURATE, hard, callous, hardened, unfeeling, insensible. (Yielding, tractable.) *Obedient*, compliant, submissive, dutiful, respectful. (Obstinate.) *Obese*, corpulent, fat, adipose, fleshy. (Attenuated.) *Obey*, v., conform, comply, submit. (Rebel, disobey.) *Object*, n., aim, end, purpose, design, mark, butt. *Object*, v., oppose, except to, contravene, impeach, deprecate. (Assent.) *Obnoxious*, offensive. (Agreeable.) *Obscure*, undistinguished, unknown. (Distinguished.) *Obstinate*, contumacious, headstrong, stubborn, obdurate. (Yielding.) *Occasion*, opportunity. *Offense*, affront, misdeed, misdemeanor, transgression, trespass. *Offensive*, insolent, abusive, obnoxious. (Inoffensive.) *Office*, charge, function, place. *Offspring*, issue, progeny. *Old*, aged, superannuated, ancient, antique, antiquated, obsolete, old-fashioned. (Young, new.) *Omen*, presage, prognostic. *Opaque*, dark. (Bright, transparent.) *Open*, candid, unreserved, clear, fair. (Hidden, dark.) *Opinion*, notion, view, judgment, belief, sentiment. *Opinionated*, conceited, egotistical. (Modest.) *Oppose*, resist, withstand, thwart. (Give way.) *Option*, choice. *Order*, method, rule, system, regularity. (Disorder.) *Origin*, cause, occasion, beginning, source. (End.) *Outlive*, survive. *Outward*, external, outside, exterior. (Inner.) *Over*, above. (Under.) *Overbalance*, outweigh, preponderate. *Overbear*, bear down, overwhelm, overpower, subdue. *Overbearing*, haughty, arrogant, proud. (Gentle.). *Overflow*, inundation, deluge. *Overrule*, supersede, suppress. *Overspread*, overrun, ravage. *Overturn*, invert, overthrow, reverse, subvert. (Establish, fortify.) *Overwhelm*, crush, defeat, vanquish.

PAIN, suffering, qualm, pang, agony, anguish. (Pleasure.) *Pallid*, pale, wan. (Florid.) *Part*, division, portion, share, fraction. (Whole.) *Particular*, exact, distinct, odd, singular, strange. (General.) *Patient*, passive, submissive, meek. (Obstinate.) *Peace*, calm, quiet, tranquillity. (War, riot, trouble, turbulence.) *Peaceable*, pacific, peaceful, quiet. (Troublesome, violent.) *Penetrate*, bore, pierce, perforate. *Penetration*, acuteness, sagacity. (Dullness.) *People*, nation, persons, folks. *Perceive*, note, observe, discern, distinguish. *Perception*, conception, notion, idea. *Peril*, danger, pitfall, snare. (Safety.) *Permit*, allow, tolerate. (Forbid.) *Persuade*, allure, entice, prevail upon. *Physical*, corporeal, bodily, material. (Mental.) *Picture*, engraving, print, representation, illustration, image. *Piteous*, doleful, woeful, rueful. (Joyful.) *Pitiless*, see merciless. *Pity*, compassion, sympathy. (Cruelty.) *Place*, n., spot, site, position, post, situation, station. *Place*, v., order, dispose. *Plain*, open, manifest, evident. (Secret.) *Play*, game, sport, amusement. (Work.) *Please*, gratify, pacify. (Displease.) *Pleasure*, charm, delight, joy. (Pain.) *Plentiful*, abundant, ample, copious, plenteous. (Scarce.) *Poise*, balance. *Positive*, absolute, peremptory, decided, certain. (Negative, undecided.) *Possessor*, owner, proprietor. *Possible*, practical, practicable. (Impossible.) *Poverty*, penury, indigence, need, want. (Wealth.) *Power*, authority, force, strength, dominion. *Powerful*, mighty, potent. (Weak.) *Praise*, commend, extol, laud. (Blame.) *Prayer*, entreaty, petition, request, suit. *Pretense*, n., pretext, subterfuge. *Prevailing*, predominant, prevalent, general. (Isolated, sporadic.) *Prevent*, obviate, preclude. *Previous*, antecedent, introductory, preparatory, preliminary. (Subsequent.) *Pride*, vanity, conceit. (Humility.) *Principally*, chiefly, essentially, mainly. *Principle*, ground, reason, motive, impulse, maxim, rule, rectitude, integrity. *Privilege*, immunity, advantage, favor, prerogative, exemption, right, claim. *Probity*, rectitude, uprightness, honesty, integrity, sincerity, soundness. (Dishonesty.) *Problematical*, uncertain, doubtful, dubious, questionable, disputable, suspicious. (Certain.) *Prodigious*, huge, enormous, vast, amazing, astonishing, astounding, surprising, remarkable, wonderful. (Insignificant.) *Profession*, business, trade, occupation, vocation, office, employment, engagement, avowal. *Proffer*, volunteer, offer, propose, tender. *Profligate*, abandoned, dissolute, depraved, vicious, degenerate, corrupt, demoralized. (Virtuous.) *Profound*, deep, fathomless, penetrating, solemn, abstruse, recondite. (Shallow.) *Profuse*, extravagant, prodigal, lavish, improvident, excessive, copious, plentiful. (Succinct.) *Prolific*, productive, generative, fertile, fruitful, teeming. (Barren.) *Prolix*, diffuse, long, prolonged, tedious, tiresome, wordy, verbose, prosaic. (Concise, brief.) *Prominent*, eminent, conspicuous, marked, important, leading. (Obscure.) *Promiscuous*, mixed, unarranged, mingled, indiscriminate. (Select.) *Prompt*, see punctual. *Prop*, v., maintain, sustain, support, stay. *Propagate*, spread, circulate, diffuse, disseminate, extend, breed, increase. (Suppress.) *Proper*, legitimate, right, just, fair, equitable, honest, suitable, fit, adapted, meet, becoming, befitting, decent, pertinent, appropriate. (Wrong.) *Prosper*, flourish, succeed, grow rich, thrive, advance. (Fail.) *Prosperity*, well-being, weal, welfare, happiness, good luck. (Poverty.) *Proxy*, agent, representative, substitute, delegate, deputy. *Prudence*, carefulness, judgment, discretion, wisdom. (Indiscretion.) *Prurient*, itching, craving, hankering, longing. *Puerile*, youthful, juvenile, boyish, childish, infantile, trifling, weak, silly. (Mature.) *Punctilious*, nice, particular, formal, precise. (Negligent.) *Punctual*, exact, precise, nice, particular, prompt, timely. (Dilatory.) *Putrefy*, rot, decompose, corrupt, decay. *Puzzle*, v., perplex, confound, embarrass, bewilder, confuse, pose, mystify. (Enlighten.)

QUACK, impostor, pretender, charlatan, empiric, mountebank. (Savant.) *Quaint*, artful, curious, far-fetched, fanciful, odd, singular. *Qualified*, competent, fitted, adapted. (Incompetent.) *Quality*, attribute, rank, distinction. *Querulous*, doubting, complaining, fretting, repining. (Patient.) *Question*, query, inquiry, interrogatory. *Quibble*, cavil, evade, equivocate, shuffle, prevaricate. *Quick*, lively, ready, prompt, alert, nimble, agile, active, brisk, expeditious, adroit, fleet, rapid, swift, impetuous, sweeping, dashing, clever, sharp. (Slow.) *Quote*, note, repeat, cite, adduce.

RABID, mad, furious, raging, frantic. (Rational.) *Race*, course, match, pursuit, career, family, clan, house, ancestry, lineage, pedigree. *Rack*, agonize, wring, torture, excruciate, distress, harass. (Soothe.) *Racy*, spicy, pungent, smart, spirited, lively, vivacious. (Dull, insipid.) *Radiance*, splendor, brightness, brilliance, brilliancy, lustre, glare. (Dullness.) *Radical*, organic, innate, fundamental, original, constitutional, inherent, complete, entire. (Superficial. In a political sense, uncompromising; antonym, moderate.) *Rancid*, fetid, rank, stinking, sour, tainted, reasty. (Fresh, sweet.) *Rancor*, malignity, hatred, hostility, antipathy, animosity, enmity, ill-will, spite. (Forgiveness.) *Rank*, order, degree, dignity, nobility, consideration. *Ransack*, rummage, pillage, overhaul, explore, plunder. *Ransom*, emancipate, free, unfetter. *Rant*, bombast, fustian, cant. *Rapacious*, ravenous, voracious, greedy, grasping. (Generous.) *Rapt*, ecstatic, transported, ravished, entranced, charmed. (Distracted.) *Rapture*, ecstasy, transport, delight, bliss. (Dejection.) *Rare*, scarce, singular, uncommon, unique. *Rascal*, scoundrel, rogue, knave, scamp, vagabond. *Rash*, hasty, precipitate, foolhardy, adventurous, heedless, reckless, careless. (Deliberate.) *Rate*, value, compute, appraise, estimate, chide, abuse. *Ratify*, confirm, establish, substantiate, sanction. (Protest, oppose.) *Rational*, reasonable, sagacious, judicious, wise, sensible, sound. (Unreasonable.) *Ravage*, overrun, overspread, desolate, despoil, destroy. *Ravish*, enrapture, enchant, charm, delight, abuse. *Raze*, demolish, destroy, overthrow, ruin, dismantle. (Build up.) *Reach*, touch, stretch, attain, gain, arrive at. *Ready*, prepared, ripe, apt, prompt, adroit, handy. (Slow, dilatory.) *Real*, actual, literal, practical, positive, certain, genuine, true. (Unreal.) *Realize*, accomplish, achieve, effect, gain, get, acquire, comprehend. *Reap*, gain, get, acquire, obtain. *Reason*, n., motive, design, end, proof, cause, ground, purpose. *Reason*, v., deduce, draw from, trace, infer, conclude. *Reasonable*, rational, wise, honest, fair, right, just. (Unreasonable.) *Rebellion*, insurrection, revolt. *Recant*, recall, abjure, retract, revoke. *Recede*, retire, retreat, withdraw, ebb. *Receive*, accept, take, admit, entertain. *Reception*, receiving, levee, receipt, admission. *Recess*, retreat, depth, niche, vacation, intermission. *Recreation*, sport, pastime, play, amusement, game, fun. *Redeem*, ransom, recover, rescue, deliver, save, free. *Redress*, remedy, repair, remission, abatement, relief. *Reduce*, abate, lessen, decrease, lower, shorten, conquer. *Refined*, polite, courtly, polished, cultured, genteel, purified. (Boorish.) *Reflect*, consider, cogitate, think, ponder, muse, ruminate. *Reform*, amend, correct, better, restore, improve. (Corrupt.) *Reformation*, improvement, reform, amendment. (Corruption.) *Refuge*, asylum, protection, harbor, shelter, retreat. *Refuse*, v., deny, reject, repudiate, decline, withhold. (Accept.) *Refuse*, n., dregs, dross, scum, rubbish, leavings, remains. *Refute*, disprove, falsify, negative. (Affirm.) *Regard*, v., mind, heed, notice, behold, view, consider, respect. *Regret*, n., grief, sorrow, lamentation, repentance, remorse. *Regular*, orderly, uniform, customary, ordinary, stated. (Irregular.) *Regulate*, methodize, arrange, adjust, organize, govern, rule. (Disorder.) *Reimburse*, refund, repay, satisfy, indemnify. *Relevant*, fit, proper, suitable, appropriate, pertinent, apt. (Irrelevant.) *Reliance*, trust, hope, dependence, confidence. (Suspicion.) *Relief*, succor, aid, help, redress, alleviation. *Relinquish*, give up, forsake, resign, surrender, quit, leave, forego. (Retain.) *Remedy*, help, relief, redress, cure, specific, reparation. *Remorseless*, pitiless, relentless, cruel, ruthless, merciless, barbarous. (Merciful, humane.) *Remote*, distant, far, secluded, indirect. (Near.) *Reproduce*, propagate, imitate, represent, copy. *Repudiate*, disown, discard, disavow, renounce, disclaim. (Acknowledge.) *Repugnant*, antagonistic, distasteful. (Agreeable.) *Repulsive*, forbidding, odious, ugly, disagreeable, revolting. (Attractive.) *Respite*, reprieve, interval, stop, pause. *Revenge*, vengeance, retaliation, requital, retribution. (Forgiveness.) *Revenue*, produce, income, fruits, proceeds, wealth. *Reverence*, n., honor, respect, awe, veneration, deference, worship, homage. (Execration.) *Revise*, review, reconsider. *Revive*, refresh, renew, renovate, reanimate, resuscitate, vivify, cheer, comfort. *Rich*, wealthy, affluent, opulent, copious, ample, abundant, exuberant, plentiful, fertile, fruitful, superb, gorgeous. (Poor.) *Rival*, n., antagonist, opponent, competitor. *Road*, way, highway, route, course, path, pathway, anchorage. *Roam*, ramble, rove, wander, stray, stroll. *Robust*, strong, lusty, vigorous, sinewy, stout, sturdy, stalwart, able-bodied. (Puny.) *Rout*, v., discomfit, beat, defeat, overthrow, scatter. *Route*, road, course, march, way, journey, path, direction. *Rude*, rugged, rough, uncouth, unpolished, harsh, gruff, impertinent, saucy, flippant, impudent, insolent, churlish. (Polished, polite.) *Rule*, sway, method, system, law, maxim, precept, guide, formula, regulation, government, standard, test. *Rumor*, hearsay, talk, fame, report, bruit. *Ruthless*, cruel, savage, barbarous, inhuman, merciless, remorseless, relentless, unrelenting. (Considerate.)

SACRED, holy, hallowed, divine, consecrated, dedicated, devoted. (Profane.) *Safe*, secure, harmless, trustworthy, reliable. (Perilous, dangerous.) *Sanction*, confirm, countenance, encourage, support, ratify, authorize. (Disapprove.) *Sane*, sober, lucid, sound, rational. (Crazy.) *Saucy*, impertinent, rude, impudent, insolent, flippant, forward. (Modest.) *Scandalize*, shock, disgust, offend, calumniate, vilify, revile, malign, traduce, defame, slander. *Scanty*, bare, pinched, insufficient, slender, meager. (Ample.) *Scatter*, strew, spread, disseminate, disperse, dissipate, dispel. (Collect.) *Secret*, clandestine, concealed, hidden, sly, underhand, latent, private. (Open.) *Seduce*, allure, attract, decoy, entice, abduct, inveigle, deprave. *Sense*, discernment, appreciation, view, opinion, feeling, perception, sensibility, susceptibility, thought, judgment, signification, import, significance, meaning, purport, wisdom. *Sensible*, wise, intelligent, reasonable, sober, sound, conscious, aware. (Foolish.) *Settle*, arrange, adjust, regulate, conclude, determine. *Several*, sundry, divers, various, many. *Severe*, harsh, stern, stringent, unmitigated, rough, unyielding. (Lenient.) *Shake*, tremble, shudder, shiver, quake, quiver. *Shallow*, superficial, flimsy, slight. (Deep, thorough.) *Shame*, disgrace, dishonor. (Honor.) *Shameful*, degrading, scandalous, disgraceful, outrageous. (Honorable.) *Shameless*, immodest, impudent, indecent, indelicate, brazen. *Shape*, form, fashion, mold, model. *Share*, portion, lot, division, quantity, quota, contingent. *Sharp*, acute, keen. (Dull.) *Shine*, glare, glitter, radiate, sparkle. *Short*, brief, concise, succinct, summary. (Long.) *Show*, v., indicate, mark, point out, exhibit, display. *Show*, n., exhibition, representation, sight, spectacle. *Sick*, diseased, sickly, unhealthy, morbid. (Healthy.) *Sickness*, illness, indisposition, disease, disorder. (Health.) *Significant*, a., expressive, material, important. (Insignificant.) *Signification*, import, meaning, sense. *Silence*, speechlessness, dumbness. (Noise.) *Silent*, dumb, mute, speechless. (Talkative.) *Simile*, comparison, similitude. *Simple*, single, uncompounded, artless, plain. (Complex, compound.) *Simulate*, dissimulate, dissemble, pretend. *Sincere*, candid, hearty, honest, pure, genuine, real. (Insincere.) *Situation*, condition, plight, predicament, state, position. *Size*, bulk, greatness, magnitude, dimension. *Slavery*, servitude, enthrallment, thraldom. (Freedom.) *Sleep*, doze, drowse, nap, slumber. *Sleepy*, somnolent. (Wakeful.) *Slow*, dilatory, tardy. (Fast.) *Smell*, fragrance, odor, perfume, scent. *Smooth*, even, level, mild. (Rough.) *Soak*, drench, imbrue, steep. *Social*, sociable, friendly, communicative. (Unsocial.) *Soft*, gentle, meek, mild. (Hard.) *Solicit*, importune, urge. *Solitary*, sole, only, single. *Sorry*, grieved, poor, paltry, insignificant. (Glad, respectable.) *Soul*, mind, spirit. (Soul is opposed to body, mind to matter.) *Sound*, a., healthy, sane. (Unsound.) *Sound*, n., tone, noise, silence. *Space*, room. *Sparse*, scanty, thin. (Luxuriant.) *Speak*, converse, talk, confer, say, tell. *Special*, particular, specific. (General.) *Spend*, expend, exhaust, consume, waste, squander, dissipate. (Save.) *Sporadic*, isolated, rare. (General, prevalent.) *Spread*, disperse, diffuse, expand, disseminate, scatter. *Spring*, fountain, source. *Staff*, prop, support, stay. *Stagger*, reel, totter. *Stain*, soil, discolor, spot, sully, tarnish. *State*, commonwealth, realm. *Sterile*, barren, unfruitful. (Fertile.) *Stifle*, choke, suffocate, smother. *Stormy*, rough, boisterous, tempestuous. (Calm.) *Straight*, direct, right. (Crooked.) *Strait*, a., narrow, confined. *Stranger*, alien, foreigner. (Friend.) *Strengthen*, fortify, invigorate. (Weaken.) *Strong*, robust, sturdy, powerful. (Weak.) *Stupid*, dull, foolish, obtuse, witless. (Clever.) *Subject*, exposed to, liable, obnoxious. (Exempt.) *Subject*, inferior, subordinate.

(Superior to, above.) *Subsequent*, succeeding, following. (Previous.) *Substantial*, solid, durable. (Unsubstantial.) *Suit*, accord, agree. (Disagree.) *Superficial*, flimsy, shallow, untrustworthy. (Thorough.) *Superfluous*, unnecessary, excessive. (Necessary.) *Surround*, encircle, encompass, environ. *Sustain*, maintain, support. *Symmetry*, proportion. *Sympathy*, commiseration, compassion, condolence. *System*, method, plan, order. *Systematic*, orderly, regular, methodical. (Chaotic.)

TAKE, accept, receive. (Give.) *Talkative*, garrulous, loquacious, communicative. (Silent.) *Taste*, flavor, relish, savor. (Tastelessness.) *Tax*, custom, duty, impost, excise, toll. *Tax*, assessment, rate. *Tease*, taunt, tantalize, torment, vex. *Temporary*, a., fleeting, transient, transitory. (Permanent.) *Tenacious*, pertinacious, retentive. *Tendency*, aim, drift, scope. *Tenet*, position, view, conviction, belief. *Term*, boundary, limit, period, time. *Territory*, dominion. *Thankful*, grateful, obliged. (Thankless.) *Thankless*, ungracious, profitless, ungrateful, unthankful. *Thaw*, melt, dissolve, liquefy. (Freeze.) *Theatrical*, dramatic, showy, ceremonious, meretricious. *Theft*, robbery, depredation, spoliation. *Theme*, subject, topic, text, essay. *Theory*, speculation, scheme, plea, hypothesis, conjecture. *Therefore*, accordingly, consequently, hence. *Thick*, dense, close, compact, solid, coagulated, muddy, turbid, misty, foggy, vaporous. (Thin.) *Thin*, slim, slender, slight, flimsy, lean, attenuated, scraggy. *Think*, cogitate, consider, reflect, ponder, contemplate, meditate, muse, conceive, fancy, imagine, apprehend, hold, esteem, reckon, consider, regard, deem, believe, opine. *Thorough*, accurate, correct, trustworthy, reliable, complete. (Superficial.) *Thought*, idea, conception, imagination, fancy, conceit, notion, supposition, care, provision, consideration, opinion, view, sentiment, reflection, deliberation. *Thoughtful*, considerate, careful, cautious, heedful, contemplative, reflective, provident, pensive, dreamy. (Thoughtless.) *Thoughtless*, inconsiderate, rash, precipitate, improvident, heedless. *Tie*, v., bind, restrain, restrict, oblige, secure, unite, join. (Loose.) *Tie*, n., band, ligament, ligature. *Time*, duration, season, period, era, age, date, span, spell. *Tolerate*, allow, admit, receive, suffer, permit, let, endure, abide. (Oppose.) *Top*, summit, apex, head, crown, surface. (Bottom, base.) *Torrid*, burning, hot, parching, scorching, sultry. *Tortuous*, twisted, winding, crooked, indirect. *Torture*, torment, anguish, agony. *Touching*, tender, affecting, moving, pathetic. *Tractable*, docile, manageable, amenable. *Trade*, traffic, commerce, dealing, occupation, employment, office. *Traditional*, oral, uncertain, transmitted. *Traffic*, trade, exchange, commerce, intercourse. *Trammel*, n., fetter, shackle, clog, bond, chain, impediment, hindrance. *Tranquil*, still, unruffled, peaceful, quiet, hushed. (Noisy, boisterous.) *Transaction*, negotiation, occurrence, proceeding, affair. *Trash*, nonsense, twaddle, trifles, dross. *Travel*, trip, ramble, peregrination, excursion, journey, tour, voyage. *Treacherous*, traitorous, disloyal, treasonable, faithless, false-hearted, perfidious, sly, false. (Trustworthy, faithful.) *Trite*, stale, old, ordinary, commonplace, hackneyed. (Novel.) *Triumph*, achievement, ovation, victory, conquest, jubilation. (Failure, defeat.) *Trivial*, trifling, petty, small, frivolous, unimportant, insignificant. (Important.) *True*, genuine, actual, sincere, unaffected, true-hearted, honest, upright, veritable, real, veracious, authentic, exact, accurate, correct. *Tumultuous*, turbulent, riotous, disorderly, disturbed, confused, unruly. (Orderly.) *Tune*, tone, air, melody, strain. *Turbid*, foul, thick, muddy, impure, unsettled. *Type*, emblem, symbol, figure, sign, kind, sort, letter. *Tyro*, novice, beginner, learner.

UGLY, unsightly, plain, homely, ill-favored, hideous. (Beautiful.) *Umbrage*, offense, dissatisfaction, displeasure, resentment. *Umpire*, referee, arbitrator, judge, arbiter. *Unanimity*, accord, agreement, unity, concord. (Discord.) *Unanimous*, agreeing, like-minded. *Unbridled*, wanton, licentious, dissolute, loose, lax. *Uncertain*, doubtful, dubious, questionable, fitful, equivocal, ambiguous, indistinct, variable, fluctuating. *Uncivil*, rude, discourteous, disrespectful, disobliging. (Civil.) *Unclean*, dirty, foul, filthy, sullied. (Clean.) *Uncommon*, rare, strange, scarce, singular, choice. (Common, ordinary.) *Unconcerned*, careless, indifferent, apathetic. (Anxious.) *Uncouth*, strange, odd, clumsy, ungainly. (Graceful.) *Uncover*, reveal, strip, expose, lay bare, divest. (Hide.) *Under*, below, underneath, beneath, subordinate, lower, inferior. (Above.) *Understanding*, knowledge, intellect, intelligence, faculty, comprehension, mind, reason, brains. *Undertake*, engage in, embark in, agree, promise. *Undo*, annul, frustrate, untie, unfasten, destroy. *Uneasy*, restless, disturbed, unquiet, stiff, awkward. (Quiet.) *Unequal*, uneven, not alike, irregular, insufficient. (Even.) *Unequaled*, matchless, unique, novel, new, unheard of. *Unfair*, wrongful, dishonest, unjust. (Fair.) *Unfit*, a., improper, unsuitable, inconsistent, untimely, incongruous. (Fit.) *Unfit*, v., disable, incapacitate, disqualify. (Fit.) *Unfortunate*, calamitous, ill-fated, unlucky, wretched, unhappy, miserable. (Fortunate.) *Ungainly*, clumsy, awkward, lumbering.

ing, unusual. (Pretty.) *Unhappy*, miserable, wretched, distressed, afflicted, painful, disastrous, drear, dismal. (Happy.) *Uniform*, regular, symmetrical, equal, even, alike, unvaried. (Irregular.) *Uninterrupted*, continuous, perpetual, unceasing, incessant, endless. (Intermittent.) *Union*, junction, combination, alliance, confederacy, league, coalition, agreement, concert. (Disunion, separation.) *Unique*, unequal, uncommon, rare, choice, matchless. (Common, ordinary.) *Unite*, join, conjoin, combine, concert, add, attach, incorporate, embody, clench, merge. (Separate, disrupt, sunder.) *Universal*, general, all, entire, total, catholic. (Sectional.) *Unlimited*, absolute, undefined, boundless, infinite. (Limited.) *Unreasonable*, foolish, silly, absurd, preposterous, ridiculous. *Unrivaled*, unequaled, unique, unexampled, incomparable, matchless. (Mediocre.) *Unroll*, unfold, open, discover. *Unruly*, ungovernable, unmanageable, refractory. (Tractable, docile.) *Unusual*, rare, unwonted, singular, uncommon, remarkable, strange, extraordinary. (Common.) *Uphold*, maintain, defend, sustain, support, vindicate. (Desert, abandon.) *Upright*, vertical, perpendicular, erect, just, equitable, fair, pure, honorable. (Prone, horizontal.) *Uprightness*, honesty, integrity, fairness, goodness, probity, virtue, honor. (Dishonesty.) *Urge*, incite, impel, push, drive, instigate, stimulate, press, induce, solicit. *Urgent*, pressing, importunate, imperative, immediate, serious, wanted. (Unimportant.) *Usage*, custom, fashion, practice, prescription. *Use*, n., usage, practice, habit, custom, avail, advantage, utility, benefit, application. (Disuse, desuetude.) *Use*, v., employ, exercise, occupy, practice, accustom, inure. (Abuse.) *Useful*, advantageous, serviceable, available, helpful, beneficial, good. (Useless.) *Useless*, unserviceable, fruitless, idle, profitless. (Useful.) *Usual*, ordinary, common, accustomed, habitual, wonted, customary, general. (Unusual.) *Usurp*, arrogate, seize, appropriate, assume. *Utmost*, farthest, remotest, uttermost, greatest. *Utter*, a., extreme, excessive, sheer, mere, pure. *Utter*, v., speak, articulate, pronounce, express, issue. *Utterly*, totally, completely, wholly, quite, altogether, entirely.

VACANT, empty, unfilled, unoccupied, thoughtless, unthinking. (Occupied.) *Vagrant*, n., wanderer, beggar, tramp, vagabond, rogue. *Vague*, unsettled, undetermined, uncertain, pointless, indefinite. (Definite.) *Vain*, useless, fruitless, empty, worthless, inflated, proud, conceited, unreal, unavailing. (Effectual, humble, real.) *Valiant*, brave, bold, valorous, courageous, gallant. (Cowardly.) *Valid*, weighty, strong, powerful, sound, binding, efficient. (Invalid.) *Valor*, courage, gallantry, boldness, bravery, heroism. (Cowardice.) *Value*, v., appraise, assess, reckon, appreciate, estimate, prize, esteem, treasure. (Despise, condemn.) *Vanish*, disappear, fade, melt, dissolve. *Vanity*, emptiness, conceit, self-conceit, affectedness. *Vapid*, dull, flat, insipid, stale, tame. (Sparkling.) *Vapor*, fume, smoke, mist, fog, steam. *Variable*, changeable, unsteady, inconstant, shifting, wavering, fickle, restless, fitful. (Constant.) *Variety*, difference, diversity, change, diversification, mixture, medley, miscellany. (Sameness, monotony.) *Vast*, spacious, boundless, mighty, enormous, immense, colossal, gigantic, huge, prodigious. (Confined.) *Vaunt*, boast, brag, puff, hawk, advertise, flourish, parade. *Venerable*, grave, sage, wise, old, reverend. *Venial*, pardonable, excusable, justifiable. (Grave, serious.) *Venom*, poison, virus, spite, malice, malignity. *Venture*, n., speculation, chance, peril, stake. *Venture*, v., dare, adventure, risk, hazard, jeopardize. *Veracity*, truth, truthfulness, credibility, accuracy. (Falsehood.) *Verbal*, oral, spoken, literal, parole, unwritten. *Verdict*, judgment, finding, decision, answer. *Vexation*, chagrin, mortification. (Pleasure.) *Vibrate*, oscillate, swing, sway, wave, undulate, thrill. *Vice*, viciousness, corruption, depravity, pollution, immorality, wickedness, guilt, iniquity, crime. (Virtue.) *Vicious*, corrupt, depraved, debased, bad, contrary, unruly, demoralized, profligate, faulty. (Virtuous, gentle.) *Victim*, sacrifice, food, prey, sufferer, dupe, gull. *Victuals*, viands, bread, meat, provisions, fare, food, repast. *View*, prospect, survey. *Violent*, boisterous, furious, impetuous, vehement. (Gentle.) *Virtuous*, upright, honest, moral. (Profligate.) *Vision*, apparition, ghost, phantom, specter. *Voluptuary*, epicure, sensualist. *Vote*, suffrage, voice. *Vouch*, affirm, asseverate, assure, aver.

WAIT, await, expect, look for, wait for. *Wakeful*, vigilant, watchful. (Sleepy.) *Wander*, range, ramble, roam, rove, stroll. *Want*, lack, need. (Abundance.) *Wary*, circumspect, cautious. (Foolhardy.) *Wash*, clean, rinse, wet, moisten, stain, tint. *Waste*, v., squander, dissipate, lavish, destroy, decay, dwindle, wither. *Wasteful*, extravagant, profligate. (Economical.) *Way*, method, plan, system, means, manner, mode, form, fashion, course, process, road, route, track, path, habit, practice. *Wave*, breaker, billow, surge. *Weak*, feeble, infirm. (Strong.) *Weaken*, debilitate, enfeeble, enervate, invalidate. (Strengthen.) *Wearisome*, tedious, tiresome. (Interesting, entertaining.) *Weary*, harass, jade, tire, fatigue. (Refresh.) *Weight*, gravity, heaviness, burden, load. (Lightness.) *Well-being*, happiness, prosperity, welfare. *Whole*, entire, complete, total, integral. (Part.)

Wicked, iniquitous, nefarious. (Virtuous.) *Will*, wish, desire. *Willingly*, spontaneously, voluntarily. (Unwillingly.) *Win*, get, obtain, gain, procure, effect, realize, accomplish, achieve. (Lose.) *Winning*, attractive, charming, fascinating, bewitching, enchanting, dazzling, brilliant. (Repulsive.) *Wisdom*, prudence, foresight, far-sightedness, sagacity. (Foolishness.) *Wit*, humor, satire, fun, raillery. *Wonder*, v., admire, amaze, astonish, surprise. *Wonder*, n., marvel, miracle, prodigy. *Word*, n., expression, term. *Work*, labor, task, toil. (Play.) *Worthless*, valueless. (Valuable.) *Writer*, author, penman. *Wrong*, injustice, injury. (Right.)

YAWN, gape, open wide. *Yearn*, hanker after, long for, desire, crave. *Yell*, bellow, cry out, scream. *Yellow*, golden, saffron-like. *Yelp*, bark, sharp cry, howl. *Yet*, besides, nevertheless, notwithstanding, however, still, ultimately, at last, so far, thus far. *Yield*, bear, give, afford, impart, communicate, confer, bestow, abdicate, resign, cede, surrender, relinquish, relax, quit, forego, give up, let go, waive, comply, accede, assent, acquiesce, succumb, submit. *Yielding*, supple, pliant, bending, compliant, submissive, unresisting. (Obstinate.) *Yoke*, v., couple, link, connect. *Yore*, long ago, long since. *Young*, juvenile inexperienced, ignorant, youthful. *Youth*, boy, lad, minority, adolescence, juvenility. *Youthful*, young, juvenile, boyish, girlish, puerile. (Old.)

ZEAL, energy, fervor, ardor, earnestness, enthusiasm, eagerness. (Indifference.) *Zealous*, warm, ardent, fervent, enthusiastic, anxious. (Indifferent, careless.) *Zest*, relish, gusto, flavor. (Disgust.)

Facts about Gold and Silver.

A ton of gold or silver contains 29,166.66 ounces.

A ton of gold is worth $602,875; silver, $37,704.84.

The United States money standard for gold and silver is 900 parts pure metal and 100 parts of alloy in 1,000 parts of coin.

The value of an ounce of pure gold is $20.67,183; 23.22 grains of pure gold equals $1.

The term karat when used to distinguish fineness of gold means one-twenty-fourth; pure gold is 24-karat gold.

A cubic foot of gold weighs 1,208 pounds, and is worth about $300,000.

In round numbers the weight of $1,000,000 in standard gold coin is 1¾ tons (3,685 lbs.); standard silver coin, 26¾ tons; subsidiary silver coin, 25 tons; minor coin, 5-cent nickel, 100 tons.

Glossary of Mining and Milling Terms.

Battery—Generally applied to a set of five stamps. *Bullion*—Ingots of gold or silver ready for the mint. *Bumping table*—A concentrating table with a jolting motion. *Cage*—A mine elevator. *Chute*—A body of ore, usually elongated, extending downward within a vein; a slide for ore or waste rock. *Cobbing*—Breaking ore for sorting. *Concentrator*—Machine for removing waste matter from mineral. *Copper plates*—Plates of copper coated with quicksilver, upon which the gold is caught as the ore flows from the stamps. *Cord*—A cord weighs about eight tons. *Country-rock*—The rock on each side of a vein. *Crevice*—A fissure, split or crack; the vein is called "the crevice." *Cribbing*—The timbers used to confine wall rock. *Cross-cut*—A level driven across the course of a vein. *Deposit*—Ore bodies not confined to a lode. *Drift*—A tunnel; a horizontal passage underground. *Dump*—A place of deposit for ore or refuse. *Feeder*—A small vein joining a larger one. *Fissure-vein*—A crack or cleft in the earth's crust filled with mineral matter. *Float*—Loose ore or rock detached from the original formation. *Flume*—A pipe or trough to convey water. *Foot-wall*—Layer of rock beneath the vein. *Free milling*—Ores containing mineral that will separate from the gangue by simple methods. *Hanging-wall*—The layer or rock, or wall, over a lode. *Ladder-way*—That part of mine-shaft containing the ladders. *Lagging*—Timbers over and upon the sides of a drift. *Ledge or Lead*—Mineral ores or gangue within fissure veins. *Mill-run*—A test of the value of a given quantity of ore. *Ore*—Compound of metals with oxygen, sulphur, arsenic, etc. *Pay-streak*—The richest streak in the vein. *Pocket*—A rich spot in the vein or deposit. *Refractory*—Resisting the action of heat and chemical re-agents. *Shaft*—A well-like passage into a mine. *Sluices*—Troughs in which ore is washed. *Smelting*—Reduction of ores in furnaces. *Spur*—A branch of a vein. *Stamps*—Weights for crushing ores. *Stope*—The part of a vein above or below the drift from which the ore has been removed. *Stoping*—Excavating the ore from the roof or floor of a drift. *Stratum*—A bed or layer. *Stulls*—A framework to support the rubbish when stoping. *Sump*—A well at the bottom of a shaft to collect water. *Tailings*—The refuse left after the washing ores containing metals not saved in the first treatment. *Tunnel*—A level driven across a vein. *Whim*—A machine used for raising ore or refuse. *Winze*—An interior shaft sunk from one level to another.

Parliamentary Law at a Glance

LIST OF MOTIONS ARRANGED ACCORDING TO THEIR PURPOSE AND EFFECT

Letters refer to Rules below.

Modifying or amending.
- 8. To amend or to substitute, or to divide the question .... K

To refer to committee.
- 7. To commit (or recommit) ...... D

Deferring action.
- 6. To postpone to a fixed time C
- 4. To lay on the table .... A E G

Suppressing or extending debate.
- 5. For the previous question ...... A E M
- To limit, or close, debate .... A M
- To extend limits of debate ...... A

Suppressing the question.
- Objection to consideration of question .... A E M N
- 9. To postpone indefinitely .... D F
- 4. To lay upon the table .... A E G

To bring up a question the second time.
- To reconsider debatable question .... D E F I
- To reconsider undebatable question .... A E F I

Concerning Orders, Rules, etc.
- 3. For the orders of the day .... A E H N
- To make subject a special order . M
- To amend the rules .... M
- To suspend the rules .... A E F M
- To take up a question out of its proper order .... A E
- To take from the table .... A E G
- Questions touching priority of business .... A

Questions of privilege.
- Asking leave to continue speaking after indecorum .... A
- Appeal from chair's decision touching indecorum .... A E H L
- Appeal from chair's decision generally .... E H L
- Question upon reading of papers A E
- Withdrawal of a motion .... A E

Closing a meeting.
- 2. To adjourn (in committees, to rise), or to take a recess, without limitation .... A E F
- 1. To fix time to which to adjourn E

ORDER OF PRECEDENCE.—*The motions above numbered 1 to 9 take precedence over all others in the order given, and any one of them, except to amend or substitute, is in order while a motion of a lower rank is pending.*

RULE A. Undebatable, but remarks may be tacitly allowed.

RULE B. Undebatable if another question is before the assembly.

RULE C. Limited debate allowed on propriety of postponement only.

RULE D. Opens the main question to debate. Motions not so marked do not allow of reference to main question.

RULE E. Cannot be amended. Motion to adjourn can be amended when there is no other business before the house.

RULE F. Cannot be reconsidered.

RULE G. An affirmative vote cannot be reconsidered.

RULE H. In order when another has the floor.

RULE I. A motion to reconsider may be moved and entered when another has the floor, but the business then before the house may not be set aside. This motion can only be entertained when made by one who voted originally with the prevailing side. When called up it takes precedence of all others which may come up, excepting only motions relating to adjournment.

RULE K. A motion to amend an amendment cannot be amended.

RULE L. When an appeal from the chair's decision results in a tie vote, the chair is sustained.

RULE M. Requires a two-thirds vote unless special rules have been enacted.

RULE N. Does not require to be seconded.

General Rules.

No motion is open for discussion until it has been stated by the chair.

The maker of a motion cannot modify it or withdraw it after it has been stated by the chair, except by general consent.

Only one reconsideration of a question is permitted.

A motion to adjourn, to lay on the table, or to take from the table, cannot be renewed unless some other motion has been made in the interval.

On motion to strike out the words, "Shall the words stand part of the motion?" unless a majority sustains the words, they are struck out.

On motion for previous question, the form to be observed is, "Shall the main question be now put?" This, if carried, ends debate.

On an appeal from the chair's decision, "Shall the decision be sustained as the ruling of the house?" the chair is generally sustained.

On motion for orders of the day, "Will the house now proceed to the orders of the day?" This, if carried, supersedes intervening motions.

When an objection is raised to considering questions, "Shall the question be considered?" objection may be made by any member before debate has commenced, but not subsequently.

Legal Advice

"Ignorance of the law excuses no one."

BLACKSTONE defines law as the rules of human action or conduct, but what is commonly understood by the term is the civil or municipal regulations of a nation as applied to a particular country. The forms of law which govern civil contracts and business intercourse are distinguished as statute and common. Statute law is the written law of the land, as enacted by State or National legislative bodies. The common law is grounded on the general customs of England, and includes the law of nature, the law of God, the principles and maxims of the law and the decisions of the superior courts. It overrides both the canon and the civil law where they go beyond or are inconsistent with it.

To the man involved in litigation the best advice is to go to the best lawyer he can find. But an ounce of prevention is worth a pound of cure, and the purpose of the following pages is to furnish the ounce of prevention. Knowledge is power in nothing so much as in business law, especially since the law presumes that no man is ignorant of the law.

Business Law in Brief.

Ignorance of the law excuses no one.

It is a fraud to conceal a fraud.

The law compels no one to do impossibilities.

An agreement without consideration is void.

Signatures made with a lead pencil are good in law.

A receipt for money paid is not legally conclusive.

The act of one partner binds all the others.

The seal of a party to a written contract imports consideration.

A contract made with a minor cannot be enforced against him. A note made by a minor is voidable.

A contract made with a lunatic is void.

A contract made on a Sunday is void.

Principals are liable for the acts of their agents.

Agents are liable to their principals for errors.

Each individual in a partnership is liable for the whole amount of the debts of the firm.

A note which does not state on its face that it bears interest, will bear interest only after due.

A lease of land for a longer term than one year is void unless in writing.

An indorser of a note is exempt from liability if notice of its dishonor is not mailed or served within twenty-four hours of its non-payment.

In case of the death of the principal maker of a note the holder is not required to notify a surety that the note is not paid, before the settlement of the maker's estate.

Notes obtained by fraud, or made by an intoxicated person, are not collectible.

If no time of payment is specified in a note it is payable on demand.

An indorser can avoid liability by writing "without recourse" beneath his signature.

A check indorsed by the payee is evidence of payment in the drawer's hands.

An outlawed debt is revived should the debtor make a partial payment.

Want of consideration—a common defense interposed to the payment of negotiable paper—is a good defense between the original parties to the paper; but after it has been transferred before maturity to an innocent holder for value it is not a defense.

Negotiable paper, payable to bearer or indorsed in blank, which has been stolen or lost, cannot be collected by the thief or finder, but a holder who receives it in good faith before maturity, for value, can hold it against the owner's claims at the time it was lost.

Sometimes the holder of paper has the right to demand payment before maturity; for instance, when a draft has been protested for non-acceptance and the proper notices served, the holder may at once proceed against the drawer and indorsers.

If a note or draft is to be paid in the State where it is made, the contract will be governed by the laws of that State. When negotiable paper is payable in a State other than that in which it is made, the laws of that State will govern it. Marriage contracts, if valid where they are made, are valid everywhere. Contracts relating to personal property are governed by the laws of the place where made, except those relating to real estate, which are governed by the laws of the place where the land is situated.

If negotiable paper, pledged to a bank as security for the payment of a loan or debt, falls due, and the bank fails to demand payment and have it protested when dishonored, the bank is liable to the owner for the full amount of the paper.

Agreements and Contracts.

A contract or agreement is where a promise is made on one side and assented to on the other, or where two or more persons enter into engagement with each other by a promise on either side. In a written contract assent is proved by the signature or mark. In verbal agreements it may be given by a word or assent, by shaking of hands, or by a sign. The old saw, "Silence gives consent," is often upheld in law.

The conditions of a contract, as applying to individuals, are: 1. Age; 2. Rationality; and 3, as to Corporations, the possession of general or special statutory powers.

Persons under age are incompetent to make contracts, except under certain limitations. Generally such persons are incapable of making binding contracts.

As to rationality, the general principle of law is that all persons not rendered incompetent by personal disability, or by considerations of public policy, are capable of making a contract.

Corporations have powers to make contracts strictly within the limits prescribed by their charters, or by special or general statute.

The first step toward a contract is the proposition or offer, which may be withdrawn at any time before it is agreed to. When the proposition is verbal, and no time is specified, it is not binding unless accepted at once. To give one the option or refusal of property at a specified price, is simply to give him a certain time to make up his mind whether he will buy the property or not. To make the option binding he must accept within the time named. The party giving the option has the right to withdraw it, and sell the property to another, at any time previous to its acceptance, if the offer is gratuitous, and there is no consideration to support it.

If a letter of acceptance is mailed, and immediately after a letter withdrawing the offer is received, the contract is binding. An acceptance takes effect from the time it is mailed, not from the time it is received; it must, however, be in accordance with the original proposition, for any new matter introduced would constitute a new offer. When the offer is accepted, either verbally or in writing, it is an express assent, and is binding.

A contract made under a mistake of law is not void. Everybody is presumed to know the law. This, however, applies only to contracts permitted by law and clear of fraud.

A refusal of an offer cannot be retracted without the consent of the second party. Once a proposition is refused, the matter is ended. And no one has the right to accept an offer except the person to whom it was made.

The consideration is the reason or thing for which the parties bind themselves in the contract, and it is either a benefit to the promisor or an injury to the other party. Considerations are technically divided into valuable and good, and it sometimes happens that the consideration need not be expressed, but is implied. A valuable consideration is either money or property or service to be given, or some injury to the contractor. A promise to marry is considered a valuable consideration. A good consideration means that the contract is entered into because of consanguinity or affection, which will support the contract when executed, but will not support an action to enforce an executory contract. Whether a consideration is sufficient or not is tested by its being a benefit to the promisor or an injury to the other party. If it has a legal value, it makes no difference how small that value may be. The promisor need not always be benefited, as, for instance, the indorser of a note, who is liable although he gets no benefit. But if a person promise to do something himself for which no consideration is to be received, there is no cause of action for breach of the contract.

There are several causes which void contracts, first among which is fraud. Fraud is defined to be "every kind of artifice employed by one person for the purpose of wilfully deceiving another to his injury." No fraudulent contract will stand in law or in equity. The party upon whom the fraud has been practiced must void the contract as soon as he discovers the fraud, for if he goes on after having knowledge of the fraud he cannot afterwards void it. But the one who perpetrates the fraud cannot plead that ground for voiding it. Contracts in restraint of trade are void, as also are contracts in opposition to public policy, impeding the course of justice, in restraint of marriage, contrary to the insolvent acts, or for immoral purposes. Any violation of the essential requisites of a contract, or the omission of an essential requisite, will void it.

DON'T enter into an agreement on a Sunday unless it is ratified on a week day.

DON'T make a contract with a person of unsound mind or under the influence of liquor, or otherwise under restraint of liberty, mind or body. Use caution in making contracts with an illiterate, blind or deaf and dumb person, and see to it that witnesses are present.

DON'T put a forced construction on a contract—the intent of the parties is a contract.

DON'T suppose that you can withdraw a proposition made in writing and sent by mail after the party to whom it was made has mailed an unconditional acceptance.

DON'T suppose that a conditional acceptance of a proposition is binding on the party making the proposition.

DON'T forget that the courts will construe a contract according to the law prevailing where it was made.

DON'T forget that the law says, "No consideration, no contract," and that the courts will not enforce a contract which is too severe in its provisions.

DON'T sign an agreement unless you have carefully weighed its provisions, which should all be fixed and certain.

Notes and Negotiable Paper.

The superstructure of business as it exists to-day rests on the broad foundation of confidence — the result of what may be called the evolution of commerce, and the principal stages in this evolution are an interesting study. First there was only barter in kind, as still practiced among savages—for example, the exchange of a bushel of corn for a handful of arrow-heads. Then came the introduction of money as a medium of exchange; and to-day we have the substitution of negotiable paper as documentary evidence of indebtedness, including promissory notes, due bills, drafts, checks, certificates of deposit, bills of exchange, bank bills, treasury notes (greenbacks), and all other evidences of debt, the ownership of which may be transferred from one person to another.

The mere acknowledgment of debt is not sufficient to make negotiable paper; the *promise* of payment or an order on some one to pay is indispensable. This promise must be for money only. The amount must be exactly specified. The title must be transferable. This feature must be visible on the face of the paper by the use of such words as "bearer" or "order." In some of the States peculiar phrases are ordered by statute, as "Payable without defalcation or discount," or "Payable at ——," naming the bank or office.

A written agreement, signed by one person, to pay another, at a fixed time, a stated sum of money, is a *promissory note*. It becomes negotiable by being made payable to an order or some one or to bearer. As it is a contract, a consideration is one of its essential elements. Yet, although it be void as between the two first parties, being negotiable and coming into the hands of another person who gives value for it, not knowing of its defect, it has full force and may be collected.

The date is of great consequence. In computing time, the day of date is not counted, but it is the fixed point beginning the time at the end of which payment must be made. Omission of the date does not destroy a note, but the holder must prove to the time of its making. The promise to pay must be precise as to time which the note is to run. It must be at a fixed period, or conditional upon the occurrence of something certain to happen, as "at sight," "five days after sight," "on demand," "three months after date," "ten days after the death of John Doe." The time not being specified, the note is considered "payable on demand."

The maker, the person who promises and whose signature the note bears, must be competent. Insane people and idiots are *naturally*, and aliens, minors and married women may be *legally*, incompetent. The maker is responsible and binds himself to pay the amount stated on the note at its maturity. He need not pay it before it becomes due, but should he do so and neglect to cancel the note, he would be again responsible if any other person, without knowledge of such payment, acquired it for value before maturity. Even a receipt for payment from the first payee would not stand good against the subsequent holder.

The payee is the person in whose favor the note is drawn; the legal holder, the person to whom the money must be paid. When a note is made payable simply to bearer, without naming the payee, any one holding the note honestly may collect.

A subsequent party, one who comes into possession of the note after the original holder, has a better claim than the first one, for the reason that between the maker and the first payee there may have been, in the contract, some understanding or condition militating against the payment when it should become due, but the third person, knowing nothing of this, gives his value and receives the note. The law will always sustain the subsequent party.

The indorser is held responsible if the maker fails to pay when the note arrives at maturity. A note payable to order must be indorsed by a holder upon passing it to another, and, as value has been given each time, the last holder will look to his next preceding one and to all the others.

A note, being on deposit as collateral security, becoming due, the temporary holder is the payee and must collect.

An indorsement is a writing across the back of the note which makes the writer responsible for the amount of the note. There are various forms of indorsement:

1. *In blank*, the indorser simply writing his name on the back of the note.

2. *General*, or *in full*, the indorser writing above his signature "Pay ———" or "Pay ——— or order."

3. *Qualified*, the words "without recourse" being used after the name of the payee in the indorsement.

4. *Conditional*, a condition being stated, as: "Pay ————, unless payment forbidden before maturity."

5. *Restrictive*, as: "Pay ———— only."

The blank indorsement, the full indorsement and the general indorsement are practically the same; each entitles the holder of the note to the money, and to look to the indorser for payment if the maker of the note defaults. It has even been held that in a general indorsement the holder had the right to fill in the words "or order" if he saw fit. The qualified indorsement relieves the indorser from any liability in case the maker of the note defaults. The conditional and restrictive indorsements are used only in special cases. Each indorser is severally and collectively liable for the whole amount of the note indorsed if it is dishonored, provided it is duly protested and notice given to each. The indorser looks to the man who indorsed it before him, and so back to the original maker of the note. As soon as a note is protested it is vitally necessary that notice should be sent to each person interested at once.

TO BE ON THE SAFE SIDE, it is well to see to it that any note offered for negotiation—

Is dated correctly;

Specifies the amount of money to be paid;

Names the person to whom it is to be paid;

Includes the words "or order" after the name of the payee, if it is desired to make the note negotiable;

Appoints a place where the payment is to be made;

States that the note is made for "value received;"

And is signed by the maker or his duly authorized representative.

In some States phrases are required in the body of the note, such as "without defalcation or discount;" but, as a general rule, that fact is understood without the statement.

Partnership.

The general rule is that every person of sound mind, and not otherwise restrained by law, may enter into a contract of partnership.

There are several kinds of partners:

1. *Ostensible* partners, or those whose names are made public as partners, and who in reality are such, and who take all the benefits and risks.

2. *Nominal* partners, or those who appear before the public as partners, but who have no real interest in the business.

3. *Dormant*, or *silent* partners, or those whose names are not known or do not appear as partners, but who, nevertheless, have an interest in the business.

4. *Special*, or *limited* partners, or those who are interested in the business only to the amount of the capital they have invested in it.

5. *General* partners, who manage the business, while the capital, either in whole or in part, is supplied by a special partner or partners. They are liable for all the debts and contracts of the firm.

A nominal partner renders himself liable for all the debts and contracts of the firm.

A dormant partner, if it becomes known that he has an interest, whether creditors trusted the firm on his account or not, becomes liable equally with the other partners.

The regulations concerning special or limited partnerships, in any particular State where recognized, are to be found in the statutes of such State; and strict compliance with the statutes is necessary in order to avoid incurring the responsibilities attaching to the position of general partner.

A person who lends his name as a partner, or who suffers his name to continue in the firm after he has actually ceased to be a partner thereof, is still responsible to third persons as a partner.

A partner may buy and sell partnership effects; make contracts in reference to the business of the firm; pay and receive money; draw, and indorse, and accept bills and notes; and all acts of such a nature, even though they be upon his own private account, will bind the other partners, if connected with matters apparently having reference to the business of the firm, and transacted with other parties ignorant of the fact that such dealings are for the particular partner's private account. The representation or misrepresentation of any fact made in any partnership transaction by one partner, or the commission of any fraud in such transaction, will bind the entire firm, even though the other partners may have no connection with, or knowledge of, the same.

If a partner sign his individual name to negotiable paper, all the partners are bound thereby, if such paper appear on its face to be on partnership account. If negotiable paper of a firm be given by one partner on his private account, and in the course of its circulation pass into the hands of a *bona fide* holder for value, without notice or knowledge of the fact attending its creation, the partnership is bound thereby.

One partner cannot bind the firm by deed, though he may by deed execute an ordinary release of a debt due the partnership.

If no time be fixed in articles of copartnership for the commencement thereof, it is presumed to commence from the date and execution of the articles. If no precise period is mentioned for continuance, a partner may withdraw at any time, and dissolve such partnership at his pleasure; and even if a definite period be agreed upon, a partner may, by giving notice, dissolve the partnership as to all capacity of the firm to bind him by contracts thereafter made. The withdrawing partner subjects himself, however, to a claim for damages by reason of his breach of the covenant.

The death of a partner dissolves the partnership, unless there be an express stipulation that, in such an event, the representatives of the deceased partner may continue the business in connection with the survivors, for the benefit of the widow and children.

A partnership is dissolved by operation of law; by a voluntary and *bona fide* assignment by any partner of his interest therein; by the bankruptcy or death of any of the partners; or by a war between the countries of which the partners are subjects.

Immediately after a dissolution, notice of the same should be published in the papers, and a special notice sent to every person who has had dealings with the firm. If these precautions be not taken, each partner will still continue liable for the acts of the others to all persons who have had no notice of such dissolution.

DON'T enter into a partnership without carefully drawn articles, and don't sign the articles until the partnership funds are on deposit.

DON'T forget that a partner may be called upon to make good partnership losses with his individual property, and that each partner may be held for the acts of the other partners as well as for his own.

DON'T enter a firm already established unless you are willing to become responsible for its debts.

DON'T do anything out of the usual run of business without the consent of your partners.

DON'T mix private matters with partnership affairs, and don't continue in a partnership where trust and confidence are lacking.

DON'T continue a partnership after expiration of articles, and don't make any change without due public notice.

DON'T dissolve a partnership without due public notice or without designating a member to settle all matters outstanding.

Agency and Attorney.

By agency is meant the substitution of one person by and for another, the former to transact business for the latter. An agency may be established by implication—an express agreement with a person that he is to become the agent of another not being necessary—or verbally, or by writing. A verbal creation of an agency suffices to authorize the agent to make a contract even in cases where such contract must be in writing.

Agency is of three kinds: special, general and professional. A special agency is an authority exercised for a special purpose. If a special agent exceed the limits of his authority, his principal is not bound by his acts.

A general agency authorizes the transaction of all business of a particular kind, or growing out of a particular employment. The principal will be bound by the acts of a general agent, though the latter act contrary to private instructions, provided he keep, at the same time, within the general limits of his authority.

Professional agents are those licensed by the proper authority to transact certain kinds of business for a compensation. The following are among this class of agents: 1. Attorneys; 2. Brokers; 3. Factors; 4. Auctioneers; 5. Masters of ships.

In regard to the subject of an agency, the general rule is, that whatever a man may do in his own right he may also transact through another. Things of a personal nature, implying personal confidence on the part of the person possessing them, cannot be delegated.

Infants, married women, lunatics, idiots, aliens, belligerents, and persons incapable of making legal contracts, cannot act as principals in the appointment of agents. Infants and married women may, however, become principals in certain cases.

Agency may be terminated in two ways: (1) by the act of the principal or agent; (2) by operation of law. In the latter case, the termination of the agency is effected by lapse of time, by the completion of the subject-matter of the agency, by the extinction of the subject-matter, or by the insanity, bankruptcy or death of either party.

DON'T do through another what would be illegal for you to do yourself.

DON'T lose any time in repudiating illegal acts of your agent.

DON'T make an illegal act of your agent's your own by accepting the benefit thereof.

DON'T transact business through an agent unless he can show that he stands in his principal's stead in the matter in hand.

DON'T, as agent, appoint sub-agents without the consent of your principal.

DON'T go beyond your authority in an agency unless you are willing to become personally responsible.

DON'T accept an agency, or act as an attorney in fact, in complicated matters, unless your powers are clearly defined in writing.

Landlord and Tenant.

Leases for one year or less need no written agreement. Leases for more than a year must be in writing; if for life, signed, sealed and witnessed in the same manner as any other important document.

Leases for over three years must be recorded. No particular form is necessary.

If no agreement in writing for more than a year can be produced, the tenant holds the property from year to year at the will of the landlord. If there is no agreement as to time, the tenant, as a rule, holds from year to year.

A tenancy at will may be terminated by giving the tenant one month's notice, requiring him to remove from the premises occupied.

A tenant is not responsible for taxes unless it is so stated in the lease.

The tenant may underlet as much of the property as he desires, unless it is expressly forbidden in the lease. Tenants at will cannot underlet.

A married woman cannot lease her property under the common law, but this provision is removed by statute in most of the States. A husband cannot make a lease which will bind his wife's property after his death.

A lease made by a minor is not binding after the minor has attained his majority. It binds the lessee, however, unless the minor should release him. Should the minor receive rent after attaining his majority, the lease will be thereby ratified. A lease given by a guardian will not extend beyond the majority of the ward.

A new lease renders void a former lease.

In case there are no writings, the tenancy begins from the day possession is taken; where there are writings and the time of commencement is not stated, the tenancy will be held to commence from the date of said writings.

Leases on mortgaged property, whereon the mortgage was given prior to the lease, terminate when the mortgage is foreclosed.

Where a tenant assigns his lease, even with the landlord's consent, he will remain liable for the rent unless his lease is surrendered or canceled.

There are many special features of the law of landlord and tenant in relation to agricultural tenancy. Generally an outgoing tenant cannot sell or take away the manure. A tenant whose estate has terminated by an uncertain event which he could neither foresee nor control is entitled to the annual crop which he sowed while his estate continued, by the law of emblements. He may also, in certain cases, take the emblements or annual profits of the land after his tenancy has ended, and, unless restricted by some stipulation to the contrary, may remove such fixtures as he has erected during his occupation for convenience, profit or comfort; for, in general, what a tenant has added he may remove, if he can do so without injury to the premises, unless he has actually built it in so as to make it an integral part of what was there originally.

The following are immovable fixtures: Agricultural erections, fold-yard walls, cart house, barns fixed in the ground, beast house, carpenter shop, fuel house, pigeon house, pineries substantially fixed, wagon house, hot houses not belonging to a gardener by trade, flowers, trees, hedges, ale-house bar, dressers, partitions, locks and keys, benches affixed to the house, statue erected as an ornament to grounds, sun dial, chimney piece not ornamental, closets affixed to the house, conduits, conservatory substantially affixed, doors, fruit trees if a tenant be not a nurseryman by trade, glass windows, hearths, millstones, looms substantially affixed to the floor of a factory, threshing-machines fixed by bolts and screws to posts let into the ground.

DON'T occupy premises until a written lease is in your possession, and don't depend on promises of a landlord unless they are part of such lease.

DON'T accept a married woman as tenant unless the law of the State permit her to make an executory contract.

DON'T think that you can legally eject subtenants unless you have given them notice of the tenant's forfeiture of his lease.

DON'T make such improvements in premises occupied by you as the law would regard as immovable fixtures, unless you are willing to turn them over to the landlord when your lease expires. A building erected on foundations sunk into the ground would become part of the realty and thus belong to the landlord.

DON'T think, however, that you have no right to remove trade fixtures erected by you.

DON'T accept less than thirty days' notice when you rent by the month.

DON'T forget that where premises are let for illegal use the law will not aid you in collecting arrears for rent.

Law Relating to Farms, Etc.

In a deed to agricultural property the boundaries should be clearly determined. The question, What does the farmer get? is answered by these boundaries; and the deed to a farm always includes the dwelling houses, barns and other improvements thereon belonging to the grantor, even though these are not mentioned. It also conveys all the fences standing on the farm, but all might not think it also included the fencing-stuff, posts, rails, etc., which had once been used in the fence, but had been taken down and piled up for future use again in the same place. But new fencing material, just bought, and never attached to the soil, would not pass. So piles of hop poles, stored away, if once used on the land, and intended to be again so used, have been considered a part of it, but loose boards or scaffold poles, merely laid across the beams of a barn and never fastened to it, would not be, and the seller of the farm might take them away. Standing trees, of course, also pass as part of the land; so do trees blown down or cut down, and still left in the woods where they fell, but not if cut and corded up for sale; the wood has then become personal property.

If there be any manure in the barnyard or in the compost heap on the field, ready for immediate use, the buyer ordinarily, in the absence of any contrary agreement, takes that also as belonging to the farm, though it might not be so if the owner had previously sold it to some other party, and had collected it together in a heap by itself, for such an act might be a technical severance from the soil, and so convert real into personal estate; and even a lessee of a farm could take away the manure made on the place while he was in occupation. Growing crops also pass by the deed of a farm unless they are expressly reserved, and when it is not intended to convey these it should be so stated in the deed itself; a mere oral agreement to that effect would not be, in most States, valid in law. Another mode is to stipulate that possession is not to be given until some future day, in which case the crops or manure may be removed before that time.

An adjoining road is, to its middle, owned by the farmer whose land is bound, unless there are reservations to the contrary in the deeds through which he derives title. But this ownership is subject to the right of the public to the use of the road.

If a tree grows so as to come over the land of a neighbor, the latter may cut away the parts which so come over, for he owns his land and all that is above or below it. If it be a fruit tree he may cut every branch or twig which comes over his land, but he cannot touch the fruit which falls to the land. The owner of the tree may enter peaceably upon the land of the neighbor and take up the branches and fruit.

Lien Laws.

Any one who, as contractor, sub-contractor or laborer, performs any work, or furnishes any materials, in pursuance of, or in conformity with, any agreement or contract with the owner, lessee, agent or one in possession of the property, toward the erection, altering, improving or repairing of any building, shall have a lien for the value of such labor or materials on the building or land on which it stands to the extent of the right, title and interest of the owner, lessee or person in possession at the time of the claimant's filing his notice with the clerk of the county court. Such lien is called a mechanic's lien.

The notice should be filed within thirty days after completion of the work or the furnishing of the materials, and should state the residence of the claimant, the amount claimed, from whom due, when due, and to whom due, the name of the person against whom claimed, the name of the owner, lessee or person in possession of the premises, with a brief description of the latter.

Liens cease in one year after the filing of the notice, unless an action is begun, or the lien is continued by an order of court.

The following classes of persons are generally entitled to liens: 1. Bailees, who may perform labor and services, on the thing bailed, at the request of the bailor. 2. Innkeepers, upon the baggage of guests they have accommodated. 3. Common carriers, upon goods carried, for the amount of their freight and disbursements. 4. Vendors, on the goods sold, for payment of the price where no credit has been expressly promised or implied. 5. Agents, upon goods of their principals, for advancements for the benefit of the latter. 6. All persons are entitled to the right of lien who are compelled by law to receive property and bestow labor or expense on the same.

The right of lien may be waived: 1. By express contract. 2. By neglect. 3. By new agreement. 4. By allowing change of possession. 5. By surrendering possession.

The manner of the enforcement of a lien, whether it be an innkeeper's, agent's, carrier's, factor's, etc., depends wholly upon the nature and character of the lien.

DON'T purchase real estate unless the records have been thoroughly searched for all liens known to the law, or until all notices of action against the same have been discharged.

DON'T think that you have no right to sell perishable property on which you have a lien. Your lien will attach to the proceeds.

DON'T foreclose a lien without proper notice.

DON'T make payments to a contractor before you have full knowledge of all liens filed.

DON'T forget that liens take precedence according to priority, and that interest always runs on a judgment.

Deeds—Transfer of Property.

A deed is a writing by which lands, tenements or hereditaments are conveyed, sealed and delivered. It must be written or printed on parchment or paper; the parties must be competent to contract; there must be a proper object to grant; a sufficient consideration; an agreement properly declared; if desired, it must have been read to the party executing it; it must be signed and sealed; attested by witnesses, in the absence of any statute regulation to the contrary; properly acknowledged before a competent officer; and recorded within the time and in the office prescribed by the State wherein executed.

The maker of a deed is the *grantor*; the party to whom it is delivered, the *grantee*. If the grantor have a wife, she must, in the absence of a statute to the contrary, sign and acknowledge the deed; otherwise, after the husband's death, she may claim the use of one-third, during her life.

By a *general warranty* deed the grantor covenants to insure the lands against all persons whatsoever; by a *special warranty* deed he warrants only against himself and those claiming under him. In deeds made by executors, administrators or guardians there is generally no warranty. A *quit-claim deed* releases all the interest which the grantor has in the land, whatever it may be.

A *deed of trust* is given to a person called a trustee, to hold in fee simple, or otherwise, for the use of some other person who is entitled to the proceeds, profits or use.

A deed may be made void by alterations made in it after its execution; by the disagreement of the parties whose concurrence is necessary; or by the judgment of a competent tribunal.

Interlineations or erasures in a deed, made before signing, should be mentioned in a note, and witnessed in proper form. After the acknowledgment of a deed the parties have no right to make the slightest alteration. An alteration of a deed after execution, if made in favor of the grantee, vitiates the deed. If altered before delivery, such alteration destroys the deed as to the party altering it.

Abstracts of title are brief accounts of all the deeds upon which titles rest, and judgments and instruments affecting such titles.

The evidences of title are usually conveyances, wills, orders or decrees of courts, judgments, judicial sales, sales by officers appointed by law, acts of the Legislature and of Congress.

DON'T accept a deed unless all the following conditions are complied with: 1. It must be signed, sealed and witnessed. 2. Interlineations must be mentioned in the certificate of acknowledgment. 3. All the partners must join in a deed from a partnership. 4. A deed from a corporation should bear the corporate seal and be signed by officers designated in the resolution of the directors authorizing it. 5. A deed from a married woman should be joined in by the husband. 6. A deed from an executor should recite his power of sale. 7. The consideration must be expressed.

DON'T deed property to your wife direct. A deed to your wife does not cut off obligations contracted previously.

DON'T pay consideration money on a conveyance of real estate until the record has been searched to the moment of passing title, and unless you know of your own knowledge that no judgments, mortgages or tax liens are outstanding against the property.

DON'T delay in having a deed or mortgage recorded.

DON'T attempt to give a better title than you have yourself.

Mortgages.

A mortgage is a conveyance of property, either real or personal, to secure payment of a debt. When the debt is paid the mortgage becomes void and of no value. In real estate mortgages the person giving the mortgage retains possession of the property, receives all the rents and other profits, and pays all taxes and other expenses. The instrument must be acknowledged, like a deed, before a proper public officer, and recorded in the office of the county clerk or recorder, or whatever officer's duty it is to record such instruments. All mortgages must contain a redemption clause and must be signed and sealed. The time when the debt becomes due, to secure which the mortgage is given, must be plainly set forth, and the property conveyed must be clearly described, located and scheduled.

Some mortgages contain a clause permitting the sale of the property without decree of court when a default is made in the payment either of the principal sum or the interest.

A foreclosure is a statement that the property is forfeited and must be sold.

When a mortgage is assigned to another person, it must be for a valuable consideration and the note or notes which it was given to secure must be given at the same time.

If the mortgaged property, when foreclosed and brought to sale, brings more money than is needed to satisfy the debt, interest and costs, the surplus must be paid to the mortgagor.

Satisfaction of mortgages upon real or personal property may be either—

1. By an entry upon the margin of the record thereof, signed by the mortgagee or his attorney, assignee or personal representative, acknowledging the satisfaction of the mortgage, in the presence of the recording officer; or—

2. By a receipt indorsed upon the mortgage, signed by the mortgagee, his agent or attorney, which receipt may be entered upon the margin of the record; or—

3. It may be discharged upon the record thereof whenever there is presented to the proper officer an instrument acknowledging the satisfaction of such mortgage, executed by the mortgagee, his duly authorized attorney in fact, assignee or personal representative, and acknowledged in the same manner as other instruments affecting real estate.

Chattel mortgages are mortgages on personal property. Most of the rules applicable to mortgages on real estate apply also to those on personal property; though in some States there are laws regulating personal mortgages. Any instrument will answer the purpose of a chattel mortgage which would answer as a bill of sale, with a clause attached providing for the avoidance of the mortgage when the debt is paid.

A chattel mortgage will not cover property subsequently acquired by the mortgagor. Mortgages of personal property should contain a clause providing for the equity of redemption. A mortgagee may sell or transfer his mortgage to another party for a consideration, but such property cannot be seized or sold until the expiration of the period for which the mortgage was given. Mortgages given with intent to defraud creditors are void.

DON'T lose any time in having a mortgage properly recorded.

DON'T pay installments on chattel mortgages unless the same are indorsed thereon.

DON'T lose sight of the fact that a chattel mortgage is a conditional bill of sale.

DON'T accept a chattel mortgage the term whereof is for more than a year.

DON'T neglect to have a chattel mortgage signed, sealed and witnessed, and don't fail to see to it that the schedule contains every article embraced under it.

DON'T fail to see to it that goods or chattels mortgaged to you are properly insured.

DON'T suppose that a chattel mortgage is valid when the debt to be secured by it is not.

DON'T give a chattel mortgage payable on demand unless you are prepared to forfeit the chattels at any moment.

DON'T think that destruction by fire or otherwise of the chattels mortgaged wipes out the debt.

DON'T forget that foreclosure in the case of a chattel mortgage is unnecessary except to cut off claims of other creditors.

Assignments.

An assignment is a transfer of property made in writing. In effect it is passing to another person all of one's title or interest in any sort of real or personal property, rights, actions or estates. However, some things are not assignable; an officer's pay or commission, a judge's salary, fishing claims, Government bounties, or claims arising out of frauds or torts. Personal trusts cannot be assigned, as a guardianship or the right of a master in his apprentice.

Unlike many other legal devices, the holder of an assignment is not bound to show that a valuable consideration was given. The owner of a cause of action may give it away if he pleases, and in the positive absence of evidence to the contrary the court will presume that the assignment was for a sufficient consideration.

Proof will be called for only when it appears that the assignment was a mere sham or fraudulent. No formality is required by law in an assignment. Any instrument between the contracting parties which goes to show their intention to pass the property from one to another will be sufficient. It may be proved, for instance, by the payee of a note, that he indorsed (or delivered without indorsement) the note to the assignee, and this is sufficient evidence of assignment.

In every assignment of an instrument, even not negotiable, the assignee impliedly warrants the validity of the instrument and the obligation of the third party to pay it. He warrants that there is no legal defence against its collection arising out of his connection with the parties; that all parties were legally able to contract, and that the amount is unpaid.

An assignment carries with it all the collateral securities and guaranties of the original debt, even though they are not mentioned in the instrument.

Where property is assigned for the benefit of creditors, an actual transfer to the assignee must be made immediately. When an assignment is made under the common law, the assignor may prefer certain creditors; but in a State where this sort of an assignment is governed by statute, no preference can be shown. An assignment for the benefit of creditors covers all of the assignor's property, wherever or whatever it may be, that is not exempt from execution.

When insured property is sold the insurance policy should be assigned. This can only be done with the consent of the insurers, and that consent must be at once obtained.

Correct schedules of the property assigned should accompany and be attached to every assignment.

Inns, Hotels and Boarding-houses.

An inn, or hotel, is a place of entertainment for travelers. If an innkeeper opens his house for travelers, it is an implied engagement to entertain all persons who travel that way, and upon this universal assumption an action will lie against him for damages if he, without good reason, refuses to admit a traveler.

Innkeepers are responsible for the safe custody of the goods of their guests, and can limit their liability only by an express agreement or special contract with their guests; but if goods are lost through negligence of the owner himself the innkeeper's liability ceases. An innkeeper may retain the goods of his guest until the amount of the guest's bill has been paid.

A boarding-house is not an inn, nor is a coffee-house or eating-room. A boarding-house keeper has no lien on the goods of a boarder, except by special agreement, nor is he responsible for their safe custody. He is liable, however, for loss caused by the negligence of his servants. An innkeeper is liable for loss without such negligence.

Bonds.

A written instrument, admitting an obligation on the part of the maker to pay a certain sum of money to another specified person at a fixed time, for a valuable consideration, is called a bond. The obligor is the one giving the bond; the beneficiary is called the obligee. This definition applies to all bonds, but generally these instruments are given to guarantee the performance or non-performance of certain acts by the obligor, which being done or left undone, as the case may be, the bond becomes void, but if the conditions are broken it remains in full force. As a rule, the bond is made out for a sum twice the amount of any debt which is apt to be incurred by the obligor under its conditions, the statement being set forth that the sum named is the penalty, as liquidated or settled damages, in the event of the failure of the obligor to carry out the conditions.

An act of Providence, whereby the accomplishment of a bond is rendered impossible, relieves the obligor of all liability.

A bond for the payment of money differs from a promissory note only in having a seal.

Bills of Sale.

A bill of sale is a formal written conveyance of personal property. If the property is delivered when sold, or if part of the purchase-money is paid, a written instrument is not necessary to make the conveyance, but it is convenient evidence of the transfer of title. But, to protect the interests of the purchaser against the creditors of the seller, the bill is not sufficient of itself; there should also be a delivery of the property. If an actual and continued change of possession does not accompany the sale it is void as against the creditors of the seller and subsequent purchasers and mortgagees in good faith, unless the buyer can show that his purchase was made in good faith, without intent to defraud, and that there was some good reason for leaving the property in the hands of the seller.

Guaranty

Is an assurance made by a second party that his principal will perform some specific act. For instance, A gives B a note, and C by indorsing the instrument guarantees to B that A will pay it at maturity. C is the guarantor; his liability is special, and if B renews the note when it becomes due he is no longer liable. A guaranty for collection is a very different thing from a guaranty of payment. The first warrants that the money is collectible; the latter, that it will be paid at maturity. In the first case the party guaranteed must be able to prove that due diligence was employed in attempting to collect the money; in the second, no such proof is necessary. The only form necessary in guaranteeing a note is writing one's name across the back of it — a process commonly called indorsing.

Corporations.

Several persons joining together for the accomplishment of any business or social purpose can legally organize themselves into a corporation, a form of partnership which combines the resources of all, and yet gives a limited pecuniary liability, amounting only to the amount of stock owned by each stockholder. In the States, the legislature of each Commonwealth enjoys the power of regulating the corporations, and in the Territories this power is, of course, vested in the General Government. The actual cost of organization amounts to something less than $10, most of which is in fees to the Secretary of State. When the stock has been subscribed a meeting is called, and each shareholder casts a vote for every share which he owns or holds a proxy for, for each person who is to be elected director, or he may give one director as many votes as the number of shares he is voting, multiplied by the number of directors to be elected, amounts to, or distribute his votes as he chooses. Thus if he owns ten shares of stock and there are six directors to be elected, he has sixty votes, which he can give, either ten for each director, or twenty for each of three, or sixty for one, or in any other way that he sees fit, so that his whole vote will not be more than sixty votes. These directors must as soon after the election as possible meet and choose a president, vice-president, secretary and treasurer, whereupon the corporation is ready for business.

The law in all the States on the subject of incorporating companies is very similar, and the necessary forms are to be obtained usually from the Secretary of State.

Wills and How to Make Them.

Every description of property, whether real or personal, may be given by will. In the case of persons dying owing debts, however, the law gives to the executors sufficient of the personal property of the deceased to pay off all existing indebtedness, irrespective of the terms of the will; and where the personal property is not sufficient for this purpose, real property may be so appropriated.

Property may be bequeathed by will to all persons, including married women, infants, lunatics, idiots, etc.

Wills may be made by any person not disqualified by age or mental incapacity. Generally speaking, a person must have attained the age of twenty-one years before he or she can make a valid will of lands, and the same age, in many States, is required for a will of solely personal property.

In New York males of eighteen and females of sixteen are competent to bequeath personal property. "Sound and disposing mind and memory" are always essential to the validity of any will. For this reason, idiots, lunatics, intoxicated persons (during intoxication), and persons of unsound or weak minds, are incompetent to make wills. A will procured by fraud is also invalid, although the testator be fully competent to make a valid will. All wills must be in writing, except those made by soldiers in active service during war, and by sailors while at sea. Such persons may make a verbal or nuncupative will, under certain restrictions, as to witnesses, etc. No particular form of words is required.

A valid will must be subscribed or signed by the testator, or some one for him, in his presence, and at his request. The signature must be affixed in the presence of each of the witnesses. In case the will be signed by some one for him, the testator must acknowledge the signature to be his own in presence of the witnesses. The testator must declare to each of the subscribing witnesses that the instrument is his "last will and testament." This is of the utmost importance, and is called the "publication." There must be at least two (three are required in some of the States) subscribing witnesses, who must act as such at the testator's request, or at the request of some one in his presence. The subscribing witnesses must not be beneficially interested in the provisions of the will. These witnesses must all sign the will in the presence of the testator, and (in New York and some of the other States) in the presence of each other.

A codicil is an appendix annexed to the will after its execution, whereby the testator makes some change in, or addition to, his former disposition, and must be signed, published and attested in the same manner as the original will.

The revocation of a will may be express or implied. Express, by the execution of a new and later will, or by the intentional destruction of the old one, or by a formal written revocation, signed and witnessed in the same manner as the will itself. An implied revocation is wrought by the subsequent marriage of the testator and the birth of children, or by either.

DON'T leave anything uncertain in a will, and don't neglect to declare it to be your last will and testament.

DON'T make a will without two (better three) witnesses, none of whom must be interested in it. See that each witness writes his full name and address.

DON'T make a new will unless you destroy or revoke the old one, and don't add a codicil unless it is executed in the same way as the original will.

DON'T neglect to make a new will if you mortgage or sell property devised or bequeathed in a prior one.

DON'T make a will which does not provide for children that may be born.

DON'T will property to a corporation whose charter does not permit it to take by devise or bequest.

DON'T fail to say "bequeath" for personal and "devise" for real property.

Heirship to Property Not Bequeathed.

In England, where the policy is to keep landed estates undivided, the law of primogeniture prevails, giving to the eldest son and his descendants superior rights to the property. In case of default, the second son and his descendants become the heirs, and so on. If there be only daughters, they inherit equally.

In the United States the property would be divided among the heirs as follows: (1). To the children. These, if of equal degree, receive the property in equal shares. If of unequal degree, the more remote descendants take the share that would have belonged to their parents, if living. Thus: A, B and C are children of the testator, and of these B and C are living and A is dead, at the testator's death. The estate, after paying all debts, will be divided into three equal parts, the descendants of A, together, receiving one-third, and B and C each another third; but in case A left no descendants, then B and C each will be awarded one-half of the property. (2) If there are no descendants the parents of the testator would receive the estate, the father being sometimes preferred to the mother. (3) If parents are not living, the brothers and sisters of the testator would take the property, sharing equally. If one or more of the brothers or sisters had died, their children would receive the share that would have descended to their parent. (4.) Grandparents would be next claimants, after which (5) uncles and aunts, and after them (6) their children, and so on. In case no heirs are found, the property inures to the State.

The above principles are stated as generally recognized in the laws of the several States. As those laws, however, vary, full information can only be obtained from the statutes of the several States.

Legacies and the Duties of Executors and Administrators.

A legacy is a gift or bequest of personal property by will or testament. Legacies are of three kinds: General, specific, and demonstrative.

A general legacy does not amount to a bequest of any particular portion of, or article belonging to, the personal estate of the testator, as distinguished from all others of the same kind; as a bequest of a sum of money, or a horse.

A specific legacy is a bequest of property specifically designated, so as to be definitely distinguished from the rest of the testator's estate; as, a bequest of all the money contained in a certain box, or the horse in the testator's stable.

A demonstrative legacy is a bequest of a certain amount of money to be paid out of a particular fund; as, a bequest of $500 to be paid out of the proceeds of the sale of certain property.

An executor should first extinguish all the lawful debts of the testator, and for this purpose all the personal property may be applied, if necessary, even though some of it has been bequeathed in specific legacies. After the debts are paid, the specific legacies are next to be satisfied; then the demonstrative legacies; and lastly, the general legacies. If there be insufficient assets to satisfy any of the legacies in either of these three classes successively, those in the same class will be paid ratably and in proportion, and subsequent classes will fail entirely.

Residuary legatees take subject to all other legacies. A residuary legatee is one to whom is bequeathed "all the rest, residue and remainder" of an estate.

Specific and general legacies are subject to ademption; thus, if the testator bequeath "the horse in his stable," and at the time of his death has no horse, the legacy fails entirely and is said to be "adeemed." Or, if the legacy bequeaths the furniture in a certain specified house, and the testator remove the furniture to another house, the legacy is adeemed.

Legacies are vested, or contingent. A vested legacy is one where the legatee acquires an absolute present right to present or future enjoyment. A contingent legacy is one where the right of enjoyment depends upon some contingency; as, a gift to a child if he attains the age of twenty-one years. A cumulative legacy is one additional to a previous legacy contained in the same will.

In New York, and several other States, a legacy given to a subscribing witness of a will is void. An executor may be a legatee. It is also provided that "no person having a husband, wife, child, or parent, shall bequeath to a corporation more than one-half of his personal estate after the payment of his debts."

Legacies are not required to be paid in less than one year from the time of the testator's death. This time is allowed to the executor to enable him to ascertain the nature and value of the property, the full liabilities of the testator, and to collect the assets.

A legacy to an infant should not be paid except under order of the court, and such order will be governed by the laws of the State.

DON'T become an executor or administrator unless you are willing and have time to attend to the duties, and don't enter upon a trust until you thoroughly understand your duties and powers.

DON'T mix trust and personal funds.

DON'T pay out a dollar of trust money without proper vouchers, and don't fail to keep accurate accounts.

DON'T liquidate any claim until you have the whole estate in hand.

DON'T pay a legacy before the time fixed in the will without deducting interest.

DON'T give a promissory note as executor or administrator.

DON'T execute a contested will, or compromise a claim due an estate, without the advice and consent of the court.

DON'T incur any other expenses than those of the burial until the will is properly probated, but do not hesitate to sell perishable property.

The Right of Dower.

Dower is one-third part of the husband's estate, and in general cannot be destroyed by the mere act of the husband. Hence, in the sale of real estate by the husband, his wife must, with the husband, sign the conveyance to make the title complete to the purchaser. In the absence of such signature, the widow can claim full dower rights after the husband's death. Creditors, also, seize the property subject to such dower rights.

The husband in his will sometimes gives his wife property in lieu of dower. In this case she may, after his death, elect to take either such property or her dower; but she cannot take both. While the husband lives the wife's right of dower is only inchoate; it cannot be enforced. Should he sell the land to a stranger, she has no right of action or remedy until his death.

In all cases the law of the State in which the *land is situated* governs it, and, as in the case of heirship, full information must be sought for in the statute which is applicable.

Marriage and Divorce.

Marriage may be entered into by any two persons, with the following exceptions: Idiots, persons of unsound mind, persons related by blood or affinity within certain degrees prohibited by law, infants under the age of consent, which varies in the different States, and persons already married and not legally divorced.

The violation of the marriage vow is cause for absolute divorce in all the States and Territories, excepting South Carolina and New Mexico, which have no divorce laws.

Physical inability is a cause in all the States except Cal., Conn., Dak., Ia., La., N. M., N. Y., S. C., Tex. and Vt. In most of these States it renders marriage voidable.

Wilful desertion, one year, in Ark., Cal., Col., Dak., Fla., Ida., Kan., Ky., Mo., Mon., Nev., Utah, Wis., W. T. and Wyo.

Wilful desertion, two years, in Ala., Ariz., Ill., Ind., Ia., Mich., Minn., Neb., Pa. and Tenn.

Wilful desertion, three years, in Conn., Del., Ga., Me., Md., Mass., Miss., N. H., N. J., O., Ore., Tex., Vt. and W. Va.

Wilful desertion, five years, in Va. and R. I., though the court may in the latter State decree a divorce for a shorter period.

Habitual drunkenness, in all the States and Territories, except Md., N. J., N. Y., N. C., Pa., S. C., Tex., Vt., Va. and W. Va.

"Imprisonment for felony" or "conviction of felony" in all the States and Territories (with limitations), except Dak., Fla., Me., Md., N. J., N. M., N. Y., N. C., S. C. and Utah.

"Cruel and abusive treatment," "intolerable cruelty," "extreme cruelty," "repeated cruelty," or "inhuman treatment," in all the States and Territories, *except* N. J., N. M., N. Y., N. C., S. C., Va. and W. Va.

Failure by the husband to provide: one year in Cal., Col., Dak., Nev. and Wyo.; two years in Ind. and Ida.; no time specified in Ariz., Mass., Mich., Me., Neb., R. I., Vt. and Wis.; wilful neglect for three years in Del.

Fraud and fraudulent contract in Ark., Conn., Ga., Ida., Kan., Ky., O., Pa. and W. T.

Absence without being heard from: three years in N. H.; seven years in Conn. and Vt.; separation five years, in Ky.; voluntary separation five years, in Wis. When reasonably presumed dead by the court, in R. I.

"Ungovernable temper," in Ky.; "habitual indulgence in violent and ungovernable temper," in Fla.; "cruel treatment, outrages or excesses as to render their living together insupportable," in Ark., Ky., La., Mo., Tenn. and Tex.; "indignities that render life burdensome," in Mo., Ore., Pa., Tenn., W. T. and Wyo.

In Ga. an absolute divorce is granted only after the concurrent verdict of two juries at different terms of the court. In N. Y. absolute divorce is granted for but one cause, adultery.

All of the causes above enumerated are for absolute or full divorce, and collusion and connivance are especially barred, and also condonation of violation of the marriage vow.

The courts of every State, and particularly of New York, are very jealous of their jurisdiction, and generally refuse to recognize as valid a divorce against one of the citizens of the State by the court of another State, unless both parties to the suit were subject at the same time to the jurisdiction of the court granting the divorce.

PREVIOUS RESIDENCE REQUIRED.—Dak., ninety days; Cal., Ind., Ida., Neb., Nev., N. M., Tex. and Wyo., six months; Ala., Ariz., Ark., Col., Ill., Ia., Kan., Ky., Mo., Miss., Minn., Mich., Mo., Mont., N. H., O., Ore., Pa., Utah, Vt. (both parties as husband and wife), W. Va., W. T. and Wis., one year; Fla., Md., N. C., R. I. and Tenn., two years; Conn. and Mass. (if, when married, both parties were residents; otherwise five years), three years.

REMARRIAGE.—There are no restrictions upon remarriage by divorced persons in Conn., Ky., Ill. and Minn. Defendant must wait two years and obtain permission from the court in Mass. The decree of the court may restrain the guilty party from remarrying in Va. Parties cannot remarry until after two years, except by permission of the court, in Me. In N. Y. the plaintiff may remarry, but the defendant cannot do so during the plaintiff's lifetime, unless the decree be modified or proof that five years have elapsed, and that complainant has married again and defendant's conduct has been uniformly good. Any violation of this is punished as bigamy, even though the other party has been married. In Del., Pa. and Tenn., no wife or husband divorced for violation of the marriage vow can marry the paramour *criminis* during the life of the former husband or wife, nor in La. at any time; such marriage in La. renders the person divorced guilty of bigamy.

Rights of Married Women.

Any and all property which a woman owns at her marriage, together with the rents, issues and profits thereof, and the property that comes to her by descent, devise, bequest, gift or grant, or which she acquires by her trade, business labor, or services performed on her separate account, shall, notwithstanding her marriage, remain her sole and separate property, and may be used, collected and invested by her in her own name, and shall not be subject to the interference or control of her husband, or be liable for his debts, unless for such debts as may have been contracted for the support of herself or children by her as his agent.

A married woman may likewise bargain, sell, assign, transfer and convey such property, and enter into contracts regarding the same on her separate trade, labor or business with the like effect as if she were unmarried. Her husband, however, is not liable for such contracts, and they do not render him or his property in any way liable therefor. She may also sue and be sued in all matters having relation to her sole and separate property in the same manner as if she were sole.

In the following cases a married woman's contract may be enforced against her and her separate estate: 1. When the contract is created in or respecting the carrying on of the trade or business of the wife. 2. When it relates to or is made for the benefit of her sole or separate estate. 3. When the intention to charge the separate estate is expressed in the contract creating the liability.

When a husband receives a principal sum of money belonging to his wife, the law presumes he receives it for her use, and he must account for it, or expend it on her account by her authority or direction, or that she gave it to him as a gift.

If he receives interest or income and spends it with her knowledge and without objection, a gift will be presumed from acquiescence.

Money received by a husband from his wife and expended by him, under her direction, on his land, in improving the home of the family, is a gift, and cannot be recovered by the wife, or reclaimed, or an account demanded.

An appropriation by a wife, herself, of her separate property to the use and benefit of her husband, in the absence of an agreement to repay, or any circumstances from which such an agreement can be inferred, will not create the relation of debtor and creditor, nor render the husband liable to account.

Though no words of gift be spoken, a gift by a wife to her husband may be shown by the very nature of the transaction, or appear from the attending circumstances.

A wife who causelessly deserts her husband is not entitled to the aid of a court of equity in getting possession of such chattels as she has contributed to the furnishing and adornment of her husband's house. Her legal title remains, and she could convey her interest to a third party by sale, and said party would have a good title, unless her husband should prove a gift.

Wife's property is not liable to a lien of a sub-contractor for materials furnished to the husband for the erection of a building thereon, where it is not shown that the wife was notified of the intention to furnish the materials, or a settlement made with the contractor and given to the wife, her agent or trustee.

The common law of the United States has some curious provisions regarding the rights of married women, though in all the States there are statutory provisions materially modifying this law. As the law now stands the husband is responsible for necessaries supplied to the wife when should he not fail to supply them himself, and is held liable if he turn her from his house, or otherwise separates himself from her without good cause. He is not held liable if the wife deserts him, or if he turns her away for good cause. If she leaves him through good cause, then he is liable. If a man lives with a woman as his wife, and so represents her, even though this representation is made to one who knows she is not, he is liable the same way as if she were his wife.

Arbitration.

Arbitration is an investigation and determination of subjects of difference between persons involved in dispute, by unofficial persons chosen by the parties in question.

The general rule is that any person capable of making a valid contract concerning the subject in dispute may be a party to an arbitration. Any matter which the parties may adjust by agreement, or which may be made the subject of a suit at law, may be determined by arbitration. Crimes cannot be made the subject matter of an arbitration. This matter is regulated by statute in the different States.

The Law of Finding.

The general rule is that the finder has a clear title against every one but the owner. The proprietor of a hotel or a shop has no right to demand property of others found on his premises. Such proprietor may make regulations in regard to lost property which will bind his employes, but they cannot bind the public. The finder has been held to stand in the place of the owner, so that he was permitted to prevail in an action against a person who found an article which the plaintiff had originally found, but subsequently lost. The police have no special rights in regard to articles lost, unless those rights are conferred by statute. Receivers of articles found are trustees for the owner or finder. They have no power in the absence of special statute to keep an article against the finder, any more than the finder has to retain an article against the owner.

Bankruptcy.

Laws have been enacted in nearly all of the States for the purpose of distributing the property of an insolvent debtor ratably among his creditors and discharging the debtor from further liability. Proceedings may be instituted by the debtor himself or by a creditor. As a general rule, proceedings in one State are not binding on a creditor residing in another State; but if Congress were to pass a national bankrupt law, this would annul all State laws on the subject, and proceedings under the national law would bind creditors in all the States and Territories.

Insolvency proceedings are generally commenced by a petition to the judge of the court of insolvency, setting forth among other things the debtor's inability to pay all his debts in full, and his desire to surrender all his property for the benefit of his creditors.

If satisfied of the truth of matters alleged in the petition, the judge issues an order commanding the proper officer to take the debtor's property and hold it until a certain time, when the creditors meet and choose an assignee.

The assignee then takes charge of the property, turns it into money, and declares a dividend for the creditors.

Pending the proceedings, the debtor may be examined on oath for the purpose of making him disclose all matters concerning his property and the disposal thereof.

If the debtor has conformed to the insolvent law in all respects he is entitled to a discharge from his debts, which is given him by the judge on the debtor's obtaining the requisite assent from the creditors.

In nearly all the States an insolvent debtor may, with the consent of his creditors, and in some States without such consent, assign all his property to a trustee for the benefit of his creditors, who converts it into money, dividing it *pro rata* among the creditors.

BUSINESS AND LEGAL FORMS

Short Form of Assignment of Written Instrument.

For Value Received, I do hereby assign, transfer and set over unto C.D., and his assigns, all my right, title and interest in and to the within written instrument, this....day of....., A.D. 1894. A. B.

Ordinary Bill of Exchange, or Draft at a Time after Sight.

$250. Chicago, January 1, 1894.

Ten days after sight, pay to the order of W. V., *two hundred and fifty* dollars, for value received, and charge the same to account of

To M. D. & Co., } J. H. C. & Co.,
New York City, N.Y. } *Chicago, Illinois.*

When a draft is payable at sight, commence thus:

"At sight, pay," etc.

General Form of Agreement.

This Agreement, made this....day of....., one thousand eight hundred and....., between A. B., of....., county of....., and State of Illinois, of the first part, and C.D., of....., in said county and State, of the second part—

Witnesseth, that the said A. B., in consideration of the covenants and agreements on the part of the party of the second part hereinafter contained, doth covenant and agree to and with the said C.D., that (here insert the agreement on the part of A. B.).

And the said C.D., in consideration of the covenants on the part of the party of the first part, doth covenant and agree to and with the said A. B., that (here insert the agreement on the part of C.D.).

In witness whereof, we have hereunto set our hands and seals, the day and year first above written.

A. B. [SEAL.]
C. D. [SEAL.]

Common Form of Bond for Payment of Money.

Know all men by these presents, that I, A. B., of....., in the county of....., and State of Illinois, am held and firmly bound unto C. D., of ....., in the county of ...... and State aforesaid, in the sum of .... dollars, to be paid to the said C D, his executors, administrators and assigns, to which payment, well and truly to be made, I bind myself, my heirs, executors and administrators, and every of them, firmly by these presents.

Sealed with my seal, the .... day of ...., A.D. 1896.

The condition of this obligation is such, that if the above bound A B, his heirs, executors and administrators, or either of them, shall well and truly pay, or cause to be paid, unto the said C D, his executors, administrators or assigns, the just and full sum of .... dollars, with interest thereon, at the yearly rate of .... per cent for the same, on or before the .... day of ....., A. D. 1896, then this obligation to be void and of no effect; otherwise to remain in full force.

A B. [SEAL.]

Form of Bill of Sale of Goods or Personal Property.

KNOW ALL MEN BY THESE PRESENTS, that I, A B, of ....., in the county of ....., and State of Illinois, in consideration of the sum of .... dollars, to me paid by C D, of ....., at and before the sealing and delivery of these presents, the receipt whereof is hereby acknowledged, have bargained, sold and delivered, and by these presents do bargain, sell and deliver unto the said C D, the following goods and chattels, to-wit: (Here insert a bill of particular goods sold or personal property).

To have and to hold the said goods and chattels unto the said C D, his executors, administrators and assigns, to his and their own proper use and benefit forever. And I, the said A B, for myself and my heirs, executors and administrators, do warrant and will defend the said bargained premises unto the said C D, his executors, administrators and assigns, from and against all persons whomsoever.

In witness whereof, I have hereunto set my hand and seal, this .... day of ....., A. D. 1896.

A B. [SEAL.]

Form of Bond for a Deed.

KNOW ALL MEN BY THESE PRESENTS, that I, A B, of the county of....., and State of Illinois, am held and firmly bound unto C D, of the county of....., and State aforesaid, in the penal sum of .....dollars, to be paid unto the said C D, his heirs, executors, administrators or assigns, to which payment, well and truly to be made, I bind myself, my heirs, executors and administrators, and every of them, firmly by these presents.

Sealed with my seal, this.....day of....., A.D. 1896.

The condition of the above obligation is such that whereas the above bounden A B has this day bargained and sold to the said C D, his heirs and assigns, for the sum of .....dollars, the following described lot or parcel of land, to-wit: (here describe the land), which sum of .....dollars is to be paid in manner following: .....dollars at the executing and delivery hereof, and.....dollars in.....from the date hereof.

Upon the payment of the said sums being made, at the time and in the manner aforesaid, the said A B, for himself, his heirs, executors and assigns, covenants and agrees, to and with the said C D, his heirs and assigns, to execute a good and sufficient deed of conveyance, in fee simple, free from all incumbrances, with full and proper covenants of warranty for the above described premises.

Now, if the said A B shall well and truly keep, observe and perform his said covenants and agreements herein contained, on his part, then this obligation to be void; otherwise to remain in full force and virtue.

A B. [SEAL.]

Power of Attorney.

KNOW ALL MEN BY THESE PRESENTS, that I, A B, of....., in the county of....., and State of Illinois, have made, constituted and appointed, and by these presents do make, constitute and appoint, C D, of ....., to be my true and lawful attorney, for me and in my name, and for my sole use, to (here state the specific purposes of the power given), hereby giving and granting unto my said attorney full power and authority in the premises to use all lawful means in my name, and for my sole benefit, for the purposes aforesaid. And generally to do and perform all such acts, matters and things as my said attorney shall deem necessary or expedient for the completion of the authority hereby given, as fully as I might and could do if I were personally present; hereby ratifying and confirming all the acts of my said attorney or his substitutes, done by virtue of these presents.

In witness whereof, I have hereunto set my hand and seal, this ..... day of ....., A.D. 1896.

A B. [SEAL.]

Warranty Deed.

The grantor (here insert name or names and place of residence), for and in consideration of (here insert consideration) in hand paid, conveys and warrants to (here insert the grantee's name or names) the following described real estate (here insert description), situated in the county of ....., in the State of Illinois.

Dated this ..... day of ....., A.D. 18..

A B. [SEAL.]

Quit Claim Deed.

The grantor (here insert grantor's name or names and place of residence), for the consideration of (here insert consideration), convey and quitclaim to (here insert grantee's name or names) all interest in the following described real estate (here insert description), situated in the county of ....., in the State of Illinois.

Dated this ..... day of ....., A.D. 18...

A. B. [SEAL.]

Mortgage.

The mortgagor (here insert name or names) mortgages and warrants to (here insert name or names of mortgagee or mortgagees), to secure the payment of (here recite the nature and amount of indebtedness, showing when due and the rate of interest, and whether secured by note or otherwise), the following described real estate (here insert description thereof), situated in the county of ....., in the State of Illinois.

A. B. [SEAL.]

Dated this ..... day of ....., A.D. 18...

Form of Certificate of Acknowledgment to Deed or other Instrument.

State of (name of State), }
County of (name of County). }

I (here give name of officer and his official title) do hereby certify that (name of grantor, and if acknowledged by wife, her name, and add "his wife,") personally known to me to be the same person whose name is (or are) subscribed to the foregoing instrument, appeared before me this day in person, and acknowledged that he (she or they) signed, sealed or delivered the said instrument as his (her or their) free and voluntary act, for the uses and purposes therein set forth.

Given under my hand and (private or official, as the case may be) seal, this ..... day of ....., A.D. 18...

(Signature of officer.) [SEAL.]

Short Form of Lease.

THIS INDENTURE, made this ..... day of ....., A.D. 18..., between A B, party of the first part, and C D, party of the second part, witnesseth, that the said party of the first part, in consideration of the covenants of the party of the second part, hereinafter set forth, do...by these presents, lease to the party of the second part, the following described property, to-wit: (here describe the premises), in the county of ....., and State of ..... To have and to hold the same, to the party of the second part, from the ..... day of ....., 18..., to the ..... day of ....., 18... And the party of the second part, in consideration of the leasing of said premises, covenants and agrees to pay the party of the first part, as ....., as rent for the same, the sum of ....., payable as follows, to-wit: (Here set forth the terms of payment.)

And the party of the second part covenants with the party of the first part that at the expiration of the term of this lease...he...will yield up the premises to the party of the first part, without further notice, in as good condition as when the same were entered upon by the party of the second part, loss by fire or inevitable accident and ordinary wear excepted, and that neither...he...nor.....legal representatives will underlet said premises, or any part thereof, or assign this lease, without the written assent of the party of the first part first had thereto.

And it is further expressly agreed between the parties hereto, that if default shall be made in the payment of the rent above reserved, or any part thereof, or any of the covenants or agreements herein contained to be kept by the party of the second part, it shall be lawful for the party of the first part or.....legal representatives, into and upon said premises, or any part thereof, either with or without process of law, to re-enter and re-possess the same at the election of the party of the first part, and to distrain for any rent that may be due thereon upon any property belonging to the party of the second part. And in order to enforce a forfeiture for non-payment of rent, it shall not be necessary to make a demand on the same day the rent shall become due, but a failure to pay the same at the place aforesaid, or a demand and a refusal to pay on the same day or at any time on any subsequent day, shall be sufficient; and after such default shall be made, the party of the second part and all persons in possession under.....shall be deemed guilty of a forcible detainer of said premises under the statute.

And it is further covenanted and agreed between said parties that (here set forth any further stipulation agreed upon.) The covenants herein shall extend to and be binding upon the heirs, executors and administrators of the parties to this lease.

Witness the hand and seals of said parties, the day and year first above written.

A B. [SEAL.]
C D. [SEAL.]

Form of Will.

I, A B, of ....., in the county of ..... and State of Illinois, of the age of ..... years, of sound mind and memory, do make, publish and declare this my last will and testament in the manner following: That is to say,

First, I give and bequeath to (here may be set forth the manner of disposition of personal property, and the names of persons and amount to each.)

Second, I give and devise to (here set forth the manner of disposition of your property, and the names of persons to whom devised, concluding as follows:) To have and to hold the same and the several tracts and parcels thereof to the said ...., his heirs and assigns forever.

And lastly, I do hereby nominate and appoint .... to be executor of this my last will and testament, hereby revoking all former wills by me made. (Add the following clause if desired:) And I do direct that my said executor shall not be obliged to give security as such.

In witness whereof, I have hereunto set my hand and seal this .... day of ...., A.D. 18..

A. B. [SEAL.]

The above instrument, consisting of one sheet (or two sheets, as the case may be) was at the date thereof signed, sealed, published and declared by the said A. B. as and for his last will and testament, in presence of us, who at his request and in his presence, and in the presence of each other, have subscribed our names as witnesses thereto (or, "the above instrument, consisting of one sheet was at the date thereof declared to us by the said A. B., the testator therein mentioned, to be his last will and testament; and at the same time acknowledged to us, and each of us, that he had signed and sealed the same, and we therefore, at his request and in his presence, and in the presence of each other, signed our names thereto as attesting witnesses.")

C. D., residing at ..... in .... county.

G. H., residing at ..... in .... county.

The foregoing is the general form of will, which can be varied in case of several devisees and legatees, according to the facts or as circumstances may require.

A *devisee* is one to whom *real* property is devised in the will.

A *legatee* is one to whom *personal* property is given in the will.

Bill of Sale.

KNOW ALL MEN BY THESE PRESENTS, that I, E. D., of the town of ...., county of ...., State of ...., of the first part, for and in consideration of the sum of one hundred dollars, lawful money of the United States, to me in hand paid, at or before the ensealing and delivery of these presents, by C. B., of the second part, the receipt whereof is hereby acknowledged, have bargained, sold, granted and conveyed, and by these presents do bargain, sell, grant and convey unto the said party of the second part, his executors, administrators and assigns (here set out the articles sold), to have and to hold the same unto the said party of the second part, his executors, administrators and assigns, forever. And I do for myself, my heirs, executors and administrators, covenant and agree to and with the said party of the second part, to warrant and defend the said described goods hereby sold unto the said party of the second part, his executors, administrators and assigns, against all and every person and persons whatsoever.

IN WITNESS WHEREOF, I have hereunto set my hand and seal this .... day of ...., 18..

E. D. [SEAL.]

Signed, sealed and delivered }
in the presence of B. R. }

Promissory Note.

$200. Baltimore, ..., 18..

Thirty days after date I promise to pay B. D., or order (or bearer), two hundred dollars, for value received. D. E.

Joint Promissory Note.

$1,050. Memphis, ..., 18..

Sixty days after date we jointly promise to pay C. D., or order (or bearer), one thousand and fifty dollars, for value received.

A. C.
B. H.

Note Payable on Demand.

$100. Mobile, ..., 18..

On demand, for value received, I promise to pay H. B., or order (or bearer), one hundred dollars (with interest). C. C.

Note Payable at Bank.

$300. St. Louis, ..., 18..

Thirty days after date, for value received, I promise to pay C. D. A., or order (or bearer), three hundred dollars, at the German-American Savings Bank. D. R. S.

Note not Negotiable.

$100. Madison, Ga., ..., 18..

Two months after date I promise to pay J. H. one hundred dollars, for value received. B. K.

Note with Surety.

$75. Columbus, Miss., ..., 18..

Six months from date I promise to pay E. G., or order (or bearer), seventy-five dollars, for value received. P. B.
K. X.

Note Payable by Installments.

$500. Albany, ..., 18..

For value received, I promise to pay A. C., or order (or bearer), five hundred dollars, in the following manner: One hundred dollars in three

months, two hundred dollars in nine months, one hundred dollars in twelve months, and one hundred dollars in fifteen months, from date, with interest on the several sums as they may become due.
W. Z.

Draft at Sight.

$100. Chicago, ..., 18..

At sight, pay J. C., or order, one hundred dollars, and charge the same to my account.

To A. K. C. B. D.

Due Bill.

$50. Cincinnati, ..., 18..

Due A. W., fifty dollars, with interest from this date. M. A.

Bill of Exchange.

$500. New York, ..., 18..

Fifteen days after sight (or as many days as may be agreed upon), pay to the order of Mr. R. B., five hundred dollars, and charge the same to the account of G. D.

To L. M., St. Louis, Mo.

MINING LAWS

WHERE papers have once been filed with the Register and Receiver, they become a part of the record, and can neither be withdrawn nor returned, but must be transmitted to the General Land Office.

An application will be rejected when the description of the premises is erroneous or insufficient.

Application for patent will be rejected because:

1. The notice was published without the knowledge of the Register.

2. The notice was not published in a newspaper designated as published nearest the claim.

3. Record title was found defective; and,

4. A previous application had been made for the same premises, which was withdrawn pending a suit in court commenced by the adverse claimant.

An application for patent will be rejected when the survey does not accurately define the boundaries of the claim;

Where the claim was not located in accordance with law.

Where several parties own separate and distinct portions of a claim, application for patent may be made by either for that portion of the claim owned by him; but where several parties own undivided interests in a mining claim, all should join in an application for a patent.

A person or association may purchase as many placer locations as the local law admits, and embrace them all in one application for a patent.

Two or more lodes cannot be embraced in one application for a patent except for placer claims embracing two or more lodes within their boundaries.

Paper sworn to before any person purporting to act as a deputy for the Register and Receiver cannot be received as evidence.

In all patents for mining claims situated within the interior boundaries of a town site a clause is inserted "excepting and excluding all town property, rights upon the surface, and all houses, buildings, structures, lots, blocks, streets, alleys or other municipal improvements not belonging to the grantee herein, and all rights necessary or proper to the occupation, possession and enjoyment of the same."

Publication of notice must be made in one newspaper for the period of sixty days.

Notice must be published ten consecutive weeks in weekly newspapers, and in daily newspapers sixty days must elapse between the first and last insertion.

Where the Register designates the daily issue of a paper for publication of notices of a mining application for patent, it is not a compliance with law to change to the weekly edition of the same paper, without authority of the Register.

The existence of a salt spring on a tract of land withdraws it from the operation of the homestead and pre-emption laws. A hearing for the purpose of proving the agricultural character of such lands is not allowed. Lands containing valuable deposits of salt may be entered under the mining acts.

Adverse Claims.—Adverse claimants must file a separate and distinct claim against each application which it is alleged conflicts with the premises owned by such adverse claimant.

The papers in an adverse claim once filed cannot be withdrawn, but become part of the record.

When an adverse claim has been filed it cannot be amended so as to embrace a larger portion of the premises than that described in the original adverse claim.

An adverse claim must be made out in proper form, and filed in the proper local office during the period of publication of the application, for the protest to be effective.

It is the duty of the adverse claimant to commence suit in proper form within the required time, and if he trusts the uncertain conditions of the United States mail, he must abide the consequences, should the delay come through misfortune or accident. Should the failure to commence suit be the result of the neglect or dis-

homesteading of his attorney; the Interior Department cannot redress the wrong.

An adverse claimant should set forth in detail the facts upon which he bases his adverse claim. A statement in general terms, embodying conclusions of law, without stating the facts generally, will not be considered in evidence.

An adverse claimant should show a compliance with the local laws in recording his claim and in regard to expenditures, and shall file a copy of the original notice of his location, and show the nature or extent of the conflict alleged.

An allegation of parties to a suit that they compose the company is sufficient, and they are not required to prove that they are the original locators or the identical parties who presented the adverse claim.

Agricultural or Mineral Lands.—Where land is of little if any value for agricultural purposes, but is essential to the proper development of mining claims, it should be disposed of under the Mining Act.

Where lands containing valuable mineral deposits have been included in an agricultural entry, said entry will be canceled at any time prior to issuance of patent, upon satisfactory evidence of the existence of such valuable deposits.

Where valuable deposits of mineral are discovered upon a tract after the same has been entered as agricultural, but before patent has been issued, the parties claiming the mine might make application for patent for same, and the agricultural entry will be canceled to that portion of the land embraced by said mining claim.

Where mineral deposits are discovered on agricultural lands after patent has been issued to an agricultural claimant, they pass with the patent.

Aliens.—A foreigner may make a mining location and dispose of it, provided he becomes a citizen before disposing of the mine. Proof that the party was not a citizen before disposing of his claim must be affirmatively shown.

Locators and intermediate owners other than applicants will not be presumed aliens in the absence of allegation or objection prior to issuance of patent.

The portion of a mining claim sold to an alien cannot be patented while such owner is an alien; but on his declaration to become a citizen his right dates back to his purchase, and he may thereupon secure a United States patent for his claim.

Tunnels.—There is no authority of law for a tunnel location 3,000 by 1,500 feet. A proper location is the width of the tunnel for 3,000 feet.

There is no provision of law for patenting tunnel location, but lodes discovered in running a tunnel may be patented in like manner as other lodes.

When a lode is struck or discovered for the first time in running a tunnel, the tunnel owners have the option of recording their claim of 1,500 feet all on one side of the point of discovery or intersection, or partly on one side thereof and partly on the other.

Prospecting for blind lodes is prohibited on the line of a located tunnel, while the tunnel is in progress, but other parties are in no way debarred from prospecting for blind lodes or running tunnels, so long as they keep without the line of such tunnel.

The right is granted to tunnel owners to 1,500 feet of each blind lode not previously known to exist, which may be discovered in their tunnel.

Cross Ledges.—Revised Statutes. Section 2336. Where two or more ledges cross or intersect each other, priority of title shall govern, and such prior location shall be entitled to all ore or mineral contained within the space of intersection, but the subsequent location shall have the right of way through the space of intersection for the purpose of the convenient working of the mine. And where two or more veins unite, the oldest or prior location shall take the vein below the point of union, including all the space of the intersection.

THE LAW OF COPYRIGHT

IT WAS formerly held that by common law an author had a perpetual right in the products of his intellect. This is now denied, and the whole matter has become the subject of statute, so that now, unless the provisions of the law designed to secure to the author the exclusive ownership of the results of his labor are strictly complied with, the product is public property. The following may be copyrighted:

First, books, meaning not only such in their ordinary sense, but such as are printed only on one sheet, as the words of a song or the music accompanying it. It may be a diagram with directions on one sheet of paper, private letters, abstracts of title, an illustrated newspaper. If the book is in manuscript, it may yet be copyrighted. A new edition of a copyrighted book is protected by the original copyright, but not to the extent of pedantic new matter in it.

Compilations may be copyrighted. Under

this head also fall dictionaries, books of chronology, gazetteers, guide books, directories, calendars, catalogues, tables, collections of statistics, receipts, designs.

Abridgments and law reports, where there is original matter, may be copyrighted.

Advertisements, as such, may not be copyrighted. Maps, charts, newspapers, magazines, musical and dramatic compositions, engravings, cuts, prints or photographs may be copyrighted.

DIRECTIONS FOR SECURING COPYRIGHTS

Under the Revised Acts of Congress, including the Provisions for Foreign Copyright

1. A *printed* copy of the title of the book, map, chart, dramatic or musical composition, engraving, cut, print, photograph, or chromo, or a *description* of the painting, drawing, statue, statuary, or model or design for a work of the fine arts, for which copyright is desired, must be delivered to the Librarian of Congress or deposited in the mail, within the United States, *prepaid*, addressed to the Librarian of Congress, Washington, D. C. This must be done on or before day of publication in this or any foreign country.

The *printed title* required may be a copy of the title page of such publications as have title pages. In other cases, the title must be printed expressly for copyright entry, with name of claimant of copyright. The style of type is immaterial, and the print of a type-writer will be accepted. But a separate title is required for each entry, and each title must be printed on paper as large as commercial note. The title of a *periodical* must include the date and number; and each number of a periodical requires a separate entry of copyright.

2. The legal fee for *recording* each copyright claim is 50 cents, and for a *copy* of this record (or certificate of copyright) an additional fee of 50 cents is required, making $1, in case certificate is wanted, which will be mailed as soon as reached in the records. In the case of publications produced by other than citizens or residents of the United States, the fee for recording title is $1, and 50 cents additional for a copy of the record. Certificates covering more than one entry in one certificate are not issued.

3. Not later than the day of publication of each book or other article, in this country or abroad, two complete copies of the best edition issued must be delivered to perfect the copyright, or deposited in the mail within the United States, addressed to the Librarian of Congress, Washington, D. C. The freight or postage must be prepaid, or the publications inclosed in parcels covered by printed penalty labels, furnished by the Librarian of Congress, in which case they will come free by mail (not express), without limit of weight. In the case of books, photographs, chromos, or lithographs, the two copies deposited must be printed from type set or plates made in the United States, or from negatives or drawings on stone, or transfers therefrom, made within the United States. Without the deposit of copies above required the copyright is void, and a penalty of $25 is incurred. No copy is required to be deposited elsewhere.

The law requires one copy of each new edition wherein any substantial changes are made, to be deposited with the Librarian of Congress.

4. No copyright is valid unless notice is given by inserting in every copy published, on the title page or the page following, if it be a book; or if a map, chart, musical composition, print, cut, engraving, photograph, painting, drawing, chromo, statue, statuary, or model or design intended to be perfected as a work of the fine arts, by inscribing upon some portion thereof, or on the substance on which the same is mounted, the following words, viz: "*Entered according to the act of Congress, in the year* ——, *by* ——, *in the office of the Librarian of Congress, at Washington*," or, at the option of the person entering the copyright, the words: "*Copyright, 18*—, *by* ——." (It is essential that the year and the name be given. The omission of either forfeits the copyright.)

The law imposes a penalty of $100 upon any person who has not obtained copyright who shall insert the notice "*Entered according to act of Congress*," or "*Copyright*," etc., or words of the same import, in or upon any book or other article.

5. The copyright law secures to authors or their assigns the exclusive right to translate or to dramatize their own works.

Since the phrase, "*All rights reserved*," refers exclusively to the right to dramatize or to translate, it has no bearing upon any publications except original works, and will not be entered upon the record in other cases.

6. The original term of copyright runs for twenty-eight years. *Within six months before* the end of that time, the author or designer, or his widow or children, may secure a renewal for the further term of fourteen years, making forty-two years in all. Applications for

renewal must be accompanied by explicit statement of ownership, in the case of the author, or of relationship, in the case of his heirs, and must state definitely the date and place of entry of the original copyright. Advertisement of renewal is to be made within two months of date of renewal certificate, in some newspaper, for four weeks.

7. The time within which any work entered for copyright may be issued from the press is not limited by any law or regulation, but the courts have held that it should take place within a reasonable time. A copyright may be secured for a projected work as well as a completed one. But the law provides for no caveat, or notice of interference — only for actual entry of title.

8. A copyright is assignable in law by any instrument of writing, and such assignment is to be recorded in the office of the Librarian of Congress within sixty days from its date. The fee for this record and certificate is one dollar, and for a certified copy of any record of assignment one dollar.

9. A copy of the record (or duplicate certificate) of any copyright entry will be furnished, under seal of the office, at the rate of fifty cents each.

10. In the case of books published in more than one volume, or of periodicals published in numbers, or of engravings, photographs, or other articles published with variations, a copyright is to be entered for each volume or part of a book, or number of a periodical, or variety, as to style, title, or inscription, of any other article. But a book published serially in a periodical, under the same general title, requires only one entry. To complete the copyright on such a work, two copies of each serial part, as well as of the complete work (if published separately), should be deposited.

11. To secure copyright for a painting, statue or model or design intended to be perfected as a work of the fine arts, a definite description must accompany the application for copyright, and a photograph of the same as large as "cabinet size" mailed to the Librarian of Congress no later than the day of publication of the work or design.

The fine arts, for copyright purposes, include only painting and sculpture, and articles of merely ornamental and decorative art are referred to the Patent Office, as subjects for design patents.

12. Copyrights cannot be granted upon trade-marks, nor upon names of companies or articles, nor upon an idea or device, nor upon prints or labels intended to be used for any article of manufacture. If protection for such names or labels is desired, application must be made to the Patent Office.

The provisions as to copyright entry in the United States by foreign authors, etc., are the same as the foregoing.

The rights of citizens or subjects of a foreign nation to copyright within the United States is not to take effect unless such nation permits to United States citizens the benefit of copyright on the same basis as to its own citizens; or unless such nation is party to an agreement providing for reciprocity in copyright, to which the United States may become a party.

14. Every applicant for a copyright should state distinctly the full name and residence of the claimant, and whether the right is claimed as author, designer, or proprietor. No affidavit or witness to the application is required.

THE LAW OF TRADEMARKS

ANY person, firm or corporation can obtain protection for any lawful trademark by complying with the following:

1. By causing to be recorded in the Patent Office the name, residence and place of business of persons desiring the trademark.

2. The class of merchandise and description of the same.

3. A description of the trademark itself with fac-similes.

4. The length of time that the said mark has already been used.

5. By payment of the required fee — $6.00 for labels and $25 for trademarks.

6. By complying with such regulations as may be prescribed by the Commissioner of Patents.

7. A lawful trademark must consist of some arbitrary word (not the name of a person or place), indicating or not the use or nature of the thing to which it is applied, of some designated symbol, or of both word and symbol.

HOW TO OBTAIN A PATENT

PATENTS are issued in the name of the United States, and under the seal of the Patent Office, to any person who has invented or discovered any new and useful art, machine, manufacture or composition of matter, or any new and useful improvement thereof, not known or used by others in this country, and not patented or described in any printed publication in this or any foreign country before his invention or discovery thereof, and not in public use or on sale for more than two years prior to his application, unless the same is proved to have been abandoned; and by any person who, by his own industry, genius, efforts and expense, has invented and produced any new and original design for a manufacture, bust, statue, alto-relievo, or bas-relief; any new and original design for the printing of woolen, silk, cotton or other fabrics; any new and original impression, ornament, pattern, print or picture to be printed, painted, cast or otherwise placed on or worked into any article of manufacture; or any new, useful and original shape or configuration of any article of manufacture, the same not having been known or used by others before his invention or production thereof, or patented or described in any printed publication, upon payment of the fees required by law and other due proceedings had.

Every patent contains a grant to the patentee, his heirs or assigns, for the term of seventeen years, of the exclusive right to make, use and vend the invention or discovery throughout the United States and the Territories, referring to the specification for the particulars thereof.

If it appear that the inventor, at the time of making his application, believed himself to be the first inventor or discoverer, a patent will not be refused on account of the invention or discovery, or any part thereof, having been known or used in any foreign country before his invention or discovery thereof, if it had not been before patented or described in any printed publication.

Joint inventors are entitled to a joint patent; neither can claim one separately. Independent inventors of distinct and independent improvements in the same machine cannot obtain a joint patent for their separate inventions; nor does the fact that one furnishes the capital and another makes the invention entitle them to make application as joint inventors; but in such case they may become joint patentees.

The receipt of letters patent from a foreign government will not prevent the inventor from obtaining a patent in the United States, unless the invention shall have been introduced into public use in the United States more than two years prior to the application. But every patent granted for an invention which has been previously patented by the same inventor in a foreign country will be so limited as to expire at the same time with the foreign patent, or, if there be more than one, at the same time with the one having the shortest unexpired term, but in no case will it be in force more than seventeen years.

Applications.—Applications for a patent must be made in writing to the Commissioner of Patents. The applicant must also file in the Patent Office a written description of the same, and of the manner and process of making, constructing, compounding and using it, in such full, clear, concise and exact terms as to enable any person skilled in the art or science to which it appertains, or with which it is most nearly connected, to make, construct, compound and use the same; and in case of a machine he must explain the principle thereof, and the best mode in which he has contemplated applying that principle, so as to distinguish it from other inventions, and particularly point out and distinctly claim the part, improvement or combination which he claims as his invention or discovery. The specification and claim must be signed by the inventor and attested by two witnesses.

When the nature of the case admits of drawings, the applicant must furnish one copy signed by the inventor or his attorney in fact, and attested by two witnesses, to be filed in the Patent Office. In all cases which admit of representation by model, the applicant, if required by the Commissioner, shall furnish a model of convenient size to exhibit advantageously the several parts of his invention or discovery.

The applicant shall make oath that he verily believes himself to be the original and first inventor or discoverer of the art, machine, manufacture, composition or improvement for which he solicits a patent; that he does not know and does not believe that the same was ever before known or used, and shall state of what country he is a citizen. Such oath may be made before any person within the United States authorized by law to administer oaths, or, when the applicant resides in a foreign country, before any minister, chargé d'affaires, consul or commercial agent, holding commission under the Government of the United States, or before any notary public of the foreign country in which the applicant may be.

On the filing of such application and the payment of the fees required by law, if, on such examination, it appears that the claimant is justly entitled to a patent under the law, and that the same is sufficiently useful and important, the Commissioner will issue a patent therefor.

Assignments.—Every patent or any interest therein shall be assignable in law by an instrument in writing; and the patentee or his assigns or legal representatives may, in like manner, grant and convey an exclusive right under his patent to the whole or any specified part of the United States.

Reissues.—A reissue is granted to the original patentee, his legal representatives, or the assignees of the entire interest, when, by reason of a defective or insufficient specification, or by reason of the patentee claiming as his invention or discovery more than he had a right to claim as new, the original patent is inoperative or invalid, provided the error has arisen from inadvertence, accident or mistake, and without any fraudulent or deceptive intention. In the cases of patents issued and assigned prior to July 8, 1870, the applications for reissue may be made by the assignees; but in the cases of patents issued or assigned since that date, the applications must be made and the specifications sworn to by the inventors, if they be living.

Caveats.—A caveat, under the patent law, is a notice given to the office of the caveator's claim as inventor, in order to prevent the grant of a patent to another for the same alleged invention upon an application filed during the life of the caveat without notice to the caveator.

Any citizen of the United States who has made a new invention or discovery, and desires further time to mature the same, may, on payment of a fee of $10, file in the Patent Office a caveat setting forth the object and the distinguishing characteristics of the invention, and praying protection of his right until he shall have matured his invention. Such caveat shall be filed in the confidential archives of the office and preserved in secrecy, and shall be operative for the term of one year from the filing thereof.

An alien has the same privilege, if he has resided in the United States one year next preceding the filing of his caveat, and has made oath of his intention to become a citizen.

The caveat must comprise a specification, oath, and, when the nature of the case admits of it, a drawing, and, like the application, must be limited to a single invention or improvement.

Fees.—Fees must be paid in advance, and are as follows: On filing each original application for a patent, $15. On issuing each original patent, $20. In design cases: For three years and six months, $10; for seven years, $15; for fourteen years, $30. On filing each caveat, $10. On every application for the reissue of a patent, $30. On filing each disclaimer, $10. For certified copies of patents and other papers, including certified printed copies, 10 cents per hundred words. For recording every assignment, agreement, power of attorney or other paper, of three hundred words or under, $1; of over three hundred and under one thousand words, $2; of over one thousand words, $3. For copies of drawings, the reasonable cost of making them.

POINTS OF CRIMINAL LAW

YOU cannot lawfully condone an offense by receiving back stolen property.

The exemption of females from arrest applies only in civil, not in criminal matters.

Every man is bound to obey the call of a sheriff for assistance in making an arrest.

The rule "Every man's house is his castle" does not hold good when a man is accused of crime.

Embezzlement can be charged only against a clerk or servant, or the officer or agent of a corporation.

Bigamy cannot be proven in law if one party to a marriage has been absent and not heard from for five years.

Grand larceny is when the value of property stolen exceeds $25.00—when less than that, the offense is petit larceny.

Arson to be in the first degree must have been committed at night, and the buildings fired must have been inhabited.

Drunkenness is not a legal excuse for crime, but delirium tremens is considered by the law as a species of insanity.

In a case of assault it is only necessary to prove an "offer or attempt at assault." Battery presumes physical violence.

Mayhem, although popularly supposed to refer to injury to the face, lips, tongue, eye or ear, applies to any injury done a limb.

A felony is a crime punishable by imprisonment in a State prison; an "infamous" crime is one punishable with death or State prison.

A police officer is not authorized to make an arrest without a warrant unless he has personal knowledge of the offense for which the arrest is made.

An accident is not a crime, unless criminal carelessness can be proven. A man shooting at a burglar and killing a member of his family is not a murderer.

Burglary in the first degree can be committed only in the night time. Twilight, if dark enough to prevent distinguishing a man's face, is the same as night in law.

Murder to be in the first degree must be willful, premeditated and malicious, or committed while the murderer is engaged in a felonious act. The killing of a man in a duel is murder, and it is a misdemeanor to accept or give a challenge.

False swearing is perjury in law only when willfully done and when the oath has been legally administered. Such qualifying expressions as "to the best of my belief," "as I am informed," may save an deponent from being perjured. The law is that the false statement sworn to must be absolute. Subornation of perjury is a felony.

CONGRESS must meet at least once a year. One State cannot undo the acts of another. Congress may admit as many new States as desired.

The Constitution guarantees every citizen a speedy trial by jury.

A State cannot exercise a power which is vested in Congress alone.

One State must respect the laws and legal decisions of another.

Congress cannot pass a law to punish a crime already committed.

U. S. Senators are chosen by the legislatures of the States by joint ballot.

Bills for revenue can originate only in the House of Representatives.

A person committing a felony in one State cannot find refuge in another.

The Constitution of the United States forbids excessive bail or cruel punishment.

Treaties with foreign countries are made by the President and ratified by the Senate.

In the U. S. Senate Rhode Island or Nevada has an equal voice with New York.

When Congress passes a bankruptcy law it annuls all the State laws on that subject.

Writing alone does not constitute treason against the United States. There must be an overt act.

Congress cannot lay any disabilities on the children of a person convicted of crime or misdemeanor.

The Territories each send a delegate to Congress, who has the right of debate, but not the right to vote.

The Vice-President, who *ex officio* presides over the Senate, has no vote in that body except on a tie ballot.

An act of Congress cannot become a law over the President's veto except on a two-thirds vote of both houses.

An officer of the Government cannot accept title of nobility, order or honor without the permission of Congress.

Money lost in the mails cannot be recovered from the Government. Registering a letter does not insure its contents.

It is the House of Representatives that may impeach the President for any crime, and the Senate hears the accusation.

If the President holds a bill longer than ten days while Congress is still in session, it becomes a law without his signature.

Silver coin of denominations less than $1 is not a legal tender for more than $5.00. Copper and nickel is not legal tender.

The term of a Congressman is two years; but a Congressman may be re-elected to as many successive terms as his constituents may wish.

Amendments to the Constitution require a two-thirds vote of each house of Congress and must be ratified by at least three-fourths of the States.

When the militia is called out in the service of the General Government, they pass out of the control of the various States under the command of the President.

The President of the United States must be 35 years of age; a U. S. Senator, 30; a Congressman, 25.

A grand jury is a secret tribunal, and may hear only one side of a case. It simply decides whether there is good reason to hold for trial. It consists of twenty-three men, twelve of whom may indict. To convict requires the unanimous vote of a trial (or petty) jury.

A naturalized citizen cannot become President or Vice-President of the United States. A male child born abroad of American parents has an equal chance to become President with one born on American soil.

VOTING AND NATURALIZATION

THE right to vote comes from the State, and is a State gift. Naturalization is a Federal right, and is a gift of the Union, not of any one State. In nearly one-half the Union aliens who have declared intentions vote and have the right to vote equally with naturalized or native-born citizens. In the other half only actual citizens may vote. The Federal naturalization laws apply to the whole Union alike, and provide that no alien male may be naturalized until after five years' residence. Even after five years' residence and due naturalization he is not entitled to vote unless the laws of the State confer the privilege upon him, and he may vote in one State (Minnesota) four months after landing, if he has immediately declared his intention, under United States law, to become a citizen.

Naturalization.— The conditions under and the manner in which an alien may be admitted to become a citizen of the United States are prescribed by sections 2165-74 of the Revised Statutes of the United States.

Declaration of Intention.— The alien must declare upon oath before a Circuit or District Court of the United States, or a District or Supreme Court of the Territories, or a court of record of any of the States having common law jurisdiction and a seal and clerk, two years at least prior to his admission, that it is, *bona fide*, his intention to become a citizen of the United States, and to renounce forever all allegiance and fidelity to any foreign prince or State, and particularly to the one of which he may be at the time a citizen or subject.

Oath on Application for Admission.—He must, at the time of his application to be admitted, declare on oath, before some one of the courts above specified, "that he will support the Constitution of the United States, and that he absolutely and entirely renounces and abjures all allegiance and fidelity to every foreign prince, potentate, state or sovereignty, and particularly, by name, to the prince, potentate, state or sovereignty of which he was before a citizen or subject," which proceedings must be recorded by the clerk of the court.

Conditions for Citizenship.—If it shall appear to the satisfaction of the court to which the alien has applied that he has resided continuously within the United States for at least five years, and within the State or Territory where such court is at the time held one year at least; and that during that time "he has behaved as a man of good moral character, attached to the principles of the Constitution of the United States, and well disposed to the good order and happiness of the same," he will be admitted to citizenship.

Titles of Nobility.—If the applicant has borne any hereditary title or order of nobility, he must make an express renunciation of the same at the time of his application.

Soldiers.—Any alien of the age of twenty-one years and upwards, who has been in the armies of the United States and has been honorably discharged therefrom, may become a citizen on his petition, without any previous declaration of intention, provided that he has resided in the United States at least one year previous to his application, and is of good moral character.

Minors.—Any alien under the age of twenty-one years who has resided in the United States three years next preceding his arriving at that age, and who has continued to reside therein to the time he may make application to be admitted a citizen thereof, may, after he arrives at the age of twenty-one years, and after he has resided five years within the United States, including the three years of his minority, be admitted a citizen; but he must make a declaration on oath and prove to the satisfaction of the court that for two years next preceding it has been his *bona fide* intention to become a citizen.

Children of Naturalized Citizens.—The children of persons who have been duly naturalized, being under the age of sixteen years at the time of the naturalization of their parents, shall, if dwelling in the United States, be considered as citizens thereof.

Citizens' Children who are Born Abroad.—The children of persons who now are or have been citizens of the United States are, though born out of the limits and jurisdiction of the United States, considered as citizens thereof.

Protection Abroad to Naturalized Citizens.—Section 2,000 of the Revised Statutes of the United States declares that "all naturalized citizens of the United States while in foreign countries are entitled to and shall receive from this government the same protection of persons and property which is accorded to native-born citizens."

When a Man Becomes of Age.—The question sometimes arises whether a man is entitled to vote at an election held on the day preceding the twenty-first anniversary of his birth. Blackstone, in his Commentaries, book I, page 463, says: "Full age in male or female is 21 years, which age is completed on the day preceding the anniversary of a person's birth, who, till that time, is an infant, and so styled in law." The late Chief Justice Sharswood, in his edition of Blackstone's Commentaries, quotes Christian's note on the above as follows: "If he is born on the 16th day of February, 1608, he is of age to do any legal act on the morning of the 15th of February, 1629, though he may not have lived twenty-one years by nearly forty-eight hours. The reason assigned is that in law there is no fraction of a day; and if the birth were on the last second of one day and the act on the first second of the preceding day twenty-one years after, then twenty-one years would be completed; and in the law it is the same whether a thing is done upon one moment of the day or another." The same high authority (Sharswood) adds in a note of his own: "A person is of full age the day before the twenty-first anniversary of his birthday."

THE PRESIDENTIAL ELECTION

THE President and Vice-President of the United States are chosen by officials termed "Electors" in each State, who are, under existing State laws, chosen by the qualified voters thereof by ballot, on the first Tuesday after the first Monday in November in every fourth year preceding the year in which the Presidential term expires.

The Constitution of the United States prescribes that each State shall "appoint," in such manner as the legislature thereof may direct, a number of electors equal to the whole number of Senators and Representatives to which the State may be entitled in Congress; but no Senator or Representative or person holding an office of trust or profit under the United States shall be an elector. The Constitution requires that the day when electors are chosen shall be the same throughout the United States. At the beginning of our government most of the electors were chosen by the legislatures of their respective States, the people having no direct participation in their choice; and one State, South Carolina, continued that practice down to the breaking out of the civil war. But in all the States now the Presidential electors are, under the direction of State laws, chosen by the people.

The manner in which the chosen electors meet and ballot for a President and Vice-President of the United States is provided for in Article XII. of the Constitution. The same article prescribes the mode in which the Congress shall count the ballots of the electors, and announce the result.

The procedure of the two houses, in case the returns of the election of electors from any State are disputed, is provided in the "Electoral Count" Act, passed by the Forty-ninth Congress.

The "Electoral Count" Act directs that the Presidential electors shall meet and give their votes on the second Monday in January next following their election. It fixes the time when Congress shall be in session to count the ballots as the second Wednesday in February succeeding the meeting of the electors.

The Presidential succession is fixed by chapter 4 of the acts of the Forty-ninth Congress, first session. In case of the removal, death, resignation or inability of both the President and Vice-President, then the Secretary of State shall act as President until the disability of the President or Vice-President is removed or a President is elected. If there be no Secretary of State, then the Secretary of the Treasury will act; and the remainder of the order of succession is: The Secretary of War, Attorney-General, Postmaster-General, Secretary of the Navy, and Secretary of the Interior. The acting President must, upon taking office, convene Congress, if not at the time in session, in extraordinary session, giving twenty days' notice.

THE INTER-STATE COMMERCE LAW

THE Inter-State Commerce Act is a law passed by Congress in 1887 for the regulation of rates and the management of inter-State commerce. It applies to carriers engaged in the transportation of passengers or property wholly by railroad or partly by railroad and partly by water, from one State, Territory or District of the United States to any other State, Territory or District, or to or from a foreign country. It provides for the appointment of a board of five commissioners, empowered to inquire into the management of the carriers and determine the reasonableness of their rates. A carrier whose line is entirely within a State is subject to the act so far as it makes or accepts through rates on inter-State commerce.

Among other things the act requires that all charges shall be just and reasonable; that charges for a shorter distance shall not exceed those for a longer distance on the same line in the same direction, when the circumstances and conditions are similar; that there shall be no unjust discrimination as between persons or classes of traffic or localities, in the charges made or in the service rendered; that the rates charged for transportation shall be printed, filed with the Commission and kept for public inspection at the several stations; and that the carriers shall annually make a complete exhibit of their business to the Commission.

The act makes exceptions from its provisions of the carriage of property for the United States or for any State or municipal government, or for charitable purposes, or to or from fairs and expositions, and it allows of the issuing of mileage, excursion or commutation tickets, and admits of the giving of reduced rates to ministers of religion and free transportation to the officers and employees of the carrier, and to the principal officers of other carriers.

INTERNAL REVENUE

THE internal revenue of the U. S. includes the taxes on spirits, tobacco, etc., and most of the receipts from national taxes, except customs duties and the receipts from the sale of public lands, patent fees, postal receipts, etc.

The Constitution declares that Congress has the power "to lay and collect taxes, duties, imposts and excises," and that they shall be uniform throughout the U. S., and provides that direct taxes shall be apportioned among the States only in proportion to the population.

At the close of the Revolution raising money by internal taxation was hardly thought of, and at that time the condition of the people and manufactures would not warrant it. The first internal revenue tax imposed by Congress was that of March 3, 1791, on distilled spirits of domestic manufacture, the enforcement of which led to the whisky insurrection. In 1798 the first direct tax of the kind, one of $2,000,000, was apportioned among the States, and it was proposed that it should be levied on dwelling-houses, slaves and land.

All internal taxes were repealed in 1802 in accordance with the recommendation of President Jefferson, and no others were authorized until 1813, when the war with England necessitated an increased revenue. These taxes were continued a few years after the war, but were abolished and none were levied until 1861.

The civil war found a renewal of the internal revenue system, and in 1861 a direct tax of $20,000,000 was apportioned among the States. On July 1, 1862, an act was passed levying taxes on all sorts and kinds of articles too numerous to mention. A few industries were taxed out of existence and all were more or less disturbed, but the people submitted without opposition. Great reductions were made after the war ceased, and at the present time the only subjects of internal revenue taxation are tobacco, spirits, fermented liquors, bank circulation and oleomargarine.

The following have always been exempt from taxation in the U. S.:

Public property of both State and Nation; the property of incorporated institutions of learning; houses of worship, cemeteries and the personal property of individuals, so far as to cover the necessities of life.

In 1792 the amount raised by internal revenue was $208,942; in 1866, $309,226,813; in 1892, $153,971,072.

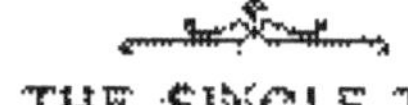

THE SINGLE TAX

THIS idea was first formulated by Mr. Henry George in his book, "Progress and Poverty," in 1879, and has grown steadily in favor. Single tax men assert as a fundamental principle that all men are equally entitled to the use of the earth; therefore, no one should be allowed to hold valuable land without paying to the community the value of the privilege. They hold that this is the only rightful source of public revenue, and they would therefore abolish all taxation, local, State and national, except a tax upon the rental value of land exclusive of its improvements, the revenue thus raised to be divided among local, State and general governments, as the revenue from certain direct taxes is now divided between local and State governments.

The single tax would not fall on all land, but only on valuable land, and on that in proportion to its value. It would thus be a tax, not on use or improvements, but on ownership of land, taking what would otherwise go to the landlord as owner.

In accordance with the principle that all men are equally entitled to the use of the earth, they would solve the transportation problem by public ownership and control of all highways, including the roadbeds of railroads, leaving their use equally free to all.

The single tax system would:

1. Dispense with a horde of taxgatherers, simplify government and greatly reduce its cost.

2. Give us with all the world that absolute free trade which now exists between the States of the Union.

3. Give us free trade in finance by abolishing all taxes on private issues of money.

4. Take the weight of taxation from agricultural districts, where land has little or no value apart from improvements, and put it upon valuable land such as city lots and mineral deposits.

5. Call upon men to contribute for public expenses in proportion to the natural opportunities they monopolize and compel them to pay just as much for holding the land idle as for putting it to its fullest use.

6. Make it unprofitable for speculators to hold land unused or only partly used, and, by thus opening to labor unlimited fields of employment, solve the labor problem, raise wages in all occupations and abolish involuntary poverty.

English education dates from Alfred the Great, who ordered that the son of every freeman who could afford it should be taught reading and writing.

The system of Pestalozzi taught that form, number and language are the elements of knowledge, and that a thorough acquaintance with them in every phase constitutes education.

Insurance

A *STOCK Insurance Company* is one whose capital is owned by stockholders, they alone sharing the profits, and they alone being liable for losses. The business of such a company, and also of a mixed company, is managed by directors chosen by the stockholders. Policy-holders, unless at the same time stockholders, have no voice in the management of the company's business or in the election of its officers.

A Mutual Insurance Company is one in which the profits and losses are shared among the policy-holders (the insured.)

Mixed Companies are a combination of the foregoing. In a mixed company all profits above a certain fixed dividend are usually divided among the policy-holders.

Some mutual and mixed companies issue what are called *non-participating policies*. The holders of these do not share in the profits or losses.

FIRE INSURANCE

Policies for fire insurance are generally issued for a period of one to five years. Ordinarily, in case of loss by fire, the insured will be paid the extent of his loss up to the amount of insurance, unless the insurance company prefer to replace or repair the damaged property, which privilege is usually reserved. If the policy contains the "average clause" the payment will cover only such portion of the loss as the amount of insurance bears to the value of the property insured.

A Floating Policy is one which covers property stored in several buildings or places. The name is applied more particularly to policies which cover goods whose location may be changed in process of manufacture, or in the ordinary course of business. The "average clause" is a usual condition of policies of this class.

Short Rates are rates for a term less than a year. If an insurance policy is terminated at the request of the policy-holder, the company retains the customary "short rates" for the time the policy has been in force, as shown by the following tables:

Policy for 1 year.	Policy for 2 years.	Policy for 3 years.	Policy for 4 years.	Policy for 5 years.	Charge this proportion of whole Premium.
1 mo.	2 mo.	3 mo.	4 mo.	5 mo.	20 per cent.
2 "	4 "	6 "	8 "	10 "	30 "
3 "	6 "	9 "	12 "	15 "	40 "
4 "	8 "	12 "	16 "	20 "	50 "
5 "	10 "	15 "	20 "	25 "	60 "
6 "	12 "	18 "	24 "	30 "	70 "
7 "	14 "	21 "	28 "	35 "	75 "
8 "	16 "	24 "	32 "	40 "	80 "
9 "	18 "	27 "	36 "	45 "	85 "
10 "	20 "	30 "	40 "	50 "	90 "
11 "	22 "	33 "	44 "	55 "	95 "

When a policy is terminated at the option of the company, a ratable portion of the premium is refunded for the unexpired term.

LIFE INSURANCE

In ordinary life policies a certain premium is to be paid every year until the death of the insured, when the policy becomes payable to the beneficiary. There are other kinds of policies, however, and these are described below:

Limited Payment Life Policy.—Conditions: Premiums to be paid annually for a certain fixed number of years, or until the death of the insured, should that occur prior to the expiration of this period. Policy payable at death of the insured. Advantages: Payments on this kind of policy may all be made while the insured is best able to make them, and, if he live to an old age, the policy will not be a continual burden, but will rather be a source of income, as the yearly dividends may be taken out in cash or added to the amount of insurance.

Term Life Policy.—In this method of insurance, the insurance company agrees to pay to the beneficiaries a certain sum on the death of the insured, should that event occur within a fixed term.

Endowment Policy.—A combination of a Term Policy and a Pure Endowment. These policies are issued for endowment periods of 10, 15, 20, 25, 30 or 35 years, and may be paid up by a single payment, by an annual premium during the endowment period, or by five or ten annual payments. Conditions: 1. Insurance during a stipulated period, payable at the death of the insured, should that event happen within said period. 2. An endowment of the same amount as the policy, payable to the insured, if still living at the end of the period fixed.

advantages: Limited term of payments; insurance during the time when the death of the insured would cause most embarrassment to his family; provision for old age, as the amount of the policy will be paid to the insured if still living, at a time when advanced age may make it of great benefit.

Annuity Policies are secured by a single cash payment and insure the holder the yearly payment of a certain sum of money during life.

Joint Life Policy.—An agreement to pay a certain sum on the death of any one of two or more persons thus insured.

Non-forfeiting Policies do not become void for non-payment of premiums. In some companies all limited-payment life policies, and all endowment policies, after premiums for three (or two) years have been paid, and the original policy is surrendered within a certain time, provide for paid-up insurance for as many parts of the original amount assured as there shall have been complete annual premiums received in cash by the company. Some companies voluntarily apply all credited dividends to the continuance of the insurance. Others apply the legal reserve to the purchase of term insurance at regular rates.

Special Forms.—The Reserve Endowment, Tontine Investment and other special policies guarantee to the holder a definite surrender value at the termination of certain periods. The surrender value of a policy is the amount in cash which the company will pay the holder of a policy on its surrender—the legal reserve less a certain per cent. for expenses.

The Reserve of life insurance policies is the present value of the amount to be paid at death, less the present value of all the net premiums to be paid in the future.

The Reserve Fund of a life insurance company is that sum in hand which, invested at a given rate of interest, together with future premiums on existing policies, should be sufficient to meet all obligations as they become due. It is the sum of the separate reserves of the several policies outstanding.

The Expectation of Life is the number of years which one may probably live. This average number of years has been determined from the experience of insurance companies:

Age.	Expectation in years.	Age.	Expectation in years.	Age.	Expectation in years.	Age.	Expectation in years
0	28.15	24	32.70	48	22.37	72	9.14
1	36.78	25	32.33	49	21.72	73	8.69
2	38.74	26	31.93	50	21.12	74	8.25
3	40.01	27	31.50	51	20.61	75	7.83
4	40.75	28	31.08	52	20.05	76	7.40
5	40.88	29	30.66	53	19.49	77	6.99
6	40.69	30	30.25	54	18.92	78	6.58
7	40.47	31	29.83	55	18.35	79	6.22
8	40.14	32	29.43	56	17.78	80	5.85
9	39.72	33	29.02	57	17.20	81	5.50
10	39.23	34	28.62	58	16.63	82	5.16
11	38.64	35	28.20	59	16.04	83	4.87
12	38.02	36	27.78	60	15.44	84	4.58
13	37.41	37	27.34	61	14.86	85	4.27
14	36.79	38	26.91	62	14.26	86	3.98
15	36.17	39	26.47	63	13.66	87	3.70
16	35.76	40	26.04	64	13.05	88	3.47
17	35.37	41	25.61	65	12.43	89	3.56
18	34.98	42	25.19	66	11.96	90	3.45
19	34.59	43	24.77	67	11.49	91	3.29
20	34.22	44	24.35	68	11.41	92	3.12
21	33.84	45	23.92	69	10.50	93	2.40
22	33.46	46	23.37	70	10.08	94	1.98
23	33.08	47	22.83	71	9.40	95	1.02

MARINE AND TRANSIT INSURANCE

Insurance of vessels and their cargoes against the perils of navigation is termed *Marine Insurance.*

Inland and Transit Insurance refer to insurance of merchandise while being transported from place to place either by rail or water routes, or both.

Insurance Certificates, showing that certain property has been insured and stating the amount of the insurance and the name of the party abroad who is authorized to make the settlement, are issued by marine companies. They are negotiable and are usually sent to the consignee of the merchandise to make the loss payable at the port of destination.

The adjustment of marine policies in case of loss is on the same principle as the adjustment of fire policies containing the "average clause."

Open Policies are such upon which additional insurances may be entered at different times.

"There is only one lamp which we can carry in our hand, and which will burn through the darkest night and make the light of a home for us in a desert place. It is sympathy with everything that breathes."—*Ouida.*

"'To be employed,' said the poet Gray, 'is to be happy.' 'It is far better to wear out than rust out,' said Bishop Cumberland. 'Have we not all eternity to rest in?' exclaimed Arnauld."—*Samuel Smiles.*

Stock Investments Explained

THE capital of corporations is always divided into shares, usually of $100 each. These are known as stock and represent an interest in the property and profits of the company. A *dividend* is the distribution of the profits, proportionate to number of shares held, among the stockholders. *Stock certificates* are written instruments, signed by the proper officers of the company, and certifying that the holder is the owner of a certain number of shares. These are transferable, and may be bought and sold the same as other property. The sum for which each share or certificate was issued is the par value, and the amount for which it can be sold the market value.

Preferred Stock takes preference of the ordinary stock of a corporation, and the holders are entitled to a stated per cent. annually out of net earnings before a dividend can be declared on common stock. Preferred stocks are generally the result of reorganization, although sometimes issued in payment of floating or unsecured debts.

Watered Stock.—Sometimes the charter of a corporation forbids the declaring of a dividend exceeding a certain per cent. of the par value of its stock. In this case the directors may find it desirable to "water" the stock—that is, issue additional shares. This increase in the number of shares of course reduces the percentage of dividend, although the same profit in the aggregate is secured to the stockholders.

DEALING IN STOCKS.—The person employing a broker to buy the stock is required to advance at the outset a certain per cent. of the purchase price of the stock, as security for possible losses by reason of a decline in the stock while in the broker's hands. The amount of the margin required is generally 10 per cent., but may be more or less, and frequently is nothing at all, depending on the broker's confidence in his customer's readiness to meet losses, if there be any.

The broker then goes into the stock exchange and buys of some selling broker the stock indicated, the buying broker himself advancing the purchase money.

The relations existing between the customer and the broker in a transaction of this kind may be briefly stated as follows:

The broker agrees: 1. That he will buy for his customer the stock indicated, at its market value. 2. That he will hold the stock for the benefit of his customer so long as the necessary margin is advanced, and kept good, or until notice is given by either party that the transaction must be closed. 3. That he will at all times have the stock in his possession or under his control, or an equal amount of other shares of the same stock, subject to the call of the customer. 4. That he will sell the shares on the order of the customer, on payment to him of the purchase price advanced by the broker, accounting to the customer for the proceeds of the sale. 5. That he will exercise proper care and competent skill in the services which he undertakes to perform.

The customer agrees: 1. To pay the margin called for at the outset. 2. To keep good such margin according to the fluctuations of the market. 3. To take the stock purchased by his order when requested to do so by the broker, paying the latter the difference between the margin advanced and the sum paid for the stock by the broker, together with his commissions for doing the business.

Although the broker's money bought the stock, it belongs to the customer, together with all its earnings and dividends while in the broker's possession, and the customer is entitled to the possession of the stock on payment to the broker of the sum of money to which he is entitled.

The broker may pledge the stock, or use it in his business, as collateral, but he must have it ready when called for by the customer, or other shares of the same stock equivalent in value.

The customer and the broker may make an express agreement that the broker may sell the stock without notice to the customer in the case of a threatened decline.

Generally speaking, when there are no directions as to selling, the broker will be protected if he can show that he followed the usual custom of brokers in like circumstances.

If the customer fails to advance the necessary margin when called for on reasonable notice, the broker may sell for his own protection.

The reasonable notice may be an hour, a day, or a week, depending on the condition of the market for that particular stock.

If a broker fraudulently converts the stock to his own use, he is guilty of embezzlement.

BONDS.—A *bond* is in the nature of a promissory note—the obligation of a corporation, state, county or city to pay a certain sum of money at a certain time, with interest payable at fixed periods or upon certain conditions.

The bond of a company may be a perfectly safe investment when the stock is not, and the stock of a prosperous and successful company, paying large dividends or having a large surplus, may sell at a higher price than the bonds of the same company, the income from which is limited to the agreed rate of interest which they bear. A much closer scrutiny should be made of a company's standing when one thinks of investing in its share capital, than when it is the intention to loan the company money on its mortgage bonds.

Generally the bonds of business corporations are secured by mortgage, but some classes of bonds are dependent on the solvency or good faith of the company issuing them.

The coupons attached to bonds represent the different installments of interest, and are to be cut off and collected from time to time as the interest becomes payable. Bonds are sometimes issued without coupons, and are then called *registered bonds*. Such bonds are payable only to the registered owner, and the interest on these is paid by check. *Convertible bonds* are such as contain provisions whereby they may be exchanged for stock, bonds or other property.

Bonds are known as First Mortgage, Second Mortgage, etc., Debentures, Consols, Convertible Land Grant, Sinking Fund, Adjustment, Income or otherwise, according to their priority of lien, the class of property upon which they are secured, etc. Income bonds are generally bonds on which the interest is only payable if earned, and ordinarily are not secured by mortgage. Bonds are also named from the rate of interest they bear, or from the dates at which they are payable or redeemable, or from both; as, U. S. 4's 1907, Virginia 6's, Western Union 7's, coupon, 1900, Lake Shore reg. 2d, 1903.

BROKERAGE AND COMMISSION. — A commission merchant, or factor, is an agent intrusted by his principal with goods to be sold, with the authority to deduct from the proceeds of the sales a certain sum agreed upon as compensation for his services, remitting the balance to his principal.

Such an agent impliedly agrees to perform his duties in a careful and diligent manner, and to obey the orders and instructions which he receives from his principal so far as he is able.

He is bound to exercise his judgment and discretion to the best advantage of his principal, and to render just and true accounts.

In the absence of special instructions to the contrary, he has an implied authority to sell at such times, and at such prices, as in the exercise of his discretion he may deem for the best interests of his principal.

He may sell on credit, if it is customary so to do, among those in the same business, unless he has received orders to the contrary.

All profits made by him in handling his principal's property or money, beyond his ordinary compensation, are for the benefit of the principal.

He cannot himself be the purchaser of the goods intrusted to him to sell, unless he deals openly and fairly with his principal, and acquaints him with all the facts and circumstances material for him to know.

TERMS USED ON THE BOARD OF TRADE

A*CCOMMODATION PAPER.* — Notes or bills not representing an actual sale or trade transaction, but merely drawn to be discounted for the benefit of drawer, acceptor or indorsers, or all combined.

Balance of Trade. — Difference in value between total imports and exports of a country.

Ballooning. — To work up a stock far beyond its intrinsic worth by favorable stories or fictitious sales.

Bear. — One who strives to depress the price of stocks, etc., and for this reason "goes short."

Buying Long. — Buying in expectation of a rise.

Breadstuffs. — Any kind of grain, corn or meal.

Broker. — An agent or factor; a middleman paid by commission.

Brokerage. — A percentage for the purchase or sale of money and stocks.

Bull. — A broker or dealer who believes that the value of stocks or breadstuffs will rise, and speculates for a rise.

Call. — Demand for payment of installments due on stocks.

Call. — A privilege given to another to "call" for delivery at a time and price fixed.

Clique. — A combination of operators controlling large capital in order to unduly expand or break down the market.

Collaterals. — Any kind of values given in pawn when money is borrowed.

Corner. — The buying up of a large quantity of stocks or grain to raise the price. When the market is oversold, the shorts, if compelled to deliver, find themselves in a "corner."

Curbstone Brokers. — Brokers or agents who

are not members of any regular organization, and do business mainly on the sidewalk.

Delivery.—When stock or grain is brought to the buyer in exact accordance with the rules of the Exchange, it is called a good delivery. When there are irregularities the delivery is pronounced bad, and the buyer can appeal to the Exchange.

Differences.—The price at which a stock is bargained for and the rate or day of delivery are not usually the same, the variation being termed the differences.

Factor.—An agent appointed to sell goods on commission.

Factorage.—Commissions allowed factors.

Flat.—Inactive; depressed; dull. The *flat* value of bonds and stocks is the value without interest.

Selling Short.—To "sell short" is to sell for future delivery what one has not got, in hopes that prices will fall.

Forcing Quotations is where brokers wish to keep up the price of a stock and to prevent its falling out of sight. This is generally accomplished by a small sale.

Gunning a stock is to use every art to produce a break when it is known that a certain house is heavily supplied and would be unable to resist an attack.

Kite-Flying.—Expanding one's credit beyond legitimate limits.

Lame Duck.—Stock-jobbers' slang for one unable to meet his liabilities.

Long.—One is *long* when he carries stock or grain for a rise.

Pointer.—A theory or fact regarding the market on which one bases a speculation.

Pool.—The stock or money contributed by a clique to carry through a corner.

Price Current.—The prevailing price of merchandise, stock or securities.

Flyer.—A small side operation, not employing one's whole capital.

Watering a stock is the act of doubling the quantity of stock without improving its quality.

Cardinal Numbers

In Seven Languages

English	*French*	*German*	*Spanish*	*Italian*	*Russian*	*Swedish*
One	Un	Eins	Uno	Uno	Odin	En
Two	Deux	Zwei	Dos	Due	Dva	Twå
Three	Trois	Drei	Tres	Tre	Tri	Tre
Four	Quatre	Vier	Cuatro	Quattro	Tschetire	Fyra
Five	Cinq	Fünf	Cinco	Cinque	Piat	Fem
Six	Six	Sechs	Seis	Sei	Schest	Sex
Seven	Sept	Sieben	Siete	Sette	Sem	Sju
Eight	Huit	Acht	Ocho	Otto	Vosem	Åtta
Nine	Neuf	Neun	Nueve	Nove	Deviat	Nio
Ten	Dix	Zehn	Diez	Dieci	Desat	Ti
Eleven	Onze	Elf	Once	Undici	Odinnatsat	Elfva
Twelve	Douze	Zwölf	Doce	Dodici	Dvenatsat	Tolf
Thirteen	Treize	Dreizehn	Trece	Tredici	Trinatsat	Tretton
Fourteen	Quatorze	Vierzehn	Catorce	Quattordici	Chetirnatsat	Fjorton
Fifteen	Quinze	Fünfzehn	Quince	Quindici	Piatnatsat	Femton
Sixteen	Seize	Sechzehn	Diez y seis	Sedici	Schestnatsat	Sexton
Seventeen	Dix-sept	Siebenzehn	Diez y siete	Diciassette	Semnatsat	Sjutton
Eighteen	Dix-huit	Achtzehn	Diez y ocho	Diciotto	Vosemnatsat	Aderton
Nineteen	Dix-neuf	Neunzehn	Diez y nueve	Diciannove	Devetnatsat	Nitton
Twenty	Vingt	Zwanzig	Veinte	Venti	Dvatsat	Tjugu
Twenty-one	Vingt-et-un	Einundzwanzig	Veinte y uno	Vent'uno	Dvatsatodin	Tjugu en
Thirty	Trente	Dreissig	Treinta	Trenta	Tridsat	Trettio
Forty	Quarante	Vierzig	Cuarenta	Quaranta	Sorok	Fyrtio
Fifty	Cinquante	Fünfzig	Cincuenta	Cinquanta	Piatdesat	Femtio
Sixty	Soixante	Sechzig	Sesenta	Sessanta	Schestdesat	Sextio
Seventy	Soixante-dix	Siebenzig	Setenta	Settanta	Semdesat	Sjuttio
Eighty	Quatre-vingts	Achtzig	Ochenta	Ottanta	Vosemdesat	Åttio
Ninety	Quatre-vingt-dix	Neunzig	Noventa	Novanta	Devianosto	Nittio
Hundred	Cent	Hundert	Ciento	Cento	Sto	Hundrade
Thousand	Mille	Tausend	Mil	Mille	Tisiatsa	Tusende

Language of Flowers

A CLUSTER of flowers can be made to express any sentiment if care is taken in the selection.

If a flower is offered reversed, its original signification is contradicted, and the opposite implied.

A rosebud divested of its thorns, but retaining its leaves, conveys the sentiment, "I fear no longer; I hope." Stripped of leaves and thorns, it signifies, "There is nothing to hope or fear."

A full-blown rose, placed over two buds, signifies "Secrecy."

"Yes" is implied by touching the flower given to the lips; "No," by pinching off a petal and casting it away.

"I am" is expressed by a laurel leaf twined around the bouquet; "I have," by an ivy leaf folded together; "I offer you," by a leaf of Virginia creeper.

In Combinations

Moss Rosebud, Myrtle.	A confession of love.
Mignonette, Colored Daisy.	Your qualities surpass your charms of beauty.
Lily of the Valley, Ferns.	Your unconscious sweetness has fascinated me.
Yellow Rose, Broken Straw, Ivy.	Your jealousy has broken our friendship.
Scarlet Geranium, Passion Flower, Purple Hyacinth, Arbor Vitæ.	I trust you will find consolation, through faith, in your sorrow; be assured of my unchanging friendship.
Columbine, Day Lily, Broken Straw, Witch Hazel, Colored Daisy.	Your folly and coquetry have broken the spell of your beauty.
White Pink, Canary Grass, Laurel.	Your talent and perseverance will win you glory.
Golden-rod, Monkshood, Sweet Pea, Forget-me-not.	Be cautious; danger is near; I depart soon; forget me not.

Single Flowers

Arbor Vitæ — Unchanging friendship.
Camelia, White — Loveliness.
Candy-Tuft — Indifference.
Carnation, White — Disdain.
China Aster — Variety.
Clover, Four-Leaf — Be mine.
Clover, White — Think of me.
Clover, Red — Industry.
Columbine — Folly.
Daisy — Innocence.
Daisy, Colored — Beauty.
Dead Leaves — Sadness.
Deadly Nightshade — Falsehood.
Fern — Fascination.
Forget-me-not.
Fuchsia, Scarlet — Taste.
Geranium, Horseshoe — Stupidity.
Geranium, Scarlet — Consolation.
Geranium, Rose — Preference.
Golden-rod — Be cautious.
Heliotrope — Devotion.
Hyacinth, White — Loveliness.
Hyacinth, Purple — Sorrow.
Ivy — Friendship.
Lily, Day — Coquetry.
Lily, White — Sweetness.
Lily, Yellow — Gayety.
Lily, Water — Purity of heart; elegance.
Lily of the Valley — Unconscious sweetness.
Mignonette — Your qualities surpass your charms.
Monkshood — Danger is near.
Myrtle — Love.
Oak — Hospitality.
Orange Blossoms — Chastity.
Pansy — Thoughts.
Passion Flower — Faith.
Primrose — Inconstancy.
Rose — Love.
Rose, Damask — Beauty ever new.
Rose, Yellow — Jealousy.
Rose, White — I am worthy of you.
Rosebud, Moss — Confession of Love.
Smilax — Constancy.
Straw — Agreement.
Straw, Broken — Broken Agreement.
Sweet Pea — Depart.
Tuberose — Dangerous pleasures.
Thistle — Sternness.
Verbena — Pray for me.
White Jasmine — Amiability.
Witch Hazel — A spell.

Handy Facts TO SETTLE ARGUMENTS

"This rule is old when I am dead: be sure you're right, then go ahead."—DAVY CROCKETT.

ARTILLERY invented in 1330.

FIRST Atlantic cable operated, 1858.

A BARREL of rice weighs 600 pounds.

THERE are 2,750 languages.

TWO persons die every second.

SOUND moves 743 miles per hour.

CHINESE invented paper, 170 B.C.

A SQUARE mile contains 640 acres.

A BARREL of pork weighs 200 pounds.

THE first steel pen was made in 1830.

HAWKS can fly 150 miles in one hour.

CALICO printing was invented in 1770.

LIGHT moves 187,000 miles per second.

SLOW rivers flow seven miles per hour.

WATCHES were first constructed in 1476.

ROME was founded by Romulus, 752 B.C.

THE first lucifer match was made in 1829.

A STORM moves thirty-six miles per hour.

GOLD was discovered in California in 1848.

BATTLES of Bunker Hill and Lexington, 1775.

PHONOGRAPH invented by T. A. Edison, 1877.

BREECH-LOADING rifles were invented in 1811.

FIRST musical notes used, 1338; printed, 1502.

KEROSENE was first used for illuminating in 1826.

NATIONAL banks first established in United States, 1816.

THE first balloon ascended from Lyons, France, 1783.

THE first fire insurance office in America, Boston, 1724.

NAPOLEON I. crowned emperor, 1804; died at St. Helena, 1820.

JET is found along the coast of Yorkshire, Eng., near Whitby.

SLAVERY in the United States was begun at Jamestown in 1619.

FIRST post-office established, between Vienna and Brussels, 1516.

THE Alexandrian Library contained 400,000 valuable books 47 B.C.

MOSCOW, Russia, has the largest bell in the world, 432,000 pounds.

THE highest denomination of United States legal tender notes is $10,000.

THE electric eel is found only in the northern rivers of South America.

COLUMBUS discovered America, Oct. 12, 1492; the Northmen A.D. 985.

HARVARD is the oldest college in the United States; established in 1638.

WAR declared with Great Britain, June 18, 1812; peace, Feb. 18, 1815.

THE harvester was invented by McCormick in 1831.

THE first theater in the United States was at Williamsburg, Va., 1752.

CONGRESS declared war with Mexico, May 13, 1846; closed Feb. 2, 1848.

MEASURE 209 feet on each side and you will have a square acre within an inch.

UNTIL 1776 cotton-spinning was performed by the hand spinning-wheel.

CARPETS were brought from the East in 1569. At first they were made by hand.

THE first complete sewing-machine was patented by Elias Howe, Jr., in 1846.

POSTAGE stamps first came into use in England in the year 1840; in the United States, in 1847.

FIRST telegraph in operation in America was between Washington and Baltimore, May 27, 1844.

FIRST sugar-cane cultivated in the United States, near New Orleans, 1751; first sugar-mill, 1758.

THE largest inland sea is the Caspian, between Europe and Asia, being 700 miles long and 270 miles wide.

GLASS mirrors first made by Venetians in the thirteenth century. Polished metal was used before that time.

THE first illumination with gas was in Cornwall, Eng., 1792; in the United States, at Boston, 1822.

PRINTING was known in China in the sixth century; introduced into England about 1474; America, 1536.

MEERSCHAUM means "froth of the sea." It is white and soft when dug from the earth, but soon hardens.

THE term "Almighty Dollar" originated with Washington Irving, as a satire on the American love for gain.

THE first railroad locomotive in America was the John Bull, imported in 1831 for the Camden and Amboy Railroad.

THE electric light was invented in 1846, and as late as 1878 was pronounced by a high scientific authority "a pretty toy."

BURNT brick were known to have been used in building the Tower of Babel. They were introduced into England by the Romans.

THE first deaf and dumb asylum was founded in England by Thomas Braidwood, 1760; and the first in the United States was at Hartford, 1817.

A FIRKIN of butter weighs 56 pounds.

A SPAN is ten and seven-eighths inches.

PLAYING-CARDS were invented in 1390.

PIANOFORTE invented in Italy about 1710.

THE value of a ton of silver is $37,704.84.

FIRST watches made in Nuremberg, 1476.

A HURRICANE moves eighty miles per hour.

MODERN needles first came into use in 1545.

ELECTRICITY moves 288,000 miles per second.

FRENCH and Indian war in America, 1754.

THE first horse railroad was built in 1826-7.

THE average human life is thirty-three years.

COACHES were first used in England in 1569.

FRENCH Revolution, 1789; Reign of Terror, 1793.

$1,000,000 in gold coin weigh 3,685.8 lbs. avoirdupois.

MORMONS arrived at Salt Lake City, Utah, July 24, 1847.

EXPERIMENTS in electric lighting, by Thomas A. Edison, 1878-80.

DAGUERRE and Niepce invented the process of daguerreotype, 1839.

FIRST American library founded at Harvard College, Cambridge, 1638.

THE first iron ore discovered in this country was found in Virginia in 1715.

"BRAVEST of the Brave" was the title given to Marshal Ney at Friedland, 1807.

THE first steam engine on this continent was brought from England in 1753.

BOOKS in their present form were invented by Attalus, king of Pergamus, in 887.

ROBERT RAIKES established the first Sunday-school at Gloucester, Eng., 1781.

ALBERT DURER gave the world a prophecy of future wood engraving in 1527.

FIRST cotton raised in the United States was in Virginia, in 1621; first exported, 1747.

ST. AUGUSTINE, oldest city in the United States, founded by the Spaniards, 1565.

JAMESTOWN, Va., founded 1607; first permanent English settlement in America.

THE first volunteer fire company in the United States was at Philadelphia, 1736.

OBERLIN College, Ohio, was the first in the United States that admitted female students.

THE first knives were used in England, and the first wheeled carriages in France in 1559.

THE first electrical signal ever transmitted between Europe and America passed over the Field submarine cable on Aug. 5, 1858.

THE shoe-pegging machine was invented in 1858. By its aid it is estimated that the labor of one man can turn out 300 pairs of shoes a day.

MORSE's telegraph was made practical in 1837. The Western Union now has 730,103 miles of wire and sends 62,000,000 messages a year.

COFFEE was brought into England in 1641.

LIGHTNING-RODS first surmounted dwellings in 1752.

ENVELOPES were first made in 1839, and sold for 10c. to 25c. apiece.

IN 1580 the first carriage was brought to England from France.

THE first medical school in the United States was founded in Philadelphia in 1764.

CHEMISTRY, as a science, was introduced into Europe by the Moors about 1240.

THE power-loom was invented in 1785. In 1893 Great Britain had 650,000 in operation.

LOCOMOTIVES were first used in 1814. In 1898 the world had 89,000, and 6,400 more are built every year.

HANDKERCHIEFS were first made for the market at Paisley, Scotland, in 1743, and sold for about $1 each.

THE aniline dyes were invented in 1856, and now over $7,000,000 worth are annually used in the United States.

DYE-WOODS were first brought to England in 1850. Last year the factories of England alone used $10,000,000 worth.

KINDERGARTENS were devised by Froebel, and practically carried out by Mr. and Mrs. Ronge in Germany, in 1849.

TEA was first brought into Europe from the East in 1610. In 1893 Europe and America consumed over 450,000,000 pounds.

THE first iron ship was launched in 1830; now the carrying power of the world's iron shipping exceeds 20,000,000 tons.

THE blast furnace was devised in 1842. In 1890 the United States alone made 9,000,000 tons of iron and 4,277,000 of steel.

THE first milch cow came to this continent in 1493. Now, in the United States, there are 16,019,591, valued at $346,000,000.

WATT's patent for a steam engine was issued in 1769. The steam engines of the world to-day equal 50,000,000 horse-power.

MATCHES were first invented in 1833; and it is estimated that 75,000,000 a day are burned by the people of the United States.

THE Bank of England, the first on the modern plan, was instituted in 1695; now the banking capital of the world is $8,197,000,000.

ELECTRIC railroads are not ten years old; in 1894 there were 485 lines, with 4,960 miles of track, and with a capital stock of $265,000,000.

THE grade of titles in Great Britain stands in the following order from the highest: Prince, Duke, Marquis, Earl, Viscount, Baron, Baronet, Knight.

THE "Valley of Death," in the island of Java, is simply the crater of an extinct volcano, filled with carbonic-acid gas. It is half a mile in circumference.

PIANOS were invented in 1710.

THE first Bible was printed in 1450.

WINDOW glass was first used in 1557.

ELECTROTYPING was first done in 1837.

COAL OIL was first used as an illuminant in 1826.

LITHOGRAPHING was first made practical in 1801.

WASHBOARDS with a metal face were patented in 1841.

YEAST for bread-making was first manufactured in 1684.

SAFETY lamps, for the use of miners, were patented in 1815.

WHEAT was first exported from the United States about 1750.

THE ice-making machine was first put into operation in 1860.

VULCANIZED rubber was first made in 1849 by a process invented by Goodyear.

THE cotton gin, which made extensive cultivation of cotton profitable, was invented in 1793.

THE first lifeboat was invented in 1802. The United States now has 242 life-saving stations.

THE first English school in America was opened in Massachusetts in 1622, with six pupils.

CURVED stereotyped plates were invented in 1815, but were little used for half a century after that date.

GAS was first made in England about 1792, and for many years was used only to illuminate the residences of royalty and the nobility.

THE first horse was brought to this continent in 1518. Now, there are, in the United States alone, 14,056,750, valued at $941,000,000.

BLACKING for boots was invented in 1836, and now the manufacturers in this country and England sell over $4,000,000 worth a year.

EVERY passenger train and many freight trains are now equipped with air-brakes, and yet the air-brake was invented as recently as 1858.

POTATOES first appear in history in 1580. In 1891 the United States raised 201,000,000 bushels. In 1884 the world raised 79,000,000 tons.

THE first horse-railroad was made in 1829. Now every country town has its street-car line, and even Constantinople and Jerusalem have such facilities.

THE first steamship crossed the Atlantic in 1819. There are now seventy lines of mail steamers. In 1889 there were 107,137 steam vessels on the high seas.

THE first practical sewing-machine was invented in 1841. Now about 600,000 are made annually in the United States, able to do the work of 7,200,000 women.

SEA signals were invented and put in operation during the reign of James II.

THE first appearance of peanuts in mercantile history was a consignment of ten bags sent from Virginia to New York for sale in 1794.

A MACHINE for making tacks was patented in 1806, but not put into practical use until near the middle of the century. Now the world consumes 50,000,000 tacks a day.

THE city of Amsterdam, Holland, is built upon piles driven into the ground. It is intersected by numerous canals, crossed by nearly three hundred bridges.

COAL was used as fuel in England as early as 852, and in 1234 the first charter to dig for it was granted by Henry III. to the inhabitants of Newcastle-on-Tyne.

TOBACCO was discovered in San Domingo in 1496; afterwards by the Spaniards in Yucatan in 1520. It was introduced in France in 1560, and into England in 1583.

THE present national colors of the United States were not adopted by Congress until 1777. The flag was first used by Washington at Cambridge, January 1, 1776.

THE Chinese Wall was completed about 200 B.C. Its length is 1,250 miles; its height, including a 5-foot parapet, 20 feet; thickness at base, 25 feet; at top, 15 feet.

BRASS pins were first made in 1540, and weighed about an eighth of a pound each. Now England, France and Germany manufacture every week 520,000,000.

STEEL pens were first made in 1803. The annual sales at present in the United States are estimated at 30,000,000 pens, while the world annually consumes 200,000,000.

QUININE, the active principle of Peruvian bark, was discovered in 1820. Now about 13,000,000 pounds of bark and 200,000 pounds of quinine are produced each year.

THE part of United States territory most recently acquired is the island of San Juan, near Vancouver's Island. It was evacuated by England at the close of November, 1873.

THE first newspaper published in this country was issued in 1704. In 1892 the United States and Canada published 19,373 papers, with an aggregate circulation of 3,481,610,000 copies.

THE first American savings bank was opened in 1778 at Philadelphia. In 1891 there were 4,781,605 depositors in the savings banks of this country, who had deposited $1,712,769,026.

"STAR ROUTES" are those over which mails are carried in other ways than by steam, by contractors in the employ of the government. They are so called from the mark (* * *) on records of the Post-office Department.

A single tobacco plant will produce 360,000 seeds.

The first English ships were the galleys built by Alfred the Great.

The screw propeller was introduced into the British navy in 1840.

Mercator's projection, which wonderfully simplified the science of navigation, was made public in 1569.

It may interest many to know that from an artistic point of view a woman's face is more beautiful when viewed from the left.

The most remarkable echo known is that in the castle of Simonetta, two miles from Milan. It repeats the echo of a pistol sixty times.

Paris was known as Lutetia until 1184, when the name of the great French capital was changed to that which it has borne ever since.

The oldest sun-picture of the human countenance was taken in 1840 by Prof. John W. Draper on the roof of the University of New York.

The mariner's compass was used for centuries by the Chinese before it was brought to Europe. Its invention or introduction is credited to Flavio Gioja, in the fourteenth century.

The first public schools in the present limits of the United States were established in Massachusetts in 1645. The first town school in this country was opened in Hartford, Conn., in 1642.

The most ancient catacombs are those of the Theban kings, begun 4,000 years ago. The catacombs of Rome contain the remains of about 6,000,000 human beings; those of Paris, 3,000,000.

The first Atlantic cable was operated in 1858. Now there are six, besides a line of cables connecting the leading countries in every part of the world, comprising over 130,000 miles of cable.

The tallest man of modern times was John Hale, of Lancashire, England, who was nine feet six inches in height. His hand was seventeen inches long and eight and one-half inches broad.

It is claimed that crows, eagles, ravens and swans live to be 100 years old; herons, 50; parrots, 60; pelicans and geese, 50; skylarks, 30; sparrow hawks, 40; peacocks, canaries and cranes, 24.

There has been no irregularity in the recurrence of leap year every four years since 1800, and will be none until 1900, which will be a common year, although it will come fourth after the preceding leap year.

The nail machine was invented in 1715. At the present day it is estimated that 4,000,000,000 nails are annually made by machinery in Great Britain alone, and from a fourth to a half this number in the United States.

China, with her 400,000,000 people, has only forty miles of railroad.

Glass was made in Egypt, 3,000 B.C.; earliest date of transparent glass, 719 B.C.

The first almanac was printed in Hungary in 1470. One patent-medicine firm in this country now prints and circulates over 3,000,000 a year, and the total number printed annually in this country is about 150,000,000.

The first printing-press, with the utmost diligence, could be made to print from twenty to thirty-five sheets an hour on one side only; newspaper printing-presses of to-day print from 25,000 to 30,000 in the same time on both sides.

The Mormon Church in Utah shows a membership of 127,294—28,000 families. The church has 12 apostles, 38 patriarchs, 3,885 seventies, 3,153 high priests, 11,000 elders, 1,500 bishops, and 4,400 deacons, being an office for each six persons.

The seven sages flourished in Greece in the sixth century B.C. They were renowned for their maxims of life, and as the authors of the mottoes inscribed in the Delphian Temple. Their names are: Solon, Chilo, Pittacus, Bias, Periander, Cleobulus, and Thales.

Needles were first made with very rude machinery in 1545. At that date a workman did well if he turned out ten a day. It is estimated that the present product of the United States exceeds 80,000,000 a year, while England makes 110,000,000.

Acid etching was first done in 1512. Little practical use was made of the process, however, until about twenty years ago, when it was improved to such an extent that "process reproductions" became the cheapest means of preparing illustrations for the press.

The infusoria, one of the lowest forms of animal life, can propagate their species in three distinct ways: first, by budding, somewhat after the manner of plants; second, by the spontaneous division of the animal into two individuals; third, by eggs.

The first forks made in England were manufactured in 1608. Their use was ridiculed by the men of the time, who argued that the English race must be degenerating when a knife and a spoon were not sufficient for table use. Last year one Sheffield firm made over 4,000,000.

The first regular effort to instruct the deaf and dumb was by Pedro de Ponce, a Spanish monk, in 1570. The first systematic effort to teach the deaf to speak was made by Dr. Thornton, of Philadelphia, in 1793. The first American Institute for the deaf and dumb was opened by Dr. Gallaudet at Hartford, Conn., in 1817.

THE "Seven Wonders of the World" are seven most remarkable objects of the ancient world. They are: The Pyramids of Egypt, Pharos of Alexandria, Walls and Hanging Gardens of Babylon, Temple of Diana at Ephesus, the Statue of the Olympian Jupiter, Mausoleum of Artemisia, and Colossus of Rhodes.

A "MONKEY WRENCH" is not so named because it is a handy thing to monkey with or for any kindred reason. "Monkey" is not its name at all, but "Moncky." Charles Moncky, the inventor of it, sold his patent for $2,000, and invested the money in a house in Williamsburgh, Kings County, New York, where he now lives.

THE American post-office was put in operation in 1710. In 1892 there were 447,591 miles of mail routes and 67,119 post-offices. The revenues of the department were $70,930,475. There were carried 3,800,000,000 letters. The world's annual mail comprises 8,000,000,000 letters and 5,000,000,000 papers.

COAL first came into use in England in 1234. During the last ten years there were produced 1,096,000,000 tons, and coal fields have been discovered in every country in the world. It is estimated that the coal-fields now known will supply the constantly increasing demand for a thousand years.

THE first Young Men's Christian Association was organized in London in 1844; first in America at Montreal and Boston, 1851. In 1893 there were in North America 1,429 associations, with a membership of 250,000 and owning property valued at $14,200,000. The number of associations throughout the world in 1893 was 4,917.

THE divorces have been about 16,400 annually in the United States for the past twenty years, but this is only one per cent. of the number of marriages, and, therefore, there is nothing in the world that human beings undertake to do that can show so small a percentage of total failures as marriage.

THE first book printed in the American colonies was the "Bay Psalm Book," from the press of the Pilgrim Fathers at Cambridge, Mass., 1640. The first dated book printed in England was "Dictes and Sayings of the Philosophers," printed by William Caxton, 1477.

THE railroad system of this country began in 1827. In 1893 there were 214,528 miles of track in the United States and 394,310 in the world. The number of passengers carried by the United States railroads in 1893 was 556,015,802, and the total earnings were $1,168,824,459. The capital stock was $4,809,176,651, and the dividends $90,719,797. The number of men employed was 786,285.

THERE is a leaning tower at Caerphilly, Glamorganshire, which stands 77 feet in height and is no less than 11 feet out of the perpendicular. The Tower of Pisa leans 13 feet in 180.

THE peach was originally a poisonous almond. Its fruity parts were used to poison arrows, and for that purpose it was introduced into Persia. Transportation and cultivation have removed its poisonous qualities, and turned it into delicious fruit.

THE flower badges of nations, etc., are as follows: Athens, violet; Canada, sugar maple; Egypt, lotus; England, rose; France, fleur-de-lis (lily); Florence, giglio (lily); Germany, corn-flower; Ireland, shamrock leaf; Italy, lily; Prussia, linden; Saxony, mignonette; Scotland, thistle; Spain, pomegranate; Wales, leek leaf.

THE oldest republic in the world, and at the same time the smallest, is San Marino, situated in Eastern Central Italy. It has an area of 22 sq. miles and 16,000 population. Another little known European republic is Andorra, situated among the high mountains of the Eastern Pyrenees, and covering an area of 149 sq. miles. It has maintained its independence since the days of Charlemagne.

THE celebrated Ferris Wheel, of the Chicago World's Fair, is 250 feet in diameter, and has a carrying capacity of 36 cars, holding 60 persons each. Diameter of axle, steel-forged and largest ever made, 33 inches; length, 45½ feet; weight, 70½ tons. Highest point of wheel, 264 feet. Total weight of wheel and cars, 2,100 tons; weight of levers and machinery, 2,200 tons; weight of people per trip, only 150 tons.

THE standard coins on the European continent are: In France, the franc; in Spain, the peseta; in Italy, the lira; in Holland and Austria, the florin; in Germany, the mark; in Russia, the ruble. Belgium and Switzerland use the French name for the piece of twenty sous. Each of these pieces is, like the American dollar, divided into one hundred parts, called kopeck in Russia, pfennig in Germany, kreutzer in Austria, cent in Holland, and in Italy, France and Spain by the word meaning hundredth.

THE first railroad was constructed at the end of the sixteenth century. The rails were made of wood, and were the invention of miners in the Hartz Mountains, Hanover. The product of the mines was carried upon the rails to the place of shipment by means of small wooden cars. The rails were round and fastened together by means of wooden pegs, which were used also, instead of nails, in the construction of the cars. Queen Elizabeth had miners brought into England, to develop the English mines, and through them the rail track was introduced into Great Britain.

*

TELEPHONE invented 1861.

THE human body has 240 bones.

MAN'S heart beats 92,160 times in a day.

TEXAS is 220 times as large as Rhode Island.

THERE are 5,000 cells in a square foot of honeycomb.

IT requires 2,700 silk worms to produce one pound of silk.

IT would take 27,000 spiders to produce one pound of web.

A HAWK flies 150 miles per hour; an eider duck, 90 miles; a pigeon, 40 miles.

A MAN can lift with both hands 256 lbs., or support on his shoulders 330 lbs.

A BODY weighing 140 lbs. produces 3 lbs. of ashes; time for burning, 55 minutes.

THE horse-power of Niagara is 3½ million nominal; equal to 10 million horses effective.

TEXAS has the largest number of counties of any State (240), and Delaware the least (3).

NINETEEN States of the Union have no sea-coast. Colorado has no sea-coast or navigable river.

MRS. GRANT received over $500,000 as royalty from the sale of "The Personal Memoirs of U. S. Grant."

PEMBINA, N. Dak., is the geographical center of North America; Atchison, Kan., of the United States.

COMPARATIVE SCALE OF STRENGTH.—Ordinary man, 100; Byron's Gladiator, 173; Farnese Hercules, 362; Horse, 750.

POUNDS of water evaporated by 1 lb. of fuel as follows: Straw, 1.9; wood, 3.1; peat, 3.5; coke or charcoal, 6.4; coal, 7.9; petroleum, 14.6.

THE average elevation of continents above sea-level is: Europe, 670 feet; Asia, 1,140 feet; North America, 1,150 feet; South America, 1,100 feet.

A SALMON has been known to produce 10,000,000 eggs. Some female spiders produce 2,000 eggs. A queen bee produces 100,000 eggs in a season.

ONE horse-power will raise 16½ tons per minute a height of 12 inches, working 8 hours a day. This is about 7,900 foot-tons daily, or 12 times a man's work.

GOOD clear ice two inches thick will bear men to walk on; four inches thick will bear horses and riders; six inches thick will bear horses and teams with moderate loads.

THE checks paid in New York and London in one month aggregate $6,860,000,000, which is greatly in excess of the value of all the gold and silver coin in existence.

IN 1884, four men were taken alive out of a mine in England, after 24 days without food. In 1880, Dr. Tanner, in New York, lived on water for 40 days, losing 36 lbs. in weight.

STORM clouds move thirty-six miles an hour.

DISTINGUISHED doctors say the seat of dyspepsia is not in the stomach, but in the head.

THE center of population, by the eleventh census, is about 20 miles east of Columbus, Ind. In 1790 it was 23 miles east of Baltimore, Md.

A MAN'S working life is divided into four decades: 20 to 30, bronze; 30 to 40, silver; 40 to 50, gold; 50 to 60, iron. Intellect and judgment are strongest between 40 and 50.

ACCORDING to Orfila, the proportion of nicotine in Havana tobacco is 2 per cent.; in French, 5 per cent., and in Virginia tobacco, 7 per cent. That in Brazilian is still higher.

ONE pair of rabbits can become multiplied in four years into 1,250,000. They were introduced in Australia a few years ago, and now that colony ships 6,000,000 rabbit skins yearly to England.

LAUTERBRUNNEN is a deep part of an Alpine pass, where the sun hardly shines in winter. It abounds with falls, the most remarkable of which is the Staubbach, which falls over the Balm precipice in spray from a height of 925 feet.

THE largest of the Pyramids, that of Cheops, is composed of four million tons of stone, and occupied 100,000 men during 20 years, equal to an outlay of $200,000,000. It would now cost $20,000,000 at a contract price of 16 cents per cubic foot.

ONE tug on the Mississippi can take, in six days, from St. Louis to New Orleans, barges carrying 10,000 tons of grain, which would require 70 railway trains of fifteen cars each. Tugs in the Suez Canal can tow a vessel from sea to sea in 14 hours.

AMERICAN life average for professions (Boston): Storekeepers, 41.8 years; teamsters, 43.6 years; laborers, 44.6 years; seamen, 46.1 years; mechanics, 47.3 years; merchants, 48.4 years; lawyers, 52.6 years; farmers, 64.2 years.

THE Spanish merino ram Challenge, owned by L. E. Shattuck, of Missouri, holds the fleece record. The first time he was sheared his wool weighed 28¾ pounds. The next spring's clip weighed 43 pounds, and the clip of April, 1898, was 43½ pounds.

BY a simple rule the length of the day and night, any time of the year, may be ascertained by simply doubling the time of the sun's rising, which will give the length of the night, and double the time of setting will give the length of the day.

ON an American 25-cent piece there are 13 stars, 13 letters in the scroll held in the eagle's beak, 13 marginal feathers in each wing, 13 tail feathers, 13 parallel lines in the shield, 13 horizontal bars, 13 arrow-heads and 13 letters in the word "quarter dollar."

A camel has twice the carrying power of an ox; with an ordinary load of 400 lbs. he can travel 12 to 14 days without water, going 40 miles a day. Camels are fit to work at 5 years old, but their strength begins to decline at 25, although they live usually till 40.

Hair which is lightest in color is also lightest in weight. Light or blonde hair is generally the most luxuriant, and it has been calculated that the average number of hairs of this color on an average person's head is 140,000, while the number of brown hairs is 110,000, and black only 108,000.

One woman in 20, one man in 30 is barren—about 4 per cent. It is found that one marriage in 20 is barren—5 per cent. Among the nobility in Great Britain, 21 per cent. have no children, owing partly to intermarriage of cousins, no less than 4½ per cent. being married to cousins.

The largest bells are the following, and their weight is given in tons: Moscow, 216; Burmah, 117; Pekin, 53; Novgorod, 31; Notre Dame, 18; Rouen, 18; Olmutz, 18; Vienna, 18; St. Paul's, 13; Westminster, 14; Montreal, 12; Cologne, 11; St. Peter's, 8½; Oxford, 8.

On the Alps the limit of the vine is an elevation of 1,600 feet; below 1,600 feet, figs, oranges and olives are produced. The limit of the oak is 3,800 feet, of the chestnut 2,800 feet, of the pine 6,500 feet, of heaths and furze 8,700 feet. Perpetual snow exists at an elevation of 8,200 feet.

The fair of Nijni-Novgorod is the greatest in the world, the value of goods sold being as follows: 1841, $15,000,000; 1867, $60,000,000; 1876, $140,000,000; the attendance in the last named year including 150,000 merchants from all parts of the world. In that of Leipsic the annual average of sales is $20,000,000, comprising 20,000 tons of merchandise, of which two-fifths is books.

The eight largest diamonds in the world weigh, respectively, as follows: The Braganza, 1,880 carats (part of the Portuguese jewels, found in 1741); Kohinoor, 106 carats; Star of Brazil, 125 carats; Regent of France, 136 carats; Austrian Kaiser, 139 carats; Russian Czar, 193 carats; Rajah of Borneo, 367 carats. The value of the above is not regulated by size, nor easy to estimate, but none of them is worth less than $500,000.

The percentage of illegitimate births for various countries, as stated by Mulhall, is as follows: Austria, 12.9; Denmark, 11.2; Sweden, 10.2; Scotland, 8.80; Norway, 8.05; Germany, 8.04; France, 7.02; Belgium, 7.0; United States, 7.0; Italy, 6.9; Spain and Portugal, 5.5; Canada, 5.3; Switzerland, 4.6; Holland, 3.5; Russia, 3.1; Ireland, 2.8; Greece, 1.3.

A man will die for want of air in five minutes; for want of sleep, in ten days; for want of water, in a week; for want of food, at varying intervals, dependent on various circumstances.

The slide of Alpnach, extending from Mount Pilatus to Lake Lucerne, a distance of eight miles, is composed of 25,000 trees, stripped of their bark, and laid at an inclination of 10 to 18 degrees. Trees placed in the slide rush from the mountain into the lake in six minutes.

In 1877 the newspaper *Nationale* of Paris had ten pigeons which carried dispatches daily between Versailles and Paris in fifteen to twenty minutes. In November, 1882, some pigeons, in face of a strong wind, made the distance of 160 miles, from Canton Vaud to Paris, in 4½ hours, or 35 miles per hour.

The University of Harvard was founded by John Harvard in the year 1638. It was the first in the present limits of the United States. The second was William and Mary, at Williamsburg, Va., in 1693; the third, Yale, at New Haven, in 1700; the fourth was the College of New Jersey, at Princeton, in 1746.

The Alps comprise about 180 mountains, from 4,000 to 15,732 feet high, the latter being the height of Mont Blanc, the highest spot in Europe. The summit is a sharp ridge, like the roof of a house, of nearly vertical granite rocks. The ascent requires two days; six or eight guides are required. It was ascended by two natives, Jacques Balmat and Dr. Paccard, August 8, 1786, at 6 A. M. They stayed up 30 minutes, with the thermometer 11 degrees below the freezing point.

The rise of the Nile commences in June, continuing until the middle of August, attaining an elevation of from 24 to 26 feet, and flooding the valley of Egypt twelve miles wide. In 1829 it rose to 26 cubits, and 30,000 persons were drowned. The Nile has a fall of six inches in 1000 miles, adds about four inches to the soil in a century, and encroaches on the sea 16 feet every year. Bricks have been found at the depth of 60 feet, showing the vast antiquity of the country. In productiveness of soil Egypt is excelled by no other land in the world.

There were 2,180 lepers in Norway in 1888, according to Mulhall. The numbers in Spain and Italy are considerable. In the Sandwich Islands the disease is so prevalent that the island of Molokai is set apart for lepers, who are under the direction of a French Jesuit priest. The death of Father Damien, in 1889, called attention to the noblest instance of self-sacrifice recorded in the nineteenth century. His place is now filled by a younger member of his order, who voluntarily sacrifices his health and life to aid the outcasts. In the Seychelles Islands leprosy is also common.

The first known dictionary was of the Chinese language, contained 40,000 characters, and was compiled by Pa-Out-She, B.C. 1100. The first Latin dictionary was compiled by Varro, about A.D. 40. The first English dictionary was Alfric's Glossary, 975. Dr. Johnson's dictionary appeared in 1755; Webster's dictionary was issued in 1828; Worcester's in 1860.

The average of human life is 33 years. One child out of every four dies before the age of 7 years, and only one-half of the world's population reach the age of 17. One out of 10,000 reaches 100 years. The average number of births per day is about 120,000, exceeding the deaths by about 15 per minute. There have been many alleged cases of longevity in all ages, but only a few are authentic.

The ratio of sickness rises and falls regularly with death rate in all countries, as shown by Dr. Farr and Mr. Edmonds at the Lisbon Congress of 1868, when the following rule was established: Of 1,000 persons, aged 30, it is probable 10 will die in the year, in which case there will be 20 of that age sick throughout the year, and 10 invalids. Of 1,000 persons, aged 75, it is probable that 100 will die in the year, in which case the sick and invalids of that age will be 300 throughout the year. For every 100 deaths let there be hospital beds for 200 sick, and infirmaries for 100 invalids.

The word *dollar* is from the German *thal* (valley) and came into use some three hundred years ago. There is a little silver-mining city or district in Northern Bohemia called Joachimsthal, or Joachim's Valley. The reigning duke of the region authorized this city in the sixteenth century to coin a silver piece which was called "Joachimsthaler." The "Joachim" was soon dropped and "thaler" only retained. The piece went into general use in Germany and Denmark, where the orthography was changed to "daler," whence it came into English and was adopted by the Americans with still further changes in the spelling.

In the small-pox epidemic of 1881, in England, the returns showed 4,475 deaths per million inhabitants—48 vaccinated to 4,380 unvaccinated, or in the proportion of 44 to 1. In the epidemic at Leipsic in 1871, the death rate was 12,700 per million, 73 per cent. of whom were unvaccinated. These figures are by Dr. Mulhall. In Boston the proportion was 15 to 50, and in Philadelphia, 17 to 65. During the Franco-German war the Germans lost only 263 men from this disease, the French 23,469, the former having been revaccinated in barracks. In the war in Paraguay, the Brazilians lost 43,000 men from malignant or black small-pox, that is, 35 per cent. of their army, nine cases in ten proving fatal.

Sunday schools for teaching the elements of English education were established by Raikes about 1781.

In the cholera visitation of 1866, the proportion of deaths per 10,000 inhabitants in the principal cities of Europe was as follows: London, 18; Dublin, 41; Vienna, 51; Marseilles, 64; Paris, 69; Berlin, 63; Naples, 89; St. Petersburg, 98; Madrid, 102; Brussels, 184; Palermo, 187; Constantinople, 198.

It is estimated that the number of insane persons in the United States is 168,000. *Causes of Insanity*—Hereditary, 24 per cent.; drink, 14 per cent.; business, 12 per cent.; loss of friends, 11 per cent.; sickness, 10 per cent.; various, 29 per cent. This result is the medium average arrived at by Mulhall on comparing the returns for the United States, England, France and Denmark.

The estimated number of religious denominations among English-speaking communities throughout the world is as follows: Episcopalians, 21,100,000; Methodists of all descriptions, 15,800,000; Roman Catholics, 14,340,000; Presbyterians of all descriptions, 10,500,000; Baptists of all descriptions, 8,180,000; Congregationalists, 6,000,000; Unitarians, 1,000,000; Free Thought, 2,100,000; minor religious sects, 2,000,000; of no particular religion, 20,000,000. Total English-speaking population, 100,000,000.

Ocean Records: *Liverpool and Queenstown to New York:* Lucania, Cunard Line, 5 days, 13 hours, 25 minutes, mean time. Left Liverpool 3:35 p.m. Oct. 1, arrived in New York 10 o'clock a.m. Oct. 7, 1893. Fastest ocean passage from Liverpool to New York. *New York to Queenstown:* 5 days, 19 hours, 57 minutes, mean time, City of New York, Inman Line; left Sandy Hook light 8:20 p.m. (Greenwich mean time) Aug. 17; arrived Daunts Rock light 4:17 p.m. (Greenwich mean time) Aug. 23, 1892; average speed 20.11 knots per hour; fastest eastward passage.

The degrees of alcohol in wines and liquors are: Beer, 4.0; porter, 4.5; ale, 7.4; cider, 8.6; Moselle, 9.6; Tokay, 10.2; Rhine, 11.0; Orange, 11.2; Bordeaux, 11.5; hock, 11.6; gooseberry, 11.8; Champagne, 12.2; claret, 13.3; Burgundy, 13.6; Malaga, 17.3; Lisbon, 18.5; Canary, 18.8; sherry, 19.0; Vermouth, 19.0; Cape, 19.2; Malmsey, 19.7; Marsala, 20.2; Madeira, 21.0; port, 23.0; Curacoa, 27.0; aniseed, 33.0; Maraschino, 34.0; Chartreuse, 43.0; gin, 51.6; brandy, 53.4; rum, 53.7; Irish whisky, 53.9; Scotch, 54.3. Spirits are said to be "proof" when they contain 57 per cent. The maximum amount of alcohol, says Parkes, that a man can take daily without injury to his health is that contained in 2 oz. brandy, ½ pt. of sherry, ½ pt. of claret, or 1 pt. of beer.

German empire re-established Jan. 18, 1871.

The first normal school was opened in Paris in 1795. The first normal college for the blind was founded in 1873.

The highest latitude ever reached in the region of the north pole was attained by the steam whaler Newport July 24, 1893. The Newport wintered at the Herschel islands and started after whale as soon as the summer opened. When the ice finally shut off further progress Captain Porter found himself in 84 degrees north latitude or within six degrees of the north pole. The highest latitude ever reached before was obtained by the Greely expedition, which mounted to 83 degrees and 30 minutes in 1882.

Capacity of the largest public buildings in the world: Coliseum, Rome, 87,000; St. Peter's, Rome, 54,000; Theater of Pompey, Rome, 40,000; Cathedral, Milan, 37,000; St. Paul's, Rome, 32,000; St Paul's, London, 31,000; St. Petronia, Bologna, 28,000; Cathedral, Florence, 24,300; Cathedral, Antwerp, 24,000; St. John Lateran, Rome, 23,000; St. Sophia's, Constantinople, 23,000; Notre Dame, Paris, 21,500; Theater of Marcellus, Rome, 20,000; Cathedral, Pisa, 13,000; St. Stephen's Vienna, 12,400; St. Dominic's, Bologna, 12,000; St. Peter's, 11,400; Cathedral, Vienna, 11,000; Gilmore's Garden, New York, 8,443; La Scala, Milan, 8,000; Mormon Temple, Salt Lake City, 8,000; St. Mark's, Venice, 7,500; Spurgeon's Tabernacle, London, 6,000; Bolshoi Theater, St. Petersburg, 5,000; Tabernacle (Talmage's), Brooklyn, 5,000; Music Hall, Cincinnati, 4,824; Auditorium, Chicago (large hall), 4,000.

There are 3,000,000 opium smokers in China. A paper read before the New York Medical Society by Dr. F. N. Hammond presents some important facts. In 1848 about 24,000 pounds of opium were consumed in the United States; in 1860, 533,450 pounds. In 1868 there were about 90,000 habitual opium eaters in the country; now they number over 500,000. More women than men are addicted to the use of the drug. The vice is one so easily contracted, so easily practiced in private, and so difficult of detection, that it presents peculiar temptations and is very insidious. The relief from pain that it gives and the peculiar exaltation of spirits easily lead the victim to believe that the use of it is beneficial. Opium and chloral are to-day the most deadly foes of women. Dr. Hammond is the better qualified to speak on this subject from having once been a consumer of opium himself. To break off from the habit, he says, the opium-eater must reduce the quantity of his daily dose, using at the same time other stimulants, and gradually eliminate the deadly drug entirely.

There were 48,930 blind people in the United States in 1880, and 33,880 deaf mutes.

The various nations of Europe are represented in the list of Popes as follows: English, 1; Dutch, 1; Swiss, 1; Portuguese, 1; African, 2; Austrian, 2; Spanish, 6; German, 6; Syrian, 8; Greek, 14; French, 15; Italian, 197. Eleven Popes reigned over 20 years; 89 from 10 to 20; 57 from 5 to 10; and the reign of 116 was less than 5 years. The reign of Pius IX. was the longest of all, the only one exceeding 25 years. Pope Leo XIII. is the 258th Pontiff. The full number of the Sacred College is 70, namely: Cardinal bishops, 6; cardinal priests, 50; cardinal deacons, 14. At present there are 62 cardinals. The Roman Catholic hierarchy throughout the world, according to official returns published at Rome in 1884, consisted of 11 patriarchs, and 1,153 archbishops and bishops. Including 12 coadjutor or auxiliary bishops, the number of Roman Catholic archbishops and bishops now holding office in the British Empire is 151. The numbers of the clergy are approximate only.

The measurement of that part of the skull which holds the brain is stated in cubic inches thus: Anglo-Saxon, 105; German, 105; Negro, 96; Ancient Egyptian, 93; Hottentot, 98; Australian native, 58. In all races the male brain is about ten per cent. heavier than the female. The highest classes of apes has only 16 oz. of brain. A man's brain, it is estimated, consists of 300,000,000 nerve cells, of which over 3,000 are disintegrated and destroyed every minute. Every man, therefore, has a new brain once in sixty days. But excessive labor, or the lack of sleep, prevents the repair of the tissues, and the brain gradually wastes away. Diversity of occupation, by calling upon different portions of the mind or body, successfully affords, in some measure, the requisite repose to each. But in this age of overwork there is no safety except in that perfect rest which is the only natural restorative of exhausted power. It has been noticed by American physicians in their European travels that the German people, who, as a rule, have little ambition and no hope to rise above their inherited station, are peculiarly free from nervous diseases; but in America, where the struggle for advancement is sharp and incessant, and there is nothing that will stop an American but death, the period of life is usually shortened five, ten or twenty years by the effects of nervous exhaustion. After the age of 50 the brain loses an ounce every ten years. Cuvier's weighed 64, Byron's 79, and Cromwell's 90 ounces, but the last was diseased. Post-mortem examinations in France give an average of 55 to 60 ounces for the brains of the worst class of criminals.

CONSUMPTION.—Of the total number of deaths, the percentage traceable to consumption in the several States and Territories is as follows: Alabama, 9.6; Arizona, 6.1; Arkansas, 6.4; California, 15.6; Colorado, 8.2; Connecticut, 15.1; Dakota, 8.8; Delaware, 16.1; District of Columbia, 18.9; Florida, 8.3; Georgia, 7.0; Idaho, 6.6; Illinois, 10.9; Indiana, 12.6; Iowa, 9.2; Kansas, 7.9; Kentucky, 15.7; Louisiana, 10.4; Maine, 19.2; Maryland, 14.0; Massachusetts, 15.7; Michigan, 13.0; Minnesota, 9.8; Mississippi, 8.8; Missouri, 9.8; Montana, 5.6; Nebraska, 9.9; Nevada, 6.3; New Hampshire, 5.6; New Jersey, 8.9; New Mexico, 2.4; New York, 8.1; North Carolina, 9.5; Ohio, 13.8; Oregon, 12.1; Pennsylvania, 12.6; Rhode Island, 14.6; South Carolina, 9.3; Tennessee, 14.5; Texas, 6.5; Utah, 2.6; Vermont, 16.1; Virginia, 12.2; Washington, 13.2; West Virginia, 15.0; Wisconsin, 13.4; Wyoming, 2.6. Average, 12.0.

FIRST public schools in America were established in the New England States about 1642.

EUCLID'S Elements of Geometry were compiled about B.C. 300.

FIRST authentic use of organs, 755; in England, 951.

THE first newspaper advertisement appeared in 1652.

THE Latin tongue became obsolete about 580.

THE great London fire occurred Sept. 26, 1666.

THE value of a ton of pure gold is $602,875.

ETHER was first used for surgical purposes in 1844.

IGNATIUS Loyola founded the order of Jesuits, 1541.

FIRST subscription library, Philadelphia 1731.

CORK is the bark taken from a species of the oak tree.

IRON horseshoes were made in 481.

BENJAMIN FRANKLIN used the first lightning rods, 1789.

GLASS windows (colored) were used in the 8th century.

AUTHENTIC history of China commenced 2,000 years B.C.

INTRODUCTION of homœopathy into the United States, 1825.

SPECTACLES were invented by an Italian in the 13th century.

MEDICINE was introduced into Rome from Greece, 200 B.C.

FIRST electric telegraph, Paddington to Drayton, Eng., 1835.

THE Chaldeans were the first people who worked in metals.

FIRST life insurance, in London, 1772; in America, Philadelphia, 1812.

EGYPTIAN pottery is the oldest known; dates from 2,000 B.C.

JULIUS CÆSAR invaded Britain, 55 B.C.; assassinated, 44 B.C.

SOAP was first manufactured in England in the 16th century.

THE largest free territorial government in the United States.

FIRST photographs produced in England, 1802; perfected, 1841.

FIRST marine insurance, A.D. 533; England, 1598; America, 1721.

PROFESSOR Oersted, Copenhagen, discovered electro-magnetism in 1819.

FIRST American express, New York to Boston—W. F. Harnden.

GLASS windows were first introduced into England in the 8th century.

DARK Ages, from the 6th to the 14th century.

A CANNON ball moves 1,000 miles per hour.

FIRST steamer crossed the Atlantic, 1819.

ASSASSINATION of Lincoln, April 14, 1865.

A HAND (horse measure) is four inches.

A BARREL of flour weighs 196 pounds.

ENVELOPES were first used in 1839.

TELESCOPES were invented in 1590.

Some Big Things

THE largest empire in the world is Great Britain, comprising more than a sixth of the land surface of the globe (8,557,658 sq. miles), and nearly a sixth of the world's population.

THE greatest grain port in the world is Chicago.

THE largest lake in the world is Lake Superior.

THE largest territory of the United States is Alaska—one-fifth of the entire national domain.

THE largest island in the world is Australia.

THE largest city in the United States not on a navigable river is Indianapolis.

THE largest university is Oxford, in England. It consists of twenty-one colleges and five halls.

THE best specimen of Grecian architecture in the world is the Girard College for Orphans, Philadelphia.

THE largest insurance company in the world is the Mutual Life of New York City, having cash assets of $176,000,000.

The tallest lighthouse in the world is the one at Hell Gate, N. Y., 250 feet high.

The greatest mass of solid iron in the world is the Iron Mountain of Missouri; it is 350 feet high and two miles in circuit.

The tallest building in Chicago, the city of tall buildings, is the Masonic Temple, 20 stories high, erected at a cost of $3,000,000.

The biggest dog in the world was Plinlimmon, a St. Bernard. In 1888 he stood 36 inches at shoulder, and weighed 214 lbs.

Twenty-eight railroad companies, operating 40,000 miles of railroad lines, enter Chicago and make it the greatest railroad center in the world.

The largest tree in the world, as yet discovered, is in Tulare County, California. It is 275 feet high, and 106 feet in circumference at its base.

The largest nugget of gold ever found was the "Welcome Nugget," found June 11, 1858, in Ballarat, Australia. It weighed 2,166 ounces, and was valued at $41,833.

The most extensive park is Deer Park in Denmark. It contains 4,200 acres. The largest park in the United States is Fairmount, at Philadelphia, and contains 2,740 acres.

The largest check ever drawn was that of the Pennsylvania Railroad Company in favor of Kidder, Peabody & Co., for $14,949,052.20, on June 1, 1881.

The largest valley in the world is the valley of the Mississippi; it contains 500,000 square miles and is one of the most fertile and profitable regions of the globe.

The longest span of wire is over the River Kistnah in India. It is used for telegraph, is over 6,000 feet long, and is stretched between two hills at an average height of about 1,200 feet.

The highest monument in the world is the Washington monument, being 555 feet. The highest structure of any kind is the Eiffel Tower, Paris, finished in 1889 and 989 feet high.

The largest and costliest library building in the world is the New Library of Congress at Washington, costing $6,000,000 and covering over four acres of ground. Storage capacity, 5,000,000 volumes.

The largest crowd that ever attended a public show of any kind was that recorded on Chicago Day, Oct. 9, 1893, at the World's Columbian Exposition, Chicago, when 754,203 people entered the gates.

The longest line of railroad in the United States is the Union Pacific, over 3,600 miles. The longest line of railroad in the world is the Russian military road from St. Petersburg to Samarcand.

The largest school in the world is the Jews' free school of Spitalfields, Eng., which has a daily attendance of 2,800 pupils.

The largest desert is Sahara, in Northern Africa. Its length is 3,000 miles and breadth 900, having an area of 2,000,000 square miles.

The largest army in the world in 1893 was the French, with 2,500,000 of all arms. In 1895, however, Germany will lead, when, with the new military laws in effect, they will have 5,000,000 men under arms.

The largest deposits of anthracite coal in the world are in Pennsylvania, the mines of which supply the market with millions of tons annually and appear to be inexhaustible.

The largest theater in the world is the Opera-house in Paris, which covers nearly four acres of ground and cost 100,000,000 francs. La Scala of Milan has the largest seating capacity.

The largest hotel in the United States, and probably the largest in the world, is located at San Francisco, Cal. It is seven stories high and cost $3,500,000. It is named the Palace and has accommodations for 1,200 guests.

The largest block of coal ever mined was dug out of the Roslyn mine, Washington, for exhibition purposes, in 1892. It is 20 feet long, 5 feet 8 inches wide, and 5 feet 4 inches high; and weighs about 25 tons.

The largest producing farm in the world lies in the southwest corner of Louisiana, owned by a Northern syndicate. It comprises 1,500,000 acres, and runs one hundred miles north and south. The fencing alone cost nearly $50,000.

The largest sun-dial in the world is Hyona Kenos, a large promontory which extends 3,000 feet above the Ægean Sea. As the sun swings round the shadow of this mountain it touches one by one a circle of islands, which act as hour-marks.

The largest cavern is Mammoth Cave in Edmondson County, Kentucky, about 28 miles from Bowling Green. It consists of a series of irregular chambers, some of which are traversed by navigable branches of the Echo river, in the waters of which blind white-fish are found.

The largest building ever erected is the temporary structure known as the Building of Manufactures and Liberal Arts at the Chicago Exposition, 1893. Cost, $1,700,000; 787 x 1,687 feet; ground area, 30.47 acres; floor space, including galleries, 44 acres; height, 236 feet.

The largest volcano in the world is Etna — its base is 90 miles in circumference; its cone, 11,000 feet high. Its first eruption occurred 474 B.C. The loftiest active volcano is Popocatapetl, 35 miles southwest of Puebla, Mexico. It is 17,748 feet above the level of the sea; its crater is three miles in circumference and 1,000 feet deep.

The largest library in the world is the National Library of France, founded by Louis XIV., which now contains 1,400,000 books, 300,000 pamphlets, 175,000 manuscripts, 300,000 maps and charts, 150,000 coins and medals, 1,300,000 engravings, and 100,000 portraits.

The largest flag ever flung to the breeze was hoisted on the central flag pole in front of the Administration Building of the World's Columbian Exposition on the morning of May 1, 1893. It was 80 feet long by 40 feet wide, and was "red, white and blue" of course, with forty-four stars in the field of blue.

The greatest cataract in the world is Niagara Falls, where the water from the great upper lakes forms a river three-quarters of a mile wide, and then, suddenly contracted, plunges over the rocks in two columns to the depth of 165 feet each. The highest fall of water in the world is that of the Yosemite in California, being 2,550 feet.

The longest railway tunnel in the world is the St. Gothard, on the line of the railroad between Lucerne and Milan, being 9¼ miles in length. Its summit is 6,600 feet beneath the peak of Kastelhorn and 990 feet below the surface at Andermatt. It is 26¼ feet wide, and 18 feet 10 inches from floor to crown of arch.

The greatest fortress, from a strategical point of view, is Gibraltar. It is considered impregnable, occupying a rocky peninsula jutting out into the sea about three miles long and three-quarters of a mile wide. One central rock rises 1,435 feet above the level of the sea. The garrison consists of 7,000 men. The largest fortress in size is Fortress Monroe.

The Union arch of the Washington Aqueduct is the largest in the world, being 220 feet; 20 feet in excess of the Chester arch across the Dee in England, 68 feet longer than that of the London Bridge, 92 feet longer than that at Neuilly on the Seine, and 100 feet longer than that of Waterloo Bridge. The height of the Washington arch is 100 feet.

The Mississippi River, from the source of the Missouri to the Eads jetties, is the longest river in the world. It is 4,300 miles in length and drains an area of 1,726,000 square miles. The Amazon, which is without doubt the widest river in the world, including the Beni, is 4,000 miles in length and drains 2,330,000 square miles of territory.

The largest anvil is that used in the Woolwich Arsenal, England. It weighs sixty tons. The anvil block upon which it rests weighs 103 tons. Altogether 600 tons of iron were used in the anvil, the block and the foundation work. It is said to have been six months cooling before it was sufficiently hard to stand the shock of the immense hammer.

The largest private house in America was begun in 1893 by Dr. Seward Webb, a relative by marriage of the Vanderbilts, and is located in the Adirondacks. Estimated cost, $1,500,000; 107 rooms. The material is granite, and the edifice covers nearly half an acre.

The highest mountain on the globe is not, as is generally supposed, Mt. Everest, that honor belonging to a lofty peak named Mt. Hercules on the Isle of Papua, New Guinea, discovered by Capt. Lawson in 1881. According to Lawson, this monster is 32,783 feet in height, being 3,781 feet higher than Mt. Everest, which is only 29,002 feet above the level of the Indian Ocean. The highest range of mountains are the Himalayas, the mean elevation being from 16,000 to 18,000 feet.

The largest State in our grand republic is Texas, which contains 274,356 square miles, capable of containing 20,000,000 of people, and then it would not be more crowded than Scotland is at present. It has been estimated that the entire population of the globe could be seated upon chairs within the boundary of Texas and each have four feet of elbow room.

The largest body of fresh water in the world is Lake Superior. It is 400 miles long and 160 miles wide; its circumference, including the windings of its various bays, has been estimated at 1,500 miles. Its area in square miles is 32,000, which is greater than the whole of New England, leaving out Maine. The greatest depth of this inland sea is 200 fathoms, or 1,200 feet. Its average depth is about 160 fathoms. It is 635 feet above sea level.

The largest ferry-boat ever constructed was named the Solano, and is now in use daily conveying trains across the Straits of Carquinez, Cal., between Benicia and Port Costa. The Solano is 420 feet long, 116 feet wide, and 20 feet depth of hold. She has eight steel boilers, four rudders, and a tonnage of 3,541 tons. On her decks are four railway tracks, with capacity for 48 ordinary freight cars and two locomotives, or 23 passenger coaches of the largest build.

The largest and costliest private mansion in the world is that belonging to Lord Bute, called Mountstuart, and situated near Rothesay, England. It covers nearly two acres; is built in Gothic style; the walls, turrets and balconies are built of stone. The immense tower in the center of the building is 120 feet high, with a balcony around the top. The halls are constructed entirely of marble and alabaster, and the rooms are finished in mahogany, rosewood and walnut. The fireplaces are all carved marbles of antique designs. The exact cost of this fairy palace is not known, but it has never been estimated at less than $8,000,000.

THE deepest artesian well is at Potsdam, 5,500 feet deep.

THE largest city in the world is London, 4,764,312 persons.

THE finest sea mirage is the Fata Morgana, in the Straits of Messina.

THE most ancient catacombs are those of Egypt, over 4,000 years old.

THE finest collection of antiquities in the world is in the British Museum.

THE best whispering gallery is in the dome of St. Paul's Cathedral in London.

THE greatest inland sea is the Caspian, which is 700 miles long by 270 in width.

THE most disastrous flood was that of Holland, 1530; 400,000 persons drowned.

THE lowest body of water is the Dead Sea, nearly 1,300 feet below the level of the sea.

THE largest locomotive was built four years ago for the Northern Pacific, 225,000 pounds in weight.

THE most extensive cemetery is in the catacombs of Rome; over 6,000,000 human beings are there interred.

THE largest animal is the whale. A whale 176 feet long and 120 in circumference was taken in the Arctic Ocean in 1847.

THE greatest jumper is the common flea. If a man could leap as far, proportioned to his size and weight, he could go from St. Louis to Chicago in two jumps.

THE largest engine is at Friedensville, Pa.; driving wheels are 35 feet in diameter, the cylinder is 110 inches, and it raises 17,500 gallons of water per minute.

THE most singular plant is the sensitive plant. Some of this family are so delicate that the passing of a cloud over the sun will cause their leaves to curl up.

THE most remarkable river is the Jordan, the Descender. Its whole course is a succession of falls and rapids, and it is not navigable in any portion of its length.

THE oldest known ruins are those of the Birs Nimroud. The great mound called by this name is supposed to be the Tower of Babel mentioned in the Book of Genesis.

THE largest building stones are those used in the cyclopean walls of Baalbec, in Syria. Some of these measure 63 feet in length by 25 in breadth and are of unknown depth.

THE most singular animal is the Ornithorhyncus Paradoxus, of Australia. It has a bill like a duck, fur like a seal, webbed feet like a goose, is amphibious and lays eggs.

THE tallest structure, compared with the size of the builder, is the hill of the Termites, or white ants. If the houses of men were proportionately lofty the humblest residence would be a mile high.

THE most wonderful insect is the common ant. The researches of natural philosophers have shown that there is not in the world a more extraordinary bit of matter than the ant's brain.

THE most valuable tree is the palm. The natives of the countries where it grows procure from it materials for their houses, clothing, baskets, mats, food and drink, fishing lines and ropes, sails and boats.

THE most remarkable stone formation in the world is the Giant's Causeway, in the north of Ireland. It consists of basalt columns, most of them as regular as though hewn by stone-cutters' chisels.

THE largest place of amusement ever constructed was the Coliseum at Rome. Its external circumference was 1,728 feet, its long diameter 615, its short 510, its height 156 feet. It had four stories, and could seat 87,000 spectators, while 20,000 more could find standing room.

THE greatest whirlpool is the maelstrom off the Norway coast. It is the eddy between the mainland and an island, and when the current is in one direction and the wind in another no ship can withstand the fury of the waves. Whales and sharks have been cast ashore and killed. The current is estimated to run thirty miles an hour.

A POLAND CHINA hog, weighing 1,300 pounds, was exhibited at the World's Fair in Chicago. He was 34 months old, measured 8 feet 9 inches from the tip of his snout to the root of his tail, 7 feet 8 inches around the body, 16 inches around the foreleg and was raised entirely on barley, wheat and oats.

THE largest bird is the condor. Condors with wings that spread 32 feet have been found in the Andes. The smallest bird is a Brazilian humming-bird, weighing but 5 grains and only a little larger than a common honey-bee. The swiftest bird is the kestrel, or sparrow-hawk. It has been known to make 150 miles an hour. The bird of greatest endurance is the albatross. One has been known to follow a ship for sixty-four days without once being seen to rest on the water.

THE largest refracting telescope in the world was presented by Charles T. Yerkes to the University of Chicago, in 1892. It has a lens 40 inches in diameter. The column and head of cast iron rise to a height of 43 feet and weigh 50 tons. The tube is of steel, 64 feet long, and 52 inches in diameter at the center, tapering towards the ends. Its weight is 6 tons. The total weight of the telescope is 75 tons. Cost $250,000. The lens of the telescope at Lick Observatory is 36 inches in diameter. The largest reflector is that of Lord Rosse in England; 72 inches.

The most extensive history is that of Gibbon. It covers the events of the world for 1,200 years.

The creature most tenacious of life is the common fresh-water polyp. One may be cut in two, and two creatures are the result. One may be slit lengthwise into half a dozen sections, making as many animals. They may be turned inside out and enjoy themselves just as well as before; if two be divided and placed end to end, the result will be a monster having a head at each end of its body.

The most pernicious winds are the simoom or hot winds of Egypt. They come from the deserts to the southeast and bring with them infinite quantities of fine dust, which penetrates even the minutest crevice. The thermometer often rises to 125 during their continuance, and thousands of human beings have been known to perish from suffocation in the fiery blast. It was one of these simooms that destroyed the army of Sennacherib. Alexander the Great nearly lost his whole force in another, and the army of Cambyses was utterly annihilated.

Height of monuments, spires, etc.: New Tower of London, 1,154 feet; Eiffel Tower, Paris, 984 feet; Washington Monument, 555 feet; Cathedral of Cologne, 511 feet; Cathedral of Rouen, 482 feet; City Hall, Philadelphia, 546½ feet; St. Stephen's Cathedral, Vienna, 470 feet; Cathedral of Strasburg, 468 feet; Pyramid of Cheops, 450 feet (original 484); St. Peter's, Rome, 448 feet; King Shafra's Pyramid, 447 feet; Notre Dame, Antwerp, 442 feet; Cathedral of Amiens, France, 422 feet; Cathedral of Salisbury, England, 404 feet; San Francisco City Hall, 400 feet; Torazzo Tower, Italy, 396 feet; Cathedral of Florence, Italy, 387 feet; St. Paul's, London, 365 feet; Hotel de Ville, Brussels, 364 feet; Cathedral of Milan, 355 feet; St. Patrick's, New York, 328 feet; Bartholdi Statue, 304 feet; Cathedral of Bremen, 324 feet; Asinelli Tower, Italy, 321 feet; Cathedral of Norwich, England, 315 feet; Board of Trade, Chicago, 303 feet; Lincoln Cathedral, England, 300 feet; Trinity Church, New York, 284 feet.

The Capitol building at Washington, D.C., is the largest building in the United States. The corner-stone was laid December 15, 1793, by President Washington, assisted by other Masons. It was partially destroyed by the British in 1814. The present dome was begun in 1855 and finished in 1863. The flag of the United States first floated from it December 12, 1863. The cost of the entire building has been something over $15,000,000. Its length is 715 feet 4 inches; width, 324 feet. It covers 3½ acres of ground. The distance from the ground to the top of the dome is 307½ feet; diameter of the dome, 135½ feet—ranking fifth as to size with the greatest domes of the world.

The most wonderful clock is that in Strasburg Cathedral.

The coldest place in the world is the region about the mouth of the McKenzie River, in British America. The thermometer there has been known to sink to 70 degrees below zero.

The highest monolith in the world is an obelisk at Karnak, in Egypt, near Luxor. The monument was erected by Hatasu, a queen who reigned 1600 B.C. It is 120 feet long and its weight is about 400 tons.

The greatest fire was that of Chicago, 1871; 17,450 buildings burned, 200 persons killed, 98,500 made homeless. Loss $200,000,000. In all 2,100 acres of land were burned over, the path of the fire having an extreme length of three and three-quarter miles, and over a mile in width. The Chicago fire swept over an area of 125 acres every hour from start to finish. It destroyed the homes of 100 people every minute. The loss in property was $1,000,000 every five minutes. Seventeen houses every minute. If all the buildings burned were placed end to end they would make an unbroken line 150 miles long.

The most extensive mines in the world are those of Freiberg, Saxony. They were begun in the twelfth century, and in 1835 the galleries, taken collectively, had reached the unprecedented length of 123 miles. A new gallery, begun in 1838, had reached a length of eight miles in 1878. The deepest perpendicular mining shaft in the world is located at Przibram, Bohemia. It is a lead mine; it was begun 1532. January, 1880, it was 3,280 feet deep. The deepest coal mine in the world is near Tournay, Belgium; it is 3,542 feet in depth, but, unlike the lead mine mentioned above, it is not perpendicular. The deepest rock-salt bore in the world is near Berlin, Prussia; it is 4,185 feet deep. The deepest hole ever bored into the earth is the artesian well at Potsdam, which is 5,500 feet in depth. The deepest coal mines in England are the Dunkirk collieries of Lancashire, which are 2,824 feet in depth. The deepest coal shaft in the United States is located at Pottsville, Pa. In 1885 it had reached a depth of 1,576 feet. From this great depth 400 cars, holding four tons each, are hoisted daily. The deepest silver mine in the United States is the Yellow Jacket, one of the great Comstock system at Virginia City, Nevada; the lower levels are 2,700 feet below the hoisting works. The Anaconda mine, Butte, Montana, is the richest in the world, rivaling and outstripping the Comstock mines in value of output. Originally bought in 1879 for $25 and a mule, it cannot now be bought at any price. Being in private hands, it has not made the stir that other mines have. The ore is silver and copper.

THE highest building in the world, not counting the iron towers and the Washington monument, is the Philadelphia City Hall, the height of which from pavement to top of tower measures 535½ feet. The height of the cathedral of Cologne from the pavement to the top of the cupola is 511 feet. It is 511 feet long, exactly the same as the height, and 231 feet wide. It was begun August 15th, 1248, and was pronounced finished August 14th, 1880, over 600 years after the corner-stone was laid.

THE largest plank ever made was exhibited by California at the World's Fair of 1893—redwood, 5 in. thick; 12⅝ feet long; 16½ feet wide. There was also shown a section of redwood tree 14 feet in diameter and 475 years old. Washington exhibited a log 24 feet long and 7 feet in diameter, and a sectional specimen of a fir-tree 410 years of age. Oregon produced a section of tide land spruce 9⅜ feet in diameter, over 300 years old. Cuba exhibited a rosewood log 25 feet long, 3 feet wide and 18 inches thick. The State of Washington exhibited a gigantic fir mast 250 feet high.

THE great pyramid of Cheops is the largest permanent structure of any kind ever erected by the hand of man. Its original dimensions at the base were 764 feet square, and its perpendicular height in the highest point 488 feet; it covers four acres, one rood and twenty-two perches of ground, and has been estimated by an eminent English architect to have cost not less than £30,000,000. Internal evidence proves that the great pyramid was begun about the year 2170 B.C., about the time of the birth of Abraham. It is estimated that about 5,000,000 tons of hewn stone were used in its construction, and the evidence points to the fact that these stones were brought a distance of about 700 miles from quarries in Arabia.

THE corner-stone of the Washington monument, the highest in the world, was laid July 4, 1848. Work progressed steadily for about six years, until the funds of the monumental society became exhausted. At that time the monument was about 173 feet high. From 1854 until 1878 nothing to speak of was done on the building. In the year last above named Congress voted an appropriation of $200,000 to complete the work. From that time forward work progressed at a rapid rate until December 6, 1884, when the aluminum apex was set at 555 feet 5⅛ inches from the foundation and the work declared finished. The foundation is 126½ feet square; number of stones used above the 150-foot level, 9,168; total weight stone used in work, 81,120 tons.

THE largest suspension bridge is that between Brooklyn and New York; the entire length is 5,989 feet; main span 1,595½ feet. The highest natural bridge in the world is at Rockbridge, Va., being 200 feet from the bottom of the arch. The largest stone bridge on earth is that finished in May, 1866, at Lagang, China. Chinese engineers had sole control of its construction. It crosses an arm of the China Sea, is nearly six miles in length, is composed entirely of stone, and has 300 arches, each 70 feet high. The largest truss iron bridge in the world crosses the Firth of Tay, Scotland. It is 10,612 feet in length and composed of eighty-five spans. The longest wooden bridge in the world is that crossing Lake Pontchartrain, near New Orleans, La. It is a trestle-work twenty-one miles in length. The highest bridge in the United States is over Kinzua Creek, near Bradford, Pa. It was built in 1882, has a total span of 2,051 feet and is 301 feet above the creek bed.

THE largest ship ever built was the Great Eastern. Work on the giant vessel was commenced in May, 1854. She was successfully launched January 31, 1858. The launching alone occupied the time from November 3, 1857, until the date above given. Her first trip of any consequence was made to New York in 1859-60. The largest ships now afloat are the Campania and her duplicate, the Lucania, both belonging to the Cunard line. The following figures show the relative sizes:

	Campania and Lucania.	Paris.	Teutonic.	Great Eastern.
Length	620	527	582	680
Beam	65	63	57.6	82
Draught	42	29	26	31
Horse power	30,000	20,100	17,000	7,650
Tonnage	17,000	10,500	9,880	22,000

THE largest cannon in the world was exhibited by Krupp at the Columbian Exposition, and left as a gift to the city of Chicago. It weighs 120.40 tons, and the carriage weighs 150 tons additional. Length of gun, 46 feet; 17-inch bore. This gun throws a projectile 5 feet long and weighing 2,300 pounds a distance of twenty miles, and has pierced steel plates two feet thick at a distance of nine miles. The cost of a single cartridge is $1,250.

"LIBERTY," Bartholdi's statue, presented to the United States by the French people in 1886, is the largest statue ever built. Its conception is due to the great French sculptor whose name it bears. It is said to be a likeness of his mother. Eight years of time were consumed in the construction of this gigantic bronze image. Its weight is 440,000 pounds, of which 176,000 pounds are copper, the remainder iron and steel. The major part of the iron and steel was used in constructing the skeleton frame-work for the inside. The monarch electric light held in the hand of the goddess is 305 feet above tide-water. The height of the figure is

152½ feet; the pedestal 91 feet, and the foundation 52 feet and 10 inches. Forty persons can find standing-room within the mighty head, which is 14¼ feet in diameter. A six-foot man standing on the lower lip could hardly reach the eyes. The index finger is eight feet in length and the nose 3¾ feet. The Colossus of Rhodes was a pigmy compared with this latter day wonder.

The largest and grandest temple of worship in the world is the St. Peter's Cathedral at Rome. It stands on the site of Nero's circus, in the northwest part of the city, and is built in the form of a Latin cross. The total length of the interior is 613½ English feet; transept, 446½ feet; height of nave, 152½ feet; diameter of cupola, 193 feet; height of dome from pavement to top of cross, 448 feet. The great bell alone without the hammer or clapper weighs 18,600 pounds, or over 9¼ tons. The foundation was laid in 1450 A.D. Forty-three popes lived and died during the time the work was in progress. It was dedicated in the year 1626, but not entirely finished until the year 1880. The cost, in round numbers, is set down at $70,000,000. Michael Angelo was the architect.

Names and Their Meaning

Abbreviations: *Br.*, British. *C.*, Celtic. *D.*, Dutch. *E.*, English. *F.*, French. *Ga.*, Gaelic. *Ger.*, German. *Gr.*, Greek. *H.*, Hebrew. *I.*, Italian. *Ir.*, Irish. *L.*, Latin. *P.*, Punic. *S.*, Saxon. *Sp.*, Spanish. *Syr.*, Syriac.

CHRISTIAN NAMES OF MEN

AARON (*H.*), a mountain, or lofty. Abel (*H.*), vanity. Abraham (*H.*), the father of many. Absalom (*H.*), the father of peace. Adam (*H.*), red earth. Adolphus (*S.*), happiness and help. Adrian (*L.*), one who helps. Alan (*C.*), harmony; or *Slavonic*, a hound. Albert (*S.*), all bright. Alexander (*Gr.*), a helper of men. Alfred (*S.*), all peace. Alonzo, form of Alphonso, q. v. Alphonso (*Ger.*), ready or willing. Ambrose (*Gr.*), immortal. Amos (*H.*), a burden. Andrew (*Gr.*), courageous. Anthony (*L.*), flourishing. Archibald (*Ger.*), a bold observer. Arnold (*Ger.*), a maintainer of honor. Arthur (*Br.*), a strong man. Augustus, Augustin (*L.*), venerable, grand.

BALDWIN (*Ger.*), a bold winner. Bardulph (*Ger.*), a famous helper. Barnaby (*H.*), a prophet's son. Bartholomew (*H.*), the son of him who made the waters to rise. Beaumont (*F.*), a pretty mount. Bede (*S.*), prayer. Benjamin (*H.*), the son of a right hand. Bennet (*L.*), blessed. Bernard (*Ger.*), bear's heart. Bertram (*Ger.*), fair, illustrious. Bertrand (*Ger.*), bright raven. Boniface (*L.*), a well-doer. Brian (*F.*), having a thundering voice.

CADWALLADER (*Br.*), valiant in war. Cæsar (*L.*), adorned with hair. Caleb (*H.*), a dog. Cecil (*L.*), dim-sighted. Charles (*Ger.*), noble-spirited. Christopher (*Gr.*), bearing Christ. Clement (*L.*), mild-tempered. Conrad (*Ger.*), able counsel. Constantine (*L.*), resolute. Cornelius (*L.*), meaning uncertain. Crispin (*L.*), having curled locks. Cuthbert (*S.*), known famously.

DAN (*H.*), judgment. Daniel (*H.*), God is judge. David (*H.*), well-beloved. Denis (*Gr.*), belonging to the God of wine. Douglas (*Ga.*), dark gray. Duncan (*S.*), brown chief. Dunstan (*S.*), most high.

EDGAR (*S.*), happy honor. Edmund (*S.*), happy peace. Edward (*S.*), happy keeper. Edwin (*S.*), happy conqueror. Egbert (*S.*), ever bright. Elijah (*H.*), God the Lord. Elisha (*H.*), the salvation of God. Emmanuel (*H.*), God with us. Enoch (*H.*), dedicated. Ephraim (*H.*), fruitful. Erasmus (*Gr.*), lovely, worthy to be loved. Ernest (*Ger.*), earnest, serious. Esau (*H.*), hairy. Eugene (*Gr.*), noble, well-born. Eustace (*Gr.*), standing firm. Evan, or Ivan (*Br.*), the same as John. Everard (*Ger.*), well reported. Ezekiel (*H.*), the strength of God.

FELIX (*L.*), happy. Ferdinand (*Ger.*), pure peace. Fergus (*S.*), manly strength. Francis (*Ger.*), free. Frederic (*Ger.*), rich peace.

GABRIEL (*H.*), the strength of God. Geoffrey (*Ger.*), joyful. George (*Gr.*), a husbandman. Gerard (*S.*), all towardliness. Gideon (*H.*), a breaker. Gilbert (*S.*), bright as gold. Giles (*Gr.*), a little goat. Godard (*Ger.*), a godly disposition. Godfrey (*Ger.*), God's peace. Godwin (*Ger.*), victorious in God. Griffith (*Br.*), having great faith. Guy (*F.*), a leader.

HANNIBAL (*P.*), a gracious lord. Harold (*S.*), a champion. Hector (*Gr.*), a stout defender. Henry (*Ger.*), a rich lord. Herbert (*Ger.*), a bright lord. Hercules (*Gr.*), the glory of Hera, or Juno. Hezekiah (*H.*), cleaving to the Lord. Horace (*L.*), meaning uncertain. Horatio (*L.*), worthy to be beheld. Howell (*Br.*), sound or whole. Hubert (*Ger.*), a bright color. Hugh, or Hugo (*D.*), high, lofty. Humphrey (*Ger.*), domestic peace.

IGNATIUS (*L.*), fiery. Ingram (*Ger.*), of angelic purity. Isaac (*H.*), laughter.

JABEZ (*H.*), one who causes pain. Jacob (*H.*), a supplanter. James, or Jacob (*H.*), beguiling. Jesse (*H.*), fatherhood. Job (*H.*), sorrowing. Joel (*H.*), acquiescing. John (*H.*), the grace of the Lord. Jonah (*H.*), a dove. Jonathan (*H.*), the gift of the Lord. Joscelin (*Ger.*), just. Joseph (*H.*), addition. Joshua (*H.*), a savior. Josiah or Josias (*H.*), the fire of the Lord. Julian (*L.*), soft-haired.

LAMBERT (*S.*), a fair lamb. Lancelot (*Sp.*), a little lance. Laurence (*L.*), crowned with laurels. Lazarus (*H.*), destitute of help. Leonard (*Ger.*), like a lion. Leopold (*Ger.*), defending the people. Lewis or Louis (*F.*), the defender of the people. Lionel (*L.*), a little lion. Llewellyn (*Br.*), like a lion. Llewellyn (*C.*), lightning. Lucius (*L.*), shining. Luke (*Gr.*), a wood or grove.

MANFRED (*Ger.*), great peace. Mark (*L.*), a hammer. Martin (*L.*), martial. Matthew (*H.*), a gift or present. Maurice (*L.*), sprung of a Moor. Meredith (*Br.*), the roaring of the sea. Michael (*H.*), who is like God? Morgan (*Br.*), a mariner. Moses (*H.*), drawn out.

NATHANIEL (*H.*), the gift of God. Neal (*F.*), somewhat black. Nicholas (*Gr.*), victorious over the people. Noel (*F.*), belonging to one's nativity. Norman (*F.*), one born in Normandy.

OBADIAH (*H.*), the servant of the Lord. Oliver (*L.*), an olive. Orlando (*I.*), counsel for the land. Orson (*L.*), a bear. Osmund (*S.*), house peace. Oswald (*S.*), ruler of a house. Owen (*Br.*), well descended.

PATRICK (*L.*), a nobleman. Paul (*L.*), small, little. Paulinus (*L.*), little Paul. Percival (*F.*), a place in France. Percy (*Eng.*), adaptation of "pierce eye." Peregrine (*L.*), outlandish. Peter (*Gr.*), a rock or stone. Philip (*Gr.*), a lover of horses. Phineas (*H.*), of bold countenance.

RALPH, contracted from Randolph, or Randal, or Ranulph (*S.*), pure help. Raymond (*Ger.*), quiet peace. Reuben (*H.*), the son of vision. Reynold (*Ger.*), a lover of purity. Richard (*S.*), powerful. Robert (*Ger.*), famous in counsel. Roderick (*Ger.*), rich in fame. Roger (*Ger.*), strong counsel. Roland or Rowland (*Ger.*), counsel for the land. Rollo, form of Roland, q. v. Rufus (*L.*), reddish.

SAMSON (*H.*), a little son. Samuel (*H.*), heard by God. Saul (*H.*), desired. Sebastian (*Gr.*), to be reverenced. Seth (*H.*), appointed. Silas (*L.*), sylvan or living in the woods. Simeon (*H.*), hearing. Simon (*H.*), obedient. Solomon (*H.*), peaceable. Stephen (*Gr.*), a crown or garland. Swithin (*S.*), very high.

THEOBALD (*S.*), bold over the people. Theodore (*Gr.*), the gift of God. Theodosius (*Gr.*), given of God. Theophilus (*Gr.*), a lover of God. Thomas (*H.*), a twin. Timothy (*Gr.*), a fearer of God. Titus (*Gr.*), meaning uncertain. Toby, or Tobias (*H.*), the goodness of the Lord.

VALENTINE (*L.*), powerful. Victor (*L.*), conqueror. Vincent (*L.*), conquering. Vivian (*L.*), living.

WALTER (*Ger.*), a conqueror. Walwin (*Ger.*), a conqueror. Wilfred (*S.*), bold and peaceful. William (*Ger.*), defending many.

ZACCHEUS (*Syr.*), innocent. Zachary (*H.*), remembering the Lord. Zebedee (*Syr.*), having an inheritance. Zechariah (*H.*), remembered of the Lord. Zedekiah (*H.*), the justice of the Lord.

CHRISTIAN NAMES OF WOMEN

ADA (*Ger.*), same as Edith, q. v. Adela (*Ger.*), same as Adeline, q. v. Adelaide (*Ger.*), same as Adeline, q. v. Adeline (*Ger.*), a princess. Agatha (*Gr.*), good. Agnes (*Ger.*), chaste. Alethea (*Gr.*), the truth. Althea (*Gr.*), hunting. Alice, Alicia (*Ger.*), noble. Alma (*L.*), benignant. Annabel (*L.*), lovable. Amy, Amelia (*F.*), a beloved. Angelina (*Gr.*), lovely, angelic. Anna, or Anne (*H.*), gracious. Arabella (*L.*), a fair altar. Aurelia (*L.*), like gold. Aurora (*L.*), morning brightness.

BARBARA (*L.*), foreign or strange. Beatrice (*L.*), making happy. Bella (*I.*), beautiful. Benedicta (*L.*), blessed. Bernice (*Gr.*), bringing victory. Bertha (*Gr.*), bright or famous. Bessie, short form of Elizabeth, q. v. Blanche (*F.*), fair. Bona (*L.*), good. Bridget (*Ir.*), shining bright.

CAMILLA (*L.*), attendant at a sacrifice. Carlotta (*I.*), same as Charlotte, q. v. Caroline, *feminine of Carolus, the Latin of Charles, noble-spirited*. Cassandra (*Gr.*), a reformer of men. Catherine (*Gr.*), pure or clean. Cecilia (*L.*), *from* Cecil. Charity (*Gr.*), love, bounty. Charlotte (*F.*), all noble. Chloe (*Gr.*), a green herb. Christina (*Gr.*), belonging to Christ. Cicely, *a corruption of* Cecilia

q. v. Clara (L.), clear or bright. Clarissa (L.), clear or bright. Constance (L.), constant.

DAGMAR (Ger.), joy of the Danes. Deborah (H.), a bee. Diana (Gr.), Jupiter's daughter. Dorcas (Gr.), a wild roe. Dorothea or Dorothy (Gr.), the gift of God.

EDITH (S.), happiness. Eleanor (S.), all fruitful. Eliza, Elizabeth (H.), the oath of God. Ellen, *another form of* Helen, *q. v.* Emily, *corrupted from* Amelia. Emma (Ger.), a nurse. Esther, Hester (H.), a star. Euodia (Gr.), prospering in the way. Eudora (Gr.), good gift. Eudocia (Gr.), good gift or well-given. Eugenia (Gr.), well-born. Eunice (Gr.), fair victory. Eva or Eve (H.), causing life.

FANNY, *diminutive of* Frances, *q. v.* Fidelia (Gr.), bright to look on. Flora (L.), flowers. Florence (L.), blooming, flourishing. Frances (Ger.), free.

GERTRUDE (Ger.), all truth. Grace (L.), favor.

HAGAR (H.), a stranger. Hadassah (H.), *form of* Esther, *q. v.* Hannah (H.), gracious. Harriet (Ger.), head of the house. Helen or Helena (Gr.), alluring. Henrietta, *fem. and dim. of* Henry, *q. v.* Hephzibah (H.), my delight is in her. Hilda (Ger.), warrior maiden. Honora (L.), honorable. Huldah (H.), a weasel.

IDA (Ger.), Godlike. Inez, Agnes. Isabel (Sp.), fair Eliza.

JANE, or Joanna *fem. of* John, *q. v.* Janet, Jeannette, little Jane. Jemima (H.), a dove. Joan (H.), *fem. of* John, *q. v.* Joanna or Johanna, *form of* Joan, *q. v.* Joyce (F.), pleasant. Judith (H.), praising. Julia, Juliana, *feminine of* Julius, *q. v.*

KATHERINE, *form of* Catherine, *q. v.* Keturah (H.), incense. Keziah (H.), cassia.

LAURA (L.), a laurel. Lavinia (L.), of Latium. Letitia (L.), joy or gladness. Lilian, Lily (L.), a lily. Lois (Gr.), better. Louisa (Ger.), *fem. of* Louis, *q. v.* Lucretia (L.), a chaste Roman lady. Lucy (L.), *feminine of* Lucius. Lydia (Gr.), descended from Lud.

MABEL (L.), lovely or lovable. Madeline, *form of* Magdalen, *q. v.* Magdalen (Syr.), magnificent. Margaret (Gr.), a pearl. Maria, Marie, *forms of* Mary, *q. v.* Martha (H.), bitterness. Mary (H.), bitter. Matilda (Ger.), a lady of honor. Maud (Ger.), *form of* Matilda, *q. v.* May (L.), month of May, *or dim. of* Mary, *q. v.* Mercy (Eng.), compassion. Mildred (S.), speaking mild. Minnie, *dim. of* Margaret, *q. v.*

NAOMI (H.), alluring. Nest (Br.), *the same as* Agnes. Nicola (Gr.), *feminine of* Nicholas. Nora, *dim. of* Honora.

OLIVE, Olivia (L.), an olive. Olympia (Gr.), heavenly. Ophelia (Gr.), a serpent.

PARNELL, or Petronilla, little Peter. Patience (L.), bearing patiently. Paulina (L.), *feminine of* Paulinus. Penelope (Gr.), a weaver. Persis (Gr.), destroying. Philadelphia (Gr.), brotherly love. Philippa (Gr.), *feminine of* Philip. Phoebe (Gr.), the light of life. Phyllis (Gr.), a green bough. Polly, *variation of* Molly, *dim. of* Mary, *q. v.* Priscilla (L.), somewhat old. Prudence (L.), discretion. Psyche (Gr.), the soul.

RACHEL (H.), a lamb. Rebecca (H.), fat or plump. Rhoda (Gr.), a rose. Rosa or Rose (L.), a rose. Rosalie or Rosaline (L.), little rose. Rosalind (L.), beautiful as a rose. Rosabella (L.), a fair rose. Rosamond (S.), rose of peace. Roxana (Per.), dawn of day. Ruth (H.), trembling, or beauty.

SABINA (L.), sprung from the Sabines. Salome (H.), perfect. Sapphira (Gr.), like a sapphire stone. Sarah (H.), a princess. Selina (Gr.), the moon. Sibylla (Gr.), the counsel of God. Sophia (Gr.), wisdom. Sophronia (Gr.), of a sound mind. Susan, Susanna (H.), a lily.

TABITHA (Syr.), a roe. Temperance (L.), moderation. Theodosia (Gr.), given by God. Tryphena (Gr.), delicate. Tryphosa (Gr.), delicious.

ULRICA (Ger.), rich. Ursula (L.), a she bear.

VICTORIA (L.), victory. Vida, (Erse), *feminine of* David.

WALBURGA (S.), gracious. Winifred (S.), winning peace.

ZENOBIA (Gr.), the life of Jupiter.

In 1552 books on geometry and astronomy were destroyed in England as savoring of magic.

The academy took its name from that of a shady grove outside the walls of Athens, where Plato and his disciples were accustomed to walk B. C. 378.

It is an error to suppose that the lion is stronger than the tiger. Dr. Haughton has proved that the strength of the lion in the fore-limbs is only 69.9 per cent. of that of the tiger, and the strength of his hind-limbs only 65.9 per cent. Five men can easily hold down a lion, but it requires nine men to control a tiger.

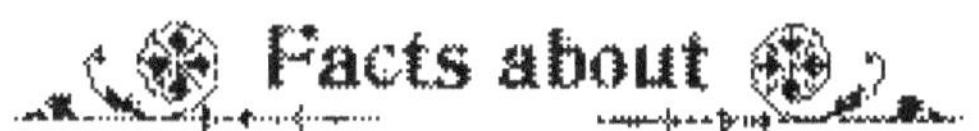

Facts about Railroads and Transportation

TWENTY POINTS ON AMERICAN RAILROADING.

1. There are in the United States 169,402.74 miles of railway—about half the mileage of the world. 2. The estimated cost is $9,000,000,000. 3. The number of people employed by American railways is more than 1,000,000. 4. The fastest time made by a train is 436 5-10 miles in 7 hours 23 minutes (443 minutes), one mile being made in 47 11-20 seconds, on the West Shore Railroad, New York. 5. The cost of a high-class eight-wheel passenger locomotive is about $8,500. 6. The longest mileage operated by a single system is that of the Atchison, Topeka & Santa Fe—about 8,000 miles. 7. The cost of a palace sleeping-car is about $15,000, or $17,000 if "vestibuled." 8. The longest railway bridge span in the United States is the Cantilever span in Poughkeepsie bridge—548 feet. 9. The highest railroad bridge in the United States is the Kinzua viaduct on the Erie road—305 feet high. 10. The first locomotive in the United States was built by Peter Cooper. 11. The road carrying the largest number of passengers is the Manhattan Elevated Railroad, New York—525,000 a day, or 191,625,000 yearly. 12. The average daily earning of an American locomotive is about $100. 13. The longest American railway tunnel is the Hoosac, on the Fitchburgh railway—4¾ miles. 14. The average cost of constructing a mile of railroad at the present time is about $30,000. 15. The first sleeping-car was used upon the Cumberland Valley Railroad of Pennsylvania, from 1836 to 1848. 16. The chances of fatal accidents in railway travel are very slight—one killed in ten million. Statistics show more are killed by falling out of windows than in railway accidents. 17. The line of railway extending farthest east and west is the Canadian Pacific, running from Quebec to the Pacific Ocean. 18. A steel rail, with average wear, lasts about eighteen years. 19. The road carrying the largest number of commuters is the Illinois Central at Chicago—4,828,128 commutation fares in 1887. 20. The fastest time made between Jersey City and San Francisco is 3 days, 7 hours, 39 minutes and 16 seconds. Special theatrical train, June, 1876.

TRAIN MANAGEMENT.

"Standard Code."

A train while running must display two green flags by day and two green lights by night, one on each side of the rear of the train.

After sunset, or when obscured by fog or other cause, must display headlight in front and two red lights in rear.

Two green flags by day and two green lights by night, displayed in the places provided for that purpose on the front of an engine, denote that the train is followed by another train running on the same schedule and entitled to the same time-table rights as the train carrying the signals.

Two white flags by day or two white lights by night, carried in the same manner, denote that the train is an extra.

A blue flag by day and a blue light by night, placed on the end of a car, denotes that car inspectors are at work under or about the car or train and that it must not be coupled to or moved until the blue signal is removed.

COLORED FLAG OR LANTERN SIGNALS—TORPEDOES.

"Standard Code."

Red signifies danger.

Green signifies caution, go slowly.

White signifies safety.

Green and white signifies stop at flag stations for passengers or freight.

One cap or torpedo on rail means stop immediately.

Two caps or torpedoes on rail means reduce speed immediately and look out for danger signal.

LOCOMOTIVE WHISTLE SIGNALS.

Just one long blast on the whistle, ———— this style,
Is a sign of nearing town,
A railroad crossing or junction, maybe,
And this —, the brakes whistled down.

Two long ——— ——— are just the reverse of the last,
And this — — the engine's reply

When word from the conductor to stop,—
A sort of cheerful "Aye! Aye!"

These three — — — will show
when the train comes apart.
This — — — means two different things:
That the train will back, or asks you to note
Some special signal it brings.

These four — — — — belong
to the flagman alone,
And these — — — — are meant for the crew;
But this one — — — —, when crossing a road at grade,
More nearly interests you.

Five short ones — — — — — say to the flagman on guard,
"Look out for a rear attack!"
And a lot like this — — — — — — that a
heedless cow
Or a deaf man is on the track!

D. B. Benjamin.

SWINGING-LAMP SIGNALS.

1. A lamp swung across the track is the signal to stop. 2. A lamp raised and lowered vertically is the signal to move ahead. 3. A lamp swung vertically in a circle across the track, when the train is standing, is the signal to move back. 4. A lamp swung vertically in a circle at arm's length across the track, when the train is running, is the signal that the train has parted.

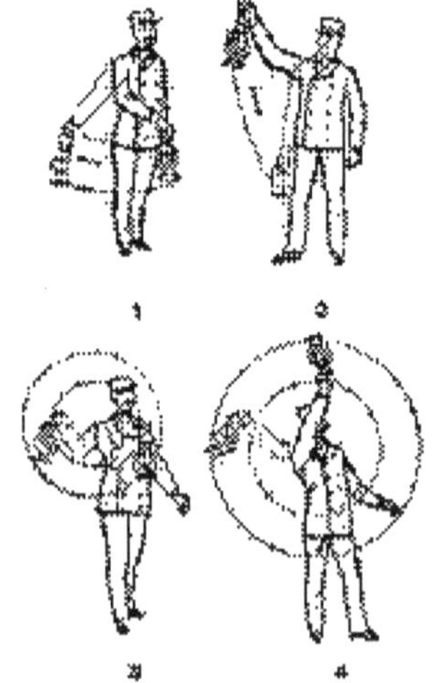

$_*$ A flag, or the hand, moved in any of the directions given above, will indicate the same signal as given by a lamp.

STEAMBOATING.

The first idea of steam navigation was contained in a patent obtained in England by Hulls, in 1736.

Fitch experimented in steam navigation on the Delaware river in 1783-4.

Oliver Evans was the next experimenter in steam navigation in 1785-6.

Rumsey was also an experimenter in Virginia in steam navigation in 1787.

W. Symington made a trial on the Forth and Clyde with a small but rudely constructed model of a steamer in 1789.

Chancellor Livingston built a steamer on the Hudson in 1797.

The first experiment in steamboating on the Thames, England, was in 1801.

Fulton built the steamer, the North River, and in 1807 made the passage up the Hudson River to Albany from New York in 33 hours — the first steam navigation on record.

Fulton built the Orleans at Pittsburg, the first steamer on Western rivers. It was completed and made the voyage to New Orleans, 2,000 miles, in 1811.

Mr. Symington repeated his experiments on the Thames with success in 1802.

The first vessels of Europe commenced plying on the Clyde in 1812.

The Savannah, the first steamer to cross the ocean, was of 350 tons burden, and sailed from Savannah, Ga., July 15, 1819.

Capt. Johnson was paid £10,000, or $50,000, for making the first steam voyage to India. The voyage was made on the steamer Enterprise, which sailed from Falmouth, England, Aug. 16, 1825.

The first war steamer was built in England in 1838.

CAPACITY OF A TEN-TON FREIGHT CAR.

Whisky	60	barrels
Salt	70	"
Lime	70	"
Flour	90	"
Eggs	130 to 160	"
Flour	200	sacks
Cattle	18 to 20	head
Hogs	50 to 60	"
Sheep	80 to 100	"
Lumber, green	6,000	feet
Lumber, dry	10,000	"
Barley	300	bush.
Wheat	340	"
Apples	370	"
Corn	400	"
Potatoes	430	"
Oats	680	"
Bran	1,000	"

Weather Forecasts

ALMANAC predictions can be nothing but conjecture, the earth's subjection to many unknowable and undeterminable forces rendering such calculations impossible. It is practicable, however, by the following rules, drawn from actual results during very many years and applied with due regard to the subjects of solar and lunar attraction with reference to this planet, to foresee the kind of weather most likely to follow the moon's change of phase.

Prognostications.

If New Moon, First Quarter, Full Moon or Last Quarter happens					In Summer.	In Winter.
Between midnight		and	2	A. M.	Fair ......(1 and 2)	Frost, unless wind is S. W. (7)
"	2	"	4	"	Cold and showers...	Snow and stormy.
"	4	"	6	"	Rain...............	Rain.
"	6	"	8	"	Wind and rain......	Stormy.
"	8	"	10	"	Changeable.........	Cold rain if wind W., snow if E.
"	10	"	12	"	Frequent showers (3)	Cold and high wind.
"	12	"	2	P. M.	Very rainy......(4)	Snow or rain.
"	2	"	4	"	Changeable.........	Fair and mild.
"	4	"	6	"	Fair...............	Fair.
"	6	"	8	"	Fair if wind N. W...	Fair and frosty if wind N. or N. E.
"	8	"	10	"	Rainy if S. or S. W..	Rain or snow if S. or S. W.
"	10	"	midnight		Fair...............	Fair and frosty.

OBSERVATIONS:—1. The nearer the moon's change, first quarter, full and last quarter to midnight, the fairer will be the weather during the next seven days.

2. The space for this calculation occupies from ten at night till two next morning.

3. The nearer to midday or noon the phase of the moon happens, the more foul or wet weather may be expected during the next seven days.

4. The space for this calculation occupies from ten in the forenoon to two in the afternoon. These observations refer principally to summer, though they affect spring and autumn in the same ratio.

5. The moon's change, first quarter, full and last quarter happening during six of the afternoon hours, i. e., from four to ten, may be followed by fair weather, but this is mostly dependent on the wind, as is noted in the table.

6. Though the weather, from a variety of irregular causes, is more uncertain in the latter part of autumn, the whole of winter and the beginning of spring, yet, in the main, the above observations will apply to those periods also.

7. To prognosticate correctly, especially in those cases where the wind is concerned, the observer should be within sight of a vane where the four cardinal points of the compass are correctly placed.

Certain phenomena in the air and peculiarities of birds have long been known to indicate a change in the weather. Many years ago the learned Dr. Jenner embodied these in verse, in reply to an invitation from a friend with whom he had planned an excursion the following day. It covers about all that is known to-day upon that branch of the subject:

The hollow winds begin to blow,
The clouds look black, the glass is low;
The soot falls down, the spaniels sleep,
And spiders from their cobwebs peep.
Last night the sun went pale to bed,
The moon in halos hid her head;
The boding shepherd heaves a sigh,
For see, a rainbow spans the sky;
The walls are damp, the ditches smell,
Closed is the pink-eyed pimpernel.
Hark! how the chairs and tables crack,
Old Betty's joints are on the rack;
Loud quack the ducks, the peacocks cry,
The distant hills are looking nigh.
How restless are the snorting swine,
The busy flies disturb the kine;
Low o'er the grass the swallow wings,
The cricket, too, how sharp he sings;
Puss, on the hearth, with velvet paws,
Sits, wiping o'er her whiskered jaws.
Through the clear stream the fishes rise,
And nimbly catch th' incautious flies;

The glow-worms, numerous and bright,
Illum'd the dewy dell last night;
At dusk the squalid toad was seen,
Hopping and crawling o'er the green;
The whirling wind the dust obeys,
And in the rapid eddy plays;
The frog has changed his yellow vest,
And in a russet coat is dressed.
Though June, the air is cold and still;
The blackbird's mellow voice is shrill;
My dog, so alter'd in his taste,
Quits mutton bones, on grass to feast;
And see yon rooks, how odd their flight;
They imitate the gliding kite,
And seem precipitate to fall—
As if they felt the piercing ball.
'Twill surely rain, I see with sorrow:
Our jaunt must be put off to-morrow.

WIND AND WEATHER SIGNALS

The new system of weather signals was introduced by the United States Signal Office of the War Department in 1887, and has since been in use at all the stations of the service. The flags adopted for this purpose are four in number, and of the form and dimensions indicated below:

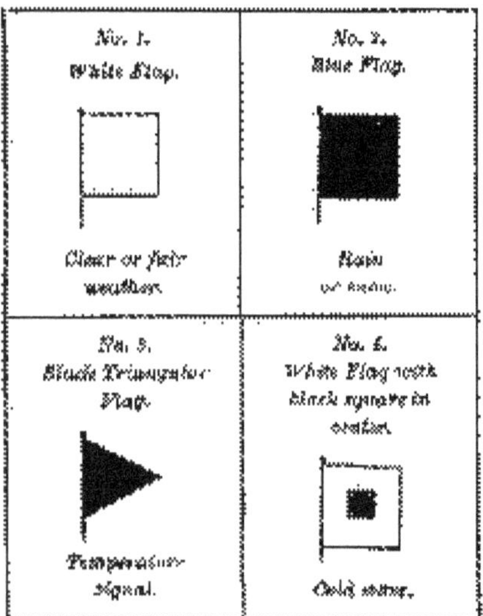

Number 1, white flag, six feet square, indicates clear or fair weather. Number 2, blue flag, six feet square, indicates rain or snow. Number 3, black triangular flag, four feet at the base and six feet in length, always refers to temperature; when placed above numbers 1 or 2 it indicates warmer weather; when placed below numbers 1 or 2 it indicates colder weather; when not displayed, the indications are that the temperature will remain stationary, or that the change in temperature will not vary five degrees from the temperature of the same hour of the preceding day. Number 4, white flag, six feet square, with black square in center, indicates the approach of a sudden and decided fall in temperature. This signal is usually ordered at least twenty-four hours in advance of the cold wave. It is not displayed unless a temperature of forty-five degrees, or lower, is expected. When number 4 is displayed, number 3 is always omitted.

When displayed on poles, the signals are arranged to read downwards; when displayed from horizontal supports, a small streamer is attached to indicate the point from which the signals are to be read.

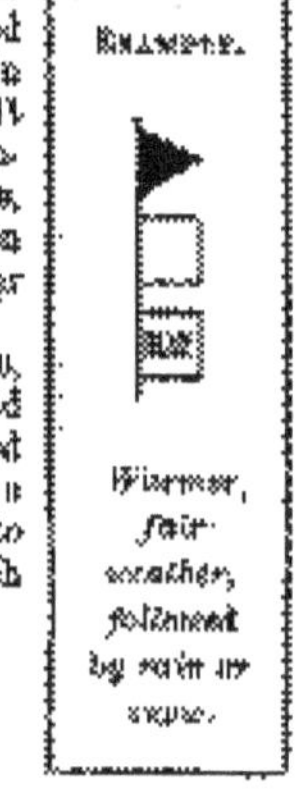
Example.
Warmer, fair weather, followed by rain or snow.

Interpretation of Displays.

No. 1, alone, indicates fair weather, stationary temperature.

No. 2, alone, indicates rain or snow, stationary temperature.

No. 1, with No. 3 below it, indicates fair weather, colder.

No. 2, with No. 3 above it, indicates warmer weather, rain or snow.

No. 1, with No. 4 below it, indicates fair weather, cold wave.

No. 3, with Nos. 1 and 2 below it, as shown in illustration, indicates warmer, fair weather, followed by rain or snow.

No. 4, followed by Nos. 2, 1 and 3, in the order given, indicates the approach of a cold wave, to be succeeded by rain or snow—this, in turn, to be followed by fair weather and colder temperature.

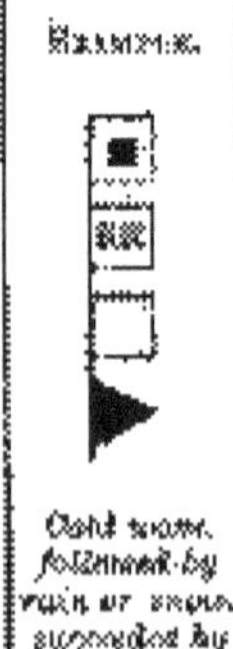
Example.
Cold wave, followed by rain or snow, succeeded by fair weather; colder.

Storm, Cautionary and Wind-Direction Signals.

A red flag with a black center indicates that the storm is expected to be of marked violence. A yellow flag with a white center indicates that the winds expected will not be so severe, but well-found, seaworthy vessels can meet them without danger. The red pennant indicates easterly winds, that is, from the northeast

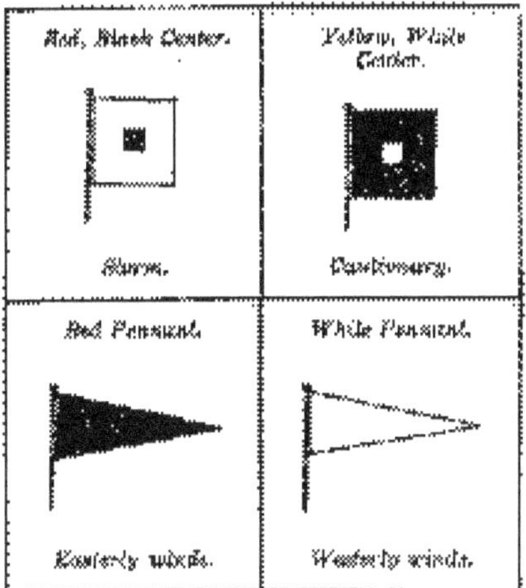

to south inclusive, and that generally the storm center is approaching. If *above* cautionary or storm-signal, winds from northeast quadrant are more probable; *below*, winds from southeast quadrant. The white pennant indicates westerly winds; that is, from north to southwest inclusive, and that generally the storm center has passed. If *above* cautionary or storm-signal, winds from northwest quadrant are more probable; if *below*, winds from southwest quadrant.

The Climates of the United States.

Mean annual temperature, Fahrenheit, at places named.

Alabama	Mobile	66°
Alaska	Sitka	46
Arizona	Tucson	69
Arkansas	Little Rock	63
California	San Francisco	55
Colorado	Denver	48
Connecticut	Hartford	50
Dakota	Fort Randall	47
Delaware	Wilmington	53
Dist. Columbia	Washington	55
Florida	Jacksonville	69
Georgia	Atlanta	58
Idaho	Fort Boise	52°
Illinois	Springfield	50
Indiana	Indianapolis	53
Indian Territory	Fort Gibson	60
Iowa	Des Moines	46
Kansas	Leavenworth	53
Kentucky	Louisville	56
Louisiana	New Orleans	69
Maine	Augusta	45
Maryland	Baltimore	54
Massachusetts	Boston	48
Michigan	Detroit	47
Minnesota	St. Paul	42
Mississippi	Jackson	64
Missouri	St. Louis	55
Montana	Helena	43
Nebraska	Omaha	49
Nevada	Cp Winfield Scott	50
New Hampshire	Concord	46
New Jersey	Trenton	53
New Mexico	Santa Fe	51
New York	Albany	48
North Carolina	Raleigh	59
Ohio	Columbus	53
Oregon	Portland	53
Pennsylvania	Harrisburg	54
Rhode Island	Providence	48
South Carolina	Columbia	62
Tennessee	Nashville	58
Texas	Austin	67
Utah	Salt Lake City	52
Vermont	Montpelier	43
Virginia	Richmond	57
Washington	Steilacoom	51
West Virginia	Romney	52
Wisconsin	Madison	45
Wyoming	Fort Bridger	41

Time Difference Between the City of New York and the Principal Foreign Cities.

Faster than New York.	H.	M.		H.	M.
Antwerp	5	13	Melbourne	9	14
Berlin	5	50	Paris	5	05
Bremen	5	31	Rio de Janeiro	2	08
Brussels	5	14	Rome	5	45
Buenos Ayres	1	02	St. Petersburg	6	57
Calcutta	10	50	Valparaiso		10
Constantinople	6	53	Vienna	6	01
Dublin	4	31	*Slower than New York.*		
Edinburgh	4	48	Canton	11	31
Geneva	5	21	Havana		38
Hamburg	5	36	Hong Kong	11	27
Liverpool	4	44	Mexico, City of	1	40
London	4	56	Panama		12
Madrid	4	42	Vera Cruz	1	28
			Yokohama	10	45

Actual New York mean time is given.

Rise of Famous Americans

ALVINZA HAYWOOD, the retired San Francisco millionaire, was in youth a farmer's "bound boy" in Northern New York, and received at 21 $100 and a "freedom suit" as his start in life.

John Shults, the millionaire baker and horseman, of Brooklyn, began life as a working baker.

Jay Gould was a poor country boy, never even learning a trade, but he had a genius for "swapping" and management.

Andrew Carnegie was a telegraph messenger.

Thomas A. Edison was a telegraph operator in the days when wages were smaller than they are now.

John Roach came penniless to New York at the age of 16 and got work in an iron foundry.

Andrew Kinsella served the Brooklyn *Eagle* as office boy and rose to be its editor.

Joseph Pulitzer came to this country with neither money nor knowledge of English, and at one time acted as coachman.

Amos Cummings and John Russell Young, like Horace Greeley, began newspaper work at the printer's case.

C. P. Huntington was a poor boy in Connecticut.

W. D. Howells was a printer in Ohio when a boy.

Erastus Wiman began life in poverty in Canada.

John D. Rockefeller was a poor boy in Ohio.

Old Joe Brown, of Georgia, began life in poverty.

Uncle Philetus Sawyer, of Michigan, many times a millionaire, began life with his "time," generously presented him by his father when he was 17.

Mark Twain, the author and millionaire, was a Mississippi pilot.

Lucy Larcom was a cotton mill hand in her early years.

Andrew D. Baird, of Brooklyn, a big stone-cutter, began life with hammer and chisel.

Professor Bowne, the Boston metaphysician, was a truck driver.

Asa Gray, the Harvard botanist, was a poor farmer's boy in Oneida County. Senator McPherson, of New Jersey, had the same humble but promising start in life.

Cardinal Gibbons was a poor Irish immigrant who served as a clerk in his youth.

Caricaturists Keppler and Nast were both poor immigrant boys.

J. Q. A. Ward, the sculptor, was a raw Ohio farm lad.

Elihu B. Washburne was a farm lad and printer's devil.

Jim McWilliams, the Detroit millionaire, began life as a clerk in a hardware store.

John W. Mackay was an apprentice in a shipyard, and went west with the gold-hunters.

Cyrus McCormick, the inventor of the reaper, thought the thing out while he was using his sickle and cradle on his father's little farm.

James G. Fair was born in Ireland and went to California, beginning as a miner with shovel and pick.

Jerry Rusk went west to grow up with the country, and took up a farm.

George William Childs left school at 10, and was an errand boy in a store in his youth.

Tom Scott, the late Pennsylvania magnate, was a choreboy in his father's inn.

Jay Cooke began clerking in a store when he was 15. F. B. Thurber was only a year older when he did the same.

Matthias Baldwin, the engine-builder, was apprenticed to a jeweler in his boyhood.

Robert Bonner started in life at the printer's case on the Hartford *Courant*.

James Gordon Bennett, Sr., reached Boston from the old country at 19 and got a job in a bookstore when he had been two days without food.

Russell Sage entered a country grocery at ten as a clerk.

A. T. Stewart began life in the new world as a teacher at $300 a year.

Elias Howe was not only born poor, but stayed poor until he was 40.

Leland Stanford literally chopped his way to the law by cutting, with the hired help of others, 2,000 cords of wood when he was eighteen years of age, for the Mohawk and Hudson River Railroad.

"In this theater of man's life it is reserved only for God and angels to be lookers-on."—*Pythagoras.*

"The greater the fool the sadder is it for the unutterable waste, the unending pain of life."—*Ouida.*

...ll-coast and lay,
...their brothers and
...they occupied the

..." said Harwood
...side with General
...ow my boots fit

...the Franc-tireurs
...either by General
...tols. They occ-
...Harwood himself
...here, and let him
...at Flourens' cas-
...eneral or on the-

...for Harwood: he
...three battalions
...plying to their
...ched. There was
...g sheets of smoke
...e gloom. Suppose
...here alone?—or

...ously; the horse
...ful live?" a voice

...ed, with a sudden
...and men shouted
...on every side, a

Curiosities of the Bible.

The following Bible curiosities are said to have been gained by a study of the good book by the Prince of Granada, heir apparent to the Spanish throne, during his thirty-three years' imprisonment at the Place of Skulls prison, Madrid:

"In the Bible the word Lord is found 1,853 times, the word Jehovah 6,855 times, and the word reverend but once, and that in the ninth verse of the 111th Psalm. The eighth verse of the 118th Psalm is the middle verse of the Bible. The ninth verse of the seventh chapter of Esther is the longest verse. The thirty-fifth verse, eleventh chapter, of St. John is the shortest. In the 107th Psalm four verses are alike, the eighth, fifteenth, twenty-first and thirty-first. Each verse of the 136th Psalm ends alike. No names or words with more than six syllables are found in the Bible. The thirty-seventh chapter of Isaiah and the nineteenth chapter of II. Kings are alike. The word girl occurs once in the Bible, and that in the third verse and third chapter of Joel, and the word boy but once, Zechariah viii., 5. There are found in both books of the Bible 3,586,483 letters and 773,692 words."—Presbyterian Review.

GEORGE WASHINGTON

Engraved from the original painting by Joseph Wright,
now owned by Mr. [illegible]

A Dictionary of Biography

EMBRACING THE EMINENT PERSONAGES OF HISTORY AND OF OUR OWN TIMES

ABBREVIATIONS: Am., American. Br., British. Dan., Danish. Eng., English. Fl., flourished. Fr., French. Ger., German. Gr., Greek. Ir., Irish. It., Italian. Nor., Norwegian. Port., Portuguese. Prus., Prussian. Rom., Roman. Scot., Scottish. Sp., Spanish. Sw., Swedish.

The numbers after each name indicate the years of birth and death. An interrogation mark denotes that the date is doubtful. After the names of the Popes the first date indicates date of accession unless otherwise stated.

"WHO?" "When?" "Where?" "What?" These four questions, to be precisely and tersely answered, were Horace Greeley's tests of the value of information. The great journalist's motto has been applied to this department. It would be impossible to give here the names of all notabilities, but it is believed that all have been included which will be met in the ordinary course of English reading. Appended to the names of the more prominent historical characters will be found such historical data as seemed desirable to supplement the historical charts, which are a special feature of this volume. Particular care has been taken to include the names of all the men and women who are making the history of to-day, especially of our own country. This will be particularly appreciated by those who fail to find this most important information in the cumbersome many-volume cyclopedias.

ABBAS PASHA, 1874-....., khedive of Egypt. ABBAS I. (the Great), 1557-1628, shah of Persia. ABBASSIDES, R. 749-1258, famous dynasty of Caliphs at Bagdad and Damascus. ABBEY, Edwin Austin, 1852-....., Am. artist. ABBOT, George, 1562-1633, Eng. prelate. ABBOTT, Rev. Jacob, 1803-79, Am. author. ABBOTT, John Stevens Cabot, 1805-77, Am. historian. ABD-EL-KADER, 1807-83, Emir of Algeria. ABDUR RAHMAN KHAN, 1845-....., Emir of Afghanistan. ABDUL-AZIZ, 1830-76, Sultan of Turkey. ABDUL HAMID II., 1842-....., Sultan of Turkey. ABELARD, Pierre, 1079-1142, Fr. orator and philosopher. ABERCROMBIE, James, 1706-81, Br. general in Am. ABERCROMBIE, John, 1781-1844, Scot. metaphysician. ABERCROMBY, Sir Ralph, 1734-1801, Br. general. ABERDEEN, John Campbell Hamilton Gordon, seventh earl of, 1847-....., Br. statesman; governor-general of Canada. ABERNETHY, John, 1764-1831, Eng. anatomist. ABOUT, Edmond, 1828-85, Fr. author. ABRAHAM (or ABRAM), born about 2000 B.C., and died at the age of 175, Hebrew prince and patriarch. ADAIR, John, 1757-1840, Am. general and statesman. ADAMS, Charles Francis, 1807-86, Am. statesman, son of J. Q. A.; negotiated treaty of Geneva. ADAMS, John, first vice-president and second president of the U. S.; one of the negotiators of the treaty of peace with Great Britain, 1782; defeated by Jefferson for the presidency in 1800, he retired to private life. ADAMS, John Quincy, 1767-1848, son of J. A., sixth president of the U. S., being elected by the House; defeated by Jackson in 1828; elected to the House in 1830, his oratory gained for him the title "Old Man Eloquent;" member of the House until 1848, in which year, while in his seat at the Capitol, he received a stroke of paralysis, which caused his death. ADAMS, Samuel, 1722-1803, Governor of Massachusetts; one of the popular leaders of the Revolution; signer of the Declaration of Independence. ADAMS, William Taylor (Oliver Optic), 1822-....., Am. story writer. ADDISON, Joseph, 1672-1719, Eng. poet, moralist and dramatist. ADELER, Max, pen name of C. H. Clark. ADRIAN I., pope from 772-95; II., 867-72; III., 884-5; IV., 1154-9; V., 1276, died same year; VI., 1521-3. ÆSCHINES, 389-14 B.C., Athenian orator. ÆSCHYLUS, 525-456 B.C., first great tragic poet and founder of the drama. ÆSOP, 619?-564 B.C., Gr. fabulist; a slave, but liberated by his master on account of his talents. ÆTION, 3. and 4th century, Gr. painter. AFFRE, Denis Auguste, 1793-1848, archbishop of Paris; killed during the insurrection of June, 1848. AGA, Mohammed, 1734-97, founder of the reigning Persian dynasty; assassinated. AGAMEMNON, ...?-.....?, generalissimo of the Gr. forces in Trojan war. AGASSIZ, Louis, 1807-73, Swiss naturalist; professor at Harvard; founded museum of comparative zoology, Cambridge. AGATHARCHUS, B. 480 B.C., Gr. painter. AGRICOLA, Cneius Julius, 37-93, Rom. general. AGRIPPA, Marcus Vipsanius, 63-12

B.C., Rom. soldier and statesman. AGRIPPINA AUGUSTA, ...-60 A.D., mother of Nero; executed by order of Nero. AIKIN, John, 1747-1822, Eng. writer. AINSWORTH, William Harrison, 1805-82, Eng. novelist. AKBAR, 1542-1605, most illustrious of the Mogul emperors. AKENSIDE, Mark, 1721-70, Eng. physician, poet and scholar. ALAEDDIN, d. 1333, son of Osman and organizer of the Janissaries. ALARIC, 350?-410, king of the Visigoths. ALBANI, Madame, 1851-....., prima donna; wife of Ernest Gye; née Emma La Jeunesse; debut at Messina, 1870. ALBERT, or ALBERT FRANCIS Augustus Charles Emmanuel, Prince of Saxe-Coburg-Gotha, 1819-61, consort of Q. Victoria. ALBERT EDWARD, Prince of Wales, 1841-....., heir-apparent to Br. crown. ALBOIN, ...-573, king of the Lombards. ALBONI, Marietta, 1824-....., It. vocalist; married Count Pepoli; retired, 1863. ALBUQUERQUE, Alfonso, Marquis de, 1453-1515, Portuguese conqueror. ALCIBIADES, 450-404 B.C., Athenian general. ALCOTT, Amos Bronson, 1799-1888, Am. philosopher and teacher. ALCOTT, Louisa May, 1832-88, Am. authoress. ALDRICH, Thomas Bailey, 1836-....., Am. poet and novelist. ALEMBERT, Jean le Rond d', 1717-83, Fr. geometer. ALEXANDER (the Great), 356-323 B.C., King of Macedon; taught by Aristotle; ascended the throne of Macedon 336, destroyed Thebes and was chosen commander of the Greeks against Persia; invaded Asia Minor in 334, defeating Darius on the banks of the Granicus; in 333 he almost annihilated the Persian army at the battle of Issus; cut the Gordian knot and caused the Ammonian oracle to declare him the son of Jupiter Ammon; captured Tyre in 332, and, having invaded Egypt, founded Alexandria; in 331 he defeated Darius at Arbela; elated by his success, he claimed the homage due to a god, stabbing his foster-brother Clitus for refusal to pay such homage; invaded India in 327, advancing as far as the Hyphasis; his death is said to have been caused by excessive drinking. ALEXANDER I., 1777-1825, emperor of Russia; II., 1818-81, assassinated by Nihilists; III., 1845-1894. ALEXANDER I., Pope from 109 to 117; II., 1061-73; III., 1159-81; IV., 1254-61; V., 1409-10; VI., 1492-1503. ALEXANDER I., ...-1124, king of Scotland; II., 1198-1249; III., 1241-86. ALEXANDER, William (Lord Stirling), 1726-83, Am. Revolutionary general. ALFIERI, Vittorio, 1749-1803, It. poet. ALFONSO XII., 1857-85, king of Spain; XIII., 1886-..... ALFRED (the Great), 849?-901, king of the West Saxons; one of the greatest and noblest of Englishmen; established schools and a system of police, and founded a navy. ALGARDI, Alessandro, 1600?-1654, It. sculptor. ALLEN, Ethan, 1737-89, Am. Revolutionary commander; captured Ticonderoga and Crown Point in 1775 with only eighty-three men. ALLEN, Ira, 1751-....., brother of Ethan A.; one of the founders of Vermont. ALLEN, William, 1784-1868, Am. writer. ALLEN, William Henry, 1784-1813, Am. naval commander. ALLIBONE, Samuel Austin, 1816-89, Am. writer. ALLISON, William B., 1829-....., Am. lawyer and statesman. ALLSTON, Washington, 1779-1843, Am. painter. ALMA-TADEMA, Lawrence, 1836-....., Dutch painter; resided in London since 1873. ALTGELD, John P., 1847-....., governor of Illinois. ALVA, Fernando Alvarez de Toledo, Duke of, 1508-82, Spanish commander in Netherlands; infamous for cruelty. AMBROSE, Saint, 340?-97, one of the fathers of the church. [illegible], see Virgilius. AMES, Fisher, 1758-1808, Am. orator and statesman. AMHERST, Jeffrey (Lord Amherst), 1717-97, Br. general and field-marshal and governor of Virginia. AMMEN, Daniel, 1820-....., Am. rear admiral. AMPÈRE, André Marie, 1775-1836, Fr. electrician and natural philosopher. ANACREON, B.C. 560?-478, Gr. lyric poet. ANAXAGORAS, B.C. 500-428, Gr. philosopher; "the father of modern science." ANAXIMANDER, B.C. 610-547, Gr. philosopher. ANDERSEN, Hans Christian, 1805-75, Dan. author. ANDERSON, Maj. Robert, 1805-71, defender of Ft. Sumter. ANDERSON, Mary, (Mme. Navarro), 1859-....., Am. actress. ANDRASSY, Julius, Count, 1823-90, Hungarian statesman. ANDRÉ, John, 1751-80, Eng. spy; hanged for connection with the Arnold treason. ANDROS, Sir Edmund, 1637-1714, Br. colonial governor of New England. ANNE, 1664-1714, queen of England; last of the Stuarts. ANTHONY, St., 251-356?, Egyptian founder of monachism. ANTHONY, Henry B., 1815-84, Am. statesman. ANTHONY of Padua, St., 1195-1231, Franciscan monk. ANTHONY, Susan Brownell, 1820-....., Am. "woman's rights" advocate. ANTIGONUS (Cyclops), B.C. 382?-301, general of Alexander the Great. ANTISTHENES, fl. 400 B.C., Gr. philosopher; founder of the Cynic school. ANTOINETTE, Marie, 1755-93, queen of Louis XVI. of France; guillotined. ANTONELLI, Giacomo, 1806-76, It. cardinal. ANTONIUS, Marcus (Mark Antony), B.C. 83?-30, Rom. general and statesman. APPLEGARTH, Robert, 1831-....., leader of the workingmen of England. AQUINAS, Thomas, Saint, (the Angelic Doctor), 1224-74, theologian, teacher and writer; member of the order of St. Dominic; the greatest of the schoolmen of the middle ages. ARABI PASHA, 1834-....., Egyptian revolutionist. ARAM, Eugene, 1704-59, Eng. scholar; executed for the murder of one Daniel Clark, whom he is said to have killed to procure means for prosecuting his studies; chief character in one of Bulwer's novels. Arbuthnot, John, 1675-1735, Scot. physician. Archimedes, B.C. 287?-12, Gr. mathematician and natural philosopher; founder of physics. Argyle (or Argyle), Archibald Campbell, eighth earl, 1598-1661, Scot. Covenanter; defeated by Montrose; executed for treason. Argyll (or Argyle), George Douglas Campbell, seventh duke, 1823-....., Eng. statesman and author. Ariosto, Lodovico, 1474-1533, It. poet. Aristides, B.C. .....-468?, Athenian general and statesman. Aristophanes, B.C. 444?-380?, Gr. comic poet; his genius and audacity in burlesque have never been equaled. Aristotle (the Stagirite), B.C. 384-22, Gr. founder of analytic philosophy. Arius, 250?-336?, patriarch of Alexandria and founder of the Arian schism. Arkwright, Sir Richard, 1732-92, Eng. manufacturer; inventor of the spinning-jenny. Arminius, Hermann, B.C. 16-21 A.D., Ger. hero; defeated the Romans A.D. 9, near the Lippe. Arminius, Jacobus (Jacob Harmen), 1560-1609, Dutch founder of Arminian theology. Armour, Philip D., 1832-....., Am. merchant and philanthropist. Armstrong, John, 1709-79, Scot. poet and physician. Armstrong, John, 1758-1843, Am. soldier, statesman and writer. Armstrong, Le Roy, 1854-....., Am. novelist. Armstrong, William George, Sir, 1810-....., Eng. inventor (Armstrong gun). Arnaud, Henri, 1641-1721, leader of the Waldenses. Arndt, Ernst Moritz, 1769-1860, Ger. poet and writer. Arnim, Harry Carl Eduard von, 1824-79, Ger. diplomatist. Arnold, Benedict, 1740-1801, Am. general and traitor; his plot to deliver West Point into the hands of the British was foiled by the capture of Major Andre, and he barely escaped; he became a colonel in the British army. Arnold of Brescia (or Arnaldo), ...-1155, It. reformer and orator. Arnold, Edwin, 1832-....., Eng. journalist and poet. Arnold, Matthew, 1822-88, Eng. author, poet and critic. Arnold, Thomas, 1795-1842, Eng. historian. Arnold von Winkelried, ...-1386, Swiss patriot, who broke the Austrian phalanx at the battle of Sempach by throwing himself against the points of their spears. Artemisia, fl. 480 B.C., queen of Halicarnassus. Artemisia, fl. 350 B.C., consort of Mausolus, prince of Caria, in whose memory she erected a tomb numbered among the seven wonders of the world. Artevelde, Jacob van, 1300?-45, leader of people of Ghent. Artevelde, Philip van, son of J. v. A., 1340-82, leader of insurrection in Flanders. Arthur, Chester Allan, 1831-86, twenty-first president of the United States, born at St. Albans, Vermont; read law, was admitted to the bar and began practice in New York City; 1860, quartermaster-general, on the staff of Gov. Morgan; 1871, collector of the port of New York, but superseded, 1878, by Gen. Merritt; 1880, nominated for vice-president by the Republicans and elected; succeeded to the presidency on the death of Garfield. Arthur, Timothy Shay, 1809-85, Am. author. Ascham, Roger, 1515-68, Eng. scholar and author. Ashburton, Alexander Baring, Lord, 1774-1848, Eng. diplomatist. Aspasia of Miletus, B.C. .....-428?, mistress of Pericles, the Athenian law not permitting a citizen to marry a foreigner; Socrates called himself one of her disciples. Astor, John Jacob, 1763-1848, Am. merchant, native of Germany; settled in New York City and entered the fur trade, establishing trading posts in the northwest as far as the Pacific and founding Astoria in 1811; he made extensive investments in real estate, and when he died his property was estimated at twenty millions. Atahualpa, ...-1533, last Inca of Peru. Athanasius, 296?-373, Gr. father of the church. Athelstan, 895?-941, king of England. Atkinson, Edward, 1827-....., Am. writer on political economy. Attila (the Scourge of God), ...-453, king of the Huns. Attucks, Crispus, ...-1770, mulatto leader of mob in Boston massacre. Auber, Daniel François Esprit, 1784-1871, Fr. composer. Audubon, John James, 1780-1851, Am. ornithologist; spent many years in studying and illustrating from life the birds of America. Auerbach, Berthold, 1812-82, Ger. Jewish author and poet. Augereau, Pierre François Charles, Duc de Castiglione, 1757-1816, Fr. general. Augustine, Saint, 354-430, Latin father of the church and founder of Roman Catholic theology. Augustus Caesar, B.C. 63-A.D. 14, first emperor of Rome. Aumale, Henri Eugene Philippe Louis d'Orleans, Duc d', 1822-....., Fr. general; son of King Louis Philippe. Aurelianus, 212-75, Rom. emperor. Aurelius Antoninus, Marcus (Marcus Aurelius), 121-80, Rom. emperor and philosopher. Aurung-Zebe, 1618-1707, emperor of Hindostan. Ausonius, 310-95?, Latin poet. Austen, Jane, 1775-1817, Eng. author. Austin, Saint, d. 607, the apostle of England. Austin, Stephen F., ...-1836, founded the first colony in Texas. Avellaneda, Nicolás, 1836-....., president Argentine Republic. Avicenna, 980-1037, Arabian physician. Aytoun, William Edmondstoune, 1813-65, Scot. poet.

Baber, Mohammed, 1483?-1530, founder of the Mogul empire in India. Baccio della Porta (Fra Bartolommeo di San Marco), 1469-1517, Italian painter, member of the order of St. Dominic. Bach, Johann Sebastian, 1685-1750, Ger. composer and director; founder of modern music. ("The

Nativity."); BACON, Francis, Baron Verulam, Viscount St. Albans (Lord Bacon), 1561-1626, Eng. statesman, jurist and philosopher, and father of experimental philosophy; from him dates the origin of all inductive science. Son of Sir Nicholas Bacon, keeper of the great seal under Elizabeth; studied at Trinity College, and at 15 began to oppose the philosophy of Aristotle; called to the bar, and made queen's counsel at 28; solicitor-general, 1607; judge of the marshal's court, 1611; attorney-general, 1613; lord keeper, 1617; lord high chancellor, 1619; charged with bribery and corruption in Parliament, 1621, he pleaded guilty (some say to save the king), and was sentenced to pay a fine of £40,000, and to be imprisoned during the royal pleasure; he regained his liberty after two days' imprisonment, his fine, too, being remitted by King James, who also allowed him a pension; he spent the rest of his life in retirement, diligently pursuing the study of literature and science. The belief that Bacon is the author or at least the principal author of the plays attributed to Shakespeare has of late years found many adherents. It is certain that unusual mystery attaches to his life and record as well as to that of his brother Anthony. The reader is referred to Hepworth Dixon's "Personal History of Francis Bacon" and Mrs. Henry Pott's remarkable work, "Francis Bacon and his Secret Society." BACON, Leonard, 1802-81, Am. divine. BACON, Nicholas, Sir, 1509-79, Eng. statesman. BACON, Roger (the Admirable Doctor), 1214-92, Eng. philosopher. BACONTHORPE, John (the Resolute Doctor), ...-1346?, Eng. monk and philosopher. BAFFIN, William, 1580-1622, Eng. navigator. BAILEY, Philip James, 1816-...., Eng. lawyer and poet. BAILLIE, Joanna, 1762-1851, Scot. poetess. BAILLIE, Matthew, 1761-1823, Scot. physician. BAILLY, Jean Sylvain, 1736-93, Fr. astronomer and philosopher; first president of the States-General; executed by the Jacobins. BAINBRIDGE, William, 1774-1833, Am. naval commander. BAJAZET (or Bayazeed), 1347-1403, sultan of the Ottomans. BAKER, Sir Samuel White, 1821-...., Eng. explorer and author; in 1847 he established a sanitarium and prosperous agricultural settlement in the mountains of Ceylon, 6,200 feet above the sea level; in 1861-4 explored the region lying around the sources of the White Nile; discovered and named Lake Albert Nyanza, and found the exit of the Nile; in 1869 another expedition was made to the great African lakes. BALBOA, Vasco Nuñez de, 1475?-1517, Sp. discoverer; discovered the Pacific Ocean, 1513; the jealousy of his superior officers caused his conviction and execution on a charge of treason.

BALFE, Michael William, 1808-70, Ir. composer; "Bohemian Girl." BALFOUR, A. J., 1848-...., Eng. statesman. BALIOL, Edward, ...-1363, king of Scotland. BALIOL, John de, 1259?-1314, king of Scotland; rival of Bruce. BALLOU, Hosea, 1771-1852, Am. theologian; founder of Universalist denomination. BALMACEDA, José Manuel, 1840-91, president of Chile. BALZAC, Honoré de, 1799-1850, Fr. novelist. BANCROFT, George, 1800-91, Am. historian and diplomate; his "History of the United States" has been translated into all the principal languages of Europe. BANCROFT, Hubert Howe, 1832-...., Am. historian. BANER (or BANIER), Johan, 1596-1641, Sw. general. BANKS, Nathaniel Prentiss, 1816-1894, Am. general and politician. BARBAROSSA, Horuk, 1476?-1518, Corsair king of Algiers. BARBAROSSA, see Frederick. BARBAULD, Anna Letitia, 1743-1825, Eng. authoress. BARBOUR, John, 1320?-95? Scot. poet. BARCLAY DE TOLLY, Michael, Prince, 1755-1818, Russian field-marshal. BARCLAY, Robert, 1648-90, Scot. Quaker author. BARHAM, Richard Harris, 1788-1845, Eng. divine and humorist; "Ingoldsby Legends." BAREBONES, Praise God, ...-1680, Eng. fanatic. BARING, Sir Francis, 1740-1810, Eng. capitalist. BARLOW, Joel, 1755-1812, Am. patriot and poet. BARNARD, John G., 1815-82, Am. general and writer. BARMECIDES, Persian family, noted for tragic fate. BARNEVELDT, John van Olden, 1549-1619, Dutch statesman. BARNUM, Phineas Taylor, 1810-91, Am. showman. BARRAS, Paul François Jean Nicolas, Count de, 1755-1829, Fr. statesman. BARRETT, Lawrence (real name, Brannigan), 1838-91, Am. actor. BARRETT, Wilson, 1846-...., Eng. actor. BARRY, James, 1741-1806, Ir. painter. BARRY CORNWALL, see Procter. BARTHÉLEMY SAINT-HILAIRE, Jules, 1805-...., Fr. statesman and writer. BAXTER, Richard, 1615-91, Eng. Dis. minister and writer. BAYARD, Pierre du Terrail de, 1475-1524, Fr. warrior, "The cavalier without fear and without reproach." BAYLE, Pierre, 1647-1706, Fr. philosopher and critic. BAZAINE, François Achille, 1811-88, Fr. general; in the Franco-German war he surrendered the fortress of Metz, with 173,000 men, 6,000 officers, 50 generals and 3 marshals, and fled to England; court-martialed and sentenced to degradation and death, but sentence was commuted to twenty years' imprisonment; confined at the isle Sainte Marguerite, he escaped and settled in Madrid. BEACONSFIELD, Benjamin Disraeli, Earl of, 1804-81, Eng. statesman and novelist. BEATON (or BETHUNE), David, Cardinal, 1494-1546, primate of Scotland. BEATTIE, James, 1735-1803, Scot. poet and philosopher. BEAUHARNAIS, Eugène de, 1781-1824, Fr. general; son of Alexander de B. and Josephine, afterwards empress of France. BEAUMONT, Francis, 1586-1616, Eng. dramatic writer; associate of John Fletcher. BEAUREGARD, Peter Gustave Toutant, 1816?-1893, Am. Confederate general, born in Louisiana; graduate of West Point; served in Mexico; commanded at Fort Sumter and at the first battle of Bull Run; defeated at Shiloh by Grant, 1862; defended Charleston, 1863. BECKET, Thomas à, 1117-70, archbishop of Canterbury; high chancellor of England; having excommunicated two bishops for complying with the king's will, he was assassinated by four barons of the royal household; canonized in 1172. BEDE (the Venerable), 673-735, Eng. monk and ecclesiastical writer. BEDFORD, John Plantagenet, duke of, 1390-1435, Eng. general; defeated by Joan of Arc. BEECHER, Henry Ward, 1813-87, Am. divine and lecturer. BEECHER, Lyman, 1775-1863, Am. divine; father of H. W. B. BEETHOVEN, Ludwig von, 1770-1827, Ger. composer and considered the greatest of musicians. BEHRING, Vitus, 1680-1741? Dan. navigator. BELISARIUS, 505?-65, Byzantine general. BELKNAP, George E., 1832-...., Am. rear admiral. BELL, Alexander Graham, 1847-...., inventor of the Bell telephone; born in Scotland, but a resident of America. BELLAMY, Edward, 1850-...., Am. author. BELLINI, Vincenzo, 1802-35, It. composer. BELVEDERE, Andrea, 1646-1732, It. painter. BENEDEK, Ludwig von, 1804-81, Hungarian general. BENEDICT I., pope from 575 to 78; II., 684-85; III., 855-58; IV., 900-3; V., chosen pope 964, driven from Rome by Otho I., died at Hamburg 965; VI., 972-74, killed by the people of Rome; VII., 975-984; VIII., 1012-24; IX., ascended the pontifical chair in 1034, but driven from Rome; X., 1058-59, deposed on account of being illegally elected; XI., 1303-4; XII., 1334-42; XIII., 1724-30; XIV., 1740-58. BENEDICT XIII. (Pedro de Luna), 1334-1424, anti-pope, chosen at Avignon 1394, while Boniface IX. reigned at Rome; both deposed 1415 by council of Constance. BENNETT, James Gordon, 1800-72, Scot.-Am. journalist. BENJAMIN, Park, 1809-64, Am. journalist and poet. BENTHAM, Jeremy, 1748-1832, Eng. jurist and utilitarian philosopher. BENTON, Thomas Hart, 1782-1858, Am. statesman; born at Hillsboro, N. C.; removed to Tennessee, where he studied law; commanded a regiment under Gen. Jackson; removed to St. Louis, where he published a political paper; elected to the U. S. Senate in 1820, he continued a member of that body for 30 years; defeated in 1850 by a division in Democratic party on slavery question; advocacy of a gold and silver currency during his second term in Senate earned for him nickname of "Old Bullion;" elected in 1852 to the House, he opposed the repeal of the Missouri Compromise; defeated for governorship of Missouri in 1856; favored Buchanan for the presidency in opposition to his son-in-law, Fremont. BÉRANGER, Pierre Jean de, 1780-1857, Fr. lyric poet. BERG, Christen Paulsen, 1829-...., Dan. statesman. BÉRIOT, Charles Auguste de, 1802-70, Belgian violinist and composer. BERKELEY, George, 1684-1753, Ir. Protestant prelate and metaphysician; founder of the philosophy of Idealism. BERLICHINGEN, Götz von (of the Iron Hand), 1480-1562, Ger. warrior. BERLIOZ, Louis Hector, 1803-69, Fr. composer. BERNADOTTE, Jean Baptiste Jules, 1764-1844, marshal of France; king of Sweden and Norway as Carl XIV. Johan. BERNARD, Saint, 1091-1153, Fr. ecclesiastic, canonized 1174; "the greatest of the monks;" abbot at Clairvaux, refusing ecclesiastical preferment, but exerting great power over Europe; preacher of the second Crusade. BERNARD DE MENTHON, Saint, 923-1008, founder of the hospices of St. Bernard. BERNARDO DEL CARPIO, fl. 9th century, Sp. soldier. BERNHARDT, Sara (Mme. Damala), 1844-...., Fr. actress. BERT, Paul, 1833-86, Fr. physician and politician. BERTHIER, Louis Alexandre, Prince of Wagram, 1753-1815, marshal of France. BERTHOLLET, Claude Louis, 1748-1822, Fr. chemist. BERWICK, James Fitz-James, Duke of, 1670-1734, marshal of France; natural son of James II. of England. BESANT, Walter, 1838-...., Eng. novelist. BESSEMER, Henry, 1813-...., Eng. engineer and inventor of Bessemer process. BEUST, Friedrich Ferdinand von, Count, 1809-86, Ger. statesman. BETSY B., pen name of Mrs. Mary Austin. BEZA, Theodore, 1519-1605, Fr. Calvinistic theologian. BICHAT, Marie François Xavier, 1771-1802, Fr. physiologist; the greatest physician of modern times and founder of general anatomy. BIDDLE, John, 1615-62, Eng. theologian; father of English Unitarians. BIDDLE, Nicholas, 1786-1844, Am. financier. BIERSTADT, Albert, 1829-...., Ger.-Am. landscape painter. BILLINGS, Josh, see Shaw. BILLINGS, William, 1746-1800, Am. musical composer. BINNEY, Amos, 1803-47, Am. naturalist. BINNEY, Horace, 1780-1875, Am. lawyer. BIRNEY, James G., 1792-1857, Am. politician. BISMARCK-SCHÖNHAUSEN, Karl Otto, Prince, 1815-...., German statesman; chancellor of the German empire; within ten years he "humbled the Austrian empire, destroyed the French empire, and established the German empire"; retired 1890. BISSELL, Wilson S., 1847-...., Postmaster-General. BJÖRNSON, Björnstjerne, 1832-...., Norwegian poet and novelist. BLACK HAWK, 1767-1838, Am. Indian chief. BLACK, Jeremiah Sullivan, 1810-83, Am. jurist. BLACK, William, 1841-...., Scot. author. BLACKBURN, Joseph Clay Stiles, 1838-

...., Am. statesman. BLACKMORE, Richard Doddridge, 1825-...., Eng. novelist. BLACKSTONE, Sir William, 1723-80, Eng. jurist. BLACKWOOD, William, 1776-1834, Scot. publisher. BLAINE, James Gillespie, 1830-93 ("the Plumed Knight"); born in Pennsylvania; removed to Maine, where he edited the *Portland Advertiser*; served four terms in the legislature; in Congress from 1862 to 1876, and speaker for three years; prominent candidate for the Republican nomination for the presidency in 1876, 1880, 1882; chosen United States senator in 1877, but resigned to accept the secretaryship of state under Garfield; secretary of state under Harrison, but resigned just before the Republican convention of 1892. BLAIR, Hugh, 1718-1800, Scot. divine and rhetorician. BLAKE, Robert, 1599-1657, Br. admiral; founder of England's naval supremacy. BLAKE, William, 1757-1828, Eng. poet and artist. BLANC, Jean Joseph Louis, 1813-82, Fr. journalist, historian and politician. BLATCHFORD, Samuel, 1820-1893, justice U. S. Supreme Court. BLAVATSKY, Helena, 1831-91, theosophist. BLENNERHASSETT, Harman, 1770-1831, friend and accomplice of Aaron Burr. BLESSINGTON, Margaret, Countess of (*née* Power), 1789-1849, beautiful and accomplished Irish lady. BLIND, Carl, 1826-...., Ger. radical. BLOOMFIELD, Robert, 1766-1823, Eng. poet. BLÜCHER, Gebhard Leberecht von (Marschall Vorwärts), 1742-1819, Prussian field-marshal; decided battle of Waterloo. BLUMENTHAL, Leonhard von, 1810-...., Prussian general and strategist. BOABDIL, ...-1538?, last Moorish king of Granada. BOADICEA, ...-62, Br. queen. BOBADILLA, Francisco de, d. 1502, Span. administrator; sent Columbus in chains to Spain. BOCCACCIO, Giovanni, 1313-75, It. novelist. BODENSTEDT, Friedrich Martin, 1819-...., Ger. poet and author. BOERHAAVE, Herman, 1668-1738, Dutch physician and philosopher. BOGARDUS, James, 1800-74, Am. inventor. BOIES, Horace, 1827-...., governor of Iowa. BOLEYN, Ann, 1507?-36, second queen of Henry VIII. of England; beheaded. BOLINGBROKE, Henry St. John, Viscount, 1678-1751, Eng. author, orator and politician. BOLIVAR, Simon, 1783-1830, liberator of the South American colonies. BONAPARTE, Charles Louis Napoleon (Napoleon III.), 1808-73, son of Louis Bonaparte; emperor of the French; as claimant to throne of France, attempted in 1836 to take Strasburg, but was banished; imprisoned in Ham 1840 for an attempted insurrection at Boulogne, but escaped to England 1846; returning to France after revolution of 1848, he was elected president, gained support of the army, and, abolishing popular representation by the *coup d'état* of 1851, was declared emperor; in 1853 he married Eugenie, Countess de Teba. Having surrendered at Sedan, after the decisive battle of the Franco-German war, he was deposed and retired to Chiselhurst, in England. BONAPARTE, Jerome, 1784-1860, king of Westphalia, youngest brother of Napoleon I. BONAPARTE, Joseph, 1768-1844, king of Spain, elder brother of Napoleon I. BONAPARTE, Louis, 1778-1846, king of Holland, brother of Napoleon I. BONAPARTE, Lucien, Prince de Canino, 1775-1840, brother of Napoleon I. BONAPARTE, Napoleon (Napoleon I.), 1769-1821, emperor of the French and greatest of modern generals. Born at Ajaccio, Corsica. Attended military school 1779 to 1784. Entered army as sub-lieutenant in 1785, and in 1793 had risen to the rank of captain of artillery. In 1793 he submitted a plan for the reduction of Toulon, held by the English and Spaniards, and was entrusted with its execution. His success won for him a commission as brigadier-general. In the spring of 1795, on the remodeling of the army, he was suspended, and placed upon half-pay, the reason given by the authorities being that he was too young to command the artillery of an army. In the fall, on the breaking out of an insurrection led by the National Guard, the convention recalled Napoleon, who gained a brilliant victory after a brief but bloody engagement. This virtually made him commander-in-chief of the army of the interior. In 1796 he was appointed to the command-in-chief of the army of Italy, and in the same year he married Josephine de Beauharnais. In his very first campaign Napoleon appeared a consummate general. In a few weeks he gained four victories, conquered Lombardy and captured Mantua, almost annihilating three Austrian armies. He then turned his arms against the Pope, compelling him to pay 30,000,000 lires and surrender many valuable works of art. After defeating another Austrian army sent to Italy, Napoleon concluded a treaty securing his success. In 1798 he was given command of a powerful expedition into Egypt, the intention being to strike at the power of Great Britain, and gained decisive victories over the Mamelukes and Turkish auxiliaries. Returning to France he overthrew the Directory and was elected first consul. In 1800 he gained the great victory of Marengo. Made peace with England, 1802, granted general amnesty, established public order, re-established the Catholic faith, and produced his Civil Code. Napoleon became emperor in 1804, and engaged in war with England, Russia, Sweden and Prussia. Divorced from Josephine in 1809, he married Maria Louisa, daughter of the emperor of Austria, in 1810. In 1812 occurred the ill-fated Russian campaign, Napoleon's loss being estimated at 450,000 men. Beaten at Leipzig, 1813, he made a disastrous retreat. In 1814 the allies entered Paris, compelled Napoleon to abdicate, and sent him to Elba, granting him the sovereignty of that island, with a yearly pension of 6,000,000 francs. Returning again to France, he was enthusiastically received and raised an army of about 125,000, but was completely defeated at Waterloo, 1815. He abdicated again; and, unable to carry out his intention of embarking for America, surrendered to the captain of a British man-of-war. Carried to the island of St. Helena, he died there in 1821. BONAPARTE, Napoleon Joseph Charles Paul (Prince Napoleon), 1822-91, son of Napoleon I. and Maria Theresa. BONAPARTE, Napoleon François Charles Joseph (Napoleon II.), 1811-32, son of Napoleon I. and Maria Theresa. BONAVENTURA, Saint, 1221-74, It. theologian. BONHEUR, Rosa (or Rosalie), 1822-...., Fr. painter of animals. BONIFACE I., pope, ruling 418-22; II., 530-2; III., elected 607 and died same year; IV., 608-15; V., 619-25, distinguished for his efforts to convert the Britons; VI., died in 896, fifteen days after election to the papacy; VII. (anti-pope), elected 974, during reign of Benedict VI.; driven from Rome but returned in 985, imprisoning John XIV., who is said to have been starved to death; died 985; VIII., 1294-1303; IX., 1389-1404. BONIFACE, Winifred, Saint, apostle of Germany, 680-755? BONNAT, Leon Joseph Florentin, 1833-...., Fr. painter. BONNER, Edmund (Bloody Bonner), 1495?-1569, bishop of London, noted for persecution of Protestants. BONNIVARD, François de, 1496-1570, hero of Byron's "Prisoner of Chillon." BOONE, Daniel, 1735-1820?, American pioneer; born in Pa., but removed in boyhood to N.C.; visited Kentucky, hitherto unexplored, in 1769, and emigrated to that State with his own and five other families in 1773, constructing a fort at Boonesborough in 1775; captured by the Indians, he was adopted by them, but escaped and returned to the fort, which was shortly after attacked by Indians under the British flag; the fort was ably defended, two of Boone's sons, however, being killed. Boone lost his lands in Kentucky in consequence of a defective title, and, removing to Missouri, pursued the occupation of a hunter and trapper. BOOTH, Edwin, 1833-93, son of Junius Brutus Booth; Am. tragedian. BOOTH, John Wilkes, 1839-65, son of Junius Brutus Booth, Am. actor; assassin of Abraham Lincoln; effected his escape, but was traced into Virginia, where, refusing to surrender, he was shot. BOOTH, Junius Brutus, 1796-1852, Eng. tragedian. BOOTH, William, 1829-...., Eng. reformer; established "Salvation Army" in 1865. BORGIA, Cesare, Duc de Valentinois, 1457-1507, natural son of Alexander VI., It. military leader; made cardinal in 1493, but afterwards murdered; notorious for cunning, perfidy and cruelty. BORGIA, Francisco; see Francis, Saint. BORGIA, Lucrezia, Duchess of Ferrara, ...-1523, sister of Cesare; distinguished for beauty and talents, and a patron of learning, but contemporaneous writers differ in their estimation of her character. BORROMEO, Carlo, Saint, 1538-84, It. cardinal. BORROW, George, 1803-81, Eng. author and traveler. BOSCAWEN, Edward, 1711-61, Eng. admiral. BOSSUET, Jacques Bénigne, 1627-1704, Fr. prelate and controversialist, and considered the greatest of Christian orators; first advocate of papal infallibility. BOSWELL, James, 1740-95, Scot. lawyer; biographer of Dr. Johnson. BOTHWELL, James Hepburn, Earl of, 1526?-77?, Scot. conspirator; husband of Queen Mary. BÖTTGER, Johann Friedrich, 1682-1719, inventor of Dresden china. BOUCICAULT, Dion, 1822-90, Ir.-Am. dramatist. BOULANGER, Geo. Ernest Jean Marie, 1837-91, Fr. gen. BOUILLON, Godfrey de, 1060?-1100, leader of first Crusade. BOURBAKI, Charles Denis Sauter, 1816-...., Fr. general. BOURBON, famous French dynasty. BOURBON, Charles, Duc de (Constable Bourbon), 1490-1527, Fr. general; a prominent character in Byron's "The Deformed Transformed." BOURDALOUE, Louis, 1632-1704, Fr. Jesuit orator. BOURNE, Hugh, 1772-1852, Eng. founder of Primitive Methodism. BOWDITCH, Nathaniel, 1773-1838, Am. mathematician. BOWDOIN, James, 1727-90, Am. statesman. BOWLES, Samuel, 1826-78, Am. journalist. BOWLES, William Lisle, 1762-1850, Eng. poet. BOYCE, William, 1710-79, Eng. organist and composer. BOYDELL, John, 1719-1804, Eng. engraver and publisher. BOYESEN, Hjalmar Hjorth, 1848-...., Nor. author in America. BOYLE, Robert, 1626-91, Ir. philosopher and philanthropist. BOZZARIS, Marco, 1790-1823, patriotic leader in Greek war for independence. BRADDOCK, Edward, 1715?-55, Eng. general in America; killed by Indians. BRADDON, Mary Elizabeth, 1837-...., Eng. novelist. BRADFORD, William, 1590-1657, governor of Plymouth colony. BRADFORD, William, 1660-1752, first printer in Pennsylvania. BRADLAUGH, Charles, 1833-91, Br. statesman. BRADLEY, Joseph P., 1813-92, Am. jurist. BRADSTREET, John, 1711-74, Am. major-general. BRAGG, Braxton, 1815-76, Confederate general. BRAHE, Tycho, 1546-1601, Sw. astronomer. BRAINERD, David, 1718-47, Am. missionary. BRANT, Joseph (Thayendanegea), 1742-1807, half-breed chief of the Mohawks. BRECKINRIDGE, John Cabell, 1821-75, Am. statesman and Confederate general; born in Kentucky; vice-president 1857-61; Democratic candidate for presidency in 1860; elected to U. S. Senate in 1861, but resigned to enter the Confederate army; Confederate secretary of war, 1865. Breitmann, Hans, pen name of Charles G. Leland. Bremer, Fredrika, 1802-65, Sw. novelist. Brentano, Clemens, 1777-1842, Ger. novelist and poet. Breughel, Jan, 1569-1625, Flemish painter. Brewer, David J., 1837-....., justice U. S. Supreme Court. Brewster, Sir David, 1781-1868, Eng. optician and physicist. Brian Boru (or Borohme), 926-1014, king of Ireland. Bridget, Saint, 1302-73, patron saint of Ireland. Bridgman, Laura, 1829-89, Am. blind deaf-mute, noted for mental acquirements. Bright, John, 1811-89, Eng. statesman and orator. Bright, Richard, 1789-1858, Eng. physician. Brillat-Savarin, Anthelme, 1755-1826, Fr. author. Broglie, Charles Jacques Victor Albert, Duc de, 1821-....., Fr. statesman and writer. Brontë, Charlotte (Currer Bell), 1816-55, Eng. novelist. Brooks, James, 1810-73, Am. journalist. Brooks, Phillips, 1835-93, Am. clergyman. Brougham, Henry, Lord, 1778-1868, Br. author, statesman and orator. Brown, Henry B., 1836-....., justice U. S. Supreme Court. Brown, John, Captain, 1800-59, born in Connecticut; a tanner by trade; removed to Kansas and became prominent as an abolitionist; gained the title of "Osawatomie" by a victory, in 1856, over a company of Missourians vastly exceeding his own force in number; in pursuance of a plan for the invasion of Virginia, he surprised Harper's Ferry in 1859, and took the arsenal and armory and forty prisoners; attacked the next day by U. S. marines and the Virginia militia, two of his sons and most of his company of twenty men were killed, and he himself wounded and taken prisoner; he was tried and hanged at Charlestown, Virginia. Brown, John Young, 1835-....., governor of Kentucky. Brown, Thomas, 1778-1820, Scot. metaphysician. Brown-Séquard, Charles Edouard, 1818-....., Fr. physiologist. Browne, Charles F. (Artemus Ward), 1835-67, Am. humorist. Browne, Sir Thomas, 1605-82, Eng. physician, philosopher and author. Browning, Elizabeth Barrett, 1809-61, wife of Robert Browning; Eng. poetess: "Aurora Leigh," "Casa Guidi Windows." Browning, Robert, 1812-89, Eng. poet: "The Ring and the Book," "Strafford," "Men and Women," "Fifine at the Fair," "A Soul's Tragedy." Brownlow, William Gannaway (Parson Brownlow), 1805-77, Am. politician. Brownson, Orestes Augustus, 1803-76, Am. theologian. Bruce, Robert, 1274-1329, the greatest of the kings of Scotland; defeated Edward II. at Bannockburn, in 1314. Brummell, George Bryan (Beau Brummel), 1778-1840, Eng. man of fashion. Brunelleschi, Filippo, 1377-1444, It. architect and sculptor. Bruno, Saint, 1030?-1101, Ger. founder of the Carthusians. Brutus, Lucius Junius, fl. 500 B.C., Rom. patriot. Brutus, Marcus Junius, 85-42 B.C., one of Cæsar's assassins; committed suicide after defeat at Philippi. Bryant, William Cullen, 1794-1878, Am. poet and journalist; born in Massachusetts; entered Williams College, read law, and was admitted to the bar in 1815; published "Thanatopsis" in 1816; became editor of the *New York Evening Post* in 1826. Bryce, James, 1838-....., Eng. writer. Buchanan, George, 1506-82, Scot. historian and poet. Buchanan, James, 1791-1868, fifteenth president of the United States; born in Pennsylvania; admitted to the bar, 1812; member of Congress, 1821-31; minister to Russia, 1832-4; U. S. senator, 1834-5; secretary of state, 1845-9; minister to England, 1853-6; signed Ostend Manifesto, 1854; president, 1857-61; in his last message, President Buchanan censured the Northern people for the imminent disruption of the Union, holding that neither the executive nor Congress had power to coerce a state. Buckland, William, 1784-1856, Eng. geologist. Buckle, Henry Thomas, 1822-62, Eng. historian. Buddha (or Boodha), Gautama, 624-523 B.C., Hindoo reformer; founder of Buddhism. Buell, Don Carlos, 1818?-....., Am. general. Buffon, Georges Louis Leclerc de, Comte, 1707-88, Fr. naturalist and philosopher. Bull, Ole Bornemann, 1810-80, Norwegian pianist. Bülow, Bernhard Ernst von, 1815-....., Ger. statesman. Bülow, Hans Guido von, 1830-....., Ger. pianist. Bulwer-Lytton, Edward George Earle Lytton, Baron Lytton, 1805-73, Eng. novelist. Bulwer-Lytton, Edward Robert, Earl of Lytton (Owen Meredith), 1831-91, son of preceding, Eng. poet. Bulwer, Sir Henry Lytton Earle, 1804-72, Eng. author and diplomatist. Bunsen, Christian Karl Josias von, Baron, 1791-1860, Ger. philologist and diplomatist. Bunyan, John, 1628-88, Eng. author; the son of a tinker, he followed that vocation and led for many years a wandering life; served in the Parliamentary army; joined the Anabaptists in 1654, and in 1655 became a Baptist minister; sentenced to transportation on a charge of promoting seditious assemblies, but sentence not enforced; was, however, imprisoned for more than twelve years, and during that time wrote his "Pilgrim's Progress." Burckhardt, Johann Ludwig, 1784-1817, Swiss traveler. Burdett-Coutts, Angela Georgina, Baroness, 1814-....., Eng. philanthropist. Bürger, Gottfried August, 1748-94, Ger. poet. Burgoyne, John, 1730-92, Brit. general and dramatist; surrendered at Saratoga. Burke, Edmund, 1730-97, Ir. orator, statesman and writer; prominent as the ablest member of the Commons to oppose the ministry's American policy; impeached Warren

Hastings in 1788. Burke, Thomas N., 1830-83, Ir. Dominican orator. Burleigh, William Cecil, Lord, 1520-98, Eng. statesman. Burlingame, Anson, 1822-70, Am. diplomatist. Burns, Robert, 1759-96, Scot. lyric poet; born at Ayr; the son of a poor farmer; worked hard on his father's farm and had little opportunity for education; began rhyming at 16, and studied mensuration and surveying; his poems brought him into society, where he acquired dissipated habits; formed a *liaison* in 1786 with Jean Armour, whom he married 1788; intended to emigrate, but the popularity of his poems, published in fall 1787, induced him to remain in Scotland; he afterward became an officer of the excise. Burnside, Ambrose Everett, 1824-81, Am. general. Burr, Aaron, 1756-1836, Am. statesman and lawyer. In 1800 Burr and Jefferson were the Democratic candidates for president and vice-president; receiving the same number of votes, the House gave the higher office to Jefferson. Burr's course in endeavoring to supplant Jefferson cost him the regard of his party. Unsuccessful as candidate for governor of New York in 1804, Burr attributed his defeat to Alexander Hamilton, whom he killed in a duel. After the expiration of his term as vice-president, Burr was tried for treason, charged with the subversion of federal authority, and with raising an expedition for the conquest of Mexico, but acquitted. Burritt, Elihu (the Learned Blacksmith), 1810-79, Am. scholar, journalist, lecturer and reformer; the son of a shoemaker, and apprenticed to a blacksmith, he devoted all his spare time to study, and eventually mastered eighteen languages. Burroughs, John, 1837- ...., Am. author. Burton, Sir Richard Francis, 1821-90, Ir. traveler in Africa. Burton, Robert, 1576-1640, Eng. philosopher. Bushnell, Horace, 1802-76, Am. divine. Butler, Benjamin Franklin, 1818-93, Am. politician, lawyer and general; born in New Hampshire; military governor of New Orleans in 1862, ruling with vigor and efficiency and preserving the city from the yellow fever; went to Congress as a Republican in 1866, and was re-elected for several terms; elected governor of Massachusetts in 1883 by the Democrats, but defeated for the same office a year later. Butler, Samuel, 1612?-80, Eng. poet. Byron, George Gordon Noel, Lord, 1788-1824, Eng. poet. In 1815 he married Anne Isabel Milbanke, but separated from her and left England in 1816; in Italy he formed a *liaison* with the beautiful Countess Guiccioli; espousing the cause of the Greeks in their struggle for liberty, he left for Greece in 1823, and died the following year at Missolonghi from the effects of exposure while preparing for the siege of Lepanto.

CABOT, George, 1751-1823, pres. Hartford convention. Cabot, John, ...-1498?, Venetian navigator in service of England; discovered North American continent 1497. Cabot, Sebastian, 1477?-1557, son of preceding; Eng. navigator. Cade, John (Jack Cade), ...-1450, Ir. rebel. Cadwalader, George, ...-1879, Am. general. Cadwalader, John, 1742-86, Am. general. Cædmon, ...-680?, Anglo-Saxon poet. Cæsar, Caius Julius, 100-44 B.C., the greatest of Roman generals. Elected consul 60 B.C.; formed a secret alliance with Pompey and Crassus known as the first triumvirate. It is said that during his Gallic wars a million of men were slain, eight hundred cities and towns captured and three hundred tribes subdued. Pompey having become his enemy through jealousy, Cæsar crossed the Rubicon 49 B.C., and in a short time became master of Italy; having conquered all his enemies, and subdued Spain and Africa, he was made perpetual dictator, and received from the senate the title of Imperator. Although beloved by the masses, the patricians feared and hated him, and the result of a conspiracy of Cassius, Brutus and others was his assassination. Cagliari, Paolo (Paul Veronese), 1530?-88, It. painter. Cagliostro, Alessandro (Joseph Balsamo), 1743-95, It. impostor and adventurer, physician and alchemist. Calderon de la Barca, Don Pedro, 1600-81, Sp. poet and dramatist. Calhoun, John Caldwell, 1782-1850, Am. statesman; born in South Carolina; elected to Congress 1810; secretary of war, 1817; vice-president 1825-32, resigning to enter the Senate; secretary of state, 1844; returned to the Senate 1845; Calhoun was an earnest champion of slavery and States' rights. Caligula, Caius Cæsar, 12-41, emperor of Rome; cruel and sensual; built a temple to himself; assassinated. Calvert, Cecilius, second Lord Baltimore, ...-1675, first proprietor of Maryland, residing in England. Calvert, George, first Lord Baltimore, 1582?-1632, father of preceding; founder of Maryland. Calvert, Leonard, 1606?-47, brother of Cecilius; first governor of Maryland. Calvin, John, 1509-64, Fr. theologian; established Presbyterian form of church government; the fundamental principle of his theology is that of predestination to eternal happiness or misery by the absolute decree of God. Cambacérès, Jean Jacques Régis de, 1753-1824, Fr. statesman. Cambyses, ...-522 B.C., king of Persia; conqueror of Egypt. Cameron, Richard, ...-1680, Scot. Covenanter. Cameron, Simon, 1799-1889, Am. politician. Camoens, Luis, 1517-79, Portuguese poet. Campbell, Alexander, 1788-1866, Ir. founder of the denomination of "Christians," or "Disciples of Christ." Campbell, Colin, Lord Clyde,

1792-1863, Br. general. CAMPBELL, John, Lord, 1779-1861, chancellor of England. CAMPBELL, Thomas, 1777-1844, Scot. poet. CAMPOS, Martinez, 1830-....., Sp. general. CANBY, Edward Richard Sprigg, 1819-73, Am. general. CANISIUS, Petrus (De Hondt), 1521-97, Dutch Jesuit theologian. CANNING, George, 1770-1827, Eng. statesman and orator. CANOVA, Antonio, 1757-1822, It. sculptor. CANROBERT, François Certain, 1809-....., Fr. marshal. CANUTE II., 995?-1035, king of Denmark; conqueror of England. CAPET, Hugh, 940?-996, founder of the Capetian dynasty. CAPRIVI DE CAPRARA DE MONTECUCCOLI, Georg Leo von, 1831-....., Bismarck's successor as chancellor of the German empire. CARACALLA, 188-217, Emperor of Rome, noted for cruelty. CAREY, Henry Charles, 1793-1879, Am. political economist. CARLETON, Will, 1845-....., Am. poet. CARLETON, William, 1794-1869, Ir. novelist. CARLISLE, John G., 1835-....., Am. statesman. CARLOS, Don, Duke of Madrid, 1848-....., claimant to Spanish throne; nephew of Charles VI. CARLYLE, Thomas, 1795-1881, Scot. essayist, biographer and historian. CARNARVON, Henry Howard Molyneux Herbert, third Earl of, 1831-....., Eng. statesman. CAROLUS DURAN (real name, Charles Auguste Emile Durand), 1837-....., Fr. painter. CARROLL, Charles, 1737-1832, Am. patriot. CARTIER, Jacques, 1494-1555?, Fr. navigator. CARTWRIGHT, Edmund, 1743-1823, Eng. inventor. CARY, Alice, 1820-70, Am. poetess. CASAS, Bartolomé de las, 1474-1566, Sp. missionary and historian. CASAUBON, Isaac, 1559-1614, Swiss scholar and critic. CASIMIR I., ...-1058, king of Poland; II., 1137-94; III., ...-1370; IV., 1425-92; V., 1609-72. CASS, Lewis, 1782-1866, Am. statesman and diplomatist. CASSAGNAC, Paul de, 1843-....., Fr. journalist. CASTELAR Y RIPOLL, Emilio, 1832-....., Sp. republican orator, essayist and statesman. CASTLEREAGH, Robert Stewart, Viscount, 1769-1822, second marquis of Londonderry; Br. statesman, prominent in suppressing the Irish rebellion of 1798; committed suicide. CASTRO, Joao de, 1500-48, Portuguese general and navigator. CATHERINE, Saint, 1347-80, It. nun at Siena; mediator between the rival popes in the great schism. CATHERINE I., 1682-1727, empress of Russia; succeeded to the throne on death of her husband, Peter the Great; II., 1729-96, notoriously immoral. CATHERINE OF ARAGON, 1485-1536, queen of Henry VIII. of England; divorced. CATHERINE DE MEDICI, 1519-89, queen of Henry II. of France; opponent of the Huguenots. CATILINE, Lucius Sergius, 108?-62 B.C., Rom. conspirator. CATO, Dionysius, fl. 3d century, Latin poet. CATO, Marcus Porcius (the Elder), 234-149 B.C., Rom. statesman and author. CATO, Marcus Porcius (the Younger), 95-46 B.C., opponent of Cæsar; famed for purity and nobility; committed suicide. CATULLUS, Caius Valerius, 87?-45? B.C., Latin poet. CAVAIGNAC, Louis Eugène, 1802-57, Fr. general. CAVOUR, Camillo Benso di, 1810-61, first prime minister of the kingdom of Italy. CAXTON, William, 1412?-92, Eng. scholar and merchant; introduced printing into England. CECIL, William, Lord Burleigh, 1520-98, lord treasurer of England. CECILIA, Saint, d. 2d century, Rom. martyr; patroness of music. CENCI, Beatrice, 1583?-99, "the beautiful parricide;" Roman lady, famous for beauty and tragic fate. CERVANTES SAAVEDRA, Miguel de, 1547-1616, Sp. novelist. CESNOLA, Louis Palma di, 1832-....., born in Italy; colonel in U. S. army during the civil war; appointed 1865 consul to Cyprus, and became famous for his excavations in that island. CHAILLU, DU, Paul Belloni, 1835-....., Fr.-Am. traveler. CHALMERS, Thomas, 1780-1847, Scot. divine. CHAMBERLAIN, Joseph, 1836-....., Eng. statesman. CHAMBERS, William, 1800-83, Scot. editor and publisher. CHAMISSO, Adelbert von, 1781-1838, Ger. traveler. CHAMPOLLION, Jean François, 1791-1832, Fr. Egyptologist. CHANNING, William Ellery, 1780-1842, Am. divine. CHAPIN, Edwin Hubbell, 1814-80, Am. divine. CHARLEMAGNE (Charles the Great, or Charles I.), 742-814, emperor of Germany and founder of the kingdom of the Franks (now France); crowned emperor of the west, with the title of Cæsar Augustus, by Pope Leo III., 800; the most powerful and enlightened monarch of his time; his empire extended from the Elbe to the Ebro, and from Calabria to Hungary; first of the Carlovingian dynasty. CHARLES II. (the Bald—Charles II. of France), 823-77, emperor of Germany; invaded Italy and was crowned emperor; III. (the Fat), 832?-88; IV., 1316-78, emperor of Germany and king of Bohemia; V., 1500-58, emperor of Germany; king of Spain as Charles I.; in 1521, summoned the Diet of Worms to check the progress of Luther's doctrines; in 1527, warring with Francis I. of France and Pope Clement VII., Rome was sacked and the pope made prisoner; convened the Diet of Augsburg to suppress the reformation, but, the Protestants having united, liberal terms were granted them; in 1535, defeated Barbarossa and captured Tunis, liberating thousands of Christian slaves; defeated in 1552 by the Protestant forces under Maurice of Saxony, he signed the treaty of Passau, establishing the Protestant church on a firm basis; three years later he retired to the monastery of St. Yuste; VI., 1685-1740; VII. (Karl Albrecht), 1697-1745. CHARLES II. (the Bald—Charles II. of Germany), 823-77, king of France; IV., 1294-1328; V., 1337-80; VI.,

1368-1422, became insane 1392; VII., 1403-61, expelled the English; IX., 1550-74; X., 1757-1836. Charles I. (Charles Stuart), 1600-49, king of England; executed after attempting to subdue his rebellious subjects; II., 1630-85, witty, but careless and voluptuous; the habeas corpus act was passed during his reign. Charles I. (Charles V. of Germany), 1500-58, king of Spain; II., 1661-1700; III., 1716-88; IV., 1748-1819. Charles IX., 1550-1611, king of Sweden; X. (Gustavus), 1622-60; XII., 1682-1718, ascended the throne in 1697; a league being formed against him by Russia, Denmark and Poland in 1700, he besieged Copenhagen, forced Denmark to make peace, and beat the Russians; he then invaded Poland, compelling King Augustus to resign; invading Russia, he was badly defeated at Pultowa; he fled to Turkey, but soon returned; marching into Norway, he was killed at the siege of Frederickshald; XIII., 1748-1818; XIV. (Bernadotte), 1764-1844; XV., 1826-72, king of Sweden and Norway. Charles Edward Stuart (the Young Pretender), 1720-88, Eng. prince. Charles the Bold, 1433-77, duke of Burgundy. Charles Martel, 694?-741, king of the Franks. Charlotte, 1840-....., ex-empress of Mexico; wife of Maximilian. Chase, Salmon Portland, 1808-73, Am. statesman and jurist. Chateaubriand, François Auguste de, Viscount, 1768-1848, Fr. author. Chatham, William Pitt, Earl of (the Great Commoner), 1708-78, Eng. statesman and orator; opposed taxation of American colonies. Chatterton, Thomas, 1752-70, Eng. literary impostor. Chaucer, Geoffrey, 1340?-1400, Eng. poet; "Father of English poetry." Cheever, George Barrell, 1807-90, Am. divine. Cheke, Sir John, 1514-57, Eng. scholar. Chénier, André Marie de, 1762-94, Fr. poet. Cherbuliez, Victor, 1832-....., Fr. novelist. Cherubini, Maria Luigi, 1760-1842, It. composer. Chesterfield, Philip Dormer Stanhope, Earl of, 1694-1773, Eng. orator and wit; distinguished as a man of fashion. Chitty, Joseph, 1776-1841, Eng. jurist. Choate, Rufus, 1799-1859, Am. lawyer and statesman. Choiseul, Étienne François de, 1719-85, Fr. statesman. Choris, Louis, 1795-1828, Russian painter and traveler. Christian (or Christiern) I., 1426-81, king of Denmark; II., 1481-1559, called "The Nero of the North;" III., 1503-59; IV., 1577-1648; V., 1646-99; VI., 1699-1746; VII., 1749-1808; VIII., 1786-1848; IX., 1818-..... Christina, 1626-89, queen of Sweden; daughter of Gustavus Adolphus; learned and eccentric; abdicated, 1654. Chrysippus, 280-207 B.C., Gr. stoic philosopher. Chrysostom, John, Saint, 350?-407, Gr. father of the church. Church, Frederick Edwin, 1826-....., Am. painter. Churchill, Charles, 1731-64, Eng. satirist. Churchill, Randolph Spencer, Lord, 1849-....., Eng. statesman. Cibber, Colley (Hughes Ross), 1671-1757, Eng. actor and dramatist. Cicero, Marcus Tullius, 106-43 B.C., Rom. author, statesman and orator; the greatest critic of antiquity; while consul, suppressed the conspiracy of Catiline; exiled 58 B.C., but recalled; was an adherent of Pompey, but enjoyed the favor of Julius Cæsar; killed by the soldiers of Antony; as an orator, Cicero is regarded second only to Demosthenes. Cid Campeador (Ruy Diaz de Bivar), 1040?-99, Castilian hero. Cimon, 510-449 B.C., Athenian general and statesman. Cincinnatus, Lucius Quintus, 520-439 B.C., Rom. patriot and dictator; elected consul while cultivating a farm, having lost his property; conquered the Æqui; twice chosen dictator, and at the expiration of each term of office he returned to the plow. Clarke, Adam, 1762-1832, Irish Methodist Bible commentator. Clara Belle, pen name of Mrs. Wm. Thompson, deceased; now name of a news syndicate. Claude Lorraine, 1600-82, Fr. painter. Claudian (Claudius Claudianus), 365?-408?, Latin poet. Claudius (Tiberius Claudius Drusus Nero), B.C. 10-54 A.D., Rom. emperor; invaded Britain. Claudius, Marcus Aurelius, 214-70, Rom. emperor. Clay, Henry, 1777-1852, Am. statesman and orator; "The Great Pacificator." Born in Virginia; removed to Kentucky, 1797; practiced law; elected to Kentucky legislature in 1804, and two years later chosen to fill a short term in the U. S. Senate; re-elected to the Senate 1809, and to the House of Representatives 1811, of which body he was made speaker; re-elected speaker 1813; signed treaty of Ghent 1815; re-elected speaker four times; in 1824, he was one of four candidates for the presidency; when the election devolved on the House, his influence decided the contest in favor of Jackson; a bloodless duel between Clay and Randolph, in 1826, was the result of charges against Clay growing out of this election; re-elected to the Senate in 1831 for six years; in 1832, defeated for the presidency as the candidate of the anti-Jackson party; again elected to the Senate 1836, but resigned 1842; Whig candidate for the presidency in 1844; re-elected senator 1846. To Clay is due the credit for the "Missouri Compromise," believed to have postponed for ten years the civil war. Clemens, Samuel Langhorn (Mark Twain), 1835-....., Am. humorist. Clement I., 30?-100, pope; IV., ...-268; V., 1264?-1314; VII. (Giulio de Medici), 1475?-1534; VIII., 1605; XI., 1649-1721; XIV., 1705-74. Clement of Alexandria, 150?-220?, father of the church. Cleon, ...-422 B.C., Athenian demagogue and general. Cleopatra,

69-30 B.C., queen of Egypt; noted for beauty and accomplishments. CLEVELAND, Stephen Grover, 1837-....., Am. statesman; born at Caldwell, N. J., the son of a Presbyterian minister, who removed to Fayetteville, N. J., in 1840; first worked in a country store, secured an education and became a teacher in the N. Y. Blind Asylum; studied law in Buffalo; admitted to the bar, 1863, and became assistant district attorney, afterwards sheriff; mayor of Buffalo, 1881, and then elected governor of New York by 192,000 majority; elected president in 1884, and again in 1892; married Miss Frances Folsom June 2, 1886. CLINTON, De Witt, 1769-1828, Am. statesman. CLINTON, George, 1739-1812, vice-president of the U. S. CLINTON, Sir Henry, 1738-95, Eng. general in America. CLIVE, Robert, Lord, 1725-74, Eng. general and founder of British empire in India. CLOOTS, Jean Baptiste, Baron (Anacharsis Cloots), 1755-94, Prussian traveler and Fr. revolutionist; guillotined. CLOUGH, Arthur Hugh, 1820-61, Eng. poet. CLOVIS (or Chlodwig), 465-511, king of the Franks; conqueror of Gaul. CLUSERET, Gustave Paul, 1823-....., Fr. general in America, and revolutionist in France and Switzerland. COBBETT, William, 1762-1835, Eng. political writer. COBDEN, Richard, 1804-65, Eng. statesman and economist. CODY, William, 1832-....., Am. scout; originator of the "Wild West" show. COKE (or Cook), Sir Edward, 1552-1633, Eng. jurist. COLBERT, Jean Baptiste, 1619-83, Fr. statesman. COLE, Thomas, 1801-48, Eng. landscape painter. COLERIDGE, Samuel Taylor, 1772-1834, Eng. poet. COLFAX, Schuyler, 1823-85, Am. politician; vice-president. COLIGNY, Gaspard de, 1517-72, Fr. admiral; leader of the Huguenots; killed in massacre of St. Bartholomew. COLLIER, Jeremy, 1650-1726, Eng. theologian. COLONNA, Vittoria, 1490-1547, It. poet. COLQUHOUN, Archibald Ross, 1848-....., Br. explorer. COLT, Samuel, 1814-62, Am. inventor of revolving pistol. COLUMBA, Saint, 521-97, the apostle of Caledonia. COLUMBUS, Christopher (It.: Cristoforo Colombo, Sp.: Cristoval Colon), 1436-1506, Genoese navigator; became a sailor at 14; studied mathematics at the University of Pavia; removed to Lisbon at the age of thirty; was employed in several expeditions to the west coast of Africa; meditated reaching India by a western route, and unsuccessfully solicited the aid of John II. of Portugal; but finally Ferdinand and Isabella of Spain furnished him two small vessels, and another was added by the efforts of friends; with one hundred and twenty men he set sail from Palos, August 3, 1492, and discovered the island of San Salvador, October 12 of same year; supposing that he had reached India, he called the natives Indians; after visiting Cuba and Hayti, he returned to Spain, where he was received triumphantly; in 1493 he again sailed across the Atlantic, this time with seventeen ships, and discovered Jamaica and Porto Rico; in 1498 he made his third voyage, with six vessels, discovering the mainland at the mouth of the Orinoco; in 1499, complaints having been made to the court of the conduct of Columbus at Hispaniola, he was carried to Spain in chains by Francisco de Bobadilla; Columbus' last voyage to America was made in 1502, to Honduras; he died neglected. COMONFORT, Ignacio, 1810?-63, president of Mexico. COMTE, Auguste, 1798-1857, Fr. philosopher. CONDÉ, Louis II., Prince de, 1621-86, Fr. general; victorious over the Spaniards at Rocroi, 1643, and over the Germans at Nördlingen, 1645; again defeated the Spanish at Lens in 1648, almost annihilating their infantry, previously regarded invincible; seeking revenge for having been imprisoned by the orders of Mazarin or the queen, he warred against the government, and next entered the service of Spain; returned to France in 1659, and defeated William of Orange in 1674. CONFUCIUS, or KONG-FOO-TSE, 551-478 B.C., Chinese philosopher; the son of a soldier, he was raised to the rank of mandarin at 19; commenced public teaching at 22; became, in 499 B.C., minister of crime, and soon after retired from public life, devoting his time to study, travel and the dissemination of his doctrines. The philosophy of Confucius relates to the present life only; he placed great importance upon the outward forms of politeness, being the first to enunciate, in substance, the golden rule; his influence has been enormous, his teachings affecting two-thirds of humanity for twenty-three centuries. CONGREVE, Sir William, 1772-1828, Eng. engineer. CONGREVE, William, 1670-1729, Eng. dramatist. CONKLING, Roscoe, 1829-88, Am. statesman, lawyer and orator. CONRAD I., ...-918, emperor of Germany; II., ...-1039; III., 1093-1152; IV., 1228-54; V., 1252-68. CONSCIENCE, Hendrik, 1812-83, Flemish novelist. CONSTANS I., 320?-50, emperor of Rome; II., 630-68. CONSTANTINE I. (the Great), 272-337, emperor of Rome; embraced Christianity, and transferred his court from Rome to Byzantium, thenceforth called Constantinople. CONTI, François Louis de, Prince, 1664-1709, Fr. general. CONWAY, Moncure Daniel, 1832-....., Am. author. COOK, Eliza, 1817-....., Eng. poetess. COOK, James, 1728-79, Eng. discoverer; killed by natives in Sandwich Islands. COOKE, George Frederick, 1756-1812, Eng. actor. COOPER, Sir Astley Paston, 1768-1841, Eng. physician. COOPER, James Fenimore, 1789-1851, Am. novelist. COPERNICUS (Kopernik), Nicholas, 1473-

1543, Ger. astronomer; father of modern astronomy; disproved the Ptolemaic theory; in his great work, "The Revolution of the Celestial Orbs," the first copy of which was handed to him on the day of his death, he demonstrated that the sun is the centre of the system. Coppée, François Édouard Joachim, 1842-....., Fr. poet. Coquelin, Benoît Constant, 1841-....., Fr. actor. Coquelin, Ernest Alexandre Honoré, 1848-....., Fr. actor. Corday, Charlotte, 1768-93, Fr. heroine; assassinated Marat. Coriolanus, Caius Marcius, fl. 490 B.C., Rom. hero. Corneille, Pierre, 1606-84, founder of the French drama. Cornell, Ezra, 1807-74, Am. philanthropist. Cornwall, Barry, see Procter. Cornwallis, Charles, Earl, 1738-1805, Br. general. Corot, Jean Baptiste Camille, 1796-1875, Fr. painter. Correggio, Antonio Allegri da, 1494-1534, It. painter; known as "the divine;" his work excels in harmony, grace and sweetness of color and form. Cortez, Hernando, 1485-1547, Sp. conqueror of Mexico. Cotton, John, 1585-1652, Puritan minister in Boston. Coues, Elliott, 1842-....., Am. naturalist. Cowley, Abraham, 1618-67, Eng. poet. Cowper, William, 1731-1800, Eng. poet. Cowper, William, 1666-1709, Eng. anatomist. Cox, Samuel Sullivan, 1824-89, Am. statesman. Crabb, George, 1778-1854, Eng. philologist. Crabbe, George, 1754-1832, Eng. poet. Craik, Dinah Maria (Mulock), 1826-87, Eng. authoress. Cranch, Christopher Pearse, 1813-....., Am. artist and poet. Crane, Walter, 1845-....., Eng. painter. Cranmer, Thomas, 1489-1556, Eng. reformer; archbishop of Canterbury; burned to death. Crawford, Francis Marion, 1845-....., Am. novelist residing in Rome. Crassus, Marcus Licinius, 105?-53 B.C., Rom. triumvir. Creasy, Sir Edward Shepherd, 1812-78, Eng. historian. Crichton, James (the Admirable Crichton), 1560-83, Scot. prodigy; stabbed by his pupil, a son of the Duke of Mantua. Crispi, Francesco, 1819-....., It. statesman. Crittenden, John Jordan, 1786-1863, Am. statesman. Crockett, David, 1786-1836, Am. backwoodsman. Croesus, 590-48 B.C., king of Lydia; famous for wealth. Croly, George, 1780-1860, Ir. poet and pulpit orator. Cromwell, Oliver, 1599-1658, Eng. general and leader of the political and religious revolution in England; entered the Parliamentary army, in 1642, as captain of cavalry; rapidly promoted, and led left wing at Marston Moor, 1644; commanded right wing at Naseby, 1645, and became leader of the independents; transferred the custody of the king from Parliament to the army, 1647; won the battle of Preston, 1648; signed the death warrant of Charles I., 1649; made commander-in-chief, 1650, and defeated the Scotch at Dunbar and Charles at Worcester; dissolved Parliament in 1653, and was, in 1654, proclaimed by the army lord protector of the commonwealth. Cruden, Alexander, 1700-70, Scot. bookseller and author; "Concordance." Cruikshank, George, 1792-1878, Eng. humorous artist. Cumberland, William Augustus, Duke of, 1721-65, conqueror at Culloden. Cunningham, Allan, 1785-1842, Scot. author and critic. Curran, John Philpot, 1750-1817, Ir. legislator and orator. Curtis, George Ticknor, 1812-....., Am. lawyer and author. Curtis, George William, 1824-92, Am. author and editor. Cushing, Caleb, 1800-79, Am. lawyer and statesman. Cushman, Charlotte Saunders, 1816-76, Am. actress. Custer, George A., 1839-76, Am. general; killed by the Sioux. Cuvier, Georges C. L. F., Baron, 1769-1832, Fr. naturalist; the greatest of zoologists and founder of comparative anatomy. Cyprian, Saint, 200?-58, Latin father; bishop of Carthage; martyr. Cyril, Saint, 315?-86, bishop of Jerusalem. Cyril, Saint, 376?-444, bishop of Alexandria. Cyrus (the Great, or the Elder), ...-529 B.C., king of Persia; conquered Babylon. Cyrus (the Younger), ...-401 B.C., hero of Xenophon's "Anabasis."

Daguerre, Louis Jacques Mandé, 1789-1851, Fr. artist; inventor of the daguerreotype. Dahlberg, Eric, 1625-1703, Sw. general and engineer. Dahlgren, John Adolph, 1809-70, Am. rear-admiral. Dallas, Alexander James, 1759-1817, Am. statesman. Dallas, George Mifflin, 1792-1864, Am. statesman. Dalton, John, 1766-1844, Eng. chemical philosopher. Daly, Augustin, 1838-....., Am. dramatist. Damiani, Peter, 990-1072, It. ecclesiastic. Damiens, Robert F., 1714-57, Fr. fanatic. Dampier, William, 1652-1712, Eng. navigator. Dana, Charles Anderson, 1819-....., Am. journalist. Dana, Francis, 1743-1811, Am. lawyer and statesman. Dana, Richard Henry, 1787-1879, Am. poet and writer. Dana, Richard Henry, 1815-82, son of R. H., Am. author and lawyer; "Two Years Before the Mast." Dancer, Daniel, 1716-94, Eng. miser. Dandelot, François de Coligny, 1521-69, Fr. general. Dandolo, Enrico, 1108-1205, blind doge of Venice. Dane, Nathan, 1752-1835, Am. lawyer and statesman. Daniel, fl. 6th century B. C., Hebrew prince and prophet. Daniel, Samuel, 1562-1619, Eng. poet. Dante Alighieri, 1265-1321, the greatest poet of Italy; "the Christian Homer." Danton, George Jacques, 1759-94, a leader of the French revolution; guillotined. D'Arblay, Mme. Frances (Burney), 1752-1840, Eng. novelist. Darboy, Georges, 1813-71, archbishop of Paris. Dare, Shirley, pen name of P. C. Dunning. Darius I. (Darius Hystaspis),

....-485 B. C., king of Persia; II., ...-405 B.C.; III. (Codomanus), ...-330 B. C., defeated by Alexander. Darius the Mede, supposed to be Cyaxares II. Darley, Felix O. C., 1822-88, Am. artist. Darling, Grace, 1815-42, Eng. heroine. Darnley, Henry Stuart, Lord, 1546?-67, husband of Mary of Scots; assassinated. Darwin, Charles Robert, 1809-82, Eng. naturalist; originator of the theory of evolution; in his "Origin of Species by Means of Natural Selection," published 1859, he propounds the theory that all forms of life have been produced by a series of gradual changes in natural descent; in his "Descent of Man," he infers that "man is descended from a hairy quadruped furnished with a tail and pointed ears, probably arboreal in its habits." Darwin, Erasmus, 1731-1802, Eng. physician and poet. D'Aubigné, Jean Henri Merle, 1794-1872, Swiss historian. D'Aubigné, Théodore, 1550-1630, Fr. soldier, poet and historian. Daudet, Alphonse, 1840-....., Fr. novelist. Davenport, Edward L., 1816-77, Am. actor. David, 1085-1015 B. C., king of Israel. David, Saint, 490?-544, patron of Wales. David, Jacques Louis, 1748-1825, Fr. historical painter. Daviess, Joseph Hamilton (Jo Daviess), 1787-1834, Am. statesman. Da Vinci, Leonardo; see Vinci. Davis, Henry Winter, 1817-65, Am. politician. Davis, Jefferson, 1808-89, Am. statesman and president of the Confederacy; born in Kentucky; graduate of West Point; served in Black Hawk and Mexican wars; elected to U. S. Senate from Mississippi, 1847; secretary of war, 1853-7; re-elected senator, 1857; inaugurated provisional president of the Confederate States, 1861, and elected for six years 1862; imprisoned in Fortress Monroe for two years after the fall of Richmond. Davitt, Michael, 1846-....., Ir. patriot. Davoust (or Davout), Louis Nicholas, Duke of Auerstadt and Prince of Eckmühl, 1770-1823, marshal of France. Davy, Sir Humphrey, 1778-1829, Eng. chemist; inventor of the safety lamp. Dayton, William Lewis, 1807-64, Am. statesman. Dearborn, Henry, 1751-1829, Am. general and statesman. Decatur, Stephen, 1779-1820, Am. naval commander; defeated the Algerines; killed in a duel. De Foe (or Defoe), Daniel, 1661-1731, Eng. novelist. De Kalb, John, Baron, 1732-80, Ger. general; accompanied Lafayette to America, and served under Washington; killed at battle of Camden. De Haas, Maurice F. H., 1832-....., Dutch marine painter. Delahaye, Ernest, 1855-....., Fr. painter. Delaroche, Paul, 1797-1856, Fr. painter. Delaware, Thomas West, Lord, ...-1618, governor of Virginia. Delmas, Antoine Guillaume, 1768-1813, Fr. general. Delorme, Marion, 1612-50, Fr. beauty and courtesan. Del Sarto, Andrea Vannuchi, 1486-1530, Fr. painter. Democritus, 460-361 B.C., "the laughing philosopher of Greece." Demosthenes, 385?-322 B.C., Athenian orator; conquered an impediment in his speech, and by perseverance and determination became the greatest of orators; opposed Philip of Macedon, against whom he delivered his *Philippics*; condemned to death by Antipater, he committed suicide by poison. Denis, Saint, ...-272, apostle and patron of France. Depew, Chauncey Mitchell, 1834-....., Am. railroad manager, lawyer and orator. De Quincey, Thomas, 1785-1859, Eng. author; his "Confessions of an Opium-Eater," an autobiography, published in 1821, created a great sensation. Derby, Edward Geoffrey Smith Stanley, Earl of, 1799-1869, Eng. statesman and orator; translated Homer's Iliad. Derby, Edward Henry Smith Stanley, Earl of, 1826-1893, Eng. statesman. Deroulède, Paul, 1846-....., Fr. poet. Descartes, René, 1596-1650, Fr. philosopher and mathematician; represented the revolt against scholasticism, re-examining all questions and discarding the authority of great names; "I think, therefore I am." Desfontaines, René Louiche, 1752-1833, Fr. botanist. De Smet, Peter John, 1801-73, Jesuit missionary to the Indians. Desmoulins, Camille, 1762-94, Fr. Jacobin; guillotined. De Soto, Ferdinand, 1496-1542, Sp. explorer; discovered the Mississippi. Dessalines, Jean Jacques, 1760-1806, negro emperor of Hayti. De Vigny, Alfred, Count, 1799-1863, Fr. novelist and poet. De Witt, Jan, 1625-72, Dutch statesman. Diaz, Porfirio, 1830-....., president of Mexico. Dick, Thomas, 1772-1857, Scot. author. Dickens, Charles, 1812-70, Eng. novelist. Dickinson, Anna Elizabeth, 1842-....., Am. lecturer. Diderot, Denis, 1713-84, Fr. philosopher and novelist; chief editor of "The Encyclopædia" and librarian of Catherine of Russia. Dilke, Sir Charles Wentworth, 1843-....., Eng. statesman, editor and author. Dillon, John, 1851-....., Ir. political leader. Diocletian, 284-305, Rom. emperor. Diogenes, died 323 B. C., Gr. cynic philosopher; lived in a tub, affecting contempt for the comforts of life. Dionysius (the Elder), 430?-367 B.C., tyrant of Syracuse. Dionysius (the Younger), 396-343? B. C., tyrant of Syracuse. Dionysius of Halicarnassus, 70?-7? B. C., Gr. historian. Disraeli, Benjamin, see Beaconsfield. Disraeli, Isaac, 1766-1848, father of B., Eng. litterateur; born of a Jewish family. Dix, John Adams, 1798-1879, Am. general and statesman. Dixon, William Hepworth, 1821-79, Eng. author and historian. Dodge, Mary Abigail (Gail Hamilton), 1830-....., Am. authoress; cousin of James G. Blaine. Dodge, Mary Mapes, 1838-....., Am. authoress. Döllinger, John Joseph Ignatius, 1799-1890, Ger. theologian and historian; leader of the "Old Catholic" movement. Dolbear, Amos Emerson, 1837-...., Am. physicist and inventor. Domenichino (Zampieri), 1581-1641, It. painter. Dominic, Saint, 1170-1221, Sp. preacher; founder of order of Dominicans. Domitian, 51?-96, Rom. emperor. Donatus, fl. 300, founder of the Donatists. Donizetti, Gaetano, 1798-1848, It. composer. Donnelly, Ignatius, 1831-...., Am. author and reformer. Doré, Paul Gustave, 1832-83, Fr. artist. Doria, Andrea, 1468-1560, Genoese patriot and commander. Dorr, Thomas Wilson, 1805-54, Am. politician. Dorset, Charles Sackville, Earl of, 1637-1706, Eng. poet and wit. Dorset, Thomas Sackville, Earl of, 1536-1608, Eng. poet and statesman. Dorsey, James Owen, 1848-...., Am. ethnologist. Dorsey, John Syng, 1783-1818, Am. surgeon. Douglas, Archibald (Bell-the-Cat), ...-1514?, "the great earl of Angus;" lord chancellor. Douglas, James, Earl of, ...-1388, Scot. patriot. Douglas, Stephen Arnold (the Little Giant), 1813-1861, Am. statesman; native of Vermont; admitted to the bar in New York; removed to Illinois and gained distinction as an orator; judge of Illinois Supreme Court, 1841; elected to Congress, 1843; senator, 1847; supported the compromise measures of Henry Clay, and advocated the doctrine known as "squatter sovereignty;" re-elected to Senate, 1853, and reported bill repealing Missouri Compromise; candidate for Democratic nomination for presidency in 1856; defeated Lincoln for U. S. Senate in 1858, they canvassing the State together; candidate of one wing of the Democratic party for president in 1860; supported the Union party in 1861. Douglass, Frederick, 1817?-...., Am. orator; formerly a slave. Dow, Lorenzo, 1777-1834, Am. preacher. Dow, Neal, 1804-...., Am. temp. reformer. Draco (or Dracon), fl. 624 B. C., Athenian lawgiver. Drake, Sir Francis, 1540-96, Eng. naval hero; first English circumnavigator of the globe. Drake, Joseph Rodman, 1795-1820, Am. poet. Draper, John William, 1811-82, Am. scientist. Drayton, Michael, 1563-1631, Eng. poet. Dreyse, Johann Nikolaus von, 1787-1867, Prussian inventor of the needle gun. Drusus, Claudius Nero, 38-9 B.C., Rom. general. Dryden, John, 1631-1700, Eng. poet, critic and dramatist. Du Chaillu, Paul Belloni, 1835-...., Fr. traveler. Dudevant, Mme. Amantine Lucile Aurore (née Dupin) (George Sand), 1804-76, Fr. novelist. Dudley, Benjamin Winslow, 1785-1870, Am. surgeon. Dudley, Charles Edward, 1780-1841, Am. senator. Dudley, Robert, Earl of Leicester, 1531?-88, favorite of Queen Elizabeth. Dufaure, Jules Armand Stanislas, 1798-1881, Fr. statesman. Dufferin, Frederick Temple Hamilton Blackwood, Earl of, 1826-...., Eng. statesman, governor-general of Canada. Dumas, Alexandre, 1802-70, Fr. novelist. Dumas, Alexandre, 1824-...., son of A. D., Fr. novelist. Dumouriez, Charles François, 1739-1823, Fr. general. Duncan I., ...-1040, Scot. king; killed by Macbeth. Dundonald, Thomas Cochrane, Earl of, 1775-1860, Br. admiral. Dunglison, Robley, 1798-1869, Am. physician. Dunois, Jean de (Bastard of Orleans), Fr. national hero; natural son of the Duke of Orleans; defeated the English at Montargis in 1427, and assisted at the siege of Orleans in 1429; expelled the English from Normandy and Guienne, and was created Count d'Orleans. Duns Scotus (the Subtle Doctor), 1265?-1308, Scot. theologian. Dunstan, Saint, 925-988, Eng. prelate. Dupanloup, Felix Antoine Philibert, 1802-78, Fr. prelate. Dupleix, Joseph, Marquis, 1697-1763, Fr. governor in India. Du Pont, Samuel Francis, 1803-65, Am. rear-admiral. Duquesne, Abraham, 1610-88, Fr. naval commander. Durer, Albrecht, 1471-1528, Ger. painter and engraver. Dvorak, Anton-in, 1841-...., Bohemian musician. Dwight, Timothy, 1752-1817, Am. author and divine. Dyck, Van, Philip, 1680-1752, Dutch painter.

EADS, James Buchanan, 1820-87, Am. engineer. Early, Jubal A., 1816-...., Confederate general. Eastlake, Sir Charles Lock, 1793-1865, Eng. painter. Ebers, George Moritz, 1837-...., Ger. novelist. Eaton, Amos, 1777-1842, Am. naturalist. Eaton, William, 1764-1811, Am. soldier. Eblé, Jean Baptiste, 1758-1812, Fr. general. Edgeworth, Maria, 1767-1849, Eng. novelist. Edgeworth, Richard Lovell, 1744-1817, Eng. author; father of Maria E. Edison, Thomas Alva, 1847-...., Am. electrician and inventor; newsboy on a railway, telegraph operator, and then an inventor, his inventions including telephone, phonograph, aerophone, phonometer, etc.; his laboratory at Orange, N. J., is the largest in the world. Edmund I., 922?-46, Anglo-Saxon king; II. (Ironside), 989-1016. Edmunds, George Franklin, 1828-...., Am. lawyer and statesman; born in Vermont; admitted to the bar, 1849; became U. S. Senator, 1866, to fill an unexpired term, and has since been continuously re-elected; pres. of Senate, 1883; retired, 1891. Edward I., ...-925, king of the Anglo-Saxons; II. (the Martyr), 962?-978; III. (the Confessor), 1004-66. Edward I. (Longshanks), 1239-1307, king of England; conquered Wales and Scotland; II., 1284-1327, defeated by Bruce at Bannockburn; dethroned by the queen and her favorite, Roger de Mortimer, 1326; murdered the following year; III., 1312-77, son of Edward II.; proclaimed king in 1327; executed Mortimer, and imprisoned the queen-mother; carried on war with France and won the great victory of Crecy; IV., 1441-83; V., 1470-83, ascended the throne at the age of 13, assassinated two months later; VI., 1537-53. Edward, Prince of Wales (the Black Prince), 1330-76, son of Edward III.; participated in invasion of France, commanding the main body of the English at Crecy; won the battle of Poitiers. Edwards, Amelia Blandford, 1831-92, Eng. novelist. Edwards, Jonathan, 1703-58, Am. theologian and metaphysician. Edwin, 586?-633, king of Northumbria. Edwy, 938-58, king of the Anglo-Saxons. Effingham, see Howard, Charles. Egbert (the Great), 775?-838, Saxon king of Wessex. Eggleston, Edward, 1837-...., Am. author. Egmont, Lamoral, Count, 1522-68, Flemish statesman and soldier. Eiffel, Alexandre Gustave, 1832-...., Fr. engineer. Elbée, Gigot d', 1752-94, Vendean general. Eldon, John Scott, Earl of, 1751-1838, Eng. statesman. Elgin, James Bruce, Earl of, 1811-63, Br. statesman; governor-general of Canada. Elgin, Thomas Bruce, Earl of, 1777?-1841, Br. diplomatist; the "Elgin Marbles" were obtained by him at Athens and sold to the British government for £35,000. Elia, pen name of Charles Lamb. Eliot, Charles William, 1834-...., Am. educator. Eliot, George, see Evans, Marian C. Eliot, John, "Apostle of the Indians," 1604-90, Eng. clergyman. Eliot, Sir John, 1590-1632, Eng. orator and statesman. Elizabeth, 1533-1603, queen of England; daughter of Henry VIII. Elizabeth Petrovna, 1709-62, empress of Russia; daughter of Peter the Great. Elizabeth, Saint, 1207-31, queen of Hungary. Ellenborough, Edward Law, Lord, 1748-1818, Eng. chief justice. Ellenborough, Edward Law, Earl of, 1790-1871, Eng. statesman. Ellery, William, 1727-1820, Am. patriot. Elliot, George Augustus, Lord Heathfield of Gibraltar, 1718-90, Br. commander. Elliott, Ebenezer, 1781-1849, Eng. poet. Elliott, Jesse Duncan, 1782-1845, Am. commodore. Ellsworth, Ephraim Elmer, 1837-61, Am. soldier. Ellsworth, Oliver, 1745-1807, Am. jurist and statesman. Ellwood, Thomas, 1639-1713, Eng. Quaker author. Elssler, Fanny, 1811-84, Viennese dancer. Elzevir, a celebrated family of printers and publishers at Leyden, 1579-1680. Emerson, Ralph Waldo, 1803-82, Am. essayist, philosopher and poet, and founder of the "Transcendental" school of philosophy. Emin Pasha (Dr. Jacob Schnitzer), Austrian explorer; killed 1892. Emmanuel (the Great), 1469-1521, king of Portugal. Emmet, Robert, 1780-1803, Ir. patriot and orator; became a leader of the "United Irishmen," and was implicated in the killing of Lord Kilwarden, chief justice of Ireland, and others; although defending himself with great eloquence, he was sentenced to death and executed. Emmet, Thomas Addis, 1764-1827, brother of R. E.; a leader of the "United Irishmen," and imprisoned from 1798 till 1802; removed to America in 1804, and was in 1812 elected attorney-general of New York. Empedocles, 475-.... B.C., Gr. philosopher. Encke, Johann Franz, 1791-1865, Ger. astronomer. Endicott, John, 1589-1665, colonial governor of Mass. Enghien, Louis Antoine Henri de Bourbon, Duc d', 1772-1804, Fr. prince; executed by order of Napoleon. Ennius, Quintus, 239-169 B.C., Rom. epic poet. Enoch (or Henoch), 3378-.... B.C., father of Methuselah; translated at the age of 365. Epaminondas, 412?-362 B.C., Theban statesman, orator and general. Epictetus, 60-...., Gr. Stoic philosopher. Epicurus, 340?-270 B.C., Gr. philosopher; founder of the Epicurean school. Erasmus, Desiderius, 1465-1536, Dutch scholar and printer of the first Greek New Testament. Erastus, Thomas, 1524-83, Ger. physician and writer. Eratosthenes, 276-196? B.C., Gr. geometer; considered the founder of the science of astronomy. Eric XIII., 1382-1459, king of Sweden (VII. or VIII. of Denmark); XIV., 1533-77. Eric the Red, fl. 1000, Scandinavian navigator; discovered Greenland. Ericsson, John, 1803-89, Sw. engineer and inventor; constructed the first "Monitor," with revolving turrets for guns, which destroyed the Confederate iron-clad Merrimac. Erigena, Joannes Scotus, fl. 850, Ir. philosopher. Ernesti, Johann August, 1707-81, Ger. scholar. Erskine, Ebenezer, 1680-1754, Scot. theologian. Erskine, Henry, 1746-1817, Scot. lawyer and orator. Erskine, Thomas, Baron, 1750-1823, Scot. lawyer and orator. Escobar y Mendoza, Antonio, 1589-1669, Sp. Jesuit and casuist. Escobedo, Mariano, 1826-...., Mexican soldier. Espartero, Joaquin Baldomero, Duke de la Vittoria, 1792-1879, Sp. statesman and general; defeated the Carlists. Essex, Robert Devereux, second Earl of, 1567-1601, a favorite of Queen Elizabeth; beheaded for high treason. Essex, Robert Devereux, third Earl of, 1592-1646, Eng. Parliamentary general. Estaing, Charles Hector, Comte d', 1729-94, Fr. admiral; beheaded. Esterhazy de Galantha, Paul, 1635-1713, Hungarian governor-general. Ethelbert, 552?-616, king of Kent. Ethelbert, ...-866, king of the Anglo-Saxons. Ethelred I., ...-871, king of the Anglo-Saxons; II. (the Unready), 968-1016, ordered massacre of Danes in 1002. Euclid of Alexandria, fl. 300 B.C., Gr. mathematician. Eudoxia (or Eudocia), 394?-461, Rom. empress. Eugene of Savoy (Prince François Eugène de Savoie-Carignan), 1663-1736, Austrian general; defeated the Turks at Peterwar-

system. At present all our silver dollars as well as the bulk of our paper money are kept in their purchasing power equal to the gold dollar. The material out of which the paper dollar is made is worth nothing, and the government keeps it equal in its purchasing power to the gold dollar by promising to pay a dollar for it when presented for payment.

The material out of which the silver dollar is made is, at present, worth in the market about 50 cents—it was 53 cents only two or three weeks ago—so that the government owes every purchaser of a silver dollar 50 cents. It meets this obligation by keeping the silver dollar in its purchasing power equal to the gold dollar—according to a solemn pledge made by the law of 1890 and reiterated by the law in 1893—that the United States will maintain the two metals at a parity upon the legal ratio.

A violation of that pledge by a neglect to maintain it would be downright repudiation and national dishonor.

How, then, does the government keep the gold and the silver dollar on a parity? First, by limiting the number of silver dollars in circulation, and, second, by keeping on hand a sufficient gold reserve so that the government shall be able to meet its obligations as they are likely to be presented. We all know that under stress of circumstances this reserve had to be replenished by obtaining gold through the sale of bonds, and if that gold had not been so obtained the government would not have been able to meet its obligations in such a way as to maintain the parity between the two metals, and would have become a repudiator.

The Bryan Democracy now proposes the free coinage of silver, which means that anybody, American or foreigner, can present silver bullion at our mints to have it coined into dollars, by which, of course, the limitation of the silver circulation will be removed. The Bryan platform further demands that there shall be no more government bonds issued in times of peace, which

"Old Abe," the War Eagle.

"Old Abe," the famous Wisconsin war eagle, was captured in the spring of 1861, on Flambeau River, near the line between Ashland and Price Counties, by a Chippewa Indian chief named Sky. The bird was then about the size of a common chickenhawk. The Indian traded the eagle to Daniel McCann, of Eagle Point, Wis., for a bushel of corn, and McCann sold it to Mr. Mills of Eau Claire for $5. Mills presented the bird to Captain J. E. Perkins, who was then organizing the Eighth Wisconsin Regiment. The bird then began the most remarkable career that has been ever known to a member of the feathered tribe. At Madison, before the regiment left for the South, the eagle was given the name of Old Abe, in honor of President Lincoln. A perch was then made for the bird, which was carried at the side of the colors of Company C of the Eighth Wisconsin. At the siege of Corinth Old Abe sat on his perch as calm as though nothing were going on—an incident which is said to have caused the Confederate General to declare that he "would rather capture that eagle bird than a whole brigade of Yankees."

Altogether Old Abe participated in thirty-eight battles and engagements. After the close of the war Barnum offered [illegible] for the eagle, and a Western millionaire "went" the prince of showmen "one better," offering to exchange [illegible] in gold for him. During the last years of his life Old Abe was kept in a large cage in the historical department of the capitol building at Madison. He died on March 26, 1881. His body was turned over to a taxidermist, who fixed the bird so that he now looks as natural as he did in life. Over a million pictures of Old Abe have been sold, and a book telling of his wonderful career had a good sale for several years.—St. Louis Republic.

adin in 1716, and at Belgrade in 1717. EUGÉNIE MARIE DE MONTIJO, 1826-....., empress of the French; wife of Napoleon III. EUGENIUS I., pope, ruled 654-8; II., 824-7; III., 1145-53; IV., 1431-39, deposed, died 1447. EULER, Leonard, 1707-83, Swiss mathematician. EURIPIDES, 480-406 B.C., Gr. tragic poet; mediator between ancient and modern drama. EUSEBIUS OF NICOMEDIA, fl. 325, Arian prelate. EUSEBIUS PAMPHILI, 266-340?, ecclesiastical historian, and bishop of Cæsarea. EVALD, Johannes, 1743-81, Danish poet. EVANS, Marian C. (George Eliot), 1820-81, Eng. novelist; the daughter of a clergyman; lived with George H. Lewes, as his wife, for several years, and after his death married J. W. Cross. EUSTACHI, Bartolommeo, 1510-74, It. anatomist. EVARTS, William Maxwell, 1818-....., Am. lawyer and statesman; leading counsel for defense in impeachment trial of President Johnson; attorney-general, 1868-9; counsel for the United States, in 1872, before the Geneva Arbitration Tribunal; senator from N.Y. EVELYN, John, 1620-1706, Eng. author. EVERETT, Edward, 1794-1865, Am. scholar, orator and statesman; elected to Congress in 1824, remaining in that body for ten years; in 1835 became governor of Massachusetts; minister to England, 1841-5; secretary of state, 1852; elected to the United States Senate, 1853, but resigned on account of illness; defeated for the vice-presidency in 1860. EWING, Thomas, 1789-1871, Am. statesman. EXMOUTH, Edward Pellew, Viscount, 1757-1833, Eng. admiral. EYCK, VAN, Hubert, 1366-1426, Flemish painter. EYCK, VAN, Jan (John of Bruges), 1390?-1440?, brother of H. E., Flemish painter. EYRE, Edward John, 1815?-....., Eng. explorer in Australia. EZEKIEL, fl. 7th century B.C., Hebrew prophet. EZRA, fl. 5th century B.C., Hebrew lawgiver.

FABIUS MAXIMUS, Quintus (Cunctator), -203 B.C., Roman consul and general; inaugurated the "Fabian" policy, carrying on only a defensive war against Hannibal. FAED, Thomas, 1826-....., Scot. painter. FAHRENHEIT, Gabriel Daniel, 1686-1736, Ger. inventor of the thermometer. FAIRFAX, Thomas, Lord, 1611-71, parliamentary general; won the battle of Naseby. FAITHFULL, Emily, 1835-....., Eng. authoress. FALCONER, William, 1735?-69, Scot. poet. FALIERO (or FALIERI), Marino, 1278-1355, doge of Venice; hero of Byron's tragedy. FANEUIL, Peter, 1700-43, Am. merchant. FANNY FERN, pen name of Mrs. James Parton. FARADAY, Michael, 1791-1867, Eng. chemist and natural philosopher; founder of science of magneto-electricity. FARNESE, Alessandro, Duke of Parma, 1546-92, It. general. FARQUHAR, George, 1678-1707, Ir. dramatist. FARRAGUT, David Glasgow, 1801-70, Am. admiral; passed the New Orleans forts and captured New Orleans in 1862. FAY CONVERSATION, pen name of A. M. Griswold. FAUST, Karl, 1825-....., Ger. composer. FAUST, Dr. Johann, fl. 1500, Ger. necromancer. FAUST, Johann, ...-1466? one of the inventors of printing. FAWCETT, Edgar, 1847-....., Am. author. FAWKES, Guy, ...-1606, Eng. conspirator. FEARNE, Charles, 1749-94, Eng. jurist. FEATHERSTONHAUGH, George William, ...-1866, Am. traveler and geologist. FECHTER, Charles Albert, 1824-79, Eng. actor. FÉNELON, François de Salignac de la Mothe, 1651-1715, Fr. prelate and author; "Telemachus." FERDINAND (of Saxe-Coburg), 1861-....., Prince of Bulgaria. FERDINAND I., 1503-64, Emperor of Germany; II., 1578-1637; King of Bohemia and Hungary; III., ...-1657. FERDINAND IV., 1751-1825, King of Naples (I. of the two Sicilies). FERDINAND II., 1810-59, king of the two Sicilies. FERDINAND I. (the Great), 1000-65, King of Castile; V., (the Catholic) (II. of Aragon, III. of Naples, II. of Sicily), 1452-1516, founded the Spanish monarchy; VI. (the Wise), 1713-59; VII., 1784-1833. FERGUSON, Adam, 1724-1816, Scot. philosopher. FERGUSON, James, 1710-76, Scot. astronomer. FERGUSSON, James, 1808-86, Scot. architect. FERNANDEZ, Diniz, fl. 1446, Port. navigator. FERNANDEZ, Juan, ...-1576, Sp. navigator. FERNEL, Jean, 1497-1558, Fr. physician and writer. FERRIS, George Washington Gale, 1859-....., Am. engineer (Ferris wheel). FERRY, Jules François Camille, 1832-1893, Fr. statesman. FERSEN, Axel von, Count, 1755-1810, Sw. field-marshal. FESCH, Joseph, cardinal, 1763-1839, Fr. prelate. FESSENDEN, William Pitt, 1806-69, Am. statesman. FEUERBACH, Paul Johann Anselm, 1775-1833, Ger. jurist. FEUILLET, Octave, 1821-90, Fr. author. FICHTE, Immanuel Hermann, 1797-1879, Ger. philosopher. FICHTE, Johann Gottlieb, 1762-1814, Ger. metaphysician. FIELD, Cyrus West, 1819-92, Am. merchant and financier; established first telegraph cable between America and Europe. FIELD, David Dudley, 1805-....., Am. jurist. FIELD, Eugene, 1850-....., Am. poet. FIELD, Roswell Martin, 1852-....., Am. poet and writer, brother of Eugene. FIELD, Stephen J., 1816-....., associate justice U. S. Sup. Ct. FIELDING, Henry, 1707-54, Eng. novelist and dramatist. FIESCHI, Joseph Marco, 1790-1836, Corsican conspirator. FIESCO (or FIESCHI), Giovanni Luigi, Count of Lavagna, 1525-47, Genoese conspirator. FIESOLE, Giovanni da (Fra Angelico), 1387-1455, It. painter. FILLMORE, Millard, 1800-74, Am. statesman; thirteenth president of the United States; born in New York; learned fuller's trade; read law and acquired a lucrative practice in Buffalo; elected to Congress, 1832, and continued a member till 1842; elected vice-president, 1848; became president on the death of Taylor, 1850; approved the Fugitive Slave Law and the compromise measures of Henry Clay, and made Daniel Webster secretary of state. FISH, Hamilton, 1808-1893, Am. statesman. FISHBACK, William M., 1831-....., governor of Arkansas. FISHER, John, 1459-1535, Eng. prelate; executed; opposed the Reformation. FITCH, John, 1743-98, Am. inventor (steamboat). FITZGERALD, Edward, Lord, 1763-98, Ir. revolutionist. FLAMINIUS, Caius, ...-217 B.C., Rom. general and consul. FLAMININUS, Titus Quintius, 230-174 B.C., Rom. general and consul. FLAXMAN, John, 1755-1826, Eng. sculptor. FLETCHER, Andrew (of Saltoun), 1653-1716, Scot. author. FLETCHER, John, 1576-1625, Eng. poet and dramatist; associate of Beaumont. FLOWER, Roswell P., 1835-....., governor of N. Y. FLOTOW, Frederick Ferdinand Adolphus von, 1812-83, Ger. composer; "Martha." FONTENELLE, Bernard de Bovier de, 1657-1757, Fr. author. FOOTE, Andrew Hull, 1806-63, Am. rear-admiral. FORD, John, 1586-1639, Eng. dramatist. FORREST, Edwin, 1806-72, Am. tragedian. FORSTER, John, 1812-76, Eng. biographer. FORSTER, William Edward, 1818-86, Eng. statesman. FORSYTH, John, 1780-1841, Am. statesman. FORTESCUE, Sir John, 1395?-1485?, Eng. jurist. FORTUNY, Mariano, 1838-74, Sp. painter. FOSCARI, Francesco, 1373-1457, doge of Venice. FOSTER, Birket, 1825-....., Eng. engraver. FOSTER, Stephen Collins, 1826-64, Am. song-writer. FOURIER, François Charles Marie, 1772-1837, Fr. socialist. FOWLER, Orson Squire, 1809-87, Am. phrenologist. FOX, Charles James, 1749-1806, Eng. orator and statesman; entered Parliament 1768 as a Tory, but joined the opposition in 1773, and became leader of the Whigs, opposing the policy of Pitt. FOX, George, 1624-90, Eng. founder of the society of Friends, or Quakers. FOXE, John, 1517-87, Eng. Protestant clergyman and author; "Book of Martyrs." FOY, Maximilian Sebastien, 1775-1825, Fr. orator and general. FRA BARTOLOMMEO, see Baccio. FRA DIAVOLO (Michael Pezza), 1760-1806, Neapolitan brigand. FRANCIA, Jose Gaspar Rodriguez, 1757?-1840, dictator of Paraguay. FRANCIS I., 1494-1547, king of France; defeated at Pavia; II., 1543-60. FRANCIS I., 1708-65, emperor of Germany; II. (I. of Austria), 1768-1835. FRANCIS II., 1836-....., king of the Two Sicilies. FRANCIS BORGIA, Saint, 1510-72, duke of Gandia and viceroy of Catalonia; joined the Society of Jesus and became general of the order. FRANCIS DE PAULA, Saint, 1416-1507, It. Franciscan monk; founded the order Fratres Minimi. FRANCIS DE SALES, Saint, 1567-1622, Fr. Jesuit writer and orator; bishop of Geneva. FRANCIS OF ASSISI, Saint, 1182-1226, It. founder of the Franciscan order, whose labors gave new life and power to the Church of Rome. FRANCIS JOSEPH CHARLES, 1830-....., emperor of Austria. FRANCIS, John Wakefield, 1789-1861, Am. physician. FRANCIS, Sir Philip, 1740-1818, Br. statesman and writer; supposed author of "Letters of Junius." FRANCIS XAVIER, see Xavier. FRANKLIN, Benjamin, 1706-90, Am. statesman and philosopher; born in Boston; the youngest of a family of seventeen children; his father was a tallow chandler; learned the trade of a printer and studied diligently; removed to Philadelphia, where he established the *Pennsylvania Gazette*; began the publication of *Poor Richard's Almanac* in 1732; discovered the identity of lightning and electricity in 1752, by means of a kite; Franklin occupied many positions of public trust and was the recipient of many honors. FRANKLIN, Sir John, 1786-1847, Eng. Arctic explorer. FRECHETTE, Louis Honoré, 1839-....., Can. poet and politician. FREDERICK I. (Barbarossa), 1121-90, emperor of Germany; crowned by Pope Adrian IV.; reduced Milan in 1158, but was defeated by the Lombards near Legnano; joined the third crusade in 1189 with 150,000 men, and defeated the Turks at Iconium; died in the Holy Land; II., 1194-1250, opposed by the Guelphs and the pope in his project to unite Italy and Germany in one empire; began a crusade against the Moslems in 1227, but turned back, and was excommunicated by Pope Gregory IX.; resumed the crusade in 1228, captured Jerusalem and made peace with the pope; defeated the Guelphs at Cortenuova, 1237, and renewed war with the pope. FREDERICK WILLIAM (the Great Elector), 1620-88, elector of Brandenburg; founder of the Prussian monarchy. FREDERICK I., 1657-1713, first king of Prussia; II. (Frederick the Great), 1712-86, subjected to inhuman treatment in youth by his father, he gave but little promise of his future greatness; ascended the Prussian throne in 1740, and invaded Silesia, which was ceded to him by Maria Theresa in 1742; an alliance having been formed against him by Austria, Russia and France, he began the Seven Years' War in 1756 by invading Saxony; gained a great victory at Prague in 1757, but was defeated at Kolin soon afterward; in the same year he defeated a French army twice as large as his own at Rossbach, and won a brilliant and decisive victory over the Austrians at Leuthen; in 1759 he was defeated at Kunersdorf, and Berlin was captured by the allies, but in 1760 he gained the victories of Liegnitz and Torgau, and peace was made in 1763, Prussian Poland being added to Frederick's dominions. Frederick was a voluminor writer, and a friend of Voltaire, who spent several years at his court. Frederick William I., 1688-1740, king of Prussia; father of Frederick the Great; II., 1744-97; III., 1770-1840, founded the Zollverein; IV., 1795-1861. Frederick III. (Frederick William), 1831-88, king of Prussia and emperor of Germany. Frederick VI., 1768-1839, king of Denmark; VII., 1808-63. Freeman, Edward Augustus, 1823-...., Eng. historian. Freiligrath, Ferdinand, 1810-76, Ger. lyric poet. Frelinghuysen, Theodore, 1787-1862, Am. statesman. Frelinghuysen, Frederick Theodore, 1817-85, nephew of T. F.; Am. statesman. Frémont, John Charles, 1813-90, Am. politician, explorer and general; Republican candidate for the presidency, 1856. Freycinet, Charles Louis de, 1828-...., Fr. statesman. Froebel, Frederick, 1782-1852, Ger. educator; founder of the "Kindergarten." Froissart, Jean, 1337-1410?, Fr. historian; "Chronicles." Froude, James Anthony, 1818-...., Eng. historian. Fry, Elizabeth (nee Gurney), 1780-1845, Eng. philanthropist. Fuller, Melville W., 1833-...., chief justice of the U. S. Fuller, Sarah Margaret, Countess d'Ossoli, 1810-50, Am. authoress. Fulton, Robert, 1765-1815, Am. engineer and inventor, born in Pennsylvania; after spending some years in London as an artist, he turned his attention to civil engineering and inland navigation; went to Paris, and there he invented a submarine torpedo; returned to New York, 1806, and, with the assistance of Robert Livingston, discovered steam navigation; in 1807 he built the steamer Clermont, which made regular trips between Albany and New York at a speed of five miles an hour; although he spent a large amount of money on his inventions the patent did not prove of pecuniary value to him. Fuseli, John H., 1742-1825, Swiss historical painter.

Gadsden, Christopher, 1724-1805, Am. statesman. Gadsden, James, 1788-1858, Am. statesman. Gage, Thomas, 1720?-87, Br. general in Am. Gaines, Edmund Pendleton, 1777-1849, Am. general. Gaines, Myra Clark, 1805-85, wife of E. P. G.; Am. heiress. Gainsborough, Thomas, 1727-88, Eng. painter. Galba, Servius Sulpicius, B.C. 3?-A.D. 69, Rom. emperor. Galen, 131-200?, Gr. physician, medical writer and philosopher, living at Rome; his works remained authority until the fifteenth century. Galerius, Caius Valerius Maximianus, ...-311, Rom. emperor. Galilei, Galileo (Galileo), 1564-1642, It. astronomer; discovered, about 1584, the isochronism of the vibrations of a pendulum, and the law by which the velocity of falling bodies is accelerated; adopted in astronomy the system of Copernicus; constructed his wonderful telescope, 1609; through it he discovered the satellites of Jupiter, and was enabled to explore the surface of the moon and view the phases of Venus; he also ascertained that the "Milky Way" was composed of myriads of stars; in 1632 he published his "Dialogues on the Ptolemaic and Copernican Systems," but was compelled by the Inquisition to abjure the theory of the motion of the earth; he was detained in prison for several years, but it does not appear that he was severely treated, as he was allowed to pursue his studies until prevented by blindness. Gall, Franz Joseph, 1758-1828, Ger. physician; founder of phrenology. Gallatin, Albert, 1761-1849, Am. statesman; native of Switzerland. Gallaudet, Thomas Hopkins, 1787-1851, Am. clergyman and instructor of deaf-mutes. Gallieni, Joseph Simon, 1849-...., Fr. officer and explorer. Gallienus, Publius Licinius Valerius, 233?-68, Rom. emperor. Gallitzin (or Galitzin), an illustrious family of Russian princes. Galt, John, 1779-1839, Scot. novelist. Galvani, Aloisio, 1737-98, It. discoverer of galvanism. Gama, Vasco da, 1450?-1524, Port. navigator. Gambetta, Leon, 1838-82, Fr. statesman. Gambier, James, Baron, 1756-1833, Br. admiral. Garcilaso de la Vega, 1503-36, Sp. poet. Gardiner, Stephen, 1483-1555, Eng. prelate and statesman. Garfield, James Abram, 1831-81, twentieth president of the United States; born in Ohio; worked on a farm in boyhood, and learned the trade of a carpenter; afterward became driver and helmsman of a canal-boat; graduated at Williams College in 1856; appointed professor of Latin and Greek in Hiram College, Ohio, and chosen president of that institution in 1858; married Miss Lucretia Rudolph, and occasionally acted as a Campbellite minister; elected to the State Senate, 1859, and in 1861 was chosen colonel of an Ohio regiment; promoted to the rank of brigadier-general; elected to Congress, 1862, and remained in that body until 1880, when he was made senator; nominated for the presidency by the Republican party in 1880, and elected; shot by Charles J. Guiteau, in Washington, July 2, 1881, and died on September 19 of same year. Garibaldi, Giuseppe, 1807-82, It. patriot and general. Garland, Hamlin, 1860-...., Am. novelist. Garnier, Jules Arsène, 1847-...., Fr. painter. Garrick, David, 1716-79, Eng. actor. Garrison, William Lloyd, 1804-79, Am. abolitionist. Garth, Sir Samuel, 1672?-1719, Eng. physician and poet. Gascoigne, George, 1535-77, Eng. poet. Gaskell, Elizabeth Cleghorn, 1810-65, Eng. authoress. Gassendi, Pierre, 1592-1655, Fr. savant. Gates, Horatio, 1728-1806, Am. Revolutionary general; born in England; captured Burgoyne's army at Saratoga. Gath, pen name of Geo. Alf. Townsend. Gatling, Richard Jordan, 1818-....., Am. inventor. Gauss, Carl Friedrich, 1777-1855, Ger. mathematician. Gautama Buddha, see Buddha. Gautier, Théophile, 1811-72, Fr. poet and novelist. Gaveston, Piers de, ...-1312, favorite of Edward II. of England; arrested by the nobles. Gay, John, 1685-1732, Eng. poet. Gay-Lussac, Joseph Louis, 1778-1850, Fr. chemist. Geikie, Cunningham, 1826-....., Eng. clergyman and author. Gellert, Christian Fürchtegott, 1715-69, Ger. poet. Geneviève, Saint, 422?-512, Fr. religious. Genghis Khan, 1162-1227, Mogul conqueror; subdued China and Persia. Genseric, 406?-477, king of the Vandals; invaded Africa, 429; defeated the Romans in numerous battles; captured Carthage, 439; captured and sacked Rome, 455; defeated the navy of the Emperor Majorian, 457. Geoffrey of Monmouth, 1100?-54, Eng. chronicler. Geoffroy, Jean, 1853-....., Fr. painter. George I. (Lewis), 1660-1727, king of Great Britain; II. (Augustus), 1683-1760, defeated the French at Dettingen in 1743; Charles Edward Stuart was defeated at Culloden, 1746, by the duke of Cumberland, and the latter part of the reign of George II. was marked by victories over the French in Canada, in India and on the ocean; III. (William Frederick), 1738-1820, arbitrary and ignorant, and through his obstinacy lost the American colonies; became insane in 1810; IV. (Augustus Frederick), 1762-1830; "the first gentleman of Europe;" led a dissipated life and incurred an immense debt; married, in 1785, Mrs. Fitzherbert; she being a Roman Catholic, the marriage was illegal; his father refusing to pay his debts unless he contracted a regular marriage, he was induced, 1795, to marry his cousin, whom he regarded with great dislike, a separation being the result; became regent, 1811; took little interest in public affairs; one year before his death an act was passed relieving Roman Catholics from political disabilities. George, Saint, fl. 3d century, bishop of Alexandria; patron saint of England; to him is attributed the destruction of a terrible dragon. George, Henry, 1839-....., Am. author and economist, and advocate of the single tax. Gerard-Tum (or Tenque), 1040?-1121, founder of the Knights of St. John of Jerusalem. Germanicus, Cæsar, B.C. 14-A.D. 19, Rom. general. Gérôme, Jean Léon, 1824-....., Fr. painter. Gerry, Elbridge, 1744-1814, Am. revolutionary statesman; signer of the Declaration of Independence; governor of Massachusetts, 1810; vice-president, 1812. Gessler, ...-1307, Austrian bailiff killed by Tell. Gesner, Conrad, 1516-65, Swiss naturalist. Gherardi, Bancroft, 1832-....., Am. rear-admiral. Ghiberti, Lorenzo, 1378-1455, Florentine sculptor. Gibbon, Edward, 1737-94, Eng. historian. Gibson, John, 1791-1866, Eng. sculptor. Giddings, Joshua Reed, 1795-1864, Am. abolitionist. Gifford, Sanford Robinson, 1823-80, Am. painter. Gifford, William, 1757-1826, Eng. writer and critic. Gilbert, Sir Humphrey, 1539-83, Eng. navigator. Gilbert, Sir John, 1817-....., Eng. artist. Gilbert, William Schwenck, 1836-....., Eng. humorous author and librettist. Gilder, Richard Watson, 1844-....., Am. editor and poet. Giles, William Branch, 1762-1830, Am. statesman. Gillray, James, 1757-1815, Eng. caricaturist. Girard, Stephen, 1750-1831, Am. merchant and banker; born in France; founded Girard College. Girardin, Emile de, 1806-81, Fr. journalist. Giulio Romano, 1492-1546, It. painter and architect. Gladden, Washington, 1836-....., Am. clergyman. Gladstone, William Ewart, 1809-....., Eng. premier. Glauber, Johann Rudolph, 1604-68, Ger. chemist. Glendower, Owen, 1349?-1415, Welsh chieftain. Gluck, Christoph Willibald von, 1714-87, Ger. composer. Gobelin, Gilles and Jean, fl. 1450, Fr. dyers. Godfrey of Bouillon, 1058?-1100, leader of first crusade. Godiva (Lady Godiva), fl. 11th century, Eng. heroine; wife of Leofric, earl of Leicester. Godman, John D., 1794-1830, Am. physician and naturalist. Godunof, Boris Fedorovitch, 1552-1605, czar of Russia. Godwin, William, 1756-1836, Eng. novelist. Goethe, Johann Wolfgang von, 1749-1832, Ger. poet and author, dramatist, novelist and statesman. Goffe, William, 1605?-79, Eng. puritan and regicide. Goldsborough, Louis M., 1805-77, Am. rear-admiral. Goldsmith, Oliver, 1728-74, Ir. poet and writer. Gomez, Sebastiano, 1646-90, Sp. painter; a slave of Murillo, who liberated him and took him into his studio. Gonsalvo de Cordova, Hernandez, 1453?-1515, Sp. commander. Goodrich, Samuel Griswold (Peter Parley), 1793-1860, Am. author. Goodyear, Charles, 1800-60, Am. inventor. Gordon, Charles George (Chinese Gordon), 1833-85, Eng. soldier. Gordon, George, Lord, 1750-93, Eng. agitator. Gordon-Cumming, Constance Frederica, Lady, 1837-....., Scot. traveler and writer. Görgei, Arthur, 1818-....., Hungarian general. Gore, Catherine Grace, 1799-1861, Eng. novelist. Gortschakoff, Alexander Michaelovitch, Prince, 1798-1883, Russian statesman and diplomatist. Gosse, Edmund William, 1849-....., Eng. poet and critic. Gottschalk, Louis Moreau, 1829-69, Am. composer. Gough, John B., 1817-86, Am. temperance lecturer; born in England. Gould, Augustus Addison, 1805-66,

Am. naturalist. GOULD, Hannah Flagg, 1789-1865, Am. poetess. GOULD, Jay, 1836-92, Am. railway financier. GOUNOD, Charles François, 1818-93, Fr. composer. GOURKO, Nicolai Vasilievitch, Count, 1828-....., Polish-Russian general. GOWER, John, 1320?-1408, Eng. poet. GRACCHUS, Caius Sempronius, 159-121 B.C., Rom. statesman. GRACCHUS, Tiberius Sempronius, brother of C. S. G., B.C. 168?-133?, Rom. statesman. GRAHAM, John, Viscount Dundee (Claverhouse), 1650?-89, Scot. officer, noted for merciless severity toward the Covenanters. GRAHAM, Sylvester, 1794-1851, Am. vegetarian. GRANGER, Gideon, 1767-1822, Am. statesman. GRANT, James, 1822-87, Scot. novelist. GRANT, Ulysses Simpson, 1822-85, eighteenth president of the United States; born in Ohio; graduated at West Point, 1843; served in Mexico; became a captain in 1853; resigned in 1854, and after passing some time in St. Louis, removed to Galena, Ill., in 1859, and engaged in business; in 1861 he was made aide-de-camp to the governor of Illinois, but soon after was chosen colonel of the Twenty-first Illinois Volunteers, and in July of same year was made brigadier-general; made commander-in-chief of the Union armies in March, 1864; elected to the presidency in 1868, and again in 1872, and after the expiration of his second term he traveled extensively in Europe and Asia. GRANVILLE, Granville George, Earl, 1815-91, Eng. statesman. GRATTAN, Henry, 1746-1820, Ir. orator and statesman. GRAY, Asa, 1810-88, Am. botanist. GRAY, Thomas, 1716-71, Eng. poet. GREELEY, Horace, 1811-72, Am. journalist; born in New Hampshire; learned the printer's trade and worked as a journeyman printer in New York for one year; founded the New York *Tribune*, 1841; a staunch Whig and Republican, he favored Frémont for the presidency in 1856, and Lincoln in 1860; accepted the Democratic nomination in 1872, but was defeated by Grant. GREEN, John Richard, 1837-83, Eng. historian. GREEN, Seth, 1817-88, Am. pisciculturist. GREENE, Nathaniel, 1742-86, Am. Revolutionary general. GREENLEAF, Benjamin, 1786-1864, Am. mathematician. GREENLEAF, Simon, 1783-1853, Am. jurist. GREENOUGH, Horatio, 1805-52, Am. sculptor. GREENWOOD, Grace, see Lippincott. GREGORY I. (Saint—the Great), 540-604, pope, ascending the pontifical chair in 590; II., ruled 715-31; III., 731-41; IV., 827-44; V., 996-99; VI., 1044-47; VII. (St. Hildebrand), 1073-85, excommunicated Henry IV.; VIII., 1187, died same year; IX., 1227-41, excommunicated Frederick II.; X., 1271-76; XI., 1370-78, condemned the doctrines of Wycliffe; XII., 1406-9; he and the anti-pope Benedict XIII., were deposed by the council of Pisa; died, 1417; XIII., 1572-85, reformed the Julian calendar; XIV., 1590-91, excommunicated Henry IV. of France; XV., 1621-23, founded the Propaganda; XVI., 1831-46, succeeded by Pius IX. GREGORY OF NYSSA, Saint, 332-94, Gr. father of the church. GREGORY OF TOURS, Saint, 540-95, Fr. prelate and historian. GREGORY, James, 1638-75, Sc. geometer. GREGORY NAZIANZEN, Saint, 328?-89, bishop of Constantinople. GRENVILLE, George, 1712-70, Eng. statesman. GRESHAM, Walter Q., 1832-....., Am. jurist and secretary of state. GRÉVY, François Paul Jules, 1807-91, Fr. president. GREY, Henry, Earl, 1802-....., Eng. statesman. GREY, Lady Jane, 1537-54, gifted Eng. lady; executed. GRIMM, Friedrich Melchior, Baron, 1723-1807, Ger. writer. GRIMM, Jakob Ludwig (1785-1863), and Wilhelm Karl (1786-1859), Ger. philologists; brothers. GRISI, Giulia, 1812-69, It. singer. GRISWOLD, Rufus Wilmot, 1815-57, Am. author. GROTIUS (De Groot), Hugo, 1583-1645, Dutch jurist and theologian. GROUCHY, Emmanuel de, Marquis, 1766-1847, Fr. general. GUARNERI, Giuseppe A., 1683-1745, It. violin-maker. GUATEMOZIN, 1497-1525, last Aztec emperor of Mexico. GUELPH (or Welf), noble German family, originally Italian. GUIDO RENI, 1575-1642, It. painter. GUILLOTIN, Joseph Ignace, 1738-1814, Fr. physician; advocate of the guillotine. GUISE, Charles de, 1525-74, cardinal of Lorraine. GUISE, Claude de Loire de, Duke, 1496-1550, Fr. general and statesman. GUISE, François de Lorraine de, Duke, 1519-63. GUISE, Henry I. of Lorraine de, Duke, 1550-88. GUIZOT, François Pierre Guillaume, 1787-1874, Fr. statesman and historian. GUSTAVUS I. (Gustavus Vasa), 1496-1560, king of Sweden; II. (Gustavus Adolphus), 1594-1632, defeated the Polish and Russian armies invading Sweden; became the head of the Protestant league in Germany and defeated Tilly at Leipsic in 1631, and on the banks of the Lech in 1632; at the great battle of Lützen, Wallenstein now commanding the imperial army, Gustavus was killed, but his troops nevertheless gained a complete victory; III., 1746-92, assassinated; IV., 1778-1837, ascended the throne in 1792, but was deposed in 1809. GUTENBERG, Johann (Gensfleisch), 1400-68, Ger. inventor of movable type and the printing-press; first books printed about 1457; died in poverty. GUZMAN, Alfonso Perez de, 1258-1309, Sp. commander.

HADING, Jeanne Alfredine Tréfouret, 1859-....., Fr. actress. HADRIAN (or Adrian), 76-138, Rom. emperor. HAFIZ, Mohammed Shems ed-Deen, 1320?-1390?, Persian poet. HAGEDORN, Friedrich von, 1708-54, Ger. poet. HAGGARD, Henry Rider, 1856-....., Eng.

novelist. Hahnemann, Samuel Christian Friedrich, 1755-1843, Ger. founder of homœopathy. Hale, Edward Everett, 1822-....., Am. clergyman and author. Hale, Sir Matthew, 1609-76, Eng. jurist. Hale, Nathan, Captain, 1755-76, Am. patriot. Halévy, Jacques F. F. E., 1799-1862, Fr. composer. Haliburton, Thomas Chandler (Sam Slick), 1796?-65, Nova Scotian jurist and humorous writer. Halifax, Charles Montague, Earl of, 1661-1715, Eng. statesman. Halifax, George Savile, Marquis of, 1630-95. Hall, Charles Francis, 1821-71, Am. Arctic explorer. Hall, James, 1811-....., Am. author and judge. Hall, Mrs. S. C. (Anna Maria Fielding), 1800-81, Ir. authoress. Hallam, Arthur Henry, 1811-33, Eng. critic and essayist. Hallam, Henry, 1777-1859, father of preceding; Eng. historian and critic. Halleck, Fitz-Greene, 1790-1867, Am. poet. Halleck, Henry Wager, 1814-72, Am. general and writer. Halley, Edmund, 1656-1742, Eng. astronomer. Halpine, Charles Graham (Miles O'Reilly), 1829-68, Ir.-Am. journalist and poet. Halstead, Murat, 1829-....., Am. journalist. Hamilton, Alexander, 1757-1804, Am. orator, statesman, financier and general; born in the West Indies; secretary and aide-de-camp to Washington in Revolutionary war; chosen to the Continental Congress, 1782, but resigned in order to practice law; leading member of the convention of 1787; secretary of the treasury, 1789-95; became recognized leader of the Federal party. Hamilton died from a wound received in a duel with Aaron Burr, and his death was deeply deplored. Hamilton, Gail, pen name of Mary A. Dodge. Hamilton, Sir William, 1788-1856, Scot. metaphysician. Hamilton, Sir William Rowan, 1805-65, Ir. astronomer. Hamlin, Hannibal, 1809-91, Am. statesman. Hampden, John, 1594-1643, Eng. statesman and reformer; entered Parliament in 1620; denied the authority of the crown to levy tonnage without the consent of Parliament, and refused to contribute to the forced loan ordered by King Charles, for which he was imprisoned; regaining his liberty and re-entering Parliament, he ably and firmly resisted the arbitrary measures of the crown; intending, with his cousin, Oliver Cromwell, to emigrate in 1636, they were detained by order of council; in 1640 he led the opposition in the Long Parliament, and was the most popular public man in England; impeached for high treason in 1642, together with four other members, the Commons refused to surrender them, although the king personally led his guard in an attempt to arrest them in their seats; Hampden afterward raised a regiment for the Parliamentary army, and, after displaying great courage in numerous engagements, was slain in a skirmish. Hampton, Wade, 1753-1835, Am. general. Hampton, Wade, 1818-....., Confederate general; elected governor of South Carolina in 1876, and U. S. senator in 1878. Hancock, John, 1737-93, Am. statesman; president of the Continental Congress. Hancock, Winfield Scott, 1824-86, Am. general; second in command at Gettysburg; Democratic candidate for president in 1880. Handel, George Frederick, 1684-1759, Ger. composer; settled in England in 1712; "The Messiah," the greatest of oratorios, was produced 1741; Handel was stricken with blindness, 1751, but continued to conduct his oratorios; buried in Westminster Abbey. Hannibal, 247-183 B.C., Carthaginian general; considered the greatest general of the world; sworn by his father, Hamilcar Barca, to eternal enmity toward Rome; became commander of the Carthaginian forces, 221 B.C.; subdued several powerful Spanish tribes, and in 219 captured Saguntum; crossed the Alps, 218; defeated the Romans near the Ticinus and on the banks of the Trebia; routed Flaminius at Lake Thrasymene, 217; almost destroyed a superior Roman army near Cannæ, 216; captured Capua; recalled to Carthage to repel a Roman invasion under Scipio Africanus, he was defeated at Zama in 202; banished from Carthage about 194, through the enmity of the aristocracy; finally ended his life by taking poison, to escape falling into the hands of the Romans. Hans Sachs, 1494-1576, Ger. poet and shoemaker. Harcourt, Sir William, 1827-....., Eng. statesman. Hardee, William J., 1815-73, Confederate general. Hardenberg, Friedrich von, see Novalis. Hardicanute, 1017?-42, king of England and Denmark. Hardinge, Henry, Viscount, 1785-1856, Eng. general. Hardwicke, Philip Yorke, Earl of, 1690-1764, Eng. jurist. Hardy, Thomas, 1840-....., Eng. novelist. Harlan, John M., 1833-....., U. S. Supreme Court justice. Harland, Marion, pen name of Mrs. M. V. Terhune. Harney, William Selby, 1798-1889, Am. general. Harold I. (Harefoot), ...-1040, king of England; II., ...-1066, defeated by William the Conqueror, and slain. Haroun al Raschid, 765?-809, caliph of Bagdad. Harper, William Rainey, 1856-....., Am. Hebraist and educator. Harris, Joel Chandler, 1848-....., Am. author. Harrison, William Henry, 1773-1841, Am. general and ninth president. Harrison, Benjamin, 1833-....., born at North Bend, O.; graduated from college at 18; studied law and began practice at Indianapolis in 1854; elected reporter of the supreme court in 1860; this office he abandoned in 1862, to aid the cause of the Union, and rose to the rank of brigadier-general; elected U. S. senator, 1881, and President, 1888. Harte, Francis Bret, 1839-....., Am. author. Harvard, John, 1608?-38, founder of Harvard College. Harvey, William, 1578-1657, Eng. physician and anatomist, and the greatest of physiologists; discovered the circulation of the blood. Hasdrubal, ...-207 B.C., Punic general; brother of Hannibal; defeated the Scipios; slain at the Metaurus. Hastings, Warren, 1732-1818, Br. general and statesman; president of the Council of Bengal, and governor-general of India; defeated Hyder Ali, king of Mysore; after perpetrating great outrages in order to replenish the treasury, he resigned in 1785 and returned to England; impeached soon afterward, and opposed in his trial by Burke, Sheridan and Fox, but acquitted. Hatton, Joseph, 1839-....., Eng. journalist. Hauck, Minnie, 1852-....., Ger.-Am. singer. Havelock, Sir Henry, 1795-1857, Br. general; defeated the Sepoys in India, and relieved Lucknow. Hawke, Edward, Lord, 1715-81, Eng. admiral. Hawkins, Sir John, 1520-95, Eng. naval officer. Hawthorne, Julian, 1846-....., son of N., Am. author. Hawthorne, Nathaniel, 1804-64, Am. author. Hay, John, 1838-....., Am. author. Haydn, Joseph, 1732-1809, Ger. musical composer; his masterpiece, the oratorio of "The Creation," was produced in 1798. Haydon, Benjamin Robert, 1786-1846, Eng. painter. Hayes, Isaac Israel, 1832-81, Am. Arctic explorer. Hayes, Rutherford Birchard, 1822-93; nineteenth president of the United States; born in Connecticut; admitted to the bar, 1845; brigadier-general in civil war; Congress, 1865-8; governor of Ohio, 1868-76; Republican candidate for the presidency, 1876; inaugurated president, 1877, the electoral commission to determine the result of the election of 1876 having decided, by a vote of eight to seven, that Hayes had received 185 electoral votes as against 184 for Samuel J. Tilden, the Democratic candidate. Hayne, Paul Hamilton, 1830-86, Am. poet. Hayne, Robert Young, 1791-1839, Am. orator and statesman; opponent of Webster in discussing the Constitution; governor of South Carolina. Hazlitt, William, 1778-1830, Eng. critic and writer. Heath, William, 1737-1814, Am. Revolutionary general. Heber, Reginald, 1783-1826, Eng. prelate and author. Hegel, Georg Wilhelm Friedrich, 1770-1831, Ger. philosopher, metaphysician and pantheist. Heine, Heinrich, 1799-1856, Ger. lyric poet and author. Heloise, 1101-64, Fr. nun; pupil and friend of Abelard. Helps, Sir Arthur, 1817-75, Eng. author. Helmholtz, Hermann L. F., 1821-....., Ger. physicist. Helvetius, Claude Adrian, 1715-71, Fr. philosopher. Hemans, Felicia Dorothea (née Browne), 1794-1835, Eng. poetess. Hendricks, Thomas Andrews, 1819-85, Am. statesman. Hengist, ...-488, Jutish chief; founded kingdom of Kent. Hennepin, Louis, 1640-1702?, Fr. Catholic missionary and explorer of the Mississippi. Henrietta Maria, 1609-69, queen of England. Henry I. (Beauclerc), 1068-1135, king of England; defeated his brother Robert and usurped the throne; II., 1133-89; first of the Plantagenets; issued constitutions of Clarendon, which were, however, repealed about ten years later; conquered Ireland; during his reign Thomas à Becket was killed; III. (of Winchester), 1207-72; warred with the barons; IV. (Bolingbroke), 1366-1413; first king of the house of Lancaster; V. (of Monmouth), 1388-1422; conquered France; VI. (of Windsor), 1421-71; his reign was made memorable by the war of the Roses; VII., 1456-1509; founded the Tudor dynasty; VIII., 1491-1547; defeated the French at Guinegate and the Scotch at Flodden, 1513; made Thomas Wolsey prime minister; applied unsuccessfully to the pope for a divorce from Catherine of Aragon, his wife; favored the Reformation; deposed Wolsey and elevated Thomas Cranmer; had himself declared head of the church; married Anne Boleyn after the archbishops of York and Canterbury had declared his marriage with Catherine invalid; declared the English Church independent of the papal see and abolished the monasteries; had Anne Boleyn executed in 1536, and married Jane Seymour the day after the execution; excommunicated by the pope, 1538; his third wife having died in 1537, he married Anne of Cleves in 1540; was divorced from her the same year and married Catherine Howard, who was executed on a charge of adultery in 1542; married Catherine Parr in 1543, she surviving him. Henry I., 1005?-60, king of France; II., 1518-59; married Catherine de Medici; III. (Henri de Valois), 1551-89, last of the Valois; IV. (le Grand), 1553-1610, king of Navarre; first of the Bourbons; assassinated. Henry I. (the Fowler), 876-936, emperor of Germany; defeated the Hungarians; II. (Saint), 972-1024; III. (the Black, or the Bearded), 1017-56; IV. 1050-1106; excommunicated by Gregory VII.; V., 1081-1125, last of the Salic line; VI., 1165-97; VII., 1262-1313. Henry, Patrick, 1736-99, Am. patriot and orator; member of the Continental Congress; governor of Virginia. Heraclitus, fl. 500 B.C., Gr. philosopher. Herbert, George, 1593-1632, Br. poet and divine. Herbert, Hilary A., 1835-....., secretary of the navy. Herder, Johann Gottfried von, 1744-1803, Ger. author. Herkomer, Hubert, 1849-....., Ger. artist in England. Hermann, see Arminius. Herod (the Great), B.C. 73-A.D. 4, king of Judea. Herodotus, 484?-408 B.C., Gr. historian; "the father of history;" his work covers the period of 240 years preceding his own time. Herrick, Robert, 1591-1674, Eng. divine and poet. Herschel,

Sir John Frederick William, 1792-1871, Eng. astronomer and philosopher. HERSCHEL, Sir William, 1738-1822, father of preceding; Ger. astronomer; born in Hanover, but moved to England at 21; discovered Uranus. HESIOD, fl. 800 B.C., Gr. poet. HEYSE, Paul Johann Ludwig, 1830- . . . ., Ger. author. HEZEKIAH, 750-698 B.C., king of Judah. HICKS, Elias, 1748-1830, Am. Quaker preacher. HIGGINSON, Thomas Wentworth, 1823- . . . ., Am. author. HILDRETH, Richard, 1807-65, Am. journalist and historian. HILL, Sir Rowland, 1795-1879; author of the Eng. penny post system. HILLERN, Wilhelmine von, 1836- . . . ., Ger. novelist. HIPPARCHUS, fl. 160 B.C., Bithynian astronomer. HIPPOCRATES, 460-357? B.C., Gr. physician; "the father of medicine;" many diseases still bear the names he gave them. HOAR, George Frisbie, 1826- . . . ., Am. lawyer and statesman. HOBART, Augustus Charles (Hobart Pasha), 1822-86, Turkish naval commander, born in England. HOBBES, Thomas, 1588-1679, Eng. philosopher. HOCHE, Lazare, 1768-97, Fr. general. HOE, Richard March, 1812-86, Am. inventor of printing presses. HOFER, Andreas, 1767-1810, Tyrolese patriot; executed. HOFFMAN, Charles Fenno, 1806-84, Am. author. HOGARTH, William, 1697-1764, Eng. painter and engraver. HOGG, James, 1772-1835, Scot. poet. HOHENLOHE, HOHENSTAUFEN, HOHENZOLLERN, princely families of Germany. HOLBEIN, Hans (the Younger), 1497-1554, Ger. painter. HOLLAND, Josiah Gilbert, 1819-81, Am. author. HOLMES, Oliver Wendell, 1809-1894, Am. physician, author and poet. HOLST, von, Hermann Eduard, 1841- . . . ., Ger. historian. HOLT, Sir John, 1642-1710, Eng. judge. HOMER, fl. 1000 B.C., Gr. poet; "the father of poets;" about his life scarcely anything is known; supposed to have been blind and poor; some maintain that the "Iliad" and "Odyssey," the two great epics ascribed to him, are collections of songs from various poets, and that Homer never existed. HONORIUS, Flavius, 384-423, Rom. emperor. HOOD, Thomas, 1798-1845, Eng. poet and humorist. HOOK, Theodore Edward, 1788-1841, Eng. author. HOOKER, Joseph, 1819-79, Am. general. HOOKER, Richard, 1553-1600, Eng. theologian. HOPKINS, John, 1795-1873, Am. philanthropist. HOPKINSON, Francis, 1738-91, Am. author; signed the Declaration of Independence. HOPKINSON, Joseph, 1770-1842, son of F.H., Am. lawyer, author of "Hail Columbia." HORACE (Quintus Horatius Flaccus), 65-8 B.C., Latin poet. HORSFORD, Eben Norton, 1818- . . . ., Am. chemist. HOSMER, Harriet Goodhue, 1830- . . . ., Am. sculptor. HOUDIN, Robert, 1805-71, Fr. conjuror. HOUDON, Jean Antoine, 1741-1828, Fr. sculptor. HOUSSAYE, Arsène, 1815- . . . ., Fr. author.

HOUSTON, Sam, 1793-1863, Am. general and statesman; governor of Tennessee, 1827-9; passed a number of years with the Cherokee Indians; commander-in-chief of the Texan forces in revolt against Mexico, and defeated and captured Santa Ana in 1836; elected president of Texas same year, and re-elected 1841; elected senator from Texas after its admission to the Union, in 1845, and governor in 1859. HOWARD, Henry, Earl of Surrey, 1516-47, Eng. poet. HOWARD, John, 1726-90, Eng. philanthropist; investigated and published horrors of English and continental prisons. HOWARD, Oliver Otis, 1830- . . . ., Am. general. HOWE, Elias, 1819-67, Am. inventor. HOWE, Samuel Gridley, 1801-76, Am. philanthropist. HOWELLS, William Dean, 1837- . . . ., Am. author. HOWITT, William, 1792-1879, Eng. author. HOYLE, Edmond, 1672-1769, Eng. author; "Games." HUC, Evariste Regis, Abbé, 1813-60, Fr. missionary. HUDSON, Henry (or Hendrik), ...-1611, Eng. navigator. HUGHES, Thomas, 1823- . . . ., Eng. author and barrister. HUGO, Victor Marie, Vicomte, 1802-85, Fr. poet, novelist and dramatist. HULL, Isaac, 1775-1843, Am. commodore. HULL, William, 1753-1825, Am. revolutionary general. HUMBERT I., 1844- . . . ., king of Italy. HUMBOLDT, Friedrich Heinrich Alexander von, Baron, 1769-1859, Ger. scientist. HUME, David, 1711-76, Scot. historian and sceptic philosopher. HUNT, James Henry Leigh, 1784-1859, Eng. poet and author. HUNT, William Henry, 1790-1864, Eng. painter in water-colors. HUNT, William Holman, 1826- . . . ., Eng. painter. HUNTER, David, 1802-86, Am. general. HUNTER, John, 1728-93, Scot. surgeon. HUSS, John, 1373-1415, Bohemian reformer; burned at the stake. HUXLEY, Thomas Henry, 1825- . . . ., Eng. scientist. HYACINTHE, Père, see LOYSON. HYDER ALI, 1718-82, Hindoo prince. HYPATIA, d. 415, female philosopher at Alexandria.

IBERVILLE, Pierre le Moyne d', Sieur, 1661-1706, Canadian military and naval commander. IGNATIEFF, Nicholas Pavlovitch, 1832- . . . ., Russian general and diplomatist. IGNATIUS, Saint (Theophorus), ...-107, bishop of Antioch. IGNATIUS, Saint, 799-877, patriarch of Constantinople. IGNATIUS DE LOYOLA, see LOYOLA. INGELOW, Jean, 1830- . . . ., Eng. poetess and novelist. INGERSOLL, Jared, 1749-1822, Am. lawyer. INGERSOLL, Robert Green, 1833- . . . ., Am. lawyer, author and lecturer. INGOLDSBY, Thomas, pen name of R. H. Barham. INGRES, Jean A. D., 1781-1867, Fr. painter. INMAN, Henry, 1801-46, Am. portrait painter. INNESS, George, 1825- . . . ., Am. landscape painter. INNOCENT I., pope, ruling 402-17; during his reign Rome was sacked by Alaric; II., 1130-43; III. (Lothario), born in 1161, and chosen pope 1198; put France under the ban, 1199, because Philip Augustus repudiated his wife; promoted the fourth crusade, the result of which was the capture of Constantinople; deposed Otho, emperor of Germany, transferring the crown to Frederick of Sicily; subjected John of England to the papal see, compelling him to pay an annual tribute; crushed the Albigenses in 1214, and died two years later; IV. (Sinibaldo de Fieschi), 1243-54; V., assumed pontificate 1276, and died same year; VI., 1352-62; VII., 1404-6; VIII., 1484-92; IX., 1591, died same year; X., 1644-55; XI., 1676-89; XII., 1691-1700; XIII., 1721-24. Iredell, James, 1751-99, Am. jurist. Irenæus, Saint, 140?-202?, bishop of Lyons, martyr. Irene, 752?-803, empress of Constantinople. Irving, Henry (John Henry Brodribb), 1838-....., Eng. actor. Irving, Washington, 1783-1859, Am. author; the purest prose-writer and humorist of America; born in New York City. Isabella I. (the Catholic), 1451-1504, queen of Castile; wife of Ferdinand of Aragon; patroness of Columbus; II. (Maria Isabel Louisa), 1830-....., ex-queen of Spain. Isabella of France, 1292-1358, queen of England, wife of Edward II., whom her adherents deposed, and with whose assassination she is charged; her son, Edward III., assumed the throne and ordered her arrest, and she died after twenty years' incarceration. Isaiah, fl. 740 B.C., Hebrew prophet. Iturbide, Don Augustin de, 1790-1824, emperor of Mexico. Ivan III. (Vasilievitch), 1438-1505, czar of Russia; IV. (Vasilievitch, the Terrible), 1529-84.

JACKSON, Andrew, 1767-1845, seventh president; born in South Carolina; son of an Irishman; received but little education; enlisted against the British in 1781; began the practice of law at Nashville, 1788; Congress, 1796; U.S. senate, 1797; judge Tennessee Supreme Court, 1798-1804; fought several duels, killing Chas. Dickinson in 1806; defeated the Creek Indians, 1814, and was commissioned brigadier-general; defeated the British at New Orleans, 1815; successfully carried on war against the Seminoles, 1817-18; Senate, 1823, and nominated for the presidency, the opposing candidates being Clay, J. Q. Adams and W. H. Crawford; Jackson had the highest number of votes, but not a majority, and Adams was elected by the House of Representatives; Jackson was elected to the presidency, however, in 1828; he was the first president to remove public officers on account of their politics; re-elected in 1832; in that year, the convention of South Carolina having declared the tariff laws of 1828 null and void, Jackson issued a proclamation declaring his intention to check by force of arms all movements tending to disunion. Jackson, Howell E., 1832-....., justice U.S. Supreme Court. Jackson, Thomas Jonathan (Stonewall), 1824-63, Confederate general, native of Virginia; defeated Gen. Banks at Cedar Mountain, and captured Harper's Ferry with 10,000 prisoners, 1862; killed by a company of his own men, mistaking him and his staff for Federal cavalry. Jacquard, Joseph Marie, 1752-1834, Fr. inventor. Jamblichus, fl. 320, Syrian Neo-Platonic philosopher. James I., 1566-1625, king of England (VI. of Scotland); executed Raleigh; a translation of the Bible was made under his direction; II., 1633-1701 (VII. of Scotland), deposed by revolution. James I., 1394-1437, king of Scotland, assassinated; II., 1430-60; III., 1453-88; IV., 1473-1513, defeated and slain at Flodden; V., 1512-42; VI. (I. of England); VII. (II. of England). James, Henry, Jr., 1843-....., Am. novelist. Jameson, Robert, 1774-1854, Scot. naturalist. Janauschek, Fanny, 1830-....., Bohemian tragedienne. Jansen, Cornelis, 1585-1638, Dutch theologian; founder of the Jansenists. Januarius, Saint, 272-305, patron saint of Naples. Jasper, William, 1750-79, brave Am. soldier. Jay, John, 1745-1829, Am. statesman; first chief justice. Jeanne d'Albret, 1528-72, queen of Navarre. Jean Paul, see Richter. Jefferson, Joseph, 1829-....., Am. actor. Jefferson, Thomas, 1743-1826, Am. statesman; third president; born in Virginia; admitted to the bar, 1767; elected to Virginia House of Burgesses, 1769, Continental Congress, 1775; drafted the Declaration of Independence; governor of Virginia, 1779-81; minister plenipotentiary, 1784, to negotiate treaties with European powers; minister at Paris, 1785-9; secretary of state, 1789-93; elected vice-president, 1796, and president in 1800, holding that office from 1801 to 1809. Jeffrey, Francis, 1773-1850, Scot. critic and judge. Jeffreys, George, Lord, 1648-89, infamous Br. judge; lord high chancellor under James II.; died in the Tower. Jenkins, Edward, 1838-....., Eng. author. Jenner, Edward, 1749-1823, Eng. physician; introduced vaccination. Jenner, Sir William, 1815-....., Eng. physician and anatomist. Jerome, Saint, 340?-420, Latin father of the church. Jerome of Prague, 1378-1416, Bohemian religious reformer; follower of Huss; burned at the stake. Jerrold, Douglas William, 1803-57, Eng. humorist and satirical writer. Jervis, John, Earl of St. Vincent, 1734-1823, Eng. admiral. Joachim, Joseph, 1831-....., Hungarian violinist. Joan of Arc (Jeanne d'Arc), 1411?-31, Fr. heroine ("the Maid of Orleans"); born in Lorraine of an humble peasant family; believing herself commissioned by heaven to liberate France, and convincing Charles VII. of her divine authority, she was given command of a considerable force, and by the victories she gained enabled Charles to be crowned at Rheims; although she wished to return home and resume her former humble life, she was induced to retain her command in the army; she was captured in 1430 by the Burgundians, delivered to the English, and burned at the stake after a mock trial. Joel, fl. 770 B.C., Hebrew prophet. John I. (Saint), pope, ruling 523-6; II., 533-5; III., 560-73; IV., 640-2; V., 685-7; VI., 701-5; VII., 705-7; VIII., 872-82; IX., 898-900; X., 915-28; XI., 931-6; XII., 956-64; XIII., 965-72; XIV., 984-5; XV., died in 985, only a few days after his accession; XVI., 986-96; XVII. (rival of Gregory V. in 997); XVIII., 1003; XIX., 1004-9; XX., 1024-33; XXI., 1276; XXII., chosen 1316, deposed 1327, died 1334; XXIII., chosen in 1410, deposed 1414. John, 1166-1216, king of England; granted Magna Charta. John II. (the Good), 1319-64, king of France. John II. (Casimir V.), 1609-72, king of Poland; III. (Sobieski), 1624-96. John I. (the Great), 1357-1433, king of Portugal. John, 1801-73, king of Saxony. John of Austria, Don, 1547?-78, Sp. general. John of Gaunt (Ghent), 1340-99, duke of Lancaster; son of Edward III. John the Baptist, B.C. 5-A.D. 28, prophet. John the Evangelist (St. John), ...-100?, apostle. Johnson, Andrew, 1808-75, Am. statesman; seventeenth president; born in N. C.; learned the trade of a tailor in Tenn.; Congress, 1843-53; governor, 1853-7; senator, 1857; military governor, 1862; elected vice-president, 1864, and succeeded to the presidency on the death of Lincoln, 1865; became involved in a bitter quarrel with the leaders of the Republican party, and was impeached in 1868, but acquitted, although thirty-five senators voted for conviction to only nineteen against, a two-thirds majority being necessary; he was subsequently elected to the Senate from Tennessee as a Democrat. Johnson, Eastman, 1824-...., Am. painter. Johnson, Reverdy, 1796-1876, Am. statesman. Johnson, Richard Mentor, 1780-1850, ninth vice-president of the United States. Johnson, Samuel, 1709-84, Eng. writer and lexicographer. Johnston, Albert Sydney, 1803-62, Confederate general. Johnston, Joseph Eccleston, 1807-91, Confederate general. Joliet, Louis, 1645-1700?, Fr. explorer of the Mississippi. Jomini, Henri, Baron, 1779-1869, Swiss military writer. Jonah, fl. 800 B.C., Hebrew prophet. Jones, George, 1811-91, Am. journalist. Jones, John Paul, 1747-92, Am. revolutionary naval commander; born in Scot.; captured the Serapis. Jones, Sir William, 1746-94, Eng. orientalist. Jones, Thomas G., 1844-...., governor of Ala. Jonson, Ben, 1574-1637, Eng. poet and dramatist. Joseffy, Rafael, 1852-...., Hungarian pianist. Joseph I., 1678-1711, emperor of Germany; II., 1741-90, abolished feudal serfdom. Josephine, 1763-1814, empress of France; wife of Napoleon Bonaparte. Josephus, Flavius, 37-95?, Jewish historian. Joshua, 1537-1427 B.C., Hebrew leader. Jovian, 331-64, Rom. emperor. Juarez, Benito Pablo, 1806-72, Mexican Aztec statesman. Judas Maccabæus, ...-160 B.C., Hebrew leader. Judson, Adoniram, 1788-1850, Am. Baptist missionary. Julian (the Apostate), 331-63, Rom. emperor. Julius I., pope, 336-52; II., 1503-13; III., 1550-55. June, Jenny, pen name of Mrs. J. C. Croly. Junot, Andoche, Duc d'Abrantes, 1771-1813, Fr. general. Justin (the Martyr), 103-167?, church father in Palestine. Justin I., 450-527, Byzantine emperor; II., ...-578. Justinian I. (the Great), 483?-565, Byzantine emperor. Juvenalis, Decimus Junius, 40?-125?, Latin poet.

KALAKAUA, David, 1836-91, king of Hawaii. Kamehameha IV., 1834-63, king of Hawaii. Kane, Elisha Kent, 1820-57, Am. Arctic explorer. Kant, Immanuel, 1724-1804, Ger. metaphysician and philosopher. Kean, Edmund, 1787-1833, Eng. tragedian. Kearney, Philip, 1815-62, Am. general. Keats, John, 1795-1821, Eng. poet. Keble, John, 1792-1866, Eng. divine and writer. Keene, Laura, 1820-73, Am. actress. Kellermann, François Christophe de, 1735-1820, Fr. general. Kellogg, Clara Louise, 1842-...., Am. vocalist. Kemble, Charles, 1775-1854, brother of J. P. K., Eng. actor. Kemble, Frances Anne, 1809-1893, Eng. actress. Kemble, John Philip, 1757-1823, Eng. tragedian. Kempis, Thomas à, 1380-1471, Ger. ascetic writer; "Imitation of Christ." Kendal, Mrs. W. H. (Madge Robertson), 1849-...., Eng. actress. Kennan, George, 1845-...., Am. traveler and author. Kent, James, 1763-1847, Am. jurist. Kepler, Johann, 1571-1630, Ger. astronomer; discovered the laws and orbits of motion of the planets. Key, Francis Scott, 1779-1843, Am. poet; author of "The Star-Spangled Banner." Khosru I., ...-579, king of Persia; II., ...-628. Kidd, William, 1650-1701, Am. pirate; executed. Kilpatrick, Hugh Judson, 1836-81, Am. general. King, Rufus, 1755-1827, Am. statesman. King, William Rufus, 1786-1853, Am. statesman. Kingsley, Charles, 1819-75, Eng. divine and author. Kitto, John, 1804-54, Eng. Biblical scholar. Kléber, Jean Baptiste, 1754-1800, Fr. general. Klopstock, Friedrich Gottlieb, 1724-1803, Ger. poet. Knott, James Proctor, 1830-...., Am. statesman. Knowles, James Sheridan, 1784-1862, Eng. dramatist and actor; subsequently be-made a Baptist minister. Knox, Henry, 1750-1806, Am. general and statesman. Knox, John, 1505-72, leader of the Scot. reformation. Koch, Robert, 1843-...., Ger. bacteriologist. Kosakov, Alexander Vissarionovitch, 1832-...., Rus. general. Kosciusko, Thaddeus, 1746?-1817, Polish patriot and general; commanded the Polish insurgent army; bravely defended Warsaw, but was defeated. Kossuth, Louis, 1802-1894, Hungarian patriot, orator and statesman; leading spirit in the insurrection of 1848-49. Krapotkin, Peter Alexeievitch, Prince, 1842-...., Russ. anarchist. Krupp, Alfred, 1810-87, Ger. manufacturer of steel guns. Kwang Hsu, 1871-...., emperor of China. Kublai-Khan, ...-1294, founder of Mongol dynasty in China.

LABLACHE, Luigi, 1794-1858, It. singer. Labouchere, Henry, 1831-...., Eng. radical journalist. La Chaise d'Aix, François (Pere la Chaise), 1624-1709, Fr. Jesuit. Lactantius, 260?-325, Latin father of the church. La Fayette, Marie Jean Paul Roch Yves Gilbert Motier de, Marquis, 1757-1834, Fr. general and patriot; came to America in 1777 to aid the Americans in their struggle for independence; and was commissioned major-general; fought at Brandywine, where he was wounded, and in numerous other engagements; visited France and obtained supplies and munitions, returning 1779; commanded the advance guard at Yorktown, 1781; returned again to France; chosen commandant of the French National Guard, 1789; visited America, 1824, and was enthusiastically received; took a prominent part in the revolution of 1830. La Fontaine, Jean de, 1621-95, Fr. poet and fabulist. Lagrange, Joseph Louis, 1736-1813, Fr. mathematician. Lamar, Lucius Quintus Cincinnatus, 1825-1893, Am. statesman and jurist. Lamartine, Alphonse de, 1790-1869, Fr. poet and statesman. Lamb, Charles (Elia), 1775-1834, Eng. essayist. Lambert, Daniel, 1770-1809, Eng. giant. Lambert, John, 1621-94, Eng. Parliamentary general. Lamont, Daniel S., 1851-...., secretary of war. Lamotte-Fouqué, Friedrich Heinrich Karl de, Baron, 1777-1843, Ger. novelist and poet. Landon, Letitia E., 1802-38, Eng. authoress. Landon, M. D. (Eli Perkins), Am. humorist. Landor, Walter Savage, 1775-1864, Eng. author. Landseer, Sir Edwin, 1802-73, Eng. animal painter. Lang, Andrew, 1844-...., Eng. essayist and poet. Langlande (or Langland), Robert, fl. 1360, Eng. monk and poet. Langtry, Mrs. L. Lillie, 1852-...., Eng. society beauty. Langton, Stephen, ...-1228, Eng. prelate. Lanier, Sidney, 1842-81, Am. poet. Lannes, Jean, Duke of Montebello, 1769-1809, Fr. marshal. Lansdowne, William Petty, Marquis of, 1737-1805, Eng. statesman. Laplace, Pierre Simon, Marquis, 1749-1827, Fr. astronomer and mathematician. Larcom, Lucy, 1826-1893, Am. poetess. Larrabee, William, 1832-...., Am. statesman and writer, governor of Iowa; "The Railroad Question." La Rochefoucauld, François de, Duke, 1613-80, Fr. moralist and statesman. La Salle, Jean Baptiste, 1651-1719, founder of the Christian Brothers. La Salle, Robert Cavelier de, 1635?-87, Fr. explorer. Lasker, Edward, 1829-84, Ger. statesman. Lassalle, Ferdinand, 1825-64, Ger. socialist. Latimer, Hugh, 1490-1555, Eng. reformer; burned. Latour d'Auvergne, Théophile Malo Corret de, 1743-1800, Fr. officer; called, by Napoleon, "The First Grenadier of France." Lauderdale, John Maitland, Duke of, 1616-82, Eng. cabal minister. Laurens, Henry, 1724-92, Am. statesman. Lavater, Johann Caspar, 1741-1801, Swiss physiognomist. Lavoisier, Antoine Laurent, 1743-94, Fr. chemist; founder of modern chemistry; guillotined by revolutionary tribunal. Law, John, 1671-1729, Scot. financier in France; promoted the "South Sea Bubble." Lawrence, Amos, 1786-1852, Am. philanthropist. Lawrence, James, 1781-1813, Am. naval hero; as commander of the Chesapeake, he engaged the British frigate Shannon off Boston and was killed in the action; his last words were: "Don't give up the ship." Lawrence, Sir Thomas, 1769-1830, Eng. painter. Lawrence, Saint, ...-258, Rom. martyr. Layard, Austen Henry, 1817-...., Eng. orientalist. Lazarus, Emma, 1849-87, Am. poetess. Lecky, William Edward Hartpole, 1838-...., Eng. author. Lecouvreur, Adrienne, 1690-1730, Fr. actress. Ledru-Rollin, Alexandre Auguste, 1808-74, Fr. socialist. Ledyard, John, 1751-89, Am. traveler. Lee, Arthur, 1740-92, Am. statesman; brother of R. H. and F. L. Lee. Lee, Charles, 1731-82, Am. general; native of Wales. Lee, Francis Lightfoot, 1734-97, Am. patriot. Lee, Henry (Light-Horse Harry), 1756-1818, Am. general and statesman; governor of Virginia. Lee, Richard Henry, 1732-94, Am. orator and patriot. Lee, Robert Edward, 1807-70, Am. general; commander-in-chief of the Confederate army; son of Henry Lee; born in Virginia; graduate of West Point; chief engineer of Gen. Scott's army in Mexico; Confederate brigadier-general, 1861, and appointed to the chief command, 1862; surrendered at Appomattox, April 9, 1865; subsequently chosen president of Washington College at Lexington, Va., where he died. Leech, John, 1816-64, Eng. caricaturist. Lefebvre, François Joseph, Duke of Dantzig, 1755-1820, Fr. general. Lemoyne,

Gottfried Wilhelm von, Baron, 1646-1716, Ger. philosopher and mathematician. LEICESTER, Robert Dudley, Earl of, 1532?-88, a favorite of Queen Elizabeth. LEIDY, Joseph, 1823-91, Am. naturalist. L'ENCLOS, Ninon de, 1616-1706, Fr. beauty. LEO I., 400?-474, Byzantine emperor; III., 680?-741; V., ...-820; VI., 866?-911. LEO I. (Saint—the Great), Pope, ruling 440-61; II., 682-4; III. (Saint), 795-816; IV., 847-55; V., 903, reigned only two months; VI., 928-9; VII., 937-9; VIII., 963-5; IX., 1049-54; X. (Giovanni de Medici), 1513-21; XI., 1605, died twenty-four days after his accession; XII., 1823-9; XIII. (Gioacchino Pecci), born at Carpineto, in the Papal States, 1810, the son of Count Lodovico Pecci; ordained a priest in 1837, and created archbishop of Damietta in 1843; nuncio to Belgium three years; cardinal, 1853; cardinal camerlengo, 1877; elected to the papacy, to succeed Pius IX., February 20, 1878. LEONIDAS, ...-480 B.C., king of Sparta; leader of the brave three hundred at Thermopylæ. LEOPOLD I. (the Great), 1640-1705, emperor of Germany; II., 1747-92. LEOPOLD I., 1790-1865, king of Belgium; II., 1835-..... LERDO DE TEJADA, Sebastian, 1827-...., president of Mexico. LE SAGE, Alain René, 1668-1747, Fr. novelist. LESLIE, Alexander, Earl of Leven, ...-1661, Scot. general. LESSEPS, Ferdinand de, Viscount, 1805-94, Fr. engineer and diplomatist; planned the Suez Canal and the inter-oceanic canal across Panama. LESSING, Gotthold Ephraim, 1729-81, Ger. author and critic; "the Luther of German literature, drama and art." LEUTZE, Emanuel, 1816-68, Ger. historical painter. LEVER, Charles James, 1806-72, Ir. novelist. LEVERRIER, Urbain J. J., 1811-77, Fr. astronomer. LEWELLING, Lorenzo D., 1846-...., governor of Kansas. LEWES, George Henry, 1817-78, Eng. author; husband of "George Eliot." LEWIS, Matthew Gregory, 1775-1818, Eng. novelist. LEWIS, Meriwether, 1774-1809, Am. explorer. LEYDEN, Lucas van, 1494-1533, Dutch painter. LIEBIG, Justus von, Baron, 1803-73, Ger. chemist. LILIUOKALANI, 1838-...., queen of Hawaii. LINCOLN, Abraham, 1809-65, sixteenth president of the United States; "with malice toward none, with charity to all;" born in Kentucky; removed to Indiana when eight years old; captain in the Black Hawk war, 1832; elected to the Illinois legislature, 1834; admitted to the bar, 1836, and removed to Springfield, Ill.; elected to Congress in 1846; Republican candidate for U. S. senator in 1858, his opponent being Stephen A. Douglas; nominated for the presidency and elected, 1860; reelected, 1864, but assassinated April 14, 1865, by John Wilkes Booth; his death was universally deplored, for his wise administration of affairs during the civil war had won for him the regard of both factions of the bloody controversy. LIND, Jenny (Mrs. Goldschmidt), 1821-87, Sw. vocalist. LINNÆUS, Charles, 1707-78, Sw. botanist, and greatest naturalist of modern times. LIPPI, Filippo, 1412-69, It. painter. LIPPINCOTT, Sara Jane (Grace Greenwood), 1823-...., Am. authoress. LISZT, Franz, Abbé, 1811-86, Hungarian pianist. LITTLETON (or Lyttleton), Sir Thomas, 1420?-81, Eng. jurist. LIVERPOOL, Robert B. J., Earl of, 1770-1828, Eng. statesman. LIVINGSTON, Edward, 1764-1836, Am. jurist. LIVINGSTONE, David, 1817-73, Scot. explorer in Africa. LIVY (Titus Livius), 59 B.C.-17 A.D., Rom. historian. LOCKE, John, 1632-1704, Eng. philosopher; founded the sensational school of philosophy, claiming that all knowledge comes through the senses. LOCKHART, John Gibson, 1794-1854, Scot. author. LODGE, Henry Cabot, 1850-...., Am. author. LOGAN (Tah-gah-jute), 1725?-80, Am. Indian chief. LOGAN, Benjamin, 1742?-1802, Kentucky pioneer. LOGAN, John Alexander, 1826-86, Am. general and statesman. LOLA MONTEZ, 1820?-61, Creole ballet dancer. LONG, Roger, 1680?-1770, Eng. astronomer. LONGFELLOW, Henry Wadsworth, 1807-82, Am. poet. LONGINUS, fl. 3d century, Gr. philosopher. LONGSTREET, James, 1821-...., Confederate general. LORNE, John George Edward Henry Douglas Sutherland Campbell, Marquis of, 1845-...., gov.-gen. Canada, 1878-83. LORRAINE, Charles IV., Duke of, 1604-75, Ger. general; V., 1643-90. LOSSING, Benson John, 1813-91, Am. historian. LOTI, Pierre, see Viaud. LOUIS I. (le Débonnaire), 778-840, emperor of the West and king of France; divided the empire among his sons; VI. (the Fat), 1078?-1137, king of France; IX. (Saint), 1215-70; led a large army against the Saracens in 1248; defeated and taken prisoner in Egypt, but effected his ransom; led another crusade in 1270, but died the same year near Tunis; a wise ruler, and noted for many virtues; XI., 1423-83, established post-office; XII., 1462-1515; XIII., 1601-43; XIV. (le Grand), 1638-1715 ("I am the state"); XV., 1710-74; XVI., 1754-93, guillotined; XVII. (Dauphin), 1785-95; XVIII. (Monsieur), 1755-1824. LOUIS I., 1786-1868, king of Bavaria. LOUIS IV. (the Bavarian), 1287?-1347, Ger. emperor. LOUIS PHILIPPE, 1773-1850, "the citizen king" of France; abdicated, 1848. LOUVOIS, François Michel Letellier de, Marquis, 1641-91, Fr. statesman; caused revocation of the edict of Nantes. LOVER, Samuel, 1797-1868, Ir. novelist. LOWELL, James Russell, 1819-91, Am. poet and critic. LOWRIE, John, 1793-1836, Am. statesman. LOYOLA, Ignatius de (Saint Ignatius), 1491-1556, Spanish founder of the Society of

Jesus, or Jesuits; entered the army at an early age; crippled by a wound in 1521, he turned his attention to religion; made a pilgrimage to Jerusalem in 1523, and subsequently studied at the University of Paris, where he met Francis Xavier and James Lainez, in conjunction with whom, in 1540, he formed the society which has since become so celebrated. Loyson, Charles (Pere Hyacinthe), 1827-....., Fr. reformer and ex-Carmelite. Lubbock, Sir John, 1834-....., Eng. naturalist and statesman. Lucanus, Marcus Annaeus, 39-65, Rom. epic poet. Lucca, Pauline, 1842-....., Ger. vocalist. Lucian, 120?-....., Gr. satirist. Lucilius, Caius, 148?-103? B.C., Rom. satiric poet. Lucretius (Titus Lucretius Carus), 95-..... B.C., Latin poet; greatest didactic poet and most profound of Latin authors. Lucullus, Lucius Licinius, 110-57 B.C., Rom. general. Luther, Martin, 1483-1546, leader of the Protestant Reformation; born at Eisleben, Germany, the son of a miner; educated at the University of Erfurt, and in 1505 entered the Augustine convent at that place; ordained a priest, 1507; became professor of philosophy at Wittenberg, 1508; visited Rome, 1510; denounced the sale of indulgences, 1517; and became involved in numerous controversies; cited to appear before Leo X., he refused to comply; burned the papal bull containing an order to destroy certain of his works, and denied the authority of the pope; excommunicated; enjoyed the support of the elector of Saxony; attended the Diet of Worms, convened for his trial, in 1521; laid aside his monastic dress in 1524, and married Catherine von Bora, an ex-nun, in 1525; enjoyed, during the latter part of his life, the greatest distinction from the princes of Germany. Luther completed, in 1522, his translation of the New Testament, and in 1534 that of the Old Testament; the central point of his theology is justification by faith. Luxembourg, François Henri de Montmorenci de, 1628-95, marshal of France. Lycurgus, fl. 850 B.C., Spartan law-giver. Lyell, Sir George, 1797-1875, Scot. geologist. Lyndhurst, John Singleton Copley, Lord, 1772-1863, lord chancellor of England; born in Boston, Mass. Lyon, Nathaniel, 1819-61, Am. general. Lysander, ...-395 B.C., Spartan general. Lysias, 458-378 B.C., Athenian orator. Lysimachus, 360?-281 B.C., king of Thrace. Lysippus, fl. 330 B.C., Gr. sculptor. Lytton, see Bulwer.

MACAULAY, Thomas Babington, Baron, 1800-59, Eng. critic, poet and essayist. Macbeth, ...-1056?, king of Scotland. McCarthy, Justin, 1830-....., Ir. writer and Home Ruler leader in Parliament. Machiavelli, Niccolo di Bernardo dei, 1469-1527, It. statesman and author; among his numerous writings are his "History of Florence" and "The Prince," the latter of which (not intended for publication, but for the private perusal of the Medici) has rendered the name Machiavelli the synonym of perfidy. McClellan, George Brinton, 1826-85, Am. general; born in Philadelphia; graduate of West Point; served in the Mexican war, and in 1855 served on a commission sent by the government to make observations on the Crimean war; became chief engineer of the Illinois Central railroad in 1857; re-entered the army, 1861, taking command of the Federal troops in Western Virginia, and gained the victories of Rich Mountain and Cheat River; November, 1861, became commander of the armies of the United States; gained a victory at Fair Oaks, 1862, but was forced to relinquish the plan of reducing Richmond; superseded by Gen. Pope, but recalled, and defeated the Confederates under Lee at Antietam; relieved of command about six weeks later; Democratic candidate for the presidency in 1864, and afterward elected governor of New Jersey. McConnell, William J., 1839-....., governor of Idaho. McCormick, Cyrus Hall, 1809-84, Am. inventor of reaping-machine. McCosh, James, 1811-1894, Scot. theologian in Am. McCulloch, Hugh, 1808-....., Am. financier and secretary of the treasury. Macdonald, Flora, 1720-90, Scot. heroine; saved the life of "the Young Pretender." Macdonald, George, 1824-....., Scot. poet and novelist. Macdonald, Sir John A., 1814-91, Canadian premier. Macchiavelli, see Machiavelli. McCloskey, John, 1810-85, first Am. cardinal. McDowell, Irvin, 1818-85, Am. general. McGlynn, Edward (Father McGlynn), 1837-....., Am. clergyman and reformer. McKinley, William, Jr., 1844-....., Am. politician. Mackenzie, Morell, Sir, 1837-92, Eng. physician. MacMahon, Marie Edme Patrice Maurice de, Duc de Magenta, 1808-93, marshal of France and president of the Fr. republic. Macpherson, James, 1737-96, Scot. poet. McPherson, James Birdseye, 1828-64, Am. general. Macready, William Charles, 1793-1873, Eng. tragedian. Madison, James, 1751-1836, fourth president of the United States; born in Virginia; member of the Virginia legislature and delegate to the convention of 1787; joint author with Jay and Hamilton of the Federalist; Congress, 1789-97; secretary of state, 1801-9; president, 1809-17. Magellan, Fernando, 1470-1521, Port. navigator. Magee, William C., 1821-91, primate of England. Mahmoud, Abool-Kasim-Yemeen-ed-Dowlah, 967-1030, Mohammedan conqueror. Mahomet, see Mohammed. Mahony, Francis (Father Prout), 1804-66, Ir. journalist. Maintenon, Françoise d'Aubigné de, Marquise,

6

1635-1719, consort of Louis XIV. Malibran, Marie Felicita (née Garcia), 1808-36, Fr. vocalist and actress. Malthus, Thomas Robert, 1766-1834, Eng. writer on political economy. Mandeville, Sir John, 1300-72, Eng. traveler. Manfred, 1231-66, king of Naples. Manning, Henry Edward, 1808-92, Eng. Catholic prelate and author; united with the Roman Catholic church in 1851; archbishop of Westminster, 1865; cardinal, 1877. Mansfeld, Ernst von, Count, 1585-1626, Ger. general. Mansfield, William Murray, Earl of, 1704-93, Br. jurist. Mantegna, Andrea, 1431-1506, It. painter. Manteuffel, Edwin Hans Carl von, Baron, 1809-85, Prussian field-marshal. Manuel I. Comnenus, 1120?-80, Byzantine emperor; II. Palaeologus, 1348-1425. Manutius, Aldus, 1450?-1515, Venetian printer. Manutius, Aldus, 1547-97, Venetian printer and author. Marat, Jean Paul, 1744-93, Fr. Jacobin demagogue, assassinated by Charlotte Corday. Marcellus, Marcus Claudius, 268?-208 B.C., Rom. consul. Margaret (Semiramis of the North), 1353-1412, queen of Norway, Sweden and Denmark. Margaret of Anjou, 1429-82, queen of Henry VI. of England. Margaret of Angoulême, 1492-1549, queen of Navarre and author. Margaret of Austria, 1480-1530, regent of the Netherlands. Margaret of Valois, 1553-1615, queen of France. Margaret, Saint, 1046-93, queen of Scotland. Margaret, Saint, ...-275, virgin of Antioch; martyr. Maria Christina, 1806-78, queen dowager of Spain. Maria II. da Gloria, 1819-53, queen of Portugal. Maria de' Medici, 1573-1642, queen of France. Maria Louisa, 1791-1847, empress of France. Maria Theresa, 1717-80, empress of Austria and queen of Hungary and Bohemia. Marie Antoinette, 1755-93, wife of Louis XVI. of France; guillotined. Mario, Giuseppe, Marquis di Candia, 1810-83, It. singer. Marion, Francis, 1732-95, Am. Revolutionary general. Mariotte, Edme, 1620-84, Fr. physicist. Marius, Caius, 157-86 B.C., Rom. general and consul. Markham, Henry H., 1840-...., governor of California. Marlborough, John Churchill, Duke of, 1650-1722, Eng. commander; commanded the English forces in the Netherlands, 1689; commanded in Ireland, 1690; accused of treason, deposed and confined in the Tower, 1692; reinstated, 1696; commanded the allied armies in Holland, 1702; won the battle of Blenheim, 1704; Ramillies, 1706; Oudenarde, 1708; Malplaquet, 1709. Marlowe, Christopher, 1564-93, Eng. dramatist. Marmont, Auguste Frederic Louis Viesse de, Duke of Ragusa, 1774-1852, Fr. marshal. Marquette, Jacques, 1637-75, Fr. missionary and discoverer; explored the Mississippi. Marryat, Frederick, 1792-1848, Eng. novelist and naval officer. Marshall, John, 1755-1835, Am. jurist and statesman; chief justice of the United States. Martial, Marcus Valerius, 43-104, Latin poet. Martel, Charles, Duke of Austrasia (the Hammer), 694-741, conquered the Saracens in the great battle of Tours, or Poictiers, 732. Martineau, Harriet, 1802-76, Eng. writer. Martinez Campos, Arsenio, 1831-...., Sp. general and statesman. Marvel, Ik, pen name of Donald G. Mitchell. Marx, Karl, 1818-83, Ger. socialist. Mary I. (bloody Mary), 1516-58, queen of England; married Philip II. of Spain; persecuted the Protestants; II., 1662-94, wife of William III. Mary Stuart, 1542-87, queen of Scots; daughter of James V. and Mary of Guise; educated in France, where she was married to the Dauphin in 1558, who the following year ascended the French throne as Francis II., but died childless, 1560; invited to the throne of Scotland, and married her cousin, Lord Darnley; suppressed, 1565, a revolt of the Protestants instigated by Queen Elizabeth; joined, 1566, a league to extirpate heresy, and, wearying of the arrogance and dissoluteness of Lord Darnley, bestowed her confidence on David Rizzio, an Italian musician, whose murder was instigated the same year by Mary's jealous husband; Lord Darnley was killed in 1567, and Queen Mary married the Earl of Bothwell the same year; public sentiment in Scotland against her became so intense that she was compelled to fly to England, where she was finally beheaded on an unproven charge of conspiracy. Masaniello, 1620-47, Neapolitan insurgent leader. Mason, James M., 1797-1871, Am. statesman. Massasoit, 1580?-1661, sachem of the Wampanoags. Massena, André, Prince of Essling, 1758-1817, Fr. marshal. Massinger, Philip, 1584-1640, Eng. dramatist. Mather, Cotton, 1663-1728, Am. divine and writer, notorious for his persecution of witchcraft. Mathew, Theobald (Father Mathew), 1790-1856, Ir. Catholic priest, called "the Apostle of Temperance." Matthews, Brander, 1852-...., Am. author. Matthews, Claude, 1845-...., governor of Indiana. Maupassant, de, Henri R. A. G., 1850-93, Fr. novelist. Maurice, 1521-53, elector of Saxony; Ger. general and Protestant leader. Maurice of Nassau, 1567-1625, Dutch warrior; prince of Orange. Maximilian I., 1459-1519, emperor of Germany. Maximilian (Ferdinand Maximilian Joseph), 1832-67, archduke of Austria and emperor of Mexico; executed by the Mexicans. Mazarin, Giulio, Cardinal, 1602-61, Fr. prime minister. Mazeppa, Ivan Stepanovitch, 1644-1709, Polish nobleman and hetman of the Cossacks; hero of Byron's poem. Mazzini, Giuseppe, 1805-72, It. patriot. Meade, George Gordon, 1815-72, Am. general; won the battle of Gettysburg. MEDICI, Alessandro de', 1510-37, first duke of Florence; assassinated. MEDICI, Cosimo de' (the Elder), 1389-1464, chief of the Florentine republic. MEDICI, Cosimo de' (the Great), 1519-74, first grand duke of Tuscany. MEDICI, Lorenzo de' (the Magnificent), 1448-92, prince of Florence; scholar and patron of literature and art. MEHEMET ALI, 1769-1849, viceroy of Egypt. MEISSONIER, Jean Louis Ernest, 1815-91, Fr. painter. MELANCHTHON, Philip, 1497-1560, Ger. reformer; leader of the Reformation after Luther's death. MELIKOFF, Loris, 1824-88, Russian general. MELVILLE, Andrew, 1545-1622, Scot. religious reformer. MENDELSSOHN-BARTHOLDY, Felix, 1809-47, Ger. composer. MENELEK, emperor (or negus) of Abyssinia; proclaimed March 12, 1889. MENNO SYMONS (Menno Simonis), 1496-1561, Friesland founder of the Mennonites. MERCADANTE, Saverio, 1797-1870, It. composer. MEREDITH, Owen, pen name of Lord E. R. Lytton. MÉRIMÉE, Prosper, 1803-70, Fr. novelist. MESMER, Friedrich Anton, 1733-1815, Ger. discoverer of "mesmerism." METELLUS, Quintus Cecilius, fl. 100 B.C., Rom. general. METTERNICH, Clemens Wenzel Nepomuk Lothar von, 1773-1859, Austrian statesman. MEYERBEER, Giacomo (Jakob Meyer-Beer), 1794-1864, Ger. composer. MICHAEL ANGELO (Michelangelo Buonarotti), 1475-1564, It. painter, sculptor, architect and poet; "the Dante of the arts;" patronized by Lorenzo the Magnificent; invited to Rome by Pope Julius II., where he designed the church of St. Peter; became architect of that magnificent structure in 1546, and devoted the rest of his life almost exclusively to its completion. MIFFLIN, Thomas, 1744-1800, Am. patriot; president of Continental Congress. MILES, Nelson A., 1839-...., Am. general. MILL, James, 1773-1836, Scot. historian and writer. MILL, John Stuart, 1806-73, Eng. philosopher and political economist. MILLAIS, John Everett, 1829-...., Eng. painter. MILLER, Hugh, 1802-56, Scot. geologist. MILLER, Joaquin (Cincinnatus Hiner Miller), 1841-...., Am. poet. MILLET, Jean François, 1814-75, Fr. painter. MILLS, Clark, 1815-83, Am. sculptor. MILTIADES, fl. 500 B.C., Athenian commander; gained the great victory of Marathon. MILTON, John, 1608-74, poet of the Puritans; educated at Cambridge; passed several years in travel; advocated the popular party, opposing prelacy and the established church; wrote many political and controversial works in prose; was appointed in 1649 Latin secretary of the Council of State; in 1654 he had become entirely blind; his "Paradise Lost" was completed in 1665, and sold for £10, half of which was not to be paid until after the sale of 1,300 copies. MINIÉ, Claude Étienne, 1810-79, Fr. inventor (Minié rifle). MIRABEAU, Honoré Gabriel de Riquetti de, Comte, 1749-91, Fr. orator and statesman; entered the army in 1770; exiled and imprisoned for debt; separating from his wife, he eloped with a young woman in 1776, for which offense he was condemned to death; escaped, however, with four years' imprisonment; led a wandering life for several years, engaging in numerous intrigues; sent to Berlin on a secret mission in 1786, and elected to the States-General in 1789, and later to the National Assembly, of which he became president in 1791. MIR KHODADAD, Khan of Baluchistan; succeeded, 1857. MITCHELL, Ormsby Macknight, 1810-62, Am. general and astronomer. MITCHELL, Donald Grant (Ik Marvel), 1822-...., American author. MITCHELL, Henry L., 1831-...., governor of Florida. MITCHELL, Margaret Julia (Maggie), 1832-...., Am. actress. MITFORD, Mary Russell, 1786-1855, Eng. authoress. MITFORD, William, 1744-1827, Eng. historian. MITHRIDATES VI. (the Great), 132-63 B.C., king of Pontus. MODJESKA, Helena, 1844?-...., Polish actress. MOHAMMED (or Mahomet), 569-632, conqueror and prophet, and founder of the Moslem religion, which threatened to subdue the Christian world; pretended, at the age of forty, to have received a revelation from Allah, and thenceforth devoted himself to the propagation of his new religion; previous to this time he had been an idolater; his new faith, which included the unity of God, was rejected at Mecca, where a conspiracy was formed against him, but was warmly embraced in Medina, to which place the prophet fled in 622; from this flight, called the Hegira, the Mussulmans compute their time; after this event Mohammed propagated the faith of Islam by the sword, gaining numerous victories, and spreading his religion over a large portion of Western Asia. MOHAMMED II. (the Victorious), 1430-81, Turkish sultan; III., 1612-42. MOLIÈRE (Jean Baptiste Poquelin), 1622-73, Fr. dramatist and actor; the French Shakespeare. MOLTKE, Carl Bernhard Hellmuth von, Count, 1800-91, commander of the German armies in the Franco-German war, and designed the entire campaign. MOMMSEN, Christian Matthias Theodor, 1817-...., Ger. historian. MONK, George, Duke of Albemarle, 1608-70, Eng. general; restored the monarchy. MONMOUTH, James Scott, Duke of, 1649?-85, natural son of Charles II.; rebelled, but was defeated and executed. MONROE, James, 1758-1831, fifth president; born in Virginia; captain in the war of 1812; studied law under Jefferson; Congress, 1783; opposed the Constitution; governor of Virginia, 1799; envoy extraordinary to France, 1802; re-elected governor, 1811;

appointed secretary of state same year by Madison; elected president, 1816, and re-elected 1820. MONTAGU, Lady Mary Wortley, 1690-1762, Eng. authoress. MONTAIGNE, Michel Eyquem de, 1533-92, Fr. philosopher and essayist; originator of the modern essay; his "Essays" have been called "the breviary of freethinkers." It is claimed by some scholars that Montaigne's name on the title page of the "Essays" was but a cover for Francis Bacon or his brother. MONTALEMBERT, Charles Forbes de, Comte, 1810-70, Fr. publicist. MONTCALM, Louis J. de St. Véran, Marquis of, 1712-59, Fr. commander in Canada. MONTEFIORE, Moses, Sir, 1784-1885, Eng. Jewish philanthropist. MONTESQUIEU, Charles de Secondat, Baron de, 1689-1755, Fr. jurist and philosopher; his "Esprit des Lois" is the first philosophy of history. MONTEZUMA II., 1480?-1520, last Aztec emperor of Mexico. MONTFORT, Simon de, 1150?-1218, Norman crusader. MONTFORT, Simon de, Earl of Leicester, 1200?-65, son of preceding; led the barons against Henry III. MONTGOLFIER, Jacques Etienne (1745-99) and Joseph Michel (1740-1810), Fr. manufacturers; invented air-balloon. MONTGOMERY, James, 1771-1854, Scot. poet. MONTGOMERY, Richard, 1736-75, Am. general. MONTGOMERY, Robert, 1807-55, Eng. poet. MONTMORENCY, Anne de, Duc, 1493-1567, Fr. constable. MONTMORENCY, Henri de, Duc, 1534-1614, constable of France. MONTROSE, James Graham, Marquis of, 1612-50, Scot. general; executed. MOODY, Dwight Lyman, 1837-...., Am. evangelist. MOORE, Sir John, 1761-1809, Br. general; fell at Corunna. MOORE, Thomas, 1779-1852, Ir. poet. MORALES, Luis, 1509-86, Sp. painter. MORAN, Thomas, 1837-...., Am. artist. MORE, Hannah, 1745-1833, Eng. authoress. MORE, Sir Thomas, 1480-1535, Eng. statesman and philosopher; educated at Oxford; entered Parliament, 1504; produced "History of Richard III.," 1513; "Utopia," 1516; became a great favorite of Henry VIII., who made him lord chancellor in 1530; being an ardent Catholic, he refused to sanction the divorce of Queen Catherine and resigned his office in 1532; imprisoned in 1534 for declining to take an oath acknowledging the validity of the king's marriage to Anne Boleyn, and executed the following year for denying the king's supremacy as head of the church. MOREAU, Jean Victor, 1763-1813, Fr. general. MORELOS, José Maria, 1780-1815, Mexican revolutionist. MORGAN, John Hunt, 1826-64, Confederate cavalry officer and major-general. MORLEY, John, 1838-...., Eng. statesman. MORNAY, Philippe de, Seigneur du Plessis-Marly, 1549-1623, Fr. Protestant statesman. MORRIS, George P., 1802-64, Am. journalist and poet. MORRIS, Gouverneur, 1752-1816, Am. statesman. MORRIS, Lewis, 1834-...., Eng. poet. MORRIS, Luzon B., 1827-...., governor of Connecticut. MORRIS, Robert, 1734-1806, Am. statesman and financier. MORRIS, William, 1834-...., Eng. poet. MORSE, Samuel Finley Breese, 1791-1872, Am. inventor of the magnetic telegraph; graduate of Yale College; studied painting in England, returning to America in 1832; constructed small recording electric telegraph in 1835; finally obtained aid from Congress in 1843, and constructed a line between Washington and Baltimore in 1844. MORTIMER, Roger, Earl of March, 1287?-1330, favorite of Isabella of England; executed. MORTON, James Douglas, Earl of, 1530-81, regent of Scotland; executed as accessory to Darnley's murder. MORTON (or Moreton), John, 1410-1500, Eng. prelate. MORTON, J. Sterling, 1832-...., secretary of agriculture. MORTON, Levi Parsons, 1824-...., Am. banker and vice-president. MORTON, Oliver Perry, 1823-77, Am. statesman. MOSCHELES, Ignaz, 1794-1870, Ger. pianist and composer. MOSES, 1570-1450 B.C., Hebrew law-giver; led the Israelites out of Egypt. MOTLEY, John Lothrop, 1814-77, Am. diplomatist and historian. MOTT, Lucretia (née Coffin), 1793-1880, Am. social reformer. MOTT, Valentine, 1785-1865, Am. surgeon. MOULTRIE, William, 1731-1805, Am. Revolutionary general. MOZART, Johann Chrysostomus Wolfgang Amadeus, 1756-1791, Ger. composer; composed short pieces at the age of six, and at seven gave concerts in Paris and London; distinguished for the universality of his genius; he gave artistic form to opera. MUHLENBERG, Henry Melchior, 1711-87, founder of the German Lutheran church in America. MUHLENBERG, John Peter Gabriel, 1746-1807, Am. general. MUKHTAR PASHA, Ghazi Ahmed, 1837-...., Turkish general and statesman. MULHALL, Michael G., 1836-...., Eng. author. MÜLLER, Friedrich Maximilian (Max Müller), 1823-...., Ger. scholar and writer in England. MULOCK, Dinah Maria, see Craik. MUNCHAUSEN, Hieronymus Karl Friedrich von, Baron, 1720-97, Ger. soldier and romancist. MUNKACSY, Mikhail, 1844-...., Hungarian painter. MÜNZER, Thomas, ...-1525, Ger. Anabaptist fanatic. MURAT, Joachim, 1771-1815, Fr. marshal and king of Italy. MURILLO, Bartolomé Esteban, 1618-82, Sp. painter; excelled as a colorist and regarded as the greatest of the Spanish school. MURRAY (or Moray), James Stuart, Earl of, 1533-70, regent of Scotland; opponent of Mary Stuart; assassinated. MURRAY, Lindley, 1745-1826, Am. grammarian. MURPHY, Nathan O., 1849-...., governor of Arizona. MUSSET, Louis Charles Alfred de, 1810-57, Fr. poet.

NADIR SHAH (Kouli Khan), 1688-1747, king of Persia. Nana Sahib, 1821-59?, leader of Sepoy mutiny. Napier, Sir Charles James, 1782-1853, Eng. general in India. Napier, Sir Charles John, 1786-1860, Br. admiral. Napier, John, 1550-1617, Scot. mathematician. Napier, Sir William Francis Patrick, 1785-1860, Br. general and writer. Napier de Magdala, Robert Cornelis Napier, Baron, 1810-90, Br. general. Napoleon, see Bonaparte. Nasby, Petroleum V., pen name of D. R. Locke. Nash, Richard (Beau Nash), 1674-1761, Eng. fop. Nasr-ed-Din, 1829-...., shah of Persia. Nast, Thomas, 1840-...., Ger.-Am. caricaturist. Nebuchadnezzar, ...-561 B.C., Chaldean king of Babylon; conquered Jerusalem, Tyre and Egypt. Necker, Jacques, 1732-1804, Fr. statesman and financier; father of Mme. de Staël. Neilson, Adelaide, 1850-80, Am. actress. Nelson, Horatio, Viscount, 1758-1805, the greatest of Britain's admirals; entered the navy at 12; post-captain, 1779; rear-admiral, 1797, his promotion having been earned by his share in the victory of St. Vincent; lost his right arm in an unsuccessful attack on Teneriffe; won the battle of the Nile in 1798, for which he was raised to the peerage as Baron Nelson of the Nile; became separated from his wife, owing to an infatuation with Lady Hamilton, which lasted until his death; created a viscount for the victory of the Baltic, where, being second in command, he disobeyed the orders directing him to retreat; fell at Trafalgar, where his fleet gained a decisive victory over the French and Spanish; his last words, "Thank God, I have done my duty." Nelson, Knute, 1843-...., governor of Minn. Nepos, Cornelius, fl. 1 B.C., Rom. historian. Neri, Filippo de Santi (St. Philip Neri), 1515-95, It. founder of the "Priests of the Oratory." Nero, Lucius Domitius, 37-68, Rom. emperor. Nerva, Marcus Cocceius, 32-98, Rom. emperor. Nesselrode, Charles Robert von, Count, 1780-1862, Russian diplomatist. Nestorius, ...-440?, Syrian prelate; founder of the Nestorian schism. Newman, John Henry, Cardinal, 1801-90, Eng. theologian; recognized leader of the High Church party until 1845, when he became a Catholic; appointed rector of Catholic University at Dublin, 1854, and made a cardinal by Pope Leo XIII. in 1879. Newton, Sir Isaac, 1642-1727, Eng. philosopher; the son of a farmer; graduated at Cambridge, 1665, about which time he invented the "method of fluxions" and discovered the law of gravitation; discovered, 1666, that light is not homogeneous, but consists of rays of different refrangibility. Ney, Michel, Duke of Elchingen and Prince of the Moskwa, 1769-1815, Fr. marshal; the son of a cooper; entered the army at 18 as a private, and was gradually promoted; Napoleon called him "the bravest of the brave," and his titles were conferred upon him for his services at Elchingen, in 1805, and his victory at the battle of Borodino; commanded the rear guard in the retreat from Moscow; defeated by Bernadotte, at Dennewitz, 1813; submitted to Louis XVIII. upon the abdication of Napoleon, against whom he was sent with an army in 1815, but united his army with that of his old commander; had five horses shot under him at Waterloo, where he fought with his usual valor; was captured soon after, and executed on a charge of treason. Nicholas I., pope, ruling 858-67; II., 1059-61; III., 1277-80; IV., 1288-92; V., 1447-55. Nicholas I., 1796-1855, emperor of Russia. Niebuhr, Barthold Georg, 1776-1831, Ger. historian. Nicot, Jean, 1530-1600, Fr. scholar; introduced tobacco. Nightingale, Florence, 1820-...., Eng. philanthropist. Nilsson, Christine (Countess de Miranda), 1843-...., Sw. vocalist. Noailles, Adrien M., Duke of, 1678-1766, Fr. general. Nordau, Max, 1849-...., Austrian author. Nordenskiöld, Adolf Erik, 1832-...., Sw. explorer. Nordhoff, Charles, 1830-...., Am. author and journalist. North, Christopher, see Wilson, John. North, Frederick, Lord, 1732-92, Eng. statesman. Northcote, Sir Stafford Henry, 1818-87, Eng. statesman. Northen, William J., 1835-...., governor of Georgia. Norton, Caroline Elizabeth Sarah (née Sheridan), 1808-77, Eng. authoress. Norton, Seymour Francis, 1841-...., Am. writer and reformer; "Ten Men of Money Island." Nostradamus (Michel de Notredame), 1503-66, Fr. astrologer. Nottingham, Heneage Finch, first Earl of, 1621-82, Eng. jurist and statesman. Novalis (Friedrich von Hardenberg), 1772-1801, Ger. author. Novello, Vincent, 1781-1861, Eng. composer. Noyes, George Rapall, 1798-1868, Am. theologian. Noyes, John Humphrey, 1811-86, Am. communist. Nuñez, Rafael, 1825-...., president of Colombia.

OATES, Titus, 1649-1705, Eng. informer; contriver of the "Popish Plot." Oberlin, Jean Frédéric, 1740-1826, Fr.-Ger. reformer and philanthropist. O'Brien, William, 1852-...., Ir. political leader. O'Brien, William Smith, 1803-64, Ir. political agitator. O'Connell, Daniel, 1775-1847, Ir. patriot and orator; advocated Catholic emancipation, but opposed resort to arms; elected to Parliament, 1828, but not allowed to take his seat until 1829, when the bill for Catholic emancipation was passed; gave up his law practice and gave his entire attention to public duties; began advocating the repeal of the union in 1840; was convicted in 1844 on a charge of treason, but sentence was reversed by the House of Lords. O'Conor, Charles, 1804-84, Am. lawyer. Ockham, William of (the Invincible Doctor), 1280?-1347, Eng. theologian. Odoacer, ...-493, Gothic king of Italy; executed. O'Donnell, Leopold, Count of Lucena, Duke of Tetuan, 1809-67, Sp. general and statesman. Oehlenschläger, Adam Gottlob, 1779-1850, Danish poet. Oersted, Hans Christian, 1777-1851, Danish natural philosopher; founder of the science of electro-magnetism. Offenbach, Jacques, 1819-80, Ger.-Fr. composer. Oglesby, Richard J., 1824-...., Am. statesman. Oglethorpe, James Edward, 1698-1785, Eng. general; colonized Georgia. Ohnet, Georges, 1848-...., Fr. novelist. Oldcastle, Sir John, Lord Cobham, 1360-1417, Eng. reformer. Oldfield, Anne, 1683-1730, Eng. actress. Oliphant, Margaret, 1818-...., Eng. novelist. Ollendorf, Henri Godefroy, 1803-65, Ger. educator. Ollivier, Olivier Emile, 1825-...., Fr. statesman. Olney, Richard, 1835-...., attorney-general. Omar I., 581-644, Arabian caliph; conquered Jerusalem. Omar Khayyam, ...-1123, Persian poet. Omar Pasha (Michael Lattas), 1806-71, Turkish commander in the Crimean war. O'Meara, Barry Edward, 1780-1836, Ir. physician and author. Opie, Mrs. Amelia, 1769-1853, Eng. authoress. Optic, Oliver, pen name of Wm. T. Adams. Orange, William, Prince of (the Silent), 1533-84, founder of the Dutch republic; leader of the insurrection which broke out when it was attempted to introduce the Inquisition into the Netherlands; assassinated. O'Reilly, John Boyle, 1844-91, Ir.-Am. poet and journalist. O'Reilly, Miles, see Halpine. Origen, 185?-253, Gr. theologian and preacher; endeavored to harmonize the teachings of Christ and Plato. Orleans, Louis Philippe Joseph, Duc d', 1747-93, took the popular side on the assembling of the States-General, renounced his titles and assumed the name of *Egalité* (Equality); voted for the death of his cousin, Louis XVI.; condemned by the revolutionary tribunal and executed; his son, Louis Philippe, afterward became king of France. Orleans, Philippe, Duc d', 1674-1723, regent of France. Orloff, Alexis, Count, 1787-1861, Russian general. Ormond, James Butler, Duke of, 1610-88, Ir. statesman. Orsini, Felice, 1819-58, It. conspirator; leader in the attempted assassination of Napoleon III. in 1858; executed. Oscar II., 1829-...., king of Sweden and Norway. Osman I., 1259-1326, founder of Ottoman dynasty. Ossoli, Margaret Fuller, Marchioness, 1810-50, Am. authoress. Otho I. (the Great), 912-73, emperor of Germany, Christianized the Danes, deposed Pope John XII.; II., 955-83; III., 980-1002; IV., 1174-1218. Otho I., 1815-67, king of Greece. Otis, James, 1725-83, Am. lawyer, orator and patriot. Otway, Thomas, 1651-85, Eng. dramatist. Oudinot, Nicholas Charles, 1767-1847, Fr. general. "Ouida" (Mlle. Louise de la Ramée), 1840-...., Eng. authoress. Outram, Sir James, 1803-63, Eng. general in India. Overbury, Sir Thomas, 1581-1613, Eng. poet. Ovid (Publius Ovidius Naso), B.C. 43-18 A.D., Rom. poet. Owen, Sir Richard, 1804-...., Eng. zoologist and anatomist. Owen, Robert, 1771-1858, Eng. socialist. Oxenstiern (Oxenstjerna), Axel, Count, 1583-1654, Sw. statesman.

Paganini, Niccolo, 1784-1840, It. violinist. Paine, Robert Treat, 1731-1814, Am. lawyer and statesman. Paine, Thomas, 1737-1809, Am. political writer and free-thinker; born in England. Pakenham, Sir Edward, 1778-1815, Br. general; fell at New Orleans. Palestrina, Giovanni Pierluigi da, 1524-94, It. composer. Paley, William, 1743-1805, Eng. theologian. Palissy, Bernard, 1506-89, Fr. potter and inventor of pottery enamel; died in the Bastile. Palladio, Andrea, 1518-80, It. architect. Palmaroli, Pietro, ...-1828, It. painter. Palmerston, Henry John Temple, Viscount, 1784-1865, Eng. statesman. Paoli, Pasquale di, 1726-1807, Corsican general. Papin, Denis, 1647-1712, Fr. physician. Papineau, Louis Joseph, 1789-1871, Canadian politician. Paracelsus, Philippus Aureolus Theophrastus Bombastus (Von Hohenheim), 1493-1541, Swiss alchemist. Parepa-Rosa, Euphrosyne, 1836-74, Scot. vocalist. Paris, Louis Albert Philippe d'Orleans, Comte de, 1838-...., Fr. prince; grandson of Louis Philippe. Park, Mungo, 1771-1805, Scot. traveler and explorer. Parker, Matthew, 1504-75, Eng. prelate. Parker, Theodore, 1810-60, Am. rationalistic theologian. Parkman, Francis, 1823-1893, Am. historian. Parnell, Charles Stewart, 1846-91, Ir. statesman. Parr, Catharine, 1509-48, surviving queen of Henry VIII. Parr, Thomas, 1483-1635, Eng. centenarian. Parrhasius, fl. 400 B.C., Gr. painter. Parrott, Robert Parker, 1804-77, Am. inventor. Parry, Sir William Edward, 1790-1855, Eng. Arctic explorer. Parsons, Theophilus, 1750-1813, 1797-1882, Am. jurists. Partington, Mrs., pen name of B. P. Shillaber. Parton, James, 1822-91, Am. historian. Pascal, Blaise, 1623-62, Fr. philosopher and mathematician. Pasteur, Louis, 1822-...., Fr. chemist and pathologist. Pater, Walter Henry, 1839-...., Eng. writer. Paton, Sir Joseph Noel, 1821-...., Eng. painter. Patrick, Saint, 372?-463?, apostle of Ireland. Patti, Adelina Maria Clorinda, Marquise de Caux, 1843-...., operatic singer, of Italian descent; born in Madrid. Pattison, Robert E., 1850-...., governor of Pennsylvania. Paul,

Saint, of Tarsus (Saul), 10?-64?, apostle and founder of the Christian church, making Christianity a world-religion in place of a Jewish religion. Paul I., pope, 757-67; II., 1464-71; III. (Alessandro Farnese), 1534-49, excommunicated Henry VIII., called Council of Trent; IV., 1555-9; V., 1605-21. Paul I., 1754-1801, emperor of Russia; assassinated. Paul Veronese (Paolo Cagliari), 1528?-88, It. painter. Pausanias, d. 479 B.C., Spartan general. Paxton, Sir Joseph, 1803-65, Eng. architect. Payne, John Howard, 1792-1852, Am. dramatist and poet. Peabody, George, 1795-1869, Am. philanthropist in England; acquired great wealth as a banker; expended over five millions in benevolent enterprises. Peale, Rembrandt, 1778-1860, Am. painter. Peck, George W., Am. comic writer; governor of Wis. Pedro (de Alcantara) I., 1798-1834, emperor of Brazil; king of Portugal as Pedro IV.; II., 1825-91; deposed 1889. Peel, Sir Robert (Orange Peel), 1788-1850, Eng. statesman; repealed the corn laws. Peixoto, Floriano, president of Brazil, elected 1891. Pelham, Henry, 1694-1754, Eng. statesman. Pellegrini, Carlos, president Argentine Rep., elected 1890. Pellico, Silvio, 1789-1854, It. poet and patriot. Pemberton, John Clifford, 1814-81, Confederate general. Penn, William, 1644-1718, Eng. Quaker, statesman, courtier, author and philanthropist; founder of Pennsylvania. Pepin (the Short), 714?-68, king of France; son of Charles Martel and father of Charlemagne. Pepys, Samuel, 1632-1703, Eng. author and scholar. Pepperell, Sir William, 1696-1759, Am. colonial general. Perceval, Spencer, 1762-1812, Eng. statesman; assassinated. Percival, James Gates, 1795-1856, Am. poet. Percy, Thomas, 1728-1811, Eng. prelate and author. Pereire, Emile (1800-75) and Isaac (1806-....), Fr. financiers; founded the "Credit Mobilier." Pergolese, Giovanni Battista, 1710-37, It. composer. Pericles, 495?-429 B.C., Athenian orator, statesman and general; became the leader of the democratic party and the first man in Athens; erected many noble public works, including the Parthenon; his age is called "the golden age of Athens." Perkins, Eli, pen name of M. D. Landon. Perrault, Claude, 1613-88, Fr. architect. Perry, Matthew Galbraith, 1794-1858, Am. commodore; commanded expedition to Japan. Perry, Oliver Hazard, 1785-1819, Am. commodore; defeated the British on Lake Erie. Persius Flaccus, Aulus, 34-62, Rom. satirist. Perugino, Pietro (Vannucci), 1446-1524, It. painter. Pestalozzi, Johann Heinrich, 1746-1827, Swiss educationist. Peter, Saint, ...-67, apostle. Peter I. (the Great), 1672-1725, czar of Russia and founder of the Russian monarchy; organized an army and entered it as a private; studied practical seamanship, and formed a navy; traveled incognito in Western Europe; worked as a ship-carpenter in Holland; founded schools and effected a number of reforms; defeated Charles XII. of Sweden, at Poltava, 1709; founded St. Petersburg; his second wife, Catharine, was a prisoner of war, of obscure parentage; the crown prince, Alexis, opposing the czar's policy, was forced to renounce the succession, and is said to have been poisoned by his father. Peter the Hermit, 1050?-1115, preacher of first crusade. Peterborough, Charles Mordaunt, Earl of, 1658-1735, Eng. general. Petion, Alexandre, 1770-1818, first president of Hayti. Petrarch (Francesco Petrarca), 1304-74, It. poet and scholar; enamored of Laura de Sade, whose name he made immortal. Pettie, John, 1839-...., Scot. artist. Phelps, Elizabeth Stuart, 1844-...., Am. authoress. Phidias, 490-432 B.C., the greatest of Greek sculptors, and architect of the Parthenon; he was never excelled in expressing the ideal majesty of the human form, and his Zeus, at Olympia, is counted among the wonders of the world. Philidor, assumed name of a Fr. family (Danican) of musicians; François André Danican (1726-95) was a celebrated chess player. Philip (Pometacom) (King Philip), ...-1676, New England Indian chief; sachem of Pokanoket. Philip II., 382-336 B.C., king of Macedonia; father of Alexander the Great. Philip II. (Augustus), 1165-1223, king of France; annexed Normandy, Anjou and Lorraine; won the battle of Bouvines; III. (the Bold), 1245-85; ascended the throne in 1270; IV. (the Fair), 1268-1314, reduced the power of the feudal nobles; imprisoned Pope Boniface VIII. and caused him to remove his seat to Avignon; suppressed the order of Knights Templar; VI. (of Valois), 1293-1350. Philip II., 1527-98, king of Spain; son of Charles V.; provoked insurrection in the Netherlands by his attempt to introduce the Spanish Inquisition; married, on the death of Mary Tudor, his second wife, Isabella of France, the betrothed of his son, Don Carlos; equipped the "Invincible Armada" for the conquest of England; III., 1578-1621; IV., 1605-65; V., 1683-1746; first of the House of Bourbon. Philip (the Good), 1396-1467, duke of Burgundy. Phillipps, Adelaide, 1833-...., Eng.-Am. vocalist. Phillips, Wendell, 1811-84, Am. orator and abolitionist. Phips (or Phipps), Sir William, 1651-95, colonial governor of Massachusetts. Phocion, 402?-317 B.C., Athenian general and statesman. Piccolomini, Ottavio, 1599-1656, Austrian general; conspirator against Wallenstein; gained great distinction in the Thirty Years' war; led Spanish army in Flanders. Pickering, Timothy, 1745-1829, Am. statesman.

PIERCE, Franklin, 1804-69, fourteenth president of the United States; born in New Hampshire; Congress, 1833-7; senator, 1837-42; brigadier-general in Mexican war; elected president on the Democratic ticket, in 1852, holding that office from 1853-7; opposed coercion of the South in 1863. PIERREPONT, Edwards, 1817-92, Am. lawyer. PILATE, Pontius, ...-36, Rom. governor of Palestine. PINCKNEY, Charles Cotesworth, 1746-1825, Am. statesman and soldier; leader of the Federalists. PINDAR, 520?-440? B.C., greatest of Greek lyric poets. PINKNEY, William, 1764-1822, Am. lawyer and orator. PINZON, Martin Alonzo, 1441?-93, Sp. navigator with Columbus. PINZON, Vicente Yanez, 1460?-1524, Sp. navigator with Columbus; discovered Brazil. PISANO, Andrea, 1270-1345, It. sculptor and architect. PISANO, Nicola, 1206?-78?, It. sculptor. PISISTRATUS, 612-527 B.C., tyrant of Athens. PITCAIRN, Maj. John, ...-1775, Eng. officer; fell at Bunker Hill. PITMAN, Benn, 1822-...., Eng. phonographer. PITMAN, Isaac, 1813-...., Eng. inventor of phonography. PITT, see Chatham. PITT, William, 1759-1806, Eng. statesman and orator; son of the earl of Chatham; head of the great coalition against Bonaparte. PIUS I., pope, 142-57; II., 1458-64; III., 1503; died same year; IV. (Giovanni Angelo de Medici), 1559-65, convoked Council of Trent; V., 1566-72; VI., 1775-99; VII., 1800-23; taken from Rome in 1809 by Napoleon, and detained at Genoa and Fontainebleau; VIII., 1829-30; IX. (Giovanni Maria Mastai-Ferretti), born 1792; chosen to the pontificate, 1846; died, 1878; during his incumbency the dogmas of the Immaculate Conception and of Papal Infallibility were promulgated, temporal power overthrown, 1870, and the Papal States annexed to Italy. PIZARRO, Francisco, 1475?-1541?, Sp. conqueror of Peru. PLANTAGENET, dynasty of English kings, 1154-1485. PLATO, 429-347 B.C., Gr. philosopher; disciple of Socrates; held that the human soul has always existed, and that an idea is an eternal thought of the divine mind; Emerson says, "Plato is philosophy, and philosophy is Plato." PLEASONTON, Alfred, 1824-...., Am. general. PLINY (the Elder), 23-79, Rom. naturalist; perished at an eruption of Vesuvius. PLINY (the Younger), 62?-116, Rom. orator and author. PLOTINUS, 205-70, Gr. Neo-Platonic philosopher. PLUNKETT, William Conyngham, Lord, 1764-1854, Ir. jurist. PLUTARCH, 50?-120?, Gr. biographer and philosopher; "father of biography." POCAHONTAS, 1595?-1617, daughter of Powhatan; saved the life of Capt. John Smith, an Eng. explorer; was converted to Christianity, and married an Englishman named Rolfe. POE, Edgar Allan, 1809-49, Am. author. POLK, James Knox, 1795-1849, Am. statesman; eleventh president; born in North Carolina; removed to Tennessee; admitted to the bar; Congress, 1825; speaker for two terms; governor of Tennessee, 1839-41; elected president on the Democratic ticket, holding that office from 1845-9. POLK, Leonidas, 1806-64, episcopal bishop and Confederate general; prominent at Shiloh and Stone River. POLLOK, Robert, 1798?-1827, Scot. poet. POLO, Marco, 1252?-1324?, Venetian traveler. POLYBIUS, 206?-124 B.C., Gr. historian. POLYCARP, Saint, 80?-169?, bishop of Smyrna; martyr. POMPADOUR, Jeanne Antoinette Poisson, Marquise de, 1721-64, mistress of Louis XV. of France. POMPEY (the Great), 106-48 B.C., Rom. general and triumvir; conquered Sertorius and Mithridates; became leader of the aristocracy and opponent of Cæsar; defeated at Pharsalia. PONCE DE LEON, Juan, 1460-1521, Sp. discoverer of Florida. PONIATOWSKI, Josef Antoni, Prince, 1762-1813, Polish commander. PONTIAC, 1712?-69, chief of the Ottawas; formed coalition of Indians against the whites, and attempted to capture Detroit. POOLE, William Frederick, 1821-...., Am. librarian. POPE, Alexander, 1688-1744, Eng. poet. PORTER, David, 1780-1843, Am. commodore. PORTER, David Dixon, 1813-91, son of preceding; Am. admiral; reduced Fort Fisher, 1865. PORTER, Fitz John, 1822-...., nephew of D. P.; Am. general. PORTER, Jane, 1776-1850, Eng. novelist. PORTER, Noah, 1811-92, Am. educator. POWERS, Hiram, 1805-73, greatest of American sculptors. POWHATAN, 1550-1618, Indian chieftain in Virginia. PRAXITELES, fl. 360 B.C., Gr. sculptor, who expressed the perfect ideal grace of the female figure. PREBLE, Edward, 1761-1807, Am. naval officer. PRENTICE, George Denison, 1802-70, Am. poet and journalist. PRENTISS, Sergeant Smith, 1808-50, Am. orator and lawyer. PRESCOTT, William Hickling, 1796-1859, Am. historian. PRICE, Sterling, ...-1867, Confederate general. PRIM, Juan, Count de Reus and Marquis de los Castillejos, 1814-70, Sp. general and statesman; assassinated. PRIOR, Matthew, 1664-1721, Eng. poet and diplomatist. PROBUS, Marcus Aurelius, 232-82, Rom. emperor. PROCTER, Adelaide Anne, 1825-64, Eng. poetess. PROCTER, Bryan Waller (Barry Cornwall), 1790-1874, Eng. poet. PROUT, Father, pen name of Francis Mahony. PRYNNE, William, 1600-69, Eng. Puritan writer. PTOLEMY I. (Soter), 367?-283 B.C., king of Egypt; II. (Philadelphus), 309-247 B.C. PTOLEMY (Claudius Ptolemæus), fl. 2d century, Gr. astronomer and geographer; believed the earth to be at rest in the center of the universe, the heavenly bodies moving around it. PUGIN, Augustus N. W., 1812-52, Eng. architect. PULASKI, Casimir, Count, 1747-79, Polish patriot; general in the Am. Revolutionary army; fell at the siege of Savannah. PULITZER, Joseph, 1847-...., Hungarian-Am. journalist. PULLMAN, George Mortimer, 1831-...., Am. inventor and capitalist. PUTNAM, Israel, 1718-90, Am. Revolutionary general; conspicuous at the battle of Bunker Hill. PYM, John, 1584-1643, Eng. republican statesman and orator. PYRRHO, 376-288? B.C., Gr. skeptic and philosopher. PYRRHUS, 318?-272 B.C., king of Epirus and one of the greatest of ancient generals; defeated the Romans and conquered Macedonia. PYTHAGORAS, 600?-510? B.C., first Gr. philosopher; taught the doctrine of transmigration of souls; basis of his philosophy, number and harmony; soul distinct from body.

QUACKENBOS, George Payn, 1826-81, Am. educationist. QUAD, M., pen name of Chas. B. Lewis. QUARLES, Francis, 1592-1644, Eng. poet. QUEENSBERRY, William Douglas, Duke of, 1724-1810, Scot. profligate. QUIN, James, 1693-1766, Eng. actor. QUINCY, Josiah, 1744-75, Am. orator and patriot. QUINCY, Josiah, 1772-1864, son of preceding; Am. statesman and scholar. QUINTILIANUS, Marcus Fabius, 40?-118?, Rom. rhetorician.

RABELAIS, François, 1495?-1553, Fr. scholar and satirist; joined the Franciscans, but left the order; afterward studied medicine; his great work, "The Pleasant Story of the Giant Gargantua," is a satire upon the different branches of society of his age, more particularly the monastic orders. RACHEL (Elisabeth Rachel Félix), 1821-58, Fr. actress, born in Switzerland. RACINE, Jean, 1639-99, Fr. dramatist. RACINE, Louis, 1692-1763, Fr. poet; son of J. B. RADCLIFFE, 1764-1823, Eng. novelist. RADCLIFFE, John, 1650-1714, Eng. physician. RAGLAN, James Henry Fitzroy Somerset, Lord, 1788-1855, Eng. general. RAIKES, Robert, 1735-1811, Eng. founder of Sunday schools. RALEIGH, Sir Walter, 1552-1618, Eng. courtier, statesman, navigator and author; a favorite of Queen Elizabeth; executed by James I. RAMEAU, Jean Philippe, 1683-1764, Fr. composer. RAMSAY, Allan, 1685-1758, Scot. poet. RANDOLPH, John (of Roanoke), 1773-1833, Am. politician and orator. RANDOLPH, Peyton, 1723-75, president of first Am. Congress. RAPHAEL (Raffaelle Sanzio, or Santi d'Urbino), 1483-1520, It. painter; "the prince of painters." RAVAILLAC, François, 1578-1610, Fr. fanatic; assassin of Henry IV. RAWLINSON, George, 1815-...., Eng. historian. READ, George, 1733-98, signer Declaration of Independence. READ, Opie Pope, 1852-...., Am. novelist. READ, Thomas Buchanan, 1822-72, Am. poet and artist. READE, Charles, 1814-84, Eng. novelist. RÉAUMUR, René Antoine Ferchault de, 1683-1757, Fr. naturalist. RÉCAMIER, Jeanne F. J. A. B., 1777-1849, Fr. lady noted for beauty and accomplishments. RED JACKET, 1760-1830, Seneca Indian chief. REED, Thomas Brackett, 1839-...., Am. lawyer and politician. REEVES, John Sims, 1822-...., Eng. oratorio singer. REGULUS, Marcus Atilius, ...-250 B.C., Rom. general and statesman. REID, Capt. Mayne, 1818-83, Ir.-Am. novelist. REID, Whitelaw, 1837-...., Am. journalist and vice-president. REMBRANDT VAN RYN, Paul, 1607-69, Dutch painter; chief of the Dutch school; the greatest master of colors and unrivaled as an etcher. RÉMUSAT, Charles François Marie, Count, 1797-1875, Fr. statesman and philosopher. RENAN, Joseph Ernest, 1823-92, Fr. philologist and writer. RETZ, Jean François Paul de Gondi, Cardinal, 1614-79, Fr. prelate. REUTER, Fritz, 1810-74, low-Ger. poet and novelist. REUTER, Julius, 1815-...., Ger. originator of Reuter's Telegraphic Agency. REVERE, Paul, 1735-1818, Am. engraver and Revolutionary patriot; carried the news of Gage's impending attack to Concord. REYNOLDS, John Fulton, 1820-63, Am. general. REYNOLDS, Robert J., 1838-...., governor of Delaware. REYNOLDS, Sir Joshua, 1723-92, Eng. portrait painter. RICARDO, David, 1772-1823, Eng. political economist. RICH, John T., 1841-...., governor of Michigan. RICHARD I. (Cœur de Lion), 1157-99, king of England; led a large army into Palestine; conquered Acre and defeated Saladin; II., 1366-1400; III., 1452-85, last of the Plantagenets. RICHARDSON, Samuel, 1689-1761, Eng. novelist. RICHELIEU, Armand Jean du Plessis, Cardinal, 1585-1642, Fr. prelate and statesman; minister to Louis XIII., but real ruler of France for eighteen years. RICHTER, Johann Paul Friedrich (Jean Paul), 1763-1825, Ger. author. RIDLEY, Nicholas, 1500?-55, Eng. bishop and reformer. RIDPATH, John Clark, 1840-...., Am. educator. RIENZI, Nicola Gabrini, 1313?-54, Rom. orator; attempted to restore republic. RILEY, James Whitcomb, 1853-...., Am. poet. RIPON, George Frederick Samuel Robinson, Earl de Grey and Marquis of, 1827-...., Eng. statesman. RISTORI, Adelaide, Marchioness del Grillo, 1821-...., It. actress. RITTENHOUSE, David, 1732-96, Am. astronomer. RIVIÈRE, Briton, 1840-...., Eng. animal painter. RIZZIO, David, 1540-66, It. musician; favorite of Mary Stuart; assassinated. ROBERT (the Devil), ...-1035, duke of Normandy; father of William the Conqueror. ROBERT I. (Robert Bruce), 1274-1329, king of Scotland; II., 1316-90, first of the Stuarts. ROBERTSON, Frederick William, 1816-53, Eng. divine. ROBESPIERRE, Maximilien Joseph Marie Isidore, 1758-94, Fr.

Jacobin communist; ruler during the Reign of Terror; guillotined. Robin Hood, fl. 12th century, Eng. outlaw. Rob Roy (Robert McGregor), 1660?-1735?, Scot. freebooter. Rochambeau, Jean Baptiste Donatien de Vimeur de, Count, 1725-1807, Fr. marshal; general in America in 1780. Rochefort, Victor Henri de Rochefort-Luçay, Comte, 1830-...., Fr. editor and communist. Rochefoucauld, François, Duc de la, 1613-80, Fr. wit and author. Rochejaquelein, Henri de la, Comte, 1772-94, Fr. royalist. Rodney, George Bridges, Lord, 1718-92, Brit. admiral. Roebling, John Augustus, 1806-69, Am. engineer. Rogers, John, 1829-...., Am. sculptor. Rogers, John, 1500?-55, Eng. divine; burned at Smithfield. Rogers, Samuel, 1763-1855, Eng. poet. Roland, Marie Jeanne Philipon, Mme., 1754-93, Fr. Girondist and writer; guillotined. Rollin, Charles, 1661-1741, Fr. historian. Rollo (or Hrolf), 860?-930?, Norwegian viking; first duke of Normandy. Romanoff, Michael Feodorovitch, 1598?-1645, founder of the Russian dynasty. Romero, Matias, 1837-...., Mexican statesman. Romulus, fl. 750 B.C., founder of Rome. Romilly, Sir Samuel, 1757-1818, Eng. statesman. Rooke, Sir George, 1650-1709, Br. admiral. Rosa, Salvator, 1615-73, It. painter. Roscius, Quintus, 61 B.C.-...., Rom. actor. Rosecrans, William Starke, 1819-...., Am. general. Ross, Sir John, 1777-1856, Br. admiral and Arctic navigator. Ross, Sir James Clark, 1800-62, nephew of preceding; Br. Arctic navigator. Rossetti, Dante Gabriel, 1828-82, Eng. painter and poet. Rossini, Gioacchino, 1792-1868, It. composer. Rothschild, Mayer Anselm, 1743-1812, Jewish banker at Frankfort; founder of the house of Rothschild. Rothschild, Nathaniel Mayer de, first Lord Rothschild, 1840-...., Eng. banker. Rouget de l'Isle, Claude Joseph, 1760-1836, Fr. poet and musician. Rouher, Eugène, 1814-84, Fr. politician. Rousseau, Jean Baptiste, 1670-1741, Fr. lyric poet. Rousseau, Jean Jacques, 1712-78, Fr. philosopher and writer. Rubens, Peter Paul, 1577-1640, Flemish painter; chief of the Flemish school. Rubinstein, Anton Gregor, 1829-1894, Russ. composer and pianist. Rückert, Friedrich, 1789-1866, Ger. orientalist and poet. Rudolph I. of Hapsburg, 1218-91, emperor of Germany; founder of the Austrian empire; II., 1552-1612. Rumford, Benjamin Thompson, Count, 1753-1814, Am. natural philosopher in France. Rupert, Prince (Prince Robert of Bavaria), 1619-82, Ger. warrior. Ruskin, John, 1819-...., Eng. writer on art. Russell, John, Earl, 1792-1878, Eng. statesman. Russell, William, Lord, 1639-83, Eng. patriot. Russell, William E., 1857-...., governor of Massachusetts. Rutledge, John, 1739-1800, Am. statesman and jurist. Ruyter, Michael Adrianszoon de, 1607-76, Dutch admiral.

SACHS, Hans, 1494-1576, Ger. cobbler and poet. Sackville, George, Viscount (Lord George Germain), 1716-85, Eng. statesman and general. Sadi-Carnot, Marie François, 1837-1894, president of France. Sadlier, Mary Anne, Mrs., 1820-...., Am. authoress. Saint Clair, Arthur, 1734-1818, Am. general. Sainte-Beuve, Charles Augustin, 1804-69, Fr. poet and critic. Saint-Pierre, Jacques Henri Bernardin de, 1737-1814, Fr. author. Saint Gaudens, Augustus, 1848-...., Ir.-Am. sculptor. Saint Simon, Claude Henri de, Count, 1760-1825, Fr. socialist. Sala, George Augustus Henry, 1828-...., Eng. littérateur. Saladin, 1137-93, sultan of Egypt and Syria; opposed the Crusaders; defeated the Christians at Tiberias. Sale, George, 1680-1736, Eng. orientalist. Salisbury, Robert Arthur Talbot Gascoyne Cecil, Marquis of, 1830-...., Eng. premier. Sallust (Caius Sallustius Crispus), 86-34 B.C., Rom. historian. Saltonstall, Sir Richard, 1586-1658?, Puritan in Massachusetts colony. Salvini, Tommaso, 1829?-...., It. tragedian. Samuel, 1170-1060 B.C., last of the Israelite judges. Sand, George, see Dudevant. Sandeau, Léonard Sylvain Jules, 1811-83, Fr. novelist. Sankey, Ira David, 1840-...., Am. evangelist. Santa Anna (or Ana), Antonio Lopez de, 1798-1876, Mexican general and statesman. Sappho, fl. 600 B.C., Gr. lyric poetess. Sardanapalus, fl. 900 B.C., king of Assyria. Sardou, Victorien, 1831-...., Fr. dramatist. Saul, ...-1055 B.C., first king of Israel. Savage, Richard, 1698-1743, Eng. poet. Savonarola, Girolamo, 1452-1498, It. religious reformer. Saxe, Hermann Maurice, Count of, 1696-1750, marshal of France; native of Saxony. Saxe, John Godfrey, 1816-87, Am. humorous poet. Say, Jean Baptiste Léon, 1826-...., Fr. statesman. Schelling, Friedrich Wilhelm Joseph von, 1775-1854, Ger. philosopher. Schenck, Robert Cumming, 1809-90, Am. general and statesman. Schiller, Johann Christoph Friedrich von, 1759-1805, the most popular of German poets. Schlegel, August Wilhelm von, 1767-1845, Ger. poet, critic and philologist. Schlegel, Karl Wilhelm Friedrich von, brother of A. W., 1772-1829, Ger. philosopher and scholar. Schliemann, Heinrich, 1822-90, Ger. archæologist. Schoeffer, Peter, 1430-1502, one of the inventors of printing; partner of Johann Faust. Schofield, John McAllister, 1831-...., Am. general. Schomberg, Friedrich A. H., Duke of, 1616?-90, Protestant general. Schopenhauer, Arthur, 1788-1860, Ger. pessimist philosopher. Schurz,

Andreas, 1552-1629, Dutch Jesuit scholar. Schubert, Franz, 1797-1828, Ger. composer. Schulte, Johann Friedrich von, 1827-....., Ger. theologian. Schumann, Robert, 1810-56, Ger. composer. Schurz, Carl, 1829-....., Ger.-Am. statesman. Schouvaloff, Peter Andreievitch, Count, 1828-....., Rus. diplomatist. Schuyler, Philip, 1733-1804, Am. general. Schwanthaler, Ludwig Michael, 1802-48, Ger. sculptor. Schwarz, Berthold, fl. 14th century, Ger. monk and alchemist; reputed inventor of gunpowder. Schwatka, Frederick, 1849-92, Am. explorer. Schweinfurth, George August, 1836-....., Ger. traveler. Scipio Africanus Major, Publius Cornelius, 235-184? B.C., Rom. general; invaded Africa and defeated Hannibal. Scipio Æmilianus Africanus Minor, Publius Cornelius, 185?-29 B.C., Rom. general; destroyed Carthage. Scott, Sir Walter, 1771-1832, Scot. novelist and poet. Scott, Winfield, 1786-1866, Am. general. Sebastian, Saint, 255?-88, Rom. soldier and martyr. Sebastian, Dom, 1554-78, king of Portugal. Secchi, Pietro Angelo, 1818-78, It. astronomer. Sedgwick, Catherine Maria, daughter of T. S., 1789-1867, Am. authoress. Sedgwick, John, 1813-64, Am. general. Sedgwick, Theodore, 1746-1813, Am. jurist. Selkirk, Alexander, 1676?-1723, Scot. sailor whose adventures suggested the story of "Robinson Crusoe." Semiramis, fl. 1250 B.C., Assyrian queen; built Babylon and greatly increased her dominions; invaded India, but was defeated. Semmes, Raphael, 1809-77, Confederate naval officer. Seneca, Lucius Annæus, 5?-65, Rom. statesman, moralist and Stoic philosopher. Sennacherib, fl. 700 B.C., Assyrian king. Sergius I., pope, 687-701; II., 844-7; III., 904-12; IV., 1009-12. Servetus, Michael, 1509-53, Sp. theologian. Sesostris (Rameses), fl. 1400 B.C., king of Egypt. Severus, Alexander, 205-35, Rom. emperor. Severus, Lucius Septimius, 146-211, Rom. emperor. Sévigné, Marie de Rabutin-Chantal, Marquise de, 1627-96, Fr. lady, celebrated for her beauty and accomplishments. Seward, William Henry, 1801-72, Am. statesman. Seymour, Horatio, 1811-86, Am. statesman; Democratic nominee for the presidency in 1868. Sforza, Ludovico (Il Moro), 1451-1510, It. general. Shaftesbury, Anthony Ashley Cooper, first Earl of, 1621-83, Eng. statesman. Shaftesbury, Anthony Ashley Cooper, third Earl of, 1671-1713, Eng. philanthropist, author and freethinker. Shaftesbury, Anthony Ashley Cooper, seventh Earl of, 1801-85, Eng. philanthropist. Shakespeare (Shakspere, or Shakespeare), William, 1564-1616, reputed author of the world's greatest dramas; born at Stratford-on-Avon; married Anne Hathaway, 1582; went to London about 1586 and became an actor and owner of a play-house; acquired a competence and retired to his native town about 1610; "Venus and Adonis" and "The Rape of Lucrece," the only works published under his own hand, appeared 1593-4; the first collective edition of the Shakespeare plays appeared in 1623. Shaw, Henry W. (Josh Billings), 1818-85, Am. humorist. Sheil, Richard Lalor, 1793-1851, Ir. orator. Shelley, Percy Bysshe, 1792-1822, Eng. poet. Sheppard, Jack, ...-1724, Eng. burglar; hanged. Sheridan, Philip Henry, 1831-88, Am. general; victorious at Winchester, Cedar Creek and Five Forks; made lieutenant-general, 1869, and promoted to the chief command on retirement of General Sherman, 1883. Sheridan, Richard Brinsley, 1751-1816, Ir. orator and dramatist. Sherman, John, 1823-....., Am. statesman; secretary of the treasury, 1877-81. Sherman, Roger, 1721-93, Am. statesman. Sherman, William Tecumseh, 1820-91, brother of J. S.; Am. general; made the celebrated "March to the Sea;" became general of the army in 1869, retiring in 1883. Shiras, George, Jr., 1832-....., justice U. S. Supreme Court. Sickingen, Franz von, 1481-1523, Ger. Prot. general. Siddons, Sarah (née Kemble), 1755-1831, Eng. actress. Sidney, Algernon, 1622-83, Eng. republican; executed on false charge of complicity in "Rye House Plot." Sidney, Sir Philip, 1554-86, Eng. soldier and poet. Siemens, Ernst Werner, 1816-....., Ger. inventor. Siemens, Charles William, 1823-83, brother of E. W. S., Ger. inventor in London. Sigismund, 1368-1437, Ger. emperor and king of Hungary. Sigismund I., 1466-1548, king of Poland; II., 1518-72. Sigourney, Mrs. Lydia Howard Huntley, 1791-1865, Am. poetess. Silliman, Benjamin, 1779-1864, Am. naturalist. Simeon Stylites, 390?-459, Syrian mystic; lived for forty-six years on the tops of pillars. Simeoni, Giovanni, 1816-92, prefect of Propaganda. Simon, Jules, 1814-....., Fr. statesman. Sixtus I., pope from 117 to 128; II., 257-58, martyr; III., 431-40; IV., 1471-84; V. (Felice Peretti), 1585-90. Skobeleff, Michael, 1843-82, Russian general. Slick, Sam, see Haliburton. Slocum, Henry Wadsworth, 1827-....., Am. general. Smiles, Samuel, 1816-....., Scot. author. Smith, Adam, 1723-90, Scot. political economist. Smith, Gerrit, 1797-1874, Am. philanthropist. Smith, Hoke, 1855-....., secretary of the interior. Smith, Horace (1780?-1849) and James (1775-1839), Eng. poets and humorists; brothers. Smith, John, Captain, 1579-1631, Eng. explorer; founder of Virginia. Smith, Joseph, 1805-44, founder of the Mormon church. Smith, Seba (Maj. Jack Downing), 1792-1868, Am. author. Smith, Sydney, 1771-1845, Eng. divine and essayist.

SMOLLETT, Tobias George, 1721-71, Scot. novelist. SOBIESKI, John, 1629-96, king of Poland and patriot; defeated the Turks and raised the siege of Vienna. SOCRATES, 470?-399 B.C., Gr. philosopher of ethics; teacher of Plato. SOLIMAN II. (the Magnificent), 1494-1566, sultan of Turkey; conquered Persia and part of Hungary. SOLOMON (the Wise), 1033?-975? B.C., king of Israel. SOLON, 638-558? B.C., Athenian law-giver and poet. SOMERS, John, Baron, 1651-1716, Eng. jurist and statesman. SONTAG, Henriette, Countess Rossi, 1806-54, Ger. vocalist. SOPHOCLES, 495-405 B.C., Gr. tragic poet. SOTHERN, Edward Askew, 1830-81, Am. comedian. SOULT, Nicholas Jean de Dieu, 1769-1851, Fr. marshal. SOUTHEY, Robert, 1774-1843, Eng. poet-laureate. SOUTHWORTH, Emma D. E. (Nevitt), 1818-...., Am. novelist. SPARKS, Jared, 1789-1866, Am. historian. SPARTACUS, ...-71 B.C. Thracian gladiator in Rome; inaugurated Servile war. SPEKE, John Hanning, 1827-64, Eng. explorer in Africa. SPENCER, Herbert, 1820-...., Eng. philosopher. SPENSER, Edmund, 1553-99, Eng. poet. SPINNER, Francis E., 1802-90, treasurer of the U.S. SPINOZA, Benedict, 1632-77, Dutch Jewish philosopher and pantheist. SPURGEON, Charles Haddon, 1834-92, Eng. pulpit-orator. SPURZHEIM, Johann Caspar, 1776-1832, Ger. phrenologist. STAËL-HOLSTEIN, Anne Louise Germaine, Baronne de (Mme. de Staël), 1766-1817, Fr. authoress. STANDISH, Miles, 1584-1656, captain of Plymouth colony. STANFORD, Leland, 1824-93, Am. lawyer and philanthropist. STANHOPE, Philip Henry, Earl of, 1805-75, Eng. historian. STANLEY, Arthur Penrhyn (Dean Stanley), 1815-81, Eng. divine and author; dean of Westminster Abbey. STANLEY, Henry Morton (John Rowlands), 1840-...., Am. explorer in Africa; born in Wales. STANTON, Edwin McMasters, 1814-69, Am. statesman; secretary of war in President Lincoln's cabinet. STANTON, Elizabeth Cady, 1815-...., Am. "woman's rights" advocate. STARK, John, 1728-1822, Am. Revolutionary general. STEDMAN, Edmund Clarence, 1833-...., Am. poet. STEELE, Sir Richard, 1671-1729, Br. essayist and dramatist. STEIN, Heinrich Friedrich Karl von, Baron, 1757-1831, Prussian statesman. STEPHEN, Saint, stoned 36?, first Christian martyr. STEPHEN I., pope, 253-7; II., 752; III., 752-7; IV., 768-72; V., 816; VI., 885-91; VII., 896-7; VIII., 928-30; IX., 939-42; X., 1057-8. STEPHEN I. (Saint), 979-1038, king of Hungary. STEPHEN, 1105-54, king of England. STEPHENS, Alexander Hamilton, 1812-83, Am. statesman and writer; the "Nestor of the Confederacy;" born in Georgia; admitted to the bar, 1834; Congress, 1843; opposed the secession of his State; vice-president of the Confederate States; elected to the U. S. Senate from Georgia, but not permitted to take his seat; member of the House of Representatives, however, from 1874 until his death. STEPHENSON, George, 1781-1848, Eng. engineer; inventor of the locomotive engine. STEPHENSON, Robert, 1803-59, son of G. S., Eng. engineer; inventor of tubular bridge. STERLING, John, 1806-44, Br. essayist. STERNE, Laurence, Rev., 1713-68, Ir. humorous writer. STEUBEN, Frederick William Augustus von, Baron, 1730-94, Ger.-Am. general in the Revolutionary war. STEVENS, Thaddeus, 1792-1868, Am. abolitionist. STEVENSON, Adlai E., 1835-...., vice-president. STEVENSON, Robert Louis, 1850-...., Scot. author. STEWART, Alexander Turney, 1803-76, Am. merchant. STEWART, Balfour, 1828-...., Scot. physicist. STOCKTON, Francis Richard, 1834-...., Am. story-writer. STODDARD, Richard Henry, 1825-...., Am. poet. STONE, Lucy, 1818-93, Am. "woman's rights" advocate. STORY, Joseph, 1779-1845, Am. jurist. STORY, William Wetmore, 1819-...., Am. sculptor. STOWE, Mrs. Harriet Elizabeth Beecher, 1812-...., Am. authoress. STRABO, 54 B.C.-21 A.D., Gr. geographer. STRADELLA, Alessandro, 1645-78, It. composer. STRADIVARI, Antonio, 1670-1735, It. violin-maker. STRAFFORD, Thomas Wentworth, Earl of, 1593-1641, Eng. statesman; beheaded. STRAKOSCH, Max, 18..-92, impresario. STRAUSS, Johann, 1804-49, Ger. composer. STRAUSS, Johann, 1825-...., son of preceding, Ger. composer. STRICKLAND, Agnes, 1806-74, Eng. authoress. STUART, Gilbert C., 1756-1828, Am. portrait painter. STUYVESANT, Peter, 1602-82, last Dutch governor of New Netherland (New York). SUE, Marie Joseph Eugene, 1804-57, Fr. novelist. SULLA (or Sylla), Lucius Cornelius, 138-78 B.C., Rom. statesman and general. SULLIVAN, Arthur Seymour, Sir, 1842-...., Eng. composer. SUMNER, Charles, 1811-74, Am. statesman. SURREY, Henry Howard, Earl of, 1516?-47, Eng. poet. SUWAROW, Alexander Vasilievitch, 1729-[illegible], Rus. general. SWEDENBORG, Emanuel, 1688-1772, Sw. theosophist; in his theosophy the central point is the correspondence of the natural and the supernatural. SWIFT, Jonathan, 1667-1745, Ir. divine and satirist. SWINBURNE, Algernon Charles, 1837-...., Eng. poet. SWINTON, William, 1833-...., Scot. author in America. SYLVESTER I. (Saint), pope, 314-35; II., 999-1003; III. (anti-pope), 1046.

TACITUS, Caius Cornelius, 55?-118?, Rom. historian; to him we owe nearly all our knowledge of the early Britains and the Germans. TAGLIONI, Marie, Countess des Voisins, 1804-84, Sw. opera dancer. TAINE, Hippolyte Adolphe, 1828-93, Fr. author.

Talbot, William Henry Fox, 1800-77, Eng. author and discoverer of photography. Talfourd, Sir Thomas Noon, 1795-1854, Eng. author. Talleyrand-Périgord, Charles Maurice de, Prince of Benevento, 1754-1838, Fr. diplomatist. Talmage, Thomas Dewitt, 1832-....., Am. clergyman. Tamerlane (or Timour), 1336-1405, Asiatic conqueror. Tancred, 1078-1112, Norman leader in the first Crusade. Taney, Roger Brooke, 1777-1864, Am. jurist. Tannahill, Robert, 1774-1810, Scot. poet. Tarquinius Superbus (Lucius Tarquinius), ...-495 B.C., last king of Rome. Tasman, Abel Janssen, 1600?-59, Dutch navigator. Tasso, Torquato, 1544-95, It. poet. Tauchnitz, Christian Bernhard, Baron, 1816-....., Ger. publisher. Taylor, Bayard, 1825-78, Am. traveler, novelist, poet and journalist. Taylor, Jeremy, 1613-67, Eng. bishop and author. Taylor, Thomas (the Platonist), 1758-1835, Eng. scholar. Taylor, Tom, 1817-80, Eng. dramatist. Taylor, Zachary, 1784-1850, Am. general and statesman; twelfth president; born in Virginia; entered the army in 1808; served in Seminole and Black Hawk wars; major-general in Mexican war, and won the battles of Resaca de la Palma and Buena Vista; elected president by the Whigs in 1848. Tecumseh, 1770-1813, chief of the Shawnee Indians; defeated by Harrison at Tippecanoe; killed in the battle of the Thames. Tell, Wilhelm, fl. 1300, legendary Swiss hero. Teniers, David (the Younger), 1610-90, Flem. painter. Tennyson, Alfred, Baron, 1809-92, Eng. poet-laureate. Terence (P. Terentius Afer), 195?-160? B.C., Rom. comic poet. Terpander, fl. 675 B.C., Gr. musician. Terry, Alfred Howe, 1827-90, Am. general. Terry, Ellen Alice, 1848-....., Eng. actress. Tertullian, 150?-230?, Latin father of the church. Tesla, Nikola, 1857-....., Austrian electrician; born in Montenegro; came to America, 1883, to study under Edison; his recent experiments and discoveries have led the scientific world to believe that a new volume of electricity is about to be opened; it is believed that he will yet produce light by vibration purely and electrical disturbance without the dynamo. Tetzel, Johann, 1460?-1519, Ger. monk; vendor of indulgences. Tewfik Pasha, 1852-....., khedive of Egypt. Thackeray, William Makepeace, 1811-63, Eng. novelist. Thalberg, Sigismond, 1812-71, Swiss pianist. Thales, 636?-546 B.C., Gr. sage and philosopher. Thaxter, Celia, 1836-....., Am. poet. Themistocles, 514?-449? B.C., Athenian general and statesman. Theocritus, fl. 275?, Gr. pastoral poet. Theodora, ...-548, empress of the East; wife of Justinian. Theodore, 1818?-68, king of Abyssinia. Theodoric (the Great), 455-526, king of the Ostrogoths. Theodosius, Flavius (the Great), 346?-395, Rom. emperor. Theophrastus, 372?-287? B.C., Gr. philosopher and moralist. Thierry, Jacques N. Augustin, 1795-1856, Fr. historian. Thiers, Louis Adolphe, 1797-1877, Fr. statesman and historian. Thomas, George H., 1816-70, Am. Federal general; won the battles of Chickamauga and Nashville. Thomas, Theodore, 1835-....., Am. musical director; born in Hanover. Thomson, James, 1700-48, Scot. poet. Thoreau, Henry D., 1817-62, Am. author. Thorwaldsen, Albert B., 1770-1844, Danish sculptor. Thucydides, 471-400 B.C., greatest of Greek historians. Tiberius, 42 B.C.-37 A.D., Rom. emperor. Tilden, Samuel Jones, 1814-86, Am. statesman; governor of New York; Democratic candidate for presidency, 1876. Tillman, B. R., 1847-....., governor of S. C. Tilly, Johann Tserklaes von, Count, 1559-1632, Ger. general in Thirty Years' War; fell at the battle of the Lech. Timoleon, 395-337 B.C., Corinthian general. Tindal, Matthew, 1657?-1733, Eng. theological writer. Tintoretto, Il (Giacomo Robusti), 1512-94, It. painter. Titcomb, Timothy, pen name of J. G. Holland. Titian (Tiziano Vecellio), 1477-1576, the greatest of Venetian painters. Titjens (or Tietjens), Theresa, 1834-77, Ger. vocalist. Titus, 40-81, Rom. emperor. Tobin, John, 1770-1804, Eng. dramatist. Tocqueville, Alexis Charles Henri Clerel de, 1805-59, Fr. statesman and author. Todleben, Franz Eduard, 1818-84, Russian general. Tolstoi, Count Lyof, ..., Russian novelist and reformer. Tone, Theobald Wolfe, 1763-98, Ir. patriot; founder of the United Irishmen. Tooke, John Horne, 1736-1812, Eng. philologist and radical. Torquemada, Tomas de, 1420-98, Sp. Dominican monk; inquisitor-general. Torricelli, Evangelista, 1608-47, It. physicist. Toussaint l'Ouverture, Francois Dominique, 1743-1803, negro leader of the Haytian rebellion. Trajan, 52-117, Rom. emperor. Tramp, Marse, Am. pen name of Henry Watterson. Trollope, Anthony, 1815-82, Eng. novelist. Tromp, Martin Harpertzoon van, 1597-1653, Dutch admiral. Tromp, Cornelis van, 1629-91, Dutch admiral. Trowbridge, John Townsend, 1827-....., Am. novelist and poet. Trumbull, John, 1750-1831, Am. poet and satirist. Trumbull, John, 1756-1843, Am. painter. Trumbull, Jonathan, 1710-1809, Am. statesman. Tupper, Martin Farquhar, 1810-89, Eng. poet and author. Turenne, Henri de la Tour d'Auvergne, Vicomte de, 1611-75, Fr. general. Turgeneff, Ivan Sergyevich, 1818-83, Russian novelist. Turner, Joseph Mallord William, 1775-1851, Eng. landscape painter. Turpin, Dick, 1711-39, Eng. highwayman. Tweed, William Marcy (Boss Tweed), 1823-78,

Am. politician and ambassador; mayor of New York city. Tyler, John, 1790-1862, tenth president of the United States; born in Va.; practiced law; Congress, 1816-21; governor of Virginia, 1825; senator, 1827; sympathized with the nullifiers and opposed Jackson; resigned, 1836; elected vice-president on Whig ticket, 1840; succeeded Harrison in 1841. Tyler, Wat, ...-1381, Eng. rebel; leader of rebellion against capitation tax. Tyndall, John, 1820-1893, Ir. scientist.

UHLAND, Johann Ludwig, 1787-1862, Ger. lyric poet. Ulloa, Antonio de, 1716-95, Sp. mathematician and naval officer; governor of Louisiana. Ulfilas (or Ulphilas), 313-83, the apostle of the Goths; translated the Scriptures into Gothic. Ulpianus, Domitius, ...-228, Rom. jurist. Unger, Johann Friedrich, 1750-1813, Ger. printer and engraver. Urban I., pope, 222-30, martyr; II., 1088-99, organized the first crusade; III., 1185-7; IV., 1261-4; V., 1362-70; VI., 1378-89; VII., 1590; VIII., 1623-44. Ure, Andrew, 1778-1857, Scot. chemist and physician. Urquhart, David, 1805-77, Scot. writer and politician. Ussher, James, 1580-1656, Ir. prelate and scholar.

VALENS, Flavius, 328?-78, emperor of the East. Valentinianus I. (Flavius), 321-75, Rom. emperor; II. (Flavius), 371-92; III. (Placidius), 419-55. Valerian (Publius Licinius Valerianus), ...-268?, Rom. emperor. Van Buren, Martin, 1782-1862, eighth president of the United States; enrolled at the bar in New York in 1803, and elected to the State Senate; state attorney-general, 1815; leader of the "Albany Regency;" U. S. senator, 1821; governor, 1828; secretary of state, 1829-31; vice-president, 1833-7; president, 1837-41. Vancouver, George, 1758?-98, Eng. navigator. Vanderbilt, Cornelius, 1794-1877, Am. capitalist. Vandyke (or Van Dyck), Sir Anthony, 1599-1641, Flemish painter; resided in England for several years before his death, where he became the most popular artist of his time. Vane, Sir Henry, 1612-62, Eng. republican statesman. Vanloo, Charles André, 1705-65, Fr. painter. Vanloo, Jean Baptiste, 1684-1745, Fr. painter. Van Rensselaer, Stephen (the Patroon), 1764-1839, Am. statesman and landholder. Varus, Publius Quintilius, fl. 7, Rom. general; defeated by Arminius. Vassar, Matthew, 1792-1868, founder of Vassar College. Vauban, Sébastien le Prestre, Seigneur de, 1633-1707, Fr. military engineer. Vedder, Elihu, 1836-...., Am. artist. Velasquez, Don Diego Rodriguez de Silva y, 1599-1660, Sp. painter. Velde, Willem van der (the Elder), 1610-93, Dutch marine painter. Velde, Willem van der (the Younger), 1633-1707, Dutch marine painter. Vendome, Louis Joseph, Duc de, 1654-1712, Fr. general. Verboeckhoven, Eugene Joseph, 1799-1881, Belgian painter. Verdi, Giuseppe, 1814-...., It. composer. Verne, Jules, 1828-...., Fr. author. Vernet, Antoine Charles Horace, 1758-1836, Fr. painter. Vernon, Edward, 1684-1757, Eng. admiral. Vespasianus, Titus Flavius, 9-79, Rom. emperor. Vespucci, Amerigo (Americus Vespucius), 1451-1512, It. navigator and astronomer. Viaud, Jean ("Pierre Loti"), 1850-...., Fr. writer. Victor, Claude Perrin, Duke of Belluno, 1764-1841, Fr. marshal. Victor I., pope, 185-198; II., 1055-7; III., 1086-7; IV. (anti-pope), recognized by Frederick I. in 1159, died 1164. Victor Emmanuel I., 1759-1824, king of Sardinia; II., 1820-78, first king of Italy; restored Italian unity. Victoria (Victoria Alexandrina), 1819-...., queen of Great Britain and empress of India. Vidocq, Eugene François, 1775-1860, Fr. detective. Villard, Henry, 1835-...., Ger.-Am. financier. Villars, Claude Louis Hector de, Duc, 1653-1734, Fr. general. Vincent de Paul, Saint, 1576-1660, Fr. priest and reformer. Vincent, John Heyl, 1832-...., Am. Methodist Episcopal bishop and educator. Vinci, Leonardo da, 1452-1519, Florentine painter. Virchow, Rudolf, 1821-...., Ger. pathologist. Virgil (or Vergil), (Publius Virgilius Maro), 70-19 B.C., Latin poet. Volta, Alessandro, 1745-1827, It. inventor of voltaic pile. Voltaire, François Marie Arouet de, 1694-1778, Fr. author, poet, wit, dramatist, historian, philosopher and skeptic, and the greatest critic of modern times; the son of a notary; imprisoned in the Bastile in 1716 on an unfounded suspicion of being the author of a libel on the regent, and there produced "Œdipe" and wrote part of the "Henriade;" in England, 1726-9, passing much time in the society of Bolingbroke; passed the years 1750-3 with Frederick the Great. Voorhees, Daniel W., 1827-...., Am. orator and statesman. Vortigern, ...-485, king of the Britons.

WADDINGTON, William Henry, 1826-...., Fr. statesman and archæologist, of Eng. descent. Wagner, Richard, 1813-83, Ger. composer, poet and critic. Waite, Davis H., 1825-...., governor of Colorado. Waite, Morrison Remick, 1816-88, Am. chief justice. Waldemar I. (the Great), 1131-81, king of Denmark. Walker, John, 1732-1807, Eng. lexicographer. Wallace, Sir William, 1270?-1305, Scot. general and patriot; defeated by Edward I. of England; betrayed and executed. Wallace, William Vincent, 1815-65, Ir. composer. Wallenstein, Albrecht Wenzel Eusebius von, Count, 1583-1634, Austrian general;

hero of one of Schiller's dramas; entered the imperial army at the beginning of the Thirty Years' war; raised an army at his own expense in 1625, invading Denmark; banished from court by Emperor Ferdinand, but recalled on the death of Marshal Tilly; defeated by Gustavus Adolphus at Lützen in 1632, but gained several victories in Silesia; again lost the emperor's favor, being charged with aspirations to the throne of Bohemia, was deprived of his command and assassinated. Walpole, Horace, Earl of Orford, 1717-97, Eng. author and wit. Walther von der Vogelweide, 1170?-1230?, greatest of Ger. minnesingers. Walton, Izaak, 1593-1683, Eng. writer; "The Complete Angler." Warbeck, Perkin, ...-1499, Eng. pretender; hanged. Ward, Artemas, 1727-1800, Am. general. Ward, Artemus, see Browne. Warner, Charles Dudley, 1829-...., Am. humorist. Warner, Susan (Elizabeth Wetherell), 1818-85, Am. authoress. Warren, Joseph, 1741-75, Am. physician; Revolutionary general and patriot; fell at Bunker Hill. Warren, Samuel, 1807-77, Eng. author. Warwick, Richard Neville, Earl of (the king-maker), 1420?-71, Eng. warrior; set up and deposed Edward IV. Washington, George, 1732-1799, commander-in-chief in the American Revolution and first president of the United States; "the father of his country;" born in Virginia; aide-de-camp to Braddock in the Indian campaign of 1755; married Martha Custis, 1759; chosen to Congress, 1774; appointed commander-in-chief, 1775; president, 1789-97. Watt, James, 1736-1819, Scot. engineer and inventor; improved and completed the steam-engine; also credited with the discovery of the composition of water. Watteau, Jean-Antoine, 1684-1721, Fr. painter. Watterson, Henry, 1840-...., Am. journalist. Watts, Isaac, 1674-1748, Eng. Dissenting minister and sacred poet. Wayne, Anthony, 1745-96, Am. Revolutionary general. Weber, Karl Maria Friedrich Ernst von, Baron, 1786-1826, Ger. composer. Webster, Daniel, 1782-1852, Am. lawyer, orator and statesman; "the expounder of the Constitution;" born in N. H.; Congress, 1812-16, 1822-8; Senate, 1828-41; secretary of state; re-entered Senate in 1844; again became secretary of state in 1850; nominated for the presidency in 1836, but defeated; candidate for the Whig nomination in 1848, but defeated by Taylor, whom he supported; Webster's reply to Hayne, of South Carolina, is considered the greatest speech ever made in Congress. Webster, Noah, 1758-1843, Am. lexicographer. Wedgwood, Josiah, 1730-95, Eng. potter. Weed, Thurlow, 1797-1882, Am. journalist. Wellington, Arthur Wellesley, first Duke of, 1769-1852, greatest of Br. generals; gained great distinction in India, in the war against the Mahrattas; major-general, 1802; Parliament, 1806; secretary for Ireland, 1807; defeated the Danes at Kioge, and was given command of an army sent to Spain against the French, 1808; triumphantly entered Madrid, 1812; defeated Jourdan and Soult, 1813; invaded France and gained numerous victories; defeated Napoleon at Waterloo, 1815; was afterward prime minister and minister of foreign affairs. Wells, Horace, 1815-48, Am. dentist. (Anæsthesia.) Wells, Samuel Roberts, 1820-75, Am. phrenologist. Wenceslaus (or Wenzel), 1361-1419, emperor of Germany and king of Bohemia. Wesley, Charles, 1708-88, Eng. Methodist divine and hymn-writer. Wesley, John, 1703-91, brother of C. W.; Eng. founder of Methodism, "the religion of feeling." West, Benjamin, 1738-1820, Am. painter in England. Wharton, Francis, 1820-89, Am. jurist and theologian. Wharton, Henry, 1664-95, Eng. ecclesiastical writer. Whately, Richard, 1787-1863, Eng. prelate and author. Wheeler, William Almon, 1819-87, Am. statesman; vice-president. Whistler, James Abbott MacNeal, 1834-...., Am. artist in England. White, Andrew Dickson, 1832-...., Am. scholar. White, Henry Kirke, 1785-1806, Eng. religious poet. White, Joseph Blanco, 1775-1841, Eng. author. White, Richard Grant, 1822-85, Am. author. Whitefield, George, 1714-70, Eng. preacher; founder of Calvinistic Methodists. Whitman, Walt, 1819-92, Am. poet. Whitney, Eli, 1765-1825, Am. inventor of the cotton-gin. Whittier, John Greenleaf, 1807-92, Am. poet; member of the Society of Friends. Wieland, Christoph Martin, 1733-1813, Ger. poet. Wilberforce, William, 1759-1833, Eng. philanthropist and statesman; secured the abolition of the slave trade. Wilcox, Ella Wheeler, 1845-...., Am. authoress. Willard, Frances Elizabeth, 1839-...., Am. temperance reformer. William I. (the Conqueror), 1027-87, king of England; duke of Normandy; conquered England; II. (Rufus), 1056-1100; III. (William Henry of Nassau, prince of Orange), 1650-1702, won battle of the Boyne; IV., 1765-1837, uncle of Queen Victoria. William I., 1772-1843, king of the Netherlands; II., 1792-1849; III., 1817-90. William I., 1797-1888, king of Prussia and emperor of Germany; II., 1859-..... William of Nassau, see Orange. Williams, Roger, 1599-1683, Eng. Puritan minister; founder of Rhode Island colony; born in Wales. Willis, Nathaniel Parker, 1806-67, Am. journalist and poet. Wilmot, David, 1814-68, Am. statesman. (Wilmot Proviso.) Wilson, Alexander, 1766-1813, Scot.-Am. ornithologist. Wilson, Henry (original name, Jeremiah Jones

Colbath), 1812-75, Am. politician; eighteenth vice-president. Wilson, John (Christopher North), 1785-1854, Scot. writer. Windom, William, 1827-91, secretary of U. S. treasury. Wiseman, Nicholas, 1802-65, Eng. cardinal. Witikind, ...-807, Saxon warrior; conquered by Charlemagne. Wolcott, John, 1738-1819, Eng. satirist. Wolfe, Charles, 1791-1823, Ir. poet. Wolfe, James, 1726-59, Eng. general; fell at Quebec. Wolseley, Garnet Joseph, Sir, 1833-...., Br. general. Wolsey, Thomas, 1471-1530, Eng. cardinal and statesman; prime minister of Henry VIII.; deposed, 1529. Wood, Mrs. Henry, 1820-87, Eng. novelist. Woodworth, Samuel, 1785-1842, Am. poet. Worcester, Edward Somerset, Marquis of, 1601?-67, Eng. nobleman; one of the inventors of the steam-engine. Worcester, Joseph Emerson, 1784-1865, Am. lexicographer. Wordsworth, William, 1770-1850, Eng. poet. Wrangel, Karl Gustaf von, Count, 1613-76, Sw. general. Wrangell, Ferdinand Petrovitch von, Baron, 1795?-1870, Russian explorer. Wren, Sir Christopher, 1632-1723, Eng. architect. (St. Paul's Cathedral, London.) Wright, Silas, 1795-1847, Am. statesman. Wycherley, William, 1640?-1715, Eng. comedy writer. Wycliffe (or Wickliffe), John de, 1324?-84, Eng. reformer.

XANTIPPE, the wife of Socrates, notorious for bad temper, but credited by her husband with many domestic virtues. Xavier, Francis, Saint, 1506-52, Sp. Jesuit missionary to India and Japan. Xenocrates, 396-314 B.C., Gr. philosopher. Xenophanes, 600?-500? B.C., Gr. philosopher. Xenophon, 445?-355? B.C., Athenian historian and general. Xerez, Francisco de, 1504?-70, Sp. historian with Pizarro. Xerxes (the Great), ...-465 B.C., king of Persia; invaded Greece, but defeated at Salamis. Ximenes de Cisneros, Francisco (Cardinal Ximenes), 1436-1517, Sp. prelate and statesman; published Polyglot Bible. Ximenez de Quesada, Gonzalo, 1495?-1546, Sp. explorer.

YALE, Elihu, 1648-1721, patron of Yale College. Yancey, William Lowndes, 1814-63, Am. politician. Yonge, Charlotte Mary, 1823-...., Eng. authoress. York, Edmund Plantagenet, first Duke of, 1341-1402, founder of the house of York. Young, Arthur, 1741-1820, Eng. agricultural writer. Young, Arthur H. (Art Young), 1866-...., Am. cartoonist. Young, Brigham, 1801-77, president of the Mormon church. Young, Charles Augustus, 1834-...., Am. astronomer. Young, Edward, 1684-1765, Eng. poet. Yves, Saint, 1253-1303, Fr. monk and jurist; patron of lawyers.

ZALEUCUS, fl. 7th century B.C., Gr. legislator and reformer; first to make a written code of laws. Zamoyski, John Sarius, 1541-1605, Polish general, statesman and scholar. Zarate, Agustin de, 1490?-1560, Sp. historian. Zechariah, fl. 6th century B.C., Hebrew prophet. Zelotti, Battista, 1532-92, It. painter. Zeno (or Zenon), 355?-263? B.C., Gr. philosopher; founder of Stoic school. Zeno (or Zenon) of Elea, 490-...., Gr. philosopher. Zenobia, Septima, ...-275, queen of Palmyra. Zephaniah, Hebrew prophet; flourished in the reign of Josiah. Zeuxis, 464?-396, Gr. painter. Zimmermann, Johann Georg von, 1728-95, Swiss physician and philosopher. Zinzendorf, Nicolaus Ludwig von, Count, 1700-60, Ger. theologian. Ziska, John, of Trocznow, 1360-1424, Bohemian general and leader of the Hussites. Zoega, Georg, 1755-1809, Danish archaeologist. Zola, Emile, 1840-...., Fr. novelist. Zollicoffer, Felix K., 1812-62, Am. general. Zoroaster, fl. 500 B.C., Persian philosopher and founder of the Magian religion. Zschokke, Johann Heinrich Daniel, 1771-1848, Ger. author. Zwingli, Ulrich, 1484-1531, Swiss reformer; killed in battle.

The Suez Canal is the most important shipping enterprise known to history. It enables two ships to do the work of three in trading between Europe and the East. From London to Bombay, by way of the Cape, is 10,595 miles; by the canal, 6,330. It cost £17,000,000, was begun in 1858 and finished in 1869. The length is 92 miles, depth 26 feet; the tolls average £800 per vessel, or 8 shillings per ton of net tonnage. The estimated saving to commerce is £3,000,000 a year. In 1889 3,425 vessels went through, the mean time of passing being twenty-seven hours. Electric lights are now used to enable ships to pass at night as readily as in the daytime.

The most singular ship in the world is the Polyphemus, of the British navy. It is simply a long steel tube, deeply buried in the water, the deck rising only four feet above the sea. It carries no masts or sails, and is used as a ram and torpedo-boat.

One towboat on the Mississippi, in a good stage of water, can take from St. Louis to New Orleans a tow carrying 10,000 tons of grain, a quantity that would require fifty railroad trains of ten cars each.

It has been calculated that the salary and expense bills of the traveling salesmen of the United States in a single year would more than pay off the entire national debt.

History at a Glance

HISTORICAL, BIOGRAPHICAL AND STATISTICAL DIAGRAMS, SUGGESTING DATES, NAMES AND EVENTS, AND DESIGNED FOR READY REFERENCE, AND TO AID THE MEMORY

B.C.	FROM THE DELUGE TO THE TIME OF CYRUS
2350	**The Deluge.** [illegible] dynasty founded in China. [illegible]. Birth of Abraham. [illegible]. Call of Abraham. [illegible]. Isaac born. [illegible]. Jacob and Esau born. [illegible]. [illegible] alphabet invented. [illegible]. Joseph sold into Egypt. [illegible]. Jacob removes into Egypt. [illegible]. [illegible], King of Egypt. [illegible]. [illegible], King of Egypt. [illegible]. Beginning of the chronology of the Arundelian marbles, brought to England A. D. [illegible]. [illegible]. Moses born. [illegible]. Aaron born. [illegible]. **The Exodus. The Law given from Sinai.** [illegible]. Moses and Aaron die. [illegible]. Joshua leads the Israelites into Canaan.

B.C.	The Hebrews	Egypt	Assyria	Greece, etc.
		The Pharaohs.		
1300				
1200				
1100		[illegible]. Cheops builds the great Pyramid.		
1000		[illegible]. Shishak. [illegible]. [illegible] Jerusalem and plunders the Temple.		
900				
800				

B.C.	Judah	Israel	Assyria	Egypt	Greece, Rome
				[illegible]. Sennacherib's invasion.	
700					
				[illegible]. Necho II. loses 120,000 men trying to cut canal to Red Sea. [illegible]. Nebuchadnezzar defeats Necho.	
600					
				[illegible]. Apries, King.	
				[illegible]. Conquered and devastated by Nebuchadnezzar.	
				Amasis. Psammenit.	
				[illegible]. Conquered by Cambyses, son of Cyrus.	

FROM CYRUS TO ALEXANDER

B.C.	Persia	Greece	Macedonia	Rome
			[illegible]. Subdued by Darius of Persia.	
500				
400				

[illegible]	Persia	Greece	Macedonia	Rome
B.C.			93. Amyntas.	
			[illegible]. Philip II.	
			38. Athenians and Thebans defeated at Chaeronea.	
			36. Murder of Philip. Accession of Alexander the Great.	
			34. Battle of the Granicus.	
		33. Battle of Issus.		
		32. Capture of Damascus. Siege of Tyre.		
	32. Alexander captures Tyre and conquers Egypt. Alexandria founded.			
	31. Battle of Arbela and subjugation of Persia.			
	30. Darius assassinated.			
	27. Alexander invades India.			
	23. Alexander dies at Babylon.			

FROM ALEXANDER TO AUGUSTUS

B.C.	Egypt	Syria	Greece	Macedonia	Rome
	23. Ptolemy I. 01. Battle of Ipsus. Final division of Alexander's dominions.				
300					
	Ptolemy Lagos. 85. Ptolemy Philadelphus.			[illegible]. Philip IV.	
				86. Lysimachus, King of Thrace, subjects Macedonia.	
	47. Ptolemy Euergetes.				
	Egyptians conquer Syria.				
	21. Ptolemy Philopator.			20. Philip V.	
				11. War with Rome.	
200	4. Ptolemy Epiphanes.				

[illegible]	Egypt	Judea	Syria	Greece	Macedonia	Rome
B. C.	[illegible] Ptolemy Philometor.	[illegible]			[illegible] Second war with Rome.	
					[illegible] Perseus.	
					[illegible] Third war with Rome.	
					[illegible] Battle of Pydna.	
					Macedonia made a Roman province.	
		[illegible] subdued by [illegible]				
	[illegible] Ptolemy Physcon.	[illegible] John Hyrcanus.		[illegible] Corinth taken by Mummius.		
	[illegible] Ptolemy Lathyrus.					
100						
	Ptolemy Alexander.					
	[illegible] Berenice.					
	[illegible] Murder of Pompey.					
	[illegible] Cleopatra.					
	[illegible] Death of Antony and Cleopatra. Egypt subdued by Rome.					
B. C.						

	FROM AUGUSTUS TO CHARLEMAGNE
A. D.	
100	
200	
300	

A.D.	The Western Empire	The Eastern Empire
300		76. Valens allows the [illegible] to settle in Thrace. 78. Constantinople threatened by the Goths. 95. Arcadius, Emperor of the East. The Huns invade the Eastern provinces.
400	86. The Franks in Gaul. 89. The Ostrogoths in Italy.	8. Theodosius II. 28. Nestor, Patriarch of Constantinople. 29. Vandals, under Genseric, invade Africa. 33. Attila, King of the Huns. 39. The Vandals surprise Carthage. 47. Attila ravages the empire and exacts tribute. 50. Marcian. 65. Great fire at Constantinople.
500	8. Kingdom of the **Franks** founded by Clovis. 30. Belisarius in Italy. 52. Ostrogoths expelled from Italy. 68. The Lombards overrun Italy.	2. The empire ravaged by the Persians. 29. The Justinian code published. 81. The Slavonians in Thrace.
600	28. Dagobert, King of France. 56. Clovis II., King of France. 62. Lombards defeat Constans II. in Italy. 89. Cadwallader, last King of the Britons. 97. Anafesto, Doge of Venice.	11. Mahomet spreads his doctrines. 15. Persians ravage Syria and Palestine. 22. The Hegira. 40. The Saracens invade Egypt. 73. Siege of Constantinople. 97. Saracens conquer Northern Africa.
700	11. Saracens invade Spain. 14. Charles Martel, Duke of France. 32. **Battle of Tours.** Saracens defeated by the Franks under Charles Martel. 52. Pepin the Short, King of France. 68. Succeeded by his sons, Charlemagne and Carloman. 72-85. Charlemagne conquers the Saxons. 74. Charlemagne conquers the Lombards. 87. The Danes in England. 91-96. Charlemagne establishes the margraviate of Austria.	20. The Saracens defeated at Constantinople. 26. Iconoclasts burn and destroy works of art.
800	[illegible]. **Charlemagne crowned Emperor of the West** by Pope Leo III.	[illegible] Haroun al Raschid, Caliph of Arabia.

VI.	FROM CHARLEMAGNE TO NAPOLEON			
A. D.	**England**	**France**	**Germany**	**Eastern Empire**
800	**The Anglo-Saxons** 27. Egbert, King. 71. Alfred the Great.	40. Charles the Bald. 61. Pillaged by Northmen.		11. Bulgarians defeat the Greek Emperor.
900	25. Athelstan. 37. Defeats Danes, Scots, etc. 79. Edward the Martyr assassinated.	12. Rollo, Duke of Normandy. **Capetian Dynasty** 87. Hugh Capet, King. 96. Paris made capital.		70. John Zimisces.
1000	Ethelred. 16. Edmund. **The Danes** 17. Canute sole ruler. 36. Canute II. 42. Saxons restored. Edward the Confessor. 66. Battle of Hastings. **The Normans** William I. (the Conqueror.) 87. William II.	1000. Robert II. 31. Henry I. 60. Philip I. 95. War with England.		54. Schism of Greek Church 81. Alexius Comnenus. 96. Desperate reception of Crusaders.
1100	Henry I. 35. Stephen. **The Plantagenets** 54. Henry II. 71. Invasion of Ireland. 89. Richard Coeur de Lion 99. John Lackland.	8. Louis the Fat. 37. Louis VII. 80. Philip II.		43. Manuel Comnenus. 47. Treachery to German Crusaders.
1200	15. **Magna Charta** signed. 16. Henry III. 63. War of the Barons. 65. Barons defeated. 72. Edward I. 83. Conquest of Wales. 97. Sir Wm. Wallace in Scotland.	14. Louis X. Battle of Bouvines. 16. Philip V. 22. Charles IV. **House of Valois** 28. Philip VI. 64. Charles V. 80. Charles VI.		4. Baldwin I. 6. Peter de Courtenay 19. Robert de Courtenay 28. Baldwin II. 61. Michael Palæologus.
1300	7. Edward II. 14. Battle of Bannockburn. 27. Edward III. 46. Battle of Cressy. 56. Battle of Poictiers. 77. Richard II. **H. of Lancaster** 99. Henry IV.	14. Louis X. 16. Philip V. 22. Charles IV. **House of Valois** 28. Philip VI. 50. John II. 64. Charles V. 80. Charles VI.		28. Andronicus III. 41. John Palæologus. 60. The Turks in Adrianople. 91. Manuel Palæologus.
1400	13. Henry V. War with France. 15. Battle of Agincourt. 22. Henry VI. 55. War of the Roses. **House of York** 61. Edward IV. 83. Richard V. **House of Tudor** 85. Henry VII.	22. Charles VII. 29. Joan of Arc raises siege of Orleans. 51. English expelled. 61. Louis XI. 83. Charles VIII. **Valois-Orleans.** 98. Louis XII.		25. John Palæologus II. 48. Constantine Palæologus. 53. Amurath captures Constantinople. **Turkey** 56. Turks defeated at Belgrade.

VII — FROM CHARLEMAGNE TO NAPOLEON

A.D.	Spain	Italy	Russia	Scandinavia	Contemporary
800	[illegible] Kingdom of Navarre founded by Basque kings.	43. Invaded by the Saracens.		800-1000, Viking period. Norwegians colonize Iceland.	[illegible] Haroun al Raschid, Caliph of Arabia, dies.
900		[illegible] becomes rich and powerful.		Eric. [illegible]. Olaf, first Christian King of Sweden.	
1000	[illegible]. Sancho II., King of Castile. [illegible]. Ramiro I., King of Aragon. [illegible]. Moors seize [illegible]. [illegible]. Henry of Besançon takes Portugal from Saracens.	16-71. Saracens expelled by the Normans. 73-85. Gregory VII. establishes universal sovereignty of Papacy.		2. Massacre of Danes by Ethelred of Eng. 3. Avenged by Sweyn, King of Denmark. 13. Sweyn conquers England. 80. Inge the Elder King of Sweden.	1. The Northmen discover America. 55. Turks take Jerusalem. 96. First Crusade. 98. Crusaders take Antioch. 99. Crusaders take Jerusalem.
1100	[illegible] Exploits of the Cid Ruy Diaz. [illegible]-1144. Dynasty of the Almoravides at Cordova. [illegible]. Alphonso of Leon defeats the Moors in several battles.	10. Rise of Lombard cities. 30. The glory of Venice. 54. Barbarossa. [illegible]. Wars of the Guelphs and Ghibellines. 76. Barbarossa defeated at Legnano. 83. Peace of Constance.		[illegible]. Eric Edwardson.	4. Crusaders take Acre. 46. Second Crusade. 71. Saladin's conquest in Asia. 89. Third Crusade. 94. Fourth Crusade.
1200	[illegible]-48. Ferdinand III. takes Cordova, Toledo, etc., from the Moors. 38. Moors found Granada. 74. Crown of Navarre passes to France.	20-50. Wars of Frederick II. 77. The Visconti at Milan. 82. The Sicilian Vespers. French expelled from Sicily.		44. Danes invade Russia; defeated by Alexander Nevski. 79. Magnus. 90. Birger.	1200. Fifth Crusade. 17. Sixth Crusade. 18. Genghis Khan, the Mogul, conquers Asia. 69. Eighth and last Crusade. 99. Osman I., Turkish empire.
1300	[illegible]. King of Granada brings 200,000 Moors from Africa. 40. Alphonso XI. of Castile defeats Moors at Tarifa.	8. Pope Clement V. removes to Avignon. 33. First Doge of Genoa appointed. 47. Rienzi [illegible] Rome. 54. Death of Rienzi.		89. Margaret offered the Swedish Crown. 97. Union of Calmar: Sweden, Norway and Denmark, Eric King.	12. Knights Templars suppressed. 96. Battle of Nicopolis. Christians defeated.
1400	69. Ferdinand II. of Aragon marries Isabella of Leon and Castile. 80-[illegible] Inquisition established. [illegible]-[illegible]. Jews persecuted. [illegible]. Ferdinand takes Granada.	95. Charles VIII. conquers Naples. 96. Charles loses Naples. 99. Louis XII., aided by Venice, conquers Milan, but loses and holds it [illegible].		14. War with Schleswig. 35. Revolt of peasantry. 48. [illegible]. 70. Sten Sture.	2. Battle of Angora. Tamerlane captures Bajazet. 28. Amurath II. consolidates Ottoman Empire. 48. Hungarians defeat Turks at [illegible]. 92. Columbus discovers America. 97. Cabot discovers Newfoundland.

England	France	Germany	America
9. Henry VIII. 13. Battle of Flodden. 15. Wolsey. 20. Field of the Cloth of Gold. 36. Ann Boleyn beheaded. 47. Edward VI. 53. Mary. 54. Marries Philip of Spain. 58. Elizabeth. 87. Mary of Scots beheaded. 88. Spanish Armada.	13. English invasion. 15. Francis I. 25. Battle of Pavia. 47. Henry II. 59. Francis II. 60. Huguenot War. 72. Massacre of St. Bartholomew. 74. Henry III. **House of Bourbon** 89. Henry IV. of Navarre.	[illegible] Luther. [illegible] Charles V. [illegible] Diet of Worms. [illegible] Augsburg Confes[illegible] [illegible] Death of John of Leyden. [illegible] Charles V. abdicat[illegible] Ferdinand I. [illegible] Maximilian II. [illegible] Rudolph II.	12. Florida discovered by Ponce de Leon. 13. Balboa discovers the Pacific Ocean. 21. Cortez conquers Mexico. 41. De Soto discovers the Mississippi. 84. First American settlement founded by Walter Raleigh.
House of Stuart 3. James I. 25. Charles I. 49. **Commonwealth** Oliver Cromwell. 60. Stuarts restored. Charles II. 66. Great London fire. 79. Habeas Corpus Act. 85. James II. 88. William and Mary. 90. Battle of the Boyne.	10. Louis XIII. 24. Richelieu. 27. Siege of Rochelle. 43. Louis XIV. 48. Wars of the Fronde. 72. Holland invaded. 85. Edict of Nantes revoked. 89. War with England. 97. Peace of Ryswick.	[illegible] Matthias. [illegible] Thirty Years' Wa[illegible] [illegible] Ferdinand II. [illegible] Battle of Prague. [illegible] Gustavus Adolph[illegible] [illegible] Sweden invades [illegible]many. [illegible] Battle of Lutzen. [illegible] of Gustavus [illegible]	7. Jamestown settlement. 14. New Amsterdam settled. 20. Pilgrims land at Plymouth Rock. 82. William Penn.
2. Anne. **House of Hanover** 14. George I. 27. George II. 39. War with Spain. 45. Stuart troubles in Scotland. Battle of Culloden. 56. War with France. 60. George III. 75. War with American Colonies. 98. Nelson destroys French fleet near Alexandria.	4. Defeated by Marlborough at Blenheim. 13. Peace of Utrecht. 15. Louis XV. 16. Speculation era. [illegible] Law. 45. Battle of Fontenoy. 46. Victories of Marshal Saxe. 48. Peace of Aix-la-Chapelle. 74. Louis XVI. 78. Aids America. 87. Assembly of Notables. 89. States General. 89. Revolution. 93. Reign of Terror. Louis beheaded. **Republic** 99. Napoleon, First Consul.		33. Oglethorpe founds Savannah. 59. Quebec captured by the English. 63. Peace of Paris. France cedes Canada to England. 75. Battle of Lexington. 76. Declaration of Independence. 89. George Washington, President. 97. John Adams, President.
1. Union with Ireland. 3. War with France. 5. Napoleon defeated at Trafalgar. 8. Peninsular War. 12. War with U. S. 14. Peace with U. S. 15. Battle of Waterloo.	4. Napoleon, Emperor. 5. Battle of Austerlitz. 6. Jena. 9. Wagram. 12. Russian campaign. 13. War with all Europe. 14. Allies enter France. Napoleon sent to Elba. **Restoration** Louis XVIII., King. 15. Napoleon returns. Battle of Waterloo. Napoleon sent to St. Helena.	[illegible] of Elba [illegible] [illegible] and Napo[illegible] [illegible] Battle of Leipzig. [illegible] Russian campaign. [illegible] [illegible] Congress of Vien[illegible] [illegible] German Confederati[illegible]	1. Thomas Jefferson, President. 4-6. Lewis and Clarke explore the Upper Missouri. 9. James Madison, President. 15. Battle of New Orleans.

x	Spain	Italy	Russia	Scandinavia	Contemporary
1500	1502-09. Mohammedans expelled. 12. Ferdinand conquers Navarre. 16. Accession House of Austria. Charles I., King of Spain. 19. Charles becomes Emperor of Germany as Charles V. 57. War with France. 71. Turks defeated at Lepanto. 80. Portugal conquered. 88. Armada defeated.	9. Venice stripped of Italian possessions. 13-21. Pope Leo X.		20. Christian II. 23. Sweden breaks loose from Union of Calmar. Gustavus Vasa. 59. Frederick II. of Denmark. 60. Eric XIV., King of Sweden. War between Denmark and Sweden. 70. Peace of Stettin. 93. Augsburg Confession accepted at Upsala.	34. Order of Jesuits founded. 72. Holland, under William of Orange, rebels against Philip's tyranny. 81. Holland a republic. 82. Reformation of calendar.
1600	1609-10. 900,000 Moors banished. 40. Portugal independent.	27-31. War of Mantuan Succession. 93. Battle of Marsaglia. French defeat Duke of Savoy.		1604. Charles IX. 11. Gustavus Adolphus. 13. [illegible] of Commerce. 17. Russia cedes Finland to Sweden. 30. Gustavus defeats Tilly. 32. Gustavus Adolphus killed at battle of Lützen. Christina. 54. Charles X. 97. Charles XII.	36. Tulip mania. 39. Van Tromp sweeps the Channel. 69. Turks take Candia. 83. Sobieski, King of Poland, defeats the Turks at Vienna. 99. Peace of Carlowitz.
1700	1700. Philip V. (Bourbon). 2. War of Succession. 4. English capture Gibraltar. 13. Siege of Barcelona. 35. Charles conquers Naples. 59. Charles III. 96. War with England. 97. Battle of Cape St. Vincent.	6. Battle of Turin. 13. Peace of Utrecht. Italy divided. 96-97. Bonaparte's first victories in Italy. 98. Pius VI. deposed by Bonaparte.		1700. Sweden defeats Russians at Narva. 9. Pultowa. Peter sends 14,000 Swedish prisoners to colonize Siberia.	40. Maria Theresa, Queen of Hungary.
1800	5. Battle of Trafalgar. 8. French take Madrid. Charles IV. abdicates. Joseph Bonaparte, King. 12. Battle of Salamanca. 12. Wellington occupies Madrid. 14. Ferdinand VII. restored.	2. Italian Republic. Bonaparte president. 5. Napoleon crowned King of Italy. 14. Fall of Napoleon. Kingdom overthrown. 15. Lombardo-Venetian Kingdom established by Austria.		9. Finland ceded to Russia. 14. Union of Sweden and Norway.	3. Humboldt traverses Mexico. 5. Mungo Park murdered in Africa. 15. Treaty of Vienna.

A.D.	England	France	Prussia	Austria	America
1800	[illegible] 20. George IV. 24. Death of Lord Byron.	24. Charles X.			17. James Monroe, President.
1825	26. Great commercial crisis. 29. Catholic relief bill. 30. William IV. 37. Victoria. Hanover separated from Great Britain. 39. War with China. 40. Penny postage. 46. Repeal of the Corn Laws. 48. Chartist riots. 49. Cholera.	27. War with Algiers. 30. Louis Philippe. Conquest of Algiers. 31. Hereditary peerage abolished. 48. Revolution. Republic proclaimed. Outbreak of Red Republicans. Louis Napoleon, President.			25. John Quincy Adams, President. 29. Andrew Jackson, President. 37. Martin Van Buren, President. 41. Wm. H. Harrison, President. John Tyler, President. 45. James K. Polk, President. 49. Zachary Taylor, President.
1850	51. First "Great Exhibition." 54. Crimean War. 56. War with China. War with Persia. 57. Indian mutiny. Great commercial crisis. 58. Jewish disabilities removed. 67. War with Abyssinia. Fenian trouble. 69. Disestablishment of Irish Church. 73. Ashantee war.	51. Coup d'état. Louis Napoleon re-elected. 52. Empire re-established by popular vote and the President-General Emperor as Napoleon III. 59. War with Austria. Magenta and Solferino. 70. War with Prussia. Battle of Sedan. Napoleon surrenders. 71. The Commune. Republic, Thiers, President. 73. MacMahon, President.		Austria withdraws from German Confederation. 67. New constitution. 73. International Exhibition, Vienna.	53. Franklin Pierce, President. 57. James Buchanan, President. 58. Atlantic cable. 61. Abraham Lincoln, President. 65. Andrew Johnson, President. 69. Ulysses S. Grant, President.
1875	76. Queen proclaimed Empress of India. 78. Great commercial depression. War in Afghanistan. 79. Zulu War. 80. Famine in Ireland. Land League. 82. War in Egypt. 86. Irish Home Rule Question. 93. Gladstone's Home Rule bill passed by the Commons but defeated by the Peers.	79. Jules Grévy, President. 87. Sadi-Carnot, President. 89. Boulanger exiled.		78. Occupation of Herzegovina and Bosnia. 79. Count Andrassy resigns. 80. Agreement with Germany on Eastern question. 98. Attempt to assassinate the Emperor.	77. R. B. Hayes, President. 81. James A. Garfield, President. 81. Chester A. Arthur, President. 85. Grover Cleveland, President. 89. Benjamin W. Harrison, President. 93. Grover Cleveland, President.
1900					

XI.	FROM NAPOLEON TO THE PRESENT TIME				
A.D.	**Spain**	**Italy**		**Scandinavia**	**Contemporary**
1800	[illegible]			18. Charles XIV. (Bernadotte).	[illegible] Sir John Ross [illegible] Baffin's Bay.
1825	23. French expedition to Cadiz. Cadiz made a free port. [illegible] abolished. 33. Isabella II. Christina, Regent. Carlist War. Don Carlos defeated. 40. Espartero, Regent. 43. Driven out. Isabella 13 years old declared of age. 54. Espartero recalled.	47. Charles Albert of Sardinia promulgates new code. 48-49. Sardinia defeated by Austria. 49. Victor Emmanuel II. Roman Republic overthrown.		44. Oscar I., King of Sweden. 48. War between Denmark and Germany.	29. Greece independent. 29-33. James Ross discovers magnetic pole. 31. Belgium independent. 45. Franklin's exp. to North Pole. 48. Liberia founded.
1850	56. Insurrection. O'Donnell dictator. 59. War with Morocco. 60. Moors defeated. 62. Prim intervention. 68. Successful revolution led by Prim and Serrano. 71. Crown accepted by Amadeus. 72-76. Carlist War. 73. Abdication. Republic. Alfonso XII.	55. Sardinia joins alliance against Russia. 59. War with Austria. 60. Garibaldi invades Naples. Sardinian army defeats Papal troops. Sicily and Naples annexed to Sardinia. 61. Victor Emmanuel King of Italy. 66. War with Germany. 70. Rome annexed.		59. Charles XV. 64. Christian IX. of Denmark renounces claim to Schleswig and Holstein. 72. Oscar II., King of Sweden.	58. Livingstone's Zambezi expedition. (Africa). 74-7. Stanley in Africa.
1875	78. Death of Queen Mercedes. 80. Slavery abolished in Cuba. 86. Posthumous son born to Queen Christina. 90. Canovas de Castillo, premier. 93. War with Moors.	78. Death of Victor Emmanuel. Humbert, King. Death of Pius IX. Leo XIII., Pope. 89. Republican agitation.			78. Montenegro independent. Servia free state. Roumania fed. 81. Thessaly ceded to Greece. 82. Greely's North Pole exp. 86. Congo Free State constituted. 87-9. Stanley penetrates to Lake Albert Nyanza. 90. Heligoland transferred to Germany.
1900					

History of America

A. D.

[illegible]. The Icelandic discovery.—Leif Erikson and the Northmen.

1400

92. Columbus discovers the island of Guanahani, of the Bahamas, which he names San Salvador, Oct. 12. He discovers Cuba, Oct. 28; Hayti, Dec. 6.

97. Cabot discovers Labrador. 99. Amerigo Vespucci's voyage.

1500

1. Negro slaves imported into Hispaniola. 6. Death of Columbus.
13. Balboa discovers the Pacific Ocean. 21. Cortez conquers Mexico. 28. Narvaez visits Florida.
34. Cartier explores the St. Lawrence. 41. De Soto conquers Louisiana.
44. De Soto discovers the Mississippi. 64. The Huguenots in Florida.
65. St. Augustine, in Florida, founded by the Spaniards.
85. First settlement, at Roanoke Island, founded by Walter Raleigh, a failure.

1600

The Colonies

1607. Settlement at Jamestown.		
9. Hendrik Hudson discovers the Hudson River.	New York	14. New Amsterdam (now New York City) settled by the Dutch.
20. The Puritans land at Plymouth Rock.	Massachusetts	20. Dutch vessel, with first negro slaves, enters James River. 30. Boston founded.
31. Settlement by Swedes and Finns at Cape Henlopen.	Delaware	38. Peter Minuit at Christina.
34. Maryland granted to Lord Baltimore.		34. Settlement by English Catholics at St. Mary's.
35. Settlements by English at Windsor, Hartford and Wethersfield.	Connecticut	
36. Settlement by English, under Roger Williams, at Providence.	Rhode Island	
64. Elizabethtown settled.	New Jersey	(First settlement by Dutch, at Bergen, 1618.)
65. Clarendon Colony settlement.		
70. First settlement, English, Ashley River.	South Carolina	80. Charleston founded.
82. First settlement in Pennsylvania by English under William Penn.	Pennsylvania	86. Odious administration of Sir Edmund Andros. 89. King William's War.
1700 33. English settlement, under Oglethorpe, at Savannah.	Georgia	2. Queen Anne's War.
41. New Hampshire separated from Massachusetts.		(First settlement in New Hampshire, Eng., Little Harbor, 1623.) 44. King George's War.

54. French and Indian War. Kentucky settled by Daniel Boone.
55. Braddock's defeat. 58. Fort Du Quesne taken by Washington.
63. France cedes Canada to England.
65. Colonial Congress at New York resists the stamp act. 66. Stamp act repealed.
67. Tax on tea. 68. General Gage sent to Boston.
70. Boston massacre. Repeal of the duties on tea. 73. Destruction of tea in Boston harbor.
74. First Continental Congress meets in Philadelphia, Sept. 5. [illegible] declaration of rights, Nov. 5.
75. **Revolutionary War** begins with battle of Lexington. Battle of Bunker Hill.
76. **Declaration of Independence.**
77. Lafayette joins the Americans. National government adopted by Congress and recognized by France. Battle of Princeton. Battle of Brandywine. Burgoyne surrenders at Saratoga.
78. Battle of Monmouth.
81. Battle of Cowpens. Cornwallis surrenders at Yorktown.
83. Treaty of peace. 85. Cotton introduced into Georgia.
87. The Constitution adopted.
88. The Constitution of the **UNITED STATES** ratified by eleven States.

DATE	United States	Canada	Spanish America
1789	**GEORGE WASHINGTON**, President. John Adams, Vice-President. 90. Indian war in Ohio. 91. **Vermont** admitted. 92. **Kentucky** admitted. 94. Whisky insurrection. 96. **Tennessee** admitted.	91. Canada is given a constitution and divided into two provinces. 94. Toronto capital of Upper Canada.	
1797	**JOHN ADAMS**, President. Thomas Jefferson, Vice-President. 00. Capital removed from Philadelphia to Washington.		
1801	**THOMAS JEFFERSON**, President. Aaron Burr, Vice-President. 02. **Ohio** admitted. 03. Louisiana purchase. War with Tripoli. 04. Burr-Hamilton duel. 05. George Clinton, Vice-President. 07. Trial of Aaron Burr.	03. Slavery abolished.	03. Hayti republic. 08. King of Portugal goes to Brazil.
1809	**JAMES MADISON**, President. George Clinton, Vice-President. 11. Battle of Tippecanoe. 12. **Louisiana** admitted. **War with England.** Canada invaded. Madison re-elected. 13. Commander Perry captures English fleet. Elbridge Gerry, Vice-President. Battle of the Thames. 14. Battle of Lundy's Lane. English capture Washington and burn public buildings. Bombardment of Fort McHenry. 15. **Battle of New Orleans.** 16. **Indiana** admitted.	12. British capture Detroit. 13. Americans capture Toronto and Fort George. Death of Tecumseh. 16. Sir John Sherbrooke, Governor of Lower Canada.	09. War of Independence in Buenos Ayres. 11. Dr. Francia dictator of Peru. Venezuela independent. 11-15. Simon Bolivar's struggles for liberty. 15. Brazil made a kingdom. 16. Buenos Ayres independent.
1817	**JAMES MONROE**, President. Daniel Tompkins, Vice-President. **Mississippi** admitted. 18. **Illinois** admitted. Seminole war in Florida. 19. **Alabama** admitted. Purchase of Florida. 20. Missouri Compromise. **Maine** admitted. 21. **Missouri** admitted. 22. South American republics acknowledged. 23. Monroe doctrine declared. 24. Visit of Lafayette.	18. Duke of Richmond, Governor of Lower Canada. 17-26. Political agitation in Upper Canada: Robert Gourlay. 20. Antagonism between French and English in Lower Canada. 24. Welland Canal incorporated.	17. Chile independent. 21. Central America independent. 22. Brazil independent: Dom Pedro, Emperor. Iturbide Emperor of Mexico. 24. Simon Bolivar dictator of Peru. 25. Bolivia founded.

The United States	Canada	Spanish America
JOHN QUINCY ADAMS, President. John C. Calhoun, Vice-President. 28. Protective tariff bill passed.	25. Agitation in Upper Canada over alien bill. 26. Mob destroys Mackenzie's printing-office.	28. Uruguay independent.
	29. Agitation for responsible government in Upper Canada. 30. Lord Aylmer Governor of Lower Canada. 31. Imperial duties surrendered to assembly. 34. Papineau party demand total separation from Great Britain.	31. Dissolution of United States of Colombia. 31. Dom Pedro abdicates. His six-year-old son Dom Pedro II, Emperor of Brazil. 35. The Texans revolt. 36. Defeat of the Mexicans.
	37-38. Insurrection. 38. End of rebellion in Upper C. 40. Union of Upper and Lower C. Lord Sydenham, Governor. 41. Responsible government established.	
WILLIAM H. HARRISON, President. John Tyler, Vice-President. Harrison dies April 4. **JOHN TYLER**, President. Vetoes bank bill. 42. Dorr rebellion in Rhode Island. 43. Texas applies for annexation.	44. Government removed to Montreal.	
	45. Great fire at Quebec. 47. Lord Elgin, Governor. Agitation over rebellion losses bill.	46. Venezuela independent. War bet. Mexico and U. S. 46. Battles of Palo Alto and Resaca de la Palma. 47. Buena Vista, Cerro Gordo, Contreras. City of Mexico captured.
ZACHARY TAYLOR, President. Millard Fillmore, Vice-President. 50. **MILLARD FILLMORE**, President. California admitted. Fugitive slave law passed.	49. Annexation to U. S. advocated. Riots in Montreal. 53. Reciprocity with U.S. signed.	50. Lopez' attempt on Cuba. 51. Lopez garroted.
FRANKLIN PIERCE, President. William Rufus King, Vice-President. 54. Kansas-Nebraska bill. Contention in Kansas.	55. Government removed to Quebec. 55. Sir Edmund W. Head, Governor.	53. Santa Ana, dictator of Mexico. 55. Walker's expedition to Nicaragua.
JAMES BUCHANAN, President. John C. Breckinridge, Vice-President. Dred Scott decision. Mormon insurrection. Financial distress. 58. Minnesota admitted. 59. Oregon admitted. 59. John Brown's insurrection. 60. South Carolina secedes. 61. Kansas admitted.		58. Juarez, President of Mexico. 60. Walker invades Honduras.

A. D.	The United States	Canada	Spanish America
1861	**ABRAHAM LINCOLN**, President. Hannibal Hamlin, Vice-President. Attack on Fort Sumter. Harper's Ferry and Norfolk seized. 62. Battle of Antietam. 63. Proclamation of Emancipation. **West Virginia** admitted. Battle of **Gettysburg**. 64. The Kearsarge sinks the Alabama. 65. Andrew Johnson, Vice-President. Surrender of Gen. Lee, April 9. Lincoln assassinated, April 14. **ANDREW JOHNSON**, Prest. The war ended. Amnesty issued by the President. 67. **Nebraska** admitted. Alaska purchased. Southern States organized as military districts. 68. Impeachment, trial and acquittal of President Johnson.	**61. Lord Monck, Governor.** **65. Great fire at Quebec.** **66. Reciprocity treaty with U. S. Fenian invasion.** **67. Canada, New Brunswick and Nova Scotia form the Dominion of Canada.**	61. France at war with Mexico. 63. The French enter City of Mexico. Archduke Maximilian of Austria invited to become Emperor. 64. He accepts. 65. Paraguay at war with Uruguay, Brazil, Argentine Republic. Chile and Spain at war. 66. Juarists in Mexico have great success. 67. Maximilian surrenders and is executed.
1869	**ULYSSES S. GRANT**, President. Schuyler Colfax, Vice-President. Pacific Railroad completed. 70. Fifteenth amendment ratified. 71. Great fire at Chicago. Tweed ring exposed. Geneva award. 72. Great fire at Boston. Political disabilities of Southern people removed. Modoc War. 73. Henry Wilson, Vice-President. The Virginius troubles with Spain. Financial panic. 75. Passage of act for specie resumption in 1879. **Colorado** admitted. 76. Centennial Exposition, Philadelphia. Custer massacre.	**71. British Columbia becomes part of the Dominion.** **73. Prince Edward's Island joins the Dominion. Lord Dufferin, Governor-General.**	68. Cuban revolt.
1877	**RUTHERFORD B. HAYES**, President. William A. Wheeler, Vice-President. Railroad riots. 78. Yellow fever epidemic along Lower Mississippi. 79. Resumption of specie payment.	**77. Great fire at St. John, N. B.** **78. Marquis of Lorne appointed Viceroy.**	79. War between Chile and Peru.

XVI	The United States	Canada	Spanish America
1881	**JAMES A. GARFIELD**, President. Chester A. Arthur, Vice-President. President Garfield shot by Guiteau. **CHESTER A. ARTHUR**, President. Treaty with China. 83. Opening of Brooklyn Bridge. Apaches subdued by General Crook. General strike of telegraph operators.	84. Dynamite explosions in Parliament buildings, Quebec.	
1885	[illegible]	85. Rebellion of Louis Riel. Riel captured and hanged. 88. Lord Stanley, Governor-General. Fisheries treaty rejected by U. S.	
1889	**BENJAMIN W. HARRISON**, President. Levi P. Morton, Vice-President. **North Dakota, South Dakota, Washington** and **Montana** admitted to the Union. Opening of Oklahoma. Johnstown flood. Pan-American Congress. 90. **Idaho** and **Wyoming** admitted. Reciprocity treaty with South American republics. McKinley tariff law goes into effect. Sioux War. Death of Sitting Bull. Eleventh census—population, 62,622,250. 92. Birth of the People's party at Omaha.	89. Great fire at Quebec. 90. Reciprocity defeated in House of Commons. Toronto University burned.	89. Civil War in Hayti. Dom Pedro of Brazil deposed. 91. Balmaceda, President of Chile, deposed. Commits suicide.
1893	**GROVER CLEVELAND**, President. Adlai E. Stevenson, Vice-President. Sandwich Islands ask to be annexed. World's Columbian Exposition at Chicago. Great financial depression. Cleveland calls special session of Congress to repeal Sherman bill. Congress of Religions, Chicago.	93. The Earl of Aberdeen, Governor-General.	93. Revolution in Brazil. Revolution in Argentina.

Political History of the United States

THAT enthusiastic little rebel, Rhode Island, was the first of the colonies to declare itself "free from all dependence on the crown of Great Britain." This she did on May 4, 1776. The Assembly of Virginia in the same month instructed her delegates to the Continental Congress to present to that body a proposition "affirming the independence of the colonies from Great Britain." In compliance with these instructions Richard Henry Lee, of Virginia, on June 7, 1776, introduced his famous resolutions: "That these united colonies are, and of right ought to be, free and independent States; that they are absolved from all allegiance to the British crown; and that all political connection between them and the state of Great Britain is, and ought to be, totally dissolved. That it is expedient forthwith to take the most effectual measures for forming foreign alliances. That a plan of confederation be prepared and transmitted to the respective colonies for their consideration and approbation." John Adams seconded these resolutions, and an animated discussion ensued. On June 8, a committee, consisting of Thomas Jefferson, John Adams, Benjamin Franklin, Roger Sherman and Robert R. Livingston, was appointed to draw up a declaration of independence embodying the sense of Lee's resolutions. On July 2, Lee's resolutions were passed by the vote of twelve of the thirteen colonies, the New York delegates refraining from voting for want of instructions from their province. On July 3, the formal declaration, almost precisely as written by Thomas Jefferson, was presented by the committee above named, and was debated with great spirit, John Adams being the chief speaker on the part of the committee. The discussion was resumed on the morning of the 4th, and at 2 o'clock in the afternoon, after one or two slight modifications, it was adopted. The announcement was hailed with the liveliest enthusiasm. "Ring! ring!" shouted the lad stationed below to give the signal to the old bellman in the State-house tower; and he did ring until the whole city shouted for joy. The King's arms were wrenched from the Court-house and burned in the streets; bonfires were lighted, the city illuminated, and the exultation was prolonged far into the night. In New York city the populace hurled the leaden statue of George III. from its pedestal and molded it into bullets, and in all the great cities similar demonstrations of enthusiasm were exhibited.

The Declaration of Independence was signed August 2, 1776, when President John Hancock said, "There must be no pulling different ways; we must all hang together," to which Franklin replied, "Yes, we must all hang together, or we shall all hang separately."

State constitutions were adopted in the same year as follows: By New Jersey (July 2), Virginia (July 5), Pennsylvania (July 15), Maryland (Aug. 14), Delaware (Sept. 20), North Carolina (Dec. 18).

1778 — Independence of United States acknowledged by France by a treaty of alliance and commerce.

1779 — Naval victory of John Paul Jones.

1781 — A French fleet in aid of the United States drives the British from Chesapeake Bay. Surrender of Cornwallis.

1782 — Independence recognized by Holland.

1783 — Independence acknowledged by Sweden, Denmark, Spain and Russia, successively. Definite treaty of peace with Great Britain, Sept. 3.

1787 — Formation and adoption of the Constitution.

American politics begin properly with the close of the Revolutionary war, out of which travail this nation was born. When the British departed they left behind them thirteen separate and independent States joined together in a feeble confederation and governed as a whole, so far as they would consent to be governed at all, by the inadequate Continental Congress. The finances were in a deplorable condition; the States were jealous of each other and of the Congress. As everything was badly defined and unsettled there were constant misunderstandings and abuses, and it seemed that after achieving freedom America was about to cast it away. During the war there had been two parties, the Tories, who were English in sympathy, and the Whigs, who were Americans to the core. These gave place to two new divisions, one of which favored a closer and lasting union in which the States should bind themselves together into a compact government — called the Federalists; and one which, while generally admitting the need for a closer and more binding union, still sought to preserve the sovereignty and independence of the States — these were known as Anti-Federalists. Our Constitution and our form of government are the result of the two opposing forces, and its great flexibility — its perfection — is to be ascribed to the wisdom with which the fathers sought out and chose what was best in the scheme of either.

It is impossible here to do more than outline

the growth of parties, but no man can be an intelligent voter who does not study the foundation of the republic. Every citizen should pursue the subject further in the pages of the *Federalist*, which argued one side of the issue, and in the writings of Thomas Jefferson, who upheld the other. It will show how high ran feeling at the time when it is pointed out that, although the Constitution was adopted in 1787, it was ratified by but eleven States in 1788. Still this was enough to set the new nation up in business.

GEORGE WASHINGTON (1789-1797) was the unanimous choice of the electoral college, and the hero of the Revolution became the first President of the United States in 1789. It is not to be imagined that even at that time the people were all of one mind about the Constitution. There is no document — not even the Bible — which is not subject to different interpretations, and the great charter of our American liberties was no exception to the rule. Parties were formed known as strict constructionists and loose constructionists, the former Federalists and the latter Anti-Federalists, the first believing in a strongly centralized government, the second jealously observant of the rights of the States. It will be found that a close analysis of the distinction made there has been and is the dividing line of American parties ever since.

Of course new issues complicated the old ones. The Anti-Federalists changed their name to the Democratic-Republican party, and warmly urged the alliance with France. In the revolution which had just ended, the French alone had first come to our aid, and on land and sea had waged war upon our common enemy. Hence there was a lively sense of gratitude to that great nation throughout the country, made none the less by the establishment of the republic, and hardly destroyed by the atrocities of the Reign of Terror. The Federalists, on the other hand, inclined toward England as the national friend, through the ties of kinship and common language. In spite of these differences of opinion, which were daily growing more bitter, there was practically no partisanship during Washington's administration. He called Federalists and Anti-Federalists into his cabinet, which was composed of men of such opposite views as Alexander Hamilton and Thomas Jefferson, and his farewell address, which every school-boy has read, is full of grave warning against the evils and dangers of party spirit.

But with Washington in retirement, the contest began. The Federalists put JOHN ADAMS (1797-1801) in the field, and elected him in spite of the English treaty which John Jay had made and which Adams had supported. Thomas Jefferson became Vice-President, because at that time the Vice-Presidency went to the man receiving the next largest vote for President, a system which was in force until 1804.

There were many reasons why the Federalist triumph could not be a permanent one. England was intensely unpopular, and the administration was accused of favoring that kingdom unduly. The alien and sedition laws caused an access of the public displeasure, and the party split into two sections, one following Adams, the other Hamilton. Nominations for the election were made by members of Congress; Adams and Pinkney were chosen as the Federal standard-bearers, Jefferson and Aaron Burr as the Republican. Jefferson and Burr were elected, but as both had received the same number of votes, the election was thrown into the house, which chose THOMAS JEFFERSON (1801-9) the third President of the United States.

The history of his administration was a quiet one. He refused to make the civil service the spoil of victory, and gave proof of the flexibility of his ideas of government by the purchase of Louisiana Territory from France in 1803, which was a measure tending strongly toward Federalism — giving a hostage, as it were, to the central government on the part of the States. Jefferson also agreed to the building of the great post road to the Ohio, which was by no means a Republican scheme.

JAMES MADISON (1809-17) was elected fourth President. He, like Jefferson, was a Republican, although, as has been pointed out, that party is more nearly akin to what is to-day called Democracy. C. C. Pinkney, the Federalist candidate who opposed him, and who had run twice against Jefferson, received 47 electoral votes, while Madison was given 122. The Federalists lost every part of the country save New England, and one result of this election was to give that sectional tone to our politics which has to a greater or less extent endured to the present time.

The country was drifting into a war with England at this time, and the public spirit was aroused by the continual outrages perpetrated upon our sailors on the high seas by British ships. The Republicans were recognized as the fighting party, and under the leadership of Calhoun, Clay and Crawford, the War of 1812 was begun. The Federalists protested, and in Massachusetts and Connecticut the Governors refused to allow the militia to go out of the State, save to repel invasion. That argument lasted but a short time, however, for the country was invaded and the city of Washington captured and burned. The treaty of peace was signed in the winter of 1814, but before the news reached this country Andrew Jackson had gained the magnificent victory at New Orleans, on January 8, 1815.

With the close of Madison's administration a new era in our politics began. The questions of Federalism and of the French or English friendship were dead, and new issues were coming up. These were the tariff, the management of finances and the development of industry. What became known as the **Era of Good Feeling** followed, which lasted from the election of JAMES MONROE (1817-25) up to 1828. Upon Monroe's second election, in 1821, there was no opposition to him, and he would have had the unanimous vote of the Electoral College had not one of the electors declared that that honor should be confined sacredly to Washington.

It was the **Slavery Question** which put an end to the era of good feeling, and which burned hotly, and more hotly, until it wrapped the whole land in the flames of civil war. It began with the application of Missouri for admission into the Union in 1820. Prior to that time Mason and Dixon's Line, which is the boundary of Maryland and Pennsylvania and the Ohio River, formed the division between slave States and free. Missouri lies beyond the Mississippi River, and out of the limits fixed, and the question was a threatening one until Henry Clay brought in his famous **Missouri Compromise**, which admitted Missouri as a slave State, and forbade slavery north of 36° 30' north latitude. To balance Missouri in the Senate, Maine was admitted at the same time as a free State.

A protective tariff had been devised by John C. Calhoun in 1816, and President Monroe strengthened and increased the protection accorded. In 1819 he purchased Florida from Spain; and in 1823, in consequence of the war made by Spain against her revolted colonies in the three Americas, he voiced that splendid declaration which will always be associated with his name—the **Monroe Doctrine**. This doctrine briefly is that the United States will not interfere in any European war, nor will it permit European interference or European control in America, North or South.

No better proof could be given of the condition of parties than the election which ended Monroe's tenure of office. The Electoral College chose a Vice-President, John C. Calhoun, but its vote for the Presidency was so scattered between Jackson, Adams, Crawford and Clay that the choice was thrown into the House. Here, by an alliance of the friends of Clay and Adams, Jackson was defeated, and JOHN QUINCY ADAMS (1825-29) became the sixth President. Clay was rewarded with the portfolio of State, and out of the alliance the "**Whig**" Party was formed. Their principles were in part those of the old Federalists. They were for a high tariff with strong protection, and they early declared for a policy of internal improvements to be paid for by the nation at large. Jackson's followers took the place of the old anti-Federalists; they were strict constructionists, opposed to the tariff, and in their principles and speeches was to be found the nucleus of the States' rights doctrine. They called themselves "**Democrats.**" The four years of Adams' presidency was passed in marshaling and organizing the two opposing forces.

ANDREW JACKSON (1829-37), the seventh President, carried everything before him. The electoral vote was 178 to 83; the popular, 647,231 for Jackson, 509,097 for Adams. As soon as he had taken up the reins of power, Jackson removed some five hundred office-holders from their places, on Marcy's famous theory that "**to the victors belong the spoils.**" Upon this principle the tenure of political office still practically, if not theoretically, depends.

The Tariff was exceedingly unpopular at the South, which was then, as now, an agricultural rather than a manufacturing region. Several States had protested, and in 1830 Senator Hayne laid down the doctrine of Nullification—that any State could declare null and void any act of Congress. Webster answered this declaration in the debate which has since been famous. The original discussion was not on the tariff regulations, but on the sale of public lands. The struggle was a hot one. Jackson took occasion to put himself on record at once with his celebrated toast, "Our Federal Union, it must be preserved." The words were first uttered at a dinner in honor of his birthday. Calhoun took the opposite view, and in 1831 the President's Cabinet was broken up by the issue. A new tariff bill was passed, but the South was still dissatisfied, and in 1832 South Carolina passed the Nullification ordinance. Jackson at once sent a naval force into Charleston harbor, and Congress passed a bill enforcing the tariff; but Henry Clay again came forward with a compromise which was accepted on both sides.

The United States Bank was the next bone of contention. It had been chartered in 1816 for twenty years. After a struggle with Congress, and with his Secretary of the Treasury, Duane, who would not remove the national deposits from the bank, Jackson dismissed Duane and appointed Taney Secretary of the Treasury. The deposits ceased. The Senate at once passed a vote of censure on the President, but the House, after investigating the bank, sustained Jackson at every point and refused a new charter. The fight with the Senate, in which there was an adverse majority, continued until the end of Jackson's term. During his administration was the first weak beginning of the Abolition party. The Anti-Slavery Society was formed in 1833. It was the target for abuse and violence, which culminated in the assassination of Lovejoy. Congress solemnly declared that it would listen to no petitions upon the question of slavery, and Jackson asked that the sending of abolition documents through the mails should be prohibited. This the Senate refused.

The Democratic candidate, MARTIN VAN BUREN (1837-1841), the eighth President, was elected over W. H. Harrison and several other opposition nominees, including Daniel Webster. He followed out Jackson's policy to the letter, one part of which, the celebrated "specie circular," brought on the Great Panic of 1837. This was an order to United States agents to receive only gold and silver for public lands. Banks collapsed, money became scarce, and failures were most frightfully numerous. In 1840 Van Buren was renominated, but the Whigs, by an attack on the Democratic financial policy, carried the country and elected W. H. HARRISON (1841) the ninth President. It was in this campaign that the abolitionists produced their first national platform, which favored the abolition of slavery in the District of Columbia and the Territories. In the same year the Democracy at Baltimore resolved that Congress had no power to interfere with or control the domestic institutions of the several States, which were the sole and proper judges of everything pertaining to their own affairs not prohibited by the Constitution, and that the efforts "by Abolitionists or others" to interfere with questions of slavery were calculated "to lead to the most alarming and dangerous consequences," "to diminish the happiness of the people and endanger the stability and permanence of the Union, and ought not to be countenanced by any friend of our political institutions." The convention also adopted a resolution to the effect that every attempt to abridge the rights or privileges of foreign-born citizens should be resisted. This was aimed at the Know-nothing tendency then just appearing, which had, however, no affiliation with the Abolition movement, already vigorous.

Harrison did not live out the year, and he was succeeded by the Vice-President, JOHN TYLER (1841-1845), the tenth President. Tyler rapidly got into trouble with his cabinet, which, save Webster, deserted him on issues connected with his attempt to carry out Harrison's financial policy. The slavery question was pressing forward more and more urgently for solution all this time. An Ohio Congressman, Giddings, brought the issue into the House of Representatives, and was censured by that body for so doing. He resigned and was at once unanimously re-elected. A new tariff bill was brought in, and the proposition then made for a division of the surplus among the States.

Finance, protection, internal improvements, and indeed every minor issue, had to give way to the great puzzle of slavery. It was coming on for adjustment, and no hand could stay it. In the campaign of 1844 it produced the dispute over the re-annexation of Texas. The Democratic platform declared the Great American Measure—the taking in of Texas and Oregon. As Texas would be a slave territory, the plan was antagonized in the North, but after a close and perplexed election JAMES K. POLK (1845-1849), the eleventh President, was elected. Henry Clay, the Whig candidate, was beaten by the vote of 62,300 which was given to Jas. G. Birney by the Liberty party.

The new administration at once took up the Texas matter, and the War with Mexico was the necessary consequence. The history of that struggle will be found in its appropriate place in this book. It is here necessary merely to point out the results. By the treaty of Guadalupe-Hidalgo, the United States acquired all that country which we now call the great West, including the treasures of California and the Sierras. The northwestern frontier was fixed at the 49th degree of north latitude, and the administration closed with the largest accession of land that had yet been made to the Republic.

The Wilmot Proviso attempted to block slavery in the new Territories, and Oregon was organized as free soil. A low tariff bill was passed, and the Whigs got through a river and harbor bill which the President promptly vetoed. This brought the country up to the campaign of 1848, in which the Whigs recovered the government. The platform of the Democracy made at Baltimore approved the Mexican war, congratulated the republic of France on achieving its liberty, and the world on the downfall of thrones and dominations everywhere. The same year, at Philadelphia, the Whigs resolved merely that Zachary Taylor was the best man for President. At Buffalo, in the same year, the Abolitionists determined that they would forget all past political differences in a common resolve to maintain the rights of free labor against the aggression of the slave power, and to secure a free soil to a free people. This convention also demanded cheap postage; river and harbor improvements when required for the general convenience; indorsed the idea of the homestead law, and inscribed on its banner, "Free soil, free speech, free labor and free men."

The magic of military success and the excellent organization of the Whigs made ZACHARY TAYLOR (1849-1850), twelfth President. He lived but a short time and was succeeded by the Vice-President, MILLARD FILLMORE (1850-1853), thirteenth President.

With 1850 what might be called the war period of American politics began. In this year was introduced the **Clay compromise**, which admitted California as a free State, but on the other hand altered the **Fugitive Slave Laws**, which inflamed the North to the point of war. Several of the States met the action of Congress by personal liberty laws, which really amounted to nullification. The old parties broke up; there were Democrats, and Free-Soil Democrats, and Whigs. Winfield Scott, the Whig candidate, carried only four States in the Union, and FRANKLIN PIERCE (1853-1857), the fourteenth President, was elected.

There was soon actual fighting on the dividing line between North and South. The **Kansas-Nebraska Bill** repealed the Missouri compromise and made all new territory open to slavery. The Whig party split in two on this issue, one of the sections becoming the Republican party of the day, the other going over finally to the Democrats, a fact which will account for much of the confusion on purely financial and tariff issues to be found in both these parties to-day. When you find a Republican who is a free trader, or a Democrat who is a protectionist, the anomaly is to be traced directly to the fissure, and the new sides taken in the 1850's on the free soil question.

Passions were at fever heat. In Kansas the "Jayhawkers" and the "Border Ruffians" were already at each other's throats. It was plain that the matter in dispute could only be settled by an appeal to the arbitrament of arms.

In 1856 the Republicans nominated their first candidate, Gen. John C. Fremont, the "Pathfinder." Their platform recites that the convention was called without regard to previous political differences, to enable all opposed to the repeal of the Missouri Compromise to come together. The platform opposed the extension of slavery into the territories; declared that Congress should prohibit in the territories "the twin relics of barbarism, polygamy and slavery;" and opposed all proscriptive legislation, thus antagonizing the Democracy on the slavery issue and the Know-nothings on nativism. The Whigs met at Baltimore. Their platform is devoted exclusively to a denunciation of "geographical parties," and a recommendation of Millard Fillmore, the American or "Know-nothing" candidate for President. The Democrats added little to former platforms, save that they declared against the Know-nothings on their war on foreigners, and agreed with them in their declaration against interference with slavery. They nominated and elected JAMES BUCHANAN (1857-61), fifteenth President. Fremont, however, polled a popular vote of 1,341,264 against Buchanan's 1,838,169, while Fillmore received 874,534.

The **Dred Scott Case** now came on to exacerbate still more bitterly public feeling. Chief Justice Taney declared that a negro was a chattel, that the compromise of 1820 was unconstitutional, and that a slave-owner might settle in any territory. Following this came John Brown's raid into Virginia, his attempt to excite a slave insurrection, and his death upon the gallows. There was nothing for it but war, and into war the country rapidly drifted.

The campaign of 1860 was the most confused in the whole history of American politics. There was talk of secession in the air. There was notoriously war preparation in the South. The North was divided. Every man felt that parties would have to be re-arranged and new political frontiers defined. The "Constitutional Union" party met at Baltimore. All it demanded was the "Constitution of the country, the union of the States, and the enforcement of the laws." The Republicans met at Chicago. The platform is the most significant in the political history of the republic, and contains the essence of all its history since that date. It denounced the threats of disunion made by Democrats in Congress as an "avowal of contemplated treason" which it was the duty of the people to "rebuke and forever silence." It asserted that the normal condition of all the territory of the United States is that of freedom; that the re-opening of the slave trade was a crime against humanity; that duties should be readjusted so as to encourage the development of the industrial interests of the whole country; that Congress should pass a complete and satisfactory homestead law; that the rights of citizenship enjoyed by foreigners should not be abridged or impaired; that the rights of all citizens, native or naturalized, should be protected abroad and at home. The Douglas Democratic platform, adopted at Charleston, favored the acquisition of Cuba; declared that State legislatures which interfered with the enforcement of the fugitive slave law were revolutionary and subversive of the Constitution; and reaffirmed the Cincinnati platform of 1856 on tariff. The Breckinridge platform, adopted at Charleston and Baltimore, reaffirmed the Democratic platform adopted at Cincinnati, with certain "explanatory resolutions," which in substance were that slave-owners had a right "to settle with their property" in the territories without being interfered with by territorial or Congressional legislation.

On these issues four candidates were put in the field. The Republicans nominated Abraham Lincoln; the Democrats, J. C. Breckinridge; the Constitutional Union party, John Bell; the Independent Democrats, Stephen A. Douglas. **ABRAHAM LINCOLN** (1861-65) was chosen sixteenth President, by a popular vote of 1,866,352; Douglas received 1,375,157; Breckinridge, 845,763; Bell, 589,581.

On December 20, 1860, South Carolina declared the Union was dissolved, and a **Secession** resolution was passed. Following, six other slave States immediately seceded. Every effort was made to stem the tide of disunion, but nothing could be done save with arms in the field. A peace congress met and proved futile. The Crittenden compromise was scoffed out of court. The Confederate States of America was formed at Montgomery, Alabama, in February, 1861, with Jefferson Davis as President, and slavery and low tariffs as its corner stone. The first ball was fired April 14, 1861, and the great issue of the century joined.

For the time politics were relegated to the background. There were only Unionists and Secessionists. The financing of the great struggle led to high tariff, the issue of treasury notes, and finally the establishment of the national banking system. The internal revenue system was developed, an income tax was imposed, greenbacks were issued, and the resources of the country stretched to meet the expenses of a war that cost $3,000,000 a day.

On Jan. 1, 1863, President Lincoln issued the **Emancipation Proclamation**, which freed the Southern slaves, and marks an epoch in the history of the world. Two years later, under the apple tree at Appomattox, Lee surrendered to Grant, and the war ended with the complete triumph of the Northern arms. There had in the meantime been another presidential election, in which Lincoln defeated George B. McClellan and John C. Fremont. Shortly after Lee's surrender Lincoln was assassinated by J. Wilkes Booth, an actor, and **ANDREW JOHNSON** (1865-69), the seventeenth President, took up the chief magistracy.

The problem of the day was the **Reconstruction** of the old slave States, upon which the new President and his party at once quarreled. The point at issue was the proper safeguarding of the newly-freed negro. Congress passed the Civil Rights bill, the Freedman's Bureau bill, and submitted the XIVth Amendment to the Constitution. The President was finally impeached by Congress, but his trial before the Senate resulted in an acquittal by one vote.

ULYSSES S. GRANT (1869-77), the eighteenth President, was elected over Horatio Seymour, on a platform adopted by the Republicans at Chicago, which denounced repudiation; favored suffrage on equal terms to all men; encouraged immigration, and declared itself in sympathy with all oppressed people who are struggling for their rights. The Democratic platform of 1868 acknowledged that the questions of slavery and secession had been forever settled by the war or by constitutional conventions; and favored amnesty for all political offenses. It made a very distinct pronouncement on tariff in the following words: "A tariff for revenue upon foreign imports, and such equal taxation under the internal revenue laws as will afford incidental protection to domestic manufactures, and as will, without impairing the revenue, impose the least burden upon, and best promote and encourage the great industrial interests of the country."

The XVth Amendment, guaranteeing negro suffrage, was passed by Congress in 1869. A Liberal Republican ticket, with **Horace Greeley** at its head, was supported by the united opposition against Grant in 1872, but was defeated easily, and Greeley, one of the greatest figures in later American politics, died shortly afterward. The South was pacified, and the **Treaty of Washington** made, which involved the payment of the Alabama claims by the English Government.

In 1876 occurred the famous **Hayes and Tilden Controversy**, which tested the flexibility of our electoral machinery so severely. Tilden was the Democratic nominee, and he had an undoubted popular majority—4,284,265, against 4,033,295 for Hayes. Rival electors claimed to have been elected in Louisiana and Florida. Intimidation, fraud and illegal voting were charged, and Congress finally appointed the **Electoral Commission** to settle the dispute, as there was nothing in the Constitution to cover the circumstances. On a party vote the commission awarded the disputed electoral votes to the Republican candidate, thus making **RUTHERFORD B. HAYES** (1877-81) nineteenth President of the United States. Specie payment was resumed during this administration, and the silver coinage act passed.

From that time on to the present the tariff issue has been the chief matter of debate in each campaign. In 1880 the Republicans elected **JAMES A. GARFIELD** (1881) twentieth President. He was assassinated by a madman, Charles J. Guiteau, and **CHESTER A. ARTHUR** (1881-85) became twenty-first President. The most important measure of this administration was the passage of the Pendleton civil service reform bill.

GROVER CLEVELAND (1885–89), the twenty-second President, was the first Democrat chosen since the war. Out of his famous tariff reform message the Democratic platform of 1888 was stated at St. Louis, and the country was invited to choose squarely between protection as represented by Benjamin Harrison, the Republican candidate, and a tariff revision as represented by Cleveland.

The result was, after one of the most remarkable struggles in American politics, already known by its well earned name of the Campaign of Intellect, that BENJAMIN HARRISON (1889–93) was elected twenty-third President of the United States. The campaign of 1892 presented no new issues as between the leading parties, but the appearance of the People's Party, a new political organization, added interest to the contest. The Republicans led off in the conventions, meeting at Minneapolis, June 7. Preceding the convention the exciting question had been as to whether Mr. Blaine would accept the nomination if tendered him. His resignation of the Secretaryship of State was deemed to answer the question of his acceptance in the affirmative. The platform adopted reaffirmed the doctrine of ultra-protection. President Harrison was nominated on the first ballot, 905 votes being cast; of these Harrison had 535 1-6, McKinley 182, Blaine 182 5-6, Reed 4, and Lincoln 1.

The Democrats met in Chicago, June 21. The convention was in many respects a peculiar one in the history of party meetings. It was evident before the convention that Mr. Cleveland was the choice of a large majority of the rank and file of the Democratic party and that he was opposed by the politicians of his party; the bitterest opposition to him being in his own State. The regular delegation from that State was unanimous for David B. Hill's nomination. Only one vote was taken in the convention. The number of delegates was 910. The vote stood: Cleveland 617⅓, Boies 103, Hill 114, Gorman 36½, Carlisle 14, Stevenson 16⅔, Morrison 3, Campbell 2, Russell 1, Whitney 1, and Pattison 1. The vote on Vice-President stood: Stevenson 402, Gray 343, Mitchell 45, Morse 86, Watterson 26, Cochran 5, Tree 1, and Boies 1.

The Prohibitionists met at Cincinnati, June 29. The important question before the convention was that of fusion with some of the new parties, but the idea met with no favor. Gen. John Bidwell was nominated on the first ballot.

The People's party convention met at Omaha, July 4, and adopted a platform favoring among other things free coinage of silver and Government control of railroads. Only one ballot was taken for President, Gen. Jas. B. Weaver, of Iowa, being the nominee. J. G. Field was nominated for Vice-President.

The election of 1892 resulted in the election of GROVER CLEVELAND. The People's party polled a surprisingly large vote for a new party, 1,055,424, or 8.67 per cent, to 5,556,562 for Cleveland (45.78 per cent), 5,162,874 for Harrison (40.49 per cent), and 264,066 for Bidwell (2.17 per cent).

The By-ways of American Politics.

The minor American parties which have appeared and disappeared during our century and over of national life are the following: **Anti-Renters**, a New York party which flourished about 1841. They resisted the collection of back rents on the Van Rensselaer manor near Albany. They had strength enough to defeat Wright, the regular Democratic candidate for Governor of New York. **Barn-Burners**, New York, 1848, seceders from the Democratic party. They were opposed to slavery extension. **Bucktails**, New York, about 1815; they supported Madison. **Conservatives**, New York and some other States, 1837; paper money Democrats. **Doughfaces**, 1820, Northern members of Congress who voted in favor of the Missouri Compromise. **Hunkers**, New York, a faction of the Democrats favoring the South, Barn-Burners being the other faction. **Know-Nothings**, New York, 1854, opposed to naturalization of foreigners unless they had been twenty-one years in the country. **Loco-Focos**, New York, 1835; a branch of the Democratic party. **Liberal Republicans**, 1872; Republicans who joined with the Democrats in support of Greeley for President. **Temperance, or Prohibition**, from 1808 down, in many States; in favor of preventing or restricting the sale of liquors. The total Prohibition vote at the presidential election in 1888 was 249,937; in 1892 264,066. **Women's Rights**, from 1860 down; those who favored granting to women the right of suffrage.

In Athens every citizen, under severe penalties, was compelled to teach his sons to read and to swim. If he did not fit them for some trade they were not obliged to support him in his old age.

"Men use rough words and harsh, sometimes, by reason of the very gentleness and pity that are in their souls."—*Ouida.*

"There is no darkness but ignorance."—*Shakespeare.*

History of the Tariff

CUSTOMS AVERAGES AND TARIFF LEGISLATION

THE first tariff act was signed by President Washington on July 4, 1789. The new Government had just been established, and the object of the law was to put money into the empty treasury of the Republic. Alexander Hamilton was the author of the measure, which was modeled on the 5 per cent. import duty that the Congress of the Confederation had tried in vain to impose. This first law imposed specific duties on forty-seven articles and ad valorem rates of 7½, 10, 12½ and 15 per cent. on four commodities or small groups. The unenumerated goods were compelled to pay 5 per cent. The second tariff act passed the House by a vote of 39 to 13, and passed the Senate without a division. It was approved by the President on August 10, 1790. This act was longer than its predecessor and the scale of duties was higher. Then followed the act of May 2, 1792, which became operative in the following July. It raised the duty on unenumerated merchandise to 7½ per cent. and that on many articles paying 7½ to 10 per cent. Another tariff bill was passed on June 7, 1794, going into effect July 1. It imposed numerous rates in addition to those already payable, some of them specific and others 2½ and 5 per cent. ad valorem. Additional tariff measures were enacted on March 3 and July 8, 1797, and on May 13, 1800. These acts imposed additional rates, and there was a further increase of 2½ per cent. on March 26, 1804, on all imports then paying ad valorem rates.

The whole industrial situation of the country was changed suddenly and radically in 1807-8. Napoleon's Berlin and Milan decrees were followed by the English Orders in Council, and Mr. Jefferson's administration retaliated for the outrages on our commerce by the celebrated Embargo in December, 1807. This was followed by the Non-Intercourse act in 1809, and by a declaration of war against England in 1812. During the progress of hostilities all commercial intercourse with Great Britain was, of course, suspended, and all import duties were doubled as a war measure.

This is known as the "Tariff of 1812." It passed the House of Representatives by a vote of 76 to 48, and received the sanction of the Senate by 20 votes in its favor to 9 against it. Amendments to it were adopted on February 25, and again on July 29, 1813. On February 15, 1816, the additional duties imposed by the act of 1812 were repealed; and additional duties of 42 per cent., to take effect July 1, were substituted, but the law did not go into operation. From 1812 to 1816 the average rate on all imports was 32.73 per cent., the range being from 6.84 per cent. in 1815 to 69.03 in 1813.

The Lowndes-Calhoun Bill.

The next great tariff measure is known as the Lowndes-Calhoun bill. It was approved April 27, 1816, took effect the following July, and may be said to be the first of the protective tariffs. It was not wholly set aside until 1846, under the administration of Mr. Polk. The ad valorem duties under it ranged from 7½ to 30 per cent. The unenumerated goods paid 15 per cent., the manufactures of iron and other metals generally 20 per cent., the majority of woolen goods 25 per cent., cotton goods 25 per cent., "with clauses establishing 'minimums'"—that is, in reckoning duties, 25 cents per square yard was to be deemed the minimum cost of cotton cloth; unbleached and uncolored yarn, 60 cents, and bleached or colored yarn, 75 cents per pound. These rates became practically prohibitory on the cheaper goods. The law was amended April 20, 1818, and again on March 3, 1819. It had the support of New England and the Middle States, but the South was opposed to it. From 1817 to 1820 the average rate on imports was 26.52 per cent.; from 1821 to 1824, 35.02 per cent.; and from 1821 to 1824, on dutiable goods only, 36.28 per cent. This general increase of duties was due to the necessity of providing for the interest on the heavy debt incurred by the second war with England.

The Clay Tariff followed in 1824. The vote in the House was close—107 to 102; and there was a majority of only 4 in the Senate. New England and the South voted against the measure, while on the other side were ranged the West and Middle States. It received the President's signature on May 22, 1824, and went into effect July 1. It remained in force in almost its entirety until 1828. It raised the duty on woolen goods from 25 to 30 per cent. for one year, and then to 33⅓ per cent. There was a "minimum" of 30 cents per square yard on cotton cloth. Wool over 10 cents a pound was rated at 20 per cent. until June 1, 1825, then 25 per cent. for one year, and then 30 per cent. The average rate on all imports from 1825 to 1828 was 47.17 per cent. and on dutiable goods 50.22 per cent.

The "Tariff of Abominations."

The "Tariff of Abominations," as it is called, was approved May 19, 1828, and went into operation part the following July and part in September. In the House 105 members voted for it and 94 members, mostly from New England and the South, against it. In the Senate the vote was 26 to 21. It had special reference to iron, wool and manufactures of wool. The duty on wool was 4 cents per pound and 40 per cent. for one year; then 4 cents and 45 per cent. for a year; then 4 cents and 50 per cent. Somewhat lower duties were provided for in an act passed on May 24, 1828; again in May, 1830, and still again on July 13, 1832. The average duty on all goods from 1829 to 1832 was 47.81 per cent., and on all dutiable articles 51.35 per cent.

The Modifying Tariff of 1832 was intended "to correct the inequalities of that of 1828." It was passed by the Whigs, or National Republicans, and levied high duties on cotton and woolen goods and other articles to which protection was meant to be applied. The vote in the House was 132 to 65 and in the Senate 32 to 16, the votes in favor of it coming from all sections of the country. The New England vote in the House was a tie. It was approved on July 14, and took effect on March 3, 1833. The existing duties were superseded by the act, some of them reduced and a few raised. In a separate act of the same date railroad iron was made free. Under its operation the average rate on imports in 1833-34, during the ten months it was in force, was 26.29 per cent., and dutiable articles 38.25 per cent.

The Compromise Tariff of 1833 provided for taking off one-tenth of the duties each year until a uniform rate on all of 20 per cent. should be reached. It passed the House by 119 to 85 and the Senate by 29 to 16. New England then joined the Middle States in voting for high protective duties. It was approved on March 2, 1833, the day before the tariff of 1832 went into operation, and took effect on January 1, 1834. The terms of the compromise were that all duties which in the tariff of 1832 exceeded 20 per cent. should have one-tenth of the excess over 20 per cent. taken off on January 1, 1834; one-tenth more on January 1, 1836; again one-tenth in 1838, and another one-tenth in 1840; so that by 1840 four-tenths of the excess over 20 per cent. would be disposed of. Then on January 1, 1842, one-half of this remaining excess was to be taken off, and on July 1, 1842, the other half of the remaining excess was to go. There would, therefore, after July 1, 1842, have been a uniform rate of 20 per cent. on all articles. The average duty on all imports from 1834 to 1842 was 18.25 per cent., and on dutiable articles 34.73 per cent.

The Tariff of 1842.

The tariff of 1842 was passed by the Whigs as a party measure, and was avowedly protective. It took effect on August 30, 1842; changed all existing rates, was amended in March, 1843, and died December 1, 1846. New England and the Middle States gave it strong support. The South was massed in opposition and the West was a tie. The average rate on all imports under it was 26.92 per cent. and on dutiable articles 33.47 per cent.

The Polk-Walker tariff of 1846 is one of the most noteworthy acts in the fiscal history of our government.

Robert J. Walker, of Mississippi, who was President Polk's Secretary of the Treasury, laid down these principles as a basis for revenue reform in his celebrated report of 1845:

"No more money shall be collected than is needed for economical administration. The duty on no article should exceed the lowest rate which will yield the largest revenue. Below such rate discrimination may be made, or for imperative reasons an article may be made free. Luxuries should be taxed at the maximum rate for revenue. Duties should be all ad valorem, and never specific. Duties should be so imposed as to operate as equally as possible throughout the Union, without respect to class or section."

The bill framed on this basis was approved by Mr. Polk on July 30, 1846. It passed the House by 114 to 95, the East being in opposition and the West and South in support. The vote in the Senate on a third reading was a tie, and Vice-President Dallas gave the casting vote in the affirmative. The Senate vote on the final passage stood 28 to 27. This act superseded the Whig tariff, and remained in force until 1861. It swept away specific and compound duties. It divided all dutiable merchandise into eight classes, which introduced greater simplicity into the whole system of custom regulations. The average duty on all imports was, from 1847 to 1856, 22.20 per cent. and on dutiable articles 26.22 per cent.

The Tariff of 1857, which was the next in order, made a still further reduction in duties. It was approved on March 3, 1857, took effect on July 1, and remained in force until April 1, 1861. New England united with the South in giving it 123 votes to 72 in the House, and in the Senate 33 to 12. The average duty on all goods, from 1856 to 1861, was 15.66 per cent. and on dutiable articles 20.12 per cent.

The Morrill Tariff.

The Morrill tariff of 1861 differed from all its predecessors in that it provided for a general system of compound and differential duties, specific and ad valorem, and also made a distinction between goods imported from different parts of the world. It passed the House on May 11, 1860, by a vote of 105 to 64, and the Senate on February 20, 1861, by a vote of 25 to 14. From the first, through all the countless legislation that has followed in its wake, it has been avowedly protective. It was frequently changed during the War of the Rebellion, ostensibly for purposes of revenue. At an early period in its history the number of rates ran up to over two thousand. From 1861 to 1869 every year produced some enlargement of the original scheme. In 1870 there was some modification of rates, generally in the line of reduction. Tea and coffee, taxed since 1861, were put on the free list, and the duties on cotton and woolen goods, wool iron, paper, glass and leather were lowered about 10 per cent. The free list was somewhat enlarged, but the reduction was rescinded in the act of March 3, 1875. The duty on quinine was abolished on July 1, 1879. The average duty on all imports, from 1862 to 1883, was 34.16 per cent. and on dutiable articles 42.74 per cent.

The Commission tariff was passed by the House on March 3, 1883, by a vote of 152 to 116, and passed the Senate on March 2, the vote being 32 to 31. This was the tariff which was in force until October 6, 1890, when it was superseded, except as to tobacco and tin-plate, by the McKinley bill.

The McKinley Bill.

The McKinley measure was prepared entirely in the interests of high protection, and raised the tariff all round to an average of at least 55 per cent. It was adopted in the Senate by 33 votes to 27, and in the House by 152 to 81. But at the Congressional election of 1892 the public condemnation of McKinleyism was almost universal, and the Democratic party, which had pledged itself to a modified form of free trade, obtained a large majority in the lower house. The anti-election promises were embodied in a bill introduced by Mr. Wilson, a Democratic representative from West Virginia.

The Wilson bill made many radical and sweeping reductions. Raw material, including wool and many other necessities, were put on the free list; the sugar bounty of two cents per pound was abolished, and many small taxes were stricken off the tariff list entirely. The strongest fight was made upon the sections relating to iron and steel. Under the McKinley bill, steel ingots, cogged ingots, blooms, slabs, billets, shafting, etc., valued at from one cent to sixteen cents per pound, paid from four-tenths of a cent to four cents and a fifth per pound, or an average of about 48 per cent. For this the Wilson bill substituted a 25 per cent. ad valorem tariff all round.

As the debates in committee went on, the tendency towards almost absolute free trade became daily stronger, and additional reductions were proposed. Hides and skins, indigo, meerschaum, most kinds of oils and many other articles were freed, or the tariff on them largely cut down, under the Wilson bill.

Ohio, Governor McKinley's home, and the great producer of wool, stuck to its tariff programme at the election in the fall of 1893, and re-elected Gov. McKinley by an overwhelming majority.

A fair estimate of the reductions made by the Wilson bill, including remissions and articles placed upon the free list, would be not less than 40 per cent. all round.

The Civil Service

THE officials and clerks — over 120,000 in all — by whom the people's business in the administration of government is carried on constitute the Civil Service. About 5,000 of these are appointed by the President alone or with the consent of the Senate; about 15,000 under what are known as the "Civil Service Rules," but the great body of officeholders are appointed by the heads of departments.

Those employed in the civil service have always been theoretically entitled to serve "during good behavior," but practically, within a few years, their positions have depended upon their allegiance to the political party in power.

In 1883 Congress passed a law for the improvement of the civil service of the United States. This act provides for the appointment by the President of three commissioners to have general charge of filling the vacancies in the civil service department, and stipulates that the fitness of all applicants for all subordinate positions in the departments at Washington, and in all custom-houses and post-offices having as many as 50 officeholders, shall be tested by examinations, and the positions assigned with reference to the capacity, education and character of the applicants, regardless of political preferences.

According to this, no absolute appointment to office can be made until the applicant has proven his or her ability to fill the position satisfactorily by six months' service; no person habitually using intoxicating beverages to excess shall be appointed to, or retained in, any office; no recommendation which may be given by any Senator or member of the House of Representatives, except as to character and residence, shall be considered by the examiners; men and women shall receive the same pay for the same work.

The general competitive examinations for admission to the service are limited to the following subjects: 1. Orthography, penmanship and copying. 2. Arithmetic—fundamental rules, fractions and percentage. 3. Interest, discount, and the elements of bookkeeping and of accounts. 4. Elements of the English language, letter-writing, and the proper construction of sentences. 5. Elements of the geography, history and government of the U. S.

A standing of 65 per cent. in the first three branches is necessary to qualify an applicant for appointment. Where special qualifications are necessary for specific work the examinations are adapted to test the knowledge of the applicant in that particular line.

No applicant will be examined who cannot furnish proof that he is of good moral character and in good health.

There is a board of examiners in each of the principal cities of the U. S., and several examinations are held each year. Applications must be made on the regular "application paper," which can be obtained of the commissioners, or any board of examiners.

Several of the States have adopted the principles laid down in the Civil Service Act and applied them to the State civil service, and it is probably only a question of time when Civil Service Reform will be consummated throughout the U.S., and the public service will thereby be rendered much more efficient.

History of the American Flag

THE Quartermaster-General of the Army has issued the following bulletin regarding the history of the American flag:

The American Congress, in session at Philadelphia, established by its resolution of June 14, 1777, a national flag for the United States of America. The resolution was as follows:

"*Resolved*, That the flag of the thirteen united States be thirteen stripes, alternate red and white; that the union be thirteen stars, white in a blue field, representing a new constellation."

Although nearly a year previous, July 4, 1776, these thirteen united States had been declared independent, this resolution is the first legislative action recorded relating to a national flag for the new sovereignty.

The use of thirteen stripes was not a new feature, as they had been introduced (in alternate white and blue) on the upper left-hand corner of a standard presented to the Philadelphia Light Horse by its captain in the early part of 1775, and, moreover, the union flag of the thirteen united colonies raised at Washington's headquarters, at Cambridge, Jan. 2, 1776, had the thirteen stripes just as they are this day; but it also had the crosses of St. George and St. Andrew on a blue ground in the corner. There is no satisfactory evidence, however, that any flag bearing the union of the stars had been in public use before the resolution of June, 1777.

It is not known to whom the credit of designing the stars and stripes is due. It is claimed that a Mrs. John Ross, an upholsterer, who resided on Arch Street, Philadelphia, was the maker of the first flag combining the stars and stripes. Her descendants assert that a committee of Congress, accompanied by General Washington, who was in Philadelphia in June, 1776, called upon Mrs. Ross and engaged her to make the flag from a rough drawing which, at her suggestion, was redrawn by General Washington, with pencil, in her back parlor, and the flag thus designed was adopted by Congress. Although the resolution establishing the flag was not officially promulgated by the secretary of Congress until Sept. 3, 1777, it seems well authenticated that the stars and stripes were carried at the battle of the Brandywine, Sept. 11, 1777, and thenceforward during all the battles of the revolution.

Soon after its adoption the new flag was hoisted on the naval vessels of the United States. The ship Ranger, bearing the stars and stripes and commanded by Captain Paul Jones, arrived at a French port about Dec. 1, 1777, and her flag received on Feb. 14, 1778, the first salute ever paid to the American flag by foreign naval vessels. The flag remained unchanged for about eighteen years after its adoption. By this time two more States (Vermont and Kentucky) had been admitted to the Union, and on Jan. 13, 1794, Congress enacted that from and after the first day of May, 1795, the flag of the United States be fifteen stripes, alternate red and white; that the union be fifteen stars, white in a blue field.

This flag was the national banner from 1795 to 1818, during which period occurred the war of 1812, with Great Britain. By 1818 five additional States (Tennessee, Ohio, Louisiana, Indiana and Mississippi) had been admitted to the Union, and therefore a further change in the flag seemed to be required. After considerable discussion in Congress on the subject, the act of April 4, 1818, was passed, which provided:

"1. That from and after the fourth day of July next the flag of the United States be thirteen horizontal stripes, alternate red and white; that the union have twenty stars, white in a blue field.

"2. That on the admission of every new State into the Union one star be added to the union of the flag and that such addition shall take effect on the 4th of July next succeeding such admission."

The return to the thirteen stripes of the 1777 flag was due in a measure to a reverence for the standard of the revolution, but it was also due to the fact that a further increase of the number of stripes would have made the width of the flag out of proportion to its length unless the stripes were narrowed, and this would have impaired their distinctness when seen from a distance. A newspaper of the time said:

"By this regulation the thirteen stripes will represent the number of States whose valor and resources originally effected American independence, and the additional stars will mark the increase of the States since the present Constitution."

No act has since been passed by Congress altering this feature of the flag, and it is the same as originally adopted, except as to the number of stars in its union. In the war with Mexico, the national flag bore twenty-nine stars in the union; during the late civil war, thirty-five. In none of the acts of Congress relating to the flag has the manner of arranging the stars been prescribed, and in consequence there has been a lack of uniformity in the matter, and flags in use by the public generally may be seen with the stars arranged in various ways. The early custom was to insert the stars in parallel rows across the blue field, and this custom has, it is believed, been observed in the navy at least since 1818, at which time the President ordered the stars to be arranged in such manner on the national flag used in the navy. In the army, too, it is believed, the stars have always been arranged in horizontal rows across the blue field, but not always in vertical rows; the effect, however, being about the same as in the naval flag. Hereafter there will be no difference in the arrangement between the army and navy, as an agreement has been arrived at between the War and Navy departments on the subject.

The national flags hoisted at camps or posts are made of bunting of American manufacture. They are of the following three sizes: The storm and recruiting flag, 8 feet in length by 4 feet 2 inches in width; the post flag, measuring 20 feet in length by 10 feet in width; the garrison, measuring 36 feet in length by 20 feet in width (this flag is hoisted only on holidays and great occasions). The union is one-third of the length of the flag and extends to the lower edge of the fourth red stripe from the top. The national colors carried by regiments of infantry and artillery and the battalion of engineers, on parade or in battle, are made of silk and are 6 feet 6 inches long and 6 feet wide and mounted on staffs. The field of the colors is 31 inches in length and extends to the lower edge of the fourth red stripe from the top.

Great Men's Works

MOHAMMED began the Koran at 38.
Shelley wrote "Queen Mab" at 18.
Keats wrote his "Endymion" at 22.
Alexandre Dumas wrote plays at 22.
Disraeli wrote "Vivian Grey" at 21.
Heine published his first songs at 23.
Swift wrote the "Tale of a Tub" at 37.
Seneca wrote "De Beneficiis" after 60.
Richardson published "Pamela" at 51.
Racine wrote the "Andromache" at 28.
Paley wrote the "Horæ Paulinæ" at 47.
Coleridge published "Christabel" at 44.
Pliny finished the "German War" at 31.
Luther wrote his ninety-five theses at 34.
Poe wrote "The Raven" in his 36th year.
Confucius began his religious works at 30.
Butler wrote "Hudibras" after he was 60.
Owen Meredith published "Lucile" at 29.

Sterne published "Tristram Shandy" at 46.

Shakespeare wrote his first play at about 24.

Machiavelli completed "The Prince" at 45.

Boileau wrote his first satirical poems at 24.

Lord Bacon wrote the "Novum Organum" at 41.

Sir Thomas More finished his "Utopia" at 38.

Spenser published the "Faerie Queene" at 35.

Persius is thought to have written his satires at 25.

Corneille wrote "Melite," his first drama, at 21.

David is said to have written his first psalm at 18.

Goldsmith finished "The Deserted Village" at 42.

Sheridan wrote his "School for Scandal" at 26.

Josephus published his "Wars of the Jews" at 56.

Calvin published his "Psychopannychia" at 25.

It is said that Horace wrote his first odes at 28.

Tacitus finished the first part of his history at 50.

Livy is said to have finished his "Annals" at 50.

Lamartine's poems appeared when the poet was 30.

Thackeray was 36 when "Vanity Fair" appeared.

Homer is said to have composed the Iliad after 80.

Dante finished the "Divina Commedia" at about 51.

Samuel Johnson published "London" when he was 29.

Solomon is said to have collected the Proverbs at 50.

The Eclogues of Virgil were written between 43 and 47.

John Bunyan finished the "Pilgrim's Progress" at 50.

George Eliot was 39 when "Adam Bede" was printed.

Baxter wrote the "Saint's Everlasting Rest" at 34.

Robert Browning wrote "The Ring and the Book" at 57.

Adam Smith published "The Wealth of Nations" at 53.

Fichte wrote the famous "Wissenschaftslehre" at 32.

Von Ranke finished his "History of the Popes" at 39.

"The Robbers," by Schiller, made the author famous at 20.

Thomas à Kempis wrote the "Imitation of Christ" at 34.

Voltaire's first tragedy came out when the author was 22.

Hannah More wrote "The Search After Happiness" at 28.

Martial is said to have written epigrams before he was 20.

Bryant was 19 when made famous by "Thanatopsis."

Joseph Addison's first essays appeared when he was 28.

Famous Poems and Their Authors.

"Elegy Written in a Country Churchyard" is the master composition of Thomas Gray (1716-1771).

"The Shipwreck" is by William Falconer (1730-1769).

"The Minstrel" is the production of James Beattie (1735-1803).

"Rock of Ages" is from the pen of Augustus Montague Toplady (1740-1778).

"The Farmer's Boy" was written by Robert Bloomfield (1766-1823).

"The Burial of Sir John Moore" is the effort of Charles Wolfe (1791-1823).

"Woodman, Spare that Tree" is the work of George P. Morris (1802-1864.)

"The Buccaneer" was composed by Richard Henry Dana (1787-1879).

"Star-Spangled Banner" was written by Francis Scott Key (1780-1843.)

"La Marseillaise" is the work of Rouget de L'Isle (1760-1836).

"Home, Sweet Home," is by John Howard Payne (1792-1852).

"From Greenland's Icy Mountains" is the composition of Reginald Heber (1783-1826).

"Battle Hymn of the Republic" was written by Julia Ward Howe (1819).

"Ben Bolt" is from the pen of Thomas Dunn English (1819).

"Rocked in the Cradle of the Deep" is by Emma C. Willard (1787-1870).

"Hail, Columbia," is the production of Joseph Hopkinson (1770-1842).

"Curfew Must Not Ring To-night" is the work of Mrs. Rose Hartwick Thorpe (1850).

Ill fares the land, to hastening ills a prey,
Where wealth accumulates and men decay.
Princes and lords may flourish and may fade;
A breath can make them as a breath has made;
But an honest peasantry, a country's pride,
When once destroyed, can never be supplied.

—Goldsmith.

AREA AND POPULATION OF THE CONTINENTS

The following table shows the area, population, and density of population in each of the divisions of the earth:

	Area: square miles.	Population.	Pop. per square mile.
Europe	3,797,410	357,351,800	94
Asia	17,039,906	855,254,000	48
Africa	11,515,104	163,430,017	14
Australasia	3,458,029	3,884,900	1.1
North America	7,252,055	69,080,084	11
South America	6,844,602	33,849,700	5
	40,300,297	1,479,717,051	29
Polar Islands	1,684,844	11,410	....
Total	42,290,461	1,479,728,151	28

STATISTICS OF ALL THE CHIEF COUNTRIES.

Countries.	Population.	Square Miles.	Capitals.
British Empire	337,845,000	9,040,677	London.
China	393,241,000	4,468,750	Peking.
Russian Empire	108,787,244	8,457,989	St. Petersburg.
France and Colonies	65,624,249	1,167,229	Paris.
France	38,218,903	204,177	....
Colonies	27,075,339	963,069	....
United States	62,622,250	3,602,990	Washington.
German Empire	46,855,704	211,168	Berlin.
Prussia	28,318,633	134,467	Berlin.
Bavaria	5,416,180	29,291	Munich.
Saxony	3,182,103	5,789	Dresden.
Wurtemberg	1,994,049	7,532	Stuttgart.
Baden	1,600,839	5,803	Karlsruhe.
Alsace-Lorraine	1,563,145	5,602	....
Hesse	956,370	2,965	Darmstadt.
Mecklenburg-Schwerin	575,140	5,137	Schwerin.
Hamburg	518,712	158	....
Brunswick	372,580	1,425	Brunswick.
Oldenburg	341,250	2,479	Oldenburg.
Saxe-Weimar	313,065	1,387	Weimar.
Anhalt	247,603	906	Dessau.
Saxe-Meiningen	214,697	953	Meiningen.
Saxe-Coburg Gotha	198,717	760	Gotha.
Bremen	165,850	99	....
Saxe-Altenburg	161,129	511	Altenburg.
Lippe	123,250	478	Detmold.
Reuss (younger line)	112,118	319	Gera.
Mecklenburg-Strelitz	98,371	1,131	Neu Strelitz.
Schwarzburg-Rudolstadt	83,939	363	Rudolstadt.
Schwarzburg-Sondershausen	73,623	333	Sondershausen.
Lubeck	67,658	115	....
Waldeck	56,565	433	Arolsen.
Reuss (elder line)	55,787	122	Greiz.
Schaumburg-Lippe	37,204	131	Buckeburg.
Austro-Hungarian Empire	41,827,700	261,681	Vienna.
Japan	38,507,254	147,669	Tokio.
Netherlands and Colonies	33,042,038	778,167	The Hague.
Turkish Empire	32,000,000	1,731,350	Constantinople.
Italy	29,699,785	110,665	Rome.
Spain and Colonies	24,873,621	861,952	Madrid.
Brazil	14,000,000	3,219,000	Rio de Janeiro.
Mexico	11,000,000	751,700	Mexico.
Corea	10,528,000	83,000	Seoul.
Congo State	8,000,000	802,000	....

STATISTICS OF ALL THE CHIEF COUNTRIES.—Concluded.

Countries.	Population.	Square Miles.	Capitals.
Persia	7,653,600	636,000	Teheran.
Portugal and Colonies	7,249,809	360,591	Lisbon.
Egypt*	6,806,381	494,000	Cairo.
Sweden and Norway	6,774,409	298,974	Stockholm.
Morocco	6,300,000	314,000	Fez.
Belgium	6,030,043	11,373	Brussels.
Annam†	6,000,000	106,200	Hue.
Siam	5,700,000	200,450	Bangkok.
Roumania*	5,376,000	46,314	Bucharest.
Argentine Republic	4,300,000	1,095,013	Buenos Ayres.
Colombia	4,000,000	331,420	Bogota.
Afghanistan	4,000,000	279,000	Cabul.
Madagascar	3,500,000	230,000	Antananarivo.
Abyssinia	3,000,000	129,000	....
Peru	2,970,000	405,040	Lima.
Switzerland	2,933,334	15,981	Berne.
Chile	2,665,926	250,810	Santiago.
Bolivia	2,300,000	472,000	La Paz.
Greece	2,187,208	24,977	Athens.
Denmark	2,172,205	14,789	Copenhagen.
Venezuela	2,121,988	566,159	Caracas.
Servia	2,096,043	18,757	Belgrade.
Bulgaria*	2,007,919	24,700	Sofia.
Nepaul	2,000,000	56,000	Khatmandu.
Cochin-China	1,649,180	23,058	Saigon.
Oman	1,600,000	81,000	Muscat.
Guatemala	1,427,116	46,774	New Guatemala.
Ecuador	1,146,000	144,000	Quito.
Liberia	1,150,000	14,000	Monrovia.
Transvaal	800,000	110,193	Pretoria.
Uruguay	700,000	72,112	Montevideo.
Khiva	700,000	22,320	Khiva.
Salvador	651,130	7,225	San Salvador.
Hayti	550,000	29,830	Port au Prince.
Paraguay	476,000	145,000	Asuncion.
Honduras	431,917	42,658	Tegucigalpa.
Nicaragua	400,000	51,600	Managua.
Dominican Republic	350,000	20,596	San Domingo.
Montenegro	245,380	3,486	Cettigne.
Costa Rica	213,785	19,985	San José.
Orange Free State	133,518	41,484	Bloemfontein.
Hawaii	80,647	6,587	Honolulu.

* Also enumerated with Turkish Empire. † Also enumerated with Colonies of France.

Errors in History.

The African king Prester John never had an existence.

There never was such a person as Pope Joan, the "female pontiff."

Portia did not swallow the burning coals. The whole story was certainly an invention.

Francis I., after the battle of Pavia, did not say, "All is lost save honor." The expression was entirely different.

The organ of the middle ages which, when moved into the sunshine, played tunes of itself, was a play of the medieval fancy.

Seneca was not a half Christian philosopher, but a grasping money-lender and miser, who died worth over $15,000,000.

The Pharaoh of the Exodus was not drowned in the Red Sea. His mummy has been found, the skull split by a large battle-ax.

Cæsar did not say "Et tu, Brute!" Eye-witnesses to the assassination depose that "he died fighting, but silent, like a wolf."

Alfred the Great did not visit the Danish camp disguised as a minstrel. There is no good reason to believe that he could either play the harp or speak Danish.

The luminous paintings said to have been common among the Japanese 200 years ago were luminous only in the imagination of travelers.

The romantic and supposedly beautiful Mary, "Queen of Scots," was cross-eyed, and had other physical blemishes that are not accounted attributes of beauty, as we view it, from our standards of beauty to-day.

Fair Rosamond was not poisoned by Queen Eleanor, but, after a long residence as a nun in the convent of Godstow, died greatly esteemed by her associates.

Philip III., of Spain, was not roasted to death by a roaring fire because court etiquette forbade any one to go to his assistance. He died a natural death, and the same story is told of a dozen different monarchs who were sticklers for ceremony.

The hanging gardens of Babylon did not hang, nor were they gardens. They were terraces supported by arches and overgrown with trees. They were erected for the amusement of a Babylonian queen who had come from a mountainous country.

Some Interesting Dates.

Fruits, Flowers, Etc.—The cherry dates back to A.D. 100; the lily, 800; jasmine, 1548; mulberry, 1520; mignonette, 1528; the plum, 1530; geranium, 1534; gooseberry, 1540; melons, 1540; hyssop, 1548; pomegranate, 1548; lemon, 1554; peach, 1562; carnation, 1567; pink, 1567; lavender, 1568; pineapple, 1568; quince, 1573; tulip, 1578; oleander, 1600; Virginia creeper, 1629; black walnut, 1629; hickory nut, 1640; nectarine, 1652; honeysuckle, 1656; sumachs, 1653; hawthorn, 1682; passion flower, 1692; raspberry, 1696; foxglove, 1696; currant, 1705; snowdrop, 1756; chrysanthemum, 1790; dahlia, 1803; camelia, 1811; petunia, 1823; verbena, 1827; fuchsia, 1888.

Foods and Cookery.—Forks first used, 1220; sugar in Europe, 1250; first English cook book, 1398; cabbages, 1510; turkeys, 1523; guineafowl, 1540; potatoes, 1565; cauliflower, 1603; tea, 1610; cattle imported to America, 1611; coffee, 1616; bread made with yeast, 1634; rice, 1690; celery, 1704; ice cream, 1760; U. S. fish culture, 1804; Liebig's extract, 1847; condensed milk, 1849; food adulteration act, 1854; aerated bread, 1858; cooking schools, 1873.

Fuel and Light.—Wood fuel, prehistoric; charcoal, B.C. 1800; oil lamps, B.C. 1000; wax candles, B.C. 200; peat, B.C. 60; rush lights, A.D. 1300; coal gas, 1792; Davy's safety-lamp, 1802; sperm candles, 1811; paraffine, 1825; petroleum, 1859; natural gas, 1870; water gas, 1873; electric heating, 1878; incandescent electric light, 1878.

The World's Clothing.—Spinning and weaving and dyeing are prehistoric. The peplos, or long cloak, was worn in Greece, B.C. 600; Tyrian purple dye used, B.C. 600-300; the Roman toga worn, B.C. 250-A.D. 100; breeches worn by the Scythians, B.C. 650; kilts and hose worn by the Celts, B.C. 100; figured weaving in Italy, A.D. 100-1000; Dutch and Flemish weaving, A.D. 1100; silk weaving at Palermo, A.D. 1146; linen cloth made in England, 1253; English wool trade flourished from A.D. 1307; Brabant looms brought to England, 1340; linen shirts in common use, 1566; silk worms brought to France, 1600; felt in common use, 1610; fly shuttles, 1738; calico printing, 1764; spinning-jenny, 1767; carding-machine, 1770; mule, 1779; power loom, 1785; cotton gin, 1793; shoddy, 1813; sewing-machine, 1841; silk worm disease, 1854; rubber coats, 1875; electric looms, 1880.

Curious Misnomers.

Arabic figures were not invented by the Arabs, but the early scholars of India.

Cleopatra's needles were not erected by that queen, neither do they commemorate any event in her history. They were set up by Rameses the Great.

The Jerusalem artichoke has no connection whatever with the holy city of the Jews. It is a species of sunflower, and gets its name from girasole, one of the scientific names of that genus of plants.

The word "pen" means a feather, and is from the Latin penna, a wing. Surely the expression "a steel pen" could be improved upon.

Galvanized iron is not galvanized at all, but is coated with zinc by being plunged into a bath of that metal and muriatic acid.

Pompey's pillar at Alexandria was neither erected by Pompey nor to his memory.

Common salt is not a salt and has long since been excluded from the class of bodies denominated "salts."

Rice paper is not made from either rice or straw, but from a pithy plant called tungtsau, found in China, Corea and Japan.

Brazil grass neither comes from nor grows in Brazil. It is strips from a species of Cuban palm.

Oh, fear not in a world like this,
And thou shalt know ere long,
Know how sublime a thing it is
To suffer and be strong.—*Longfellow.*

Sweet are the uses of adversity,
Which, like the toad, ugly and venomous,
Wears yet a precious jewel in his head;
And this our life, exempt from public haunt,
Finds tongues in trees, books in the running brooks,
Sermons in stones, and good in everything.
—*Shakespeare.*

Truth, crushed to earth, shall rise again;
The eternal years of God are hers;
But Error, wounded, writhes with pain
And dies among his worshippers.—*Byron.*

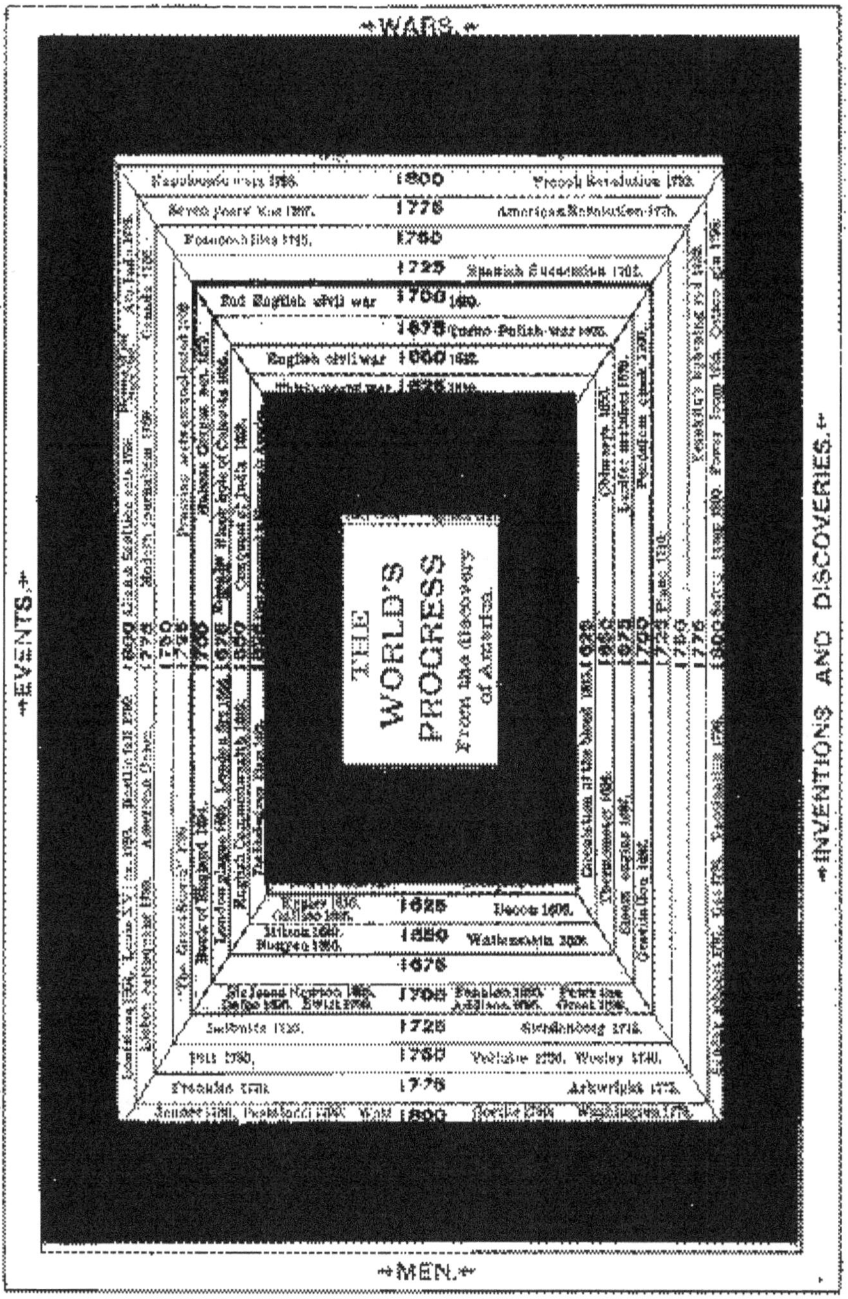

→WARS.←

Napoleonic wars 1796.	1800	French Revolution 1789.
Seven years' war 1756.	1775	American Revolution 1775.
Louisburg taken 1745.	1750	
	1725	Spanish Succession 1702.
End English civil war	1700 1689.	
	1675 Turko-Polish war 1672.	
English civil war	1650 1642.	
Thirty years' war	1625 1618.	

→EVENTS.←

→INVENTIONS AND DISCOVERIES.←

THE
WORLD'S
PROGRESS
From the discovery
of America.

Kepler 1610. Galileo 1609.	1625	Bacon 1605.
Milton 1640. Bunyan 1660.	1650	Wallenstein 1626.
	1675	
Sir Isaac Newton 1686. Defoe 1690. Swift 1700.	1700	Fenelon 1690. Addison 1705. Peter the Great 1700.
Leibnitz 1700.	1725	Swedenborg 1719.
Pitt 1750.	1750	Voltaire 1750. Wesley 1740.
Franklin 1755.	1775	Arkwright 1775.
Schiller 1790. Pestalozzi 1790. Watt	1800	Goethe 1780. Washington 1775.

→MEN.←

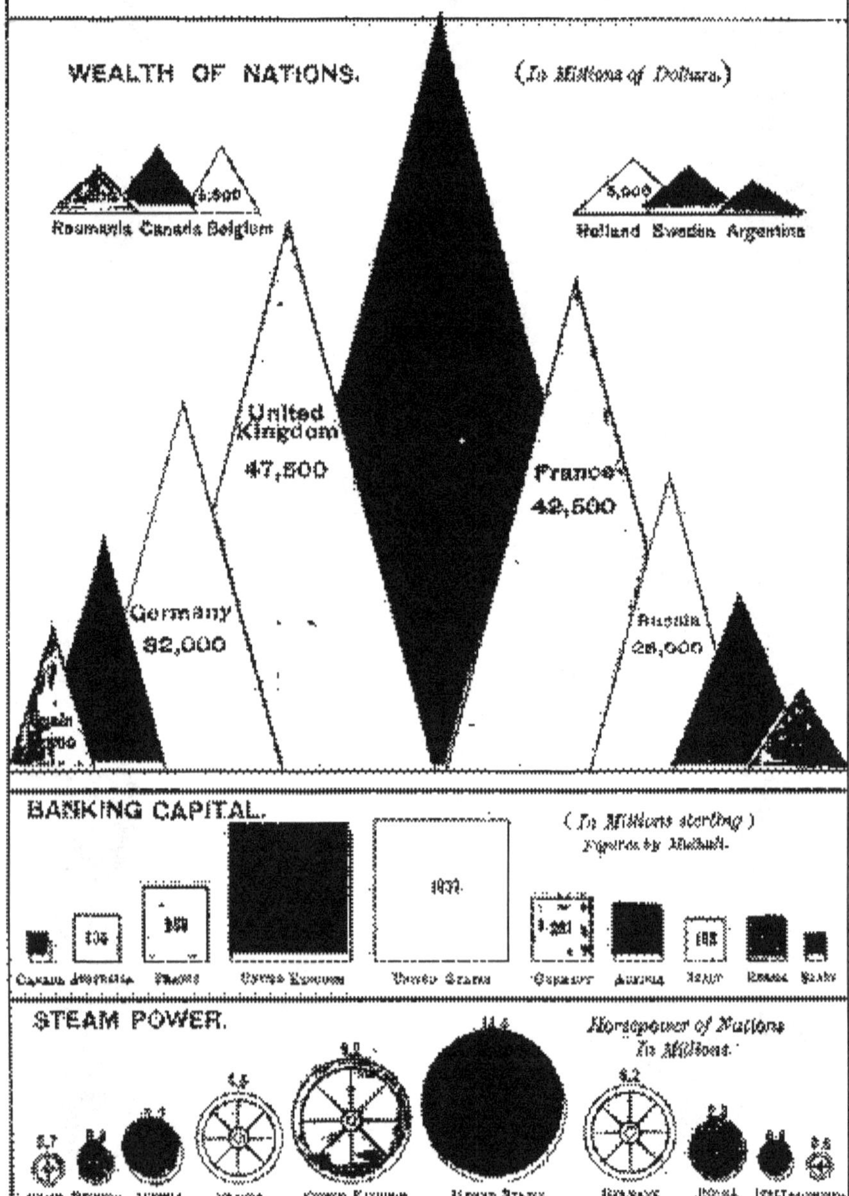
THE WORLD'S GREAT NATIONS.
WEALTH OF NATIONS.
(In Millions of Dollars.)
Roumania Canada Belgium
Holland Sweden Argentina
United Kingdom
47,500
France
42,500
Germany
32,000
Russia
26,000
BANKING CAPITAL.
(In Millions sterling)
Figures by Mulhall.
STEAM POWER.
Horsepower of Nations
In Millions.

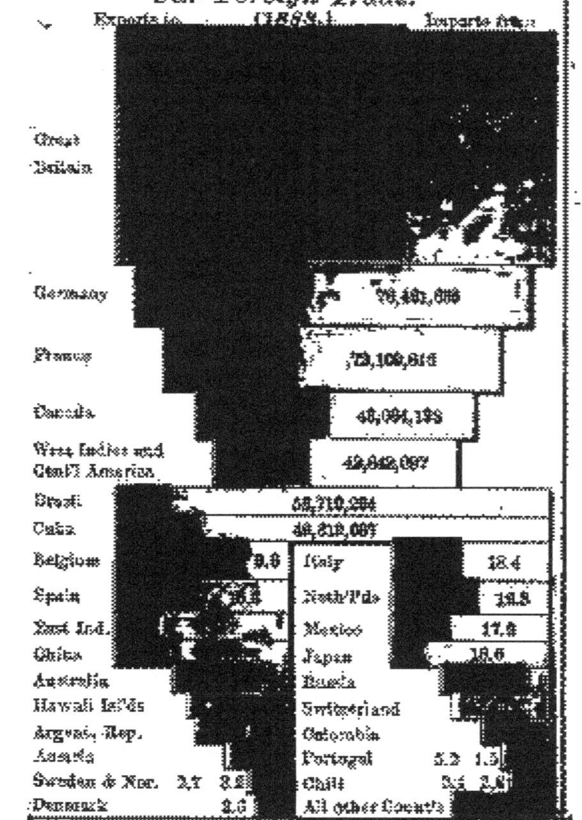

Our Foreign Trade.
Exports to
Imports from
Great Britain
Germany
France
Canada
West Indies and Cent'l America
Brazil
Cuba
Belgium
Spain
East Ind.
China
Australia
Hawaii Isl'ds
Argent. Rep.
Denmark
Sweden & Nor.
Italy
Neth'l'ds
Mexico
Japan
Russia
Switzerland
Colombia
Portugal
Chili
All other Countr's
70,401,000
73,109,616
46,094,193
42,042,097
18.4
17.8
5.2

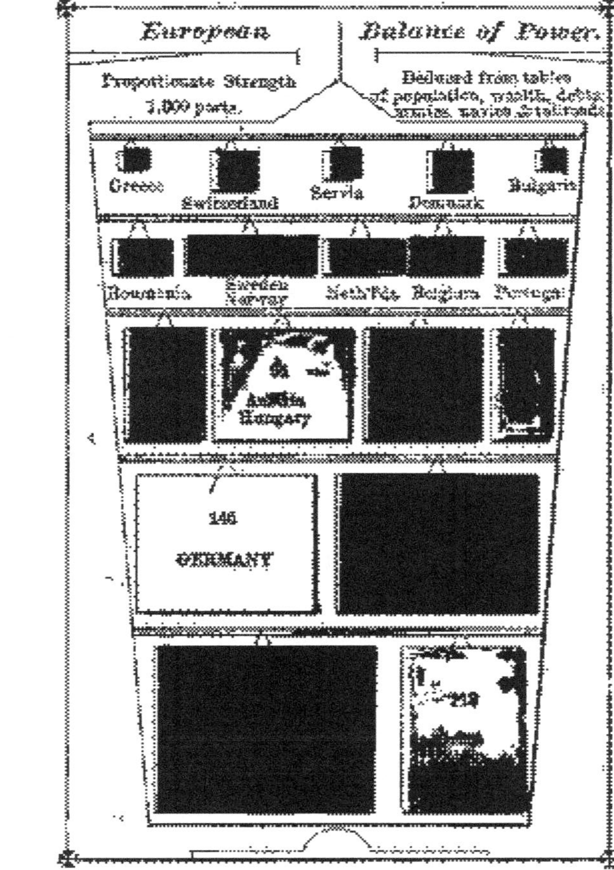

European Balance of Power.
Proportionate Strength
1,000 parts.
Deduced from tables of population, wealth, debts, armies, navies & railroads.
Greece
Switzerland
Servia
Denmark
Bulgaria
Roumania
Sweden Norway
Neth'l'ds
Belgium
Portugal
Austria Hungary
146
GERMANY

DENSITY OF POPULATION.

Inhabitants per Square Mile in 1820 and in 1890.

(Red for 1820. Yellow for 1890.)

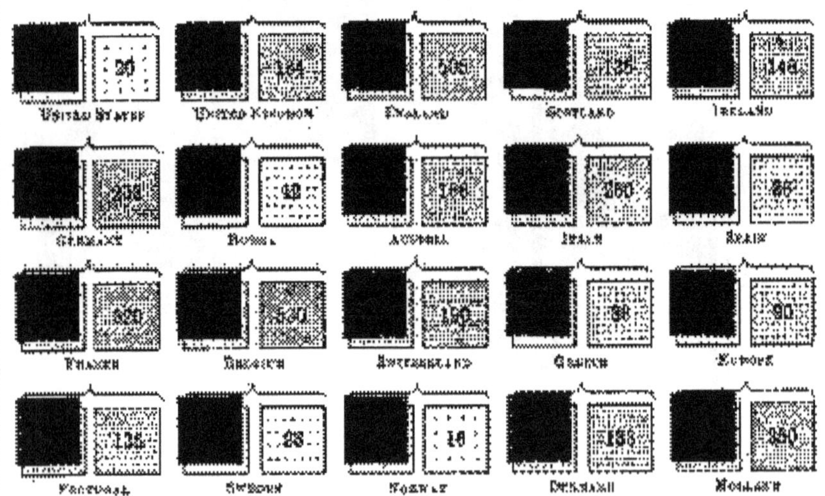

EDUCATION AND ILLITERACY.

The numbers on the right and the red Columns show the percentage of Adults able to write. The numbers on the left (1 to 21) and the blue columns show the percentage of the population attending school—average attendance.

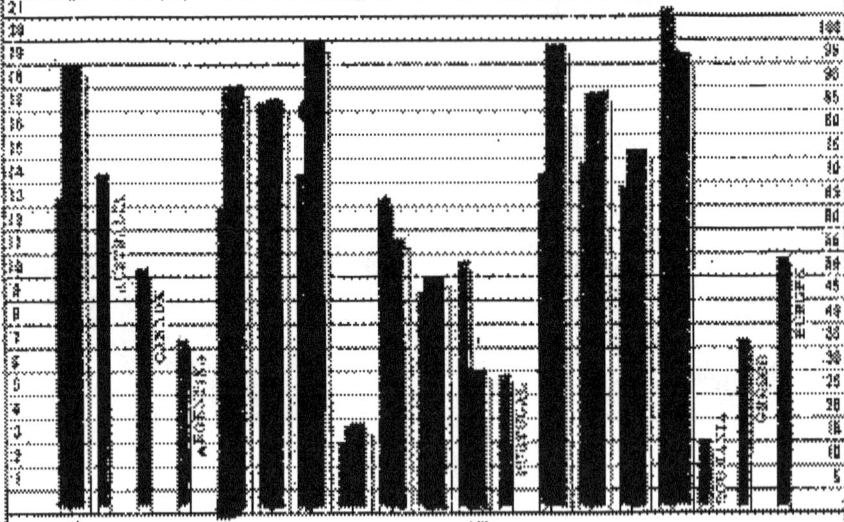

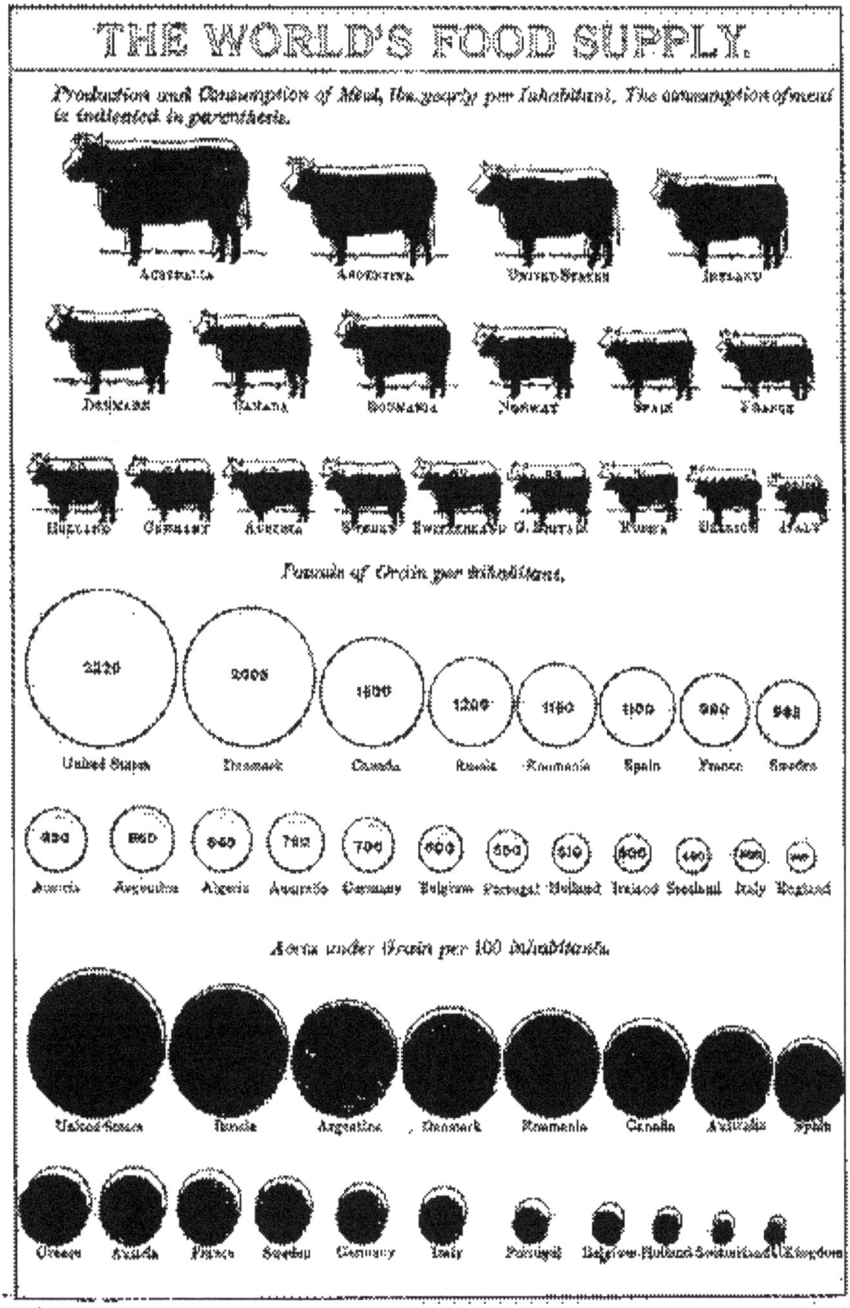

THE WORLD'S FOOD SUPPLY.

Production and Consumption of Meat, lbs. yearly per Inhabitant. The consumption of meat is indicated in parenthesis.

Australia — Argentina — United States — Ireland

Denmark — Canada — Roumania — Norway — Spain — France

England — Germany — Austria — Sweden — Switzerland — G. Britain — Russia — Belgium — Italy

Pounds of Grain per Inhabitant.

United States	Denmark	Canada	Russia	Roumania	Spain	France	Sweden
2220	2005	1600	1200	1150	1100	990	945

Austria	Argentina	Algeria	Australia	Germany	Belgium	Portugal	Holland	Ireland	Scotland	Italy	England
[illegible]	860	[illegible]	[illegible]	700	600	550	510	500	490	[illegible]	[illegible]

Acres under Grain per 100 Inhabitants.

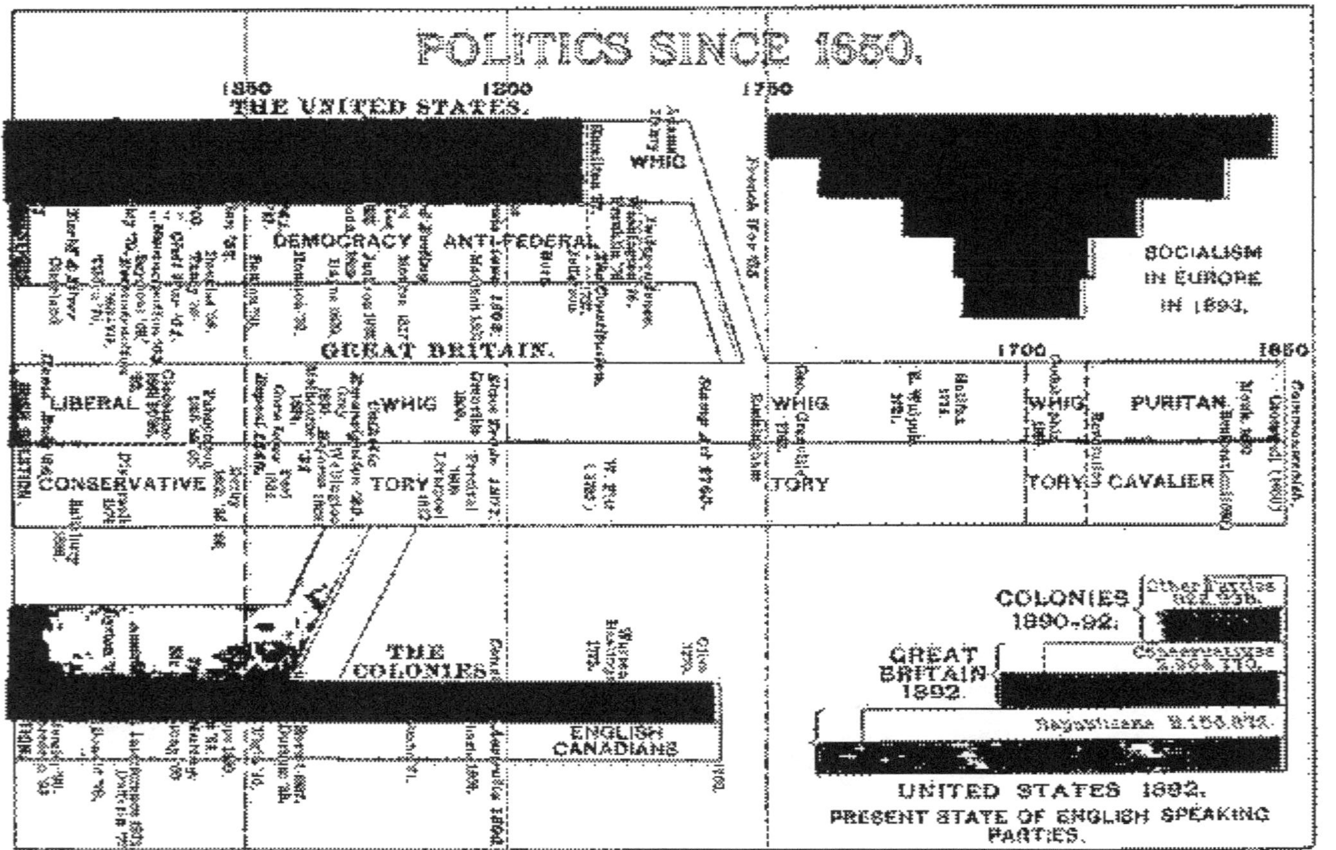

POLITICS SINCE 1650.
1850
1800
1750
1700
1650
THE UNITED STATES.
WHIG
DEMOCRACY
ANTI-FEDERAL
GREAT BRITAIN.
LIBERAL
CONSERVATIVE
WHIG
TORY
PURITAN
CAVALIER
SOCIALISM IN EUROPE IN 1893.
THE COLONIES
ENGLISH CANADIANS
COLONIES 1890-92.
GREAT BRITAIN 1892.
UNITED STATES 1892.
PRESENT STATE OF ENGLISH SPEAKING PARTIES.

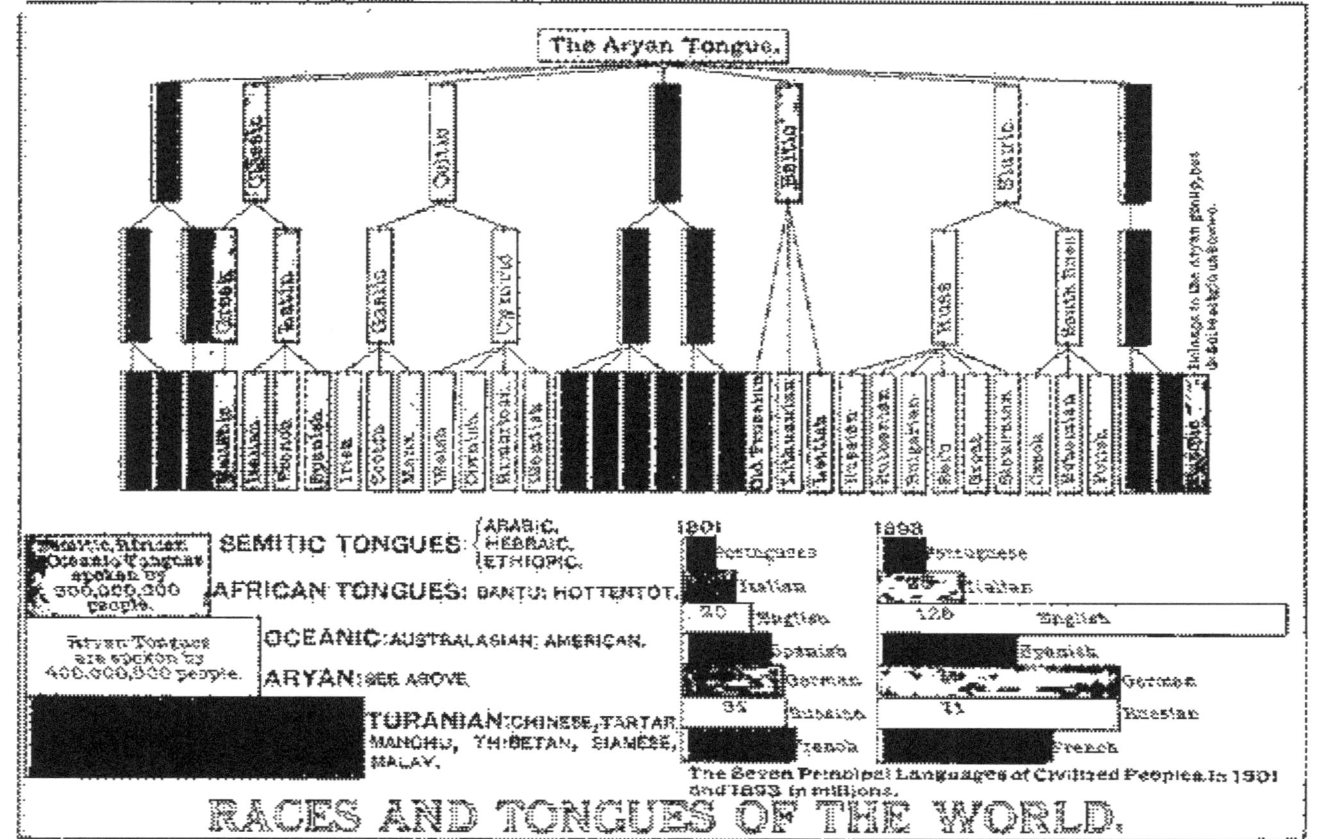

The Seven Principal Languages of Civilized Peoples in 1801 and 1893 in millions.

RACES AND TONGUES OF THE WORLD.

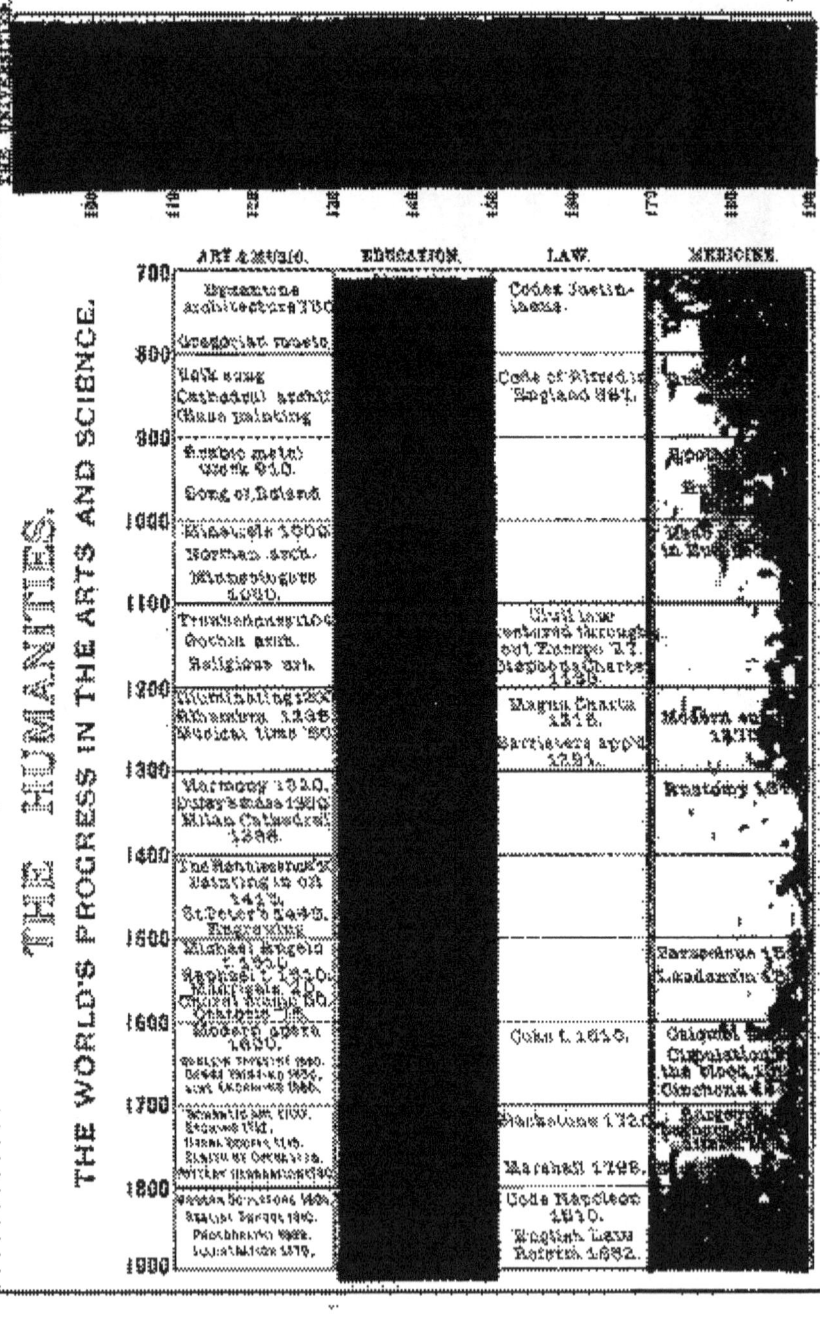
THE HUMANITIES.
THE WORLD'S PROGRESS IN THE ARTS AND SCIENCE.
ART & MUSIC.
EDUCATION.
LAW.
MEDICINE.
700
800
900
1000
1100
1200
1300
1400
1500
1600
1700
1800
1900
Byzantine architecture
Gregorian music
Folk song
Glass painting
Song of Roland
Norman arch.
Gothic arch.
Religious art.
Milan Cathedral
St. Peter's
Engraving
Modern opera
Codex Justinianeus.
Magna Charta
Code Napoleon 1810.
Anatomy
Circulation of the blood
Cinchona

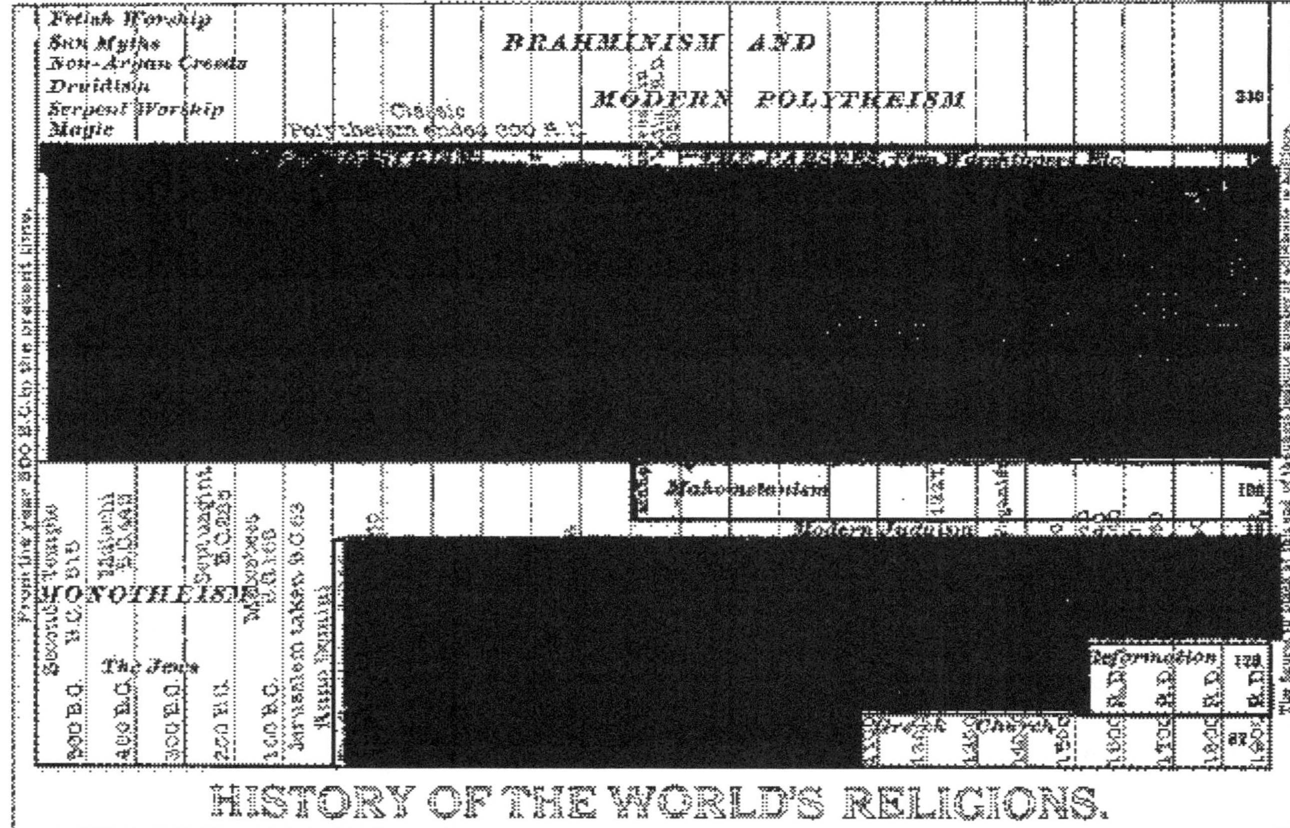
Fetish Worship
Sun Myths
Non-Aryan Creeds
Druidism
Serpent Worship
Magic
BRAHMINISM AND
MODERN POLYTHEISM
Classic
Polytheism ended 600 A.D.
Mahometanism
Modern Judaism
MONOTHEISM
The Jews
Second Temple
Malachi
Septuagint
Maccabees
Jerusalem taken B.C. 63
900 B.C.
400 B.C.
300 B.C.
200 B.C.
100 B.C.
Greek Church
Reformation
HISTORY OF THE WORLD'S RELIGIONS.

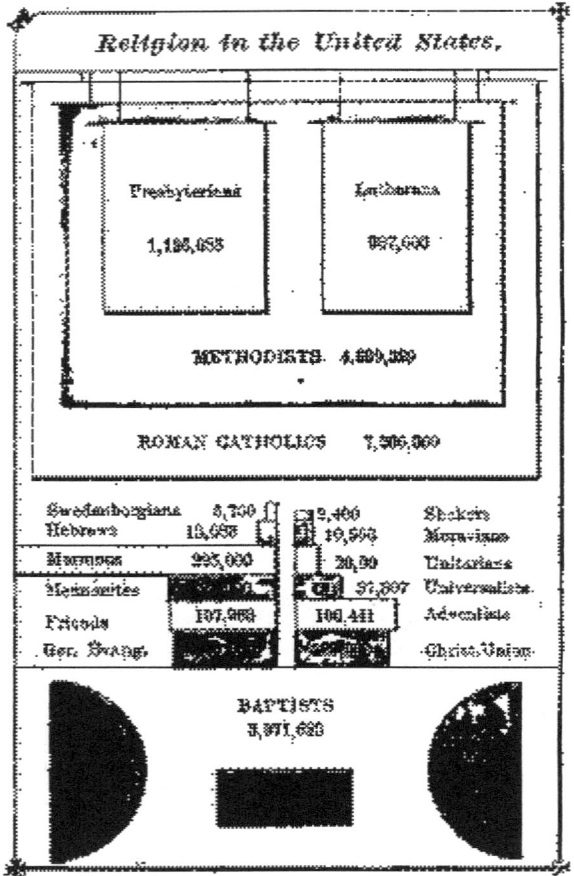

Religion in the United States.

Presbyterians 1,196,053

Lutherans 997,600

METHODISTS 4,699,389

ROMAN CATHOLICS 7,306,500

Swedenborgians 5,700

Hebrews 13,055

Mormons 995,000

Mennonites

Friends 107,968

Ger. Evang.

9,400 Shakers

19,503 Moravians

20,90 Unitarians

57,807 Universalists

100,441 Adventists

Christ. Union

BAPTISTS 3,971,623

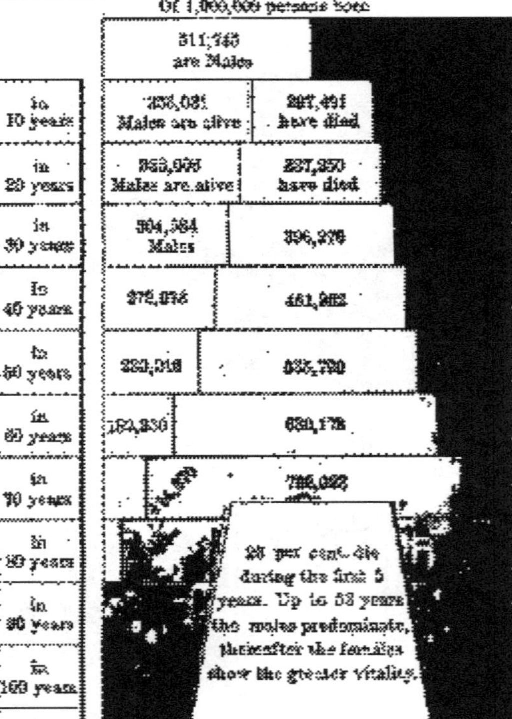

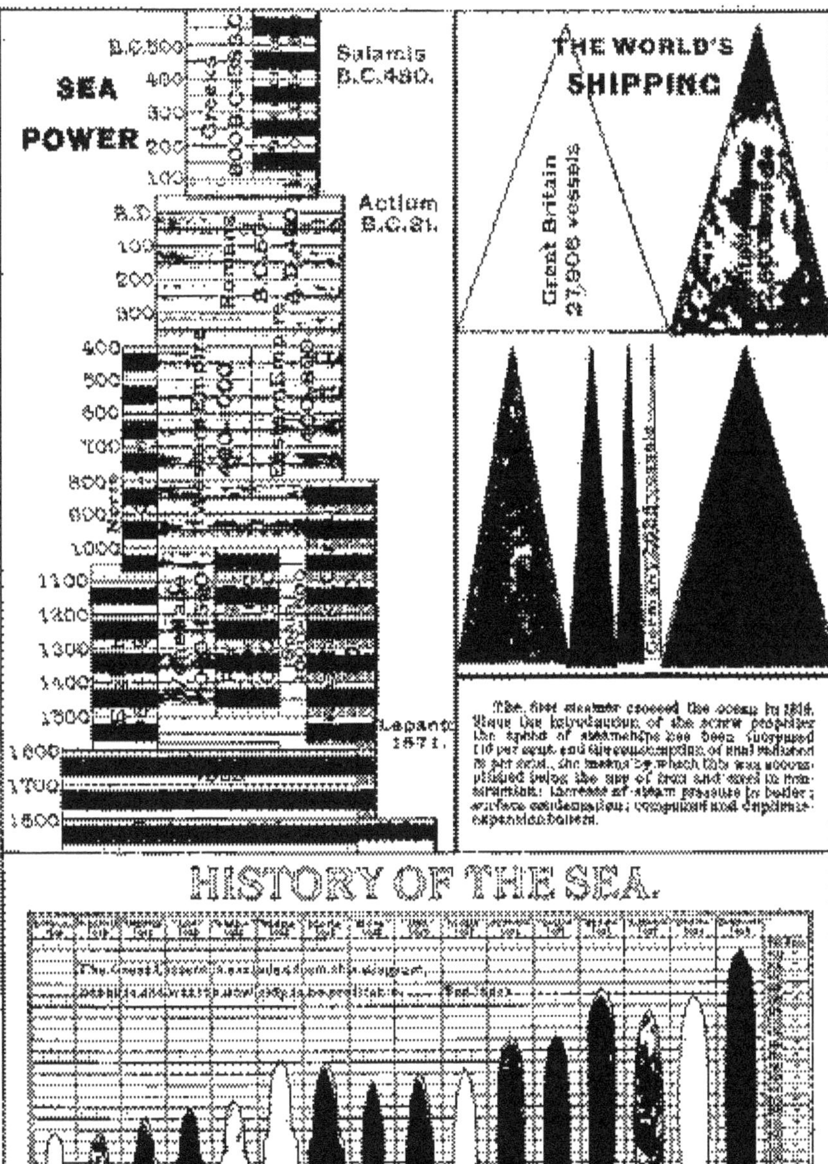

EVOLUTION OF STEAMSHIP DIMENSIONS FROM 1840 TO THE PRESENT TIME.

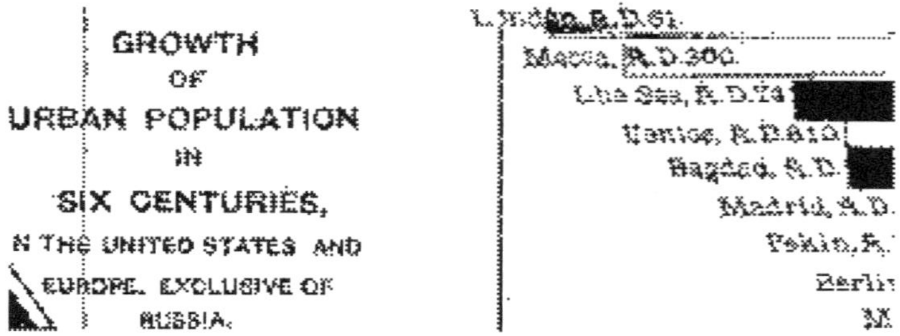

GROWTH
OF
URBAN POPULATION
IN
SIX CENTURIES,
IN THE UNITED STATES AND
EUROPE, EXCLUSIVE OF
RUSSIA.

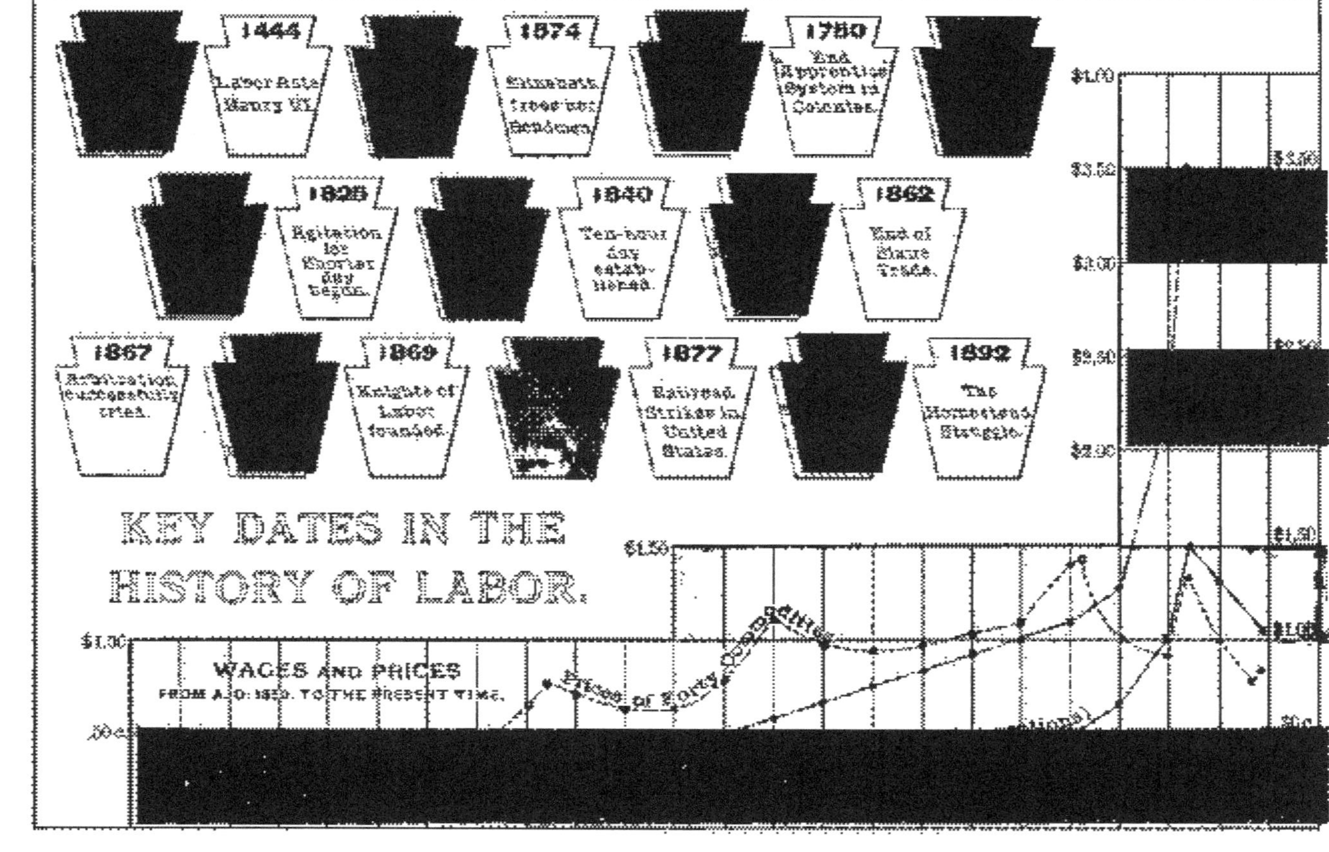

1444
1874
1780
End Apprentice System in Colonies.
1825
Agitation for Shorter day begun.
1840
Ten-hour day established.
1862
End of Slave Trade.
1867
1869
Knights of Labor founded.
1877
Railroad Strikes in United States.
1892
The Homestead Struggle.
KEY DATES IN THE HISTORY OF LABOR.
WAGES AND PRICES
FROM A.D. 1350. TO THE PRESENT TIME.
$4.00
$3.50
$3.00
$2.50
$2.00
$1.50
$1.00

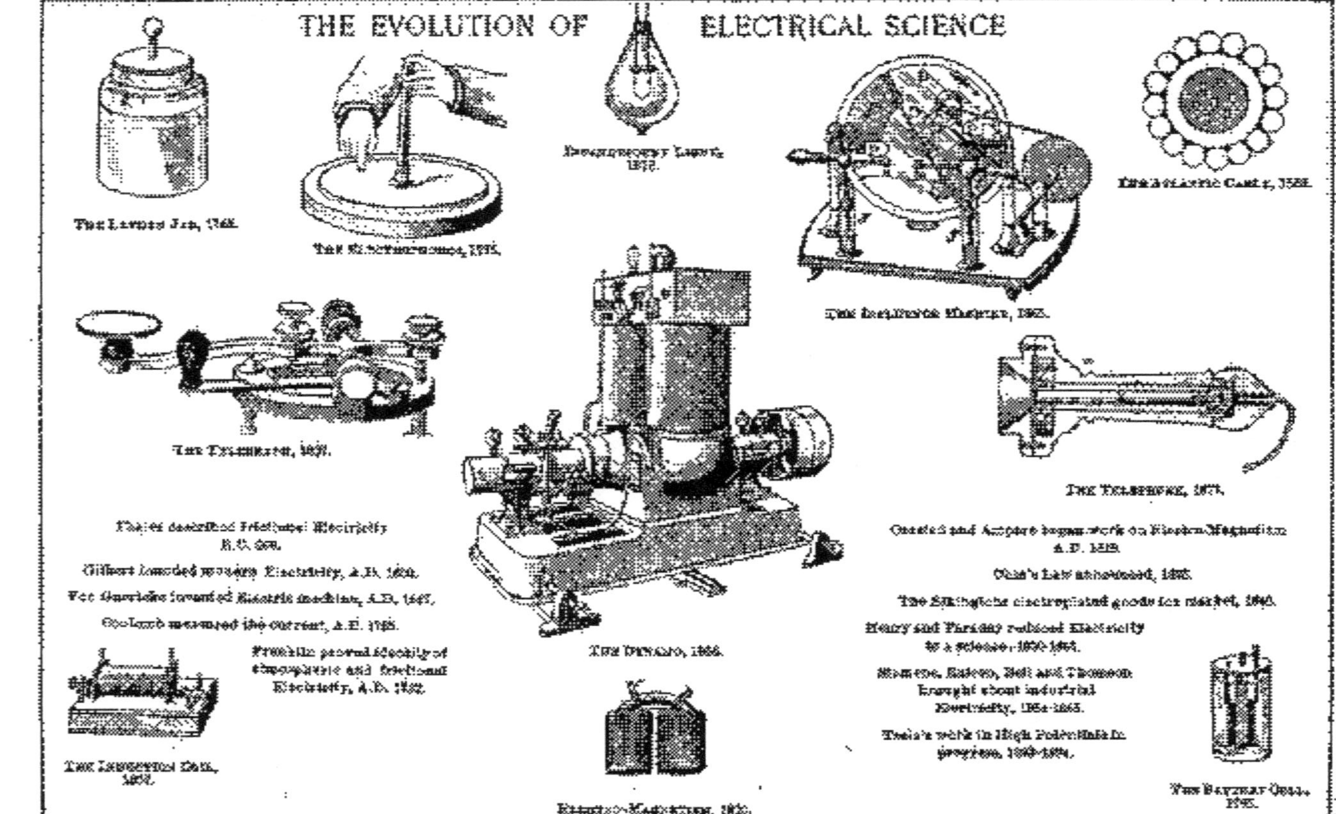
THE EVOLUTION OF ELECTRICAL SCIENCE

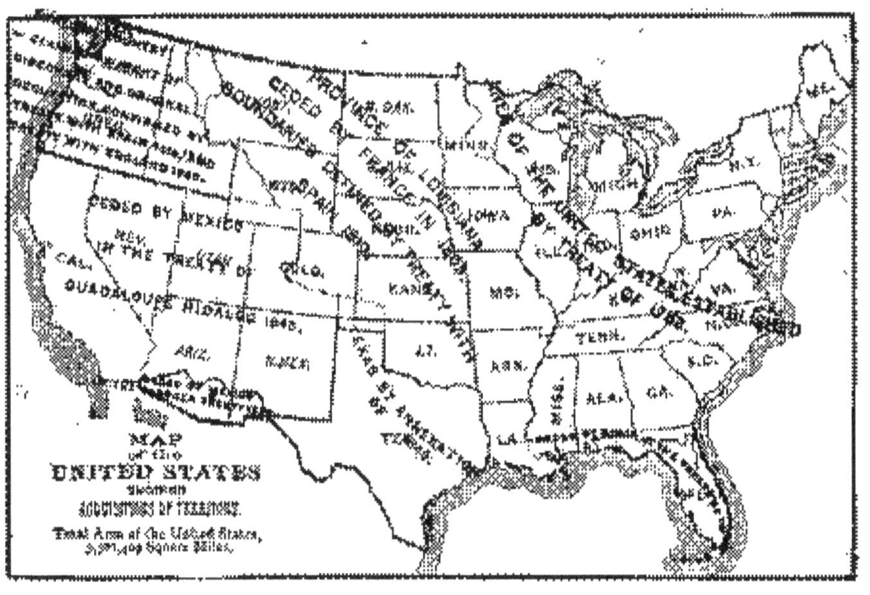
MAP
of the
UNITED STATES
showing
ACQUISITIONS OF TERRITORY.
Total Area of the United States,
3,571,492 Square Miles.
CEDED BY MEXICO
IN THE TREATY OF
GUADALOUPE HIDALGO 1848.
PROVINCE OF LOUISIANA
CEDED BY FRANCE IN 1803
TEXAS
TENN.
IOWA
OHIO
PA.
N.Y.
MO.
KANSAS
COLO.
ARIZ.
N.MEX.
MICH.
MINN.
VA.
S.C.
GA.
ALA.
MISS.
ARK.
LA.
CAL.
NEV.

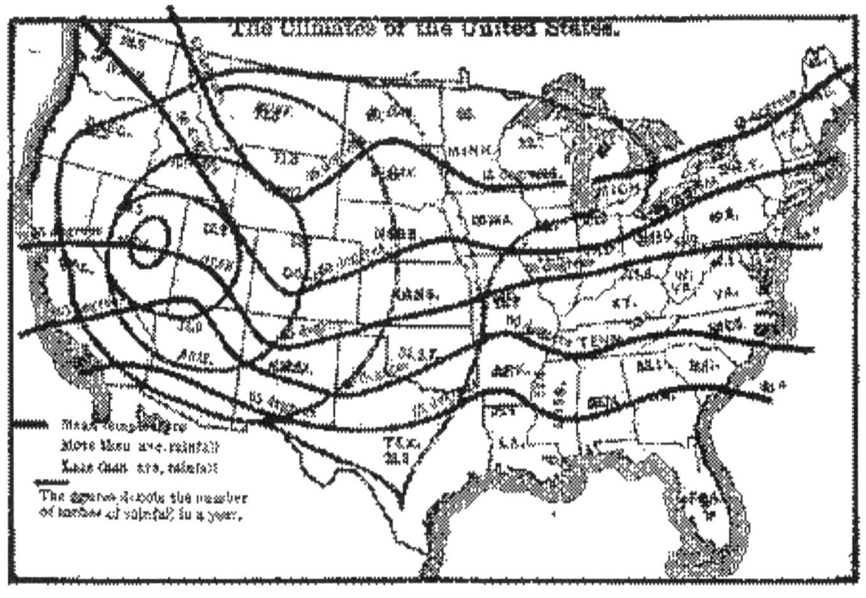
The Climates of the United States.
TEX.
IOWA
PA.
OHIO
KY.
VA.
TENN.
KANS.
ARIZ.
ARK.
MINN.
MICH.
N.Y.

TELEGRAPHIC ALPHABET

Morse		Needle and Mirror	Morse		Needle and Mirror
A	[illegible]	[illegible]	S	[illegible]	[illegible]
Ä (ae)	[illegible]	[illegible]	T	[illegible]	[illegible]
B	[illegible]	[illegible]	U	[illegible]	[illegible]
C	[illegible]	[illegible]	Ü (ue)	[illegible]	[illegible]
D	[illegible]	[illegible]	V	[illegible]	[illegible]
E	[illegible]	[illegible]	W	[illegible]	[illegible]
F	[illegible]	[illegible]	X	[illegible]	[illegible]
G	[illegible]	[illegible]	Y	[illegible]	[illegible]
H	[illegible]	[illegible]	Z	[illegible]	[illegible]
I	[illegible]	[illegible]	Ch	[illegible]	[illegible]
J	[illegible]	[illegible]	1	[illegible]	[illegible]
K	[illegible]	[illegible]	2	[illegible]	[illegible]
L	[illegible]	[illegible]	3	[illegible]	[illegible]
M	[illegible]	[illegible]	4	[illegible]	[illegible]
N	[illegible]	[illegible]	5	[illegible]	[illegible]
O	[illegible]	[illegible]	6	[illegible]	[illegible]
Ö (oe)	[illegible]	[illegible]	7	[illegible]	[illegible]
P	[illegible]	[illegible]	8	[illegible]	[illegible]
Q	[illegible]	[illegible]	9	[illegible]	[illegible]
R	[illegible]	[illegible]	0	[illegible]	[illegible]

The Morse alphabet is the one ordinarily used in telegraphing, but messages by cable are generally sent by the Needle and Mirror system. About 25 words, averaging five letters each, can be sent per minute by the Morse signals, about 20 words per minute can be sent by the "Needle and Mirror" on short cables. Errors and ambiguities in the transmission of telegraphic dispatches may generally be detected by a study of the alphabet—by noting such combinations as may easily be confounded with others.

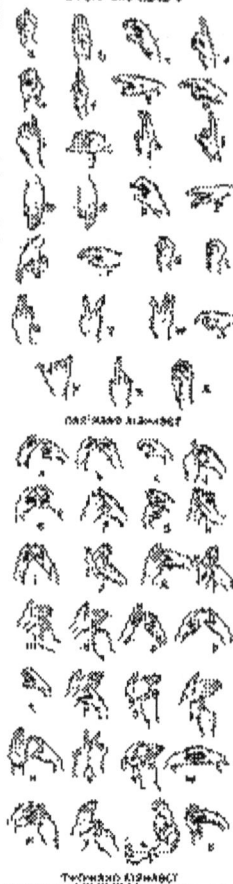

DEAF AND DUMB ALPHABET

ONE-HAND ALPHABET

TWO-HAND ALPHABET

ALPHABET FOR THE BLIND

MOON'S SYSTEM

A B C D E F G H I J K L M N O P

Q R S T U V W X Y Z &

1 2 3 4 5 6 7 8 9 0

Medicine and Hygiene

DISEASES AND THEIR REMEDIES

PRESCRIPTIONS BY EMINENT PRACTITIONERS

IT should be clearly understood that in all cases of disease the advice of a skillful physician is of the first importance. It is not, therefore, intended to supersede the important and necessary practice of the medical man; but rather, by exhibiting the treatment required, to show in what degree his aid is imperative. In cases, however, where the disorder may be simple or transient, or in which remote residence, or other circumstances, may deny the privilege of medical attendance, the following particulars will be found of the utmost value. Moreover, the hints given upon what should be avoided will be of great service to the patient, since the *physiological* is no less important than the medical treatment of disease. The numbers refer to prescriptions on pages 195-197.

APOPLEXY — Lay the head upon a bag of pounded ice; immediate and large bleeding from the arm; cupping neck; leeches to the temple; aperients Nos. 1 and 7; one or two drops of croton oil rubbed or dropped on the tongue. Avoid excesses, intemperance, animal food.

BILE, BILIOUS, OR LIVER COMPLAINTS — Abstinence from malt liquor, cool homœopathic cocoa for drink, no tea or coffee, few vegetables, no broths or soups; lean, juicy meat not overcooked for dinner, with stale bread occasionally and a slice of toasted bacon for breakfast. Nos. 44 and 45.

CHICKEN POX — Mild aperients, No. 4, succeeded by No. 7, and No. 8, if much fever accompany the eruption.

CHILBLAINS — Warm, dry woolen clothing to exposed parts in cold weather, as a preventive. In the first stage, friction with No. 40, used cold. When ulcers form they should be washed twice daily with carbolic soap and dressed with benzoated zinc ointment. Or, chilblains in every stage, whether of simple inflammation or open ulcer, may always be successfully treated by Goulard's extract, used pure or applied on lint twice a day.

COMMON CONTINUED FEVER — Aperients; in the commencement No. 1, followed by No. 7; then diaphoretics, No. 8, and afterwards tonics, No. 15, in the stage of weakness. Avoid all excesses.

COMMON COUGH — The linctus, No. 42 or No. 43, abstinence from malt liquor, and protection from cold, damp air. Avoid cold, damp and draughts.

CONSTIPATION — The observance of a regular period of evacuating the bowels, which is most proper in the morning after breakfast. The use of mild aperients, No. 37, and brown bread instead of white. There should be an entire change in the dietary for a few days while taking opening medicine.

CONSUMPTION — The disease may be complicated with various morbid conditions of the lungs and heart, which require appropriate treatment. Take cod liver oil, malt and whisky. To allay the cough, No. 32 is an admirable remedy. Avoid cold, damp, excitement and over-exertion.

CONVULSIONS (CHILDREN) — If during teething, free lancing of the gums, the warm bath, cold applications to the head, an emetic, and a laxative clyster, No. 20.

CROUP — Hot fomentations as long as the attack lasts; the emetic No. 16, afterwards the aperient No. 5. Avoid cold and damp. Keep the air in the sick-room moistened with steam.

A SIMPLE CROUP REMEDY — Take the white of an egg, stir it thoroughly into a small quantity of sweetened water, and give it in repeated doses until a cure is effected. If one egg is not enough, a second, or even a third, should be used.

DROPSY — Evacuate the water by means of No. 10, and by rubbing camphorated oil into the body night and morning.

EPILEPSY — If accompanied or produced by fullness of the vessels of the head, leeches to the temples, blisters, and No. 1 and No. 7. If from debility or confirmed epilepsy, the mixture No. 18. Avoid drinking and excitement. Let the patient alone during the convulsion.

ERUPTIONS ON THE FACE — The powder No. 30, internally, sponging the face with the lotion No. 31. Avoid excesses in diet.

ERYSIPELAS — Aperients, if the patient be strong, No. 1, followed by No. 7, then tonics, No. 27. No. 27 may be used from the commencement for weak subjects.

Fainting — Effusion of cold water on the face, stimulants to the nostrils, pure air, and the recumbent position; afterwards avoidance of the exciting cause. Avoid excitement.

Frost-bite and Frozen Limbs — No heating or stimulating liquors must be given. Rub the parts affected with ice, cold, or snow water, and lay the patient on a cold bed.

Gout — The aperient No. 1, followed by No. 34, bathing the parts with gin-and-water; for drink, weak tea or coffee. Warmth by flannels. Abstain from wines, spirits and animal food.

Gravel — No. 5, followed by No. 7, the free use of magnesia as an aperient. The pill No. 22. Abstain from fermented drinks and hard water. Another form of gravel must be treated by mineral acids, given three times a day.

Whooping Cough — Whooping cough may be complicated with congestion or inflammation of the lungs, or convulsions, and then becomes a serious disease. If uncomplicated, No. 48.

Hysterics — The fit may be prevented by the administration of thirty drops of laudanum, and as many of ether. When it has taken place, open the windows, loosen the tight parts of the dress, sprinkle cold water on the face, etc. A glass of wine or cold water when the patient can swallow. Avoid excitement and tight lacing.

Indigestion — The pills No. 2, with the mixture No. 16, at the same time abstinence from veal, pork, mackerel, salmon, pastry and beer; for drink, homoeopathic cocoa, a glass of cold spring water the first thing every morning. Avoid excesses.

Inflammation of the Bladder — Aperients No. 5 and No. 7, the warm bath, afterwards opium; the pill No. 11 three times a day till relieved. Avoid fermented liquors, etc. Large quantities of water should be taken, especially spring water containing lithia.

Inflammation of the Bowels — Leeches, blisters, fomentations, hot baths, iced drinks, the pills No. 19; move the bowels with clysters, if necessary, No. 20. Avoid cold, indigestible food, etc.

Inflammation of the Brain — Application of cold to the head, bleeding from the temples or back of the neck by leeches or cupping; aperient No. 4, followed by No. 7, No. 15. Avoid excitement, study, intemperance.

Inflammation of the Kidneys — Leeches over the seat of pain, aperients No. 5, followed by No. 49; the warm bath. Avoid violent exercise, rich living.

Inflammation of the Liver — Leeches over the right side, the seat of pain, blisters, aperient No. 4, followed by No. 7, afterwards the pills No. 19, till the gums are slightly tender. Avoid cold, damp, intemperance and anxiety.

Inflammation of the Lungs — Leeches to seat of pain, succeeded by a blister; the demulcent mixture, No. 16, to allay the cough, with the powders No. 15, whisky and milk. Avoid cold, damp and draughts.

Inflammation of the Stomach — Leeches to the pit of the stomach, followed by fomentations, cold iced water for drink, bowels to be evacuated by clysters; abstinence from all food except cold gruel, milk and water. Avoid excesses and condiments.

Inflammatory Sore Throat — Leeches and blisters externally, aperient No. 1, followed by No. 7; gargle to clear the throat, No. 17. Avoid cold, damp and draughts.

Inflamed Eyes — The bowels to be regulated by No. 5; drop 5 per cent. cocaine solution in the eye every three or four hours, the eye to be bathed with No. 25.

Influenza — No. 4 as an aperient and diaphoretic. No. 16 to allay fever and cough. No. 28 as a tonic, when weakness only remains. Avoid cold and damp; use clothing suited to the changes of temperature.

Intermittent Fever, or Ague — Take No. 18 during the intermission of the paroxysm of the fever, keeping the bowels free with a wine glass of No. 7. Avoid bad air, stagnant pools, etc.

Itch — The ointment No. 28, or lotion No. 29.

Jaundice — The pills No. 1, afterwards the mixture No. 7, drinking freely of dandelion tea.

Looseness of the Bowels (Bilious Choleraic) — One pill No. 19, repeated if necessary; afterwards the mixture No. 21. Avoid unripe fruits, acid drinks, ginger beer; wrap flannel around the abdomen.

Measles — A well-ventilated room, aperient No. 4, with No. 14 to allay the cough and fever.

Menstruation (Excessive) — No. 40 during the attack, with rest in the recumbent position; in the intervals, No. 39.

Menstruation (Scanty) — In strong patients, cupping the loins, exercise in the open air, No. 40, the feet in warm water before the expected period, the pills No. 36; in weak subjects No. 39. Gentle and regular exercise. Avoid hot rooms and too much sleep. In cases of this description, it is desirable to apply to a medical man for advice. It may be useful to many to point out that pennyroyal tea is a simple and useful medicine for inducing the desired result.

Menstruation (Painful) — No. 41 during the attack; in the intervals, No. 38 twice a week, with No. 19. Avoid cold, mental excitement, etc.

MUMPS — Fomentation with a decoction of camomiles and poppy heads; No. 4 as an aperient, and No. 9 during the stage of fever. Avoid cold, and attend to the regularity of the bowels.

NERVOUSNESS — Cheerful society, early rising; exercise in the open air, particularly on horseback, and No. 12. Avoid excitement, study and late meals.

PALPITATION OF THE HEART — The pills No. 2, with the mixture No. 12.

PILES — The paste No. 31, at the same time a regulated diet. When the piles are external, or can be reached, one or two applications of Goulard's extract, with an occasional dose of lenitive electuary, will generally succeed in curing them.

QUINSY — A blister applied all around the throat; an emetic, No. 16, commonly succeeds in breaking the abscess; afterwards the gargle No. 17. Avoid cold and damp.

RHEUMATISM — Bathe the affected parts with No. 23, and take internally No. 24, with No. 25 at bedtime, to ease pain, etc. Avoid damp and cold; wear flannel.

RICKETS — The powder No. 33, a dry, pure atmosphere, a nourishing diet.

RINGWORM — The lotion No. 32, with the occasional use of the powder No. 5. Fresh air and cleanliness.

SCARLET FEVER — Well-ventilated room, sponging the body when hot with cold or tepid vinegar, or spirits and water; aperient, No. 4; diaphoretic, No. 8. If dropsy succeed the disappearance of the eruption, frequent purging with No. 5, succeeded by No. 7.

SCROFULA — Pure air, light but warm clothing; diet of fresh animal food; bowels to be regulated by No. 6 and No. 26, taken regularly for a considerable time.

SCURVY — Fresh animal and vegetable food, and the free use of ripe fruits and lemon juice. Avoid cold and damp.

SMALLPOX — A well-ventilated apartment, mild aperients; if fever be present, No. 7, succeeded by diaphoretic No. 8, and tonic No. 13 in the stage of debility, or decline of the eruption.

ST. VITUS' DANCE — The occasional use, in the commencement, of No. 5, followed by No. 7, afterwards No. 46.

THRUSH — One of the powders No. 6 every other night; in the intervals a dessertspoonful of the mixture No. 18 three times a day; white spots to be dressed with the honey of borax.

TIC DOLOREUX — Regulate the bowels with No. 3, and take, in the intervals of pain, No. 27. Avoid cold, damp and mental anxiety.

TOOTHACHE — Continue the use of No. 3 for a few alternate days. Apply liquor ammonia to reduce the pain, and when that is accomplished, fill the decayed spots with silver succedaneum without delay, or the pain will return. A drop of creosote, or a few drops of chloroform on cotton, applied to the tooth, or a few grains of camphor placed in the decaying opening, or camphor moistened with turpentine, will often afford instant relief.

TYPHUS FEVER — Sponging the body with cold or tepid water, a well-ventilated apartment, cold applications to the head and temples. Aperient No. 4, with refrigerant No. 9, tonic No. 13 in the stage of debility.

WATER ON THE BRAIN — Local bleeding by means of leeches, blisters, aperient No. 5, and mercurial medicines, No. 15.

WHITES — The mixture No. 36, with the injection No. 37. Clothing light but warm, moderate exercise in the open air, country residence.

WORMS IN THE INTESTINES — The aperient No. 5, followed by No. 7, afterwards the free use of lime water and milk in equal parts, a pint daily. Avoid unwholesome food.

... Prescriptions ...

TO BE USED IN CASES ENUMERATED ON PAGES 193-195

THE following prescriptions, originally derived from various prescribers' pharmacopœias, and now carefully revised, embody the favorite remedies employed by the most eminent physicians:

1. Take of powdered aloes, nine grains; extract of colocynth, compound, eighteen grains; calomel, nine grains; tartrate of antimony, two grains; mucilage, sufficient to make a mass, which is divided into six pills: two to be taken every twenty-four hours, till they act thoroughly on the bowels; in cases of inflammation, apoplexy, etc.

2. Powdered rhubarb, Socotrine aloes, and gum mastic, each one scruple; make into twelve pills; one before and one after dinner.

3. Compound extract of colocynth, extract of jalap, and Castile soap, of each one scruple; make into twelve pills.

4. James' powder, five grains; calomel, three grains; in fevers, for adults. For children, the following: Powdered camphor, one scruple; calomel and powdered scammony, of each nine grains; James' powder, six grains; mix and divide into six powders. Half of one powder twice a day for an infant a year old; a whole powder for two years; and for four years, the same three times a day.

5. James' powder, six grains; powdered jalap, ten grains; mix, and divide into three or four powders, according to the child's age; in one powder if for an adult.

6. Powdered rhubarb, four grains; mercury and chalk, three grains; ginger in powder, one grain; an alterative aperient for children.

7. Fluid extract cascara, six drams; tincture aloes, four drams; tincture hyoscyamus, four drams; neutralising cordial, two ounces; dessertspoonful every four hours until the bowels move freely.

8. Nitrate of potash, one dram and a half; spirits of nitric ether, half an ounce; camphor mixture, and the spirit of mindererus, each four ounces; in fevers, etc.; two tablespoonfuls, three times a day, and for children a dessertspoonful every four hours.

9. Spirit of nitric ether, three drams; dilute nitric acid, two drams; syrup, three drams; camphor mixture, seven ounces: in fevers, etc., with debility; dose as in preceding prescription.

10. Decoction of broom, half a pint; cream of tartar, one ounce; tincture of squills, two drams; in dropsies; a third part three times a day.

11. Pills of soap and opium, five grains for a dose, as directed.

12. Ammoniated tincture of valerian, six drams; camphor mixture, seven ounces; a fourth part three times a day; in spasmodic and hysterical disorders.

13. Bisulphate of quinia, half a dram; dilute sulphuric acid, twenty drops; compound infusion of roses, eight ounces; two tablespoonfuls every four hours, in intermittent and other fevers, during the absence of the paroxysm.

14. Almond mixture, seven ounces and a half; wine of antimony and ipecacuanha, of each one dram and a half; a tablespoonful every four hours; in cough with fever; etc.

15. Calomel, one grain; powdered white sugar, two grains; to make a powder to be placed on the tongue every two or three hours. Should the calomel act on the bowels, powdered kino is to be substituted for the sugar.

16. Antimony and ipecacuanha wines, of each an ounce; a teaspoonful every ten minutes for a child till vomiting is produced; but for an adult a large tablespoonful should be taken.

17. Compound infusion of roses, seven ounces; tincture of myrrh, one ounce.

18. Infusion of orange peel, seven ounces; tincture of hops, half an ounce, and a dram of carbonate of soda; two tablespoonfuls twice a day. Or infusion of valerian, seven ounces; carbonate of ammonia, two scruples; compound tincture of bark, six drams; spirits of ether, two drams; one tablespoonful every twenty-four hours.

19. Blue pill, four grains; opium, half a grain; to be taken three times a day.

20. For a Clyster.—A pint and a half of gruel or fat broth; a tablespoonful of castor oil, one of common salt, and a lump of butter; mix, to be injected slowly. A third of this quantity is enough for an infant.

21. Chalk mixture, seven ounces; aromatic and opiate confection, of each one dram; tincture of catechu, six drams; two tablespoonfuls every two hours.

22. Carbonate of soda, powdered rhubarb, and Castile soap, each one dram; make thirty-six pills; three twice a day.

23. Lotion.—Common salt, one ounce; distilled water, seven ounces; spirits of wine, one ounce; mix.

24. Dried sulphate of magnesia, six drams; heavy carbonate of magnesia, two drams; wine of colchicum, two drams; water, eight ounces; take two tablespoonfuls every four hours.

25. Compound powder of ipecacuanha, ten grains; powdered guaiacum, four grains; in a powder at bedtime.

26. Brandish's solution of potash; thirty drops twice a day in a wineglass of beer.

27. Bisulphate of quinia, half a dram; dilute sulphuric acid, ten drops; compound infusion of roses, eight ounces; two tablespoonfuls every eight hours, and as a tonic in the stage of weakness succeeding fever.

28. Flowers of sulphur, two ounces; hog's lard, four ounces; white hellebore powder, half an ounce; oil of lavender, sixty drops.

29. Iodide of potash, two drams; distilled water, eight ounces.

30. Flowers of sulphur, half a dram; carbonate of soda, a scruple; tartarized antimony, one-eighth of a grain; one powder night and morning, in eruptions of the skin on face.

31. Milk of bitter almonds, seven ounces; bichloride of mercury, four grains; spirits of rosemary, one ounce; bathe the eruption with this lotion three times a day.

32. Sulphate of zinc, two scruples; sugar of lead, fifteen grains; distilled water, six ounces; the parts to be washed with the lotion three times a day.

33. Carbonate of iron, six grains; powdered rhubarb, four grains; one powder night and morning.

34. Aromatic powder and pepsin, each one dram; make twelve powders; one three or four times a day.

35. Sulphate of zinc, twelve grains; wine of opium, one dram; rosewater, six ounces.

36. Sulphate of magnesia, six drams; sulphate of iron, ten grains; diluted sulphuric acid, forty drops; tincture of cardamoms (compound), half an ounce; water, seven ounces; a fourth part night and morning.

37. Decoction of oak bark, a pint; dried alum, half an ounce; for an injection; a syringe full to be used night and morning.

38. Compound gamboge pill and a pill of assafœtida and aloes, of each half a dram; make twelve pills; two twice or three times a week.

39. Griffith's mixture—one tablespoonful three times a day.

40. Ergot of rye, five grains, in a powder, to be taken every four hours. This should only be taken under medical advice and sanction.

41. Powdered opium, half a grain; camphor, two grains, in a pill; to be taken every three or four hours whilst in pain.

42. Syrup of balsam of tolu, two ounces; the muriate of morphia, two grains; muriatic acid, twenty drops; a teaspoonful twice a day.

43. Salts of tartar, two scruples; twenty grains of powdered cochineal; ¼ lb of honey; water, half a pint; boil and give a tablespoonful three times a day.

44. Calomel, ten grains; Castile soap, extract of jalap, extract of colocynth, of each one scruple; oil of juniper, five drops; make into fifteen pills; one three times a day.

45. Infusion of orange peel, eight ounces; carbonate of soda, one dram, and compound tincture of cardamoms, half an ounce; take a tablespoonful three times a day succeeding the pills.

46. Carbonate of iron, three ounces; syrup of ginger sufficient to make an electuary; a teaspoonful three times a day.

47. Take of Castile soap, compound extract of colocynth, compound rhubarb pill and the extract of jalap, each one scruple; oil of caraway, ten drops; make into twenty pills, and take one after dinner every day whilst necessary.

48. Spirit of rosemary, five parts; spirit of wine, or spirit of turpentine, one part.

49. Take of thick mucilage, one ounce; castor oil, twelve drams; make into an emulsion; add mint water, four ounces; spirit of nitre, three drams; laudanum, one dram; mixture of squills, one dram; and syrup, seven drams; mix; two tablespoonfuls every six hours.

LARGEST SAFE DOSES OF POISONOUS DRUGS.

Every person should know the largest doses, which it is safe to take, of active medicines. The following table shows the largest doses admissible, in grammes, and also the equivalent in grains for solids, and in minims for liquids. The doses are expressed in fractions, thus: 1-13, 1-64, meaning one-thirteenth, one-sixty-fourth. In non-professional hands it is the safest plan to strictly observe the rule of never giving the maximum dose of any medicine:

Medicines.	Grammes.	Grains.
Arsenious Acid	.006	1-13
Acid, Carbolic	.05	¾
" Hydrocyanic	.06	1
Aconitia	.004	1-16
Aconite Root	.15	2¼
Arsenic, Iodide	.025	⅜
Atropia	.001	1-64
Atropia Sulph	.001	1-64
Barium, Chlor	.12	1¾
Belladonna Herb	.2	3
" Root	.1	1½
Codia	.05	¾
Conia	.001	1-64
Digitalis	.3	4½
Extract Aconite Leaves	.1	1½
" " Root	.025	⅜
" Belladonna	.1	1½
" Cannabis Indica	.1	1½
" Conium	.18	2¾
" Digitalis	.2	3
" Nux Vomica Alc.	.05	¾
" Opium	.1	1½
" Stramon. Seed	.05	¾
Fowler's Solution	.4	6 min.
Lead, Sugar of	.06	9-10
Mercury, Corrosive Chlor	.03	9-20
" Red Iodide	.03	9-20
Morphia and its Salts	.03	9-20
Nitrate Silver	.03	9-20
Oil, Croton	.06	9-10
Opium	.15	2¼
Phosphorus	.015	2-9
Potassa, Arsenite	.006	1-13
" Cyanide	.03	9-20
Santonine	.1	1½
Soda, Arsenite	.005	1-13
Strychnia and Salts	.01	1-6
Tartar Emetic	.2	3
Veratria	.005	1-13
Veratrum Viride	.3	4½
Zinc, Chloride	.015	2-9
" Valerianate	.06	9-10

The Spanish Armada consisted of 132 ships, 3,165 cannon, 8,766 sailors, 2,088 galley slaves, 21,855 soldiers, 1,355 volunteers, and 150 monks.

The progress of education in Europe since 1840 has been wonderful. The population has increased 33 per cent., and the school attendance 145 per cent.

Additional Recipes and Suggestions

RHEUMATISM—There is no better specific for rheumatism than earth-worm oil. It is commonly made by taking two or three dozen of the largest earth-worms that can be found, and placing them in a tin or iron cup over the fire. In a few moments the worms will dissolve into a fine oil, which is then strained and may be bottled, tightly corked, and set away in a cool place for use. It should be employed as a liniment, and the stiffest rheumatic joints, well rubbed with this natural lubricant, will recover their former flexibility.

A cure for INFLAMMATORY RHEUMATISM that is said to be unfailing, when properly carried out, is to fill a large-sized tub, one sufficiently large to admit of placing within it a cane-seat chair, with hay, and pour over it a wash-boiler full of boiling water. The water must be boiling, not simply hot. Now place the patient on the chair and cover quickly with something heavy and close so no steam will escape. Keep the patient over the tub one hour, then wrap in warm blankets and put to bed. Renew the blankets three times within twenty-four hours. Three of these vapor baths are sufficient. They are weakening, but very effectual.

NEURALGIA of the face, it is claimed, has been cured by applying a mustard plaster to the elbow. For neuralgia of the heart, apply the plaster to the back of the neck. The reason for this is that mustard is said to touch the nerves the moment it begins to draw or burn, and to be of most use must be applied to the nerve centers, or directly over the place where it will touch the affected nerve most quickly.

SLEEPLESSNESS—Insomnia comes to be a habit, often, especially with the elderly, very hard to cure or break up. Anodynes all lose their effect after a while. Sometimes sleeplessness may be overcome by drinking a glass of milk just before retiring—hot or cold. Sometimes a "good square meal" at the same hour will have a good effect, for it draws the blood from the brain by giving the stomach something to do. Dipping the feet in cold water several times and then rubbing them briskly till warm, with a coarse towel, will sometimes have the desired effect. So also will laying a wet compress under the back of the neck. Sleep can also be induced, too, by partaking liberally of common celery. The same may be said of lettuce. Eating a generous allowance of white onions will also produce sleep.

DIPHTHERIA—The negroes of the South use the juice of the pineapple for diphtheria, and it is said to be a sure cure. The pineapple must be thoroughly ripe. The juice is of so corrosive a nature that it instantly cuts the diphtheria mucus.

DRINK FOR HEARTBURN, ETC.—Orange juice (of one orange), water and lump sugar to flavor, and, in proportion to acidity of orange, bicarbonate of soda, about half a teaspoonful. Mix orange juice, water and sugar together in a tumbler, then put in the soda, stir, and the effervescence ensues.

TO CURE A FELON—If the felon is not more than three days' duration it can be cured by the following simple remedy: Take one gill of strong vinegar and heat it as hot as the finger can bear, put into it, when heated, one tablespoonful of saleratus and dip the finger or the part affected into this. Repeat it as often as possible, and the felon will be sure to disappear.

RING WORM—To one part sulphuric acid add sixteen to twenty parts water. Use a brush and feather, and apply it to the parts night and morning. A few dressings will generally cure. If the solution is too strong and causes pain, dilute it with water, and if the irritation is excessive, rub on a little oil or other softening application, but always avoid the use of soap.

NERVOUS HEADACHE—Bathe the head freely in water as hot as can be borne. This should be applied not alone to the temples, but to the back of the ears and the back of the neck, where the nerves are very numerous. The effect is, in most cases, soothing and beneficial. If convenient a simultaneous application of hot water to the feet and back of the neck is to be recommended.

BILIOUS OR SICK HEADACHE—Soak the feet in hot water, drink herb tea and take a sweat. An acid or overloaded stomach causes the headache.

COLD IN THE HEAD—May be relieved by the inhalation of vapors arising from a solution of pulverized camphor or compound tincture of benzoine, about a teaspoonful in a pint of boiling water, which should be put into a pitcher having closely fitted over it a cone of thick paper, with an opening at the top, through which the patient may breathe. He should inhale by the mouth and exhale through the nose.

FACE-ACHE—Dissolve as much camphor as will fill a small thimble in half a teacupful of the best brandy. This will cure face-ache when it arises from cold in the jaw. Dip cotton cloth or paper in this mixture and place it on the cheek or gum. An ounce of laudanum added to five ounces of opodeldoc may be similarly used. Warm applications of any kind are also good.

APERIENT FRUIT SALTS.—Half pound powdered lump sugar; ¼ lb. bicarbonate of soda; ¼ lb. tartaric acid; ¼ lb. epsom salts; ¼ lb. cream tartar. Dose: Heaped teaspoonful to half a glass of water. This is an excellent aperient and pleasant to the taste.

HYDROPHOBIA.—In case any one is bitten by a dog whose condition is suspicious, the most effective and beneficial treatment is to cauterize the wound, at once, with a stick of silver nitrate, commonly called "lunar caustic." The stick of caustic should be sharpened to a pencil point, introduced quite to the bottom of the wound, and held in contact with every part of the wounded surface until it is thoroughly cauterized and insensible. This destroys the virus by which the disease could be communicated. It is well known to physicians that in every instance where a person is bitten by a mad dog small pustules make their appearance sooner or later on the under side of the tongue, but generally in from six to nine days. These pustules must be opened by a sharp-pointed instrument, as they are too tough to break of themselves and the matter must be discharged and spit out or it will be reabsorbed, which reabsorption is said to cause the paroxysms termed hydrophobia. This is the course recommended by Prof. Marochetti of Moscow in 1820. It was also published in an English magazine some forty years ago by a gentleman from Tartary, where mad dogs are common, and this method of treatment usual and successful.

POISON IVY.—Dr. J. M. Ward recommends the following remedy for poisoning by *Rhus radicans*, or "poison ivy": "Use in all cases of poisoning by this plant Labarraque's solution of chloride of soda. The acid poison requires an alkaline antidote, and this solution meets the indication fully. When the skin is unbroken it may be used clear 3 or 4 times a day, or in other cases diluted with from 2 to 5 parts of water." The most exasperating thing about poison ivy is its resemblance to the harmless and beautiful woodbine or Virginia creeper. Their leaves are very similar. They both seek stumps and fences and low bushes for their embraces, and haunt clearings in the woods. They both bear tiny flowers and berries. There are, however, several marked differences. The poison ivy has three leaves in each cluster, while the Virginia creeper has five. If the vine's leaves are clustered in five you may handle it with impunity. If only three leaves spring together from each stem do not even approach it, for sometimes it will poison by its breath.

BLEEDING FROM THE NOSE.—Any determination of blood to the head easily ruptures the net-work of delicate blood-vessels spread over the internal surface of the nostrils, covered only with a thin tegument. Great heat, violent exertion, a blow, and postures of the body which send the blood to the head, are all likely to occasion bleeding from the nose. It sometimes comes on without any previous warning, but at other times its coming will be preceded by pains in the head, accompanied by heaviness, flushings of the face, itching in the nostrils, together with costiveness, or shivering. It should not be suddenly stopped in persons who are healthy and strong; but where weakness exists, and the discharge of blood is at all large, it will be as well to get into cool air, in a somewhat erect position, with the head reclining a little back, to drink freely of cold water, and apply ice as nearly as possible in contact with the bleeding surface.

SWOLLEN FEET.—A powder is used in the German army for sifting into the shoes and stockings of the foot-soldiers, called "Fusstreupulver," and consists of 3 parts salicylic acid, 10 parts starch and 87 parts pulverized soapstone. Blisters on the feet occasioned by walking are cured by drawing a needleful of worsted thread through them; clip it off at both ends, and leave it till the skin peels off.

HOARSENESS.—A baked lemon is an excellent remedy for hoarseness and one that is often resorted to by singers and public speakers. The lemon is baked like an apple and a little of the heated and thickened juice squeezed over lump sugar.

HAY FEVER.—A wash made of witch hazel and cocaine, applied to the nasal passages when the asthma comes on, will stop the wheezing almost instantly.

ASTHMA.—Asthma may be greatly relieved by soaking blotting or tissue paper in strong saltpetre water; dry it, then burn it at night in the sleeping-room.

HICCOUGH.—Sit erect and inflate the lungs fully. Then, retaining the breath, bend forward slowly until the chest meets the knees. After slowly arising again to the erect position, slowly exhale the breath. Repeat this process a second time, and the nerves will be found to have received an access of energy that will enable them to perform their natural functions.

SCURF IN THE HEAD.—Into a pint of water drop a lump of fresh quicklime, the size of a walnut; let it stand all night, then pour the water off clear from sediment or deposit, add a quarter of a pint of the best vinegar, and wash the head with the mixture, which is perfectly harmless, and forms a simple and efficacious remedy.

CHILBLAIN REMEDY.—White wax, 2 drachms; spermaceti, 2 drachms; balsam peru, 2 drachms; olive oil, 2 ounces; muriatic acid, 2 drachms; water, 6 drachms. Apply at night.

CHILBLAIN CREAM.—Balsam tolu, ½ drachm; rectified spirit, 1½ ounces; dissolve and add hydrochloric acid, ½ drachm; compound tincture benzoin, ½ drachm. Apply at night.

ARNICA LINIMENT.—Add to one pint of sweet oil two tablespoonfuls of tincture of arnica. Good for wounds, stiff joints, rheumatism, and all injuries.

TOBACCO ANTIDOTE.—Buy two ounces or more of gentian root, coarsely ground. Take as much of it after each meal, or oftener, as amounts to a common quid of "fine-cut." Chew it slowly and swallow the juice. Continue this a few weeks, and you will conquer the insatiable appetite for tobacco.

POULTICES AND OINTMENTS.—Sometimes a simple poultice, applied in time, will save calling in a physician. A poultice of a pint or two of boiled cranberries, mixed with powdered elm bark or wheat flour, spread upon a cloth and applied to the face, is a specific for erysipelas. A poultice of dried hop yeast is excellent also. For ulcers or sores which emit an offensive smell, make a poultice of two ounces of bread and five ounces of hot water, keep it hot until soaked well, then add five drachms of powdered flaxseed, two drachms of powdered charcoal and form a soft poultice. Yeast poultices are also good for this purpose. An ointment made of the bark of the root of climbing bittersweet and lard is excellent for cuts and sores of all kinds.

WHITE LINIMENT.—For burns, scalds, etc. Melt together, stirring constantly, ½ pint of olive oil, 1½ ounces spermaceti, ¾ ounce white wax.

OINTMENT FOR SORE NIPPLES.—Take of tincture of tolu, two drachms; spermaceti ointment, half an ounce; powdered gum, two drachms. Mix these materials well together to make an ointment. The white of an egg mixed with brandy is the best application for sore nipples; the person should at the same time use a nipple shield.

OINTMENT FOR PILES.—Take of good lard, four ounces; camphor, two drachms; powdered galls, one ounce; laudanum, half an ounce. Apply the ointment made with these ingredients every night at bed-time.

VOLATILE LINIMENT.—Mix well together an ounce each of Florence oil and spirits of hartshorn, or, if the skin of the patient be tender, one ounce of the oil and half an ounce of the spirits. Excellent for inflammation or tension of any kind, and especially for inflammatory quinsy. Apply with a flannel cloth, and renew every four or five hours.

DRINK FOR FEVERS.—One pint of water, into which mix the juice of a lemon and one teaspoonful of cream of tartar; sweeten with loaf sugar and drink freely.

TO PRODUCE PERSPIRATION.—Twelve drachms of antimonial wine and two drachms of laudanum. Of this mixture eighteen drops may be taken in water every five or six hours.

DYSPEPSIA, HEARTBURN, AND ACIDITY.—Pure water, five ounces; carbonate of ammonia, two drachms; syrup of orange peel, one ounce. Mix. For a six-ounce mixture.

WARMING PLASTER.—Burgundy pitch, seven parts; and add plaster of cantharides, one part. Some add a little camphor. Used in chest complaints, local pains, etc.

PURE STIMULANTS.

For cases of spasmodic pain from flatulency or other cause, where brandy is often recommended, it is much safer to use pure stimulants.

1. *Ginger.*—Grate 1 teaspoonful of good sound ginger and add a teacupful of water, milk and sugar to taste. Drink as hot as possible.

2. *Pure Cayenne Pepper.*—This is a powerful, but valuable remedy, used judiciously, as tea, using a small pinch in a tablespoonful of hot water, and repeat the dose if necessary for violent pains where ginger only alleviates distress.

3. *Hot Water* is also very useful for indigestion, and to allay craving for drink. Taken in sips as hot as possible after a meal, for indigestion, or when the craving comes on for other cases. When there is real exhaustion from over-work or illness, it is important to remember that it is rest that is called for, not a stimulus to more work. The following is a good restorative in cases of extreme exhaustion:

RESTORATIVE DRAUGHT.—Carbonate of ammonia, 2 drachms; syrup of ginger, 1 fluid ounce; chloroform water, 1 fluid ounce; pure water, to make 6 fluid ounces. Dose, 1 tablespoonful, three times a day.

FOR SINKING AND LASSITUDE, giving food and renewed strength. Hot water, as hot as can be swallowed, cup after cup until the mischief is gone, is the best remedy for pain from indigestion. Hot milk, not boiling, but hot as can be sipped in spoonfuls. From a small teacupful to a ½ pint, as the patient may be able to bear, done repeated four times daily if needed. (A brown whole-meal biscuit, or small piece of brown bread, will greatly add to nutriment and help digestion in many cases.) When milk alone causes acidity, add lime-water, (which may be made or bought at druggist's) in proportion of ¼.

EXTERNAL STIMULANTS.—1. For violent chills, sore throat, severe headaches, neuralgic pains in any part, and almost any case where local inflammatory action from the above or kindred causes is set up, use mustard and water to the feet, as hot as can be borne, adding boiling water cautiously every few minutes while the patient is covered with a blanket and sitting with feet in the bath. Keep the feet in for 10 or 15 minutes, or more, and repeat it when fit of pain returns. If possible let the patient go to bed immediately after using it.

SORE THROAT.—In addition to medicines as named, or camphor, aconite or belladonna, according to special symptoms and directions for use always given with these medicines, apply a cold water compress on going to bed at night, as follows: Take a strip of old linen or soft calico about 6 inches wide and long enough to go round the neck and wrap well over 5 or 6 inches. Fold into 4 or 5 thicknesses lengthwise, to suit long or short neck, and squeeze it out of cold water as dry as possible. Then have also a strip of oil-silk, gutta-percha tissue, or mackintosh sheeting, wide enough to cover the folded cloth (2 to 2½ inches), and from 12 to 18 inches in length, and a strip of new flannel about ¾ of a yard long, and folded treble or four-fold. First put the wet linen on so as to be wrapped over the throat; next quickly put the waterproof round the neck, carefully covering the wet bandage; then put on the folded flannel and secure with a safety-pin, and keep it on all night. In most cases, this, and the proper medicine internally, will remove any ordinary sore throat by one night's use. If not quite cured, repeat each night; or in severe cases, renew the wet cloth in morning and evening, and keep the patient in bed one, two or three days.

CARE OF THE EARS.

Serious injury often results to the delicate mucous membrane lining the canal of the ears from the pushing of wash cloths, sponges and the like inside the delicate canal. Nothing should ever be pushed inside the canals of the ears. The contents or wax, which is naturally found there should not be removed until it can be washed away with ordinary washing; this should not include a doubling or twisting of the end of a wash cloth for the purpose of pushing it inside the auditory canal.

EARACHE.—At the first symptoms of earache, let the patient lie on the bed with the painful ear uppermost. Fold a thick towel and tuck it around the neck; then with a teaspoon fill the ear with warm water. Continue doing this for fifteen or twenty minutes; the water will fill the ear orifice, and flow over on the towel. Afterward turn over the head, let the water run out, and plug the ear with warm glycerine and cotton. This may be done every hour until relief is obtained. It is almost an invariable cure, and has saved many cases of acute inflammation. The water should be quite warm, but not too hot.

TO REMOVE FOREIGN BODIES FROM THE EAR.—Make a loop of six inches of very fine flexible wire; pass it down to the tympanum and turn it carefully around. This is preferable to a scoop or the use of the syringe.

TO REMOVE INSECTS.—Lay the head upon the table and pour into the ear a little sweet oil or oil of almonds. A drop or two of oil will kill the insect, and the pain will cease. Afterwards syringe the ear with warm water.

CARE OF THE EYES.

It will always be found that good sight depends to a great extent upon good health, and one should never, under any circumstances, neglect his general condition. A good rule to remember in caring for the eyes is: *Never read in bed*, or when lying on a sofa; and another, *Never read on the cars*, never rub your eyes, nor allow your children to do so from their cradles. Veils are bad for the sight, especially those spotted or covered with a pattern. Pale blues or greens are the most restful wall papers for the eyes, whereas red is exceedingly fatiguing. Do not read, write or work longer than two hours together without resting your eyes and closing them fully five minutes. Be most careful to live in a dry house, on dry soil; attend to the digestion, for did not Milton declare his blindness to proceed from the effects of dyspepsia? If the eyes be weak bathe them in a basin of soft water to which a pinch of table-salt and a dessertspoonful of cologne have been added. Avoid all sudden changes between light and darkness. Never begin to read or write or sew for several minutes after coming from darkness to a bright light. Never read by twilight, or moonlight, or on a very cloudy day. Never read or sew directly in front of the light or window or door. It is best to have the light fall from above, obliquely over the left shoulder. Never sleep so that on first awaking the eyes shall open on the light of a window. Do not use the eyesight by light so scant that it requires an effort to discriminate.

SUGGESTIONS TO TEACHERS.—In consequence of the increase of affections of the eye, a specialist has formulated the following rules to be observed in the care of the eyes for school work: A comfortable temperature, dry and warm feet, good ventilation; clothing at the neck and on other parts of the body loose; posture erect, and never read lying down or stooping. Little study before breakfast or directly after a heavy meal; none at all at twilight or late at night; use great caution about studying after recovery from fevers; have light abundant but not dazzling, not allowing the sun to shine on desks or on objects in front of the scholars, and letting the light come from the left hand or left and rear; hold book at right angles to the line of sight or nearly so; give eyes frequent rest by looking up. The distance of the book from the eye should be about fifteen inches. The usual indication of strain is redness of the rim of the eyelid, betokening a congested state of the inner surface, which may be accompanied with some pain. When the eye is excessively red is not the proper remedy, but the use of glasses of sufficient power to aid in accommodating the eye to vision.

CINDERS IN THE EYES—The best method in all such cases, if the flow of tears does not soon wash out the foreign substance, as it usually will unless it be a sharp cinder, is to turn back the eyelid, have the eyeball rolled by looking downward or otherwise, to bring the cinder or dust to view, and remove it with the corner of a clean linen handkerchief. If it cling too tightly for this it can be loosened and removed with the moistened end of a wooden toothpick. The irritation caused is much modified if not entirely relieved by holding the closed eye in cold water for a few minutes. If it continues severe drop in the eye a solution of sugar of lead, say what will lie on a silver half-dime, in half a tumbler of pure water, preferably using very clean rain water.

Putting a flaxseed under the lid of the eye to get out a cinder is quite effective. After the seed has been moistened by the secretions of the eye, it exudes a mucilage which not only alleviates the irritation of a foreign body, but also frequently surrounds it and prevents pain from the motion of the eyeball against the cinder and ultimately assists in its removal. The remedy may seem novel to many persons, but there are commercial travelers who never start on a journey without a pinch of flaxseed somewhere in their satchels.

HOW TO CURE A STY—Put a teaspoonful of soda in a small bag, pour on just enough boiling water to moisten it. Place it on the eye pretty warm, keeping it there all night. In the morning the sty will have disappeared; if not, a second application will surely remove it.

HOW TO CURE A BLACK EYE—Apply at once a cloth wet in water just as hot as you can bear it. Continue the application for 15 or 20 minutes, and although the eye may be a little swollen, the blackness will disappear.

WHEN SPECTACLES ARE NEEDED—When it is necessary to remove objects from the eye to see them distinctly. When one is obliged to have more light than formerly; when one is inclined to put the light between the eye and the object. If, looking for some time at a near object, the eye becomes fatigued and there is a dimness or a mist before it. If small printed letters run into each other, and appear double or treble when looked at for any length of time. When, by a little exertion, the eyes are so fatigued that one has to shut them to relieve them by looking at different objects.

Homœopathic Remedies

AS homœopathy is now practiced so widely, this department could scarcely lay claim to be considered complete without a brief mention of the principal remedies used and recommended by homœopathic practitioners. The principle of homœopathy is set forth in the Latin words, "*Similia similibus curantur*," the meaning of which is, "Likes are cured by likes." The homœopathist, in order to cure a disease, administers a medicine which would produce in a perfectly healthy subject symptoms like but not *identical* with, or the same as, the symptoms to counteract which the medicine is given. He, therefore, first makes himself thoroughly acquainted with the symptoms that are exhibited by the sufferer; having ascertained these, in order to neutralize them and restore the state of the patient's health to a state of equilibrium, so to speak, he administers preparations that would produce symptoms of a like character in persons in good health. It is not said that the drug can produce in a healthy person the disease from which the patient is suffering; it is only advanced by homœopathists that the drug given has the power of producing in a person in health symptoms similar to those of the disease under which the patient is languishing, and that the correct mode of treatment is to counteract the disease symptoms by the artificial production of similar symptoms by medical means, or, in other words, to suit the medicine to the disorder by the previously acquired knowledge of the effects of the drug by experiment on a healthy person.

HOMŒOPATHIC REMEDIES are given in the form of globules or tinctures, the latter being generally preferred by homœopathic practitioners. When contrasted with the doses of drugs given by allopathists, the small doses administered by homœopathists must at first sight appear wholly inadequate to the purpose for which they are given; but homœopathists, whose dilution and trituration diffuse the drug given throughout the vehicle in which it is administered, argue that by this *extension of its surface* the active power of the drug is greatly increased.

Great stress is laid by homœopathists on attention to diet. The reader will find on a succeeding page a list of articles of food that may and may not be taken. Below are given briefly a few of the more common ailments, with the symptoms by which they are indicated and the medicines by which they may be alleviated and eventually cured.

ASTHMA.—An ailment which should be referred in all cases to the medical practitioner. *Symptoms.* Difficulty in breathing, with cough, either spasmodic and without expectoration, or accompanied with much expectoration. *Medicines.* Aconitum napellus, especially with congestion or slight spitting of blood; Antimonium tartaricum for rattling and wheezing in the chest; Arsenicum for chronic asthma; Ipecacuanha; Nux vomica.

BILIOUS ATTACKS, if attended with diarrhœa and copious evacuations of a bright yellow color. *Medicines.* Bryonia, if arising from sedentary occupation, or from eating and drinking too freely; or Nux vomica and Mercurius in alternation, the former correcting constipation and the latter nausea, fullness at the pit of the stomach and a foul tongue.

BRONCHITIS.—*Symptoms.* Catarrh, accompanied with fever; expectoration dark, thick, and sometimes streaked with blood; urine dark, thick and scanty. *Medicines.* Aconitum napellus, especially in earlier stages; Bryonia for pain in coughing and difficulty in breathing; Antimonium tartaricum, loose cough, with much expectoration, and a feeling of, and tendency to, suffocation; Ipecacuanha, accumulation of phlegm in bronchial tubes and for children.

BRUISES AND WOUNDS.—For all bruises, black eyes, etc., apply Arnica lotion; for slight wounds, after washing well with cold water, apply Arnica plaster; to stop bleeding, when ordinary means fail, and for larger wounds, apply concentrated tincture of Calendula.

COLD IN THE HEAD OR CATARRH.—*Symptoms.* Feverish feeling generally, and especially about the head, eyes and nose, running from, and obstruction of, nose; soreness and irritation of the throat and bronchial tubes. *Medicines.* Aconitum napellus for feverish symptoms; Belladonna for sore throat and headache with inclination to cough; Mercurius for running from nose and sneezing; Nux vomica for stoppage of nostrils; Chamomilla for children and women, for whom Pulsatilla is also useful in such cases.

CHILBLAINS.—*Symptoms.* Irritation and itching of the skin, which assumes a bluish red color. *Medicines.* Arnica montana, taken internally or used as outward application, unless the chilblain be broken, when Arsenicum should be used. If the swelling and irritation do not yield to these remedies, use Belladonna and Rhus toxicodendron.

CHOLERA.—1. Bilious cholera. *Symptoms.* Nausea, proceeding to vomiting, griping of the bowels, watery and offensive evacuations, in which much bile is present, accompanied with weakness and depression. *Medicines.* Bryonia, with Ipecacuanha at commencement of attack. 2. Malignant or Asiatic cholera. *Symptoms* as in bilious cholera, but in a more aggravated form, followed by what is called the "cold stage," marked by great severity of griping pain in the stomach, accompanied with frequent and copious watery evacuations, and presently with cramps in all parts of the body, after which the extremities become chilled, the pulse scarcely discernible, the result of which is stupor and ultimately death. *Medicines.* Camphor in the form of tincture, in frequent doses, until the sufferer begins to feel warmth returning to the body, and perspiration ensues. In the latter stages, Cuprum and Veratrum.

TINCTURE OF CAMPHOR is one of the most useful of the homœopathic remedies in all cases of colic, diarrhœa, etc. In ordinary cases fifteen drops on sugar may be taken every quarter of an hour until the pain is allayed. In more aggravated cases, and in cases of cholera, a few drops may be taken at intervals of from two to five minutes. A dose of fifteen drops of camphor on sugar tends to counteract a chill if taken soon after premonitory symptoms show themselves, and act as a prophylactic against cold.

Colic or Stomach-Ache.—This disorder is indicated by griping pains in the bowels, which sometimes extend upwards into and over the region of the chest. Sometimes the pain is attended with vomiting and cold perspiration. A warm bath is useful, and hot flannels, or a jar or bottle filled with hot water should be applied to the abdomen. *Medicines.* Aconitum napellus, especially when the abdomen is tender to the touch, and the patient is feverish; Belladonna for severe griping and spasmodic pains; Bryonia for bilious colic and diarrhœa; Chamomilla for children.

Constipation.—Women are more subject than men to this confined state of the bowels, which will, in many cases, yield to exercise, plain, nutritious diet, with vegetables and cooked fruit, and but little bread, and an enema of milk and water, or thin gruel if it is some time since there has been any action of the bowels. *Medicines.* Bryonia, especially for rheumatic patients, and disturbed state of the stomach; Nux vomica, for persons of sedentary habits, especially males; Pulsatilla, for women; Sulphur, for constipation that is habitual or of long continuance.

Convulsions.—For convulsions, arising from whatever cause, a warm bath is desirable, and a milk and water enema, if the child's bowels are confined. *Medicines.* Belladonna and Chamomilla, if the convulsions are caused by teething, with Aconitum napellus if the little patient be feverish; Aconitum napellus, Cina and Belladonna, for convulsions caused by worms; Aconite and Coffea, when they arise from fright; Ipecacuanha and Nux vomica, when they have been caused by repletion, or food that is difficult of digestion.

Cough.—For this disorder, a light farinaceous diet is desirable, with plenty of out-door exercise and constant use of the sponging-bath. *Medicines.* Aconitum napellus, for a hard, dry, hacking cough; Antimonium, for cough with wheezing and difficulty of expectoration; Belladonna, for spasmodic cough, with tickling in the throat, or sore throat; Bryonia, for hard, dry cough, with expectorations streaked with blood; Ipecacuanha, for children.

Croup.—As this disorder frequently and quickly terminates fatally recourse should be had to a duly qualified practitioner as soon as possible. The disease lies chiefly in the larynx and bronchial tubes, and is easily recognizable by the sharp, barking sound of the cough. A warm bath and mustard poultice will often tend to give relief. *Medicines.* Aconitum napellus, in the earlier stages of the disorder, and Spongia and Hepar sulphuris, in the more advanced stages, the latter medicine being desirable when the cough is not so violent and the breathing easier.

Diarrhœa.—The medicines to be used in this disorder are those mentioned under colic and bilious attacks.

Dysentery is somewhat similar to diarrhœa, but the symptoms are more aggravated in character, and the evacuations are chiefly mucous streaked with blood. As a remedy hot flannels or a stone jar filled with hot water and wrapped in flannel should be applied to the abdomen. *Medicines.* Colocynthis and Mercurius in alternation.

Dyspepsia or Indigestion arises from weakness of the digestive organs. *Symptoms.* Chief among these are habitual costiveness, heartburn and nausea, disinclination to eat, listlessness and weakness, accompanied with fatigue after walking, etc., restlessness and disturbed sleep at night, bad taste in the mouth, with white tongue, especially in the morning, accompanied at times with fullness in the region of the stomach, and flatulence, which causes disturbance of the heart. The causes of indigestion are too numerous to be mentioned here, but they may be inferred when it is said that scrupulous attention must be paid to diet; that meals should be taken at regular and not too long intervals; that warm drinks, stimulants and tobacco should be avoided; that early and regular hours should be kept, with a cold or chilled sponge bath every morning; and that measures should be taken to obtain a fair amount of exercise, and to provide suitable occupation for both body and mind during the day. *Medicines.* Arnica montana for persons who are nervous and irritable, and suffer much from headache; Bryonia for persons who are bilious and subject to rheumatism, and those who are listless and disinclined to eat, and have an unpleasant bitter taste in the mouth; Hepar sulphuris for chronic indigestion and costiveness, attended with tendency to vomit in the morning; Mercurius in cases of flatulence, combined with costiveness; Nux vomica for indigestion that makes itself felt from 2 a.m. to 4 a.m., or thereabouts, with loss of appetite and nausea in the morning, and for persons with a tendency to piles, and those who are engaged in sedentary occupations; Pulsatilla for women generally, and Chamomilla for children.

Fevers.—For all fevers of a serious character, such as scarlet fever, typhus fever, typhoid fever, gastric fever, intermittent fever, or ague, etc., it is better to send at once for a medical man. In cases of ordinary fever, indicated by alternate flushes and shivering, a hot, dry skin, rapid pulse, and dry, foul tongue, the patient should have a warm bath, take but little nourishment, and drink cold water. *Medicine.* Aconitum napellus.

FLATULENCY.—This disorder, which arises from, and is a symptom of indigestion, frequently affects respiration, and causes distention and quickened action of the heart. The patient should pay attention to diet, as for dyspepsia. *Medicines.* Cina and Nux vomica; Pulsatilla for women, and Chamomilla for children. See *Dyspepsia.*

HEADACHE.—This disorder proceeds from so many various causes, which require different treatment, that it is wise to apply at once to a regular homœopathic practitioner, and especially in headache of frequent occurrence. *Medicines.* Nux vomica when headache is caused by indigestion; Pulsatilla being useful for women; Belladonna and Ignatia, for sick headache; Aconitum napellus and Arsenicum for nervous headache.

HEARTBURN.—For this unpleasant sensation of heat, arising from the stomach, accompanied by a bitter taste, and sometimes by nausea, Nux vomica is a good medicine. Pulsatilla may be taken by women.

INDIGESTION.—See *Dyspepsia.*

MEASLES.—This complaint, which seldom attacks adults, is indicated in its early stage by the usual accompaniments and signs of a severe cold in the head—namely, sneezing, running from the nose and eyelids, which are swollen. The sufferer also coughs, does not care to eat, and feels sick and restless. About four days after the first appearance of these premonitory symptoms, a red rash comes out over the face, neck and body, which dies away, and finally disappears in about five days. The patient should be kept warm, and remain in one room during the continuance of the disorder, and especially while the rash is out, lest, through exposure to cold in any way, the rash may be checked and driven inwards. *Medicines.* Aconitum napellus and Pulsatilla, which are sufficient for all ordinary cases. If there be much fever, Belladonna, and if the rash be driven in by a chill, Bryonia.

MUMPS.—This disorder is sometimes consequent on measles. It is indicated by the swelling of the glands under the ear and lower jaw. It is far more painful than dangerous. Fomenting with warm water is useful. *Medicines.* Mercurius generally; Belladonna may be used when mumps follow an attack of measles.

NETTLERASH.—This rash, so called because in appearance it resembles the swelling and redness caused by the sting of a nettle, is generally produced by a disordered state of the stomach. *Medicines.* Aconitum napellus, Nux vomica, or Pulsatilla, in ordinary cases; Arsenicum is useful if there is much fever; Belladonna if the rash is accompanied with headache.

PILES.—The ordinary homœopathic remedies for this painful complaint are Nux vomica and Sulphur.

SPRAINS.—Apply to the part affected a lotion of one part of tincture of Arnica in two of water. For persons who cannot use Arnica, in consequence of the irritation produced by it, a lotion of tincture of Calendula may be used in the proportion of one part of the tincture to four of water.

TEETHING.—Infants and very young children frequently experience much pain in the mouth during dentition, and especially when the tooth is making its way through the gum. The child is often feverish, the mouth and gums hot and tender, and the face flushed. There is also much running from the mouth, and the bowels are disturbed, being in some cases confined, and in others relaxed, approaching to diarrhœa. *Medicines.* These are Aconitum napellus, in ordinary cases; *Nux vomica,* when the bowels are confined; Chamomilla, when the bowels are relaxed; Mercurius, if the relaxed state of the bowels has deepened into diarrhœa; Belladonna, if there be symptoms of disturbance of the brain.

WHOOPING COUGH.—This disease is sometimes of long duration, for if it shows itself in the autumn or winter months, the little patient will frequently retain the cough until May, or even June, when it disappears with return of warmer weather. Change of air when practicable is desirable, especially when the cough has been of long continuance. In this cough there are three stages. In the first the symptoms are those of an ordinary cold in the head and cough. In the second the cough becomes hard, dry and rapid, and the inhalation of air, after or during the paroxysm of the coughing, produces a peculiar sound from which the disease is named. In the final stage the cough recurs at longer intervals, and the paroxysms are less violent and ultimately disappear. In this stage the disease is subject to fluctuation, the cough again increasing in frequency of occurrence and intensity if the patient has been unduly exposed to cold or damp, or if the weather is very changeable. Children suffering from whooping cough should have a light, nourishing diet and only go out when the weather is fine and worm. *Medicines.* Aconitum napellus in the very commencement of the disorder, followed by Ipecacuanha and Nux vomica when the second stage is just approaching and during its continuance. These medicines may be continued if necessary during the third stage.

WORMS.—The presence of worms is indicated by irritation of the membrane of the nose, causing the child to thrust its finger into the nostrils; by irritation of the lower part of the body; by thinness, excessive appetite and restlessness in sleep. Children suffering from worms should eat meat freely and not take so much bread, vegetables and farinaceous food as children generally do. They should have as much exercise as possible in the open air, and be sponged with cold water every morning. The worms that mostly trouble children are the thread worms, which are present chiefly in the lower portion of the intestines, and the round worm. *Medicines, etc.* Administer an injection of weak salt-and-water, and give Aconitum napellus, to be followed by Ignatia and Sulphur in the order in which they are here given. These are the usual remedies for thread worms. For round worms, whose presence in the stomach is indicated by great thinness, sickness and discomfort, and pain in the stomach, Aconitum napellus, Cina, Ignatia and Sulphur are given.

EXTENT OF DOSES IN HOMŒOPATHY.—Homœopathic medicines are given in the form of globules, pilules, or tincture, the last-named being generally preferred. The average doses for adults are from half a drop to one drop of the tincture given in a tablespoonful of water, from two to four pilules, or from three to six globules. In using the tincture it is usual to measure out a few tablespoonfuls of water and to add to it a certain number of drops, regulated by the quantity of water that is used. For children medicine is mixed at the same strength, but a less quantity is given. The proper quantity for a dose is always given in books and manuals for the homœopathic treatment of disease. Small cases of the principal medicines used in homœopathy can be procured from most druggists, and with each case a little book showing the symptoms and treatment of all ordinary complaints is usually given.

DIET IN HOMŒOPATHY.—The articles of food that are chiefly recommended when attention to diet is necessary are stale bread, beef, mutton, poultry, fresh game, fish, chiefly cod and flat fish, avoiding mackerel, etc., eggs and oysters. Rice, sago, tapioca and arrowroot are permitted, as are also potatoes, carrots, turnips, broccoli, cauliflower, asparagus, French beans and Lima beans. Water, milk, cocoa and chocolate may be drunk. It is desirable to avoid all things that are not specified in the foregoing list. Ripe fruit may be eaten, but unripe fruit, unless cooked, should be scrupulously avoided.

Valuable Hygienic Suggestions

RULES FOR THE PRESERVATION OF HEALTH

PURE *atmospheric air* is composed of nitrogen, oxygen and a very small proportion of carbonic acid gas. Air once breathed has lost the chief part of its oxygen and acquired a proportionate increase of carbonic acid gas. Therefore, health requires that we breathe the same air once only.

The solid part of our bodies is continually wasting and requires to be repaired by fresh substances. Therefore, food which is to repair the loss should be taken with due regard to the exercise and waste of the body.

The fluid part of our bodies also wastes constantly; there is but one fluid in animals, which is water. Therefore, water only is necessary, and no artifice can produce a better drink.

The fluid of our bodies is to the solid in proportion as nine to one. Therefore, a like proportion should prevail in the total amount of food taken.

Light exercises an important influence upon the growth and vigor of animals and plants. Therefore, our dwellings should freely admit the solar rays.

Decomposing animal and vegetable substances yield various noxious gases which enter the lungs and corrupt the blood. Therefore, all impurities should be kept away from our abodes, and every precaution be observed to secure a pure atmosphere.

Warmth is essential to all the bodily functions. Therefore, an equal bodily temperature should be maintained by exercise, by clothing or by fire.

Exercise warms, invigorates and purifies the body; clothing preserves the warmth the body generates; fire imparts warmth externally. Therefore, to obtain and preserve warmth, exercise and clothing are preferable to fire.

Mental and bodily exercise are equally essential to the general health and happiness. Therefore, labor and study should succeed each other.

Man will live most healthily upon simple solids and fluids, of which a sufficient but temperate quantity should be taken. Therefore, over-indulgence in strong drinks, tobacco, snuff, opium, and all mere indulgences, should be avoided.

Sudden alternations of heat and cold are dangerous (especially to the young and the aged). Therefore, clothing, in quality and quantity, should be adapted to the alternations of night and day and of the seasons; and drinking cold water when the body is hot, and hot tea and soups when cold, are productive of evil results.

The skin is a highly organized membrane full of minute pores, cells, blood vessels and nerves; it imbibes moisture or throws it off, according to the state of the atmosphere and the temperature of the body. It also "breathes," as do the lungs (though less actively). All the internal organs sympathize with the skin. Therefore, it should be repeatedly cleansed.

Fire consumes the oxygen of the air and produces noxious gases. Therefore, the air is less pure in the presence of candles, gas or coal fire, than otherwise, and the deterioration should be repaired by increased ventilation.

Late hours and anxious pursuits exhaust the nervous system and produce disease and premature death. Therefore, the hours of labor and study should be short.

Moderation in eating and drinking, short hours of labor and study, regularity in exercise, recreation and rest, cleanliness, equanimity of temper and equality of temperature—these are the great essentials to that which surpasses all wealth: health of mind and body.

Onions as Medicine.—Onions are really sweeteners of the breath after the local effects have passed away. They correct stomach disorders and carry off the accumulated poisons of the system. They provide a blood purifier that all may freely use, and do perfect work in constipation troubles. As a vermifuge the onion cannot be surpassed, and, eaten raw, will often check a cold in the head. One small onion eaten every night before retiring is a well-known doctor's prescription for nervous affections of the head, and is highly recommended for sleeplessness; it acts on the nerves in a soothing way, without the injurious effects of drugs. The heart of an onion, heated and placed in the ear, will often relieve the agony of earache, while the syrup produced from sprinkling a sliced onion with sugar and baking in the oven will work wonders in a "croupy" child.

Apple as Medicine.—Chemically, the apple is composed of vegetable fiber, albumen, sugar, gum, chlorophyl, malic acid, gallic acid, lime, and much water. It contains a larger percentage of phosphorus than any other fruit or vegetable. The phosphorus is admirably adapted for renewing the essential nervous matter, lecithin, of the brain and spinal cord. The acids of the apple are of signal use for men of sedentary habits, whose livers are sluggish in action, those acids serving to eliminate from the body noxious matters which, if retained, would make the brain heavy and dull, or bring about jaundice or skin eruptions and other allied troubles. Some such experience must have led to our custom of taking apple sauce with roast pork, rich goose, etc. The malic acid of ripe apples, either raw or cooked, will neutralize any excess of chalky matter engendered by eating too much meat. Such fresh fruits as the apple, the pear and the plum, when taken ripe and without sugar, diminish acidity in the stomach rather than provoke it. Their vegetable salts and juices are converted into alkaline carbonates, which tend to counteract acidity.

Burnt Alum.—*An Invaluable Household Remedy.*—Several years ago the writer lived on a ranch fifteen miles from the nearest town, and in case of sickness or accident the services of a physician could not be obtained for less than $25 a visit. After being forced in emergencies to resort to some kind of treatment, I soon accumulated quite a stock of knowledge of simple household medicines. My experience proved the best all-around medicine to be burnt alum, which destroys all animal or insect poison and fungus growth.

Croup readily succumbs when the patient takes a few doses of molasses into which is mixed a pinch of burnt alum. Rub the chest well with lard, turpentine and coal oil mixed.

For diphtheria gargle the throat with a mixture of burnt alum, sugar and chlorate of potash, dissolved in a half glass of water.

For an ordinary *sore throat* gargle with water in which has been placed a teaspoonful of sugar and a large pinch of burnt alum.

La grippe can be cured by taking quinine in doses of from 2 to 3 grains *every other night* for a week, and using a powder of sugar and burnt alum. Take only in small doses, when the cough is tight and croupy, as alum has a tendency to constipate, and in this disease it is very essential to keep the bowels open.

When a person is bitten by *a dog* or any animal, after the wound has bled a little, wash in warm water, and immediately apply a salve made of burnt alum, vaseline or lard. The alum will destroy the poison, and no wound will follow. It is also a preventive of hydrophobia. *Hemorrhages* of all kinds can be stopped by water strongly impregnated with alum. T.

Ordinary *toothache* can be cured by inserting in the cavity cotton saturated with vaseline dipped in burnt alum.

How to Sleep.—It is a common expression that to take food immediately before going to bed and to sleep is unwise. Such a suggestion is answered by a reminder that the instinct of animals prompts them to sleep as soon as they have eaten; and in summer an after-dinner nap, especially when that meal is taken at mid-day, is a luxury indulged in by many. Neither darkness nor season of the year alter the conditions. If the ordinary hour of the evening meal is six or seven o'clock, and the morning meal at seven or eight o'clock, an interval of twelve hours or more elapses without food, and for persons whose nutrition is at fault this is altogether too long a period for fasting. That such an interval without food is permitted explains many a restless night and much of the languor and headache, and the languid, half-rested condition on rising which is accompanied by no appetite for breakfast. This meal itself often dissipates those conditions. It is, therefore, desirable, if not essential, when nutriment is to be crowded, that the last thing before going to bed should be the taking of food. Sleeplessness is often caused by starvation, and a tumbler of milk, if drunk in the middle of the night, will often put people to sleep when hypnotics would fail of their purpose. Food before rising is an equally important expedient. It supplies strength for bathing and dressing, laborious and wearisome tasks for the enfeebled, and is a better morning "pick-me-up" than any hackneyed "tonic."

To Avoid Ague.—1. Choose for sleeping-apartments rooms on the sunny side of the house. 2. As soon as the dew begins to fall, build a fire, as the heat will do much to kill the malaria. 3. Do not expose yourself to the malarial air after sunset or before sunrise. 4. Take a thorough bath every day on rising, in a warm room, with friction enough to produce a reaction. 5. This will keep the skin healthy and active. Regulate the bowels by a proper diet. In many cases ague is caused by the accumulation of morbid matters in the system.

Fruit as Medicine.—Grape fruit is almost as good as quinine for malarial troubles, and pineapple is a sure cure for sore throat and diphtheria. Tomatoes are perfect liver regulators—they contain a very small portion of mercury. Oranges act on the kidneys very beneficially, while lemons and grapes are efficacious in curing and preventing cutaneous troubles. Watercresses act on the lungs, and are said to be a cure for incipient consumption. They certainly have marvelous tonic power, and refresh one after great fatigue. A diet of grapes as a cure-all has been proved valuable in hundreds of cases, and, if taken in time, a case of jaundice can be cured by eating nothing but lettuce and lemon juice.

What They Should Do.—Women who would retain the beauty with which they have been endowed should avoid peppered soups, stews, game patés, ragouts and spices. Women of nervous and sanguine temperament should restrict themselves to a diet of eggs, milk, bread, fruit, light broths and crustacea. Malt and spirituous liquors should be let severely alone, and tonics containing iron, phosphoric acid and other drugs are so harmful to the complexion that they should not be tampered with, but only resorted to on medical advice.

To Avoid Sunstrokes.—Those who abstain from the use of spirituous drinks during hot weather, and have regular hours for sleeping and eating, need have little fear of sunstroke. Bathing, washing, or sponging the skin all over in the morning is a wholesome precaution. Light, easy-fitting, broad-brimmed hats should be worn by those who work outdoors. Those who have to work in the sun for any length of time should have a shed or shade of some kind handy, where they can rest a few minutes at a time occasionally. Those who have to go about the streets should keep on the shady side, wear light and porous hats, and, if possible, carry sun umbrellas.

To Keep Cool During Hot Nights.—Bathe the body with cool water just before retiring, and lie down without drying it off. The water absorbs the heat, and in evaporating throws the heat off with it. It will be most effectual in hot countries, and those who have tried it say there is absolutely no danger of taking cold.

What Lemons Will Do.—Lemon juice, with water and very little sugar, taken every morning, will keep the stomach in order and prevent dyspepsia.

If you have dark hair, and it seems to be falling out, cut off a slice of lemon and rub it on your scalp. It will stop the trouble promptly.

Squeeze a lemon into a quart of milk (this is for the ladies), and it will give you a mixture to rub on your face night and morning, and get a complexion like a primrose. Pour lemon juice into an equal quantity of glycerine, and rub your hands with the mixture before going to bed. If you don't mind sleeping with gloves on, that is better still. In the morning wash your hands thoroughly in warm water, and apply the lemon juice again pure, but only a few drops. You must not keep this up too long, or your hands will show too decided a whiteness.

If you have a bad headache, cut a lemon into slices and rub these along your temples. The pain will not be long disappearing, or at least in growing easier to bear.

If a bee or an insect stings you, apply a few drops of lemon juice.

If you have a troublesome corn the lemon can be again put to good account by rubbing it on the toe after you have taken a hot bath and cut away as much as possible of the troublesome intruder.

Rules for Fat People and for Lean.—To increase the weight: Eat, to the extent of satisfying a natural appetite, of fat meats, butter, cream, milk, cocoa, chocolate, bread, potatoes, peas, parsnips, carrots, beets, farinaceous foods, as Italian corn, rice, tapioca, sago, corn starch, pastry, custards, oatmeal, sugar. Avoid acids. Exercise as little as possible, and sleep all you can.

To reduce the weight: Eat, to the extent of satisfying a natural appetite, of lean meat, poultry, game, eggs, milk moderately, green vegetables, turnips, succulent fruits, tea or coffee. Drink lime juice, lemonade, and acid drinks. Avoid fat, butter, cream, sugar, pastry, rice, etc.

Dangers of Foul Air.—If the condensed breath collected on the cool window panes of a room where a number of persons have been assembled be burned, a smell as of singed hair will show the presence of organic matter, and if the condensed breath be allowed to remain on the windows a few days, it will be found, on examination by the microscope, that it is alive with animalcula. It is the inhalation of air containing such putrescent matter which causes half of the sick-headaches, which might be avoided by a circulation of fresh air.

A Mistaken Idea.—The old adage, "Feed a cold and starve a fever," is very silly advice. If anything, the reverse would be nearer right. When a person has a severe cold it is best for him to eat very lightly, especially during the first few days of the attack.

Tomato in Bright's Disease.—When Thomas Jefferson brought the tomato from France to America, thinking that if it could be induced to grow bountifully it might make good feed for hogs, he little dreamed of the benefit he was conferring upon posterity. A constant diet of raw tomatoes and skim-milk is said to be a certain cure for Bright's disease. Gen. Schenck, who, when Minister to England, became a victim to that complaint, was restored to health

14

by two years of this regimen. With many persons the tomato has much the same effect upon the liver as a small blue pill.

How and When to Drink Water.—According to Doctor Leuf, when water is taken into the full or partly full stomach, it does not mingle with the food, as we are taught, but passes along quickly between the food and lesser curvature toward the pylorus, through which it passes into the intestines. The secretion of mucus by the lining membrane is constant, and during the night a considerable amount accumulates in the stomach; some of its liquid portion is absorbed, and that which remains is thick and tenacious. If food is taken into the stomach when in this condition, it becomes coated with this mucus, and the secretion of the gastric juice and its action are delayed. These facts show the value of a goblet of water before breakfast. This washes out the tenacious mucus and stimulates the gastric glands to secretion. In old and feeble persons water should not be taken cold, but it may be with great advantage taken warm or hot. This removal of the accumulated mucus from the stomach is probably one of the reasons why taking soup at the beginning of a meal has been found so beneficial.

To Straighten Round Shoulders.—A stooping figure and a halting gait, accompanied by the unavoidable weakness of lungs incidental to a narrow chest, may be entirely cured by a very simple and easily-performed exercise of raising one's self upon the toes leisurely in a perpendicular position several times daily. To take this exercise properly one must take a perfectly upright position, with the heels together and the toes at an angle of forty-five degrees. Then drop the arms lifelessly by the sides, animating and raising the chest to its full capacity of muscularity, the chin well drawn in, and the crown of the head feeling as if attached to a string suspended from the ceiling above. Slowly rise upon the balls of both feet to the greatest possible height, thereby exercising all the muscles of the legs and body; come again into a standing position without swaying the body backward out of the perfect line. Repeat this same exercise, first on one foot, then on the other. It is wonderful what a straightening-out power this exercise has upon round shoulders and crooked backs, and one will be surprised to note how soon the lungs begin to show the effect of such expansive development.

Diet of Business Men.—Business men should diet themselves so as to be able to do the maximum of work between the lunch hour and evening, and not work for a few minutes after eating. Such foods as plain soups, cold chicken, milk, drunk slowly, cocoa, lettuce, rice, rice pudding, sandwiches, beef or lamb, bread and butter will be ample nutrition, and yet so readily assimilated that brain work will not interfere with their digestion. Alcohol in any form should not be taken by brain workers, and pastry and ice cream should be avoided. Fifteen minutes should be spent in light reading or conversation before severe mental labor is begun. A light cigar immediately after lunch aids digestion. It is in the evening, when the work of the day is done, that a substantial meal should be taken.

To Produce the Habit of Nose-Breathing.—It has long been known that if people would only keep their mouths shut and breathe through their nose, nature's respirator, they would avoid a variety of serious ailments. Dr. F. A. A. Smith now insists that a large proportion of diseases of the throat are attributable to the neglect of this habit. He says that mothers should see to it that their little ones do not acquire the habit of mouth-breathing, and if they have acquired it, steps should immediately be taken to rid them of it. One of the simplest ways in which Dr. Smith suggests that this can be done is the placing of a four-tail bandage under the chin, causing the mouth to be closed, both by day and night, for several weeks. It must first, however, be ascertained whether there are any impediments in the nostrils, and if so these should be removed.

Overshoes or "Rubbers."—Carelessness in the wearing of overshoes is one of the most fruitful causes of colds and winter ills. When worn too long they "draw" the feet to an extent which is often painful and sometimes productive of "frost-bite." Where the ordinary shoes are of proper stoutness it is best not to wear "rubbers" at all, and under no circumstances should they be worn in two widely different temperatures on the same day. Remove them immediately on entering a house, even if you remain inside but a short time. The same remarks apply to mufflers and other throat wrappings.

A Cup of Cheer.—For those who wish to keep the imagination fresh and vigorous, chocolate is the beverage of beverages. However copiously you have lunched, a cup of chocolate immediately afterward will produce digestion three hours after, and prepare the way for a good dinner. It is recommended to every one who devotes to brain work the hours he should pass in bed; to every wit who finds he has become suddenly dull; to all who find the air damp, the time long, and the atmosphere unsympathetic; and, above all, to those who, tormented with a fixed idea, have lost their freedom of thought.

Simple Relief for Lung Troubles.—It has long been known that pine needle pillows would alleviate persons afflicted with lung troubles, and a Florida editor relates an incident in support of the fact as follows: During a visit to the house of a most estimable lady living on Indian River, this editor was told of a discovery that had been made which may prove a boon to sufferers from lung or bronchial troubles. This lady having heard that there was peculiar virtue in a pillow made from pine straw, and having none of that material at hand, made one from fine, soft pine shavings, and had the pleasure of noting immediate benefit. Soon all the members of the household had pine-shavings pillows, and it was noticed that all coughs, asthmatic or bronchial troubles abated at once after sleeping a few nights on these pillows. An invalid suffering with lung trouble derived much benefit from sleeping upon a mattress made from pine shavings. The material is cheap and makes a very pleasant and comfortable mattress, the odor of the pine permeating the entire room, and absorbing or dispelling all unpleasant odors.

A Simple Home Remedy.—Did you ever give asafetida tea to the baby for colic, or to the older ones for nervousness? For colic, pour half a cup of boiling water on a piece of asafetida as large as a pea, let it stand until cool enough to drink, sweeten a little, and give baby as much as it will drink of it; and you will be surprised how soon it will cease its cries and drop off into a quiet sleep.

If the older children are fretful, peevish and worrisome without any seeming cause, ten chances to one it is nervousness of some kind, and a half cup or more, according to their age, will work wonders in their deportment. If they do not sleep well at night, give them a good drink at bedtime; and if you are tired and worn out, and nature is vainly calling for the rest you fain would take, but cannot from nervousness, drink a generous draught of it yourself and see what a help it will be to you.

Of course the odor is disagreeable, but the taste is not, and, if properly sweetened, children never object to it. Indeed, they seem rather to relish it.

Sunshine.—Equally important with pure air in living-apartments is sunshine. It carries with it radiance and cheer and vigor and good health. It is the great purifier, warding off mould, moisture, gloom, depression and disease. It should be admitted to every apartment of the house, and made welcome at all times. It is a strong preventive to the disorders that visit shaded and musty places. It brings health and happiness that can not be obtained from any other source. It is nature's own health-giving agent, and nothing can be substituted for it. It has no artificial counterpart. It does not only touch the physical body, but it reaches the mind and soul and purifies the whole existence of man. It may fade a carpet or upholstery, but it will bring color to the cheeks, light to the eye and elasticity to the step. The closed and shaded window may throw a richness of color upon the room, but it will bring paleness and feebleness to the occupants.

Tea and Coffee.—Tea is a nerve stimulant, pure and simple, acting like alcohol in this respect, without any value that the latter may possess as a retarder of waste. It has a special influence upon those nerve centers that supply will power, exalting their sensibility beyond normal activity, and may even produce hysterical symptoms, if carried far enough. Its active principle, theine, is an exceedingly powerful drug, chiefly employed by nerve specialists as a pain-destroyer, possessing the singular quality of working toward the surface. That is to say, when a dose is administered hypodermically for sciatica, for example, the narcotic influence proceeds outward from the point of injection, instead of inward toward the center, as does that of morphia, atropia, etc. Tea is totally devoid of nutritive value, and the habit of drinking it to excess, which so many American women indulge in, particularly in this country, is to be deplored as a cause of our American nervousness.

Coffee, on the contrary, is a nerve food. Like other concentrated foods of its class, it operates as a stimulant also, but upon a different set of nerves from tea. Taken strong in the morning, it often produces dizziness and that peculiar visual symptom of overstimulation which is called muscæ volitantes — dancing flies. But this is an improper way to take it, and rightly used it is one of the most valuable liquid additions to the morning meal. Its active principle, caffeine, differs in all physiological respects from theine, while it is chemically very closely allied, and its limited consumption makes it impotent for harm.

What Causes Coughs.—Colds and coughs are prevalent throughout the country, but throat affections are by far more common among business men. Every unfortunate one mutters something about the abominable weather and curses the piercing wind. Much of the trouble, however, is caused by overheated rooms, and a little more attention to proper ventilation would remove the cause of suffering. Dr. J. Ewing Mears said to an inquirer: "The huskiness and loss of power of articulation so common among us are largely due to the use of steam for heating. The steam cannot be properly regulated, and the temperature becomes too high. A person living in this atmosphere has all the cells of the lungs open, and when he passes into the open air he is unduly exposed. The affliction is quite common among the men who occupy offices in the new buildings which are fitted up with all modern improvements. The substitution of electric light for gas has wrought a change to which people have not yet adapted themselves. The heat arising from a number of gas jets will quickly raise the temperature of a room, and unconsciously people relied upon that means of heating to some extent. Very little warmth, however, is produced by the electric light, and when a man reads by an incandescent light he at times finds himself becoming chilly, and wonders why it is. Too hot during the day and too cold at night are conditions which should be avoided."

Care of the Feet.—Ill-health is often caused by carelessness about the feet. The largest pores in the system are in the bottom of the feet, and the most offensive matter is discharged through the pores. The feet and armpits should be washed every day with pure water only, as from them an offensive odor is emitted unless daily bathing is practiced. The pores, instead of being repellants, are absorbents, and the fetid matter is taken back into the system unless quickly removed from the surface. Stockings should not be worn more than one or two days at a time.

The Dark Sick-Room.—The first words of most physicians when they enter sick-rooms in private houses should be Goethe's dying exclamation: "More light! more light!" It certainly is true that generally before the doctor can get a good look at the patient, he has to ask that the curtains be raised, in order that the rays of a much greater healer than the ablest physician may ever hope to be may be admitted. If the patient's eyes are so affected that they cannot bear the light, a little ingenuity will suffice to screen them, and at the same time allow the cheerful light to enter. A dark sick-room must be an unhealthful one, and now that it is known that light is one of the most potent microbe-killers, let us have it in abundance.

Sick-Room Disinfectants.—One of the simplest disinfectants of a sick-room is ground coffee burnt on a shovel, so as to fill the atmosphere of the room with its pungent aromatic odor. If two red-hot coals are placed on a fire-shovel, and a teaspoonful of ground coffee is sprinkled over them at a time, using three teaspoonfuls in all, it will fill the room with its aroma, and is said to have the hygienic effect of preventing the spread of various epidemic diseases. The odor is very agreeable and soothing to a sick person, where other disinfectants prove disagreeable. Physicians who doubt the power of coffee as a disinfectant frequently recommend it as a deodorizer, and it certainly is one of the very best and most agreeable. Most of the disinfectants sold have no special power as such, but are simply deodorizers, the two being frequently confounded. It is best, however, to obtain from a physician in cases of dangerous epidemics something that will certainly destroy the germs of the disease as well as deodorize the room.

When Quinine Will Break Up a Cold.—It is surprising, says a family physician, how certainly a cold may be broken up by a timely dose of quinine. When first symptoms make their appearance, when a little languor, slight hoarseness and ominous tightening of the nasal membranes follow exposure to draughts or sudden chill by wet, five grains of this useful alkaloid are sufficient in many cases to end the trouble. But it must be done promptly. If the golden moment passes, nothing suffices to stop the weary sneezing, handkerchief-using, red nose and woebegone-looking periods that certainly follow.

Ways to Avoid Colds.—Before the cold weather comes on, and colds, sore throats and all other attendant evils of our variable climate are fairly with us, mothers should see that their children accustom themselves to the use of cold water on the throat and chest. A vigorous washing and scrubbing with cold water every morning, followed by friction with a coarse towel, will do much to prevent any throat trouble later on. A child should also be taught to gargle the throat well with cold water every time it washes its teeth.

Milk as a Dressing for Wounds.—Milk has been found to contain remarkable healing qualities if applied to wounds in an early stage, and excellent results have been obtained by its use in the dressing of burns. Compresses are soaked in milk and laid on the burn, to be renewed night and morning. An extensive burn has in this way been reduced in three days to one-quarter of its original size. Another burn, which had been treated for eight days with olive oil and oxide of zinc, healed rapidly under a milk dressing.

The Care of Children

DON'T do everything for and with the baby that you are advised to do; consider well the advice, and then rely most on your own judgment.

Don't neglect to have the little fellow's clothing light, warm, loose and free from pins.

Don't wake the baby to exhibit the tints of his eyes to admiring friends. Sleep is his most unquestionable right.

Don't spoil the infant by walking or rocking it to sleep, and do not let any one else do so; it will sleep best and most naturally when lying upon a comfortable bed.

Don't strain the baby's eyes by allowing strong lights to shine directly into them, especially when he first wakes.

Don't lay the child down with his ears bent away from his head; the result will be a deformity.

Don't try to prevent a teething child from sucking his thumb; it helps the work of dentition, and if the habit is acquired it can easily be broken up by the application of some bitter tincture to the thumbs, two or three applications only being necessary.

Don't fail to feel of baby's hands and feet during cold weather, both day and night. If they become cold, rub them gently till warm; if that does not have the desired result, wrap them in warm flannels.

Don't forget that small socks, tight clothing—anything which interferes with the circulation—will produce coldness of the hands and feet.

Don't forget that baby's lungs need plenty of pure, fresh air; but that they are still delicate, and ought not to be exposed to raw winds or sudden changes.

Don't have the room too warm; seventy degrees is about the right temperature, and there should be as little change as possible.

Don't take the baby out in severe cold, in damp or unhealthy weather, with the supposition that it will be the means of "hardening" him; it may do that—it may cost the little life.

When to Give Baby a Drink.—Infants, generally, whether brought up at breast or artificially, will, in warm, dry weather, take water every hour with advantage, and their frequent fretfulness and rise of temperature are often due to their not having it. In teething, spoonfuls of water, given every hour or oftener, cool and soothe the gums, and this, with larger, cooling evaporation, often stops the fretting and restlessness so universal at this period.

In teething and other disturbances the feverish condition demands more water to meet the extra evaporation from skin and lungs and to keep the body cool. The young child may be parched with thirst, but be unable to make known its wants. It is well to always test this—that is, whenever a child is uneasy give it a few teaspoonfuls of water, and if this is at all quieting, immediately, or after a few minutes, give more as often and as long as it is accepted and appears useful. If the water is reasonably pure no harm can come if not enough cold water is taken at one time to produce a chill of the internal organs.

Artificial Feeding of Infants.—The following formula, by a physician of high standing, has been found beneficial in numerous cases where everything else failed to produce satisfactory results. In the author's own family, it saved the life of an infant daughter who had been given up by an old practitioner, but who, it seems, was dying simply from lack of proper nourishment. She is now a rosy, robust child. The virtue of this formula consists in the fact that it most nearly corresponds to the natural nourishment from a healthy mother's breast. In using the formula care should be taken to use only absolutely pure water, and all bottles and vessels should be scrupulously clean. The cream and milk should be from one cow only:

Take two tablespoonfuls of cream, two tablespoonfuls of lime water; one tablespoonful of good milk, three tablespoonfuls of a solution of sugar of milk containing eighteen drams to one pint of pure water.

This quantity warmed is enough for once feeding a child of four months. For an older child add one teaspoonful of milk to the mixture for each month over four. For a younger child, diminish the quantity of milk in the same ratio.

The child should be fed every two hours and a half during the day and evening and as little as possible at night.

If the child be constipated, substitute barley water for lime-water. In preparing the barley water a porcelain-lined kettle should be employed if possible. Use the best pearl barley, and boil to a very thin gruel, which strain.

Each feeding must, of course, be made fresh, although the barley water and the sugar-of-milk solution may be made in quantities.

Teething.—Young children, whilst cutting their first set of teeth, often suffer severe constitutional disturbance. At first there is restlessness and peevishness, with slight fever, but not unfrequently these are followed by convulsive fits, as they are commonly called, which are caused by the brain becoming irritated; and sometimes under this condition the child is either cut off suddenly, or the foundation of serious mischief to the brain is laid. The remedy, or rather the safeguard against these frightful consequences, is trifling, safe, and almost certain, and consists merely in lancing the gum covering the tooth which is making its way through. When teething is about it may be known by the spittle constantly drivelling from the mouth and wetting the frock. The child has its fingers often in its mouth, and bites hard any substance it can get hold of. If the gums be carefully looked at, the part where the tooth is pressing up is swollen and redder than usual; and if the finger be pressed on it the child shrinks and cries, showing that the gum is tender. When these symptoms occur, the gum should be lanced, and sometimes the tooth comes through the next day, if near the surface; but if not so far advanced the cut heals and a scar forms, which is thought by some objectionable as rendering the passage of the tooth more difficult. This, however, is not so, for the scar will give way much more easily than the uncut gum. If the tooth does not come through after two or three days, the lancing may be repeated; and this is more especially needed if the child be very fractious and seems in much pain. Lancing the gums is further advantageous because it empties the inflamed part of its blood, and so relieves the pain and inflammation. The relief children experience in the course of two or three hours from the operation is often very remarkable, as they almost immediately become lively and cheerful.

Care of Children's Teeth.—The close connection between the malignant form of sore throat, so common among little children, and decayed teeth has already attracted the attention of wise physicians. It is a too common thing for mothers to allow their children to grow up without any care of their teeth, under the impression that the first teeth are only temporary, and it is natural that they should decay. It is now known, however, that these teeth, if allowed to decay, become the habitation of the toxless bacteria, and it is already conjectured that this is a frequent cause of diphtheria and kindred diseases, which attack little children more violently than they do adults.

It is the greatest mistake to allow a child to be careless about its teeth. From the moment a child is born its mouth should be washed out daily or semi-daily with cold water, and as soon as teeth appear a soft baby brush should be used. When the child is able to use a brush for himself he should be taught to brush his teeth at the back as well as the front, for the foulest accretions of tartar, which causes the decay of the teeth, usually find a resting-place at the back of the teeth.

Any spot of decay in a child's teeth should be promptly attended to, cleaned out and filled with some soft cement to arrest its growth. There is probably no more fruitful cause of disease of the throat and stomach than foul teeth in childhood. Clear cold water and a brush are all that a child needs for his teeth regularly. Once a week the teeth should be scrubbed out thoroughly with white castile soap and water, using a brush. The soap tends, it is said, to destroy any animalcules, but it should not be used oftener, as it causes the enamel to turn yellow.

To Cure a Cold.—It is wise to check a cold at the outset, and not allow it to gain too much hold.

A cold in the head may sometimes be arrested in its first stages by camphor, but this, like all other drugs, should only be given by a physician's order.

In a feverish cold, aconite, mixed in the proportion of half a drop of the medicine to a teaspoonful of water, taken by the child every hour, is often marvelously efficacious; but this, too, should not be administered unless prescribed by the doctor, as it is said to be very dangerous to some constitutions.

It is always safe, however, to fight against a cold by external applications, as camphorated oil rubbed upon the throat and chest and between the shoulders—this is admirable for children; or vaseline similarly applied.

In influenza a little relief is sometimes obtained by painting the inside of the nostrils with a camel's-hair brush or a tiny swab dipped in melted vaseline. This process will answer for young children; but older persons may snuff up the vaseline.

A mustard foot bath is often helpful in the first stages of a cold. A good handful each of mustard and coarse salt should be stirred into the water, and all chills must be avoided afterwards.

For an ordinary sore throat the outside of the throat may be rubbed at night with wet salt and the neck then bound with a narrow strip of flannel. Rubbing with camphorated oil is often beneficial to inflamed sore throats.

The old-fashioned pork and pepper may also be used for this trouble in children. For congestion of the lungs a mustard plaster should be applied, and the surface of this should be spread with sweet oil or white of an egg to prevent blistering the skin.

A hot bath is valuable in the first stages of congestion of the lungs, as it is also in infantile convulsions and in sudden brain trouble. In the last-named attack ice should be applied to the head and a hot water-bag to the feet.

The Function of the Tonsils.—Many a mother who has found in the tonsils of her children the seat of frequent trouble has wondered for what purpose these masses of sensitive blood vessels are included in the anatomy of the throat. Late researches by Dr. Lovell Gulland have developed some interesting facts about them, which ought to change opinion from skeptical curiosity to grateful welcome.

The tonsils are, it seems, glands in which the white blood corpuscles are developed. Now, the white blood corpuscles are the natural enemy of malignant microbes and bacteria, attacking them wherever encountered and always coming off victorious.

It will be seen, therefore, that a workshop for the manufacture of white corpuscles is a valuable plant, and its location just at the junction of the mouth and nasal passage, two sources of disease-germ supply, is only another evidence of the admirable economy of nature.

While the larger portion of the white corpuscles created by the tonsils pass right on into the circulation, patrolling and protecting the entire blood system, many more remain on the tonsil surfaces to catch the insidious bacillus at the very threshold as he has stolen through the mouth or slipped in by way of the nostrils. By the time the invading germ has passed the tonsil quarantine it is harmless, and thus, equally with the blood, are the throat, stomach and lungs protected.

Cholera Infantum.—This disease is caused generally by bad milk. Milk must therefore be kept fresh, and this can be done as follows: As soon as the milk comes put it in a glass bottle; put the bottle in a kettle with a block of wood under it to prevent the bottom coming in contact with the kettle; put water enough in the kettle to come half way up the side of the bottle; heat the water as hot as possible without boiling; then take the kettle from the fire and cork the bottle; let the bottle remain in the kettle for half an hour; then put the bottle in a cool place. This makes the milk safe without boiling. If possible use a rubber stopple instead of cork. The bottle and stopple must be cleansed every day with boiling water.

A Warning.—Cuffing the ears of children is a wicked and dangerous practice. The concussion of the air in the ear passage is extremely likely to fracture the tympanum of the ear and thus render the child permanently deaf. Dullness of hearing arising from cold, catarrh and other afflictions may be alleviated and often cured, but when the drum of the ear is ruptured nothing whatever can be done. There are many permanently deaf persons whose affliction has been brought on by boxing the ears, and the practice should be carefully avoided by parents and teachers. There are many ways of proper punishment without embittering a whole life.

Children Need Sleep.—Children, until they are 12 or 13 years old, should have at least 10 hours sleep, 11 is better; until 18 or 19, 9 hours is none too much. In this country children inherit nervous temperaments. No hygienic measure soothes, quiets and strengthens the nerves like plenty of sleep. Children should never be awakened in the morning. Yet the demands of the household convenience and the claims of school make it necessary that they should be out of bed at a certain hour, usually not later than seven. To make this possible, and give them their fair share of sleep so that they will be ready to waken of their own accord, they must be in bed between 8 and 10, according to their ages. If bedtime is made pleasant to them, as a mother love can make it, with a story, a little talk over the events of the day, with loving words and ministrations, the hardship of banishment to bed will be robbed of its bitterness.

A Hint for Mothers.—Mothers, whose babies toe in, rub (at least twice a day) the outer side of the little legs with a firm stroke upward. You can do it regularly when putting baby to bed and at such other times as may be convenient. When the little one climbs into your lap for a "cuddle" or a story is a good time. Hold the little foot sometimes in your hand in a correct position. Recollect, do not rub down and not the inner side of the leg. The object is to nourish and strengthen the outer muscles, which are proportionately weak. Begin below the ankle and rub to the knee slowly and quietly, but not too lightly. The treatment, faithfully persevered in, it will soon correct the trouble.

Infant's Syrup.—The syrup is made thus: One pound best box raisins, half an ounce of anise-seed, two sticks licorice; split the raisins, pound the anise-seed, and cut the licorice fine; add to it three quarts of rain water, and boil down to two quarts. Feed three or four times a day, as much as the child will willingly drink. The raisins are to strengthen, the anise is to expel the wind, and the licorice as a physic.

Ointment for Scurf in the Heads of Infants.—Lard, two ounces; sulphuric acid, diluted, two drachms; rub them together, and anoint the head once a day.

Remedy for Worms.—Bruise ½ oz. of Carolina pink-root, ½ oz. of senna leaf, ½ oz. of manna, and ½ oz. of American worm-seed. Pour on 1 pt. of boiling water, and steep without boiling. Add half as much milk and sweeten well. To a child 5 years old give 1 gill 3 times a day, before meals.

Croup Remedy.—In an attack of croup, before a physician can arrive, no time should be lost in waiting. An emetic is the first thing to be given, and nothing is better than a teaspoonful of the wine or syrup of ipecac, either clear or diluted in a little water. Repeat in fifteen or twenty minutes, if necessary. But sometimes there is no ipecac in the house; in such a case give a teaspoonful of powdered alum in honey or syrup. Keep the air in the room continually moistened by steam; the vapor of unslaked lime is excellent. Keep the temperature of the room as high as eighty degrees, and avoid draughts.

Whooping Cough Cure.—The juice of 1 lemon, 1 tablespoonful of sweet oil, 2 oz. loaf sugar, white of 1 egg, 1 teaspoonful paregoric. Beat together in a bowl and give a teaspoonful after coughing.

Contagious Diseases

SCARLET FEVER, a contagious disease producing a large annual mortality, is produced by a specific poison which emanates from the person of the patient, and can be caused by no other means, and this poison is remarkable for the tenacity with which it affixes itself to objects which, if portable, may convey it long distances, and for its tenacity of life, which renders it difficult to destroy. Diphtheria, also a contagious disease, and largely fatal, may also arise from other causes than contagion, notably from fermenting filth, and requires not only isolation, but cleanliness for its extinction. Typhoid fever and Asiatic cholera, while not directly communicable from person to person, are spread by the dejecta of their victims, which contaminate the water supply, and thus an efficient disinfection of these dejecta is a very desirable thing to accomplish.

The following points will help to determine the nature of a suspicious illness:

CHICKEN-POX.—Small rose pimples, changing to vesicles, appear the second day of fever or after 24 hours' illness; scabs form about the fourth day of fever; duration, 6 or 7 days.

ERYSIPELAS.—Diffuse redness and swelling second or third day of illness.

MEASLES.—Small red dots, like flea bites, fourth day of fever or after 72 hours' illness; rash fades on seventh day; duration, 6 to 10 days.

SCARLET FEVER.—Bright scarlet, diffused, second day of fever or after 24 hours' illness. Rash fades on fifth day; duration, 8 to 10 days.

SMALL-POX.—Small red pimples, changing to vesicles, then pustules, third day of fever or after 48 hours' illness; scabs form ninth or tenth day, fall off about fourteenth day; duration, 2 to 3 weeks.

TYPHOID FEVER.—Rose-colored spots, scattered, appear eleventh to fourteenth day, accompanied by diarrhea; duration, 22 to 30 days.

It will often relieve a mother's anxiety to know how long there is danger of infection after a child has been exposed to a contagious disease. The following table gives the information concerning the more important diseases:

Disease.	Symptoms appear	Period ranging from	Patient is infectious
CHICKEN-POX	On 14th day	10 to 18 days	Until all scabs have fallen off.
DIPHTHERIA	On 2d day	2 to 5 days	14 days after throat trouble disappears
MEASLES*	On 14th day	10 to 14 days	Until scaling and cough cease.
MUMPS	On 19th day	16 to 21 days	14 days from commencement.
ROTHELN	On 14th day	12 to 26 days	10-14 days from commencement
SCARLET FEVER	On 4th day	1 to 7 days	Until all scaling has ceased.
SMALL-POX	On 12th day	1 to 14 days	Until all scabs have fallen off.
TYPHOID FEVER	On 21st day	1 to 23 days	Until diarrhea ceases.
WHOOP. COUGH†	On 14th day	7 to 14 days	Six weeks after beginning to whoop.

*In measles the patient is infectious three days before the eruption appears.

†In whooping cough the patient is infectious during the primary cough, which may be three weeks before the whooping begins.

Valuable Advice on Cholera.—The following plain thesis on cholera was recently prepared by Dr. Heinz Marks of St. Louis, at the request of the Mayor:

Asiatic cholera is caused by Koch's cholera germs. Regarding this germ the following is true: First, its best soil is in the intestines of man; second, thrives best at a temperature between 88 and 104 degrees Fahrenheit; third, prospers best in an alkaline solution, but may sustain itself for months in neutral solution; fourth, requires moisture for its sustenance; fifth, is not transmissible to lower animals in epidemic form; sixth, above 158 degrees Fahrenheit it is killed with a certainty in short time; seventh, chemical agents, especially mineral acids, kill it; eighth, gastric juice (the acids of) destroys it absolutely; ninth, drying at temperature over 150 Fahrenheit kills it in a short time, sometimes in a few hours; tenth, putrescent fluids kill it; eleventh, enters the body only by way of digestion, in food and drink; twelfth, leaves the body by the fecal discharges; thirteenth, is found in the vomit only when intestinal contents have entered the stomach before the vomit.

Milk.—In warm milk it grows and thrives with rapidity. Boiling the milk kills the germ. It grows rapidly in milk which has been previously boiled and allowed to stand, hence the milk should be boiled immediately before each meal.

Water.—In ordinary drinking water it usually soon dies from the presence of other bacteria, acids, etc., but in exceptional cases it has sustained itself for a long time in such water. In water which has been boiled it sustains itself for a long time; sometimes for months.

Food.—Many articles of food are favorable soil for it, and any article, food, furniture or otherwise, under proper circumstances, may carry the germ to non-infected persons. Flies, cockroaches, mice, rats, mosquitoes, bedbugs, etc., after feasting on or being about infected material, carry the germs that have attached themselves to the insects, etc., and transmit same to food supplies by feeding on the food or passing over it.

Prevention of Disease.—Render free from cholera germs all food immediately before it is taken into the stomach by subjecting it to cooking. Live on such articles of food which digest completely and most easily in the stomach. Avoid eating shortly before retiring. Keep the stomach acid by taking diluted muriatic acid after meals and drinking a sulphuric acid lemonade during the day. Avoid overwork, exhaustion, excessive loss of sleep, etc. Disinfect the hands before meals.

Discharges.—From the discharges, and sometimes the vomit, all infection takes place, hence they should be immediately and thoroughly disinfected. The soiled linen should immediately be immersed in bichloride of mercury solution, 10 grains of bichloride to a quart of water. The patient should be bathed with a mild bichloride of mercury solution — two grains to a quart of water—after discharges from the bowels or vomit. The discharges from the patient should immediately be disinfected with bichloride of mercury and potassium permanganate, 80 grains to a quart of water.

In the city, where lead pipes are used for drainage, bichloride of mercury will have to be dispensed with in disinfecting the discharges, because the bichloride corrodes the pipe. The most effective disinfectant for the discharges is chloride of lime.

Nurses.—Attendants on cholera patients should not wash their faces in water that is not free from cholera germs, and should disinfect their hands before washing their faces. They should avoid putting anything in their mouths except properly prepared foods. When their garments become soiled with choleraic discharges or vomits they should be treated immediately like the soiled linen.

The Sick-Room.—Beds should be cleansed with bichloride solution, 15 grains to a quart of water; or carbolic acid, one-half pint of carbolic acid to a quart of water. The sick-chamber should be kept free from all flies, roaches, mice, rats, etc., and perfectly dry. After the patient has recovered or has died, the room should be fumigated; the floor and immovable furniture and such furniture as will permit should be washed with 15 grains of bichloride of mercury solution to a quart of water. Such furniture as will not bear the bichloride should be disinfected with carbolic acid, one-half pint to a quart of water. All linen and clothing should be boiled or disinfected.

Disinfectants.—Heat is the best disinfectant and should be employed wherever it is possible. Chloride of lime is the best disinfectant for foul places, streets, yards, closets, etc. All mud holes and damp spots should be dried and disinfected. Sidewalks and streets should not be watered in time of epidemic. All foul material should be removed.

Disinfection of Food.—All the food, knives, forks, dishes, etc., can readily be disinfected shortly before meals by dry heat or boiling water. All food should be cleansed well before cooking.

Pitting in Smallpox.—The following is a simple process that has been adopted most successfully, not only in cases of smallpox, in which it completely prevented pitting, but in all eruptive diseases generally, such as measles, scarlatina, nettlerash, chickenpox, etc., relieving the itching, tingling and irritation of these complaints, and thereby affording great relief, especially in the case of children. It consists in smearing the whole surface of the body, after the eruption is fairly out, with bacon fat; and the simplest way of employing it is to boil thoroughly a small piece of bacon with the skin on, and when cold to cut off the skin with the fat adhering to it, which is to be scored crosswise with a knife, and then gently rubbed over the surface once, twice or thrice a day, according to the extent of the eruption and the recurrence of itching and irritation. Another plan, practised by Dr. Allshorn, of Edinburgh, is to mix three parts of oil with one of white wax, by heat, and while warm and fluid to paint over the face and neck with a camel-hair brush. As this cools and hardens it forms a mask, which effectually excludes the air, and prevents pitting. It is said that if light is admitted into the patient's room through yellow blinds, so that the red and blue rays of the sun are excluded, pitting will be prevented.

Protection Against Bacteria.—It is fortunate that only few bacteria are disease-producing; the great majority of them are harmless and beneficent objects in nature. They are the principal agents of oxidation of organic matter, and it is to them that we owe the phenomena of fermentation and decay. They are the common scavengers of the earth. Were it it not for their constant and beneficent work the world would soon be choked up with decaying animal and vegetable matter, and all the higher orders of life would perish.

But the infectious bacteria have the power of elaborating nitrogenous poisons, known as ptomaines, and the question whether zymotic diseases are produced by bacteria themselves or by these ptomaines can not, in our present imperfect state of knowledge, be answered with certainty. In some cases, however, the disease seems to come from organic poison. Thus tyrotoxicon, which is the alkaloid produced by bacteria in the fermentation of milk, produces a complexus of symptoms in the human system resembling those of cholera infantum, so it is very probable that tyrotoxicon is the chemical irritant producing the disease. What is true of cholera infantum is perhaps also true of typhoid fever and other filth diseases, but not at the same stage of life.

All bacteria feed upon organic matter, and develop in great numbers in fermenting solutions of it. Their number is generally approximately proportional to the amount of impurity, and therefore may represent the relative danger of potable waters. A water that contains a large number of them should not be used for drinking without first being boiled. By boiling polluted water for half an hour all the infectious (but not the harmless) bacteria in it will be destroyed. If it is then filtered to remove the vegetable substances, and aerated to render it potable, such water can be used with perfect safety for drinking. Since the infectious bacteria are the agents of all filth diseases, it should be the aim in all sanitary analysis of water to determine whether they have actual existence in the water, or, what answers the same purpose, to determine the conditions favorable for their development. Whenever a chemical analysis reveals the presence of sewage in a water its use should be discontinued for drinking, without an expensive bacteriological examination.

Accidents and Emergencies

IF an artery is cut, red blood spurts. Compress it above the wound. If a vein is cut, dark blood flows. Compress it below and above.

If choked, go upon all fours and cough.

For slight burns, dip the part in cold water; if the skin is destroyed, cover with varnish or linseed oil.

For apoplexy, raise the head and body; for fainting, lay the person flat.

Send for a physician when a serious accident of any kind occurs, but treat as directed until he arrives.

Scalds and Burns.—The following facts cannot be too firmly impressed on the mind of the reader; that in either of these accidents the *first, best, and often the only remedies required* are sheets of wadding, fine wool, or carded cotton, and in the default of these, violet powder, flour, magnesia, or chalk. The object for which these several articles are employed is the same in each instance; namely, to exclude the air from the injured part; for if the air can be effectually shut out from the raw surface, and care is taken not to expose the tender part till the new cuticle is formed, the cure may be safely left to nature. The moment a person is called to a case of scald or burn, he should cover the part with a sheet, or a portion of a sheet, of wadding, taking care not to break any blister that may have formed, or stay to remove any burnt clothes that may adhere to the surface, but as quickly as possible envelop every part of the injury from all access of the air, laying one or two more pieces of wadding on the first, so as effectually to guard the burn or scald from the irritation of the atmosphere; and if the article used is wool or cotton, the same precaution, of adding more material where the surface is thinly covered, must be adopted; a light bandage finally securing all in their places. Any of the popular remedies recommended below may be employed when neither wool, cotton nor wadding are to be procured, it being always remembered that that article which will best exclude the air from a burn or scald is the best, quickest and least painful mode of treatment. And in this respect nothing has surpassed cotton loose or attached to paper as in wadding.

If the skin is much injured in burns, spread some linen pretty thickly with chalk ointment, and lay over the part, and give the patient some brandy and water if much exhausted; then send for a medical man. If not much injured, and very painful, use the same ointment, or apply carded cotton dipped in lime water and linseed oil. If you please, you may lay cloths dipped in ether over the parts, or cold lotions. Treat scalds in same manner, or cover with scraped raw potato; but the chalk ointment is the best. In the absence of all these, cover the injured part with molasses, and dust over it plenty of flour.

Body in Flames.—Lay the person down on the floor of the room, and throw the table cloth, rug or other large cloth over him, and roll him on the floor.

Dirt in the Eye.—Place your forefinger upon the cheek-bone, having the patient before you; then slightly bend the finger; this will draw down the lower lid of the eye, and you will probably be able to remove the dirt; but if this will not enable you to get at it, repeat this operation while you have a knitting-needle or bodkin placed over the eyelid; this will turn it inside out, and enable you to remove the sand, or eyelash, etc., with the corner of a fine silk handkerchief. As soon as the substance is removed, bathe the eye with cold water, and exclude the light for a day. If the inflammation is severe, let the patient use a refrigerant lotion.

Lime in the Eye.—Syringe it well with warm vinegar and water in the proportion of one ounce of vinegar to eight ounces of water; exclude light.

Iron or Steel Spiculæ in the Eye.—These occur while turning iron or steel in a lathe, and are best remedied by doubling back the upper or lower eyelid, according to the situation of the substance, and, with the flat edge of a silver probe, taking up the metallic particle, using a lotion made by dissolving six grains of sugar of lead and the same of white vitriol in six ounces of water, and bathing the eye three times a day until the inflammation subsides. Another plan is —Drop a solution of sulphate of copper (from one to three grains of the salt to one ounce of water) into the eye, or keep the eye open in a wineglassful of solution. Bathe with cold lotion, and exclude light to keep down inflammation.

Dislocated Thumb.—This is frequently produced by a fall. Make a clove hitch, by passing two loops of cord over the thumb, placing a piece of rag under the cord to prevent it cutting the thumb; then pull in the same line as the thumb. Afterwards apply a cold lotion.

Cuts and Wounds.—In all recent wounds, the first consideration is to remove foreign bodies, such as pieces of glass, splinters of wood, pieces of stone, earth or any other substance that may have been introduced by the violence of the act which caused the wound.

Where there is much loss of blood, an attempt should be made to stop it with dry lint, and compression above the part wounded, if the blood be of a florid color; and below, if of a dark color. *In proportion to the importance of the part wounded will be the degree of the discharge of blood, and the subsequent tendency to inflammation and its consequences.

Clean cut wounds, whether deep or superficial and likely to heal by the first intention, should always be washed or cleaned, and at once evenly and smoothly closed by bringing both edges close together, and securing them in that position by adhesive plaster. Cut thin strips of sticking-plaster, and bring the parts together; or, if large and deep, cut two broad pieces, so as to look like the teeth of a comb, and place one on each side of the wound, which must be cleaned previously. The pieces must be arranged so that they shall interlace one another; then, by laying hold of the pieces on the right side with one hand, and those on the other side with the other hand, and pulling them from one another, the edges of the wound are brought together without any difficulty.

Ordinary Cuts are dressed by thin strips, applied by pressing down the plaster on one side of the wound, and keeping it there and pulling in the opposite direction, then suddenly depressing the hand when the edges of the wound are brought together.

Contusions are best healed by laying a piece of folded lint, well wetted with arnica oil lotion, or boracic acid, on the part, and, if there is much pain, placing a hot bran poultice over the dressing, renewing both, if necessary, every two hours. When the injuries are very severe, lay a cloth over the part, and suspend a basin over it filled with cold lotion. Put a piece of cotton into the basin, so that it shall allow the lotion to drop on the cloth, and thus keep it always wet.

Hemorrhage, when caused by an artery being divided or torn, may be known by the blood issuing out of the wound in leaps or jerks, and being of a bright scarlet color. If a vein is injured the blood is darker, and flows continuously. To arrest the latter, apply pressure by means of a compress and bandage. To arrest arterial bleeding, get a piece of wood (part of a broom handle will do), and tie a piece of tape to one end of it; then tie a piece of tape loosely over the arm, and pass the other end of the wood under it; twist the stick round and round until the tape compresses the arm sufficiently to arrest the bleeding, and then confine the other end by tying the string around the arm. A compress made by enfolding a 50-cent piece in several folds of lint or linen should, however, be first placed under the tape and over the artery. If the bleeding is very obstinate, and it occurs in the arm, place a cork underneath the string, on the inside of the fleshy part, where the artery may be felt beating by any one; if in the leg, place a cork in the direction of a line drawn from the inner part of the knee towards the outer part of the groin. It is an excellent thing to accustom yourself to find out the position of these arteries, or, indeed, any that are superficial, and to explain to every person in your house where they are, and how to stop bleeding. If a stick cannot be got take a handkerchief, make a cord bandage of it, and tie a knot in the middle; the knot acts as a compress, and should be placed over the artery, while the two ends are to be tied around the thumb. *Observe always to place the ligature between the wound and the heart.* Putting your finger into a bleeding wound, and making pressure until a surgeon arrives, will generally stop violent bleeding.

Violent Shocks will sometimes stun a person, and he will remain unconscious. Untie strings, collars, etc.; loosen anything that is tight and interferes with the breathing; raise the head; see if there is bleeding from any part; apply smelling-salts to the nose, and hot bottles to the feet.

In **Concussion**, the surface of the body is cold and pale, and the pulse weak and small, the breathing slow and *gentle*, and the pupil of the eye generally contracted or small. You can get an answer by speaking loud, so as to arouse the patient. Give a little brandy and water, keep the place quiet, apply warmth, and do not raise the head too high. If you tickle the feet the patient feels it.

In **Compression of the Brain** from any cause, such as apoplexy, or a piece of fractured bone pressing on it, there is loss of sensation. If you tickle the feet of the injured person he does not feel it. You cannot arouse him so as to get an answer. The pulse is slow and labored; the breathing deep, labored and snorting; the pupil enlarged. Raise the head, loosen strings or tight things, and send for a surgeon. If one cannot be got at once, apply mustard poultices to the feet and thighs, leeches to the temples, and hot water to the feet.

Choking.—When a person has a fish bone in the throat, insert the forefinger, press upon the root of the tongue, so as to induce vomiting; if this does not do, let him swallow a large piece of potato or soft bread; and if these fail, give a mustard emetic. A piece of food lodged in the throat may sometimes be pushed down with the finger, or removed with a hair-pin quickly straightened and hooked at the end, or by two or three vigorous blows on the back between the shoulders.

Fainting, Hysterics, Etc.—Loosen the garments, bathe the temples with water or eau-de-cologne; open the window, admit plenty of fresh air, dash cold water on the face, apply hot bricks to the feet, and avoid bustle and excessive sympathy.

Drowning.—Attend the following *essential rules:* 1. Lose no time. 2. Handle the body gently. 3. Carry the body face downwards, with the head gently raised, and never hold it up by the feet. 4. Send for medical assistance immediately, and in the meantime act as follows: 5. Strip the body; rub it dry, then wrap it in hot blankets, and place it in a warm bed in a warm room. 6. Cleanse away the froth and mucus from the nose and mouth. 7. Apply warm bricks, bottles, bags of sand, etc., to the armpits, between the thighs, and to the soles of the feet. 8. Rub the surface of the body with the hands inclosed in warm, dry worsted socks. 9. If possible, put the body into a warm bath. 10. To restore breathing, put the pipe of a common bellows into one nostril, carefully closing the other and the mouth, at the same time drawing downwards, and pushing gently backwards, the upper part of the windpipe, to allow a more free admission of air; blow the bellows gently, in order to inflate the lungs, till the breast be raised a little; then set the mouth and nostrils free, and press gently on the chest; repeat this until signs of life appear. The body should be covered the moment it is placed on the table, except the face, and all the rubbing carried on under the sheet or blanket. When they can be obtained, a number of tiles or bricks should be made tolerably hot in the fire, laid in a row on the table, covered with a blanket, and the body placed in such a manner on them that their heat may enter the spine. When the patient revives, apply smelling-salts to the nose, give warm wine or brandy and water. Cautions.—1. Never rub the body with salt or spirits. 2. Never roll the body on casks. 3. Continue the remedies twelve hours without ceasing.

Lightning and Sunstroke.—Treat the same as apoplexy.

Suffocation by Noxious Vapors.—Remove to the cold air; dash cold water or water and vinegar on the face and body at intervals. If the body feel cold, employ gradual warmth. If necessary, apply mustard poultices to the soles of the feet and to the spine, and try artificial respiration as in drowning, with electricity.

Suspended Animation from Intense Cold.—Rub the body with snow, ice or cold water. Restore warmth by degrees, and after some time, if necessary, employ the means for restoring the drowned.

Suspension by Hanging.—Loosen the cord or whatever it may be by which the person has been suspended. A few ounces of blood may be taken from the jugular vein, or by cupping-glasses applied to the head or neck, or by leeches applied to the temples. It is positively necessary to have medical aid, as the treatment must vary according to circumstances.

Suspended Animation through Intoxication.—Lay the body on a bed, with the head a little raised; then remove the neckcloth, and procure medical assistance. Warm fluids may be conveyed to the stomach by means of a flexible tube and a gum-elastic bottle. On signs of returning life, a teaspoonful of warm water may be given, and, if swallowed, some warm wine or diluted spirits. Then the person, conveyed to a warm bed, may go to sleep if so inclined, and if carefully watched so as to guard against any sinking in the powers of life during sleep. The restorative process should be used for four or six hours. It is a wrong opinion that persons are irrecoverable because life does not speedily reappear. Electricity and bleeding should never be employed unless by the direction of a physician.

Frozen Limbs.—Rub with snow or very cold water until the frozen part becomes red. Wipe dry, rub briskly with the hand and cover with flannel.

Fainting.—Loosen the clothing and place the person upon the back, with the head low. Let plenty of fresh air into the room, and do not allow a crowd to collect around the patient. Use gentle friction and apply camphor or ammonia upon the forehead and about the nostrils. Often all that is necessary is to lay the person full length upon his back and let him alone, only giving him plenty of fresh air.

Sprained Ankle.—Wash the ankle frequently with cold salt water, which is far better than warm vinegar or decoctions of herbs. Keep your foot as cold as possible to prevent inflammation, and sit with it elevated on a cushion. Live on very low diet, and take every day some cooling medicine. By obeying these directions only, a sprained ankle has been cured in a few days.

A Simple Cure for Sprains.—A lady who can testify to the efficacy of the following cure for a sprain or bruise gives it to the public: Make a plaster by stirring salt enough into hot molasses to make it of a consistency to remain in place when confined by a muslin bandage. Suit the size of your plaster to the spot to be covered, and pack it securely around the injured member.

How to Raise the Body of a Drowned Person.—In a recent failure to recover the body of a drowned person in New Jersey, a French-Canadian undertook the job, and proceeded as follows: Having supplied himself with some glass gallon jars and a quantity of unslacked lime, he went in a boat to the place where the man was seen to go down. One of the jars was filled half full of lime, and then filled up with water and tightly corked. It was then dropped into the water and soon after exploded at the bottom of the river with a loud report. After the third trial, each time at a different place, the body rose to the surface and was secured.

Bites of Insects.—A free application of ammonia to the part bitten will give instant relief from bites of bees, wasps, hornets, scorpions, etc. The part may afterward be covered with sweet oil.

To Remove a Bee-Sting.—Remove the sting at once with a needle or the fingers; press a key tightly over the stung part, and the pressure will force the poison out. Wipe the place with clean linen, suck it and then dab with the blue-bag.

Bites of Snakes.—These are dangerous and require powerful remedies. The bites of the various kinds of snakes do not have the same effects, but people suffer from them in different ways. It is of the greatest importance to prevent the poison mixing with the blood and to remove the whole of it instantly from the body. Take a piece of tape or anything that is near and tie tightly around the part bitten; if it be the leg or arm, immediately above the bite and between it and the heart. The wound should be sucked several times by any person near. There is no danger to the person performing this kindness providing his tongue or any part of the mouth has no broken skin. Having sucked the poison, immediately spit it out. A better plan is to cut out the central part bitten with a sharp instrument. This may not be a very pleasant operation for an amateur, but, as we have to act promptly in such an emergency, courage will come. After the operation bathe the wound for some time to make it bleed freely. Having done this rub the wound with a stick of lunar caustic or, still better, a solution composed of sixty grains of lunar caustic dissolved in an ounce of water. This solution should be dropped into the wound. Of course the band tied round the wound in the first place must be kept on during the time these means are being adopted. The wound afterwards must be covered with lint dipped in cold water. There is generally great depression of strength in these cases; it is necessary, therefore, to give some stimulant, a glass of hot brandy and water, or twenty drops of sal-volatile. When the patient has somewhat recovered give him a little mustard in hot water to make him vomit; if, on the other hand, the vomiting is continuous, a large mustard poultice should be applied to the stomach and one pill given composed of a grain of solid opium. Note.—Only one of these pills must be given without medical advice. All these remedies can be acted upon until a surgeon arrives.

Capt. Crawford's Snake Remedy.—Capt. Jack Crawford, the "Poet Scout," tells the writer that he guards against rattlesnake poisoning by carrying in his saddlebags a small vial of turpentine. He says that he has extracted the poison from a rattlesnake bite by simply pressing the mouth of the bottle down on the wound after removing the stopper, the turpentine drawing the poison upward from the wound into the bottle.

"A conceited young man one day, conversing with the celebrated Dr. Parr, observed that he would believe nothing that he could not understand. 'Then, young man, your creed will be the shortest of any man's I know.'"—*Helps.*

Poisons and their Antidotes

ALWAYS send immediately for a medical man. Save all fluids vomited, and articles of food, cups, glasses, etc., used by the patient before taken ill, and lock them up.

As a rule give emetics after poisons that cause sleepiness and raving;—chalk, milk, eggs, butter and warm water, or oil, after poisons that cause vomiting and pain in the stomach and bowels, with purging; and when there is no inflammation about the throat, tickle it with a feather to excite vomiting.

Vomiting may be caused by giving warm water, with a teaspoonful of mustard to the tumblerful, well stirred up. Sulphate of zinc (white vitriol) may be used in place of the mustard, or powdered alum. Powder of ipecacuanha, a teaspoonful rubbed up with molasses, may be employed for children. *Tartar emetic* should never be given, as it is excessively depressing and uncontrollable in its effects. The stomach pump can only be used by skillful hands, and even then with caution.

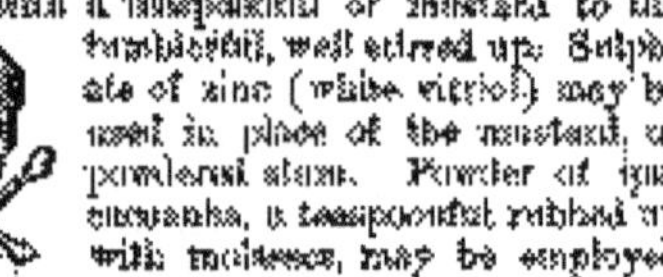

Opium and Other Narcotics.—After vomiting has occurred, cold water should be *dashed* over the face and head. The patient must be kept awake, walked about between two strong persons, made to grasp the handles of a galvanic battery, tinkled with strong nails, and vigorously slapped. *Belladonna* is an antidote for opium and for morphia, etc., its active principles; and, on the other hand, the latter counteracts the effects of belladonna. But a knowledge of medicine is necessary for dealing with these articles.

Strychnia.—After emetics have been freely and successfully given, the patient should be allowed to breathe the vapor of sulphuric ether, poured on a handkerchief and held to the face, in such quantities as to keep down the tendency to convulsions. Bromide of potassium, twenty grains at a dose, dissolved in syrup, may be given every hour.

Alcoholic Poisoning should be combated by emetics, of which the sulphate of zinc, given as above directed, is the best. After that, strong coffee internally, and stimulation by heat externally, should be used.

Acids are sometimes swallowed by mistake. Alkalies, lime water, magnesia, or common chalk mixed with water, may be freely given, and afterward mucilaginous drinks, such as thick gum water or flaxseed tea.

Alkalies are less frequently taken in injurious strength or quantity, but sometimes children swallow lye by mistake. Common vinegar may be given freely, and then castor or sweet oil in full doses—a tablespoonful at a time, repeated every half hour or two.

Nitrate of Silver when swallowed is neutralized by common table salt freely given in solution in water.

The Salts of Mercury or Arsenic (often kept as bedbug poison), which are powerful irritants, are apt to be very quickly fatal. Milk or the whites of eggs may be freely given, and afterward a very thin paste of flour and water. In these cases an emetic is to be given *after* the poison is neutralized.

Phosphorus paste, kept for roach poison or in parlor matches, is sometimes eaten by children, and has been willfully taken for the purpose of suicide. It is a powerful irritant. The first thing to be done is to give freely of magnesia and water; then to give mucilaginous drinks, as flaxseed tea, gum water or sassafras pith and water; and lastly to administer freely powdered bone-charcoal, either in pill or in mixture with water.

In no case of poisoning should there be any avoidable delay in obtaining the advice of a physician, and, meanwhile, the friends or bystanders should endeavor to find out exactly what has been taken, so that the treatment adopted may be as prompt and effective as possible.

❧

The National Bank Law.—The National bank act provides for a limit of capital in establishment of the national banks proportioned to the importance of their locality. To start a bank in a town of 6,000 population or less requires a capital of not less than $50,000. In a town between 6,000 and 50,000 people, the capital of the bank must be $100,000, while not less than $200,000 is required in a town of more than 50,000 inhabitants. Each bank must deposit with the United States Treasury bonds to the extent of at least one-third of its entire capital as security for its creditors. The Government then issues to the bank 90 per cent. of its deposits in blank notes, which, when properly filled and signed, become the circulation of the bank. Each bank must report its condition quarterly to the Comptroller of the Currency, and must at all times have on hand in lawful money of the United States an amount equal to at least 25 per cent. of its circulation and deposits. The notes issued by the national banks are thus secured, but depositors run the same risk of loss through dishonesty or mismanagement of funds as with other banks.

Hygienic Toilet Recipes

Bathing.—The surface of the skin is punctured with millions of little holes called pores. The duty of these pores is to carry the waste matter off. For instance, perspiration. Now, if the pores are stopped up the body has to find some other way to get rid of its impurities. Then the liver has more than it can do. Then we take a liver pill when we ought to clean out the pores instead. The housewife is very particular to keep her sieves in good order; after she has strained a substance through them they are washed out carefully with water, because water is the best thing known. That is the reason water is used to bathe in. But the skin is a little different from a sieve, because it helps along the process itself. All it needs is a little encouragement. What the skin wants is rubbing. If you should quietly sit down in a tub of water and as quietly get up and dry off without rubbing, your skin wouldn't be much benefited. The water would make it a little soft, especially if it was warm. But rubbing is the great thing. Stand where the sunlight strikes a part of your body, then take a dry brush and rub it, and you will notice that countless little flakes of cuticle fly off. Every time one of these flakes is removed from the skin your body breathes a sigh of relief.

Too much bathing is a bad thing. Soap and water are good things to soften up the skin, but rubbing is what the skin wants. Every morning or every evening, or when it is most convenient, wash the body all over with water and a little ammonia, or anything which tends to make the water soft; then rub dry with a towel, and after that go over the body from top to toe with a dry brush. Try this for two or three weeks, and your skin will be like velvet.

A little ammonia in bath water for the entire body is refreshing, and removes any disagreeable smell of perspiration. It must not, however, be used in washing the eyes.

Best Things for the Complexion.—Cleanliness, perfect cleanliness, usually means a healthy and, therefore, a beautiful skin. Pure white castile is generally acknowledged to be the best soap for the complexion unless expensive toilet soaps can be used. The highly-colored and highly-perfumed soaps will spoil the best of complexions in short order. Some ladies use no soap at all, believing that it irritates and roughens the skin. Hot water, they argue, answers every purpose so far as the face is concerned. It is not wise to use soap on the face during the day, but just before retiring a thorough washing with plenty of hot water, castile soap and a soft cloth is imperative. Vaseline or cold cream may be applied for the night and washed off in the morning with a little ammonia in hot water.

Soft water is the best to wash in, but where it cannot be had a good substitute may be made by adding a few drops of ammonia or borax to the hard water in common use. The Princess of Wales uses distilled water which costs about 20 cents a gallon. To whiten the skin a few drops of spirits of camphor may be added to hot water once or twice a week.

Very often bad complexions are caused by indigestion. For the indigestion, correct the diet and take a charcoal tablet before each meal. The teeth should be thoroughly brushed and the mouth rinsed after each meal. This cleansing of the mouth is of the greatest importance in dyspepsia of any degree. There is as much dyspepsia in the mouth as in the rest of the alimentary canal, for dyspepsia is really ferment, with corroding effects on the live tissues of membrane and nerves.

To correct acidity after eating, let a bit of magnesia the size of a large pea dissolve in the mouth and swallow it. The acidity has everything to do with spoiling complexion and temper. The face is the index of the condition of the internal economy. Lime water may be beneficial for poor digestion, or lemon drops, or a third of a teaspoonful of baking-soda in half a glass of hot water, flavored with tincture of cinnamon, which is a good stomachic in itself. These should be tried to see which suits best. It is often best to alternate these simple remedies.

Freckles.—Drinking the juice of a lemon in a little water every morning before eating will efface freckles. Lemon juice taken in this way, and a vapor bath given the face at night, using boiling water and a Turkish towel, will reduce the flesh of the face or the double chin.

Ointment for Blackheads.—For blackheads or fleshworms the following ointment applied every day will prove efficacious: Iodide of potash, one ounce; cologne, two ounces; white brandy, four ounces.

Lotion for Humors and Eruptions.—Rose water, 1 ounce; glycerine, 50 drops; tannic, 20 grains. Mix. Apply morning and night.

To Remove Pimples.—1. Mix 3 oz. of spirits of wine and ½ dr. of liquor of potassa. This mixture should be applied to the pimples with a camel's-hair pencil. If too strong, ½ oz. pure water may be added to it. 2. A weak solution of carbolic acid in rose water will cure summer pimples and simple eruptions.

Cure of Warts.—The easiest way to get rid of warts is to pare off the thickened skin which covers the prominent wart; cut it off by successive layers; shave it till you come to the surface of the skin, and till you draw blood in two or three places. When you have thus denuded the surface of the skin, rub the part thoroughly over with lunar caustic. One effective operation of this kind will generally destroy the wart; if not, cut off the black spot which has been occasioned by the caustic, and apply the caustic again, or *acetic acid* may be applied in order to get rid of it.

Wrinkles may be removed from the face by the persistent use of hot fomentations and the massage treatment.

An Excellent Lotion.—A mixture of equal parts of bay rum, rosewater and glycerine is soothing to chapped skin, and will be found an excellent lotion to keep constantly on hand in cold weather.

A Good Cold Cream.—Melt together a dram of white beeswax, an ounce of spermaceti and two ounces of almond oil, to which add a small quantity of green camphor. Pour, while warm, into small pomade jars, and set away to cool.

Almond Paste.—Take of blanched almonds four ounces, and the white of one egg; beat the almonds to a smooth paste in a mortar, then add the white of egg, and enough rosewater, mixed with one-half its weight of spirits of wine, to give the proper consistency. This paste is used as a cosmetic, to beautify the complexion, and is also a remedy for chapped hands, etc.

A Harmless Lotion.—For whitening and softening the skin a harmless lotion may be prepared from two grains of cascarilla powder, two grains muriate of ammonia and eight ounces emulsion of almonds.

Care of the Hands.—If the hands become blistered, rub in the following mixture: Oil of almonds one part, rectified spirits one part, rose or elderflower water one part.

For stained hands, try citric acid, spirits of rosemary and glycerine; afterwards remove with distilled water.

Danish women use pure cream and buttermilk for their thin, delicate skins, so liable to become dry and discolored.

Madame Sara Bernhardt's unguent may be found serviceable for the hands: Equal parts of lemon and glycerine, a small quantity of borax, and the whole sweetened with triple extract of violets.

Bernhardt says in regard to the hands: "Learn to know what suits you best and use this unguent occasionally, not for all times and seasons."

If you are going into the pine woods or to camp out, to strike up an intimate acquaintance with nature, don't forget to take along a bottle of tar oil. The gnat, mosquito and the countless assiduous denizens of air, earth and water will soon make your acquaintance. Rub the tar oil well in and keep it there as long as possible. Experienced woodsmen claim that not only do insects object strenuously to both its taste and odor, but that beyond this it is an antidote to freckles, tan, sunburn and a parched skin, and that poor complexions have left the woods richly beautified by its use.

Cream for the Hands.—A very simple and efficacious cream for the hands may be prepared as follows: Take two ounces of lanoline and two ounces of glycerine, place in a small jelly can and stand in a warm oven until the lanoline is entirely melted; then add a few drops of otto of roses, lavender or rosewater, and stir the whole briskly while cooling, otherwise the lanoline and glycerine will separate.

Camphor Tablet for Chapped Hands, etc.—Melt tallow, and add a little powdered camphor and glycerine, with a few drops of oil of almonds to scent. Pour in moulds and cool.

Finger-Nails.—Our finger-nails grow out about three times a year; they should be trimmed with scissors once a week, not so close as to leave no room for the dirt to gather, for then they do not protect the ends of the fingers, as was designed by nature; besides, if trimmed too close at the corners, there is danger of their growing into the flesh, causing inconvenience and sometimes great pain. The collections under the ends of the nails should not be removed by anything harder than a brush or a soft piece of wood; nor should the nails be scraped with a penknife or other metallic substance, as it destroys the delicacy of their structure and will at length give them an unnatural thickness.

Most persons are familiar with those troublesome bits of skin which loosen at the roots of the finger-nails. It is caused by the skin adhering to the nail, which, growing outward, drags the skin along with it, stretching it until one end gives way. To prevent this, the skin should be loosened from the nail once a week, not with a knife or scissors, but with something blunt, such as the end of an ivory paper cutter. This is best done after soaking the fingers in warm water, then pushing the skin back gently and slowly.

Biting off the finger-nails is an uncleanly practice, for thus the unsightly collections at the ends are kept often clean. Children may be broken of such a filthy habit by causing them to dip the ends of their fingers several times a day in wormwood bitters, without letting them know the object. If this is not sufficient, cause them to wear caps on each finger until the practice is discontinued.

To Whiten the Finger-Nails.—Take two drams of dilute sulphuric acid, one dram of tincture of myrrh, four ounces of spring-water, and mix them in a bottle. After washing the hands, dip the fingers in a little of the mixture and it will give a delicate appearance to the hand. Rings with stones or pearls in them should always be removed from the fingers when the hands are washed, as soap and water spoils jewelry set with precious stones.

CARE OF THE TEETH.

Regard should be had to the quality of the tooth powder used. It should not be of a hard, gritty nature, else the enamel will be destroyed. Many of the most expensive prepared powders are bad. If any portion of the enamel be destroyed decay will soon do its deadly work. The simplest tooth powders are therefore the best. The peasant girls in some parts of Scotland wet the forefinger, and, putting it up the chimney, secure a portion of soot. Lady readers will hardly follow such an example. Charcoal is good; camphorated chalk also. What is really wanted is a powder that shall clean without scrubbing, and, while cleaning, also disinfect. The brush should never be hard, and it ought to be worked up and down as well as horizontally.

A Simple Tooth Wash.—Dip the brush in water, rub it over genuine castile soap, then dip it in prepared chalk. There is no danger of scratching the teeth, as the chalk is prepared; but with a good stiff brush and the soap, it is as effectual as soap and sand on a floor.

Borax Tooth Wash.—Dissolve two ounces of borax in three pints of water; before quite cold, add thereto one teaspoonful of tincture of myrrh, and one tablespoonful of spirits of camphor; bottle the mixture for use. One wineglassful of the solution, added to half a pint of tepid water, is sufficient for each application. This solution, applied daily, preserves and beautifies the teeth, extirpates tartarous adhesion, produces a pearl-like whiteness, arrests decay, and induces a healthy action in the gums.

Camphorated Dentifrice.—Prepared chalk, one pound; camphor, one or two drams. The camphor must be powdered by moistening it with a little spirit of wine, and then intimately mixing it with the chalk.

Myrrh Dentifrice.—Powdered cuttlefish, one pound; powdered myrrh, two ounces.

American Tooth Powder.—Coral, cuttlefish bone, dragon's blood, of each eight drams; burnt alum and red sanders, of each four drams; orris root, eight drams; cloves and cinnamon, of each half a dram; vanilla, eleven grains; rosewood, half a dram; rose-pink, eight drams. All to be finely powdered and mixed.

Quinine Tooth Powder.—Rose-pink, two drams; precipitated chalk, twelve drams; carbonate of magnesia, one dram; quinine (sulphate), six grains. All to be well mixed together.

Charcoal Tooth Powder.—Powdered charcoal, four ounces; powdered yellow bark, two ounces; powdered myrrh, one ounce; orris root, half an ounce.

Rose Tooth Paste.—Cuttlefish bone, three ounces; prepared chalk, two ounces; orris, one ounce; lake or rose-pink to give it a pale rose color; attar of roses, sixteen drops; honey of roses in sufficient quantity.

Wash to Harden the Gums.—Mix ½ pint of Jamaica spirits, ½ teaspoonful of powdered alum, ½ of pulverized saltpetre, and 1 ounce of pulverized myrrh.

CARE OF THE HAIR.

Dandruff is not only very disagreeable, but it is apt to cause the hair to fall out. A reliable remedy is made of a thimbleful of borax dissolved in a teacupful of water. Brush the hair thoroughly, and wet with the solution every day for a week, and an improvement is sure to follow.

Long hair should never be shampooed more than once a month. Some people think that by brushing and caring well for the hair a shampoo once a year is sufficient, but few people, especially those whose hair is naturally oily, believe in this advice. Brushing stimulates the growth of the hair, and makes it glossy and soft. It also stops the hair from falling out, and is the best tonic for the scalp.

To brush and brush and still to brush is the best medicine for the hair, remembering always that it is the hair and not the scalp which is to receive this treatment. Upon the brush used depends a great deal. In the first place it must be immaculately clean, and one's brushes should be washed as religiously as one's face. The comb should be coarse, so that it will disentangle the hair if it is snarled, but if the hair is well brushed the comb really is of very little use. A fine-comb is never advised. The brush should have long, soft bristles that go through the hair, taking with them every particle of dust and leaving behind them a glow that is beautiful.

A dermatologist of high standing says that the proper way to shampoo the head is to use some pure soap, such as castile of the best quality, or glycerine soap, made into a "good lather on the head," with plenty of warm water, and rubbed into the scalp with the fingers, or with either a stiff brush that has long bristles. When the scalp is very sensitive borax and water, or the yolk of three eggs beaten in a pint of lime water, are recommended instead of soap and water. After rubbing the head thoroughly in every direction and washing out the hair with plenty of warm water, or with douches of warm water, alternating with cold, and drying the hair and scalp with a bath-towel, a small quantity of vaseline or sweet-almond oil should be rubbed into the scalp. The oil thus applied is used to take the place of the oil that has been removed by washing, and to prevent the hair from becoming brittle.

Good Hair Wash.—Dissolve one part of camphor and two of borax pulverized in a quart of boiling water. This preserves and beautifies the hair. Use as often as you please when cool.

An Excellent Hair Renewer is made of mace and alcohol, using half an ounce of oil of mace to one pint of alcohol. Rub the bald spot with a piece of flannel until the skin is red, and then apply the mixture with a small brush three or four times a day.

Lotion for Baldness.—Eau-de-Cologne, two ounces; tincture of cantharides, two drams; oil of rosemary, oil of nutmeg, and oil of lavender, each ten drops. To be rubbed on the bald part of the head every night.

Hair Tonic.—To prevent the hair from falling off: One ounce each of neatsfoot oil and spirits of turpentine; active solution of cantharides, thirty drops. Mix. Apply to the roots of the hair two or three times a week.

Hair Wash.—To cleanse the scalp and at the same time promote the growth of the hair. Rosewater, seven ounces; aromatic spirits of ammonia, one ounce; tincture of cantharides, one and one-half drams; glycerine, one-half ounce. Mix and shake before using. Apply to the scalp with an old tooth-brush.

To Clean Long Hair.—Beat up the yolk of an egg with a pint of soft water; apply it warm, and afterward wash it out with warm water.

Superfluous Hair.—Any remedy is doubtful; many of those commonly used are dangerous. The safest plan is as follows: The hairs should be perseveringly plucked up by the roots, and the skin, having been washed twice a day with warm soft water, without soap, should be treated with the following wash, commonly called Milk of Roses: Beat four ounces of sweet almonds in a mortar, and add half an ounce of white sugar during the process; reduce the whole to a paste by pounding; then add, in small quantities at a time, eight ounces of rose water. The emulsion thus formed should be strained through a fine cloth, and the residue again pounded, while the strained fluid should be bottled in a large stoppered vial. To the pasty mass in the mortar add half an ounce of sugar, and eight ounces of rose water, and strain again. This process must be repeated three times. To the thirty-two ounces of fluid add twenty grains of the bichloride of mercury, dissolved in two ounces of alcohol, and shake the mixture for five minutes. The fluid should be applied with a towel, immediately after washing, and the skin gently rubbed with a dry cloth till *perfectly* dry. Wilson, in his work on *Healthy Skin*, writes as follows: "Substances are sold by the perfumers called depilatories, which are represented as having the power of removing hair. But the hair is not destroyed by these means, the root and that part of the shaft implanted within the skin still remain, and are ready to shoot up with increased vigor as soon as the depilatory is withdrawn. The effect of the depilatory is the same, in this respect, as that of a razor, and the latter is, unquestionably, the better remedy. It must not, however, be imagined that depilatories are negative remedies, and that, if they do no permanent good, they are, at least, harmless; that is not the fact; they are violent irritants, and require to be used with the utmost caution."

Hair Dye, usually styled Colombian, Argentine, etc., etc.—Solution No. 1—Hydrosulphuret of ammonia, one ounce; solution of potash, three drams; distilled or rain water, one ounce (all by measure). Mix, and put into small bottles, labeling it No. 1. Solution No. 2—Nitrate of silver, one dram; distilled or rain water, two ounces. Dissolve and label No. 2. Directions for application: The solution No. 1 is first applied to the hair with a tooth brush, and the application continued for fifteen or twenty minutes. The solution No. 2 is then brushed over, a comb being used to separate the hairs, and allow the liquid to come in contact with every part. Care must be taken that the liquid does not touch the skin, as the solution No. 2 produces a permanent dark stain on all substances with which it comes in contact. If the shade is not sufficiently deep, the operation may be repeated. The hair should be cleansed from grease before using the dye.

Walnut Hair Dye.—The simplest form is the expressed juice of the bark or shell of green walnuts. To preserve this juice, a little rectified spirits may be added to it, with a few bruised cloves, and the whole digested together, with occasional agitation for a week or fortnight, when the clear portion is decanted, and, if necessary, filtered. Sometimes only a little common salt is added to preserve the juice. It should be kept in a cool place.

To Restore Hair when Removed by Ill-health or Age.—Rub onions frequently on the part requiring it. The stimulating powers of this vegetable are of service in restoring the tone of the skin and assisting the capillary vessels in sending forth new hair; but it is not infallible. Should it succeed, however, the growth of these new hairs may be assisted by the oil of myrtle-berries, the repute of which, perhaps, is greater than its real efficacy. Even if they do no good, these applications are harmless.

Baldness.—The decoction of boxwood, which has been found successful in some cases of baldness, is thus made: Take of the common box, which grows in garden borders, stems and leaves four large handfuls; boil in three pints of water, in a closely covered vessel, for a quarter of an hour, and let it stand in a covered earthenware jar for ten hours or more; strain, and add an ounce and a half of eau-de-cologne or lavender water, to make it keep. The head should be well washed with this solution every morning.

TOILET MISCELLANY.

Eyelashes.—To increase the length and strength of the eyelashes, simply clip the ends with a pair of scissors about once a month. In eastern countries mothers perform the operation on their children, both male and female, when they are mere infants, watching the opportunity whilst they sleep. The practice never fails to produce the desired effect.

To Cure Enlargement and Redness of the Nose.—Muriate of ammonia, one dram; tannic acid, one-half dram; glycerine, two ounces; rosewater, three ounces. Saturate a piece of cotton with the mixture, and bind it on the nose nightly until a cure is effected.

Uses of Borax Water.—Borax water will instantly remove all soils and stains from the hands, and heal all scratches and chafes. To make it, put some crude borax in a large bottle and fill with water. When the borax is dissolved, add more to the water, until at last the water can absorb no more and a residuum remains at the bottom of the bottle. To the water in which the hands are to be washed, pour enough from this bottle to make it quite soft. It is very cleansing and very healthy. By its use the hands will be kept in excellent condition—smooth, soft and white.

To Sweeten the Breath After Using Tobacco.—Chlorate of sodium, twenty-four grains; powdered sugar, one ounce; gum-tragacanth, twenty grains; perfumer's essential oil, two drams. Powder the chlorate in a glass mortar; put the powder in a cup and pour in a little water, let it settle and pour off. Repeat the process three times with fresh water, filtering what is poured off each time; and mix the gum and sugar with it, adding the perfume last.

Offensive Breath.—For this purpose, almost the only substance that should be admitted at the toilet is the concentrated solution of chloride of soda—from six to ten drops of it in a wineglassful of pure spring-water, taken immediately after the operations of the morning are completed. In some cases the odor arising from carious teeth is combined with that of the stomach. If the mouth be well rinsed with a teaspoonful of the solution of the chloride in a tumbler of water, the bad odor of the teeth will be removed.

SCENTS AND PERFUMES.

French Milk of Roses.—Two and one-half pints of rosewater, one-half pint of rosemary water, two ounces of tincture of storax, two ounces of tincture of benzoin, one-half ounce of esprit de rose. First mix the rosewater and rosemary water, and then add the other ingredients. This is a useful wash for the complexion.

Violet Powder.—Wheat starch, six parts by weight; orris-root powder, two. Having reduced the starch to an impalpable powder, mix thoroughly with the orris root, and then perfume with otto of lemon, otto of bergamot and otto of cloves, using twice as much of the lemon as either of the other ottos.

Perfume for Handkerchiefs.—Oil of lavender, three fluid drams; oil of bergamot, three fluid drams; extract of ambergris, six minims; camphor, one grain; spirits of wine, one pint. To be well shaken every day for a fortnight, and then filtered.

Bouquet de la Reine.—Take one ounce of essence of bergamot, three drams of English oil of lavender, one-half dram of oil of cloves, one-half dram of aromatic vinegar, six grains of musk, and one pint and a half of rectified spirits of wine. Distill.

Cosmetic.—Melt one pound of soft soap over a slow fire, with one-half pint of sweet oil, and add a teacupful of fine sand. Stir the mixture together until cold.

Scent Bag.—This will prevent moths injuring clothes: One ounce of cloves, caraway seeds, nutmeg, mace, and of orris root as much as will equal the other ingredients when put together. Grind the whole well to powder and put it into little silk bags.

Scent Powder. — A good recipe for scent powder to be used for wardrobes, boxes, etc., far finer than any mixture sold at the shops, is the following: Coriander, orris root, rose leaves and aromatic calamus, each one ounce; lavender flowers, ten ounces; rhodium, one-fourth of a dram; musk, five grains. These are to be mixed and reduced to a coarse powder. This scents clothes as if fragrant flowers had been pressed into their folds.

Lavender Water. — Best English lavender, four drams; oil of cloves, one-half dram; musk, five grains; best spirits of wine, six ounces; water, one ounce. Mix the oil of lavender with a little spirits first, then add the other ingredients and let it stand, being kept well corked for at least two months before it is used, shaking it frequently.

A very good lavender water may be made at home by the following recipe: One pint proof spirits, one ounce essential oil of lavender, two drams essence of ambergris. Put into a quart bottle and shake well.

Lavender Scent Bag. — One-half pound of lavender flowers free from stalk, one-half ounce of dried thyme and mint, a quarter of an ounce of ground cloves and caraways, one ounce of dried common salt. Mix them well together; and put them into silk or cambric bags.

Memory Rhymes

The Months.

Thirty days hath September,
April, June, and November;
All the rest have thirty-one,
But February, which has twenty-eight alone,
Except in leap year, then's the time
When February's days are twenty-nine.

Birthdays.

Monday for health,
Tuesday for wealth,
Wednesday best of all;
Thursday for crosses,
Friday for losses,
Saturday no luck at all.

Short Grammar.

Three little words you often see
Are Articles — *a*, *an*, and *the*.
A Noun's the name of any thing,
As *school*, or *garden*, *hoop* or *swing*.
Adjectives tell the kind of noun,
As *great*, *small*, *pretty*, *white*, or *brown*.
Instead of nouns the pronouns stand —
His head, *her* face, *your* arm, *my* hand.
Verbs tell something to be done —
To *read*, *count*, *laugh*, *sing*, *jump*, or *run*.
How things are done the adverbs tell —
As *slowly*, *quickly*, *ill*, or *well*.
Conjunctions join the words together,
As men *and* women, wind *or* weather.
The preposition stands before
The noun, as *in* or *through* the door.
The interjection shows surprise —
As *Oh*, how pretty! *Ah*, how wise!
The whole are called nine parts of speech,
Which reading, writing, speaking, teach.

To Tell the Age of Horses.

To tell the age of any horse,
Inspect the lower jaw, of course;
The six front teeth the tale will tell,
And every doubt and fear dispel.

Two middle "nippers" you behold
Before the colt is two weeks old.
Before eight weeks two more will come;
Eight months the "corners" cut the gum.

The outside grooves will disappear
From middle two in just one year.
In two years, from the second pair;
In three, the corners, too, are bare.

At two the middle "nippers" drop;
At three, the second pair can't stop.
When four years old the third pair goes;
At five a full new set he shows.

The deep black spots will pass from view
At six years from the middle two;
The second pair at seven years;
At eight the spot each "corner" clears.

From middle "nippers," upper jaw,
At nine the black spots will withdraw.
The second pair at ten are white;
Eleven finds the "corners" light.

As time goes on, the horsemen know,
The oval teeth three-sided grow;
They longer get, project before
Till twenty, when we know no more.

Bees.

A swarm of bees in May
Is worth a load of hay;
A swarm of bees in June
Is worth a silver spoon;
A swarm of bees in July
Is not worth a fly.

Rules for Riding.

Keep up your head and your heart,
Your hands and your heels keep down.
Your knees press close to your horse's side,
And your elbows close to your own.

The Cuckoo.

May — sings all the day;
June — changes his tune;
July — prepares to fly;
August — go he must.

Physical Exercise

THE principal methods of developing the physique now prescribed by trainers are exercise with dumbbells, the bar bell and the chest weight. The rings and horizontal and parallel bars are also used, but not nearly to the extent that they formerly were. The movement has been all in the direction of the simplification of apparatus; in fact, one well-known teacher of the Boston Gymnasium, when asked his opinion, said: "Four bare walls and a floor, with a well-posted instructor, is all that is really required for a gymnasium."

Probably the most important as well as the simplest appliance for gymnasium work is the wooden dumbbell, which has displaced the ponderous iron ball of former days. Its weight is from three-quarters of a pound to a pound and a half, and with one in each hand a variety of motions can be gone through, which are of immense benefit in building up or toning down every muscle and all vital parts of the body.

The first object of an instructor in taking a beginner in hand is to increase the circulation. This is done by exercising the extremities, the first movement being one of the hands, after which come the wrists, then the arms, and next the head and feet. As the circulation is increased the necessity for a larger supply of oxygen, technically called "oxygen-hunger," is created, which is only satisfied by breathing exercises, which develop the lungs. After the circulation is in a satisfactory condition, the dumbbell instructor turns his attention to exercising the great muscles of the body, beginning with those of the back, strengthening which holds the body erect, thus increasing the chest capacity, invigorating the digestive organs, and, in fact, all the vital functions. By the use of very light weights an equal and symmetrical development of all parts of the body is obtained, and then there are no sudden demands on the heart and lungs.

After the dumbbell comes exercise with the round, or bar bell. This is like the dumbbell, with the exception that the bar connecting the balls is four or five feet, instead of a few inches in length. Bar bells weigh from one to two pounds each, and are found most useful in building up the respiratory and digestive systems, their especial province being the strengthening of the exterior muscles and increasing the flexibility of the chest.

Of all fixed apparatus in use the pulley weight stands easily first in importance. These weights are available for a greater variety of objects than any other gymnastic appliance, and can be used either for general exercise or for strengthening such muscles as most require it. With them a greater localization is possible than with the dumbbell, and for this reason they are recommended as a kind of supplement to the latter. As chest-developers and correctors of round shoulders they are most effective. As the name implies, they are simply weights attached to ropes, which pass over pulleys, and are provided with handles. The common pulley is placed at about the height of the shoulder of an average man, but recently those which can be adjusted to any desired height have been very generally introduced.

When more special localization is desired than can be obtained by means of the ordinary apparatus, what is known as the double-action chest weight is used. This differs from the ordinary kind in being provided with several pulleys, so that the strain may come at different angles. Double-action weights may be divided into three classes—high, low and side pulleys—each with its particular use.

The highest of all, known as the giant pulleys, are made especially for developing the muscles of the back and chest, and by stretching or elongating movements to increase the interior capacity of the chest. If the front of the chest is full and the back or side chest deficient, the pupil is set to work on the giant pulley. To build up the side walls he stands with the back to the pulley-box and the left heel resting against it; the handle is grasped in the right hand if the right side of the chest is lacking in development, and then drawn straight down by the side; a step forward with the right foot as long as possible, is taken, the line brought as far to the front and near the floor as can be done, and then the arm, held stiff, allowed to be drawn slowly up by the weight. To exercise the left side the same process is gone through with, the handle grasped in the left hand. Another kind of giant pulley is that which allows the operator to stand directly under it, and is used for increasing the lateral diameter of the chest. The handles are drawn straight down by the sides, the arms are then spread and drawn back by the weights. Generally speaking, high pulleys are most used for correcting high, round shoulders; low pulleys for low, round shoulders; side pulleys for individual high or low shoulders, and giant pulleys for the development of the chest and to correct spinal curvature.

The traveling rings, a line of iron rings covered with rubber and attached to long ropes fastened to the ceiling some ten feet apart, are also valuable in developing the muscles of the back, arms and sides. The first ring is grasped in one hand and a spring taken from an elevated platform. The momentum carries the gymnast to the next ring, which is seized with the free hand, and so the entire length of the line is traversed. The parallel bars, low and high, the flying rings, the horizontal bar and the trapeze all have their uses, but of late years they have been relegated to a position of distinct inferiority to that now occupied by the dumbbells and pulley weights.

1. The bar bell—chest expander. 2. Anterior muscular developer. 3. Developing the loins and lumbar region—aid to digestion. 4. Side and loin development. 5. Giant pulley exercise—for elevating right side of chest. 6. Developing muscles that hold the shoulders back. 7. Developing muscles of front upper chest. 8. Posterior development—to make one erect.

 Exercises for Girls 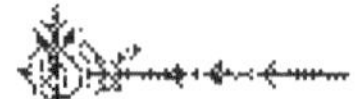

Here are a few exercises for girls, prescribed by a prominent physician, for physical development and for the relief of dyspepsia and kindred ailments. After counseling moderation in eating and a thorough mastication of food, the physician says:

Take these exercises nightly after resting a little while from the day's work:

1. Stand in walking position, one foot in advance of the other, your hands on your hips, and twist the trunk to the side of the rear foot as far as possible; then change feet and twist to the opposite side. Repeat fifteen times to each side. Do the same twisting with your hands clasped behind your back, your shoulders well held back.

2. Stride standing. Rise on your toes and bend your knees outward and downward. Repeat ten times slowly.

3. Stand on one foot, your hips firm, and slowly raise your other leg, extended in front. Keep a steady balance. Change feet and repeat.

4. Stand with your heels together, your hands on your hips. Bend your body forward, to the side, backward, and to the opposite side, then forward to complete the circle. Repeat, and rotate your body in opposite directions.

5. Lie on your back, with your hips firm and your feet held under a bureau; try to raise your head and shoulders as far as possible with deep inspiration. Repeat, turning your body.

6. Bend your body over a bar in the doorway, or the stair railing, backward, forward and sidewise, with your hands clasped behind your neck.

7. Place your bar low, hang under it with your body extended stiffly and resting on your heels. Slowly draw your chest up to touch the bar by bending your elbows outward. Repeat.

Combine these movements with deep respiration, opening a window for good, pure air; make each exercise as useful to the muscles as possible; they are corrective exercises — not merely amusing.

Rub your stomach with cool water after the exercises.

. Original . and . Tested . Recipes .

BY KATHRYN ARMSTRONG

FROM the richest to the poorest, the selection and preparation of food often becomes one of the chief objects in life. The resources of every family may be greatly increased by the knowledge of what may be called trifling details, and refinement in the art of cookery depends much more on the manner of doing a thing than on the cost attending it. To cook well is immensely more important to the middle and working classes than to the rich, for they who live by the "sweat of their brow," whether mentally or physically, must have the requisite strength to support their labor. Every wife, mother or sister should be a good plain cook. If she has servants she can direct them, and if not, so much the more must depend upon herself.

An old saying, to be found in one of the earliest cookery books—"First catch your hare," etc.—has more significance than is generally supposed. To catch your hare well, you must spend your income judiciously. This is the chief thing. In our artificial state of society, every income, to keep up appearances, has at least half as much more to do as it can afford. In the selection of provisions the *best* is generally the *cheapest*. Half a pound of good meat is more nutritious than three times the amount of inferior. As to vegetables, buy them fresh. Above all, where an income is small and there are many to feed, be careful that all the nourishment is retained in the food that is purchased. This is to be effected by careful cooking. Cleanliness is an imperative condition. Let all cooking utensils be clean and in order. Uncleanliness produces disorder, and disorder confusion. In the cooking of meat by any process whatever, remember, above all, to cook the juice in it, not out of it.

Boiling.

In boiling, put the meat, if fresh, into cold water, or, if salt, into luke-warm. Simmer it very gently until done. It is a general rule to allow a quarter of an hour to every pound of meat; but in this, as in everything else, judgment must be used according to the bone and shape of the joint, and according to the taste of the eaters. All kinds of meat, fish, flesh and fowl, should be boiled very slowly, and the scum taken off just as boiling commences. If meats are allowed to boil too fast they toughen, all their juices are extracted, and only the fleshy fiber, without sweetness, is left; if they boil too long they are reduced to a jelly, and their nourishing properties are transferred to the water in which they are boiled. Nothing is more difficult than to boil meat exactly as it should be; close attention and good judgment are indispensable.

Roasting.

In roasting meat the gravy may be retained in it by pricking the joint all over with a fork and rubbing in pepper and salt. Mutton and beef may be underdone; veal and pork must be well cooked. Young meat generally requires more cooking than old; thus lamb and veal must be more done than mutton and beef. In frosty weather meat will require a little more time for cooking. All joints for roasting will improve by hanging a day or so before cooking.

Broiling.

Broiling is the most nutritious method of cooking mutton and pork chops, or beef and rump steaks, kidneys (which should never be cut open before cooking), etc. Have the gridiron clean, and put over a clear fire; put the meat on it; "keep it turned often." This last is a common direction in books, but the reason why is never stated; it is to keep the gravy in the meat. By letting the one side of a steak be well done before turning, you will see the red gravy settled on the top of the steak, and so the meat is hard and spoiled. This is cooking the gravy out, instead of keeping it in to nourish the consumer. Never stick the fork in the meaty part; you will lose gravy if you do. Be sure to turn often, and generally the chop or steak is done if it feels firm to the fork; if not done, it will be soft and flabby.

Frying.

Although very bad for chops or steaks, the frying-pan is indispensable for some things, such as veal cutlets, lamb chops (sometimes), fish, pancakes, etc. Most meats and fish are usually fried with egg and bread-crumbs. The frying-pan must be kept clean. This is very essential, as the dirt that sticks to the pan absorbs the fat, prevents the meat browning and turns it black. Have a clear, brisk fire, for the quicker meat is fried the tenderer it is. According to what is to be fried, put little or much fat in the pan; fish and pancakes require a considerable quantity. The fat must always boil before putting the meat into it; if not, it coddles. For veal cutlets a little butter is best and most economical, as it helps to make the gravy. Some cooks have a few slices of bacon with cutlets or liver; the fat from this, if the bacon be not rank, will do very nicely; and if the meat be well flavored and fried quickly, and some nice gravy made to it, few persons would know the difference. Some like thickened and some plain gravy to these fried meats; some a large quantity, others very little; all these must be accommodated. To make these gravies, have ready a little burnt sugar to brown with; empty the pan of the fat, if it be, as is most likely, too rank to use; put warm water in the pan; mix very smoothly sufficient flour and water to thicken it to taste; into this put as much butter as you like to use (a little will do; more will make it richer); pepper and salt it sufficiently; stir it very smoothly into the pan while the water is only warm; stir it well until it boils, and brown it with the burnt sugar to your taste. Care must be taken, after the gravy boils, not to let it boil fast for any length of time, as all thickened gravies, hashes, etc., boil away very fast and dry up; neither must it stand still in the pan; a whitish scum then settles on the top and spoils the appearance of it.

N. B.—For all frying purposes be particular that the pan is thoroughly hot before using.

Cooking Time-Table.

Baking Meats.

Beef Sirloin—Rare, 8 minutes for each pound; well-done, 10 to 15 minutes for each pound.

Beef Ribs or Rump—10 to 15 minutes for each pound.

Beef Fillet—20 to 30 minutes.

Lamb—Well done, 15 minutes for each pound.

Mutton—Rare, 10 to 12 minutes for each pound; well done, 15 to 18 minutes for each pound.

Pork—Well done, 25 to 30 min. for each pound.

Veal—Well done, 18 to 20 min. for each pound.

Braised Meat—3½ to 4 hours.

Chickens—Weighing from 3 to 5 pounds, 1 to 1½ hours.

Turkeys—Weighing from 9 to 12 pounds, 3 to 3½ hours.

Fish—Of average thickness, weighing from 6 to 8 pounds, 1 hour.

Cake and Pastry.

Sponge Cake—45 to 60 minutes.

Plain Cake—30 to 40 minutes.

Cookies—10 to 15 minutes.

Gingerbread—20 to 30 minutes.

Plum Pudding—2½ to 3 hours.

Tapioca or Rice Pudding—1 hour.

Bread Pudding—45 minutes.

Pies with two crusts—30 to 40 minutes.

Graham Rolls—½ hour.

Wheat Rolls—10 to 15 minutes.

Bread—40 to 60 minutes.

Biscuit—10 to 15 minutes.

Broiling.

Beefsteak—Cut 1½ inches thick, 5 to 8 minutes.

Beefsteak—1 inch thick, 3 to 5 minutes.

Mutton Chops—8 to 10 minutes.

Chickens—15 to 25 minutes.

Fish—Thin, 4 to 6 minutes.

Fish—Thick, 10 to 15 minutes.

Ham—8 to 10 minutes.

Boiling Fish.

Bass—10 minutes for each pound.

Bluefish—10 minutes for each pound.

Fresh Cod or Haddock—6 minutes for each pound.

Halibut—In square, 15 minutes for each pound.

Salmon—In square, 15 minutes for each pound.

Small Fish—6 to 8 minutes for each pound.

Oysters—3 to 4 minutes, or until the edges curl.

Boiling Meats.

Veal—2 or 3 hours.

Beef—3 to 4 hours.

Mutton—2 or 3 hours.

Ham—5 to 5½ hours.

Sweetbreads—20 to 25 minutes.

Chickens—1 to 1½ hours.

Fowls—2 to 3 hours.

Tongue—2 to 3 hours.

Vegetables.

String Beans—1½ to 2 hours.

Shell Beans—1 to 2 hours.

Cauliflower—30 to 40 minutes.

Cabbage, New—30 to 45 minutes.

Corn, Young—8 to 12 minutes.

Carrots—30 to 60 minutes.

Asparagus—15 to 18 minutes.

Onions—25 to 45 minutes.

Oyster Plant—40 to 60 minutes.

Peas—15 to 20 minutes.

Potatoes—Boiled, 20 to 30 minutes.

Potatoes—Steamed, 30 to 45 minutes.

Turnips—25 to 30 minutes.

Parsnips—35 to 45 minutes.

SOUPS

THE true economy of soups lies in the fact that so many things which might otherwise be wasted may be utilized in making them. In households where expenditure is not so much a consideration, it may be deemed expedient always to purchase fresh meat for the sole purpose of making soup, but, in such instances, the soup could certainly not be regarded as an *economical* addition to a dinner. Still, where Economy must rule, the resources from which she may draw a tureen of good soup, without having recourse to the butcher, are ample. Almost everything that is used as food may be converted into soup. Scraps of meat, bread, vegetables, rice, sago, spice, milk, and, better still, bones left from the meat after cooking, may, with a little ingenuity, be made into excellent, nourishing soup.

The basis of all good soup is stock. This may be made from meat or bones and flavored with vegetables. Let it be borne in mind that no good stock can be made the day it is required for soup. It should be made the previous day, strained into a basin, and allowed to stand until required, when the fat, which would render the soup so objectionable, will have cooled on the top and may be taken off entirely. The stock may then be used as the basis of any kind of soup.

In making stocks or soups care must be taken to simmer gently, not boil, or they will be found wanting both in flavor and nourishment. The lid of the stock-pot must be kept tightly closed, or there will be considerable waste during the long time which the contents must of necessity simmer. It will be necessary to remove the lid a few times in order to take off the scum as it rises.

When preparing the stock, all the meat used should be cut into small pieces and the bones broken or crushed. Cold water and salt should be added, and the whole brought very gradually to simmering point, the vegetables being added after the stock has been well skimmed.

On no account must stock be left in an iron stock-pot any length of time, or it will contract a very unpleasant flavor. It must be poured into an earthenware vessel and remain uncovered. To those about to purchase a stock-pot we would recommend an earthenware rather than an iron one as being more cleanly and not necessitating the emptying out of the stock when finished.

To Color Soups—To obtain a green color pound spinach leaves and add the juice obtained to the stock. For a red color use tomatoes, without the skins and seeds. For amber grate a carrot and mix with the soup, and for a rich brown use burnt sugar or burnt onions.

Macaroni Soup—Five cents' worth of bones, 1 tablespoonful salt and peppercorns, 1 good-sized turnip and 4 leeks, 2 carrots, 4 onions, 2 cloves, 1 blade of mace, 1 bunch of herbs (marjoram, thyme, lemon-thyme and parsley), ½ lb. macaroni.

Time required, about 2½ hours. Break up the bones and put them into a stew-pan with cold water enough to cover them and 1 quart more. When on the point of boiling put in a tablespoonful of salt to help the scum to rise, then take the turnip, peel it and cut it in quarters; then take 2 carrots, wash and scrape them; take also 4 leeks, wash and shred them up finely; now take 4 onions, peel them and stick 2 cloves into them; then skim the soup well and put in the vegetables, add a blade of mace and a teaspoonful of peppercorns, then allow soup to simmer for 2½ hours, then take ½ lb. of macaroni, wash and put in a stewpan with plenty of cold water and a little salt. Allow it to boil until tender, then strain off the water and pour some cold water on, to wash the macaroni again; then cut in small pieces and it is ready for the soup. When the soup is ready for use strain it over the macaroni.

Milk Soup—4 potatoes, 2 leeks or onions, 2 oz. butter, pepper, ½ oz. salt, 1 pint milk, 3 tablespoonfuls tapioca.

Put 2 quarts of water into a stewpan, then take 4 potatoes, peel and cut in quarters, take also 2 leeks, wash well in cold water and cut them up; when the water boils put in potatoes and leeks, then add the butter, salt and pepper to taste. Allow it to boil to a mash, then strain the soup through a colander, working the vegetables through also; return the pulp and the soup to the stewpan, add one pint of milk to it and boil; when boiling sprinkle in by degrees tapioca, stirring all the time; then let it boil for 15 minutes gently.

Spring Vegetable Soup—2 lbs. shin of beef, 2 lbs. knuckle of veal, a little salt, 2 young carrots, 1 turnip, 1 leek, ½ head of celery, 1 cauliflower, 1 gill of peas, ½ saltspoonful of carbonate of soda.

Cut the meat from the bone—do not use the fat; break the bones in halves; do not use the marrow. Put the meat and bones into a stock-pot with five pints of cold water, a teaspoonful of salt will assist the scum to rise; boil quickly and remove scum as it rises, then simmer gently 5 hours. Cut carrots and turnips in slices; the head of celery and leek wash well and cut in squares; cut the cauliflower in sprigs after washing. One hour before serving add vegetables; the sprigs of cauliflower can be put in 15 minutes before serving. Put one gill of peas, a teaspoonful of salt, a quarter of a saltspoonful of soda into boiling water and boil 15 minutes, then put peas in tureen and put soup over them.

Good Gravy Soup—1 lb. beef, 1 pound veal, 1 lb. mutton, 3 quarts water, 1 crust of bread, 1 carrot, 1 onion, a little summer savory, 4 cloves, pepper and a blade of mace.

Cut the meat in small pieces and put into the water, with the crust of bread toasted very crisp. Peel the carrot and onion, and, with a little summer savory, pepper, 4 cloves and a blade of mace, put in the stewpan. Cover it and let it stew slowly until the liquid is reduced to 2 qts. Then strain it, take off the fat, and serve with sippets of toast.

Scotch Mutton Broth—2 qts. of water, neck of mutton, 4 or 5 carrots, 4 or 5 turnips, 3 onions, 4 large spoonfuls of Scotch barley, salt to taste, some chopped parsley.

Soak a neck of mutton in water for an hour; cut off the scrag, and put it into a stew-pot with two quarts of water. As soon as it boils skim it well, and then simmer it an hour and a half; then take the best end of the mutton, cut it into pieces (two bones in each); take some of the fat off, and put in as many as you think proper; skim the moment the fresh meat boils up and every quarter of an hour afterwards. Have ready 4 or 5 carrots, the same number of turnips, and 3 onions, all cut, but not small, and put them in soon enough to get quite tender; add 4 large spoonfuls of Scotch barley, first wetted with cold water. The meat should stew three hours. Salt to taste, and serve all together. Twenty minutes before serving put in some chopped parsley. It is an excellent winter dish.

A Roast Beef and Boiled Turkey Soup—Bones of a turkey and beef, 2 or three carrots, 2 or 3 onions, 2 or 3 turnips, ½ doz. cloves, pepper, salt, tomatoes, 3 tablespoonfuls of flour, some bread.

The liquor that the turkey is boiled in, and the bones of the turkey and beef, put into a soup-pot with 2 or 3 carrots, turnips and onions, ½ dozen cloves, pepper, salt and tomatoes, if you have any; boil it 4 hours, then strain and cool. Put the soup back into the pot, mix 3 tablespoonfuls of flour into a little cold water; stir it into the soup; give it one boil. Cut some bread dice-form, lay it in the bottom of the tureen, pour the soup on it, and color with a little soy.

White Soup—3 potatoes, 3 leeks or a few green onions, 2 quarts water or stock, a small teacupful sago, 1 pint milk, 2 oz. butter.

Boil the potatoes and onions in the stock until quite tender, then mash them through a sieve with a little of the stock. Return the whole to the saucepan, add the milk. Sprinkle in the sago gradually, stirring well. When the sago has boiled clear and tender, stir in the butter and serve. If water be used instead of stock, ½ teaspoonful of salt should be added with the potatoes and leeks, and pepper to taste.

Greek Soup—4 lbs. lean beef, 1 lb. lean mutton, 1 lb. veal, 4 oz. lean ham, 4 carrots, 4 onions, 1 head celery, a little soy, a few allspice and a few coriander seeds, some pepper and salt, 10 quarts water.

Cut up the beef, mutton and veal into small pieces, and throw into a stewpan with 10 quarts of cold water; add a little salt and then place on the stove to boil; take off the scum, add a little cold water, and take off the second scum; then cut up the carrots, onions and celery and throw in the pot; add a little more salt, a few allspice and coriander seeds; let it simmer 6 hours, color the soup with a little soy, and strain it through a fine cloth; take off any fat that may be on the soup with a sheet of paper; before sending to table boil the soup, and place in the tureen a little fried lean ham cut into small pieces.

Giblet Soup—3 sets of ducks' giblets, 2 lbs. beef, some bones, shank bones of two legs of mutton, 3 onions, some herbs, pepper and salt, carrots, 3 quarts water, ¼ pint cream, 1 oz. butter, 1 spoonful flour.

Thoroughly clean 3 sets of ducks' giblets, cut them in pieces, and stew with 2 lbs. of beef, some bones, the shank bones of 2 legs of mutton, 3 small onions, some herbs, pepper and salt to taste, and carrots, for 3 hours in 3 quarts of water. Strain and skim, add ¼ pint of cream mixed with one ounce of butter kneaded with a spoonful of flour, and serve with the giblets. (Only the gizzard should be cut).

Potato Soup—2 lbs. potatoes, a pinch of celery seed, a sprig of parsley, 2 quarts white stock, pepper and salt to taste.

Boil or steam the potatoes very dry, mash them very finely with a fork, and add them gradually to the boiling stock. Pass through a sieve, add the seasoning, and simmer 5 minutes, adding 1 oz. of butter and ½ pint of milk. Serve with fried bread or toast.

Oyster Soup a la Reine—2 or 3 doz. small oysters, some pale veal stock, mace, cayenne, 1 pint boiling cream.

Two or 3 dozen small oysters to each pint of soup should be prepared. Take the beards and simmer them separately in a little very pale veal stock 20 minutes. Heat 2 quarts of the stock, flavor with mace and cayenne, and add the strained stock from the oyster beards. Simmer the fish in their own liquor, add to it the soup and 1 pint of boiling cream. Put the oysters in a tureen, pour over the soup and serve. If not thick enough thicken with arrowroot or butter mixed with flour.

Chicken Soup (Brown)—1 or 2 fowls, a bunch of herbs, 1 carrot, 1 onion, 2 oz. lean ham, 2 oz. butter, pepper and salt, 2 quarts good stock, and a little roux, a few allspice, a little grated nutmeg and mace.

Cut up the carrot and onion, and fry in 2 oz. of good butter, a nice light brown; add the ham and fowls cut up small, taking care to break up the bones with a chopper, add the stock, and boil until the fowl is cooked to rags; thicken with a little roux, add the allspice and mace and a little grated nutmeg, color with a little soy, add seasoning to taste. Serve with the soup some plain boiled rice.

Beef Gravy Soup—Some beef water, 2 oz. salt to every gallon of water, 4 turnips, 3 carrots, some celery, 4 young leeks, 6 cloves, 1 onion, ½ teaspoonful peppercorns, some savory herbs.

Various parts of beef are used for this; if the meat, after the soup is made, is to be sent to the table, rump steak or the best parts of the leg are generally used, but if soup alone is wanted, part of the shin with a pound from the neck will do very well. Pour cold water on the beef in the soup pot and heat the soup slowly, the slower the better, letting it simmer beside the fire, strain it carefully, adding a little cold water now and then, put in 2 oz. of salt for every gallon of water, skim again, and put in four turnips, two carrots, some celery, 4 young leeks, 6 cloves stuck into an onion, half a teaspoonful of peppercorns, and some savory herbs; let the soup boil gently for six hours; strain.

Milk Soup with Vermicelli—Salt, 5 pints boiling milk, 5 oz. fresh vermicelli.

Throw a small quantity of salt into 5 pints of boiling milk, and then drop lightly into it 5 oz. of good fresh vermicelli; keep the milk stirred as this is added, to prevent its gathering into lumps, and continue to stir it very frequently from 15 to 20 minutes, or until it is perfectly tender. The addition of a little pounded sugar and powdered cinnamon makes this a very palatable dish. For soup of this description, rice, semolina, sago, cocoa-nut, sago and macaroni may all be used, but they will be required in rather smaller proportions to the milk.

Green Pea Soup—4 lbs. beef, ½ pk. green peas, 1 gal. water, ½ cup rice-flour, salt, pepper and chopped parsley.

Four lbs. beef, cut into small pieces, ½ pk. green peas, 1 gallon water, ½ cup of rice-flour, salt, pepper and chopped parsley; boil the empty pods of the peas in the water 1 hour before putting in the beef. Strain them out, add the beef, and boil slowly for 1½ hour longer; ½ hour before serving, add the shelled peas, and 20 minutes later, the rice-flour with salt, pepper and parsley. After adding the rice-flour, stir frequently, to prevent scorching. Strain into a hot tureen.

Celery Soup—The white part of 3 heads of celery, ½ lb. rice, 1 onion, 1 quart stock, 2 quarts milk, pepper and salt, and a little roux.

Cut up the celery and onions very small, boil them in the stock until quite tender, add the milk and the rice, and boil together until quite a pulp, add pepper and salt and a little roux, strain through a fine hair sieve or a metal strainer, and boil a few minutes, taking care it does not burn. Serve some small croutons or fried bread with it.

Tomato Soup—4 lbs. tomatoes, 2 onions, 1 carrot, 2 quarts of stock or broth, pepper and salt and a little roux, 2 oz. fresh butter.

Cut up the onions and carrot; place them in a stewpan with the butter, and lightly fry them. Take the seeds out of the tomatoes, then put them in the stewpan with the fried onions and carrot, add the stock, pepper and salt, and let them boil for 1 hour, occasionally stirring them; add a little roux to thicken the soup, and strain through a fine hair sieve. Serve the soup very hot, and send to the table with it some small pieces of fried bread, sprinkled with chopped parsley.

Tomato Soup without Meat—1 can tomatoes, 2 large onions, ½ pint milk, 1 tablespoonful flour, 2 tablespoonfuls butter, salt, pepper.

Take 1 can of tomatoes, press through the colander and set on the fire where it will stew gently. Slice 2 large onions very thin and add to the tomatoes. Let it stew ½ hour, then add ½ pint of milk, 1 tablespoonful of flour rubbed in 2 of butter, and salt and pepper to taste. Let it boil 3 minutes, when it is done. Serve with bits of toasted bread.

Soup à la Dauphine—6 lbs. of lean beef, 4 carrots, 2 turnips, 4 onions, 1 head celery, 4 oz. lean ham, pepper and salt, a little soy, 2 bay leaves, a bunch of herbs, a few allspice, 2 blades of mace, 3 qts. water.

Cut up the onions, carrots, turnips and celery into small pieces, and lay in the bottom of a large stewpan; cut up the 6 lbs. of lean beef, and lay on the top of the vegetables, sprinkle a little salt over it, and cook over the fire (taking care it does not burn) for 2 hours; add 3 qts. of water, and bring it to the boil; take off the fat and scum, add a little more cold water, and throw in 2 blades of mace, 2 bay leaves, a bunch of herbs, 4 oz. of lean ham cut up very fine, and a few allspice, color a light brown with a little soy, and simmer for 5 hours, and then strain through a fine cloth, and with a sheet of paper take off any floating fat; boil again, and before serving throw in the soup some green tarragon leaves and a little chervil.

Julienne Soup—1 carrot, 1 turnip, 1 stick of celery, 3 parsnips, 2 or 3 cabbage leaves, butter, lettuce, 1 handful of sorrel and chervil, stock, salt and pepper.

Cut in very small slices a carrot, a turnip, a stick of celery, 3 parsnips, and 2 or 3 cabbage leaves, put them in a saucepan with butter, and give them a nice color, shaking the saucepan to prevent them from sticking to the bottom, then add a lettuce and a handful of sorrel and chervil torn in small pieces, moisten these with stock and leave them on the fire for a few minutes, then boil up, add the whole of the stock and boil gently for 3 hours; season with salt and pepper.

Mrs. President Harrison's Clear Soup—4 lbs. lean beef, 4 qts. water, 1 teaspoonful celery seed, 2 small onions, 2 small carrots, 1 bunch parsley, 3 blades mace, 16 whole cloves, the whites of 4 eggs, salt and pepper to taste.

Cut the beef in pieces of the size of a walnut, taking care not to leave a particle of fat on them. Pour on it the water and let it boil up 3 times, skimming well each time; for if any of the grease is allowed to go back into the soup it will be impossible to get it clear. Scrape the carrots, stick 4 cloves firmly into each onion, and put them in the soup. Then add the celery seed, parsley, mace, pepper and salt. Let this boil until the vegetables are tender, then strain through a bag, return to the soup-pot, and stir in the well-beaten whites of the eggs. Boil until the eggs gather to one side, skim off, and color a delicate amber by burning a dessertspoonful of brown sugar and stirring it into the soup until sufficiently cleared. Wash the bag in warm water, pour the soup through again, and serve.

Clear Soup—1 quart brown stock, ½ lb. very lean beef, 1 onion, 1 carrot, 2 whites of eggs.

Carefully remove the fat from the meat, chop it fine and put it in a basin of cold water, just stirring it to separate it. Let it stand 5 minutes, then pour it into a saucepan with the vegetables cut in pieces, the whites and broken shells of the eggs, and the stock; whisk while heating over the fire, whisk well until it begins to rise, then cease, and let it boil 2 minutes. Cover closely and let it stand quietly until there is a thick crust on top, then strain through a jelly bag or soup-cloth. Vegetables cut into small strips, or wafers, and boiled for 10 minutes, may be added before serving.

Barley Soup—½ pint pearl barley, 1 qt. white stock, the yolk of 1 egg, 1 gill cream, ½ pat fresh butter, bread.

Boil half a pint of pearl barley in a quart of white stock till it is reduced to a pulp, pass it through a hair sieve, and add to it as much well-flavored white stock as will give a purée of the consistency of cream; put the soup on the fire; when it boils stir into it, off the fire, the yolk of an egg beaten up with a gill of cream; add half a pat of fresh butter, and serve with small dice of bread fried in butter.

A Delicate and Delicious Soup—Three carrots, 2 turnips, 2 onions, 2 leeks, 1 stick of celery, 2 oz. butter, a little mutton broth, seasoning to taste.

Cut up the vegetables small and fry them in the butter till tender and of a light brown color. Add enough to keep them from burning, and stew them for an hour. Then rub through a sieve with a little more broth. Stew for a few minutes longer; salt and cayenne to taste.

If properly done the soup will be as thick as cream.

Onion Soup—Water that has boiled a leg or neck of mutton, 1 shank bone, 6 onions, 4 carrots, 2 turnips, salt.

Into the water that has boiled a leg or neck of mutton put the carrots and turnips and shank bone, and simmer 2 hours, then strain it on six onions, first sliced and fried a light brown, simmer 3 hours, skim carefully, and serve. Put into it a little rice or fried bread.

Eel Soup—3 lbs. eels, 1 onion, 1 oz. butter, 3 blades mace, 1 bunch sweet herbs, ¼ oz. peppercorns, salt, 2 tablespoonfuls flour, ¼ pt. cream, 2 qts. water.

Wash the eels, cut them into thin slices and put them in the stewpan with the butter; let them simmer for a few minutes, then pour the water to them, and add the onion cut in small slices, the herbs, mace and seasoning. Simmer till the eels are tender, but do not break the flesh. Remove them carefully, mix flour smoothly to a batter with the cream, bring it to a boil, pour over the eels, and serve.

Asparagus Soup—Twenty-five heads of asparagus, 1 qt. stock, 1 tablespoonful flour, 1 oz. butter, sugar, pepper and salt, some spinach greening, 1 pat of fresh butter or 1 gill of cream, small dice of bread.

Put 25 heads of asparagus in a saucepan with a qt. of stock, free from fat, let them boil till quite done; remove the asparagus, pound it in a mortar, then pass it through a sieve; mix a tablespoonful of flour and 1 oz. of butter in a saucepan on the fire; add a little sugar, pepper and salt, quantity sufficient for the asparagus pulp, and the stock in which the asparagus was originally boiled; let the whole come to a boil, then put in a little spinach greening, and lastly a pat of fresh butter, or stir in a gill of cream. Serve over small dice of bread fried in butter.

Cream of Asparagus Soup—One bundle asparagus, 1 qt. milk, butter, flour.

Wash the asparagus, cut it into pieces, put in a saucepan, cover with 1 pt. of boiling water, boil gently for ¾ of an hour, remove the tips and put aside until wanted; press the remaining part through a colander, using the water in which it was boiled; put 1 qt. of milk into a double boiler; rub together one large tablespoonful of butter and two tablespoonfuls of flour; stir this carefully into the milk; stir constantly until smooth and partly thick. If, by any carelessness, it should look the slightest lumpy, put it through a sieve; return to the double boiler, and add the asparagus that has been pressed through the colander. Season to taste with salt and pepper, add the asparagus tips, and as soon as the whole is smoking hot, serve. You can not fail, unless you allow the mixture to stand; then the vegetable will separate from the milk and give it a curdled appearance.

Cream of Tomato Soup—One pt. can tomatoes, 1 qt. milk, parsley, mace, butter, flour, bay leaf, sugar, soda.

To the tomatoes add a sprig of parsley, a blade of mace and a bay leaf, and stew together for 15 minutes. Rub together 1 tablespoonful of butter and 2 tablespoonfuls of flour; add to 1 qt. boiling milk and stir constantly until it thickens. When ready to use the soup, press the tomatoes through a sieve and add 1 teaspoonful of sugar and ½ teaspoonful of soda, then the boiling milk. It must not go on the fire after the tomatoes and milk are mixed, or it will curdle.

Mulligatawney Soup—One chicken (or 3 rabbits), 2 small onions, butter, curry powder, ½ lemon, cloves.

Cut up a good-sized chicken as for a fricassee; cut 2 small onions in slices, put a tablespoonful of butter in a frying-pan, add the chicken and onion, and stir till a nice brown; mix well with these a tablespoonful of curry powder, 4 whole cloves, the juice of ½ a lemon, and salt to taste. Put all in the soup kettle with 3 qts. of water, bring slowly to a boil, skim and let it simmer gently for 2 hours. Three rabbits may be used in place of the chicken, if preferred.

Corn Soup—One can green corn, 1 pt. milk, flour, butter, 1 egg.

Take one can of green corn and put it on the back of the stove with 2 qts. of hot water; let it cook gently ½ hour, then put where it will cook more rapidly. When the corn is tender, put in 1 pt. of milk, season to taste, let it boil up, then add 2 tablespoonfuls of flour mixed with 2 of butter. If you like you may, after removing the soup from the fire, stir in one well-beaten egg, beating rapidly to prevent curdling.

Bean Soup—One qt. dried white beans, a cup milk or cream, butter, soda.

Soak 1 qt. of dried white beans over night. In the morning, drain; add 3 qts. of water; when it comes to the boiling point, pour off and add 3 qts. of fresh boiling water, also about ¼ of a teaspoonful of soda. Boil until the beans are soft; then press through a sieve and return it to the kettle. Add salt and pepper to taste and a cup of cream or a cup of milk and a bit of butter. If still too thick, add more milk. Crackers buttered and browned in the oven or squares of bread browned in butter are nice to serve with this.

Oyster Soup—Fifty oysters, 1 pt. milk, a blade of mace, 1 tablespoonful butter, 1 teaspoonful flour, powdered cloves, salt, pepper, chopped parsley.

Put in a stewpan a pint of milk, a blade of mace, with a heaping tablespoonful of butter; put in another stewpan the juice from 50 oysters; place them on the stove. When the milk begins to boil thicken it with a heaping teaspoonful of flour previously mixed with milk; then stand it back on the range where it does not boil. When the scum begins to rise on the top of the oyster juice skim it off; then add a pinch of powdered cloves and some salt and black pepper. When it begins to boil pour it into the stewpan with the milk, stirring gently, so it does not curdle or lump. Then turn in the oysters. Let them boil about 1 minute or until the edges curl; then turn into a soup tureen, where you have previously placed a tablespoonful of chopped parsley. Serve at once.

FISH

FRESH water fish have often a muddy smell and taste. To take this off soak the fish in strong salt and water after it is nicely cleaned, then dry and dress it. The fish must be put in the water while cold and set to do very gently, or the outside will break before the inner part is done. Crimp fish should be put into boiling water, and when it boils up put a little cold water in, to check extreme heat, and simmer it a few minutes. Small fish nicely fried, covered with egg and crumbs, make a dish far more elegant than if served plain. Great attention should be paid to the garnishing of fish. Use plenty of horse-radish, parsley and lemon. If fish is to be fried or broiled it must be wrapped in a clean cloth after it is well cleaned. When perfectly dry, wet with an egg (if for frying) and sprinkle the finest bread crumbs over it; then, with a large quantity of lard or dripping, boiling hot, plunge the fish into it and fry a light brown; it can then be laid on blotting-paper to receive any grease. Butter gives a bad color; oil fries the finest color for those who will allow for the expense. Garnish with raw or fried parsley, which must be thus done: When washed and picked throw it again into clean water; when the lard or dripping boils, throw the parsley into it immediately from the water, and instantly it will be green and crisp and must be taken up with a slice. If fish is to be broiled, it must be seasoned, floured and put on a gridiron that is very clean, which, when hot, should be rubbed with a piece of suet to prevent the fish from sticking. It must be broiled on a very clear fire and not too near, or it may be scorched.

Cod's Head and Shoulders (to Boil)—One cod's head and shoulders, salt water, 1 glass of vinegar, horseradish.

Wash and tie it up, and dry with a cloth. Salt the water, and put in a glass of vinegar. When boiling, take off the scum; put the fish in, and keep it boiling very briskly about ½ hour. Parboil the milt and roe, cut in thin slices, fry, and serve them. Garnish with horseradish; for sauce, oysters, eggs, or drawn butter.

Stewed Codfish in Brown Sauce—Slice the fish, take off the skin and fry quickly a fine brown, lift it out and place in a stewpan with boiling brown gravy; add the juice of a lemon and some salt. Stew the fish gently until it begins to break, lift it on a hot dish, stir into the gravy 1½ oz. of butter with 1 teaspoonful of flour and a little mace. Boil the sauce 1 minute, pour it over the fish and serve.

Salmon Croquettes—The contents of 1 can of salmon from which the oil has been poured and which have been shredded fine, 1 cupful of fine bread crumbs, 1 egg and cayenne pepper to taste; mix well, make into balls, dip first into beaten egg and then into bread crumbs or cracker dust; fry in plenty of boiling lard and drain on coarse brown paper before serving. Garnish the dish with parsley and, if you like, slices of lemon.

Salt Cod—Cod, vinegar (1 glass), parsnips, cream, butter, flour.

Soak and clean the piece you mean to dress, then lay it all night in water, with a glass of vinegar. Boil it enough, then break it into flakes on the dish; pour over it parsnips boiled, beaten in a mortar, and then boiled up with cream and a large piece of butter rubbed with a little flour. It may be served as above with egg sauce instead of the parsnips, and the root sent up whole; or the fish may be boiled and sent up without flaking, and the sauces as above.

Cod's Roes—One or more cod's roes, 1½ oz. of butter, 2 eggs, 1 teaspoonful of salt, 1 pinch of cayenne pepper, 1 grate of nutmeg, 1 dessertspoonful of tomato sauce or vinegar.

Boil 1 or more cod's roes, according to size, till quite set and nearly done. Take them out of the water, and when cold cut them into slices

¾ of an inch thick. Now put into a small stewpan 1½ oz. of butter; when made liquid over the fire, take it off and stir into it the yolks of 2 eggs, a small teaspoonful of salt, a pinch of cayenne pepper, a grain of nutmeg, and a dessertspoonful of tomato or Mogul sauce, or the vinegar from any good pickle. Mix all well together and stir it over the fire for 2 or 3 minutes to thicken. Dip the slices of cod's roe in this sauce to take up as much as they will, lay them in a dish, pour over them any of the sauce that may be left, put the dish into the oven for 10 minutes, and send to table very hot.

Codfish Balls—Equal quantities of potatoes and boiled codfish, 1 oz. butter, 1 egg.

Equal quantity of mashed potatoes and boiled codfish minced fine; to each ½ lb. allow 1 oz. of butter and a well-beaten egg; mix thoroughly. Form into balls between 2 spoons; drop into hot lard, and fry till brown.

Salt Salmon (to Souse)—One salt salmon, cayenne, whole allspice, a little mace, cold vinegar.

Wash a salt salmon, and cover it with plenty of clean water. Let it soak 24 hours, but be careful to change the water several times. Then scale it, cut it into 4 parts, wash, clean, and put on to boil. When half done change the water; and when tender, drain it, put it in a stone pan, sprinkle some cayenne, whole allspice, a few cloves, and a little mace over each piece; cover with cold vinegar. This makes a nice relish for tea.

Fish Pie—Any remains of cold fish, such as cod or haddock. Clear the fish from the bones, put a layer of it in a pie-dish, sprinkle with pepper and salt, then put a layer of bread crumbs, some grated nutmeg and chopped parsley. Repeat this until the dish is quite full, pour in some white sauce, cover with a layer of bread crumbs or mashed potatoes. Bake ½ to ¾ an hour.

Salmon (Fried, with Anchovy Sauce)—Some thin slices from the tail end of a salmon, anchovy sauce, flour, bread crumbs, eggs, water, a little roux, a little cayenne pepper, lard.

Scrape the scales off the tail end of a salmon, cut in thin slices, dip them in flour, then in 2 eggs whisked up with a tablespoonful of water and a tablespoonful of anchovy sauce, then dip them in bread crumbs, and fry in boiling lard for 8 or 10 minutes; dish them up on a napkin in a nice heap, and sprinkle a little chopped parsley over them, and serve in a sauce-boat some sauce.

Salmon (Dressed, Italian Sauce)—Two slices about 2 in. thick of good salmon, 2 onions, 1 carrot, 1 shalot, 2 gherkins, a few preserved mushrooms and a few capers, 3 oz. of butter, a little chopped parsley, 1 tablespoonful of anchovy sauce, and a pint of good stock, and a little roux.

Cut up 2 onions and 1 carrot into thin slices, and lay them in the bottom of a baking dish with a little pepper and salt and 1 oz. of butter; lay the slices of salmon on the top of the vegetables, cover them with buttered paper, and bake for 35 minutes in a warm oven; when cooked, serve with sauce made as follows: Cut up 1 shalot very fine, and lightly fry in 2 oz. of butter; throw in a little chopped parsley, 2 gherkins chopped fine, and a few capers and mushrooms, cut up very fine, and 1 pt. of good stock, a little roux to thicken, and one tablespoonful of anchovy sauce and a little pepper; boil these ingredients together for 20 minutes; lift the salmon carefully onto a dish (taking care no onion or carrot hang to it), pour the boiling sauce over it and serve very hot.

Perch and Tench—Put them into cold water, boil them carefully and serve with melted butter and soy. Perch is a most delicate fish. They may be either fried or stewed, but in stewing they do not preserve so good a flavor.

Trout and Grayling (to Fry)—Scale, gut, and wash well; then dry them, and lay them separately on a board before the fire, after dusting some flour over them. Fry them of a fine color with fresh dripping; serve with crisp parsley and plain butter. Perch and tench may be done the same way.

Perch and Trout (to Broil)—Split them down the back, notch them two or three times across, and broil over a clear fire; turn them frequently, and baste with well salted butter and powdered thyme.

Mackerel—Boil, and serve with butter and fennel.

To broil them, split, and sprinkle with herbs, pepper and salt; or stuff with the same, crumbs and chopped fennel.

Potted: Clean, season, and bake them in a pan with spice, bay leaves and some butter; when cold, lay them in a potting-pot, and cover with butter.

Pickled: Boil them, then boil some of the liquor, a few peppers, bay leaves, and some vinegar; when cold, pour it over them.

Mackerel (Pickled, called Caveach)—Six mackerel, 1 oz. of pepper, 2 nutmegs, a little mace, 4 cloves, 1 handful of salt.

Clean and divide them; then cut each side into three, or, leaving them undivided, cut each fish into five or six pieces. To six large mackerel, take nearly an ounce of pepper, 2 nutmegs, a little mace, 4 cloves and a handful of salt, all in the finest powder. Mix, and, making holes in each piece of fish, thrust the seasoning into them; rub each piece with some of it; then fry them brown in oil; let them stand till cold, then put them into a stone jar and cover with vinegar; if to keep long, pour oil on the top. Thus done, they may be preserved for months.

Mullet with Tomatoes—One-half doz. red mullet, pepper, salt and chopped parsley, 5 or 6 tablespoonfuls of tomato sauce.

Butter a baking dish plentifully, lay on it side by side ½ doz. red mullet, sprinkle them with pepper, salt and chopped parsley, then add about 5 or 6 tablespoonfuls of tomato sauce. Cover the whole with a sheet of well-oiled paper, and bake for about ½ hour.

Soles—If boiled, they must be served with great care to look perfectly white, and should be well covered with parsley. If fried, dip in egg, and cover them with fine crumbs of bread; set on a frying-pan that is just large enough, and put into it a large quantity of fresh lard or dripping, boil it, and immediately slip the fish into it; do them of a fine brown. Soles that have been fried are very nice when cold with oil, vinegar, salt and mustard.

Soles au Gratin—Soles, a little stock, 1 lemon, a little anchovy, pepper and salt, bread crumbs, a small piece of butter, and a little vinegar.

Place a sole in an oval tin baking dish, lay on the top a piece of butter, and round it the juice of ½ a lemon and a little anchovy sauce, a teaspoonful of vinegar and a little pepper, and then bake it for 15 minutes in a hot oven; when nearly cooked sprinkle some bread crumbs over it and color the top with a salamander. Serve in the tin it was baked in, with a little chopped parsley on the top.

Sturgeon (Fresh)—Sturgeon, egg, bread crumbs, parsley, pepper, salt.

Cut slices, rub egg over them, then sprinkle with crumbs of bread, parsley, pepper, salt; fold them in paper, and broil gently. Sauce: butter, anchovy and soy.

Turbot en Mayonnaise—Some fillets of turbot, oil, tarragon vinegar, salt and pepper, eggs, cucumbers, anchovies, tarragon leaves, beets, capers, aspic jelly.

Cut some fillets of cooked turbot into moderate-sized round or oblong pieces, carefully taking off the skin and extracting all bones. Place these pieces of fish into a bowl, with a dressing made of oil, tarragon vinegar, salt and pepper. As soon as the fish is well flavored with this seasoning, arrange the pieces round a dish like a crown. Place a circle of chopped hard-boiled eggs, tiny pickled cucumbers, anchovies, tarragon leaves, beetroot and capers round the dish, and then arrange a wall of aspic jelly round the edge of the dish. Fill up the center of the crown of the fish with good mayonnaise sauce.

Turbot au Gratin (a nice Dish for Luncheon)—Cold cooked turbot, anchovy sauce, a little stock, cayenne pepper, 2 oz. butter, a little flour and some bread crumbs.

Place a piece of butter, about 2 oz., in a stewpan and melt it on the fire; add a little flour, then a little anchovy sauce and a little cayenne pepper; stir these well together and then drop in the sauce any cold turbot you may have left from dinner the evening before, place some of the turbot out of the sauce in large patty pans, and cover it with bread crumbs and bake it in a hot oven; if the top does not get brown enough, heat a salamander and finish off that way. Serve the patty-pans upon a napkin or paper.

Smelts (to Fry)—Smelts, egg, bread crumbs, lard.

They should not be washed more than is necessary to clean them. Dry them in a cloth, then lightly flour them, but shake it off. Dip them into plenty of egg, then into bread-crumbs, grated fine, and plunge them into a good pan of boiling lard; let them continue gently boiling, and a few minutes will make them a bright yellow-brown. Take care not to take off the light roughness of the crumbs, or their beauty will be lost.

Eel Pie—One or two eels, seasoning, gravy, gelatine.

Cut up 1 or 2 eels and stew gently until tender in a little good brown gravy, seasoned to taste; when done enough, strain the gravy through muslin, add gelatine and pour over the fish. A few sprigs of parsley placed about the mould will much improve the appearance.

Eels (to Boil)—Clean, cut off the heads, and dry them. Joint them into suitable lengths, or coil them on your fish-plate; boil them in salted water. Use drawn butter and parsley for sauce.

Haddock with Tomatoes—One dried haddock, 1 onion, 1 oz. butter, 1 ripe tomato, pepper, parsley.

Soak a dried haddock in plenty of cold water for half a day, drain off the water and replace it with boiling water; when the haddock has been in this for 2 hours, take it out, carefully remove all the bones and skin, and break the meat into flakes; slice a moderate-sized onion, put it into a saucepan with 1 oz. of butter; as soon as the onion is soft, add one ripe tomato, cut into slices; after a couple of minutes add the flesh of the haddock, a sprinkling of pepper and some finely minced parsley; shake the saucepan on the fire, until the contents are thoroughly heated, then draw it aside, to be kept warm till the time for serving.

Fish Croquettes—Remnants of turbot, brill, haddock, or salmon, butter, pinch of flour, some milk, pepper, salt, nutmeg, parsley.

From some remnants of boiled turbot, brill, haddock, or salmon, pick out the flesh carefully, and mince it, not too finely; melt a piece of butter in a saucepan, add a small pinch of flour and some hot milk; stir on the fire until the mixture thickens, then put in pepper, salt, and a little grated nutmeg, together with some finely chopped parsley, and, lastly, the minced fish. As soon as the whole is quite hot, turn it out on a dish to get cold, then fashion and finish the croquettes as in the first recipe.

Halibut (Boiled)—Halibut, salted water.

Allow the fish to lie in cold salt water for an hour. Wipe dry in a clean cloth and score the skin, then put into the fish-kettle with cold salted water sufficient to cover it. Let it come slowly to the boil, and allow from ½ to ¾ of an hour for a piece weighing 4 or 5 lbs. When ready, drain, and serve with egg sauce.

Halibut (Baked)—Halibut, a little butter, salt and water, a tablespoonful of walnut catsup, a dessertspoonful of Worcestershire sauce, the juice of a lemon, a little brown flour.

A piece of halibut weighing 5 or 6 lbs., lay in

salt water for 2 hours. Wipe in a clean cloth and score the skin. Have the oven tolerably hot, and bake about 1 hour. Melt a little butter in hot water and baste the fish constantly. It should be of a fine brown color. Any gravy that is in the dripping-pan mix with a little boiling water, then stir in the walnut catsup and Worcestershire sauce, the juice of the lemon, and thicken with the brown flour (the flour should be mixed with a little cold water previously); give one boil and serve in sauce-boat.

Baked Herrings or Sprats — Herrings, allspice, salt, black pepper, 1 onion and a few bay leaves, vinegar.

Wash and drain without wiping them; season with allspice in fine powder, salt, and a few whole cloves; lay them in a pan with plenty of black pepper, 1 onion, and a few bay-leaves; add vinegar enough to cover them. Put paper over the pan, and bake in a slow oven. If you like throw saltpetre over them the night before, to make them look red. Gut, but do not open them.

Fish Chowder — Two lbs. solid fish-shreds, ½ lb. salt pork, 4 onions, 10 potatoes, salt and pepper, 2 tablespoonfuls farina, milk.

Take ½ lb. fat salt pork, cut into slices, and fry out well. Slice four large onions and fry in the pork fat until they are a light brown. Stir constantly to prevent burning, and thus make the chowder bitter. Put this into a pot with 3 qts. of boiling water and let it boil 20 minutes. Skim out the pieces of pork and onion and add 10 potatoes, sliced, not too thin, and boil 20 minutes. Then add 2 lbs. of solid fish-shreds and boil 10 minutes if the fish is not cooked. Add salt and pepper to taste. When cooked stir in slowly a thickening made of 2 tablespoonfuls of farina mixed in cold milk, and let it boil up once only. Put the pot back on the fire, and after letting it stand a few moments skim off the scum which will rise to the top, and serve.

Planked Shad — Secure a handsome, thick oak board, and have some brass bored, with stout wooden pegs to fit; spread the dressed fish open on the board, securing it with the pegs. Heat the end of the plank in a shallow pan and set all before a clear fire; put a little salt and water in the pan and baste the fish often, adding when it is nearly done a tablespoonful of melted butter and half as much walnut catsup. If the board is handsome serve the shad on it, but it can be laid on a hot dish and the gravy, with a little walnut catsup added, poured over. Serve with pickled walnuts.

OYSTERS, SHELLFISH, ETC.

Lobsters (Potted) — Lobsters, mace, white pepper, nutmeg, salt and butter.

Half boil them, pick out the meat, cut it into small pieces, season with mace, white pepper, nutmeg, and salt, press close into a pot, and cover with butter, bake ½ hour; put the spawn in. When cold, take the lobster out, and put it into the pots with a little of the butter. Beat the other butter in a mortar with some of the spawn, then mix that colored butter with as much as will be sufficient to cover the pots, and strain it. Cayenne may be added if approved.

Lobster Croquettes — Lobster, pepper, salt, powdered mace, bread crumbs, 2 tablespoonfuls of butter, egg, biscuit, parsley.

To the meat of a well-boiled lobster, chopped fine, add pepper, salt, and powdered mace. Mix with this one quarter as much bread crumbs, well rubbed, as you have meat; make into pointed balls, with 2 tablespoonfuls of butter melted; roll these in beaten egg, then in biscuit powdered fine, and fry in butter or very nice sweet lard. Serve dry and hot, and garnish with crisped parsley. This is a delicious supper dish or entrée.

Crabs (Hot) — One good-sized crab, pepper, salt, bread crumbs, milk, cream, or oiled butter, parsley.

For this, 1 good-sized crab or 3 or 4 small ones may be used. The meat must be picked from the claws and the soft inside from the body; season with pepper and salt, add a small quantity of bread crumbs, and moisten with milk, or, better still, a few spoonfuls of cream or oiled butter. When well mixed, put it into the large shell, strewing fresh bread crumbs over the top, and sprinkling some oiled butter over them; let it remain in the oven just long enough to get hot through and to be a nice golden-brown color. It should be served very hot on a napkin garnished with parsley.

Crabs (Boiled) — Crabs, salt water, sweet oil.

Boil them in salt and water 20 minutes; take them out, break off the claws, wipe the crabs, throw away the small claws, and crack the large ones and send to table. Rub a little sweet oil on the shells.

Oysters on Toast — Drain the liquor from a qt. of oysters; cut each into 4 pieces, and strain through coarse muslin back into the sauce. When it boils again, dip out a small cupful and keep it hot. Stir into that left on the range a heaped teaspoonful of butter rolled in a scant tablespoonful of cornstarch. In another vessel heat ½ cup of milk. Stir the oysters into the thickened liquor; season with pepper and salt, and cook, after they are scalding hot, 3 minutes before adding the milk. Line a hot platter with neat slices of crustless toast, buttered; wet with the reserved liquor, and cover with the oysters.

Oysters (Stewed) — Oysters, a blade of mace, some lemon peel, a few white peppers, cream, butter, and flour.

Open and separate the liquor from them, then wash them from the grit; strain the liquor, and put with the oysters a piece of mace and lemon peel, and a few white peppers. Simmer them very gently, and put some cream and a little flour and butter. Serve with sippets.

Oysters (Stewed) — Liquor from 2 qts. of oysters, one teacupful of hot water, salt, pepper, 2 tablespoonfuls of butter, 1 cupful of milk.

Drain the liquor from 2 qts. of firm, plump oysters; mix with it a small teacupful of hot water, add a little salt and pepper, and set over the fire in a saucepan. Let it boil up once, put in the oysters, let them boil for 5 minutes or less—not more. When they "ruffle," add two tablespoonfuls of butter. The instant it is melted and well stirred in, put in a large cupful of boiling milk, and take the saucepan from the fire. Serve with oyster or cream biscuits as soon as possible. Oysters become tough and tasteless when cooked too much or left to stand too long after they are withdrawn from the fire.

Oyster Sausages—One doz. large oysters, ½ lb. rump steak, a little seasoning of herbs, pepper and salt.

Chop all fine, and roll them into the form of sausages.

Angels on Horseback.—Oysters, bacon.

Trim the beards from as many oysters as may be required, wrap each in a very thin shaving of fat, streaky bacon (cold boiled bacon is the best); run them one after the other onto a silver skewer, and hold them over a toast in front of a clear fire until the bacon is slightly crisp; serve on the toast immediately.

Escalloped Lobster—Select lobsters that are rather above the medium size; plunge them in boiling water for half an hour. When cool enough to handle, split in two and remove the entrails; cut the meat into dice, being careful to pick out all the meat from the claws. Prepare in a farina kettle a pint of rich gravy made from equal parts of cream and milk, thickened with a heaping tablespoonful of flour, creamed with 2 tablespoonfuls of butter. Season well with salt, cayenne pepper and a tiny pinch of grated nutmeg; add the lobster to the sauce thus made, place in a buttered baking dish, cover with bread crumbs; place in a hot oven for 10 minutes to brown.

Barbecued Oysters—Drain a dozen large oysters, dust them over with pepper and cut an equal number of thin slices of bacon of about the same size. First put a slice of bacon and then an oyster and bacon and so on, alternating, on an iron skewer, taking care not to crowd them, and roast in a very hot oven until the bacon begins to crisp. Serve hot in a covered dish.

Panned Oysters—Select large, fat oysters, split and toast round crackers, and spread in the bottom of a pan; drain the liquor from the oysters, put in a saucepan and set on the stove to boil; skim, and season with pepper, salt and a little butter; moisten the toasted crackers with hot liquor, and lay the oysters over; spread with bits of butter and set in a hot oven for 15 minutes.

Scalloped Oysters—Butter a baking-dish; fill it with alternate layers of rolled crackers and oysters; over each layer of oysters spread bits of butter and dash pepper—not salt, as it will shrivel them. Heat the liquor of the oysters, add to it 1 teacupful of cream, season to taste and pour over the oysters. Set in a moderate oven and bake nearly an hour.

Oysters (Fried)—Carefully dry in a clean cloth a dozen large oysters. In a bright frying-pan put 2 heaping tablespoonfuls of good butter, and as soon as this comes to a boil throw in the oysters and whip them out with a strainer as soon as they begin to curl up, and serve immediately. Oysters cooked in this manner are delicious, but the butter must be heated to the point when the blue smoke hovers over the pan. To 3 well-beaten eggs add ½ pt. of oyster juice, a teaspoonful of salt and black or cayenne pepper, according to taste. Work into this a gill of sweet oil, until the whole becomes a batter. On a bed of cracker dust on the table lay your oysters, then take them one by one by the beard, dip them in the mixture and then in the bread crumbs. Repeat this three or four times, first in the egg mixture, then in the bread crumbs. Place each oyster on the table by itself. Do not pile one on top of the other or they will become heavy. Now fry in a pan of hot butter and serve on a hot dish.

Oysters (Roast)—Take a dozen large oysters, wash them clean and place them on the coals of a bright fire. As soon as the shells open, pour the juice into a hot soup-plate, remove the oysters from the shells with a knife, put them in the plate with a lump of butter and serve while hot. Oysters treated in this manner retain more of their flavor and are easier digested than when cooked in any other way.

Oysters (Stewed)—To a pint of milk add the juice of 25 oysters, a teaspoonful of salt, pepper according to taste. Let it boil for 1 or 2 minutes, then add your oysters and a generous lump of butter.

Oyster Patties—Make a rich paste, roll it out ½ in. thick, then turn a teacup down on the paste, and, with the point of a sharp pen-knife, mark the paste lightly round the edge of the cup. Then with the point of the knife make a circle about ½ in. from the edge; cut this circle half way through. Place them on tins, and bake in a quick oven. Remove the center, and fill with oysters seasoned and warmed over the fire.

Oyster Omelet—Six eggs, whites and yolks beaten separately; 1 tablespoonful of cream, ½ teaspoonful of corn starch wet with the cream, a saltspoonful of salt and a dust of pepper; a dozen fine oysters broiled.

Beat yolks well, adding the cream and corn-starch; stir in the stiffened whites lightly; have ready a tablespoonful of butter in a frying-pan, hissing hot, but not browned. Pour in the omelet, and as soon as it sets at the edges, loosen with a knife and shake gently with a uniform motion from side to side, until the center is almost set. The oysters should have been broiled before you began the omelet. To do this, roll them in fine cracker-dust, salted and peppered, broil quickly over a clear fire, transfer to a hot dish, put a bit of butter on each, and cover and keep hot while the omelet is cooking. When this is done, lay one-half of it, as it lies on the pan, with the oysters, fold the other over dexterously and reverse the frying-pan quickly upon the heated dish in which it is to be served.

POULTRY AND GAME

IN choosing ducks, be careful to secure those with plump bodies and thick and yellowish feet, and, to insure their being tender, it is advisable to let them hang a day or two. In choosing turkeys, the hens are preferable for boiling on account of their whiteness and tenderness.

Partridges in perfection will have dark-colored bills and yellowish legs; the time they should be kept entirely depends upon the taste of those for whom they are intended, as what some people consider delicious, to others would be disgusting and offensive.

Rabbits when young have smooth and sharp claws.

In selecting a goose, choose one with a clean white skin, plump breast and yellow feet. Charcoal is considered as an admirable preventive for decomposition.

Chicken Patties—Cold chicken, milk, flour, pepper, salt and butter, puff paste.

Mince cold chicken, and stir it into a white sauce, made of milk thickened with flour and flavored with pepper, salt and butter; line small patty pans with puff paste, bake first, and then fill with the mixture, and set in a hot oven for a few minutes to brown.

Fowl (to Boil)—For boiling, choose those that are not black-legged. Pick them nicely, singe, wash and truss them. Flour them, and put them into boiling water. Serve with parsley and butter, oyster, lemon, liver or celery sauce.

Fowls (Roast)—Butter, flour, gravy, lemon-juice, sausages, bacon.

Fowls require constant attention in dredging and basting, and the last ten minutes let butter rolled in flour be stuck over them in little bits, and allowed to melt without basting. The gravy for fowls should always be thickened, and slightly flavored with lemon-juice. Sausages or rolled bacon should be served on the same dish, and white mashed potatoes should always be handed with poultry.

Chicken Cutlets (with Rice)—A teacupful of rice, some good stock, 1 onion, salt and pepper, some cold ham and chicken, egg, bread-crumbs.

Boil a teacupful of rice in some good stock, and pound it in a mortar with an onion that has been cooked in butter, with salt and pepper. Pound separately in equal portions cold ham and chicken; form this into cutlets; cover them with egg and bread-crumbs and fry. Serve with a sharp sauce.

Chicken a la Jardiniere—2 young chickens, butter, 1 onion, some savory herbs, carrots, turnips, onions, beef stock, mushrooms, 2 cabbages, some heads of asparagus, pepper, sugar.

Put two young chickens in a saucepan with some butter, a large onion chopped up, some savory herbs, some salt and sufficient water; the chickens should be dropped in the mixture when it is boiling, and left in the saucepan until the liquid is reduced by half; cut up in good shapes some carrots and turnips, some whole onions skinned and blanched, and put them in a saucepan with some butter, some beef stock, some mushrooms, two very young cabbages and some heads of asparagus; season with salt, pepper, and a little sugar; cook very gently, and fifteen minutes before serving add a piece of butter kneaded with flour. Serve with vegetables well arranged around the dish.

Chicken Rissoles—Some remnants of fowls, ham and tongue, butter, a pinch of flour, white pepper, salt, nutmeg, parsley, eggs, a few drops of lemon-juice, flour, water, 2 pinches of sugar.

Mince very finely some remnants of fowls, free from skin, add an equal quantity of ham or tongue, as well as a small quantity of truffles, all finely minced; toss the whole in a saucepan with a piece of butter, mixed with a pinch of flour; add white pepper, salt, and nutmeg to taste, as well as a little minced parsley; stir in off the fire the yolks of one or two eggs beaten up with a few drops of lemon-juice, and lay the mixture on a plate to cool. Make a paste with some flour, a little water, two eggs, a pinch of salt, and two or three of sugar; roll it out to the thickness of a penny piece, stamp it out in round pieces three inches in diameter; put a piece of the above mince on each, then fold them up, fastening the edges by moistening them with water. Trim the rissoles neatly with a fluted cutter, dip each one in beaten-up egg, and fry a golden color in hot lard.

Chicken (Jellied)—A chicken, 1 oz. of butter, pepper and salt, ½ packet of gelatine.

Boil the chicken until the water is reduced to a pint; pick the meat from the bones in fair-sized pieces, removing all gristle, skin and bone. Skim the fat from the liquor, add an ounce of butter, a little pepper and salt, and half a packet of gelatine. Put the cut-up chicken into a mould, wet with cold water; when the gelatine has dissolved pour the liquor hot over the chicken. Turn out when cold.

Chicken Loaf—A chicken, 2 oz. of butter, pepper, salt, egg.

Boil a chicken in as little water as possible until the meat can easily be picked from the bones; cut it up finely, then put it back into the saucepan with two ounces of butter, and a seasoning of pepper and salt. Grease a square china mould and cover the bottom with slices of hard-boiled egg; pour in the chicken, place a weight on it, and set aside to cool, when it will turn out.

Chicken Croquettes—Breast of a roast fowl, tongue, truffles, butter, flour, stock, parsley, pepper, salt, nutmeg, eggs, lemon-juice, parsley.

The breast of a roast fowl, two parts; of boiled tongue, one part, and of truffles, one part; mince all these very finely, and mix them together. Melt a piece of butter in a saucepan, stir a little flour into it, then put in the above mixture, and moisten with a small quantity of stock; add some finely minced parsley, pepper, salt, and nutmeg to taste. Stir it on the fire for a few minutes, then stir in it, off the fire, the yolks of one or two eggs beaten up with the juice of a lemon and strained. Spread out this mince (which should be pretty stiff) on a marble slab, and when it is nearly cold fashion it into small portions in the shape of balls or of corks. Dip each in a beaten-up egg, and then roll it in very fine baked bread-crumbs; repeat this operation after the lapse of an hour, and after a similar interval fry the croquettes in hot lard to a golden color. Serve on a napkin, with plenty of fried parsley.

Pressed Chicken—Two chickens, boiled until the meat leaves the bones easily, then pull to pieces and chop fine, letting the liquor in which they were cooked boil down until only a cupful remains. Add about one-half as much chopped ham as chicken; roll two soda crackers, pour the stock over, seasoning highly. Mix well together, put in a deep, long pan, pressing down hard with the hand. Fold a cloth several times, put over the top, and put on a weight. It will slice nicely if prepared the day before using.

Braised Chicken — Draw and prepare a chicken as for roasting. Truss it without liking and place in a baking-pan over ½ of a small carrot and 1 onion, chopped fine, 4 cloves, 1 sprig of parsley and a little salt and pepper. To this add 1 pint of rich meat stock, cover closely and bake in a quick oven for 1½ hours. Then dish the fowl and place it where it will keep hot. Put one tablespoonful of butter in a frying-pan, let it brown, and rub smooth in it one tablespoonful of flour; add to this the liquor in which the chicken was braised and then twelve mushrooms, chopped fine. Stir this continually until it boils.

Wild Duck (Roast) — Duck, bread-crumbs, carrot, pepper and salt, sage and onions, currant jelly, 1 pinch of cayenne, browned flour.

Before roasting, parboil with a small carrot pared and put inside. This will absorb the fishy taste. If you have no carrot at hand, an onion will have the same effect, but unless you mean to use onion in the stuffing a carrot is preferable. When parboiled, throw away the carrot or onion, lay in fresh water for half an hour, stuff with bread-crumbs seasoned with pepper, salt, sage and an onion, and roast till brown and tender, basting half the time with butter and water, then with drippings. Add to the gravy, when you have taken up the duck, one tablespoonful of currant jelly and a pinch of cayenne. Thicken gravy with browned flour and serve in a tureen.

Quail Pie — Puff paste, salt pork or ham, 6 eggs, butter, pepper, 1 bunch parsley, juice of 1 lemon.

Clean and dress the birds, loosen the joints, but do not divide them; put on the stove to simmer, while you prepare puff paste. Cover a deep dish with it, then lay in the bottom some shreds of pork or ham, then a layer of hard boiled eggs, a little butter and pepper. Take the birds from the fire, sprinkle with pepper and minced parsley. Squeeze lemon juice upon them, and upon the breasts of the birds a few pieces of butter rolled in flour. Cover with slices of egg, then shred some ham and lay upon this. Pour in a little of the gravy in which the quails were parboiled, and put on the lid. Leave a hole in the middle and bake a little over 1 hour.

Rabbit Pie — Two rabbits, ½ lb. fat pork, 4 eggs, pepper, butter, a little powdered mace, a few drops of lemon juice, puff paste.

Cut a pair of rabbits into ten pieces, soak in salt and water half an hour and simmer until half done, in enough water to cover them. Cut a quarter of a pound of pork into slices, and boil four eggs hard. Lay some pieces of pork in the bottom of the dish, then next a layer of rabbit. Upon this spread slices of boiled egg, and pepper and butter. Sprinkle, moreover, with a little powdered mace, a few drops of lemon juice upon each piece of meat. Proceed in this manner until the dish is full, the top layer being pork. Pour in water in which the rabbit was boiled; when you have salted it and added a few lumps of butter rolled in flour, cover with puff paste, make a hole in the middle and bake for 1 hour. Cover with paper if it should brown too fast.

Rabbit (Stewed) — One rabbit, dripping or butter, flour, 6 onions.

Cut a rabbit in pieces; wash in cold water, a little salted. Prepare in a stewpan some flour and clarified dripping or butter; stir it until it browns. Then put in the pieces of rabbit, and keep stirring and turning until they are tinged with a light color; then add 6 onions, peeled but not cut up. Serve all together in a deep dish.

A German Dish — A tender fowl, salt, pepper, mace, flour, yolk of 1 egg, hot lard, liver, gizzard, parsley.

Quarter a tender fowl, season the pieces with pepper, salt and mace; flour, and then dip them in the beaten-up yolk of an egg; fry a golden color in hot lard; dish them, garnished with the liver and gizzard fried separately, and with fried parsley. Serve either with a salad garnished with hard-boiled eggs or tomato sauce.

Giblets (to Stew) — Salt and pepper, butter, 1 cup of cream, 1 teaspoonful of flour.

Treat them as directed for giblet-pie (under the head "Pies"); season them with salt and pepper, and a very small piece of mace. Before serving give them one boil with a cup of cream, and a piece of butter rubbed in a teaspoonful of flour.

Pigeons — May be dressed in many ways. The flavor depends very much on their being cropped and drawn as soon as killed. No other bird requires so much washing. Pigeons left from dinner the day before may be stewed or made into a pie; in either case care must be taken not to overdo them, which will make them stringy. They need only be heated up in gravy, made ready; and force-meat balls may be fried and added, instead of putting a stuffing into them. If for a pie, let beefsteaks be stewed in a little water, and put cold under them, and cover each pigeon with a piece of fat bacon, to keep them moist. Season as usual.

Pigeons (Roast) — Should be stuffed with parsley, either cut or whole, and seasoned within. Serve with parsley and butter. Peas or asparagus should be dressed to eat with them.

Turkey (to Roast) — The sinews of the legs should be drawn, whichever way it is dressed. The head should be twisted under the wing; and in drawing it take care not to tear the liver, nor let the gall touch it. Put a stuffing of sausage-meat, or, if sausages are to be served in the dish, a bread stuffing. As this makes a large addition to the size of the bird, observe that the heat of the fire is constantly to that part; for the breast is often not done enough. A little strip of paper should be put on the bone to hinder it from scorching, while the other parts roast. Baste well and froth it up. Serve with gravy in the dish, and plenty of bread-sauce in a sauce-tureen. Add a few crumbs and a beaten egg to the stuffing of sausage-meat.

Roast Turkey — Plain force-meat, 1 turkey, bacon, butter, salt, pork sausages, gravy.

Pluck, singe, draw, wipe thoroughly and truss a fine turkey; stuff it with plain force-meat, pack it up in some thin slices of fat bacon, and over that a sheet of buttered paper; put in oven, basting frequently with butter. A quarter of an hour before it is done, remove the paper and slices of bacon. Sprinkle with salt just before serving. Garnish with pork sausages, and serve with a tureen of gravy. Time of roasting, 2 or 3 hours, according to size.

Partridge — Dress 1 doz. nice partridges; put them in a baking-pan with 1 lb. good butter, a small teacupful vinegar, 1 teaspoonful water, 2 pods red pepper, ½ teaspoonful ground black pepper, and salt to suit your taste. Put the pan into the stove, which must be hot enough to cook them at once; ¾ of an hour is generally sufficient. When the birds are brown all over, which they will be if you have basted them diligently as you turned them, set the pan on the top of the stove, pour in at once 1 quart of fresh sweet cream, adding ½ teacupful of grated biscuit crumbs; stir well to keep from scorching, and serve in a few minutes on a warm platter.

To Cook Ducks — Prepare as many ducks as you wish for a meal and cut them up as you would to stew. Cover with cold water and let it come to a boil, then pour off the water, adding a fresh supply. Boil until tender, season with pepper and salt, then, pouring off the water, fry brown in butter. This is a splendid dish; the parboiling takes out all the wild taste which ducks usually have. Old prairie chickens may be treated in the same way.

Roast Goose — Prepare the goose the same as a chicken. Fill with potato or onion stuffing, being careful not to fill it too full, as this dressing will always swell in cooking. Place it in a baking-pan with 1 cupful of water and 2 teaspoonfuls of salt. Bake in a quick oven, allowing 18 minutes for each pound, basting it frequently. When the goose has been roasting an hour, cool the oven and finish the roast at a moderate heat. Goslings may be cooked in the same manner, allowing 15 minutes to each pound.

Potato Stuffing for Goose or Ducks — Mix together 2 cupfuls hot mashed potatoes, 1 teaspoonful salt, 1 teaspoonful onion juice, 4 tablespoonfuls of cream, ¼ teaspoonful black pepper, 1 tablespoonful chopped parsley, 1 tablespoonful butter and the yolks of 2 eggs. Beat until light.

Truffle and Chestnut Stuffing — One lb. fat bacon, 2 shallots, 1 lb. chestnuts, ½ lb. truffles, pepper, salt, spices, thyme, marjoram.

Mince 1 lb. of fat bacon and a couple of shallots, give them a turn on the fire in a saucepan; then put in 1 lb. of chestnuts, boiled and peeled, and ½ lb. of truffles, both cut up in moderate-sized pieces; add pepper, salt and spices to taste; also a little powdered thyme and marjoram. Give the mixture another turn or two on the fire, and it is ready.

Truffle Sauce — Rub a saucepan with a shallot, melt a piece of butter in it, add a very small quantity of flour and the trimmings of the truffles chopped coarsely; moisten with some good stock free from fat, and season with pepper, salt and the least pinch of nutmeg. Let the sauce simmer about 10 minutes, and it is ready.

To Boil a Turkey — Pick, singe, draw and wash it. Truss it by drawing the legs in under the skin; fasten them with a piece of tape round the joints, and tie it round the rump. Make a stuffing of bread-crumbs, pepper and salt, or of chopped oysters, and put it where the crop was taken out. Boil slowly for 2 hours, take off the tape, and serve with either oyster, celery or plain white sauce.

Chestnut Sauce (for Roast Turkey) — Remove the outer skin from a number of chestnuts (carefully excluding any that may be the least tainted), put them to boil in salted water with a handful of coriander seeds, and a couple of bay leaves. When thoroughly done, remove the outer skin, and pound the chestnuts in a mortar, adding a little stock (free from fat) now and then. When a smooth paste is obtained, fry an onion in butter to a light color, add the chestnut paste and sufficient stock to get the sauce of the desired consistency; add salt and pepper to taste, pass through a hair sieve, and serve.

Roast Haunch of Venison — Butter, salt, flour and water.

Trim the joint neatly, wipe it well with a cloth, rub it over with butter, and sprinkle it with salt; then wrap it up in a sheet of buttered kitchen-paper. Make a paste with flour and water, roll it out to the thickness of about half an inch, wrap the joint in this, and close up all the openings carefully by wetting the edges of the sheet of paste; lastly, pack up the haunch in a sheet of well buttered paper, put in the oven for about three hours, basting occasionally, then remove the paste and paper coverings, baste the haunch plentifully with butter, and when nearly done dredge some flour over it and some salt. Serve on a hot water dish.

Breast of Venison (Stewed).—One onion, 1 carrot, a bundle of sweet herbs, a few cloves, pepper and salt, common stock, butter, 1 tablespoonful of flour, 1 squeeze of lemon.

Remove the bones and skin, roll it up and tie it with a string in the shape of a round of beef, put it into a stewpan with an onion and carrot, sliced, a bundle of sweet herbs, a few cloves and pepper and salt to taste, add common stock sufficient to come up to the piece of venison, cover up the stewpan and let the contents simmer gently for about three hours, turning the meat occasionally; when done strain as much of the liquor as will be wanted for sauce, into a saucepan containing a piece of butter, previously melted and well mixed with a tablespoonful of flour, stir the sauce on the fire until it thickens, then add a squeeze of lemon; pour it over the meat in a dish and serve.

Wild Ducks (Stewed).—Pepper, salt, flour, butter, gravy made of the giblets, neck, and some pieces of veal, 1 shallot, 1 bunch of sweet herbs, ½ cup of cream or rich milk in which an egg has been beaten, brown flour, one tablespoonful of wine, juice of half a lemon.

Prepare to parboil for ten minutes. Lay in cold water for half an hour. Cut into joints, pepper, salt and flour them. Fry a light brown in some butter. Put them in a stewpan and cover with gravy made from the giblets, necks, and some pieces of veal. Add a minced shallot, bunch of sweet herbs, salt and pepper. Cover and stew for half an hour or until tender, take out the duck, skim the gravy and strain; add half a cup of cream, or some rich milk in which an egg has been beaten, thicken with brown flour, and add the juice of half a lemon. The lemon juice must be beaten in slowly, or the cream may curdle. Boil up and pour over the ducks and serve.

MEATS

In purchasing beef secure meat of a deep red color, with the fat mingled with the lean, giving it a marbled appearance. The fat will be firm, and the color resembling grass butter. The smaller the breed, so much sweeter the meat. It will be better for eating, if kept a few days. Veal, lamb and pork (being white meat), will not keep more than a day or two.

BEEF.—For roasting, the sirloin and rib pieces are the best. The chief object is to prevent the escape of the juices, and if you are roasting in an oven, it is a very good plan to throw a cup of *boiling* water over the meat when it is first put in the oven. This will prevent the escape of the juices for a while, and will thoroughly warm through the meat.

MUTTON.—Choose this by the fineness of its grain, good color, and firm white fat. It is not the better for being young; if of a good breed and well-fed, it is better for age; but this only holds with wether-mutton; the flesh of the ewe is paler, and the texture finer. Ram-mutton is very strongly-flavored; the flesh is of a deep red, and the fat is spongy.

LAMB.—Observe the neck of a fore-quarter; if the vein is bluish it is fresh; if it has a green or yellow cast it is stale. In the hind-quarter, if there is a faint smell under the kidney, and the knuckle is limp, the meat is stale. If the eyes are sunken, the head is not fresh. Grass-lamb comes in season in April or May, and continues till August. House-lamb may be had in great towns almost all the year, but is in highest perfection in December and January.

PORK.—Pinch the lean, and if young it will break. If the rind is tough, thick, and cannot easily be impressed by the finger, it is old. A thin rind is a merit in all pork. When fresh, the flesh will be smooth and cool; if clammy, it is tainted. What is called measly pork is very unwholesome, and may be known by the fat being full of kernels, which in good pork is never the case. Pork fed at still-houses does not answer for curing any way, the fat being spongy. Dairy-fed pork is the best. A sucking pig, to be eaten in perfection, should not be more than three weeks old, and should be dressed the same day it is killed.

VEAL.—Veal should be perfectly white; if purchasing the loin, the fat enveloping the kidney should be white and firm. Veal will not keep so long as older meat, especially in hot or wet weather. Choose small and fat veal. It is in season from March to August.

Beef-Steak Pudding.—¾ lb. of flour, 6 oz. of beef suet, 2½ lbs. of rump or beefsteak, pepper and salt, 1 doz. oysters, ½ pint of stock.

Chop the suet finely, and rub it into the flour with your hands, sprinkling a little salt, then mix with water to a smooth paste; roll the paste to an eighth of an inch; line a quart pudding basin with the paste; cut the steak into thin slices, flour them, and season with pepper and salt; put the oysters and the liquor that is with them into a saucepan and bring it to the point of boiling; then remove from the fire and strain the liquor into a basin; then cut off the beards and the hard parts, leaving only the soft, roll the slices of steak, filling the basin with the meat and oysters; pour in the stock and liquor from the oysters. Cover with paste and boil three hours.

N. B.—Be sure the water is boiling before putting the pudding in.

Fillets of Beef (with Olives).—A piece of rump steak, pepper, salt, olives, onions, flour, stock, sauce.

Cut a piece of rump-steak into slices ½ of an inch thick, and trim them into shape. Melt plenty of butter in a baking-tin, lay the fillets of beef in this, and let them stand in a warm place for an hour or so; then sprinkle them with pepper and salt, and fry them in some very hot butter, turning them to let both sides color. Stone a quantity of olives and parboil them. Fry some onions a brown color in butter, add a little flour, and, when that is colored, as much stock as you want sauce, pepper, salt and spices to taste. Let the sauce boil, then strain it, add the olives, and serve when quite hot, with the fillets in a circle round them.

Grenadins of Beef.—Rump steak, bacon fat, rich stock of gravy, carrots, turnips, butter, flour, milk, pepper, salt and nutmeg.

Cut some rump steak in slices a little more than half an inch thick, trim them all to the same size in the shape of cutlets, and lard them thickly on one side with fine lardoons of bacon fat. Lay them out, the larded side uppermost, into a flat pan, and put into it as much highly-flavored rich stock or gravy as will come up to the grenadins without covering them. Cover the pan and place it in the oven to braise gently for an hour. Then remove the cover, baste the grenadins with the gravy, and let them remain uncovered in the oven till the larding has taken color; they are then ready. Take equal quantities of carrots and turnips cut into the shape of olives. Boil all these vegetables in salted water, then melt a piece of butter in a saucepan, add a tablespoonful of flour, stir in sufficient milk to make a sauce, add pepper, salt and a little grated nutmeg. Put all the vegetables into this sauce, of which there should be just enough to hold them together; toss them gently in it till quite hot. Dress them in the middle of a dish, round them dispose the grenadins in a circle; and, having removed the superfluous fat from their gravy, pour this round the grenadins, and serve.

Beefsteak Pie.—Forcemeat, 2 oz. of fat bacon, 2 oz. of bread crumbs, parsley, thyme, a small onion, mushrooms, seasoning for forcemeat, salt, pepper and nutmeg, 2 eggs, a tender rump-steak, shallot, gravy.

Make some forcemeat with 2 oz. of fat bacon, 2 oz. of bread crumbs, a little chopped parsley, thyme, a small onion and some mushrooms; add seasoning of salt, pepper and nutmeg, pound in mortar, moistening with the yolks of 2 eggs. Take a tender rump steak or the under cut of a sirloin of beef, cut it in thin slices, season with salt, pepper and a little shallot. Roll each slice like a sausage with some forcemeat inside, border a pie dish, put in the beef and forcemeat, fill it up with good gravy, flavored with Harvey sauce. Cover with puff paste; bake in a moderate oven. Make a hole in the top, and add some reduced gravy.

Fillets of Beef (a la Chateaubriand).—A piece of sirloin of beef, pepper, salt, oil.

A piece of the under cut of the sirloin of beef; trim off the fat neatly, and the skin next to it; cut it across the grain into slices 1½ in. thick, sprinkle them with pepper, dip them in oil, and broil over a clear fire, sprinkle with salt, and serve very hot in a dish garnished with potatoes sautées or soufflés. For potatoes sautées or soufflés see recipe under "Vegetables."

Corn Beef.—Four gal. of fresh water, ½ lb. of coarse brown sugar, 2 oz. of saltpetre, 7 lbs. of common salt.

Put 4 gal. of fresh water, ½ lb. of coarse brown sugar, 2 oz. saltpetre, 7 lbs. of common salt into a boiler, remove the scum as it rises, and, when well boiled, leave it to get cold. Put in the meat in the pickle, lay a cloth over it, and press the meat down with bricks or any weight.

Beef Cake (Cold Meat Cookery).—To each lb. of cold roast meat allow ¼ lb. of bacon or ham, a little pepper and salt, 1 bunch of minced savory herbs, 2 eggs.

Have your meat underdone and mince very finely, add the bacon, which must also be well minced; mix together, stir in the herbs and bind with 2 eggs; make into square cakes about ½ inch thick, fry in hot dripping, drain on blotting paper, and serve with gravy poured round.

Beef Croquettes.—One cupful cold beef, chopped fine, 1 cupful mashed potatoes, 2 tablespoonfuls finely minced parsley and 1 onion; season to taste; then add 1 well-beaten egg and mix thoroughly. Mould into balls, dip first in bread crumbs, then into beaten egg, fry in plenty of hot lard until a delicate brown. Eat very hot.

Bubble and Squeak (Cold Meat Cookery).—A few thin slices of cold boiled beef, a little butter, small cabbage, 1 sliced onion, pepper and salt to taste.

Fry the beef gently in the butter, place on a flat dish, and cover with fried greens. Savoys may be used. Boil until tender, press in colander, mince and then put in frying pan with butter and sliced onion, and a little salt and pepper.

Roast Bullock's Heart.—One bullock's heart, ¼ lb. suet, 5 oz. bread crumbs, ¼ pt. of milk, 1 tablespoonful of chopped parsley, 1 dessertspoonful of chopped mixed herbs, ¼ lb. of dripping or butter, 1 pt. of gravy or beef-tea. For the sauce: One small onion, a dessertspoonful of flour, salt and pepper, butter the size of an egg, a large spoonful of mushroom catsup.

Wash the heart in salt water, taking care to remove all the blood; wash in second water and dry with a clean cloth; be careful to dry it thoroughly; chop the suet as finely as possible, mix with some bread crumbs the suet, parsley, herbs, salt and pepper; lastly, put in the milk, then proceed to fill all the cavities of the heart with the stuffing; take a piece of paper, grease it well with butter or dripping, place this over the cavities and tie it on tightly with string; put 1 oz. of dripping into the pan, and baste the heart occasionally; when gravy boils, cut up the onion, sprinkling with pepper and salt, and add to the gravy; allow it to stew gently until about 5 minutes before the heart is done; skim occasionally; when done strain the liquor into another saucepan, put the butter, and allow it to melt a minute or two; then add the flour and mix smoothly together; then pour in slowly the liquor, stirring until it boils and thickens. Then dish up, remove paper, and add to the sauce the mushroom catsup. Immediately pour this sauce round the heart and serve.

Stuffed Steak—Take a good sized steak—either round or flank will do—pound until tender. Have ready a dressing made of bread crumbs well seasoned, with bits of butter and onion or parsley chopped through it. Spread the steak with this, roll and tie firmly. Brown 3 tablespoonfuls of flour in your pan, work in a little butter and thin with cold water. Put the steak in the pan, and baste frequently as it bakes in a moderate oven.

Beef Omelet—Three lbs. of beefsteak, ½ lb. of suet, salt and pepper, a little sage, eggs, 6 Boston crackers.

Three lbs. of beefsteak, ½ lb. of suet, chopped fine; salt, pepper, and a little sage, 3 eggs, 6 Boston crackers rolled; make into a roll and bake.

Beef (Stewed)—One tablespoonful of butter, 2 sliced onions, 12 whole cloves, allspice, ½ teaspoonful salt, ¼ teaspoonful of black pepper, 1 pt. of cold water, 2 or 3 lbs. of tender beef, a little flour, a few sprigs of sweet basil.

In a stewpan place a large tablespoonful of butter, in which fry until quite brown two sliced onions, adding, while cooking, 12 whole cloves; ditto allspice; ½ teaspoonful of salt, and half that quantity of black pepper; take from the fire, pour 1 pt. of cold water, wherein lay 2 or 3 lbs. of tender lean beef cut in small, thick pieces; cover closely, and let all stew gently 2 hours, adding, just before serving, a little flour thickening. A few sprigs of sweet basil is an improvement.

Irish Stew—Cut three pounds of the neck of beef into small pieces, put in a saucepan and cover with half a gallon of boiling water, add a teaspoonful of salt, 2 sliced onions and 3 or 4 pepper-corns, and simmer gently for 2 hours. Pare and quarter half a dozen potatoes, add to the meat, and cook half an hour longer; thicken with the beaten yolk of an egg and a tablespoonful of butter rolled in flour.

Hamburg Steak—This is a nice way to cook Hamburg steak: Chop fine 1 pound of round steak, add 2 small onions, chopped fine, and pepper and salt to taste. Flour your hands, take two tablespoonfuls of the mixture and make into small flat cakes. Have a large lump of butter very hot in your frying-pan, drop in the cakes and fry brown on either side. Some people make a gravy by adding a couple teaspoonfuls of flour to the butter in the pan, stirring in half a pint of cold water, with salt and pepper, and letting it boil up.

Hash—Put 1½ teacups of boiling water into a saucepan, and make a thin paste with a teaspoonful of flour and a tablespoonful of water. Stir and boil it for 5 minutes. Add half a teaspoonful of black pepper, rather more of salt, and 1 tablespoonful of butter. Chop cold beef into fine hash, removing all tough, gristly pieces; put the meat into a tin pan; pour over it the gravy above mentioned, and let it heat ten minutes or so, but not cook. If preferred, add equal quantity of chopped boiled potatoes, and if you have the gravy of yesterday's dinner, you may use it instead of the made gravy, and you will need less pepper and salt and butter.

Beef Tongue—If it has been dried and smoked before it is dressed it should be soaked over night, but if only pickled, a few hours will be sufficient. Put it in a pot of cold water over a slow fire for an hour or two before it comes to a boil; then let it simmer gently for from three to four hours, according to its size; ascertain when it is done by probing it with a skewer. Take the skin off, and before serving surround the root with a paper frill.

Jellied Tongue—Boil until done one large beef's tongue, saving a pint of the liquor; remove the skin, allow it to get perfectly cold and slice as for the table. In half a pint of water dissolve thoroughly two ounces of gelatine; carefully take from a teacupful of browned veal gravy all the grease, stir in a small tablespoonful of sugar, one tablespoonful of burned sugar to color the jelly, and three tablespoonfuls of vinegar, then the liquor in which the tongue was boiled; mix in well the dissolved gelatine, then a pint of boiling water; strain through a jelly-bag. As soon as it begins to set, pour a little jelly into the bottom of the mould, add a layer of tongue, then more jelly, until it is full; set in a cold place. When wanted, dip the mould an instant into hot water, and turn the contents into a dish, which should be garnished with lettuce leaves, nasturtium flowers or sprigs of celery.

PORK

Pork Pie—½ lb. of lard, 1 lb. of pork (leg or loin), seasoning, 1 lb. of flour and an egg, ½ glass of cold water.

Put the lard and water into rather a large saucepan; place upon the fire and allow to boil (take care it does not boil over, or it will catch fire). Cut the pork into pieces about an inch square; when the lard and water are quite boiling pour into the middle of the flour and mix with a spoon. When the paste is cool enough knead it well, it must be rather stiff; cut off a quarter of the paste, and the remainder mould into the shape of a basin, pressing it inside; shape it evenly all round, it should be about ½ inch in thickness; dip the pieces of pork in cold water, seasoning well with pepper and salt, then place in the mould of paste as closely as possible. If liked, a little chopped sage can be sprinkled over the pork; then take the rest of the paste, roll it, and cut to the size of the top of the mould, taking care to have it the same size as the inside; break an egg and divide the yolk from the white; with a paste-brush dip into the white of egg and brush the edge of the paste; then place this on the top of the pie, pressing the edges well. Any trimmings of paste that are left cut into little leaves, dip into the white of egg, and stick them on top of the pie; then wet the pie all over with the yolk of the egg and bake for about 2 hours.

Pork (Hashed)—Some remains of cold roast pork, pepper and salt to taste, 2 onions, 2 blades of mace, 1 teaspoonful of flour, 1 teaspoonful of vinegar, 2 cloves, ½ pint of gravy.

Take the onions, chop and fry them a nice brown; then take the pork and cut it into thin slices, seasoning with pepper and salt to taste, and add these to the rest of the above ingredients; stew it for about half an hour gently, and serve with sippets of toasted bread.

Sucking Pig (Roast)—Pig, 8 oz. of bread-crumbs, 16 sage leaves, pepper and salt, tablespoonful of butter, salad oil to baste with, tablespoonful of lemon juice, ½ pint of gravy.

Stuff the pig with finely grated bread-crumbs, minced sage, pepper and salt, and a tablespoonful of butter. Take care these are well blended. After stuffing the pig sew up the slit neatly, truss the legs back, to allow the inside to be roasted, put in oven, and directly it is dry have ready some butter tied in a piece of thin cloth, and rub the pig with this in every part. Continue this operation several times while roasting; do not allow the pig to burn in any part. Then take ½ pint of gravy, 1 tablespoonful of lemon juice, add the gravy that flowed from the pig; pour a little of this over the pig, and the remainder send to the table in a tureen. Instead of butter for basting many cooks use salad oil, as this makes the crackling crisp. Before dishing cut off the head and part the body down the middle, and lay on the dish back to back. Take care that it is sent to table very hot, and serve with apple sauce. It will take about 2 hours for a small pig to roast.

Pork Cheese—About 2 lbs. of cold roast pork, a dessertspoonful of chopped-up parsley, 5 sage leaves, pepper and salt, a bunch of savory herbs, 2 blades of mace, a little nutmeg, ½ teaspoonful of minced lemon peel, sufficient gravy to fill the mould.

Cut the pork into pieces, but do not chop; there should be about ¼ of fat to 1 pound lean; sprinkle with pepper and salt, pound the spices thoroughly and mince as finely as possible the parsley, sage, lemon peel and herbs; then mix all this nicely together. Place in mould and fill with gravy. Bake a little over an hour. When perfectly cold turn out.

To Boil a Ham—Let it soak in cold water for 24 hours before putting it on the fire, cover it with cold water and boil slowly. When it can be easily probed with a skewer lift it out and take off the skin, boiling it again for 1 hour. Leave it in the water it is boiled in till quite cold, then grate burnt bread over it and trim with frills of cut paper.

VEAL

Roast Veal (Stuffed)—Eight oz. of bruised bread crumbs, 4 oz. of chopped suet, shallot, thyme, marjoram and winter savory, 2 eggs, salt and pepper.

To 8 oz. of bruised crumbs of bread add 4 oz. of chopped suet, shallot, thyme, marjoram and winter savory, all chopped fine; 2 eggs, salt and pepper to season; mix all these ingredients into a firm, compact kind of paste, and use this stuffing to fill a hole or pocket which you will have cut with a knife in some part of the piece of veal, taking care to fasten it in with a skewer. A piece of veal weighing 4 lbs. would require rather more than an hour to cook it thoroughly before a small fire.

Veal (Stewed)—Two qts. of water, 1 peeled onion, a few blades of mace, a little salt, ½ lb. of rice, butter, chopped parsley.

Break the shank bone, wash it clean, and put it into 2 qts. of water, 1 onion peeled, a few blades of mace and a little salt; set over a quick fire, and remove the scum as it rises; wash carefully ½ lb. of rice, and when the veal has cooked for about an hour skim it well and throw in the rice; simmer for ¾ of an hour slowly; when done put the meat in a deep dish and the rice around it. Mix a little drawn butter, stir in some chopped parsley, and pour over the veal.

Veal and Ham Pie—Forcemeat balls, 2 or 3 eggs, ham and veal, mushrooms, gravy, pie crust, jelly, onions, herbs, lemon peel, salt, cayenne, parsley, whites of eggs.

Cut some thin slices off the leg or neck of veal, free them from skin and gristle, lard them well, and season with salt and pepper. Have some eggs boiled hard and thin slices of ham. Make some forcemeat balls with fat bacon, the trimmings of the veal, chopped onions, parsley and sweet herbs, grated lemon peel, salt, cayenne, and pounded mace. Pound all in a mortar, and bind with 1 or 2 eggs. Line a pie with good paste, and fill it with layers (not too close), first one of ham, then one of veal, of forcemeat balls, of the eggs (cut in halves), and so on; a few mushrooms may be added; pour in some gravy; lastly, a layer of thin bacon, and cover all with tolerably thick crust, glaze. Bake for about 4 hours in a moderate oven. Make a hole in the top, and insert some good savory jelly—made with an ox or calf's foot, knuckle of veal, and trimming of bacon and ham well flavored with onions, sweet herbs and lemon peel, and cleared with the whites of egg. Leave till quite cold, then it can be cut with a sharp knife into slices.

Veal Pudding—Slice boiled veal about ½ an inch in thickness; butter a pudding dish and have ready 2 cupfuls of boiled rice; put first a layer of rice, then one of meat; season to taste, and add, if you like, a little chopped sage. Beat 1 egg into 1 cupful of milk; add a little salt and pour over the pudding; bake ¾ of an hour.

Veal Cake—One-half lb. veal cutlets, 1 rasher of ham, 2 hard-boiled eggs, a little veal stuffing, and ½ oz. of gelatine.

Cut the eggs into slices and arrange them at the bottom and sides of a pie-dish. Cut the veal and ham into rather small pieces; arrange them in layers, with a little stuffing and egg between, and a small quantity of water, pepper and salt. Cover with a plain crust, in which make two holes. Bake very slowly for 2 hours.

Before it is done have ready the gelatine dissolved in ½ teacupful of boiling water, with pepper and salt. Pour this into the holes in the crust. Shake it down well to mix together. Turn out when cold.

Veal (Marbled)—Spice, butter, tongue and veal.

Some cold roasted veal, season with spice, beat in a mortar; skin a cold boiled tongue, cut up and pound it to a paste, adding to it nearly its weight of butter; put some of the veal into a pot, and strew in lumps of the pounded tongue; put in another layer of the veal and then more tongue; press it down and pour clarified butter on top; this cuts very prettily like veined marble. White meat of fowls may be used instead of veal.

Veal Scallop—Pepper and salt, crackers, milk and gravy from meat, 2 eggs, butter.

Chop some cold roast or stewed veal very fine; put a layer on the bottom of a pudding dish well buttered; season with pepper and salt; next have a layer of finely-powdered crackers; wet with a little milk or some of the gravy from the meat. Proceed until the dish is full; spread over all a thick layer of cracker-crumbs, seasoned with salt and wet into a paste with milk and 2 beaten eggs. Stick pieces of butter all over it, cover closely, and bake half an hour; then remove the cover and bake long enough to brown nicely. Do not get it too dry.

Veal Cutlets—Four lbs. of the best end of the neck of veal, ½ teaspoonful of minced thyme, rind of a small lemon, 1 bunch of parsley, 1 tablespoonful of butter, 1 teaspoonful of lemon juice, 1 egg, pepper and salt, bread-crumbs, ½ lb. of bacon.

To shape the cutlets, saw off the end of the rib bone, cut off the chine bone also, which lies at the back of the cutlets; then form the cutlets to a neat shape. Mince thyme and lemon rind and parsley as finely as possible; melt the butter, and add these ingredients to it; add also the egg, pepper and salt, and beat all up together; then rub very finely some crumbs of bread; dip each cutlet into the mixture, then cover with bread-crumbs; when the gridiron is perfectly warm arrange the cutlets upon it. Have the fire clear and bright, but do not allow them to cook too fast or the bread-crumbs will burn before the cutlets are cooked through; allow them to brown nicely on both sides; about 15 minutes will be the time. Serve on a wall of mashed potatoes in a circle; fill the center of dish with rolls of bacon and with a nice brown sauce. (See "Sauces.")

For Rolls—Cut some neat slices of bacon, roll them up and run a skewer through each; place this in the oven for about 5 minutes, then remove the skewer and arrange in center of dish.

Veal Croquettes—Boil 1½ lbs. of veal—or use that left from roast. Mince very fine, add two eggs, ½ cup of rolled crackers, salt and pepper. Make into small balls or cakes, roll in flour and fry in butter, or put in wire basket and fry in lard. Serve on napkin.

Hashed Calf's Head (à la Poulette)—Calf's head, 1 oz. of butter, 2 tablespoonfuls of flour, ½ pint of white stock, a few button mushrooms, white pepper and salt to taste, 2 eggs, juice of a lemon, parsley.

Cut the remnants of a boiled head into uniform pieces the size of half an apple. Melt in a saucepan 1 or 2 ounces of butter, according to the quantity of meat to be hashed; amalgamate with it 1 or 2 tablespoonfuls of flour, then stir in ½ pint, more or less, of white stock. Stir well, then add a few button mushrooms, white pepper and salt to taste, and let the sauce boil for 10 minutes. Put the saucepan by the side of the fire, and lay the pieces of calf's head in it; let them get hot slowly, but not boil. Just before serving stir in off the fire the yolks of two eggs, beaten up with the juice of a lemon, and strained; also a small quantity of either tarragon or parsley very finely minced.

Veal (Braised Loin of)—Veal, 2 oz. of butter, 1 carrot, 1 onion, a little parsley, sweet herbs, a leaf or two of basil, a bay leaf, a crust of bread browned brown, a little flour, and a little stock.

About 2 oz. of butter, 1 carrot, 1 onion, a little parsley, sweet herbs, a leaf or two of basil, and a bay leaf; brown a large crust of bread and put it in a stewpan with the above things, and fry them until they are brown; then flour the meat and brown it well, putting it back in the saucepan; add a little stock, and baste it in the gravy till done, and keep turning the meat. Simmer 4 pounds for 3 or 4 hours.

MUTTON

Mutton Cutlets—This is an entrée always ready to hand, but it must be carefully and neatly prepared. A dish of well-dressed mutton cutlets is truly "a dish to put before a king;" whereas greasy, fat, gristly meats, called for the nonce cutlets, offend the taste of the least fastidious. The first thing to attend to is the cutting and trimming of the cutlets neatly. Take a piece of the best end of the neck of mutton, saw off the bones short, remove gristle and fat, and the cutlets about one-third of an inch in thickness, shape and trim them neatly, beat them with a cutlet bat dipped in water, and then proceed to cook them by any of the following recipes:

Pepper, salt, and broil them over a brisk fire; serve them with mashed or sauté potatoes in the center of the dish.

Season as above, and before broiling dip them in oil or oiled butter. Serve with

Soubise Sauce—Peel and blanch 4 onions, cool in water; drain, put them in a stewpan with enough water or white stock to cover; add some cayenne, bay leaf, a little mace, a small piece of ham or bacon; keep the lid closely shut and simmer gently until tender; take them out, drain them thoroughly, press through a sieve or tammy-cloth, add ½ pt. of bechamel sauce made thick. Put in a stewpan a little parsley, 1 clove, a small piece of bay leaf, sweet herbs, and 1 pt. of white stock freed from fat; when boiled long enough to extract the flavor of the herbs, etc., strain it, boil up quickly till reduced to half the quantity; mix a tablespoonful of arrowroot with ½ pt. of milk or cream, pour on the reduced stock and simmer for 10 minutes.

A Dainty Dish — For a dainty dish of cold meat, boil a leg of lamb in water enough to cover, to which add a handful of cloves and whole allspice and a stick or two of cinnamon. Let it stand in the water in which it was boiled to become cold. Slice very thin. Beef can be cooked in the same style.

Mutton Pudding — 2 lbs. of the chump end of the loin, weighed after being boned; suet crust (proportions — 6 oz. of suet to each lb. of flour), 1 tablespoonful of minced onion, pepper and salt.

Cut the meat into thin slices, sprinkling with pepper and salt. For the suet crust use the above proportions of flour and suet, mixing with a little salt and pepper, milk or water, to the proper consistency. Line your dish with the crust, lay in the meat, nearly fill the dish with water; add the minced onion and cover with the crust.

Irish Stew (Mutton) — 2 lbs. thick mutton cutlets, 4 lbs. potatoes, 1 onion, pepper and salt, ½ pint of water.

Prepare the potatoes as for boiling, cut them in halves. Slice the onion very thinly. Place a layer of potatoes at the bottom of the stewpan, then a layer of cutlets, and a sprinkling of onion, pepper and salt; then another layer of potatoes and so on until all is used up. Pour in the water, cover the pan closely and simmer gently for 2 hours.

Mutton (Roast Leg of, Stuffed) — A leg weighing 7 or 8 pounds, 2 shallots, forcemeat.

Make forcemeat, to which add the minced shallots. Get the butcher to take the bone from the mutton, as he can do it without spoiling the skin; if very fat, cut off some of it. Fill up the hole with the forcemeat, then sew it up to prevent it falling out, tie up neatly and roast about 2½ hours or a little longer. When ready to serve, remove the string and serve with a good gravy.

Lamb (Stewed) — A breast of lamb, 1 tablespoonful of salt, 1 qt. of canned peas, 1 tablespoonful of wheat flour, 3 tablespoonfuls of butter, pepper to taste.

Cut the scrag, or breast of lamb, in pieces, and put in a stewpan with water enough to cover it. Cover the stewpan closely and let it simmer or stew for fifteen or twenty minutes; take off the scum, then add a tablespoonful of salt and a quart of canned peas; cover the stewpan and let them stew for half an hour; work a small tablespoonful of wheat flour with three tablespoonfuls of butter, and stir it into the stew; add pepper to taste; let it simmer together for ten minutes.

Lamb Chops — A little butter, a little water, enough potatoes to fill a small dish, 1 teacupful of cream.

Lamb chops are excellent cooked this way: Put them in a frying-pan with a very little water, so little that it will boil away by the time the meat is tender; then put in lumps of butter with the meat and let it brown slowly; there will be a brown, crisp surface, with a fine flavor. Serve for breakfast with potatoes cooked thus: Choose the small ones and let them boil till they are tender; drain off the water, and pour over them, while still in the kettle, at least one teacupful of cream; mash them smoothly in this.

Shoulder of Mutton (Rolled with Oysters) — A little pepper, a piece of mace, about 2 dozen oysters, a little water, an onion, a few peppercorns, about ½ pint of good gravy, a tablespoonful of flour and butter.

Hang it some days; then salt it well for two days; bone it, and sprinkle it with pepper and a piece of mace pounded; lay some oysters over it, and roll the meat up tight and tie it. Stew it in a small quantity of water, with an onion and a few peppercorns, till quite tender. Have ready a little good gravy, and some oysters stewed in it; thicken this with flour and butter, and pour over the mutton, when the tape is taken off. The stewpan should be kept covered.

Sweetbreads — Half boil them, and stew them in a white gravy; add cream, flour, butter, nutmeg, salt and white pepper. Or do them in brown sauce seasoned. Or parboil them, and then cover them with crumbs, herbs and seasoning, and brown them in a Dutch oven. Serve with butter and mushroom catsup or gravy. N. B. — If there is no oven at hand, they may be toasted before the fire upon a toasting fork.

Fried Sweetbreads — After they are parboiled and cold, split in halves and cut into pieces as large as very large oysters, wipe dry and dip in beaten egg, then in fine cracker crumbs; fry in hot lard or butter same as oysters; sprinkle with salt before dipping in egg. Serve hot; garnish with parsley.

Sweetbreads (Larded) — A couple of sweetbreads, a few strips of bacon, onions, carrots, sweet herbs, pepper, salt, spice to taste, a small quantity of rich stock.

Trim a couple of sweetbreads, soak them half an hour in tepid water, then parboil them for a few minutes, and lay them in cold water; when quite cold take them out, dry them and lard them quickly with fine strips of bacon. Put a slice of fat bacon in a stewpan with some onions, carrots, a bunch of sweet herbs, pepper, salt and spices to taste, and a small quantity of rich stock; lay the sweetbreads on this, and let them gently stew till quite done, basting the top occasionally with the liquor. When cooked, strain the liquor, skim off superfluous fat, reduce it almost to a glaze, brown the larded side of the sweetbreads with a salamander, and serve with sauce over them.

Kidneys (a la Brochette) — Plunge some mutton kidneys in boiling water; split them down the center, but do not separate them; peel and pass a skewer across them to keep them open, pepper, salt, and dip them into melted butter, broil them over a clear fire on both sides, doing the cut side first; remove the skewers, have ready some maître d'hôtel butter, that is butter beaten up with chopped parsley, salt, pepper, and a little lemon juice. Put a small piece in the hollow of each kidney, and serve very hot.

Stewed Kidneys — 4 kidneys, ½ a small onion, 1 oz. butter, 2 teaspoonfuls of flour, pepper and salt to taste.

Cut the kidneys in small pieces, and roll them in flour; chop the onion small, and fry with the pieces of kidney in the butter until brown. Then add the pepper, salt, and enough cold water to cover them, and stew very gently for an hour. Thicken with the flour a few minutes before done, and serve very hot.

CURRIES.

MOST people have a liking for a really good curry; but how very rarely it is to be obtained in America, unless at the house of some one who has passed a good many years in India. The dish miscalled a curry is frequently set before people, but too often as far as possible removed from the real and appetizing plat which a good Indian cook will send to table. The meat is tough, has most likely been boiled instead of gently simmered, the sauce, or thick gravy, is hot enough in all conscience, but it tastes only of curry powder of an inferior kind; the rice is a sloppy mess, and the result is a fiery, leathery sort of indigestible hash, instead of a sweet, acid, highly but agreeably flavored, perfectly cooked and digestible dish, fit to set before a prince. Any cook, of whatever nationality, who has really mastered the art of stewing properly, that is, very gently and slowly, can cook a curry; the real difficulties lie in procuring good curry powder or curry paste.

Curry Powder — 1 lb. pale turmeric seed, ½ lb. cumin seed, ½ lb. black pepper, ½ lb. coriander seed, 2 oz. cayenne pepper, ½ lb. Jamaica ginger, 10 oz. caraway seed, ½ oz. cardamoms.

Purchase the ingredients of a first-class druggist. Additional heat can be obtained by those who like very hot curries, if red Chile powder be added according to taste. Mix together all the ingredients well powdered, and place before the fire or in the sun, stirring occasionally. Keep in well corked bottles.

Indian Curry — 2 large tablespoonfuls of curry powder, a dessertspoonful of salt, the same of black pepper, 4 onions, ½ lb. butter, 1½ lbs. meat, ½ pint of milk, lemon juice or Chile vinegar.

Two large tablespoonfuls of curry powder, a dessertspoonful of salt, the same of black pepper. Fry and chop very fine four onions, then moisten the curry powder with water, and put it in a stewpan with all the above ingredients, and a quarter of a pound of butter. Let it stew for twenty minutes, stirring all the time to prevent burning, then add one and a half pounds of cold or fresh meat, or any fowl or rabbit, cut into short, thick pieces, without fat, add half a pint of milk or good stock to make the curry thick. Boil all up at once, and let it stew gently for three or four hours. When ready add lemon juice or Chile vinegar.

Curried Rabbit — 1 rabbit, ½ lb. butter, 1 apple, 2 onions, 2 tablespoonfuls curry powder, ½ pint of cream, 1 pint stock, 1 lemon, a saltspoonful of salt.

Melt the butter over the fire, peel and chop the onions as finely as possible, then put them into the melted butter to fry a light brown. After the rabbit has been properly prepared for cooking, wash well and dry in a cloth, cut in pieces of equal size. After straining the butter from the onions, return the former to the stewpan, put in pieces of rabbit, and allow to fry for ten or fifteen minutes, turning occasionally. Peel and core the apple, and chop as finely as possible. When the meat is done add to it two tablespoonfuls of curry powder and the salt, stirring for five minutes, then add the fried onion, chopped apple and a pint of good stock. Allow to simmer for two hours, at the end of the time add the cream, squeeze the juice from the lemon into the stewpan. It is then ready to serve.

N. B.—Veal or chicken can be used, if preferred.

Curry of Mutton — Mutton, 1 onion, butter the size of an egg, curry powder, a little salt, a cup of cream.

Slice a medium-sized onion, and put it with a large lump of butter in a saucepan; let it cook slowly for five minutes. Cut the mutton in neat pieces; sprinkle curry powder over them, also a little salt, and just before putting in the saucepan pour a part of a cup of sweet cream over them. Let this all simmer gently for half an hour, so that the ingredients will become thoroughly mixed.

A Dry Malay Curry — A cauliflower, 2 onions, a sour apple, a pint of shrimps, slices of cold mutton, 2 oz. butter, a large tablespoonful of curry powder, a lemon, a small teaspoonful of salt.

Pick a cauliflower into small pieces and well wash them; chop two onions and one sour apple, pick a pint of fresh boiled shrimps, cut some slices of cold mutton about half an inch thick, knead two ounces of butter with a large tablespoonful of curry powder, and a small teaspoonful of salt. Put the butter, onions and apple into a stewpan, and fry till brown, then add the cauliflower and shrimps. Shake the saucepan frequently, and let it simmer for an hour and a half, adding the slices of mutton towards the end of the time, that they may be heated through. Finally, add the juice of a lemon. Place the slices of mutton round the dish with the cauliflower, etc., in the middle. Serve very hot, with a separate dish of boiled rice.

Curried Lobster.—Lobster, cream, rice.

Take the flesh of a lobster (or a tin of lobster does very well for this dish), make curry gravy with plenty of cream; pour into a saucepan with the lobster, warm it just to boiling point; serve with rice round.

Boiled Rice for Curry.—Put the rice on the stove in cold water, and allow it to come to a boil for a minute or two. Strain, dry and put in stewpan without lid at the back of the stove, to allow the steam to evaporate; shake into dish very light; a few drops of lemon juice put in directly after it boils will make the grains separate better.

Curried Eggs.—6 eggs, 2 onions, butter, a tablespoonful of curry powder, 1 pint of broth, a cup of cream, arrowroot.

Slice the onions and fry in butter a light brown, add curry powder, and mix with the broth, allowing to simmer till tender; then put in cream, and thicken with arrowroot; simmer for five minutes, then add 6 hard-boiled eggs, cut in slices.

Curried Beef.—Beef, 2 oz. butter, 2 onions, a tablespoonful of curry powder, ½ pint milk, lemon juice.

Slice the onions and fry in butter a light brown, mix well with the curry powder, adding the beef, cut into small pieces about an inch square, pour in milk and allow to simmer for thirty minutes, stirring frequently; when done add lemon juice. It greatly improves the dish to build a wall of mashed potatoes or boiled rice around it.

Potato Curry (1).—Cold potatoes, onion, salt and pepper, curry powder to taste, egg, bread crumbs, and gravy.

Mash cold potatoes with minced onion, salt, pepper, and curry powder to taste; form into small balls with egg and bread crumbs, fry crisp, serve with rich gravy flavored with curry powder.

Potato Curry (2).—Potatoes, onions, butter, curry powder, a little starch, cream, lemon juice.

Fry some sliced raw potatoes and onions slightly in butter with a little curry powder, then simmer until done in a very little stock; add some cream, butter and lemon juice before serving.

Potato Curry (3).—Curry powder, mashed potatoes, milk.

Put a good pinch of curry powder in mashed potatoes, allowing rather more butter and milk than usual. This last is a delicious accompaniment to chicken.

Curry (Dry).—A few onions, ¼ lb. butter, 1½ lbs. steak, a little flour and curry powder, salt to taste, juice of 1 lemon.

Slice up a good-sized onion, and fry it a golden color in ¼ lb. of butter; cut up 1½ lbs. of fresh steak into pieces the size of dice. Dredge them well with flour and curry powder, add a little salt, and squeeze the juice of a lemon over them; then fry them lightly in the butter in which the onions have been previously cooked. Add all together, and stew gently in a saucepan for ½ hour.

GRAVIES.

GRAVY may be made quite as good of the skirts of beef, and the kidney, as of any other meat, prepared in the same way.

An ox-kidney, or milt, makes good gravy, cut all to pieces, and prepared as other meat; and so will the shank end of mutton that has been dressed, if much be not wanted.

The shank-bones of mutton are a great improvement to the richness of gravy; but first soak them well, and scour them clean.

A Good Beef Gravy (for Poultry or Game).—½ lb. lean beef, ½ pint cold water, 1 small onion, a saltspoonful of salt, a little pepper, a tablespoonful of mushroom catsup or sauce, ½ teaspoonful of arrowroot.

Cut the beef into small pieces and put it and the water into a stewpan. Add the onion and seasoning, and simmer gently for three hours. A short time before it is required, mix the arrowroot with a little cold water, pour into the gravy while stirring, add the mushroom catsup and allow it just to come to a boil. Strain into a tureen and serve very hot.

Savory Gravy (Thick).—1 onion, butter, a tablespoonful of flour, ½ pint of broth or stock, pepper and salt, a small quantity of Worcestershire sauce.

Mince one onion fine, fry it in butter to a dark brown, and stir in a tablespoonful of flour. After one minute add ½ pint of broth or stock, pepper and salt, and a very small quantity of Worcester sauce.

Gravy for General Use.—1 lb. of lean beef cut in small pieces and floured, put into a saucepan with 12 cloves, 24 peppercorns, 6 blades of mace, some nutmeg, pepper, salt, and 1½ pints of water.

Simmer gently for 2 hours, stirring frequently. Strain before using. Add a little of the browning for soups and gravies.

Plain Gravy.—An onion, a little butter, ½ pint of stock, pepper and salt, a small piece of lean ham or bacon, a dessertspoonful of Worcester sauce, a sprig of parsley and thyme.

Mince an onion finely, fry it in butter to a dark brown color, then add ½ of a pint of stock, pepper and salt to taste, a small piece of lean ham or bacon minced small, a little Worcester sauce, a sprig of thyme and one of parsley. Let it boil five or ten minutes; put it by till wanted, and strain it before serving.

Gravy for Hashes.—Remnants and bones of the joint intended for hashing, a pinch of salt and pepper, ½ teaspoonful of whole allspice, a bunch of savory herbs, a saltspoonful of celery salt or ½ a head of celery, an onion, a small piece of butter, a little corn flour, and boiling water.

Put the bones (having previously chopped them), with the remnants of the meat, salt, pepper, spice, herbs and celery into a stewpan. Cover with boiling water and allow it to simmer for two hours. Cut up the onion in neat slices and fry in butter to a pale brown. Then mix slowly with the gravy from bones. Boil fifteen minutes, strain, then return to stewpan. Flavor with catsup or any flavoring that may be preferred. Thicken with butter and flour and just allow it to come to the boil. Serve very hot.

Gravy for a Fowl (when there is no meat to make it from)—The feet, liver, gizzards and neck of the fowl, a little browned bread, a slice of onion, a sprig of parsley and thyme, some pepper and salt, 1 teaspoonful of mushroom catsup, a little flour and butter.

Wash the feet nicely, and cut them and the neck small; simmer them with a little bread browned, a slice of onion, a sprig of parsley and thyme, some pepper and salt, and the liver and gizzards in ½ pint water, till half wasted. Take out the liver, bruise it, and strain the liquor to it. Then thicken it with flour and butter, and add 1 teaspoonful of mushroom catsup.

Veal Gravy—Bones, any cold remnants of veal, 1½ pints water, 1 onion, 1 saltspoonful minced lemon peel, a little salt, a blade of mace, a few drops of the juice of the lemon, butter and flour.

Place all the ingredients (excepting the lemon juice and flour) into a stewpan, and allow them to simmer for 1 hour. Strain into a basin. Add a thickening of butter and flour mixed with a little water, also the lemon juice. Give one boil and serve very hot. Flavor with tomato sauce or catsup.

Cheap Gravy for Fowls, Etc.—Boil the neck and feet of the fowl in ½ pint water with any slight seasonings of spices or herbs, or salt and pepper only; stew very slowly for 1 hour. Just before serving, take the gravy from the dripping-pan, drain off the fat, and strain the liquor from the neck to it; pass the gravy again through a strainer, add salt and pepper, heat it, and serve very hot.

Gravy for a Goose or Duck—Prepare in same way as for general use, with the addition of an onion and some sage.

SAUCES.

THE appearance and preparation of sauces are of the highest importance. Brown sauces should not be as thick as white ones, and should possess a decided character, so that, both whether sweet or sharp, plain or savory, they would bear out their names. Care is also to be taken that they blend and harmonize with the various dishes they are to accompany.

White Sauce—One pint milk, 2 or 3 mushrooms, 1 onion, 1 carrot, 1 bundle sweet herbs, whole pepper and salt to taste, a few cloves, a little mace, 1 oz. butter, and 1 gill cream.

Put into 1 pint milk 2 or 3 mushrooms, 1 onion and a carrot cut into pieces, 1 bundle of sweet herbs, whole pepper and salt to taste, a few cloves and a little mace; let the whole gently simmer for about an hour; put 1 ounce of butter into a saucepan, and stir on the fire until it thickens. Finish by stirring in 1 gill cream.

Horseradish Sauce—Two oz. horseradish, 5 tablespoonfuls milk or cream, 2 dessertspoonfuls vinegar, 1 teaspoonful sugar, ½ do. pepper.

Grate the horseradish, mix it with milk, sugar and pepper. Add the cream or milk very gradually, and heat the whole over the fire, stirring well all the time. If allowed to boil it will spoil. Serve with hot roast beef.

Sauce for Wild Fowl—Half pint gravy, 1 small onion, 3 or 4 leaves basil, a piece of the thin rind of a lemon, 1 dessertspoonful lemon juice.

Boil the gravy, onion and basil together for a few minutes, strain, and add the lemon juice. Seville orange juice may be used instead of lemon.

Standard Sauce for Fish—Maitre d'hotel butter is prepared by mixing together, cold, 1 tablespoonful each of butter and finely chopped parsley; add 1 teaspoonful of lemon juice and a little pepper and salt. Work well together, and when ready to serve the fish, spread it generously with the butter and set the dish in the mouth of the oven for a minute or two. The parsley must be as fine as powder.

Egg Sauce for Fish—Boil 2 eggs for 10 minutes, and then lay them in cold water for 5 minutes. Remove the shells, and mince them very fine. Heat ¼ lb. butter, mix eggs and butter well together, make them hot, and serve with salt fish.

Egg Sauce for Puddings—Beat yolk of 1 egg with a little sugar and cream, stir till it boils, then add a few drops of flavoring to taste.

Liver Sauce—Livers of any kind of poultry, butter, flour, minced shallots, gravy stock, a small pinch of sweet herbs, pepper, spices and salt, and juice of ½ lemon.

Scald the livers of the poultry, rabbits or hares and mince them finely. Melt a piece of butter in a saucepan, add a little flour to it and a small quantity of minced shallots. Let the whole fry for a minute or two, then add gravy stock in sufficient quantity to make a sauce, and a small pinch of powdered sweet herbs, and pepper, spices and salt to taste. Put in the minced livers and let the sauce boil 20 minutes, and at the time of serving add a small piece of fresh butter and the juice of ½ lemon.

Fennel Sauce—Fennel, 3 oz. butter, flour, pepper and salt, yolks of 2 eggs, juice of 1 lemon.

Blanch a small quantity in boiling salted water, take it out, dry it in a cloth, and chop it finely; melt 3 oz. fresh butter, add rather more than a tablespoonful flour, mix well, and put in pepper and salt to taste, and about a pint hot water; stir on the fire till the sauce thickens, then stir in the yolks of 2 eggs beaten up with the juice of a lemon and strained. Add plenty of chopped fennel, and serve.

Shrimp Sauce—Half pint shrimps, juice of ½ lemon, butter, a dust of cayenne.

Take ½ pint shrimps, pick out all the meat from the tails, pound the rest in a mortar with the juice of ½ lemon and a piece of butter; pass the whole through a sieve. Make 1 pint melted butter, put the meat from the tails into it, add a dust of cayenne, and when the sauce boils stir into it the shrimp butter that has come through the sieve, with or without a tablespoonful of cream.

Mock Cream Sauce — Pour ½ pint boiling milk on 1 teaspoonful arrowroot, previously mixed in a small quantity of cold milk. Stir the mixture well, and, when moderately warm, add the white of 1 egg well beaten. Place the whole over the fire, and stir it till it nearly boils.

Fruit Sauce — Half pint sugar, cinnamon, bay leaf, cloves, and any kind of fruit.

Put ½ lb. sugar and ½ pint water over the fire to boil, skim and boil 5 minutes, add to this a piece of stick cinnamon about 2 inches long, 1 bay leaf and 3 cloves; at the end of 5 minutes add ½ pint any kind of mashed fruit; for instance, apricots, stewed apples; in fact, any fruit that will go nicely with the pudding with which you expect to serve the sauce. Strain the whole through a sieve, flavor, and it is ready to serve.

Cauliflower Sauce — Two small cauliflowers, 1½ oz. butter, 1 tablespoonful flour, pepper and salt, yolks of 2 eggs, juice of a lemon.

Boil 2 small cauliflowers; when done, pick them out into sprigs and arrange them, heads downward, in a pudding basin, which must have been made quite hot; press them in gently, then turn them out dexterously on a dish, and pour over them the following sauce, boiling hot: Melt 1½ oz. butter in a saucepan, mix with it a tablespoonful of flour, and then add ½ pint of boiling water; stir till it thickens; add salt and white pepper to taste; then take the saucepan off the fire, and stir in the yolks of 2 eggs beaten up with the juice of a lemon and strained.

Dutch Sauce — Three tablespoonfuls vinegar, 1 lb. butter, yolks of 2 eggs, pepper and salt.

Put 3 tablespoonfuls vinegar in a saucepan, and reduce it on the fire to a third; add ¼ lb. butter and the yolks of 2 eggs. Place the saucepan on a slow fire, stir the contents continuously, and as fast as the butter melts add more, until 1 lb. is used. If the sauce becomes too thick at any time during the process, add a tablespoonful of cold water and continue stirring. Then put in pepper and salt to taste, and take great care not to let the sauce boil. When it is made — that is, when all the butter is used and the sauce is of the proper thickness — put the saucepan containing it into another filled with warm (not boiling) water until the time of serving.

Sweet Sauce — One tablespoonful flour, sugar or molasses, 1 oz. butter, 1 tablespoonful lemon juice.

Mix a tablespoonful of flour quite smooth in 4 tablespoonfuls water, then stir into it ½ pint boiling water, sugar or molasses to taste; stir over the fire until the sauce boils, when, if allowed, an ounce of butter may be added, with a tablespoonful of lemon juice. When sweetened with sugar, a little nutmeg or ground cinnamon may be used instead of lemon juice, if preferred. A tablespoonful of raspberry jam or any fruit syrup may be used to flavor the sauce, and is generally much liked.

Mayonnaise Dressing — Yolks of 2 hard-boiled eggs, mustard, vinegar, olive oil or butter.

Take the yolks of 2 hard-boiled eggs and mash smooth with ½ teaspoonful mustard and 2 tablespoonfuls olive oil; then add slowly ½ teacup vinegar; if olive oil is not liked, melted butter may be used instead.

Poor Man's Sauce — A good-sized onion, butter, ½ pint common stock or water, vinegar, parsley, pepper and salt, flour.

Mince a good-sized onion, not too finely, put it into a saucepan with a piece of butter equal to it in bulk. Fry till the onion assumes a light brown color, add ½ pint common stock or water and a small quantity of vinegar, pepper and salt to taste, and some minced parsley; then stir the sauce into another saucepan, in which a tablespoonful of flour and a small piece of butter have been mixed, over the fire. Let the sauce boil up, and it is ready.

A Cheap Brown Sauce — One pint brown stock, 1½ oz. flour, 2 oz. butter, 4 mushrooms, salt and pepper.

Put the butter into a stewpan and put it on the fire to melt; wash the mushrooms in cold water, cut off the stalks and peel them; when the butter is melted stir in the flour and mix to a smooth paste; then add the stock and mushrooms, and stir the sauce smoothly until it boils and thickens, then remove the stewpan to the back of the stove and let it simmer gently for 8 or 10 minutes; season with pepper and salt; be careful to skim off the butter as it rises to the top of the sauce. Should the sauce be not brown enough, a teaspoonful of caramel might be stirred into it; strain and serve.

Onion Sauce (Brown) — Two oz. butter, rather more than ½ pint of rich gravy, 6 large onions, pepper and salt.

Put into your stewpan the onions, sliced, fry them of a light brown color, with 2 oz. of butter; keep them stirred well to prevent them turning black; as soon as they are of a nice color, pour over the gravy, and simmer gently until tender; skim off all fat, add seasoning and rub the whole through a sieve; then put in a saucepan, and when it boils, serve.

Tomato Sauce — Ten lbs. ripe tomatoes, 1 pint best brown vinegar, 2 oz. salt, ½ oz. cloves, 1 oz. allspice, ½ lb. white sugar, 1 oz. garlic, ½ oz. black pepper, ¼ oz. cayenne pepper.

Wipe the tomatoes clean, and boil or bake till soft; then strain and rub through a sieve that will retain the seeds and skins. Boil the juice for an hour, then add the above ingredients (all the spices must be ground). Boil all together for a sufficient time, which may be known by the absence of any watery particle, and by the whole becoming a smooth mass; 5 hours will generally suffice. Bottle without straining into perfectly dry bottles, and cork securely when cold. The garlic must be peeled. The proportions of spice may be varied according to taste.

Oyster Sauce—Oysters, butter, flour, milk, blade of mace, bay leaf, pepper and salt, cayenne, a few drops of lemon juice.

Parboil the oysters in their own liquor, beard them, and reserve all the liquor. Melt a piece of butter in a saucepan, add a little flour, the oyster liquor, and enough milk to make as much sauce as is wanted. Put in a blade of mace and a bay leaf tied together, pepper and salt to taste, and the least bit of cayenne. Let the sauce boil, add the oysters, and as soon as they are quite hot remove the mace and bay leaf, stir in a few drops of lemon juice, and serve.

Worcester Sauce—Two tablespoonfuls Indian soy, 2 ditto walnut catsup, 1 dessertspoonful of salt, 1 teaspoonful cayenne pepper, 1 nutmeg (sliced thin); 1 doz. cloves, ½ oz. root ginger pounded, a little lemon peel, a small head of garlic divided into cloves, 1 pint vinegar, 3 oz. lump sugar.

Dissolve the sugar in a little of the vinegar over the fire, add the other ingredients; put all into a wide-necked bottle. It should stand for a month before using, and is better if shaken every day. At the end of the month pour off clear into bottles.

Chestnut Sauce—Remove the outer shell from some fine chestnuts, scald them in boiling water, and remove the inner skin. Stew them in good white stock till quite tender, drain, and while hot press them through a sieve. Put the pulp into a saucepan, add a small piece of butter, a little sugar, pepper and salt. Stir over the fire till quite hot, but do not let it boil, and serve.

Mushroom Sauce—Remove the stalks and gritty part from ½ pint of mushrooms; wash, drain, and put them into ½ pint of well-flavored gravy, simmer them till quite tender, drain them, and keep them hot. Melt 1 oz. butter in a saucepan, add to it 1 oz. flour, stir over the fire till brown; pour in the gravy, stirring till it boils. Arrange the mushrooms in the centre of the dish, the cutlets round them, and pour the sauce over.

Chile Sauce—One bu. ripe tomatoes, 2 doz. large onions; chop very fine and boil 1 hour; then add 1 pint salt, 2½ quarts vinegar, 6 red peppers chopped fine, 2 tablespoonfuls each of ground ginger and cinnamon, and 1 each of cloves and nutmeg. Boil steadily for about 2 hours; bottle and seal tightly.

Bread Sauce (for Poultry or Game)—Giblets, ½ lb. stale bread, 1 onion, 10 white peppers, 1 blade mace, salt, 2 tablespoonfuls cream.

Put the giblets into 1 pint water, add the onion, pepper, mace, salt. Allow it to simmer for 1 hour, then strain the liquor over the bread crumbs. Cover the stewpan and let it stand on the stove for 1 hour (do not allow it to boil), then beat the sauce up with a fork until it is nice and smooth. Allow it to boil 5 minutes, stirring well until it is thick, then add cream and serve hot.

Caper Sauce—Two oz. butter, 1 tablespoonful flour, 1 pint stock, pepper and salt, Worcester sauce, capers.

Put 2 oz. butter and 1 tablespoonful flour into a saucepan; stir the mixture on the fire until it acquires a brown color; add rather less than 1 pint boiling stock, free from fat; season with pepper, salt and a little Worcester sauce. When the sauce boils throw in plenty of capers; let it boil once more, and it is ready.

Sauce Hollandaise—Take a scant ½ cup good butter. Beat the butter to a cream and add the yolks of 3 eggs, beating them into the butter with the juice of ½ lemon. Add 1 sliced onion, 6 peppercorns and 1 bay leaf. Set the bowl containing the sauce in a basin of boiling water and stir it continually for a few moments. Then add a little boiling stock with a little grated nutmeg and 1 teaspoonful of salt. Continue stirring it for about 5 minutes longer, when it should be of the consistency of a custard and perfectly smooth. Strain it through a sieve, add 1 teaspoonful butter and serve.

Mint Sauce—Chop 1 bunch fresh mint fine, mix with 1 tablespoonful sugar, a pinch of salt and pepper, rub well together, and add ½ cup vinegar, with a squeeze of lemon juice.

STOCKS.

Common Stock—Take all the bones of joints, etc., that are available, carcasses and bones of poultry and game (not high), chop them all into convenient pieces and put them into a saucepan together with any scraps of meat, cooked or uncooked, resulting from remnants, the trimming of cutlets, etc. Add a couple of carrots, 1 onion, 1 bunch parsley, 1 bay leaf, a small sprig thyme, and 1 marjoram; salt to taste, a small quantity of white pepper and allspice mixed, and 2 or 3 cloves. Fill the saucepan with cold water until it covers the contents by 1 inch, and set it on the fire to boil slowly for about 4 hours; strain the liquor through a cloth into a basin and when cold, the cake of fat on the top being removed, the stock will be fit for use.

Gravy Stock—Place a layer of slices of onion in a saucepan holding 1 gal., over this a layer of fat bacon, and over all about 2 lbs. shin of beef chopped in small pieces; 1 pint common stock, or even water, being poured on the whole, set the saucepan on the fire for 1 hour, until the liquor is almost evaporated—what is called reduced to a "glaze"—then add sufficient cold common stock or cold water to cover contents of the saucepan, and 2 or 3 carrots cut in slices, 1 leek, 1 head celery (when in season), or some celery seed; 1 handful parsley, ½ clove garlic, 1 sprig marjoram and 1 of thyme, 1 bay leaf, 4 or 5 cloves, white pepper and salt to taste. After boiling for about 3 hours strain off the liquor, and, being absolutely freed from fat, it is ready for use.

Veal Stock — Fry a couple of onions, sliced, and 1 lb. lean veal cut in pieces in a saucepan with some butter until they assume a light color, then add ½ lb. ham chopped up small; and moisten with 1 pint common stock cold and perfectly free from fat. Let the liquor reduce almost to a "glaze" — then add 2 quarts cold common stock, 1 knuckle veal, or 2 calves' feet, a couple of carrots, head of celery, parsley, bay leaf, thyme, mace, pepper and salt, all in due proportion. After boiling 2 or 3 hours, strain free from fat.

VEGETABLES.

VEGETABLES should be carefully cleaned from insects, and nicely washed. Boil in plenty of water, and drain the moment they are done enough. If overboiled, they lose their beauty and crispness. To dress them with meat is wrong, except carrots with boiled beef.

To boil vegetables green, be sure the water boils when you put them in. Make them boil very fast. Don't cover, but watch them; and if the water has not slackened, you may be sure they are done when they begin to sink. Then take them out immediately. Hard water, especially if chalybeate, spoils the color. To boil green in hard water, put a teaspoonful of salt of wormwood into the water when it boils, before the vegetables are put in.

Vegetable Marrow (to Boil or Stew) — This excellent vegetable may be boiled as asparagus. When boiled, divide it lengthwise into two, and serve it on toast accompanied by melted butter; or when nearly boiled, divide it as above, and stew gently in gravy. Care should be taken to choose young ones not exceeding 6 in. in length.

Spinach — Wash and pick your spinach very carefully; drop into boiling water and cook 15 minutes. Drain thoroughly through a colander, then chop quite fine. Return to the stove, add 1 tablespoonful of butter, pepper and salt to taste; put in a vegetable dish and garnish with hard-boiled eggs.

To Stew Celery — Wash, cut into neat slices, removing the green parts. Plunge into sufficient boiling water to cover it, adding salt in the proportion of a dessertspoonful to 2 qts. of water. Stew until tender, serve in a dish with white sauce over. The celery may be stewed in stock if preferred.

How to Serve Potatoes — A great deal of ignorance is often shown by excellent housekeepers in putting potatoes on the table. The usual practice of bringing them up in a porcelain or deep dish, with a close-fitting cover, would utterly destroy the best potatoes in ten minutes, however carefully cooked. They should be placed in a wooden dish, or served in a porcelain dish with towels above and below to absorb the moisture.

Potatoes (Stuffed) — Five medium-sized potatoes, ½ oz. butter, 1 tablespoonful grated cheese, pepper, salt, and yolk of 1 egg.

Bake the potatoes in their skins; and when done cut off a small slice from one end, scoop out the inside, and rub through a wire sieve. Add to it ½ an oz. butter, 1 tablespoonful grated cheese, pepper, salt, and the yolk of an egg. Mix well, refill the skins, fit on the slices which were cut off, and put into the oven again for 10 minutes before serving.

Lyonnaise Potatoes — Into a saucepan put a large lump of butter and a small onion finely chopped, and when the onion is fried to an amber color, throw in slices of cold boiled potatoes, which must be thoroughly stirred until they are turning brown; at that moment put in a spoonful of finely chopped parsley, and as soon as it is cooked, drain through a colander, so that the potatoes retain the moisture of the butter, and many particles of parsley.

Potatoes (Sautées au Beurre) — Cut with a vegetable cutter into small balls about the size of a marble; put them in a stewpan with plenty of butter and a good sprinkling of salt; keep the saucepan covered, and shake it occasionally until they are quite done, which will be in about an hour.

Savory Potatoes — Peel as many potatoes as you require. Put them in a pie-dish with a good-sized onion chopped fine, ½ teaspoonful of dried sage powdered, 2 oz. butter and 2 tablespoonfuls olive oil, and enough water to cover the bottom of the dish. Pepper and salt to taste, and bake in a slow oven.

Saratoga Potatoes — Saratoga chips are prepared in thin, paper-like slices (a slaw-cutter is required for this), and crisped, but not browned, in hot fat. The secret of preparing them properly lies in cutting them first in the thinnest slices possible, and soaking them for at least 1 hour in cold salt water. This last process draws the starch out of the potato, and is positively necessary to success. Before frying, each piece must be thoroughly dried on a towel. When taken out of the fat they may be drained on a sieve a moment in a very hot oven or over the stove, then cooled quickly in a draft.

Potatoes (Virginia Style) — Slice as for Saratoga potatoes, but thicker, soak in cold water, drain, and fry in covered pan with 2 or 3 spoonfuls of suet, letting it brown before they are put in. Salt and pepper thickly while cooking at leisure.

Potato Pancakes — Grate 6 large potatoes in a porcelain bowl, add 4 eggs, not beaten, 1 teacup flour, ½ cup milk and 1 even teaspoonful baking-powder; stir all lightly together, taking care not to beat the eggs up too much. Fry the same as ordinary pancakes, but longer, to cook thoroughly.

Potatoes (à la Crème) — Slice the potatoes as for frying and soak in cold water ½ hour. Parboil in a frying-pan, pour the water off and let them stand on the fire uncovered till the steam is driven off; brown 1 spoonful of butter or fat and pour over them a minute after; then cover the potatoes with milk, in which they should boil till done. Salt and pepper while cooking and watch lest they burn. There should be just milk enough when done for a creamy gravy, thickened by the starch of the potatoes.

Fried Potatoes—American fried potatoes are boiled first and sliced cold to fry. They need a large frying-pan, or are best cooked on a griddle which has surface enough to let each piece lie next to the fire. Slice them ¼ inch thick so as not to break in turning. Salt and pepper, and when the large spoonful of fat is turning brown in the hot pan lay them in, brown quickly and turn with a broad griddle-cake turner.

Potatoes of secondary quality are best pared and sliced raw and fried. The heat of boiling fat, which is stronger than that of boiling water, drives the water out of them. Small, deep kettles are sold for frying, and the lard is kept in them and used many times over.

Potato Balls—Four large, mealy potatoes, cold; mash them in a pan with 2 tablespoonfuls of melted butter, a pinch of salt, a little pepper, 1 tablespoonful of cream and the beaten yolk of 1 egg; rub it together for about 5 minutes, or until very smooth; shape the mixture into balls about the size of a walnut or small rolls, dip them into an egg well beaten and then into the finest sifted bread crumbs; fry them in boiling lard.

Potato Croquettes—Boil 1 dozen potatoes, strain and mash well; add 2 yolks of eggs, beat well and season. When cold, mould in the shape of long corks and dip each piece into beaten eggs; then roll in crumbs and fry a golden brown.

Scalloped Potatoes—Cut 4 good-sized boiled or steamed potatoes into dice; put 2 tablespoonfuls of butter in a frying-pan, and, when melted, add 2 tablespoonfuls of flour; mix until smooth; then add 1 pint of milk, and stir continually until it boils; add a teaspoonful of salt and 3 dashes of black pepper; take from the fire. Put a layer of this sauce in the bottom of a baking-dish, then a layer of potatoes, then another layer of sauce, and so on until all is used, having the last layer sauce; sprinkle the top lightly with bread crumbs and put in the oven for 15 minutes to brown. Serve in the dish in which it was baked.

Cabbage (à la Cauliflower)—Cut the cabbage fine as for slaw; put it into a stewpan, cover with water and keep closely covered; when tender, drain off the water, put in a small piece of butter with a little salt, ½ cup cream, or 1 cup milk. Leave on the stove a few minutes before serving.

Farci (or Stuffed Cabbage)—Veal stuffing, slices of sausage meat, gravy.

Cook the cabbage in salt and water sufficiently to open the leaves, and insert between them layers of ordinary veal stuffing and slices of sausage meat; then tie it securely round with thread to prevent the meat falling out. Replace in the stewpan and cook briskly at first, then simmer till completely tender. Serve in the same manner as ragout—that is to say, with a little gravy poured over the whole.

Cabbage for Roast Meats—Take a medium-sized head of well-blanched cabbage and chop very fine. Put in a stew-kettle with just enough water to cook it tender, which will depend somewhat upon the strength of the fire. Add salt to taste, and when it is cooked, if any water remains in the kettle, drain it off; then add a lump of butter the size of a small egg, a little white pepper and enough milk to just about cover the cabbage. This is a very delicate way of preparing this vegetable, and it goes nicely with roast meats.

Stuffed Cucumbers—Boil large, firm cucumbers until tender, scoop out the seeds and in their place put a filling made of fine bread crumbs, well-seasoned, and a little minced ham or veal. Fasten the cucumbers together with strings and put in a baking-pan with a large cupful of water and a good-sized piece of butter; baste frequently and bake ½ hour. A delicate and delicious dish.

Aux Pommes—One red cabbage, 3 or 4 moderate-sized apples, butter, salt, pepper, walnut, cloves, vinegar, red currant jelly, flour.

Put a red cabbage into a saucepan, having previously washed it well; just cover it with water; peel, halve and core 3 or 4 moderate-sized apples and add them to the cabbage with a piece of butter about the size of a walnut, salt, pepper and 3 or 4 cloves. Cook very gently over a slow fire for 3 hours. When ready to be served, add 1 dessertspoonful of vinegar, the same quantity of red currant jelly, and sufficient flour to thicken the sauce; pour over and send to table.

Tomatoes (Baked)—Half dozen tomatoes, bread crumbs, pepper, salt and butter.

Cut ½ dozen tomatoes in halves, remove the pips, and fill the insides with a mixture of bread crumbs, pepper and salt in due proportions; place a small piece of butter on each half tomato and lay them close together in a well-buttered tin; bake in a slow oven about ½ hour and serve. They may be eaten hot or cold.

Tomatoes (Stuffed)—Tomatoes, shallot, butter, bread crumbs, ham, parsley, sweet herbs, pepper, salt and toast.

Dip some tomatoes in hot water, peel them, cut them in halves and remove the pips; rub a baking-sheet with shallot; butter it well, and lay the tomatoes in it, filling each half with the following composition: Two parts bread crumbs, 1 part ham finely minced, and, according to taste, parsley and sweet herbs also finely minced, and pepper and salt. Put a small piece of butter on each half tomato; and bake them 15 minutes. Have ready some round pieces of buttered toast; on each of these put a half tomato, and serve.

Tomatoes with Macaroni—Tomatoes, butter, pepper, salt, bay leaf, thyme, stock or gravy, macaroni.

Cut up a quantity of tomatoes and remove from each the pips and watery substance; put them into a saucepan with a small piece of butter, pepper, salt, a bay leaf, and some thyme; add a few spoonfuls of either stock or gravy; keep stirring on the fire until they are reduced to a pulp, pass them through a hair sieve, and dress the macaroni with this sauce and plenty of Parmesan cheese freshly grated.

Tomato Fritters—One quart stewed tomatoes, 1 egg, soda, flour, lard.

Use 1 quart stewed tomatoes, 1 egg, 1 small teaspoonful of soda; stir in flour enough to make a batter like that for griddle cakes. Have some lard very hot on the stove, drop the batter in, a spoonful at a time, and fry.

Tomatoes (Broiled)—Large, fresh tomatoes, butter, pepper, salt, sugar, an eggspoonful of made mustard.

In buying tomatoes for broiling, be careful to select large and fresh ones. Do not pare them. Slice in pieces about ½ inch thick and broil them for a few minutes upon a gridiron; while they are broiling, prepare some hot butter in a cup, seasoning with pepper, salt, an eggspoonful of made mustard and a little sugar; when the tomatoes are finished, dip each piece into this, and then dish (the dish must be hot). If any of the seasoning remains, heat to the point of boiling and pour over the dish; serve immediately. This is a very nice dish if cooked well.

Onions (Boiled)—Skin them thoroughly. Put them to boil; when they have boiled a few minutes, pour off the water and add clean, cold water, and then set them to boil again. Pour this away and add more cold water, when they may boil till done. This will make them white and clear and very mild in flavor. After they are done, pour off all the water and dress with a little cream, salt and pepper to taste.

Spanish Onions (à la Grecque)—Peel off the very outer skins and cut off the pointed ends; put the onions in a deep dish, and put a piece of butter and a little salt and pepper on the place where the point has been cut off, cover with a plate or dish, and let them bake for not less than 2 hours. They will throw out a delicious gravy.

Peas and Carrots—Take 5 or 6 good-sized carrots, scrape, cut into small dice and soak for 1 hour in cold water, then boil for 1½ hours in three times enough water to cover them, with salt to season well. When thoroughly cooked, drain off the water and add 1 can of peas, well drained, and 1 cup of milk, and place on the stove again. Mix a heaping teaspoonful flour with a good heaping teaspoonful butter, and add when the milk boils up. Cook for a few moments, adding salt to taste, and a good shake of pepper.

Onions (Stuffed)—Very large Spanish onions, cold fat pork or bacon, bread crumbs, pepper, salt, mace, cream, 1 egg, butter, juice of ½ lemon, browned flour, milk.

Wash and skin the onions. Lay in cold water 1 hour. Parboil in boiling water ½ hour. Drain, and while hot extract their hearts, taking care not to break the outside layers. Chop the inside thus obtained very fine, with a little cold fat pork or bacon. Add bread crumbs, pepper, salt, mace, and wet with 1 or 2 spoonfuls cream or milk. Bind with 1 well-beaten egg, and work into a smooth paste. Stuff the onions with this; put into a dripping-pan with a very little hot water, and simmer in the oven for 1 hour, basting often with butter melted. When done, take the onions up carefully, and arrange the open ends upwards in a vegetable dish. Add to the gravy in the dripping-pan the juice of ½ lemon, 4 tablespoonfuls cream or milk, and a little browned flour wet with cold milk. Boil up once, and pour over the onions.

Mushrooms—The cook should be well acquainted with the different sort of things called by this name by ignorant people, as the deaths of many persons have been caused by carelessly using the poisonous kinds. The eatable mushrooms first appear very small and of a round form on a very small stalk. They grow very fast, and the upper part and stalk are white. As the size increases the under part gradually opens and shows a fringy fur of a very fine salmon color, which continues more or less till the mushroom has been picked, when it turns to a brown. The skin can be more easily peeled from the real mushroom than the poisonous kind. A good test is to sprinkle a little salt on the spongy part or gills of the sample to be tried; if they turn black they are wholesome, if yellow they are poisonous. Give the salt a little time to act before you decide as to their quality.

Mushrooms (Stewed)—Gather those that have red gills; cut off that part of the stem which grew in the earth; wash, and take the skin from the top; put them in a stewpan with some salt; stew them till tender; thicken with 1 spoonful butter and browned flour.

Mushrooms (Broiled)—Prepare them as directed for stewing. Broil them on a griddle; and when done, sprinkle salt and pepper on the gills, and put a little butter on them.

Mushrooms (Baked)—Pare the top and cut off part of the stalk, wipe them carefully with a piece of flannel or cloth and a little fine salt. Then put them into a baking-dish and put a piece of butter on each mushroom. Sprinkle with pepper to taste and bake for 20 minutes or ½ hour. When done serve on a hot dish with the gravy poured over the mushrooms.

Mushrooms (à la Crème)—Cut the mushrooms in pieces, and toss them over a brisk fire in butter seasoned with salt, a very little nutmeg, and 1 bunch herbs. When they are done enough, and the butter nearly all wasted away, take out the herbs, add the yolk of 1 egg beaten up in some good cream; make very hot and serve.

Parsnips—Boil, mash, season with butter, pepper and salt, make into little cakes; roll in flour and brown in hot lard.

Parsnips (American Fashion)—Scrape and boil some parsnips, then cut each lengthwise in four, and fry them very brown, and dish in pairs.

Parsnips (Buttered)—Boil the parsnips tender and scrape; slice lengthwise. Put 3 tablespoonfuls butter into a saucepan, with pepper, salt, and a little chopped parsley. When heated put in the parsnips. Shake and turn until mixture boils, then lay the parsnips in order upon a dish, and pour the butter over them and serve.

Parsnips (Fricasseed)—Scrape them, boil in milk till they are soft; then cut them lengthwise into pieces 2 or 3 inches long, and simmer in a white sauce, made of 2 spoonfuls broth, 1 piece mace, ½ cupful cream, a piece of butter, and some flour, pepper and salt.

Cucumbers (to Dress)—Pare and cut the cucumbers into slices as thin as a wafer (it is better to commence at the thick end). Place in a glass dish; sprinkle with salt and pepper and pour over it ½ teacupful vinegar and 3 tablespoonfuls salad oil. This is a nice accompaniment to boiled salmon, and is useful in completing a salad. It is also an excellent garnish for lobster salad.

Cucumbers (Stewed)—Three large cucumbers, a little butter, ½ pint brown gravy, a little flour.

Cut the cucumbers lengthwise, removing the seeds. Have the pieces a convenient size for the dish they are served in. Plunge them into boiling water with a little salt. Allow it to simmer for 5 minutes. Put the gravy into another saucepan, and when the cucumbers are done, remove from the water and place in the gravy, and allow to boil until they are tender. If there should be a bitter taste, add 1 teaspoonful granulated sugar. Dish carefully, skim the sauce, and pour over the cucumbers.

Cucumbers (Fried)—Pare cucumbers, cut in slices, press the slices upon a dry clean cloth; dredge with flour; have ready a pan of boiling oil or butter, put the slices into it, and keep turning them until they are brown; remove them from pan and lay upon a sieve to drain. Serve on a hot dish.

Lima Beans—One qt. of Lima beans, wash and soak them over night in cold water; simmer over a slow fire 4 hours; then add salt, pepper, butter (the size of an egg), and 1 qt. of sweet milk; boil for ½ hour.

Lima and Butter Beans—Shell and place in cold water, allowing them to remain in the water ½ hour; then put into boiling water with a little salt and cook until tender; drain, and butter and pepper.

French Beans—Top, tail and string the beans carefully; cut in pieces about an inch long; lay in cold salt water for a quarter of an hour; drain, plunge into saucepan of boiling water and boil until tender; drain in a colander; dish with lump of of butter stirred in.

Turnips (Boiled)—Pare and cut in pieces; put them into boiling water well salted, and boil until tender; drain thoroughly and then mash and add a piece of butter, pepper and salt to taste, and a small teaspoonful of sugar; stir till they are thoroughly mixed, and serve hot.

Turnips (German Recipe)—Six large turnips, 3 oz. butter, ½ pint weak stock, 1 tablespoonful flour, pepper and salt.

Heat the butter in a stewpan, pare and cut the turnips into pieces the size of dice and season with pepper and salt; then place in the hot butter, toss over the fire for 5 minutes, add the stock and simmer gently until the turnips are tender. Brown the flour with a little butter; add this to the turnips and simmer 5 minutes. Boiled mutton may be served with this dish.

Turnips (a la Creme)—Small new turnips: peel and boil in salted water; drain thoroughly. Melt 1 oz. butter in a saucepan, add to it a dessertspoonful of flour, pepper, salt, grated nutmeg, and a small quantity of milk or cream; put in the turnips; simmer gently a few minutes, and serve.

Turnips (a la Maitre)—Boil some small new turnips as in the preceding recipe; drain them thoroughly, and melt some butter in the saucepan; put the turnips in, give them a toss or two, add a little chopped parsley, pepper and salt, a squeeze of lemon juice, and serve.

Carrots (to Boil)—Place upon the stove two quarts of warm water with a tablespoonful of salt; bring to a boil; wash and scrape six young carrots, remove any black specks, cut in halves, plunge into the boiling water, and boil until tender; drain, and serve upon a hot dish.

Carrots (Stewed)—Wash and scrape the carrots; split the largest. Then whiten them in hot water, and drain them on a sieve; then boil them in weak broth, with salt; then put some butter in a saucepan, with a dessertspoonful of flour; stir it and brown it. Add the carrots to it, broth and pepper. Stir, and let all simmer together.

Salsify (Boiled)—Scrape the roots, cut them in short lengths, and throw them into vinegar and water as they are being done. Boil them till tender in salted water, drain them, toss them into a saucepan with a piece of butter, a little lemon juice, and some minced parsley, add salt and serve.

Egg Plant (Baked)—Parboil 15 minutes. Then make a triangular cut in the top; remove the piece and take out the seeds. Let it lie for an hour in water, to which a tablespoonful of salt has been added. Make a stuffing of one cup of crumbs, two ounces of salt pork, and an onion chopped fine, 1 teaspoonful salt, ½ teaspoonful pepper and nutmeg mixed; wet with half a cup of boiling water or stock, and fill the egg plant, tying a string around it to keep the piece in place. Bake an hour, basting often with a spoonful of butter in a cup of water.

Hotch-Potch—Put a pint of peas into a stewpan with a quart of water, and boil them until they will pulp through a sieve; then take the lean end of a loin of mutton, cut into small pieces and put it into a stewpan with a gallon of water, the carrots and turnips cut into small pieces, and a seasoning of pepper and salt; boil it until all the vegetables are quite tender, put in the pulped peas and a head of celery (or lettuce) and one onion, sliced; let it boil 15 minutes and serve.

Green Corn (Stewed)—Having cut the corn from the cob, put into boiling water and allow to stew ½ hour; remove nearly all the water and cover with milk, and allow to stew until tender; before dishing, roll some pieces of butter in flour and mix with the corn, adding a little pepper and salt; give one boil and serve.

Green Corn (Boiled)—Strip off all the outer husks, allowing the innermost to remain; remove the silk and re-cover the ear with the remaining husk, secure with a piece of thread, plunge into boiling salted water, and boil ½ hour. Cut off stalks and dish upon a napkin.

Green Corn (Roasted)—Open the husks, remove the silk, close the husks closely, and roast in the ashes of a wood fire until tender; serve with butter, pepper and salt. This is frequently eaten in camp.

Summer Squash—Pare the outer rind, remove the seeds; quarter, and lay in ice water 10 minutes; put into boiling water, a little salt, and cook until tender; press all the water from them. Mash smooth, season with butter and pepper and serve hot.

Winter Squash—Proceed as above, allowing more time to cook; before putting into the boiling water, allow it to soak in cold water 3 hours.

Cauliflower (Boiled)—Wash in 2 or 3 waters. Cut off the end of stalk and outer leaves, allow to lie in salt and water 5 minutes, plunge into boiling salted water, and boil 15 or 20 minutes; drain and serve hot.

Cauliflower (Fried)—Pick out all the green leaves from a cauliflower, and cut off the stalk close; put it head downward in a saucepan full of boiling salted water; do not overboil it; drain it on a sieve; pick it out into small sprigs, and place in a deep dish with plenty of vinegar, whole pepper, salt, and a few cloves. When it has lain about an hour in this drain it, dip in batter, and fry in hot lard to a golden color.

Cauliflower (Scalloped)—Choose a cauliflower of medium size, boil it 20 minutes; put into a saucepan 1 oz. butter, ½ gill milk, and 1 oz. bread crumbs; add cayenne and salt to taste, and stir till the bread has absorbed the milk and butter. Beat an egg and add this to the sauce, but be sure that it does not simmer after the egg has been added. Butter a flat tin dish, take off the fine leaves of the cauliflower and place them all round on it, break up the flower carefully and lay in the center, making it as high as possible; pour the sauce over this, sprinkle a few bread-crumbs on the top, and bake 10 minutes.

Green Peas (to Keep)—Shell, and put them into a kettle of water when it boils; give them 2 or 3 warmings only, and pour them in a colander; when the water drains off, turn them out on a table covered with cloth, and pour them on another cloth to dry perfectly; then bottle them in wide-mouthed bottles, leaving only room to pour clarified mutton-suet upon them an inch thick, and for the cork. Resin it down, and keep it in the cellar or in the earth. When they are to be used, boil them till tender, with a piece of butter, a spoonful of sugar, and a little mint.

Green Peas (Stewed)—Put a quart of peas, a lettuce and an onion, both sliced, a piece of butter, pepper, salt, and no more water than hangs round the lettuce from washing; stew them 2 hours very gently. When to be served, beat up an egg and stir it in, or a little flour and butter. Some think a teaspoonful of white powdered sugar is an improvement.

Green Peas (à la Française)—Put the required quantity of peas necessary for your dish into a perfectly clean and bright stewpan, with some water and butter in the following proportion: For every pint of peas 1 gill water and 1 oz. butter. When this is thoroughly amalgamated, add a little bouquet, tied together, of parsley, also salt, pepper, and another ½ oz. butter, then 8 or 9 small white onions, and a whole lettuce. Simmer the whole well for an hour, or more if the peas and other vegetables are not completely tender. The time, in fact, must be regulated according to the judgment of the cook. When done, take out the bunch of parsley, the lettuce, and the onions, which are very serviceable for íneltes, stews or soups, even when cooked as above. The peas, when once cooking, must not be touched by a spoon or a fork, as it would bruise them and spoil the appearance of the entrée, but well tossed constantly to prevent them sticking to the stewpan, always kept briskly simmering, but never boiling; otherwise they will harden.

Baked Beans—Beans should be carefully looked over, thoroughly washed and put to soak over night in about twice their bulk of water. Put them in the kettle soon after breakfast the next morning, add about as much water as at first, place them where they will not burn, and let them cook slowly and without stirring until about ten o'clock. Then add half a pound of salt pork thoroughly washed and cut across the rind in small dice. Place the pork on the top of the beans and let it boil for an hour or more. Then lift the meat out, turn the beans and liquor into a baking-pan, press the water down until only the rind is out of the pork, and bake in a slow oven for several hours.

Asparagus—After scraping the stalks to cleanse them, place them in a vessel of cold water. Tie them up neatly into bundles of about 25 heads each, then place them in a saucepan of boiling water, sprinkling a handful of salt over it. When it is boiling remove any scum there may be; the stalks will be tender when they are done; they will take about twenty minutes or half an hour; be careful to take them up the minute they are done; have ready some toast, dip it in the liquor in which the asparagus was boiled; dish upon toast, and serve with a boat of melted butter.

Asparagus in Ambush.—Two bunches of asparagus, 6 stale biscuits (or rolls may be used), 4 eggs, about ½ pint of milk, butter the size of an egg, flour, pepper and salt to taste.

Take the green tops of the two bunches of asparagus, boil them tender and mince finely. While they are boiling, take the biscuits or rolls, divide them, keeping the top half for a cover; place them all in the oven to crisp; make the milk hot, and then pour in the eggs, beaten; stir over the fire until it thickens, then add the butter rolled in flour, and lastly add the asparagus; spread the rolls with this mixture, put on the tops and serve hot.

Asparagus and Eggs.—Twenty-five or 30 heads of asparagus, good rich butter, salt and pepper, 5 or 6 eggs.

Boil the asparagus (after cutting them into pieces of about ½ an inch) for 15 minutes; take a cup of rich butter and put it into a saucepan; drain the asparagus, and put it with the butter; heat them to a boil, seasoning with pepper and salt, and then pour into a buttered baking-tin or dish; break five or six eggs neatly over the surface of this, sprinkle with pepper and salt, and put it in the oven until the eggs are set nicely. Serve hot.

Asparagus Pudding.—Green tops of 2 bunches of asparagus, 3 tablespoonfuls of prepared flour, 4 or 5 well-beaten eggs, 2 dessertspoonfuls of melted butter, 1 teacup of milk, 1 pinch of soda, pepper and salt to taste.

Boil the asparagus and when cool chop finely; take the eggs, butter, pepper and salt, and beat them up together, then put in the flour; stir the soda into the milk, and add gradually; lastly put in the asparagus. Put this into a buttered mould with a lid, or if it has no lid tie it down tightly with a floured cloth; boil for two hours. When done, turn out on a dish, and pour melted butter round it.

Artichokes, with White Sauce.—Wash them well, peel and shape them to a uniform size; throw them into boiling salted water, and let them boil fifteen to twenty minutes; drain them at once thoroughly; put them on a dish and serve with the following sauce poured over them: Mix over the fire 1½ oz. butter with a tablespoonful of flour; add ½ pint of boiling water, white pepper and salt to taste; stir till the sauce thickens, then take the saucepan off the fire, and stir in the yolks of two eggs, beaten up with the juice of a lemon, and strained.

Artichokes, with Cream.—Prepare and parboil them as in the preceding recipe; then put them into a saucepan with a due allowance of white sauce, and let them finish cooking in this, adding at the last a small quantity of cream and grated nutmeg.

Artichokes, with Gravy.—Prepare them as above, cutting them to the size of pigeon's eggs. Parboil them for ten minutes, drain them and toss them in a saucepan with a piece of butter; then add a small quantity of good clear gravy and a dust of pepper. Let them simmer very gently till wanted.

Artichokes (Mashed).—Salted water, a piece of butter, a little cream, white pepper, nutmeg and salt.

Wash, peel and boil them in salted water; drain, and pass them through a hair sieve. Squeeze all the water out of the pulp; put it into a saucepan, and work it on the fire, with a piece of butter and a little cream, adding white pepper, nutmeg and salt if necessary. When quite hot and sufficiently dry, serve.

Artichokes (Fried).—Wash, peel and parboil them whole for ten minutes, then cut them in strips the size of a little finger. Flour them carefully, and fry in hot lard; or they may be dipped in batter and fried. Serve piled up on a napkin.

Artichokes (Stewed).—Mince a couple of shallots and fry them in plenty of butter; put in the artichokes parboiled and cut into pieces, moisten with a little stock, season with pepper, salt, and a little lemon juice; lastly add some finely-chopped parsley, and let the whole stew gently till quite done. A small quantity of Parmesan cheese may be added.

Artichokes, au Gratin.—Wash, peel and boil them whole; cut them in slices the thickness of a cent. Butter a dish previously rubbed with a shallot; arrange the slices on it, strew over them some baked bread-crumbs, seasoned with pepper, salt and a little powdered thyme, add a squeeze of lemon, put a few pieces of butter on the top, and bake for ten or fifteen minutes.

Pumpkin (Stewed).—Halve, remove the seeds, pare and slice neatly. Soak for an hour in cold water; then place in a saucepan of boiling water on the fire. Allow it to stew gently until it falls to pieces. Stir often. Then take it out, drain, squeeze, and rub through a colander, then put it back in the saucepan, adding two dessertspoonfuls of butter, pepper and salt to taste. Stir quickly, and when nearly boiling dish, adding more pepper if required.

Pumpkin (Baked).—Cut the pumpkin into quarters; remove seeds, cut into slices lengthwise about half an inch thick. Place in a baking-dish suitable for the purpose and arrange in layers about three slices deep. Put a very little water in the bottom of the dish and bake very slowly until done (the water must have evaporated). It takes a long time to bake. Butter the slices on both sides and dish.

SALADS.

ANY cold vegetable can be made into salad. I wonder that any one eats asparagus hot, it is so good cold. Scrape it thoroughly, boil till soft (about thirty-five minutes), lay away carefully till cold, then make French or mayonnaise dressing and pour over.

In making tomato salad scald the tomatoes first, then plunge in cold water, and the skins will come off easily. Set on the ice till cold, slice with a sharp knife, set the slices back upon each other so that each tomato shall retain its shape.

Avoid breaking the lettuce leaves, and see that they are perfectly drained. Arrange the lettuce prettily in a glass dish, and set the vegetable that accompanies it in the center. Never add the dressing till it comes to the table.

Sliced bananas or oranges with lettuce and mayonnaise dressing are delicious. The former are, however, a trifle rich for any one whose digestion is only moderately reliable.

In making cucumber salad, if the cucumbers are quite young, cut up one with the rind on. The peculiar slight bitter taste is very welcome to the palate of an epicure. Cucumbers should always lie in very salt ice water for a while to make them crisp and should not be seasoned until the last minute. Flabby cucumbers are as mean as cold batter-cakes.

Lettuce Salad (1)—Take 4 or 5 heads of cabbage lettuce, remove all outside leaves and cut off the stalks close; then cut each head apart into 4 or 5 "quarters," that is, cut through the stalk and then tear the rest. Put 4 tablespoonfuls olive oil into the salad bowl, with 1½ tablespoonfuls tarragon vinegar, pepper and salt according to taste, and beat the mixture with a fork some minutes; then put in the lettuce and keep it turning over swiftly for 5 minutes, adding a small pinch of mint, chopped as finely as possible.

Lettuce Salad (2)—Wash 2 heads lettuce, dry them thoroughly and break the leaves or cut them into convenient pieces. Put the yolks of 2 hard-boiled eggs into a basin with a teaspoonful of French mustard, pepper and salt to taste, and a tablespoonful of oil; work the mixture into a smooth paste, and add successively 3 tablespoonfuls of oil, 1 of tarragon and 1 of plain vinegar; then a little chervil, garden cress and tarragon finely chopped. Stir the mixture well, and lastly add the lettuce; turn it or work it well. Garnish the top with hard-boiled eggs.

Herring Salad—Heat through by turning on the stove 3 well-smoked herring, then tear off the heads and pull the skin away; split, take out the backbone, and cut up into small bits, or to shred them is better. Put in a salad bowl, add 1 small chopped onion, 2 hard-boiled chopped eggs, and 1 boiled potato; cut fine with a teaspoonful of chopped parsley; season with a teaspoonful of salt, 1 of pepper, 3 tablespoonfuls vinegar and 2 of oil. Mix well, and, if you have it, decorate with a boiled beet.

Potato Salad—Slice 8 cold boiled potatoes; disperse between the slices 1 silver-skinned onion cut quite fine; beat together 3 parts oil and 1 part, more or less, according to the strength of it, tarragon vinegar, with pepper and salt to taste. Pour this over the potatoes, and strew over all a small quantity of any of the following: Powdered sweet herbs, mint, parsley, chervil, tarragon or capers, or a combination of these all, finely minced.

Cold Slaw—To 1 quart cut cabbage, use ½ cupful cream (either sweet or sour), 2 tablespoonfuls vinegar, 2 eggs, 1 teaspoonful salt, 1 tablespoonful butter and a little pepper; put the vinegar on to boil, add the beaten eggs to the cream and butter, and stir these into the boiling vinegar till the butter is melted and the whole mass smooth and creamy; add the pepper and salt and pour, while hot, over the cabbage; when cold, it is ready for use.

Lobster Salad—Clean thoroughly some lettuce, endives and beetroots, cut them up and mix them with the following dressing: 4 tablespoonfuls oil, 2 tablespoonfuls vinegar, 1 teaspoonful made mustard, the yolks of 2 eggs, ½ teaspoonful anchovy sauce, and cayenne and salt. Pick out from the shells the flesh of 1 hen lobster, cut into well-shaped pieces, put ½ in the salad and garnish with the rest, also with the whites of 2 hard-boiled eggs chopped fine, and the yolks mixed with the coral and rubbed through a sieve.

Sardine Salad—Allow 2 sardines for each person; bone and fillet these, carefully removing all the skin, and set them aside until required. Boil 2 eggs for 3 minutes; shell them and break them up in your salad bowl with a spoon; mix with them a teaspoonful each French mustard and essence of anchovies, the strained oil from the tin of sardines with as much Lucca oil as will make 3 tablespoonfuls in all; add Chili, shallot, and good malt vinegar to taste (vinegar varies so much in quality that it is difficult to specify the exact proportions). Cut up some nice crisp lettuce, and mix it well with the dressing, but only just before it is to be served. Put a little heap of mustard and cress in the center of the salad, with a whole red capsicum upon it, arrange the sardines round, and outside these a border of mustard and cress, dotted here and there with thin slices of red capsicum.

Cabbage Salad—Chop fine 1 firm head cabbage, sprinkle lightly in a dish. Make the dressing as follows: Stir together 2 raw eggs, 1 teaspoonful white pepper, 1 teaspoonful mustard, a little salt, 2 teaspoonfuls melted butter and 1 cupful strong vinegar. Put this mixture in a small vessel set inside of another full of boiling water and stir 5 minutes; set aside to cool, then beat in ½ cup cream, pour over the cabbage and serve.

Tomato Salad—Peel some good-sized tomatoes, not over-ripe, cut them in slices and remove the pips, lay them in a dish with oil and vinegar in the proportion of 2 to 1, sprinkle pepper and salt over them according to taste, a few leaves basil finely minced, and some onions very finely sliced. They should lie in the sauce for a couple of hours before serving.

Egg Salad—Boil ½ dozen eggs until hard, shell them and cut them into slices and pour over them, while hot, the following dressing: Put in a soup plate ½ teaspoonful salt and ¼ teaspoonful black pepper, add 3 tablespoonfuls olive oil and stir until the salt is dissolved. Stir in 1 tablespoonful tarragon vinegar, 1 tablespoonful onion juice and 1 tablespoonful chopped parsley. Stand away in a cold place for 2 hours and serve.

Chicken Salad—Draw, singe and boil the chicken. When done and perfectly cold remove the skin and cut the meat into dice. If you want it very nice, use only the white meat; save the dark for croquettes. After you have cut it set it away in a cold place until wanted. Wash and cut the white parts of celery into pieces about a half inch long, throw them into a bowl of cold water and also set them away until wanted. To every pint of chicken allow two-thirds of a pint of celery and a cup and a half of mayonnaise dressing. When ready to serve, dry the celery and mix with the chicken; dust lightly with salt, white pepper or cayenne, then mix with it the mayonnaise. Serve on a cold dish garnished with white celery tips. One cup of whipped cream may be added to every ½ pint of mayonnaise when ready to use it. It makes the dressing lighter, with less of the oily flavor.

Celery Salad—Two heads of celery, 1 tablespoonful salad oil, ½ lemon or vinegar, a teaspoonful granulated sugar, pepper and salt to taste.

Well wash the celery, removing any unsightly parts, lay in iced water until wanted; then cut into pieces about an inch in length. Season with remaining ingredients, mix well and serve in salad bowl.

Red Cabbage Salad—One small red cabbage, 1 small dessertspoonful salt, ½ pint vinegar, 1½ dessertspoonfuls oil, a little cayenne pepper.

Secure a nice fresh cabbage, remove the outer leaves and cut the cabbage into nice thin slices, then mix in the above ingredients and allow to stand for two days, when it will be fit for use. This salad will keep good for several days.

Rev. Sidney Smith's Recipe for Salad Dressing.

"Two boiled potatoes, strained through a kitchen sieve,
Softness and smoothness to the salad give;
Of mordant mustard take a single spoon —
Distrust the condiment that bites too soon,
Yet deem it not, thou man of taste, a fault
To add a double quantity of salt;
Four times the spoon with oil of Lucca crown,
And twice with vinegar procured from town;
True taste requires it, and your poet begs
The pounded yellow of two well boiled eggs.
Let onions' atoms lurk within the bowl,
And, scarce suspected, animate the whole;
And, lastly, in the flavored compound toss
A magic spoonful of anchovy sauce.
Oh! great and glorious, and herbaceous treat,
'Twould tempt the dying anchorite to eat;
Back to the world he'd turn his weary soul,
And plunge his fingers in the salad bowl."

Boiled Salad Dressing—Put ½ pint of milk in a double boiler, and when it boils stir in 2 tablespoonfuls corn starch moistened with a little cold water. Stir until it boils and thickens, then add the yolks of 3 eggs, well beaten; stir a minute longer, take it from the fire and add a tablespoonful of butter, a teaspoonful of salt, and stir in by degrees 2 tablespoonfuls of vinegar. Stand it aside to get cold, and it is ready for use.

French Dressing—Half teaspoonful salt, the same of pepper, mixed with 1 tablespoonful vinegar or lemon juice; add 3 tablespoonfuls oil; beat together briskly and pour over the salad; before passing on the different plates toss and turn the salad so that it may mix well.

Mayonnaise Dressing—The yolks of 2 well-beaten eggs, 1 teaspoonful each of sugar and salt, ½ teaspoonful pepper and 1½ teaspoonfuls mustard; mix well. Heat to the boiling point 1 cupful vinegar and a lump of butter the size of a pigeon's egg; while this is heating beat to a stiff froth the whites of the 2 eggs and mix with the other ingredients, beating well; then add the boiling vinegar, a few drops at a time. Set on the fire 2 or 3 minutes, stirring constantly; beat a few minutes after removing it from the fire, and set away to cool.

PICKLES

ENAMELED kettles should always be used in preference to those of brass or copper, as the verdigris produced by the vinegar on these metals is extremely poisonous. For some pickles use cold vinegar, as in boiling most of the strength is lost by evaporation. For French beans, broccoli, cauliflower, gherkins, etc., it is better to heat the vinegar, for which the following process is recommended: Put the vinegar and spice in a jar, cover it tightly, let it simmer on the back of the stove. Shake occasionally. Pickles should never be put into glazed jars, as salt and vinegar penetrate the glaze and produce a poison.

Glass or stone jars are preferable to any other; a small piece of alum in each jar will make the pickles firm and crisp. One tablespoonful of sugar to each quart of vinegar will be found a very great improvement to all pickles. Always use the very best cider vinegar.

Pickled Onions—In the month of September, choose the small, white, round onions, take off the brown skin, have ready a very nice tin stewpan of boiling water, throw in as many onions as will cover the top; as soon as they look clear on the outside, take them up as quick as possible with a slice, and lay them on a clean cloth, cover them close with another, and scald some more, and so on. Let them lie to be cold, then put them in a jar, or glass, or wide-mouthed bottles, and pour over them the best vinegar, just hot but not boiling. To each gallon of vinegar add 1 oz. allspice and 1 oz. black pepper. When cold, cover them. Should the outer skin shrivel, peel it off. They must look quite clear.

Pickled Walnuts—Fifty walnuts (seasonable for pickling early in July). To each pint of vinegar allow 1 oz. black pepper, ½ oz. allspice, and ½ oz. bruised ginger.

Prick the walnuts with a fork, and put them in a brine (compound of 1 lb. salt to each quart of water). Let them remain in this 9 days, changing the brine three times. Put them in the sun until they turn black; put them into jars, allowing sufficient room to cover them with vinegar: boil (or scald) vinegar and spices in the above proportions. Cover closely and keep dry. They can be used in 6 weeks.

Jumbo Pickle—Chop fine a head of cabbage, sprinkle with salt; let it remain thus for 12 hours; then mix 1 onion finely minced with the cabbage), drain through a colander; add a good quantity of pepper and celery seed. Put it in a jar and cover with vinegar. Ready for use in 3 days.

Red Cabbage—Slice into a colander, and sprinkle each layer with salt; let it drain 2 days, then put it into a jar, and pour hot vinegar enough to cover, and put in a few slices of red beetroot. Observe to choose the purple red cabbage. Those who like the flavor of spice will boil it with the vinegar. Cauliflower cut in branches, and thrown in after being salted, will look a beautiful red.

Green Tomato Pickles—One peck green tomatoes; 1 dozen large white onions, sliced crosswise to fall into rings; 2 oz. whole pepper, 1 oz. white mustard seed, 1 oz. cloves, 1 oz. allspice. Put a layer of tomatoes and onions, then a good handful of salt, etc., till all are in a stone jar; then put a plate on top and weight down over night; in morning squeeze out with hand and put to boil in kettle, putting in layers with spices; add 1 gal. best malt vinegar, and boil 20 minutes. Put in stone jar to keep.

Damson and Cherry Pickles—To 6 pounds fruit put 3 pounds sugar, 1 qt. vinegar, 4 tablespoonfuls or 2 oz. cinnamon, 1 tablespoonful cloves, as much mace. Put the fruit in a jar. Boil the vinegar, sugar and spices, and pour them boiling hot on the fruit. Tie the spices loosely in muslin before boiling.

Ripe Peaches Pickle—Pare them and drop them in vinegar that has been boiled, with 1 teacup sugar to 1 qt. vinegar, and 12 cloves, a teaspoon of whole allspice and three large sticks of cinnamon. Always tie spices in cheese cloth or muslin loosely before boiling.

Piccalilli—Small cucumbers, button onions, small branches of cauliflower, carrots, ginger, grapes, strips of horse-radish, radishes, bean pods, cayenne pods, 4 qts. best vinegar, 4 tablespoonfuls salt, mustard and flour, 2 tablespoonfuls ground ginger, pepper, allspice and turmeric.

The brine for this pickle is made by putting a pint of rock salt into a pail of boiling water. Put the vegetables for pickling into the brine and cover tightly to prevent the steam escaping. Allow them to stand a night and a day. Change the brine a second time and allow them to remain the same length of time. The second brine may be used a second time if skimmed and scalded. Choose pickles from the brine of an equal size and of various colors. Great taste may be displayed in the arrangement of the pickles when putting them in bottles. To 4 qts. of best vinegar add the spices. Simmer these together (the mustard and turmeric must be blended together with a little vinegar before they are added to the liquor); when the liquor is on the point of boiling, pour into a vessel; cover tightly. When sufficiently cold pour into the bottles containing the pickle, and make air-tight. It will be ready for use in 5 or 6 months.

Beets—Vinegar, beets, 2 oz. whole pepper, 2 oz. allspice to every gallon of vinegar.

Carefully remove all dirt from the beets. Let them simmer in boiling water for 1½ hours, then take them out and leave to cool. Boil the remaining ingredients for 10 or 15 minutes and leave to cool. When cold pour it over the beets (which you have previously pared and cut into thin slices). Make air-tight and they will be ready for eating in a week or 10 days.

EGGS.

ABOUT one-third of the entire weight of an egg may be regarded as nitrogenous and nutritious matter; a greater proportion than that of meat, which is rated at only from 25 to 28 per cent. The lightest way of cooking eggs is by poaching. The yolk of an egg alone is better for invalids and will be frequently relished when the white would be rejected. When cream cannot be procured for coffee the yolk of a soft-boiled egg is a very good substitute. To prevent the juice of fruit pies from soaking into the bottom crust wash the crust over with beaten egg before putting in the fruit. When making frosting in warm weather, set the whites of the eggs on ice a short time before using. If the eggs you have to use for frosting are not quite as fresh as you could desire, a pinch of salt will make them beat stiffer. The white of an egg, an equal quantity of cold water and confectioners' sugar sufficient to make the required consistency, make a nice frosting which, as it requires no beating, is very easily made. When beaten eggs are to be mixed with hot milk, as in making gravies or custards, dip the hot milk into the beaten eggs a spoonful at a time, stirring well each time until the eggs are well thinned, then add both together. This will prevent the eggs from curdling.

The whites or yolks of eggs which are left after making cake, etc., will keep well for a day or two if set in a cool place—the yolks well beaten and the whites unbeaten. Whites or yolks of eggs may be used with whole eggs in any cake or other recipe calling for eggs, counting two yolks or two whites as one egg. When eggs are cheap and plentiful in summer, wash all those used in cooking before breaking, save the shells, and when a quantity are dry, crush them fine; beat half a dozen eggs well and stir them into the shells. Spread them where they will dry quickly, and when thoroughly dry, put in a thin cotton bag and hang in a dry place. In the winter, when eggs are dear, a tablespoonful of this mixture put in a cup, a little cold water poured over it and left to stand over night, or for half an hour or so in the morning before breakfast, will answer every purpose of a whole egg in making cakes.

It is a good plan in testing eggs to apply the tongue to the large end of the egg, and if perfectly fresh the egg will feel warm, or they can be held to the light and if perfectly clear will be good; or try them in water—the freshest will sink first. Always keep them in a cool place.

Poached Eggs (on Toast)—If the eggs are not new-laid they will not poach well. Fill a shallow saucepan with water and salt, add a little vinegar, a few peppercorns, and some leaves of parsley. When the water is on the point of boiling (it should never be allowed to boil) break 2 or more eggs into it (according to the size of the pan); when done, take them out carefully, lay them on slices of hot buttered toast, and serve.

Poached Eggs (on Ham Toast)—Make some buttered toast, cut in pieces of uniform shape, spread over them a small quantity of grated ham, put a poached egg on each piece of toast, and serve hot.

Poached Eggs and Minced Chicken—Free some remnants of fowl from skin, etc., mince them with an equal quantity of ham or tongue, as well as a small quantity of truffles or mushrooms, all finely minced; toss the whole in a saucepan with a good-sized piece of butter mixed with a pinch of flour, add white pepper, salt and powdered spices to taste, and moisten with a little white stock; lastly, stir in, off the fire, the yolk of 1 egg beaten up with the juice of ½ lemon, and strained; serve within a border of bread sippets fried in butter, and dispose the poached eggs on the top.

Stuffed Eggs—Cut some hard-boiled eggs in half, mince the yolks with a few olives and capers, some anchovies thoroughly washed, a few truffle trimmings, and a little tarragon, add some pepper, and fill each half egg with this mixture. Pour some liquefied butter over, and warm them in the oven. Then place each half-egg on a round sippet of bread fried in butter to a light yellow color, and serve.

Buttered Eggs—Break 4 eggs into a basin, and beat them well; put 2 oz. butter and 2 tablespoonfuls cream into a saucepan; add a little grated tongue, pepper and salt to taste; when quite hot, add the eggs, stir till nearly set, then spread the mixture on pieces of buttered toast and serve.

Fried Eggs—Melt a piece of butter in a small frying-pan, break 2 eggs in it carefully so as not to break the yolks; when nearly set, slip them out on a hot dish, pour the butter over them, sprinkle with salt and pepper, and serve.

Fried Eggs with Tomatoes—Melt a small piece of butter in a saucepan, put in it a small quantity of French tomato sauce, add pepper and salt to taste, and when quite hot turn it out on a dish, disposing on it the eggs fried in butter.

Scrambled Eggs—Beat up 4 eggs, with salt and pepper to taste; put 1 oz. butter into a saucepan; directly it is melted pour in the eggs, and keep constantly stirring with a spoon until they are nearly set, adding at the last a little finely-minced parsley.

Scrambled Eggs with Asparagus—Parboil some asparagus points, cut the size of peas, in salted water, drain them and toss them in a little butter till quite hot. Scramble some eggs as in the preceding recipe, and, when nearly set, add the asparagus points instead of the parsley.

Scrambled Eggs with Tomatoes—Beat up 4 eggs with a tablespoonful of French tomato sauce, or one large tomato, peeled, freed from pips, and chopped small, and proceed as above.

Scrambled Eggs with Onions—Chop coarsely 2 slices of Spanish onion; put them into a saucepan with plenty of butter, and when they are thoroughly cooked, without having taken any color, throw in 4 eggs beaten together with pepper and salt to taste; keep on stirring till the eggs are nearly set, and then serve.

Scrambled Eggs with Fish—Pick out the meat of any remnants of fish, such as salmon, turbot, cod, haddock or whiting, and with a silver fork break it up small; take 2 tablespoonfuls of this and 4 eggs; beat the whole together with a little pepper and salt to taste, and a little parsley finely minced; then proceed as in first recipe.

Scrambled Eggs with Ham—Beat up a tablespoonful of grated ham with 4 eggs, and pepper to taste; put them into a saucepan with a piece of butter, and stir till nearly set.

Scrambled Eggs with Cheese—Put 4 eggs and 2 tablespoonfuls of Parmesan cheese into a basin with a sprinkling of pepper; beat all together, and proceed as in the first recipe, omitting the parsley.

Scrambled Eggs (on Toast)—Any of the foregoing may be served on slices of buttered toast, but if so served they must be even less set, at the time of serving, than when served plain; or neat bread sippets, fried in butter, may be served round them.

Sippets (Fried)—Cut out of a loaf slices from ¼ to ⅜ in. thick, shape them into triangles or arrowheads, all of a size; put some butter in a frying-pan, and when quite hot lay the sippets in it; turn them frequently, adding more butter as it is wanted, and taking care that they are all fried to the same golden color. A readier way, but producing not so nice a sippet, is to lay the pieces of bread in the frying-basket, and dip it in a saucepan full of boiling fat. They must afterwards be laid in front of the fire to drain.

Omelet (Plain) — Beat up 3 or 4 eggs with 1 dessertspoonful of parsley very finely minced, and pepper and salt to taste; put a piece of butter, the size of an egg, into a frying-pan; as soon as it is melted pour in the omelet mixture, and, holding the handle of the pan with one hand, stir the omelet with the other by means of a spoon. The moment it begins to set cease stirring, but keep on shaking the pan for a minute or so; then with the spoon double up the omelet and keep shaking the pan until the under side of the omelet has become of a golden color. Turn it out on a hot dish and serve.

Omelet — One-half cupful sweet milk, 1 of fine bread crumbs, 3 eggs, whites and yolks beaten separately, ½ teaspoonful chopped sage or a whole one of parsley; pepper and salt to taste. Mix well, adding the white of egg last; melt a lump of butter in a large frying-pan, pour in your mixture, and, taking a silver knife, gently lift it away from the sides as the egg "sets." Then put in the oven until it browns on top, fold over and serve on a hot plate.

Omelet — The following makes a delicious omelet for four persons: Break 5 eggs, putting the whites in one dish and the yolks in another. Beat the yolks to a froth, then add a saltspoonful of salt, a little pepper, a heaping tablespoonful of finely chopped parsley, and 5 tablespoonfuls of cream. Beat all together for a moment and then add the whites, previously beaten to a stiff froth. Mix gently together and pour immediately into a hot spider containing a level tablespoonful of melted butter. Cook rather slowly in order not to burn the bottom before the omelet is cooked through, and when nicely browned fold half over. Place on a warm platter, and serve immediately.

Omelet (Savory) — Beat up 3 or 4 eggs with ½ shallot very finely minced, some parsley similarly treated, and a very small pinch of powdered sweet herbs; add pepper and salt to taste; then proceed as above.

Omelet (Cheese) — Beat up 3 eggs with 1 or 2 tablespoonfuls grated Parmesan cheese. Cook as above, and serve with some more grated cheese strewn over the omelet.

Omelet (Tomato) — Equal parts of sliced onions and tomatoes peeled and freed from pips; chop them both coarsely. Fry the onions in butter. When cooked, without being colored, add the tomatoes, with pepper and salt, and keep stirring the mixture on the fire till it forms a sort of purée. Make a plain omelet, and insert this in the fold on dishing it.

Omelet (Mushroom) — Parboil a small quantity of button mushrooms, slice them small, and stew them just long enough to cook them in a small quantity of either white or brown sauce (see Sauces); then use as in preceding recipe.

Omelet (Fish) — Beat up 3 eggs with a quantity equal in bulk to 1 egg of the remnants of any cold fish (salmon or turbot) finely shredded with a fork, a pinch of minced parsley, pepper and salt to taste.

Omelet (Oyster) — See "Oysters."

CATSUPS, ETC.

Lemon Catsup — One doz. lemons, ½ breakfast cupful white mustard seed, 1 eggcupful turmeric and white pepper, ½ eggcupful cloves and mace, ½ a small teacupful white sugar, 1 tablespoonful cayenne, ½ a small teacupful horse-radish, ½ a small teacupful salt, 4 shallots.

Finely grate the rind of lemons, pound the spices in a mortar, grate the horse-radish. Thoroughly blend these ingredients, then sprinkle the salt over all, extract the juice from the lemons and add to the mixture. Allow to stand in a cool place for 3 or 4 hours. Boil in an enameled kettle 30 minutes, pour into a stone jar, cover tightly. Stir every day for 14 days, then strain, bottle and seal.

Tomato Catsup (1) — To 1 peck tomatoes allow 1 tablespoonful salt, mace, black pepper, cloves powdered, and 1 of celery seed; a teaspoonful cayenne, ½ lb. tin of mustard.

Make a small incision in each tomato, put into an enameled saucepan, and boil until perfectly soft, and the pulp dissolved; work through a colander, then through a hair sieve. Place upon the stove, adding the remaining ingredients (the celery seed must be confined in a muslin bag), and boil 6 hours. Stir continually for the first 5 hours, and all the last hour. Pour into a stone jar; allow to stand from 12 to 14 hours in a cold place. When perfectly cool add a pint of strong vinegar, remove the celery seed, bottle, cork, and seal. Keep in a dry, dark place.

Tomato Catsup (2) — Ripe tomatoes; to every lb. of juice add a pint of vinegar, a dessertspoonful sliced garlic, a small teaspoonful of salt and white pepper.

Place a number of ripe tomatoes in a jar; cover and bake till tender. Strain and work through a sieve, and add the above ingredients. Pour into a stewpan and boil until the ingredients are perfectly soft. Work through the sieve a second time, and to every pound squeeze the juice of three lemons. Boil again until of the thickness of cream. Set aside to get cold. Bottle, cork and seal, and keep in a dry, dark place.

Walnut Catsup — Mash the shells of walnuts, bruise them slightly, put them with salt in a stone jar for two or three weeks until they ferment, then boil them up, strain off the liquor; add to every 2 quarts 1 oz. each of allspice, ginger, black pepper, cloves and mace; boil the whole 1 hour; let it cool, bottle it, and tie a bladder over the corks.

French Mustard — One quart of brown mustard seed, 1 handful each of parsley, chervil, tarragon and burnet, 1 teaspoonful of celery seed, cloves, mace, garlic, salt to taste, enough vinegar to cover.

Put the whole into a basin with enough vinegar to cover the mixture. Let it steep 24 hours, then pound it in a marble mortar. When thoroughly pounded pass it through a fine sieve; add enough vinegar to make the mustard of the desired consistency, and put into jars for use.

Mint Vinegar—A wide-mouthed bottle or bottles. Fill them (loosely) with nice, fresh mint leaves, then add good vinegar to fill the bottle or bottles; cork well. Allow to stand for two or three weeks, and at the expiration of this time strain into fresh bottles and cork securely. Useful when mint is not in season.

Herbs (to Dry)—Gather the herbs for drying before they begin to flower. Free from dirt and dust and tie in bunches, having previously removed the roots. Dry in the oven or before the fire; in either case, dry quickly, as the flavor is better preserved by quick drying. Upon no consideration allow them to burn. Tie up in paper bags and hang in a dry place. N. B.—Take care to gather the herbs on a dry day.

Herb Powder (for winter use)—Take 2 oz. each of winter savory, sweet marjoram, lemon, thyme, lemon peel and 4 oz. of parsley.

Thoroughly dry the herbs and take off the leaves. Grind to a powder and pass through a sieve. Dry the lemon peel and pound as finely as possible, then mix all together thoroughly. Keep in glass bottles tightly corked.

Parsley (to keep for winter use)—Take fresh bunches of parsley; plunge into boiling water slightly salted, boiling for 3 or 4 minutes. Remove from the water, and drain dry very quickly before the fire, and put in bottles for use. Soak in tepid water 5 minutes when required for cooking.

Garlic Vinegar—Steep an ounce of garlic in 2 quarts of the best white vinegar; add a nutmeg scraped. This vinegar is much esteemed by the French.

A Useful Catsup—One and one-half pints mushroom catsup, ½ pint walnut pickle, 3 tablespoonfuls Chili vinegar, 2 shallots.

Take 1½ pints of freshly-made mushroom catsup, peel the shallots and add them to the catsup and allow it to simmer for 20 minutes, then add the pickle and vinegar and boil again for 10 minutes. Stand in a cool place, and when perfectly cold, bottle, and, having placed a small piece of shallot in each bottle, cork and set by for use.

FORCEMEATS.

WHETHER in the form of stuffing-balls or for patties, forcemeat makes a considerable part of good cooking, by the flavor it imparts to the dish it accompanies, and considerable care should be taken in preparing it. It is often the case, at many excellent tables where everything else is well done, to find very bad forcemeat or stuffing.

Forcemeat (for Fowls)—Quarter lb. suet, 2 oz. ham, the grated rind of ½ lemon, a dessertspoonful of minced parsley, 1 tablespoonful of minced sweet herbs, cayenne, salt, grounded mace to taste, 7 oz. bread-crumbs, 2 eggs.

Cut the ham into small, thin strips, chop the suet finely, also the lemon peel; add the seasoning, then the crumbs; thoroughly blend, and after the eggs have been well beaten add to the other ingredients, and it is ready for use. If wished for balls, fry a golden brown in hot lard.

Forcemeat (Balls for Soup)—Eight oz. bread-crumbs, sweet herbs, salt and pepper to taste, 5 eggs.

Have the bread-crumbs finely grated, and the herbs pounded to a powder; sprinkle with pepper and salt; boil 2 eggs hard and mince finely. Mix all together and bind the whole with the remaining eggs. Form into little balls, and drop into the soup about 5 or 6 minutes before serving.

Oyster Forcemeat (for Roast or Boiled Turkey)—Two teacupfuls bread-crumbs, ½ oz. minced suet, 1 tablespoonful savory herbs, a sprinkle of nutmeg, salt and pepper to taste, 2 eggs, 1½ doz. oysters.

Have the bread-crumbs and suet finely minced, add the herbs chopped as finely as possible; mix well. Having opened the oysters, beard and chop them (not very small) and add to the other ingredients; beat up the eggs, and with the hand work all together thoroughly; it is then ready for use.

Sage and Onion Stuffing (for Pork, Ducks, Geese)—Two teacups bread-crumbs, 4 large onions, 12 sage leaves, butter the size of an egg, pepper and salt to taste, 1 egg.

Peel and boil the onions for 5 or 6 minutes, dip the sage leaves in the same water (while boiling) for a minute or two, then chop finely; add seasoning, the bread-crumbs and butter; beat up the egg, and work all together. It is then ready for use.

Quenelles—Moisten 1 cup of finely-crumbled bread with 3 tablespoonfuls of milk, add 2 tablespoonfuls of melted butter and as much finely-chopped meat (stewed veal or fowl, cold) as you wish, work in 1 well-beaten egg, and season all thoroughly with salt and pepper; flour your hands, and shape mass into round balls, rolling them into flour when shaped. Bring to a boiling heat in a saucepan 1 large cup well-seasoned gravy, drop in the balls, and boil fast for about 5 minutes. The gravy can be thickened and poured over them, or they can be rolled in flour or cracker crumbs, and fried in lard or butter.

BREAD AND CAKES.

OF all articles of food, bread is perhaps the most important; therefore it is necessary to be well acquainted with the quality of the ingredients and the art of making it. Flour ought to be a few weeks old before being used, and care must be taken to keep it perfectly dry. It is of the utmost importance to purchase only the best quality of flour, for it is the truest economy. Patent flour should be more scantily measured than winter wheat, as it contains more gluten. Do not place the sponge or dough too near the fire, as some cooks are liable to do in cold weather, or the quality of bread will be endangered. The proper heat should be gentle and equal for fermentation. Care must also be taken to mix and knead (brisk and long kneading will fully repay for the trouble) when it has reached the point for either. Bread requires a brisk oven, and should take about 1 to 1½ hours to bake. The cook must be guided by experience as to the exact degree of heat.

The secret of biscuit-making is precision and dispatch. Laggards and lazy people are not successful biscuit-makers. The best cooks always say they simply throw their biscuits together, and certainly they are not long about it. The cause of success is that biscuits begin to bake before the effervescent qualities of the powder or soda are exhausted.

For good cake (as in bread) it is of great importance to use no ingredients but those of the finest quality. The flour must be dry and sifted. It will be found a good plan, after purchasing currants, to wash in three waters, pick and dry in a cloth. Then look them carefully over, discarding any stone, stalk or grit. Lay before the fire or in the sun to dry. Put by in a jar, and they will always be ready for use. Eggs should be well whisked, the whites and yolks beaten separately and strained. Butter must not be allowed to oil. Lemon peel should be cut thinly as possible. Sugar should be finely powdered. When soda is used it is a good plan to dissolve it in warm water. When all the ingredients are mixed, vigorous and patient beating will greatly add to the lightness of the cake. The heat of the oven is of great importance for cakes, especially those that are large. If the oven is not very quick, the batter will not rise. Should you fear scorching, put some paper over the cake. If the fire is not long enough lighted to have a body of heat, or if it has become slack, the cake will be heavy. To know when the cake is done, take a broom straw and pierce into the very center, draw it instantly out, and if the least stickiness adheres, put the cake back immediately and shut the oven.

Fine sugar should be used in cake-making to give good texture. Cake pans with movable bottoms are more easily managed, for they may be placed on a teacup and the rim will fall off. The milk in cake-making should be added slowly. Butter the tins, then flour them.

Yeast (1) — A double handful of hops, ½ doz. potatoes, ½ gal. water, 1 or ½ cupful ginger, small cup flour, a cup brown sugar, ½ cup salt, a cupful good yeast.

Allow the hops and potatoes to boil together in ½ gallon of water till done; strain and mash the ginger, then add remaining ingredients, excepting the yeast. Let stand until cool, then add the yeast. Next day cork up tight in a jug.

Yeast (2) — Two oz. hops, 1 gal. water, a handful salt, 1 lb. best flour, 3 lbs. potatoes.

Boil the hops in a gallon of water for ½ hour; strain it, and let it cool down to the heat of new milk; then put the salt and brown sugar; beat the flour with some of the liquor, and then mix all together. Two days after, add the potatoes, boiled and then mashed, to stand for 24 hours; then put into bottles, and it will be ready for use. Stir it frequently while making, and keep it warm. Before using, shake the bottle up well. It will keep in a cool place for two months.

To Make Baking-Powder — Take ½ lb. of ground rice, ½ lb. carbonate of soda, 2 oz. tartaric acid. Mix them very thoroughly and smoothly. Allow 2 teaspoonfuls to 1 lb. of flour.

Another Way — Mix well together 6 oz. carbonate of soda, 4 oz. tartaric acid, 1 teaspoonful salt, and 1 teaspoonful powdered sugar.

Home-Made Bread (1) — Four lbs. flour, 1 tablespoonful solid brewers' yeast, 1½ pints lukewarm milk and water, salt.

Put the flour into a deep pan, sprinkle a little salt into it, hollow out the middle with a wooden spoon (taking care to leave the bottom of the pan well covered with flour). Next take the yeast, which has been made solid by liberally mixing with cold water, and allowing it to settle 24 hours. Then proceed to pour the yeast into the hole in the flour, and mix with it as much flour as is round about it until it is of the consistency of thick batter; be careful there are no lumps. Sift plenty of flour over the top, cover with a clean cloth, and set it where the air is warm and equal. Allow to stand an hour or a little longer, and if the yeast has broken through it is then ready to be made into dough. Pour into the sponge the remaining milk and water. Mix into it as much of the flour as you can with the spoon. Now take plenty of the flour, sprinkle on the top of the leaven, and proceed to knead briskly, and when perfectly free from the lumps and it does not adhere to the hands, it may be covered with a cloth and left to rise a second time. When it begins to crack, which will be in about ¾ of an hour, it can be formed into loaves and baked. In forming the loaves divide in two and make up the shape and size required, and with a sharp knife make incisions in the top of each loaf. If baked in tins, take care to grease them before using. When baked stand on end to allow the steam to evaporate. The dough can be made without making a sponge (if desired) by mixing the yeast with the best part of the milk and water, and after a little salt has been added, proceed to work up the whole of the flour at once, and then set as above. The dough will soften in the rising, so it should be made firm at first.

Home-Made Bread (2) — Put the flour into a large pan; mix in a dessertspoonful of salt; make a hole in the middle, and pour in the yeast (half a teacup of yeast to two quarts of flour), with about a pint of water or milk (which use warm in winter and cold in summer), and mixing in all the flour; then put a blanket, or towel, over the pan, and let it stand to rise near the fire, in winter. This is "putting bread in sponge." When it has risen, mix all the flour with the sponge; knead it well, and let it stand 2 hours till quite light. Then mold the dough on a board till elastic, and put the loaves into greased or floured baking-tins; prick them two or three times through with a fork; let them rise again for a quarter of an hour, and bake them in a quick oven.

White Bread — Sponge, a pan of buttermilk, or sour milk, flour, 1 teacupful of yeast.

For the sponge take a pan of buttermilk or sour milk which has just turned thick. Put it on the stove and scald. When the curd is well separated from the whey strain or skim it out. Let the whey cool until it will not scald, then stir in the flour, beating thoroughly. It should be about as thick as batter for griddle cake. Sweet milk, or even water, may be used as a wetting for the sponge, if good sour milk or buttermilk cannot be had. But fresh buttermilk is, perhaps, the best of all. When the sponge is about milkwarm, beat in a teacupful of yeast. One teacupful of the yeast is enough for three ordinary white loaves, one loaf of brown bread and a tin of rolls. The sponge should be made at night. Let it stand until morning. Unless the weather is very cold, it is not necessary to put it near the fire. In the morning, when the sponge is light, take out enough for your loaf of brown bread. Mix the remainder with flour, taking care not to put in too much, as that will make the bread dry and hard. Knead ½ an hour. The whiteness and delicacy of the bread will be much increased by thorough kneading. Put the dough away to rise again. When it is light, if you wish to make rolls, save enough of the dough for that purpose. Make the remainder into loaves. Set them away to rise. When light, bake.

Fine Wheat Bread — For 4 loaves: 1 pint water, 1 cake compressed yeast, 1 tablespoonful salt, 1 tablespoonful sugar.

Mix hard or stiff, as for baking, at first. Set it to rise; when it has risen, knead it again; let rise again. If mixed in the morning — which is the best when using compressed yeast — after the second rising, put it in the pans, and it will be ready to bake in the afternoon. Be sure and knead it when it first rises, and then let it rise again.

Plain Bread — Half lb. white flour, 1 teaspoonful baking-powder, a pinch of salt, ½ pint milk and water.

The simplest way of making bread in small quantities is as follows: Take ½ lb. of white flour, and, while in a dry state, mix in thoroughly a small teaspoonful baking-powder and a pinch of salt. Then add about a quarter of a pint of milk and water, or water alone; knead it as quickly as possible, and put immediately into a very hot oven; the whole secret of making light bread after this fashion lies in attention to these last rules. If the oven is well heated, it will rise almost directly, and it should be baked until the outside is quite crisp and hard. I generally knead mine into the desired shape, but they can be baked in tins if preferred. For brown bread, I use three parts of brown and one of white flour, and a little extra baking-powder; also adding a little more water, if necessary, to mix it.

Rice and Wheat Bread — One lb. rice, 2 quarts water, 4 lbs. flour, 4 large spoonfuls yeast, salt.

Simmer 1 lb. rice in 2 quarts water till it becomes perfectly soft; when it is of a proper warmth, mix it extremely well with 4 lbs. flour, and yeast and salt as for other bread, of yeast about 4 large spoonfuls; knead it extremely well; then set it to rise before the fire. Some of the flour should be reserved to make up the loaves. If the rice should require more water, it must be added, as some rice swells more than others.

French Bread — One-fourth pk. fine flour; yolks of 3 and whites of 2 eggs, salt, ½ pt. good yeast, ½ pt. milk.

With ¼ pk. fine flour mix the yolks of 3 and whites of 2 eggs, beaten and strained, a little salt, ½ pt. of good yeast, that is not bitter, and as much milk, made a little warm, as will work into a thin, light dough; stir it about, but don't knead it; have ready 3 wooden quart dishes, divide the dough among them, set to rise, then turn them out into the oven, which must be quick. Rasp when done.

Sago Scones — Take a teacupful of sago and soak in cold water, put it on with 1 qt. sweet milk, let it boil till quite dissolved, stirring occasionally; add a little salt, then pour out on the baking-board and let it lie till cold. Mix up with flour, taking care not to make it too stiff; roll out quite thin, cut to the size wanted, and bake.

Brown Bread — One pt. corn meal, 1 pt. rye flour, 1 tablespoonful brown sugar, 1 teaspoonful salt, 2 of baking-powder, 1 tablespoonful lard, ¾ pt. milk.

Sift together the above ingredients, excepting the lard and milk; rub into the mixture the lard and add the milk. Mix into a batter-like cake and bake 1 hour. Protect it with brown paper if it should brown too fast at first.

Boston Brown Bread — One and one-half cups yellow cornmeal, 1 cup rye flour, 1 cup Graham flour, 1 cup New Orleans molasses, 2 full teaspoonfuls baking-powder and a little salt.

Mix all to a consistency of a thick batter with either milk or water, pour into a buttered mold or tin pail, and steam in boiling water 4 hours.

Rye Bread — Two cups Indian meal, scalding water, a small cup of white bread sponge, sugar, salt, a teaspoonful of soda, rye.

Make the Indian meal into a thick batter with scalding water; when cool add the white bread sponge, a little sugar and salt, and the soda, dissolved. In this stir as much rye as is possible with a spoon; let it rise until it is very light; then work in with your hand as much rye as you can, but do not knead it, as that will make it hard; put it in buttered bread tins, and let it rise for about 15 minutes; then bake it for 1½ hours, cooling the oven gradually for the last 30 minutes.

Corn Bread—Take 2 cups flour, 1 cup cornmeal, ½ cup sugar, 1 egg, 2 tablespoons butter, 1½ cups sweet milk, 3 teaspoons baking-powder; quick oven.

Corn Bread Steamed—Three cups cornmeal, boiling water, 1 cup flour, 2 cups sour milk, 1 cup molasses, 1 teaspoonful soda, a little salt.

Scald 2 cups cornmeal with boiling water, add another cup of meal and remaining ingredients. Mix thoroughly, and steam 3 hours.

Bread Omelet—A teacupful bread-crumbs, 1 teacupful sweet milk, 5 eggs, pepper, salt, a small lump of butter.

Let the milk come to the boiling point, pour it over the crumbs and let it stand a few minutes; take the eggs, beat them well and pour into the bread mixture; season with salt and pepper and a small lump of butter; when thoroughly mixed, butter a hot skillet and pour the mixture in, letting it fry slowly; when one side is browned nicely, cut it in squares and turn. Serve at once.

Barley Scones—Take 1 quart sweet milk and put it on in a pan with a little salt. When it boils, stir in barley-meal until it is as thick as porridge, pour out on the baking-board and let it stand till cold. Knead up with barley-meal to a nice soft dough, roll out and cut to the size wanted, and bake.

Rusks—One pint new milk, 2 tablespoonfuls yeast, flour, 2 tablespoonfuls butter, 1 cupful sugar, 2 eggs, 2 saltspoonfuls salt.

Rusks require a longer time for rising than ordinary rolls or biscuits. Prepare a sponge of the yeast, milk and flour (sufficient to make a thin batter) and allow it to rise all night. Next morning add eggs, butter and sugar (which must have been mixed well together), milk and flour enough to produce a soft dough. Shape into round balls of equal size, place in a pan and allow to rise until very light. Flavor according to taste. Bake in a quick, steady oven till of a pretty brown color, glaze with the yolk of an egg and sprinkle with powdered white sugar.

Butter Rolls—One quart flour, ½ teaspoonful salt, 2 teaspoonfuls baking-powder, 1 egg, 1 pint milk, 1 tablespoonful lard.

Sift the flour, salt and baking powder together, rub in the lard cold, then add the egg and milk; mix as soft as possible. Roll it out ½ inch in thickness and cut with a plain, round biscuit cutter. Dip them in melted butter, fold ½ of each piece over the remainder and bake in a quick oven for 15 minutes.

Vienna Rolls—One quart milk, ½ teaspoonful salt, 3 teaspoonfuls baking-powder, 1 tablespoonful lard, 1 pint milk.

Mix into a dough easily to be handled without sticking to the hands; turn on the board and roll out to the thickness of ½ inch, cut it out with a large cake cutter, spread very lightly with butter, fold one-half over the other and lay them in a greased pan without touching. Wash them over with a little milk, and bake in a hot oven.

French Rolls—Two eggs, ½ pint milk, 1 tablespoonful yeast, 1 oz. butter.

Beat 2 eggs and mix with them ½ pint milk and a tablespoonful yeast; knead well and let stand till morning; then work in 1 oz. butter; mold into small rolls, and bake at once.

Cinnamon Rolls—Save a piece of dough, about enough to make a loaf, out of your bread before you make it out for baking. To this dough add 1 egg, 1 tablespoonful butter, ½ cupful milk, 1 cupful sugar and 1 tablespoonful cinnamon. Work thoroughly, make into rolls and set to rise. When almost done draw to the oven-door, spread lightly with butter and cover with a mixture made of 3 tablespoonfuls butter and 1 tablespoonful cinnamon. Good hot or cold.

Parkin—One and three-fourths lbs. flour, ½ lb. oatmeal, 4 oz. butter, 2 lbs. molasses, a teacupful milk, 6 teaspoonfuls baking-powder, 1 dessertspoonful ground ginger.

Mix the dry ingredients well together, warm the molasses with milk (do not make it hot) and mix the whole. Bake in a well-buttered tin for 1 hour. Cut into squares before taking out of the tin. It should be 1½ inches thick.

Breakfast Rolls—Two quarts flour, 1 tablespoonful sugar, 1 tablespoonful butter, ½ cupful yeast, 1 pint scalded milk, or water if milk be scarce, and a little salt.

Set to rise until light; then knead until hard and set to rise, and when wanted make in rolls; place a piece of butter between the folds and bake in a slow oven.

Graham Biscuits—One quart water or milk, butter the size of an egg, 3 tablespoonfuls sugar, 2 tablespoonfuls baker's yeast, and a pinch of salt; enough white flour to use up the water, making it the consistency of batter cakes, and as much Graham flour as can be stirred in with a spoon.

Set it away till morning; in the morning grease pan, flour hands; take a lump of dough the size of a large egg; roll lightly between the palms; let them rise 20 minutes and bake in a tolerably hot oven.

Sally Lunn—Two lbs. flour, ½ lb. butter, 3 eggs, 1 pint milk, ½ gill yeast, salt according to taste.

Cut up the butter in the flour, and with your hands rub it well together; beat the eggs; add them gradually to the flour alternately with the milk; stir in the yeast and salt. Bake it in an earthen mold, or iron pan, 1 hour.

Breakfast Muffins—Three eggs, 1 breakfast-cupful milk, 1 tablespoonful butter melted, 1 tablespoonful sugar, a pinch of salt, 2 heaped teaspoonfuls baking-powder.

Whisk the eggs and salt with the milk; put the melted butter into a basin with the above ingredients, mixing in flour enough to make a batter. Bake in round tins, and when almost done wash the top of each with a feather dipped in milk.

Graham Muffins—One quart Graham flour, 2 teaspoonfuls baking-powder, a piece of butter the size of a walnut, 1 egg, 1 tablespoonful sugar, ½ teaspoonful salt, milk enough to make a batter as thick as for griddle cakes.

Bake in muffin-rings, about 20 minutes, in a quick oven.

Rice Muffins—Two cups cold boiled rice, 1 pint flour, 1 teaspoonful salt, 1 tablespoonful sugar, 2 teaspoonfuls baking-powder, ½ pint milk, 3 eggs.

Mix into a smooth and rather firm batter, and bake as above.

Oatmeal Muffins—One cup oatmeal, 1½ pints flour, 1 teaspoonful salt, 2 teaspoonfuls baking-powder, 1 pint milk, 1 tablespoonful lard, 2 eggs.

Mix smoothly into a batter rather thinner than for cup cakes. Fill the muffin-rings ⅔ full and bake in a hot oven.

Crumpets—Two eggs, 1 teaspoonful each of salt and sugar; 4 teaspoonfuls baking-powder, 1 qt. milk, 3 pts. flour.

Mix into a stiff batter and bake in greased muffin rings on a hot greased griddle.

Waffles—Two eggs, 1 pt. milk, ¼ oz. butter, ½ gill yeast, salt to taste, and flour enough to form a thick batter.

Warm the milk and butter together; beat the eggs, and add them by turns with the flour; stir in the yeast and salt. When they are light, heat your waffle-irons and butter them, pour in some of the batter, and brown them on both sides; butter them, and serve them with or without sugar and cinnamon.

Waffles (without Yeast)—Three eggs, 1 pt. milk, 1 teaspoonful butter, as much flour as will make a batter.

Beat the yolks and whites separately; melt the butter, and while lukewarm stir it into the milk; whisk the yolks very light, add to them the milk and flour alternately; beat it well; lastly stir in the whites, which should be whisked very dry. The batter should not be beaten after the whites are in. Grease your waffle-irons after having heated them; fill them nearly full of the batter, close them, and place them over the fire; turn the irons so as to bake the waffle on both sides. When done, take it out and butter it. These must be baked the moment they are mixed.

Rice Waffles—One gill rice, 3 gills flour, salt to taste, 1 oz. butter, 3 eggs, as much milk as will make it a thick batter.

Boil the rice in very little water until it is soft; drain it and mash it fine. Then add the butter to the rice while it is warm; whisk the eggs very light, the yolks and whites separately. Add the yolks to the rice, and as much milk as will form a batter. Beat the whole very hard, then stir the whites of the eggs gently into the mixture. Grease your waffle-irons, and bake them. If the batter should be too thin, add a little more flour.

Italian Bread—Mix 1 pt. each of milk and water and bring to a boil, add 1 teaspoon salt, and sprinkle in gradually 1 pt. meal and 2 tablespoonfuls of flour. Cook 2 hours. Pour in the depths of ½ inch in shallow pans to cool; when cold cut in round cakes; put in overlapping rows in pan; pour melted butter over, then grated cheese; brown in oven.

Crackers—One qt. flour, 1 dessertspoon butter, a pinch of salt and milk enough to make a stiff dough. Beat well, cut out and bake.

Beaten Biscuit—One qt. flour, 2½ oz. lard, 1 teacup milk, 1 teaspoon salt. Mix the greater part of the flour with the other ingredients and beat 15 minutes, adding the rest of the flour by degrees. They require a steady heat, but not too hot an oven. They should bake ½ hour, otherwise they will be heavy and dark in the middle.

Puff Biscuit—One and one-half pts. flour, 3 teaspoonfuls baking-powder and 1 teaspoonful salt, 1 tablespoonful lard, 1½ cups milk. Chop the lard through the flour; sift in salt and add the milk. Roll out quickly, touching as little as possible. Cut in rather large circles; spread one-half of the circle with butter, then fold the other over it; bake 15 minutes. If you choose, you can sprinkle sugar on the top.

Pop-Overs—Make of equal proportions (say 2 cups) milk and flour, 2 eggs, a little salt, butter the size of an egg.

Mix the salt in the flour; mix well, melt the butter and add to other ingredients; the last thing, grease and half fill the tins; bake quickly.

Crullers—Take 2 cups sugar, 1 cup sweet milk, 3 eggs and 1 tablespoonful butter; beat all together, then add a good pinch of salt, 1 teaspoon level full of grated nutmeg; 1 heaping tsp. of cinnamon and the grated rind of a lemon. Now mix thoroughly together 3 cupfuls flour and 2 heaping teaspoonfuls baking-powder; sift into the bowl containing the other ingredients and mix them. Add enough more flour to give them the proper consistency for rolling out. Fry in hot lard, which must be exactly hot enough to brown at once. If too hot they are burned; if not hot enough, as is so often the case, your crullers slowly take up the lard and become greasy and indigestible.

Mush Cakes—One qt. milk, ¼ pound butter, flour enough to make a dough, salt according to taste, Indian meal sufficient to thicken the milk, ½ pint of yeast.

Boil the milk, and stir into it as much Indian meal, mixed with cold milk, as will make a mush as thick as batter; add the butter and salt while the mush is hot; as soon as it becomes lukewarm stir in the yeast and as much flour as will form a dough; cover it and stand it to rise. When light, make it out into biscuits, put them in buttered pans, and as soon as they rise again, bake them in a hot oven.

Buckwheat Cakes—One pint buckwheat flour, 1 qt. water, salt according to taste, 1 gill home-made yeast.

Mix the water (which should be lukewarm if the weather is cold) with the meal; add the salt and yeast; beat it well; when light, bake them on a griddle. Grease the griddle; pour on a little of the batter; spread it so as to form a cake about the size of a breakfast-plate; the cakes should be very smooth at the edges. When they are done on one side, turn them; when brown on both sides, put some butter on the plate; put the cake on it, butter the top, bake another and put on it, butter hot, and send them to the table. Buckwheat cakes are much better if they are sent to the table with only 1 or 2 on the plate.

Rye Batter Cakes—One pint of rye meal, milk, salt according to taste, 1 gill home-made yeast.

Add enough lukewarm milk to the rye to make a thin batter, with salt; beat it well, then add the yeast; when they are light, bake them on a griddle, as buckwheat cakes.

Plain Currant Cake—Take 1/2 lb. flour, 2 teaspoonfuls baking-powder, 1/4 lb. butter, 1/4 lb. sugar, 6 oz. currants, milk.

Rub the butter into the flour, add the other ingredients, and mix with milk into a thick dough. Bake in a well greased tin for about 40 minutes.

Icing for Cakes—Beat up the whites of 3 eggs with 3/4 lb. of powdered white sugar till light; pour it over the cake, smoothing it with a knife. Set the cake in a warm place till the sugar becomes hard.

Sponge Jelly Cake—Three eggs, 4 oz. sugar, 1 cup flour, 1 dessertspoonful baking-powder, 3 tablespoonfuls boiling water.

Mix the baking-powder with the flour, and beat each of the eggs separately. Then mix all the ingredients together, and bake in jelly tins in a brisk oven. When cool, chocolate frosting put between the cakes makes them very delicious or jelly if preferred.

Jelly Rolls—Three eggs, 1/2 cupful butter, 1 1/2 teaspoonfuls baking-powder, 3/4 of a cup of pulverized sugar, 1 cupful flour, a little salt.

Bake in shallow pans—a dripping-pan well buttered is good for this purpose; put in the dough till it is about 1/2 inch thick; take it carefully from the tins when baked and lay on a cloth; spread jelly over it evenly with a knife; roll while hot; if this is not done the cake will crumble.

Sponge Jelly Cake (Rolled)—Five eggs, 1 cup sugar, 1 cup flour, 1 teaspoonful baking-powder.

Beat the yolks and sugar to a cream, add the whites, beaten to a stiff froth; then the flour, to which the baking-powder has been mixed. Bake in a dripping-pan. When done, turn out on a cloth, spread jelly on the bottom of the cake, and roll from the side.

Johnny Cake—One pt. corn meal, 1 teacupful sugar, 1 pt. milk, 2 eggs, 1 teaspoonful butter, salt to taste, 1 teaspoonful dissolved saleratus.

Mix the butter and sugar with the meal; boil half the milk. Add the dissolved saleratus and the eggs, after they have been well beaten, to the remaining half of the cold milk. Pour the boiling milk over the meal and let it cool. Then add the cold milk and mixture. Bake in a shallow pan.

Icing for Cakes (1)—Four eggs, 1 lb. finely powdered white sugar, vanilla, strawberry, lemon, or any other flavoring.

Beat well the whites of the eggs, adding the sugar to stiffen in small quantities; continue until you have beaten the eggs to a stiff froth; it will take about 1/2 an hour if well beaten all the time; if not stiff enough then, add more sugar; spread carefully on the cake with a broad-bladed knife; to color icing yellow put the grated peel of a lemon (or orange) into a piece of muslin, strain a little juice through it and press hard into the other ingredients. Strawberry juice or cranberry syrup colors a pretty pink color.

Icing for Cakes (2)—The whites of 2 eggs, 1/2 lb. castor sugar, and the juice of a lemon or a few drops of orange-flower water.

Beat the mixture until it hangs upon the fork in flakes, then spread over the cake, dipping the knife in cold water occasionally; stand it before the fire, and keep turning the cake constantly, or the sugar will catch and turn brown. As soon as it begins to harden it may be removed. The icing must not be put on until the cake itself is cold; otherwise it will not set. A few drops of cochineal will color it if desired.

Lemon Icing—Squeeze the juice of 2 lemons into a basin with 1/2 lb. of powdered white sugar, and beat it for a short time. If wanted pink, add cochineal.

Eggless Icing—Take 1 cupful confectioner's sugar and 2 tablespoonfuls water; beat thoroughly and spread on your cake, which should be ice-cold. The icing will whiten when it has stood a little while. You may color it with pink sugar or chocolate if you like.

Excellent Frosting—Boil together 1 cup granulated sugar and 4 tablespoonfuls hot water until it threads from the spoon, stirring often. Beat the white of 1 egg until firm; when the sugar is ready set it from the stove long enough to stop boiling, then pour onto the egg slowly, but continuously, beating rapidly; continue to beat until of the right consistency to spread on the cake, and flavor while beating. It hardens very quickly after it is ready to put on the cake, so it is best to have the white of another egg ready to add a little if it gets too hard to spread smoothly. Boil the sugar the same as for candy; when right for candy it is right for frosting; if at last it hardens very rapidly it has been boiled too hard, but a little white of egg will rectify it. Or if not boiled enough (that is, if it remains too thin after beaten until cold) pan in pulverized sugar, adding a little and beating hard; then, if not just right, a little more, and beat again until thick enough.

The one thing is to have the sugar boiled just right; if you hit that point you will not have a bit of trouble; if not, it will require "doctoring." A good deal depends upon stirring the sugar into the white of the egg at first; if too fast or too slow it will cook the egg in lumps. If you should not get it just right at first do not be discouraged; when once you get it perfect you will never make it any other way. This quantity is for one cake.

Almond Icing—Put in a brass or copper pan 4 lbs. moist sugar, with 1 pint of water. Boil 5 minutes, draw off the fire, and mix 2 lbs. ground sweet almonds, stirring till thick, then pour over the cake and dry slowly.

Chocolate Icing—One-quarter cake chocolate, ½ cup sweet milk, 2 dessertspoonfuls corn starch, 1 teaspoonful vanilla.

Mix together the chocolate, milk and starch; boil for 2 minutes, flavor with the vanilla, and sweeten with powdered white sugar to taste.

Plain Fruit Cake—One lb. flour, ¼ lb. dripping, 2 teaspoonfuls baking-powder, a little allspice and salt, ½ lb. currants, ¼ lb. white sugar, and ½ pt. milk.

Mix into the flour the baking powder and salt, then with the hands rub the dripping in the flour until it resembles bread-crumbs. Add the currants, allspice and sugar. Take care that the ingredients are well mixed; pour in the milk and mix with a wooden spoon. Grease a quartern tin and pour the mixture into it; bake 1 hour. To insure the cake being done stick a piece of broom straw into it. This answers the same purpose as a knife and is better, as the knife is apt to make the cake heavy. Turn the cake on end to allow the steam to evaporate.

Plain Fruit Cake (2)—One lb. flour, ½ lb. raisins, 4 oz. dripping, 4 oz. white sugar, 1 teacup milk, 1 egg, 2 teaspoonfuls baking-powder, a little salt, 1 oz. lemon peel.

Add to the flour the baking-powder and salt; rub the dripping into the flour with your hands. Take care it is well incorporated. Stone the raisins, grate the lemon rind, and with the sugar add to the other ingredients. Well whisk the egg, and mix in the milk, adding to the mixture; thoroughly mix. Grease a cake tin and bake 1 hour. Proceed to test as above.

Economical Fruit Cake—Five oz. butter, 2 lbs. flour, ½ lb. sugar, 1 lb. currants, 1 gill yeast, enough milk to make a thick batter, 1 tablespoonful of powdered cinnamon.

Mix the flour, leaving out ¼ lb., with the butter cut in small pieces, the sugar, cinnamon and fruit; add milk enough to form a thick batter, and lastly stir in the yeast. Mix it over night, and set it away to rise; in the morning stir in the remainder of the flour, and let it rise; when light, mould it out very lightly; butter your pan, and bake it in an oven about as hot as for bread.

Plum Cake—One lb. each of butter, sugar and flour, 10 eggs, 2 lbs. raisins, ½ lb. each of currants and sliced citron, 1 teaspoonful of ground cloves, 1 of mace, 1 nutmeg, the juice and grated peel of 1 lemon, ½ coffeecup of molasses.

Beat the butter till it is soft and creamy, then add the sugar. Beat the whites and the yolks of the eggs separately; stir the yolks in with the butter and sugar; stir the flour in gradually (having first mixed 1 heaping teaspoonful of cream of tartar with it). When the flour is about half worked in, put in ½ teaspoonful soda dissolved in as little water as is possible to use; then add the whites of the eggs, and lastly the fruit, which is well covered with the rest of the flour. Bake in a large tin, with a buttered paper on the sides as well as on the bottom; it will need to bake slowly for 5 hours. Then do not attempt to lift it from the tin until it is perfectly cold. This cake should be made several days before it is used.

Delicious Coffee Cake—Sift 1½ pints of flour with 2 teaspoonfuls of baking-powder. Cut into this a heaping tablespoonful of butter and mix it through the flour. Stir in a cupful of syrup, and mix it with cold coffee to the consistency of soft dough. Work into the dough a teaspoonful of ground cloves, one of cinnamon and one of allspice, also half a pound of seeded raisins, and half a pound of currants well floured. Bake in oblong pans in moderate oven for an hour. This cake should stand about two days before cutting.

Johnny Cake—One pint of flour, 1 pint of corn meal (yellow is best), 1 pint of sweet milk, 2 large tablespoonfuls of molasses, a teaspoonful of salt, 2 well-beaten eggs, and 2 tablespoonfuls of melted butter. Beat thoroughly, and when ready to bake add two heaping teaspoonfuls of baking-powder. Have your pans well greased and warm, and bake in quick oven about twenty-five minutes.

Cheese Sticks—Mix well ½ cup of butter into 1 cup of flour, add 1 teaspoonful each of salt and sugar; mix with enough water to make a soft dough and roll out very thin. Have ready ½ cup of grated cheese, sprinkle a little on the dough with a very little cayenne pepper and roll out again; do this until the cheese is all used up, then cut it into strips, lay in greased pans and bake in quick oven.

Aunt Patty's Egg Bread—Two cups white Indian meal, 1 cup cold boiled rice, 3 eggs well beaten, 1 tablespoonful melted butter, 2 cups sweet milk, 1 teaspoonful salt, and pinch of soda. Stir the beaten eggs into the milk, add meal, salt, butter, last of all the rice. Beat well a few minutes, and bake in shallow pan.

Seed Cake—Ten oz. flour, 3 oz. sugar, 2 teaspoonfuls baking-powder, and 1 teaspoonful caraway seeds, 1 egg, 3 oz. butter, a little salt, and ½ glass milk.

Mix the baking-powder and salt in the flour, rub in the butter also (with the hands). Add the sugar and caraway seeds, taking care to thoroughly blend them. Well whisk the egg and add the milk to it; add to the other ingredients and beat well for about 10 minutes. Grease a baking-tin and pour the mixture in. It will take about 1 hour to bake.

Cookies—Take 4 cupfuls flour, 2 cupfuls sugar, ½ cupful butter, ½ nutmeg, 3 eggs, 1 teaspoonful soda, 2 teaspoonfuls cream of tartar, sufficient milk to make dough soft enough to drop on a tin.

Mix the flour, butter, sugar and spices together, add the eggs, dissolve the soda and tartar in the milk, and mix the whole well together. Drop dessertspoonfuls on a greased baking-sheet and bake in a good oven.

Rice Cake—Two handfuls rice, a little less than a quart of milk, sugar to taste, rind of lemon cut in 1 piece, a small stick of cinnamon, 4 eggs, a small quantity of candied citron.

Pick and wash in 2 or 3 waters the rice and put it to cook in the milk, sweeten to taste, add the lemon rind and cinnamon. Let the rice simmer gently until it is tender and has absorbed all the milk. Turn it into a basin to cool, and remove the lemon rind and cinnamon. Then stir into it the yolks of 4 and the white of 1 egg. Add a little candied citron cut in small pieces. Butter and bread-crumb a plain cake-mould, put the mixture into it and bake in a quick oven ½ hour.

Rice Cakes—Eight oz. rice flour, 4 oz. white sugar, 4 oz. butter, 2 eggs.

Work the butter to a creamy substance, add the sugar and flour, and mix in the well-whisked eggs. Roll upon pastry-board and shape into cakes with a cake-cutter. Bake in a slow oven.

Indian Loaf Cake—One lb. Indian meal, ½ lb. butter, 3 eggs, ½ lb. sugar, ½ lb. raisins, ½ lb. currants.

Cut up the butter in the Indian meal; pour over it as much boiling milk as will make a thick batter; beat the eggs very light; when the batter is cool pour them into it. Seed the raisins; wash, pick and dry the currants; mix them with the raisins, and dredge as much wheat flour on them as will adhere to them. Stir the fruit into the batter, and add the sugar. Bake it in a moderate oven 2 hours.

Queen Cakes—One lb. dried flour, 1 lb. sifted sugar, 1 lb. washed currants, 1 lb. butter, 8 eggs.

Mix the flour, sugar and currants; beat the butter to a cream, beat it well, then mix with it the eggs, yolks and whites beaten separately, and put in the dry ingredients by degrees; beat the whole for 1 hour; butter little tins and put the mixture in, only filling half full, and bake; sift a little fine sugar over just as you put into the oven.

Ginger Cup Cake—Two cupfuls butter, 2 cupfuls sugar, 1 cupful molasses, 1 cupful cream, 3 eggs, 1 tablespoonful dissolved saleratus, 4 heaping cupfuls flour, ½ cupful ginger.

Beat the butter and sugar to a cream; whisk the eggs light, and add to it; then stir in the other ingredients. Butter a pan or earthen mould, and pour in the mixture. Bake in a moderate oven, or it may be baked in queen-cake pans.

Ginger Nuts—Half lb. butter, ½ lb. sugar, 1 pint molasses, 2 oz. ginger, 2 tablespoonfuls cinnamon, as much flour as will form a dough, ½ oz. ground cloves and allspice mixed.

Stir the butter and sugar together; add the spice, ginger, molasses, and flour enough to form a dough. Knead it well, make it out in small cakes, bake them on tins in a very moderate oven. Wash them over with molasses and water before they are put in to bake.

Ginger Bread—Half lb. moist sugar, 2 oz. ground ginger, 1 lb. flour, ½ lb. butter, ½ lb. molasses.

Put the butter and molasses into a jar near the fire; when the butter is melted mix it with the flour while warm, and spread the mixture thinly on buttered tins, mark it in squares before baking, and as soon as baked enough separate it at the marks before it has time to harden. Time to bake, 15 minutes.

Honeycomb Ginger Bread—Half lb. flour, ½ lb. coarsest brown sugar, ½ lb. butter, 1 dessertspoonful allspice, 2 dessertspoonfuls ground ginger, the peel of ½ lemon, grated, and the whole of the juice; mix all these ingredients together, adding about ½ lb. molasses so as to make a paste sufficiently thin to spread upon sheet tins.

Beat well, butter the tins, and spread the paste very thinly over them, bake it in a rather slow oven, and watch it till it is done; withdraw the tins, cut it in squares with a knife to the usual size of wafer biscuits (about 4 inches square), and roll each piece round the fingers as it is raised from the tin.

Drop Ginger Cakes—Put in a bowl 1 cupful brown sugar, 1 cupful molasses, 1 cupful butter, then pour over them 1 cupful boiling water, stir well; add 1 egg, well beaten, 2 teaspoonfuls soda, 2 tablespoonfuls each of ginger and cinnamon, ½ teaspoonful ground cloves, 5 cupfuls flour. Stir all together and drop with a spoon on buttered tins; bake in a quick oven, taking care not to burn them.

Yorkshire Tea Cakes—Six handfuls flour, 1 egg, 1 oz. yeast, a piece of lard about the size of 2 eggs, a little salt, and about a pint of new milk.

Mix the yeast with a little sugar, flour and water. Rub the lard into the flour, and when the yeast has risen stir it in with a little warm milk. Leave it to rise before the fire, then stir it all together with the rest of the milk warmed, and add to the egg beaten up. Knead it well together and leave it to rise before the fire, but not too near; cover it with a cloth. When risen enough, knead it into cakes, let them stand before the fire until they rise, and bake in a moderate oven.

Currant tea cakes are made by adding currants and a little brown sugar to the dough.

Metropolitan Cake—Light part: 2 cups sugar, ½ cup butter, 1 cup sweet milk, 2½ cups flour, whites of 5 eggs, 2 teaspoonfuls baking-powder. Dark part: ½ cup molasses, ½ cup flour, 1 cup raisins, 1 teaspoonful cinnamon, ½ teaspoonful cloves, 2 large spoonfuls of the light part.

Bake the light part in 2 cakes. Bake the dark part in 1 cake and place between the 2 light cakes with jelly or frosting.

Almond Biscuits—One-quarter lb. almonds, ½ lb. flour, ¼ lb. sugar, ¼ lb. butter, a very small egg.

Blanch and mince the almonds, add them to the flour and sugar, moisten with the egg, and mix with the butter, previously melted. Roll out rather thin, cut with a biscuit-cutter, and bake for ¼ hour.

Virginia Silver Cake—Three-fourths lb. butter; 1 lb. white sugar (loaf sugar pounded and sifted in the best mode), ¾ lb. flour, ¼ lb. corn starch, whites of 16 eggs, 1 teaspoonful cream tartar. Cream the butter, then sift the flour, corn starch and cream tartar gradually into the butter; add last of all the beaten whites; flavor with almond. This cake requires much watching in baking, and a slow oven.

Sponge Cake—Five eggs, ½ lb. loaf sugar, the grated rind and juice of one lemon, ¼ lb. flour.

Separate the yolks from the whites. Beat the yolks and sugar together until they are very light; then add the whites, after they have been whisked to a dry froth; alternately with the flour stir in the lemon, put the mixture in small pans, sift sugar over them and bake.

Hickory Nut Cake—One and one-half cupfuls sugar, ½ cupful butter, a scant ½ cupful sweet milk, 2 cupfuls flour, 3 eggs, 2 teaspoonfuls cream tartar, 1 of soda or 3 teaspoonfuls baking-powder.

Bake in layers. Filling for same: 1 cupful sweet cream or milk; let it come to a boil; then stir in 1 tablespoonful of corn starch which has previously been wet with cold milk; sweeten to taste; let it just boil up; remove from the fire, and stir in 1 pint of pulverized hickory nut meats. Flavor to taste, and when partially cool spread between each 2 layers.

Strawberry Shortcake—Butter, flour, strawberries, sugar, whipped cream.

Make a rich, short crust with butter and flour, allowing 1 ounce more of flour than butter; bake in flat tins of equal size (the pastry when baked should be about an inch thick); open the shortcake, butter it well, and cover ½ with a layer of strawberries previously mixed with sugar; have alternate layers of berries and pastry, finishing with the former, over which place a layer of whipped cream.

Shortcake (Spanish)—Three eggs, ½ cup butter, 1 cup sugar, ¾ cup sweet milk, a little cinnamon, 2 cups flour and 1 teaspoonful baking-powder.

Stir the flour in, do not knead it; the eggs, butter and sugar should be beaten together till very light; bake in a shallow tin; when it is done spread a thin frosting over the top; make this of the white of 1 egg, a little pulverized sugar and a teaspoonful of cinnamon; set it in the oven to brown.

Blackberry Shortcake—Two qts. flour, 3 tablespoonfuls butter, 3 of lard, 2½ cups buttermilk or thick sour milk, yolks of 2 eggs, a teaspoonful of soda and salt.

Mix the salt in the flour, then work in the shortening; beat the yolks of the eggs; dissolve the soda in a little hot water and add to the above proportion of milk; add these to the first mixture; quickly make into a paste, roll out half an inch thick, having upper and under crust. Lay the paste in a well greased baking-tin, cover thickly with berries, sprinkle with sugar, cover with the top crust. Bake about half an hour; cut into squares and eat (splitting these open) with sugar and butter.

Short-Cake (Scotch)—Four ozs. white sugar, ½ lb. slightly salted butter, 1 lb. flour.

Mix the flour and butter with the hands; then add the sugar, and work all into a smooth ball; then roll out until it is an inch thick; prick over with a fork and pinch round the edges, and bake for ½ hour in an oven with a moderate fire, in a round or square pan, according to taste.

Chocolate Cake—Half lb. butter, yolks of 12 eggs, ½ lb. white sugar, same of ground almonds, ¼ lb. chocolate, 2 tablespoonfuls cinnamon, ½ teaspoonful pounded cloves.

Melt the butter and stir it until it froths, beat the yolks of the eggs and stir into the butter; add the sugar and pounded almonds, grated chocolate, cinnamon and pounded cloves, beat well for 15 minutes; then beat the whites of the eggs to a froth, and add these to the above mixture; butter the mould, and bake the above in a moderate oven for 1½ hours.

Almond Macaroons—Blanch and skin 8 oz. of Jordan almonds and 1 oz. of bitter ones; dry them on a sieve, and pound them to a smooth paste in a mortar, adding occasionally a very little water, to prevent them from getting oily; add to them 8 oz. pulverized sugar, 1 teaspoonful rice flour, and the whites of 3 eggs beaten to a stiff froth; put this on paper in drops the size of walnuts, bake in a slow oven until they are of a light color and firmly set; take them from the paper by wetting the under side of it.

Cocoanut Macaroons—Stir together the whites of 4 eggs beaten to 1 lb. of desiccated cocoanut and 1 cupful powdered sugar. Work till it becomes a soft paste and drop in spoonfuls on a buttered tin. Bake in a slow oven.

Silver Cake—Three-fourths lb. sugar, ½ lb. flour, ¼ lb. butter, whites of 8 eggs, 1 heaped teaspoonful essence of bitter almonds.

Cream the butter and sugar; whisk the eggs to a stiff froth and add; lastly the flour and flavoring. Flavor icing of this cake with rose-water.

Cocoanut Cake—Six oz. butter, 1 lb. sugar, 1 lb. flour, 1 large cupful milk, 1 teaspoonful soda, 2 of cream-of-tartar.

Rub the butter into the flour; add the sugar and cream-of-tartar; well whisk the eggs; dissolve the soda in a little warm water, adding these to other ingredients. Bake in layers as for jelly cake. Icing to place between the layers: 6 oz. white sugar, whites of two eggs. Well whisk the eggs and sugar, add the grated cocoanut and place between the layers.

Scotch Snow Cake—Seven oz. white sugar, 1 lb. arrowroot, ½ lb. butter, whites of 7 eggs, any flavoring that is preferred.

Beat the butter until like cream, and while beating add gradually the arrowroot and sugar. When the whites of the eggs are beaten to a stiff froth, mix with the other ingredients and beat for a quarter of an hour. Flavor to taste, pour into buttered mould and bake for 1½ hours.

White Bride Cake—Put 1 lb. of butter into a basin and beat it with your hand till it comes to a fine cream; add 1½ lbs. pulverized sugar, and beat together until it is fine and white; then add 1 lb. sifted flour, give it a stir, and then add the whites of 14 eggs; continue to beat it and add another pound of flour and 14 more whites; beat well; mix all together, paper your dish around the sides and bottom, put in your batter and bake in a moderate oven.

Shrewsbury Cake—One lb. sugar, pounded cinnamon, a little grated nutmeg, 2 lbs. flour, a little rosewater, 3 eggs, melted butter.

Sift the sugar, cinnamon and nutmeg into the flour (which must be of the finest kind); add the rosewater to the eggs and mix with the flour, etc.; then pour in enough melted butter to make it a good thickness and roll out. Mould well, roll thinly, and cut into such shapes as you like.

Marble Spice Cake—Three-quarters of a pound of flour, well dried; 1 lb. white sugar, ½ butter, whites of 14 eggs, 1 tablespoonful cream tartar mixed with flour.

When the cake is mixed, take out about a teacupful of batter and stir into it 1 teaspoonful of cinnamon, 1 of mace, 1 of cloves, 2 of spice and 1 of nutmeg. Fill your mould about an inch deep with the white batter, and drop into this, in several places, a spoonful of the dark mixture; then put in another layer of white, and add the dark as before; repeat this until your batter is used up. This makes one large cake.

Corn-Starch Cake—Four eggs, whites only; 1 cup butter, ⅔ cup corn-starch, ½ cup sweet milk, 2 cup flour, 2 teaspoonfuls baking-powder, lemon or rosewater flavoring.

Cream the butter and sugar thoroughly either with the hand or a silver spoon; mix the corn-starch with the milk and add; then add the eggs, beaten stiff, next the sifted flour, into which the baking-powder has been stirred. Put into well greased mould and bake.

Cracknels—One qt. flour, ½ nutmeg, 4 eggs, 4 spoonfuls rosewater, 1 lb. butter.

Mix the flour, the nutmeg, grated, the yolks of the eggs, beaten, and the rosewater, into a stiff paste with cold water; then roll in the butter and make into cracknel shape; put them into a kettle of boiling water, and boil them till they swim; then take them out and put them into cold water; when hardened, lay them out to dry and bake on tin plates.

Lemon Biscuits—One lb. flour, ¾ lb. white sugar, ¼ lb. fresh butter, 1 oz. lemon peel, 1 tablespoonful lemon juice, 3 eggs.

Add the butter to the flour and rub finely with the hands; mince the lemon peel and stir it and the sugar into the former mixture; well whisk the eggs and lemon juice, and thoroughly mix the whole. Drop from a spoon to a greased baking-tin about 2 inches apart. Bake for 20 minutes.

Cocoanut Biscuits—Six oz. cocoanut grated, 9 oz. white sugar, 3 eggs.

Whisk the eggs for about 12 minutes, then sprinkle in the sugar gradually, lastly the cocoanut; form with your hands into little pyramids; place upon white paper, and the paper on tins. Bake in a cool oven until slightly brown.

Rice Biscuits—One-half lb. ground rice, 5 oz. white sugar, 4 oz. butter, 2 eggs.

Well beat the butter; stir in gradually the ground rice and sugar; well whisk the eggs and add to the other ingredients. Roll out on the paste-board and cut into shapes with paste cutter. Place upon greased tin and bake a quarter of an hour in a slow oven.

Delicious Rolls—One and one-half pints new milk, 1 cupful hop yeast, ½ teaspoonful salt, and flour for forming dough, which must be covered and left to rise over night. In the morning add the whites of 2 well-beaten eggs, ½ cupful butter and flour, and knead the dough briskly for 10 minutes; roll to the thickness of ½ an inch, cut in 4-inch squares, brush the tops with sweet milk and fold them over cornerwise; place them close together in buttered pans. Set in a warm place until light, when bake in a quick oven.

Graham Gems—Two tablespoonfuls sugar, 1 tablespoonful butter, well stirred together; add 1 coffeecupful sweet milk, graham to make a stiff batter, then 1 well-beaten egg, saltspoonful of salt and 2 teaspoonfuls good baking-powder. This makes a dozen gems. Bake 15 or 20 minutes.

PASTRY

A GOOD hand at pastry will use less butter and produce lighter crust than others. Salt butter is very good, and if well washed makes a good, flaky crust. If the weather is warm the butter should be placed in ice water to keep it as firm as possible; when lard is used take care that it is perfectly sweet.

In making pastry, as in other arts, "practice will make perfect;" it should be touched as lightly as possible, made in a cool place, and with hands perfectly cool; if possible, use a marble slab instead of pastry board; if the latter is used, it is better to procure it made of hard wood.

It is important to use great expedition in the preparation of pastry, and care must be taken not to allow it to stand long before baking, or it will become flat and heavy. A brisk oven will be required for puff pastry; a good plan to test the proper heat is to put a small piece of the paste in before baking the whole. Be sure that the oven is as near perfection as possible; for an oven in which the heat is not evenly distributed can never produce a well-baked pie or tart; where there is an unequal degree of heat the pastry rises on the hottest side in the shape of a large bubble and sinks into a heavy, indigestible lump on the coolest. Raised pie crust should have a good soaking heat, and glazed pastry rather a slack heat. When suet is used it must be perfectly free from skin and minced as finely as possible; beef suet is considered the best.

All moulds, pie-dishes, patty-pans, and vessels of all descriptions used for baking or boiling must be well buttered.

The outside of a boiled pudding often tastes disagreeably, which arises from the cloth not being nicely washed and kept in a dry place. It should be dipped in boiling water, squeezed dry, and floured when to be used. If bread, it should be tied loosely; if batter, tightly over. The water should be boiling briskly when the pudding is put in. Batter pudding should be strained through a coarse sieve when all is mixed. In others the eggs separately. A pan of cold water should be ready, and the pudding dipped in as soon as it comes out of the pot, and then it will not adhere to the cloth.

Snow is an excellent substitute for eggs either in puddings or pancakes. Two large spoonfuls will supply the place of one egg, and the article it is used in will be equally good. This is a useful piece of information, especially as snow often falls at the season when eggs are the dearest.

Apple Pudding (Boiled) — Suet or butter crust, apples, sugar to taste, a little minced lemon peel, 2 tablespoonfuls lemon juice.

Butter a pudding mould, line with the paste, pare, core and cut the apples into small pieces. Fill the basin and add the sugar, finely minced lemon peel and juice. Cover with the crust, press the edges firmly, cover with a floured cloth. Tie securely and plunge into boiling water. Allow to boil 3 hours. Remove from basin and send to table quickly.

Apple Charlotte — Soak ½ box gelatine 2 hours in 2 small cups of cold water. Pare and steam 8 medium-sized apples; when they are tender press through the colander and add 2 cups of sugar and the juice of 1 large lemon. Mix the gelatine with the hot apples and stir until they are cool, then set on ice to harden. Serve very cold with whipped cream. This is an old English dainty.

Currant Dumplings — One lb. flour, 6 oz. beef suet, ½ lb. currants, 1 glass of water.

Mince the suet finely, mix with the flour and currants, which of course have been washed, picked and dried; mix with the above proportion of water or milk, divide into dumplings about the size of an orange; tie in cloths, plunge into boiling water, and boil from 1 to 1¼ hours. Serve with butter and white sugar.

Lemon Dumplings — Ten oz. fine bread-crumbs, 1 large tablespoonful flour, ½ lb. finely chopped beef suet, the grated rinds of 2 small lemons, 4 oz. powdered sugar, 3 large eggs beaten and strained, and last of all the juice of the 2 lemons also strained.

Mix the ingredients well, divide into four dumplings, tie them in well-floured cloths, and let them boil an hour.

Apple Pudding (Baked) — Ten apples, 4 oz. brown sugar, 3 oz. butter, 4 eggs, 2½ breakfast cups of bread-crumbs.

Pare and cut into quarters the apples, removing the cores. Boil them to a pulp. Well whisk the eggs and put them and the butter into the apple pulp. Stir the mixture for 5 minutes. Grease a pie dish and place a sprinkling of bread-crumbs, then of apple, and proceed in this manner until all are used. Bake for ¾ of an hour. The top layer must be of bread-crumbs.

Batter Pudding — One and one-half cupfuls flour, 1 teaspoonful baking-powder, ½ teaspoon salt, 1 tablespoon butter, 2 eggs, 1 pint milk.

Steam 1 hour and serve with sauce. Adding a cupful of raisins, or any other desirable fruit, either fresh or dried, to the above pudding, makes a most delicious dish.

Bread Pudding — Bread and boiling milk, allowing ½ a pint to 1 lb. soaked bread, 2 beaten eggs, a little nutmeg, sugar.

Soak the bread in cold water, then squeeze it very dry, take out any lumps, and add the milk, beat up the eggs, sweeten to taste, add nutmeg, and bake the pudding slowly until firm. If desired, a few sultanas may be added to the pudding; or, if the bread is light, such as the crusts of French rolls, it may be soaked in as much cold milk as it will absorb, and when it is perfectly soft have sugar, eggs and flavoring added to it.

Caramel Pudding — A handful of white sugar, ½ pint water, yolks of 8 eggs, 1 pint milk.

Boil the sugar and water until of a deep brown color, warm a small basin, pour the syrup in and keep turning the basin in your hand until the inside is completely coated with the syrup, which, by that time, will have set. Take the yolks of the eggs and mix gradually and effectually with the milk. Pour this mixture into the prepared mould. Lay a piece of paper on the top. Set it in a saucepan full of cold water, taking care that the water does not come over the top of the mould, put on the cover, and let it boil gently by the side of the fire for 1 hour. Remove the saucepan to a cool place, and when the water is quite cold take out the mould, and turn out the pudding very carefully.

Creamed Sponge Cake—Cut the top from a stale sponge cake loaf in 1 piece, ½ an inch thick. Dig and scrape the crumbs from inside of loaf and upper slice, leaving enough to keep the outside firm. Spread a thick layer of fruit jelly on the inside. Heat a cup of milk to a boil, stir in a tablespoonful of cornstarch wet with cold milk, and the cake crumbs rubbed fine. Stir until thick, take from the fire, beat in 2 whipped eggs and 2 tablespoonfuls of sugar. Make all into smooth batter; set in boiling water on the range and stir for 5 minutes after the mixture is really hot enough. Turn into a bowl, flavor with almond or vanilla, and let it get cold. Fill the cake with it, fit on the top, wash all over with whipped white of egg; sift powdered sugar evenly over it until no more will adhere to the surface, and let it harden.

Martha's Pudding—One-half pint milk, 1 laurel leaf, a piece of cinnamon, 1 teacup bread-crumbs, 3 eggs, nutmeg and lemon-peel, 1 tea-spoonful orange-flower water.

Put the laurel leaf and cinnamon into the milk and boil, then pour over the bread-crumbs, add the eggs well beaten, the nutmeg, lemon-peel and flower-water. Sweeten to taste, butter a basin, stick currants and split raisins in rows upon it. Stir all the ingredients well together and pour into the basin. Cover with a cloth and boil 1½ hours.

Chocolate Pudding—One quart milk, 14 even tablespoonfuls grated bread-crumbs, 12 table-spoonfuls grated chocolate, 6 eggs, 1 tablespoon-ful vanilla, sugar to make very sweet.

Separate the yolks and whites of 4 eggs; beat up the 4 yolks and 2 whole eggs together very light with sugar. Put the milk on the range, and when it comes to a perfect boil pour it over the bread and chocolate; add the beaten eggs, sugar and vanilla; be sure it is sweet enough; pour into a buttered dish; bake 1 hour in a moderate oven. When cold, and just before it is served, have the 4 whites beaten with a little powdered sugar, and flavor with vanilla and use as a meringue.

Currant Pudding (Boiled)—Fourteen oz. flour, 7 oz. suet, 7 oz. currants, a little milk.

Have the currants washed and dried, mixed with the finely minced suet and flour. Moisten the whole with sufficient milk to form a stiff batter. Place in a floured cloth and plunge into boiling water. Boil 4 hours and serve with butter and sugar.

Gingerbread Pudding—Two oz. lard or butter, 2 tablespoonfuls brown sugar, 2 ditto golden syrup, 1 egg, 1 teacupful milk, 1 tea-spoonful ground ginger, 8 oz. flour, 1 teaspoon-ful baking-powder.

Work the butter and sugar together, then add the egg beaten well, the ginger, syrup and milk, and then the flour and baking-powder. Steam 4 hours.

Ginger Pudding—Nine oz. flour, 3 oz. suet, 3 oz. sugar, 1 large tablespoonful grated ginger.

Chop the suet finely, add to the flour, sugar and ginger; mix well. Butter a mould and put the ingredients in perfectly dry. Cover securely with a cloth and boil 3 hours. To be eaten with sweet sauce.

Cherry Pudding—One pint flour, 1 cup milk, butter the size of an egg, 2 eggs, ½ cup sugar, 2 teaspoonfuls baking-powder, a little salt and a pint of cherries which have been stoned. Boil 1 hour. If one has not a regular boiler, the batter may be turned into a 5-pound lard pail, or any tin pail holding about 2 quarts. Cover tightly, and place in a large kettle of boiling water, which should also be covered. Never let the pudding stop boiling for a second until it is removed.

Orange Pudding—The rind of 1 Seville orange, 6 oz. fresh butter, 6 oz. white sugar, 6 eggs, 1 apple, puff paste.

Grate the rind and mix with the butter and sugar, adding by degrees the eggs well beaten; scrape a raw apple and mix with the rest; line the bottom and sides of a dish with paste, pour in the orange mixture and lay it over crossbars of paste. It will take half an hour to bake.

Lemon Pudding—Two eggs, 2 cupfuls sugar, 2 tablespoonfuls corn-starch, 2 lemons, butter.

Beat the yolks of the eggs light, add the sugar; dissolve the corn-starch in a little cold water, stir into it 2 teacupfuls of boiling water; put in the juice of the lemons, with some of the grated peel. Stir all together with a teaspoonful of butter. Bake about 15 minutes. When done spread over the top the beaten whites of the eggs, and brown.

Fairy Pudding—Over ½ box gelatine pour 1 cup of cold water and let it soak 1 hour. Let 1 pint of rich milk come to a boil and add to it 3 well-beaten eggs and ½ cup of sugar; when it thickens stir in the gelatine and in 2 minutes take from the fire and flavor with almond extract. Line a mould with stale cake, pour in the mixture and set away on ice. Whip 1 pint of cream and pile on the top; serve very cold.

Marmalade Pudding—Two oz. lard or butter, 2 tablespoonfuls brown sugar, 4 oz. marma-lade, 1 egg, 1 teacup milk, 9 oz. flour, 1 teaspoon-ful baking-powder.

Well mix the butter and sugar, then add the eggs well beaten, the marmalade and milk, then the flour and baking-powder. Steam 4 hours.

Boiled Batter Pudding—Three-fourths lb. flour, 3 eggs, a pinch of salt, a pint of milk.

Put the flour and salt in a basin and break the eggs in it and mix well. Then add the milk gradually, stirring well to make the batter smooth. Beat it with a wooden spoon for a few minutes, put it into a well-buttered basin, tie over with a well-floured cloth and boil for 1½ hours.

Holiday Pudding—A plain sponge cake, strawberry jam, icing, a rich custard, some pre-served ginger.

Make the sponge cake in a round mould; take out the inside of the cake with a cutter, not too near the edge; put in a layer of strawberry jam, not too thickly spread. Cut the inside of the cake you have taken out in slices, spread some jam between each slice (different sorts of jam may be used, but strawberry does very nicely), and replace the cake. Ice it nicely over; put it into a very slow oven to dry the icing. Then make the custard and pour into it small pieces of preserved ginger. Pour into the cake and serve hot.

Cabinet Pudding—One and one-half pints new milk, white sugar, 1 lemon, cinnamon, mace, cloves, 3 eggs and the yolks of 4, butter, 4 or 5 sponge cakes.

Boil the milk with enough white sugar to sweeten it, the peel of a fresh lemon cut thinly, the cinnamon, mace and cloves. Boil these ingredients as for a custard. Beat up the eggs. Pour the boiling milk, etc., on to these, stirring continually, then strain the whole through a hair sieve and leave to cool. Take a good-sized pudding mould, butter it well and line it with sponge cake cut into thin slices. Pour the custard into the mould and tie it close. It will take 1½ hours to boil. It is an improvement, after buttering the mould and before placing the sponge cakes, to arrange some stoned raisins, slices of candied peel and nutmeg. Serve hot with sauce.

Fig Pudding—One lb. flour, 3 oz. bread crumbs, 2 oz. finely-chopped suet, 3 oz. sugar, 1 egg, ½ lb. figs cut in slices.

Flavor with nutmeg; mix all with milk and boil 3 hours.

Steamed Pudding—One cupful suet chopped fine, 1 cupful molasses, 1 cupful currants washed and dried, 1 cupful sour milk, 1 teaspoonful soda, a little salt, flour.

Mix well, using flour enough to make a stiff dough; pour into a mold and steam 4 hours.

Oxford Dumplings—Two oz. grated bread, 4 oz. currants, 4 oz. suet chopped fine, 1 large spoonful flour, 1 oz. pounded sugar, 3 eggs, grated lemon peel and a little spice.

Mix with the yolks of the eggs well beaten and a little milk. Divide into 4 dumplings ½ inch thick, and fry a nice brown in plenty of lard. Serve with white sauce and sifted sugar on them.

Fruit Pudding—Crust: One-fourth oz. suet to 6 oz. flour; pinch of salt, and water enough to make a thick paste; fruit and sugar.

Make the crust of suet, flour, salt and water; roll it out thin before putting into a buttered basin, then add the fruit mixed with the sugar, except in the case of apples, which are sometimes sweetened by boiling with sugar; put on a lid of paste, and boil the pudding 1½ hours. Care should be taken to roll the crust thin, in order to get as much fruit as possible into the pudding. It is a good plan to stew a little fruit, and serve it with the pudding, as it should be given to children in large proportion to the crust.

Strawberry Saracen—Toast very thin slices of stale bread and line the bottom and sides of a China dish with them, after buttering generously. Trim the bread to fit the dish neatly. Fill the space with strawberries packed and heaped as full as the dish will hold; sift plenty of sugar all through and over them, and set the dish in a moderate oven for about half an hour. It will be found that the berries melt a great deal, so they must be plentiful. Serve very cold with rich, thick cream. This is one of the most delicious desserts imaginable; notwithstanding that there are people who consider it almost a crime to cook strawberries in any way.

Mince Pies—The sooner the Christmas mince meat is prepared and set away to ripen so much better will the pies made of it be. Take 3 lbs. lean beef from the round and boil it in enough water to cover it. When very tender, set it away till cold, and then chop very fine, carefully removing any piece of gristle or fat. Next weigh out 5 lbs. Greening apples; after peeling and coring them, chop fine and add to the meat. Chop fine 1 lb. kidney suet and 2 lbs. seeded raisins and add to the above with 2 lbs. clean currants, ¾ lb. citron, finely shredded, and 4 oz. each of candied orange and lemon peel (or the grated rind of 2 oranges and 2 lemons), and the pulp of 2 oranges and 2 lemons chopped and freed from seeds and tough bits. To these ingredients add enough sugar to sweeten to taste, also 2 even tablespoonfuls cinnamon, 1 tablespoonful mace, 1 tablespoonful allspice and 1 tablespoonful cloves, together with a grated nutmeg and a good teaspoonful salt. Now add enough sweet cider to secure the right consistency—3 pints or two quarts. Any fruit juice is an improvement, especially the juice from spiced pears or peaches. Some liberally disposed housewives contribute a jar of preserved strawberries, or raspberries, or cherries, to their pot of mince, which is a rare improvement. When all has been thoroughly mixed, place the stone pot containing the mince meat on the back of the range to warm slowly through, gradually moving it forward till it boils; then push it back to simmer for a few moments, after which it should be set away to cool. Keep in a cool place till wanted, and in making the pies sprinkle in about a dozen seeded raisins to each one.

Plum Pudding—Two lbs. beef suet, 1½ lbs. bread crumbs, 1½ lbs. flour, 2 lbs. raisins, 2½ lbs. currants, ½ lb. mixed peel, 2½ lbs. [illegible] sugar, [illegible] eggs, a little nutmeg, ginger, allspice (powdered), a large pinch of salt, ½ pint milk.

Chop the suet as finely as possible, and any stale pieces of bread can be used for grating, allowing the above quantity; mix with the suet and flour. Stone the raisins, and have the currants perfectly washed and dried, the peel cut into thin slices and added to the suet, bread and flour, mixing well for some minutes; then add the sugar and continue working with the hands for 5 minutes. Put the eggs into a bowl (breaking each into a cup first to ascertain that it is fresh and to remove the speck), add to them grated nutmeg, powdered ginger and powdered allspice, according to taste, and a large pinch of salt; then stir in ½ pint milk; beat all up together, and pour it gradually into another bowl, working the whole mixture with the hand for some time. If the mixture be too stiff add more milk, and continue to work it with a wooden spoon for at least ½ hour. Scald 2 pudding cloths, spread each in a bowl and dredge them well with flour. Divide the composition in 2 equal parts, put each in its cloth and tie it up tightly. To boil the pudding, place 2 inverted plates in saucepans filled with water, and when the water boils fast put each pudding into its saucepan. Let them boil 6 hours, keeping the saucepan full by adding more water as it is required, and taking care that it never ceases boiling. Then take the puddings out and hang them up till the next day, when the cloth of each pudding should be tightened and tied afresh, and 3 hours' boiling, as in the first instance, will make them ready for table.

Baked Custard—Five eggs, 3 tablespoonfuls sugar, 1 quart milk, 2 teaspoonfuls almond or other flavoring extract. Beat the whites and yolks of the eggs separately, to the yolks add the sugar, then, a little at a time, the milk, then the flavoring, and lastly the whites of the eggs, stir well together and bake in thick cups set in a pan of water in rather quick oven until firm—this usually takes about 30 minutes.

A Teetotaler's Christmas Pudding—Pick and stone 2 lbs. good Valencias; pick, wash and dry 1 lb. currants; chop 2 lbs. beef suet; have ready ½ lb. brown sugar, 6 oz. candied peel, cut thin, 2½ lbs. flour, 6 eggs, a quart or more of milk, 1 oz. mixed spice, and a tablespoonful salt.

Put the flour into a large pan, add the plums, currants, suet, sugar, peel, spice and salt, and mix them well together while dry. Beat the eggs well in a large basin, and add a portion of the milk, stirring it at the same time. Make a well in the middle of the flour and pour in the milk and eggs. Keep stirring till all the ingredients are thoroughly mixed. Add more milk, if necessary, and stir up again; the batter should be rather stiff. Have a good stout cloth ready; wet and flour it well, lay it over a pan, pour in the batter, and tie it firmly up. When the water in the copper or large kettle boils, put the pudding in and let it boil gently for 8 or 9 hours. Turn it carefully out of the cloth. Serve with or without sauce.

Dutch Boiled Pudding—Mix well together 1 cupful suet, 1 cupful milk, 1 cupful molasses, 1 tablespoonful ginger, 1 teaspoonful ground cloves, ½ nutmeg; add flour to make a stiff batter, and 1 teaspoonful baking-powder, and last of all mix in the batter 1½ cupfuls of any kind of fruit well floured. Wet a cloth bag—an old napkin makes a good bag—and sprinkle conscientiously with flour; then pour in the batter and tie up the neck of the bag very tightly, leaving a generous room for the pudding to swell; for it is as expansive as gossip. Have a kettle of boiling water and dump in the bag. You must turn the bag every 10 minutes for the first hour, then boil it for two hours longer, and if you have not let the supply of water run too low, or forgot to turn it, or excited yourself in the manipulations and thus left too much of the pudding above water in your haste, or pricked the bag with your basting fork, or done anything else ruinous, you will have a pudding not nearly so indigestible as you might suppose.

Puff Puddings—One pint flour, 2 teaspoonfuls baking-powder and a teaspoonful salt, enough milk to make a soft batter, and 1 pint of any kind of ripe berries. Make your batter, grease cups thoroughly, and into each one put a tablespoonful of the batter and one of the berries, covering them with more batter. Set the cups in a steamer and steam 20 minutes. Make the sauce as follows: Mix 1 cup sugar and ½ cup butter; to this add 2 eggs; beat well and add 1 cup milk and one of the berries. Set inside of a vessel of boiling water until ready to use, stirring often.

Roly Poly Jam Pudding—Suet crust and 12 oz. of any kind of jam.

Having made a nice suet crust, roll to the thickness of about ½ inch. Place the jam in the center and spread equally over the paste, allowing a margin of about ½ inch for the pudding to join. Roll up lightly, join the ends securely, place upon a floured cloth, and fasten with tape, allowing a little for the pudding to swell. Plunge into boiling water and boil 2 hours.

Red Currant Pudding—Some red currants and raspberries, sugar, slices of bread.

Stew the red currants and raspberries with sugar till thoroughly done, pour off all the juice, and put the fruit while hot into a pudding basin lined with bread made to fit exactly; fill the basin up with fruit, and cover it with a slice of bread made to fit exactly; let it stand till quite cold with a plate on it. Boil up the juice which was poured off with a little more sugar, and let that get cold. When served the pudding must be turned out on a dish and the juice poured all over it so as to color the bread thoroughly. It can be served with custard or cream.

Raspberry Pudding—One pint bread-crumbs, 1 quart milk, 2 cupfuls sugar, 1 lemon, butter, a cupful of preserved raspberries, 4 eggs.

Mix the bread-crumbs, milk, 1 cupful sugar, the peel of the lemon grated, the yolks of the eggs, and a small piece of butter, and bake. When done spread over the top a cupful of preserved raspberries; put over that a meringue made with the whites of the eggs, a cupful of sugar and the juice of the lemon. Return it to the oven to color; let it partly cool and serve it with rich cream.

Sweet Potato Pudding—Two cups mashed sweet potato (the potato must first be boiled); a cup of sugar, a small cup of butter, 3 eggs, ½ teaspoonful soda dissolved in a little hot water, a teaspoonful lemon extract, and ½ teaspoonful grated nutmeg.

Beat the eggs until they are very light, rub the butter and sugar to a cream, and mix all with the potato; cover a deep plate or shallow pudding dish with a thick crust; then put in the mixture and bake slowly for ¾ of an hour.

Rice and Raisin Pudding—Five eggs, 1 cup rice, 1 cup sugar, butter the size of an egg, 2 handfuls of raisins.

Simmer the rice in a quart of milk until tender; remove from the stove to cool. Well whisk the yolks of the eggs and add to the rice, also the rest of the milk, sugar, and butter; then well beat the whites of the eggs, stone the raisins, and add to the other ingredients. Grate nutmeg on the top and bake 1 hour.

Raspberry Bavarian Cream — Cover ½ box gelatine with ½ cupful cold water and let soak ½ hour; set over boiling water and stir until dissolved; add 6 tablespoonfuls sugar and a pint of raspberry juice; strain into a tin pan. Set on ice and stir until thick; add a pint of whipped cream. Mix thoroughly, pour in a mold, and stand aside to harden.

Arrowroot Blanc Mange — Moisten 2 dessertspoonfuls of best arrowroot with water, rub to a smooth paste and throw it into 1 cupful of boiling milk; stir steadily and boil until it thickens. Serve cold, sweetened and flavored to taste.

Baked Lemon Pudding — Three oz. crumbs, 3 oz. sugar, 3 oz. butter, the grated rind and juice of a lemon, ½ pint milk, 3 eggs, some good paste.

Mix the dry ingredients, pour over them the milk, made hot. When cold, add the eggs and lemon juice. Line a greased dish with this paste, putting a double strip round the edge; pour the mixture into it, and bake in a moderate oven.

Rice and Apple Pudding — A cupful of rice, 6 apples, a little chopped lemon peel, 2 cloves, sugar.

Boil the rice for 10 minutes; drain it through a hair sieve until quite dry. Put a cloth into a pudding basin and lay the rice round it like a crust. Cut the apples into quarters, stuffing them in the middle of the rice with a little chopped lemon peel, cloves and some sugar. Cover the fruit with rice, tie up tight, and boil for an hour. Serve with melted butter, sweetened and poured over it.

Cream Tapioca Pudding — Three tablespoonfuls tapioca, 4 eggs, 3 tablespoonfuls sugar, 3 tablespoonfuls prepared cocoanut, 1 quart milk.

Soak the tapioca in water over night, put it in the milk and boil ¾ of an hour. Beat the yolks of the eggs into a cup of sugar, add the cocoanut, stir in and boil 15 minutes longer; pour into a pudding dish; beat the whites of the eggs to a stiff froth, stir in 3 tablespoonfuls of sugar; put this over the top and sprinkle with cocoanut, and brown 5 minutes.

French Tapioca — Two oz. fine tapioca, ½ pint milk, 1 well-beaten egg, sugar and flavoring.

Take the tapioca de la couronne, and boil it in ½ pint water until it begins to melt, then add the milk by degrees, and boil until the tapioca becomes very thick; add the egg, sugar and flavoring to taste, and bake gently for ¾ of an hour. This preparation of tapioca is superior to any other, is nourishing, and suitable for delicate children.

Velvet Pudding — Five eggs, 1½ cupfuls sugar, 4 tablespoonfuls corn starch, 3 pints milk.

Dissolve the corn starch in a little cold milk, and add 1 cupful of sugar and the yolks of the eggs beaten. Boil 3 pints of milk and add the other ingredients while boiling; remove from the fire when it becomes quite thick; flavor with vanilla and pour into a baking-dish; beat the whites of the eggs to a stiff froth, add ½ cup sugar, turn over the pudding, and place it in the oven and let brown slightly.

Sauce for Velvet Pudding — Yolks of 2 eggs, 1 cupful sugar, 1 tablespoonful butter, 1 cup milk.

Well beat the yolks, sugar and butter; add to the milk (boiling), and set on the stove till it comes to boiling heat; flavor with vanilla.

Florentine Pudding — 1 quart milk, 3 tablespoonfuls corn starch dissolved in a little cold milk, 3 eggs, ½ teacupful sugar; flavoring, lemon or vanilla, etc. according to taste, white sugar.

Put the milk in a saucepan and allow it to boil. Add to the corn starch (mixed in the milk) the yolks of the 3 eggs beaten, the sugar and flavoring; stir in the scalding milk, continue stirring until the mixture is of the consistency of custard. Pour into baking tin; beat the whites of the eggs in a teacup of pulverized sugar and when the pudding is cooked spread on the top; place in the oven to brown. Can be eaten with cream, but is very nice without.

Sweet Macaroni — One-quarter lb. best macaroni, 3 quarts water, a pinch of salt, 1 teacupful milk, ¼ lb. white sugar, flavoring.

Break up the macaroni into small lengths, and boil in the water (adding the salt) until perfectly tender; drain away the water, add to the macaroni, in a stewpan, the milk and sugar, and keep shaking over the fire until the milk is absorbed. Add any flavoring and serve with or without stewed fruit.

Gingerbread Pudding — One-quarter lb. suet, 2 oz. ground ginger, ½ lb. sugar, 3 tablespoonfuls molasses, 1 teaspoonful baking-powder, 1 lb. flour, about ½ pint milk.

Mix the dry ingredients, dissolve the molasses in the milk, beat all well together, and boil in a well-floured cloth for 3 hours.

Oatmeal Pudding — Two oz. fine Scotch oatmeal, ½ pint cold milk, 1 pint boiling milk, sugar to taste, 2 oz. bread crumbs, 1 oz. shred suet, 1 or 2 beaten eggs, lemon flavoring or grated nutmeg.

Mix with the oatmeal first, the cold milk, and then add the boiling milk; sweeten and stir over the fire for 10 minutes, then add the bread crumbs; stir until the mixture is stiff, then add the suet and eggs; add flavoring. Put the pudding in a buttered dish and bake slowly for an hour.

Apple Snowballs — One-half lb. rice, 5 or 6 large apples, a little butter and sugar.

Wash the rice, put it into plenty of water, and boil quickly for 10 minutes, drain it and let it cool. Pare the apples, take out the core with a vegetable cutter, and fill the hole with a small piece of butter and coarse sugar. Enclose each apple in rice, tie in separate cloths, and boil for 1 hour. Serve with sweet sauce.

Sunday Pudding — One-quarter lb. bread-crumbs, ½ pint milk, sugar and flavoring to taste, 2 eggs, strawberry jam.

Boil the bread-crumbs in the milk, sweeten and flavor, and when the bread is thick stir in the yolks of the eggs. Put the pudding into a buttered tart dish, bake slowly for ¾ of an hour. Then spread over the top a layer of strawberry jam, and on this the whites of the eggs beaten with a tablespoonful of sifted sugar to a strong froth. Dip a knife in boiling water, and with it smooth over the whites; put the pudding again into a moderate oven until the top is a light golden brown. Serve immediately.

Yorkshire Pudding — One egg, a pinch of salt, milk, 4 tablespoonfuls flour.

Beat the egg and salt with a fork for a few minutes. Add to this 4 tablespoonfuls of milk and the flour; beat (with a spoon) very well, while in a batter, for 10 minutes. Then add the milk till it attains almost the consistency of cream. Take care to have the dripping hot in the pudding tin. Pour the batter into the tin to the thickness of about a quarter of an inch, then bake under the roasting joint. The above will make a pudding of moderate size, perhaps one dozen squares. The great secret of a pudding being light is to mix it 2 hours before cooking it.

Malvern Pudding—Some thin slices of dry bread, fresh fruit, sugar, custard.

Line a basin with the slices of bread. Boil some fresh, juicy fruit with sugar, in the proportion of ½ lb. to 1 lb. of fruit. Pour into the lined basin, and cover with slices of bread. Put a saucer on the top with a heavy weight on it. Turn out next day and pour custard round it.

Orange Custard — The juice of 12 oranges, the yolks of 12 eggs, 1 pint of cream, sugar to taste.

Sweeten the juice, and stir it over a slow fire until the sugar dissolves, taking off the scum as it rises. When nearly cold stir in the yolks, well beaten, and the cream. Stir again over the fire until it thickens. Be careful not to boil it, or it will curdle.

Apple Solid — Take 3 lbs. sliced apples, 1½ lbs. lump sugar, the juice and grated rind of 2 lemons.

Dip the lumps of sugar in water, and boil with the apples and lemon until stiff. Put into a mould, and, when cold, turn out. May be served with custard poured round.

Apple Snow — Take 4 apples, 3 dessert-spoonfuls of sugar, the grated rind of a lemon, the whites of 3 eggs.

Peel, core and stew the apples, mix with them the sugar and lemon rind. Beat the whites of eggs to a stiff froth, mix with the apples, and beat the whole until quite white. Pile on a glass dish.

Preserve Sandwiches — One-half lb. sifted sugar, ½ lb. butter, 2 eggs, 2 oz. ground rice; work them well together, then add 7 oz. flour.

Spread half this mixture upon buttered paper in a shallow tin, then a layer of preserve, and cover with the other half of the paste. Bake in a quick oven, and when cold and ready for use cut it into pieces like sandwiches, and sprinkle sugar over.

Graham Pudding — Two cups Graham flour, 2 eggs, 1 quart milk, butter the size of an egg, salt to taste.

Put a pint of milk into a buttered stewpan, and allow to heat slowly. Mix the rest of the milk in the flour, and beat lightly with the butter, eggs and salt. Then pour the hot milk upon it, mix well, return to the fire surrounded by boiling water, and stir constantly for ½ hour; grate nutmeg upon it. Serve in uncovered dish, and eat with butter and sugar.

Cottage Pie — Two lbs. potatoes, scraps of cold meat, 1 onion, 1½ oz. butter, pepper and salt to taste, ½ glass milk.

Boil and mash potatoes (or, if there are any cold ones at hand, they will do as well); put the milk and butter on the fire to boil, and when boiling pour upon the mashed potatoes and mix to a paste; place the meat in a pie dish with a little fat in layers, mince the onion and sprinkle each layer with it, also pepper and salt; half fill the dish with water or gravy and cover with the potatoes, smoothing neatly and marking with a fork into a pattern; bake ½ hour.

Boiled Bread Pudding — One-half lb. bread-crumbs, 2 oz. powdered loaf sugar, 1 pint milk, 2 oz. currants, 1 oz. candied peel cut very small, 3 eggs.

Mix the crumbs and sugar; make the milk hot, and pour it over them. When nearly cold add the other ingredients, and boil in a mould for 2 hours, or steam 3 hours. Serve with lemon sauce.

Eel Pie — Eels, salt, pepper and nutmeg, puff paste, 1 onion, a few cloves, a little stock, 1 egg, butter, flour and lemon juice.

Skin and wash some eels, remove the heads and tails, cut up the fish into pieces about three inches long, season them with salt, pepper and nutmeg. Border a pie-dish with puff paste, put in the eels with a chopped onion, and a few cloves; add a little clear stock; cover with puff paste, brush over the crust with the yolk of an egg, and bake. Make a sauce with the trimmings of the eels, some white stock seasoned with salt and pepper; thicken it with butter and flour, add some lemon juice, strain, and pour it quite hot through a funnel into the pie.

Pigeon Pie—Pigeons, pepper and salt, a piece of butter, a bunch of parsley, a beefsteak, 3 hard-boiled eggs, 1 cup water, a few pieces of ham, crust.

Rub the pigeons with pepper and salt, inside and out; in the former put a piece of butter, and, if approved, some parsley chopped with the livers, and a little of the seasoning; lay the steak at the bottom of the dish, and the birds on it; between every two a hard egg. Put the water in the dish, and if you have any ham in the house, lay a piece on each pigeon; it is a great improvement to the flavor. Observe, when the ham is cut for gravy or pies, to take the under part rather than the prime. Season the gizzards, and the two joints of the wings, and put them in the center of the pie, and over them, in a hole made in the crust, three feet nicely cleaned, to show what pie it is.

Chicken Pie—Two young fowls; seasonings: white pepper, salt, a little mace and nutmeg, all of the finest powder, and cayenne. Some fresh ham cut in slices, or gammon of bacon, some forcemeat balls, and hard eggs. Gravy from knuckle of veal or a piece of scrag, shank bone of mutton, herbs, onion, mace, and white pepper.

Cut up the fowls; add the seasoning. Put the chicken, slices of ham, or gammon of bacon, forcemeat balls and hard eggs by turn in layers. If it be baked in a dish put a little water, but none if in a raised crust. By the time it returns from the oven have ready a gravy made of the veal or scrag, shank bones of mutton and seasoning. If to be eaten hot you may add truffles, morels, mushrooms, etc., but not if to be eaten cold. If it is made in a dish put as much gravy as will fill it; but in raised crust the gravy must be nicely strained, and then put in cold as jelly. To make the jelly clear, you may give it a boil with the whites of two eggs, after taking away the meat, and then run it through a fine lawn sieve.

Giblet Pie—Some goose or duck giblets, water, onion, black pepper, a bunch of sweet herbs, a large teacupful of cream, sliced potatoes, plain crust, salt.

Line the edge of a pie dish with a plain crust. Stew the giblets in a small quantity of water with the seasoning till nearly done. Let them grow cold, and, if not enough to fill the dish, lay a beef, veal or two or three mutton steaks at the bottom. Add the giblets and the liquor was boiled in. Lay slices of cold potatoes on the top and cover with the crust; bake for 1½ hours in a brisk oven.

Lemon Pie (1)—Crust, 1 lemon, 1½ cups white sugar, 1 cup water, a piece of butter the size of an egg, 1 tablespoonful flour, 1 egg.

Make your crust as usual; cover your pie-tins (I use my jelly-cake tins) and bake exactly as for tart crusts. If you make more than you need, never mind, they will keep. While they are baking, if they rise in the center, take a fork and open the crust to let the air out. Now make the filling as follows: For one pie take a nice lemon and grate off the outside, taking care to get only the yellow; the white is bitter. Squeeze out all the juice; add white sugar, water and butter. Put in a basin on the stove. When it boils stir in the flour, and the yolk of one egg, beaten smooth with a little water. When it boils thick take off the stove and let it cool. Fill your pie crust with this. Beat the white of an egg stiff, add a heaping tablespoonful of sugar; pour over the top of the pie. Brown carefully in the oven.

Lemon Pie (2)—One cup sugar, 1 tablespoonful butter, 1 egg, 1 lemon, juice and rind, 1 teacupful boiling water and 1 tablespoonful corn-starch.

Dissolve the corn-starch in a little cold water, then stir it into the boiling water; cream the butter and sugar, then pour over them the hot mixture; cool, add the lemon juice, rind and beaten egg; bake with or without upper crust.

Peach Pie—Puff or short crust, peaches, sugar.

Line a dish with a nice crust, skin the peaches, remove the stones, and put the fruit into the dish, with a little sugar and water. Cover with crust and bake a golden brown.

Rhubarb Pie—Rhubarb, a little lemon peel, sugar, water, short crust.

Use a deep pie dish, wipe the stalks with a clean, damp cloth, cut into pieces about an inch in length, mince the lemon peel, line the edge of the dish with the crust, then fill the dish with rhubarb, sugar and lemon, adding a cup of water. Cover with crust, making a hole in the middle. Bake about ¾ of an hour.

Gooseberry Pie—Top and tail the berries, line the edge of a deep dish with short crust. Put the berries into it with at least 6 ounces of moist sugar and a little water. Cover with upper crust and bake from ½ to ¾ of an hour.

Damson Pie—Damsons, ¼ lb. moist sugar, crust.

Line the edge of a deep dish with crust, place a small cup in the middle, fill the dish with the fruit, sprinkling the sugar over; cover with crust and bake about ¾ of an hour. If puff paste is used, just before it is done remove from the oven and brush over with the white of an egg, beaten to a froth. Sift a little white sugar over and return to the oven till finished.

Cocoanut Pie—One cup grated cocoanut, ½ pint milk, 2 crackers, 3 eggs, butter, salt, rind of ½ lemon, sugar if desired, puff crust.

Make a nice puff crust, line a dish and bake; when done, set aside to cool; soak the cocoanut in the milk, pound the crackers well, whisk the eggs, and grate the rind of the half lemon. Mix all together, adding a little salt, sugar and butter. When well mixed place in the pie dish, and put in the oven to slightly brown.

Pumpkin Pie (1)—One pint well-stewed and strained pumpkin, 1 quart scalding hot rich milk, 1½ cups sugar, 4 eggs, 1 teaspoonful salt, 1 tablespoonful ginger and 1 of ground cinnamon.

Bake in pie-plate lined with good paste; do not let mixture stand after it is put together, but bake at once.

Pumpkin Pie (2)—One quart stewed pumpkin, pressed through a sieve, 9 eggs, whites and yolks beaten separately, 2 quarts milk, 1 teaspoonful mace, 1 of cinnamon and 1 of nutmeg, 1½ cups sugar.

Beat all together and bake with one crust.

Pumpkin Pie (3)—A pumpkin, 1 good cupful molasses; to a whole pumpkin allow 3 pints rich milk, 4 eggs, some salt, a little cinnamon, brown sugar to taste, crust.

Prepare the pumpkin by cutting into small pieces; stew rapidly until it is soft and the water is stewed out, then let it simmer on the stove to simmer all day. When well cooked, add the molasses, and cook all down until dry; then sift through a colander; it will nearly all go through if properly cooked; then add the milk, spice and eggs. Too much spice destroys the flavor of the pumpkin. Sweeten to taste; then bake in a crust the same as for custard. Let it cook until of a dark brown color. This is a very wholesome dish.

French Pancakes—Five eggs, nearly a pint of cream, 1 oz. butter.

Beat the cream till it is stiff, and the yolks and whites separately and add to the cream, and beat the mixture for 5 minutes; butter the pan and fry quickly; sugar and roll, and place on a hot dish in the oven. Serve very hot.

Rice Pancakes—One-half lb. rice, 1 pint cream, 8 eggs, a little salt and nutmeg, ½ lb. butter, flour.

Boil the rice to a jelly in a small quantity of water; when cold, mix it with the cream, well-whisk the eggs and add also with a little salt and nutmeg. Then stir in the butter, just warmed, and add, slowly stirring all the time, as much flour as will make the batter thick enough. Fry in as little lard as possible.

Irish Pancakes—Eight eggs, 1 pint cream, nutmeg and sugar to taste, 3 oz. butter, ½ pint flour.

Beat 8 yolks and 4 whites of eggs, strain them into the cream, put in grated nutmeg and sugar to taste; set 3 oz. fresh butter on the fire, stir it, and as it warms pour it to the cream, which should be warm when the eggs are put to it; then mix smooth almost ½ pint flour. Fry the pancakes very thin, the first with a piece of butter, but not the others. Serve several on one another.

Apple Pie—Puff paste, apples, sugar (brown will do), a small quantity of finely minced lemon peel, and lemon juice.

Prepare the paste (see recipe *Puff Paste*), spread a narrow strip round the edge of your baking-dish and put in the fruit, which you have previously pared, cored and cut into convenient slices. Sweeten according to taste and add the flavoring; cover with a pie crust, making a small hole in the middle, and place in the oven to bake. When nearly done, rub the crust with the white of an egg beaten to a froth and spread lightly over it. Sprinkle with white sugar and replace in the oven until done.

Orange and Apple Pie—Puff paste, oranges, apples, sugar.

Cover a tin pie-plate with puff pastry and place a layer of sliced oranges, with the pips removed, on it, and scatter sugar over them; then put a layer of sliced apples, with sugar, and cover with slices of oranges and sugar. Put an upper crust of nice pastry over the pie, and bake it for ½ hour, or until the apples are perfectly soft. Take the pie from the tin plate while it is warm, put into a china plate and scatter sugar over the top.

To Ice or Glaze Pastry—The whites of 3 eggs, 4 oz. sugar.

Place the whites upon a plate (beaten with a knife to a stiff froth); just before the pastry is done, remove from the oven; brush with the beaten egg and sprinkle the white sugar upon it. Return to the oven to set.

Glaze—The yolks of 3 eggs, a small piece of warm butter, white sugar.

Beat the yolks and butter together, and, with a pastry brush, brush the pastry just before it is finished baking; sift white sugar upon it and return to the oven to dry.

Light Paste for Tarts—One egg, ¾ lb. flour, ½ lb. butter.

Beat the white of an egg to a strong froth, then mix it with as much water as will make the flour into a very stiff paste; roll it very thin, then lay the third part of half a pound of butter upon it in little pieces; dredge with some flour left out at first and roll up tight. Roll it out again, and put the same proportion of butter, and so proceed till all be worked up.

Strawberry Tart—One lb. sifted flour, yolks of 3 eggs, 1 gill ice water, ½ lb. fresh butter, 1 tablespoonful sifted sugar, strawberries.

Rub the butter into the flour and sugar, add the yolks of eggs, and mix well with a knife; then add just enough ice water to make a paste that will roll out. It must be a firm paste, rather dry. Be careful that the flour is dry and the butter cold. Roll out the paste about one-third of an inch thick; line with it a pie-dish at least 1 inch deep with straight sides; trim the edges neatly, and bake the empty crust in a quick oven for 10 to 12 minutes. When the tart is to be served, fill it neatly with strawberries, pour some of the syrup over and serve with a pitcher of cream. The strawberries should not be allowed to stand long in the crust, or its crispness will be destroyed. The crust should be firm, brittle and crisp, not flaky.

Sponge Cake—Three cups granulated flour, 7 eggs beaten separately, 1 cup lukewarm water, 1 lemon, juice and grated rind, 3 cups flour and 3 teaspoonfuls baking-powder.

Put the yolks of the eggs in your cake bowl and beat them very light with a silver fork; then add your sugar a little at a time, beating thoroughly; next add the lemon, then alternately the water and the flour, into which the baking-powder has been sifted; lastly add the whites of the eggs beaten very stiff and merely stirred in lightly, not beaten. Bake in a moderate oven, and do not open the pan once put in.

Puff Paste—One lb. flour; ¾ lb. butter; 1 egg, with water.

Mix the flour with a lump of butter the size of an egg to a very stiff paste with cold water; divide the butter into six equal parts, roll the paste and spread on one part of the butter, dredging it with flour; repeat until all the butter is rolled in.

Short Crust—Half lb. flour, 8 oz. butter, 2 oz. white sugar, a pinch of salt, yolks of 2 eggs.

Rub into the butter the flour and the powdered loaf sugar; beat up the yolks of the eggs, the salt, and enough milk or water to make the flour into a paste; work the paste lightly, and roll to cut thin. If not wanted sweet, the sugar may be left out.

Suet Crust for Meat Puddings—Eight oz. flour, 5 oz. beef suet, a little salt.

Remove all skin from the suet, chop finely, and mix with the flour, adding a little salt; mix well, add by degrees a little cold water and make into a paste; flour the paste board and place the paste upon it, roll out to the thickness of ¼ inch. It is then ready for use.

Potato Paste — Pound boiled potatoes very fine, and add, while warm, a sufficiency of butter to make the mash hold together, or you may mix it with an egg; then, before it gets cold, flour the board pretty well to prevent it from sticking, and roll it to the thickness wanted. If it becomes quite cold before it be put on the dish, it will be apt to crack.

Cocoanut Potato Pie—Three eggs, one large potato, ½ cup cocoanut, 1 pint milk, 1 tablespoonful butter, sugar to taste, and a little salt.

Boil and mash the potato and add the sugar, butter and salt, then the beaten eggs, and lastly the milk, in which part of the cocoanut has been soaked. Reserve the white of an egg for frosting; add to it the rest of the cocoanut and spread a little red sugar over the top.

Cream Fritters — Three tablespoonfuls potato flour, 1 pint new milk, 3 whole eggs, yolks of 4 eggs, a pat of very fresh butter, powdered white sugar to taste, a few drops essence of almonds, bread-crumbs.

Make a smooth paste with the flour and a part of the milk; then gradually add the remainder of the milk, the eggs and yolks, the butter, white sugar to taste, and essence of almonds. Put the mixture into a saucepan on the fire, stirring all the while till it is quite thick. Spread out on a dish until of thickness of ½ an inch. When quite cold cut into lozenges; egg and bread-crumb them, or dip in the batter; fry a nice color in lard and serve sprinkled with white sugar.

Cheese Fritters — About a pint of water, a piece of butter the size of an egg, the least piece of cayenne, plenty of black pepper, ¼ lb. ground Parmesan cheese, yolks of 2 or 3 eggs, and whites of 2 beaten to a froth, salt, flour.

Put the water into a saucepan with the butter, cayenne and black pepper. When the water boils throw gradually into it sufficient flour to form a thick paste; then take it off the fire and work into it the Parmesan cheese, and then the yolks and whites of the eggs. Let the paste cool for a couple of hours, and proceed to fry by dropping pieces of it the size of a walnut into plenty of hot lard. Serve sprinkled with very fine salt.

Puffs for Dessert — One pint milk and cream, the whites of 4 eggs beaten to a stiff froth, 1 heaping cup sifted flour, 1 scant cup powdered sugar; add a little grated lemon peel and a little salt.

Beat these all together till very light, bake in gem pans, sift pulverized sugar over them and eat with sauce flavored with lemon.

Plain Puffs—Yolks of 6 eggs, 1 pint sweet milk, a large pinch of salt, whites of 4 eggs, flour.

Beat the yolks of the eggs till very light, stir in the milk, salt, and the whites beaten to a stiff froth, and flour enough to make a batter about as thick as a boiled custard. Bake in small tins in a quick oven.

Banana Fritters — Sift 2 cups flour and 1½ teaspoonfuls baking powder; to this add the yolks of 2 eggs, a little salt, ½ cup sugar and enough milk to make a moderate batter; whip the whites of the eggs and then add a tablespoonful of melted butter. Slice ½ dozen bananas and stir into the batter; fry at once in plenty of boiling lard, and drain on coarse brown paper before serving.

Spanish Puffs — A teacupful water, a tablespoonful white sugar, a pinch of salt, 2 oz. butter, flour, yolks of 4 eggs.

Put the water into a saucepan with the sugar, salt and butter; while it is boiling add sufficient flour for it to leave the saucepan; stir one by one the yolks of the four eggs; drop in a teaspoonful at a time into boiling lard; fry them a light brown.

Cream Puffs — One pint water, ½ lb. butter, ¾ lb. sifted flour, 10 eggs, 1 small teaspoon soda. Mock cream: 1 cup sugar, 4 eggs, 1 cup flour, 1 quart milk, flavoring.

Boil the water; rub the flour with the butter; stir into the water while boiling. When it thickens like starch remove from the fire. When cool stir into it the well-beaten eggs and the soda. Drop the mixture onto the buttered tins with a large spoon. Bake till a light brown, in a quick oven. When done, open one side and fill with mock cream made as follows in the above proportions: Beat eggs to a froth; stir in the sugar, then flour; stir them into the milk while boiling; stir till it thickens, then remove from the fire and flavor with lemon or vanilla. It should not be put into the puffs until cold.

Orange Puffs—Rind and juice of 4 oranges, 2 lbs. sifted sugar, butter.

Grate the rind of the oranges, add the sugar, pound together and make into a stiff paste with the butter and juice of the fruit; roll it, cut into shapes and bake in a cool oven. Served piled up on a dish with sifted sugar over.

Orange Fritters — Six large oranges peeled and sliced, two well-beaten eggs, 3 tablespoonfuls of sugar, and enough flour to make a batter about as stiff as it for flannel cakes; dip the oranges into the batter, being sure that they are well covered by it, then fry in plenty of boiling lard; drain on coarse brown paper, sift powdered sugar over the fritters and serve.

Apple Fritters — Sift together 1 cupful flour, 2 tablespoonfuls sugar, 1 teaspoonful baking-powder and ½ saltspoonful salt. Beat 1 egg very light, and add ¾ cupful milk; pour this gradually into the dry mixture, beating well; add 2 apples cut fine. Drop by spoonfuls into hot fat and fry; drain and sprinkle with powdered sugar. Pastry flour should be used for fritters, as bread flour contains too much gluten. Bread flour should be used only when yeast is added. The apples should be cut fine or chopped; the fritters are also very good if the apples are cut in thick slices, dipped in the batter, and then fried.

Charlotte Russe—Soak ½ box gelatine in ½ cup cold milk 1 hour; when dissolved, set up in hot water, using gelatine lukewarm; into 1 pint whipped cream add ½ cup pulverized sugar, a little salt and the beaten whites of 2 eggs, and flavor with vanilla; then add gelatine and strain while pouring in; stir until gelatine is well mixed with the cream, and, when nearly stiff enough to drop, turn into moulds lined with lady fingers or narrow slices of sponge cake, first dipping the cake into white of egg.

Apple Jelly—One lb. apples, 1 lemon, ½ lb. lump sugar, 1 oz. gelatine, ½ pint water and a little cochineal.

Peel and core the apples, put them in a stewpan with the sugar, water, grated rind and juice of the lemon; stew till tender, rub through a sieve, then stir in the gelatine, previously melted in a gill of boiling water. Color part of the apples with cochineal, and pour into a mould with alternate layers of colored and plain apple. May be served with or without whipped cream.

Apple Turnovers—One lb. flour, 5 oz. dripping or butter, small teaspoonful baking-powder, 4 apples (allowing 1 for each turnover), 4 teaspoonfuls brown sugar.

Pare, core and slice the apples. Mix the baking-powder into the flour, then add the dripping or butter, mixing well together. Moisten with cold water and stir to a paste. Roll out; cut into circles about 8 inches in diameter. Put the apple on one of the rounds and sprinkle with sugar. Moisten the edges of the paste and shape in the form of a turnover.

Snow Cream—One-half oz. gelatine, 1 tumbler water, the juice of 1 lemon, ½ lb. loaf sugar, and 2 eggs.

Soak the gelatine in half the water for 1 hour, and fill up with the other half boiling; add to it the lemon juice and sugar. Whisk the whites of the eggs well; put them to the other ingredients, and whisk the whole for ½ of an hour. Put into a mould to set. With the yolks of the eggs and nearly ½ pint of milk, make a custard, sweetened and flavored with lemon. Pour it round the cream when turned out.

Lemon Sponge—One oz. gelatine, 1 pint water, the juice of 3 lemons, the thin rind of 2, ½ lb. lump sugar, and whites of 2 eggs.

Boil all, except the eggs, together for 10 minutes, and let it stand until cold and beginning to set. Beat the whites well, add them to it, and whisk the whole until it becomes a stiff froth. May be put into a mould or piled in glass dishes.

Chocolate Blanc Mange—One qt. of rich fresh milk or cream, 3 oz. chocolate, ½ lb. white sugar, 1 2-oz. box of gelatine dissolved in ½ pint water.

Boil milk, chocolate and sugar together a few minutes, after first dissolving the chocolate and rubbing it smooth in a little of the milk. Then add the gelatine and 10 drops of vanilla. Stir well and remove from the fire in about 5 minutes. When lukewarm pour through a strainer into moulds that have been previously dipped into a bath of cold water.

Russian Cream—Jelly.—To 1 package Cox's gelatine add 1 pint cold water. When dissolved add 1 pint hot water, 2 cups sugar, juice of 6 lemons. Stir slowly until well dissolved, then strain into moulds.

Cream.—Cover 1 package gelatine with cold water. When dissolved add 1 cup new milk, 1 cup sugar; heat to boiling point, stirring frequently, then set away to cool. Whip 1 quart of thick cream until light, beat the whites of 6 eggs, and add both to the mixture; when cool flavor with vanilla. Place the jelly in the bottom of the moulds, and when stiff and cold add the cream; turn out of moulds and serve in slices.

Flummery—Three large handfuls of small white oatmeal, 1 large spoonful of white sugar, 2 large spoonfuls of orange-flower water.

Put 3 large handfuls of very small white oatmeal to steep a day and night in cold water; then pour it off clear, and add as much more water, and let it stand the same time. Strain it through a fine hair-sieve, and boil it till it be as thick as hasty-pudding, stirring it well all the time. When first strained, put to it the white sugar and flower water. Pour it into shallow dishes, and serve to eat with milk or cream and sugar.

Isinglass Blanc Mange—One oz. isinglass, 1 qt. water, whites of 4 eggs, 2 spoonfuls rice water, sugar to taste, 2 oz. sweet and 1 oz. bitter almonds.

Boil the isinglass in the water till it is reduced to a pint; then add the whites of the eggs with the rice water to prevent the eggs poaching, and sugar to taste; run through the jelly-bag; then add the almonds; give them a scald in the jelly, and pour them through a hair-sieve; put in a china bowl; the next day turn it out, and stick it all over with almonds, blanched and cut lengthwise. Garnish with green leaves or flowers.

Orange Fool—Juice of 3 Seville oranges, 3 well-beaten eggs, ½ pint cream, a little nutmeg and cinnamon, white sugar to taste.

Mix the orange juice with the eggs, cream and spices. Sweeten to taste. The orange juice must be carefully strained. Set the whole over a slow fire, and stir it until it becomes about the thickness of melted butter; it must on no account be allowed to boil; then pour into a dish for eating cold.

Gooseberry Fool—One quart gooseberries, water, sugar, 1 quart cream.

Pick 1 quart of quite young gooseberries, and put them into a jar with a very little water and plenty of sugar; put the jar in a saucepan of boiling water till the fruit be quite tender, then beat it through a colander, and add gradually 1 quart of cream with sufficient sugar to sweeten.

Stewed Apples and Rice.—Some good baking apples, syrup, 1 lb. sugar to 1 pint water, lemon peel, jam, some well-boiled rice.

Peel the apples, take out the cores with a scoop so as not to injure the shape of the apples, put them in a deep baking-dish, and pour over them a syrup made by boiling sugar in the above proportion; put a little piece of shred lemon peel inside each apple, and let them bake very slowly until soft, but not in the least broken. If the syrup is thin, boil it until it is thick enough; take out the lemon peel, and put a little jam inside each apple, and between each a little heap of well-boiled rice; pour the syrup gently over the apples, and let it cover the rice. This dish may be served either hot or cold.

Spiced Apples.—Four lbs. apples (weigh them after they are peeled), 2 lbs. sugar, ½ oz. cinnamon in the stick, ½ oz. cloves, and 1 pt. vinegar.

Let the vinegar, spices and sugar come to a boil; then put in the whole apples, and cook them until they are so tender that a broom-splint will pierce them easily. These will keep for a long time in a jar. Put a clean cloth over the top of the jar before putting the cover on.

Apple Charlotte.—Some good cooking apples, sugar (1 lb. apple pulp to ½ lb. sugar), lemon flavoring, fried bread.

Bake good cooking apples slowly until done; scrape out all the pulp with a teaspoon, put it in a stewpan in the above proportions; stir it until the sugar is dissolved and the pulp stiff. Take care it does not burn. Add a little lemon flavoring, and place the apple in the center of a dish, arranging thickly and tastefully around it neatly cut pieces of the carefully fried bread. If it is desired to make this dish very nice, each piece of fried bread may be dipped in apricot jam. Rhubarb charlotte may be made in the same manner. The rhubarb must be boiled and stirred until a good deal of the watery portion has evaporated, and then sugar, ½ lb. to 1 lb. of fruit, being added, it should be allowed to boil until it is thick.

DESSERT.

Oranges.—Oranges may be prepared for table in the following manner: Cut gently through the peel only, from the point of the orange at the top to a point made at the bottom, dividing the outside of orange into eleven or sections, seven or eight in number. Loosen the peel carefully, and take each section off, leaving it attached only at the bottom. Scrape the white off the orange itself, and turn in each section double to the bottom of the orange, so that the whole looks like a dahlia or some other flower.

Almonds and Raisins.—Serve in a glass dish; the raisins piled high in the center. Blanch the almonds and strew over them.

Frosted Currants.—Froth the white of an egg or eggs, dipping the bunches into the mixture. Drain until nearly dry, then roll in white sugar. Lay upon white paper to dry.

Impromptu Dessert.—Cover the bottom of a large glass dish with sliced orange; strew over it powdered sugar, then a thick layer of cocoanut. Alternate orange and cocoanut till the dish is full, heaping the cocoanut on the top.

Dessert of Apples.—One lb. sugar, 2 lb. finely flavored ripe sour apples, 1 pint rich cream, 2 eggs, ½ cup sugar.

Make a rich syrup of the sugar; add the apples nicely pared and cored. Stew till soft, then mix smoothly with the syrup and pour all into a mould. Stir into the cream (or if there is none at hand, new milk must answer) the eggs well beaten; also the sugar, and let it just boil up in a farina kettle; then set aside to cool. When cold take the apples from the mould and pour this cream custard around it and serve. If spice or flavoring is agreeable, nutmeg, vanilla or rose water can be used.

Dish of Figs.—One cup sugar, ½ cup water, ½ teaspoonful cream of tartar.

Let the sugar and water boil until it is a pale brown color; shake gently the basin in which it is boiling, to prevent it burning, but do not stir it at all until just before you take it from the fire; then stir in the cream of tartar. Wash and cut open some figs; spread them on a platter, then pour the sugar over them. Take care to have each fig covered; set them in a cool place till the sugar has time to harden.

A Dish of Nuts.—Arrange them piled high in the center of a dish; a few leaves around the edge of the dish will greatly improve the appearance. In dishing filberts serve them with the outer skin on. If walnuts, wipe with a damp cloth before serving.

HOME-MADE CANDIES.

MEN, women and children—not to mention dogs and horses—like sugar, and the taste is entirely defensible. These white crystals, the frost of honey, feed the ever-burning flame of the body, supplying animal heat, which is life, and rousing the nervous energies like phosphorus, or better than phosphates in some cases. I have had brain-fag so entire that it seemed as if I never could write or had written a line, relieved by taking a syrupy small glass of eau sucrée, when shortly ideas gathered and took shape and the black brain resumed its work. I can't help fancying that the sweets craved so ardently by children have much to do with furnishing nerve aliment to their fast-growing systems. Sugar contributes both animal heat and nervous force, and seems to be a transformation of the elements of heat, as the diamond is transformed carbon.

In the terrible retreat from Moscow, the few of Napoleon's army who needed a few pounds of sugar to eat were enabled to support the intense cold. In tropic countries Europeans learned to drink eau sucrée before long walks as a preventive of sunstroke and paralysis, and the French Algerian troops carry sugar on their marches to enable them to withstand the desert heat. Persons with spinal inflammation and paralytic tendencies often have a craving for sweets, which is nature teaching instinctively for help, and indulgence in such cases is followed by improvement.

As much pure sugar or sweets as can be eaten without producing acidity is not only safe but beneficial for any one who craves it. Disturbance seldom follows in any ordinary case when the sweets are perfectly pure and are taken at proper times, not nibbled constantly between meals.

Confectionery is one of the perquisites of childhood, and as choice French candies are beyond the capacity of many a mother's purse, and cheap ones are often made unwholesome, if not positively dangerous, by adulteration, home-made candies have become very popular, many delicious and attractive varieties being as easily made as any other toothsome dainties. As a preventive of "graining," glucose (grape sugar or syrup) is much used in the manufacture of candy. But as it is not always convenient to procure, and often imparts a bitter flavor, the recipes here given are for the use of cream of tartar instead.

A preparation called "fondant"—made by removing boiled syrup from the fire just before it will harden—is the foundation of nearly all French candies, and when once the art of making this is mastered a large variety of candies are easily made.

Fondant—To 1 lb. sugar add ½ pint cold water and ⅛ teaspoonful cream of tartar, and boil rapidly for 10 minutes without stirring. Dip the fingers into ice water, drop a little of the syrup into cold water, then roll it between the fingers, and if it forms a soft, creamy ball that doesn't adhere it is done. If not hard enough boil a little longer, and if too hard add a little water, boil up and test again. Set aside in the kettle to become lukewarm, then stir the mass with a knife until it is white and dry at the edges. It should then be taken out and kneaded exactly as one would knead bread dough, until it is creamy and soft. By covering with a damp cloth and keeping in a cool place it will keep well for several days, and several times this amount may be made at one time. In making several pounds it is better to divide the mass before kneading, and each part may be flavored differently.

Chocolate Creams—Dust the moulding-board with as little flour as possible and roll a piece of fondant into a cylindrical shape. Cut it into regular-shaped pieces, roll between the palms of the hands until round, lay on paraffine paper and let harden until the next day. Melt a cake of chocolate in a rather deep vessel that has been set in a pan of hot water; add a piece of paraffine half as large as a walnut, the same amount of butter, and ½ teaspoonful vanilla. Roll the creams in this, by using a steel fork or crochet needle, and place again on paraffine paper.

Nut Rolls—Take equal parts of walnut, butternut, or whatever variety of nut meats you prefer, and fondant, mix well, and form into a roll. Cover this with plain fondant, roll in granulated sugar and let harden until next day, then slice crosswise.

Molasses Nut Balls and Bars—Boil 2 cupfuls brown sugar, 1 of New Orleans molasses, and ½ cup water until it will snap when tested in cold water. Take from the stove, add 2 cupfuls chopped walnut meats, stir until nearly cold, and then roll into balls between the palms of the hands; wrap in paraffine paper.

For walnut or peanut bars boil together a cupful of New Orleans molasses, 1 of brown sugar, and half a cup of water. When it stands the test of water add a tablespoonful each of butter and vinegar. When it boils up remove from the fire, add 3 teacupfuls peanut or walnut meats, pour into buttered shallow pans, smooth the top, and when nearly cold cut in bars or squares with a buttered knife.

Cocoanut bars are made in the same way, using fresh cocoanut that has been dried out 2 hours after being grated, or shredded cocoanut.

Crystallizing Syrup—Any variety of bonbon made with fondant may be crystallized to make another attractive variety by the following process. Boil 1½ lbs. sugar and ½ pint water until it forms a thread that will snap easily. Remove from the fire, and when nearly cold sprinkle a tablespoonful of water on the top to dissolve the film. Have the candies in a shallow pan, pour the syrup carefully over, covering each part; cover with a damp cloth, resting on the syrup to prevent the formation of a crust. After standing 6 hours, with a hat pin remove the candies, place on paraffine paper, spread a damp cloth over, and leave until dry.

Jelly Rolls—Roll out evenly a piece of plain fondant, spread with any variety of fruit jelly or marmalade preferred, and when hard cut into slices and crystallize as above.

Chocolate Caramels—Half lb. Baker's chocolate, 3 lbs. sugar, half granulated and half brown, the latter not too moist, ½ lb. butter, 1 small cup milk.

Mix the ingredients and boil until it hardens in cold water, which should be about 20 minutes. Stir all the time if you wish the caramels to be "crumbly."

Cocoanut Bon-bons—To the white of one egg and an equal quantity of water add enough pulverized sugar and grated cocoanut to enable you to make into balls; lay the balls on greased plates. Take two cups of sugar and one of water and boil until it creams, then add one teaspoonful of vanilla or rose water; set the dish containing this mixture on another containing boiling water, so it will not get too hard; then roll the balls in it as you would chocolate creams, and lay on greased plates to harden.

Almond Taffy — Boil together ½ pint water and 1 lb. brown sugar for 10 minutes. Blanch and slice through the middle 1½ oz. almonds; stir them in the syrup with 2 oz. of butter. Let the mixture boil hard for 10 minutes. Pour on a well-buttered dish to the thickness of ¼ inch.

Everton Taffy — Put a pound of brown sugar in a buttered pan, together with 3 tablespoonfuls of water. Let it boil until it becomes a smooth, thick syrup. Add ¼ pound of butter, stirring well. Let this boil ½ hour; add lemon flavoring.

Butterscotch — Use 2 cupfuls of New Orleans molasses, 2 cupfuls granulated sugar, ¾ cupful butter, and a very little water. Cook quickly about 20 minutes. Try a little in cold water, to see when it becomes crisp. Just before taking up add ½ teaspoonful baking-soda well mashed and smooth. Pour into buttered tins and cut as soon as it becomes perfectly cool.

Sugar Candy — Put in a shallow pan 3 cupfuls granulated sugar, ½ cupful water, ½ cupful vinegar, and at the last, ½ tablespoonful butter, with ¼ teaspoonful cooking-soda, dissolved in hot water. Cook quickly, without stirring, for 1 hour, or until it crisps in cold water. Pull while quite hot with buttered finger tips, and continue pulling until the candy is white. Chop into small pieces.

Candied Fruit — Boil 1 cupful granulated sugar, 4 tablespoonfuls water, 2 tablespoonfuls vinegar and ¼ spoonful soda. Avoid stirring. When the mixture is boiled to a syrup, dip into it cherries, grapes, pine-apple, oranges, pears, etc. When well dipped place the fruit on paraffine paper and put in a warm place to dry. Chestnuts and filberts thus candied are delicious.

Hoarhound Candy — Hoarhound candy is a favorite cough remedy. To 1 quart of water add a small handful of hoarhound herb, and boil ½ hour. Strain, pressing all the liquid from the herbs. Add 3 lbs. of brown sugar, and boil to the "hard crack." Put in a piece of butter as large as a walnut. When the butter is dissolved, pour the mass on a greased platter or marble slab. When almost cold, square off with a knife.

Molasses Taffy — Boil together 2 cupfuls of brown sugar, 1 of New Orleans molasses, ½ cupful of water, and 2 tablespoonfuls of vinegar; when crisp, add a tablespoonful of butter, stir 1 minute, then remove from the fire, add ½ teaspoonful soda; when nearly cold pull until a beautiful golden color.

French Almond Rock — Put 1 lb. of loaf sugar and a teacupful of water into a saucepan, stir it until the sugar is melted, take off the scum that comes to the top, and when boiled for ¼ hour add 1 tablespoonful vinegar or lemon juice. Stir in sliced almonds to taste, pour out on a well-buttered tin and cut into slices.

Lemon Candy — Into a bright tinned kettle put 3½ lbs. of sugar, 1½ pints of water, and a full teaspoonful of cream of tartar. Place over a hot fire and stir until the lumps disappear. Boil briskly until the candy is hard and brittle when a little is thrown into cold water. Take the candy from the fire and pour it on a large platter, greased with a little butter. When cooled sufficiently to be handled, add a teaspoonful of finely powdered tartaric acid, and the same quantity of extract of lemon, and work them into the mass. The acid should be fine and free from lumps. The mass must be worked enough to distribute the acid and lemon extract evenly, but no more, as too much handling destroys its transparency. It may now be formed into sticks or drops, or spread out flat on tins in thin sheets.

Molasses Candy — Dissolve 1 cupful of sugar in ½ cupful of vinegar, mix with 1 quart of molasses, and boil, stirring often, until it hardens when dropped from a spoon into cold water; then stir in a piece of butter the size of an egg and 1 teaspoonful of saleratus, the latter dissolved in hot water. Flavor to your taste, give a hard final stir, and pour into buttered dishes. As it cools, cut into squares for "taffy," or, while soft enough to handle, pull white into sticks, using only the buttered tips of your fingers for that purpose.

"Old-Fashioned" Molasses Candy — Into a kettle holding 4 times the amount of molasses to be used, pour a convenient quantity of good New Orleans molasses. Boil over a slow fire half an hour, stirring all the time, and taking off the kettle if there is any danger of the contents running over. Do not let the candy burn. When a little dropped in cold water becomes quickly hard and brittle, add a teaspoonful of carbonate of soda, free from lumps, to every 2 quarts, stir quickly to mix, and pour on greased platters to cool. When sufficiently cool, pull back and forth, the hands being rubbed with butter to prevent the candy from sticking to them, until the candy is of a bright yellowish brown color. If you wish, flavor with vanilla or lemon.

Cocoanut Kisses — Beat together the whites of 2 eggs with as much granulated sugar as they will take up, making a rather stiff batter. Add a piece of butter the size of an English walnut and half a teaspoonful of vanilla or lemon extract. When beaten perfectly smooth, add grated cocoanut, which should be fresh and carefully prepared. Stir in the cocoanut, beating for some minutes. Then drop the prepared confection upon buttered tins and place them in a current of air to dry. Many confectioners put them at once in the oven; but they sometimes spread out if the heat is applied too soon. They may remain in the oven until slightly brown, or may merely be allowed to heat through and dry.

Mrs. Senator Cullom's Candy—Mix together the whites of 2 eggs, an equal quantity of cold water, and enough confectioners' sugar to make a stiff dough. It will require about 2 lbs. To prepare fruits and nuts, take seeds out of dates and fill with the cream; blanch almonds and cover with cream. Candied cherries are nice, taking little balls of the cream and putting a cherry on each. English walnuts are used in the same way as cherries.

Marshmallows—Dissolve 1 lb. clear white gum-arabic in 1 quart water; strain, add 1 lb. refined sugar, place on fire. Stir continually until sugar is dissolved and the mixture becomes of the consistency of honey. Next add gradually the beaten whites of 8 eggs; stir the mixture all the time until it thickens and does not adhere to the finger, pour into a tin slightly dusted with starch, and when cool divide with a sharp knife.

Peppermint Drops—The peppermint and wintergreen drops which follow the ice cream course to prevent possible disturbance from chilling with the frozen dainties are made of pure sugar with half the quantity of arrowroot used for the cream drops, and essence of wintergreen or mint to taste, rolled on a marble slab and cut out in disks the size of a quarter dollar. Confectionery is a pretty art for ladies and a very convenient one where there are children with the traditional sweet tooth. And what adds more repute to a hostess' table than that it is furnished with tempting fresh bonbons of her own making?

Harmless Colorings for Candies—Vegetable colorings are always to be used, the juice of blood beet for deepest red, cranberry juice tinging a delicate pink, and cochineal—the sole exception—giving a lovely rose. In coloring yellow, carrot juice or a very little yolk of egg answers better than gamboge. Spinach furnishes the best green, and is prepared by cutting fresh spinach into alcohol and using a few drops to color with. A quarter oz. cochineal will color confectionery for a lifetime, and should be kept in a bottle closely corked. One bug is used at a time, pounding it and pouring on 2 or 3 teaspoonfuls of boiling water, after which the liquid is bottled and will keep three months, only a drop or two being needed for any common quantity of confectionery or frosting. Blue is rarely used, and the drop of indigo needed will not hurt any one. The petals of yellow roses, infused in boiling water, yield a delicate dye which is charming with old-fashioned rosewater desserts.

ICE CREAM, ICES, Etc.

Frozen Custard—One quart rich milk, 1 large cup sugar, 1 teaspoonful salt, yolks of 6 eggs, 1½ teaspoonfuls almond flavoring, 1 cup cream.

Let the milk come to a boil; beat the sugar, salt and eggs together, and add the milk, a few drops at a time; return to the double boiler and cook 5 minutes, stirring all the time. Set away to get cold, and freeze.

Grape Sherbet—One quart grape juice, obtained by boiling the grapes half an hour and straining through a jelly bag, juice of 3 good-sized oranges, 1½ cups sugar.

Mix the orange and grape juice, strain and pour into your freezer. Freeze for 5 minutes, pour out and add the whites of 2 well-beaten eggs; return to the freezer and freeze for 20 minutes. Remove the dasher and pack away for an hour, then serve.

Peach Ice Cream—Two quarts ripe peaches, 1 cup sugar, mix well and set away in a covered dish. Take one pint of milk and one of cream; let them come to a boil; mix together 1 cup sugar, 2 scant tablespoonfuls flour and a teaspoonful salt, beat the eggs well, mix all; then add the boiling milk and cream. Return to your boiler and boil gently 20 minutes, stirring often to prevent sticking. When quite cold stir in the peaches, which must be mashed fine, and freeze.

Lemon Water Ice—Half a box of gelatine, dissolved in 1 pint cold water. Take the juice of 6 lemons and mix with 1½ lbs. white sugar, then pour 1 quart of hot water on the sugar and lemons; pour 1½ pints of boiling water over the gelatine, and when it is quite dissolved add to the rest of the ingredients. Strain and set away to cool; when cold whip 15 minutes, and freeze.

Caramel Ice Cream—Burnt sugar ice cream is a favorite dish in Virginia, and it is often called caramel cream on account of its peculiar color, though it requires neither chocolate nor vanilla. It is made by pouring boiled custard, a little at a time, over a frying-pan in which brown sugar has been burned until it is a dark brown color. Keep on adding the custard, stirring all the time until the whole is smooth and the pan is full, then pour the contents back into the main bowl of custard, which should be the color of strong coffee when it is all mixed. The art in making this cream is in burning the sugar until it is exactly right. If this is properly prepared you have only to freeze it like any other custard. For 1 gallon it requires 1 gallon of milk, 2 cups of white sugar, the yolks of 16 eggs and 2 cups of brown sugar well burned.

Chocolate Ice Cream—Six tablespoonfuls grated chocolate, 2 breakfast cups cream, 1 of fresh milk, ½ lb. sugar.

Stir the chocolate into the milk, mixing well, add remaining ingredients and freeze.

Fruit Cream—One and one-quarter lbs. of any kind of preserved fruit, 1 quart cream, juice of 2 lemons, sugar to taste.

Take the whole of the ingredients and work through a sieve. Then freeze in a freezing-can, and work until it is frozen. Then turn out and serve.

Ice Cream — One quart milk, 3 eggs, ¾ lb. sugar, 2 tablespoonfuls corn-starch or arrowroot, 1 qt. cream.

Scald the milk, yolks of eggs, sugar, and corn-starch or arrowroot, until it is of the consistency of custard. Then allow to cool. When cool add the cream whipped, and the whites of the eggs whisked to a stiff froth. Sweeten to taste, flavor, and freeze in the usual way.

Vanilla Ice Cream — Beat the yolks of 6 eggs with ¾ of a pound of sugar until very light. Put 1½ pints of rich milk on the fire to scald, highly flavored with vanilla. When the milk is scalded, stir it into the egg as soon as it is cool enough not to curdle. Now stir the mixture constantly until it has slightly thickened. Do not let it remain too long and curdle, or it will be spoiled. When taken off the fire again, mix in ¼ box of gelatine which has been soaked ½ hour in 2 tablespoonfuls of lukewarm water near the fire. The heat of the custard will be sufficient to dissolve it if it is not already dissolved. Cool the custard well before putting it into the freezer, however; stir it almost constantly until it begins to set; then stir in lightly a pint of cream, whipped. Stir it for 2 or 3 minutes longer; put it into a mould, and return it to a second relay of ice and salt.

Strawberry Water Ice — Boil 1 pint of water and 3 teacupfuls of granulated sugar for about 10 minutes, skimming carefully. Remove from the fire and allow it to grow cold, then add 2 pints of strawberry juice. Many people think the flavor is improved by adding a little currant juice. Beat the mixture well together and freeze. Red raspberry ice made in the same way is also excellent.

Orange Water Ice — Rub sugar on the peel of 2 oranges and 1 lemon. Squeeze and strain the juice of the lemon and 6 oranges. Dissolve the flavored sugar with a little hot water, and mix with ½ pint of syrup. If too sweet, add a little water. Strain into the freezing-pot, and finish as lemon water ice.

Crystal Palace Cream — A rich custard, ½ oz. gelatine dissolved in a little boiling water, 2 sponge cakes, 2 macaroons, 3 tablespoonfuls milk.

Make the custard, dissolve the gelatine, and when it is nearly cold pour into the custard, which must also be cool; soak the cakes and macaroons in the milk (or, if preferred, any fruit syrup, which must be rich and sweet. Put the cakes into a mould and gently pour the cream over them; let it stand till cold. A few glacé cherries may be added.

Lemon Cream — One pint of thick cream, yolks of 2 eggs, 4 oz. fine sugar, rind of 1 lemon cut thinly, juice of the lemon.

Well beat the yolks and add to the cream, sugar and rind of the lemon; boil, and then stir it till almost cold; put the juice of a lemon into a dish and pour the cream upon it, stirring until quite cold.

Lemon Cream, Solid — Half a pint of cream, the juice of 2 lemons and the rind of 2, ¾ lb. loaf-sugar in small lumps.

Rub the sugar on the lemons, and lay them at the bottom of the dish, pour the lemon-juice over, make the cream a little warm; then, standing on a chair and with the dish on the ground, pour the cream on so as to froth it.

Lemon Cream (without cream) — Four lemons, 12 tablespoonfuls water, 7 oz. powdered white sugar, yolks of 9 eggs.

Peel the lemons very thinly into the above proportion of water, then squeeze the juice into the sugar. Beat the yolks thoroughly and add the peel and juice together, beating for some time. Then strain into your saucepan, set over a gentle fire and stir one way till thick and scalding hot. Do not let it boil or it will curdle. Serve in jelly glasses.

Cherry Cream — Take 2 qts. cherries, heaping quarts, and bruise them without removing the pits, throw over them ½ cupful sugar and let them stand in a cool place for 2 hours. Then strain. Sweeten the juice after straining, beat a pint of cream, gradually add the juice and the beaten whites of 2 eggs, continually whisking it till no more froth arises. The secret of success is to have cream and eggs all thoroughly chilled on ice, and in adding the juice a little at a time to prevent curdling.

Nesselrode Pudding — Make a custard with 1 pint milk, 6 tablespoonfuls sifted sugar, and yolks of 7 eggs (or use ½ pint milk and ½ pint cream); let the milk come to the boil, then mix it with the other ingredients; after stirring for some time put the mixture in a pan over the fire and go on stirring till it thickens, but it must not boil, or it will curdle; strain and flavor it with vanilla or any other flavor. Divide the custard in two separate basins; flavor and color the one to taste, partly freeze it, and add a small tumblerful of whipped cream, slightly sweetened with powdered sugar. Meanwhile brown, in ½ oz. fresh butter, 4 oz. blanched almonds and 1 oz. sifted sugar; pound this quite smooth, mix with the other half of the custard, strain and freeze. Mold the two ices in layers and freeze for 2 hours.

Tutti Frutti — When a rich cream is partly frozen, candied cherries, English currants, chopped raisins, or any other candied fruits, chopped rather fine, are added; add about the same quantity of fruit as there is of ice-cream. Mould and imbed in ice and salt. Serve with whipped cream.

Strawberry Ice Cream — Sprinkle sugar over the strawberries, mash them well and rub them through a sieve. To a pint of the juice add a pint of good cream. Make it very sweet. Freeze it in the usual way, and, when beginning to set, stir in lightly 1 pint cream, whipped, and lastly a handful of whole strawberries, sweetened. Put it into a mould which is imbedded in ice. Or, when fresh strawberries can not be obtained, there is no more delicious cream than that made with the French bottled strawberries. Mix the juice in the mold with the cream, and add the whipped cream and the whole strawberries when the juice, etc., have partly set in the freezer.

Pineapple Ice Cream — Make a plain vanilla ice cream and when partially frozen stir in ½ can grated pineapple. Mix well and complete the freezing. The remainder of the pineapple may be converted into a most delicious trifle.

Pineapple Trifle — Line a pretty dish with stale sponge cake and spread upon it the grated pineapple. Whip 1 pint sweet cream, sweeten and flavor with vanilla; stir in 1-5 box Nelson's gelatine which has been previously soaked in ½ cup cold water, then dissolved by adding ½ cupful boiling water. Pour this over the cake and set on ice to stiffen.

Grape Sherbet — Lay a square of cheese-cloth over a bowl; put in a pound of ripe grapes; mash very thoroughly with a wooden masher; squeeze out all the juice; add an equal amount of cold water, the juice of 1 lemon, and sugar enough to make it very sweet. Freeze as usual.

Currant Ice — Boil 1 quart of water and a pound of sugar until reduced to a pint, skim it, take it off the fire, add a pint of currant juice; when partly frozen, stir in the whites of 2 eggs. Mould, and freeze again. A good ice for fever patients.

Lemon Sherbet — Soak 1 teaspoonful gelatine in ½ cup cold water, and dissolve with ½ cup boiling water. Add the juice of 6 lemons, 1 pint sugar, and 3½ cups water. Strain and freeze. If the lemons have become dry by being kept in the house, let them soak in cold water for a little time. A good way is to pour boiling water over the fruit, and then drop into cold water. This would destroy any insects which might be in the peel. Lemons may be kept in sour milk with good results. The gelatine is not used for nutriment, but to give a better consistency to the sherbet. If it is not convenient to use a freezer, the sherbet may be frozen in a pail. Put the lemon mixture in the pail and pack into a pail of ice and rock salt, using half salt and half finely-cracked ice in alternate layers. When it becomes hardened, scrape the sherbet from the side of the pail, and beat with a Dover egg-beater. Pack down again, and keep closely covered until ready to serve. If the sherbet is to be frozen in an ice-cream freezer, use two-thirds of ice and one-third of rock salt, in alternate layers. Turn the crank very slowly, as the slower it is turned the faster the cream is frozen and the smoother it is. If the crank is turned rapidly, the liquid is stirred about so that it does not come in contact with the sides of the can long enough to freeze.

Peaches and Cream Frozen — Peel and quarter the fresh peaches; mix them with sugar and cream to taste. Arrange some of the quarters of the peaches tastefully in the bottom of a basin, then fill, and freeze the mass solid, without stirring. Turn it out to serve.

Iced Pudding — One and one-half pints of custard, composed of the yolks of 4 eggs, 4 tablespoonfuls of sugar, a flavoring of vanilla, 2 oz. fruits, consisting of equal parts of dried cherries, pine-apple, dried pears, or apricots, all cut into very small pieces. These fruits may be selected, or perhaps it would be more convenient to purchase ¼ lb. of the French preserved dried fruits; or add 1 oz. candied citron sliced, 2 oz. currants, 2 oz. stoned and chopped raisins, and ½ pint cream whipped. Freeze the custard in the usual manner, then mix in the fruits and whipped cream. Put into a mould, and place it on ice and salt. Serve whipped cream around it.

Frozen Custard with Fruit — Two pints milk, same of cream, 6 eggs, 3 teacups sugar, 1 pint berries or peaches cut up small.

Let the milk nearly boil; beat the yolks of the eggs with the sugar and add the milk by degrees. Whip the whites of the eggs to a froth and add to the mixture; put all in a saucepan, stirring until it is a nice thick and smooth custard. When perfectly cold whisk in the cream and freeze. If the custard is allowed to freeze itself, stir in the fruit after the second beating.

Custard — One and a half quarts rich milk, 1 cup sugar, ½ box gelatine, 4 eggs, vanilla to taste.

Dissolve the gelatine in the milk; add the yolks and sugar; let it come to a boil, then remove from the fire. When cool, add whites of eggs, etc. Pour into mould. To be eaten with cream, if preferred.

Chocolate Custard — One quart milk, yolks of 6 eggs, 4 tablespoonfuls sugar, ½ cup grated vanilla chocolate.

Boil the ingredients until thick enough, stirring all the time. When nearly cold flavor with vanilla. Pour into cups, and put the whites of the eggs beaten with some powdered sugar on top.

PRESERVES.

FRUIT for preserving must be gathered in dry weather, and should be carefully selected, discarding all bruised fruit, and purchasing only that of the largest and finest quality. Use only the best white sugar. There is no economy in using common sugar, because it causes a greater amount of scum, which must of course be taken off. In making syrups the sugar must be pounded and dissolved in the syrup before setting on the fire; no syrups or jellies should be boiled too high. Fruits must not be put into a thick syrup at first. Fruits preserved whole or sliced may be boiled in a syrup made of two pounds of sugar to every pound of water, the quantity of syrup differing in some cases, but the general rule is one and a half the substance of fruit. The following has been found very good: To thirty six pounds of sugar, put into a preserving-pan, and pour into it five pints of cold spring water; in another pint beat lightly up the white of one small egg, but do not froth it very much; add it to the sugar, and give it a stir to mix it well with the whole. Set the pan over a gentle fire when the sugar is nearly dissolved, and let the scum rise without being disturbed; when the syrup has boiled five minutes take it from the fire, let it stand a couple of minutes, and then skim it very clean; let it boil again, then throw in half a cup of cold water, which will bring the remainder of the scum to the surface; skim it until it is perfectly clear, strain it through a thin cloth, and it will be ready for use, or for further boiling.

All unripe fruit must be rendered quite tender by gentle scalding, before it is put into syrup, or it will not imbibe the sugar; and the syrup must be thin when it is first added to it, and be thickened afterwards by frequent boiling, or with additional sugar, or the fruit will shrivel instead of becoming plump and clear. A pound of sugar boiled for ten minutes in one pint of water will make a very light syrup; but it will gradually thicken if rapidly boiled in an uncovered pan. Two pounds of sugar to the pint of water will become thick with a little more than half an hour's boiling, or with three or four separate boilings of eight or ten minutes each; if too much reduced it will candy instead of remaining liquid.

In making jams many cooks, after allowing the proper proportion of sugar, put the fruit into the preserving-pan without removing the stones or skins until after boiling, as the flavor is thought to be finer by adopting this method. Glass bottles are preferable to any other, as they allow inspection to detect incipient fermentation, which may be stayed by reboiling. Copper or brass preserving-pans are the best kind to use, but they require a great deal of care to keep clean; the enameled are very nice and easily kept in order. Jams should be kept in a dry, cool place, and if properly made will only require a small round of writing-paper oiled, and laid on to fit, and tied down securely with a second paper brushed over with the white of egg to exclude the air.

Plum Jam.—Allow ¾ lb. of white sugar to 1 lb. of fruit. It is difficult to give the exact quantity of sugar to be used in plum jam; in fact, it entirely depends upon the quality of the plums used; therefore your own judgment will be necessary. After weighing the plums halve them and remove the stones; then place on a large dish and sprinkle with the sugar; leave them thus for 24 hours; then put into a preserving-pan and let them simmer gently on the back of the stove for about 20 or 30 minutes, then boil very quickly for ½ hour, skimming carefully, and stirring with a wooden spoon to prevent the jam sticking. It greatly improves the jam to put some kernels from the plum stones into it.

To Preserve Fruit in Syrup.—To every lb. of fruit allow 1 lb. of lump sugar, ½ tumbler of cold water. Boil the water and sugar together until it thickens slightly, which will take about ½ hour if the sugar be good. Take off the scum as it rises. Add the fruit and boil for ½ hour (rather longer if stone fruit), stirring very slightly, or the fruit will break. Take off the scum as it rises, but if both sugar and fruit be good there will be very little. Put into jars and tie over.

N. B.—To keep well, fruit must be perfectly sound and dry when gathered.

Currant Jam.—Three-quarters of a lb. of white sugar to every pound of fruit.

Let the fruit be very ripe, remove from the stalks with a silver fork; dissolve the sugar over the fire, then put in the currants and boil for ¾ hour, stirring and skimming all the time. Put into jars and cover air-tight.

Raspberry Jam.—Allow 1 lb. white sugar to 1 lb. fruit, and ½ cup red currant juice.

Directly this fruit is purchased preserve it; if allowed to stand the jam and the flavor will not be so good; place in preserving-pan and allow to boil for ¾ hour. Be particular to skim well, as this will make the jam nice and clear. When done, place in pots and cover in the usual manner.

Gooseberry Jam.—Some fine full-grown, unripe gooseberries, their weight in sugar; to 1 pint of liquor allow 1 lb. of sugar.

Cut, and pick out the seeds of the gooseberries; put them into a pan of water, green, and put them into a sieve to drain; beat them in a marble mortar, with their weight in sugar. Boil a quart of them to a mash in a quart of water; squeeze, and add to the liquor sugar in the above proportions; then boil and skim it, put in your green gooseberries, and having boiled them till very thick, clear, and of a nice green, put them into bottles.

Damson Jam.—Equal quantities of fruit and jelly.

Choose the fruit without blemish; remove the stones from the fruit, and put it and the sugar into your preserving-pan; stir slowly until the sugar is melted, and remove all scum. After the jam has begun to simmer, allow it to boil for an hour. It is necessary to stir diligently, or the jam will burn. When done, pot in the usual way.

Tomato Preserves.—Select small, green tomatoes, wipe carefully and prick the skins in several places. To ½ peck of them take 4 lbs. sugar, juice of 2 large lemons, and 2 oz. green ginger root and 1 of mace; put on the rest of the ingredients and let them boil ½ hour, skimming carefully; then put on the tomatoes and let them cook gently. When the tomatoes are clear and can be pierced with a straw take them up and lay carefully on plates to cool, allowing the syrup to simmer on the back of the stove. Put the tomatoes into jars, pour over the syrup and seal. Small yellow tomatoes may be preserved in the same way.

Tomato Jelly—One peck yellow tomatoes cut into pieces and boiled until soft; strain through a jelly bag; put on the fire and boil 20 minutes; to every cup of juice measure one of sugar; set the sugar in the oven, being careful that it is only heated through, not scorched. At the end of the 20 minutes add the sugar and the juice of a dozen lemons which has been strained through your jelly bag; boil 15 minutes more, then pour into your jelly glasses. Have the glasses just washed in hot water and wiped dry, and put a teaspoon in each one as you are ready to fill it. This will prevent the hot liquid from breaking the glasses.

Quince Marmalade—Four lbs. peeled and thinly sliced quinces in 2 quarts acidulated water, 2 lbs. peeled, cored and sliced apples, 3 lbs. sugar.

Place the fruit on the fire to boil until soft; then add the sugar, and stir the marmalade with a clean wooden spoon over a brisk fire until reduced to a rather thick paste—running rather slowly off the spoon when lifted out of the pan; the marmalade must then be immediately removed from the fire and poured into pots.

Green Grape Jam—To 1 lb. grapes allow ¾ lb. sugar.

Pick the grapes carefully and reject any that are injured; wash them. Put the grapes into a preserving-pan, then a layer of sugar, then a layer of grapes. Boil on a moderate fire, stirring it all the time to prevent its burning, and as the grape stones rise take them out with a spoon, so that by the time the fruit is sufficiently boiled—about 1 hour—the stones will all have been taken out. Put into jars and cover in the usual way.

Blackberry Jam—To every lb. of picked fruit allow 1 lb. loaf sugar and ½ lb. apples peeled and cored and cut quite small. Boil the fruit for 10 minutes, add the sugar, boil, stir and remove all scum. It will take from ½ to ¾ of an hour.

Strawberry Jam—To 1 lb. fruit allow ¾ lb. of 1 lb. sugar; to 6 lbs. strawberries add 1 pint red currant juice.

Put the currant juice and strawberries on to boil for 20 minutes, and stir carefully all the time; then put in the sugar and boil up very quickly for 20 or 25 minutes, removing any scum that arises; put into your jars, covering airtight. If a pound of sugar is used there will be more jelly.

Apple Marmalade—Pare, core and quarter some apples; put into a preserving-pan with sufficient water to prevent burning. Boil till it is a pulp. Take an equal weight of sugar in large lumps, dip in water and boil till it is a thick syrup; put it in the pulp, and simmer on a quick fire quarter of an hour. Grate in lemon peel before it is boiled.

Apple Cheese—Dissolve 1 lb. sugar in ½ pint water; add 1½ lbs. apples cut in quarters, and the rind of 1 lemon grated. Boil 2 hours; 10 minutes before that time add the juice of the lemon; stir all the time after the lemon is added, and boil quickly.

To Preserve Raspberries—To 1 lb. fruit, quite ripe, add 1 lb. finely-sifted sugar. Make the sugar as hot as possible without scorching, put it to the fruit, and stir till every particle of sugar is dissolved; put it in jars, and tie down with bladder. It will keep for a year, and looks just like fresh raspberries crushed with sugar.

Quince Jam—To 1 lb. quinces allow ¾ lb. sugar.

Peel and quarter the quinces, leaving the seeds in, as they readily impart their mucilage to the water and thus thicken the syrup. Put the fruit and sugar into a preserving-pan, and ½ teacupful water to moisten the bottom of the pan; stir the fruit and sugar frequently, and when it boils keep it boiling rapidly until the fruit is soft and of a clear red color. It will take about an hour, reckoning from the first boiling-up. Put into jam pots and cover when cold.

Apple Jam—Allow to every pound of pared and cored fruit ¾ lb. white sugar, the rind of 1 lemon, and juice of ½ lemon.

Having peeled and cored the apples, weigh them, and slice them very thin. Place in a stone jar and surround with boiling water; allow them to boil until tender; when tender place in a preserving-pan, add the sugar, grated lemon and juice. Boil slowly ½ hour from the time it begins to simmer, remove the scum, and put into jars and cover in the usual manner.

Green Fig Preserves—Equal quantity of fruit and syrup, peel of 1 large lemon, a little ginger.

Lay the figs in cold water for 24 hours, then simmer them till tender; put them again into cold water, and let them remain for two days, changing the water each day. If not quite soft, simmer again, and replace in cold water until next day. Take their weight in loaf sugar, and with ⅔ of it make a syrup, in which simmer the figs for 10 minutes. In 2 days take the third of the sugar, pound fine, and pour the syrup from the figs on it. Make a rich syrup with the peel of the lemon and a little raw ginger, and boil the figs in it; then mix all together and put into large jam pots. The figs may be cut in half, if preferred, after they have simmered until soft.

Preserved Pumpkins—Equal proportions of sugar and pumpkins, 1 gill lemon juice.

Cut the pumpkin in two, peel and remove the seed, cut in pieces about the size of a 25 cent piece; after weighing place in a deep vessel in layers, first sprinkling a layer of sugar, then of pumpkin, and so on, until it is finished; now add the lemon juice and set aside for 3 days; now for every 3 lbs. of sugar add ½ a pint of water and boil until tender. Pour into a pan, setting aside for 6 days, pour off the syrup and boil till thick; skim and add the pumpkin while boiling; bottle in the usual manner.

Quinces Preserved Whole — Some ripe quinces; to every pint of water allow 2 lbs. white sugar.

Pare the quinces and put them into the preserving pan, three-fourths covered with cold water (if they should float while the water is being poured on them, press them down with a plate until you have gauged the exact height of the water); take out the quinces, measure the water and add the sugar. Let this boil rapidly in the preserving-pan for 5 minutes, and then put in quinces. The syrup should not cover them at first, but when they are half cooked it will then simply cover the fruit. Boil the quinces rapidly, until soft enough for a knitting-needle to pierce them easily, which should be in an hour and a half, reckoning from the first boiling-up. Take the quinces out carefully, so as not to break them, and lay them on dishes to cool. Run the syrup through a jelly bag, or a piece of new flannel, put in a gravy strainer; this frees it of all odd little bits that may boil from the outside of the quinces, and makes it clearer. Put the syrup back in the preserving-pan, and boil it rapidly until it will jelly when dropped on a plate; put the quinces into the boiling syrup, and let them simmer gently for 10 minutes. Place each quince carefully in wide-necked jars, pour the hot syrup over them, and when cold cover in the usual way.

Preserved Oranges — Any number of oranges, with rather more than their weight in sugar; allow rather more than ½ pint of water to each lb. sugar.

Slightly grate undercut the oranges round and round with a knife, but not very deeply. Put them into cold water for 3 days, changing the water twice each day. Tie them up in a cloth and boil them until they are quite soft; that is, soft enough to be penetrated by the head of a pin. While they are boiling place the sugar on the fire with the water; let it boil for a few minutes, then strain it through muslin. Put the oranges into the syrup and boil till it jellies and is of a yellow color. Try the syrup by putting some to cool; it should not be too stiff. The syrup need not cover the oranges completely, but they must be turned so that each part gets thoroughly done. Place the oranges in pots, cover with syrup, and tie down with paraffine papers. This is an excellent way of preserving oranges or shaddocks whole. Only they should be looked at now and then, and boiled up again in fresh syrup, if what they are in has become too hard, which, however, if they have been properly done, will not be the case. They form a nice dish for dessert, or for serving, filled with whipped cream or custard, either cold or gently warmed through in the syrup in a stewpan.

To Cover Preserves — Cut a round of thin paper the size of your jar, brush it over with white of egg, and place on the preserves egg downwards. See that it lies flat so as to keep out the air. Cut a round of white cooking-paper rather larger than your jar. Snip round the edge. Brush well over with white of egg, place on your jar, and stick down the edges round the jar with a dry cloth. Let your jam be cold before done, and let the paper on the top dry well before putting away.

Apple Marmalade — Some good cooking apples, ¾ lb. fruit, ½ teacupful water to 1 lb. sugar, a few cloves, cinnamon or lemon peel for flavor.

Peel, core and thinly slice the apples (apples that cook to a smooth pulp easily); put the sugar in a preserving-pan (a tin or iron saucepan will turn them black) with the water; let it gradually melt, and boil it for 10 minutes; then put in the sliced apple, and a few cloves, cinnamon or lemon peel to flavor, if liked. Boil rapidly for an hour, skim well, and put in jam pots; it should be quite a smooth pulp, clear, and a bright amber color. Will keep good for 12 months.

Grape Marmalade — Take 10 lbs. of nice ripe grapes and wash them carefully; squeeze the pulps into one dish and throw the skins into another, put the pulps through a colander to remove seeds, then put pulps and skins together with ¾ lb. sugar to 1 lb. of fruit and cook thoroughly until jellied.

Sweet Tomato Pickle — Three and ½ lbs. tomatoes, 1½ lbs. sugar; ½ oz. each of cinnamon, mace and cloves mixed, 1 pint vinegar.

Peel and slice the tomatoes, sticking into them the cloves; put all together into a stewpan and stew an hour. When done pack in glass jars, and pour the syrup over boiling hot.

Sweet Peach Pickle — To 4 lbs. peaches allow 2 lbs. white sugar, ½ oz. each of mace, cinnamon and cloves mixed, and 1 pint of the best white vinegar.

Pour scalding water over the peaches and remove the skins with a butter knife; drop into cold water; stick four cloves in each peach. Lay the peaches in preserving-pan with the sugar sprinkled over them; bring gradually to the boil, add vinegar and spice, boil 5 or 6 minutes. Remove the peaches and place in bottles. Boil the syrup thick and pour over boiling hot.

How to Ice Fruit — Any desirable fruit may be iced by dipping first in the beaten white of an egg, then in pulverized sugar. Do this until the icing is sufficiently thick. Peaches should be pared and cut in halves, and sweet, juicy pears are treated in the same way. Cherries, strawberries and other small fruits are iced with the stems on, only the largest being chosen. Pineapples should be cut into thin slices and these again divided into quarters. Oranges and lemons should be carefully pared, and all the white skin removed. Lemons are cut into horizontal slices, and oranges are divided into quarters.

Salted Peanuts — Buy one quart of unroasted peanuts, break the shells carefully to prevent crushing; then drop the nuts into very hot water and rub gently until the red skin is off. Dry carefully, lay on flat tin plates and pour melted butter over them — a couple of teaspoonfuls will suffice; then set in rather quick oven until a nice brown; then take up and sprinkle liberally with salt, turning them so that both sides will receive a coat.

CANNED FRUITS, ETC.

To Can Peaches — First prepare the syrup. For canned fruits, 1 quart granulated sugar to 2 quarts water is the proper proportion; to be increased or lessened, according to the quantity of fruit to be canned, but always twice as much water as sugar. Use porcelain kettle, and, if possible, take care that it is kept solely for canning and preserving — nothing else. Have another porcelain kettle by the side of the first, for boiling water (about 3 quarts). Put the peaches, a few at a time, into a wire basket, such as is used to cook asparagus, etc. See that it is perfectly clean and free from rust. Dip them, when in the basket, into a pail of boiling water for a moment, and transfer immediately into a pail of cold water. The skin will then at once peel off easily, if not allowed to harden by waiting. This, besides being a neat and expeditious way of peeling peaches, also saves the best part of the fruit, which is so badly wasted in the usual mode of paring fruit. As soon as peeled, halve and drop the peaches into boiling water, and let them simmer — not boil hard — till a silver fork can be passed through them easily. Then lift each half out separately with a wire spoon and fill the can made ready for use; pour in all the boiling syrup which the jar will hold; leave it a moment for the fruit to shrink while filling the next jar; then add as much more boiling syrup as the jar will hold, and cover and screw down tightly immediately. Continue in this way, preparing and sealing one jar at a time, until all is done. If any syrup is left over, add to it the water in which the peaches were simmered, and a little more sugar; boil it down till it "ropes" from the spoon and you have a nice jelly, or, by adding some peaches or other fruit, a good dish of marmalade. Peaches or other fruit, good, but not quite nice enough for canning, can be used in this way very economically. Peaches to be peeled as directed above should not be too green or too ripe, else, in the first place, the skin cannot be peeled off, or, if too ripe, the fruit will fall to pieces.

Another Way — After peeling and halving as above directed, lay a clean towel or cloth in the bottom of a steamer over a kettle of boiling water and put the fruit on it, half filling the steamer. Cover tightly and let it steam while making the syrup. When this is ready, and the fruit steamed till a silver fork will pass through easily, dip each piece gently into the boiling syrup; then as gently place in the hot jar, and so continue till all have been thus scalded and put in the jar. Then fill full with syrup, cover and seal immediately. While filling, be sure and keep the jars hot.

Pears — The skin will not peel off so easily as that of peaches by dipping them in boiling water, but it will loosen or soften enough to be taken off with less waste of the fruit than if pared without scalding. Prepare the syrup and proceed as for peaches. They will require longer cooking; but as soon as a silver fork will pass through easily, they are done. Longer cooking destroys the flavor.

Pineapples — Pare very carefully with a silver knife, as steel injures all fruit. With the sharp point of the knife dig out as neatly and with as little waste as possible all the "eyes" and black specks, then cut out each of the sections in which the "eyes" were, in solid pieces clear down to the core. By doing this all the real fruit is saved, leaving the core a hard, round, woody substance, but containing considerable juice. Take this core and wring it with the hands as one wrings a cloth till all the juice is extracted, then throw it away. Put the juice thus saved into the syrup; let it boil up 5 minutes, skim till clear, then add fruit. Boil as short a time as possible, and have the fruit tender. The pineapple loses flavor by over-cooking more rapidly than any other fruit. Fill into well-heated jars, add all the syrup the jar will hold; cover and screw down as soon as possible.

Plums — Plums should be wiped with a soft cloth as desired, never washed. Have the syrup all ready, prick each plum with a silver fork to prevent the skin from bursting, and put them into the syrup. Boil from 5 to 10 minutes, judging by the size of the fruit. Dip carefully into the hot jars, fill full, and screw on the cover immediately. Cherries may be put up in the same way.

Strawberries (Canned) — Allow to each 1 lb. of fruit ⅜ lb. of sugar.

Put berries and sugar into a large, flat dish and allow to stand about 3 hours, then draw off the juice and put into preserving-pan and allow to come to a boil, removing the scum as it rises; then put in the berries, and let them come to a boil. Put into warm bottles and seal quickly.

Cherries (Canned) — To every 1 lb. of fruit ¼ lb. of sugar, 3 gills of water.

Put the sugar and water on the fire to heat, and as soon as it comes to a boil put in the cherries and allow them to scald for ½ hour; put into bottles boiling hot and seal. A few of the kernels put in to scald with the fruit impart a fine flavor. Note — Be sure to skim well.

Preserved Crab Apples — Select large, fine crab apples, prick the skins in several places; put into your preserving-kettle ¾ lb. of sugar to each pound of fruit and a cupful of water; let the syrup boil 10 minutes, skimming off the scum which rises to the top; then put in your fruit and cook gently until the apples can be pierced with a straw; then take them out and lay on plates; boil the juice ½ hour longer; then put the fruit in jars, fill up with juice and seal.

Fruit Jellies — The fruit should be placed in a jar, and the jar set in a stewpan of warm water, covered and allowed to boil until the fruit is broken; take a strong jelly bag and press a little of the fruit at a time, turning out each time the skins; allow 2 lbs. of sugar to 1 quart of juice, set on the stove to boil again. Many good cooks heat the sugar by placing in the oven and stirring now and then to prevent burning. When the juice begins to boil (watch that it does not boil over 15 minutes), then add the heated sugar; stir well and just bring to a boil, remove directly from the stove, dip the glasses to contain it in hot water, and set them upon a dish cloth wrung out of warm water, pouring the boiling liquid into them; cover in the usual manner.

Rhubarb Jelly — Soak 2 oz. gelatine in a pint of water with ¾ lb. best lump sugar; well wash and slice about 2½ lbs. of rhubarb of a nice bright color, put it into a stewpan to boil with a quart of water, leave it to get thoroughly stewed, but not long enough to let the juice get thick; strain the latter, and add 1½ pints of it to the dissolved gelatine, with the whites and shells of 3 eggs. Whisk it all quickly on the fire, pass it through the jelly-bag, and pour it into a mould and leave it to set.

Orange and Tapioca Jelly — Soak 6 tablespoonfuls of tapioca for 3 hours in 3 cupfuls of salted water; set in hot water and boil, adding 4 teaspoonfuls of sugar and a little boiling water if too thick. When clear remove, add the juice of 1 orange. Cover the bottom of the mould with sliced oranges, and when the jelly is cool pour it over the fruit.

Quince Jelly — Ripe quinces, allowing 1 pint of water to each pound of fruit, ¾ lb. of sugar to each pound of juice.

Prepare the quinces and put them in water in the above proportions; simmer gently till the juice becomes colored, but only very pale; strain the juice through a jelly bag, but do not press the fruit; allow it to drain itself. Put the strained juice in a preserving-pan and boil 20 minutes; then stir in the sugar in the above proportions and stir over the fire for 20 minutes, taking off the scum, and pour into glasses to set. It should be rich in flavor, but pale and beautifully transparent. Long boiling injures the color.

Raspberry Jelly — Ripe, carefully picked raspberries; allow ¾ lb. of pounded sugar to every pound of fruit.

Boil the raspberries for 10 minutes, strain and weigh the juice and add the sugar in the above proportions and boil for 15 or 20 minutes. Skim and stir well.

Cherry Jelly — Mayduke or Kentish cherries (allowing ½ pint of water to 1 lb. of fruit).

Boil the cherries in the water, strain the juice and proceed as for raspberry jelly.

Red Currant Jelly — Red currants; ¾ lb. of sugar to 1 lb. of juice.

Pick the fruit and simmer it in water for about an hour, or until the juice flows freely; strain, boil up the juice, add the sugar, and boil again, skimming and stirring well for 15 minutes. Put into small pots, and when cold and firm cover it.

Black Currant Jelly — Make in the same way, but use a larger proportion of sugar.

White Currant Jelly — Pick the fruit carefully, weigh it, and put into the preserving-pan equal quantities of fruit and sugar. Boil quickly for 10 minutes, and strain the juice into the pots; when cold and stiff cover them.

Blackberry Jelly — Make as directed for red currants, but use only 10 oz. of sugar to each pound of juice. The addition of a little lemon juice is an improvement.

Barberry Jelly — Barberries, a little water, ¾ lb. of sugar to every pound of juice.

Take ripe barberries, carefully reject any spotted or decayed ones, wash, drain them and strip off the stalks. Boil with a very little water till quite tender, press out and strain the juice, boil up the juice, add the sugar, and boil for 10 minutes, skimming and stirring as above.

Green Gooseberry Jelly — Carefully picked gooseberries, allowing to each pound of fruit ¾ pint of water; to every pound of juice allow 1 lb. of white sifted sugar.

Boil the fruit in the water, reduce to a pulp — it will take ¾ hour — strain through a jelly-bag, weigh the sugar in the above proportions; boil up the juice quickly and add the sugar; boil till reduced to a jelly (about 20 minutes), skim and stir well; pour into pots.

Red Gooseberry Jelly — Make it in the same way as the green, but ¾ lb. of sugar will be sufficient for each pound of juice. In straining the juice be careful not to press the fruit. The surplus fruit, with the addition of some currant juice, can be made into common jam.

Mixed Fruit Jelly — Fruit, strawberries, currants, cherries, etc.; ¾ lb. of sugar to each pound of juice.

Take ripe fruit, strip off the stalks and remove the stones from the cherries, boil all together for ¾ hour, strain the juice. Boil up the juice, add the sugar in the above proportions, stirring well till quite dissolved, boil again for 15 or 20 minutes till it jellies, stirring frequently, and carefully removing all scum as it rises.

Quince Jelly — Ripe quinces; to every pound of quince allow 1 lb. of crushed sugar.

Peel, cut up and core the quinces. Put them in sufficient cold water to cover them, and stew gently till soft, but not red. Strain the juice without pressure, boil the juice for 20 minutes, add the sugar and boil again till it jellies — about ¼ hour — stir and skim well all the time. Strain it again through a napkin, or twice-folded muslin, pour into pots or moulds, and when cold cover it. The remainder of the fruit can be made into marmalade with ¾ lb. sugar and ½ lb. juicy apples to every pound of quinces, or it can be made into compotes or tarts.

Quince and Apple Jelly — Equal quantities of quinces and apples; to every pound of juice allow ¾ lb. white sugar.

Stew the fruit separately till tender (the quinces will take longer), strain the juice, mix it and add the sugar. Proceed as in quince jelly.

Apple Jelly — Some sound apples; allow ¾ lb. sugar to each pound of juice.

Peel, core and quarter the apples, and throw them into cold water as they are done; boil them till tender, then strain the juice from them through a fine sieve, and afterwards through a jelly bag—if necessary pass it through twice, as the juice should be quite clear; boil up the juice, add the sugar, stir till melted, and boil for another 10 minutes; add the strained juice of a lemon to every 1½ lbs. of juice just before it is finished.

Apple Jelly (2)—One lb. moist sugar, 1 lb. apples, 1 lemon—the juice of the lemon to be used and the rind added, cut very fine.

Boil the whole until it becomes a perfect jelly; let it stand in a mould till quite firm and cold, turn it out and stick it with almonds, cut crosswise round. If for dessert, use a small plain mould.

Orange Jelly—Put 1 package of gelatine to soak in 1 pint of cold water; when it is dissolved add 3 pints of boiling water and juice of ½ dozen oranges and 2 lemons, as well as 1 pound of sugar; when all is dissolved, strain through a jelly bag and set away to harden. Cider or other fruit juice may be substituted for the oranges and lemons.

Sago Jelly—Two lbs. picked red currants, 1 pint cold water, ½ lb. white sugar, a cupful of sago.

Put the currants into the water and boil till soft, pass them through a sieve; put the juice to boil again with the sugar; when quite boiling add the sago, previously soaked in cold water; boil 30 minutes until quite transparent, put into a mould, and when cold turn out. Serve with or without custard around it.

Currant Sponge—Cover ½ box of gelatine with cold water and let soak ½ hour; pour over a pint of boiling water, add ½ pint of sugar and stir over the fire for 5 minutes. Pour in ½ pint of red currant juice, strain into a tin pan, set on ice until the mixture begins to thicken, beat to a froth, add the well-beaten whites of 4 eggs, mix, and pour into a mould to harden. Serve with whipped cream.

DAIRY DISHES.

GREAT attention and cleanliness are required in the management of a dairy. The cows should be regularly milked at an early hour, and their udders perfectly emptied.

The quantity of milk depends on many causes; as the goodness, breed and health of the cow, the pasture, the length of time from calving, the having plenty of clean water in the field she feeds in, etc. A change of pasture will tend to increase it.

When a calf is to be reared, it should be removed from the cow in ten days at the farthest. It should be removed in the morning and no food given to it till the following morning, when, being extremely hungry, it will drink readily; feed it regularly morning and evening, and let the milk which is given to it be just warm; skimmed milk will be quite good enough.

The milk when brought in should always be strained into the pans. The cans containing the recently drawn milk should be placed in water about 58° F., which should rise a little above the level of the milk; the animal heat is thus reduced to between 56° and 58° F., and the milk will keep sweet for thirty-six hours even in the hottest weather. This temperature allows the cream to rise with greater facility and with less admixture of other constituents than can be obtained in any other way. Some butter-makers allow the milk to stand for thirty-six hours; others say that twenty-four hours is sufficient for all the cream to rise. After the cream has risen it is to be removed by skimming, and after standing a suitable time is placed in the churn. The kind of churn generally preferred by the best butter-makers is the common dash-churn, made of white oak. Much depends upon the manner in which the operation is performed, even with the same churn. The motion should be steady and regular, not too quick nor too slow. The time occupied in churning 12 or 15 gallons of cream should be from 40 to 60 minutes. When removed from the churn, it should be thoroughly washed in cold water, using a ladle and not the hands. It should then be salted with about one-twentieth of its weight of the purest and finest salt, which should be thoroughly incorporated with it, by means of a butter-worker, or ladle, the hands being never allowed to touch the butter. Twelve hours afterwards another working should be performed and the butter packed in strong and perfectly tight white oak firkins. When filled they should be headed up and a strong brine poured in at the top. It should then be placed in a cool, well-ventilated cellar.

Dr. Ure gives the following directions for curing butter, known as the Irish method: "Take one part of sugar, one part of nitre, and two of the best Spanish great salt, and rub them together into a fine powder. This composition is to be mixed thoroughly with the butter as soon as it is completely freed from the milk, in the proportion of 1 ounce to 1 lb; and the butter thus prepared is to be pressed tight into the vessel prepared to receive it, so as to leave no vacuities. This butter does not taste well till it has stood at least a fortnight; it then has a rich, marrowy flavor that no other butter ever acquires."

Preserving Butter—Two lbs. of common salt, 1 lb. loaf-sugar, and 1 lb. saltpetre. Beat the whole well together, then to 16 lbs. of butter put 1 lb. of this mixture, work it well, and when cold and firm put it into glazed earthen vessels that will hold 14 lbs. each. Butter thus preserved becomes better by being kept, but it must be kept from the air, and securely covered down. If intended for winter use, add another ounce of the mixture to every pound of butter, and on the top of the pans lay enough salt to cover them with brine.

Clouted Cream — In order to obtain this, the milk is suffered to stand in a vessel for 24 hours. It is then placed over a stove, or slow fire, and very gradually heated to an almost simmering state, below the boiling point. When this is accomplished (the first bubble having appeared), the milk is removed from the fire, and allowed to stand for 24 hours more. At the end of this time the cream will have arisen to the surface in a thick or clouted state, and is removed. In this state it is eaten as a luxury; but it is often converted into butter, which is done by stirring it briskly with the hand or a stick. The butter thus made, although more in quantity, is not equal in quality to that procured from the cream which has risen slowly and spontaneously; and in the largest and best dairies in the Vale of Honiton the cream is never clouted, except when intended for the table in that state.

Rennet — Take out the stomach of a calf just killed, and scour it well with salt and water, both inside and out; let it drain, and then sew it up with two large handfuls of salt in it, or keep it in the salt wet, and soak a piece in fresh water as it is required.

Maître d'Hotel Butter — Two oz. fresh butter, juice of 1 lemon, white sugar and salt to taste, parsley blanched, freed from moisture and finely minced.

Put the butter in a basin with the other ingredients, incorporate the whole effectually and quickly, and put it by in a cool place until wanted.

Butter (to serve as a little dish) — Roll butter in different forms, either like a pine, making the marks with a teaspoon, or in crimping cutters, work it through a colander, or scoop with a teaspoon, and mix it with grated beef tongue or anchovies. Make a wreath of curled parsley to garnish.

Curled Butter — Procure a strong cloth, and secure it by two of its corners to a nail or hook in the wall; knot the remaining two corners, leaving a small space. Then place your butter into the cloth; twist firmly over your serving dish, and the butter will force its way between the knots in little curls or strings. Garnish with parsley and send to table.

Fairy Butter — Two tablespoonfuls white sugar; yolks of 2 hard-boiled eggs, 2 tablespoonfuls orange-flower water, ¼ lb. fresh butter.

Pound the yolks with the orange-flower water (in a mortar) to a smooth paste, then mix in the sugar and butter. Now place in a clean cloth, and force the mixture through by wringing. The butter will fall upon the dish in pieces according to the size of the holes in the cloth.

Melted Butter — Five oz. butter, 1 tablespoonful flour, 2 tablespoonfuls water, salt to taste.

Put all the ingredients into a stew-pan, and stir one way over the fire until all the ingredients are well mixed. Allow it just to boil, and it is ready to serve.

Cheese (to make) — Warm the milk till equal to new; but observe it must not be too hot; now add a sufficiency of rennet to turn it, and cover it over; let it remain till well turned, then strike the curd well down with the skimming-dish, and let it separate, observing to keep it still covered. Put the vat over the tub, and fill it with curd, which must be squeezed close with the hand, and more is to be added as it sinks; and at length left about three inches above the edge of the vat. Before the vat is in this manner filled, the cheese cloth must be laid at the bottom of it, and, when full, drawn smoothly over on all sides. The curd should be salted in the tub after the whey is out. When everything is prepared as above directed, put a board under and over the vat, then place it in the press; let it remain 2 hours, then turn it out, put on a fresh cheese cloth, and press it again 10 hours; then salt it all over, and turn it again into the vat; then press it again 24 hours. The vat should have several small holes in the bottom to let the whey run off.

Cheese (to preserve sound) — Wash in warm whey, when you have any, wipe it once a month, and keep it on a rack. If you want to ripen it, a damp cellar will bring it forward. When a whole cheese is cut, the larger quantity should be spread with butter inside, and the outside wiped to preserve it. To keep those in daily use moist, let a clean cloth be wrung out from cold water, and wrapped round them when carried from table. Dry cheese may be used to advantage to grate for serving with macaroni.

Cream Cheese — Put 5 quarts of strippings, that is, the last of the milk, into a pan with 2 spoonfuls of rennet. When the curd is come, strike it down two or three times with the skimming-dish just to break it. Let it stand 2 hours, then spread a cheese-cloth on a sieve, put the curd on it, and let the whey drain; break the curd a little with your hand, and put it into a vat with a 2-lb. weight upon it. Let it stand 12 hours, take out, and bind a fillet round. Turn every day till dry, from one board to another; cover them with nettles, or clean dock leaves, and put between two pewter plates to ripen. If the weather be warm, it will be ready in 2 weeks.

Sage Cheese — Bruise some young red sage and spinach leaves, press out the juice, and mix it with the curd; then proceed as with other cheese.

Cheese Straws — Six oz. flour, 4 oz. butter, 3 oz. grated Parmesan cheese, a little cream, salt, white pepper, and cayenne.

Roll it out thin, cut into narrow strips, bake in a moderate oven, and serve piled high and very hot and crisp.

Roast Cheese—Three oz. Cheshire cheese, yolks of 2 eggs, 4 oz. grated bread-crumbs, 3 oz. butter, a dessertspoonful of mustard, salt and pepper.

Grate the cheese, add the yolks, bread-crumbs and butter; beat the whole well in a mortar and add the mustard, salt and pepper. Make some toast cut into neat slices and spread the paste thickly on. Cover with a dish and place in the oven till hot through, then uncover and let the cheese color a light brown. Serve immediately.

Ramequins—Beat 2 eggs, whites and yolks separately; to the yolks of the eggs add 2 tablespoonfuls flour, 2 oz. melted butter and 2 oz. cheese, grated; to this add the stiff whites of the eggs. Mix well and bake in buttered gem-pans, in quick oven, about 15 minutes. Eat hot.

Cheese Dish—Quarter lb. good, fresh cheese, 1 cup sweet milk, ½ teaspoonful dry mustard, a little pepper and salt, 1 tablespoonful butter.

Cut the cheese into thin slices, put it into a "spider" or saucepan, and pour over it the milk; mix in the other ingredients. Stir this mixture all the time while over the fire. Turn the contents into a hot dish and serve immediately.

Cheese Toast—Some rich cheese, pepper to taste, a beaten egg, with sufficient milk to make it of the consistency of cream.

Grate the cheese and mix with the other ingredients; warm the mixture on the fire, and when quite hot pour it over some slices of hot buttered toast. Serve immediately.

BEVERAGES

THE making of tea depends upon the brand. Always scald the pot just as you make the tea. A general rule is: "One teaspoonful for each person and one for the pot." Pour on a little boiling water to wet the tea. A minute or two later add a cup or two of boiling water. Allow to stand and add what boiling water is necessary for the amount of tea desired. This develops the strength of the tea and keeps it hot. Ceylon tea must not wait more than five minutes, as after that it takes on an unpleasant taste. Make a little, and often.

To make good coffee is the simplest and yet one of the most important things that pertain to cooking, but comparatively few know how to do it. For a family of five or six, take ¾ cup good ground coffee and mix with it the white of 1 egg and a little water; put it in the coffee-pot, and add to that about a pint of cold water. When it comes to a boil, set it on the back of the stove and add boiling water sufficient for use. This, with cream and sugar, makes most delicious coffee.

Remember in making coffee:

That the same flavor will not suit every taste, but that every one may be suited to a nicety by properly blending two or more kinds.

That equal parts of Mocha, Java and Rio will be relished by a good many people.

That a mild coffee can be made dangerously strong and still retain the mildness of flavor.

That the enjoyment of a beverage and slavish devotion thereto are quite different things.

That the flavor is improved if the liquid is turned from the dregs as soon as the proper strength has been obtained.

That where the percolation method is used the coffee should be ground very fine or the strength will not be extracted.

That if the ground coffee is put into the water and boiled, it should be rather coarse; otherwise it will invariably be muddy.

That a good coffee will always command a fair price, but that all high-priced coffees are not necessarily of high quality.

That, in serving, the cups and cream should be warm; the cream should be put in the cup before the coffee is poured in, but it is immaterial when the sugar is added.

That a level teaspoonful of the ground coffee to each cup is the standing allowance, from which deviation can be made in either direction, according to the strength desired.

Cocoa—Two tablespoonfuls cocoa, 1 breakfast cupful boiling milk and water.

Put sufficient cold milk in to form the cocoa into a smooth paste. Then add equal proportions of boiling milk and boiling water, mixing well. Great care must be taken that the milk does not burn, as it will impart a disagreeable flavor.

Chocolate—Allow 2 sticks of chocolate to 1 pint of new milk. After the chocolate is scraped, either let it soak an hour or so, with a tablespoonful of milk to soften it, or boil it a few moments in 2 or 3 tablespoonfuls water; then, in either case, mash into a smooth paste. When the milk, sweetened to taste, is boiling, stir in the chocolate paste, adding a little of the boiling milk to it first to dilute it evenly. Let it boil half a minute, stir it well and serve immediately.

Ginger Beer—One and one fourth lbs. loaf sugar, 1 lemon, 2 oz. best white ginger, 1 gallon boiling water, 1 tablespoonful German yeast, and ¼ oz. cream of tartar.

Peel the lemon; cut the inside in pieces. Crush the ginger, add the sugar and cream of tartar; pour over all the boiling water; stir well until the sugar is melted. Let it stand 24 hours to be quite cold, then stir in the yeast, which ought to be previously dissolved. Stir, and strain through a coarse cloth; then bottle, taking care the corks are secured. Keep in a cool place in hot weather.

Oatmeal Drink—(Dr. Parkes)—"The proportions are ¼ lb. oatmeal to 2 or 3 quarts water, according to the heat of the day and the work and thirst; it should be well boiled, and then 1 or 1½ oz. brown sugar added. If you find it thicker than you like, add 3 quarts water. Before drinking it, shake up the oatmeal well through the liquid. In summer drink this cold; in winter, hot. You will find it not only quenches thirst, but will give you more strength and endurance than any other drink. If you cannot boil it, you can take a little oatmeal mixed with cold water and sugar, but this is not so good; always boil it if you can. If at any time you have to make a very long day, as in harvest, and cannot stop for meals, increase the oatmeal to ½ lb., or even ¾ lb., and the water to 3 quarts if you are likely to be very thirsty. If you cannot get oatmeal, wheat flour will do, but not quite so well."

Those who try this recipe will find that they can get through more work than when using beer, and that they will be stronger and healthier at the end of the harvest. Cold tea and skim milk are also found to be better than beer, but not equal to the oatmeal drink.

Lemonade (1)—Six large lemons and 1 lb. loaf sugar.

Rub the sugar over the rinds to get out the flavor, then squeeze out all the juice on the sugar; cut what remains of the lemons into slices, and pour on them a quart of boiling water; when this has cooled, strain it onto the juice and sugar, and add as much more water (cold) as will make it palatable.

Lemonade (2)—One oz. tartaric acid, 1 lb. loaf sugar, 1 pint boiling water, and 20 or 30 drops essence of lemon.

To be kept in a bottle and mixed with cold water, as desired.

Lemon Syrup—Boil until clear 1 pint lemon juice, strained, and 2 lbs. loaf sugar, stirring constantly, and add ½ pint water to prevent its boiling too thick. The juice of a dozen lemons will give about a pint.

To Keep Lemon Juice—Buy the fruit when cheap, when not quite ripe; cut off the peels, and roll the fruit in your hand, so as to make them part with the juice readily. Squeeze the juice into a china basin, strain through a muslin which will not allow the least pulp to pass. Have ready ½- and ¼-oz. phials (quite dry), fill with the juice so as to allow ½ teaspoonful sweet oil in each. Cork tightly, and set them upright in a cool place. When wanted for use, wind some clean cotton round a skewer, and, dipping it in, the oil will be attracted. The juice will be quite clear; the rinds can be dried for grating.

Peppermint Cordial—One lb. loaf sugar, 1 pint boiling water.

Simmer 15 minutes, then stir in 1 tablespoonful honey; when nearly cold, add 30 drops essence of peppermint. Bottle for use. Four tablespoonfuls to a tumbler of cold or hot water makes a delicious drink. Essence of ginger can be used in the same way.

Raspberry Syrup—Fill a ½-gallon fruit jar with ripe red raspberries, pour over them good cider vinegar; cover tightly, and set away in a cool, dark place for a week. Put on the fire and let come to a scalding point, strain through a jelly bag; to the juice add pint for pint of sugar. Boil gently about 20 minutes, skimming constantly. Bottle, seal, and keep in a cool place. Add a wineglassful to a glass of iced water. It is excellent.

Ginger Pop—Allow 4 quarts warm water, 2 oz. white ginger root, 2 lemons, 1 lb. white sugar, ½ tablespoon cream tartar, and ½ cup soft yeast. Cut the ginger root fine and boil in a little of the water; grate in the yellow rind only of the lemons, and put in the pulp and juice; when nearly cold, add the yeast. Put all in a stone jar in a warm place 24 hours, then bottle for use.

Currant Vinegar—Two quarts black currants, 1 pint best vinegar, 1½ lbs. white sugar.

Well bruise the currants and place into a basin with the vinegar; let it stand 3 or 4 days, and then strain into an earthen jar; add the sugar, set the jar in a saucepan of cold water and boil for an hour. When cold, bottle; it is the better for keeping.

Raspberry Vinegar—To 4 quarts red raspberries put enough vinegar to cover, 1 lb. sugar to every pint of juice.

Let the raspberries and vinegar stand for 24 hours; scald and strain; add sugar, boil 20 minutes, skim well, and when cold bottle.

Koumiss—Put 1 gill buttermilk into a quart of new, rich milk, and add 4 lumps white sugar; see that the sugar is dissolved. Put in a covered vessel, in a warm place, for 10 hours; it will then be thick. Pour from one pitcher to another, so that it may become uniformly thick; then bottle and set away in a warm place. It will be good in 24 hours in summer and 36 in winter. The bottles must not only be tightly corked, but the corks tied down. Shake the bottles well before opening. This is an excellent drink for people with weak digestion, and is also good for children.

Temperance Cup—Pare the yellow rind very thinly from twelve lemons; squeeze the juice over it in an earthen bowl, and let it stand over night, if possible. Pare and slice thinly a very ripe pineapple, and let it lie over night in ½ lb. powdered sugar. If all these ingredients cannot be prepared the day before they are used, they must be done very early in the morning, because the juices of the fruit need to be incorporated with the sugar at least 12 hours before the beverage is used. After all the ingredients have been properly prepared, as above, strain off the juice, carefully pressing all of it out of the fruit; mix it with 2 lbs. powdered sugar and 3 quarts ice water, and stir it until the sugar is dissolved. Then strain it again through a muslin or bolting-cloth sieve, and put it on the ice or in a very cold place until it is wanted for use.

SICK-ROOM COOKERY

WITHIN the last few years great changes have occurred in the ideas entertained by the medical profession as to what is proper food for invalids. As a rule, patients are allowed to eat about what is desired, care being taken of course not to overload the stomach. There are cases, however, where there is little wish for food, and where the thoughtful nurse must look for something which is daintily appetizing as well as nourishing, and at the same time easy of digestion. To meet this want the recipes below are given.

Never set before the sick a large quantity of food; tempt with a very small portion delicately cooked and tastefully served. If not eaten directly, remove from the sick-room without delay, as no food should be allowed to stand there. Do not give the same food often, as variety is charming. Never keep the sick waiting; always have something in readiness—a little jelly, beef-tea, stewed fruit, gruel, etc. It will be found more tempting to serve any of these in glasses. If much milk is used, keep it on ice. Let all invalid cookery be simple; be careful to remove every particle of fat from broth or beef-tea before serving.

Beef-Tea.—Take 1 lb. lean beef, 1 pint water, and ½ saltspoonful salt.

Cut the meat into very small pieces, carefully removing the fat. Put into a stone jar with the salt and water; cover with the lid, and tie over a piece of thick brown paper. Put it into a moderate oven, simmer slowly for 4 hours, and strain.

Beef-Tea Custard.—This may be served alone, either hot or cold, or a few small pieces can be put in a cup of beef-tea, which is thus transferred into a kind of soupe royale. Beat up an egg in a cup, add a small pinch of salt, and enough strong beef-tea to half fill the cup; butter a tiny mould and pour in the mixture. Steam it for 20 minutes, and turn it out in a shape.

Mutton Broth.—Cut in small pieces 1 lb. of lean mutton or lamb, and boil it, unsalted, in 1 quart cold water, keeping it closely covered until it falls to pieces. Strain it and add 1 tablespoonful of rice or barley, soaked in a little warm water. Simmer for ½ hour, stirring often, then add 4 tablespoonfuls milk, salt and pepper, and a little chopped parsley, if liked. Simmer again 5 minutes, taking care that it does not burn. Chicken broth may be prepared in the same way. Crack the bones well before putting them into the water.

Veal Broth.—One and ½ lbs. veal, 1 doz. sweet almonds, 1 qt. water, a little salt, 1 pt. boiling water.

Remove all the fat from the veal, and simmer gently in the water till it is reduced to a pint; blanch and pound the almonds till they are a smooth paste, then pour over them the boiling water very slowly, stirring it all the time till it is as smooth as milk; strain both the almond and veal liquors through a fine sieve and mix well together; add the salt, and boil up again.

Chicken Broth.—An old fowl, 2 pints water, a pinch of salt, a blade of mace, 6 or 8 peppercorns, a very small chopped onion, a few sprigs sweet herbs.

Cut up the fowl and put it, bones as well, in a saucepan with the water, salt, mace, peppercorns, onion and sweet herbs; let it simmer very gently till the meat is very tender, which will take about 3 hours, skimming well during the time. Strain carefully and set aside to cool.

Egg Broth.—An egg, ½ pint good unflavored veal or mutton broth quite hot, salt, toast.

Beat the egg well in a broth basin; when frothy add the broth, salt to taste, and serve with toast.

Beef Broth.—One lb. good lean beef, 2 quarts cold water, ½ teacup tapioca, a small piece of parsley, an onion, if liked, pepper and salt.

Soak the tapioca 1 hour, cut in small pieces the beef, put in a stew pan the above proportion of water, boil slowly (keeping well covered) 1½ hours, then add the tapioca, and boil ½ hour longer. Some add with the tapioca a small piece of parsley and a slice or two of onion. Strain before serving, seasoning slightly with pepper and salt. It is more strengthening to add, just before serving, a soft poached egg. Rice may be used instead of tapioca, straining the broth, and adding 1 or 2 tablespoonfuls of rice (soaked for a short time), and then boiling ½ hour.

Scotch Broth.—The liquor in which a leg of mutton, piece of beef or old fowl has been boiled, barley, vegetables chopped small, a cup of rough oatmeal mixed in cold water, salt and pepper to taste.

Add to the liquor some barley and vegetables, chopped small, in sufficient quantity to make the broth quite thick. The necessary vegetables are carrots, turnips, onions and cabbage, but any others may be added; old (not parched) peas and celery are good additions. When the vegetables are boiled tender add the oatmeal to the broth, salt and pepper to taste. This very plain preparation is genuine Scotch broth as served in Scotland; with any coloring or herbs, etc., added, it is not real Scotch broth. It is extremely palatable and wholesome in its plain form.

Broth (Beef, Mutton and Veal).—Two lbs. lean beef, 1 lb. scrag of veal, 1 lb. scrag of mutton, some sweet herbs, 10 peppercorns, 5 quarts water, 1 onion.

Put the meat, sweet herbs and peppercorns into a nice tin saucepan, with the water, and simmer till reduced to 3 quarts. Remove the fat when cold. Add the onion, if approved.

Mutton Cutlets (Delicate) — Two or 3 small cutlets from the best end of a neck or loin of mutton, 1 cupful of water or broth, a little salt, and a few peppercorns.

Trim the cutlets very nicely, cut off all the fat, place them in a flat dish with enough water or broth to cover them; add the salt and peppercorns and allow them to stew gently for 2 hours, carefully skimming off every particle of fat which may rise to the top during the process. At the end of this time, provided the cutlets have not been allowed to boil fast, they will be found extremely tender. Turn them when half done.

Rabbit (Stewed) — Two nice young rabbits, 1 quart of milk, 1 tablespoonful of flour, a blade of mace, salt and pepper.

Mix into a smooth paste the flour with ½ glass of milk, then add the rest of the milk; cut the rabbits up into convenient pieces; place in a stewpan with the other ingredients and simmer gently until perfectly tender.

Meat Jelly (1) — Beef, isinglass, 1 teacupful of water, salt to taste.

Cut some beef into very small pieces and carefully remove all the fat. Put it in an earthen jar with alternate layers of the best isinglass (it is more digestible than gelatine) until the jar is full. Then add a teacupful of water with a little salt, cover it down closely, and cook it all day in a very slow oven. In the morning scald a jelly mould and strain the liquor into it. It will be quite clear, except at the bottom, where will be the brown sediment such as is in all beef tea, and it will turn out in a shape. It is, of course, intended to be eaten cold, and is very useful in cases where hot food is forbidden, or as a variety from the usual diet.

Meat Jelly (2) — A calf's foot, 1½ lbs. neck of veal or beef, a slice or two of lean ham, 1 small onion, a bunch of parsley, a teaspoonful of salt, a little spice, 3 quarts of water.

Simmer slowly 5 or 6 hours, and strain. The above makes a strong but not highly flavored jelly. More ham or any bones of unboiled meat, game or poultry will improve it. The liquor in which chicken or veal has been boiled should, when at hand, be used instead of water. Meat jellies keep better when no vegetables are stewed in them.

Baked Hominy — To a cupful of cold boiled hominy (small kind) allow 2 cups of milk, a heaping teaspoonful of white sugar, a little salt, and 3 eggs.

Beat the eggs very light, yolks and whites separately. Work the yolks into the hominy, alternately with the butter. When thoroughly mixed, put in the sugar and salt, and go on beating while you soften the batter gradually with milk. Be careful to leave no lumps in the batter. Lastly, stir in the whites and bake in a buttered pudding-dish until light, firm and delicately browned. It may be used as a dessert.

Strengthening Blanc-Mange — One pint milk, ½ oz. isinglass, rind of ½ small lemon, 2 oz. sugar, yolks of 3 fresh eggs.

Dissolve the isinglass in the water, strain through muslin, put it again on the fire with the rind of the half lemon cut very thin, and the sugar; let it simmer gently until well flavored, then take out the lemon peel, and stir the milk to the beaten yolks of the eggs; pour the mixture back into the saucepan, and hold it over the fire, keeping it stirred until it begins to thicken; put it into a deep basin and keep it moved with a spoon until it is nearly cold, then pour it into the moulds, which have been laid in water, and set it in a cool place till firm.

Milk Punch — One-half pint new milk and 1 new-laid egg.

Set the milk in a clean saucepan over a moderate fire; while it is heating beat the egg to a froth in a basin or a large cup. When the milk begins to bubble, skim off the froth as it forms, and pour it into the whipped egg, quickly beating the milk in; repeat until the egg is well mixed (without curdling) with about half the new boiled milk. Pour the remainder from the saucepan into the mixture in basin, and quickly pour the whole back into the pan, then again into the basin, and so on until it is all frothy and well mixed. This cooks the eggs sufficiently. Add a pinch of salt, a lump or more of loaf-sugar, a few gratings of nutmeg or ginger according to taste, and serve in a tumbler, to be taken while hot. For cases of spasmodic pain from flatulency, or other cause, where brandy is often recommended, this is much safer to use.

Pure Stimulants — See *Medicine and Hygiene*, p. 260.

A Fever Drink (1) — A little tea sage, 2 sprigs of balm, a very small quantity of wood sorrel, a small lemon, 2 pints of boiling water.

Put the sage, balm and wood sorrel into a stone jug, having previously washed and dried them; peel thin the lemon, and clear from the white; slice and put a piece of the peel in; then pour on the water, sweeten and cover.

A Fever Drink (2) — One oz. pearl barley, 3 pints water, 1 oz. sweet almonds, a piece of lemon peel, a little syrup of lemons and capillaire.

Wash well the barley; stir it twice, then add the water, sweet almonds beaten fine, and the lemon peel; boil till you have a smooth liquor, then add the syrup.

Apple Water — Some well flavored apples, 3 or 4 cloves, a strip of lemon peel, boiling water.

Slice the apples into a large jug (they need be neither peeled nor cored). Add the cloves and lemon peel, and pour boiling water over. Let it stand a day. It will be drinkable in 12 hours or less.

Currant Water — One quart red currants, ½ pint raspberries, 2 quarts water, syrup—1 quart of water, about ½ lb. of sugar.

Put the fruit with the water over a very slow fire to draw the juice, for ½ hour. They must not boil. Strain through a hair sieve and add syrup. Other fruits may be used in the same way.

Sago Jelly. — Boil a teacupful of sago in 4 pints of water until quite thick; when cold add a pint of raspberry juice pressed from fresh fruit, or half the quantity of raspberry syrup; add enough white sugar to sweeten to the taste, and boil fast for 5 minutes. Pour into the mould. Use a little cream with the jelly.

Flax-Seed Lemonade. — Into a covered vessel pour 1 quart of boiling water upon 4 tablespoonfuls of flax-seed. Steep it for 3 hours, and then add the juice of 2 lemons and sweeten to the taste. If too thick, add cold water. Good for colds.

Bread Panada. — Toast to a light brown several slices of stale baker's bread. Pile them in a bowl with sugar and a little salt sprinkled between them. Cover with boiling water; cover tightly and set into a pan of boiling water, letting it simmer gently until the contents of the bowl are like jelly. Eat while warm, with a little powdered sugar and nutmeg.

Slippery-Elm Bark Tea. — Break the bark into bits, pour boiling water over it, cover it closely and let it stand until cold. Put sugar and ice in for summer diseases, or add lemon juice for colds.

Rice Milk. — Two tablespoonfuls rice, 1 pint milk, 1 tablespoonful ground rice (if wanted thick, 2 will be required), a little cold milk.

Put the rice into the pint of milk; boil it until done, stirring to prevent it burning. Put the ground rice with a little cold milk, mix smooth, and stir it in; boil for about 15 minutes.

Thick Milk may be made in the same way as "rice milk," only substituting flour for rice, thickening and sweetening to taste. Five minutes' boiling will do.

Chamomile Tea. — One oz. dried chamomile flowers, ½ oz. dried orange peel, 1 quart boiling water.

Put the chamomile into a jug with the orange peel. Pour over it the boiling water, and stand in the back of the stove, just close enough to the fire to keep it simmering till the strength of the peel and flower is drawn out; then strain off for use.

Dandelion Tea. — Six or 8 dandelion roots, according to size, 1 pint boiling water.

Pull up the dandelion roots and cut off the leaves; wash the roots well and scrape off a little of the skin. Cut them up into small pieces and pour the boiling water on them. Let stand all night; then strain through muslin. It should be quite clear and the color of brown sherry. About ½ glassful should be taken at a time. This decoction should be made only in small quantities, as it will keep fresh only two or three days.

Jelly Water. — Stir a tablespoonful of currant or other jelly into ½ pint water; keep it cold and give as occasion requires. Excellent in fevers.

Toast Water. — Toast a large slice of wheat bread so that it is a deep brown all over, but not blackened or burnt. Lay in a covered earthenware vessel, cover it with boiling water, and let it steep until cold. Strain it and add a little lemon juice, unless forbidden by the physician.

FOR CHILDREN.

For Diarrhea. — If the child has symptoms of diarrhea or summer complaint, take the caul of mutton or lamb, and simmer in a pint of water, dusting in a little flour and a little salt. This soup is nutritious, and allays the irritation of the bowels.

Arrowroot, made quite thin, with a teaspoonful of sweet cream, is nutritious and harmless. Do not make the food for infants too rich.

Milk Porridge. — Take 1 spoonful of Indian meal, and 2 of white flour; wet to a paste with cold water; put the paste into 2 cups of boiling water, and boil 30 minutes; add 2 cups of milk and a pinch of salt, and cook 20 minutes more, stirring often. Eat with sugar and milk stirred in while hot.

For Teething. — Tie a teacup of flour closely in a cloth, and boil for 1 hour. When cold, grate fine — enough to thicken a pint of half milk and half water the consistency of porridge. Add a little salt.

Barley Water. — Pick over and wash 2 tablespoonfuls of pearl barley; soak in ½ hour in a very little lukewarm water, and stir, without draining, into 3 cupfuls of boiling water, salted a very little. Simmer 1 hour, stirring often. Strain and add 2 teaspoonfuls white sugar. When milk disagrees with infants, barley water can often be used.

Digestion of Various Foods.

Easy of Digestion. — Arrowroot, asparagus, cauliflower, baked apples, oranges, grapes, strawberries, peaches.

Moderately Digestible. — Apples, raspberries, bread, puddings, custards, chocolate, coffee, porter.

Hard to Digest. — Nuts, pears, plums, cherries, cucumbers, onions, carrots, parsnips.

TIME REQUIRED FOR DIGESTION.

	Hrs.	Min.
Apples, sweet	1	30
" sour	2	00
Beans, pod, boiled	2	30
Beef, fresh, lean, roasted	3	00
" " dried	3	30
" " fried	4	00
Beets, boiled	3	45
Bread, wheat, fresh	3	30
" corn	3	15
Butter (melted)	3	30
Cabbage, with vinegar, raw	2	00
" boiled	4	30
Cheese (old, strong)	3	30
Codfish	2	00
Custard, baked	2	45
Duck, domestic, roasted	4	00
" wild, "	4	30
Eggs, fresh, hard-boiled	3	30
" " soft	3	00

	Hrs.	Min.
Eggs, fresh, fried	3	30
Goose, roast	2	30
Lamb, fresh, boiled	2	30
Liver, beef, broiled	2	00
Milk, boiled	2	00
" raw	2	15
Mutton, roast	3	15
" broiled	3	00
" boiled	3	00
Oysters, raw	2	55
" roast	3	15
" stewed	3	30
Parsnips, boiled	3	30
Pork, fat and lean, roast	5	15
" " " boiled	4	15
" " " raw	3	00
Potatoes, boiled	3	30
" baked	2	30
Rice, boiled	1	00
Sago, "	1	45
Salmon, salted, boiled	4	00
Soup, beef, vegetable	4	00
" chicken	3	00
" oyster	3	30
Tapioca, boiled	2	00
Tripe, soused, boiled	1	00
Trout, fresh, boiled or fried	1	30
Turkey, domestic, roast	2	30
" wild, roast	2	18
Turnips, boiled	3	30
Veal, fresh, broiled	4	00
" fresh, fried	4	30
Venison steak, broiled	1	35

Fat, Water and Muscle Properties of Food.

100 parts	Water.	Muscle.	Fat.
Cucumbers	97.5	1.5	1.0
Turnips	91.4	1.1	4.0
Cabbage	90.0	4.0	5.0
Milk, cows'	86.0	5.0	8.0
Apples	84.0	5.0	10.0
Eggs, yolk of	52.0	16.0	27.0
Potatoes	75.2	1.4	22.8
Veal	66.5	19.2	1.65
Eggs, white of	53.0	27.0	.0
Lamb	50.5	11.0	35.0
Beef	50.0	15.0	30.0
Chicken	46.0	26.0	32.0
Mutton	44.0	12.5	40.0
Pork	39.5	10.0	50.0
Bacon	14.8	24.0	57.5
Buckwheat	14.8	8.6	76.4
Barley	14.0	15.0	63.9
Corn	14.0	16.0	72.0
Peas	14.0	23.4	60.0
Wheat	14.0	14.6	69.4
Oats	18.5	17.0	66.4
Rice	13.5	6.5	79.5
Cheese	10.0	62.0	29.0
Butter			100.0

Percentage of Nutrition.

Raw cucumbers, 2; raw melons, 3; boiled turnips, 4½; milk, 7; cabbage, 7½; currants, 10; whipped eggs, 13; beets, 14; apples, 16; peaches, 20; boiled codfish, 21; broiled venison, 22; potatoes, 22½; fried veal, 24; roast pork, 24; roast poultry, 26; raw beef, 26; raw grapes, 27; raw plums, 29; broiled mutton, 30; oatmeal porridge, 75; rye bread, 79; boiled beans, 87; boiled rice, 88; barley bread, 88; wheat bread, 90; baked corn bread, 91; boiled barley, 92; butter, 93; boiled peas, 93; raw oils, 96.

Relative Value of Food (Beef par).

Oysters, 22; milk, 24; lobsters, 30; cream, 53; codfish, 68; eggs, 72; turbot, 84; mutton, 87; venison, 89; veal, 92; fowl, 94; herring, 100; beef, 100; duck, 104; salmon, 108; pork, 116; butter, 124; cheese, 130.

Percentage of Carbon in Food.

Cabbage, 3; beer, 4; carrots, 5; milk, 7; parsnips, 8; fish, 9; potatoes, 12; eggs, 13; beef, 27; bread, 27; cheese, 36; peas, 36; rice, 38; corn, 38; biscuit, 42; oatmeal, 42; sugar, 42; flour, 46; bacon, 64; cocoa, 69; butter, 79.

Foot-Tons of Energy per Ounce of Food.

Cabbage, 15; carrots, 20; milk, 21; ale, 30; potatoes, 38; porter, 42; beef, 55; egg, 57; ham, 65; bread, 88; egg (yolk), 127; sugar, 130; rice, 143; flour, 148; arrowroot, 151; oatmeal, 152; cheese, 168; butter, 281.

Loss of Meat in Cooking.

100 lbs.	raw beef	=	67	lbs.	roast.
100	" "	=	74	"	boiled.
100	" raw mutton	=	75	"	roast.
100	" raw fowl	=	80	"	roast.
100	" "	=	87	"	boiled.
100	" raw fish	=	94	"	boiled.

The Percentage of Starch

In common grains is as follows, according to Prof. Yeomans: Rice flour, 84 to 85; Indian meal, 77 to 80; oatmeal, 70 to 80; wheat flour, 39 to 77; barley flour, 67 to 70; rye flour, 50 to 61; buckwheat, 52; peas and beans, 42 to 43; potatoes, (75 per cent. water), 13 to 15.

The Degrees of Sugar

In various fruits are: Peach, 1.6; raspberry, 4.0; strawberry, 5.7; currant, 6.1; gooseberry, 7.2; apple, 7.9; mulberry, 9.2; pear, 9.4; cherry, 10.3; grape, 14.9.

Measures for Housekeepers.

Wheat flour	1 lb. is	1 quart.
Indian meal	1 lb. 2 oz. is	1 quart.
Butter (soft)	1 lb. is	1 quart.
Granulated sugar	1 lb. is	1 quart.
Powdered sugar	1 lb. 1 oz. is	1 quart.
Best brown sugar	1 lb. 2 oz. is	1 quart.
Eggs	10 eggs are	1 lb.
Flour	8 quarts are	1 peck.
Flour	4 pecks are	1 bush.

Liquids.—Thirty-two large tablespoonfuls make a pint; 8 large tablespoonfuls, 1 gill. Four gills make 1 pint; 2 pints, 1 quart; 4 quarts, 1 gallon. An ordinary-sized tumbler holds half a pint; a wine-glass, half a gill. Thirty-five drops are equal to one teaspoonful.

THE CENSUS OF 1890.

THE POPULATION OF THE UNITED STATES—OFFICIAL TABULATION.

The population of the United States on June 1, 1890, as shown by the official count, completed in 1891, exclusive of white persons in the Indian Territory, Indians on reservations, and Alaska, was 62,622,250. The following comparative table gives the figures for each State. The black figures after the name of the State show that State's rank as regards population. New York still heads the list, as in 1880, and is followed by Pennsylvania. Illinois changes places with Ohio, and is now third. Of the other changes in the list the most marked are those of Texas, which rises from No. 11 to No. 7; Kentucky, which drops from 8 to 11; Minnesota, which rises from 26 to 20; Nebraska, which rises from 30 to 26; Maryland, which drops from 23 to 27; Colorado, which rises from 35 to 31; Vermont, which drops from 32 to 36; Washington, which rises from 42 to 34; Delaware, which drops from 38 to 42; Nevada, which drops from 43 to 49, and Arizona, which drops from 44 to 48.

STATES AND TERRITORIES.	POPULATION. 1890.	1880.	1870.	INCREASE FROM 1880 TO 1890. Percentage.	INCREASE FROM 1870 TO 1880. Percentage.
The United States	62,622,250	50,155,783	38,558,371	24.86	30.08
North Atlantic Div.	17,401,545	14,507,407	12,298,730	19.95	17.96
Maine **30**	661,086	648,936	626,915	1.87	3.51
New Hampshire **33**	376,530	346,991	318,300	8.51	9.01
Vermont **36**	332,422	332,286	330,551	0.04	0.52
Massachusetts **6**	2,238,943	1,783,085	1,457,351	25.57	22.35
Rhode Island **35**	345,506	276,531	217,353	24.94	27.23
Connecticut **29**	746,258	622,700	537,454	19.84	15.86
New York **1**	5,997,853	5,082,871	4,382,759	18.00	15.97
New Jersey **18**	1,444,933	1,131,116	906,096	27.74	24.83
Pennsylvania **2**	5,258,014	4,282,891	3,521,951	22.77	21.61
South Atlantic Div.	8,857,920	7,597,197	5,853,610	16.59	29.79
Delaware **42**	168,493	146,608	125,015	14.93	17.27
Maryland **27**	1,042,390	934,943	780,894	11.49	19.73
District of Columbia **39**	230,392	177,624	131,700	29.71	34.87
Virginia **15**	1,655,980	1,512,565	1,225,163	9.48	23.46
West Virginia **28**	762,794	618,457	442,014	23.34	39.92
North Carolina **16**	1,617,947	1,399,750	1,071,361	15.59	30.65
South Carolina **23**	1,151,149	995,577	705,606	15.63	41.09
Georgia **12**	1,837,353	1,542,180	1,184,109	19.14	30.24
Florida **32**	391,422	269,493	187,748	45.24	43.54

POPULATION OF THE UNITED STATES.—(*Continued.*)

STATES AND TERRITORIES.	POPULATION. 1890.	1880.	1870.	INCREASE FROM 1880 TO 1890. Percentage.	INCREASE FROM 1870 TO 1880. Percentage.
Northern Central Div.	22,362,279	17,364,111	12,981,111	28.78	33.76
Ohio **4**	3,672,316	3,198,062	2,665,260	14.83	19.99
Indiana **8**	2,192,404	1,978,301	1,680,637	10.82	17.71
Illinois **3**	3,826,351	3,077,871	2,539,891	24.32	21.18
Michigan **9**	2,093,889	1,636,937	1,184,059	27.92	38.25
Wisconsin **14**	1,686,880	1,315,497	1,054,670	28.23	24.73
Minnesota **20**	1,301,826	780,773	439,706	66.74	77.57
Iowa **10**	1,911,896	1,624,615	1,194,020	17.68	36.06
Missouri **5**	2,679,184	2,168,380	1,721,295	23.56	25.97
North Dakota **41**	182,719	36,909	14,181	395.05	853.23
South Dakota **37**	328,808	98,268		234.60	
Nebraska **26**	1,058,910	452,402	122,993	134.06	267.82
Kansas **19**	1,427,096	996,096	364,399	43.27	173.35
Southern Central Div.	10,972,893	8,919,371	6,434,410	23.02	38.62
Kentucky **11**	1,858,635	1,648,690	1,321,011	12.73	24.80
Tennessee **13**	1,767,518	1,542,359	1,258,520	14.60	22.55
Alabama **17**	1,513,017	1,262,505	996,992	19.84	26.63
Mississippi **21**	1,289,600	1,131,597	827,922	13.96	36.67
Louisiana **25**	1,118,587	939,946	726,915	19.01	29.31
Texas **7**	2,235,523	1,591,749	818,579	40.44	94.45
Indian Territory (*b*)					
Oklahoma **46**	61,834				
Arkansas **24**	1,128,179	802,525	484,471	40.58	65.65
Western Div.	3,027,613	1,767,697	990,510	71.27	78.46
Montana **44**	132,159	39,159	20,595	237.49	90.14
Wyoming **47**	60,705	20,789	9,118	192.01	128.00
Colorado **31**	412,198	194,327	39,864	112.12	387.47
New Mexico **43**	153,593	119,565	91,874	28.46	30.14
Arizona **48**	59,620	40,440	9,658	47.43	318.71
Utah **40**	207,905	143,963	86,786	44.42	65.88
Nevada **49**	45,761	62,266	42,491	*a* 26.51	46.54
Idaho **45**	84,385	32,610	14,999	158.77	117.42
Alaska (*c*)					
Washington **34**	349,390	75,116	23,955	365.13	213.57
Oregon **38**	313,767	174,768	90,923	79.53	92.22
California **22**	1,208,130	864,694	560,247	39.72	54.34

a Decrease.

b The number of white persons in the Indian Territory is not included in this table. The total Indian population of the United States, exclusive of Alaska, but including 58,806 counted in the general census, being the taxed or taxable Indians, numbers 249,273.

c Including 5,338 persons in Greer County (in Indian Territory) claimed by Texas.

d The number of white persons in Alaska is not included in this table, as the census of Alaska, which was made a subject of special investigation by law, has not yet been completed.

POPULATION OF CITIES.

Fifty Principal Cities of the United States in 1890.

In the Order of their Rank.

CITIES.	1890.	1880.	CITIES.	1890.	1880.
New York, N. Y.	1,515,301	1,206,299	Denver, Colo.	106,713	35,629
Chicago, Ill.	1,099,850	503,185	Indianapolis, Ind.	105,436	75,056
Philadelphia, Pa.	1,046,964	847,170	Allegheny, Pa.	105,287	78,682
Brooklyn, N. Y.	806,343	566,663	Albany, N. Y.	94,923	90,758
St. Louis, Mo.	451,770	350,518	Columbus, Ohio	88,150	51,647
Boston, Mass.	448,477	362,839	Syracuse, N. Y.	88,143	51,792
Baltimore, Md.	434,439	332,313	Worcester, Mass.	84,655	58,291
San Francisco, Cal.	298,997	233,959	Toledo, Ohio	81,434	50,137
Cincinnati, Ohio	296,908	255,139	Richmond, Va.	81,388	63,600
Cleveland, Ohio	261,353	160,146	New Haven, Conn.	81,298	62,882
Buffalo, N. Y.	255,664	155,134	Paterson, N. J.	78,347	51,031
New Orleans, La.	242,039	216,090	Lowell, Mass.	77,696	59,475
Pittsburg, Pa.	238,617	156,389	Nashville, Tenn.	76,168	43,350
Washington, D. C.	230,392	177,624	Scranton, Pa.	75,215	45,850
Detroit, Mich.	205,876	116,340	Fall River, Mass.	74,398	48,961
Milwaukee, Wis.	204,468	115,587	Cambridge, Mass.	70,028	52,669
Newark, N. J.	181,830	136,508	Atlanta, Ga.	65,533	37,409
Minneapolis, Minn.	164,738	46,887	Memphis, Tenn.	64,495	33,592
Jersey City, N. J.	163,003	120,722	Wilmington, Del.	61,431	42,478
Louisville, Ky.	161,129	123,758	Dayton, Ohio	61,220	38,678
Omaha, Neb.	140,452	30,518	Troy, N. Y.	60,956	56,747
Rochester, N. Y.	133,896	89,366	Grand Rapids, Mich.	60,278	32,016
Saint Paul, Minn.	133,156	41,473	Reading, Pa.	58,661	43,278
Kansas City, Mo.	*132,716	55,785	Camden, N. J.	58,313	41,659
Providence, R. I.	132,146	104,857	Trenton, N. J.	57,458	29,910

Cities and Towns of 8,000 and over in 1890

Arranged Alphabetically and Compared with the Census of 1880.

CITIES AND TOWNS.	1890.	1880.	CITIES AND TOWNS.	1890.	1880.
Adams, Mass.	9,213	5,591	Athens, Ga.	8,639	6,099
Adrian, Mich.	8,756	7,849	Atlanta, Ga.	65,533	37,409
Akron, Ohio	27,601	16,512	Atlantic City, N. J.	13,055	5,477
Alameda, Cal.	11,165	5,708	Auburn, Me.	11,250	9,555
Albany, N. Y.	94,923	90,758	Auburn, N. Y.	25,858	21,924
Alexandria, Va.	14,339	13,659	Augusta, Ga.	33,300	21,891
Allegheny, Pa.	105,287	78,682	Augusta, Me.	10,527	8,665
Allentown, Pa.	25,228	18,063	Aurora, Ill.	19,688	11,873
Alpena, Mich.	11,283	6,153	Austin, Texas	14,575	11,013
Alton, Ill.	10,294	8,975	Baltimore, Md.	434,439	332,313
Altoona, Pa.	30,337	19,710	Bangor, Me.	19,103	16,856
Amesbury, Mass.	9,798	3,355	Bath, Me.	8,723	7,874
Amsterdam, N. Y.	17,336	9,466	Baton Rouge, La.	10,478	7,197
Anderson, Ind.	10,741	4,126	Battle Creek, Mich.	13,197	7,063
Ann Arbor, Mich.	9,431	8,061	Bay City, Mich.	27,839	20,693
Anniston, Ala.	9,998	942	Bayonne, N. J.	19,033	9,372
Appleton, Wis.	11,869	8,005	Beatrice, Neb.	13,836	2,447
Arkansas City, Kans.	8,347	1,012	Beaver Falls, Pa.	9,735	5,104
Asheville, N. C.	10,235	2,616	Bellaire, Ohio	9,934	8,025
Ashland, Wis.	9,956	....	Belleville, Ill.	15,361	10,683
Ashtabula, Ohio	8,338	4,445	Beverly, Mass.	10,821	8,456
Atchison, Kans.	13,963	15,105	Biddeford, Me.	14,443	12,651

* Includes [illegible] which, by a recent decision of Missouri Supreme Court, is now outside the limits.

Cities and Towns of over 8,000 Population.—Continued.

CITIES AND TOWNS.	1890.	1880.	CITIES AND TOWNS.	1890.	1880.
Binghamton, N. Y.	35,005	17,317	Denver, Colo.	106,713	35,629
Birmingham, Ala.	26,178	3,086	Des Moines, Iowa	50,093	22,408
Bloomington, Ill.	20,484	17,180	Detroit, Mich.	205,876	116,340
Boston, Mass.	448,477	362,839	Dover, N. H.	12,790	11,687
Braddock, Pa.	8,561	3,310	Dubuque, Iowa	30,311	22,254
Bradford, Pa.	10,514	9,197	Duluth, Minn.	33,115	3,483
Bridgeport, Conn.	48,866	27,643	Dunkirk, N. Y.	9,416	7,248
Bridgeton, N. J.	11,424	8,722	Dunmore, Pa.	8,315	4,311
Brockton, Mass.	27,294	13,608	East Liverpool, Ohio	10,956	5,568
Brookline, Mass.	12,103	8,057	Easton, Pa.	14,481	11,924
Brooklyn, N. Y.	806,343	566,663	East Portland, Oreg.	10,532	2,934
Brunswick, Ga.	8,459	[illegible]	East Providence, R. I.	8,422	5,056
Buffalo, N. Y.	255,664	155,134	East St. Louis, Ill.	15,169	9,185
Burlington, Iowa	22,565	19,450	Eau Claire, Wis.	17,415	10,119
Burlington, N. J.	[illegible]	[illegible]	Elgin, Ill.	17,823	8,787
Burlington, Vt.	14,590	11,365	Elizabeth City, N. J.	37,764	28,229
Butler, Pa.	8,734	3,163	Elkhart, Ind.	11,360	6,953
Butte, Mont.	10,723	3,363	Elmira, N. Y.	30,893	20,541
Cairo, Ill.	10,324	9,011	El Paso, Texas	10,338	736
Cambridge, Mass.	70,028	52,669	Erie, Pa.	40,634	27,737
Camden, N. J.	58,313	41,659	Evansville, Ind.	50,756	29,280
Canton, Ohio	26,189	12,258	Everett, Mass.	11,068	4,159
Carbondale, Pa.	10,833	7,714	Fall River, Mass.	74,398	48,961
Cedar Rapids, Iowa	18,020	10,104	Findlay, Ohio	18,553	4,633
Charleston, S. C.	54,955	49,984	Fitchburg, Mass.	22,037	12,429
Charlotte, N. C.	11,557	7,094	Flint, Mich.	9,803	8,409
Chattanooga, Tenn.	29,100	12,892	Flushing, N. Y.	[illegible]	[illegible]
Chicago, Ill.	1,099,850	503,185	Fond du Lac, Wis.	12,024	13,094
Chicopee, Mass.	14,050	11,286	Fort Scott, Kans.	11,946	5,372
Chillicothe, Ohio	11,288	10,938	Fort Smith, Ark.	11,311	3,099
Chippewa Falls, Wis.	8,670	3,068	Fort Wayne, Ind.	35,393	26,880
Chelsea, Mass.	27,909	21,782	Fort Worth, Texas	23,076	6,663
Chester, Pa.	20,226	14,997	Framingham, Mass.	9,239	6,235
Cheyenne, Wyo.	11,690	3,456	Frederick, Md.	8,193	8,659
Cincinnati, Ohio	296,908	255,139	Freeport, Ill.	10,189	8,516
Cleveland, Ohio	261,353	160,146	Fresno, Cal.	10,818	1,112
Clinton, Iowa	13,619	9,052	Galesburg, Ill.	15,264	11,437
Clinton, Mass.	10,424	8,029	Galveston, Texas	29,084	22,248
Cohoes, N. Y.	22,509	19,416	Gardner, Mass.	8,424	4,988
Colorado Springs, Colo.	11,140	4,226	Gloucester, Mass.	24,651	19,329
Columbia, Pa.	10,599	8,312	Gloversville, N. Y.	13,864	7,133
Columbia, S. C.	15,353	10,036	Grand Rapids, Mich.	60,278	32,016
Columbus, Ga.	17,303	10,123	Green Bay, Wis.	9,069	7,464
Columbus, Ohio	88,150	51,647	Greenville, S. C.	8,607	6,160
Concord, N. H.	17,004	13,843	Greenwich, Conn.	10,131	7,892
Corning, N. Y.	8,550	4,802	Hagerstown, Md.	10,118	6,627
Council Bluffs, Iowa	21,474	18,063	Hamilton, Ohio	17,565	12,122
Covington, Ky.	37,371	29,720	Hannibal, Mo.	12,857	11,074
Cranston, R. I.	8,099	5,940	Harrisburg, Pa.	39,385	30,762
Cumberland, Md.	12,729	10,693	Harrison, N. J.	8,338	6,898
Cumberland, R. I.	8,090	6,445	Hartford, Conn.	53,230	42,015
Dallas, Texas	38,067	10,358	Hastings, Neb.	13,584	2,817
Danbury, Conn.	16,552	11,666	Haverhill, Mass.	27,412	18,472
Danville, Ill.	11,491	7,733	Hazleton, Pa.	11,872	6,935
Danville, Va.	10,305	7,526	Helena, Mont.	13,834	3,624
Davenport, Iowa	26,872	21,831	Henderson, Ky.	8,835	5,365
Dayton, Ohio	61,220	38,678	Hoboken, N. J.	43,648	30,999
Decatur, Ill.	16,841	9,547	Holyoke, Mass.	35,637	21,915
Delaware, Ohio	8,224	6,894	Hornellsville, N. Y.	10,996	8,195
Denison, Texas	10,958	3,975	Hot Springs, Ark.	8,086	3,554

Cities and Towns of over 8,000 Population — Continued.

CITIES AND TOWNS.	1890.	1880.	CITIES AND TOWNS.	1890.	1880.
Houston, Texas	27,557	16,513	Macon, Ga.	22,746	12,749
Hudson, N. Y.	9,970	8,670	Madison, Ind.	8,936	8,945
Huntington, W. Va.	10,108	3,174	Madison, Wis.	13,426	10,324
Hutchinson, Kans.	8,682	1,540	Mahanoy, Pa.	11,286	7,181
Hyde Park, Mass.	10,193	7,088	Malden, Mass.	23,031	12,017
Indianapolis, Ind.	105,436	75,056	Manchester, Conn.	8,222	6,462
Ironton, Ohio	10,939	8,857	Manchester, N. H.	44,126	32,630
Iron Mountain, Mich.	8,599	......	Manchester, Va.	9,246	5,729
Ishpeming, Mich.	11,197	6,039	Manistee, Mich.	12,812	6,930
Ithaca, N. Y.	11,079	9,105	Mankato, Minn.	8,838	5,550
Jackson, Mich.	20,798	16,105	Mansfield, Ohio	13,473	9,859
Jackson, Tenn.	10,039	5,377	Marblehead, Mass.	8,202	7,467
Jacksonville, Fla.	17,201	7,650	Marietta, Ohio	8,273	5,444
Jacksonville, Ill.	12,935	10,927	Marinette, Wis.	11,523	2,750
Jamestown, N. Y.	16,038	9,357	Marion, Ind.	8,769	3,182
Janesville, Wis.	10,836	9,018	Marion, Ohio	8,327	3,899
Jeffersonville, Ind.	10,666	9,357	Marlborough, Mass.	13,805	10,127
Jersey City, N. J.	163,003	120,722	Marquette, Mich.	9,093	4,690
Johnstown, N. Y.	7,768	5,013	Marshalltown, Iowa	8,914	6,240
Johnstown, Pa.	21,805	8,380	Massillon, Ohio	10,092	6,836
Joliet, Ill.	23,264	11,657	Meadville, Pa.	9,520	8,860
Joplin, Mo.	9,943	7,038	Medford, Mass.	11,079	7,573
Kalamazoo, Mich.	17,853	11,937	Memphis, Tenn.	64,495	33,592
Kankakee, Ill.	9,025	5,651	Menominee, Mich.	10,630	3,288
Kansas City, Kans.	38,316	3,200	Meriden, Conn.	21,652	15,540
Kansas City, Mo.	132,716	55,785	Meridian, Miss.	10,624	4,008
Kearney, Neb.	8,074	1,782	Michigan City, Ind.	10,776	7,366
Keokuk, Iowa	14,101	12,117	Middletown, Conn.	9,013	6,826
Key West, Fla.	18,080	9,890	Middletown, N. Y.	11,977	8,494
Kingston, N. Y.	21,261	18,344	Milford, Mass.	8,780	9,310
Knoxville, Tenn.	22,535	9,693	Millville, N. J.	10,002	7,660
Kokomo, Ind.	8,261	4,042	Milwaukee, Wis.	204,468	115,587
La Crosse, Wis.	25,090	14,505	Minneapolis, Minn.	164,738	46,887
Lafayette, Ind.	16,243	14,860	Moberly, Mo.	8,215	6,070
Lancaster, Pa.	32,011	25,769	Mobile, Ala.	31,076	29,132
Lansing, Mich.	13,102	8,319	Moline, Ill.	12,000	7,800
Lansingburg, N. Y.	10,550	7,432	Montgomery, Ala.	21,883	16,713
Laredo, Texas	11,319	3,521	Mount Carmel, Pa.	8,254	2,378
La Salle, Ill.	9,855	7,847	Mount Vernon, N. Y.	10,830	4,586
Lawrence, Kans.	9,997	8,510	Muncie, Ind.	11,345	5,219
Lawrence, Mass.	44,654	39,151	Muscatine, Iowa	11,454	8,295
Leadville, Colo.	10,384	14,820	Muskegon, Mich.	22,702	11,262
Leavenworth, Kans.	19,768	16,546	Nanticoke, Pa.	10,044	3,884
Lebanon, Pa.	14,664	8,778	Nashua, N. H.	19,311	13,397
Lewiston, Me.	21,701	19,083	Nashville, Tenn.	76,168	43,350
Lexington, Ky.	21,567	16,656	Natchez, Miss.	10,101	7,058
Lima, Ohio	15,987	7,567	Natick, Mass.	9,118	8,479
Lincoln, Neb.	55,154	13,003	Nebraska City, Neb.	11,494	4,183
Lincoln, R. I.	20,355	13,765	New Albany, Ind.	21,059	16,423
Little Falls, N. Y.	8,783	6,910	Newark, N. J.	181,830	136,508
Little Rock, Ark.	25,874	13,138	Newark, Ohio	14,270	9,600
Lockport, N. Y.	16,038	13,522	New Bedford, Mass.	40,733	26,845
Logansport, Ind.	13,328	11,198	New Brighton, N. Y.	16,423	12,679
Long Island City, N. Y.	30,506	17,129	New Britain, Conn.	19,007	11,800
Los Angeles, Cal.	50,395	11,183	New Brunswick, N. J.	18,603	17,166
Louisville, Ky.	161,129	123,758	Newburg, N. Y.	23,087	18,049
Lowell, Mass.	77,696	59,475	Newburyport, Mass.	13,947	13,538
Lynchburg, Va.	19,709	15,959	Newcastle, Pa.	11,600	8,418
Lynn, Mass.	55,727	38,274	New Haven, Conn.	81,298	62,882
McKeesport, Pa.	20,741	8,212			

Cities and Towns of over 8,000 Population — Continued.

CITIES AND TOWNS.	1890.	1880.	CITIES AND TOWNS.	1890.	1880.
New London, Conn.	13,757	10,537	Quincy, Mass.	16,723	10,570
New Orleans, La.	242,039	216,090	Racine, Wis.	21,014	16,031
Newport, Ky.	24,918	20,433	Raleigh, N. C.	12,678	9,265
Newport, R. I.	19,457	15,693	Reading, Pa.	58,661	43,278
New Rochelle, N. Y.	9,057	5,268	Richmond, Ind.	16,608	12,742
Newton, Mass.	24,379	16,995	Richmond, Va.	81,388	63,600
New York, N. Y.	1,515,301	1,206,299	Roanoke, Va.	16,159	......
Norfolk, Va.	34,871	21,966	Rochester, N. Y.	133,896	89,366
Norristown, Pa.	19,791	13,063	Rockford, Ill.	23,584	13,129
North Adams, Mass.	16,074	10,191	Rock Island, Ill.	13,634	11,659
Northampton, Mass.	14,990	12,172	Rockland, Me.	8,174	7,599
Norwalk, Conn.	17,747	13,956	Rome, N. Y.	14,991	12,194
Norwich, Conn.	16,156	15,112	Rutland, Vt.	11,760	12,149
Oakland, Cal.	48,682	34,555	Sacramento, Cal.	26,386	21,420
Ogden, Utah	14,889	6,069	Saginaw, Mich.	46,322	29,541
Ogdensburg, N. Y.	11,662	10,341	Saint Joseph, Mo.	52,324	32,431
Oil City, Pa.	10,932	7,315	Saint Louis, Mo.	451,770	350,518
Omaha, Neb.	140,452	30,518	Saint Paul, Minn.	133,156	41,473
Orange, N. J.	18,844	13,207	Salem, Mass.	30,801	27,563
Oshkosh, Wis.	22,836	15,748	Salt Lake City, Utah	44,843	20,768
Oswego, N. Y.	21,842	21,116	San Antonio, Texas	37,673	20,550
Ottawa, Ill.	9,985	7,834	San Diego, Cal.	16,159	2,637
Ottumwa, Iowa	14,001	9,004	Sandusky, Ohio	18,471	15,838
Owensborough, Ky.	9,837	6,231	San Francisco, Cal.	298,997	233,959
Paducah, Ky.	12,797	8,036	San Jose, Cal.	18,060	12,567
Paris, Texas	8,254	3,980	Saratoga Springs, N. Y.	11,975	8,421
Parkersburg, W. Va.	8,408	6,582	Savannah, Ga.	43,189	30,709
Passaic, N. J.	13,028	6,532	Schenectady, N. Y.	19,902	13,655
Paterson, N. J.	78,347	51,031	Scranton, Pa.	75,215	45,850
Pawtucket, R. I.	27,633	19,030	Seattle, Wash.	42,837	3,533
Peabody, Mass.	10,158	9,028	Sedalia, Mo.	14,068	9,561
Peekskill, N. Y.	9,676	6,893	Shamokin, Pa.	14,403	8,184
Pensacola, Fla.	11,750	6,845	Sheboygan, Wis.	16,359	7,314
Peoria, Ill.	41,024	29,259	Shenandoah, Pa.	15,944	10,148
Perth Amboy, N. J.	9,512	4,808	Shreveport, La.	11,979	8,009
Petersburg, Va.	22,680	21,656	Sing Sing, N. Y.	9,352	6,578
Philadelphia, Pa.	1,046,964	847,170	Sioux City, Iowa	37,806	7,366
Phillipsburg, N. J.	8,644	7,181	Sioux Falls, S. Dak.	10,177	2,164
Phoenixville, Pa.	8,514	6,682	Somerville, Mass.	40,152	24,933
Pine Bluff, Ark.	9,952	3,203	South Bend, Ind.	21,819	13,280
Piqua, Ohio	9,090	6,031	South Bethlehem, Pa.	10,302	4,925
Pittsburg, Pa.	238,617	156,389	South Omaha, Neb.	8,062	......
Pittsfield, Mass.	17,281	13,364	Spencer, Mass.	8,747	7,466
Pittston, Pa.	10,302	7,472	Spokane Falls, Wash.	19,922	350
Plainfield, N. J.	11,267	8,125	Springfield, Ill.	24,963	19,743
Plymouth, Mass.	7,314	[illegible]	Springfield, Mass.	44,179	33,340
Plymouth, Pa.	9,344	6,065	Springfield, Mo.	21,850	6,522
Port Huron, Mich.	13,543	8,883	Springfield, Ohio	31,895	20,730
Port Jervis, N. Y.	9,327	8,678	Stamford, Conn.	15,700	11,297
Portland, Me.	36,425	33,810	Steelton, Pa.	9,250	2,447
Portland, Ore.	46,385	17,577	Steubenville, Ohio	13,394	12,093
Portsmouth, N. H.	9,827	9,690	Stillwater, Minn.	11,260	9,055
Portsmouth, Ohio	12,394	11,321	Stockton, Cal.	14,424	10,282
Portsmouth, Va.	13,268	11,390	Streator, Ill.	11,414	5,157
Pottstown, Pa.	13,285	5,305	Superior, Wis.	11,983	......
Pottsville, Pa.	14,117	13,253	Syracuse, N. Y.	88,143	51,792
Poughkeepsie, N. Y.	22,206	20,207	Tacoma, Wash.	36,006	1,098
Providence, R. I.	132,146	104,857	Taunton, Mass.	25,448	21,213
Pueblo, Colo.	24,558	3,217	Terre Haute, Ind.	30,217	26,042
Quincy, Ill.	31,494	27,268	Tiffin, Ohio	10,801	7,879

Cities and Towns of over 8,000 Population—Concluded.

CITIES AND TOWNS.	1890.	1880.	CITIES AND TOWNS.	1890.	1880.
Titusville, Pa.	8,073	9,046	Westfield, Mass.	9,805	7,587
Toledo, Ohio	81,434	50,137	West Troy, N. Y.	12,967	8,820
Topeka, Kans.	31,007	15,452	Weymouth, Mass.	10,866	10,570
Trenton, N. J.	57,458	29,910	Wheeling, W. Va.	34,522	30,737
Troy, N. Y.	60,956	56,747	Wichita, Kans.	23,853	4,911
Union, N. J.	10,643	3,620	Wilkesbarre, Pa.	37,718	23,339
Utica, N. Y.	44,007	33,914	Williamsport, Pa.	27,132	18,934
Vernon, Conn.	8,808	6,915	Willimantic, Conn.	8,648	6,608
Vicksburg, Miss.	13,373	11,814	Wilmington, Del.	61,431	42,478
Vincennes, Ind.	8,853	7,680	Wilmington, N. C.	20,056	17,350
Waco, Texas	14,445	7,295	Winona, Minn.	18,208	10,208
Waltham, Mass.	18,707	11,712	Winston, N. C.	8,018	2,854
Warwick, R. I.	17,761	12,164	Woburn, Mass.	13,499	10,931
Washington, D. C.	230,392	177,624	Woonsocket, R. I.	20,830	16,050
Waterbury, Conn.	28,646	17,806	Worcester, Mass.	84,655	58,291
Watertown, N. Y.	14,725	10,697	Yonkers, N. Y.	32,033	18,892
Watertown, Wis.	8,755	7,883	York, Pa.	20,793	13,940
Wausau, Wis.	9,253	4,277	Youngstown, Ohio	33,220	15,435
West Bay City, Mich.	12,981	6,397	Zanesville, Ohio	21,009	18,113
West Chester, Pa.	8,028	7,046			

The Wonderful Growth of Chicago.

The population of Chicago in 1830, was 70; 1840, 4,853; 1845, 12,088; 1850, 29,963; 1855, 80,023; 1860, 112,172; 1865, 178,900; 1870, 298,977; 1872, 364,377; 1880, 503,185; 1884, (estimated) 675,000; 1885, (estimated) 727,000; 1886, (estimated) 750,000; 1887, (estimated) 760,000; 1889, (estimated) 1,000,000; 1890, 1,099,133.

THE NAMES OF THE STATES.

Alabama—Indian; meaning "Here we rest." *Arkansas*—"Kansas," the Indian name for "smoky water," with the French prefix "arc," bow or bend in the principal river. *California*—*Caliente fornalla*, Spanish for "hot furnace," in allusion to the climate. *Colorado*—Spanish; meaning "colored," from the red color of the Colorado river. *Connecticut*—Indian; meaning "long river." *Delaware*—Named in honor of Lord Delaware. *Florida*—Named by Ponce de Leon, who discovered it in 1512, on Easter Day, the Spanish *Pascua de Flores*, or "Feast of Flowers." *Georgia*—In honor of George II. of England. *Illinois*—From the Indian "illini," men, and the French suffix "ois," together signifying "tribe of men." *Indiana*—Indian land. *Iowa*—Indian; meaning "beautiful land." *Kansas*—Indian; meaning "smoky water." *Kentucky*—Indian; for "at the head of the river;" or "the dark and bloody ground." *Louisiana*—In honor of Louis XIV. of France. *Maine*—From the province of Maine, in France. *Maryland*—In honor of Henrietta Maria, queen of Charles I. of England. *Massachusetts*—The place of the great hills (the blue hills southwest of Boston).

NAMES OF THE STATES.

Michigan—The Indian name for a fish weir. The lake was so called from the fancied resemblance of the lake to a fish trap. *Minnesota*—Indian; meaning "sky-tinted water." *Mississippi*—Indian; meaning "great father of waters." *Missouri*—Indian; meaning "muddy." *Nebraska*—Indian; meaning "water valley." *Nevada*—Spanish; meaning "snow-covered," alluding to the mountains. *New Hampshire*—From Hampshire county, England. *New Jersey*—In honor of Sir George Carteret, one of the original grantees, who had previously been governor of Jersey Island. *New York*—In honor of the Duke of York. *North and South Carolina*—Originally called Carolina, in honor of Charles IX. of France. *Ohio*—Indian; meaning "beautiful river." *Oregon*—From the Spanish "oregano," wild marjoram, which grows abundantly on the coast. *Pennsylvania*—Latin; meaning Penn's woody land. *Rhode Island*—From a fancied resemblance to the island of Rhodes in the Mediterranean. *Tennessee*—Indian, meaning "river with the great bend." *Texas*—Origin of this name is unknown. *Vermont*—French; meaning green mountain. *Virginia*—In honor of Elizabeth, the "Virgin Queen." *Wisconsin*—Indian; meaning "gathering of the waters," or "wild rushing channel."

MOTTOES OF THE STATES.

Arkansas—*Regnant populi*: The people rule. *California*—*Eureka*: I have found it. *Colorado*—*Nil sine numine*: Nothing without the Divinity. *Connecticut*—*Qui transtulit sustinet*: He who has transferred, sustains. *Delaware*—Liberty and Independence. *Florida*—In God is our trust. *Georgia*—Wisdom, Justice, Moderation. *Illinois*—State Sovereignty and National Union. *Iowa*—Our liberties we prize, and our rights we will maintain. *Kansas*—*Ad astra per aspera*: To the stars through rugged ways. *Kentucky*—United we stand, divided we fall. *Louisiana*—Union and Confidence. *Maine*—*Dirigo*: I direct. *Maryland*—*Crescite et multiplicamini*: Increase and multiply. *Massachusetts*—*Ense petit placidam sub libertate quietem*: By her sword she seeks under liberty a calm repose. *Michigan*—*Si quaeris peninsulam amoenam circumspice*: If thou seekest a beautiful peninsula, look around. *Minnesota*—*L'Etoile du Nord*: The Star of the North. *Missouri*—*Salus populi suprema lex esto*: Let the welfare of the people be the supreme law. *Nebraska*—Popular Sovereignty. *Nevada*—*Volens et potens*: Willing and able. *New Jersey*—Liberty and Independence. *New York*—*Excelsior*: Higher. *Ohio*—*Imperium in imperio*: An empire within an empire. *Oregon*—*Alis volat propriis*: She flies with her own wings. *Pennsylvania*—Virtue, Liberty, Independence. *Rhode Island*—Hope.

South Carolina—*Animis opibusque parati:* Ready with our lives and property. *Tennessee*—Agriculture, Commerce. *Vermont*—Freedom and Unity. *Virginia*—*Sic semper tyrannis:* So be it ever to tyrants. *West Virginia*—*Montani semper liberi:* The mountaineers are always free. *Wisconsin*—Forward. *United States*—*E pluribus unum:* From many, one. *Annuit cœptis:* God has favored the undertaking; *Novus ordo seclorum:* A new order of ages. The first named on one side of the great seal, the other two on the reverse.

GEOGRAPHICAL NICKNAMES.

STATES AND TERRITORIES.

Alabama, Cotton State; Arkansas, Toothpick and Bear State; California, Eureka and Golden State; Colorado, Centennial State; Connecticut, Land of Steady Habits, Freestone State and Nutmeg State; Dakota, Sioux State; Delaware, Uncle Sam's Pocket Handkerchief and Blue Hen State; Florida, Everglade and Flowery State; Georgia, Empire State of the South; Idaho, Gem of the Mountains; Illinois, Prairie and Sucker State; Indiana, Hoosier State; Iowa, Hawkeye State; Kansas, Jayhawker State; Kentucky, Corn-cracker State; Louisiana, Creole State; Maine, Timber and Pine Tree State; Maryland, Monumental State; Massachusetts, Old Bay State; Michigan, Wolverine and Peninsular State; Minnesota, Gopher and North Star State; Mississippi, Eagle State; Missouri, Puke State; Nebraska, Antelope State; Nevada, Sage State; New Hampshire, Old Granite State; New Jersey, Blue State and New Spain; New Mexico, Vermin State; New York, Empire State; North Carolina, Rip Van Winkle, Old North and Turpentine State; Ohio, Buckeye State; Oregon, Pacific State; Pennsylvania, Keystone, Iron and Oil State; Rhode Island, Plantation State and Little Rhody; South Carolina, Palmetto State; Tennessee, Lion's Den State; Texas, Lone Star State; Utah, Mormon State; Vermont, Green Mountain State; Virginia, Old Dominion; Wisconsin, Badger and Copper State.

NATIVES OF STATES AND TERRITORIES.

Alabama, lizards; Arkansas, toothpicks; California, gold-hunters; Colorado, rovers; Connecticut, wooden nutmegs; Dakota, squatters; Delaware, muskrats; Florida, fly-up-the-creeks; Georgia, buzzards; Idaho, fortune seekers; Illinois, suckers; Indiana, hoosiers; Iowa, hawkeyes; Kansas, jayhawkers; Kentucky, corn-crackers; Louisiana, creoles; Maine, foxes; Maryland, clam-humpers; Massachusetts, Yankees; Michigan, wolverines; Minnesota, gophers; Mississippi, tadpoles; Missouri, pukes; Nebraska, bugeaters; Nevada, sage-hens; New Hampshire, granite boys; New Jersey, blues, or clam-catchers; New Mexico, Spanish Indians; New York, Knickerbockers; North Carolina, tarheels; Ohio, buckeyes; Oregon, hard cases; Pennsylvania, pennamites, or leather-heads; Rhode Island, gun-flints; South Carolina, weasles; Tennessee, whelps; Texas, beef-heads; Utah, polygamists; Vermont, green-mountain boys; Virginia, beagles; Wisconsin, badgers.

NICKNAMES OF CITIES.

Atlanta, Gate City of the South; Baltimore, Monumental City; Bangor, Lumber City; Boston, Modern Athens, Literary Emporium, City of Notions, and Hub of the Universe; Brooklyn, City of Churches; Buffalo, Queen of the Lakes; Burlington (Iowa), Orchard City; Charleston, Palmetto City; Chicago, Prairie, or Garden City; Cincinnati, Queen of the West and Porkopolis; Cleveland, Forest City; Denver, City of the Plains; Detroit, City of the Straits; Hartford, Insurance City; Indianapolis, Railroad City; Keokuk, Gate City; Lafayette, Star City; Leavenworth, Cottonwood City; Louisville, Falls City; Lowell, Spindle City; McGregor, Pocket City; Madison, Lake City; Milwaukee, Cream City; Nashville, Rock City; New Haven, Elm City; New Orleans, Crescent City; New York, Empire City, Commercial Emporium, Gotham, and Metropolis of America; Philadelphia, City of Brotherly Love, City of Penn, Quaker City, and Centennial City; Pittsburgh, Iron City and Smoky City; Portland (Me.), Hill City; Providence, Roger Williams's City, and Perry Davis's Pain Killer; Raleigh, Oak City; Richmond (Va.), Cockade City; Richmond (Ind.), Quaker City of the West; Rochester, Aqueduct City; Salt Lake City, Mormon City; San Francisco, Golden Gate; Savannah, Forest City of the South; Sheboygan, Evergreen City; St. Louis, Mound City; St. Paul, North Star City; Vicksburg, Key City; Washington, City of Magnificent Distances, and Federal City.

The English Sparrow.

The first English sparrow was brought to the United States in 1850, but it was not until 1870 that the species can be said to have firmly established itself. Since then it has taken possession of the country. Its fecundity is amazing. In the latitude of New York and southward it attains, as a rule, five or six broods in a season, with from four to six young in a brood. Assuming the average annual product of a pair to be twenty-four young, of which half are females and half males, and assuming further, for the sake of computation, that all live, together with their offspring, it will be seen that in ten years the progeny of a single pair would be 275,716,983,698.

WARS OF THE UNITED STATES.

Statement of the Number of United States Troops Engaged.

WARS.	FROM	TO	REGULARS.	MILITIA AND VOLUNTEERS.	TOTAL.
War of the Revolution	Apr 19, 1775	Apr 11, 1783	130,711	164,080	309,781
Northwestern Indian wars	Sept 19, 1790	Aug 3, 1795	......	......	8,983
War with France	July 9, 1798	Sept 30, 1800	......	......	4,593*
War with Tripoli	June 10, 1801	June 4, 1805	......	......	3,330*
Creek Indian war	July 27, 1813	Aug 9, 1814	600	13,181	13,781
War 1812 with G. Britain	June 18, 1812	Feb 17, 1815	85,000	471,622	576,622
Seminole Indian war	Nov 20, 1817	Oct 21, 1818	1,000	6,911	7,911
Black Hawk Indian war	Apr 21, 1831	Sept 30, 1832	1,341	5,126	6,465
Cherokee disturbance or removal	1836	1837	......	9,494	9,494
Creek Indian war or disturbances	May 5, 1836	Sept 30, 1837	935	12,483	13,418
Florida Indian war	Dec 23, 1835	Aug 14, 1843	11,169	29,953	41,122
Aroostook disturbance	1836	1839	......	1,500	1,500
War with Mexico	Apr 24, 1846	July 4, 1848	30,954	73,776	112,230
Apache, Navajo, and Utah war	1849	1855	1,500	1,061	2,561
Seminole Indian war	1856	1858	......	3,687	3,687
Civil war†	1861	1865	......	......	2,772,408

* Naval forces engaged. † The number of troops on the Confederate side was about 600,000.

The number of casualties in the volunteer and regular armies of the United States, during the war of 1861-65, was reported by the Provost Marshal General in 1866: Killed in battle, 61,362; died of wounds, 34,727; died of disease, 183,287; total died, 279,376; total deserted, 199,105. Number of soldiers in the Confederate service who died of wounds or disease (partial statement), 133,821. Deserted (partial statement), 104,428. Number of United States troops captured during the war, 212,608; Confederate troops captured, 476,169. Number of United States troops paroled on the field, 16,431; Confederate troops paroled on the field, 248,599. Number of United States troops who died while prisoners, 29,725; Confederate troops who died while prisoners, 26,774.

The Bible.

There is no date from beginning to end in the Bible. It comprises some 60 documents, and is supposed to have been written by about 40 men; 54 miracles are recorded in the Old and 41 in the New Testament; total, 105. The shortest verse in the Old Testament is "Remember Lot's wife." There is one in the New Testament as short as John xi. 35, in point of words, but not in letters, viz: Thessalonians v. 16, "Rejoice evermore." There are 2 chapters in the Bible alike verbatim, and 1 book, Esther, in which the Deity is not mentioned.

THE CIVIL WAR OF 1861-65.

Number of Men in the Union Army Furnished by Each State and Territory, from April 15, 1861, to Close of War.

STATES AND TERRITORIES.	NUMBER OF MEN FURNISHED.	AGGREGATE REDUCED TO A THREE YEARS' STANDARD.	STATES AND TERRITORIES.	NUMBER OF MEN FURNISHED.	AGGREGATE REDUCED TO A THREE YEARS' STANDARD.
Alabama	2,576	1,611	New York	448,850	392,270
Arkansas	8,289	7,836	North Carolina	3,156	3,156
California	15,725	15,725	Ohio	313,180	240,514
Colorado	4,903	3,697	Oregon	1,810	1,773
Connecticut	55,864	50,623	Pennsylvania	337,936	265,517
Delaware	12,284	10,322	Rhode Island	23,236	17,878
Florida	1,290	1,290	South Carolina	......	......
Georgia	......	......	Tennessee	31,092	26,394
Illinois	259,092	214,133	Texas	1,965	1,632
Indiana	196,363	153,576	Vermont	33,288	29,068
Iowa	76,242	68,630	Virginia	......	......
Kansas	20,149	18,706	West Virginia	32,068	27,714
Kentucky	75,760	70,832	Wisconsin	91,327	79,260
Louisiana	5,224	4,654	Dakota	206	206
Maine	70,107	56,776	Dist. of Columbia	16,534	11,506
Maryland	46,638	41,275	Indian Territory	3,530	3,530
Massachusetts	146,730	124,104	Montana	......	......
Michigan	87,364	80,111	New Mexico	6,561	4,432
Minnesota	24,020	19,675	Utah	......	......
Mississippi	545	545	Washington Ter.	964	964
Missouri	109,111	86,530	U.S. Army	......	......
Nebraska	3,157	2,175	U.S. Volunteers	......	......
Nevada	1,080	1,080	U.S. Col'd Troops	93,441	91,789
New Hampshire	33,937	30,849			
New Jersey	76,814	57,908	Total	2,772,408	2,320,258

The armies of the United States were commanded during the war of the Rebellion by President Lincoln as commander-in-chief under the constitutional provision; and under him, as general commanders, by Brevet Lieutenant General Winfield Scott until Nov. 6, 1861; by Major General George B. McClellan from Nov. 6, 1861, to March 11, 1862; by Major General Henry W. Halleck from July 11, 1862, to March 12, 1864 (there being no general commander between March 11 and July 11, 1862); and Lieutenant General and General U. S. Grant from March 12, 1864, to March 4, 1869. The first of the principal armies into which the force of the United States was divided was the Army of the Potomac. This army was called into existence in July, 1861, and was organized by Major General George B. McClellan, its first commander, Nov. 5, 1862. Major General A. E. Burnside took command of it, Jan. 26, 1863, Major General Joe Hooker was placed in command, and June 27, 1863, Major General George G. Meade succeeded him. The Army of the Ohio was organized by General D. C. Buell, under a general order from the

THE CIVIL WAR OF 1861-65.

War Department dated Nov. 9, 1861, from troops in the military department of the Ohio. General Buell remained in command until Oct. 30, 1862, when he was succeeded by General W. S. Rosecrans. At this time the Army of the Ohio became the Army of the Cumberland and a new department of the Ohio was formed and Major General H. G. Wright assigned to the command thereof. He was succeeded by Major General Burnside, who was relieved by Major General J. G. Foster of the command of both department and army. Major General Schofield took command Jan. 26, 1864, and Jan. 17, 1865, the department was merged into the Department of the Cumberland. The Army of the Cumberland was formed of the Army of the Ohio, as above noted. It continued under the command of General Rosecrans until October, 1863, when General George H. Thomas took command of it. The Army of the Tennessee was originally the Army of the District of Western Tennessee, fighting as such at Shiloh. It became the Army of the Tennessee on the concentration of troops at Pittsburgh Landing under General Halleck, and when the Department of the Tennessee was formed Oct. 16, 1862, the troops serving therein were placed under command of Major General U. S. Grant. Oct. 27, 1863, Major General William T. Sherman was appointed to the command of this army; March 12, 1864, Major General J. B. McPherson succeeded him; July 30, 1864, McPherson having been killed, Major General O. O. Howard was placed in command, and May 19, 1865, Major General John A. Logan succeeded him. Other minor armies were the Army of Virginia, which was formed by the consolidation of the forces under Major Generals Fremont, Banks and McDowell by order of the War Department, Aug. 12, 1862. Major General John Pope was placed in command, but after the disastrous defeat of this general at Manassas the army as such was discontinued and its troops transferred to other organizations. The Army of the James was formed of the Tenth and Fourteenth corps and cavalry, and was placed under the command of Major General Butler. Its operations were carried on in conjunction with the Army of the Potomac. Other temporary arrangements of the troops formed the Army of the Mississippi in the Mississippi River operations in 1862; the Army of the Gulf in Louisiana in May, 1863; the Army of West Virginia, in the valley of the Shenandoah, in May, 1864, and the army of the Middle Military Division in Virginia in the fall of 1864.

A horse will live 25 days without solid food, merely drinking water; 17 days without either eating or drinking; and only 5 days when eating solid food without drinking.

PRINCIPAL BATTLES OF THE CIVIL WAR.

Date.		Place.	Federal Loss.	Confed. Loss.
Apr. 12, 1861		Bombardm't Ft. Sumter	no one hurt	5 w
"	19	Riot, Baltimore	3 k, 7 w	[illegible] k, 3 w
June	10	Big Bethel, Va	16 k, 34 w, 5 m	No report
July	5	Carthage, Mo	13 k, 31 w	200 k, [illegible] w
"	12	Rich Mountain, W. Va	11 k, 35 w	[illegible] k, 140 w
"	21	Bull Run, Va	4500 k, w, & m, 28 [illegible] / 481 k, 1011 w, 700 p	1852 k & w
Aug.	10	Wilson's Creek, Mo	223 k, 721 w, 292 m	421 k, 1317 w, 3 m
Sept.	12-14	Cheat Mountain, W. Va	13 k, 20 w, 60 p	100 k & w, 20 p
"	20	Lexington, Mo	42 k, 108 w, 1624 p	25 k, 75 w
"	21	Ball's Bluff, Va	223 k, 226 w, 500 p	36 k, 223 w, 2 p
Nov.	7	Belmont, Mo	84 k, 288 w, 235 m	261 k, 427 w, 278 m
"	7	Port Royal, S. C.	8 k, 23 w, 236 p	k and w no report
"	8	Piketon, Ky	6 k, 24 w	400 k and w, 2000 p
Dec.	18	Milford, Mo	2 k, 17 w	1300 p
Jan. 19, 1862		Mill Spring, Ky	39 k, 207 w	192 k, 140 p
Feb.	8	Roanoke Island, N. C.	50 k, 200 w	30 k, 50 w, 2500 p
"	6	Fort Henry, Tenn		
"	16	Fort Donelson, Tenn	446 k, 1735 w, 150 p	231 k, 1007 w, 13500 p
Mar.	8	Pea Ridge, Ark	1383 k, w and m	1300 k, 2850 w, 1600 p
"	14	Newbern, N. C.	91 k, 466 w	[illegible] k, 200 w, 200 p
"	23	Winchester, Va	110 k, 400 w	400 k & w, 300 p
Apr.	6-7	Pittsburg Landing, Tenn	1614 k, 7721 w, 3963 m	1728 k, 8012 w, 959 m
"	10	Island No. 10		17 k, 6000 p
May	5	Williamsburg, Va	2073 k & w, 623 p	700 k, 1500 w, 300 p
"	25	Winchester, Va		
"	27	Hanover C. H., Va	[illegible]	200 k & w, 600 p
"	30	Corinth, Miss		
"	31	Fair Oaks, Va	890 k, 3627 w, 1222 p	2800 k, 3897 w
June	1	Fair Oaks, Va	6000 k & w	8000 k & w
"	8	Cross Keys, Va	125 k, 500 w	500 k & w
"	9	Port Republic, Va	67 k, 361 w, 574 m	1500 k, w & m
"	25	Chickahominy, Va	50 k, 150 w	1600 k & w
"	26	Gaines' Mills, Va	7000 k, w and m	About the same
July	1	Malvern Hill, Va	[illegible] k, w and m	Nearly 5000
Aug.	5	Baton Rouge, La	250 k, w and m	800 k, w & m
"	9	Cedar Mountain, Va	1500 k, w and m	1300 k, 1500 w
"	27	Gallatin, Tenn	64 k, 100 w, 200 p	118 k & w
"	29	Kettle Run, Va	300 k, w and m	300 k & w, 100 p
"	28	Groveton, Va	[illegible] k, w and m	1250 k, [illegible]
"	30	Bull Run 2nd	800 k, 4000 w, 3000 p	700 k, 3000 w
"	29-30	Richmond, Ky	500 k, 700 w, 2000 p	250 k, 500 w
Sept.	1	Chantilly, Va	1300 k and w	800 k & w
"	14	South Mountain, Md	443 k, 1806 w, 76 m	500 k, 2343 w, 1500 p
"	15	Harper's Fy, (by siege)	80 k, 120 w, 11583 p	500 k & w
"	17	Antietam, Md	12469 k, w & m	[illegible]
"	19-20	Iuka, Miss	135 k, 527 w	[illegible] k, 600 w, 300 p
Oct.	3-4	Corinth, Miss	315 k, 1812 w, 232 m	1423 k, 2268 w, [illegible]
"	8	Perryville, Ky	2600 k, w and m	2500 k, 3000 w, 200 p
Dec.	7	Prairie Grove, Ark	195 k, 799 w	1650 k & w
"	13	Fredericksburg, Va	1512 k, 6000 w, 524 p	1800 k & w
"	27-29	Vicksburg	191 k, 982 w, 756 m	no report
Jan. 2, 1863		Stone River, Tenn	1533 k, 6079 w, [illegible]	[illegible] k & w, 1500 p
"	11	Fort Hindman, Ark	1000 k, w & m	[illegible] k & w, 4800 p
Feb.	3	Fort Donelson, Tenn	12 k, 30 w	150 k, 400 w, 300 p
May	3	Suffolk, Va	300 k, 718 w, 5 m	1500 k, w & m

PRINCIPAL BATTLES OF THE CIVIL WAR.—Continued.

Date.		Place.	Federal Loss.	Confed. Loss.
May	1	LaGrange, Ark.	200 k, w & m	
"	2	Fredericksburg, Va.	2000 k & w	
"	2-3	Chancellorsville, Va.	1660 k & w, 1760 p	10000 k & w, 2000 p
"	12	Jackson, Miss.	40 k, 240 w, & m	400 k & w
"	14	Champion Hills, Miss.	426 k, 1842 w	1000 k, w & m
"	16	Big Black River, Miss.	29 k, 242 w	2600 k, w & m
"	18-22	Vicksburg, Miss.	2600 loss	no report
"	27	Port Hudson	300 k, w & m	600 k, w & m
June	6	Milliken's Bend, Miss.	127 k, 287 w, 137 m	200 k, 500 w
"	9	Beverly Ford, Va.	500 k, w & m	750 k, w & m
"	14	Winchester, Va.	3000 k, w & m	850 k, w & m
"	27	Shelbyville, Tenn.	50 k, 363 w, 33 m	1634 p and 300 k & w
July	1-3	Gettysburg, Pa.	total loss 23186	total loss 27000
"	4	Vicksburg surrenders	245 k, 3688 w, 303 p	9000 k & w, 30000 p
"	4	Helena, Ark.	250 k, w & m	500 k & w, 1000 p
"	5	Bolton, Miss.		2000 p
"	8	Port Hudson surrenders		5500 p
"	10-18	Ft. Wagner, S. C.	700 k, w & m	600 k, 331 w
Sept.	9	Cumberland Gap		2000 p
"	19-20	Chickamauga	1644 k, 9262 w, 4945 m	17000 k, w & m
"	14	Bristow Station, Va.	51 k, 329 w	1200 k & w, 500 p
Dec.	4	Knoxville, Tenn.	925 k & w	1000 p
"	23-25	Chattanooga	4000 k & w	10000 k, w & m
"	25	Missionary Ridge		
"	26	Ringgold, Ga.	500 k, w & m	360 p
"	27-28	Locust Grove, Va.	1000 k, w & m	1200 k, w & m
Mar. 25, 1864		Paducah, Ky.	14 k, 46 w	300 k & w
Apr.	8-9	Mansfield, La.	500 k & w, 1500 p	4000 p
"	17-20	Plymouth, N. C.	150 k, 1600 p	1500 k & w
May	5-7	Wilderness, Va.	loss 20000	loss 11400
"	8	Spottsylvania, Va.	loss 10000	loss 10000
"	12	Spottsylvania, Va.		4000 p
"	12-16	Ft. Darling, Va.	5000 k, w & m	no report
"	13-15	Resaca, Ga.	200 k, 2800 w	no report
"	25-28	Dallas, Ga.	1000 k & w	300 p, 4000 k & w
June	1-3	Cold Harbor, Va.	3000 k, w & m	1500 k, w & m
"	15-18	Petersburg, Va.	loss 9000	no report
"	22	Weldon R. R., Va.	600 k & w, 1000 p	no report
"	27	Kenesaw Mt., Ga.	3000 k & w	no report
July	9	Monocacy, Md.	1000 k & w	no report
"	20	Peach Tree Creek, Ga.	1700 k, w & m	5000 k & w, 1000 p
"	22	Atlanta, Ga.	3521 k & w	10000 k & w
"	30	Petersburg, Va.	4000 k, w & m	1000 k, w & m
Aug.	5-23	Mobile Bay, Ala.	335 k, 88 w	[illegible]
"	18-21	Deep Bottom, Va.	loss 1000	loss 3000
"	21	6 Mile Station, Va.	3000 k & w	3600 p
"	25	Weldon R. R., Va.	1000 k & w, 2000 p	1500 k & w
"	31	Atlanta, Ga.	50 k, 5 m, 431 w	3000 k & w
Sept.	19	Winchester, Va.	3000 k & w	3000 k, 4000 w, 3000 p
"	22	Fishers Hill	400 k & w	400 k & w, 1100 p
"	25	Ironton, Mo.	9 k, 60 w	1500 k & w
30—Oct.	1	Petersburg, Va.	500 k & w	1000 k & w
Oct.	19	Cedar Creek, Va.	4000 k & w, 1000 m	3000 k & w, 1500 p
"	26	Mine Creek, Mo.	1000 m, 2000 k & w	300 k, 1000 p
"	27	Hatcher's Run, Va.	156 k, 400 w, 1200 m	1000 k, w & m
Nov.	30	Franklin, Tenn.	189 k, 1033 w, 1104 m	1750 k, 3800 w, 702 p
Dec.	15	Nashville, Tenn.	3000 k, w & m	20000 k, w & m

PRINCIPAL BATTLES OF THE CIVIL WAR.—Concluded.

Date.		Place.	Federal Loss.	Confed. Loss.
Jan. 15, 1865		Ft. Fisher	110 k, 536 w	400 k & w, 2500 p
"	19-22	Wilmington, N. C.	200 k & w	1000 p
Feb.	27	Waynesboro, Va.	25 k & w	5 k, 1300 p
"	8	Kingston, N. C.	loss 1000	1200 k & w, 2800 p
"	16	Averasboro, N. C.	74 k, 774 w	322 k, 670 p
Mar.	19	Bentonville, N. C.	loss 1600	267 k, 1625 p
"	25-27	Petersburg, Va.	130 k, 1340 w, 971 m	2500 k & w, 2500 p
Apr.	1	Five Forks, Va.	loss 2000	5000 p
"	2	Selma, Ala.		3000 p
"	2-3	Petersburg & Richmond	5000 k, w & m	3000 k, w & m
"	6	Farmville & Sailors Cr.		6000 p
"	9	Surrender of Gen. Lee		26115 p
"	11	Ft. Blakely, Mobile	2000 k & w	500 k & w, 4300 p
"	12	Surrender of Mong'y, Ala.		2700 p, 100 g
"	12	Salisbury, N. C.		1000 p
"	26	Surrender of Gen. Johnston		27000 p
May	1	Surrender of Gen. Morgan		1200 p
"	4	Surrender of Gen. Taylor		10000 p
"	10	Surrender of Thompson's Co.	30 k	8000 p
"	13	Near Brazos, Chica, Tex.	70	
"	10	Capture of Jeff. Davis		
"	26	Surrender of Gen. Smith		20000 p

In addition to the battles given above there were 2,000 battles, engagements and skirmishes.

Principal Naval Battles of the Civil War.

1862, Feb. 6—Fort Henry, Tenn., captured by Commodore Foote.

Feb. 8—Roanoke Island, N. C., captured by Commodore Goldsborough and Gen. Burnside.

16—Fort Donelson, Tenn., combined forces of Gen. Grant and Commodore Foote.

Mar. 8—Confederate ram Merrimac "sinks" U. S. Frigates Cumberland and Congress, Hampton Roads, Va.

9—Federal Monitor disables the Merrimac.

April 6—Pittsburgh Landing.

8—Capture of Island No. 10.

11—Fort Pulaski, Ga., captured by land and naval forces.

24—Forts Jackson, St. Philip and New Orleans.

May 13—Natchez, Miss., captured by Admiral Farragut.

July 1—Malvern Hill.

1863, Jan. 11—Fort Hindman, Ark., Admiral Porter.

11—U. S. steamer Hatteras sunk by Confederate Alabama.

17—Monitor Weehawken captures Confederate ram Atlanta.

THE CIVIL WAR OF 1861–65.

May 18—Vicksburg, Miss., Admiral Porter.
July 8—Port Hudson, Miss., captured.
8—Natchez, Miss.
1864, June 19—U. S. steamer Kearsarge "sinks the Alabama" off Cherbourg, France.
Aug. 5—Mobile, Ala., Admiral Farragut.
1865, Jan. 15—Fort Fisher, N. C., captured by Gen. Terry and Commodore Porter.

During the Civil War the Federal Navy was increased in two years to over 400 vessels, the greater part of which were used in blockading Southern ports; notwithstanding their vigilance and effectiveness, many Confederate cruisers managed to escape the blockade and destroy the Northern merchant vessels.

At the present time (1880) not one-half the vessels belonging to the navy are in active service; the greater portion of those in commission are employed in what is called squadron service. There are seven squadrons, viz., the European, the Asiatic, the North Atlantic, the South Atlantic, the North Pacific, the South Pacific and the Gulf squadrons. These squadrons are under command of a high naval officer of the rank of commodore or rear admiral, whose ship is called the flag-ship of the squadron.

Federal Vessels Captured or Destroyed by Confederate "Cruisers."

Ships	39	Steamboats	4
Brigs	46	Gunboats	2
Barks	34	Cutter	1
Schooners	87	Tug	1

Vessels Captured or Destroyed for Violation of the Blockade, or in Battle, from May, 1861, to May, 1865.

Schooners	725	Gunboats	2
Sloops	153	Propellers	4
Steamers	282	Pilot boats	2
Barks	27	Boats	8
Brigs	30	Yachts	9
Ships	13	Tugs	3
Ironclads and rams	16	Barkentine	1
Brigantines	2	Pungy	1
Miscellaneous	96		

Tin, when compressed in powder, becomes solid under a pressure of ten tons on the square inch, zinc at thirty-eight tons, antimony at thirty-eight tons, aluminum at thirty-eight tons, bismuth at thirty-eight tons, and copper at thirty-three tons.

Cost of Recent Wars.

Crimean war	£340,000,000
Italian war of 1859	60,000,000
American civil war—North	940,000,000
" " " —South	460,000,000
Schleswig-Holstein war	7,000,000
Austrian and Prussian war, 1866	66,000,000
Expeditions to Mexico, Morocco, Paraguay, etc., (estimated)	40,000,000
Franco-Prussian war	500,000,000
Russian and Turkish war, 1877	250,000,000
Zulu and Afghan wars, 1879	30,000,000
	£2,663,000,000

This would allow $30 for every man, woman and child on the habitable globe. It would make two railways all around the world at $250,000 per mile each. These figures are furnished by the Peace Society, London.

Losses from War in Twenty-Five Years (1855–80.)

	Killed in battle, or died of wounds and disease.
Crimean war	750,000
Italian war, 1859	45,000
War of Schleswig-Holstein	3,000
American civil war—the North	280,000
" " " —the South	200,000
War between Prussia, Austria and Italy, 1866	45,000
Expeditions to Mexico, Cochin China, Morocco, Paraguay, etc.	65,000
Franco-German war of 1870–71—France	155,000
" " " " —Germany	60,000
*Russian and Turkish war of 1877	225,000
Zulu and Afghan wars, 1879	40,000
Total	1,868,000

Length and Cost of American Wars.

War.	Length.	Cost.
1. War of the revolution	7 years—1775–1782	$ 135,193,703
2. Indian war in Ohio Ter.	1790	....
3. War with the Barbary St	1803–1804	....
4. Tecumseh Indian war	1811	....
6. War with Great Britain	3 years—1812–1815	107,159,003
6. Algerine war	1815	....
7. First Seminole war	1817	....
8. Black Hawk war	1832	....
9. Second Seminole war	1835	....
10. Mexican war	2 years—1846–1848	66,000,000
11. Mormon war	1856	....
12. Civil war	4 years—1861–1865	$6,500,000,000

*About thirty thousand skeletons of Russian and Turkish soldiers were shipped to England in 1881, as manure, in the form of bones or bone dust.

GREAT BATTLES OF HISTORY.

The number placed *hors-de-combat* in battle are not relatively as large as formerly, as the table below will show:

	Men Engaged.	Hors-de-combat.	Ratio.
Trasymene	65,000	17,500	27 per cent.
Cannæ	146,000	52,000	36 "
Bannockburn	135,000	38,000	28 "
Agincourt	62,000	11,400	18 "
Cressy	117,000	31,200	27 "
Marengo	58,000	13,000	22 "
Austerlitz	170,000	33,000	19 "
Borodino	230,000	78,000	31 "
Waterloo	145,000	51,000	35 "
Alma	102,000	8,400	8 "
Sadowa	422,000	32,000	8 "
Gravelotte	310,000	45,500	15 "
Gettysburg	140,000	8,000	6 "

According to Napoleon, the proportions of an army should be 70 per cent. infantry, 15 per cent. cavalry, and 15 per cent. between artillery, engineers and train.

The proportion of men capable of bearing arms is estimated at 25 per cent. of the population.

At the close of the Franco-German war the Germans took from the French 7,441 pieces of cannon, including 2,485 field pieces and 5,000 fortress guns. At the battle of Waterloo the British artillery fired 9,467 rounds, or one for every Frenchman killed.

The Decisive Battles of History.

Actium, B.C. 31. The combined fleets of Antony and Cleopatra defeated by Octavius, and imperialism established in the person of Octavius.

Philippi, B.C. 42. Brutus and Cassius defeated by Octavius and Antony. The fate of the Republic decided.

Metaurus, B.C. 207. The Carthaginians, under Hasdrubal, were defeated by the Romans, under Caius and Marcus Livius.

Arbela, B.C. 331. The Persians defeated by the Macedonians and Greeks under Alexander the Great. End of the Persian empire.

Syracuse, B.C. 414. The Athenians defeated by the Syracusans and their allies, the Spartans, under Gylippus.

Marathon, B.C. 490. The Athenians, under Miltiades, defeated the Persians under Datis. Free government preserved.

Winfeld-Lippe, A.D. 9. Teutonic independence established by the defeat of the Roman legions under Varus at the hands of the Germans under Arminius (Hermann).

Chalons, A.D. 451. The Huns, under Attila, called the

DECISIVE BATTLES OF HISTORY.

"Scourge of God," defeated by the confederate armies of Romans and Visigoths.

Tours, A.D. 732. The Saracens defeated by Charles Martel and Christendom rescued from Islam.

Hastings, A.D. 1066. Harold, commanding the English army, defeated by William the Conqueror, and a new regime established in England by the Normans.

Siege of Orleans, A.D. 1429. The English defeated by the French under Joan of Arc.

Defeat of the Spanish Armada, A.D. 1588. England saved from Spanish invasion.

Lutzen, A.D 1632. Decided the religious liberties of Germany. Gustavus Adolphus killed.

Blenheim, A.D. 1704. The French and Bavarians, under Marshal Tallard, defeated by the English and their allies, under Marlborough.

Pultowa, A.D. 1709. Charles XII., of Sweden, defeated by the Russians under Peter the Great.

Saratoga, A.D. 1777. Critical battle of the American War of Independence. The English defeated by the Americans under Gen. Gates.

Valmy, A.D. 1792. An invading army of Prussians, Austrians and Hessians, under the Duke of Brunswick, defeated by the French under Kellermann. The first success of the Republic against foreigners.

Trafalgar. On the 21st of October, A.D. 1805, the great naval battle of Trafalgar was fought. The English defeated the French and destroyed Napoleon's hopes to successfully invade England.

Waterloo, A.D. 1815. The French, under Napoleon, defeated by the allied armies of Russia, Austria, Prussia and England, under Wellington.

Siege of Sebastopol, A.D. 1855. The Russians succumbed to the beleaguering armies of England, France and Turkey, and the result was delay in the expansion of the Russian Empire.

Gettysburg, July, A.D. 1863. The deciding battle of the war for the Union. The Confederates under Gen. Lee defeated by the Union forces under Meade.

Sedan, A.D. 1870. The decisive battle of the Franco-German war.

Slavery and Serfdom.

Some of the wealthy Romans had as many as 10,000 slaves. The minimum price fixed by the law of Rome was $80, but after great victories they could sometimes be bought for a few shillings on the field of battle. The day's wages of a Roman gardener were about 16 cents, and his value about $300, while a blacksmith was valued at about $700, a cook at $2,000, an actress at $4,000, and a physician of $11,000.

The number of slaves emancipated in the British Colonies in 1834 was 786,993, the indemnity aggregating, in round figures, $100,000,000. In Brazil, in 1856, there were 1,510,800 slaves, 15 per cent. of the entire population. These were held by 41,000 owners, averaging 37 to each owner. In 1880 the number of slaves was 1,300,000. Owing to the gradual abolition of slavery in Brazil by law it is expected that it will be entirely obsolete in 1900.

Slavery in the United States.

Year.	Number.	Year.	Number.
1790	697,890	1830	2,009,030
1800	893,046	1840	2,487,380
1810	1,151,400	1850	3,204,300
1820	1,698,100	1860	3,975,700

Serfdom in Russia.

There were 47,933,000 serfs in Russia in 1861, as follows: Crown serfs, 23,651,000; appanage, 3,326,000; held by nobles, 21,755,000. The cost of redemption was, in round numbers, about $395,000,000, as follows:

Mortgages remitted	$150,000,000
Government scrip	101,000,000
Paid by serfs	52,000,000
Balance due	90,000,000

The indemnity to the nobles was $22 per serf. The lands are mortgaged to the state till 1912. The lands ceded to Crown serfs are mortgaged only till 1902. The item of "mortgages remitted" is the amount due by nobles to the Imperial Bank and canceled.

Austrian Servitude (1840).

	Value.
Labor (two days per week)	$175,000,000
Tithe of crops, etc.	60,000,000
Male tribute, timber	7,000,000
Female tribute, spun wool	8,000,000
Fowl, eggs, butter	6,000,000
Total	$256,000,000

There were 3,000,000 serfs, whose tribute averaged more than $85 per head, which was, in fact, the rent of their farms. Some Bohemian nobles had as many as 10,000 serfs. The redemption was effected by giving the nobles 5 per cent. Government scrip, and land then rose 50 per cent. in value.

German Serfs.

In 1848 the state took 60,000,000 acres from the nobles, leaving them still 22,000,000 acres, and gave the former among the serfs. Indemnity as follows: 1. Government scrip, $500 for each serf family, to nobleman. 2. Land tax, $15 per annum, transferred to peasant. 3. Interest, $35 per annum for 47 years, to be paid by peasant to the state, being 4 per cent. on cost of redemption.

Famous Giants and Dwarfs.

The most noted giants of ancient and modern times are as follows:

Name.	Place.	Height, Feet.	Period.
Goliath	Palestine	11.0	B.C. 1063.
Gabbara	Rome	9.2	Claudius Cæsar.
John Middleton	England	9.2	A.D. 1578.
Frederick's Swede	Sweden	8.4	
Cajanus	Finland	7.9	
Gilly	Tyrol	8.1	
Patrick Cotter	Cork	8.7	1806.
Chang Gow	Pekin	7.8	1880.

Many of the great men of history have been rather small in stature. Napoleon was only about 5 ft. 4 in., Washington was 6 ft. 2 in. One of the greatest of American statesmen, Alexander H. Stephens, never exceeded 115 pounds in weight, and in his old age his weight was less than 100 pounds.

The more notable human mites are named below:

Name.	Height, inches.	Date of Birth.	Place of Birth.
Count Borowlaski	39	1739	Warsaw.
Tom Thumb (Chas. S. Stratton)	31	1837	New York.
Mrs. Tom Thumb	32	1842	"
Che-Mah	25	1838	China.
Lucia Zarate	20	1863	Mexico.
General Mite	21	1864	New York.

Evictions in Ireland.

The total number of families evicted in Ireland for 33 years is 482,000 as below:

Years.	Evicted.	Re-admitted.	Net Evictions.
1849–51	263,000	13,000	250,000
1852–60	110,000	28,000	82,000
1861–70	47,000	8,000	39,000
1871–80	41,000	8,000	25,000
1881–82	21,000	4,000	17,000
Total	482,000	119,000	363,000

The number of persons actually evicted was over two millions (say 70,000 per annum).

Great Financial Panics.

The most remarkable crises since the beginning of the present century have been as follows:

1814. England, 240 banks suspended.
1825. Manchester, failures 2 millions.
1831. Calcutta, failures 15 millions.
1837. United States, "Wild-cat" crisis; all banks closed.
1839. Bank of England saved by Bank of France. Severe also in France, where 93 companies failed for 6 millions.
1844. England. State loans to merchants. Bank of England reformed.
1847. England, failures 20 millions; discount 13 per cent.
1857. United States, 7,200 houses failed for 111 millions.
1866. London, Overend-Gurney crisis; failures exceeded 100 millions.
1869. Black Friday in New York (Wall street), September 24.

Excessive Heat in the Past.

In 1303 and 1304 the Rhine, Loire and Seine ran dry. The heat in several French provinces during the summer of 1705 was equal to that of a glass furnace. Meat could be cooked by merely exposing it to the sun. Not a soul dare venture out between noon and 4 p.m. In 1718 many shops had to close. The theaters never opened their doors for three months. Not a drop of water fell during six months. In 1773 the thermometer rose to 118 degrees. In 1778 the heat at Bologna was so great that a great number of people were stifled. There was not sufficient air for the breath, and people had to take refuge under the ground. In July, 1793, the heat again became intolerable. Vegetables were burned up, and fruit dried on the trees. The furniture and wood-work in dwelling-houses cracked and split up; meat went bad in an hour.

Summer Heat in Various Countries.

The following figures show the extreme summer heat in the various countries of the world: Bengal and the African desert, 150° Fahrenheit; Senegal and Guadaloupe, 130°; Persia, 125°; Calcutta and Central America, 120°; Afghanistan and the Arabian desert, 110°; Cape of Good Hope and Utah, 105°; Greece, 104°; Arabia, 103°; Montreal, 103°; New York, 102°; Spain, India, China, Jamaica, 100°; Sierra Leone, 95°; France, Denmark, St. Petersburg, Shanghai, the German Empire, Buenos Ayres, and the Sandwich Islands, 90°; Great Britain, Siam, and Peru, 85°; Portugal, Pekin and Natal, 80°; Siberia, 77°; Australia and Scotland, 75°; Italy, Venezuela and Madeira, 73°; Prussia and New Zealand, 70°; Switzerland and Hungary, 66°; Bavaria, Sweden, Tasmania and Moscow, 65°; Patagonia and the Falkland Isles, 55°; Iceland, 45°; Nova Zembla, 34°.

Severest Cold on Record.

1034. Mediterranean frozen; traffic with carts.
1420. Bosphorus frozen.
1468. Wine at Antwerp sold in blocks.
1658. Swedish artillery crossed the Sound.
1756. Snow knee-deep at Naples.
1789. Fahrenheit thermometer marked 23° below zero at Frankfort, and 36° below at Basle.
1809. Moscow, 43° below zero, greatest cold recorded there; mercury frozen.
1829. Jakoutsk, Siberia, 75° below zero on the 25th of January; greatest cold on record.
1846. December marked 25° below zero at Pontarlier; lowest ever marked in France.
1864. January, Fahrenheit stood at zero in Turin; greatest cold recorded in Italy.

Captain Parry, in his Arctic explorations, suffered for some time 51 degrees below zero. Frost is diminishing in Canada with the increase of population, as shown by the fact that Hudson's Bay was closed, from 1816-35, 184 days per annum, and from 1871-80 only 179 days per annum.

The Great Famines of History.

Walford mentions 350 famines since the 11th century, namely: England, 201; Ireland, 34; Scotland, 12; France, 10; Germany, 14; Italy, etc., 95. The worst in modern times have been:

Country.	Date.	No. of Victims.
France	1770	48,000
Ireland	1847	1,000,000
India	1866	1,450,000

Deaths from hunger and want were recorded as follows in 1879, according to Mulhall: Ireland, 3,269; England, 222; London, 101; France, 260. The proportion per 1,000 deaths was, respectively, 37.6, 6, 40, 9.

Remarkable Plagues of Modern Times.

Date.	Place.	Deaths.	Weeks.	Deaths per Week.
1656	Naples	300,000	28	10,400
1665	London	68,600	32	2,160
1720	Marseilles	60,100	36	1,700
1771	Moscow	87,800	32	2,700
1778	Constantinople	179,200	28	6,400
1799	Cairo	88,400	25	3,500
1812	Constantinople	144,000	13	11,100
1834	Cairo	57,000	18	3,200
1835	Alexandria	14,900	17	900
1871	Buenos Ayres	26,200	11	2,400

Great Fires and Conflagrations.

London, Sept. 2–6, 1666.—Eighty-nine churches, many public buildings and 13,200 houses destroyed; 400 streets laid waste; 200,000 persons homeless. The ruins covered 436 acres.

New York, Dec. 16, 1835.—600 buildings; loss, $20,000,000. Sept. 6, 1839.—$10,000,000 worth of property.

Pittsburgh, April 10, 1845.—1,000 buildings; loss, $6,000,000.

Philadelphia, July 9, 1850.—350 buildings; loss, $1,500,000; 25 persons killed, 9 drowned, [illegible] wounded.

St. Louis, May 4, 1851.—Large portion of the city burned; loss, $15,000,000.

San Francisco, May 3–5, 1851.—2,500 buildings; loss, $3,500,000; many lives lost. June 22, 1851.—500 buildings; loss, $3,000,000.

Santiago (Spain), Dec. 8, 1863.—A fire in the church of the Compania, beginning amid combustible ornaments; 2,000 persons killed, mostly women.

Charleston, S. C., Feb. 17, 1865.—Almost totally destroyed, with large quantities of naval and military stores.

Richmond, Va., April 2 and 3, 1865.—In great part destroyed by fire at time of Confederate evacuation.

Portland, Me., July 4, 1866.—Almost entirely destroyed; loss, $15,000,000.

Chicago, Oct. 8 and 9, 1871.—3⅓ square miles laid waste; 17,450 buildings destroyed; 200 persons killed; 98,500 made homeless. July 14, 1874.—Another great fire; loss, $4,000,000.

Great forest fires in Michigan and Wisconsin, October 8–14, 1871.—1,500 lives lost.

Boston, Nov. 9–11, 1872.—800 buildings; loss, $73,000,000; 15 killed.

Fall River, Mass., Sept. 19, 1874.—Great factory fires; 60 persons killed.

St. John, N. B., June 21, 1876.—Loss, $12,500,000.

Brooklyn Theater burned, Dec. 5, 1876.—300 lives lost.

Seattle and Spokane, Wash., 1889.—About $10,000,000 each.

Great Floods and Inundations.

An inundation in Cheshire, England, A.D. 353.—3,000 persons perished.

Glasgow, A.D. 758.—More than 400 families drowned.

Dort, April 17, 1421.—72 villages submerged; 100,000 people drowned.

Overflow of the Severn, A.D. 1483, lasting ten days.—Men, women and children carried away in their beds, and the waters covered the tops of many mountains.

General inundation in Holland, A.D. 1530.—By failure of dikes; 400,000 said to have been drowned.

At Catalonia, A.D. 1617.—50,000 drowned.

Johnstown, Pa., May 31, 1889.—By the bursting of a huge reservoir on the mountain, the town was almost entirely destroyed, and about 6,000 persons perished. The water in its passage to Johnstown descended about 250 feet. The theoretical velocity due to this descent would be about 127 feet per second, or between 86 and 87 miles an hour. According to the best accounts from 15 to 17 minutes were occupied in the passage to Johnstown, a distance of about twelve miles. Thus the average velocity could not have been far short of [illegible] miles an hour. The impetus of such a mass of water was irresistible. As the flood burst through the dam it [illegible] away as if they were stalks of [illegible].

Qualifications of Voters in the States.

States.	Requirement as to Citizenship.	Residence in: State.	County.	Precinct.	Registration.
Alabama	Citizen or declared intent.	1 y	3 m	1 m	Legis. may require
Arkansas	Citizen or declared intent.	1 y	6 m	1 m	Prohib., as bad to [illegible]
California	Actual citizen	1 y	90 d	30 d	Required by law
Colorado	Citizen or declared intent.	6 m	....	....	Req. by constitution
Connecticut	Actual citizen	1 y	6 m	6 m	Required by law
Delaware	Actual county taxpayer	1 y	1 m	....	No reg. required
Florida	U. S. citizen or declared intention	1 y	6 m	....	Req. by constitution
Georgia	Actual citizen	1 y	6 m	....	Legis. may regulate
Illinois	Actual citizen	1 y	90 d	30 d	Required by law
Indiana	Citizen or declared intent.	6 m	60 d	30 d	No law for reg.
Iowa	Actual citizen	6 m	60 d	....	Required by law
Kansas	Citizen or declared intent.	6 m	....	30 d	Req. in cities only
Kentucky	Citizen or declared intent.	2 y	1 y	60 d	No reg. required
Louisiana	Citizen or declared intent.	1 y	6 m	30 d	Legis. may regulate
Maine	Actual citizen	3 m	....	....	Required by law
Maryland	Actual citizen	1 y	6 m	....	Req. by constitution
Massachusetts	Citizen	1 y	....	6 m	Required by law
Michigan	Citizen or declared intent.	3 m	....	10 d	Required by law
Minnesota	Citizen or declared intent.	4 m	....	10 d	Required by law
Mississippi	Actual citizen	6 m	1 m	....	Req. by constitution
Missouri	Citizen or declared intent.	1 y	60 d	....	Req. by constitution in cities only
Nebraska	Citizen or declared intent.	6 m	....	....	Required by law
Nevada	Citizen or declared intent.	6 m	30 d	....	Req. by constitution
N. Hampshire	Actual citizen	....	....	6 m	Required by law
New Jersey	Actual citizen	1 y	5 m	....	Req. cities of [illegible]
New York	Actual citizen	1 y	4 m	30 d	Req. cities of [illegible]
N. Carolina	Actual citizen	1 y	90 d	....	Req. by constitution
Ohio	Actual citizen	1 y	....	....	No reg. required
Oregon	Citizen or declared intent.	6 m	....	....	....
Pennsylvania	Actual citizen	1 y	....	2 m	Req. by constitution
R. Island	Actual tax-paying citizen	1 y	....	6 m	Required by law
S. Carolina	Actual citizen	1 y	60 d	....	Req. by constitution
Tennessee	Actual citizen	1 y	6 m	....	No reg. required
Texas	Citizen or declared intent.	1 y	6 m	6 m	Prohibited
Vermont	Actual citizen	1 y	....	....	Required by law
Virginia	Actual citizen	2 y	....	3 m	Required by law
W. Virginia	Actual citizen	1 y	60 d	....	Prohibited
Wisconsin	Citizen or declared intent.	1 y	....	....	Required by law

State elections are held in the various States as follows: Alabama and Kentucky, first Monday in August; Arkansas, first Monday in September; Georgia, first Wednesday in October; Louisiana, Tuesday after third Monday in April; Maine, second Monday in September; Oregon, first Monday in June; Rhode Island, first Wednesday in April; Vermont, first Tuesday in September. All others are on Tuesday after first Monday in November. State Presidential elections are all on Tuesday after first Monday in November.

RODERIGO DE TRIANA was the name of the sailor with Columbus who first saw the "New World"—at 2 A. M., Oct. 12, 1492, on board the Pinta.

Interest Laws and Statutes of Limitations.

States and Territories.	Interest Laws.		Statutes of Limitations.		
	Legal Rate.	Rate Allowed by Contract.	Judgments, Years.	Notes, Years.	Open Accounts, Years.
	Per Ct.	Per Cent.			
Alabama	8	8	20	6	3
Arkansas	6	10	10	5	3
Arizona	10	12	5	5	3
California	7	Any rate	5	4	2
Colorado	10	Any rate	6	6	6
Connecticut	6	†	..	6	6
Dakota	7	Any rate	20	6	6
Delaware	6	6	20	6	3
District of Columbia	6	10	12	3	3
Florida	8	Any rate	20	5	2
Georgia	7	8	7	7	4
Idaho	10	18	6	6	4
Illinois	6	8	7	20	5
Indiana	6	8	10	10	6
Iowa	6	10	10	10	5
Kansas	7	12	5	5	2
Kentucky	6	8	15	15	5
Louisiana	5	8	10	5	3
Maine	6	Any rate	20	6	6
Maryland	6	6	12	3	3
Massachusetts	6	Any rate	20	6	6
Michigan	7	10	6	6	6
Minnesota	7	10	10	6	6
Mississippi	6	10	7	6	3
Missouri	6	10	20	10	5
Montana	10	Any rate	6	6	5
Nebraska	7	10	5	5	4
Nevada	10	Any rate	6	6	4
New Hampshire	6	6	20	6	6
New Jersey	6	6	20	6	6
New Mexico	6	12	15	6	4
New York	6	6*	20	6	6
North Carolina	6	8	10	3	3
Ohio	6	8	5	15	6
Oregon	8	10	10	6	6
Pennsylvania	6	6	5	6	6
Rhode Island	6	Any rate	20	6	6
South Carolina	7	10	10	6	6

* New York has by a recent law legalized any rate of interest on call loans of $5,000 or upward, on collateral security. † No usury, but over six per cent. cannot be collected by law.

Interest Laws and Statutes of Limitations.—*Concluded.*

States and Territories.	Interest Laws.		Statutes of Limitations.		
	Legal Rate.	Rate Allowed by Contract.	Judgments, Years.	Notes, Years.	Open Accounts, Years.
	Per Ct.	Per Cent.			
Tennessee	6	6	10	6	6
Texas	8	12	10	4	2
Utah	10	Any rate	5	4	2
Vermont	6	6	8	6	6
Virginia	6	6	10	5	2
Washington	10	Any rate	6	6	3
West Virginia	6	6	10	10	5
Wisconsin	7	10	20	6	6
Wyoming	12	Any rate	5	5	4

† No usury, but over six per cent. cannot be collected by law.

A TRIP AROUND THE WORLD.

From Atlantic cities to Omaha, Neb., via the great trunk lines of railway—about 1,400 miles, in 2 days and 2 hours.

From Omaha to San Francisco, Cal., via Union and Central Pacific railroads—1,914, in 4 days and 6 hours.

From San Francisco to Yokohama, Japan, by Pacific Mail line of steamers—4,800 miles, in 22 days.

From Yokohama to Hong Kong, China, by Pacific Mail or Peninsular and Oriental steamers—1,600 miles, in 6 days.

From Hong Kong to Calcutta, India, by Peninsular and Oriental steamers—3,500 miles in 15 days.

From Calcutta to Bombay, India, by the East Indian and Great Indian Peninsular railways—1,400 miles, in 3 days.

From Bombay to Suez, Egypt, by Peninsular and Oriental steamers—3,600 miles, in 14 days.

From Suez to Alexandria, Egypt, by rail—225 miles, in 10 hours.

From Alexandria to Brindisi, Italy, by Peninsular and Oriental steamers—850 miles, in 3 days.

Brindisi to London, Eng., by rail, via Paris or the Rhine—1,300 miles, in 3 days.

From London to Liverpool, Eng., by railway—200 miles, in 6 hours.

From Liverpool to the Atlantic cities, America, by either of the great Atlantic steamship lines—3,060 miles, in 10 days.

Total distance, 23,659 miles. Time, 82 days. Fare, about $1,100, with $4 per day for meals and incidentals; the total cost of the trip, $1,400.

300 FACTS ABOUT POULTRY.

Characteristics of the Various Breeds Concisely Stated.

No.	Races.	Weight of Chick one day old.	Daily increase of the Weight of Chick during ten days.	Annual Laying.	Weight of Eggs.	Quantity of Food Daily.	Average Weight of Flesh at 6 months.	Average Weight of Bone.
		oz.	oz.	Eggs.	oz.	oz.	lbs. oz.	oz. dr.
1	Crevecoeur	[illegible]	[illegible]	[illegible]	[illegible]	[illegible]	[illegible]	[illegible]
2	Houdan	[illegible]	[illegible]	[illegible]	[illegible]	[illegible]	[illegible]	[illegible]
3	La Bresse, black	[illegible]	[illegible]	[illegible]	[illegible]	[illegible]	[illegible]	[illegible]
4	La Bresse, gray	[illegible]	[illegible]	[illegible]	[illegible]	[illegible]	[illegible]	[illegible]
5	Dorking	[illegible]	[illegible]	[illegible]	[illegible]	[illegible]	[illegible]	[illegible]
6	La Fleche	[illegible]	[illegible]	[illegible]	[illegible]	[illegible]	[illegible]	[illegible]
7	Le Mans	[illegible]	[illegible]	[illegible]	[illegible]	[illegible]	[illegible]	[illegible]
8	Gournay	[illegible]	[illegible]	[illegible]	[illegible]	[illegible]	[illegible]	[illegible]
9	Courtes Pattes	[illegible]	[illegible]	[illegible]	[illegible]	[illegible]	[illegible]	[illegible]
10	Andalusian	[illegible]	[illegible]	[illegible]	[illegible]	[illegible]	[illegible]	[illegible]
11	Brahma	[illegible]	[illegible]	[illegible]	[illegible]	[illegible]	[illegible]	[illegible]
12	Campine, silver-spangled	[illegible]	[illegible]	[illegible]	[illegible]	[illegible]	[illegible]	[illegible]
13	Cochin, cinnamon	[illegible]	[illegible]	[illegible]	[illegible]	[illegible]	[illegible]	[illegible]
14	Game	[illegible]	[illegible]	[illegible]	[illegible]	[illegible]	[illegible]	[illegible]
15	[illegible]	[illegible]	[illegible]	[illegible]	[illegible]	[illegible]	[illegible]	15
16	Padouique	[illegible]	[illegible]	[illegible]	[illegible]	[illegible]	[illegible]	[illegible]
17	Dorking	[illegible]	[illegible]	[illegible]	[illegible]	[illegible]	[illegible]	[illegible]
18	Spanish	[illegible]	[illegible]	[illegible]	[illegible]	[illegible]	[illegible]	[illegible]
19	Hamburg, silver spangled	[illegible]	[illegible]	[illegible]	[illegible]	[illegible]	[illegible]	[illegible]
20	Dutch, black	[illegible]	[illegible]	[illegible]	[illegible]	[illegible]	[illegible]	[illegible]
21	Langshan	[illegible]	[illegible]	[illegible]	[illegible]	[illegible]	[illegible]	[illegible]
22	Leghorn, silver spangled	[illegible]	[illegible]	120	[illegible]	[illegible]	[illegible]	[illegible]
23	Hamburg, golden spangled	[illegible]	[illegible]	[illegible]	[illegible]	[illegible]	[illegible]	[illegible]
24	Scotch Gray	[illegible]	[illegible]	[illegible]	[illegible]	[illegible]	[illegible]	[illegible]
25	Bantam, silver spangled	[illegible]	......	[illegible]	[illegible]	[illegible]	......	......
26	Game Bantam	[illegible]	......	[illegible]	[illegible]	[illegible]	......	......
27	[illegible]	[illegible]	......	[illegible]	[illegible]	[illegible]	......	......
28	Silkies	[illegible]	......	[illegible]	[illegible]	[illegible]	......	......

Below are given soil and climate best adapted for the various breeds, rate of development, quality of flesh, etc., etc. The numbers in first column of preceding table refer to further description and characteristics of same breeds in paragraphs following:

1. Gravelly, mild climate, hardy fowl, develops rapidly and fattens easily, does not set, flesh exquisite, white and delicate.

2. Calcareous soil, any climate, very rapid development, incubation nil, flesh delicate.

FACTS ABOUT POULTRY.

3. Great, hardy in all climates, fattens quickly, good layers, does not set, flesh exquisite.

4. Any climate, fattens quickly, incubation nil, flesh very good.

5. Mild climate, dry soil, development slow, incubation good, flesh delicate.

6. Mild climate, dry soil, development slow, fattens easily, incubation nil, flesh very delicate.

7. Dry soil, any climate, rapid development, incubation rarely, delicate flesh.

8. Grass soil, any climate, pretty rapid development, incubates rarely, flesh good.

9. Dry soil, hardy in all climates, development middling, incubation good but little, good flesh.

10. Dry soil and warm climate, development middling, incubation nil, flesh delicate.

11. Hardy, dry soil, any climate, development slow, incubation excellent, good mother, flesh fair.

12. Hardy race, any climate, require much space, development middling, incubation nil, flesh good.

13. Hardy in any climate, develop very slowly, incubation excellent, good mother but heavy, flesh stringy.

14. Hardy in any climate, development rapid, incubation capital, good mother, flesh excellent.

15. Very hardy race in any climate, development rapid, incubation nil, flesh delicate.

16. Hardy in any climate, development middling, incubation very good, excellent mothers, flesh good.

17. Grass soil and mild climate, develop very rapidly, incubate well, very good mothers, flesh very delicate and juicy.

18. Delicate race, sandy soil and warm climate, develop slowly, long time feathering, incubation rare, flesh delicate.

19. Any soil or climate, development middling, incubation very rare, flesh delicate.

20. Delicate breed, requires grass soil, development middling, incubation nil, flesh pretty good.

21. Very hardy in any climate, develop rapidly, incubation good, most excellent mothers, flesh excellent.

22. Very hardy in any climate, develop rapidly, incubate very rarely, flesh indifferent.

23. Delicate race, fear damp, development not very rapid, incubation rare, flesh delicate.

24. Delicate race, grass soil, development middling, incubation nil, flesh good.

25. Very delicate breed, dry soil, development middling, incubation pretty good.

26. Delicate, dry soil, development middling, incubation good, should not be [illegible].

27. Sandy soil, development middling, incubation indifferent, flesh good.

28. Very hardy race in any climate, develop rapidly, excellent incubation, flesh very bad.

THE "POOR MAN'S REGION," in the Pine Barrens of the Southern States, is a belt of country more than seventeen hundred miles long and about one hundred and seventy miles broad, stretching from Richmond, Va., along the Atlantic and Gulf coasts, to beyond the western bank of Louisiana. The soil is sandy and the principal tree is the long-leaf pine. These forests, while affording a valuable article of lumber, also yield pitch, tar and turpentine.

THE first proposer of secession in the United States Congress was Josiah Quincy, of Massachusetts, in 1811, who said that, if Louisiana were admitted into the Union, "it will be the right of all and the duty of some to definitely prepare for a separation, amicably if they can, violently if they must." Mr. Poindexter, of Mississippi, called him to order, appealing to the Speaker of the House; but on appeal the Speaker's decision was reversed, and Mr. Quincy sustained by a vote of fifty-three ayes to fifty-six noes, on the point of order.

DUCKS, GEESE AND TURKEYS.

Breeds.	Live weight in pounds.	Live weight of Hen	Age at maturity, mos.	Cost of raising to maturity.	Annual cost of keeping.	Av. No. of eggs laid per year.
Ducks, common	3	3	10	75	1.00	60
Ducks, Aylesbury	7	6	10	1.00	1.00	60
Ducks, Cayuga	6	6½	10	94	1.00	1.25
Ducks, Pekin	6	6¾	14	1.00	1.00	75
Ducks, Rouen	7¼	7½	13	1.00	1.00	80
Geese, common	8	7	12	1.20	1.50	30
Geese, African	16	18	24	1.50	2.08	30
Geese, Egyptian	7	8	12	1.50	1.50	40
Geese, Embden	18	15	30	1.75	2.50	25
Geese, Toulouse	22	20	28	2.00	2.00	40
Turkeys, common	15	10	15	1.25	1.56	50
Turkeys, black	15	12	18	1.55	1.75	50
Turkeys, bronze	24	15	30	2.00	2.50	50
Turkeys, buff	15	12	24	1.25	1.50	50
Turkeys, Narragansett	22	14	30	1.15	1.28	80

The annual supply of eggs in the United States is estimated at over [illegible] dozen, and, at the low price of fifteen cents per dozen, represents a value of over $150,000,000—double the value of the product of our silver mines.

Fate of the Apostles.

The following brief history of the fate of the Apostles may be new to those whose reading has not been evangelical:

St. Matthew is supposed to have suffered martyrdom or was slain with the sword at the city of Ethiopia.

St. Mark was dragged through the streets of Alexandria, in Egypt, till he expired.

St. Luke was hanged upon an olive tree in Greece.

St. John was put into a caldron of boiling oil at Rome and escaped death. He afterward died a natural death at Ephesus in Asia.

St. James the Great was beheaded at Jerusalem.

St. James the Less was thrown from a pinnacle or wing of the temple and then beaten to death with a fuller's club.

St. Philip was hanged up against a pillar at Hierapolis, a city of Phrygia.

St. Bartholomew was flayed alive by the command of a barbarous king.

St. Andrew was bound to a cross, whence he preached unto the people till he expired.

St. Thomas was run through the body with a lance at Coromandel, in the East Indies.

St. Jude was shot to death with arrows.

St. Simon Zealot was crucified in Persia.

St. Matthias was first stoned and then beheaded.

St. Barnabas was stoned to death by Jews at Salonica.

St. Paul was beheaded at Rome by the tyrant Nero.

How to Tell the Age of a Horse.

The safest way of determining the age of a horse is by the appearance of the teeth, which undergo certain changes in the course of years.

Eight to fourteen days after birth the first middle nippers of the set of milk teeth are cut (Fig. 1). Four to six weeks afterwards the pair next to them (Fig. 2), and finally, after six or eight months, the last (Fig. 3).

All these milk teeth have a well defined body and neck, and a slender fang, and on their front surface grooves or furrows, which disappear from the middle nippers at the end of one year, from the next pair in two years, and from the incisive teeth (corner) in three years.

At the age of two the nippers become loose and fall out, in their places appear two permanent teeth, with deep, black cavities, and full, sharp edges (Fig. 4).

At the age of three, the next pair (Fig. 5) fall out.

At four years old, the corner teeth fall out (Fig. 6).

At five years old, the horse has his permanent set of teeth.

The teeth grow in length as the horse advances in years, but at the same time his teeth are worn away by use about one-twelfth of an inch every year, so that the black cavities of the center nippers below disappear in the sixth year (Fig. 7), those of the next pair in the seventh year (Fig. 8), and those of the corner teeth in the eighth year (Fig. 9). Also the outer corner teeth of upper and lower jaw just meet at eight years of age.

At nine years old, cups leave the two center nippers above, and each of the two upper corner teeth has a little sharp projection at the extreme outer corner (Fig. 10).

At the age of ten, the cups disappear from the adjoining teeth.

At the age of eleven, the cups disappear from the corner teeth above, and are only indicated by brownish spots.

The oval form becomes broader, and changes, from the twelfth to the sixteenth year, more and more into a triangular form, and the teeth lose, finally, with the twentieth year, all regularity. There is nothing remaining in the teeth that can afterwards clearly show the age of the horse, or justify the most experienced examiner in giving a positive opinion.

The tushes, or canine teeth, conical in shape, with a sharp point, and curved, are cut between the third and fourth year, their points become more and more rounded until the ninth year, and after that, more and more dull in the course of years, and lose, finally, all regular shape. Mares have, frequently, no tushes, or they very faintly indicated.

Age of Sheep and Goats. At one year old they have eight front teeth of uniform size. At two years the two middle ones are supplanted by two large ones. At three a small tooth appears on each side. At four there are six large teeth. At five all the front teeth are large, and at six all begin to get worn.

Age of Cattle. A cow's horn is supposed to furnish a correct indication of the age of the animal, but this is not always true. For ordinary purposes, however, the following will be found approximately correct: At two years of age a circle of thicker matter begins to form on the animal's horn, which becomes clearly defined at three years of age, when another circle begins to form, and an additional circle every year thereafter. The cow's age, then, can be determined by adding two to the number of circles. The rings on a bull's horns do not show themselves until he is five years old—so in the case of a bull five must be added to the number of rings.

MEDICINES FOR THE HORSE.

Name of Drug.	Action and Use.	Dose.	Antidote.
Aloes	Laxative and Tonic	½ to 1 oz	
Alum	Astringent	2 to 3 drs	
Anise Seed	Aromatic and Stomachic	½ to 1 oz	
Aqua Ammonia	Stimulant and Antacid	1 to 4 drs	Vinegar
Arsenic	Alterative and Tonic. For Paralysis, Mange, etc.	2 to 5 grs	Magnesia and oil
Assafœtida	Antispasmodic. Coughs, etc.	2 to 3 drs	
Bicarbonate of Potash	Diuretic and Antacid. For Rheumatism	2 to 4 drs	Vinegar and raw Linseed Oil
Belladonna	For Lockjaw, Diarrhea, etc.	½ to 1 dr	
Black Antimony	Promotes the Secretions	¼ to ½ dr	Infusion of oak bark. Give also Linseed Oil
Blue Vitriol	Astringent and Tonic	½ to 1 dr	Eggs, Milk, etc.
Calomel	Cathartic	20 to 40 grs	Eggs and Milk
Camphor	Antispasmodic	½ to 1 dr	
Cantharides	Diuretic and Stimulant	3 to 6 grs	
Carbolic Acid	Externally used Disinfectant		Eggs, magnesia, gruel
Castor Oil	Cathartic	½ to 1 pt	
Cayenne	Stimulant and Carminative	5 to 15 grs	
Chlorate of Potash	Diuretic. For Bleeding, etc.	½ to 2 drs	
Copperas	Tonic and Astringent	½ to 1½ drs	
Croton Oil	Powerful Purgative	10 to 15 drops	Opium
Digitalis Leaf	Sedative and Diuretic	10 to 20 grs	Stimulants
Epsom Salts	Cathartic and Febrifuge	1 to 8 oz	
Ether	Antispasmodic	½ to 2 oz	
Fowler's Solution	Used for Skin Diseases	1 to 4 drs	Hydrated Peroxide of iron
Gentian Root	Tonic	1 to 4 drs	
Ginger	Tonic, Stimulant & Stomachic. For Flatulent Colic, Dyspepsia, etc.	2 to 4 drs	
Glauber's Salts	Cathartic	4 to 12 drs	
Iodide of Potassium	Diuretic and Alterative. For Rheumatism, Dropsy, Enlarged Glands, etc.	½ to 1½ drs	Give freely starch or flour, with water largely
Linseed Oil, Raw	Cathartic and Nutritive	1 to 2 pts	
Magnesia	For using as an Antacid and Laxative	½ to 1 oz	
Mercurial Ointment	For Mange, Itch, Lice, and other Parasites		Whites of eggs with milk, freely
Nux Vomica	Nervous Stimulant. For Paralysis	15 to 25 grs	[illegible], followed quickly by [illegible], dissolved in water
Opium	Anodyne and Antispasmodic. Given in Colic, Inflammation of Bowels, Diarrhea, etc.	½ to 2 drs	Belladonna, strong coffee, brandy & ammonia. Dash cold water on and keep horse moving
Prepared Chalk	Antacid	½ to 1 oz	
Quinine	Tonic During Convalescence	15 to 30 grs	
Saltpetre	Diuretic and Febrifuge	1 to 2 drs	Linseed oil largely, etc.
Soda Bicarb.	Similar to Bicarb. Potash	4 to 8 drs	
Soda Sulphite	Antiseptic and Alterative. For Blood Diseases	½ to 1 oz	
Sulphite of Lime	Antacid. An antidote in poisoning by acids	4 to 6 drs	
Spts of Chloroform	Anodyne & Antispasmodic	1 to 2 ozs	

MEDICINES FOR THE HORSE.—*Continued.*

Name of Drug.	Action and Use.	Dose.	Antidote.
Strychnia	Tonic & Stimulant. For Paralysis	¼ to 1 gr	Tobacco
Sulphur	Alterative and Laxative. Skin Diseases, Rheumatism	½ to 2 oz	
Sweet Spts. Nitre	Diuretic and Diaphoretic	½ to 1½ oz	
Tannic Acid	Astringent	20 to 40 grs	
Tartar Emetic	Sedative and Alterative	¼ to ½ dr	Tannic Acid
Tin. Aconite Root	Sedative. For Lung Fevers, etc.	5 to 35 drops	Small doses of Nux Vomica, stimulants largely, & keep moving
Tin. Cantharides	Stimulant and Tonic	1 to 4 drs	
Tincture Ergot	Parturient	1 to 2 oz	
Tincture Iodine	Used externally		
Tincture Iron	Tonic and Astringent. For Typhoid Diseases	½ to 1 oz	
Tr. Nux Vomica	Tonic. Stimulant in Paralysis and Dyspepsia	1 to 4 drs	See Nux Vomica
Tincture Opium	Anodyne and Antispasmodic	1 to 2 ozs	See Opium
White Vitriol	Astringent. For Wounds, Cuts & Sores, in solution	1 to 2 drs	Milk, eggs & flour

For a colt one month old, give one twenty-fourth of the full dose for an adult horse; if given about three months old, one-twelfth; six months old, one-sixth; one year old, one-third; two years old, one-half; three years old, three-fourths.

The Seven Bibles of the World

Are the Koran of the Mohammedans, the *Eddas* of the Scandinavians, the *Try Pitikes* of the Buddhists, the *Five Kings* of the Chinese, the Three Vedas of the Hindoos, the Zendavesta, and the Scriptures of the Christians. The Koran is the most recent of these seven Bibles, and not older than the seventh century of our era. It is a compound of quotations from the Old and New Testaments, the Talmud, and the Gospel of St. Barnabas. The Eddas of the Scandinavians were first published in the fourteenth century. The Pitikes of the Buddhists contain sublime morals and pure aspirations, and their author lived and died in the sixth century before Christ. There is nothing of excellence in these sacred books not found in the Bible. The sacred writings of the Chinese are called the Five Kings, king meaning web of cloth, or the warp that keeps the threads in their place. They contain the best sayings of the best sages on the ethico-political duties of life. These sayings cannot be traced to a period higher than the eleventh century B.C. The Three Vedas are the most ancient books of the Hindoos, and it is the opinion of Max Muller, Wilson, Johnson, and Whitney that they are not older than eleven centuries B.C. The Zendavesta of the Persians is the grandest of all the sacred books next to our Bible. Zoroaster, whose sayings it contains, was born in the twelfth century B.C. Moses lived and wrote his Pentateuch fifteen centuries B.C., and, therefore, has a clear margin of 300 years older than the most ancient of the sacred writings.

CANARY BIRDS.

HOW TO KEEP THEM HEALTHY AND IN GOOD SONG.

Place the cage so that no draught of air can strike the bird.

Give nothing to healthy birds but rape, hemp, canary seed, water, cuttle-fish bone, and gravel paper or sand on floor of cage.

A bath three times a week.

The room should not be overheated.

When moulting keep warm and avoid all draughts of air.

Give plenty of German summer rape seed. A little hard boiled egg mixed with cracker grated fine, once or twice a week, is excellent.

Feed at a certain hour in the morning.

DISEASES AND CURES.

Husk or Asthma. The curatives are aperients, such as endive, water cresses, bread and milk and red pepper.

Pip. Mix red pepper, butter and garlic and swab out the throat.

Sweating. Wash the hen in salt and water, and dry rapidly.

Costiveness. Plenty of green food and fruit.

Obstruction of the Rump Gland. Pierce with a needle. Press the inflamed matter out, and drop fine sugar over the wound.

Lice. Keep a saucer of fresh water in the cage and the bird will free itself.

Overgrown Claws or Beak. Pare carefully with a sharp knife.

Moulting. Give plenty of good food and keep warm. Saffron and a rusty nail put in their drinking water is excellent.

Loss of Voice. Feed with paste of bread, lettuce and rape seed with yolk of egg. Whisky and sugar is an excellent remedy.

What a Horse Can Draw.

On metal rails a horse can draw:

One and two-thirds times as much as on asphalt pavement.
Three and one-third times as much as on good Belgian blocks.
Five times as much as on ordinary Belgian blocks.
Seven times as much as on good cobble-stone.
Thirteen times as much as on ordinary cobble-stone.
Twenty times as much as on an earth road.
Forty times as much as on sand.

A superb compilation of engineering maxims states that a horse can drag, as compared with what he can carry on his back, in the following proportions: On the worst earthen road, three times as much; on a good macadamized road, nine; on plank, twenty-five; on a stone trackway, thirty-three; and on a good railway, fifty-four times as much.

Test for Glue.

The following simple and easy test for glue is given: A weighed piece of glue (say one-third of an ounce) is suspended in water for twenty-four hours, the temperature of which is not above fifty degrees Fahrenheit. The coloring material sinks, and the glue swells from the absorption of the water. The glue is then taken out and weighed; the greater the increase in weight the better the glue. If it then be dried perfectly and weighed again, the weight of the coloring matter can be learned from the difference between this and the original weight.

WEIGHTS AND MEASURES.

TROY WEIGHT.—24 grains make 1 pennyweight, 20 pennyweights make 1 ounce. By this weight gold, silver and jewels only are weighed. The ounce and pound in this are same as in Apothecaries' weight.

APOTHECARIES' WEIGHT.—20 grains make one scruple; 3 scruples make 1 dram, 8 drams make 1 ounce, 12 ounces make 1 pound.

AVOIRDUPOIS WEIGHT.—16 drams make 1 ounce, 16 ounces make one pound, 25 pounds make 1 quarter, 4 quarters make 1 hundredweight. 2,000 pounds make 1 ton.

DRY MEASURE.—2 pints make 1 quart, 8 quarts make 1 peck, 4 pecks make 1 bushel, 36 bushels make 1 chaldron.

LIQUID OR WINE MEASURE.—4 gills make 1 pint, 2 pints make 1 quart, 4 quarts make 1 gallon, 31½ gallons make 1 barrel, 2 barrels make 1 hogshead.

TIME MEASURE.—60 seconds make 1 minute, 60 minutes make 1 hour, 24 hours make 1 day, 7 days make 1 week, 4 weeks make 1 lunar month, 28, 29, 30 or 31 days make 1 calendar month (30 days make a month in computing interest), 52 weeks and 1 day, or 12 calendar months, make 1 year, 365 days, 5 hours, 48 minutes and 49 seconds make 1 solar year.

CIRCULAR MEASURE.—60 seconds make 1 minute, 60 minutes make 1 degree, 30 degrees make 1 sign, 90 degrees make 1 quadrant, 4 quadrants or 360 degrees make 1 circle.

LONG MEASURE—DISTANCE.—3 barleycorns 1 inch, 12 inches 1 foot, 3 feet 1 yard, 5½ yards 1 rod, 40 rods 1 furlong, 8 furlongs 1 mile.

CLOTH MEASURE.—2¼ inches 1 nail, 4 nails 1 quarter, 4 quarters 1 yard.

MISCELLANEOUS.—3 inches one palm, 4 inches 1 hand, 6 inches 1 span, 18 inches 1 cubit, 21.8 inches 1 Bible cubit, 2½ feet 1 military pace.

SQUARE MEASURE.—144 square inches 1 square foot, 9 square feet 1 square yard, 30¼ square yards 1 square rod, 40 square rods 1 rood, 4 roods 1 acre.

SURVEYORS' MEASURE.—7.92 inches 1 link, 25 links 1 rod, 4 rods 1 chain, 10 square chains or 160 square rods 1 acre, 640 acres 1 square mile.

CUBIC MEASURE.—1,728 cubic inches 1 cubic foot, 27 cubic feet 1 cubic yard, 128 cubic feet 1 cord (wood), 40 cubic feet 1 ton (shipping), 2,150.42 cubic inches 1 standard bushel, 268.8 cubic inches 1 standard gallon, 1 cubic foot four-fifths of a bushel.

METRIC WEIGHTS.—10 milligrams 1 centigram, 10 centigrams 1 decigram, 10 decigrams 1 gram, 10 grams 1 dekagram, 10 dekagrams 1 hektogram, 10 hektograms 1 kilogram.

METRIC MEASURES.—(One milliliter—Cubic centimeter.)—10 milliliters 1 centiliter, 10 centiliters 1 deciliter, 10 deciliters 1 liter, 10 liters 1 dekaliter, 10 dekaliters 1 hektoliter, 10 hektoliters 1 kiloliter.

METRIC LENGTHS.—10 millimeters 1 centimeter, 10 centimeters 1 decimeter, 10 decimeters 1 meter, 10 meters 1 dekameter, 10 dekameters 1 hektometer, 10 hektometers 1 kilometer.

Relative Value of Apothecaries' and Imperial Measure.

Apothecaries.	Imperial.							
1 gallon equals	6 pints,	13	ounces,	1	drams,	23	minims.
1 pint "		16	"	5	"	18	"
1 fluid ounce equals		1	"	0	"	20	"
1 fluid dram "				1	"	2½	"

Handy Metric Tables.

The following tables give the equivalents of both the metric and common systems, and will be found convenient for reference:

	Approximate Equivalent.	Accurate Equivalent.
1 inch .... (length)	2½ centimeters	2.540
1 centimeter	0.4 inch	0.393
1 yard	1 meter	0.914
1 meter (39.37 inches)	1 yard	1.093
1 foot	30 centimeters	30.479
1 kilometer (1,000 meters)	⅝ mile	0.621
1 mile	1⅗ kilometers	1.609
1 gramme .... (weight)	15⅖ grains	15.432
1 grain	0.065 gramme	0.065
1 kilogramme (1,000 grammes)	2.2 pounds avoirdupois	2.204
1 pound avoirdupois	½ kilogramme	0.453
1 ounce avoirdupois (437½ grains)	28⅓ grammes	28.349
1 ounce troy, or apothecary (480 grains)	31 grammes	31.103
1 cubic centimeter .... (bulk)	1/16 cubic inch	0.061
1 cubic inch	16⅓ cubic centimeters	16.386
1 liter (1,000 cubic centimeters)	1 United States standard quart	0.946
1 United States quart	1 liter	1.057
1 fluid ounce	29½ cubic centimeters	29.570
1 hectare (10,000 square meters) (surface)	2½ acres	2.471
1 acre	0.4 hectare	0.405

It may not be generally known that we have in the nickel five-cent piece of our coinage a key to the tables of linear measures and weights. The diameter of this coin is two centimeters, and its weight is five grammes. Five of them placed in a row will, of course, give the length of the decimeter, and two of them will weigh a decagram. As the kiloliter is a cubic meter, the key of the measure of length is also the key to the measures of capacity. Any person, therefore, who is fortunate enough to own a five-cent nickel, may carry in his pocket the entire metric system of weights and measures.

Handy Weights and Measures.

One quart of wheat flour is one pound. One quart of corn meal weighs eighteen ounces. One quart of butter, soft, weighs fourteen to sixteen ounces. One quart of brown sugar weighs from a pound to a pound and a quarter, according to dampness. One quart of white sugar weighs 2 pounds. Ten medium-sized eggs weigh one pound. A tablespoonful of salt is one ounce. Eight tablespoonfuls make a gill. Two gills or sixteen tablespoonfuls are half a pint. Sixty drops are one teaspoonful. Four tablespoonfuls are one wineglassful. Twelve tablespoonfuls are one teacupful. Sixteen tablespoonfuls, or half a pint, are one tumblerful.

The Meaning of Measures.—A square mile is equal to 640 acres. A square acre is 208.71 feet on one side. An acre is 43,560 square feet. A league, 3 miles. A span, 10⅞ inches. A hand, 4 inches. A palm, 3 inches. A great cubit, 11 inches. A fathom, 6 feet. A mile, 5,280 feet.

Domestic and Drop Measures Approximated.—A teaspoonful, one fluid drachm, 4 grams. A dessertspoonful, two fluid drachms, 8 grams. A tablespoonful, half fluid ounce, 15 grams. A wineglassful, two fluid ounces, 64 grams. A tumblerful, half pint, 256 grams.

The original Mrs. Partington was a respectable old lady who lived at Sidmouth, in Devonshire, England. Her cottage was on the beach, and during a terrible storm (November, 1824) the sea rose to such a height as every now and then to invade the old lady's residence. The old lady persistently mopped out the water with such help as she could command, until finally she was compelled to retreat to an upper story.

PRACTICAL CALCULATIONS.

Short Cuts in Arithmetic.—Handy Tables for Ready Reckoning:

To Ascertain the Weight of Cattle.—Measure the girt close behind the shoulder, and the length from the fore part of the shoulder-blade along the back to the bone at the tail, which is in a vertical line with the buttock, both in feet. Multiply the square of the girt, expressed in feet, by five times the length, and divide the product by seven; the quotient is the weight, nearly, of the four quarters, in pounds avoirdupois. It is to be observed, however, that in very fat cattle the four quarters will be about one-twentieth more, while in those in a very lean state they will be one-twentieth less than the weight obtained by the rule.

Rules for Measuring Corn in Crib, Vegetables, etc., and Hay in Mow.—This rule will apply to a crib of any size or kind. Two cubic feet of good, sound, dry corn in the ear will make a bushel of shelled corn. To get, then, the quantity of shelled corn in a crib of corn in the ear, measure the length, breadth and height of the crib, inside the rail; multiply the length by the breadth and the product by the height; then divide the product by two, and you have the number of bushels of shelled corn in the crib.

To find the number of bushels of apples, potatoes, etc., in a bin, multiply the length, breadth and thickness together, and this product by eight, and point off one figure in the product for decimals.

To find the amount of hay in a mow, allow 512 cubic feet for a ton, and it will come out very generally correct.

To Measure Bulk Wood.—To measure a pile of wood, multiply the length by the width, and that product by the height, which will give the number of cubic feet. Divide that product by 128, and the quotient will be the number of cords. A standard cord of wood, it must be remembered, is four feet wide; that is, the wood must be four feet long. Farmers usually go by surface measure, calling a pile of stove wood eight feet long and four feet high a cord. For such measurement thirty-two feet would be the divisor.

How to Measure a Tree.—Very many persons, when looking for a stick of timber, such as a spar is, cannot estimate either the height of the tree or the length of timber it will cut. The following rule will enable any one to approximate nearly to the length from the ground to any position desired on the tree: Take a stake, say six feet in length, and place it against the tree you wish to measure. Then step back some rods, twenty or more if you can, from which to do the measuring. At this point a light pole and a measuring rule are required. The pole is raised between the eyes and the tree, and the rule is brought into position against the pole. Then by sighting and observing what length of the rule is required to cover the stake at the tree, and what the entire tree, dividing the latter length by the former and multiplying by the number of feet the stake is long, you reach the approximate height of the tree. For example, if the stake at the tree be six feet above ground and one inch on the rule corresponds exactly with this, and if then the entire height of the tree corresponds exactly with say nine inches on the rule, this would show the tree to possess a full height of fifty-four feet. In practice it will thus be found an easy matter to learn the approximate height of any tree, building, or other such object.

To Measure Casks or Barrels.—Find mean diameter by adding to head diameter two-thirds (if staves are but slightly curved, three-fifths) of difference between head and bung diameters, and dividing by two. Multiply square of mean diameter in inches by .7854, and the product by the height of the cask in inches. The result will be the number of cubic inches. Divide by 231 for standard or wine gallons, and by 282 for beer gallons.

Grain Measure.—To find the capacity of a bin or wagon-bed, multiply the cubic feet by 8 (tenths). For great accuracy, add ⅜ of a bushel for every 300 cubic feet. To find the cubic feet, multiply the length, width and depth together.

Cistern Measure.—To find the capacity of a round cistern or tank, multiply the square of the average diameter by the depth, and take 5⅞ of

PRACTICAL CALCULATIONS.

the product. For great accuracy, multiply by .1805. For square cisterns or tanks, multiply the cubic feet by .1[illegible]. The result is the contents in barrels.

LAND MEASURE.—To find the number of acres in a body of land, multiply the length by the width (in rods), and divide the product by 160. When the opposite sides are unequal, add them, and take half the sum for the mean length or width.

MEASURES OF CAPACITY.—The following table, showing contents of boxes, will often be found convenient, taking inside dimensions:

[illegible] in. x [illegible] in. x [illegible] will require a barrel of 31½ gallons.
[illegible] in. x [illegible] in. x [illegible] in. will contain 10 gallons.
8½ in. x 7 in. x 4 in. will contain a gallon.
4 in. x 4 in. x 3.6 in. will contain a quart.
24 in. x 28 in. x 16 in. will contain 5 bushels.
16 in. x 12 in. x 11.2 in. will contain a bushel.
12 in. x 11.2 in. x 8 in. will contain a half bushel.
7 in. x 6.4 in. x 12 in. will contain a peck.
8.4 in. x 8 in. x 4 in. will contain a half peck, or 4 dry quarts.
6 in. x 5.6 in. and 4 in. deep, will contain a half gallon.
4 in. x 4 in. and 4.2 in. deep, will contain a quart.

Food for Stock.

One hundred pounds of good hay for stock are equal to: Beets, white silesia, 669; turnips, 469; rye straw, 429; clover, red, green, 373; carrots, 371; mangolds, 368; potatoes, kept in pit, 350; oat straw, 347; potatoes, [illegible]; carrot leaves, [illegible]; hay, English, 100; Lucerne, 89; clover, red, dry, 88; buckwheat, 78½; corn, 62½; oats, 59; barley, 58; rye, 53½; wheat, 44½; oilcake, linseed, 43; peas, dry, 37½; beans, 28.

Number of Shrubs, Plants or Trees in an Acre.

Distance apart.	No. of Plants.	Distance apart.	No. of Plants.	Distance apart.	No. of Plants.
1 by 1	43,560	5 by 2	4,356	15 by 15	193
1½ " 1½	19,360	5 " 3	2,904	16 " 16	170
2 " 1	21,780	5 " 4	2,178	17 " 17	150
2 " 2	10,890	5 " 5	1,742	18 " 18	134
2½ " 2½	6,969	5½ " 5½	1,417	19 " 19	120
3 " 1	14,520	6 " 6	1,210	20 " 20	108
3 " 2	7,260	6½ " 6½	1,031	24 " 24	75
3 " 3	4,840	7 " 7	888	25 " 25	69
3½ " 3½	3,555	8 " 8	680	27 " 27	60
4 " 1	10,890	9 " 9	537	30 " 30	48
4 " 2	5,445	10 " 10	435	40 " 40	27
4 " 3	3,630	11 " 11	360	50 " 50	17
4 " 4	2,722	12 " 12	302	60 " 60	12
4½ " 4½	2,151	13 " 13	257	66 " 66	10
5 " 1	8,712	14 " 14	222		

The city of Ghent, Belgium, stands on twenty-six islands, connected with each other by eighty bridges. The city of Venice is built on eighty islands, connected by nearly 400 bridges. In Venice canals serve for streets and gondolas for carriages.

Bricks and common pottery owe their red color to the iron naturally contained in the clay of which they are formed, the iron, by the action of the heat, being converted into red oxide of iron. Some varieties of clay, like that found near Milwaukee, contain little or no iron, and bricks made from such clay are consequently of a light yellow color.

Quantity of Seeds Required for Planting.

	Seeds per ounce.	Length of Drill, per oz.	Vitality, Years.
Asparagus	1,300 to 1,800	50 feet	4 to 5
Beet	1,200 to 1,500	100 "	6 " 8
Carrot	20,000 to 24,000	400 "	4 " 5
Cabbage, Cauliflower	8,500 to 12,000	Transplant	4 " 5
Celery	50,000 to 70,000	Transplant	3 " 5
Egg plant	6,300 to 6,000	Transplant	6 " 8
Endive	20,000 to 24,000	Transplant	8 " 10
Lettuce	25,000 to 30,000	150 feet	5 " 8
Okra	500 to 600	50 "	3 " 5
Onion	7,000 to 8,000	100 "	2 " 3
Parsnip	5,000 to 6,000	200 "	2 " 3
Radish	3,000 to 4,000	100 "	4 " 5
Salsify	2,500 to 3,000	150 "	2 " 3
Spinach	2,500 to 3,000	100 "	4 " 5
Tomato	About 20,000	Transplant	4 " 5
Turnip	8,000 to 12,000	200 feet	4 " 5

Number of Pounds to the Bushel, Legal Weight, in the Different States.

STATES.	Wheat.	Rye.	Oats.	Barley.	Buckwheat.	Shelled Corn.	Corn in the Ear.	Corn Meal.	Potatoes.	Sweet Potatoes.	Onions.	Beans.	Peas.	Dried Apples.	Anthracite Coal.
Arkansas	[illegible]	[illegible]	[illegible]	[illegible]	[illegible]	...	70	50	60	50	57	60	60	24	80
California	[illegible]	[illegible]	[illegible]	[illegible]	[illegible]	52	...	...	...	...	...	...	...	...	...
Connecticut	[illegible]	[illegible]	[illegible]	[illegible]	[illegible]	56	...	50	60	...	50	60	60	...	...
Georgia	[illegible]	[illegible]	[illegible]	[illegible]	[illegible]	56	70	48	60	55	57	60	60	24	80
Illinois	[illegible]	[illegible]	[illegible]	[illegible]	[illegible]	56	70	48	60	55	57	60	...	24	80
Indiana	[illegible]	[illegible]	[illegible]	[illegible]	[illegible]	56	68	50	60	...	48	60	...	25	...
Iowa	[illegible]	[illegible]	[illegible]	[illegible]	[illegible]	56	70	...	60	46	57	60	...	24	80
Kansas	[illegible]	[illegible]	[illegible]	[illegible]	[illegible]	56	70	50	60	50	57	60	...	24	80
Kentucky	[illegible]	[illegible]	[illegible]	[illegible]	[illegible]	56	70	50	60	55	57	60	60	24	76
Maine	[illegible]	[illegible]	[illegible]	[illegible]	[illegible]	56	...	50	60	...	52	64	60	...	...
Massachusetts	[illegible]	[illegible]	[illegible]	[illegible]	[illegible]	56	...	50	60	55	52	...	...	...	...
Michigan	[illegible]	[illegible]	[illegible]	[illegible]	[illegible]	56	70	50	60	56	54	60	60	28	...
Minnesota	[illegible]	[illegible]	[illegible]	[illegible]	[illegible]	56	...	...	60	...	...	...	...	28	...
Missouri	[illegible]	[illegible]	[illegible]	[illegible]	[illegible]	56	...	...	60	...	57	60	...	24	...
New Hampshire	[illegible]	[illegible]	[illegible]	[illegible]	[illegible]	56	...	50	60	...	...	60	60	...	...
New Jersey	[illegible]	[illegible]	[illegible]	[illegible]	[illegible]	56	...	...	60	54	57	60	60	25	...
New York	[illegible]	[illegible]	[illegible]	[illegible]	[illegible]	58	...	...	60	...	...	62	60	...	...
North Carolina	[illegible]	[illegible]	[illegible]	[illegible]	[illegible]	54	...	46	...	...	...	...	60	...	...
Ohio	[illegible]	[illegible]	[illegible]	[illegible]	[illegible]	56	70	...	60	50	50	60	60	22	...
Pennsylvania	[illegible]	[illegible]	[illegible]	[illegible]	[illegible]	56	...	...	56	...	...	...	...	...	...
Rhode Island	[illegible]	[illegible]	[illegible]	[illegible]	[illegible]	56	...	50	...	...	50	...	...	...	...
South Carolina	[illegible]	[illegible]	[illegible]	[illegible]	[illegible]	56	70	50	60	50	57	60	60	25	...
Tennessee	[illegible]	[illegible]	[illegible]	[illegible]	[illegible]	56	72	50	60	50	56	60	60	26	...
Vermont	[illegible]	[illegible]	[illegible]	[illegible]	[illegible]	56	...	...	60	...	52	60	60	...	...
Virginia	[illegible]	[illegible]	[illegible]	[illegible]	[illegible]	56	70	50	60	55	57	60	60	28	80
Wisconsin	[illegible]	[illegible]	[illegible]	[illegible]	[illegible]	56	58	...	60	...	50	60	...	28	...

Ants never sleep. Emerson mentions this as "a recently observed fact."

Barbed Wire Required for Fences.

Estimated number of pounds of barbed wire required to fence space or distances mentioned, with one, two or three lines of wire, based upon each pound of wire measuring one rod (16½ feet).

	1 Line	2 Lines	3 Lines
1 square acre	50⅔ lbs.	101⅓ lbs.	152 lbs.
1 side of a square acre	12⅔ lbs.	25⅓ lbs.	38 lbs.
1 square half-acre	36 lbs.	72 lbs.	108 lbs.
1 square mile	1280 lbs.	2560 lbs.	3840 lbs.
1 side of a square mile	320 lbs.	640 lbs.	960 lbs.
1 rod in length	1 lb.	2 lbs.	3 lbs.
100 rods in length	100 lbs.	200 lbs.	300 lbs.
100 feet in length	6 1-16 lbs.	12⅛ lbs.	18 3-16 lbs.

To Measure Corn or Similar Commodity on a Floor.—Pile up the commodity in the form of a cone; find the diameter in feet; multiply the square of the diameter by .7854, and the product by one-third the height of the cone in feet; from this last product deduct one-fifth of itself, or multiply it by .80364, and the result will be the number of bushels.

Contents of Fields and Lots.—An acre is 43,560 square feet. The following table will assist farmers in making an accurate estimate of the amount of land in different fields under cultivation:

10 rods	×	16 rods	= 1	A.	105 ft.	×	105 7/10 ft.	= ¼	A.
8 "	×	20 "	= 1	"	25 "	×	100 "	= .0574	"
5 "	×	32 "	= 1	"	25 "	×	110 "	= .0631	"
4 "	×	40 "	= 1	"	25 "	×	120 "	= .0688	"
5 yards	×	968 "	= 1	"	25 "	×	125 "	= .0717	"
10 "	×	484 yds.	= 1	"	25 "	×	150 "	= .109	"
20 "	×	242 "	= 1	"	2178 square feet			= .05	"
40 "	×	121 "	= 1	"	4356 "		"	= .10	"
80 "	×	60½ "	= 1	"	6534 "		"	= .15	"
70 "	×	69 1/7 "	= 1	"	8712 "		"	= .20	"
220 feet	×	198 feet	= 1	"	10890 "		"	= .25	"
440 "	×	99 "	= 1	"	13068 "		"	= .30	"
110 "	×	396 "	= 1	"	15246 "		"	= .35	"
60 "	×	726 "	= 1	"	17424 "		"	= .40	"
120 "	×	363 "	= 1	"	19602 "		"	= .45	"
240 "	×	181½ ft.	= 1	"	21780 "		"	= .50	"
200 "	×	108 9/10 "	= ½	"	32670 "		"	= .75	"
100 "	×	108 9/10 "	= ¼	"	[illegible] "		"	= [illegible]	"

There is a lake of pitch in the island of Trinidad, about a mile and a half in circumference. While the substance near the shores is sufficiently hard to bear [illegible], [illegible] and quadrupeds, it grows soft and warm toward the center, and there it is in a boiling state.

GRADE PER MILE, TIMBER, ETC.

Grade per Mile.—The following table will show the grade per mile as thus indicated:

An inclination of—

1 foot in 16	is 330 feet per mile	1 foot in 40	is 132 feet per mile
1 " 20	is 264 " "	1 " 50	is 106 " "
1 " 25	is 211 " "	1 " 100	is 53 " "
1 " 30	is 176 " "	1 " 125	is 42 " "
1 " 35	is 151 " "		

To Find the Quantity of Lumber in a Log.—Multiply the diameter in inches at the small end by one-half the number of inches, and this product by the length of the log in feet, which last product divide by 12.

Example. How many feet of lumber can be made from a log 30 inches in diameter and 14 feet long?

30 × 15 = 450 × 14 = 6300 ÷ 12 = 525 feet. Ans.

To Tell the Soundness of Timber.—Apply the ear to the middle of one of the ends, while another party strikes the other end. The blow will be clearly and distinctly heard, however long the beam may be, if the wood is sound and of good quality, but if decay has set in, the sound will be muffled and indistinct. The toughest part of a tree will always be found on the side next the north.

The Number of Cubic Feet in a Round Log of Uniform Diameter.—Square the diameter in inches, multiply by .7854, and multiply this product by the length in feet, divide by 144, and the quotient is the number of cubic feet.

Number of Cubic Feet in the Trunk of a Standing Tree.—Find the circumference in inches, divide by 4, square the quotient, multiply by the length in feet, divide by 144, deduct [illegible] for thickness of bark, and the result will be, approximately, the number of cubic feet.

Following are some curious facts about fishes. While naturalists have generally accepted Cuvier's view that the existence of fishes is strictly [illegible] and [illegible], recent observations tend to show that many fishes [illegible] sounds. The [illegible], the climbing perch of India, [illegible] and [illegible] considerable distances and is [illegible] to climb trees and bushes. At Tranquebar, Hindostan, [illegible] the strange spectacle of fish and shell-fish dwelling high on lofty trees. The perch [illegible] in pursuit of certain shell-fish which form his favorite food. Covered with viscid slime, he glides smoothly over the rough bark. Spines, which he may sheathe and unsheathe at will, serve him like hands to hang by, and with the aid of his fins and a powerful tail he pushes himself upward. One species of fish, the stickleback, are [illegible] build nests. There are several varieties of this fish, all natives of fresh water, with one or two exceptions. They are found in the Green River. The [illegible] is a sightless fish which grows in the dreary waters of the Mammoth Cave of Kentucky.

Abraham's purchase of the cave of Machpelah is the first recorded commercial transaction.

BOARD AND PLANK MEASUREMENT AT SIGHT.

This table gives the square feet and inches in boards or planks from 2 to 25 inches wide, and 4 to 20 feet long. If a board be longer than 20 feet, or wider than 25 inches, unite two of the numbers.

LENGTH. — WIDTH.	4 ft. ft. in.	5 ft. ft. in.	6 ft. ft. in.	7 ft. ft. in.	8 ft. ft. in.	9 ft. ft. in.	10 ft. ft. in.	11 ft. ft. in.	12 ft. ft. in.	13 ft. ft. in.	14 ft. ft. in.	15 ft. ft. in.	16 ft. ft. in.	17 ft. ft. in.	18 ft. ft. in.	19 ft. ft. in.	20 ft. ft. in.
2 in.	[illegible]	[illegible]	[illegible]	[illegible]	[illegible]	[illegible]	[illegible]	[illegible]	[illegible]	[illegible]	[illegible]	[illegible]	[illegible]	[illegible]	[illegible]	[illegible]	[illegible]
3 in.	[illegible]	[illegible]	[illegible]	[illegible]	[illegible]	[illegible]	[illegible]	[illegible]	[illegible]	[illegible]	[illegible]	[illegible]	[illegible]	[illegible]	[illegible]	[illegible]	[illegible]
4 in.	[illegible]	[illegible]	[illegible]	[illegible]	[illegible]	[illegible]	[illegible]	[illegible]	[illegible]	[illegible]	[illegible]	[illegible]	[illegible]	[illegible]	[illegible]	[illegible]	[illegible]
5 in.	[illegible]	[illegible]	[illegible]	[illegible]	[illegible]	[illegible]	[illegible]	[illegible]	[illegible]	[illegible]	[illegible]	[illegible]	[illegible]	[illegible]	[illegible]	[illegible]	[illegible]
6 in.	[illegible]	[illegible]	[illegible]	[illegible]	[illegible]	[illegible]	[illegible]	[illegible]	[illegible]	[illegible]	[illegible]	[illegible]	[illegible]	[illegible]	[illegible]	[illegible]	[illegible]
7 in.	[illegible]	[illegible]	[illegible]	[illegible]	[illegible]	[illegible]	[illegible]	[illegible]	[illegible]	[illegible]	[illegible]	[illegible]	[illegible]	[illegible]	[illegible]	[illegible]	[illegible]
8 in.	[illegible]	[illegible]	[illegible]	[illegible]	[illegible]	[illegible]	[illegible]	[illegible]	[illegible]	[illegible]	[illegible]	[illegible]	[illegible]	[illegible]	[illegible]	[illegible]	[illegible]
9 in.	[illegible]	[illegible]	[illegible]	[illegible]	[illegible]	[illegible]	[illegible]	[illegible]	[illegible]	[illegible]	[illegible]	[illegible]	[illegible]	[illegible]	[illegible]	[illegible]	[illegible]
10 in.	[illegible]	[illegible]	[illegible]	[illegible]	[illegible]	[illegible]	[illegible]	[illegible]	[illegible]	[illegible]	[illegible]	[illegible]	[illegible]	[illegible]	[illegible]	[illegible]	[illegible]
11 in.	[illegible]	[illegible]	[illegible]	[illegible]	[illegible]	[illegible]	[illegible]	[illegible]	[illegible]	[illegible]	[illegible]	[illegible]	[illegible]	[illegible]	[illegible]	[illegible]	[illegible]
12 in.	[illegible]	[illegible]	[illegible]	[illegible]	[illegible]	[illegible]	[illegible]	[illegible]	[illegible]	[illegible]	[illegible]	[illegible]	[illegible]	[illegible]	[illegible]	[illegible]	[illegible]
13 in.	[illegible]	[illegible]	[illegible]	[illegible]	[illegible]	[illegible]	[illegible]	[illegible]	[illegible]	[illegible]	[illegible]	[illegible]	[illegible]	[illegible]	[illegible]	[illegible]	[illegible]
14 in.	[illegible]	[illegible]	[illegible]	[illegible]	[illegible]	[illegible]	[illegible]	[illegible]	[illegible]	[illegible]	[illegible]	[illegible]	[illegible]	[illegible]	[illegible]	[illegible]	[illegible]
15 in.	[illegible]	[illegible]	[illegible]	[illegible]	[illegible]	[illegible]	[illegible]	[illegible]	[illegible]	[illegible]	[illegible]	[illegible]	[illegible]	[illegible]	[illegible]	[illegible]	[illegible]
16 in.	[illegible]	[illegible]	[illegible]	[illegible]	[illegible]	[illegible]	[illegible]	[illegible]	[illegible]	[illegible]	[illegible]	[illegible]	[illegible]	[illegible]	[illegible]	[illegible]	[illegible]
17 in.	[illegible]	[illegible]	[illegible]	[illegible]	[illegible]	[illegible]	[illegible]	[illegible]	[illegible]	[illegible]	[illegible]	[illegible]	[illegible]	[illegible]	[illegible]	[illegible]	[illegible]
18 in.	[illegible]	[illegible]	[illegible]	[illegible]	[illegible]	[illegible]	[illegible]	[illegible]	[illegible]	[illegible]	[illegible]	[illegible]	[illegible]	[illegible]	[illegible]	[illegible]	[illegible]
19 in.	[illegible]	[illegible]	[illegible]	[illegible]	[illegible]	[illegible]	[illegible]	[illegible]	[illegible]	[illegible]	[illegible]	[illegible]	[illegible]	[illegible]	[illegible]	[illegible]	[illegible]
20 in.	[illegible]	[illegible]	[illegible]	[illegible]	[illegible]	[illegible]	[illegible]	[illegible]	[illegible]	[illegible]	[illegible]	[illegible]	[illegible]	[illegible]	[illegible]	[illegible]	[illegible]
21 in.	[illegible]	[illegible]	[illegible]	[illegible]	[illegible]	[illegible]	[illegible]	[illegible]	[illegible]	[illegible]	[illegible]	[illegible]	[illegible]	[illegible]	[illegible]	[illegible]	[illegible]
22 in.	[illegible]	[illegible]	[illegible]	[illegible]	[illegible]	[illegible]	[illegible]	[illegible]	[illegible]	[illegible]	[illegible]	[illegible]	[illegible]	[illegible]	[illegible]	[illegible]	[illegible]
23 in.	[illegible]	[illegible]	[illegible]	[illegible]	[illegible]	[illegible]	[illegible]	[illegible]	[illegible]	[illegible]	[illegible]	[illegible]	[illegible]	[illegible]	[illegible]	[illegible]	[illegible]
24 in.	[illegible]	[illegible]	[illegible]	[illegible]	[illegible]	[illegible]	[illegible]	[illegible]	[illegible]	[illegible]	[illegible]	[illegible]	[illegible]	[illegible]	[illegible]	[illegible]	[illegible]
25 in.	[illegible]	[illegible]	[illegible]	[illegible]	[illegible]	[illegible]	[illegible]	[illegible]	[illegible]	[illegible]	[illegible]	[illegible]	[illegible]	[illegible]	[illegible]	[illegible]	[illegible]

EXPLANATION.—To ascertain the number of feet, multiply the number of feet in length by the number of inches in width, and divide the product by 12; the result will be the number in feet and inches. Thus, multiply 9 inches wide by 26 feet long, and the result will be 234. Divide this by 12 and we have the product 19 feet and 6 inches.

BANKERS' TIME TABLE.

To Find the Number of Days Between Any Two Dates of the Same Year, or Two Consecutive Years.

Consult the following table. The numbers in black letter at head of the columns represent the months—1, January; 2, February, etc. In leap years, add one to the corresponding numbers of all dates after February 28.

	1	2	3	4	5	6	7	8	9	10	11	12
1	1	[illegible]	[illegible]	[illegible]	[illegible]	[illegible]	[illegible]	[illegible]	[illegible]	[illegible]	[illegible]	[illegible]
2	[illegible]	[illegible]	[illegible]	[illegible]	[illegible]	[illegible]	[illegible]	[illegible]	[illegible]	[illegible]	[illegible]	[illegible]
3	[illegible]	[illegible]	[illegible]	[illegible]	[illegible]	[illegible]	[illegible]	[illegible]	[illegible]	[illegible]	[illegible]	[illegible]
4	[illegible]	[illegible]	[illegible]	[illegible]	[illegible]	[illegible]	[illegible]	[illegible]	[illegible]	[illegible]	[illegible]	[illegible]
5	[illegible]	[illegible]	[illegible]	[illegible]	[illegible]	[illegible]	[illegible]	[illegible]	[illegible]	[illegible]	[illegible]	[illegible]
6	[illegible]	[illegible]	[illegible]	[illegible]	[illegible]	[illegible]	[illegible]	[illegible]	[illegible]	[illegible]	[illegible]	[illegible]
7	[illegible]	[illegible]	[illegible]	[illegible]	[illegible]	[illegible]	[illegible]	[illegible]	[illegible]	[illegible]	[illegible]	[illegible]
8	[illegible]	[illegible]	[illegible]	[illegible]	[illegible]	[illegible]	[illegible]	[illegible]	[illegible]	[illegible]	[illegible]	[illegible]
9	[illegible]	[illegible]	[illegible]	[illegible]	[illegible]	[illegible]	[illegible]	[illegible]	[illegible]	[illegible]	[illegible]	[illegible]
10	[illegible]	[illegible]	[illegible]	[illegible]	[illegible]	[illegible]	[illegible]	[illegible]	[illegible]	[illegible]	[illegible]	[illegible]
11	[illegible]	[illegible]	[illegible]	[illegible]	[illegible]	[illegible]	[illegible]	[illegible]	[illegible]	[illegible]	[illegible]	[illegible]
12	[illegible]	[illegible]	[illegible]	[illegible]	[illegible]	[illegible]	[illegible]	[illegible]	[illegible]	[illegible]	[illegible]	[illegible]
13	[illegible]	[illegible]	[illegible]	[illegible]	[illegible]	[illegible]	[illegible]	[illegible]	[illegible]	[illegible]	[illegible]	[illegible]
14	[illegible]	[illegible]	[illegible]	[illegible]	[illegible]	[illegible]	[illegible]	[illegible]	[illegible]	[illegible]	[illegible]	[illegible]
15	[illegible]	[illegible]	[illegible]	[illegible]	[illegible]	[illegible]	[illegible]	[illegible]	[illegible]	[illegible]	[illegible]	[illegible]
16	[illegible]	[illegible]	[illegible]	[illegible]	[illegible]	[illegible]	[illegible]	[illegible]	[illegible]	[illegible]	[illegible]	[illegible]
17	[illegible]	[illegible]	[illegible]	[illegible]	[illegible]	[illegible]	[illegible]	[illegible]	[illegible]	[illegible]	[illegible]	[illegible]
18	[illegible]	[illegible]	[illegible]	[illegible]	[illegible]	[illegible]	[illegible]	[illegible]	[illegible]	[illegible]	[illegible]	[illegible]
19	[illegible]	[illegible]	[illegible]	[illegible]	[illegible]	[illegible]	[illegible]	[illegible]	[illegible]	[illegible]	[illegible]	[illegible]
20	[illegible]	[illegible]	[illegible]	[illegible]	[illegible]	[illegible]	[illegible]	[illegible]	[illegible]	[illegible]	[illegible]	[illegible]
21	[illegible]	[illegible]	[illegible]	[illegible]	[illegible]	[illegible]	[illegible]	[illegible]	[illegible]	[illegible]	[illegible]	[illegible]
22	[illegible]	[illegible]	[illegible]	[illegible]	[illegible]	[illegible]	[illegible]	[illegible]	[illegible]	[illegible]	[illegible]	[illegible]
23	[illegible]	[illegible]	[illegible]	[illegible]	[illegible]	[illegible]	[illegible]	[illegible]	[illegible]	[illegible]	[illegible]	[illegible]
24	[illegible]	[illegible]	[illegible]	[illegible]	[illegible]	[illegible]	[illegible]	[illegible]	[illegible]	[illegible]	[illegible]	[illegible]
25	[illegible]	[illegible]	[illegible]	[illegible]	[illegible]	[illegible]	[illegible]	[illegible]	[illegible]	[illegible]	[illegible]	[illegible]
26	[illegible]	[illegible]	[illegible]	[illegible]	[illegible]	[illegible]	[illegible]	[illegible]	[illegible]	[illegible]	[illegible]	[illegible]
27	[illegible]	[illegible]	[illegible]	[illegible]	[illegible]	[illegible]	[illegible]	[illegible]	[illegible]	[illegible]	[illegible]	[illegible]
28	[illegible]	[illegible]	[illegible]	[illegible]	[illegible]	[illegible]	[illegible]	[illegible]	[illegible]	[illegible]	[illegible]	[illegible]
29	[illegible]	...	[illegible]	[illegible]	[illegible]	[illegible]	[illegible]	[illegible]	[illegible]	[illegible]	[illegible]	[illegible]
30	[illegible]	...	[illegible]	[illegible]	[illegible]	[illegible]	[illegible]	[illegible]	[illegible]	[illegible]	[illegible]	[illegible]
31	[illegible]	...	[illegible]	...	[illegible]	...	[illegible]	[illegible]	...	[illegible]	...	[illegible]

	1	2	3	4	5	6	7	8	9	10	11	12
1	[illegible]	[illegible]	[illegible]	[illegible]	[illegible]	[illegible]	[illegible]	[illegible]	[illegible]	[illegible]	[illegible]	[illegible]
2	[illegible]	[illegible]	[illegible]	[illegible]	[illegible]	[illegible]	[illegible]	[illegible]	[illegible]	[illegible]	[illegible]	[illegible]
3	[illegible]	[illegible]	[illegible]	[illegible]	[illegible]	[illegible]	[illegible]	[illegible]	[illegible]	[illegible]	[illegible]	[illegible]
4	[illegible]	[illegible]	[illegible]	[illegible]	[illegible]	[illegible]	[illegible]	[illegible]	[illegible]	[illegible]	[illegible]	[illegible]
5	[illegible]	[illegible]	[illegible]	[illegible]	[illegible]	[illegible]	[illegible]	[illegible]	[illegible]	[illegible]	[illegible]	[illegible]
6	[illegible]	[illegible]	[illegible]	[illegible]	[illegible]	[illegible]	[illegible]	[illegible]	[illegible]	[illegible]	[illegible]	[illegible]
7	[illegible]	[illegible]	[illegible]	[illegible]	[illegible]	[illegible]	[illegible]	[illegible]	[illegible]	[illegible]	[illegible]	[illegible]
8	[illegible]	[illegible]	[illegible]	[illegible]	[illegible]	[illegible]	[illegible]	[illegible]	[illegible]	[illegible]	[illegible]	[illegible]
9	[illegible]	[illegible]	[illegible]	[illegible]	[illegible]	[illegible]	[illegible]	[illegible]	[illegible]	[illegible]	[illegible]	[illegible]
10	[illegible]	[illegible]	[illegible]	[illegible]	[illegible]	[illegible]	[illegible]	[illegible]	[illegible]	[illegible]	[illegible]	[illegible]
11	[illegible]	[illegible]	[illegible]	[illegible]	[illegible]	[illegible]	[illegible]	[illegible]	[illegible]	[illegible]	[illegible]	[illegible]
12	[illegible]	[illegible]	[illegible]	[illegible]	[illegible]	[illegible]	[illegible]	[illegible]	[illegible]	[illegible]	[illegible]	[illegible]
13	[illegible]	[illegible]	[illegible]	[illegible]	[illegible]	[illegible]	[illegible]	[illegible]	[illegible]	[illegible]	[illegible]	[illegible]
14	[illegible]	[illegible]	[illegible]	[illegible]	[illegible]	[illegible]	[illegible]	[illegible]	[illegible]	[illegible]	[illegible]	[illegible]
15	[illegible]	[illegible]	[illegible]	[illegible]	[illegible]	[illegible]	[illegible]	[illegible]	[illegible]	[illegible]	[illegible]	[illegible]
16	[illegible]	[illegible]	[illegible]	[illegible]	[illegible]	[illegible]	[illegible]	[illegible]	[illegible]	[illegible]	[illegible]	[illegible]
17	[illegible]	[illegible]	[illegible]	[illegible]	[illegible]	[illegible]	[illegible]	[illegible]	[illegible]	[illegible]	[illegible]	[illegible]
18	[illegible]	[illegible]	[illegible]	[illegible]	[illegible]	[illegible]	[illegible]	[illegible]	[illegible]	[illegible]	[illegible]	[illegible]
19	[illegible]	[illegible]	[illegible]	[illegible]	[illegible]	[illegible]	[illegible]	[illegible]	[illegible]	[illegible]	[illegible]	[illegible]
20	[illegible]	[illegible]	[illegible]	[illegible]	[illegible]	[illegible]	[illegible]	[illegible]	[illegible]	[illegible]	[illegible]	[illegible]
21	[illegible]	[illegible]	[illegible]	[illegible]	[illegible]	[illegible]	[illegible]	[illegible]	[illegible]	[illegible]	[illegible]	[illegible]
22	[illegible]	[illegible]	[illegible]	[illegible]	[illegible]	[illegible]	[illegible]	[illegible]	[illegible]	[illegible]	[illegible]	[illegible]
23	[illegible]	[illegible]	[illegible]	[illegible]	[illegible]	[illegible]	[illegible]	[illegible]	[illegible]	[illegible]	[illegible]	[illegible]
24	[illegible]	[illegible]	[illegible]	[illegible]	[illegible]	[illegible]	[illegible]	[illegible]	[illegible]	[illegible]	[illegible]	[illegible]
25	[illegible]	[illegible]	[illegible]	[illegible]	[illegible]	[illegible]	[illegible]	[illegible]	[illegible]	[illegible]	[illegible]	[illegible]
26	[illegible]	[illegible]	[illegible]	[illegible]	[illegible]	[illegible]	[illegible]	[illegible]	[illegible]	[illegible]	[illegible]	[illegible]
27	[illegible]	[illegible]	[illegible]	[illegible]	[illegible]	[illegible]	[illegible]	[illegible]	[illegible]	[illegible]	[illegible]	[illegible]
28	[illegible]	[illegible]	[illegible]	[illegible]	[illegible]	[illegible]	[illegible]	[illegible]	[illegible]	[illegible]	[illegible]	[illegible]
29	[illegible]	...	[illegible]	[illegible]	[illegible]	[illegible]	[illegible]	[illegible]	[illegible]	[illegible]	[illegible]	[illegible]
30	[illegible]	...	[illegible]	[illegible]	[illegible]	[illegible]	[illegible]	[illegible]	[illegible]	[illegible]	[illegible]	[illegible]
31	[illegible]	...	[illegible]	...	[illegible]	...	[illegible]	[illegible]	...	[illegible]	...	[illegible]

Scantling and Timber Measure Reduced to One-inch Board Measure.

To ascertain the number of feet of scantling or timber, say 18 feet long and 2 by 4 inches: Find 2 by 4 in the top column, and 18 in the left hand column, and under 2 by 4 and against 18 is 12 feet. If the scantling is longer than contained in the table, add two lengths together. If thicker, take part of same length.

Feet	THICKNESS AND WIDTH IN INCHES.															
	[illegible]	[illegible]	[illegible]	[illegible]	[illegible]	[illegible]	[illegible]	[illegible]	[illegible]	[illegible]	[illegible]	[illegible]	[illegible]	[illegible]	[illegible]	[illegible]
6	[illegible]	[illegible]	[illegible]	[illegible]	[illegible]	[illegible]	[illegible]	[illegible]	[illegible]	[illegible]	[illegible]	[illegible]	[illegible]	[illegible]	[illegible]	[illegible]
7	[illegible]	[illegible]	[illegible]	[illegible]	[illegible]	[illegible]	[illegible]	[illegible]	[illegible]	[illegible]	[illegible]	[illegible]	[illegible]	[illegible]	[illegible]	[illegible]
8	[illegible]	[illegible]	[illegible]	[illegible]	[illegible]	[illegible]	[illegible]	[illegible]	[illegible]	[illegible]	[illegible]	[illegible]	[illegible]	[illegible]	[illegible]	[illegible]
9	[illegible]	[illegible]	[illegible]	[illegible]	[illegible]	[illegible]	[illegible]	[illegible]	[illegible]	[illegible]	[illegible]	[illegible]	[illegible]	[illegible]	[illegible]	[illegible]
10	[illegible]	[illegible]	[illegible]	[illegible]	[illegible]	[illegible]	[illegible]	[illegible]	[illegible]	[illegible]	[illegible]	[illegible]	[illegible]	[illegible]	[illegible]	[illegible]
11	[illegible]	[illegible]	[illegible]	[illegible]	[illegible]	[illegible]	[illegible]	[illegible]	[illegible]	[illegible]	[illegible]	[illegible]	[illegible]	[illegible]	[illegible]	[illegible]
12	[illegible]	[illegible]	[illegible]	[illegible]	[illegible]	[illegible]	[illegible]	[illegible]	[illegible]	[illegible]	[illegible]	[illegible]	[illegible]	[illegible]	[illegible]	[illegible]
13	[illegible]	[illegible]	[illegible]	[illegible]	[illegible]	[illegible]	[illegible]	[illegible]	[illegible]	[illegible]	[illegible]	[illegible]	[illegible]	[illegible]	[illegible]	[illegible]
14	[illegible]	[illegible]	[illegible]	[illegible]	[illegible]	[illegible]	[illegible]	[illegible]	[illegible]	[illegible]	[illegible]	[illegible]	[illegible]	[illegible]	[illegible]	[illegible]
15	[illegible]	[illegible]	[illegible]	[illegible]	[illegible]	[illegible]	[illegible]	[illegible]	[illegible]	[illegible]	[illegible]	[illegible]	[illegible]	[illegible]	[illegible]	[illegible]
16	[illegible]	[illegible]	[illegible]	[illegible]	[illegible]	[illegible]	[illegible]	[illegible]	[illegible]	[illegible]	[illegible]	[illegible]	[illegible]	[illegible]	[illegible]	[illegible]
17	[illegible]	[illegible]	[illegible]	[illegible]	[illegible]	[illegible]	[illegible]	[illegible]	[illegible]	[illegible]	[illegible]	[illegible]	[illegible]	[illegible]	[illegible]	[illegible]
18	[illegible]	[illegible]	[illegible]	[illegible]	[illegible]	[illegible]	[illegible]	[illegible]	[illegible]	[illegible]	[illegible]	[illegible]	[illegible]	[illegible]	[illegible]	[illegible]
19	[illegible]	[illegible]	[illegible]	[illegible]	[illegible]	[illegible]	[illegible]	[illegible]	[illegible]	[illegible]	[illegible]	[illegible]	[illegible]	[illegible]	[illegible]	[illegible]
20	[illegible]	[illegible]	[illegible]	[illegible]	[illegible]	[illegible]	[illegible]	[illegible]	[illegible]	[illegible]	[illegible]	[illegible]	[illegible]	[illegible]	[illegible]	[illegible]
21	[illegible]	[illegible]	[illegible]	[illegible]	[illegible]	[illegible]	[illegible]	[illegible]	[illegible]	[illegible]	[illegible]	[illegible]	[illegible]	[illegible]	[illegible]	[illegible]
22	[illegible]	[illegible]	[illegible]	[illegible]	[illegible]	[illegible]	[illegible]	[illegible]	[illegible]	[illegible]	[illegible]	[illegible]	[illegible]	[illegible]	[illegible]	[illegible]
23	[illegible]	[illegible]	[illegible]	[illegible]	[illegible]	[illegible]	[illegible]	[illegible]	[illegible]	[illegible]	[illegible]	[illegible]	[illegible]	[illegible]	[illegible]	[illegible]
24	[illegible]	[illegible]	[illegible]	[illegible]	[illegible]	[illegible]	[illegible]	[illegible]	[illegible]	[illegible]	[illegible]	[illegible]	[illegible]	[illegible]	[illegible]	[illegible]
25	[illegible]	[illegible]	[illegible]	[illegible]	[illegible]	[illegible]	[illegible]	[illegible]	[illegible]	[illegible]	[illegible]	[illegible]	[illegible]	[illegible]	[illegible]	[illegible]
26	[illegible]	[illegible]	[illegible]	[illegible]	[illegible]	[illegible]	[illegible]	[illegible]	[illegible]	[illegible]	[illegible]	[illegible]	[illegible]	[illegible]	[illegible]	[illegible]
27	[illegible]	[illegible]	[illegible]	[illegible]	[illegible]	[illegible]	[illegible]	[illegible]	[illegible]	[illegible]	[illegible]	[illegible]	[illegible]	[illegible]	[illegible]	[illegible]
28	[illegible]	[illegible]	[illegible]	[illegible]	[illegible]	[illegible]	[illegible]	[illegible]	[illegible]	[illegible]	[illegible]	[illegible]	[illegible]	[illegible]	[illegible]	[illegible]
29	[illegible]	[illegible]	[illegible]	[illegible]	[illegible]	[illegible]	[illegible]	[illegible]	[illegible]	[illegible]	[illegible]	[illegible]	[illegible]	[illegible]	[illegible]	[illegible]
30	[illegible]	[illegible]	[illegible]	[illegible]	[illegible]	[illegible]	[illegible]	[illegible]	[illegible]	[illegible]	[illegible]	[illegible]	[illegible]	[illegible]	[illegible]	[illegible]

Feet	THICKNESS AND WIDTH IN INCHES.															
	[illegible]	[illegible]	[illegible]	[illegible]	[illegible]	[illegible]	[illegible]	[illegible]	[illegible]	[illegible]	[illegible]	[illegible]	[illegible]	[illegible]	[illegible]	[illegible]
[illegible]	[illegible]	[illegible]	[illegible]	[illegible]	[illegible]	[illegible]	[illegible]	[illegible]	[illegible]	[illegible]	[illegible]	[illegible]	[illegible]	[illegible]	[illegible]	[illegible]

Logs Reduced to Inch Board Measure

Find the length of the log in feet in the left hand column, and its mean diameter in inches (found by adding the two end diameters and dividing their sum by two) at the heads of the other columns, and trace them until they meet, and the figures so found will express the number of feet board measure of inch boards the log will measure.

L. Feet	Diam. [illegible]	Diam. [illegible]	Diam. [illegible]	Diam. [illegible]	Diam. [illegible]	Diam. [illegible]	Diam. [illegible]	Diam. [illegible]	Diam. [illegible]	Diam. [illegible]	Diam. [illegible]	Diam. [illegible]	Diam. [illegible]	Diam. [illegible]	Diam. [illegible]	Diam. [illegible]	Diam. [illegible]
[illegible]	[illegible]	[illegible]	[illegible]	[illegible]	[illegible]	[illegible]	[illegible]	[illegible]	[illegible]	[illegible]	[illegible]	[illegible]	[illegible]	[illegible]	[illegible]	[illegible]	[illegible]

L. Feet	Diam. [illegible]	Diam. [illegible]	Diam. [illegible]	Diam. [illegible]	Diam. [illegible]	Diam. [illegible]	Diam. [illegible]	Diam. [illegible]	Diam. [illegible]	Diam. [illegible]	Diam. [illegible]	Diam. [illegible]	Diam. [illegible]	Diam. [illegible]	Diam. [illegible]	Diam. [illegible]	Diam. [illegible]
[illegible]	[illegible]	[illegible]	[illegible]	[illegible]	[illegible]	[illegible]	[illegible]	[illegible]	[illegible]	[illegible]	[illegible]	[illegible]	[illegible]	[illegible]	[illegible]	[illegible]	[illegible]

THE Falls of Niagara have cut a channel through the solid rock [illegible] feet deep, [illegible] feet wide and seven miles long. The evidence is conclusive that the falls were formerly at Queenstown, seven miles below their present location. It has been shown that they have receded not more than a foot a year for the past half century.

ALEXANDER THE GREAT was born in Europe, died in Asia, and was buried in Africa. The preparations for his funeral consumed two years' time. The immense car containing the golden sarcophagus was drawn by sixty-four white mules, richly caparisoned, a distance of a thousand miles—from the Euphrates to the Nile.

Table For Gold Miners.

To ascertain the quantity of gold in any bulk of ore it is not necessary to reduce the mass. A proportional reduction will suffice, and the following table is based on trials of four hundred grains of ore:

If 400 Grains of Ore give Fine Gold,	One Ton of Ore Will Yield			If 400 Grains of Ore give Fine Gold,	One Ton of Ore Will Yield		
Grains.	Oz.	Dwts.	Grs.	Grains.	Oz.	Dwts.	Grs.
.001	0	1	16	.200	16	6	16
.002	0	3	6	.300	24	10	0
.003	0	4	21	.400	32	13	8
.004	0	6	13	.500	40	16	16
.005	0	8	4	.600	49	0	0
.006	0	9	19	.700	57	3	8
.007	0	11	10	.800	65	6	16
.008	0	13	1	.900	73	10	0
.009	0	14	16	1.000	81	13	8
.010	0	16	8	2.000	163	6	16
.020	1	12	16	3.000	245	0	0
.030	2	9	0	4.000	326	13	8
.040	3	5	8	5.000	408	6	16
.050	4	1	16	6.000	490	0	0
.060	4	18	0	7.000	571	13	8
.070	5	14	8	8.000	653	6	16
.080	6	10	16	9.000	735	0	0
.090	7	7	0	10.000	816	13	8
.100	8	3	8	20.000	1633	6	16

The sayings of the Seven Wise Men are the famous mottoes inscribed in the temple of Apollo at Delphi. Solon of Athens—"Know thyself." Chilo of Sparta—"Consider the end." Thales of Miletus—"Everything is the province of man." Bias of Priene—"Most men are bad." Cleobulus of Lindus—"Avoid excess." Pittacus of Mitylene—"Know thy opportunity." Periander of Corinth—"Nothing is impossible to industry."

The "Wandering Jew" was last seen in the seventeenth century. On January 1, 1644, he appeared at Paris and created a great sensation among all ranks. He claimed to have lived sixteen hundred years and to have traveled through all regions of the world. He was accosted by many prominent personages, and no one could accost him in a language of which he was ignorant. He replied readily and without embarrassment to any questions addressed to him, and he was never seen to take any amount of money or anything. He seemed familiar with the history of persons and events from the time of Christ, and claimed an acquaintance with all the celebrated characters of sixteen centuries. Of himself he said that he was usher of the court of judgment in Jerusalem, where all criminal cases were tried at the time of our Saviour; that his name was Michob Ader; and that for thrusting Jesus out of the hall with these words, "Go, why tarriest thou?" the Messiah answered him, "I go, but tarry thou till I come," thereby condemning him to live till the day of judgment. The learned looked upon him as an impostor or madman, yet both their departure bewildered and astonished.

NAILS AND SPIKES.

SIZE, LENGTH AND NUMBER TO POUND.

COMMON.			CLINCH.		FINISHING.		
Size.	Length Inches.	No. to Lb.	Length Inches.	No. to Lb.	Size.	Length Inches.	No. to Lb.
2d	1	716	2	152	4d	1⅜	384
3 fine	1⅛	588	2¼	138	5	1⅝	256
3	1¼	448	2½	98	6	2	204
4	1⅜	336	2¾	72	8	2½	102
5	1¾	216	3	66	10	3	98
6	2	169	3¼	43	12	3⅛	63
7	2¼	118			20	3½	46
8	2½	94	FENCE.		CASK.		
10	2¾	72	2	90	6d	2	143
12	3⅛	60	2¼	60	8	2½	68
20	3¾	32	2½	58	10	2⅞	60
30	4¼	20	2¾	50	12	3⅛	48
40	4¾	17	3	40	20	3¾	33
60	5	14	SPIKES.		30	4¼	18
65	5½	10	3½	19	40	4¾	14
LIGHT.			4	15			
4d	1⅜	373	4½	13	W H	2¼	69
5	1¾	272	5	10	W H	1⅞	72
6	2	196	5½	9	FLAT.		
BRADS.			6	7	3d	1⅛	265
6d	2	163	BOAT.		4	1¼	250
8	2½	96	1⅝	900	5	1¾	197
10	2¾	74			6	2	146
12	3⅛	50					

In the above table *d* stands for penny. This term penny, as applied to nails, is generally supposed to have been derived from pound. It originally meant so many pounds to the thousand; that is, six-penny means six pounds of nails to the thousand.

TACKS.

Size.	Length.	Number to Pound.	Size.	Length.	Number to Pound.	Size.	Length.	Number to Pound.
1 oz.	⅛	16000	4 oz.	7/16	4000	14 oz.	13/16	1143
1½	3/16	10666	6	9/16	2666	16	⅞	1000
2	¼	8000	8	⅝	2000	18	1	888
2½	5/16	6400	10	11/16	1600	20	1	800
3	⅜	5333	12	¾	1333	22	1 1/16	727

RAILROAD SPIKES.

Size Measured Under Head.	Average No. per keg of 200 lbs.	Ties two feet between centers, Four spikes per tie, Makes per Mile.	Rail used. Wt. per Yard.
5½ x 9/16	300	5870 lbs.—29⅓ kegs.	45 to 70
5 x 9/16	400	5170 " —26 "	40 to 56
5 x ½	450	4660 " —23¼ "	35 to 40
4½ x ½	530	3960 " —20 "	28 to 35
4 x ½	600	3520 " —17⅗ "	24 to 35
4½ x 7/16	680	3110 " —15½ "	20 to 30
4 x 7/16	720	2940 " —14⅔ "	
3½ x 7/16	900	2350 " —11¾ "	16 to 25
4 x ⅜	1000	2080 " —10½ "	
3½ x ⅜	1190	1780 " — 8 "	
3 x 5/16	1240	1710 " — 8½ "	16 to 20
2½ x ⅜	1342	1575 " — 7⅞ "	12 to 16

RAILS REQUIRED PER MILE

OF FOLLOWING WEIGHT PER YARD.

Weight per yard.	Tons of 2,240 lbs. per Mile.	Weight per yard.	Tons of 2,240 lbs. per Mile.
16 lbs.	25 tons, 320 lbs.	35 lbs.	55 tons, 0 lbs.
20 "	31 " 960 "	40 "	62 " 1920 "
25 "	39 " 640 "	45 "	70 " 1600 "
28 "	44 " 0 "	56 "	88 " 0 "
30 "	47 " 320 "	60 "	94 " 640 "
		65 "	102 " 320 "
		70 "	110 " 0 "

CROSS TIES, PER MILE.

Centre to Center.	No. Ties.
1½ Feet	3520
1¾ "	3017
2 "	2640
2¼ "	2348
2½ "	2112

SPLICE JOINTS, PER MILE.

Two Bars and Four Bolts and Nuts to each Joint.

Rails, 20 feet long,	528 joints.
" 24 " "	440 "
" 26 " "	406 "
" 28 " "	377 "
" 30 " "	352 "

Nails Required for Different Kinds of Work.

For 1,000 shingles, 3½ to 5 lbs. 4d. nails, or 3 to 3½ lbs. 3d.
1,000 laths, about 7 lbs. 3d. fine.
1,000 feet clapboards, about 18 lbs. 6d. box.
1,000 feet covering boards, about 20 lbs. 8d. common, or 25 lbs. 10d.
1,000 feet upper floors, square edged, about 38 lbs. 10d. floor, or 42 lbs. 12d. floor.
1,000 feet upper floors, matched and blindnailed, 38 lbs. 10d., or 42 lbs. 12d. common.
10 feet partitions, block or studding, 1 lb. 10d. common.
1,000 feet furring, 1 x 3, about 45 lbs. 10d. common.
1,000 feet furring, 1 x 2, about 65 lbs. 10d. common.
1,000 feet pine finish, about 30 lbs. 8d. finish.

Brick Required to Construct Any Building.

(Reckoning 7 brick to each superficial foot.)

Superficial Feet of Wall.	Number of Bricks to Thickness of 4 in.	8 in.	12 in.	16 in.	20 in.	24 in.
1	7	15	23	30	38	45
2	15	30	45	60	75	90
3	23	45	68	90	113	135
4	30	60	90	120	150	180
5	38	75	113	150	188	225
6	45	90	135	180	225	270
7	53	105	158	210	263	315
8	60	120	180	240	300	360
9	68	135	203	270	338	405
10	75	150	225	300	375	450
20	150	300	450	600	750	900
30	225	450	675	900	1125	1350
40	300	600	900	1200	1500	1800
50	375	750	1125	1500	1875	2250
60	450	900	1350	1800	2250	2700
70	525	1050	1575	2100	2625	3150
80	600	1200	1800	2400	3000	3600
90	675	1350	2025	2700	3375	4050
100	750	1500	2250	3000	3750	4500
200	1500	3000	4500	6000	7500	9000
300	2250	4500	6750	9000	11250	13500
400	3000	6000	9000	12000	15000	18000
500	3750	7500	11250	15000	18750	22500
600	4500	9000	13500	18000	22500	27000
700	5250	10500	15750	21000	26250	31500
800	6000	12000	18000	24000	30000	36000
900	6750	13500	20250	27000	33750	40500
1000	7500	15000	22500	30000	37500	45000

Facts for Builders.

1,000 shingles, laid 4 inches to the weather, will cover 100 sq. ft. of surface, and 5 lbs. of shingle nails will fasten them on.

One-fifth more siding and flooring is needed than the number of square feet of surface to be covered, because of the lap in the siding and matching.

1,000 laths will cover 70 yards of surface, and 7 lbs. of lath nails will nail them on. Eight bushels of good lime, 16 bushels of sand, and 1 bushel of hair will make enough good mortar to plaster 100 square yards.

A cord of stone, 3 bushels of lime, and a cubic yard of sand, will lay 100 cubic feet of wall.

Cement 1 bushel and sand 2 bushels will cover 3½ square yards 1 inch thick, 4½ square yards ¾ inch thick, 6¾ square yards ½ inch thick. 1 bu. cement and one of sand will cover 2¼ square yards 1 inch thick, 3 square yards ¾ inch thick, and 4½ square yards ½ inch thick.

FACTS FOR BUILDERS.

Five courses of brick will lay 1 foot in height on a chimney. 8 bricks in a course will make a flue 4 inches wide and 12 inches long, and 6 bricks in a course will make a flue 8 inches wide and 16 inches long.

Twenty-two cubic feet of stone, when built into the wall, is 1 perch.

Three pecks of lime and four bushels of sand are required to each perch of wall.

There are 20 common bricks to a cubic foot when laid, and 15 common bricks to a foot of 8-inch wall when laid.

Fifty feet of boards will build one rod of fence five boards high; first board being 10 inches wide, second 8 inches, third 4 inches, fourth 5 inches, fifth 5 inches.

Useful Facts for Bricklayers and Plasterers.

The average weight of smaller-sized bricks is about 4 lbs.; of the larger about 5 lbs.

Dry bricks will absorb about one-fifteenth of their weight in water.

A load of mortar measures a cubic yard, or 27 cubic ft.; requires a cubic yard of sand and 9 bus. of lime, and will fill 30 hods.

A bricklayer's hod 1 ft. 4 in. by 9 in. by 9 in. equals 1,296 cubic in. in capacity, and contains 20 bricks.

A single load of sand and other materials equals a cubic yard, or 27 cubic ft.; a double load twice that quantity.

One thousand bricks, closely stacked, occupy about 56 cubic ft. One thousand old bricks, cleaned and loosely stacked, occupy about 72 cubic feet.

One superficial foot of gauged arches requires ten bricks.

One superficial foot of facings requires seven bricks.

One yard of paving requires 36 stock bricks laid flat, or 52 on edge, and 36 paving bricks laid flat, or 82 on edge.

The bricks of different makers vary in dimensions, and those of the same maker vary also, owing to varying degrees of heat in burning. The calculations given above are therefore approximate.

One hundred yards of plastering will require 1,400 laths, 4½ bus. lime, four-fifths of a load of sand, 9 lbs. hair, and 9 lbs. nails, for two-coat work.

Three men and one helper will put on 450 yards, in a day's work, of two-coat work, and will put on a hard finish for 300 yards.

A bushel of hair weighs, when dry, about 14 lbs.

PUTTY FOR PLASTERING is a very fine cement made of lime only. It is thus prepared: Dissolve in a small quantity of water, as two or three gallons, an equal quantity of fresh lime, constantly stirring it with a stick until the lime is entirely slacked, and the whole becomes of a suitable consistency, so that when the stick is taken out of it, it will but just drop therefrom; this, being sifted or run through a hair sieve, to take out the gross parts of the lime, is fit for use. Putty differs from fine stuff in the manner of preparing it, and its being used without

ESTIMATES OF MATERIALS.

TO FIND THE NUMBER OF BRICKS REQUIRED IN A BUILDING. —Rule.—Multiply the number of cubic feet by 22½. The number of cubic feet is found by multiplying the length, height and thickness (in feet) together. Bricks are usually made 8 inches long, 4 inches wide and 2 inches thick; hence it requires 27 bricks to make a cubic foot without mortar, but it is generally assumed that the mortar fills 1-6 of the space.

ESTIMATES OF MATERIALS.—6½ barrels of lime will do 100 square yards plastering, two coats.

2 barrels of lime will do 100 square yards plastering, one coat.

1½ bushels of hair will do 100 square yards plastering.

2½ yards good sand will do 100 square yards plastering.

½ barrel of plaster [illegible] will hard-finish 100 square yards plastering.

1 barrel of lime will lay 1,000 bricks. (It takes good lime to do it.)

2 barrels of lime will lay 1 cord rubble stone.

¾ barrel of lime will lay 1 perch rubble stone (estimating ¼ cord to perch).

To every barrel of lime estimate about ⅝ yards of good sand for plastering and brick work.

MASON WORK—BRICK.—1⅛ barrels lime and ⅝ yard sand will lay 1,000 brick.

One man with 1½ tenders will lay 1,000 to 2,000 brick per day.

RUBBLE.—1¼ barrels lime and 1 yard of sand will lay 100 feet of stone.

One man will lay 150 feet of stone per day with one tender.

CEMENT.—1½ barrels cement and ⅝ yard sand will lay 100 feet rubble stone. [illegible]

FLOOR, WALL AND ROOF MEASURE.—To find the number of square yards in a floor or wall. Rule.—Multiply the length by the width or height (in feet) and divide the product by 9; the result will be square yards.

BIG SALARIES.—There are a score of men in New York who are paid as much for their services each year as the President of the United States. Fifty thousand dollars a year is a very tidy salary. There are hundreds of men who get $5,000 a year salary, and the number who get from $10,000 to $20,000 are legion. Very ordinary men get from $3,000 to $8,000 a year, or as much as a Cabinet officer. Mr. Norvin Green, president of the Western Union Telegraph Company, is paid $[illegible]. So is Chauncey M. Depew, president of the New York Central Railroad. Richard M. McCurdy, president of the Mutual Life Insurance Company, gets a like amount. John Hoey, president of Adams Express Company, [illegible]. President Henry B. Hyde, of the Equitable Life Insurance Company, is [illegible] the list. George G. Williams, president of the Chemical National Bank, the richest banking institution in America, with nearly $[illegible] surplus, $[illegible] average deposits, is paid a salary of $25,000 yearly. President [illegible] of the Park Bank and President Tappan of the Gallatin National Bank receive a like sum each twelve months. The best paid minister in New York is Dr. John Hall, a [illegible] man from the north of Ireland, who preaches to [illegible] every Sunday. His is the wealthiest church in town. He owes his rise in life to Robert Bonner of the *Ledger*, who heard him preaching to a small delegation in Dublin, and induced him to come to America. He gets a salary of $[illegible] a year and makes $[illegible] by his newspaper and magazine articles. He is given a handsomely furnished house as well. Dr. Morgan Dix, the third pastor of Trinity Church corporation, the wealthiest in America, receives $[illegible] yearly. Dr. William M. Taylor, of the Broadway Tabernacle, gets the same amount. He does literary work and lecturing that brings his income up to $[illegible]. Dr. Charles Hall, of the Fifth Avenue Presbyterian Church, is paid $[illegible]. He is very eloquent, and his church is crowded at all services. Dr. Parkhurst, of Madison Square Church, gets $[illegible]. He has a large and distinguished congregation. Cyrus W. Field is one of the pillars of the church. Dr. Paxton, who preaches to Jay Gould and others less wealthy, is paid $15,000. The Rev. Robert Collyer, the blacksmith preacher, is paid $[illegible].

BUILDERS' ESTIMATING TABLES.

Quantity of material in every four lineal feet of exterior wall in a balloon frame building, height of wall being given:

Length of Studs.	Size of Sills.	Size of Studs, Braces, etc.	Quantity of Lumber.	Quantity of Boarding.	Siding (6 in.).	Tar Paper, sq. feet.
8	6x 6	2x4 Studs	42	35	40	64
10	6x 8	2x4 Braces	58	44	50	80
12	6x10	4x4 Plates	62	53	60	96
14	6x10	1x6 Ribbons	68	62	70	112
16	8x10		82	71	80	128
18	8x12	Studs	87	80	90	144
20	8x12	16 inches from	99	88	100	160
22	8x12	centers	108	97	110	176
24	10x12		118	106	120	192
16	10x10	2x6 Studs	322	80	90	144
18	10x12	6x6 Braces	337	88	100	160
20	12x12	4x6 Plates	345	97	110	176
22	12x12	1x6 Ribbons	362	106	120	192
24	12x14		368	114	130	208
26	12x14	Studs 16 inch centers	376	123	140	224
28	14x14		398	132	150	240

Amount of lumber in rafters, collar-pieces and boarding, and number of shingles to four lineal feet of roof, measured from eaves to eaves over ridge. Rafters 16-inch centers.

Width of House, Feet.	Size of Rafters.	Size of Collar-pieces.	Quantity of Lumber in Rafter and Collar-pieces.	Quantity of Boarding, Feet.	No. of Shingles.
14	2x4	2x4	[illegible]	[illegible]	560
16	2x4	2x4	[illegible]	[illegible]	640
18	2x4	2x4	[illegible]	[illegible]	720
20	2x4	2x4	[illegible]	[illegible]	800
22	2x4	2x4	[illegible]	[illegible]	880
24	2x5	2x4	[illegible]	[illegible]	960
26	2x6	2x5	54	[illegible]	1040
28	2x6	2x6	68	[illegible]	1120
30	2x6	2x6	100	126	1200
32	2x6	2x6	110	145	1280
34	2x6	2x6	111	124	1360
36	2x6	2x6	120	138	1440

COMPARATIVE STRENGTH OF TIMBER AND CAST IRON.

Table showing the transverse strength of timber and of cast iron one foot long and one inch square.

MATERIAL.	Breaking Weight, lbs.	Weight Borne with Safety, lbs.
Ash, seasoned	178	105
Chestnut, seasoned	133	115
Hickory, seasoned	220	208
White Oak, seasoned	220	150
White Pine, seasoned	133	95
Yellow Pine, seasoned	250	150
Iron (cast)	5,740	4,200

HOW TO USE CEMENT.

The following general rules referring to the practical use of cement will be found convenient for reference:

Quantity of Sand.—The sand should be clean, sharp and coarse. When the sand is mixed with loam the mortar will set comparatively slow, and the work will be comparatively weak. Fine sand, and especially water-worn sand, delays the setting of the cement, and deteriorates strength. Damp sand should not be mixed with dry cement, but the cement and sand should be mixed thoroughly and uniformly together, when both are dry, and no water should be applied until immediately before the mortar is wanted for use.

Proportion of Sand.—The larger the proportion of cement the stronger the work. One part of good cement to two parts sand is allowable for ordinary work, but for cisterns, cellars, and work requiring special care, half and half is the better proportion. For floors, the cement should be increased toward the surface.

Water in Concrete.—Use no more water in cement than absolutely necessary. Cement requires but a very small quantity of water in crystallizing. Merely dampening the material gives the best results. Any water in excess necessarily evaporates and leaves the hardened cement comparatively weak and porous.

Concrete in Water.—Whenever concrete is used under water, care must be taken that the water is still. So say all English and American authorities. In laying cellar floors or constructing cisterns or similar work, care must also be taken to avoid pressure of exterior water. Cement will not crystallize when disturbed by the force of currents, or pressure of water, but will resist currents and pressure after hardening only. In still water, good cement will harden quicker than in air, and when kept in water will be stronger than when kept in air. Cements which harden especially quick in air are usually slow or worthless in water.

How to Put Down Concrete.—When, as when work is wanted, for cellar floors and cistern work, the concrete should be dampened and tamped down in place, with the back of a spade, or better, with the end of a plank or rammer, then finished off with a trowel, thus leveling and compacting the work. Only persons ignorant of the business will lay a floor or walk with soft, cement mortar. All artificial stone is made in a similar way to that described, and, when set, is strong and hard as stone.

Delay in Use.—Do not permit the mortar to exhaust its setting properties by delaying its use when ready. Inferior cement only will remain standing in the mortar-bed any length of time without serious injury.

Stone and Brick Work.—In buildings constructed of stone or brick, the best protection from dampness and decay, and also from the danger of cyclones, is a mortar of cement and coarse sand. The extra cost is inconsiderable, and the increased value of the structure very great. Chimneys laid in this manner never blow down, and cellars whose foundations are thus laid are always free from atmospheric moisture. Cement may also be mixed with lime mortar for plastering and other purposes, to great advantage.

Effect of Frost and Cold.—At a temperature less than 60 degrees Fahrenheit, all good cements set slowly, though surely, but if allowed to freeze, its value is seriously impaired. In cold weather or cold water, do not fear to wait for your concrete to crystallize.

Damage from Moisture.—Good cement is not injured by age, if carefully preserved from moisture. Lumps in bags or barrels of cement are caused by exposure to moisture. They prove the originally good quality of the cement.

THE Rhamphorhynchus, the remains of which have been found in the quarries of Solenhofen, Germany, was a curious intermediate link between birds and reptiles. Its tail, a singular appendage, was long, reptile-like, and dragged upon the ground, while its footprints were bird-like.

JOHN VERRAZANI, an eminent Florentine navigator, in 1524, landed where the lower extremity of New York City is, and giving the inhabitants spirituous liquors made many of them drunk. The Indians called the place Manna-ha-ta, or "place of drunkenness," and they were afterwards called Manhattans.

USEFUL TABLES FOR PLUMBERS, ETC.

SIZES AND WEIGHTS OF LEAD PIPE.

Calibre.	Weight per foot: lbs.	oz.	Calibre.	Weight per foot: lbs.	oz.
3/16 inch Tubing		1¼	1¼ inch Strong	4	12
1/4 inch Tubing		7	Ex. Strong	6	
5/16 inch Tubing		4	Ex. Ex. Strong	8	12
3/8 inch Tubing		6	1½ inch Aqueduct	3	
Fish String		13	Ex. Light	3	8
3/8 inch Aqueduct		8	Light	4	
Ex. Light		9	Medium	5	
Light		12	Strong	6	
Medium	1		Ex. Strong	7	8
Strong	1	2	Ex. Ex. Strong	9	
Ex. Strong	2		1¾ inch Ex. Light	4	12
1/2 inch Aqueduct		10	Light	5	8
Ex. Light		12	Medium	6	8
Light	1		Strong	7	8
Medium	1	4	Ex. Strong	8	
Strong	1	12	2 inch Waste	3	
AA	2		Ex. Light	4	
Ex. Strong	2	5	Light	5	
Ex. Ex. Strong	3		Medium	6	
5/8 inch Aqueduct		12	Strong	8	
Ex. Light	1	4	Ex. Strong	9	
Light	1	12	Ex. Ex. Strong	10	8
Medium	2		2½ inch Waste	4	
Strong	2	3	Light	6	
Ex. Strong	3		3/16 thick	8	
Ex. Ex. Strong	3	8	1/4 thick	11	
3/4 inch Aqueduct	1		3/16 thick	14	
Ex. Light	1	5	1/4 thick	17	
Light	2		3 inch Waste	3	
Medium	2	4	Waste	8	12
Strong	3		Light	9	
Ex. Strong	3	8	3/16 thick	9	
Ex. Ex. Strong	4		1/4 thick	12	
7/8 inch Aqueduct	1	8	3/16 thick	16	
Ex. Light	2		1/4 thick	20	
Light	2	8	3½ inch Waste	5	
Medium	3		1/8 thick	13	
Strong	3	5	1/4 thick	18	
1 inch Aqueduct	1	8	4 inch Waste	5	
Ex. Light	2		Waste	6	
Light	2	8	Waste	8	
Medium	3	4	Waste	10	
Strong	4		1/8 thick	16	
Ex. Strong	4	12	3/16 thick	21	
Ex. Ex. Strong	6	8	1/4 thick	25	
1¼ inch Aqueduct	2		4½ inch Waste	6	
Ex. Light	2	8	5 inch Waste	8	
Light	3		6 inch Waste	10	
Medium	3	12			

SHALT thou a man diligent in his business? He shall stand before kings; he shall not stand before mean men.—Old Testament.

SIZES AND WEIGHTS OF PURE BLOCK TIN PIPE.

3-16 in.	4 oz.	3/4 in.	7 oz. and 12 oz.
1/4 "	4 oz. and 6 oz.	1 "	10 " " 16 "
5-16 "	5 " " 8 "	1¼ "	1½ lb. and 1¾ lb.
3/8 "	4 " " 6 "	1½ "	1½ " " 2 "
1/2 "	6 " " 9 "	2 "	2 " " 4 "
5/8 "	8 " " 12 "		

WEIGHT PER SQUARE FOOT OF SHEET LEAD.

1-32 in. thick	2 lbs.	1-10 in. thick	7 lbs.
3-64 " "	2½ "	1/8 " "	8 "
1-20 " "	3 "	5-32 " "	10 "
1-16 " "	4 "	3-16 " "	12 "
1-14 " "	5 "	7-32 " "	14 "
1-12 " "	6 "	1/4 " "	16 "

WEIGHT PER JOINT OF LEAD AND GASKET FOR STREET MAINS.

	Lead.	Gasket.		Lead.	Gasket.
2-inch Pipe,	3.25 lbs.,	0.060 lbs.	10-inch Pipe,	15 lbs.,	0.30 lbs.
3-inch "	4.73 "	0.075 "	12-inch "	20 "	0.35 "
4-inch "	6. "	0.115 "	16-inch "	28 "	0.45 "
6-inch "	8. "	0.173 "	18-inch "	33 "	0.62 "
8-inch "	12. "	0.235 "	20-inch "	43 "	0.85 "

CAPACITY OF DRAIN-PIPE.

Size of Pipe.	Gallons per Minute: ½ in. Fall per 100 feet.	1 in. Fall per 100 feet.	2 in. Fall per 100 feet.	3 in. Fall per 100 feet.	4 in. Fall per 100 feet.	6 in. Fall per 100 feet.	9 in. Fall per 100 feet.	12 in. Fall per 100 feet.
3-inch.	21	30	42	52	60	74	85	104
4 "	36	52	76	92	108	132	148	184
6 "	84	120	169	206	240	294	338	414
9 "	232	330	470	570	660	810	930	1140
12 "	470	680	960	1160	1360	1670	1920	2350
15 "	830	1180	1680	2040	2370	2920	3340	4100
18 "	1300	1850	2630	3200	3740	4600	5270	6470
20 "	1760	2450	3450	4180	4860	6000	6880	8410

The maximum rainfall is about one inch per hour (except during very heavy storms)—equal to 22,633 gallons an hour for each acre, or 377 gallons a minute per acre.

AVOID shame, but do not seek glory—nothing so expensive as glory.—SYDNEY SMITH.

THAT this nation, under God, shall have a new birth of freedom, and that government of the people, by the people, for the people, shall not perish from the earth.—ABRAHAM LINCOLN.

The average width of a shingle is four inches. Hence, when shingles are laid four in. to the weather each shingle averages 16 sq. in., and 900 are required for a square of roofing (100 sq. ft.). If 4½ in. to the weather, 800; 5 in., 720; 5½ in., 655; 6 in., 600. In hip roofs, where the shingles are cut more or less to fit the roof, 5% should be added to these figures.

One thousand shingles laid four inches to the weather will require five pounds of shingle nails. Six pounds of 4d nails will lay 1000 split pine shingles.

A carpenter will carry up and lay on the roof from 1,500 to 2,000 shingles per day, or two squares to two squares and a half of plain gable-roofing.

The pitch of a slated roof should be about one in height to four in length. The usual lap is about 3 in., sometimes 4 in. Each slate should be fastened by two 3d slate nails, either of galvanized iron, copper or zinc. On roofs of gas-houses the nails should be of copper or yellow metal.

The sides and bottom edges of roof slates should be trimmed, and the nail-holes punched as near the head as possible. When slates are not of uniform size they should be sorted, and the smallest placed near the ridge.

In a first-class slate roof the top course on ridge, and the slate from two to four feet from gutters, and one foot each way from valleys and hips, should be bedded in elastic cement.

Roof-boards for slate roofs should be covered with one or two thicknesses of tarred felt roofing paper before slates are laid. Dry or rosin-sized felt should not be used on roofs.

Number of Slates per Square.

Size in Inches.	Slates per Square.	Size in Inches.	Slates per Square.	Size in Inches.	Slates per Square.
6 x 12	533	8 x 16	277	12 x 20	141
7 x 12	457	9 x 16	246	14 x 20	121
8 x 12	400	10 x 16	221	11 x 22	137
9 x 12	355	9 x 18	213	12 x 22	126
7 x 14	374	10 x 18	192	14 x 22	108
8 x 14	327	12 x 18	160	12 x 24	114
9 x 14	291	10 x 20	169	14 x 24	98
10 x 14	261	11 x 20	154	16 x 24	86

Number of Shingles Required in a Roof.

To the square foot, it takes 9 if exposed 4 inches; 8 if exposed 4½ inches, and 7 1-5 if exposed 5 inches to the weather.

Find the number of shingles required to cover a roof 38 ft. long and the rafters on each side 14 ft. Shingles exposed 4½ inches.

28×38=1064 (sq. ft.) ×8=8512 shingles. Ans.

To find the length of rafters, giving the roof one-third pitch, take three-fifths of the width of the building. If the building is 30 feet wide, they must be 18 feet long, exclusive of projection.

A tin roof, properly put on, and kept painted, will last thirty years. It ought not to be painted for the first time until it has been on about thirty days, so as to get the grease off the tin, and all the rosin should be carefully scraped off.

It is sometimes necessary, on buildings where there is much dampness or steam, as stables, blacksmith shops, round-houses, etc., to paint the roof tin one coat on the under side before laying.

Tin roofs should be laid with cleats, and not by driving the nails through the tin itself.

There are two kinds of tin—"bright tin," the coating of which is all tin, that is, the tin proper; and "terne," "leaded," or "roofing" tin, the coating of which is a composition, part tin and part lead. This last is a little cheaper, and will not rust any quicker, but the sulphur in soft coal smoke eats through the "leaded" coating sooner than through the "tinned."

There are two sizes of tin, 10x14 and 14x20, and two grades of thickness—IC light, and IX, heavy. For a steep roof (one-sixth pitch or over) the IC 14x20 tin ("leaded" if high up where little smoke will get to it; "bright" if low down), put on with a standing groove, and with the cross-beams put together with a double lock, makes as good a roof as can be made. For flat roofs IX 10x14 "bright" is best, laid with cleats, but the others make good roofs and any of them will last 25 years at least.

Number of Square Feet a Box of Roofing Tin Will Cover.—For flat seam roofing, using ½-inch locks, a box of "14x20" size will cover about 192 square feet, and for standing seam, using ⅜-inch locks and turning 1¼ and 1½ inches edges, making 1-inch standing seams, it will lay about 168 square feet.

For flat seam roofing, using ½-inch locks, a box of "20x28" size will cover about 399 square feet, and for standing seam, using ⅜-inch locks and turning 1¼ and 1½ inch edges, making 1-inch standing seams, it will lay about 365 square feet.

Every box of roofing plates (IC or IX "14x20" or "20x28" sizes) contains 112 sheets.

Facts About Gas.

A cubic foot of good gas, from a jet one thirty-third of an inch in diameter and a flame of four inches, will burn 65 minutes.

Internal lights require four cubic feet, and external lights about five cubic feet, per hour. Large or Argand burners will require from six to ten feet.

In distilling 56 pounds of coal, the volume of gas produced in cubic feet, when the distillation was effected in three hours, was 41.5; in seven hours, 39.5; in twenty hours, 33.5; in twenty-five hours, 31.7.

A retort produces about 600 cubic feet of gas in five hours, with a charge of about one and a half cwt. of coal, or 2,800 cubic feet in twenty-four hours.

PAINTING AND GLAZING.

Painters' work is generally estimated by the square yard, and the cost depends on the number of coats applied, quality of work and material to be painted.

One coat, or *priming*, will take, per 100 yards of painting, 20 pounds of lead and 4 gallons of oil. Two-coat work, 40 pounds of lead and 4 gallons of oil. Three-coat, the same quantity as two-coat, so that a fair estimate for 100 yards of three-coat work would be 100 pounds of lead and 16 gallons of oil.

One gallon priming color will cover 50 superficial yards; white zinc, 50 yds.; white paint, 44 yds.; lead color, 50 yds.; black paint, 50 yds.; stone color, 44 yds.; yellow paint, 44 yds.; blue color, 45 yds.; green paint, 45 yds.; bright emerald green, 25 yds.; bronze green, 75 yds.

One pound of paint will cover about 4 superficial yards the first coat, and about 6 each additional coat. One pound of putty, for stopping, every 20 yards. One gallon of tar and 1 lb. of pitch will cover 12 yards superficial the first coat, and 17 yards each additional coat. A square yard of new brick wall requires, for the first coat of paint in oil, ⅓ lb.; for the second, ¼ lb.; for the third, ¼ lb.

A day's work on the outside of a building is 100 yards of first coat, and 80 yds. of either second or third coat. An ordinary door, including casings, will, on both sides, make 8 to 10 yds. of painting, or about 5 yds. to a door without the casings. An ordinary window makes about 2½ or 3 yds.

WINDOW GLASS is sold by the box, which contains, as nearly as possible, 50 sq. ft., whatever the size of the panes. The thickness of ordinary, or "single thick" window glass is about one-sixteenth of an inch, and of "double thick" nearly ⅛ in. The tensile strength of common glass varies from 2,000 to 3,000 lbs. per sq. in., and its crushing strength from 6,000 to 10,000 lbs.

Where SKYLIGHTS are glazed with clear or double thick glass, it may be used in lengths of from 16 to 30 in. by a width of from 9 to 15 in. A lap of at least an inch and a half is necessary for all joints. This is the cheapest mode of glazing. The best, however, for skylight purposes is fluted or rough plate glass. The following thicknesses are recommended as proportionate to sizes: 12x48, 3-16 in.; 15x60, ¼ in.; 20x100, ⅜ in.; 94x156, ½ in.

POLISHED FRENCH PLATE WINDOW GLASS, which is the highest grade of window glass in the market, may be obtained in lights ranging in size from one inch square upwards. Owing to the extra cost of cutting large lights the price of these per square foot is sometimes double that of smaller lights.

FAITH is the substance of things hoped for, the evidence of things unseen.—NEW TESTAMENT.

PANES OF WINDOW GLASS IN A BOX OF 50 FEET.

Size, in inches.	Panes in box.	Size, in inches.	Panes in box.	Size, in inches.	Panes in box.	Size, in inches.	Panes in box.
6 x 8	150	12 x 19	33	[illegible]	[illegible]	24 x 44	[illegible]
7 x 9	115	12 x 20	30	[illegible]	[illegible]	[illegible]	[illegible]
8 x 10	90	[illegible]	[illegible]	[illegible]	[illegible]	[illegible]	[illegible]
8 x 11	82	[illegible]	[illegible]	[illegible]	[illegible]	[illegible]	[illegible]
[illegible]	[illegible]	[illegible]	[illegible]	[illegible]	[illegible]	[illegible]	[illegible]
9 x 10	80	[illegible]	[illegible]	[illegible]	[illegible]	[illegible]	[illegible]
9 x 11	73	[illegible]	[illegible]	[illegible]	[illegible]	[illegible]	[illegible]
9 x 12	67	[illegible]	[illegible]	[illegible]	[illegible]	[illegible]	[illegible]
9 x 13	62	[illegible]	[illegible]	[illegible]	[illegible]	[illegible]	[illegible]
9 x 14	57	[illegible]	[illegible]	[illegible]	[illegible]	[illegible]	[illegible]
9 x 15	53	[illegible]	[illegible]	[illegible]	[illegible]	[illegible]	[illegible]
9 x 16	50	[illegible]	[illegible]	[illegible]	[illegible]	[illegible]	[illegible]
10 x 10	72	[illegible]	[illegible]	[illegible]	[illegible]	[illegible]	[illegible]
10 x 12	60	[illegible]	[illegible]	[illegible]	[illegible]	[illegible]	[illegible]
10 x 13	55	[illegible]	[illegible]	[illegible]	[illegible]	[illegible]	[illegible]
10 x 14	52	[illegible]	[illegible]	[illegible]	[illegible]	[illegible]	[illegible]
10 x 15	48	[illegible]	[illegible]	[illegible]	[illegible]	[illegible]	[illegible]
10 x 16	45	[illegible]	[illegible]	[illegible]	[illegible]	[illegible]	[illegible]
10 x 17	43	[illegible]	[illegible]	[illegible]	[illegible]	[illegible]	[illegible]
10 x 18	40	[illegible]	[illegible]	[illegible]	[illegible]	[illegible]	[illegible]
11 x 11	60	[illegible]	[illegible]	[illegible]	[illegible]	[illegible]	[illegible]
11 x 12	55	[illegible]	[illegible]	[illegible]	[illegible]	[illegible]	[illegible]
11 x 13	50	[illegible]	[illegible]	[illegible]	[illegible]	[illegible]	[illegible]
11 x 14	47	[illegible]	[illegible]	[illegible]	[illegible]	[illegible]	[illegible]
11 x 15	44	[illegible]	[illegible]	[illegible]	[illegible]	[illegible]	[illegible]
11 x 16	41	[illegible]	[illegible]	[illegible]	[illegible]	[illegible]	[illegible]
11 x 17	39	[illegible]	[illegible]	[illegible]	[illegible]	[illegible]	[illegible]
11 x 18	36	[illegible]	[illegible]	[illegible]	[illegible]	[illegible]	[illegible]
12 x 12	50	[illegible]	[illegible]	[illegible]	[illegible]	[illegible]	[illegible]
12 x 13	46	[illegible]	[illegible]	[illegible]	[illegible]	[illegible]	[illegible]
12 x 14	43	[illegible]	[illegible]	[illegible]	[illegible]	[illegible]	[illegible]
12 x 15	40	[illegible]	[illegible]	[illegible]	[illegible]	[illegible]	[illegible]
12 x 16	38	[illegible]	[illegible]	[illegible]	[illegible]	[illegible]	[illegible]
12 x 17	35	[illegible]	[illegible]	[illegible]	[illegible]	[illegible]	[illegible]
12 x 18	33	[illegible]	[illegible]	[illegible]	[illegible]	40 x 60	[illegible]

CARPENTERS' WORK AND MEASURING.

What is called *Naked Flooring* in carpentry are the joists which support the flooring boards and ceiling of a room. There are different kinds, but they may all be comprised in the three following—viz.: single joisted floors, double floors, and framed floors.

A single joisted floor consists of only one series of joists; sometimes every third or fourth joist is made deeper, with ceiling joists nailed across at right angles. This is a good method, as ceilings stand better than when the laths are nailed to the joists alone.

A double floor consists of binding, bridging, and ceiling joists; the binding joists are the chief support of the floor, and the bridging joists are nailed upon the upper side of them; the ceiling joists are either notched to the under side or framed between with chased mortices. The best method is to notch them.

Framed floors differ from double floors only in having the binding joists framed into large pieces of timber called *girders*.

Single joisted floors, when the bearing exceeds ten feet, should be cross-bridged between the joists to prevent them from turning or twisting sideways, and also to stiffen the floor; when the bearing exceeds fifteen feet, two rows will be necessary, and so on, adding another row for each five feet bearing.

Single joisting may be used to any extent for which timber can be got deep enough; but where it is desirable to have a perfect ceiling, the bearing should not exceed 18 ft., nor the distance from center to center be more than 16 inches; otherwise the bearing for the laths become too long to produce good work.

To find the depth of a joist, the length of bearing and the thickness being given—

RULE.—Divide the square of the length in feet by the thickness in inches, and the cube root of the quotient, multiplied by 2.2 for pine, or 2.3 for oak, will be the depth in inches.

Example.—Suppose a joist whose bearing is 10 feet, and the thickness two inches, what will be the depth?

Here 10×10=100, divided by 2, the thickness=50, the cube root of which is 3.684×2.2=8.1048=equals 8 inches, the depth.

To find the scantlings of joists for different bearings from 5 to 20 feet, at several thicknesses, refer to the table on following page.

Girders are the chief support of a framed floor, and their depth is often limited by the size of the timber; therefore the method of finding the scantling may be divided in two cases—

CASE 1.—To find the depth of a girder when the length of bearing and thickness of girder are given.

Rule.—Divide the square of the length in feet by the thickness in inches, and the cube root of the quotient, multiplied by 4.2 for pine, or 4.34 for oak, will give the depth required in inches.

CASE 2.—To find the thickness when the length of bearing and depth are given.

Rule.—Divide the square of the length in feet by the cube of the depth in inches, and the quotient multiplied by 74 for pine, or by 80 for oak, will give the thickness in inches.

In these rules the girders are supposed to be ten feet apart, and this distance should never be exceeded, but should the distance apart be more or less than 10 feet, the thickness should be made proportionate thereto.

Length of bearing in feet.	Thickness 2 inches. Depth in inches.	Thickness 2½ inches. Depth in inches.	Thickness 3 inches. Depth in inches.	Thickness 3½ inches. Depth in inches.	Thickness 4 inches. Depth in inches.
5	5⅜	4¾	4⅝	4½	4
6	6⅜	5½	5	4¾	4½
7	6½	6	5½	5¼	5
8	7	6½	5¾	5⅝	5¼
9	7½	6¾	6¼	6	5¾
10	8	7¼	7	6¾	6¼
11	8¾	8	7⅝	7	6½
12	9¼	8½	8	7½	7¼
13	9¾	9	8½	8	7¾
14	10	9½	9	8¼	8
15	10½	9¾	9¼	8¾	8¼
16	11	10¼	9½	9¼	8¾
17	11½	10¾	10¼	9¾	9¼
18	12	11¼	10½	10	9¾
19	12½	11½	10¾	10¼	10
20	13	12	11¼	10¾	10¼

When the breadth of girders is considerable it is an excellent method to saw them down the middle and bolt them together, with the sawn sides outward.

Partitions unsupported from underneath the floors should be supported from the walls by means of a simple truss. This can be made by setting two pieces of scantling into the walls on either side at the floor to abut against each other at the ceiling or against a collar-beam over the doors. This plan will obviate the sinking of floors so often seen under partitions.

Weight of Lumber, Etc., Dry.

FLOORING—Dressed and matched, per 1,000 ft.	1,800 lbs.
SIDING—Dressed per 1,000 ft.	800 "
CEILING—⅞ inch thick, per 1,000 ft.	800 "
" ½ " " " "	900 "
BOARDS—Dressed one side, per 1,000 ft.	2,100 "
" and dimensions, rough, per 1,000 ft.	2,500 "
SHINGLES—per 1,000	250 "
LATH—per 1,000 pieces	500 "
PICKETS—Dressed, per 1,000 pieces	1,800 "
" Rough, per 1,000 pieces	2,500 "

WEAR AND TEAR OF BUILDING MATERIALS.

The figures given below are averages deduced from replies made by eighty-three competent builders in twenty-seven cities and towns of Western States:

Material of Buildings.	Frame Dwellings: Average Life, years.	Frame Dwellings: Percentage of Depreciation per Annum.	Brick Dwellings, (Shingle roof): Average Life, years.	Brick Dwellings, (Shingle roof): Percentage of Depreciation per Annum.	Frame Stores: Average Life, years.	Frame Stores: Percentage of Depreciation per Annum.	Brick Stores, (Shingle roof): Average Life, years.	Brick Stores, (Shingle roof): Percentage of Depreciation per Annum.
Brick	..	..	75	1⅓	..	..	80	1¼
Plastering	20	5	50	2½	16	6	30	3¼
Painting, outside	5	20	7	14	5	20	6	16
Painting, inside	7	14	7	14	5	20	6	16
Shingles	16	6	16	6	16	6	16	6
Cornice	40	2½	40	2½	30	3⅓	40	2½
Weather-boarding	30	3⅓	..	..	30	3⅓	..	..
Sheathing	50	2	50	2	40	2½	50	2
Flooring	20	5	20	5	18	6	18	5
Doors, complete	30	3⅓	30	3⅓	25	4	30	3⅓
Windows, complete	30	3⅓	30	3⅓	25	4	30	3⅓
Stairs and newel	30	3⅓	30	3⅓	20	5	30	3⅓
Base	40	2½	40	2½	30	3⅓	30	3⅓
Inside blinds	30	3⅓	30	3⅓	30	3⅓	30	3⅓
Building hardware	20	5	20	5	18	5	15	6
Piazzas and porches	20	5	20	5	20	5	25	4
Outside blinds	16	6	16	6	16	6	16	6
Sills and first floor joists	25	4	40	2½	25	4	30	3⅓
Dimension lumber	60	2	75	1⅓	40	2½	60	1⅔

In Java the "Valley of the Upas Tree" is sometimes called the "Valley of Death," and its deadly influence was formerly ascribed to the malignant properties of a peculiar vegetable production of the island, called the "upas tree," which especially flourishes in this locality. Recent travelers, however, declare that accounts of the fatality attending a passage of this famous valley have been greatly exaggerated.

A MAN may fish with the worm that hath eat of a king, and eat of the fish that hath fed of that worm.—*Shakspeare.*

Sizes of Chairs and Desks for Schools.

Desks for Single Scholar, 2 ft. long; For Two Scholars, 3 ft. 10 in.

Age of Scholar.	Height of Chair.	Height of Desk (next Scholar).	Space Occupied by Desk and Chair.
16 to 18 years.	16¾ inches.	29½ inches.	2 feet 9 inches.
14 to 16 "	15½ "	28 "	2 " 9 "
12 to 14 "	15½ "	27½ "	2 " 9 "
10 to 12 "	14¼ "	26½ "	2 " 7 "
8 to 10 "	13½ "	25½ "	2 " 6 "
7 to 8 "	12¾ "	24 "	2 " 4 "
6 to 7 "	11½ "	22½ "	2 " 3 "
5 to 6 "	10½ "	21 "	2 " 2 "
4 to 5 "	9½ "	19 "	2 " 0 "

WEIGHT OF FLOORS, AND THE LOAD UPON SAME.

The dead weight of a fire-proof floor will average for the arches, concrete, plastering and flooring, 70 lbs. per sq. foot. The live weight, equal to a dense crowd of people, 80 lbs. per sq. foot, or a total for an office building of 150 lbs. per sq. foot.

The following loads are exclusive of weight of arches and beams:

Dense crowd of people .... 80 lbs. per sq. foot
For floors of houses .... 60 " " " "
Theaters and churches .... 80 " " " "
Ball rooms .... 90 " " " "
Ware houses .... 250 " " " "
Factories .... 200 to 400 " " " "
Snow 30 inches deep .... 15 " " " "
Brick walls .... 112 " " cubic "
Stone (Chicago lime stone, dressed) .... 160 " " " "

The dead weight of a wooden floor, including wood joists:

Double flooring and plastering will average .25 lbs. per sq. foot
If deafened .... 25 " " " "
Stud partition of wood plastered each side ... 20 " " " "

In estimating the weight of a flat ceiling and roof it will be safe to assume the following:

Ceiling of wooden construction .... 15 lbs. per sq. foot.
Ceiling of iron construction .... 25 to 65 " " " "
Roof of wooden construction .... 45 " " " "
Roof of iron construction .... 60 to 100 " " " "

The weight of roof includes the wind pressure and snow.

STRENGTH OF PIERS.—Granite will sustain 40 tons per sq. ft.; Berea (sand stone), 30 tons per sq. ft.; limestone (magnesium), 20 tons per sq. ft.; Portland (sand stone), 15 tons per sq. ft.; brick in cement, 3 tons per sq. ft.; rubble masonry, 2 tons per sq. ft.; lime, cement foundation, 2½ tons per sq. ft.

WEIGHT OF VARIOUS MATERIALS.

WEIGHT OF STONES.—Granite, (averages) per cubic foot, 170 lbs.; limestone (magnesium), 144 lbs.; Berea (sand stone), 140 lbs.; free stone, 140 lbs.; gypsum, natural state, 140 lbs.

One ton of vein marble is 13 cubic feet; of statuary marble, 13½; granite, 13⅛; of Berea stone, 14⅓; of limestone, magnesium, 13¾.

WEIGHT OF MASONRY.—Granite, per cubic foot, 160 lbs.; of Berea stone range, 140; of limestone rubble, 140; of brick, dry, 115; of brick, dry (press), 130; of brick, dry (fire), 150; of brick masonry in mortar, 110; of brick masonry cement, 112.

WEIGHT OF MARBLE SLABS.—One-half inch thick, per sq. foot, 7.19 lbs.; ¾ inch thick, 10.75; 1 inch thick, 14.32; 1¼ inch thick, 17.92; 1½ inch thick, 21.05; 1¾ inch thick, 25.05; 2 inch thick, 28.67; 2½ inch thick, 35.84.

CEMENT AND LIME.—One bushel of Portland cement weighs 96 lbs.; of Rosendale, 70; of Louisville, 62; of quick lime well shaken, 80; of quick lime, loose, 70.

IRON AND WOOD.—One cubic foot of wrought iron weighs 480 lbs.; of cast iron, 450; of oak (seasoned), 48; of pine (seasoned), 36.

COAL.—One bushel of Anthracite weighs 66 lbs.; of Bituminous, 80; of coke (Connellsville), 40; of charcoal (hardwood) 30.

MISCELLANEOUS WEIGHTS.—Per cubic foot: Ordinary quick lime, 55 lbs.; old mortar, 90; new mortar, well tempered, 113; new mortar, 110; river sand (average), 107; river sand (screened), 95; clay with gravel, 130; earth—vegetable, 90; earth—loamy, 100; earth—sand field, 116.

SAN MARINO, in Italy, on the coast of the Adriatic Sea, is the oldest Republic in the world. It is, next to Monaco, the smallest State in Europe. The exact date of the establishment of this Republic is not known, but according to tradition, it was in the fourth century, by Marinus, a Dalmatian hermit, and has ever since remained independent. It is mountainous, and contains four or five villages. The word "LIBERTY" is inscribed on its capitol.

Is life so dear, or peace so sweet, as to be purchased at the price of chains and slavery? Forbid it, Almighty God! I know not what course others may take; but as for me, give me liberty or give me death!—*Patrick Henry.*

THE law is a sort of hocus-pocus science, that smiles in yer face while it picks yer pocket; and the glorious uncertainty of it is of mair use to the professors than the justice of it.—*Macklin.*

KNOWLEDGE is of two kinds: we know a subject ourselves or we know where we can find information upon it.—*Johnson.*

Crushing and Tensile Strength, in Lbs., per Sq. inch of Natural and Artificial Stones.

DESCRIPTION.	Weight per Cubic ft. in lbs.	Crushing Force. Lbs. per Square Inch.
Aberdeen Blue Granite	164	5,400 to 10,214
Quincy Granite	166	15,300
Freestone, Belleville	......	3,823
Freestone, Conn.	......	1,098
Freestone, Connecticut	......	3,319
Sandstone, Acquia Creek, used for Capitol, Washington	......	5,340
Limestone, Magnesian, Grafton, Ill.	......	17,000
Marble, Hastings, N. Y.	......	18,941
Marble, Italian	......	12,624
Marble, Stockbridge, City Hall, N. Y.	......	10,382
Marble, Statuary		3,216
Marble, Veined	168	11,651
Slate	......	9,800
Brick, Red	135.5	808
Brick, Pale Red	130.3	562
Brick, Common	......	800 to 4,500
Brick, Machine Pressed	......	6,222 to 14,216
Brick, Stock	......	2,177
Brick-work, set in Cement, bricks not very hard	......	521
Brick, Masonry, Common	......	500 to 800
Cement, Portland	......	3,000 to 6,200
Cement, Portland, Cement 1, Sand 1	......	1,280
Cement, Roman	......	342
Mortar	......	120 to 240
Crown Glass	......	31,000
		TENSION.
Portland Cement	......	427 to 711
Portland Cement, with Sand	......	62 to 284
Glass, Plate	......	9,420
Mortar	......	50
Plaster of Paris	......	72
Slate	......	11,000

ERROR of opinion may be tolerated where reason is left free to combat it.—*Thomas Jefferson.*

VIRTUE is like precious odors, most fragrant when they are incensed or crushed.—*Lord Bacon.*

WEIGHT OF CAST IRON COLUMNS.

PER LINEAL FOOT OF PLAIN SHAFT.

Diam.	Thickness of Metal											
	¼ in.	⅜ in.	½ in.	⅝ in.	¾ in.	⅞ in.	1 in.	1⅛ in.	1¼ in.	1½ in.	1¾ in.	2 in.
2	4.3	6.0	7.4	8.4	9.2	9.7	9.8	.....	.....	.....	.....	.....
2½	5.5	7.8	9.8	11.5	12.9	14.0	14.7	.....	.....	.....	.....	.....
3	6.7	9.7	12.3	14.6	16.6	18.2	19.6	.....	.....	.....	.....	.....
3½	8.0	11.5	14.7	17.6	20.2	22.5	24.5	.....	.....	.....	.....	.....
4	9.2	13.3	17.2	20.7	23.9	26.8	29.5	.....	.....	.....	.....	.....
4½	10.4	15.2	19.6	23.8	27.6	31.1	34.4	37.3	39.9	.....	.....	.....
5	11.7	17.0	22.1	26.8	31.3	35.4	39.3	42.8	46.0	.....	.....	.....
5½	12.9	18.9	24.5	29.9	35.0	39.7	44.2	48.3	52.2	.....	.....	.....
6	14.1	20.7	27.0	33.0	38.7	44.0	49.1	53.8	58.3	.....	.....	.....
6½	15.3	22.6	29.5	36.1	42.3	48.3	54.0	59.4	64.4	.....	.....	.....
7	16.6	24.4	31.9	39.1	46.0	52.6	58.9	64.9	70.6	81.0	.....	.....
7½	17.8	26.2	34.4	42.2	49.7	56.9	63.8	70.4	76.7	88.4	.....	.....
8	19.0	28.1	36.8	45.2	53.4	61.2	68.7	75.9	82.8	95.7	.....	.....
8½	20.2	29.9	39.3	48.3	57.1	65.5	73.6	81.5	89.0	103.1	.....	.....
9	21.5	31.8	41.7	51.4	60.7	69.8	78.5	87.0	95.1	110.4	.....	.....
9½	22.7	33.6	44.2	54.5	64.4	74.1	83.4	92.5	101.2	117.8	133.2	.....
10	23.9	35.4	46.6	57.5	68.1	78.4	88.4	98.0	107.4	125.2	141.7	157.1
10½	25.2	37.3	49.1	60.6	71.8	82.7	93.3	103.5	113.5	132.5	150.3	166.9
11	26.4	39.1	51.5	63.7	75.5	87.0	98.2	109.1	119.7	139.9	158.9	176.7
11½	27.6	41.0	54.0	66.7	79.2	91.3	103.1	114.6	125.8	147.3	167.5	186.5
12	28.8	42.8	56.5	69.8	82.8	95.6	108.0	120.1	131.9	154.6	176.1	196.3
12½	.....	44.6	58.9	72.9	86.5	99.9	112.9	125.6	138.1	162.0	184.7	206.2
13	.....	46.5	61.4	75.9	90.2	104.2	117.8	131.2	144.2	169.4	193.3	216.0
13½	.....	.....	63.8	79.0	93.9	108.5	122.7	136.7	150.3	176.7	201.9	225.8
14	.....	.....	66.3	82.1	97.6	112.7	127.6	142.2	156.5	184.1	210.5	235.6
14½	.....	.....	68.7	85.1	101.2	117.0	132.5	147.7	162.6	191.4	219.1	245.4
15	.....	.....	71.2	88.2	104.9	121.3	137.4	153.2	168.7	198.8	227.6	255.3
16	.....	.....	76.1	94.3	112.3	129.9	147.3	164.3	181.0	213.5	244.8	274.9
17	.....	.....	81.0	100.5	119.7	138.5	157.1	175.3	193.3	228.3	262.0	294.5
18	.....	.....	85.9	106.6	127.0	147.1	166.9	186.4	205.6	243.0	279.2	314.2
19	.....	.....	90.8	112.7	134.4	155.7	176.7	197.4	217.8	257.7	296.4	333.8
20	.....	.....	95.7	118.9	141.7	164.3	186.5	208.5	230.1	272.4	313.6	353.4

Increase in Weight per ½ in. Increase in Diameter.

¼ in.	⅜ in.	½ in.	⅝ in.	¾ in.	⅞ in.	1 in.	1⅛ in.	1¼ in.	1½ in.	1¾ in.	2 in.
1.2	1.8	2.5	3.1	3.7	4.3	4.9	5.5	6.1	7.4	8.6	9.8

WEIGHT OF CAST IRON BALLS.

Diameter, Inches.	Weight, Lbs.	Diameter, Inches.	Weight, Lbs.	Diameter, Inches.	Weight, Lbs.
2	1.09	5	17.04	8	69.81
2½	2.13	5½	22.68	8½	83.75
3	3.68	6	29.45	9	99.40
3½	5.84	6½	37.44	10	136.36
4	8.73	7	46.78	11	181.48
4½	12.43	7½	57.52	12	235.65

To Find the Weight of Cast Iron Balls When the Diameter is Given—*Rule:* Multiply the cube of the diameter by .1364.

To Find the Diameter of Cast Iron Balls When the Weight is Given—*Rule:* Multiply the cube root of the weight by 1.94.

To Find the Weight of a Spherical Shell—From the weight of a ball of the outer diameter subtract the weight of one of the inner diameter.

Cast Iron—Assumed Weight in Estimating

A cubic foot . . . . = 450 lbs.
A square foot, 1 inch thick . . . . . = 37½ "
A bar 1 inch square and 1 foot long . . . = 3.125 "

TABLE OF WEIGHT PER LINEAL FOOT OF ROUND CAST IRON.

Diameter, Inches.	Weight, Lbs.	Diameter, Inches.	Weight, Lbs.	Diameter, Inches.	Weight, Lbs.
1	2.45	5	61.36	9	198.80
1¼	3.84	5¼	67.65	9½	221.51
1½	5.52	5½	74.25	10	245.44
1¾	7.52	5¾	81.15	10½	270.60
2	9.82	6	88.36	11	296.98
2¼	12.43	6¼	95.87	11½	324.59
2½	15.34	6½	103.70	12	353.43
2¾	18.56	6¾	111.83	13	414.79
3	22.09	7	120.26	14	481.06
3¼	25.92	7¼	129.01	15	552.23
3½	30.07	7½	138.06	16	628.32
3¾	34.52	7¾	147.42	17	709.31
4	39.27	8	157.08	18	795.22
4¼	44.33	8¼	167.05	20	981.75
4½	49.70	8½	177.33	22	1187.93
4¾	55.38	8¾	187.91	24	1413.72

Rules for Obtaining Approximate Weight of Cast Iron.

Square of diameter multiplied by 2.46 equals weight of cast iron round bar 1 foot long.

To ascertain weight of cast iron columns or pipe subtract weight of inside diameter of shell from weight of outside diameter.

Square of the diameter divided by 5 equals approximately the weight of a circular cast iron plate 1 inch thick.

Rules for Obtaining Approximate Weight of Wrought Iron.

FOR ROUND BARS—*Rule*: Multiply the square of the diameter in inches by the length in feet, and that product by 2.6. The product will be the weight in pounds, nearly.

FOR SQUARE AND FLAT WROUGHT BARS—*Rule*: Multiply the area of the end of the bar in inches by the length in feet, and that by 3.32. The product will be the weight in pounds, nearly.

To find the sectional area of a bar of wrought iron, given the weight per foot, multiply by 3 and divide by 10.

To find the weight per foot, given the area, divide by 3 and multiply by 10.

To Convert Weight of

Wrought Iron into Cast Iron	× 0.928
" " " Steel	× 1.014
" " " Zinc	× 0.918
" " " Brass	× 1.082
" " " Copper	× 1.144
" " " Lead	× 1.468
Square Iron into Round	× .7854

Decimal Approximations Useful in Calculations.

Cubic inches	× .257	= lbs.	average	cast iron.
" "	× .281	= "	"	wrought iron.
" "	× .283	= "	"	cast steel.
" "	× .3225	= "	"	copper.
" "	× .3037	= "	"	brass.
" "	× .26	= "	"	zinc.
" "	× .4103	= "	"	lead.
" "	× .2636	= "	"	tin.
" "	× .4908	= "	"	mercury.
Cylin. "	× .2023	= "	"	cast iron.
" "	× .2168	= "	"	wrought iron.
" "	× .2227	= "	"	cast steel.
" "	× .2533	= "	"	copper.
" "	× .2385	= "	"	brass.
" "	× .2042	= "	"	zinc.
" "	× .3223	= "	"	lead.
" "	× .207	= "	"	tin.
" "	× .3854	= "	"	mercury.

Weight of a Lineal Foot of Flat Bar Iron, in Lbs.

BIRMINGHAM GAUGE.

Breadth of Inches.	Thickness in Fractions of Inches.								
	¼	5-16	⅜	7-16	½	⅝	¾	⅞	1
1	[illegible]	[illegible]	[illegible]	[illegible]	[illegible]	[illegible]	[illegible]	[illegible]	[illegible]
1⅛	[illegible]	[illegible]	[illegible]	[illegible]	[illegible]	[illegible]	[illegible]	[illegible]	[illegible]
1¼	[illegible]	[illegible]	[illegible]	[illegible]	[illegible]	[illegible]	[illegible]	[illegible]	[illegible]
1⅜	[illegible]	[illegible]	[illegible]	[illegible]	[illegible]	[illegible]	[illegible]	[illegible]	[illegible]
1½	[illegible]	[illegible]	[illegible]	[illegible]	[illegible]	[illegible]	[illegible]	[illegible]	[illegible]
1⅝	[illegible]	[illegible]	[illegible]	[illegible]	[illegible]	[illegible]	[illegible]	[illegible]	[illegible]
1¾	[illegible]	[illegible]	[illegible]	[illegible]	[illegible]	[illegible]	[illegible]	[illegible]	[illegible]
1⅞	[illegible]	[illegible]	[illegible]	[illegible]	[illegible]	[illegible]	[illegible]	[illegible]	[illegible]
2	[illegible]	[illegible]	[illegible]	[illegible]	[illegible]	[illegible]	[illegible]	[illegible]	[illegible]
2⅛	[illegible]	[illegible]	[illegible]	[illegible]	[illegible]	[illegible]	[illegible]	[illegible]	[illegible]
2¼	[illegible]	[illegible]	[illegible]	[illegible]	[illegible]	[illegible]	[illegible]	[illegible]	[illegible]
2⅜	[illegible]	[illegible]	[illegible]	[illegible]	[illegible]	[illegible]	[illegible]	[illegible]	[illegible]
2½	[illegible]	[illegible]	[illegible]	[illegible]	[illegible]	[illegible]	[illegible]	[illegible]	[illegible]
2⅝	[illegible]	[illegible]	[illegible]	[illegible]	[illegible]	[illegible]	[illegible]	[illegible]	[illegible]
2¾	[illegible]	[illegible]	[illegible]	[illegible]	[illegible]	[illegible]	[illegible]	[illegible]	[illegible]
2⅞	[illegible]	[illegible]	[illegible]	[illegible]	[illegible]	[illegible]	[illegible]	[illegible]	[illegible]
3	[illegible]	[illegible]	[illegible]	[illegible]	[illegible]	[illegible]	[illegible]	[illegible]	[illegible]
3⅛	[illegible]	[illegible]	[illegible]	[illegible]	[illegible]	[illegible]	[illegible]	[illegible]	[illegible]
3¼	[illegible]	[illegible]	[illegible]	[illegible]	[illegible]	[illegible]	[illegible]	[illegible]	[illegible]
3⅜	[illegible]	[illegible]	[illegible]	[illegible]	[illegible]	[illegible]	[illegible]	[illegible]	[illegible]
3½	[illegible]	[illegible]	[illegible]	[illegible]	[illegible]	[illegible]	[illegible]	[illegible]	[illegible]
3⅝	[illegible]	[illegible]	[illegible]	[illegible]	[illegible]	[illegible]	[illegible]	[illegible]	[illegible]
3¾	[illegible]	[illegible]	[illegible]	[illegible]	[illegible]	[illegible]	[illegible]	[illegible]	[illegible]
3⅞	[illegible]	[illegible]	[illegible]	[illegible]	[illegible]	[illegible]	[illegible]	[illegible]	[illegible]
4	[illegible]	[illegible]	[illegible]	[illegible]	[illegible]	[illegible]	[illegible]	[illegible]	[illegible]
4⅛	[illegible]	[illegible]	[illegible]	[illegible]	[illegible]	[illegible]	[illegible]	[illegible]	[illegible]
4¼	[illegible]	[illegible]	[illegible]	[illegible]	[illegible]	[illegible]	[illegible]	[illegible]	[illegible]
4⅜	[illegible]	[illegible]	[illegible]	[illegible]	[illegible]	[illegible]	[illegible]	[illegible]	[illegible]
4½	[illegible]	[illegible]	[illegible]	[illegible]	[illegible]	[illegible]	[illegible]	[illegible]	[illegible]
4⅝	[illegible]	[illegible]	[illegible]	[illegible]	[illegible]	[illegible]	[illegible]	[illegible]	[illegible]
4¾	[illegible]	[illegible]	[illegible]	[illegible]	[illegible]	[illegible]	[illegible]	[illegible]	[illegible]
4⅞	[illegible]	[illegible]	[illegible]	[illegible]	[illegible]	[illegible]	[illegible]	[illegible]	[illegible]
5	[illegible]	[illegible]	[illegible]	[illegible]	[illegible]	[illegible]	[illegible]	[illegible]	[illegible]
5⅛	[illegible]	[illegible]	[illegible]	[illegible]	[illegible]	[illegible]	[illegible]	[illegible]	[illegible]
5¼	[illegible]	[illegible]	[illegible]	[illegible]	[illegible]	[illegible]	[illegible]	[illegible]	[illegible]
5⅜	[illegible]	[illegible]	[illegible]	[illegible]	[illegible]	[illegible]	[illegible]	[illegible]	[illegible]
5½	[illegible]	[illegible]	[illegible]	[illegible]	[illegible]	[illegible]	[illegible]	[illegible]	[illegible]
5⅝	[illegible]	[illegible]	[illegible]	[illegible]	[illegible]	[illegible]	[illegible]	[illegible]	[illegible]
5¾	[illegible]	[illegible]	[illegible]	[illegible]	[illegible]	[illegible]	[illegible]	[illegible]	[illegible]
5⅞	[illegible]	[illegible]	[illegible]	[illegible]	[illegible]	[illegible]	[illegible]	[illegible]	[illegible]
6	[illegible]	[illegible]	[illegible]	[illegible]	[illegible]	[illegible]	[illegible]	[illegible]	[illegible]

Wrought Iron, Assumed Weight.

A cubic foot	= 480 lbs.
A square foot, 1 inch thick	= 40 "
A bar 1 inch square, 1 foot long	= 3⅓ "
A " 1 " " 1 yard long	= 10 "

GAUGES AND THEIR EQUIVALENTS.

No. 27, equal to $\frac{1}{64}$ inch.	No. 12, equal to $\frac{7}{64}$ inch.
" 21, " " $\frac{1}{32}$ "	" 10, " " $\frac{1}{8}$ "
" 18, " " $\frac{3}{64}$ "	" 8, " " $\frac{11}{64}$ "
" 16, " " $\frac{1}{16}$ "	" 6, " " $\frac{3}{16}$ "
" 14, " " $\frac{5}{64}$ "	" 5, " " $\frac{7}{32}$ "
" 13, " " $\frac{3}{32}$ "	" 4, " " $\frac{1}{4}$ "

TRUTH is as impossible to be soiled by any outward touch as the sunbeam.—*Lord Bacon.*

AMERICAN AND BIRMINGHAM WIRE GAUGES.

THICKNESS IN INCHES.

Revised.

Gauge.	Thickness American Gauge.	Thickness Birmingham Gauge.	Gauge.	Thickness American Gauge.	Thickness Birmingham Gauge.
0000	.46	.454	17	.0453	.058
000	.4096	.425	18	.0403	.049
00	.3648	.38	19	.0359	.042
0	.3249	.34	20	.0320	.035
1	.2893	.30	21	.0285	.032
2	.2576	.284	22	.0253	.028
3	.2294	.259	23	.0226	.025
4	.2043	.238	24	.0201	.022
5	.1819	.22	25	.0179	.02
6	.1620	.203	26	.0159	.018
7	.1443	.18	27	.0142	.016
8	.1285	.165	28	.0126	.014
9	.1144	.148	29	.0113	.013
10	.1019	.134	30	.01	.012
11	.0907	.12	31	.0089	.01
12	.0808	.109	32	.0080	.009
13	.0720	.095	33	.0071	.008
14	.0641	.083	34	.0063	.007
15	.0571	.072	35	.0056	.005
16	.0508	.065	36	.005	.004

The Area of a Circle.

Of all plane figures, the circle is the most capacious, or has the greatest area within the same limits. It is geometrically demonstrable that it has the same area as a right-angled triangle with a base equal to its circumference, and a perpendicular equal to its radius, that is, half the product of the radius and circumference. It is obviously larger than any figure, of however many sides, inscribed within its perimeter, and smaller than any circumscribed polygon. As a result of laborious calculations on this basis (pushed in one instance to 600 places of decimals without reaching the end), it has been ascertained that the ratio of the diameter to the circumference of any circle (sufficiently exact for all practical purposes), is as 1 : 3.1416 (3.14159265359+) or in whole numbers, approximately, as 7 : 22, or more nearly as 113 : 355. Hence, to find the circumference or diameter, the other quantity being known, multiply or divide by 3.1416; and to find the area, multiply half the diameter by half the circumference, or the square of the diameter by .7854 (.7853981634).

To find the surface of a globe, multiply the square of the diameter by 3.1416.

To find the solidity of a globe, multiply the cube of the

AREAS OF CIRCLES.

Advancing by eighths.

Diam.	Areas 0	1/8	1/4	3/8	1/2	5/8	3/4	7/8
0	.0	.0123	.0491	.1104	.1963	.3068	.4418	.6013
1	.7854	.9940	1.227	1.485	1.767	2.074	2.405	2.761
2	3.1416	3.547	3.976	4.430	4.909	5.412	5.940	6.492
3	7.069	7.670	8.296	8.946	9.621	10.32	11.04	11.79
4	12.57	13.36	14.19	15.03	15.90	16.80	17.72	18.67
5	19.63	20.63	21.65	22.69	23.76	24.85	25.97	27.11
6	28.27	29.46	30.68	31.92	33.18	34.47	35.78	37.12
7	38.48	39.87	41.28	42.72	44.18	45.66	47.17	48.71
8	50.27	51.85	53.46	55.09	56.75	58.43	60.13	61.86
9	63.62	65.40	67.20	69.03	70.88	72.76	74.66	76.59
10	78.54	80.52	82.52	84.54	86.59	88.66	90.76	92.89
11	95.03	97.21	99.40	101.6	103.9	106.1	108.4	110.8
12	113.1	115.5	117.9	120.3	122.7	125.2	127.7	130.2
13	132.7	135.3	137.9	140.5	143.1	145.8	148.5	151.2
14	153.9	156.7	159.5	162.3	165.1	168.0	170.9	173.8
15	176.7	179.7	182.7	185.7	188.7	191.7	194.8	197.9
16	201.1	204.2	207.4	210.6	213.8	217.1	220.4	223.7
17	227.0	230.3	233.7	237.1	240.5	244.0	247.5	250.9
18	254.5	258.0	261.6	265.2	268.8	272.4	276.1	279.8
19	283.5	287.3	291.0	294.8	298.6	302.5	306.4	310.2
20	314.2	318.1	322.1	326.0	330.1	334.1	338.2	342.2
21	346.4	350.5	354.7	358.8	363.1	367.3	371.5	375.8
22	380.1	384.5	388.8	393.2	397.6	402.0	406.5	411.0
23	415.5	420.0	424.6	429.1	433.7	438.4	443.0	447.7
24	452.4	457.1	461.9	466.6	471.4	476.3	481.1	486.0
25	490.9	495.8	500.7	505.7	510.7	515.7	520.8	525.8
26	530.9	536.0	541.2	546.4	551.5	556.8	562.0	567.3
27	572.6	577.9	583.2	588.6	594.0	599.4	604.8	610.3
28	615.8	621.3	626.8	632.4	637.9	643.5	649.2	654.8
29	660.5	666.2	672.0	677.7	683.5	689.3	695.1	701.0
30	706.9	712.8	718.7	724.6	730.6	736.6	742.6	748.7
31	754.8	760.9	767.0	773.1	779.3	785.5	791.7	798.0
32	804.2	810.5	816.9	823.2	829.6	836.0	842.4	848.8
33	855.3	861.8	868.3	874.8	881.4	888.0	894.6	901.3
34	907.9	914.6	921.3	928.1	934.8	941.6	948.4	955.3
35	962.1	969.0	975.9	982.8	989.8	996.8	1003.8	1010.8
36	1017.9	1025.0	1032.1	1039.2	1046.3	1053.5	1060.7	1068.0
37	1075.2	1082.5	1089.8	1097.1	1104.5	1111.8	1119.2	1126.7
38	1134.1	1141.6	1149.1	1156.6	1164.2	1171.7	1179.3	1186.9
39	1194.6	1202.3	1209.9	1217.7	1225.4	1233.2	1241.0	1248.8
40	1256.6	1264.5	1272.4	1280.3	1288.2	1296.2	1304.2	1312.2
41	1320.3	1328.3	1336.4	1344.5	1352.7	1360.8	1369.0	1377.2
42	1385.4	1393.7	1402.0	1410.3	1418.6	1427.0	1435.4	1443.8
43	1452.2	1460.7	1469.1	1477.6	1486.2	1494.7	1503.3	1511.9
44	1520.5	1529.2	1537.9	1546.6	1555.3	1564.0	1572.8	1581.6
45	1590.4	1599.3	1608.2	1617.0	1626.0	1634.9	1643.9	1652.9

CIRCUMFERENCES OF CIRCLES.

Advancing by eighths.

Diam.	0	⅛	¼	⅜	½	⅝	¾	⅞
0		.3927	.7854	1.178	1.570	1.963	2.356	2.748
1	3.141	3.534	3.927	4.319	4.712	5.105	5.497	5.890
2	6.283	6.675	7.068	7.461	7.854	8.246	8.639	9.032
3	9.424	9.817	10.21	10.60	10.99	11.38	11.78	12.17
4	12.56	12.95	13.35	13.74	14.13	14.52	14.92	15.31
5	15.70	16.10	16.49	16.88	17.27	17.67	18.06	18.45
6	18.84	19.24	19.63	20.02	20.42	20.81	21.20	21.59
7	21.99	22.38	22.77	23.16	23.56	23.95	24.34	24.74
8	25.13	25.52	25.91	26.31	26.70	27.09	27.48	27.88
9	28.27	28.66	29.05	29.45	29.84	30.23	30.63	31.02
10	31.41	31.80	32.20	32.59	32.98	33.37	33.77	34.16
11	34.55	34.95	35.34	35.73	36.12	36.52	36.91	37.30
12	37.69	38.09	38.48	38.87	39.27	39.66	40.05	40.44
13	40.84	41.23	41.62	42.01	42.41	42.80	43.19	43.58
14	43.98	44.37	44.76	45.16	45.55	45.94	46.33	46.73
15	47.12	47.51	47.90	48.30	48.69	49.08	49.48	49.87
16	50.26	50.65	51.05	51.44	51.83	52.22	52.62	53.01
17	53.40	53.79	54.19	54.58	54.97	55.37	55.76	56.15
18	56.54	56.94	57.33	57.72	58.11	58.51	58.90	59.29
19	59.69	60.08	60.47	60.86	61.26	61.65	62.04	62.43
20	62.83	63.22	63.61	64.00	64.40	64.79	65.18	65.57
21	65.97	66.36	66.75	67.15	67.54	67.93	68.32	68.72
22	69.11	69.50	69.90	70.29	70.68	71.07	71.47	71.86
23	72.25	72.64	73.04	73.43	73.82	74.22	74.61	75.00
24	75.39	75.79	76.18	76.57	76.96	77.36	77.75	78.14
25	78.54	78.93	79.32	79.71	80.11	80.50	80.89	81.28
26	81.68	82.07	82.46	82.85	83.25	83.64	84.03	84.43
27	84.82	85.21	85.60	86.00	86.39	86.78	87.17	87.57
28	87.96	88.35	88.75	89.14	89.53	89.92	90.32	90.71
29	91.10	91.49	91.89	92.28	92.67	93.06	93.46	93.85
30	94.24	94.64	95.03	95.42	95.81	96.21	96.60	96.99
31	97.38	97.78	98.17	98.56	98.96	99.35	99.74	100.13
32	100.53	100.92	101.31	101.70	102.10	102.49	102.88	103.28
33	103.67	104.06	104.45	104.85	105.24	105.63	106.02	106.42
34	106.81	107.20	107.60	107.99	108.38	108.77	109.17	109.56
35	109.95	110.35	110.74	111.13	111.52	111.92	112.31	112.70
36	113.10	113.49	113.88	114.27	114.67	115.06	115.45	115.84
37	116.24	116.63	117.02	117.42	117.81	118.20	118.59	118.99
38	119.38	119.77	120.17	120.56	120.95	121.34	121.74	122.13
39	122.52	122.92	123.31	123.70	124.09	124.49	124.88	125.27
40	125.66	126.06	126.45	126.84	127.23	127.63	128.02	128.41
41	128.81	129.20	129.59	129.98	130.38	130.77	131.16	131.55
42	131.95	132.34	132.73	133.13	133.52	133.91	134.30	134.70
43	135.09	135.48	135.87	136.27	136.66	137.05	137.45	137.84
44	138.23	138.62	139.02	139.41	139.80	140.19	140.59	140.98
45	141.37	141.76	142.16	142.55	142.94	143.34	143.73	144.12

Table of Decimal Equivalents of 8ths, 16ths, 32nds and 64ths of an Inch.

8ths.

⅛ =	.125
¼ =	.250
⅜ =	.375
½ =	.500
⅝ =	.625
¾ =	.750
⅞ =	.875

16ths.

1/16 =	.0625
3/16 =	.1875
5/16 =	.3125
7/16 =	.4375
9/16 =	.5625
11/16 =	.6875
13/16 =	.8125
15/16 =	.9375

32nds.

1/32 =	.03125
3/32 =	.09375
5/32 =	.15625
7/32 =	.21875
9/32 =	.28125
11/32 =	.34375
13/32 =	.40625
15/32 =	.46875
17/32 =	.53125
19/32 =	.59375
21/32 =	.65625
23/32 =	.71875
25/32 =	.78125
27/32 =	.84375
29/32 =	.90625
31/32 =	.96875

64ths.

1/64 =	.015625
3/64 =	.046875
5/64 =	.078125
7/64 =	.109375
9/64 =	.140625
11/64 =	.171875
13/64 =	.203125
15/64 =	.234375
17/64 =	.265625
19/64 =	.296875
21/64 =	.328125
23/64 =	.359375
25/64 =	.390625
27/64 =	.421875
29/64 =	.453125
31/64 =	.484375
33/64 =	.515625
35/64 =	.546875
37/64 =	.578125
39/64 =	.609375
41/64 =	.640625
43/64 =	.671875
45/64 =	.703125
47/64 =	.734375
49/64 =	.765625
51/64 =	.796875
53/64 =	.828125
55/64 =	.859375
57/64 =	.890625
59/64 =	.921875
61/64 =	.953125
63/64 =	.984375

Handy Facts for Architects and Builders.

Pitch of tin, copper or tar-and-gravel roofs five-eighths of an inch to the foot and upwards.

The average weight of 20,000 men and women weighed at Boston was: Men, 141½ lbs.; women, 124½ lbs.

Smallest convenient size of slab for a 14-in. wash bowl, 21 by 24 in. Height of slab from floor, 2 ft. 6 in.

Urinals should be 2 ft. 2 in. between partitions; partitions 6 ft. high.

Space occupied by water-closets, 2 ft. 6 in. wide; 2 ft. deep.

Dimensions of double bed, 6 ft. 6 in. by 4 ft. 6 in.

Dimensions of single bed (in dormitories), 2 ft. 8 in. by 6 ft. 6 in.

Dimensions of a bureau, 5 ft. 2 in. wide, 1 ft. 6 in. deep, and upwards.

Dimensions of a common wash-stand, 2 ft. 9 in. wide, 1 ft. 6 in. deep.

HANDY FACTS FOR ARCHITECTS, ETC.

Dimensions of a Barrel.—Diameter of head, 17 in.; bung, 19 in.; length, 28 in.; volume, 7,680 cubic in.

Dimensions of billiard tables (Callender)—4 ft. by 8 ft.; 4 ft. 2 in. by 9 ft.; and 5 ft. by 10 ft. Size of room required respectively, 13 by 17; 14 by 18; 15 by 20.

Horse-stalls.—Width, 5 ft. 10 in. to 4 ft., or else 5 ft. or over in width—nine feet long. Width should never be between 4 and 5 ft., as in that case the horse is liable to cast himself.

HORSE POWER OF STEAM ENGINES, ETC.

The unit of nominal power for steam-engines, or the usual estimate of dynamical effect per minute of a horse, called by engineers a "horse power," is 33,000 pounds at a velocity of 1 foot per minute, or, the effect of a load of 200 pounds raised by a horse for 8 hours a day, at the rate of 2½ miles per hour, or 150 pounds at the rate of 220 feet per minute.

Rule.—Multiply the area of the piston in square inches by the average force of the steam in pounds and by the velocity of the piston in feet per minute; divide the product by 33,000, and 7/10 of the quotient equal the effective power.

Another Rule.—The diameter of the piston in inches, multiplied by itself, multiplied by the stroke in inches, multiplied by the revolutions per minute (not the strokes), multiplied by the mean effective (average pressure per square inch on piston), multiplied by .0000238, gives the gross or indicated horse power.

For the net effective horse power, deduct from the above about ¼ for friction of the working parts.

The mean effective pressure can be accurately determined only by the aid of an indicator. When the indicator is not used, and in the calculation the boiler pressure is substituted for the mean effective pressure, deduct from the result obtained from 40 to 60 per cent. for loss by condensation and friction of steam pipes and passages, decrease of pressure in cylinder due to expansion, back pressure of exhaust, and friction of the working parts.

For engines from 20 to 60 horse-power, an average of 50 per cent. may be deducted; for smaller engines, more.

The mean pressure in the cylinder when cutting off at

¼	stroke equals boiler pressure multiplied by	.597
⅓	" " " " "	.670
⅜	" " " " "	.748
½	" " " " "	.847
⅝	" " " " "	.919
⅔	" " " " "	.937
¾	" " " " "	.966
⅞	" " " " "	.992

Best designed boilers, well set, with good draft and skillful firing, will evaporate from 7 to 10 lbs. of water per pound of first-class coal. The average results from 50 to 60 per cent. below this.

In calculating horse power of Tubular or Flue boilers, consider 15 square feet of heating surface equivalent to one *nominal* horse power.

One square foot of grate will consume on an average 12 lbs. of coal per hour.

Steam engines, in economy, vary from 20 to 60 lbs. of feed water and from 2 to 7 lbs. of coal per hour per indicated H. P.

HORSE POWER OF BELTING.

A simple rule for ascertaining transmitting power of belting, without first computing speed per minute that it travels, is as follows: Multiply diameter of pulley in inches by its number of revolutions per minute; and this product by width of the belt in inches; divide the product by 3,300 for single belting, or by 2,100 for double belting, and the quotient will be the amount of horse power that can be safely transmitted.

Table for Single Leather, Four Ply Rubber and Four Ply Cotton Belting, Belts not Overloaded.

1 INCH WIDE, 800 FEET PER MINUTE=1 HORSE POWER.

Speed in Feet per Min.	WIDTH OF BELTS IN INCHES. 2	3	4	5	6	8	10	12	14	16	18	20
	H.P.	H.P.	H.P.	H.P.	H.P.	H.P.	H.P.	H.P.	H.P.	H.P.	H.P.	H.P.
400	1	1½	2	2½	3	4	5	6	7	8	9	10
600	1½	2¼	3	3¾	4½	6	7½	9	10½	12	13½	15
800	2	3	4	5	6	8	10	12	14	16	18	20
1000	2½	3¾	5	6¼	7½	10	12½	15	17½	20	22½	25
1200	3	4½	6	7½	9	12	15	18	21	24	27	30
1500	3¾	5⅝	7½	9⅜	11¼	15	18¾	22½	26¼	30	33¾	37½
1800	4½	6¾	9	11¼	13½	18	22½	27	31½	36	40½	45
2000	5	7½	10	12½	15	20	25	30	35	40	45	50
2400	6	9	12	15	18	24	30	36	42	48	54	60
2800	7	10½	14	17½	21	28	35	42	49	56	63	70
3000	7½	11¼	15	18¾	22½	30	37½	45	52½	60	67½	75
3500	8¾	13	17½	22	26	35	44	52½	61	70	79	88
4000	10	15	20	25	30	40	50	60	70	80	90	100
4500	11¼	17	22½	28	34	45	57	68	79	90	102	114
5000	12½	19	25	31	37½	50	62½	75	87½	100	112	125

Double leather, six-ply rubber or six-ply cotton belting will transmit 50 to 75 per cent. more power than is shown in this table. (One inch wide, 550 feet per minute=one horse power.)

Diameter of Wheel in Ft.	Number of Revolutions.	Trade No. of Rope.	Diameter of Rope.	Horse Power.	Diameter of Wheel in Ft.	Number of Revolutions.	Trade No. of Rope.	Diameter of Rope.	Horse Power.
4	80	23	3/8	3.3	10	80	19 / 18	5/8 / 11/16	58.0 / 56.4
4	100	23	3/8	4.1	10	100	19 / 18	5/8 / 11/16	66.7 / 73.0
4	120	23	3/8	5.0	10	120	19 / 18	5/8 / 11/16	82.5 / 87.6
4	140	23	3/8	5.8	10	140	19 / 18	5/8 / 11/16	96.2 / 102.2
5	80	22	7/16	6.9	11	80	19 / 18	5/8 / 11/16	61.9 / 75.6
5	100	22	7/16	8.6	11	100	19 / 18	5/8 / 11/16	81.1 / 94.4
5	120	22	7/16	10.3	11	120	19 / 18	5/8 / 11/16	97.8 / 113.3
5	140	22	7/16	12.1	11	140	19 / 18	5/8 / 11/16	112.6 / 132.1
6	80	21	1/2	10.7	12	80	18 / 17	11/16 / 3/4	93.4 / 99.8
6	100	21	1/2	13.4	12	100	18 / 17	11/16 / 3/4	116.7 / 124.4
6	120	21	1/2	16.1	12	120	18 / 17	11/16 / 3/4	140.1 / 149.9
6	140	21	1/2	18.7	12	140	18 / 17	11/16 / 3/4	163.5 / 173.7
7	80	20	9/16	16.9	13	80	18 / 17	11/16 / 3/4	112.0 / 133.8
7	100	20	9/16	21.1	13	100	18 / 17	11/16 / 3/4	140.0 / 152.2
7	120	20	9/16	25.3	13	120	18 / 17	11/16 / 3/4	168.0 / 193.9
7	140	20	9/16	29.6	14	80	17 / 16	3/4 / 7/8	134.0 / 141.0
8	80	19	5/8	22.0	14	100	17 / 16	3/4 / 7/8	168.0 / 176.0
8	100	19	5/8	27.5	14	120	17 / 16	3/4 / 7/8	202.0 / 211.0
8	120	19	5/8	33.0	15	80	17 / 16	3/4 / 7/8	207.0 / 217.0
8	140	19	5/8	38.5	15	100	17 / 16	3/4 / 7/8	250.0 / 258.0
9	80	20 / 19	9/16 / 5/8	40.0 / 41.0	15	120	17 / 16	3/4 / 7/8	300.0 / 306.0
9	100	20 / 19	9/16 / 5/8	50.0 / 51.0					
9	120	20 / 19	9/16 / 5/8	60.0 / 62.2					
9	140	20 / 19	9/16 / 5/8	70.0 / 72.0					

A gallon of water (U. S. standard) weighs 8⅓ pounds and contains 231 cubic inches. A cubic foot of water weighs 62½ pounds, and contains 1,728 cubic inches or 7½ gallons.

Doubling the diameter of a pipe increases its capacity four times. Friction of liquids in pipes increases as the square of the velocity.

The mean pressure of the atmosphere is usually estimated at 14.7 pounds per square inch, so that with a perfect vacuum it will sustain a column of mercury 29.9 inches or a column of water 33.9 feet high.

To find the pressure in pounds per square inch of a column of water, multiply the height of the column in feet by .434. Approximately we say that every foot elevation is equal to ½ pound pressure per square inch; this allows for ordinary friction.

To find the diameter of a pump cylinder to move a given quantity of water per minute (100 feet of piston being the standard of speed), divide the number of gallons by 4, then extract the square root, and the product will be the diameter in inches of the pump cylinder.

To find quantity of water elevated in one minute running at 100 feet of piston speed per minute: Square the diameter of the water cylinder in inches and multiply by 4. Example: Capacity of a 5-inch cylinder is desired. The square of the diameter (5 inches) is 25, which, multiplied by 4 gives 100, the number of gallons per minute (approximately).

To find the horse power necessary to elevate water to a given height, multiply the total weight of the water in lbs. by the height in feet and divide the product by 33,000 (an allowance of 25 per cent. should be added for water friction, and a further allowance of 25 per cent. for loss in steam cylinder).

The area of the steam piston, multiplied by the steam pressure, gives the total amount of pressure that can be exerted. The area of the water piston multiplied by the pressure of water per square inch gives the resistance. A margin must be made between the power and the resistance to move the pistons at the required speed—say from 20 to 40 per cent., according to speed and other conditions.

To find the capacity of a cylinder in gallons. Multiplying the area in inches by the length of stroke in inches, will give the total number of cubic inches; divide this amount by 231 (which is the cubical contents of a U. S. gallon in inches), and the product is the capacity in gallons.

With the efficient working of pumps certain precautions are necessary. Following are a few hints that will be of service to persons interested in the subject:

Care should be exercised to prevent foreign substances from entering the suction

USEFUL HYDRAULIC INFORMATION.

pipe. In case of such danger a strainer should be used and the total area of the strainer holes should be from two to five times the area of the pipe.

It is of great advantage to have the suction pipe as straight and free as possible. Elbows and valves obstruct the flow of water much more than usually supposed.

Above all other things, the suction pipe should be perfectly air-tight, as a very small leak will supply the pump with so much air that little or no water will be obtained.

It is advantageous, and, when high speed is desired, becomes a necessity, to connect a vacuum chamber to the suction pipe near the pump.

A foot valve should be used on long or high suctions. Its area should be at least as much as the pipe.

If in an exposed position, the pump should be thoroughly drained after stopping, to prevent injury by frost, by means of the drain-cocks provided for the purpose.

When a pump is to remain idle for some time the steam cylinder should be well oiled before stopping.

The working parts should be carefully packed so as not to necessitate them being screwed down too tight.

The most economical speed to run a pump is 100 feet per minute.

The friction of liquids in pipes increases as the square of the velocity.

To find the capacity of a Double-Acting Pump in U. S. gallons per minute; multiply together: the area of the water cylinder in inches; the length of the stroke in inches; the number of single strokes per minute. Divide the product by 231. For a Single-Acting Pump take half the number of single strokes.

For domestic use water should be kept in wooden or iron tanks. Zinc can be used to advantage. The use of lead-lined tanks is exceedingly dangerous, especially for keeping rain water.

CAPACITY OF CYLINDRICAL CISTERNS OR TANKS

For Each Foot of Depth (U. S. Gallons).

Diameter in Feet.	Gallons.	Pounds.	Diameter in Feet.	Gallons.	Pounds.
2.0	23.5	196	9.0	475.9	3,965
2.5	36.7	306	9.5	530.2	4,422
3.0	52.9	441	10.0	587.5	4,900
3.5	72.0	600	11.0	710.9	5,929
4.0	94.0	784	12.0	846.0	7,056
4.5	119.0	992	13.0	992.9	8,281
5.0	146.9	1,225	14.0	1,151.5	9,604
5.5	177.7	1,482	15.0	1,321.9	11,025
6.0	211.5	1,764	16.0	1,504.1	12,544
6.5	248.2	2,070	20.0	2,350.1	19,600
7.0	287.9	2,401	25.0	3,672.0	30,625
7.5	330.5	2,756	30.0	5,287.7	44,100
8.0	376.0	3,136	35.0	7,197.1	60,025
8.5	424.5	3,540	40.0	9,400.2	78,400

The great philosopher, Plato, defined man as a featherless biped. Thereupon the shrewd old cynic, Diogenes, plucked the feathers from a goose, and, having labeled it "Plato's man," threw it over into the philosopher's classroom.

SIZE, CAPACITY, ETC., OF BOILERS.

LOCOMOTIVES.

Length.		Diam.	Fire Box.	Dome.	Flues.		Length.		Area Chimney.	Capacity.
ft.	in.	inches.	inches.	inches.		in.	ft.	in.	sq. inches.	sq. in.
7	3	36	30x30	16x16	44	2	4	6	135	939
7	8	42	33x36	15x30	42	2¼	4	8	240	1300
8	3	42	36x30	16x30	48	2¼	5		250	1350
10	8	42	39x36	20x24	48	2¼	7		240	1725
12	8	42	38x42	24x24	40	3	8	6	230	2000
14	3	42	36x42	24x24	40	3	10	0	280	2500
10	3	42	42x30	24x24	50	3	7		280	2000
14	8	48	42x42	24x30	50	3	10	6	230	3000
16		48	42x48	30x36	50	3	11	3	250	3000

Shell ¼-in. C. H. No. 1 iron; heads and fire-box, 5/16-in. C. H. No. 1 flange; wrought iron rings around fire door and in legs.

HORIZONTAL TUBULARS.

Length.	Diam.	Dome.	No. Flues.		Area Chimney.	Heating S.	Capacity.
Feet.	inches.	inches.		in.	sq. inches.	sq. inches.	sq. inches.
10	36	20x20	30	3	230	250	1400
12	36	20x24	30	3	200	330	1650
10	42	20x24	40	3	250	390	1900
12	42	24x24	40	3	250	440	2200
14	42	24x24	40	3	300	490	2400
16	42	24x30	40	3	350	560	2800
14	48	24x30	50	3	440	650	3150
12	48	24x30	50	3	440	725	3625
16	54	30x36	38	3½	525	850	4250
16	60	30x36	50	4	800	975	4875
18	60	30x36	56	4	800	1250	6250

Small boilers: Shell 5/16-in. C. H. No. 1 iron; heads, 3/8-in. C. H. No. 1 flange iron.

Large boilers (54 in. and upwards): Shell 3/8-in. C. H. No. 1 iron; heads, ½-in. C. H. No. 1 flange iron.

BRICK CHIMNEYS.

Thickness of brick-work, one brick from top to twenty-five feet from top; a brick and a half from 25 to 50 ft. from top, increasing by half a brick for each additional 25 feet to bottom. The diameter at base should be not less than one-tenth the height. If the inside diameter at top exceed 4½ feet, the top length should be a brick and a half thick.

combined area of all the flues or tubes. Where boilers are provided with other means of draught the dimensions of the chimney are not so important.

Diameter and Height of Boiler Chimneys.

Horse power of Boiler.	Height of Chimney.	Inside Diam. at Top.	Horse power of Boiler.	Height of Chimney.	Inside Diam. at Top.
10	80 ft.	14 inches.	70	140 ft.	30 inches.
12	86 "	16 "	90	150 "	34 "
16	90 "	18 "	120	155 "	38 "
20	99 "	19 "	160	160 "	42 "
30	105 "	21 "	200	165 "	45 "
50	120 "	22 "	250	170 "	48 "
60	130 "	24 "	300	180 "	54 "

Table of the Principal Alloys.

A combination of copper and tin makes bath metal.
A combination of copper and zinc makes bell metal.
A combination of tin and copper makes bronze metal.
A combination of tin, antimony, copper and bismuth makes britannia metal.
A combination of tin and copper makes cannon metal.
A combination of copper and zinc makes Dutch gold.
A combination of copper, nickel and zinc, with sometimes a little iron and tin makes German silver.
A combination of gold and copper makes standard gold.
A combination of gold, copper and silver makes old-standard gold.
A combination of tin and copper makes gun metal.
A combination of copper and zinc makes mosaic gold.
A combination of tin and lead makes pewter.
A combination of lead and a little arsenic makes sheet metal.
A combination of silver and copper makes standard silver.
A combination of tin and lead makes solder.
A combination of lead and antimony makes type metal.
A combination of copper and arsenic makes white copper.

How to Mix Printing Inks and Paints in the Preparation of Tints.

THE FIRST NAMED COLOR ALWAYS PREDOMINATES.
Mixing dark green and purple makes bottle green.
Mixing white and medium yellow makes buff tint.
Mixing red, black and blue makes dark brown.
Mixing bronze, blue, lemon yellow and black makes dark green.
Mixing white, medium yellow and black makes drab tint.
Mixing white, lake and lemon yellow makes flesh tint.
Mixing white and purple makes lavender tint.
Mixing red, black and medium yellow makes maroon.
Mixing lake and purple makes magenta.
Mixing medium yellow and purple makes olive green.
Mixing medium yellow and red makes orange.
Mixing white, ultramarine blue and black makes pearl tint.
Mixing white and lake makes pink.
Mixing ultramarine blue and lake makes purple.
Mixing orange, lake and purple makes russet.
Mixing medium yellow, red and white makes sienna.
Mixing white and ultramarine blue makes sky blue.
Mixing ultramarine blue, black and white makes slate.
Mixing vermilion and black makes Turkey red.
Mixing white, yellow, red and black makes umber.

Durability of Different Woods.

Experiments have been lately made by driving sticks, made of different woods, each two feet long and one and one-half inches square, into the ground, only one-half an inch projecting outward. It was found that in five years all those made of oak, elm, ash, fir, soft mahogany, and nearly every variety of pine, were totally rotten. Larch, hard pine and teak wood were decayed on the outside only, while acacia, with the exception of being also slightly attacked on the exterior, was otherwise sound. Hard mahogany and cedar of Lebanon were in tolerably good condition; but only Virginia cedar was found as good as when put in the ground. This is of some importance to builders, showing what woods should be avoided, and what others used by preference in underground work.

The duration of wood when kept dry is very great, as beams still exist which are known to be nearly 1,100 years old. Piles driven by the Romans prior to the Christian era have been examined of late, and found to be perfectly sound after an immersion of nearly 2,000 years.

The wood of some tools will last longer than the metals, as in spades, hoes and plows. In other tools the wood is first gone, as in wagons, wheelbarrows and machines. Such wood should be painted or oiled; the paint not only looks well, but preserves the wood; petroleum oil is as good as any other.

Hard wood stumps decay in five or six years; spruce stumps decay in about the same time; hemlock stumps in eight to nine years; cedar, eight to nine years; pine stumps, never.

Cedar, oak, yellow pine and chestnut are the most durable woods in dry places.

Timber intended for posts is rendered almost proof against rot by thorough seasoning, charring and immersion in hot coal tar.

Specific Gravity of Various Substances.

A gallon of water or wine weighs 10 lbs., and this is taken as the basis of the following table.

LIQUIDS.		WOODS.		METALS.	
Water	100	Cork	24	Zinc	719
Sea water	103	Poplar	38	Cast iron	721
Dead Sea	124	Fir	55	Tin	729
Alcohol	84	Cedar	61	Bar iron	778
Olive oil	92	Pear	66	Steel	788
Turpentine	99	Walnut	67	Copper	895
Wine	100	Cherry	72	Brass	840
Urine	101	Maple	75	Silver	1,051
Cider	101	Apple	79	Lead	1,135
Beer	102	Ash	84	Mercury	1,357
Woman's milk	102	Beech	85	Gold	1,925
Cow's "	103	Mahogany	106	Platina	2,000
Goat's "	104	Oak	117		
Porter	104	Ebony	133		

PRECIOUS STONES.

Emerald	277.5	Diamond	353.0	Garnet	406.3
Crystal	286.3	Topaz	401.1	Ruby	428.3

SUNDRIES.

Indigo	77	Peat	133	Porcelain	226
Gunpowder	93	Opium	134	Stone	252
Butter	94	Honey	145	Marble	270
Ice	92	Ivory	183	Granite	278
Glue	126	Brick	200	Chalk	279
Coal	130	Sulphur	203	Glass	289

Weight in Cubic Feet.

	Lbs. per Cub. Ft.		Lbs. per Cub. Ft.
Cork	15	Brick	125
Cedar	35	Stone	160
Birch	51	Granite	165
Pine	54	Glass	172
Water	63	Iron	450
Mahogany	66	Copper	550
Ice	58	Silver	655
Oak	73	Lead	710
Clay	75	Gold	1,255
Coal	80		

Tensile and Transverse Strength

A crushing force of 1,000 lbs. per square inch on a bar 1 inch square, and 12 inches long, gives the following ratios of strength:

	Tensile.	Transverse.		Tensile.	Transverse.
Stone	196	10	Cast iron	158	20
Glass	150	12	Timber	1,300	85

Tensile Test of Steel.

SIX ½ INCH SPECIMENS.

Sq. Inch Section.	Strain, Tons per Sq. Inch.	Extension, Inches.	Sq. Inch Section.	Strain, Tons per Sq. Inch.	Extension, Inches.
1.0000	18.91	.21	.4996	26.35	1.40
.8799	16.66	.23	.3906	42.28	2.00
.9852	21.44	.49	.3641	25.06	2.30
.3746	27.58	1.00			

Elastic limit	17.82 tons.	Cohesion	45.51 tons.
Maximum strain	25.34 "	Extension	27½ per cent.
Breaking load	26.55 "	Contraction	44½ "

TENSILE STRENGTH OF STEEL.—Continued.

Taking the strength of Swedish iron at 100, the tensile strength of steel compares thus:

Swedish iron	100	Cast steel	173
Boiler steel	115	Spring steel	202

Pecuniary Value of Metals.

Few people have any idea of the value of precious metals other than gold, silver and copper, which are commonly supposed to be the most precious of all. There are many metals more valuable and infinitely rarer. The following table gives the names and prices of all the known metals of probability worth:

	Price per Av. pound.		Price per Av. pound.
Vanadium	$12,600 00	Gold	$ 300 00
Rubidium	9,206 00	Molybdenum	225 00
Zirconium	7,200 00	Thallium	225 00
Lithium	7,000 00	Platinum	120 00
Cerium	5,400 00	Manganese	120 00
Calcium	4,500 00	Tungsten	115 00
Strontium	4,200 00	Magnesium	64 00
Terbium	4,000 00	Cadmium	64 00
Yttrium	4,000 00	Aluminum	8 00
Erbium	3,400 00	Silver	20 00
Cerium	3,400 00	Cobalt	16 00
Didymium	3,200 00	Sodium	3 00
Indium	2,800 00	Nickel	4 00
Ruthenium	2,400 00	Cadmium	4 00
Rhodium	2,300 00	Bismuth	2 00
Niobium	2,000 00	Mercury	[illegible]
Barium	1,900 00	Arsenic	[illegible]
Palladium	1,400 00	Tin	[illegible]
Osmium	1,300 00	Copper	[illegible]
Iridium	1,300 00	Antimony	[illegible]
Uranium	900 00	Zinc	.11
Titanium	896 00	Lead	.09
Chromium	500 50		

VALUE OF METALS AS CONDUCTORS.

	Heat.	Electricity.		Heat.	Electricity.
Gold	100	94	Iron	37	16
Platinum	98	16	Zinc	36	29
Silver	97	94	Tin	30	15
Copper	90	100	Lead	18	8

TENACITY OF METALS.

A wire, 0.08 of a line in diameter, will sustain weights as follows:

Lead	55 lbs.	Silver	187 lbs.
Tin	46 "	Platinum	274 "
Zinc	110 "	Copper	302 "
Gold	150 "	Iron	549 "

FLUID DENSITY OF METALS.

Zinc	6.48	Copper	8.22
Iron	6.88	Silver	9.24
Tin	7.03	Lead	10.37

TABLE OF SQUARES AND CUBES OF ALL NUMBERS FROM 1 TO 540.

No.	Squares.	Cubes.	No.	Squares.	Cubes.
1	1	1	55	30 25	166 375
2	4	8	56	31 36	175 616
3	9	27	57	32 49	185 193
4	16	64	58	33 64	195 112
5	25	125	59	34 81	205 379
6	36	216	60	36 00	216 000
7	49	343	61	37 21	226 981
8	64	512	62	38 44	238 328
9	81	729	63	39 69	250 047
10	1 00	1 000	64	40 96	262 144
11	1 21	1 331	65	42 25	274 625
12	1 44	1 728	66	43 56	287 496
13	1 69	2 197	67	44 89	300 763
14	1 96	2 744	68	46 24	314 432
15	2 25	3 375	69	47 61	328 509
16	2 56	4 096	70	49 00	343 000
17	2 89	4 913	71	50 41	357 911
18	3 24	5 832	72	51 84	373 248
19	3 61	6 859	73	53 29	389 017
20	4 00	8 000	74	54 76	405 224
21	4 41	9 261	75	56 25	421 875
22	4 84	10 648	76	57 76	438 976
23	5 29	12 167	77	59 29	456 533
24	5 76	13 824	78	60 84	474 552
25	6 25	15 625	79	62 41	493 039
26	6 76	17 576	80	64 00	512 000
27	7 29	19 683	81	65 61	531 441
28	7 84	21 952	82	67 24	551 368
29	8 41	24 389	83	68 89	571 787
30	9 00	27 000	84	70 56	592 704
31	9 61	29 791	85	72 25	614 125
32	10 24	32 768	86	73 96	636 056
33	10 89	35 937	87	75 69	658 503
34	11 56	39 304	88	77 44	681 472
35	12 25	42 875	89	79 21	704 969
36	12 96	46 656	90	81 00	729 000
37	13 69	50 653	91	82 81	753 571
38	14 44	54 872	92	84 64	778 688
39	15 21	59 319	93	86 49	804 357
40	16 00	64 000	94	88 36	830 584
41	16 81	68 921	95	90 25	857 375
42	17 64	74 088	96	92 16	884 736
43	18 49	79 507	97	94 09	912 673
44	19 36	85 184	98	96 04	941 192
45	20 25	91 125	99	98 01	970 299
46	21 16	97 336	100	1 00 00	1 000 000
47	22 09	103 823	101	1 02 01	1 030 301
48	23 04	110 592	102	1 04 04	1 061 208
49	24 01	117 649	103	1 06 09	1 092 727
50	25 00	125 000	104	1 08 16	1 124 864
51	26 01	132 651	105	1 10 25	1 157 625
52	27 04	140 608	106	1 12 36	1 191 016
53	28 09	148 877	107	1 14 49	1 225 043
54	29 16	157 464	108	1 16 64	1 259 712

TABLE OF SQUARES AND CUBES—*Continued.*

No.	Squares.	Cubes.	No.	Squares.	Cubes.
109	1 18 81	1 295 029	169	2 85 61	4 826 809
110	1 21 00	1 331 000	170	2 89 00	4 913 000
111	1 23 21	1 367 631	171	2 92 41	5 000 211
112	1 25 44	1 404 928	172	2 95 84	5 088 448
113	1 27 69	1 442 897	173	2 99 29	5 177 717
114	1 29 96	1 481 544	174	3 02 76	5 268 024
115	1 32 25	1 520 875	175	3 06 25	5 359 375
116	1 34 56	1 560 896	176	3 09 76	5 451 776
117	1 36 89	1 601 613	177	3 13 29	5 545 233
118	1 39 24	1 643 032	178	3 16 84	5 639 752
119	1 41 61	1 685 159	179	3 20 41	5 735 339
120	1 44 00	1 728 000	180	3 24 00	5 832 000
121	1 46 41	1 771 561	181	3 27 61	5 929 741
122	1 48 84	1 815 848	182	3 31 24	6 028 568
123	1 51 29	1 860 867	183	3 34 89	6 128 487
124	1 53 76	1 906 624	184	3 38 56	6 229 504
125	1 56 25	1 953 125	185	3 42 25	6 331 625
126	1 58 76	2 000 376	186	3 45 96	6 434 856
127	1 61 29	2 048 383	187	3 49 69	6 539 203
128	1 63 84	2 097 152	188	3 53 44	6 644 672
129	1 66 41	2 146 689	189	3 57 21	6 751 269
130	1 69 00	2 197 000	190	3 61 00	6 859 000
131	1 71 61	2 248 091	191	3 64 81	6 967 871
132	1 74 24	2 299 968	192	3 68 64	7 077 888
133	1 76 89	2 352 637	193	3 72 49	7 189 057
134	1 79 56	2 406 104	194	3 76 36	7 301 384
135	1 82 25	2 460 375	195	3 80 25	7 414 875
136	1 84 96	2 515 456	196	3 84 16	7 529 536
137	1 87 69	2 571 353	197	3 88 09	7 645 373
138	1 90 44	2 628 072	198	3 92 04	7 762 392
139	1 93 21	2 685 619	199	3 96 01	7 880 599
140	1 96 00	2 744 000	200	4 00 00	8 000 000
141	1 98 81	2 803 221	201	4 04 01	8 120 601
142	2 01 64	2 863 288	202	4 08 04	8 242 408
143	2 04 49	2 924 207	203	4 12 09	8 365 427
144	2 07 36	2 985 984	204	4 16 16	8 489 664
145	2 10 25	3 048 625	205	4 20 25	8 615 125
146	2 13 16	3 112 136	206	4 24 36	8 741 816
147	2 16 09	3 176 523	207	4 28 49	8 869 743
148	2 19 04	3 241 792	208	4 32 64	8 998 912
149	2 22 01	3 307 949	209	4 36 81	9 129 329
150	2 25 00	3 375 000	210	4 41 00	9 261 000
151	2 28 01	3 442 951	211	4 45 21	9 393 931
152	2 31 04	3 511 808	212	4 49 44	9 528 128
153	2 34 09	3 581 577	213	4 53 69	9 663 597
154	2 37 16	3 652 264	214	4 57 96	9 800 344
155	2 40 25	3 723 875	215	4 62 25	9 938 375
156	2 43 36	3 796 416	216	4 66 56	10 077 696
157	2 46 49	3 869 893	217	4 70 89	10 218 313
158	2 49 64	3 944 312	218	4 75 24	10 360 232
159	2 52 81	4 019 679	219	4 79 61	10 503 459
160	2 56 00	4 096 000	220	4 84 00	10 648 000
161	2 59 21	4 173 281	221	4 88 41	10 793 861
162	2 62 44	4 251 528	222	4 92 84	10 941 048
163	2 65 69	4 330 747	223	4 97 29	11 089 567
164	2 68 96	4 410 944	224	5 01 76	11 239 424
165	2 72 25	4 492 125	225	5 06 25	11 390 625
166	2 75 56	4 574 296	226	5 10 76	11 543 176
167	2 78 89	4 657 463	227	5 15 29	11 697 083
168	2 82 24	4 741 632	228	5 19 84	11 852 352

TABLE OF SQUARES AND CUBES—*Continued.*

No.	Square.	Cubes.	No.	Square.	Cubes.
[illegible]	[illegible]	[illegible]	[illegible]	[illegible]	[illegible]

TABLE OF SQUARES AND CUBES—*Continued.*

No.	Square.	Cubes.	No.	Square.	Cubes.
[illegible]	[illegible]	[illegible]	[illegible]	[illegible]	[illegible]

TABLE OF SQUARES AND CUBES—*Concluded.*

No.	Squares.	Cubes.	No.	Squares.	Cubes.
469	21 99 61	103 161 709	485	23 52 25	[illegible]
470	22 09 00	103 823 000	486	[illegible]	[illegible]
471	[illegible]	[illegible]	487	[illegible]	[illegible]
472	[illegible]	[illegible]	488	[illegible]	[illegible]
473	[illegible]	[illegible]	489	[illegible]	[illegible]
474	[illegible]	[illegible]	490	[illegible]	[illegible]
475	[illegible]	[illegible]	491	[illegible]	[illegible]
476	[illegible]	[illegible]	492	[illegible]	[illegible]
477	[illegible]	[illegible]	493	[illegible]	[illegible]
478	[illegible]	[illegible]	494	[illegible]	[illegible]
479	[illegible]	[illegible]	495	[illegible]	[illegible]
480	[illegible]	[illegible]	496	[illegible]	[illegible]
481	[illegible]	[illegible]	497	[illegible]	[illegible]
482	[illegible]	[illegible]	498	[illegible]	[illegible]
483	[illegible]	[illegible]	499	[illegible]	[illegible]
484	[illegible]	[illegible]	500	25 00 00	125 000 000

LENGTH OF CIRCULAR ARC.

Huygens' approximation to length of a circular arc:

A = Chord of any circular arc.
B = Chord of half that arc.
R = Radius of the circular arc.
L = Length of the circular arc.
Then

$$L = \frac{8B - A}{3}$$

Or, as it is usually written,

$$L = 2B + \tfrac{1}{3}(2B - A).$$

WEDDING ANNIVERSARIES.

First, cotton; second, paper; third, leather; fifth, wooden; seventh, woolen; tenth, tin; twelfth, silk and fine linen; fifteenth, crystal; twentieth, china; twenty-fifth, silver; thirtieth, pearl; fortieth, ruby; fiftieth, golden; seventy-fifth, diamond.

YOUR BIRTHDAY.

Born on Monday, fair in face;
Born on Tuesday, full of God's grace;
Born on Wednesday, the best to be had;
Born on Thursday, merry and glad;
Born on Friday, worthily given;
Born on Saturday, work hard for a living;
Born on Sunday, shall never know want.

An indenture is a deed or instrument in writing. Originally such writings were made in duplicate upon a sheet of paper which was afterward bisected or cut apart in a waving or notched line. One piece was given to each of the parties to the contract, and when the two were put together they would, of course, fit into each other exactly. This mode of indenture has passed out of use, but the term survives.

NATURAL SINES, ETC.

Deg.	Sine.	Covers.	Cosecant.	Tang.	Cotang.	Secant.	Versin.	Cosine.	Deg.
0	.0	1.00000	Infinite.	.0	Infinite.	1.00000	.0	1.00000	90
1	.01745	[illegible]	[illegible]	[illegible]	[illegible]	[illegible]	[illegible]	[illegible]	89
2	[illegible]	[illegible]	[illegible]	[illegible]	[illegible]	[illegible]	[illegible]	[illegible]	88
3	[illegible]	[illegible]	[illegible]	[illegible]	[illegible]	[illegible]	[illegible]	[illegible]	87
4	[illegible]	[illegible]	[illegible]	[illegible]	[illegible]	[illegible]	[illegible]	[illegible]	86
5	[illegible]	[illegible]	[illegible]	[illegible]	[illegible]	[illegible]	[illegible]	[illegible]	85
6	[illegible]	[illegible]	[illegible]	[illegible]	[illegible]	[illegible]	[illegible]	[illegible]	84
7	[illegible]	[illegible]	[illegible]	[illegible]	[illegible]	[illegible]	[illegible]	[illegible]	83
8	[illegible]	[illegible]	[illegible]	[illegible]	[illegible]	[illegible]	[illegible]	[illegible]	82
9	[illegible]	[illegible]	[illegible]	[illegible]	[illegible]	[illegible]	[illegible]	[illegible]	81
10	[illegible]	[illegible]	[illegible]	[illegible]	[illegible]	[illegible]	[illegible]	[illegible]	80
11	[illegible]	[illegible]	[illegible]	[illegible]	[illegible]	[illegible]	[illegible]	[illegible]	79
12	[illegible]	[illegible]	[illegible]	[illegible]	[illegible]	[illegible]	[illegible]	[illegible]	78
13	[illegible]	[illegible]	[illegible]	[illegible]	[illegible]	[illegible]	[illegible]	[illegible]	77
14	[illegible]	[illegible]	[illegible]	[illegible]	[illegible]	[illegible]	[illegible]	[illegible]	76
15	[illegible]	[illegible]	[illegible]	[illegible]	[illegible]	[illegible]	[illegible]	[illegible]	75
16	[illegible]	[illegible]	[illegible]	[illegible]	[illegible]	[illegible]	[illegible]	[illegible]	74
17	[illegible]	[illegible]	[illegible]	[illegible]	[illegible]	[illegible]	[illegible]	[illegible]	73
18	[illegible]	[illegible]	[illegible]	[illegible]	[illegible]	[illegible]	[illegible]	[illegible]	72
19	[illegible]	[illegible]	[illegible]	[illegible]	[illegible]	[illegible]	[illegible]	[illegible]	71
20	[illegible]	[illegible]	[illegible]	[illegible]	[illegible]	[illegible]	[illegible]	[illegible]	70
21	[illegible]	[illegible]	[illegible]	[illegible]	[illegible]	[illegible]	[illegible]	[illegible]	69
22	[illegible]	[illegible]	[illegible]	[illegible]	[illegible]	[illegible]	[illegible]	[illegible]	68
23	[illegible]	[illegible]	[illegible]	[illegible]	[illegible]	[illegible]	[illegible]	[illegible]	67
24	[illegible]	[illegible]	[illegible]	[illegible]	[illegible]	[illegible]	[illegible]	[illegible]	66
25	[illegible]	[illegible]	[illegible]	[illegible]	[illegible]	[illegible]	[illegible]	[illegible]	65
26	[illegible]	[illegible]	[illegible]	[illegible]	[illegible]	[illegible]	[illegible]	[illegible]	64
27	[illegible]	[illegible]	[illegible]	[illegible]	[illegible]	[illegible]	[illegible]	[illegible]	63
28	[illegible]	[illegible]	[illegible]	[illegible]	[illegible]	[illegible]	[illegible]	[illegible]	62
29	[illegible]	[illegible]	[illegible]	[illegible]	[illegible]	[illegible]	[illegible]	[illegible]	61
30	[illegible]	[illegible]	[illegible]	[illegible]	[illegible]	[illegible]	[illegible]	[illegible]	60
31	[illegible]	[illegible]	[illegible]	[illegible]	[illegible]	[illegible]	[illegible]	[illegible]	59
32	[illegible]	[illegible]	[illegible]	[illegible]	[illegible]	[illegible]	[illegible]	[illegible]	58
33	[illegible]	[illegible]	[illegible]	[illegible]	[illegible]	[illegible]	[illegible]	[illegible]	57
34	[illegible]	[illegible]	[illegible]	[illegible]	[illegible]	[illegible]	[illegible]	[illegible]	56
35	[illegible]	[illegible]	[illegible]	[illegible]	[illegible]	[illegible]	[illegible]	[illegible]	55
36	[illegible]	[illegible]	[illegible]	[illegible]	[illegible]	[illegible]	[illegible]	[illegible]	54
37	[illegible]	[illegible]	[illegible]	[illegible]	[illegible]	[illegible]	[illegible]	[illegible]	53
38	[illegible]	[illegible]	[illegible]	[illegible]	[illegible]	[illegible]	[illegible]	[illegible]	52
39	[illegible]	[illegible]	[illegible]	[illegible]	[illegible]	[illegible]	[illegible]	[illegible]	51
40	[illegible]	[illegible]	[illegible]	[illegible]	[illegible]	[illegible]	[illegible]	[illegible]	50
41	[illegible]	[illegible]	[illegible]	[illegible]	[illegible]	[illegible]	[illegible]	[illegible]	49
42	[illegible]	[illegible]	[illegible]	[illegible]	[illegible]	[illegible]	[illegible]	[illegible]	48
43	[illegible]	[illegible]	[illegible]	[illegible]	[illegible]	[illegible]	[illegible]	[illegible]	47
44	[illegible]	[illegible]	[illegible]	[illegible]	[illegible]	[illegible]	[illegible]	[illegible]	46
45	.70710	.29289	1.4142	1.00000	1.0000	1.4142	.2928	.70710	45
	Cosine.	Versin.	Secant.	Cotang.	Tang.	Cosecant.	Covers.	Sine.	

The term bankrupt originated in connection with the money-changers of Italy. They sat in the market-place with their money displayed on a bench (or *banc*, still so called) before them. When one of these financial gentlemen failed his bench (or *banc*) was said to be broken, and he was styled a bankrupt. The modern bank inherits its name from the money-changers' bench (*banco*) of mediæval Italy.

Useful Information for Printers and Publishers.

Standard Newspaper Measure.

The standard newspaper measure, as recognized and now in general use, is 13 ems pica. The standard of measurement of all sizes of type is the em quad, not the letter m.

Leads and Slugs.

Leads are designated as "—to-pica," the number being that fraction of a pica which the lead is, viz.: a 6-to-pica lead is one-sixth of a pica in thickness, or six 6-to-pica's are equal to one pica; four 4-to-pica's one pica, and so with other sizes or thicknesses of leads.

SLUGS—"Leads" of nonpareil thickness and greater are called slugs, viz.: nonpareil slugs, brevier slugs, pica slugs, etc.

Average Weight of Matter.

A "piece" of solid matter 13 ems pica wide and 6 inches long will weigh about 4⅜ lbs., but, in order to allow for the sorts usually remaining in case 4⅞ lbs. of type would be required to set that amount of solid matter. When the matter is to be leaded the weight of the type may be reduced about one-quarter, i. e., a single column of six-column folio, solid, will weigh 12½ lbs., requiring about 13 lbs. of type, while the same length column, leaded with 6-to-pica leads, will contain but 7⅞ lbs. solid matter, requiring about 10 lbs. of type to set the same.

EXAMPLE.—A single page of regular six-column folio or quarto (13x56¾) contains 256¾ square inches of matter:

256¾×4⅞÷13 (square inches of 4⅞ lbs. of type) =58⅔,

the number of pounds of type required to set that amount of matter, including sorts in case.

How to Estimate for Body Type.

To estimate the quantity of type (solid) necessary to fill a given space, multiply the number of square inches by 1⅝ (estimated weight, in ounces, of one square inch of matter, including sorts in case) divide the product by 16, and the result will be the weight of type required. If leaded, a reduction in weight of type may be made as above.

EXAMPLE.—A single page of regular six-column folio or quarto (13x59¾) contains 256¾ square inches of matter:

256¾×1⅝÷16=26⅛,

the number of pounds of type required to set that amount of matter, including sorts in case.

Miscellaneous Information.

The following table gives the number of "ems" in a space 6x13 ems pica, also the average number of "ems" in a square:

Number of Ems in	Pearl	Agate	Nonpl	Minion	Brevier	Bourgeois	Long Primer	Small Pica	Pica
6x13 Ems Pica	467⅞	388⅛	312	286½	177	146⅛	132¼	92	78
1 Column	196	166	138	106	78	61	51	48	36

Newspaper Measurement.

Table showing the number of ems of the different sizes of newspaper type in a line, the number of lines necessary to make 1,000 ems, and the length in inches. Also the number of ems in the regular lengths of columns:

13 Ems Pica, Width of Newspaper Column.	[illegible]	[illegible]	[illegible]	[illegible]	[illegible]	[illegible]	[illegible]	[illegible]	[illegible]
Agate	[illegible]	[illegible]	25½	5,040	6,566	7,350	7,900	8,800	9,250
Nonpareil	[illegible]	[illegible]	8½	4,256	5,555	6,360	6,785	7,418	8,400
Minion	[illegible]	[illegible]	4⅞	3,375	4,335	4,516	4,975	5,440	5,985
Brevier	[illegible]	[illegible]	6⅞	2,460	3,260	3,819	4,445	4,826	4,575
Bourgeois	[illegible]	[illegible]	7½	1,950	2,735	3,120	3,400	3,920	3,615
Long Primer	[illegible]	[illegible]	9	1,610	2,385	2,580	2,520	2,744	2,996

Leads for Newspapers.

Table showing the number of leads, 13 ems pica long, contained in one pound, and the number required to lead 1,000 ems of matter; together with the number of leads in a single column of matter, regular sizes of newspapers:

Size of Body Type to be Leaded with 6-to-Pica Leads.	No. Leads [illegible]	No. Leads [illegible]	[illegible] Column	[illegible] Column	[illegible] Column	[illegible] Column	[illegible] Column	[illegible] Column
Agate	52	96	128	170	256	276	224	248
Nonpareil	46	80	136	182	199	121	248	233
Minion	60	84	169	140	274	169	166	201
Brevier	50	40	90	123	341	168	132	183
Bourgeois	60	42	86	114	125	152	150	162
Long Primer	60	52	84	108	119	135	148	164

Book Work Measurement.

Table showing the number of ems in a line, and the number of lines contained in 1,000 ems of matter, standard book measure. Also, the space, in inches, filled by 1,000 ems of matter of the different measures:

Size of Type.	21 Ems Pica.			23 Ems Pica.			25 Ems Pica.		
	No. Ems in Line.	No. Lines 1,000 Ems.	No. Inches 1,000 Ems.	No. Ems in Line.	No. Lines 1,000 Ems.	No. Inches 1,000 Ems.	No. Ems in Line.	No. Lines 1,000 Ems.	No. Inches 1,000 Ems.
Nonpareil	42	24	3	46	21⅞	2¾	50	20	2½
Brevier	31½	31¾	3½	35	28½	[illegible]	36¼	27½	3
Long Primer	27¾	36½	4½	27⅜	36	4	30	33⅓	4⅛
Small Pica	25	42½	4¾	28	36	4½	27½	36¼	4½
Pica	21	48	6	23	43½	5¼	25	40	5¼

Leads for Book-work.

Number of 4-to-pica and 6-to-pica leads, standard book measures, contained in one pound, and number required to lead 1,000 ems of matter of the standard sizes of book type:

18 ems. No. Leads to Pound.	20 ems. No. Leads to Pound.	22 ems. No. Leads to Pound.	[illegible]		Nonpareil.	Brevier.	Lg. Primer.	Small Pica.	Pica.
31	34	37	4-to-Pica	[illegible]	[illegible]	[illegible]	[illegible]	[illegible]	[illegible]
46	50	56	6-to-Pica	[illegible]	[illegible]	[illegible]	[illegible]	[illegible]	[illegible]

Sizes of Newspapers.

NAME.		SIZE.
Five-column	Folio	20 x 25 inches
Six-column	Folio	22 x 31 inches
Six-column	Folio, extra margin	22 x 29 inches
Seven-column	Folio	24 x 35 inches
Seven-column	Folio, extra margin	24 x 36 inches
Eight-column	Folio	26 x 40 inches
Nine-column	Folio	28 x 44 inches
Four-column	Quarto	22 x 31 inches
Five-column	Quarto	26 x 40 inches
Six-column	Quarto	30 x 44 inches
Seven-column	Quarto	33 x 48 inches

Common Sizes of Flat Papers.

NAME.	SIZE.	NAME.	SIZE.
Flat Letter	10 x 16	Medium	18 x 23
Small Cap	13 x 16	Double Small Cap	16 x 26
Flat Cap	14 x 17	Royal	19 x 24
Demy	16 x 21	Double Cap	17 x 28
Folio	17 x 22		

MEASUREMENT BY SQUARE INCHES.

With the following table the printer dispenses entirely with a type measure proper, resorting to the common inch rule. After getting the square inches in his job, he may take the figures directly from the table, or, if the square inches are in excess of the table, add two or more of the numbers together; as, for instance, 79 square inches of brevier, the seventh line gives 567 ems for 7 inches, add a cipher and you have 5,670 ems for 70 inches, and in the ninth line add 729 ems to the 5,670 ems, and you have a total of 6,399 ems in 79 square inches.

SQUARE-INCH TYPE MEASUREMENT.

NUMBER OF EMS IN SQUARE INCHES.

(Adapted to the Point System.)

	Pica.	Small Pica.	Long Primer.	Bour-geois.	Brevier.	Minion.	Nonpa-reil.
1 square inch	36	44	52	64	81	106	144
2 square inches	[illegible]	[illegible]	[illegible]	[illegible]	[illegible]	[illegible]	[illegible]
3 " "	[illegible]	[illegible]	[illegible]	[illegible]	[illegible]	[illegible]	[illegible]
4 " "	[illegible]	[illegible]	[illegible]	[illegible]	[illegible]	[illegible]	[illegible]
5 " "	[illegible]	[illegible]	[illegible]	[illegible]	[illegible]	[illegible]	[illegible]
6 " "	[illegible]	[illegible]	[illegible]	[illegible]	[illegible]	[illegible]	[illegible]
7 " "	[illegible]	[illegible]	[illegible]	[illegible]	[illegible]	[illegible]	[illegible]
8 " "	[illegible]	[illegible]	[illegible]	[illegible]	[illegible]	[illegible]	[illegible]
9 " "	[illegible]	[illegible]	[illegible]	[illegible]	[illegible]	[illegible]	[illegible]
10 " "	[illegible]	[illegible]	[illegible]	[illegible]	[illegible]	[illegible]	[illegible]
11 " "	[illegible]	[illegible]	[illegible]	[illegible]	[illegible]	[illegible]	[illegible]
12 " "	[illegible]	[illegible]	[illegible]	[illegible]	[illegible]	[illegible]	[illegible]
13 " "	[illegible]	[illegible]	[illegible]	[illegible]	[illegible]	[illegible]	[illegible]
14 " "	[illegible]	[illegible]	[illegible]	[illegible]	[illegible]	[illegible]	[illegible]
15 " "	[illegible]	[illegible]	[illegible]	[illegible]	[illegible]	[illegible]	[illegible]
16 " "	[illegible]	[illegible]	[illegible]	[illegible]	[illegible]	[illegible]	[illegible]
17 " "	[illegible]	[illegible]	[illegible]	[illegible]	[illegible]	[illegible]	[illegible]
18 " "	[illegible]	[illegible]	[illegible]	[illegible]	[illegible]	[illegible]	[illegible]
19 " "	[illegible]	[illegible]	[illegible]	[illegible]	[illegible]	[illegible]	[illegible]
20 " "	[illegible]	[illegible]	[illegible]	[illegible]	[illegible]	[illegible]	[illegible]
21 " "	[illegible]	[illegible]	[illegible]	[illegible]	[illegible]	[illegible]	[illegible]
22 " "	[illegible]	[illegible]	[illegible]	[illegible]	[illegible]	[illegible]	[illegible]
23 " "	[illegible]	[illegible]	[illegible]	[illegible]	[illegible]	[illegible]	[illegible]
24 " "	[illegible]	[illegible]	[illegible]	[illegible]	[illegible]	[illegible]	[illegible]
25 " "	[illegible]	[illegible]	[illegible]	[illegible]	[illegible]	[illegible]	[illegible]
26 " "	[illegible]	[illegible]	[illegible]	[illegible]	[illegible]	[illegible]	[illegible]
27 " "	[illegible]	[illegible]	[illegible]	[illegible]	[illegible]	[illegible]	[illegible]
28 " "	[illegible]	[illegible]	[illegible]	[illegible]	[illegible]	[illegible]	[illegible]
29 " "	[illegible]	[illegible]	[illegible]	[illegible]	[illegible]	[illegible]	[illegible]
30 " "	[illegible]	[illegible]	[illegible]	[illegible]	[illegible]	[illegible]	[illegible]
31 " "	[illegible]	[illegible]	[illegible]	[illegible]	[illegible]	[illegible]	[illegible]
32 " "	[illegible]	[illegible]	[illegible]	[illegible]	[illegible]	[illegible]	[illegible]
33 " "	[illegible]	[illegible]	[illegible]	[illegible]	[illegible]	[illegible]	[illegible]
34 " "	[illegible]	[illegible]	[illegible]	[illegible]	[illegible]	[illegible]	[illegible]
35 " "	[illegible]	[illegible]	[illegible]	[illegible]	[illegible]	[illegible]	[illegible]
36 " "	[illegible]	[illegible]	[illegible]	[illegible]	[illegible]	[illegible]	[illegible]
37 " "	[illegible]	[illegible]	[illegible]	[illegible]	[illegible]	[illegible]	[illegible]
38 " "	[illegible]	[illegible]	[illegible]	[illegible]	[illegible]	[illegible]	[illegible]
39 " "	[illegible]	[illegible]	[illegible]	[illegible]	[illegible]	[illegible]	[illegible]
40 " "	[illegible]	[illegible]	[illegible]	[illegible]	[illegible]	[illegible]	[illegible]
41 " "	[illegible]	[illegible]	[illegible]	[illegible]	[illegible]	[illegible]	[illegible]
42 " "	[illegible]	[illegible]	[illegible]	[illegible]	[illegible]	[illegible]	[illegible]
43 " "	[illegible]	[illegible]	[illegible]	[illegible]	[illegible]	[illegible]	[illegible]
44 " "	[illegible]	[illegible]	[illegible]	[illegible]	[illegible]	[illegible]	[illegible]
45 " "	[illegible]	[illegible]	[illegible]	[illegible]	[illegible]	[illegible]	[illegible]
46 " "	[illegible]	[illegible]	[illegible]	[illegible]	[illegible]	[illegible]	[illegible]
47 " "	[illegible]	[illegible]	[illegible]	[illegible]	[illegible]	[illegible]	[illegible]
48 " "	[illegible]	[illegible]	[illegible]	[illegible]	[illegible]	[illegible]	[illegible]
49 " "	[illegible]	[illegible]	[illegible]	[illegible]	[illegible]	[illegible]	[illegible]
50 " "	1800	[illegible]	[illegible]	[illegible]	[illegible]	[illegible]	[illegible]

SIZES OF BOOK AND PRINT PAPERS.

TO FIND WEIGHT OF A GIVEN SIZE TO CORRESPOND WITH ANY OTHER SAMPLE.

RULE.—To find weight required for a given size to correspond in thickness with a given sample, multiply the weight of sample by the dimensions of sheet required, and divide by the product of the dimensions of sample. The table below gives all the regular sizes.

Size and Weight of Sample.		22 × 32	24 × 36	25 × 38	26 × 40	28 × 42	32 × 44	36 × 48
	lbs.	lbs.	lbs.	lbs.	lbs.	lbs.	lbs.	lbs.
22x32—	25	—	31	34	37	40	49	68
	30	—	37	40	43	50	61	82
	35	—	43	47	52	59	66	95
	40	—	49	54	59	67	85	109
24x36—	20	16	—	22	23	41	40	67
	35	29	—	38	42	48	45	78
	40	33	—	44	48	54	58	89
	45	37	—	49	54	61	62	105
	50	41	—	55	60	68	65	111
	60	49	—	66	72	82	84	133
25x38—	35	26	32	—	38	43	44	71
	40	30	38	—	44	50	51	81
	50	37	42	—	55	62	63	101
	60	44	55	—	66	74	76	121
	70	52	64	—	77	87	88	141
	80	59	72	—	88	99	101	162
28x42—	40	24	30	32	35	—	41	65
	45	27	33	36	40	—	46	73
	50	30	37	40	44	—	51	82
	60	36	44	48	53	—	61	98
	70	42	51	57	62	—	71	114
	80	48	59	65	71	—	82	131
	90	54	66	74	80	—	92	147
	100	60	74	82	88	—	102	163
32x44—	40	25	29	32	35	39	—	64
	50	28	36	40	44	48	—	80
	60	35	43	48	52	59	—	96
	70	41	50	56	61	68	—	112
	80	47	58	63	69	78	—	128
	90	53	65	71	78	88	—	144
	100	58	72	79	87	98	—	160

For paper (which is just double royal) multiply the figures of royal by 2. Likewise [illegible] is double [illegible], etc. For odd sizes proceed as per rule above.

HOW TO MAKE CHANGE QUICKLY.

Always consider the amount of purchase as if that much money were already counted out, then add to amount of purchase enough small change to make even dollars, counting out the even dollars until full amount is made up.

If the purchase amounts to 63 cents, and you are handed $2.00 in payment, count out 37 cents first to make an even dollar. Then lay out the other dollar.

Should the purchase be $3.69, to be taken out of $10.00, begin with $3.69 as the basis and make up even $4.00 by laying out 31 cents. This 31 cents with the amount of the purchase you will consider as $4.00, and count out even dollars to make up the $10.00 which the customer has handed in.

MERCHANTS' COST AND PRICE MARKS.

All merchants use private cipher marks to note cost or selling price of goods. The cipher is usually made up from some short word or sentence of nine or ten letters, as:

C O R N E L I U S A.
1 2 3 4 5 6 7 8 9 0.

Five dollars, according to this key, would be *e.aa*. But generally an extra letter is used to prevent repeating the mark for 0. If the sign for a second 0 in this case were *y*, we would have *e.ay* instead of *e.aa*.

TIME IN WHICH MONEY DOUBLES.

Per Cent.	Simple Int.	Comp. Int.	Per Cent.	Simple Int.	Comp. Int.
2	50 years.	35 years.	5	20 years.	14 yrs. 75 da.
2½	40 years.	28 yrs. 26 da.	6	16 yrs. 8 mos.	11 yrs. 327 da.
3	33 yrs. 4 mos.	23 yrs. 164 da.	7	14 yrs. 104 da.	10 yrs. 89 da.
3½	28 yrs. 208 da.	20 yrs. 54 da.	8	12½ years.	9 yrs. 2 da.
4	25 years.	17 yrs. 246 da.	9	11 yrs. 40 da.	8 yrs. 16 da.
4½	22 yrs. 81 da.	15 yrs. 273 da.	10	10 years.	7 yrs. 100 da.

"A Dollar Saved, a Dollar Earned."

The way to accumulate money is to save small sums with regularity. A small sum saved daily for fifty years will grow at the following rate:

Daily Savings.	Result.	Daily Savings.	Result.
One cent	$ 950	Sixty cents	$ 57,024
Ten cents	9,504	Seventy cents	66,528
Twenty cents	19,008	Eighty cents	76,032
Thirty cents	28,512	Ninety cents	85,537
Forty cents	38,015	One Dollar	95,041
Fifty cents	47,520		

Electricity Up to Date

IN THEORY AND IN PRACTICE

THE one who comes to the study of modern electricity — of the science which we are bringing with full hands to the twentieth century — should, as a first step, divest himself as far as possible of the impressions and the prejudices left upon his mind by the school-books of even so late a period as a decade ago.

What electricity is, science is not yet prepared to say. If we could imagine this world and all that it contains — all that we can see and touch and weigh — afloat in an ocean of ether, in which all matter is a-swim, then are lines of disturbance in this ether ocean fill out the definitions which we give electricity. It is not a thing; it is not matter; it is not a fluid. It is a force that touches and sways, that shatters and builds matter, but it is not matter. When a wind blows over a field of grain, setting the stalks waving in the flowing current, we have a vague simulacrum of the action of electricity upon the atoms of the solid copper or steel conductor whose behavior science watches with such interest. Electricity is a movement in ether which affects the atomic relations of matter, and thus its whole mass; but we can only examine it and judge it, not in itself, but in its results upon the grosser things we can examine and judge.

Leaving electricity, with its close kin, light and heat, as a problem for the future to solve, let us see how this modern mystery is produced.

The ancient Greeks observed that if amber, which they called *elektron*, were rubbed with a cloth, it possessed the curious property of attracting light articles, chaff and feathers. Here man laid his hand upon the secret titanic forces of nature, but it was twenty-two hundred years before any one seriously began the study of the phenomena. Dr. Gilbert, in A.D. 1600, commenced the investigation which has ended in the Atlantic cable, the telephone, the electric light, the dynamo. He laid the foundations of static electricity, and out of the system of experimental research inaugurated by him came speedily the friction machines, the Leyden jars, the electrophorus, and the most unfortunate "two-fluid theory," which delayed electrical discovery fifty years.

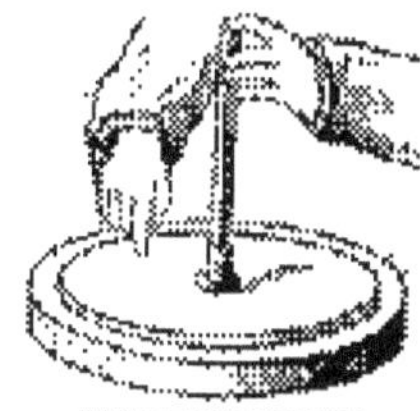

THE ELECTROPHORUS.

If you rub a piece of sealing-wax with a silk handkerchief, you get electricity, and this, broadened and widened, was the subject of the science for two centuries. Static electricity it was called. Later Galvani — and, immediately after him, Volta — produced continuous or current electricity.

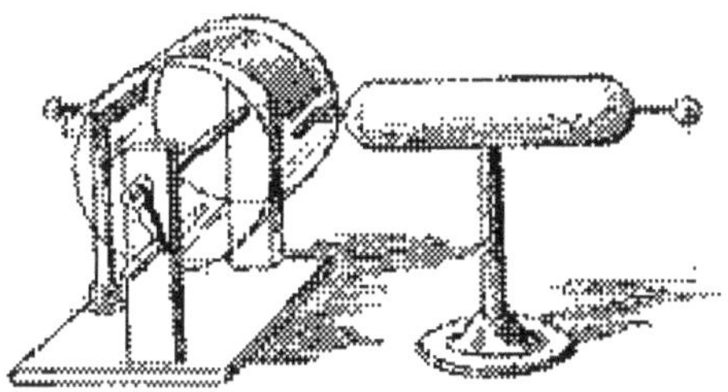

FRICTIONAL ELECTRICAL MACHINE.

WET CELL.

The voltaic pile, almost at once improved into the voltaic cell, develops electricity by the chemical action of zinc and copper in dilute acid. The cell is simply, as we know now, a fire-place where zinc is burned. Electricity moves from the copper to the zinc along any conducting contact between them. The zinc dissolves in the acid, and forces a passage of electricity through the fluid to the copper. Thus there is a motion of electricity from the copper to the zinc outside the cell, and from the zinc to the copper within it, when a complete circuit is made and chemical action is going on. Out of the battery cell came the telegraph and the whole range of electrolytic work.

If you move a wire through a magnetic field, cutting across the imaginary lines of force, you produce electricity in the wire. Take any magnet and any bit of conducting metal and move one of them in the neighborhood of the other, and electricity is developed in the conductor. Take a specially prepared powerful electro-magnet, and spin between its poles a bundle of wires, and you have the dynamo.

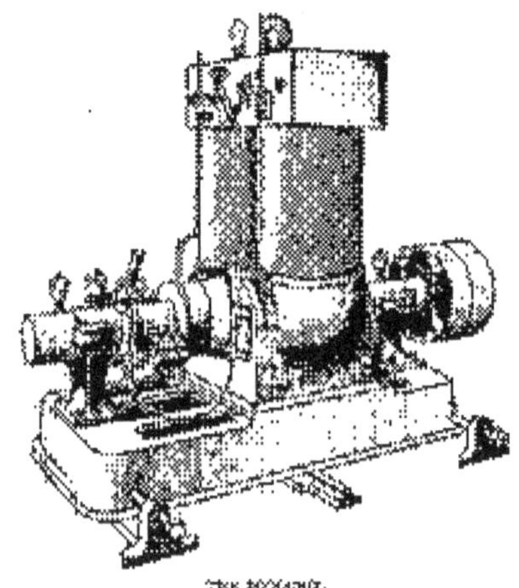

THE DYNAMO.

Here, thus, are the three chief sources of electricity: (1) Friction, (2) chemical action, (3) movement in a magnetic field. Induction is a subject which will be treated more properly later. The other principal sources of electrical disturbances are: (1) Percussion. A blow of one substance upon another always produces electrification. (2) Vibration. A rod of metal coated with sulphur produces electricity while vibrating. (3) Tearing, breaking and crushing a substance electrifies it. Sugar crushed in the dark emits a flash. (4) Crystallization and solidification. Sulphur newly crystallized is highly electrical; so is chocolate, arsenic, etc. (5) Combustion. All bodies while burning will affect the electroscope. (6) Evaporation. This is the chief cause of atmospheric electricity. (7) Pressure. Colespar squeezed in the hand is electrified. (8) Heat. Warming tourmaline and many other minerals makes them electric. (9) Animal. The torpedo, the gymnotus and the silurus can produce electricity at will. All common muscular contractions and nerve excitations produce feeble discharges. (10) Vegetable. Several plants produce electricity. (11) Contact. Dissimilar metals, upon touching each other, are electrified. This list might be greatly increased, but it suffices to say, broadly, that any act which produces a change in the relations of arrangements between themselves of the atoms of matter is accompanied by electrical phenomena. And the reader must remember that, no matter from what source electricity comes, it is the one same force.

The early investigators who rubbed sealing wax on rabbit's fur and watched the action of pith balls when the wax was presented to them saw the balls attracted and repelled. They saw the balls behave oppositely when glass was substituted for sealing wax, and they concluded that there were two fluids instead of one, which existed in exactly equal quantities in all bodies until the balance was disturbed by friction. Franklin modified this theory by supposing that upon friction the electric fluid broke up and distributed itself unequally between the rubber and the

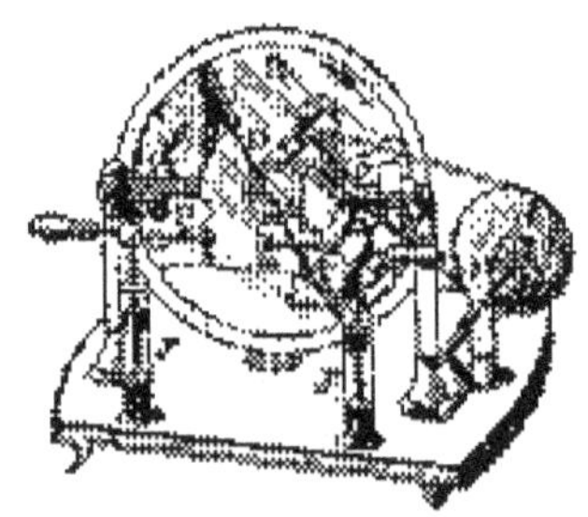

THE ELECTRICAL MACHINE.

thing rubbed. The body which was supposed to have the excess was said to be charged with positive electricity; the other was called negative. We know now that we do not know and cannot tell which of the two bodies has more and which less electricity, and, further than this, we know that electricity is not a fluid, in any material sense, whatever else it may be. Proceeding, however, upon this theory and its modifications, the early electricians filled bodies with electricity as one would fill cups with water. They thought of it, and handled it, and built up a misleading system of mathematics upon it, as a fluid, and this ridiculous beginning has left its deep mark on the science.

Any body can be charged with electricity. If the charge remains upon its surface we have before us the science of static electricity. If the electricity flows through the substance of the body we have the phenomena of current electricity. Matter may be roughly divided into substances which conduct electricity easily, and those which oppose a great resistance to the passage of the force. For instance, the resistance of glass is more than a billion times that of silver. All of the phenomena of static electricity could be produced with silver instead of glass, were it not that the charge flows off to earth at once, before it could be investigated.

Inasmuch as space is limited, and it is the purpose to put the reader as nearly *au fait* as possible with modern electricity, we will abridge unsparingly, and omit relentlessly, all of those discussions, experiments and apparatus that do not lead directly to the lucid explanation of the new marvels which science has given to the world. The reader will accordingly take it for granted that electricity may be produced in any of the ways set forth above — and, perhaps, in many others of which we do not dream as yet. That, having come into existence, having touched the plane of the matter as we know it, it follows certain well defined laws, and gives rise to certain phenomena, which make it highly probable that within less than a century hence the world's work, its light and its heating, will be torn by man out of the ether vibrations and poured directly from this mobile energy into our life.

Measuring the Force.

You can take the two wires from an ordinary Daniell cell which is producing a constant current of about one volt, in your hands, thus completing the circuit, and, unless you are a person of an abnormally sensitive constitution, you will feel absolutely nothing. A current strong enough to ring a bell violently can have a man as part of the circuit without his suspecting the fact. We are dealing here with a force so delicate and so immense that its table of measurements ranges from the shifting of a phantom ray of light upon a cobweb-supported mirror, to distances in which 180,000 statute miles make the unit. The first electroscope was the pith ball; this gave place to the straw-needle, this to the gold-leaf electroscope, this to the torsion balance, which first began to open the eyes of science to the wonder of the new age. Coulomb proved with the torsion balance that the force exerted between two electrified bodies varied inversely as the square of the distance between them, when the distance varied, and thus the path was finally cleared to the definition of a unit of electricity. *It is that quantity which, when placed at a distance of one centimetre in air from a similar and equal quantity, repels it with the force of one dyne.* A dyne is the unit of force. It is the push which, acting for one second upon a mass of one gramme, gives it a velocity of one centimetre per second.

There are three terms in common use in modern electricity which few people take the trouble to understand: The volt, the ampere, and the ohm.

The VOLT, which is equal to 100,000,000 electrical units, is about the electro-motive force produced by one Daniell cell.

The OHM is the resistance represented in theory by a velocity equal to one earth quadrant per second (10,000,000 metres — about 6,000 miles). The legal ohm is the resistance of a column of mercury one millimetre in cross-section and 106 centimetres in height.

The AMPERE measures current. It is the unit furnished by the potential of one volt through one ohm.

Imagine a large pipe, in the end of which a windmill has been fitted, and fancy that the vanes are moving so as to drive air into the pipe. Now the pressure with which this air moves forward is the volt. The resistance which the pipe makes to the passage of the air is the ohm; and the amount of air, the size of the current, which, of course, depends on the force with which the air is moved forward, and the friction and resistance of the pipe, is the ampere. It is misleading to try to find a similarity to electric movements or measurements in the manner in which water seeks its level in a pipe system, because most people find it hard to get away from the idea of weight, and there is no weight. A battery cell, or a friction machine, or a dynamo, gathers electricity out of the ether and crowds it, and packs it, and stuffs it, in so many volts, upon the end of a conductor. This conductor, if it is of silver, will have a specific resistance of 1,609, and if it is of annealed selenium, of 60,000,000,000,000. It depends wholly upon the material of which the conductor consists, just as though our pipe in the illustration were filled with marbles, or sawdust, or wool. The resistance is measured in ohms. A mile of ordinary telegraph wire is about thirteen times as hard for the current to pass through as one yard of mercury; and the amount of current which has worked its way through during a given time is told off in amperes.

If you imagine a woman combing her hair, the force she applies to the comb is like the voltage, the tangle of the hair and its reluctance to the passage of the comb could be stated as the ohm. The result of the force against the reluctance could be fancied as the ampere.

The electrical units, as determined by the Congress of Electricians, which met under the Presidency of Prof. Helmholtz during the World's Fair in Chicago in 1893, are as follows:

"The several governments represented in this Congress are recommended to formally adopt as legal units of electrical measure the following:

"Unit of Resistance. The international ohm, equal to 10^9 units of resistance of the C. G. S. scale. It is represented by the resistance offered to an unvarying electric current by a column of mercury at the temperature of melting ice, 14.4521 grammes in mass, of a constant cross-sectional area, and of the length of 106.3 centimeters.

"Unit of Current. The international ampere, equal to one-tenth of the C. G. S. unit of current. It is represented by the unvarying current which, when passed through a solution of nitrate of silver in water, deposits silver at the rate of 0.001118 of a gramme per second.

"Unit of Electro-motive Force. The international volt, which is the force that, steadily applied to a conductor whose resistance is one international ohm, will produce a current of one international ampere, equal to $\frac{1000}{1434}$ of the electromotive force between the electrodes of the cell known as Clark's cell, at a temperature of 15 degrees C.

"Unit of Quantity. The international coulomb, equal to a current of one international ampere in one second.

"Unit of Capacity. The capacity of a conductor charged to a potential of one international volt, by one international coulomb of electricity.

"Unit of Work. The joule, which is 10^7 C. G. S. units of work, being the energy expended in one second by an international ohm.

"Unit of Power. The international watt, equal to 10^7 C. G. S. units of power, equal to work done by one joule per second.

"Unit of Induction. The henry, which is the induction in the circuit when the electromotive force induced in this circuit is one international volt, while the inducing current varies at the rate of one ampere per second."

It was resolved that no international unit of light be adopted at the Congress.

Magnetism.

The reader must now again turn back almost into the night of time, to pick up the second part of modern electricity. Before history began to be written the shepherds in Magnesia, in Asia Minor, had noticed that certain curious heavy black stones had the property of attracting to them bits of iron and steel. With a great many of the other earlier phenomena of nature the wise men of those and the succeeding ages classed the work of the magnet as magic, and let it go at that. About the tenth century it was discovered that a lodestone hung on a thread, or floating on a bit of wood in water, always pointed north and south, and thus the marine magnet came into general use. The lodestone itself for a long time resisted research. It was a common ore of iron, its chemical composition being Fe_3O_4. It is found, besides Asia Minor, in Sweden,

Spain, Arkansas, and the Isle of Elba, and is at its best when discovered in the shape of regular octohedron crystals.

Dr. Gilbert, in 1600, published his *De Magnete*, which was the beginning of our modern science. He discovered that the attractive power resided chiefly in the ends, and that the middle of a magnet did not attract iron filings so strongly as the poles.

It was found that the quality of being a magnet was transmissible; that by rubbing a needle or a nail on a lodestone, the virtue, as they used to call it, passed into the thing rubbed, and that it then for some time acted just as the original lodestone.

Once begun, the study was earnestly pushed, and the behavior of magnetic needles was closely watched. It was found that their poles were opposite in their nature, and that like poles repelled each other, while unlike ones attracted. Here, too, for a time there was a two-fluid theory, in which north-seeking magnetism was distinguished as something distinct from south-seeking magnetism.

There were many similarities and many contradictions between early magnetism and early electricity. Both attracted light articles. Magnetism would not work across a screen of iron, but it would across a screen of glass. Electricity acted exactly contrary. Indeed, though the connection between the two was suspected, it was

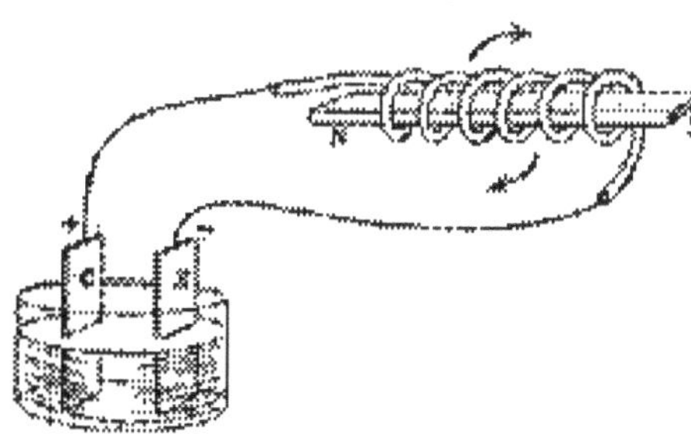

MAKING A MAGNET.

not until this century had opened that we were able to pick up the strings which bind the two classes of phenomena together.

Besides iron, nickel, cobalt, chromium, cerium and manganese are magnetic, and a feeble magnetism is perceived in other bodies and gases; and a number of bodies are diamagnetic, as it is called, and are repelled by magnets, such as bismuth, antimony, phosphorus and copper. The earth, as a whole, is a magnet, and so are

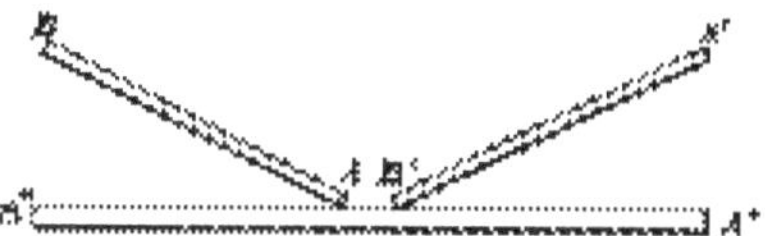

each of the planets; in fact, we can gather the whole subject of terrestrial magnetism well in hand by understanding once and for all that our earth is merely an armature spinning in the field of magnetic force of the sun, and that that fact explains its electric control.

Magnetism is induced in bodies that are touched to a magnet, but to make one properly the bar to be magnetized should be laid down horizontally; two bar magnets are then placed down upon it, their opposite poles being together. They are then drawn asunder from the middle of the bar towards its ends, and back, several times. The bar is then turned over, and the operation repeated, taking care to leave off at the middle. The process is more effectual if the ends of the bar are meanwhile supported on the poles of other bar magnets, the poles being of the same names as those of the two magnets above them used for stroking the steel bar.

The process of making electro-magnets will be explained later, and these, of course, are much stronger than either the lode-stone or rubbed magnets.

The lifting power of a magnet depends both upon the form of the magnet and on its magnetic strength. A horse-shoe magnet will lift a load three or four times as great as a bar magnet of the same weight will lift. The lifting power is greater if the area of contact between the poles and the armature is increased. Also the lifting power of a magnet grows in a very curious and unexplained way by gradually increasing the load on its armature day by day until it bears a load which at the outset it could not have done. Nevertheless, if the load is so increased that the armature is torn off, the power of the magnet falls at once to its original value. The attraction between a powerful electro-magnet and its armature may amount to 200 lbs. per square inch, or 14,000 grammes per square centimetre. Small magnets lift a greater load in proportion to their own weight than large ones. A good steel horse-shoe magnet, weighing itself one pound, ought to lift twenty pounds' weight. Sir Isaac Newton is said to have possessed a little lode-stone, mounted in a signet ring, which would lift a piece of iron 200 times its own weight.

Magnetic Field.

In any ordinary magnet, as stated above, the greatest magnetism is found at the poles, which are very near, but not quite at the end of the magnet. The space all around the magnet is filled and saturated with the pull or attraction of the force, which runs along certain well-marked lines and curves, each starting from one pole and making its way to the other. The distribution of these lines can be easily shown by dusting iron filings on a piece of paper and then bringing a horse-shoe magnet up underneath. The filings arrange themselves as shown in the cut.

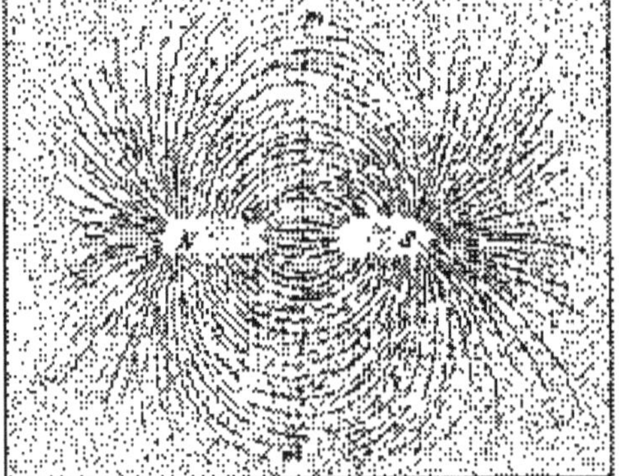

THE LINES OF FORCE.

When the armature is on, or when by any arrangement the magnetic circuit is closed, these lines of force cannot be detected, because they pass from pole to pole within the armature. But when the circuit is open, the lines are always reaching out, something like the antennae of an insect, into the free space about them. The field is the more intense the nearer we come to the magnet, and fades rapidly as we recede from it. It is out of this field, this area of disturbed conditions of the ether that lies near magnet poles, that we have drawn the great electric advance of the century.

Still, magnetism is a secret to us. We do not know what has happened to an iron bar when it is magnetized. Its volume remains as before, but its length increases by one 720,000th of itself. That is the only outward and material sign of its changed condition. A faint metallic "click" can by some people be heard within a bar at the moment of electric magnetization, as though the atoms were beating upon each other in unison. A jar of water, studded with magnetic oxide and magnetized, becomes clearer as the particles seem to arrange themselves end on. A piece of iron quickly magnetized and demagnetized grows hot as though from external friction. A ray of polarized light passing through substances in a magnetic field has the direction of its vibrations changed.

All these various phenomena point to a theory of magnetism very different from the old notion of fluids. It appears that every particle of a magnet is itself a magnet, and that the magnet only becomes a magnet, as a whole, by the particles being so turned as to point one way. This conclusion is supported by the ob-

MAGNETS AND THEIR POLES.

servation that if a glass tube full of iron filings is magnetized, the filings can be seen to set themselves endways, and that, when thus once

end, they act as a magnet until shaken up. It appears to be harder to turn the individual molecules of solid steel, but, when once so set, they remain end-on unless violently struck or heated. It follows from this theory that when all the particles were turned end-on, the limit of possible magnetization would have been attained. Some careful experiments of Beetz on iron deposited by electrolysis entirely confirm this conclusion, and add weight to the theory. The optical phenomena led Clerk Maxwell to the further conclusion that these longitudinally-set molecules are rotating round their long axes, and that in the "ether" of space there is also a vortical motion along the lines of magnetic induction; this motion, if occurring in a perfect medium (as the "ether" may be considered), producing tensions along the lines and pressures at right angles to them, would afford a satisfactory explanation of the magnetic attractions and repulsions which apparently act across empty space. Hughes has lately shown that the magnetism of iron and steel is intimately connected with the molecular rigidity of the material. His researches with the "induction balance" and "magnetic balance" tend to prove that each molecule of a magnetic metal has an absolutely constant inherent magnetic polarity; and that when a piece of iron or steel is apparently neutral, its molecules are internally arranged so as to satisfy each other's polarity, forming closed magnetic circuits amongst themselves. Thus magnetism would mean to cause the molecules of a body to assume a new and symmetrical "end-on" position.

Current Electricity.

It has been already mentioned how electricity flows away from a charged body through any conducting substance, such as a wire or a wetted string. If, by any arrangement, electricity could be supplied to the body just as fast as it flowed away, a continuous current would be produced. Such a current always flows through a conducting wire, if the ends are kept at different electric potentials. In like manner, a current of heat flows through a rod of metal if the ends are kept at different temperatures, the flow being always from the high temperature to the lower. It is convenient to regard electricity as flowing from positive to negative; or, in other words, the direction of an electric current is from the high potential to the low. It is obvious that such a flow tends to bring both to one level of potential. The "current" has sometimes been regarded as a double transfer of positive electricity in one direction, and of negative electricity in the opposite direction. The only evidence to support this very unnecessary supposition is the fact that, in the decomposition of liquids by the current, some of the elements are liberated at the point where the potential is highest, others at the point where it is lowest.

THE TELEGRAPH.

The whole purpose of the battery cell is to provide electricity for one end of the wire as rapidly as it flows off from the other, and the chemical actions and reactions between the different bodies placed in the cell set the electricity in motion. Copper and zinc have already been spoken about, platinized silver has been substituted for the copper, and much better than either are plates or columns of hard carbon with zinc. Iron can be used. Then the same result is got again from two-fluid cells like Daniell's, in which dilute sulphuric acid, working upon the zinc, and blue vitriol in water, working upon the copper, set up a steady electro-motive push. Grove's and Bunsen's batteries are modifications of the Daniell, and the Leclanché and Minudet batteries may be taken as the ideal types of this idea.

For working electric bells and telephones, and also to a limited extent in telegraphy, a zinc-carbon cell is employed, invented by Leclanché, in which the exciting liquid is not dilute acid, but a solution of sal-ammoniac. In this the zinc dissolves, forming a double chloride of zinc and ammonia, while ammonia gas and hydrogen are liberated at the carbon pole. To prevent polarization the carbon plate is packed inside a porous pot along with fragments of carbon and powdered binoxide of manganese, a substance which slowly yields up oxygen and destroys the hydrogen bubbles. If used to give a continuous current for many minutes together, the power of the cell falls off owing to the accumulation of the hydrogen bubbles; but if left to itself for a time the cell recovers itself, the binoxide gradually destroying the polarization. As the cell is in other respects perfectly constant, and does not require renewing for months or years, it is well adapted for domestic purposes. Three Leclanché cells are shown joined in series in the accompanying illustration. In more recent forms the binoxide of

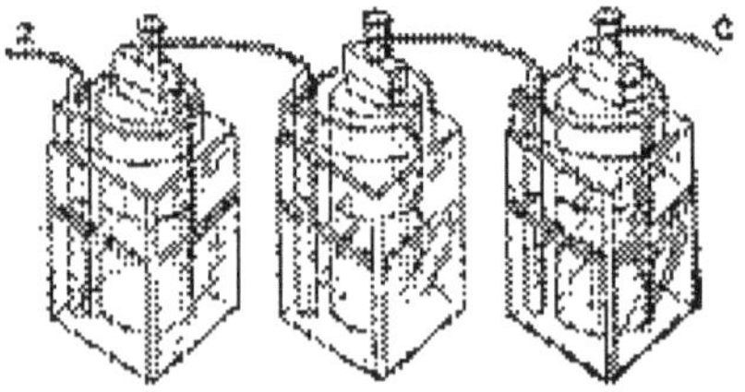

manganese is applied in a conglomerate attached to the face of the carbon, thus avoiding the necessity of using a porous inner cell.

Mons. Niaudet has also constructed a zinc-carbon cell in which the zinc is placed in a solution of common salt (chloride of sodium), and the carbon is surrounded by the so-called chloride of lime (or bleaching powder), which readily gives up chlorine and oxygen, both of which substances will destroy the hydrogen bubbles and prevent polarization. This cell has a higher electro-motive power and a less resistance than the Leclanché. De Lalande and Chaperon propose a cell in which oxide of copper is used as a solid depolarizer in a solution of caustic potash.

It is possible to measure very exactly the strength of current. The electro-motive force of each of the ordinary cells ranges from three-quarters of a legal volt up to two and a quarter volts. The strength of current is the quantity of electricity which flows past any point in the circuit in one second of time—a definition which makes clear Ohm's law: "The strength of the current varies directly as the electro-motive force, and inversely as the resistance of the circuit."

Magnetic Action of Current Electricity.

Romagnosi of Trente, in 1802, deflected a magnetic needle by holding a voltaic pile near it, but nothing followed the experiment. In 1819 Oersted of Copenhagen showed that a magnet will try to set itself at right angles to a wire carrying an electric current. He also saw that the needle turned to the left or the right according as the wire was held above or below it. The next step was to so bend the wire that it would pass both above and below the needle carrying the current forward and back.

A little consideration will show that if a current be carried below a needle in one direction, and then back in the opposite direction above the needle by bending the wire round, as in the engraving, the forces exerted on the needle by both portions of the current will be in the same direction. For let *a* be the N.-seeking, and

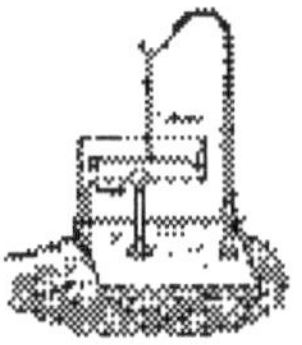

b the S.-seeking, pole of the suspended needle, then the tendency of the current in the lower part of the wire will be to turn the needle so that *a* comes toward the observer, while *b* retreats; while the current flowing above, which also deflects the N.-seeking pole to its left, will equally urge *a* toward the observer, and *b* from him. The needle will not stand out completely at right angles to the direction of the wire conductor, but will take an oblique position. The directive forces of the earth's magnetism are tending to make the needle point north and south. The electric current is acting on the needle, tending to make it set itself west and east. The resultant force will be in an oblique direction between these, and will depend upon the relative strength of the two conflicting forces. If the current is very strong the needle will turn widely round; but could only turn completely to a right angle if the current were infinitely strong. If, however, the current is feeble in comparison with the directive magnetic force, the needle will turn very little. Of course we have the machinery or foundation for the galvanoscope.

Electro-Magnetics.

The next step naturally was to coil the current-conveying wire about the magnet, and when this was done the whole science of modern electricity was born. When a current of electricity takes a coiled form magnetism is born. Wrap a wire around a bit of iron and force electricity through the circuit, and a powerful electro-magnet results. Wrap a coil of wire about an empty open space and all of the phenomena of a strong magnetic field are developed immediately upon the passage of the force. If a piece of steel has been used as the core of the coil it remains a magnet long after being brought to that condition; soft iron, however, loses its magnetism almost immediately upon the ending of the circuit.

ELECTRO-MAGNET.

The more turns are made about the core, up to a certain limit, the more powerful will be the resulting magnet; the bigger and the more conductive the wire used for wrapping, the more powerful will be the magnet. So that, by careful preparation, a magnet may be made which will support 200 to 226 pounds to the square inch of surface. Out of the powerful field following the creation of such a magnet continuous electricity may be drawn by a moving armature of insulated wires. It must be remembered, too, that after the magnet is first made by a current from a battery it can be kept up by a very small part of the electricity produced in its own field.

Now, any motion on the part of a conductor, no matter what its material may be, in a magnetic field produces or induces electricity. And any passage of electricity produces or induces a magnetic field. If an ordinary magnet is pushed down into a coil of wire, a current flows in the wire. When the magnet is pulled out of the coil a current flows again in an opposite direction. If into a large coil is plunged a smaller coil in which a current is flowing, an opposite current flows in the outer coil. In a word, there is no production of electricity anywhere or in any way which is not immediately the cause of the production of other and, as it were, balancing electricity. Even in the whirling armatures of dynamos, and in the bodies of magnets, reverse currents are always pushing, sometimes to the destruction of the usefulness of the machine.

The induction coil is one of the means of taking advantage of this fact. Around a piece of soft iron a rather thick wire, well insulated, should be wrapped; a great many turns of a smaller wire, also well insulated, should be taken about the first wrapping, and in a reverse direction. Now when a current passes through the primary there is at once born in the secondary coil a reverse current. With an automatic interrupter, which makes and breaks the current, very often powerful secondary currents are induced. In Spottiswoode's coil, which gives a spark of forty-two inches, the primary is a short wrapping of thick wire, and the secondary consists of 280 miles of wire, wound in 340,000 turns. The primary may be outside or inside the secondary. A very strong induction coil can be made at home by wrapping about a wire spool from a telegraph sounder a couple of yards of thick copper wire. With an instrument like this bright sparks can be got from one cell of battery.

THE INDUCTION COIL.

In 1867 the suggestion was made simultaneously, but independently, by Siemens and by Wheatstone, that a coil rotating between the poles of an electro-magnet might from the feeble residual magnetism induce a small current, which, when transmitted through the coils of the electro-magnet, might exalt its magnetism, and so prepare it to induce still stronger currents. Magneto-electric machines constructed on this principle, the coils of their field-magnets being placed in circuit with the coils of the rotating armature, so as to be traversed by the whole or by a portion of the induced currents, are known as dynamo-electric machines or generators, to distinguish them from the generators in which permanent steel magnets are employed. In either case the current is due to

magneto-electric machines; and in either case, also, the energy of the currents so induced is derived from the dynamical power of the steam engine or other motor, which performs the work of moving the rotating coils of wire in the magnetic field. Of the many modern machines on this principle the most famous are those of Siemens, Gramme, Brush and Edison. They differ chiefly in the means adopted for obtaining practical continuity in the current. In all of them the electro-motive force generated is proportional to the number of turns of wire in the rotating armature, and (within certain limits) to the speed of revolution. When currents of small electro-motive force, but of considerable strength, are required, as for electroplating, the rotating armatures of a generator must be made with small internal resistance, and, therefore, of a few turns of stout wire or ribbon of sheet copper. For producing currents of high electro-motive force for the purpose of electric lighting, the armature must be driven very fast, and must consist of many turns of wire, or, where very small resistance is necessary (as in a system of lamps arranged in parallel arc), of rods of copper suitably connected. The dynamos of 1895 are but improvements on this central idea.

Electric Bells.

The common form of *Electric Bell*, or Trembler, consists of an electro-magnet, which moves a hammer backward and forward by alternately attracting and releasing it, so that it beats against a bell. The arrangements of the instrument are shown in the illustration, in which *E* is the electro-magnet and *H* the hammer. A battery, consisting of one or two Leclanché cells placed at some convenient point of the circuit, provides a current when required. By touching the "push" *P*, the circuit is completed, and a current flows along the line and round the coils of the electro-magnet, which forthwith attracts a small piece of soft iron attached to the lever, which terminates in the hammer *H*. The lever is itself included in the circuit, the current entering it above and quitting it at *C* by a contact-breaker, consisting of a spring tipped with platinum resting against the platinum tip of a screw, from which a return wire passes back to the zinc-pole of the battery. As soon as the lever is attracted forward the circuit is broken at *C* by the spring moving away from contact with the screw; hence the current stops, and the electro-magnet ceases to attract the armature. The lever and hammer therefore fall back, again establishing contact at *C*, whereupon the hammer is once more attracted forward, and so on. The push *P* is shown in section on the right. It usually consists of a cylindrical knob of ivory or porcelain capable of moving loosely through a hole in a circular support of porcelain or wood, and which, when pressed, forces a platinum-tipped spring against a metal pin, and so makes electrical contact between the two parts of the interrupted circuit.

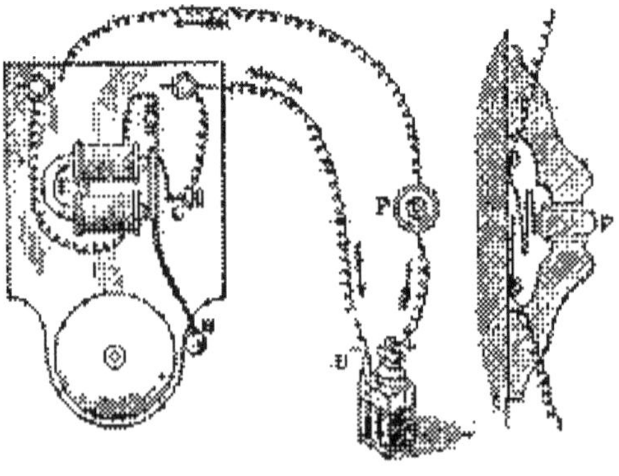

Electric Clocks.

Clocks may be either driven or controlled by electric currents. Bain, Hipp, and others, have devised electric clocks of the first kind, in which the ordinary motive power of a weight or spring is abandoned, the clock being driven by its pendulum, the "bob" of which is an electro-magnet alternately attracted from side to side. The difficulty of maintaining a perfectly constant battery current has prevented such clocks from coming into use.

Electrically controlled clocks, governed by a standard central clock, have proved a more fruitful invention. In these the standard time-keeper is constructed so as to complete a circuit periodically once every minute or half minute. The transmitted currents set in movement the hands of a system of dials placed at distant points, by causing an electro-magnet placed behind each dial to attract an armature, which, acting upon a ratchet wheel by a pawl, causes it to move forward through one tooth at each specified interval, and so carries the hands round at the same rate as those of the standard clocks.

The Telephone.

In 1876 Graham Bell invented the magneto-telephone. In this instrument the speaker talks to an elastic plate of thin sheet-iron, which vibrates and transmits its every movement electrically to a similar plate in a similar telephone at a distant station, causing it to vibrate in an identical manner, and therefore to emit identical sounds. The transmission of the vibrations depends upon the principles of magneto-electric induction. The cut herewith shows Bell's Telephone in its latest form, and its internal parts in section. The disc *D* is placed behind a conical mouthpiece, to which the speaker places his mouth or the hearer his ear.

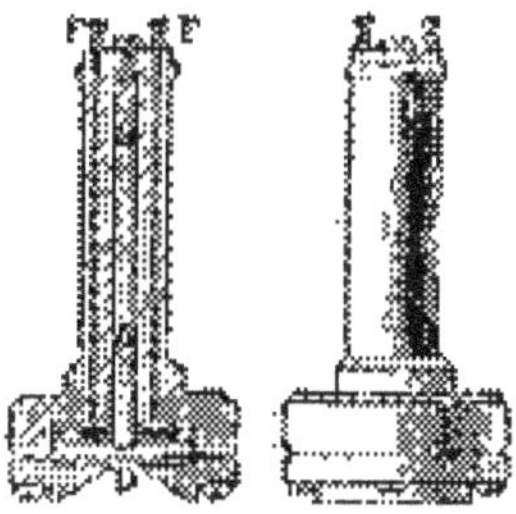

BELL'S TELEPHONE.

Behind the disc is a magnet *AA* running the length of the instrument; and upon its front pole, which nearly touches the disc, is fixed a small bobbin, on which is wound a coil *C* of fine insulated wire, the ends of the coil being connected with the terminal screws *FF*. One such instrument is used to transmit, and one to receive the sounds, the two telephones being connected in simple circuit. No battery is needed, for the transmitting instrument itself generates the induced currents as follows: The magnet *AA* induces a certain number of lines-of-force through the coil *C*. Many of these pass into the iron disc. When the iron disc in vibrating moves towards the magnet-pole, more lines-of-force meet it; when it recedes, fewer lines-of-force meet it. Its motion to and fro will therefore *alter the number of lines-of-force which pass through the hollow of the coil C*, and will therefore generate in the wire of the coils currents whose strength is proportional to the rate of change in the number of the lines-of-force which pass through the coil. Bell's telephone, when used as a transmitter, may therefore be regarded as a sort of magneto-electric generator, which, by vibrating to and fro, pumps currents in alternate directions into the wire. At the distant end the currents as they arrive flow round the coil either in one direction or the other, and therefore either add momentarily to or take from the strength of the magnet. When the current in the coils is in such a direction as to reinforce the magnet,

THE TELEPHONE.

the magnet attracts the iron disc in front of it more strongly than before. If the current is in the opposite direction the disc is less attracted and flies back. Hence, whatever movement is imparted to the disc of the transmitting telephone, the disc of the distant receiving telephone is forced to repeat, and it therefore throws the air into similar vibrations, and so reproduces the sound.

The Study of Electricity.

The student will have noticed the constant dependence put in this review of the subject upon the work of Prof. Sylvanus Thompson, who is easily the first and best teacher of the science living to-day. Every book which he has written should be in the collection of the electrician, and, having these, with some good electrical paper, he will soon be and keep abreast of progress.

Much dependence should, of course, be put in actual apparatus and work, and all that is needed may be had very cheaply. A few battery cells, say three, a coil of wire, and a knack for putting things together should give any man an electrical laboratory. He can set bells to his doors, arrange burglar alarms, and make many a handy and useful appliance for domestic purposes, out of a total expenditure that need not exceed $5; nor can there be more instructive or more interesting work.

DIRECTIONS FOR SETTING UP AND MAINTAINING BATTERIES.

In all except the blue vitriol batteries the zincs should be kept well amalgamated.

In the selection of a battery for any purpose, due consideration should be given to the relation between the work to be performed and the quantity and electro-motive force of the current required. This is a most essential point, upon which, in a great degree, depend the results obtained. The following table of batteries is arranged to show the class of work for which they are best suited:

1. For all open circuit work, such as call-bells, gas lighting, annunciators, etc., use Disque Leclanché, carbon cylinder or dry.

2. For closed circuit work, such as telegraph lines, use the Crowfoot Gravity.

3. For laboratory and experimental work, requiring powerful current for a few hours, use LaClede, carbon cylinder or dry.

Crowfoot Gravity Battery.—Open out the copper, spread it out so as to present all of its surface to the action of the solution, place it at the bottom of the jar, run the insulated wire out of the top of the jar for connecting up.

Suspend the zinc above the copper by hanging the hooked neck on the rim of the glass. The neck of the zinc is provided with a connecting clamp to receive the wire from the copper of the next cell.

Pour clean, soft water into the jar until it covers the zinc, then drop in six or eight ounces of copper sulphate, or blue vitriol, in small crystals.

To hasten the action of the battery, dissolve two or three ounces of zinc sulphate (or white vitriol) in as many ounces of water, and gently pour it on top of the copper solution.

For ordinary purposes, connect the zinc of one cell to the copper of the next, and so on; finally connect the two electrodes of the series and let them so remain for a couple of hours, until the separation of the two solutions, which will be known by the blue observed in the bottom of copper solution; this blue line should be maintained midway between the zinc and the copper; when that "blue line" is too low, drop in a few crystals of copper sulphate; if it is too high, connect the battery in short circuit as before described until it goes down, or reach down with syringe and draw out some of the copper solution and add zinc solution and fresh water.

As long as the battery remains in action there is an increase in quantity of zinc sulphate solution in the upper part of the jar.

The specific gravity of this solution should be maintained at 25 degrees; when the hydrometer indicates a lower degree there is too little zinc sulphate solution; when a higher degree than 25, there is too much zinc sulphate, and a portion of it must be taken out, and that remaining must be diluted with pure water.

A hydrometer is essential to properly maintain a large battery.

When zinc oxide forms on the surface of the zinc it must be taken out and washed in clean water with a brush.

Leclanché Battery.—Put six ounces of sal-ammoniac into the jar and pour one-third full of water, and stir. Put in the porous cell and fill jar with water to neck. Pour a few spoonfuls of water into the holes in the porous cell, put in the zinc and connect up the battery. The inside rim of the jar should be coated with beeswax or paraffine to prevent salts from overrunning.

The battery should be kept in a dry place and does not require any attention to maintain, except to add a little water occasionally, to supply loss by evaporation.

Dry Batteries are usually charged and ready for work. When they become exhausted the cheapest and best method of renewing is to return the old cell to the maker, who should replace the same with a new battery at a nominal cost. When buying dry batteries procure one that can be exchanged.

Carbon Cylinder (Sal-Ammoniac Battery).—Put about five ounces sal-ammoniac in a jar, fill jar about one-half full of water and stir. When the sal-ammoniac is dissolved insert the carbon cylinder and zinc. Should the battery become exhausted by short circuiting or continuous work, remove the dry cylinder and wash the surface with warm water. Allow the cylinder to thoroughly dry, when it can be replaced in jar with new charge of sal-ammoniac and zinc. The carbon cylinder is practically indestructible.

Carbon Cylinder (Acid) Battery.—Fill the jar about one-half full of electropoion fluid; insert the carbon cylinder. The zinc to be lowered into the fluid only when battery is in use. When the zinc is consumed by use it will be necessary to recharge the battery with new solution and zinc. This battery will run constant about two hours without recharging. The carbon cylinder is practically indestructible. The same solution as used for the Grenet Battery is equally as good for the Carbon Cylinder Acid Battery.

Grenet Battery Solution.—To make solution: To three pints of cold water add five fluid ounces of sulphuric acid; when this becomes cold add six ounces (or as much as the solution will dissolve) of finely pulverized bichromate of potash. Mix it well. To charge the battery: Pour the above solution into the glass cell until it nearly reaches the top of the spherical part. The fluid should not quite reach the zinc when it is drawn up.

Carbon (Porous Cup) Battery.—Fill the glass jar with water; the porous cell should be about the same.

Bunsen Battery.—Same directions apply as carbon battery, except instead of electropoion fluid use 40° nitric acid in the porous cell.

Electropoion Fluid.—Mix one gallon of sulphuric acid and three gallons of water. Then in a separate vessel dissolve six pounds of bichromate of potash in two gallons of boiling water, mixing the whole thoroughly together. When cold it is ready for use.

Solution for Amalgamating Zinc.—Mix one pound nitric with two pounds hydrochloric acid and add eight ounces of mercury. When the mercury is dissolved add three pounds more hydrochloric acid. To amalgamate the zinc dip it in this solution for one or two seconds, then remove it quickly to a dish of clean water and rub it with a brush or cloth, when it will be found covered with a fine, even coat of mercury. This solution can be kept in a covered jar and used many times.

Another method of amalgamating zincs is to clean them by dipping in a solution of dilute sulphuric acid and rubbing on the mercury with a cloth or brush.

Formula for Charging One Phonograph or Chromic Battery.—To four pounds (or pints) of water, add gradually one and one-half pounds (or three-fourths of a pint) of sulphuric acid, and stir while doing so, as considerable heat is generated. After this solution has cooled, add one-half pound of chromic acid. When the battery is fully charged the liquid should fill the jar to a point indicated by the arrows. When the battery is not in use the elements should always be raised out of the liquid, in order to prevent chemical action and consequent loss of material. *Do not allow the zinc to touch the carbon.*

TWENTY QUESTIONS CONCERNING ELECTRICITY.

1. How strong a current is used to send a message over the Atlantic cable?—Thirty cells of battery only. Equal to thirty volts.

2. What is the longest distance over which conversation by telephone is maintained?—Nearly 1,200 miles, between Boston and Chicago.

3. What is the fastest time made by an electric railway?—A mile a minute by a small experimental car. Twenty miles an hour on street railway system.

4. How many miles of submarine cable are there in operation?—Over 120,000 miles.

5. What is the maximum power generated by an electric motor?—Eight hundred horse-power.

6. How is a break in submarine cable located?—By measuring the electricity needed to charge the remaining unbroken part, through the device called "Wheatstone's bridge."

7. How many miles of telegraph wire in operation in the United States?—Over a million, or enough to encircle the globe forty times.

8. How many messages can be transmitted over a wire at one time?—Six, by the sextuplex system in use.

9. How is telegraphing from a moving train accomplished?—Through a circuit from the car roof inducing a current in the wire on poles along the track.

10. What are the most widely separated points between which it is possible to send a telegram?—British Columbia and New Zealand, via America and Europe.

11. How many miles of telephone wire in operation in the United States?—More than 240,000, over which 1,000,000 messages are sent daily.

12. What is the greatest candle-power of arc light used in a lighthouse?—Two million, at Hanstholm, Denmark.

13. How many persons in the United States are engaged in business depending solely on electricity?—250,000.

14. How long does it take to transmit a message from San Francisco to Hong Kong?—About fifteen minutes, via New York, Canso, Penzance, Aden, Bombay, Madras, Penang and Singapore.

15. What is the fastest time made in sending messages by the Morse system?—About forty-two words per minute.

16. How many telephones are in use in the United States?—About 300,000.

17. What war vessel has the most complete electrical plant?—U. S. man-of-war Chicago.

18. What is the average cost per mile of a transatlantic submarine cable?—About $1,000.

19. How many miles of electric railway are there in operation in the U. S.?—About 1,000 miles, and much more under construction.

20. What strength of current is dangerous to human life?—Five hundred volts, but depending on physical conditions.

Hill Banking System

THIS is a proposed plan for banking, first suggested by Thomas E. Hill in a communication to the Chicago *Inter-Ocean*, in March, 1890, in which he advocated government ownership and control of banks.

Soon after the appearance of the article on government banks, the *Farmer's Voice*, at that time edited by Lester C. Hubbard, very warmly espoused the idea as proposed by the author, and named it the Hill Banking System.

The plan suggested is very simple, easily understood, and could be readily introduced. It is this: That the Government open its own banks at all central points in the United States, to the number of 3,000, being one bank for each 24,000 inhabitants.

That 40,000 post offices in the back districts, where there are no banks, be made postal savings banks, where all persons could deposit their money in any amount, which money should be forwarded to the nearest bank, each bank being a loaning depository.

That 3 per cent. interest shall be allowed on long-time deposits, and money shall be loaned at 4 per cent. interest on any security which will sell, at forced sale, for twice the amount which is loaned. The immediate advantage of this system is shown to be the following:

1. No bonds necessary to be issued, in order to supply money to the people. No money borrowed by the government for this purpose. Not a dollar invested in banking by the government. The government simply opens its rooms at various central points, and becomes the custodian of the people's money, every depositor being guaranteed against loss. The consequence is, the bank immediately fills with money—good money, consisting of gold, silver and paper, which is now being hidden by the people through lack of confidence in banks.

2. The bank is continuously filled with money, as there is never a run on the bank, never a bank failure, never a financial panic, never a widespread business depression, throwing hundreds of thousands of people out of work, and compelling the poor, thus deprived of employment, to sell little properties for a tenth of their value, while the rich buy at their own price and rapidly become millionaires.

3. Loaning money at 4 per cent. will permit the farmer, now groaning under an interest burden ranging from 7 to 20 per cent. to pay off the mortgage, and save money enough to begin the erection of a new dwelling, barn, etc. Hundred of thousands of farmers, thus saving their interest and investing the same in improvements throughout the rural districts, will make a demand for great armies of men now in idleness, reviving all the industries, relieving all the vexations of competition and making better wages for all.

4. The government, doing its own banking, will acquire an enormous revenue, as seen in the following: Smith borrows a thousand dollars of the bank and immediately deposits the same to his credit, takes a check-book and draws checks on the bank in the payment of his debts. He gets no interest on his short-time deposit, but pays 4 per cent. An hour afterwards Jones may borrow a like amount, deposit it, and take a check-book. Thus ten persons, one after the other, may each borrow that thousand dollars, each will deposit, get no interest on short time deposit, but each pay 4 per cent.; thus making 40 per cent. for the government. In a work recently issued by Mr. Hill, entitled "Money Found," in which the system is fully elaborated, it is shown that the revenue to the government from doing its own banking may be near $400,000,000 per annum.

5. Another advantage of the system is shown to be in the absolute security afforded to life and property. Perfect confidence existing, and all money being in the bank, business only being done with checks, good only when they are signed, no money is carried about the person, except, possibly, a small amount of silver change. Under these circumstances no footpad follows after dark, no highwayman holds up the stage or railroad train, and as no money is kept about the house there is no temptation for the burglar to rob and murder the inmates of the home.

6. The proposed plan does not lower interest so much as to distress people and corporations who are dependent for revenue on interest. It fits immediately into present methods of doing business without creating any financial shock; it continues all bankers in place at good salaries, and makes a place for many more; it relieves the banker from anxiety concerning a run on his bank; it relieves the people from any anxiety as to whether they will lose their money in the bank. It makes an even and regular flow of money, bringing universal prosperity to the people and to the nation.

Useful Recipes and Trade Secrets

A COLLECTION OF PRACTICAL FORMULAS FOR ALL TRADES AND OCCUPATIONS

IN the following pages will be found a vast amount of practical knowledge for mechanics, merchants, manufacturers, architects, builders, contractors, farmers, gardeners, beekeepers, nurserymen, stock-breeders, housekeepers, surveyors, professional men, and, in fact, all classes of workers. These recipes and suggestions, together with the other departments of this volume, it is believed, comprise the whole circle of practical knowledge. The various items have been, as nearly as possible, arranged alphabetically. The seeker after information, however, should first consult the alphabetical index, at the end of the volume, as many items of information are capable of classification under various headings, and repetition has been carefully avoided.

ALABASTER or Marble — To Clean.

Muriatic acid, 1 part; soft water, 3 parts. Mix. Wash the marble well with this mixture; then rinse well with pure water, dry, and apply pure olive oil, or almond oil, to revive the color, rubbing well. Greasy marble is easily cleaned with a mixture of bi-carbonate soda, whiting and water, equal parts.

ALUM in Bread — To Discover.

Heat a knife and stick it into a loaf. If alum is in it, it will slightly coat the knife. Alum may also be discovered in bread (if it be present) by dipping a slice of the loaf into an infusion of logwood. The logwood will turn a purplish carmine if there is alum in it.

ANTI-BILIOUS PILLS.

Compound extract of colocynth, 60 grains; rhubarb, 30 grains; soap, 10 grains. Make into 24 pills. Dose, 2 to 4.

ANTS — To Destroy.

Drop quicklime on the mouth of their nest and wash it in with boiling water, or dissolve some camphor in spirits of wine, then mix with water, and pour into their haunts; or tobacco water, which has also been found effectual. They are averse to strong scents. Camphor, or a sponge saturated with creosote, will prevent their infesting a cupboard. To prevent their climbing up trees, place a ring of tar about the trunk, or a circle of rag moistened occasionally with creosote.

ANTS AND WATERBUGS.

Burn a piece of brimstone about the size of an egg in the room that is infested by ants and waterbugs. Do this at night, when through using the room. Close the room as tight as possible, so the gas will not escape.

AQUARIA — Cement for.

Take 10 parts by measure of litharge, 10 parts plaster of Paris, 10 parts dry white sand, and 1 part of finely-powdered resin. Mix, when wanted for use, into a pretty stiff paste with boiled linseed oil. This cement will stick to wood, stone, metal or glass, and hardens under water. On account of its resistance to the effect of salt water, it is a useful preparation for marine aquaria. Do not use the aquarium for two or three days after it has been cemented.

AROMATIC SPIRIT OF VINEGAR.

Acetic acid, No. 8, pure, 8 oz.; camphor, ½ oz. Dissolve and add oil lemon, oil lavender flowers, each 2 drams; oil cassia, oil cloves, ½ dram each. Thoroughly mix and keep in well-stoppered bottle.

AXLE GREASE.

1. Water, 1 gal.; soda, ½ lb.; palm oil, 10 lbs. Mix by heat, and stir till nearly cold.

2. Water, rape-oil, of each 1 gal.; soda, ½ lb.; palm oil, ¼ lb.

3. Water, 1 gallon; tallow, 3 lbs.; palm oil, 6 lbs.; soda, ½ lb. Heat to 210° Fahrenheit and stir until cool.

4. Tallow, 8 lbs.; palm oil, 10 lbs.; plumbago, 1 lb. Makes a good lubricator for wagon axles.

Excellent Axle Grease.—Take 1 part good plumbago (black lead) sifted through a coarse muslin so as to be perfectly free from grit, and stir into it 3 qts. of lard, warmed so as to be stirred easily without melting. Stir vigorously until it is smooth and uniform. Then raise the heat until the mixture melts. Stir constantly, remove from the fire, and keep stirring until cold. Apply cold to the axle or any other bearing with a brush. If intended for use where the axle or bearing is in a warm apartment, as the interior of mills, etc., 2 oz. of hard tallow or 1 oz. of beeswax may be used to every 10 lbs. of the mixture. This grease is cheaper in use than oil, tallow or tar, or any compound of them, and can be sold at a good profit in any thickly settled country.

BAD BREATH.

Bad breath from catarrh, foul stomach, or bad teeth, may be temporarily relieved by diluting a little bromo chloralum with 8 or 10 parts of water, and using it as a gargle, and swallowing a few drops before going out. A pint of bromo chloralum costs 50 cents, but a small vial will last a long time.

BAKING-POWDER.

Take by weight 6 parts of bicarbonate of soda to 5 parts of tartaric acid, which, being much purer than cream of tartar, is greatly to be preferred. Get the ingredients in this proportion from a reliable wholesale druggist. See that they are perfectly dry, roll the lumps out, mix thoroughly together, bottle tightly, and keep in a dry place. This has been used for months with much satisfaction.

BAY RUM.

French proof spirit, 1 gallon; extract bay, 6 oz. Mix and color with caramel; needs no filtering.

BED-BUGS.

Spirits of naphtha, rubbed with a small painter's brush into every part of the bedstead, is a certain way of getting rid of bugs. The mattress and binding of the bed should be examined, and the same process attended to, as they generally harbor more in these parts than in the bedstead. Ten cents' worth of naphtha is sufficient for one bed.

BED TICKS—To Clean.

Apply Poland starch, by rubbing it on thick with a cloth. Place in the sun. When dry, rub if necessary.

BEESWAX—To Bleach.

Melt the wax, and add for each pound 2 oz. of nitrate of soda and 1 oz. of sulphuric acid diluted with 8 parts of water. The latter should be added very slowly while the melted wax is constantly stirred with a glass rod. Then cool and set aside after filling the vessel with boiling water. Washing the wax with boiling water until no trace of the acid remains completes the process.

BILIOUSNESS—Remedy for.

Stir a little baking-soda into half a glass of cold water, into which has previously been squeezed the juice of a lemon. Drink while it foams.

BIRDS—To Prevent Destruction of Fruit Buds by.

Just before the buds are ready to burst, and again when they have begun to expand, give them a plentiful dusting with chimney soot. The soot is unpalatable to the birds, and they will attack no buds that it thus sprinkled. It in no way injures the nascent blossoms or leaf, and is washed off in due course of time by the rain.

BLACKBOARD—To Make.

The following directions for this work are given us by an experienced superintendent: The first care must be to make the wall surface or boards to be blacked perfectly smooth. Fill all the holes and cracks with plaster of Paris, mixed with water; mix but little at a time; press in and smooth down with a case-knife. The cracks between sheathing boards may be filled in the same way. Afterward use sand-paper. The ingredients used for slating are (1) liquid gum shellac, sometimes called shellac varnish; (2) lampblack or drop black. Gum shellac is cut in alcohol, and the liquid can be obtained of any druggist. Pour some shellac into an open dish, and stir in lampblack to make a heavy paint. With a clean brush, spread on any kind of surface but glass. Put on a little and test it. If it is glossy and the chalk slips over it, reduce the mixture with alcohol. Alcohol can be bought of any druggist. If it rubs off, let the druggist put in more gum to make the liquid thicker. One quart of the liquid and a 5-cent paper of lampblack are sufficient to slate all the blackboards in any country school with two coats.

BLACKING FOR HARNESS.

Melt 2 oz. mutton-suet with 6 oz. beeswax, add 6 oz. sugar candy, 2 oz. soft soap, dissolved in water, and 1 oz. finely-powdered indigo. When well mixed add to the whole 1 gill turpentine. Apply with a sponge; polish with a dry brush.

BLACKING FOR SHOES.

Three oz. ivory black, 2 oz. molasses, 1 oz. sulphuric acid, 1 oz. gum arabic, dissolved in water, a tablespoonful sweet oil, and a pint vinegar. Mix and stir together thoroughly. This makes a liquid blacking. A paste may be made by reducing the quantity of vinegar to little more than ½ pint.

XXL Blacking.—Put 1 gallon vinegar into a stone jug, and 1 lb. ivory black well pulverized, ½ lb. loaf sugar, ½ oz. oil of vitriol, and 7 oz. sweet oil. Incorporate the whole by stirring.

BLACKING FOR STOVES.

Mix the whites of 3 eggs, well beaten, with ½ lb. black lead; dilute to a thin paste by stirring in sour beer or porter. Apply with cloth or brush, and rub with dry brush.

BLADDERS—To Prepare.

Soak them for 24 hours in water, to which a little chloride of lime or potash has been added, then remove the extraneous membranes, wash them well in clean water and dry them.

BLEACHING FLUID—For Washing.

Into a bucket of boiling water put a pound of lime, and let it stand overnight. Next day put over the fire 2 lbs. sal soda in 2 gal. water. Let simmer until all is thoroughly dissolved; then pour the lime water into the soda water, mix thoroughly, cool and put away in glass, as it will eat holes in stone jars. A half teacupful of this fluid to three pails of water, when clothes are boiled, will make them beautifully clear and white. If any crumbs of lime fall on the clothes they will leave yellow spots.

BLEACHING with Chloride of Lime.

Two ounces of lime to each pound of cloth. Boil the cloth in strong soapsuds 5 to 10 minutes. Wring out. Pour a little hot water on the lime and stir till the lumps are out, then add gradually enough more hot water to cover the goods without crowding. Put cloth in, stir continually for 20 to 30 minutes; wring out, rinse until the water looks clear, then boil in suds again, rinse and dry. It takes more soap than one would think to make a good suds for new muslin, especially after it has been in the lime, but be sure and have the suds strong and to stir all the time while in the lime water, as that prevents any particles of lime, not dissolved, from settling on the cloth and eating a hole in it. Use clothes-sticks to stir with.

BLIGHT in Fruit Trees—To Cure.

Early in October, when the weather is calm, build a smouldering straw fire under each tree, and keep it up for an hour or more. After this scrape the trunk and branches carefully, so as to remove the moss and all impurities, and take also every web or nidus of insects that may be upon the few leaves on the trees. If very bad, wash the trunk and large branches with a solution of lime and manure. Destroy the insects and eggs dropped upon the ground, and loosen the soil under the tree. In the spring examine every branch carefully. Pick off all blights by hand, and wash off carefully, and repeat each month.

BOOTS AND SHOES.

To Make Water-Proof.—Melt together, in a pipkin, equal quantities of beeswax and mutton suet. While liquid rub it over the leather, including the soles.

To Mend.—Raw gutta percha, 1 oz.; resin, the size of a hen's egg; bisulphuret of carbon, 1 lb. Dissolve the gutta percha in the bisulphuret; add the resin; when dissolved, bottle for use. The leather must be clean and scraped a little to make it adhere.

To Soften.—Kerosene will soften boots and shoes which have been hardened by water, and render them as pliable as new.

BORERS in Peach Trees—To Destroy.

Are your young peach trees troubled with borers? Paint them with white lead and linseed oil mixed a little thicker than you would have it for ordinary housepainting. Remove the soil so as to paint an inch or two below the surface, and then paint 12 to 18 inches above ground. Paint in the spring and autumn.

BOTTLES—To Cap.

Purified resin, 7 drams; sulphuric ether, 10 drams; collodion, 15 drams; aniline red, sufficient. Dissolve the resin in the ether, mix with the collodion, and color to suit. All that is necessary is to dip the cork and the top of the bottle in it, turning it for an instant in the hand while the composition dries.

BOTTLES—To Clean.

There is no easier method of cleaning bottles than putting into them fine coal-ashes, and well shaking, either with water or not, hot or cold, according to the substance that fouls the bottle. Charcoal left in a bottle or jar for a little time will take away disagreeable smells.

Bottles that have contained oil may be cleaned by putting in them a little powdered bi-chromate of potassa, then as much in bulk of sulphuric acid. Let it run well around till all the organic particles turn black; then add a little water and rinse out.

BRANDRETH'S PILLS.

Take 2 lbs. of aloes, 1 lb. of gamboge, 4 oz. extract of colocynth, ½ lb. castile soap, 2 fluid drams oil of peppermint, and 1 fluid dram of cinnamon. Mix, and make into pills.

BRASS—To Clean.

Mix 1 oz. oxalic acid, 6 oz. rotten stone, all in powder, 1 oz. sweet oil, and sufficient water to make a paste. Apply a small proportion, and rub dry with a flannel or leather. The liquid dip most generally used consists of nitric and sulphuric acids, but this is more corrosive.

Brass work that is so dirty by smoke and heat as not to be cleaned with oxalic acid should be thoroughly washed or scrubbed with soda, or potash water, or lye. Then dip in a mixture of equal parts of nitric acid, sulphuric acid and water; or, if it cannot be conveniently dipped, make a swab of a small piece of woolen cloth upon the end of a stick, and rub the solution over the dirty or smoky parts; leave the acid on for a moment and then wash clean and polish.

BREAD, Hot—To Cut.

If you heat your knife you can cut hot bread as smoothly as cold.

BRICK OVENS—To Make.

A brick oven built in the old style, out of doors, entirely separate from the dwelling-house, is more desirable and more safe, so far as danger from fire is concerned, than if built by the side of the fireplace in the house. A good brick oven for baking bread, pies and cakes is worth all the ranges and cook-stoves that one could store in his kitchen. In such an oven everything will be baked just right, above and below, through and through. After a foundation has been prepared, let two courses of hard brick be laid for the bottom of the oven. Then build the mouth and part of the sides, until it is desirable to begin to draw the sides inward, when sand or mellow earth may be placed on the foundation, and the surface smoothed off and pressed down to the desired form of the oven. Now build the brick work over this form of sand. Lay two courses of hard bricks over the form with the best mortar. After the last bricks have been laid, the sand may be removed. The bricks should be soaked for several hours previous to being laid, so that they will not absorb the moisture of the mortar until it has set. Such an oven will cost but a few dollars, and any intelligent man, though only half a mechanic, can build it about as well as a mason.

BROADCLOTH—To Judge the Quality of.

To judge the quality of broadcloth, particular attention must be paid to the fineness of the fiber and the closeness of the texture. If, on passing the hand lightly in a direction contrary to the nap, there be a general silkiness of feel, uninterrupted by harsh roughness, these are grounds for concluding the cloth is made of fine wool. The texture should not only be composed of fine threads, but it should have an even consistency, produced by the operation of felting, by which the fibers of the wool are so perfectly incorporated that they conceal the tissue of the threads and give the entire web the appearance of felt, or, to use a familiar comparison, a piece of cloth made of fine wool and well wrought and finished should exhibit no more indication of the loom than a sheet of woven paper does of the apparatus employed in its fabrication. Dealers judge of its quality by an expedient which is more easily understood by observation than description. A portion of the cloth is taken up loosely with both hands, a fold of it being then pressed strongly between the thumb and forefinger of one hand, a sudden pull is given with the other, and according to the peculiar sharpness and vibrating clearness of the sound produced by the slipping or escape of the fold the merit of the cloth is judged. Another way is the comparison of various lines of different fabrics and of different prices; the soft, even consistency, together with the flexibility of fine broadcloth, will be rendered more evident on being contrasted with that of an inferior cloth.

BROADCLOTH—To Remove Stains from.

Mix, with 12 drops each of alcohol and spirits of turpentine, 1 oz. pipe clay, ground fine. Rub the spots with a little of this mixture moistened with alcohol, and let remain until dry; then rub with a woolen cloth.

BRONZE—To Clean.

Sweet oil will clean bronze; it must be well rubbed with a brush into all the crevices, then rubbed off thoroughly with a brush.

BRONZING IRON CASTINGS.

After having thoroughly cleaned the castings, immerse them in a solution of sulphate of copper. The castings will then take on a coating of copper. Then wash thoroughly in water.

BRONZING PLASTER CASTS.

To make a good green bronze, such as is used for French statuary, dissolve 1 oz. sal ammoniac, 3 oz. cream tartar and 6 oz. common salt in 1 pint hot water; add 3 oz. copper nitrate in a pint of hot water. Mix well together, and apply with a brush.

BROOMS—To Preserve.

To preserve brooms, dip them for a minute or two in a kettle of boiling suds once a week, shake them until almost dry, and hang them up or stand them with the handle down. This makes them tough and pliable, and they will last twice as long. A carpet wears much longer if swept with a broom cared for in this manner.

BUNIONS—To Cure.

A bunion may be cured by bathing the affected part in hot water to which a teaspoonful of salt, a tablespoonful of starch and a few drops of arnica have been added; then wipe dry with a soft linen towel and apply iodine with a camel's-hair brush. Wear a loose shoe all the time, or one which has the leather covering the bunion cut out. Bunions are caused by undue pressure. A good plan, if you have to be out a great deal, is to have the shoemaker cut a piece from your shoe where it presses upon the bunion, and replace it with an invisible patch.

BUTTER, RANCID — To Sweeten.

If butter which has become rancid be washed with new milk, and afterwards with water, it will become as good as ever. The rancid flavor of butter that has been long exposed to the air is due to what the chemists call butyric acid, which, being soluble in milk, accounts for that fluid removing the bad taste of rancid butter. The water with which the butter is afterward rinsed is used to take away any of the superfluous milk which, if left on the butter, would become sour. The manner of "washing" butter or any greasy substance is to knead it in the cold fluid after the fashion of kneading dough.

BUTTER, RANCID — To Restore.

Melt the butter in a water-bath with some fresh burnt and coarsely powdered animal charcoal (freed from dust by sifting) and strain it through clean flannel.

CALCIMINING — (See also Whitewashing).

Soak over night 1 lb. of white calcimine glue in sufficient water to cover; dissolve in boiling water; add 20 lbs. of whiting and dilute with water until the mixture is of the consistency of cream. To obtain various tints add to this as follows:

Lilac. — Add 1 pint of vermilion and 2 of Prussian blue.

Lavender. — Mix a light blue and tint slightly with vermilion.

Grey. — Raw umber and a little lampblack.

Rose. — One part red lead and 3 parts of vermilion.

Buff. — One part burned sienna and 2 parts spruce or Indian yellow.

Straw. — Chrome yellow with a touch of Spanish brown.

Be careful, in mixing tints, to stir thoroughly, and to put in the coloring gradually until you have the desired shade.

CANADA THISTLES — To Destroy.

For a small quantity, put a tablespoonful of salt on each stalk or stub, and the plant will wilt and disappear. Or cut the plant off just below the surface of the ground. Upon large farms, however, either of these methods would involve too much labor, and the best way is to turn the plants under with a plow. A strong pair of horses will turn over a sod 8 inches deep, and much lower than the knife in the hand will go; and if the work is thoroughly done, and no balks left, the plants will stay under the inverted sod for 3 or 4 weeks, unless in a very porous or light soil, which must be plowed oftener. If this is thoroughly done it is effective.

CANE-BOTTOM CHAIRS — To Clean.

Turn the chair bottom upwards, and with hot water and a sponge wash the cane-work well, so that it may become completely soaked. Should it be very dirty you must add soap. Let it dry in the open air, or in a place where there is a thorough draft, and it will become as tight and firm as when new, provided none of the strings are broken.

CANDLE-POWER.

The candle-power of a light may be approximately calculated by comparing the shadow cast by a rod in the light of a standard candle with the shadow cast by the light to be tested. By moving the latter toward or away from the rod, a point will be reached at which the shadow cast by both lights will be of the same intensity. The intensities of the two lights are directly proportional to the squares of their distances from the shadows; for example, suppose the light to be tested is three times the distance of the candle, its illuminating power is nine times as great.

CARPETS — To Brighten.

Carpets, after the dust has been beaten out, may be brightened by scattering upon them cornmeal mixed with salt and then sweeping it off. Mix salt and meal in equal proportions. Carpets should be thoroughly beaten on the wrong side first and then on the right side, after which spots may be removed by the use of ox-gall or ammonia and water.

CARPETS AND FLOORS — To Dust.

Sprinkle tea leaves on them (or freshly cut grass), then sweep carefully. Carpets should not be swept frequently with a whisk brush, as it wears them fast; only once a week, and the other times with leaves and a hair-brush. Fine carpets should be gently done with a hand-brush (such as is used for clothes) on the knees. Those parts of the carpet that are most soiled may be at any time scrubbed with a small hand-brush, when it is not considered necessary to undertake a general washing of the whole; always adding a little gall to the water to preserve the colors. A little ammonia in the water is also a good thing.

CARPETS — To Prevent Moth in.

Before putting down the carpet, wash the floor with spirits of turpentine or benzine. This must not be done with a fire in the room or with any matches or lights near.

CARPETS — To Extract Grease From.

Dissolve a piece of pearl-ash, of the size of a pea, in ½ teacupful of warm water. Pour some of the solution on a grease spot, and continue to rub it hard with a clean brush or woolen cloth, until it is nearly dry, and your carpet or garment will be as clean as ever.

CARPETS — To Renovate.

Any carpet that has a pile, such as Wilton or Brussels, should always be swept with the pile and not against it. Sweeping against the pile makes the carpets rough. Bits of dampened paper scattered about over the floor just before sweeping will assist in taking up dust and make the carpet brighter. After a carpet has become a little dingy it may be considerably improved by sweeping it with a broom dampened with water in which a little ammonia has been poured. Have the water in a basin or pail ready for use, dip the broom in it and shake off the drops of water. Then sweep down the carpets for three or four yards and dip the broom as before. If the water becomes very dirty it should be changed.

An old carpet which has become soiled may be cleaned and made to look almost as good as new by washing it with warm water and fresh beef's gall, using a pint of gall to a gallon of water; or by scrubbing it with warm soapsuds. In either case the carpet should be first well beaten so that it is free from dust, and properly laid on the floor. Scrub with ordinary scrubbing-brush with and against the grain over a small space, and immediately wipe it as dry as possible with rough cloths. If soapsuds be used rinse quickly so that the water will not soak through. Leave the windows open and do not use the room for a few hours or until the carpet is dry.

CARPETS — To Select.

There are many things to learn about carpets and their purchase. The manufacture of them is full of catches and tricks, and in the desire to make cheap goods quality and everything else are sacrificed to looks.

The regular tapestry carpet is printed like old-fashioned calico. It is made all in one color, which is the color of the ground; it is then run through presses on the same general principle as any other printed article. The color merely strikes through the outside of the wool. The pile is held in place only by single light binding thread, and a single strand of the wool may be drawn out for a yard or more by giving a gentle pull at one end. While this sort of carpet may have its uses, it is the most unprofitable thing imaginable to buy. A chair drawn over it may pull the threads out, and any roughness in the heel of the shoe is almost certain to do it, and ordinary use in a short time works the threads all out of place.

In body Brussels every color is dyed in the skein, then woven in, being thrown upon the surface only where this special color is required. In this class of goods the variety of colors is necessarily limited, as with present machinery only a certain number can be handled independently of each other. Body Brussels carpets are usually designated by the number of frames, which signify the number of colors used. In all carpets of this kind, the wool surface is thrown through the fabric, and shows to some extent on the back.

Unscrupulous manufacturers often so arrange their machinery that the back of the tapestry carpet is stained or clouded to follow as nearly as possible the colors on the surface. By this means unsophisticated persons are imposed upon. Of course, such goods are a most barefaced fraud, and should be treated as such. That reputable dealers sometimes handle them is not at all to their credit. What is known as velvet carpet is merely a tapestry with the pile cut. Wilton carpets have the interwoven back of the body Brussels, are yarn-dyed, and unquestionably the most durable carpets made. Moquettes and Axminsters are very thick, and sometimes very durable, but the purchase of such carpets may be said to be almost a lottery. For ordinary use and moderate cost, body Brussels is by far the best investment.

CARRIAGES — Rattling.

Do not allow your carriages to rattle like a threshing-machine, but, as fast as nuts or bolts get loose, fix them. Washers of sole-leather on the spindles of the axletrees will stop the clatter caused by too much "play." A piece of rubber put in between the shaft iron and clip will silence matters there; and a little coal oil on the circle, or fifth wheel, will stop squeaking. Where nuts work loose, cut a thread in front of them with a cold chisel, after screwing them up tight. A monkey wrench should be carried, that the nuts of different sizes may be attended to. To look over a carriage before going out to ride in it is as necessary as the sounding of wheels on a railroad train. A great number of lives have been lost, and thousands of dollars, in runaways caused by the sudden giving-out of some part of a vehicle.

CARRIAGES — To Wash.

Particular caution should be exercised against using a broom, brush, cloth, or even the hand, to rub off the mud, for the grit will scratch the surface of the varnish and mar the luster. Water should be dashed on if a hose is not at hand.

Use water plentifully before applying cloth or sponge. Where the mud has been allowed to dry on, wet it thoroughly; let it remain until soaked up soft, then dash on water until the dirt disappears. Apply the sponge carefully at first, well saturated with water. If it can be avoided, mud should not be allowed to dry on. Do not use hot water in winter. It destroys the varnish luster.

CASE-HARDENING.

Case-hardening is a process of hardening the surface of iron by converting it into steel. The articles to be thus hardened are put in an iron case, together with animal charcoal — that is, bones, skins, etc., burned and reduced to a powder. The box is coated with sand or clay, and exposed from 2 to 6 hours, according to the amount of iron contained, to a dull red heat. The articles are then taken out of the bone-dust and further hardened by being plunged into oil or cold water. Sometimes they are allowed to cool in the case and are afterward tempered. Prussiate of potash is frequently used for case-hardening iron. It is sprinkled or rubbed upon the iron while at a dull red heat, and this, after being put in the fire for a few minutes, is taken out and tempered in water. This process is a convenient one for small articles which are to be subjected to much wear, these being easily made of soft iron and then externally hardened.

CASTINGS—Shrinkage of.

In making allowances for shrinkage in casting, pattern-makers understand that different shapes will shrink differently. The standard of allowance for shrinkage in use in the best shops in the country is as follows, per foot: Loam castings, 1-12 inch.; green sand castings, 1-10 inch; dry castings, 1-10 inch; brass castings, 3-16 inch; copper castings, 3-16 inch; bismuth castings, 5-32 inch; tin castings, 1-4 inch; zinc castings, 5-16 inch; lead castings, 5-16 inch.

CATERPILLARS and APHIDES.

A garden syringe or engine, with a cap on the pipe full of very minute holes, will wash away these disagreeable visitors very quickly. You must bring the pipe close to the plant, and pump hard, so as to have considerable force on, and the plant, however badly infested, will soon be cleared, without receiving any injury. Afterwards rake the earth under the trees, and kill the insects that have been dislodged, or many will recover and climb up the stems of the plants. Aphides may also be cleared by means of tobacco smoke, but after this has been applied the plant should be well syringed.

CELERY.

Don't throw away the green leaves of celery. Wash the perfect ones and dry on a plate in a warming-oven or on the back of your stove, turning frequently; then keep in a tightly-covered tin box, and when celery is out of season they will prove a great addition to soups, stews and dressings.

CELLARS — To Disinfect.

A damp, musty cellar may be sweetened by sprinkling upon the floor pulverized copperas, chloride of lime, or even common lime. The most effective means to disinfect decaying vegetable matter is chloride of lime in solution. One pound may be dissolved in two gallons of water. Plaster of Paris has also been found an excellent absorbent of noxious odors. If used one part with three parts of charcoal it will be found still better.

A good agency for keeping the air of the cellar sweet and wholesome is whitewash made of good white lime and water only. The addition of glue or size is only a damage by furnishing organic matter to speedily putrefy. The use of lime in whitewash is not simply to give a white color, but it greatly promotes the complete oxidation of effluvia in the cellar air. Any vapors that contain combined nitrogen in the unoxidized form contribute powerfully to the development of disease germs.

CELLULOID.

Most celluloid is made in France, and this is the process of manufacture: A roll of paper is slowly unwound, and at the same time is saturated with a mixture of 5 parts of sulphuric acid, which falls upon the paper in a fine spray. This changes the cellulose of the paper into pyroxyline (gun cotton). The excess of the acid having been expelled by pressure, the paper is washed with plenty of water until all traces of acid have been removed. It is then reduced to a pulp and passes on to the bleaching trough. It is this gun cotton which gives it its explosive nature. Most of the water having been got rid of by means of a strainer, the pulp is mixed with from 20 to 40 per cent. of its weight of camphor, and the mixture thoroughly triturated under mill-stones. The necessary coloring having been added in the form of powder, a second mixture and grinding follows. This pulp is spread out in thin slabs, which are squeezed in a hydraulic press until they are as dry as chips. Then they are rolled in heated rollers and come out in elastic sheets. They are from that point worked up into every conceivable form. You can get celluloid collars, cuffs, hairpins, shirt fronts, cravats, penholders, brushes and combs, inkstands, knife-handles, jewelry and everything else choice that you can imagine.

CEMENTS—For All Purposes.

Hints for Cementing.—First, properly prepare the cement. If it be fused for use, warm the article to be repaired. When broken parts are closely brought together, there is but very little space for cement, and that very little is much better than none, for the molecules bind the two broken parts together, but if the two parts are separated a little, the space is filled by a sheet of cement, which is not a hard substance of itself, and this soft line gives way. Third, have the parts clean—perfectly clean, when the cement is applied. Fourth, pressure upon the two parts is of the utmost importance, for the complete exclusion of air.

Cement for Glass.—Boil isinglass in water to a consistency of cream, and add a little alcohol. Warm the cement before using, but do not heat the glass.

Diamond Cement.—Soak isinglass in water till it is soft; then dissolve it in the smallest possible quantity of proof spirits, by the aid of a gentle heat; in 2 ounces of this mixture dissolve 10 grains of ammoniacum, and while still liquid add ½ dram of mastic, dissolved in 3 drams of rectified spirits; stir well together, and put into small bottles for sale. *Directions:* Liquefy the cement by plunging the bottle in hot water, and use it directly. The cement improves the oftener the bottle is thus warmed; it resists the action of water and moisture perfectly.

Heat- and Moisture-Proof Cement.—Pure white lead, or zinc-white, ground in oil and used very thick, is an excellent cement for mending broken crockery-ware; but it takes a very long time to harden. It is well to put the mended object in some store-room, and not to look after it for several weeks or even months. It will then be found so firmly united that, if ever again broken, it will not part on the line of the former fracture.

Glycerine Cement.—A cement said to be capable of use where resistance to the action of both water and heat is required is composed by mixing ordinary glycerine with dry litharge, so as to constitute a tough paste.

Pitch Cement.—To make a splendid cement that will hold together with a wonderful tenacity wood, stone, iron, ivory, leather, porcelain, silk, woolen or cotton, take 2 parts (by weight) of pitch and 1 part of gutta percha, and melt together in an iron vessel.

Cementing Paper to Metals.—A French glue for making paper adhere to metals is made by dissolving 12 parts of gum tragacanth and 48 parts of acacia gum in 200 parts of water. After filtering add 1 part of thymol suspended in 48 parts of glycerine, and then add to the solution sufficient water to make 400 parts. This will keep a long time and can be used for metals, glass or wood.

Cement to Mend China.—Take a thick solution of gum arabic, and stir into it plaster of Paris, until the mixture is of proper consistency. Apply it with a brush to the fractured edges of the chinaware, and stick them together. In a few days it will be impossible to break the article in the same place.

Turkish Cement for Jewelry.—The jewelers in Turkey ornament watch cases and other trinkets with gems, by gluing them on with the following cement: Isinglass, soaked in water till it swells up and becomes soft, is dissolved in French brandy or rum, so as to form a strong glue; two small bits of gum galbanum, or gum ammoniacum, are dissolved in 2 oz. of this by trituration, and 5 or 6 bits of mastic as big as peas, being dissolved in as much alcohol as will render them fluid, are to be mixed with this by means of a gentle heat.

Tin Box Cement.—To fix labels to tin boxes either of the following will answer: 1. Soften good glue in water, then boil it in strong vinegar, and thicken the liquid, while boiling, with fine wheat flour, so that a paste results. 2. Starch paste, with which a little Venice turpentine has been incorporated while warm.

Acid-Proof Cement.—A cement that is acid-proof is made with a concentrated solution of silicate of soda, formed into a paste with powdered glass. This simple mixture is said to be invaluable in the operations of the laboratory where a luting is required to resist the action of acid fumes.

Elastic Cement.—Ordinary collodion is made by mixing 6 parts of gun cotton with 125 parts of ether and 8 parts of alcohol. When used as a cement it becomes very hard, cracks easily and peels off. It may be rendered elastic by the addition of 4 parts of Venetian turpentine and 2 parts of castor-oil. For surgical purposes, where perfectly close-fitting plaster is wanted, it has been found that the addition of some glycerine to the ordinary collodion, in which it is dissolved to a small extent, makes a varnish which adheres strongly to the skin, does not crack, and, on account of its elasticity, does not crease the skin.

Architectural Cement.—Take equal parts of paper paste and size, and finely powdered plaster of Paris, to make it of a proper consistency. Must be used as soon as mixed. This can be used in making architectural statues, columns, busts, etc. It receives a good polish, is very light, but will not stand the weather.

Armenian Cement (Keller's).—Soak ½ oz. of isinglass in 4 oz. of water for 24 hours; evaporate it in a water bath to 2 oz., then, after adding 2 oz. of rectified spirits, strain it through a linen cloth, and while warm mix it with ½ oz. of gum mastic dissolved in 2 oz. of rectified spirits; add 1 dram of powdered gum ammoniac; triturate them rapidly, to avoid evaporation of spirits, until thoroughly incorporated.

Liquid Cement.—Cut gum shellac in 70 per cent. alcohol. Apply to the broken dish with a feather, and hold it in a spirit lamp as long as the cement will simmer; then join together evenly, and when cold the dish will break in another place first.

Cement for Mahogany.—Add as much yellow ochre as is needed to give the right color to 4 parts of beeswax or shellac melted with 1 part of Indian red. This can be used for stopping holes and seams in mahogany furniture.

Cement for Cutlery.—1. Melt together 1 lb. of colophony and 8 oz. of sulphur, and either keep in bars or reduce to a powder. Mix 1 part of the powder with ½ part of iron filings, fine sand, or brick-dust, and fill the cavity of the handle with the mixture. Heat the stem of the knife or fork and insert into the cavity, and when cold it will be as strong as when new.

2. Melt together 4 lbs. of black resin, 1 lb. of beeswax, and add 1 lb. of finely powdered and well-dried brick-dust.

Cement for Earthenware.—Melt shellac and run it into small sticks the size of a quill. Heat the edges to be joined hot enough to soften the cement, smear them over and hold tightly together until cold.

Rubber Cement.—A cement made by dissolving rubber cut fine in benzine may be used to mend rubber boots and shoes. This cement will firmly fasten on the rubber patch. Put the pieces of rubber in a wide-mouthed bottle and fill it about half full of the purest benzine; the rubber will swell up almost immediately, and if well shaken will, in a few days, assume the consistency of honey. If the rubber does not dissolve, add more benzine. If, when dissolved, the cement is too thin, add more gum. A piece of rubber 1 inch in diameter will make a pint of cement. This dries in a few minutes and is very useful in uniting pieces of leather, as it is both elastic and durable.

Cement for Cloth.—To fasten cloth to the top of tables, desks, etc.: Make a mixture of 2½ lbs. wheat flour, 2 tablespoonfuls powdered resin, and 2 tablespoonfuls powdered alum. Rub the mixture in a suitable vessel, with water, to a uniform, smooth paste; transfer this to a small kettle over a fire, and stir until the paste is perfectly homogeneous without lumps. As soon as the mass has become so stiff that the spoon will remain upright in it, transfer it to another vessel and cover it up so that no skin may form on its surface. This cement is applied in a very thin layer to the surface of the table; the cloth, or leather, is then laid and pressed upon it, and smoothed with a roller. The ends are cut off after drying.

Cement for Leather and Cloth.—An adhesive material for uniting the parts of boots and shoes, and for the seams of articles of clothing, may be made thus: Take 1 lb. gutta percha, 4 oz. India rubber, 2 oz. pitch, 1 oz. shellac, 2 oz. oil. The ingredients are to be melted together, and used hot.

Heat-Proof Leather Cement.—This will stand both heat and alcohol: Take the best kind of glue, pour on an equal quantity of water, and let it soak over night; next morning melt it over a gentle heat, and add fine Paris white, or white lead. Mix well, and add a little acetic acid, carbolic acid, oil of cloves, or any other ethereal oil, to prevent putrefaction. This cement is well adapted for flexible objects. It will not withstand boiling water well, however, as this softens the glue.

Cement for Belting.—A cement for leather belting: Common glue and isinglass, equal parts, soaked for 10 hours in just enough water to cover them; bring gradually to a boiling heat, and add pure tannin until the whole becomes ropy or appears like the white of eggs. Buff off the surfaces to be joined, apply this cement, and clamp firmly.

Cement for Marble.—Sift plaster of Paris through muslin, and mix it with shellac dissolved in alcohol or naphtha. As soon as mixed, apply quickly and squeeze out as much of the composition as possible, wiping off that which squeezes out before it sets. The cement will hold better if the parts to be joined are roughened by a pointed tool before cementing. This can be done without breaking off the edges of the fractured parts. Plaster of Paris used with white of egg also makes a good cement, but it must be used with expedition.

Cement for Iron.—Since the late discoveries of welding by electricity, the new process has been generally preferred to soldering or cementing. A cement, however, that can be readily used for mending broken tools, and that will resist the blow of a sledge-hammer, is made thus: Take equal parts of sulphur and white lead, with about a sixth of borax; incorporate the three thoroughly. When about to apply it, wet it with strong sulphuric acid, place a thin layer of it between the two pieces of iron and press them together. In 5 days it will be dry.

Fire-Proof Iron Cement.—A cement for filling up cracks and holes in stoves is finely pulverized binoxide of manganese, mixed with a strong solution of silicate of soda (water glass), so it forms a thick paste; fill the cracks and heat the stove slowly.

Cement for Stoves.—Wood ashes and common salt, wet with water, will stop the crack of a stove.

Cement for Steam-Pipe Joints.—White lead ground in oil, a sufficient quantity. Add dry red lead enough to make a stiff putty. Put the mass in a mortar or on a block of iron or smooth stone, and pound it till it becomes soft; continue to add red lead and pound until the mass will no longer become soft by pounding, nor stick to the fingers. At this time it should be of sufficient tenacity to stretch out 3 or 4 inches when pulled, without parting. The more protracted the pounding, the finer and more tenacious the cement becomes. Interpose the putty between the flanges of the steam-pipe joints, taking care to put a thin grommet of packing or wicking around the diameter of the bore, to keep the cement from squeezing through when the flanges are screwed together. It is indestructible by steam or water, and makes one of the best joints known to the engineer.

Roof Cement.—Four parts of coal tar, 1 of air-slaked stone or shell lime and 1 of hydraulic cement or water-lime. The cost of materials is only about 3 or 4 cents per gallon. Pour the tar into an iron pot over a slow fire, and, when moderately hot, stir in the lime and the cement. Stir and mix well; apply it warm. A second coat will be well, to make sure of the covering of all the leaky cracks and to increase its durability. To improve the color and utility, sift on a coat of dry sand, white or yellow, soon, or about as fast as it is put on, as it soon becomes hard.

Cement for Iron and Stone.—Take equal parts of infusorial silica (which is imported from Germany) and oxide of lead, and mix together. Then add ½ part of freshly slaked lime and make the whole into a paste with boiled linseed oil. This forms a cement of extraordinary power, and is very useful in such work as fixing iron in stone. It is said not to expand in setting, so that there is no danger of splitting the stone.

For Mending Stone, Etc.—Mix in fine dry powder 20 parts of well washed and sifted sand, 2 of litharge, and 1 of freshly burned and slaked quicklime. This is suitable for filling up cracks, etc. It sets in a few hours, and has the appearance of light stone.

Red Cement.—The red cement for uniting glass to metals is made by melting 5 parts of black resin and 1 part of yellow wax; when entirely melted, stir in gradually 1 part of red ochre, or Venetian red, in fine powder, and previously well dried. This cement should be melted before it is used, and it adheres better if the objects to which it is applied are warmed.

Hydraulic Cement.—Hydraulic cements are those which set or become hard under water. Common lime does not possess this property, but limestone containing 8 to 25 per cent. of alumina, magnesia and silica yields a lime when burned that does not slake when moistened with water, but forms a mortar with it. This does not become solid in the air, but hardens with great rapidity under water, becoming more and more insoluble the longer it is immersed. This cement is prepared by burning the stone, breaking it in a crushmill, and then pulverizing it between millstones. When it is to be used it is made into a paste with water; no definite rules as to proportion can be given, the best plan being to add just such a quantity as to form a paste readily manipulated with a trowel. If it is to be used for filling in walls, it is necessary to make it thinner. Artificial hydraulic cements are sometimes made by mixing sand with caustic lime.

CHANDELIERS—To Renew.

Apply a mixture of bronze powder and copal varnish. The druggist of whom they are purchased will tell you in what proportion they should be mixed.

CHARCOAL TOOTH PASTE.

Chlorate of potash, ½ dram; mint water, 1 oz. Dissolve, and add powdered charcoal, 2 oz.; honey, 1 oz.

CHEESE—To Test.

Prof. Vaughan says: "I think I can positively state that any cheese which will instantaneously and intensely redden blue litmus paper should not be eaten. This is the test of 'sour cheese.' Blue litmus paper is very cheaply and easily obtained, and makes a very ready test for a cheese which is probably called 'sick' because it has undergone some change in the direction of decomposition, developing unwholesome acids as well as other relics of decay."

CHEWING-GUM.

Take 2 oz. prepared balsam of tolu — which is made of 4 oz. tolu, 1½ oz. white resin, and 1¼ oz. sheep's suet — 1 oz. white sugar, and 2 oz. oatmeal. After softening the gum in a water-bath, mix in the ingredients, and make it into sticks by rolling in finely powdered sugar or flour.

CHIMNEYS—To Stop Leaks Around.

A durable and cheap plan is to go to a painter and get his "paint skins" (skins that form on paint left standing for some time), with as much linseed oil, and boil them together; while hot, thicken, to a proper consistency, with clean sand, and apply at once.

CHINA—To Mend.

Make a light paste of the white of an egg and flour. Clean the broken edges from dust, spread them with the paste, and hold the parts together while wet, wiping off all that comes out. It must be held or fastened in position until dry. A perfectly colorless cement is made by dissolving ½ oz. of gum arabic in a wineglassful of boiling water, and adding plaster of Paris to form a thick paste. Use at once, applying with a thick brush.

CIDER—To Keep Sweet.

Put into the barrel ¼ oz. of bisulphate of lime, or before the cider works put in ½ pint of fresh mustard seed, tied up in a coarse muslin bag.

CIDER—To Keep Sweet for Years.

The process is very simple. All the early fruit should be made into vinegar. When the weather is sufficiently cool, say by the first or middle of October, make the cider of sound but mellow apples; put the cider in sweet liquor barrels, with a ⅝-in. tap-hole in the head of the barrel, about 1½ inches from the chime, and in a straight line from the bung-hole. Then place the cider in a cool, dry cellar. After it has worked sufficiently, which will probably be in a week or less, draw it off carefully, so as to not disturb the sediment at the bottom, in perfectly clean barrels, and place back upon the skids as before. If the temperature of the cellar is sufficiently cool, it may not require drawing again in a month, or longer. Then repeat the process, and after a few days bung up the barrels. Then about the latter part of March draw again, when, if properly managed before, there will be but a very little sediment. Fill the barrels full, bung up tight, and cider can be kept sweet and good for two years if thus treated.

CIDER without Apples.

Five gallons of hot water, 30 lbs. brown sugar, ¾ lb. tartaric acid, 25 gallons cold water, 3 pints of hop or brewer's yeast worked into a paste with ¾ lb. of flour and one pint of water. Put all into a barrel, which it will fill, and let it work 24 hours, the yeast running out all the time at the bung, by putting in a little water occasionally to keep it full. Then bottle, putting a couple of broken raisins to each bottle, and you will have cider that will equal champagne in flavor.

CLINKERS

May be removed from stoves or fire-brick by putting about half a peck of oyster shells on top of a hot fire.

CLOCK MOVEMENTS—To Clean.

Put them for from 15 to 30 minutes in a bath made of a quart of water and a teaspoonful of liquid ammonia or alkali, into which has been grated 5 grains of soap. Remove the articles, wipe them dry and polish with a brush and polishing powder.

CLOTH—To Clean.

Moisten a sponge with pure water, press it in a very clean towel till it becomes nearly dry; then sponge the cloth, one place after the other; all the dust will enter into the sponge; wash the sponge afterwards in water. This method of cleaning wears out the clothes less than brushing. Many spots also disappear with pure water.

CLOTH—Renovation of.

The article undergoes the process of scouring, and, after being well rinsed and drained, it is put on a board and the threadbare parts rubbed with a half-worn hatter's card, filled with flocks, or with a teazle or a prickly thistle, until a nap is raised. It is next hung up to dry, the nap laid the right way with a hard brush, and finished as before. When the cloth is much faded, it is usual to give it a dip, as it is called, or to pass it through a dye-bath, to freshen up the color.

CLOTH—To Revive Color of Black.

If a coat, clean it well, then boil from 2 to 4 ounces of logwood in your copper or boiler for ½ hour; dip your coat in warm water, and squeeze it as dry as you can; then put it into the copper and boil it for ½ hour. Take it out, and add a piece of green copperas, about the size of a horse-bean; boil it another ½ hour, then draw it, and hang it in the air for an hour or two; take it down, rinse it in 2 or 3 cold waters; dry it, and let it be well brushed with a soft brush, over which a drop or two of the oil of olives has been rubbed; then stroke your coat regularly over.

CLOTHING — To Make Watertight.

Immerse the cloth in a mixture of solutions of acetate of lead and sulphate of alumina. The salts will decompose, and when the cloth is dried, basic acetate of alumina adheres to the fiber, and thus protects it from moisture.

COCKROACHES — To Exterminate.

1. Spread molasses lightly over pieces of board, cover with borax, and place the boards where the roaches congregate.

2. Cut up green cucumbers and place them at night where the vermin come. Place fresh ones next morning, and three or four applications will do the work.

3. A teaspoonful of well bruised plaster of Paris mixed with double the quantity of oatmeal, to which a little sugar may be added, although this last-named ingredient is not essential. Strew it on the floor, or into the chinks where they frequent.

COINS — To Clean.

Silver coins may be cleaned with almost any of the silver powders in the market. Copper, bronze and nickel coins may be cleaned with a weak solution of vinegar. Put the coins for 10 minutes in the solution, let them dry, and then rub them with a piece of dry chamois skin.

COINS — To Develop Inscription on.

In almost all cases gradually heating the coins will cause the inscription to appear.

COLOGNE — Home-Made.

Into a quart of best spirits of wine put 10 drops of oil cassia, ½ dram oil of rosemary and 3 drams each of the oil of lavender, lemon and bergamot. Shake well, and let the bottle stand for several days before the gradual and cautious addition of 2 oz. of rose-water; shake thoroughly, and let it stand for a week. If the mixture is not clear by that time, put a little cotton-wool in the mouth of a clean funnel and strain the scent through it.

COLORED FIRES.

Red.—Nitrate of strontia 4 parts, chlorate of potash 1 part, shellac 1 part. *White.*—Chlorate of potash 12 parts, nitre 4 parts, sugar 4 parts, stearine 1 part, carbonate of baryta 1 part. *Green.*—Chlorate of potash 2 parts, nitrate of baryta 1 part, sugar 1 part. *Yellow.*—Chlorate of potash 6 parts, nitre 3 parts, oxalate of soda 5 parts, shellac 3 parts. The nitrate of strontia must be melted before use, so as to drive off the water of crystallization. The chlorate of potash should be powdered separately, for if struck when mixed with sulphur it explodes violently. Neither must the chlorate of potash and the other ingredients be rubbed together in a mortar, otherwise they will explode. These colored fires should not be prepared before they are required for use, as they are very apt to ignite spontaneously. By "parts," we mean parts by weight, not by measure.

COMPASS — To Tell the Points of the.

Hold your watch in such a position that the hour hand is pointed in the direction of the sun. Then the point midway between the position of the hour hand and XII. will be due south. If, for instance, the hour hand points to V, due south will be between II and III, or half way between XII and V.

COPYING PAD.

Put 1 oz. glue to soak in cold water until pliable and soft. Drain off the surplus water and place the dish in another dish containing hot water. When the glue is thoroughly melted, add 6 oz. glycerine which has been previously heated, and mix the two, adding a few drops of carbolic acid to prevent molding. Pour out this mixture into a shallow pan (9x12 inches) and set away to cool, taking care that the surface is free from blisters. After standing 12 hours it is ready for use. To use, write on a sheet of paper what you wish to duplicate with a sharp steel pen and strong aniline ink. When dry, lay the paper face down on the pad, pressing it lightly, and allow it to remain for a moment. On removing the paper, an impression will be found on the face of the pad, and if another paper is placed upon it, it will receive a similar impression. When enough impressions have been taken, the face of the pad should be immediately washed with a sponge and cold water until the ink impression is wholly removed. If the surface of the pad becomes dry, wipe it with a moist sponge, and, if uneven, melt over a slow fire.

COPYING PAPER — Magic.

To make copying paper, mix lampblack, Venetian red, Prussian blue or chrome green with cold lard, according to the color you desire. Apply the mixture, which should be of the consistence of thick paste, to the paper with a rag. Then rub the paper with a flannel rag till the color ceases to come off. By alternating these papers with writing-paper and using a solid pen, several copies of a letter can be produced at once.

COPYING PENCILS — To Make.

Make a thick paste of graphite, finely pulverized kaolin, and a very concentrated solution of aniline blue, soluble in water. Press this mixture into cylinders of proper size, and let them dry, when they will be ready for use. You may substitute gum arabic for the kaolin.

CORK—To Remove from the Inside of a Bottle.

If, in drawing a cork, it breaks, and the lower part falls down into the liquid, tie a long loop in a bit of twine or small cord, and put it in, holding the bottle so as to bring the piece of cork near to the lower part of the neck. Catch it in the loop, so as to hold it stationary. You can then easily extract it with a corkscrew.

CORKSCREW—Substitute for.

Insert in the cork a common screw, to which is attached a string to pull the cork. Or you may stick two steel forks into the cork on opposite sides, a little distance from the edge, run the blade of a knife through the two, and give a little twist, which will generally bring out the cork.

CORN REMEDIES.

1. Tincture of iodine, 4 drams; iodide of iron, 12 grains; chloride of antimony, 4 drams. Mix, and apply with a camel-hair pencil after paring the corn. It is said to cure them in three applications.

2. Soak a piece of copper in strong vinegar for 24 hours. Pour the liquid off, and bottle. Apply frequently, till the corn is removed.

3. Supercarbonate of soda, 1 oz., finely pulverized and mixed with ½ oz. lard. Apply on a linen rag every night until cured.

Corns between the Toes.—These are generally more painful than any others, and are frequently situated as to be almost inaccessible to the usual remedies. Wetting them several times a day with hartshorn will, in most cases, cure them.

COTTAGES—Cheap Wash for.

For outside of wooden cottages, fences, etc.: Take a clean barrel, put in it ½ bushel fresh quicklime, and slake it by pouring over it boiling water sufficient to cover it 4 or 5 inches deep, and stirring till slaked. When quite slaked, dissolve in water, and add 2 lbs. sulphate of zinc (white vitriol), which, in a few weeks, will cause the whitewash to harden on the wood. Add sufficient water to make a thick whitewash—this is *white*. To make a pleasing *cream color*, add 4 lbs. yellow ochre. For *fawn color*, 4 lbs. umber, 1 lb. Indian red and ¼ lb. lampblack; first dissolve the lampblack in alcohol. For *gray* or *stone color*, 1 lb. umber and 2 lbs. lampblack. This is very durable, as the zinc sets and hardens the wash.

COUGH SYRUP.

Put 1 quart hoarhound to 1 quart water, and boil it down to a pint; add 2 or 3 sticks of licorice and a tablespoonful of essence of lemon. Take a tablespoonful of the syrup three times a day, or as often as the cough may be troublesome. The above recipe has been sold for $100. Several firms are making much money by its manufacture.

COURT-PLASTER.

Court-plaster is made by repeatedly brushing over stretched sarcenet with a solution of 1 part isinglass in 8 parts of water, mixed with 8 parts of proof spirits, and finishing with a coat of tincture of benzoin or balsam of Peru.

CRAYON DRAWINGS—To Fix.

The best method is to dissolve strong isinglass in water, and brush it over the paper before commencing the drawing. Allow it to dry, when the surface is in good condition for making the drawing. When done, the paper should be held horizontally over steam. This will melt the size, which absorbs the charcoal or crayon. When allowed again to dry, the drawing has become fixed.

CREMATION.

The Siemens furnace, which has been adopted by the advocates of this mode of disposing of the dead in Germany, England and elsewhere, is probably the best known. The body is placed in an oblong brick or iron-cased chamber, underneath which is a furnace. The air of the chamber is raised to a very high temperature before the body is put in, and a stream of heated hydro-carbon from a gasometer is then admitted, which, on contact with the intensely heated air within, immediately bursts into flame. The chamber is, of course, so constructed as neither to admit draughts of air from without nor to permit the escape of gases from within. The noxious gases which are evolved in the beginning of the combustion process are passed through a flue into a second furnace, where they are entirely consumed. By this process a body weighing 144 pounds can be reduced in about 50 minutes to not more than 4 pounds of fine dust. Not more than 200 pounds of fuel are required. The cost of constructing one of these furnaces is probably about $2,000.

CURCULIO—To Get Rid of.

Make a solution of gas-tar and water so strong that after standing a few days it will be dark-colored and as pungent as creosote. When the curculio first appears, drench the trees thoroughly with the solution, using a small hand forcing-pump, and repeat it every three days for two weeks. Destroy all the fruit as it falls, as a preventive measure, which may be done by giving your fowls possession of the orchard.

CUT GLASS—To Clean.

Wash in warm water and let dry thoroughly; then polish with a soft brush and prepared chalk.

DAMPNESS—To Absorb.

For a damp closet or cupboard, which is liable to cause mildew, place in it a saucerful of quicklime. This will not only absorb all apparent dampness, but sweeten and disinfect the place. Renew the lime once a fortnight, or as often as it becomes slaked. Another good way is to put common rock salt in the saucer, which will have the same effect.

DEER SKINS—To Dress.

Take 8 qts. of rain water and put into it 1 pt. of soft soap. Warm the liquid and put the skin in while warm. Pound the hide or work it with a soft stick; let it lie in the liquid a day, and then take it out and roll it between two logs or pass it through a wringing-machine. Stretch it out to dry either in the sun or by a hot fire, and when dry oil it with any oil that you have; good fresh tallow, however, is better than anything else for the purpose. Repeat the operation, and when the skin is dry a second time, rub it with ochre to give it a fine yellow color.

DISINFECTANTS.

Copperas dissolved in water, ½ lb. to a gallon, and poured into sinks and water drains occasionally, will keep such places sweet and wholesome. A little chloride of lime, say ½ lb. to a gallon of water, will have the same effect, and either of these costs but a trifle.

A preparation may be made at home which will answer about as well as the chloride of lime. Dissolve a bushel of salt in a barrel of water, and with the salt water slake a barrel of lime, which should be made wet enough to form a thin paste or wash.

A little charcoal mixed with clear water thrown into a sink will disinfect and deodorize it. Chloride of lime and carbolic acid, considerably diluted, if applied in a liquid form, are good disinfectants, and carbolic powder is both useful and effective. The air of a bedroom may be pleasantly sweetened by throwing some ground coffee on a fire shovel previously heated.

"When plumbers discover a material for pipes which will not become coated with slime from water or sewage, then disinfection will be unnecessary, but not till then. The best plumbing known requires regular flushing and cleansing, and the best plumbers instruct their clients to use disinfectants weekly at least. All the powerful and really useful disinfectants corrode metal and stain crockery more or less. Copperas is the best for household use, 1 lb. dissolved in 12 qts. of boiling water and used hot, being more effective than cold. The valve should be open when it is poured down closets, so that it need not settle in the pan, which should be washed daily with a long-handled dish mop kept for the purpose, and scalding strong suds, when it will need no further disinfection. A large funnel should be set in the pipe of stationary wash-bowls, which, by the way, are unfit for human habitations, and unknown in the best modern houses. When the first Astor mansion was built the owner positively forbade a single stationary bowl in the dressing-rooms, an example which has since been followed in other high-class houses. With the funnel the pipes can be flushed with copperas without staining the bowls. Concentrated lye is only useful in the interest of plumbers, as it will eat out the pipes in a very short time if faithfully applied. No grease or greasy water should ever be allowed in a sink. Lye or soap enough to change the grease should be added before the water is poured away, when flushing the pipe daily with boiling water will keep it clean. A quart of copperas water poured in a closet daily, with a teaspoonful of germicide, will keep it in safe and acceptable condition, provided the closet is ventilated. An unventilated closet or bath without a window or skylight opening to the outer air is a dangerous indecency."—*Shirley Dare.*

DOGS—Training and Care of.

Growing young dogs should have plenty of sour milk.

Dogs never should be washed with soap and water. An occasional bath of milk and liver oil will cleanse the skin without producing the injurious effects which follow the liberal use of soap and water.

To make the coat glossy and the skin healthy, confine the dog in a dark place and use a brush and coarse towel on his coat freely.

To break a dog of the disagreeable habit of jumping on you, grab him quickly by the paws as soon as they touch you, and at the same moment trip him with the foot and let him fall on his back. Do this gently and good-naturedly. It will surprise the dog and break him without cowing him. To make the lesson more effectual, endeavor by playing with the dog to induce him to jump up and put his paws on you, tripping him whenever he does it. After a few lessons of this kind, the dog will express his good feeling by jumping up without touching you with his feet.

To break a dog of sucking eggs, force into his mouth a raw egg "loaded" with red pepper.

To break a dog of killing chickens, thrash him with a dead chicken.

Newly made deal-shavings make the best bed, as they clean the dog and drive away the fleas.

DRAINING LAND.

Adjust a strong metal pipe in a slanting position over the lot to be drained. It must be 20 feet in length and 6 inches in diameter. Join another pipe firmly to the opening at the bottom of this pipe, inclining it backwards at an angle sufficient to allow its end to rest upon the ground line. With the principal pipe connect a strong canvas hose down which a current of water flows and comes out of the mouth of the pipe. A vacuum is thus formed in the second pipe which sucks up the water from the ground and discharges it with the current flowing through the principal pipe.

DRAWINGS—To Fix.

Dissolve isinglass in spirits of wine, and a small portion of it, put into water, forms a good fixing for pencil drawings. Also, a weak solution of gum arabic in water, as strong as it can be without in the least glazing the paper. Or use skim milk. See *Crayon Drawings*.

DRESSES—To Make Uninflammable.

Put an ounce of alum or sal-ammoniac in the last water in which muslins or cottons are rinsed, or in the starch in which they are stiffened. This renders them uninflammable; at least, they will with difficulty take the fire, and, if they do, will burn without flame. This may save the lives of your children.

DRYING OIL.

Boil together, until it will scorch a feather, 2 gals. linseed oil, 2 oz. sulphate of zinc, 2 oz. sugar of lead, and 4 oz. each of red lead and umber. This is as good as many of the patent driers which cost a great deal more.

DYES AND DYEING.

Any article to be dyed should first be made clean. Goods should be scoured in soap and the soap rinsed out. Dip them into water just before putting them into the preparation, to prevent spotting. Use soft water always—enough to cover the goods well—this is always understood where quantity is not given. After dyeing, air, rinse well, and hang up to dry. Silk or merinos should never be wrung. Cotton goods should first be bleached if it is intended to dye them a light color.

Black Silk, Cotton, Lace or Wool Goods.—For 4 lbs. of goods take 2 oz. of blue vitriol, and 8 oz. extract of logwood, or, if preferred, 3 lbs. of logwood chips. Put each separately in 12 quarts of water. Put the vitriol water in a brass kettle if possible. Bring both kettles to the boiling point. Have the cloth thoroughly washed out in warm water; dip first in the vitriol water, then in the logwood water, and alternately from one to the other until it has been dipped in each three times. Dry, wash in strong suds, rinse in soft water twice, that it may not "crock." Put a little salt to the last water. Wring out, roll up and leave an hour or so before pressing; press on the wrong side until perfectly dry. A small piece of copperas is good to add to the logwood water. This will not fade, and answers for all materials, but best for woolen goods.

Brown Cotton, Woolen or Silk.—Wash the goods first in strong soap-suds, rinse well, then follow directions. For 5 lbs. cloth or yarn take 1 lb. gum catechu, 3 oz. blue vitriol, and 4 oz. bichromate of potash. Dissolve catechu and blue vitriol in sufficient soft water to cover the goods; bring to a scalding heat. Wring the goods out of clear hot water, shake out, put in the catechu and vitriol bath. Let them remain 3 hours, stirring and airing quite often. Dissolve the bichromate of potash in enough warm water to cover the goods; lift from the catechu dye, and put in the potash dye, scald until the desired color. Put them in all at once, but do not crowd them. Stir frequently; 15 minutes is usually enough. Rinse in clear, warm water; dry in the shade; use brass, copper or porcelain kettles, but not iron.

Blue for Cotton.—A lasting and beautiful color. Dissolve 5 oz. of copperas in water sufficient to cover the goods. When it reaches scalding point, put the goods in and scald ½ hour; take out and air; put clean water in the kettle, enough to cover the goods, together with 3 oz. of prussiate of potash. Put in the goods 30 minutes. Remove and add to the kettle 2 oz. oil of vitriol, return the goods and let remain 20 minutes or longer, if the color is to be dark. This will color 5 lbs. of cloth.

Green for Cotton.—First, color the goods blue, then take 4 oz. sugar of lead, and 2 oz. bichromate of potash, and dissolve each separately in ½ pailful of water. Dip the goods from one to the other until the desired shade is obtained. This will color 5 lbs. of goods. Or, dye blue first, and dip in the yellow dye.

Yellow for Cotton.—For 5 lbs. of goods dissolve ½ lb. sugar of lead in hot water. Dissolve ¼ lb. bi-chromate of potash. Dip in the lead dye, then in the potash until the desired shade is obtained.

Orange for Cotton.—Dye the goods yellow and dip in a very strong boiling lime-water. Wring out and dip in clear, hot rain water.

Madder Red.—This is a good, durable, but not brilliant, red. For 6 or 7 lbs. of goods, 4 gallons water, ½ lb. madder, 3 oz. alum, 1 oz.

cream tartar. Heat half the water scalding hot in a brass, copper or porcelain kettle, and dissolve in it the alum and cream tartar. When it boils put in the goods and boil 2 hours, then rinse. Empty the kettle, break the madder small and add to the other 3 gallons of water. Put in the goods and keep scalding hot 1 hour, stirring pretty constantly; then increase the fire until they boil 5 minutes. Drain and rinse in clear water without wringing. Wash in suds and dry in the shade.

Cochineal.—Take for each pound of goods 2½ oz. of alum, 1½ oz. white tartar, put in a brass or porcelain kettle, not iron, with sufficient water to cover the goods. Let boil briskly several minutes, then put in the goods, which should have been washed clean and rinsed in clear water. When the goods have boiled ½ hour take out, without wringing, and hang where they will all cool alike, without drying. Empty out the alum and tartar water, put in fresh for each pound of goods to be dyed, add an ounce of finely powdered cochineal. Let this boil 15 minutes; add sufficient cold water to make lukewarm and to just cover the goods as before. Boil 1½ hours. Remove the goods without wringing and dry in the shade.

Orange and Salmon.—Take as much strong soft soap-suds (plain bar soap will do) as will cover the quantity of goods. Tie a quantity of annotto in a bag and soak in the suds until it is soft, so that enough can be squeezed out to make the suds a deep yellow. Put in the articles, which should be clean and bleached free from color. Boil until the shade wished. See that the goods are well covered with dye. This dye will make a salmon or orange color, according to the strength or the length of time the goods are kept in. Drain out of the dye, dry quickly in the shade, then wash in soap-suds. Do not rinse.

Straw or Lemon Color.—Fustic or saffron makes a good straw or lemon color, according to the strength of the dye. Steep in soft water in an earthen or tin vessel, strain and set the dye with alum. To stiffen the goods, dissolve a little gum-arabic in the dye. When it is dissolved steep the goods in it.

Slate Color.—Tea grounds set with copperas make a good slate color. Strain, boil the goods in this and hang up to drain and dry.

To Bleach Goods for Dyeing.—Where it is necessary to remove the color in an article before dyeing, wash in hot soap-suds or boil in soap-suds until faded. Rinse thoroughly; any soap left in will ruin the dye. Goods for dyeing should be clean and free from grease.

Scarlet for Wool (Very Fine).—For 1 lb. of goods, take ½ oz. cream tartar, ½ oz. well pulverized cochineal, 2½ oz. muriate of tin. Boil up the dye and enter the goods. Work them briskly 10 or 15 minutes, then boil 1½ hours, stirring the goods slowly while boiling. Wash in clear water and dry in the shade.

Blue for Wool (Quick Process).—For 2 lbs. goods, 6 oz. alum, 3 oz. cream tartar. Boil goods in this one hour, then put them into warm water that has more or less extract of indigo in it, according to depth of color desired, and boil again until the tint suits, adding more indigo if needed.

Sky Blue (on Silk or Cotton).—Give the goods color from a solution of blue vitriol, 2 oz. to 1 gal. water, by dipping 15 minutes. Then run it through lime-water. This will make a beautiful and durable sky blue.

Aniline Blue.—Aniline is preferred to all other materials for coloring, and it is easily prepared. Blue aniline comes in crystals, and in this state has a very rich purple shade, and is generally soluble only in alcohol; at least, it is best to always use alcohol to cut the crystal. Dissolve 2 drams of aniline in 4 oz. of alcohol and bottle up; this amount of the solution is enough to make two gallons of dye.

After the fabric has been prepared for coloring by washing clean, first put into the amount of water used for the bath enough sulphuric acid to give it a sour taste, then add the solution in amount as above directed, or to obtain desired shade; put in the cloth or yarn and heat gradually until it boils. Make the rinsing water a little sour with sulphuric acid; it is better than alum, at least, for making blue permanent. It should be used only for wool and silk. Cotton or linen goods should never be put into any dye containing sulphuric acid, for it will rot the fabric, but it has no injurious effect upon silk and wool. To color cotton or linen, leave out the acid and use a little alum; but a good color cannot be insured.

To Dye Olive Color.—By combining red, yellow and blue, olive color is produced. Cotton and linen receive an olive color by being passed through a blue, yellow, and then madder bath.

To Dye Silk Stockings Black.—Dye like other silk or woolen garments. At first they will look like an iron gray; but to finish and black them they must be put on wooden legs, laid on a table and rubbed with an oily rubber or flannel upon which is oil of cloves, and then the more they are rubbed the better. Each pair of stockings will require half a tablespoonful of oil at least, and half an hour's rubbing, to finish them well. Sweet oil is the best in this process, as it leaves no disagreeable smell.

To Dye Chip and Straw Hats Black.—Put in a boiling bath of logwood for four hours.

Remove and give an airing; add a little copperas to the solution, and repeat the boiling, and allow the liquid to cool down with hat in. After drying, dress over with a sponge moistened with sweet or olive oil. Use but little oil. Dress both sides, and press into shape.

To Dye Furs.—Take lye that will bear up an egg. To 1 gal. of lye add 2 qts. soft water; boil in an iron kettle. Take 1 oz. of acetate of lead, 1 oz. of sulphate of iron, 2 oz. litharge; pulverize the ingredients and dissolve one at a time in the lye. When the fluid is blood warm, put in the furs a few moments only, then air them and dip into strong vinegar, then slick them off and hang up to dry. Hides should always be well handled. The dye can be made stronger by adding more of the ingredients, and brushing on if not dark enough.

EARWIGS.

These are very destructive insects, their favorite food being the petals of roses, pinks, dahlias, and other flowers. They may be caught by driving stakes into the ground and placing on each an inverted flower-pot, for the earwigs will climb up and take refuge under the pot, when they may be taken out and killed. Clean bowls of tobacco pipes, placed in like manner on the tops of smaller sticks, are very good traps, or very deep holes may be made in the ground with a crowbar, into which they will fall, and may be destroyed by boiling water.

EBONY—Artificial.

Dry and grind charcoal obtained by treating sea-weed for 2 hours in dilute sulphuric acid. Take 15 parts of this and add to it 10 parts of glue, 5 of gutta percha, 2½ of India rubber, the last two dissolved in naphtha; add 10 parts of coal tar, 5 parts of pulverized sulphur, 2 parts of pulverized alum, 5 parts of powdered resin, and heat the mixture to 300° Fahr. This is the same color and hardness as ebony, and, when hard, will take a polish equal to it.

EBONIZING WOOD.

Logwood chips, 8 oz.; copperas, ½ oz.; lampblack, ½ oz.; water sufficient. Boil the logwood for ½ hour in a gallon of water, and then add the copperas and lampblack. Apply to the wood hot, giving a number of coats. In varnishing ebonized wood, a little drop-black must be added to the varnish, or it will give a brown shade.

EGGS—How to Keep.

To 1 pail or 3 gallons of water, put 1 lb. fresh, unslaked lime and 1 lb. rock salt. Let it stand 2 or 3 weeks, stirring frequently, till the strong smell of the lime has passed off and there is a thin scale or crust formed on the top. Great care must be taken not to put the eggs in too soon, or any raking of the lime will cook them. I use a large butter-tub holding 8 pailfuls, and have sometimes found eggs imbedded in the sediment that have been in two seasons, perfectly fresh. The shells will be slightly crusted over, which perfectly excludes the air. They should be put in the pickle as fresh as possible. It is not necessary to strain the liquid.

To Test Eggs.—One way to test the freshness of eggs is to put them into a bucket of cold water. The fresh ones will sink immediately. Beware of those that float.

Various Uses of Eggs.—To clean vinegar bottles and cruets, crushed egg shells in a little water are as good as shot, besides being healthier and handier. *To mend broken china*, use a cement made by stirring plaster of Paris into the white of an egg. Eggs are valuable *remedies for burns*, and may be used in the following ways: The white of the egg simply used as a varnish to exclude the air, or the white beaten up for a long time with a tablespoonful of fresh lard till a little water separates. Or an excellent remedy is the mixture of the yolk of an egg with glycerine, equal parts; put in a bottle and cork tightly; shake before using; will keep for some time in a cool place. *For inflamed eyes or eyelids*, use the white of an egg beaten up to a froth with 2 tablespoonfuls rosewater. Apply on a fine rag, changing as it grows dry. Or stir 2 drams of powdered alum into the beaten whites of 2 eggs till a coagulum is formed; place between a fold of a soft linen rag and apply. *For a boil*, take the skin of a boiled egg, moisten it, and apply. It will draw off the matter and relieve the soreness in a few hours. *To cleanse the hair and promote its growth*, rub the yolk of an egg well into the scalp and rinse out thoroughly with soft warm water.

ELECTRIC BELTS.

There is no doubt that, when it is applied properly, electricity will do much in a certain class of diseases. But, in order to secure the requisite results, it is necessary to have a thorough understanding of the physics of electricity, to be able to rightly diagnose disease, and to know which current to apply, and where and how often to apply it.

Taking advantage of popular superstitious beliefs, a number of manufacturers have made so-called electric belts, guaranteed to cure every disease to which flesh is heir. Many of these belts consist either of a piece of magnetized steel, which cannot possibly have any influence on the patient, or of pieces of copper and zinc connected by wires. This is supposed to receive its excitant from the perspiration of the body. As a proof that there is electricity in this first kind of belt, they place a magnet near it and show that it will deflect the needle. This, to a great many people, is proof positive; but when they stop to consider that an ordinary steel jack-knife will also cause a needle to deflect, it ought to appear clear to them that wearing the jack-knife about their person would have the same effect as the belt.

ENAMELING.

Enamel is a vitreous substance which can be applied in a thin stratum to any smooth metallic surface, on which it is fused by the flame of a lamp, urged by the blow-pipe, or by the heat of a small furnace. The base of all enamels is a transparent and fusible glass, which readily unites with other substances. It can be colored in various tints by the use of metallic oxides. To prepare iron for enameling it should be first carefully cleaned by scouring with sand and diluted sulphuric acid, next a somewhat thick magma or mineral paste, made of pulverized quartz, borax, feldspar, kaolin and water, is brushed over the clean metallic surface as evenly as possible, and immediately after a finely powdered mixture of the enamel constituents is thickly laid over, and this exposed to the fusing heat of a furnace. It becomes strongly adherent to the iron surface in its molten state, and cools with a perfectly smooth, glassy surface. There are various formulæ for the enamel coating. One of the most simple consists of 130 parts of flint glass, 20½ parts of carbonate of soda, and 12 parts of boric acid fused together and afterward ground to a fine powder.

ENGINEERS—Points for.

When using a jet condenser let the engine make three or four revolutions before opening the injection valve, and then open it gradually, letting the engine make several more revolutions before it is opened to the full amount required.

Open the main stop-valve before you start the fires under the boilers.

When starting fires don't forget to close the gauge-cocks and safety-valve as soon as steam begins to form.

An old Turkish towel cut in two lengthwise is better than cotton-waste for cleaning brass-work.

Always connect your steam valves in such a manner that the valve closes against the constant steam pressure.

Turpentine well mixed with black varnish makes a good coating for iron smoke-pipes.

Ordinary lubricating oils are not suitable for use in preventing rust.

You can make a hole through a glass by covering it with a thin coating of wax—by warming the glass and spreading the wax on it; scrape off the wax where you want the hole, and drop a little fluoric acid on the spot with a wire. The acid will cut a hole through the glass, and you can shape the hole with a copper wire covered with oil and rotten-stone.

A mixture of 1 oz. sulphate of iron, ¼ oz. alum, ½ teaspoonful powdered salt, 1 gill of vinegar and 20 drops of nitric acid will make a hole in steel that is too hard to cut or file easily. Also if applied to steel and washed off quickly, it will give the metal a beautiful frosted appearance.

It is a fact that 35 cubic feet of sea-water is equal in weight to 36 feet of fresh water, the weight being 1 ton (2,240 pounds).

Remember that coal loses from 10 to 40 per centum of its evaporative power if exposed to the influence of sunshine and rain.

ENGRAVINGS—To Clean.

To clean and whiten engravings which have become dirty by hanging in a smoky room, soak in a weak, clear solution of chloride of lime until white, and then soak in running water. Steep for ½ an hour in water containing a very little hyposulphite of soda to neutralize any trace of adhering bleach, and dry between blotting-paper under pressure.

To Transfer Engravings. — Engravings may be transferred on white paper as follows: Place the engraving a few seconds over the vapor of iodine. Dip a slip of white paper in a weak solution of starch, and, when dry, in a weak solution of oil of vitriol. When again dry, lay a slip upon the engraving and place both for a few minutes under a press. The engraving will be reproduced in all its delicacy and finish.

ERASING-FLUID.

Recently written matter may be completely removed by a solution of chlorine gas in water. Wash the written paper repeatedly with this, and afterward wash it with lime-water, to neutralize any acid which may be left. The writing will thus be removed.

EXTRACT OF MEAT (Prof. Liebig's Recipe).

Take a pound of good, lean beef, from which all skin and fat have been cut away. Chop it up fine and mix thoroughly with an exact pint of cold water; then place it near the fire, so that it will heat very slowly, giving an occasional stir. It may stand 2 or 3 hours before it is allowed to simmer, and then will require at the utmost but 15 minutes of gentle boiling. Salt should be added when the boiling first commences. After boiling pour the extract from the meat into a bowl, and allow it to stand until any particles of fat which may show on the surface can be skimmed off, and the sediment has settled and left the soup quite clear. Then pour off gently, heat in a saucepan, and serve at once.

EYE-WATER—Camphorated.

Sulphate of copper, 15 grains; French bole, 15 grains; camphor, 4 grains; boiling water, 4 oz. Infuse, strain and dilute with 2 quarts of cold water.

FEATHERS.

To Clean White Feathers.—Draw the feathers gently through a warm soap lather several times, then pass them through tepid, and finally through cold water, to rinse them; then hold them a short distance from the fire, and curl the separate parts of the feather as it dries by holding a steel knitting-pin in the hand and drawing each portion of the feather briskly between the pin and the thumb.

To Clean Ostrich Feathers.—Pour boiling water on some white curd soap, cut in small pieces; to this add a little pearlash. As soon as the soap is dissolved, and the mixture cool enough for the hand to bear, put the feathers into it and draw them through the hand till the dirt is squeezed out of them. Next pass them through a clean lather with some blue in it, and afterward rinse in cold water with blue, to give them a good color. Shake off the water, and dry them by shaking near the fire. Curl each feather separately, when perfectly dry, with a blunt knife or ivory paper-folder, or hold the feather for an instant over glowing coals.

FENCE POSTS—To Preserve.

Coal tar, 5 gallons; quicklime (stone lime freshly slaked), and finely pulverized charcoal, of each 1 lb. The charcoal and the stone lime are both to be finely pulverized, and the tar made hot in an iron kettle, then the powders stirred in, keeping these proportions for all that may be necessary to use. Apply hot.

FILES—To Renew.

Thoroughly cleanse the files from grease or oil by alkali, soda or potash; then dip them into a solution made of 1 part nitric acid, 3 parts sulphuric acid, 7 parts water, by weight: 5 seconds to 5 minutes, according to fineness of cut. Then wash in hot water, dip in lime-water, dry and oil.

FIRE-KINDLER—Economical.

An excellent fire-kindler may be made by dipping corn-cobs in a mixture of melted resin and tar, and drying.

FLANNEL.

The Shrinkage of Flannel.—To keep flannels as much as possible from shrinking and felting, the following is to be recommended: Dissolve 1 oz. of potash in a bucket of water, and leave the fabric in it for 12 hours. Next warm the water, with the fabric in it, and wash without rubbing; also draw through repeatedly. Next immerse the flannel in another liquid containing 1 spoonful of wheat flour to 1 bucket of water, and wash in a similar manner.

To Shrink New Flannel.—Lay the flannel all night in a tub of cold salt water. In the morning pour off the whole of the water, and drain, but do not wring the flannel. Make a slight suds of water quite warm (but not hot), and of white soap or whitish Castile. Wash the flannel thoroughly through the suds, and wring it out as dry as possible. Then, having shaken it, stretched it, and folded it smoothly down on a clean table to make it straight and even, hang it out immediately. When about half dry, go to it, stretch, shake, and turn it. Take it in while it is still damp, fold it smooth, cover it with a clean towel, and after it has lain about ½ hour, iron it with a rather cool iron.

To Wash Flannel.—Flannel should always be washed with white soap; otherwise, it will neither look well nor feel soft. The water must be warm, but not boiling, as it shrinks flannel to scald it. Wash it in clean water, and entirely by itself. Rub the soap to a strong lather in the water, before the flannel is put in; for if the soap is rubbed on the flannel itself, it will become hard and stiff. Wash it in this manner through two warm waters, with a strong lather in each. Rinse it in another warm water, with just sufficient soap in it to give the water a slight whitish appearance. To this rinsing-water it is better to add a little blue from the indigo bag. Cold rinsing-water is found to harden the flannel. When it has been rinsed thoroughly, wring it hard, shake it well, and spread it out on the clothes-line. While drying, shake, stretch, and turn it several times. It should dry slowly. Flannel always washed precisely in this manner will look white and feel soft as long as it lasts, retaining a new appearance, and scarcely shrinking at all. But if once badly washed with scalding water, rubbed with brown soap, and rinsed in cold water, it may never again look well.

To Whiten Flannel when Yellow.—Boil 4 tablespoonfuls of flour in 4 quarts of water, stirring it well. Then pour one-half of the boiling liquid over the flannel, let it remain till the water cools, rub the flannel, but use no soap. Rinse it through several waters, then repeat the process with the remainder of the flour and water in a boiling state; again rinse it through several waters and hang it up to drain and dry. Do not wring it.

FLIES—To Banish.

It is not generally known that placing certain herbs in a room will banish flies from it. Sweet clover, for instance, which is not difficult to obtain, as it is found thriving luxuriantly on every country roadside, will put flies to rout. This sweet, pungent odor it exhales is quite unobjectionable, but it is still abhorred by flies.

To Destroy Flies in a room take ½ teaspoonful of black pepper in 1 teaspoonful of brown sugar, and 1 tablespoonful of cream; mix them well together, and place them in the room on a plate, where the flies are troublesome, and they will soon disappear. See *Fly Poison* and *Fly Paper*.

FLOORS—To Polish.

To polish stained floors, rub them thoroughly once a week with beeswax and turpentine.

FLOUR—The Patent Process.

By the old grinding process a large proportion of the most valuable constituent parts of the wheat was carried off as "middlings." By the patent process the wheat, cleaned by blasts, is separated into lots of similar sizes; the fuzzy tails are removed by emery-stones. The grain is then passed through corrugated, chilled-iron rollers, their corrugations ranging from 8 to 40 to the square inch, which bruise the grain without grinding it. This is on the ground floor. The bruised grain is then raised to the bolting-machines, where it is passed through gauze cloths of different textures, and thence sent down between finer corrugated rollers running at a speed of from 150 to 300 revolutions per minute. These processes of reduction are repeated six or seven times, the third giving more flour than the first two reductions, and the fifth giving the best-rising flour and the richest in albuminoids.

To Test Flour.—Prime wheat flour should have the following characteristics: When handled, none should adhere to the fingers. If a handful should be squeezed, it should not sift through the fingers, but should cling together, forming a little ball, which will show the fine lines of the palm for some time after release; if a little ball of flour be dropped on a table, it should even then preserve its form and continuity, at least in a large measure.

FLOWERS.

To Change Color by Means of Charcoal.—If roses are of a faded hue, cover the earth in the pot about 1 inch thick with pulverized charcoal, and in a few days they will be of a fine lively rose-color. The same effect is produced upon petunias, and it gives great vigor to all red or violet-colored flowers. Under its influence the white petunias become veined with red or violet tints, and the violets are covered with irregular spots of a bluish or almost black tint. These are often supposed to come from choice new varieties of seed. The only flowers insensible to the influence of charcoal are yellow.

To Keep Flowers Fresh.—Freshly cut flowers may be preserved alive for a long time by placing them in a glass or vase with fresh water in which a little charcoal has been steeped or a small piece of camphor dissolved. The vase should be set upon a plate or dish and covered with a bell glass, around the edges of which, when it comes in contact with the plate, a little water should be poured to exclude the air.

FLY PAPER.

1. Paint heavy manilla paper with common glue, and allow it to dry; then spread with the following mixture, made by melting the oil and resin over a fire, stirring constantly: Castor oil, 4 oz.; resin, 18 oz.

2. Melt resin, and add thereto, while soft, sufficient sweet oil, lard or lamp oil to make it, when cold, about the consistency of honey. Spread on writing-paper and place in a convenient spot. It will soon be filled with ants, flies and other vermin.

FLY POISON.

1. Chloride of cobalt, ½ oz.; brown sugar, 2 oz.; hot water, 1 pint.

2. Black pepper, 1 oz.; sugar, 1 oz.; cream, 2 oz. Mix into thin paste, and place wherever the flies gather most.

3. Boil quassia chips in water into a very strong decoction, and then sweeten the liquid with molasses or sugar. This fly poison is not injurious to human beings.

FRAMES—To Restore Gilt.

Rub with a sponge moistened in turpentine, then carefully dusting them. Gilt frames may also be revived by dusting them, and then washing with 1 oz. soda beaten up with the whites of 3 eggs. Scraped patches should be touched up with gold paint.

FRUITS—Medical Value of.

Edible fruits may be understandingly used to bring about remedial effects. They are invaluable adjuncts for the table, and should always be used in their ripe and perfect condition. They may be roughly classed as follows:

Laxatives.—Figs, oranges, nectarines, tamarinds, prunes, plums, mulberries, dates.

Astringents.—Pomegranates, cranberries, barberries, wild cherries, blackberries, sorbs, quinces, medlars, dewberries, raspberries, pears.

Diuretics.—Strawberries, prickly pears, whortleberries, grapes, black currants, peaches, melon seeds.

Refrigerants and Sedatives.—Pumpkins, red and white currants, melons, lemons, limes, apples.

Taken early in the morning, an orange acts very decidedly as a laxative, sometimes amounting to a purgative, and may generally be relied on.

Pomegranates are very astringent, and relieve relaxed throat and uvula. The bark of the root, in the form of a decoction, is a good anthelmintic, especially obnoxious to tape-worm.

Figs, split open, form excellent poultices for boils and small abscesses. Strawberries and lemons, locally applied, are of some service in the removal of tartar from teeth.

Apples are corrective, useful in nausea. They immediately relieve the nausea due to smoking. Bitter almonds contain hydrocyanic acid, and are useful in simple cough; but they frequently produce a sort of urticaria or nettlerash. The persimmon, or diospyros, is palatable when ripe, but the green fruit is highly astringent, containing much tannin, and is used in diarrhoea and incipient dysentery. The oil of the cocoanut has been recommended as a substitute for cod liver oil, and is much used in Germany for phthisis. Tamarinds are very agreeable to fever patients in the form of a drink. Dutch medlars are astringent and not very palatable. Grapes and raisins are nutritive and demulcent, and very grateful in the sick-chamber. A so-called "grape cure" has been much lauded for the treatment of congestions of the liver and stomach, enlarged spleen, scrofula, tuberculosis, etc. Nothing is allowed but water and bread and several pounds of grapes per diem. Quince seeds are demulcent and astringent; boiled in water they make an excellent soothing and sedative lotion in inflammatory diseases of the eyes and eyelids.

FRUITS—Seedless.

Vegetable physiologists have never made plain to the average man the conditions causing trees and vines to produce seedless fruit. The Thompson and Sultana grape and the "currant" of commerce are striking examples. As a rule, fruits are not formed without pollenization. The navel and some other varieties of oranges are seedless also, as well as the banana in general. Such fruits of course must be propagated from cuttings or buds, not from seeds. It is sometimes alleged that the seedless condition of fruits results from natural and artificial selection occurring in the course of long cultivation. Thus the banana, it is alleged, is seedless because during the thousands of years of its known cultivation such varieties have been encouraged as yield no seeds. This, however, cannot be the case with the Thompson's seedless grapes, for example, whose known cultivation extends back only a few years. We may easily believe, however, in the final evolution of the most delicious fruits from wholly unpromising originals, when we are told that the orange has been evolved from a pod containing seeds, much like the pea with its enclosing woody envelope, and that the bitter almond and the peach were once the natural product of the same tree.

FUMIGATING PASTILES.

Gum benzoin and styrax, of each 4 oz.; sandalwood and labdanum, of each 1 oz.; charcoal, 24 oz. Mix with gum-water to form the paste.

FURNACE HEAT—To Moisten.

Hang a wet towel in front of the register and allow the lower edge of the towel to dip in a shallow vessel of water. This simple arrangement will moisten the hot, dry air of the furnace, which is so productive of throat and lung diseases.

FURNITURE.

To Clean Furniture.—Mix 3 parts of linseed oil and 1 of turpentine. Apply with woolen rag.

How to Take Stains out of Mahogany.—Mix 6 oz. spirits of salt and ½ oz. rock salt of lemons (pulverized) together. Place a few drops on the spot, and rub it briskly till it is removed. Wash off with cold water.

To Remove Finger Marks from Furniture.—Apply sweet oil to varnished and kerosene to oiled furniture.

Oil for Furniture.—1. One gal. linseed oil; 12 oz. alkanet root; 2 oz. rose pink. Mix.

2. In 1½ pints linseed oil boil 4 oz. of resin.

3. Dissolve, by a gentle heat, some yellow beeswax in oil of turpentine, till the consistency, when cold, of a jelly. A little red ochre may be mixed with it.

4. French formula: One pint linseed oil, 1 oz. shellac varnish, 2 drams alkanet root, and ½ oz. gum arabic. Put together in a bottle in a warm place, and strain at the end of a week. Apply with a wad covered with fine muslin or soft linen. Rub the furniture in a circular manner, a small surface at a time. Afterward polish with a silk handkerchief.

Furniture Polish.—One pint linseed oil, 2 oz. yellow resin, 12 oz. beeswax, 2 oz. turmeric root, or alkanet root. Melt all together by a gentle heat, and strain while hot through linen. Make into balls when cold.

Furniture Cream.—1. Dissolve an ounce of pearlash in a little water, and by heat dissolve 2½ oz. white wax. Add 1 quart of water by degrees.

2. Boil together in 3 pints of rain-water 2 oz. soap, ½ lb. beeswax and 1 oz. pearlash.

The two recipes above may be diluted by water and then used in a liquid state, or, the water evaporating, the wax may be left as a polish.

FURS—To Preserve.

For the preservation of furs dryness is essential. After exposure to dampness or rain furs should be dried at a moderate distance from the fire. Before putting furs by for the summer they should be carefully combed and beaten with a small cane. During the summer they should be kept well wrapped in dry brown paper, or in a box secure from the incursion of moths, and taken out occasionally to be dried, if at all damp, and again well shaken, combed and beaten. With these precautions, the most valuable furs may be preserved uninjured for many years.

GAS ENGINE—To Silence.

A French engineer describes a simple method which he has successfully adopted for silencing the exhaust of a gas engine. His plan is to take the exhaust to a tube outside the building, which tube is slit by a saw for a length of about 6 feet, and two semi-circular portions opened out so as to give a V-shaped slot on each side of the tube, through which the gases escape. The gradually increasing opening thus provided for the exhaust gases completely silences the troublesome noise and vibration so common with this type of motor.

GAS LEAKAGE—To Detect.

Dr. Bunte suggests the use of paper dipped in palladium chloride solution. Such paper changes its color in presence of gas coming from the leaks imperceptible by the odor, and which produces no effect upon the earth covering the pipes. Dr. Bunte suggests the following method of practically applying the test to street mains: Above the pipes are excavated, at intervals of two or three yards, holes 12 to 16 inches deep, corresponding to the joints and sleeves. In each opening is placed an iron tube ½ in. in diameter, within which is a glass tube containing a roll of the test paper. The air from about the main enters the iron tube, and the trace of gas which may be present reveals itself by coloring the paper brown or black, according to the quantity. If, after 10 or 20 minutes, the paper is still white, it may be certainly concluded that at the point tested there is not the smallest escape of gas. Various authorities who have experimented with Bunte's method certify to its efficacy.

GAS PIPE—To Thaw.

Mr. F. H. Shelton says: "I took off from over the pipe some 4 or 5 inches; just a crust of earth, and then put a couple of bushels of lime in the space, poured water over it, and slaked it, and then put canvas over that, and rocks on the canvas, so as to keep the wind from getting underneath. Next morning, on returning there, I found that the frost had been drawn out from the ground for nearly 3 feet. Since then we have tried it several times."

GILDING—Without a Battery.

Clean the silver or other article to be gilded with a brush and a little ammonia water, until it is evenly bright and shows no tarnish. Take a small piece of gold and dissolve it in about four times its volume of metallic mercury, which will be accomplished in a few minutes, forming an amalgam. Put a little of the amalgam on a piece of dry cloth, rub it on the article to be gilded. Then place on a stone in a furnace, and heat to the beginning of redness. After cooling, it must be cleaned with a brush and a little cream of tartar, and a beautiful and permanent gilding will be found.

GINGER BEER.

Five lbs. sugar, 4½ oz. lemon juice, 4 oz. honey, 5½ oz. bruised ginger root, 4½ gals. water, 1½ pints yeast. Boil the ginger in ½ gal. water for 1 hour, then add the rest and strain. Add the white of an egg beaten, and ¼ oz. essence of lemon. Let this mixture stand four days and bottle.

GLASS.

Glass Bubbles.—Since glass cans have come into such general use for fruits less is heard about "danger in the can." Still there may be danger even in glass cans, as appeared of late when a little child was helped to freshly opened canned plums. His teeth were heard to grate on some hard substance, which proved to be a flake of glass he had broken with his teeth into bits. In a minute more, if unchecked, he would have innocently swallowed the glass, which would have caused serious injury and perhaps death. An inspection of the empty can discovered the rough edge of a broken air-bubble on the inside. Air-bubbles are very common in the cheap grade of glass of which fruit cans are usually made, and are less noticeable on the inside than on the outside. When the boiling fruit is poured into the can these thin shells, if on the inside, are almost sure to crack off. A tablespoonful of small shot well shaken about in the can will break these dangerous bubbles and smooth their edges; better still for this purpose is a light chain dish-cloth.

To Keep Glass from Cracking.—Place tumblers, chimneys, etc., which you wish to toughen, in a pot filled with cold water; add a little salt; boil well and then cool very slowly. The same process may be applied to porcelain, crockery, stoneware, etc.

Cleaning Fine Glass.—It is among the oldest of notions that bird-shot is useful for cleaning bottles, decanters, etc., and it may be in some cases; but one must not use it for fine glass or that which is in any way delicate. For very fine glass, a potato cut in pieces the size of small dice is preferable as a cleaning agent. This cannot possibly scratch, and, although it takes more time to achieve the desired result, it is done with no risk to the finish of the article. Good, clean, sifted sand has many uses. If one cannot obtain that which is perfectly clean, ordinary sand that has been washed down by the roadside may be used. Throw a pailful of this into a tub and pour in water, stirring the sand vigorously until all of the muddy look is washed out. When the water shows perfectly clear, after being stirred up, the sand is clean. It may then be dried and put away in a box or bag for future use. See also Cut Glass.

To Remove a Tight Glass Stopper.—Expand the neck of the bottle by heating for a few seconds with a lighted match or warm water.

To Frost Glass.—A strong solution of sulphate of zinc in water is used upon the inside of glass, which, after it becomes dry, is covered with a coat of varnish. It prevents people from looking in, and yet does not materially obstruct the light.

To Letter Glass Jars.—Cut out from a paper the letters wanted, and then paste it upon the decanter or jar. Into this pour a mixture of chalk dissolved to the consistence of milk in aquafortis and add to that a strong solution of silver. The jar must be kept closely corked and turned towards the sun in such a way that the rays will pass through the spaces of paper and fall upon the surface of the liquor. The part of the glass under the paper will remain white, while the other will turn black, thus forming the lettering. The bottle must not be shaken during the operation.

GLOVES.

To Clean Gloves.—Dry cornmeal will clean gloves nicely, but if much soiled it is better to send them to a reputable cleaner. Benzine will clean white gloves, but it is not to be recommended where there is any color. Where black kids have become rusty about the finger ends, they can be restored by adding a few drops of black ink to a tablespoonful of olive oil and applying with a feather or camel's-hair brush.

To Prevent Injury from Perspiration.—Those whose hands perspire freely can prevent their gloves being injured by rubbing their hands with ordinary cornstarch or pulverized soap-stone before putting on their gloves. Some prefer to use powder, as they think it is better for the hands.

How to Put on Gloves.—A great deal depends on the first putting-on of gloves. Have the hands perfectly clean, dry and cool, and never put on new gloves while the hands are warm or damp. When a person is troubled with moist hands, it is well to powder them before trying on the gloves; but in most cases, if the hands are cool and dry, this is not needed. First, work on the fingers, keeping the thumb outside of the glove, and the wrist of the glove turned back. When the fingers are in smoothly, put in the thumb and work the glove on very carefully; then, placing the elbow on the knee, work on the hand. When this is done, smooth down the wrist, and button the second button first, then the third, and so on to the end. Then smooth down the whole glove and fasten the first button. Fastening the first button last, when putting on a glove for the first time, makes a great deal of difference in the fit, although it may seem but a very little thing. It does not strain the part of the glove that is easiest to strain at first, and prevents the enlarging of the buttonhole, either of which is sure to take place if you begin at the first button to fasten the glove.

When removing your gloves, never begin at the tips of the fingers to pull them off, but turn back the wrist and pull off carefully, which will, of course, necessitate their being wrong side out. Turn them right side out, turn the thumbs in, smooth them lengthwise to as near as possible the shape they would be if on the hands, and place them away with a strip of white Canton flannel between if the gloves are light, but if dark-colored the flannel may be omitted. Never roll gloves into each other in a wad, for they will never look as well after. There is always some moisture in them from the hands; consequently, when rolled up this moisture has no chance of drying, and must work into the gloves, making them hard and stiff, and of very little use after, as far as looks or fit is concerned.

GLUE—For All Purposes.

Test for Glue.—The following simple and easy test for glue is given: A weighed piece of glue (say ¼ of an ounce) is suspended in water for 24 hours, the temperature of which is not above 50 degrees Fahrenheit. The coloring material sinks, and the glue swells from the absorption of the water. The glue is then taken out and weighed; the greater the increase in weight the better the glue. If it then be dried perfectly and weighed again, the weight of the coloring matter can be learned from the difference between this and the original weight.

Glue that does not Crack.—To prevent the cracking of glue by heat or extreme dryness, the addition to the solution of some calcium chloride is recommended, which retains sufficient moisture to obviate the inconvenience. By this method glue can be used upon glass or metallic surfaces.

Flexible Glue.—1. A German chemist has discovered that if glue or gelatine be mixed with about ¼ of its weight of glycerine, it loses its brittleness, and becomes useful for many purposes for which it is otherwise unfit, such as dressing leather, giving elasticity to porcelain parchment or emery paper, and for bookbinding.

2. Incorporate together 1 part of glycerine, by weight, to 4 parts of glue, and it will lose its brittleness, and can be used for various purposes, such as dressing leather, bookbinding, etc.

Fire-proof Glue.—To make a glue for resisting fire, proceed as follows: Mix a handful of quicklime in 4 oz. of linseed oil; boil to a good thickness, then spread on plates in the shade, and it will become exceedingly hard, but may easily be dissolved over the fire, and used as ordinary glue. It resists fire after having been used in gluing substances together.

Glue which Resists Moisture.—1. Dissolve ½ oz. of sandarac and ½ oz. of mastic in 8 fluid oz. of strong methylated spirits, and add ½ oz. of turpentine to the solution. Make a hot, thick solution of glue and a little isinglass; to this add the above solution, and filter the whole, while hot, through a good sieve or a piece of cloth.

2. Glue, 5 parts; resin, 4 parts; red ochre, 2 parts; mix with smallest possible quantity of water.

3. A glue which is proof against moisture may be made by dissolving 16 oz. of glue in 3 pints of skim milk. If a stronger glue be wanted, add powdered lime.

Marine Glue.—One part India rubber, 12 parts mineral naphtha. Mix, heat gently and add 20 parts of shellac, powdered fine. Cool on a slab. Heat to 250 degrees when wanted for use.

Mouth Glue.—To unite papers and other small, light objects, dissolve, with the aid of heat, pure glue and ½ its weight of coarse brown sugar, in as small a quantity of boiling water as possible; when perfectly liquid, cast into thin cakes, on a flat surface, slightly oiled, and as it cools cut into small pieces. When required for use moisten one end slightly and rub on any substance you wish to join.

Rice Glue.—Rice glue is a very delicate and suitable article for fancy work. Thoroughly mix rice flour with cold water, let it simmer gently over a slow fire. This is excellent for joining paper, etc., and, if properly made and applied, the joining will be found very strong. When dry it is almost transparent.

Liquid Glue.—1. Dissolve good, hard glue, in nitric ether. This solution can not be made too thick, as the ether will take up only a certain amount of glue. Add to the mixture a few bits of India rubber, and it will resist dampness when dry.

2. Liquid glue may also be made by dissolving glue in strong, hot vinegar, and adding ⅓ as much alcohol and a little alum. This will keep any length of time when placed in a closely stoppered bottle, and will mend horn, wood and mother-of-pearl.

3. Take a wide-mouthed bottle, and dissolve in it 8 oz. of the best glue in ½ pint of water, by setting it in a vessel of water, and heating until dissolved. Then add, slowly, 2½ oz. of strong aqua fortis (nitric acid), stirring all the while. Keep it well corked, and it will be ready for use at any moment. The preparation does not gelatinize, nor undergo putrefaction or fermentation.

GLYCERINE — Uses for.

Glycerine is excellent for rubbing into shoes as a preventive of wet feet, as well as to soften the leather and keep it in good condition.

If you want to show your husband a little attention, place a bottle at his hand of equal parts of glycerine and bay rum, for use after his morning shave, and he will rise up and bless you.

Another use may be added, which is not generally known. When you are about to seal fruit-jars, drop in half a dozen drops of glycerine, and it will help to keep the contents and prevent mould from gathering on the top.

GOLD AND SILVER — Test for.

One test for gold and silver is a piece of lunar caustic. Slightly wet the metal to be tested and rub it gently with the caustic. If gold or silver, the mark will be faint; but if an inferior metal, it will be quite black.

GOLD FISH — Preservation of.

Allow not more than one fish to a quart of water. Use the same kind of water — either spring or river — continually; change daily in summer, every other day in winter. Use deep rather than shallow vessels, with green pebbles at the bottom. Keep the fish in an even and rather cool temperature. Use a small net in handling them, and, when the water is to be changed, draw it out with a syphon. Feed the fish cracker, yolk of an egg, lettuce, flies, etc. Do not feed them with bread or cake. They require little or no food from November until March. Where there is room in the aquarium always have a few water plants growing to preserve the equilibrium. This will save changing the water so often.

GRAFTING-WAX.

Two lbs. resin, $1\frac{1}{2}$ lbs. beeswax, $\frac{1}{2}$ lb. tallow.

GRAVEL WALKS — To Make.

Lay the bottom 8 or 10 inches deep with lime rubbish, large flint stones, or other hard material, to prevent the weeds growing through; over this the gravel should be laid 6 or 8 inches thick. The gravel should be laid rounding up in the middle, so that the larger stones will run off to the sides and may be raked away. These walks should not be laid too round, as that makes them hard to walk on and lessens their apparent breadth. The rise in the middle should not be more than 1 inch in 5 feet — a walk 20 feet wide being only 4 inches higher at the middle than at the edges. When the gravel has been laid, it should be raked and the large stones thrown away; then roll the walk, both crosswise and lengthwise. If the walks are rolled three or four times after very hard showers, it will bind them more firmly together than could be done in any other way.

GREASE.

To Take Grease out of Velvet or Cloth. — Pour some turpentine over the part that is greasy; rub it till quite dry with a piece of flannel; if the grease is not quite removed, repeat the application, and when done, brush the part well and hang up the garment in the open air, to take away the smell.

Grease Extractor. — Aqua ammonia, 2 oz.; soft water, 1 quart; saltpeter, 1 teaspoonful; shaving soap in shavings 1 oz.; mix together; dissolve the soap well, and any grease or dirt that cannot be removed with this preparation, nothing else need be tried for it.

Paste for Removing Grease from Silk. — Rub together fine French chalk and lavender to the consistency of a thin paste, and apply thoroughly to the spots with the fingers; place a sheet of brown or blotting paper above and below the silk, and smooth it with a moderately heated iron. The French chalk may then be removed by brushing.

GRINDSTONE — How to Use.

Instead of running the stone in water, or letting it stand in water when not used, which will waste the stone and cause a soft spot in it, let water drop on it from a pot suspended above the stone, and stop the dropping of the water when the stone is not in use. The stone must not be allowed to get out of order, but must be kept perfectly round by the use of gas pipe or a hacker. All grease should be cleaned from tools before sharpening, as it destroys the grit.

GRUBS.

Grubs on orchard trees and gooseberry and currant bushes will sometimes be sufficiently numerous to spoil a crop; but if a bonfire be made with dry sticks and weeds on the windward side of the orchard, so that the smoke may blow among the trees, you will destroy thousands, for the grubs have such an objection to smoke that very little of it makes them roll themselves up and fall off. They must be swept up afterwards and destroyed.

GUANO — Liquid.

To Hasten the Blooming of Flowers. — Dissolve 4 oz. sulphate or nitrate of ammonia, 2 oz. nitrate of potash, 1 oz. sugar, 1 pint hot water, and put the solution in a well corked bottle; add a few drops to the water used to moisten flowering plants that are in pots. For bulbous-rooted plants, put 8 or 10 drops of the liquid into the water of a hyacinth glass or jar, changing the water every 10 or 12 days.

GUN BARRELS — To Brown.

Mix 16 parts sweet spirits niter, 12 parts saturated solution of sulphate of iron, 12 parts chloride of antimony. Bottle and cork the mixture for a day, then add 500 parts of water and thoroughly mix. Clean the barrel to a uniform grain, free from grease and finger stains. Wipe with the staining mixture on a wad of cotton. Let it stand for 24 hours, scratch-brush the surface, and repeat twice. Rub off the last time with leather moistened with olive oil. Let dry a day, and rub down with a cloth moistened with oil to polish.

GUNPOWDER.

Making Gunpowder. — All gunpowder is made of niter or saltpeter, charcoal and sulphur, and in all nations by almost the same formula, that is, by using 75 lbs. of niter, 15 lbs. of charcoal and 10 lbs. of sulphur for 100 lbs. of gunpowder. The materials are first made as pure as possible, the niter being soaked in spring water, then boiled and cooled, then filtered through canvas bags and allowed to harden again. This is done until it becomes perfectly white. The sulphur is purified by being kept melted for several hours in gun-metal pots. The charcoal is made from special woods burned in close vessels, and must be thoroughly charred and soft. The three substances are first ground separately to a fine powder and then ground together with a little water until they are thoroughly mixed. The mixture is then, by a hydrostatic press, made into thin, smooth cakes that are afterward broken up between toothed rollers into grains and rubbed through sieves until the grains are the right size. These are then put in a revolving cylinder, and by rubbing against each other are worn round and smooth. This is called glazing, and is an important process, because glazed powder keeps dry and bears shaking much better than unglazed powder. The powder is then thoroughly dried in rooms heated by steam pipes. Giant powder is the same as dynamite, and is made by mixing nitro-glycerine with infusorial earth.

White Gunpowder.—White gunpowder is commonly known as blasting powder. What is known as Melville & Gillon's blasting powder is made of chlorate of potassa, 2 parts; red sulphuret of arsenic, 1 part; reduce to a powder separately and mix together lightly, carefully avoiding the use of iron instruments, percussion, much friction, the slightest contact with acids, or exposure to heat. Another blasting compound, of less explosive force than the above, is made of equal parts of chlorate of potassa and ferro-cyanide of potassium. Still another is made by taking 1 part each of yellow prussiate of potash and of white sugar, and 2 parts of chlorate of potassa; powder each carefully and mix well but very gently with a wooden knife. These powders are not injured permanently by wetting, as they regain their explosive character when again dried. They have fully eight times the explosive force of ordinary charcoal gunpowder, but the extreme readiness with which they explode by rubbing, contact with acid, or a slight elevation of temperature, renders them altogether unsuited for the uses of ordinary gunpowder. On this account they should be prepared in very small quantities and handled in combining with the utmost caution.

GUNS—How to Handle.

1. Empty or loaded, never point a gun toward yourself or any other person.

2. When a-field, carry your gun at the half-cock. If in cover, let your hand shield the hammers from whipping twigs.

3. When riding from one shooting-ground to another, or whenever you have your gun in any conveyance, remove the cartridges, if a breech-loader, it being so easy to replace them. If a muzzle-loader, remove the caps, brush off the nipples and place a wad on the nipple, letting down the hammers on wads; simply removing caps sometimes leaves a little fulminate on the nipple, and a blow on the hammer when down discharges it.

4. Never draw a gun toward you by the barrels.

5. More care is necessary in the use of a gun in a boat than elsewhere, the limited space, confined action and uncertain motion making it dangerous at the best. If possible, no more than two persons should occupy a boat. Hammerless guns are a constant danger to persons boating.

6. Always clean your gun thoroughly as soon as you return from a day's sport, no matter how tired you feel; the consequence of its always being ready for service is ample return for the few minutes' irksome labor.

HAIR-BRUSHES—To Clean.

Put a teaspoonful or dessertspoonful of aqua ammonia into a basin half full of warm water, comb the loose hairs out of the brush, then agitate the water briskly with the brush, and rinse it well with clear water and dry in the sun. It is well to clean two brushes at the same time, as they can be rubbed together.

HAMS—To Cure.

1. To each green ham of 18 lbs., 1 dessertspoonful saltpeter; ¼ lb. brown sugar applied to the fleshy side of the ham and about the hock; cover the fleshy side with fine salt ½ inch thick, and pack away in tubs, to remain from 3 to 6 weeks, according to size. Before smoking, rub off any salt that may remain on the ham, and cover well with ground pepper, particularly about the bone and hock. Hang up and drain for 2 days; smoke with green wood for 6 weeks, or until the rind assumes a light chestnut color. The pepper is an effectual preventive of the fly.

2. When the hams are cool, rub them down in a tight cask, putting a bushel of salt, well mixed with 6 oz. saltpeter, to about 1,000 lbs. pork. After it has been salted down 4 or 5 days, make a strong brine, sufficient to float an egg, and cover the meat with it, and then let it remain 3 weeks longer; then hang it up, dusting the fresh sides with black pepper; then smoke with green wood.

HAND GRENADES.

Chloride of calcium, crude, 20 parts; common salt, 5 parts; and water, 75 parts. Mix and put in thin bottles. In case of fire, a bottle so thrown that it will break in or very near the fire will put it out. This mixture is better and cheaper than many of the high-priced grenades sold for the purpose of fire protection.

HANDKERCHIEFS.

A unique method of treating fine handkerchiefs, extensively practiced by European ladies, contemplates washing in the usual careful manner, wringing out of either hot or cold rinsing-water, but not wringing very dry. The handkerchiefs are then very carefully and smoothly spread upon a mirror, marble table, or, if necessary, even a window pane, from which dust has been carefully removed, being pressed into place so that all wrinkles are removed and every part adheres closely to the surface. They are then left in place, and in a few hours the handkerchiefs will be dry and beautifully smooth, the process being far preferable to the use of a sad-iron.

HARNESS.

Blacking.—Three oz. beeswax, 4 oz. ivory black, 1 pint neatsfoot oil, 2 oz. castile soap, 2 oz. lard, and 1 oz. alum; to be boiled together.

Blacking for Heavy Harness.—A good blacking for harness exposed to the weather is made of ½ lb. ivory black, ¼ lb. brown sugar, ½ lb. beef tallow, and a small piece of gum arabic. Make a paste of a tablespoonful of wheat flour, and while hot put in the tallow; after it is melted, add the sugar, then add the remaining ingredients and 1 quart of hot water, stirring it until quite mixed. This is not to be commended for light wearing, as it will rub off more or less when being handled.

Grain Black for Harness.—When harness loses its luster and turns brown, it should be given a new coat of grain black. Before using the grain black, the grain surface should be thoroughly washed with potash-water until all the grease is killed, and after the application of the grain black, oil and tallow should be applied to the surface. This will not only "fasten the color," but make the leather flexible. After the harness has had a good oiling, an occasional rubbing with tallow and lampblack will keep the leather tough and pliable, and prevent it from cracking.

To Make Harness Look New.—To give the leather the characteristic color of new, add to 1 pint of oil a large tablespoonful of lampblack and an ounce or two of beeswax. Leather varnishes, as a rule, are not to be recommended, as most of them are hurtful to leather.

Varnish for Harness.—Take 98 per cent. alcohol, 1 gal.; white pine turpentine, 1½ lbs.; gum shellac, 1½ lbs.; Venice turpentine, 1 gill. Let these stand in a jug in the sun or by the stove till the gums are dissolved, then add sweet oil, 1 gill, and lampblack, 2 oz.; rub the lampblack first with a little of the varnish. Proportions may be reduced for a smaller quantity. This makes a good polish, and it does not crack when the harness is twisted or knocked around.

How to Oil a Harness.—One way is to rub with a woolen cloth, saturated with oil, every part of the harness, save those of patent leather; another way is to put 2 or 3 quarts of neatsfoot oil in a long, shallow pan, and draw each piece of leather through it slowly, bending the leather backward and forward, and rubbing the oil in with a cloth or sponge. In either case be careful that where the buckle holes are a little more is applied; the belly-bands, breechings and the straps that buckle in the bits also need an extra allowance. On an old harness that is very dry, damp with warm water before oiling; this will prevent penetration of water, which resists oil. After oiling, the harness should not be exposed to high temperature of heat, either in a room or by exposure to the direct rays of the sun. In summer time let it hang in the barn; in winter, in a moderately warm room, until the oil has well penetrated. Rub off with a dry woolen rag any oil that may remain on the surface after drying.

HATS, SILK—To Renovate.

Take some soap and boiling water. Rub a brush lightly with the soap, dip it into the water and brush the hat around with the nap. If the latter is crinkled, brush it until it is smooth and the soap all out; then take the back of a knife and scrape it around. This will clean it nicely. Then beat it gently with a cane, and let it dry. Never smooth spots with your fingers, as that takes off the nap.

HIDES—To Cure.

A great many butchers do not use proper care in this branch, and the consequence is that the hides will not pass city inspection. The proper way to salt hides is to lay them flat, flesh side up, and form a nearly square bed, say 12x15 feet, folding in the edges so as to make them as nearly solid as possible. Split the ear in the cords that run up the ear in each one, so as to make them lie out flat. Sprinkle the hide with 2 or 3 shovelfuls of coarse salt, as the size may require—say, for a 60- or 80-lb. hide, from 10 to 15 lbs. of salt. At any rate, cover the hide well, as it need not be wasted. Then let them lie in this from 12 to 20 days, after which take them up, shake the salt out and use it again.

HONEY.—To Keep.

To keep honey all the year round without candying, it is only necessary to place the honey, which has previously been nicely strained, in a pan or pail, which may be placed inside of another one, putting 2 or 3 bits of wood under the pail containing the honey to prevent it from burning upon the bottom; then fill the outer one with water and just bring to the boiling point, skimming off the wax and all foam which gathers upon the top. As soon as it comes to the boiling point, remove from the stove, and, after a few minutes, skim and pour into jars to cool. Cover tightly and place in a cool cellar.

HORNS.—To Polish.

First boil the horn to remove the pith, if it has been freshly taken from the animal. If it is an old, dry horn, the pith may be dried out, and boiling is not necessary; but it may be laid in hot water for a short time to make it soft. Then scrape off all the roughnesses with a coarse file, a knife, or a piece of glass. When the rough spots are removed, rub around the horn with coarse sandpaper, then with a finer kind. After this, rub the horn lengthwise with a flannel cloth which has been dipped in powdered pumice-stone or rotten stone and moistened in linseed oil. This rubbing should continue until all the sandpaper marks are removed; then give a final rubbing with a clean flannel cloth, and lastly with a piece of tissue paper.

HOUSE PLANTS.

Plants that have blossomed through the winter, and which you intend to use another season in the house, should not go on blossoming. See that they get at their summer's work as soon as possible. That work is to rest. Encourage them to do nothing but recuperate. Do not give rich soil or large amounts of water, for these encourage vigorous growth. The plants should remain as nearly dormant as is consistent with health. Cut back well; prune into something like symmetrical form, and keep watch of them as growth is made. Pinch back whenever it seems necessary to do so to secure good form.

ICE.—To Preserve.

Wrap it in several thicknesses of newspaper. See also *Refrigerator*.

Ice in the Sick-room.—A saucerful of shaved ice may be preserved for 24 hours with the thermometer in the room at 90° F., if the following precautions are observed: Put the saucer containing the ice in a soup plate and cover it with another. Put the soup plate thus arranged on a good, heavy pillow, and cover it with another pillow, pressing the pillows so that the plates are completely imbedded in them. An old jack plane set deep is a most excellent thing with which to shave ice. It should be turned bottom upward, and the ice shoved backward and forward over the cutter.

ICE-HOUSE.—Extemporaneous.

An ice-house can be extemporized without making a tenon or sawing a board. Construct a pen near the pond or stream where the ice is to be gathered, choosing, if possible, a gravel bank where there will be good drainage. The pen may be made of rails 12 feet long, or of any desired length. The larger the pen, the better the ice will keep. Lay up two rails upon each of the four sides. Make the bottom level, and cover it a foot or more with straw, sea-weed, or any convenient refuse vegetable matter. Sawdust is better than straw, if it can be had. Spent tan-bark is a good material for this foundation. Cut the cakes of ice in the usual manner, and pack them closely, filling the interstices with pounded ice, and if the weather is freezing pour on a little water to make it solid. Pack the outside with a foot of straw, sawdust, or other material, and put up the fence as the pile of ice rises. The pile can be conveniently made about 8 feet high. Cover the top with at least 18 inches of sawdust, or 2 feet of straw trodden down closely. Make a roof of boards or slabs sloping to the north, sufficiently steep to shed water, and fasten with a few nails. Such a pile of ice as this can be secured by a couple of men and a team in a day.

A Cheap Ice-box, made with double sides and packed with sawdust, will be wanted. The inner chamber should be about 2 feet long, 2 feet deep, and 18 inches wide. This will hold a single cake of ice weighing 100 lbs. or more, and leave room on top to keep milk, fresh meat, fruit and other matters. It will last from four days to a week, according to the quantity that is used in drinking-water. If the extemporaneous ice-house is not disturbed more than once a week, it will probably supply the family through the summer with abundance of ice.

ICE-WATER.—To Preserve.

Cover the entire pitcher with a hat-shaped cover of two thicknesses of paper, with a layer of cotton batting ½ inch thick between them.

Ice-water Without Ice.—Here is a way to get ice-cold water in places where there is no ice. Wrap a porous jug in wet flannel; wrap it all round, leaving no place exposed to the air; place it, filled with water, in an open window exposed to all the air there is. Keep the flannel wet. In an hour the contents of that jug will be almost as cold as if they had been iced.

INKS.

Good Black Writing Ink.—Two gallons of strong decoction of logwood, strained, $1\frac{1}{2}$ lbs. blue galls in coarse powder, 6 oz. sulphate of iron, 1 oz. acetate of copper, 6 oz. pounded sugar, 8 oz. gum arabic. Set on the stove until it commences to boil, then strain and set away until it becomes settled, and you will have a good black ink.

A Quart of Ink for a Dime.—Buy extract of logwood, which may be had at 8 cents an ounce, or cheaper by the quantity. Buy also, for 3 cents, an ounce of bi-chromate of potash. Do not make a mistake and get the simple chromate of potash. The former is orange red, and the latter clear yellow. Now, take $\frac{1}{2}$ oz. of extract of logwood and 10 grains of bi-chromate of potash and dissolve them in a quart of hot rain-water. When cold, pour it into a glass bottle, and leave it uncorked for a week or two. Exposure to the air is indispensable. The ink is then made, and has cost 5 to 10 minutes' labor, and about 3 cents, besides the bottle. The ink is at first an intense steel blue, but becomes quite black.

Jet Black Ink.—To make jet black ink, that is shiny and glistening when applied, dissolve $\frac{1}{2}$ pint of soft water, $\frac{3}{4}$ oz. of potassium bichromate and add 60 oz. of logwood extract dissolved in 1 gallon of water; then dissolve in 1 gallon of water, by continued boiling; borax 6 oz., shellac $1\frac{1}{2}$ oz. Mix all together while warm and add ammonia 8 oz.

Violet Ink.—Boil 16 oz. of logwood in 8 quarts of rain-water to 5 pints, add 3 oz. of clean gum arabic and 5 oz. of alum (powdered). Shake till well dissolved. It would be well to strain through a wire sieve.

Copying Ink.—Take 2 gallons of rain-water and put into it $\frac{1}{4}$ lb. of gum arabic, $\frac{1}{4}$ lb. clean copperas, $\frac{1}{4}$ lb. nutgalls pulverized. Mix and shake occasionally for 10 days, and strain. If needed sooner, let it steep in an iron kettle until the required strength is obtained.

Indelible Ink.—An indelible ink that cannot be erased, even with acids, can be obtained from the following recipe: To good gall ink add a strong solution of Prussian blue dissolved in distilled water. This will form a writing fluid which cannot be erased without destruction of the paper. The ink will write a greenish blue, but afterwards will turn black.

Red Copying Ink.—Dissolve 30 parts of extract of logwood in a vessel in 750 parts of distilled water without the aid of heat; add 2 parts of chromate of potassium, and set aside. After 24 hours add a solution of 8 parts of oxalic acid, 20 parts of oxalate of ammonium, and 40 parts of sulphate of aluminum in 250 parts of distilled water, and again set aside for 24 hours. Now raise it once to boiling in a bright copper kettle, add 50 parts of vinegar, and, after cooling, fill into bottles and cork. After a fortnight decant. This ink is red in thin layers, writes red, gives excellent copies in brownish color, and turns blackish brown upon the paper.

Violet Copying Ink.—Dissolve 40 parts of extracts of logwood, 5 of oxalic acid, and 30 parts of sulphate of aluminum, without heat, in 800 parts of distilled water and 10 parts of glycerine; let stand 24 hours; then add a solution of 5 parts of bi-chromate of potassium in 100 parts of distilled water, and again set aside for 24 hours. Now raise the mixture once to boiling in a bright copper boiler; mix with it, while hot, 50 parts of wood vinegar, and when cold, put into bottles. After a fortnight decant it from the sediment. In thin layers this ink is reddish violet; it writes dark violet, and furnishes bluish violet copies.

Marking Ink.—1. Nitrate of silver, $\frac{1}{2}$ oz.; hot distilled water, 7 fl. dr.; dissolve, and add mucilage, $\frac{1}{2}$ oz., previously rubbed with sap green or syrup of buckthorn, q. s. to color. The linen must be first moistened with "liquid pounce," or "the preparation," as it is commonly called, and, when it has again become dry, written on with a clean quill pen. The ink will bear dilution if the writing is not required very black.

The Pounce or Preparation: A solution of carbonate of soda, $1\frac{1}{4}$ oz.; in water, 1 pint, slightly colored with a little sap green or syrup of buckthorn, to enable the spots wetted with it to be afterwards known.

2. (Without Preparation): Take of nitrate of silver, $\frac{1}{4}$ oz.; water, $\frac{3}{4}$ oz.; dissolve, add as much of the strongest liquor of ammonia as will dissolve the precipitate formed on its first addition, then further add mucilage $1\frac{1}{2}$ dr., and a little sap green, syrup of buckthorn, or finely-powdered indigo, to color. Writing executed with this ink turns black on being passed over a hot iron, or held near the fire.

3. Terchloride of gold, $1\frac{1}{2}$ dr.; water, 7 fl. dr.; mucilage, 2 dr.; sap green, q. s. to color. To be written with on a ground prepared with a weak solution of protochloride of tin, and dried. Dark purple.

4. Nitrate of silver, 1 oz.; tartaric acid (pure), 3 dr.; are triturated together in a mortar in a dry state; a little water is then added, by which crystals of tartrate of silver are formed, and the nitric acid set free; the latter is then saturated with liquor of ammonia, sufficient being added to dissolve all the newly-formed tartrate of sil-

ter, avoiding unnecessary excess; lastly, a little gum and coloring-matter is added.

5. To the last is added an ammoniacal solution of a salt of gold. For this purpose may be used the "purple of Cassius," the hyposulphate, the ammonio-iodide, the ammonia-peroxide of gold, but any other compound of gold which is soluble in ammonia will do as well. This ink is unacted on by nearly all those reagents which remove writing executed with solutions of salts of silver alone, as cyanide of potassium, the chlorides of lime and soda, etc.

The last two are used in the same manner as No. 2.

6. Green sulphate of iron, 1 dr.; vermilion, 4 dr.; boiled linseed oil, 1 oz.; triturated together until perfectly smooth. Used with type.

7. A strong solution of chloride of platinum with a little potassa, and sugar and gum, to thicken.

8. Sulphate of manganese, 2 parts; all in the fine powder, and triturated to a paste with a little water. Used with type and stencil-plates, the part, when dry, being well rinsed with water. Brown.

9. (Aniline Black.) This ink is prepared by means of two solutions, one of copper, the other of aniline, prepared as follows: (1) Copper solution, 8.52 grams of crystallized chloride of copper, 10.65 grams of chlorate of soda, and 5.35 grams of chloride of ammonia are dissolved in 60 grams of water. (2) Aniline solution: 20 grams of hydrochlorate of aniline are dissolved in 30 grams of distilled water, and to this are added 20 grams of solution of gum arabic (1 part of gum to 2 of water), and 10 grams of glycerine. By mixing in the cold 4 parts of the aniline solution with 1 part of the copper solution a greenish liquid is obtained, which can be employed directly for the marking; but as this liquid can only be preserved for a few days without decomposition, it is advisable to keep the solution separately until the ink is required for use.

The ink may be used either with a pen or a stencil-plate and brush; if it does not flow freely from the pen it may be diluted with a little water without fear of weakening the intensity of the color. At first the writing appears of a pale green color, but after exposure to the air it becomes black, or it may be changed to a black color immediately, by passing a hot iron over the back of the fabric, or heating it over the flames of a spirit lamp. As, however, a dry heat is apt to make brittle the fiber saturated with the ink, it is preferable to hold the marked fabric over a vessel containing water in full ebullition; the heat of the vapor is sufficient to determine almost immediately the reaction by which aniline black is formed. After the steaming, the writing should be washed in hot soapsuds, which gives the ink a fine blue shade. The ink is not acted upon by acids or alkalies, and if care be taken that the fibers are well saturated with it, there is no danger of its being removed by washing.

The products of the first two of the above formulas constitute the marking inks usually sold as indelible inks, "which no art can extract without injuring the fabric." They are not indelible, however. On the contrary, they may be discharged with almost as much facility as common iron-moulds. This may be easily and cheaply effected by means of ammonia, cyanide of potassium, the chlorides of lime and soda, and some of the hyposulphites, without, in the least injuring the texture of the fabric to which they may be applied. The only precaution required is that of rinsing the part in clean water immediately after the operation. The "marking ink without preparation" is more easily extracted than that "with preparation." The former has also the disadvantage of not keeping so well as the latter, and of depositing a portion of fulminating silver, under some circumstances, which renders its use dangerous. The thinner inks, when intended to be used with type or plates, are thickened by adding a little more gum, or some sugar.

Packer's Inks. (Used by packers for marking bales, boxes, etc.)—1. Pitch, 3 lbs.; melt over the fire, and add of lampblack, ¾ lb.; mix well.

2. Take lampblack and mix thoroughly with sufficient turpentine to make it thin enough to flow from the brush. Powdered ultramarine blue makes a fine blue marking ink.

Purple Ink.—A strong decoction of logwood, to which a little alum or chloride of tin has been added.

Red Ink.—1. Brazil wood (ground), 4 oz.; white wine vinegar (hot), 1½ pint. Digest in glass or a well tinned, copper or enamel saucepan until the next day, then gently simmer for ½ hour, adding, towards the end, gum arabic and alum, of each ½ oz.

2. Ground Brazil wood, 10 oz.; white vinegar, 10 pints; macerate for 4 or 5 days, then boil as before to one-half, and add of roach alum, 4½ oz.; gum, 5 oz., and when dissolved, bottle for use.

3. Cochineal (in powder), 1 oz.; hot water, ½ pint; digest, and when quite cold add of spirit of hartshorn, ½ pint (or liquor of ammonia, 1 oz., diluted with 3 or 4 oz. water); macerate for a few days longer, and then decant the clear. Very fine.

Sympathetic Ink.—Fluids which, when used for writing, remain invisible until the paper be heated, or acted on by some other chemical agent. Sympathetic inks have been frequently employed as the instruments of secret correspondence, and have often escaped detection; but by heating the paper before the fire until it begins to grow discolored by the heat, the whole of them may be rendered visible. The following are the most common and amusing sympathetic inks:

1. Sulphate of copper and sal ammoniac, equal parts, dissolved in water. Writes colorless, but turns yellow when heated.

2. Onion juice; like the last.

3. A weak infusion of galls. Turns black when moistened with weak copperas water.

4. Solution of chloride or nitromuriate of cobalt. Turns green when heated, and disappears again on cooling. If the salt is pure, the marks turn blue.

5. Solution of acetate of cobalt, to which a little nitre has been added. Becomes rose-colored when heated, and disappears on cooling.

6. A weak solution of mixed chlorides of cobalt and nickel. Turns green.

Yellow Ink.—From gamboge (in coarse powder), 1 oz.; hot water, 5 oz. Dissolve, and, when cold, add of spirits, ¼ oz.

Ink for Zinc Labels.—Dissolve 100 grains of bichloride of platinum in a pint of water. A little mucilage and lampblack may be added.

Ink Powders.—1. Aleppo galls, 4 oz.; sulphate of iron, 1½ oz.; gum arabic, 1 oz.; lump sugar, ½ oz. (all quite dry and in powder); mix and divide into three packets. A pint of boiling water poured over one of them produces, in a few hours, a pint of excellent ink.

2. Aleppo galls, 3 lbs.; copperas, 1 lb.; gum arabic, ½ lb.; white sugar, ¼ lb.; all in powder; mix, and divide into two-ounce packets, to be used as the last.

Lithographic Ink.—1. Mastic (in tears), 8 oz.; shellac, 12 oz.; Venice turpentine, 1 oz.; melt together; add, of wax, 1 lb.; tallow, 6 oz.; when dissolved, further add of hard tallow soap (in shavings), 6 oz.; and when the whole is perfectly combined add of lampblack 4 oz.; lastly, mix well, cool a little, and then pour it into moulds, or upon a slab, and when cold cut it into square pieces.

2. (Autographic.)—Take of white wax, 8 oz., and white soap, 2 to 3 oz.; melt, and when well combined, add of lampblack, 1 oz.; mix well, heat it strongly, and then add of shellac, 2 oz.; again heat it strongly, stir well together, cool a little, and pour it out as before. With this ink lines may be drawn of the finest to the fullest class, without danger of its spreading, and the copy may be kept for years before being transferred.

The above inks are rubbed down with a little water in a small cup or saucer for use in the same way as common water color cakes or India ink. In winter the operation should be performed near the fire, or the saucer should be placed over a basin containing a little tepid water. Either a steel pen or a camel's hair pencil may be employed with the ink.

INSECTS.

How to Destroy Insects.—The Bureau of Entomology, Washington, sends out the following, for use as insecticides on or about plants, etc.: London Purple.—To 20 lbs. of flour from ½ to 1 lb. is added and well mixed. This is applied with a sifter or blower. With 40 gallons of water ¼ to ½ lb. is mixed for spraying. Paris Green.—With 20 lbs. of flour from ½ to 1 lb. is mixed and applied by sifting or by a blower. The same amount of the insecticide to 40 gallons of water is used as a spray. Bisulphide of Carbon.—For use in the ground a quantity is poured or injected among the roots that are being infested. Against insects damaging stored grain or museum material a small quantity is used in an air-tight vessel. Carbolic Acid.—A solution of 1 part in 100 of water is used against parasites on domestic animals and their barns and sheds; also on the surface of plants and among the roots in the ground. Hellebore.—The powder is sifted on alone or mixed 1 part to 20 of flour. With 1 gallon of water ¼ lb. is mixed for spraying. Kerosene-Milk Emulsion.—To 1 part milk add 2 parts kerosene and churn by force-pump or other agitator. The butter-like emulsion is diluted ad libitum with water. An easier method is simply to mix 1 part kerosene with 3 of milk. Soap Emulsion.—In 1 gallon hot water ½ lb. whale oil soap is dissolved. This, instead of milk, is mixed to an emulsion with kerosene in the same manner and proportion as above. Pyrethrum, Persian Insect Powder.—Is blown or sifted on dry, also applied in water 1 gallon to a tablespoonful of the powder, well stirred and then sprayed. Tobacco Decoction.—This is made as strong as possible as a wash or spray to kill insect pests on animals and plants.

How to Get Rid of Household Pests.—In a lecture before the Lowell Institute recently, Professor Riley discussed the ever timely subject of household pests. For certain of the commoner pests, such as the bed-bug, the carpet-beetle and the clothes-moth, benzine, applied in a fine spray by means of a hand atomizer, was stated to be the best remedy, as in most cases it destroys the insect in all stages, including the egg. In using benzine, however, care must be taken that no fire or artificial light is in the room at the same time, the vapor of benzine being highly explosive. For cockroaches, bristle-tails, or fish-moths, and fleas, the lecturer recommended a liberal use of pyrethrum powder, in the form of either Persian or Dalmatian powder or Buhach. Fleas, he said, are generally introduced into houses by dogs or cats, and the presence of bed-bugs is not always a sign of uncleanliness, as they have been found under the bark of trees in the woods, and in country houses may sometimes be traced to this source. Keeping premises clean and dry was said to be in general a good preventive of insect pests. The common house-fly, with its complicated mouth and its microscopic eyes with 4,000 facets, was next discussed, and the lecturer then passed on to an interesting account of the mosquito. The eggs of this insect are laid in the water, and the larva, when hatched, passes through several molts in the same element, the perfect mosquito finally breaking out from the pupal skin and flying away on her bloodthirsty mission. The female mosquito is the form which stings, the male seldom leaving the swamp where he dwells, and contenting himself with vegetable juices. In dealing with the mosquito as a household pest, good pyrethrum powder is probably the best preventive of its annoyances. Moistened and made into little cones, allowed to dry, and then burned in a closed chamber, this powder will either stupefy or kill, and is one of the best means of freeing chambers from mosquitoes.

Insect Exterminator.—Quassia chips, 8½ oz.; stavesacre seed, 3 drams. Boil in 7 pints of water until reduced to 5; when cool, strain it and use with a watering-pot.

IRON.

To Test Quality of Iron.—A soft, tough iron is indicated by the fracture giving long, silky fibers of a grayish hue, the fibers cohering and twisting together before breaking. Badly refined iron is indicated by short, blackish fiber. Good iron is indicated by a medium, even grain mixed with fibers. Brittle iron is indicated by coarse grain with brilliant crystallized fracture, brown or yellow spots. It works easily when heated, and welds easily. Hot short iron is indicated by cracks on the edge of bars. Good iron heats easily, throws few sparks, and is soft when hammered.

Polished Iron Work may be preserved from rust by an inexpensive mixture, consisting of copal varnish intimately mixed with as much olive oil as will give it a degree of greasiness, adding thereto nearly as much spirit of turpentine as of varnish.

Cast Iron Work is best preserved by the common method of rubbing with black lead.

If rust has made its appearance on grates or fire-irons, apply a mixture of two parts of tripoli to one of sulphur, intimately mingled on a marble slab, and laid on with a piece of soft leather. Or emery and oil may be applied with excellent effect; not laid on in the usual slovenly way, but with a spongy piece of fig wood fully saturated with the mixture. This will not only clean but impart a polish to the metal as well.

IRONING.

There are a great many housekeepers to whom a few hints about starching and ironing cuffs, collars and shirt-bosoms would be acceptable. Many have tried to give their linen a laundry finish, and have given up in despair. If such will follow these directions they will be delighted, not only with the beautiful gloss on the linen, but also with its stiffness and elasticity:

Always dry the linen before starching.

To make the starch, wet 2 tablespoons of starch, smooth in a little cold water, pour on a quart of boiling water, stirring rapidly till it boils. Add a piece of "enamel" the size of a hazelnut. To make the "enamel," melt together with gentle heat 1 oz. white wax and 2 oz. spermaceti.

Let the starch boil ten minutes. While hot put in collars, cuffs, etc., work them thoroughly through the starch, and wring. To ½ cup of the boiled starch add a teaspoon of starch wet; smooth in 2 tablespoons of cold water. Take each piece of linen that has been through the hot starch, spread on a clean table or sheet, and with the fingers rub this mixture of boiled and raw starch on and into each piece, stretching and smoothing, running the fingers under pleats in shirt-bosoms, and smoothing out all wrinkles; dry, wring a towel not too dry out of cold water, lay each piece on this separately, and roll tight.

In half an hour they are ready to iron. After ironing them smooth with an ordinary iron, lay them on a hardwood board and rub with a polishing iron—the one with a round end of "Mrs. Potts's irons" can be used. A great deal depends on the dexterity with which you use the "heel" of this iron. A little practicing, however, will secure surprising results. Perhaps it would be well to add one hint more: everything should be perfectly clean.

Ironing Cuffs.—Cuffs ironed at home often wrinkle and blister. To avoid this, do not iron the cuffs until perfectly dry, and then, taking the front end of a flat-iron, press very hard on the edge, placing it first at one end of the cuff and slowly going over the length of it. The cuff will roll as the iron leaves it.

To Make Flat-Irons Smooth.—Beeswax and salt will make flat-irons as clean and smooth as gloss. Tie a lump of wax in a rag, and keep it for that purpose. When the irons are hot, rub them with the wax-rag, then scour with paper or rag sprinkled with salt.

To Give a Fine Polish to Starch.— Dissolve a teaspoonful of alum in a pint of starch. This holds the colors and luster.

IVORY.

The osseous portion of the tusks and teeth of the male elephant, the hippopotamus, wild boar, etc. That of the narwhal or seahorse is the most esteemed, on account of its superior hardness, toughness, translucency and whiteness. The dust or shavings (*ivory dust, ivory shavings*) of the former form a beautiful size or jelly when boiled in water. *Vegetable ivory* is the hard albumen of the seed of the *Phytelephas macrocarpa*, one of the palm family.

Ivory may be dyed or stained by any of the ordinary methods employed for woolen, after being freed from dirt and grease; but more quickly as follows:

1. Black: The ivory, well washed in an alkaline lye, is steeped in a weak, neutral solution of nitrate of silver, and then exposed to the light, or dried and dipped into a weak solution of sulphide of ammonium.

2. Blue: Steep in a weak solution of sulphate of indigo which has been nearly neutralized with salt of tartar, or in a solution of soluble Prussian blue. A still better plan is to steep it in the dyer's green indigo-vat.

3. Brown: As for black, but using a weaker solution of silver.

4. Green: Dissolve verdigris in vinegar, and steep the pieces therein for a short time, observing to use a glass or stoneware vessel; or, in a solution of verdigris, 2 parts, and sal ammoniac, 1 part, in soft water.

5. Purple: Steep in a weak neutral solution of terchloride of gold, and then expose to the light.

6. Red: Make an infusion of cochineal in liquor of ammonia, then immerse the pieces therein, having previously soaked them for a few minutes in water very slightly acidulated with aquafortis.

7. Yellow: Steep the pieces for some hours in a solution of sugar of lead, then take them out, and when dry, immerse them in a solution of chromate of potassa.

Ivory is etched or engraved by covering it with an etching ground or wax, and employing oil of vitriol as the etching fluid.

Ivory is rendered flexible by immersion in a solution of pure phosphoric acid (sp. gr. 1.13), until it loses, or partially loses, its opacity, when it is washed in clean cold soft water, and dried. In this state it is as flexible as leather, but gradually hardens by exposure to air. Immersion in hot water, however, restores its softness and pliancy. According to Dr. Ure, the necks of some descriptions of infants' feeding bottles are thus made.

Ivory is whitened or bleached by rubbing it with finely powdered pumice-stone and water, and exposing it to the sun whilst still moist, under a glass shade, to prevent desiccation and the occurrence of fissures; observing to repeat the process until a proper effect is produced.

For the preparation of ivory intended for miniature painting Hydn says: "The bleaching of ivory may be more expeditiously performed by placing the ivory before a good fire, which will dispel the wavy lines, if they are not very strongly marked, that frequently destroy the uniformity of surface."

Ivory may be gilded by immersing it in a fresh solution of proto-sulphate of iron, and afterward in a solution of chloride of gold.

Ivory is wrought, turned and fashioned in a similar manner and with similar tools to those used for bone and soft brass.

Horn for ornamental purposes is treated in a similar way to ivory, but less carefully, owing to its inferior value. The bones of living animals may be dyed by mixing madder with their food. The bones of young pigeons may thus be tinged of a rose color in 24 hours, and of a deep scarlet in 3 or 4 days; but the bones of adult animals take fully a fortnight to acquire a rose color. The bones nearest the heart become tinged the soonest. In the same way logwood and extract of logwood will tinge the bones of young pigeons purple.

IVORY—Artificial.

1. Let a paste be made of isinglass, egg-shell in very fine powder, and brandy. Give it the desired color, and pour it while warm into oiled moulds. Leave the paste in the moulds until it becomes hard.

2. Two parts of caoutchouc are dissolved in 36 parts of chloroform, and the solution is saturated with pure gaseous ammonia. The chloroform is then distilled off at a temperature of 85 degrees C. The residue is mixed with phosphate of lime or carbonate of zinc, pressed into moulds and dried. When phosphate of lime is used the product possesses to a considerable degree the nature of the composition of ivory.

JAPANNING.

The art of covering paper, wood or metal with a coating of hard, brilliant and durable varnish. The varnishes or lacquers employed for this purpose in Japan, China and the Indian Archipelago are resinous juices derived from various trees belonging to the natural order

Anacardiaceae, and species of *Rhus* (*sumach*). For use, they are purified by a defecation and straining, and are afterward mixed with a little oil, and with coloring matter, as required. In this country varnishes of amber asphaltum, or copal, or mixtures of them, pass under the names of 'Japan' and 'Japan Varnishes.'

Process: The surface is colored or painted with designs, etc., as desired, and covered with a highly transparent varnish (amber or copal), then dried at a high temperature (135° to 165° Fahr.) and lastly polished. Wood and paper are first sized, polished and varnished. For plain surfaces, asphaltum varnish, or Japan is used.

JARS.

To Clean Preserve Jars.—Sweetmeat jars or bottles may be cleaned without scraping them, by pouring in the jars hot water and a teaspoonful or two of pearlash. The contents which remain sticking to the sides and bottom of the jar will be disengaged by the pearlash and float loose in the water.

Sweetening Stone Jars.—A housekeeper writes: "Having some stone jars in which lard had been packed until they became unfit for use, I made them perfectly sweet by packing them full of fresh earth and letting it remain two or three weeks. This is an experiment with me, and I suspect it would be equally effective in any case of foul earthen or stone ware."

To Clean Jars and Buckets.—A convenient method of cleansing a jar, bucket, tub or barrel is to place a small quantity of lime on the bottom, and then slaking it with hot water in which as much salt has been dissolved as it will take up. It will purify it like a charm. Cover vessel to keep steam in.

JEWELRY.

The gold in articles of jewelry, whether solid or plated, which are not intended to be exposed to very rough usage, is generally 'colored,' as it is called in the trade. This is done as follows:

1. (Red Gold Color.) The article, after being coated with amalgam, is gently heated, and, whilst hot, is covered with gilder's wax; it is then flamed over a wood fire, and strongly heated, during which time it is kept in a state of continual motion, to equalize the action of the fire on the surface. When all the composition has burned away, the piece is plunged into water, cleansed with the 'scratch-brush,' and vinegar, and then washed and burnished. To bring up the beauty of the color, the piece is sometimes washed with a strong solution of verdigris in vinegar, next gently heated, plunged whilst hot into water, and then washed, first in vinegar, or water soured with nitric acid, and then in pure water; it is, lastly, burnished, and again washed and dried.

2. (Ormolu Color.) This is given by covering the parts with a mixture of powdered hematite, alum, common salt and vinegar, and applying heat until the coating blackens, when the piece is plunged into cold water, rubbed with a brush dipped in vinegar, or in water strongly soured with nitric acid; again washed in pure water, and dried. During this process, the parts not to be dyed in "ormolu color" should be carefully protected.

KALEIDOSCOPE.

This pleasing philosophical toy, invented by Sir David Brewster, is made as follows: Two slips of silvered glass, from 6 to 10 inches long, and from one to one and one-half inches wide, and rather narrower at one end than the other, are joined together lengthwise, by one of their edges, by means of a piece of silk or cloth glued on their backs; they are then placed in a tube of tin or pasteboard, blackened inside, and a little longer than is necessary to contain them, and are fixed by means of small pieces of cork, with their faces at an angle to each other that is an even aliquot part of 4 right angles (as the one-sixth, one-eighth, one-tenth, etc.) The other end of the tube is then closed with an opaque screen or cover, through which a small eyehole is made in the center; and the other end is fitted, first with a plate of common glass, and at the distance of about one-eighth of an inch, with a plain piece of slightly ground glass, parallel to the former; in the intermediate place or cell are placed the objects to form the images. These consist of colored pieces of glass, glass beads, or any other colored diaphanous bodies, sufficiently small to move freely in the cell, and to assume new positions when the tube is shaken or turned round. A tube so prepared presents an infinite number of changing and symmetrical pictures, no one of which can be exactly reproduced. This toy is easily constructed, is very inexpensive, and at the same time capable of affording an almost inexhaustible fund of amusement to the young. Any common tube of tin or pasteboard may be used, and strips of glass smoked on one side will answer for mirrors.

KEROSENE.

Uses of Kerosene.—Wash-day is robbed of half its terror by the use of kerosene. A tablespoonful, put into the boiler with the week's washing, results in the clothes coming out snow-white; nor is it the least bit harmful to the finest white clothes. On the contrary it cleans them without injury, and without the tiresome and destructive washboard rubbing. Again, kerosene is useful in the laundry, for it takes the rust from flat-irons better than anything else tried. It will remove iron rust and fruit stains from almost any kind of goods without injury to the coloring or fabric. The spots must be washed in kerosene before they have been put into the soap and water. As a polisher of furniture it is without a peer. It will even remove stains caused by careless hands setting hot dishes on polished table tops. In house-cleaning time it proves a blessing, for it will give window panes, mirrors and lamp chimneys a luster which nothing else can. Kerosene also prevents iron rust.

Test for Kerosene.—Into a tumblerful of water at 110° Fahr., stir a tablespoonful of the oil to be tested, and leave till the oil reaches about the same temperature. As the oil floats on the surface, pass a lighted match over it. If the oil does not ignite it can be safely used; but if it does ignite, do not use it, whatever the price may be. Another test is to fill a narrow test-tube with the oil to be tested; close it with the finger, invert it, and plunge entirely in water of 140° Fahr.; if, when the temperature has descended to 110°, any gas bubbles are seen in the closed upper part of the test-tube, the oil contains dangerous inflammable vapors.

Kerosene Stains in Carpets may be removed by sprinkling buckwheat flour over the spot. If one sprinkling is not enough, repeat.

KEYS—To Fit into Locks.

Take a lighted match or candle and smoke the new key in the flame, introduce it carefully into the key-hole, press firmly against the opposing wards of the lock, and withdraw it. The indentations on the smoked part of the key will then show you exactly where to file.

KNIVES—To Clean.

After being used all knives should be wiped on a coarse cloth, so as to insure their freedom from grease previous to being cleaned. The practice of dipping the blades in hot water not only fails to remove any grease that may be on them, but is almost sure to loosen the handles. It is very essential to remove any grease from them, since if this remain it will spoil the knife-board.

To Keep Knives from Rusting.—Steel knives which are not in general use may be kept from rusting if they are dipped in a strong solution of soda—one part water to four of soda; then wipe them dry, roll in flannel and keep them in a dry place; or the steel may be well covered with mutton tallow, then wrapped in paper and put away.

Charcoal for Table Knives.—Powdered charcoal is a good thing to use in scouring knives and forks, as it will not wear them out near so fast as brick dust, which is most commonly used.

To Clean Rusty Table Knives.—When the knives have got rusty by neglect, rub the blades over thoroughly with coal oil; allow this to remain as long as possible, a day or so at least, then rub the steel with finely powdered, unslaked lime or pumice stone. To keep them from rusting when not in daily use, dry them thoroughly and roll up in a flannel cloth and keep it in a dry place.

KOUMISS.

A liquor prepared by the Calmucs, by fermenting mare's milk, previously kept until sour, and then skimmed. By distillation it yields a spirit called rack, racky, or araka. Twenty-one pounds of fermented milk yield about ¾ pint of low wines, and this, by rectification, gives fully ¼ pint of strong alcohol. It has lately come into use as a remedy for phthisis and general debility.

The following formula for the preparation of so-called "Koumiss Extract" is said to be a good one: Powdered sugar of milk, 100 parts; glucose (prepared from grapes), 100 parts; cane sugar, 300 parts; bicarbonate of potassium, 36 parts; common salt, 24 parts. Dissolve these ingredients in 600 parts of boiling fresh whey of milk, allow the solution to cool, then add 150 parts of rectified spirits, and afterward 150 parts of strained fresh beer yeast. Stir the mixture well and put into bottles containing a half pint each. The bottles must be well corked and kept in a cool place.

For the preparation of koumiss add 5 to 6 tablespoonfuls of this extract to a quart of skimmed, luke-warm milk, contained in a bottle of thick glass; cork well, keep the bottle for half a day in a moderately warm room (16° to 20° C.), and afterward in a cool cellar, shaking occasionally. The bottle should be filled to within about 1½ in. of the cork. After two days the koumiss is ready for use.

LAC—Bleached.

By dissolving lac in a boiling lye of pearlash or caustic potassa, filtering and passing chlorine through the solution until all the lac is precipitated; this is collected, well washed and melted in hot water, and, finally, twisted into sticks, and thrown into cold water to harden. Used to make pale varnishes and the more delicate-colored sealing-wax.

LAC DYE.

A coloring substance used to dye scarlet, imported from India. It is made by dissolving out the color of genuine stick-lac by means of a weak alkaline solution, and then precipitating it along with alumina by adding a solution of alum.

To prepare the lac for dyeing, it is ground and mixed with diluted "lac spirit," and the whole allowed to stand for about a week. The cloth is first mordanted with a mixture of tartar and "lac spirit," and afterward kept near the boil for three-quarters of an hour, in a bath formed by adding a proportion of the prepared lac dye to the mixture used for mordanting. Lac dye is only applicable to woolen and silk. The colors it yields are similar to those obtained from cochineal, but less brilliant.

LACE.

To Clean Gold and Silver Lace.—Reduce to fine crumbs the interior of a 2-lb. stale loaf, and mix with them ¼ lb. of powder blue. Sprinkle some of this mixture plentifully on the lace, afterward rubbing it on with a piece of flannel. After brushing off the crumbs rub the lace with a piece of crimson velvet.

To Scour Lace.—Take a perfectly clean wine bottle; wind the lace smoothly and carefully round it; then gently sponge it in tepid soap and water; and when clean, and before it becomes dry, pass it through a weak solution of gum and water. Next pick it out and place it in the sun to dry. If it be desired to bleach the lace, it should be rinsed in some very weak solution of chloride of lime, after removal from which it must be rinsed in cold water. Starch and expose it; then boil and starch, and again expose it if it has not become sufficiently white.

The following method is also said to whiten lace: It is first ironed slightly, then folded and sewn into a clean linen bag, which is then placed for 24 hours in pure olive oil. Afterward the bag, with the lace in it, is to be boiled in a solution of soap and water for 15 minutes, then well rinsed in luke-warm water, and finally dipped in water containing a small quantity of starch. The lace is then to be taken from the bag and stretched on pins to dry.

In the cleaning of lace, borax will be found an admirable agent. Where the goods are not much soiled they may be immersed over night in a weak solution, which will so cleanse them that they will require in the morning but two or three gentle rinsings, from which they will emerge clean.

To Scour Point Lace proceed as follows: Fix the lace in a prepared tent, draw it tight and straight, make a warm lather of Castile soap, and with a fine brush dipped in rub over the lace gently, and when clean on one side do the same on the other; then throw some clean water on it, in which a little alum has been dissolved, and take off the suds; and, having some thin starch, go over with it on the wrong side, and iron it on the same side when dry; then open with a bodkin and set it in order.

To Restore Black Lace.—Mix ox-gall perfumed with musk in hot water; squeeze, but do not rub the lace in it; take it out, rinse through one pure cold water and a blued (with a blue-bag) water; squeeze it dry; pin it out very carefully to dry on a linen cloth; when nearly dry, lay a cloth over the ironing blanket, stretch the lace on it, and iron it on the right side; or dry without ironing.

Some recommend pursuing the same plan with strong green tea instead of ox-gall. Sal volatile and water also answer very well; then the lace must be dipped in thin starch and ironed between muslin.

LACQUERING.

Remove the last vestige of oil or grease from the goods to be lacquered, and do not touch the work with the fingers. A pair of spring tongs or a taper stick in some of the holes is the best way of holding.

Heat the work sufficiently hot to cause the brush to smoke when applied, but do not make hot enough to burn the lacquer.

Fasten a small wire across the lacquer cup from side to side to scrape the brush on; the latter should have the ends of the hairs trimmed exactly even with a pair of sharp scissors.

Scrape the brush as dry as possible on the wire, making a flat, smooth point at the same time.

Use the very tip of the brush to lacquer with, go very slow, and carry a steady hand.

Put on two coats at least. In order to make a very durable coat, blaze off with a spirit lamp or Bunsen burner, taking special pains not to burn the lacquer.

If the work looks gummy, the lacquer is too thick; if prismatic colors show themselves, the lacquer is too thin. In the former case, add a little alcohol; in the latter, place over the lamp, and evaporate to the desired consistency.

If the work is cheap, like lamp burners, curtain fixtures, etc., the goods may be dipped. For this purpose use a bath of nitric acid, equal parts, plunge the goods in, hung on wire, for a moment, take out and rinse in cold water thoroughly, dip in hot water, the hotter the better, remove and put in alcohol, rinse thoroughly and dip in lacquer, leaving in but a few minutes; shake vigorously to throw off all surplus lacquer, and lay in a warm place; a warm metal plate is the best to dry. Do not touch till cool, and the job is done. Lacquered work should not be touched till cold; it spoils the polish.

Sometimes drops will stand on the work, leaving a spot. These drops are merely little globules of air, and can be avoided by shaking when taken out.

The best lacquer for brass is bleached shellac and alcohol; simply this, and nothing more.

In the preparation of goods for lacquering, care should be taken to polish gradually, *i. e.*, carefully graduate the fineness of materials until the last or finest finish. Then, when the final surface is attained, there will be no deep scratches, for, of all things to be avoided in fine work, are deep scratches beneath a high polish.

LAMPS.

Care of Lamps.—The burner should be kept carefully free from oil and dust. If a soft rag is used to clean it, apply afterward a stiff brush to remove bits of lint that the cloth has probably left. To brush off the charred part with a stiff piece of card or a folded paper "lamplighter" is the best way to trim the wick. A little alcohol on a cloth is much more efficient than soap and water to clean the chimney. Use the soap and water first, and the alcohol to remove obstinate bits of dust and to give the glass a crystal polish. Rub the metal work bright with its own oil, kerosene, applied on a cloth. Have a care over your lamp cloths and brushes; they should be frequently washed and cleansed to insure cleanly service.

To Prevent Lamps from Smoking.—Soak wick in vinegar and dry well before using.

To Toughen Lamp Chimneys, etc.—Immerse the article in a pot filled with cold water, to which some common salt has been added. Boil the water well, then cool slowly.

LARD.

To Keep Sweet.—Even during the warmest weather lard can be kept sweet by the following plan: When rendering (melting) it, throw into each kettle a handful of fresh slippery elm bark. No salt must be added to it at any time. The jars in which the lard is to be kept must be thoroughly cleansed.

To Bleach.—Lard may be bleached by applying a mixture of bichromate of potash and muriatic acid, in minute proportions, to the fat.

To Try Out.—This should be done in the open air. Set a large kettle over the fire, in some sheltered place, on a still day. It will cook much quicker in large quantities. Put into the kettle, while the lard is cold, a little saleratus, say 1 tablespoonful to every 20 lbs.; stir almost constantly when nearly done till the scraps are brown and crisp, or until the steam ceases to rise; then there is no danger of its moulding; strain out into pans, and the first will be ready to empty into crocks when the last is strained.

LAVENDER.

The flowers or flowering tops of *Lavandula vera* or common garden lavender. An essential oil, spirit and tincture prepared from it are official in the pharmacopœias.

Lavender Dye for Cotton.—For 100 yards of material, take 2 lb. of logwood and 2 lbs. of sumach, and scald them separately. Then decant them into a proper-sized tub, let them cool to 150° Fahr., and add 2 gills of vitriol. Winch the goods in this 20 minutes; lift, and run them slightly through acetate of iron; wash them in two waters; then give 1 lb. of logwood as before; raise with a pint of chloride of tin, wash in two waters; then in a tub of cold water put 4 oz. extract of indigo, enter and winch in this 15 minutes, lift; give one water, and dry.

Lavender Dye for Wool.—Boil 5½ lbs. of logwood with 2 lbs. of alum. Then add 10 oz. of extract of indigo. When cold put in the goods and gradually raise to the boiling point. For 50 lbs.

Lavender Dye for Silks.—Into a vessel with warm water, as hot as the hand can bear, dissolve a little white soap, enough to raise a lather; then add 1 gill of archil liquor, and work the goods in this for 15 minutes; ring out and dry.

Boil 1 oz. of cudbear, and add the solution to the soap and water instead of archil, which will give a lavender having a redder tint than the archil. If a still redder shade of lavender be required the soap may be dispensed with.

Fine Lavender Water.—Mix together, in a clean bottle, a pint of inodorous spirit of wine, 1 oz. of oil of lavender, a teaspoonful of oil of bergamot, and a tablespoonful of oil of ambergris.

Smith's British Lavender.—English oil of lavender, 2 oz.; essence of ambergris, 1 oz.; eau de Cologne, 1 pint; rectified spirit, 1 quart. Very fragrant.

LEAD PENCILS—To Improve.

After immersing a lead pencil in a jar of linseed oil until it is thoroughly saturated, lead, wood and all, it will be found that the lead has been toughened and softened and the pencil will outwear two of the untreated.

LEATHER.

To Make Leather Wear.—It is said 2 parts of tallow and 1 of resin, melted together and applied to the soles of new boots or shoes, as much as the leather will absorb, will double their wear.

Waterproof Leather.—An Austrian chemist is reported to have solved the problem of waterproofing leather by a cheap and efficient method. He employs a solution of 15 parts of gelatine and 5 parts of bichromate of potash, dissolved in 1,200 parts of water. Impregnating the leather with this solution causes the albumen to coagulate in the pores.

LEAVES—To Dissect.

"For the dissection of leaves," says Mrs. Cussons, "I find the process of maceration too long and tedious, to say nothing of the uncertainty of the results. I have, therefore, adopted the use of alkali in saturated solution, the specimens to be introduced while the liquid is heated to the boiling point; the time of immersion to be regulated by the character of the various leaves and the nature of the epidermis to be removed. When the specimen is freed from epidermis and cellular tissue, it must be subjected to the action of chlorine to destroy the coloring matter. The introduction of peroxide of hydrogen not only serves to render the lace-like specimen purer in color, but also preserves it. In destroying the coloring matter in ferns this also is invaluable; added to the chlorine it gives a solidity to the bleached fronds, and appears to equalize the action of the chlorine. For skeletonizing capsules the slow process of maceration by steeping in rain water is alone available; a moderate heat may be applied to hasten the process, but alkali is useless. The only known flower which can be dissected is the *Hydrangea japonica*. The fibrous nature of the petals renders it easy to skeletonize in the perfect truss in which it grows. Skeletonized leaves and capsules appear to gain in the process a toughness and durability not possessed by them in their natural state."

LICE.

Chicken Lice.—Two hard kinds of lice to fight are the very small gray lice and the little red ones. These stay on the roosts and chicken houses in the day-time, and fairly swarm on the fowls at night. Worst of all, they are so very small as scarcely to be seen, and a house may be fairly overrun before their presence is detected. Watch closely; take your roosts out into the sunlight and look on the underside. Kerosene will dispatch these, but at from 15 to 25 cents a gallon it is too expensive. Crude petroleum will answer, but it can't always be had. The most economical method, both of time and cash, is to save all the strong soapsuds after washing, re-heat it boiling hot and scald the roosts and every nook and corner of the house.

To Free Plants from Leaf Lice.—1. The following is recommended as a cheap and easy method: Mix 1 oz of flour of sulphur with 1 bushel of sawdust; scatter this over the plants infected with these insects; they will soon be freed, though a second application may possibly be necessary.

2. Sprinkle some common fine-cut smoking tobacco, strong, over the top of the earth about the plant, and keep the plant well watered. The strength of the tobacco passing through the earth and about the roots will kill all creeping things and is a great benefit to the plant. If this remedy is tried the plants will soon begin to grow very fast.

LIME WATER—To Prepare.

Put a stone of fresh, unslaked lime, about the size of a half-peck measure, into a large stone jar or unpainted pail and pour over it slowly and carefully four gallons of hot water. Stir thoroughly; let it settle, and then stir again two or three times in twenty-four hours. Then bottle carefully all that can be poured off in a clear and limpid state.

Lime water is useful in many ways. It is used as a remedy for children's summer complaints, especially for diarrhea caused by acidity of the stomach, one teaspoonful being added to one cup of milk. It adds no unpleasant taste, but rather improves the flavor of milk, and prevents curdling. There is nothing better for cleansing bottles or small milk vessels, especially nursing-bottles. A cupful mixed in the sponge of bread or cakes made over night prevents souring.

LIMING LAND.

After the fall plowing is finished it is a good time to apply lime. If done then the effect will be felt on the next year's crops. Lime should never be plowed under, but always applied on the surface. Forty to fifty bushels to the acre is usually enough for each application.

LINEN—To Gloss.

Let the linen to be glossed receive as much starch as it is possible to charge it with. To each pound of starch add a piece of sperm or white wax about the size of a walnut. Before ironing lay the linen on the table and moisten very lightly on the surface with a clean wet cloth. After ironing in the usual way, the gloss is produced by means of a peculiar heavy flat-iron, rounded at the bottom and bright as a mirror, which is pressed firmly on the linen and rubbed with much force.

LINIMENT.

A semi-fluid ointment or soapy application to painful joints, swellings, burns, etc. The term is also occasionally extended to various spirituous and stimulating external applications. A preparation of a thinner consistence, but similarly employed, is called an "embrocation." These terms are, however, frequently confounded together and misapplied. Liniments are generally administered by friction with the hand or fingers, or with some substance (as a piece of flannel) capable of producing a certain amount of irritation of the skin. Sometimes a piece of linen rag is dipped in them and simply laid on the part. In most cases in which liniments are found beneficial, the advantage obtained from them is attributable rather to the friction or local irritation than to any medicinal power in the preparation itself. The greater number of cerates and ointments may be converted into liniments by simply reducing their consistency with almond or olive oil, or oil of turpentine.

Acid Liniment.—1. (Sir B. Brodie.) Salad oil, 3 oz.; oil of vitriol, 1 dram; mix, then add of oil of turpentine, 1 oz., and agitate the whole well together. As a counter-irritant, in rheumatism, stiff joints, etc.

2. (Hosp. F.) Olive oil, 3 oz.; sulphuric acid, 1 fluid dram. An excellent alterative, stimulant, discutient and counter-irritant in chronic rheumatism, stiff joints, indolent tumors, and various chronic diseases of the skin.

Liniment of Amber Oil.—1. From olive oil, 3 parts; oils of amber and cloves, of each 1 part.

2. (Opiated.) From rectified oil of amber and tincture of opium, of each 2 fluid oz.; lard, 1 oz. Anodyne, anti-spasmodic and stimulant. A once popular remedy in cramps, stiff joints, etc.

Liniment of Ammonia.—1. Solution of ammonia, 1; olive oil, 3; mix.

2. Liquor of ammonia (sp. gr. .960), 1 fluid oz.; olive oil, 2 fluid oz.; shake them together until they are mixed.

3. To the last add of olive oil, 1 fluid oz. Stimulant and rubefacient. Used in rheumatism, lumbago, neuralgia, sore throat, sprains, bruises, etc. When the skin is irritable more oil should be added, or it should be diluted with a little water.

4. (Camphorated.) *a.* Olive oil, 2 oz.; camphor, ½ oz.; dissolve by a gentle heat, and when cold, add of liquor of ammonia, 1 fluid oz.

5. (With turpentine.) Liniment of ammonia, 1½ fluid oz.; oil turpentine, ½ fluid oz.; mix.

Anti-spasmodic Liniment.—Oils of cajeput and mint, of each 1 part; tincture of opium, 3 parts; compound camphor liniment, 24 parts. Anodyne, stimulant and rubefacient.

Liniment of Arnica.—Dissolve by heat, castile soap, 4 parts, and camphor, 1 part, in rectified spirit, 30 parts. Add tincture of arnica, 5 parts.

Liniment of Belladonna.—Prepared the same as *Linimentum Aconiti*. A fluid ounce is equal to a solid ounce. Prescribed with equal parts of soap liniment, or compound camphor liniment, and is an excellent topical application for neuralgic pain.

2. Extract of belladonna, 1 dram; oil of almonds, 2 oz.; lime water, 4 fluid oz. In eczema and other cutaneous affections, to allay irritation, etc.

3. Extract of belladonna, 4 drams; glycerine, 1 oz.; soap liniment, 6 oz. As the last.

4. (Phœbus.) Extract of belladonna, 40 grains; rectified ether, 1 dram; cherry laurel water, 2 fluid oz. As a friction to the abdomen in lead colic.

Liniment of Belladonna and Chloroform.—Belladonna liniment, 7 fluid drams; belladonna chloroform (made by percolating the root with chloroform), 1 fluid dram. Sprinkled on piline and applied to the loins; excellent in lumbago.

Liniment of Borax.—Borax, 2 drams; tincture of myrrh, 1 oz.; distilled water, 1 oz.; honey of roses, 2 oz.; mix.

Liniment of Cajeput Oil.—1. Compound camphor liniment and soap liniment, of each 1½ fluid oz.; oil of cajeput, 1 fluid oz.

2. Oil of cajeput, ½ fluid dram; castor oil, 1 fluid dram; olive oil, 4½ fluid drams. A warm, antispasmodic, diffusible stimulant and rubefacient; in spasmodic asthma, colic, chronic rheumatism, spasms, chest affections, etc.

Linimentum Calcis.—Solution of lime, 1; olive oil, 1. Mix. The best liniment for burns and scalds.

Liniment of Camphor.—1. Camphor, 1 oz.; olive oil, 4 fluid oz.; gently heat the oil, add the camphor (cut small), and agitate until dissolved. Stimulant, anodyne and resolvent; in sprains, bruises, rheumatic pains, glandular enlargements, etc.

2. (Wholesale.) Camphor (clean), 21 oz.; English oil of lavender, 3½ oz.; liquor of ammonia, 2½ lbs.; rectified spirit, 7 pints; mix, close the vessel, and agitate occasionally, until the camphor is dissolved. Powerfully stimulant and rubefacient. It closely resembles, and is now almost universally sold for, Ward's "Essence for the Headache."

Liniment of Chloride of Lime.—1. Chloride of lime, 1 dram; water (added gradually), 1 fluid oz.; triturate together in a glass mortar for 10 minutes, pour off the liquid portion and add of oil of almonds, 1 fluid oz.

2. Solution of chloride of lime (ordinary), 1 part; olive oil, 2 parts.

3. Chloride of lime (in fine powder), 1 part; soft soap, 9 parts; soft water, quantity sufficient to make a liniment.

The above are cleanly and excellent applications in itch, scaldhead, foul ulcers, etc.

Liniment of Chloroform.—1. Chloroform, 1; liniment of camphor, 1; mix. The oil in the camphor liniment prevents the evaporation of the chloroform. Stimulating on application to a tender skin.

2. Chloroform, 1 fluid dram; almond oil, 7 fluid drams; mix in a phial and agitate it until the two unite.

3. Chloroform, 1 fluid dram; soap liniment, 2 fluid oz.; as the last. Used as an application in neuralgic pains, rheumatism, etc.

Liniment of Cod-liver Oil.—Cod-liver oil, 2 fluid oz.; liquor of ammonia, 1 fluid oz.; mix. Resolvent, dispersive; applied to glandular tumors, scrofulous enlargements, etc.

Liniment of Croton Oil.—Croton oil and liquor of potassa, of each 1 fluid dram; agitate until mixed, then add of rose water, 2 fluid oz. Used as a counter-irritant, in rheumatism, neuralgia, bronchial and pulmonary affections, etc. When rubbed on the skin, redness and pustular eruption ensue, and in general the bowels are acted on.

Emollient Liniment.—Camphor, 1 dram; Peruvian balsam, ½ dram; oil of almonds, 1 fl. oz.; dissolve by heat; add of glycerine, ½ fl. oz.; agitate well, and when cold, further add of oil of nutmeg, 12 drops. Excellent for chapped hands, lips, nipples, etc.

Liniment of Glycerine.—(Mr. Startin.) Soap liniment, 8 oz.; glycerine, 1 oz.; extract of belladonna, 1 oz.; mix. For gouty, rheumatic and neuralgic pains. A little veratrine is sometimes added.

Liniment of Iodine.—1. Iodine, 5; iodide of potassium, 2; camphor, 1; rectified spirit, 40; dissolve.

2. Compound tincture of iodine and laudanum, equal parts.

3. Soap liniment, 1 oz.; iodine, 8 to 10 grains.

4. Iodide of potassium, 1 dram; water, 1 fl. dram; dissolve, and add to it white soap (in shavings) and oil of almonds, of each 10 drams, previously melted together. Some perfume may be added. In scrofula, glandular enlargements, rheumatism, etc.

Liniment of Lime.—1. Olive oil and lime water, equal parts, shaken together until they are mixed. Very useful in scalds and burns.

Liniment of Mustard.—1. Flour of mustard (best), 1 oz.; water, tepid, 2 fl. oz.; mix, and add glycerine, liquor of ammonia and olive oil, of each 1 fl. oz.

2. (Hand). Carbonate of ammonia (in fine powder), 1 part; camphor (in powder), 2 parts; oil of lavender, 4 parts; tincture of mustard, 6 parts; mix; dissolve by agitation, add of simple liniment (warm), 56 parts; and again agitate until the whole is perfectly incorporated.

3. Black mustard seed (ground in pepper-mill or otherwise well bruised), ½ lb.; oil of turpentine, 1 pint; digest, express the liquid, filter, and dissolve in it camphor, ½ lb. Stimulant and rubefacient. A popular and useful remedy in rheumatic pains, lumbago, colic, chilblains, etc.

Narcotic Liniment.—Anodyne balsam, 6 parts; compound wine of opium, cold cream, of each 1 part; mix.

Liniment of Nux Vomica.—(Magendie.) Tincture of nux vomica, 1 fl. oz.; liquor of ammonia, 2 fl. drams; mix. As a stimulating application to paralyzed limbs. The addition of ½ fl. dram of glycerine and olive oil renders it an excellent application in chronic rheumatism and neuralgia.

Liniment of Oil of Ergot.—Oil of ergot, 1 dram; oil of almonds, or sulphuric ether, 3 drams; mix.

Liniment of Opium.—1. Tincture of opium, 1; liniment of soap, 3; mix.

2. Tincture of opium, 2 fl. oz.; soap liniment, 6 fl. oz.; mix.

3. Castile soap, 6 oz.; opium, 1½ oz.; rectified spirit, 1 quart; digest for 3 days, then filter, add of camphor, 3 oz.; oil of rosemary, 6 fl. drams, and agitate briskly.

5. (Wholesale.) Soft soap, 1½ lbs.; powdered opium and camphor, of each ½ lb.; rectified spirit, 1 gal.; digest a week. An excellent anodyne in local pains, rheumatism, neuralgia, sprains, etc.

Liniment of Phosphorus.—(Augustin.) Phosphorus, 6 grains; camphor, 12 grains; oil of almonds, 1 oz.; dissolve by heat; when cold decant the clear portion and add of strongest liquor of ammonia, 10 drops. A useful friction in gout, chronic rheumatism, certain obstinate cutaneous affections, etc.

Liniment of Soap.—Hard soap (cut small), 2½ oz.; camphor, 1¼ oz.; English oil of rosemary, 3 drams; rectified spirit, 18 oz.; distilled water, 2 oz.; mix the water and spirit, add the other ingredients, digest at a temperature not exceeding 70° Fahr., agitating occasionally for seven days, and filter. Soap liniment is stimulant, discutient and lubricating, and is a popular remedy in rheumatism, local pains, swellings, bruises, sprains, etc.

Liniment of Turpentine.—1. Oil of turpentine, 16; camphor, 1; soft soap, 2; dissolve the camphor in the turpentine, then add the soap, and rub till thoroughly mixed.

2. Oil of turpentine, 3 fl. oz.; resin ointment, 6 oz.; mix by a gentle heat. This forms Dr. Kentish's celebrated application to burns and scalds. The parts are first bathed with warm

oil of turpentine or brandy, and then covered with pledgets of lint, smeared with the liniment.

3. (Compound.) *a.* Oil of turpentine, 1; acetic acid, 1; liniment of camphor, 1; mix.

b. Oil of turpentine, 3 oz.; rosewater, 2½ fl. oz.; acetic acid, 5 drams; oil of lemons, 1 dram; yolk of egg, 1; make an emulsion. As a counter irritant in phthisis.

c. (Ammoniated.) Lard, 3 oz.; melt, and add, of oil of turpentine and olive oil, each 1 oz.; when cold, further add, of camphorated spirit, 4 fl. drams; liquor of ammonia, 1 fl. dram. In sciatica, lumbago, etc.

d. (Opiated.) Oil of turpentine, 1 fl. oz.; oil chamomile, 3 fl. oz.; tincture of opium, 1 fl. dram. In neuralgia, etc.

e. (Sulphuric.) Oil of turpentine, 2 oz.; olive oil, 5 oz.; mix, and add of dilute sulphuric acid, 1½ drams.

White Liniment. — Rectified oil of turpentine, 2 oz.; solution of ammonia, 2 oz.; soap liniment, 3 oz.; spirit of rosemary, 1 oz.; mix in the above order, and gradually add, with continual agitation, 8 oz. distilled vinegar. For chapped hands.

Veterinary Liniment. — Two oz. oil of spike, 2 oz. origanum, 2 oz. hemlock, 2 oz. wormwood, 4 oz. sweet oil, 2 oz. spirit of ammonia, 2 oz. gum camphor, 2 oz. spirits of turpentine. Add 1 quart strong alcohol. Mix well together and bottle tight. This is an unequaled horse liniment, and one of the best ever made for human ailments, such as rheumatism, sprains, etc.

LINT.

White linen cloth, scraped by hand or machinery, so as to render it soft and woolly. The hand-made lint is now little used. It was prepared from pieces of old linen cloth. The machine-made lint is prepared from a fabric woven on purpose. A lint made from cotton (cotton-lint) is now largely manufactured; it is much inferior to the true lint, being a bad conductor of heat. Lint is used for dressing ulcers, either alone or smeared with some suitable ointment or cerate.

Medicated Lint. — 1. Nitrate of silver, 20 to 30 grains; distilled water, 1 fl. oz.; dissolve, saturate dry lint, ½ oz., with the solution, and expose it in a saucer or capsule to the light and air until it has become black and dry.

2. Nitrate of silver and nitrate of copper, of each ½ dram; lint, 1 oz.; water, 1½ fl. oz.; as the last. Used to dress old and indolent ulcers.

LITHOGRAPHY.

The art of tracing letters, figures and other designs on stone and transferring them to paper by impression. There are two methods of lithography in general use. In the one, a drawing is made on the stone with a lithographic crayon, or with lithographic ink; in the other method, the design is made on lithographic paper, which, on being moistened and passed through the press, leaves its design on the surface of the stone, reversed. In either method, water acidulated with nitrous acid, oil of vitriol or hydrochloric acid is poured over the stone, and this, by removing the alkali from the chalk or ink, leaves the design on it in a permanent form at the same time that it "etches" away a portion of the lights, and renders the surface more absorbent of water.

The process of lithographic printing is as follows: Water is thrown over the stone; the roller charged with printing ink is passed over the surface, the paper is applied, and a copy is obtained by the action of the lithographic press. The same process must be had recourse to for each copy. The nature of the stone is such that it retains with great tenacity the resinous and oily substances contained in the ink or crayon employed for the design and also absorbs water freely; this, combined with the peculiar affinity between resinous and oily substances, and their mutual power of repelling water, occasions the ink on the printing roller to adhere to the design and to leave untouched the lights.

The stones are prepared for lithography by polishing the ordinary way, the style of work for which they are intended determining the degree of labor bestowed upon them.

For crayon drawings, the surface should have a fine grain, but the finish of the stone must depend upon the desired softness of the intended drawing. For writing or drawing on in ink the surface must receive a higher polish, and must be finished off with pumice-stone and water. The best lithographic stones are obtained from Solenhofen, near Munich, and from Pappenheim, on the banks of the Danube.

LOTIONS.

External applications or washes, consisting of water holding in solution medicinal substances. Lotions may be prepared of any soluble medicaments that are capable of exerting their action by contact with the skin. Writers on pharmacology have arranged them in classes, as sedative, anodyne, stimulant, etc., according to their effects. Sedative and refrigerant lotions are commonly employed to allay inflammation; anodyne and narcotic lotions, to relieve pain; stimulant lotions to induce the maturation of tumors, etc.; detergent lotions, to clean foul ulcers; repellent and resolvent lotions, to discuss tumors, remove eruptions, etc.; counter irritant lotions, to excite a secondary morbiaction, with the intention of relieving one already existing. Lotions are usually applied by wetting a piece of linen with them and keeping it on the part affected; or, in slight cases, by moistening the part with the fingers previously dipped into them. Lotions are more agreeable if made with rosewater, but are not thereby rendered more efficacious. In all cases, distilled water, or filtered soft water, is alone admissible as the solvent.

LUBRICATORS.

Lubricating Oil.—Take olive oil and dissolve it in boiling alcohol; add it drop by drop to the hot alcohol, until it is no longer taken into solution. Upon cooling, it will let fall crystals, and leave a considerable portion still fluid; the fluid part is to be poured off, filtered through a piece of white blotting-paper, and either used in this form, or the alcohol may be distilled off for fresh processes, and the pure lubricating oil, which will remain, can be obtained for oiling watches and delicate machinery. This will not oxidize or gum up, and will remain perfectly fluid, even when exposed to great cold.

Economical Lubricators.—1. India rubber, 2 lbs., dissolved in spirits turpentine; common soda, 5 lbs.; glue, ½ lb.; water, 5 gals.; oil 5 gals. Dissolve the soda and glue in the water by heat, add the oil, and then the dissolved rubber.

2. To Lessen Friction in Machinery: Grind together black lead with four times its weight of lard or tallow. Camphor is sometimes added, 7 lbs. to the hundredweight.

3. Anti-friction Grease: Tallow, 50 lbs.; palm oil, 30 lbs.; boil together, when cooled to 80°, strain through a sieve, and mix with 14 lbs. soda and 3 gals. water.

4. Booth's Railway Axle Grease: Water, 1 gal.; clean tallow, 3 lbs.; palm oil, 6 lbs.; common soda, ½ lb.; or: tallow 8 lbs.; palm oil, 10 lbs. Heat to about 212°; and stir well until it cools to 70°.

5. Drill Lubricator: For wrought iron, use 1 lb. soft soap mixed with 1 gal. of boiling water.

6. For Wood: Tallow and plumbago thoroughly mixed make the best lubricator for surfaces when one is wood, or when both are wood. Oil is not so good as tallow to mix with plumbago for the lubrication of wooden surfaces, because oil penetrates and saturates the wood to a greater degree than tallow, causing it to swell more.

MANURES.

The food of vegetables, as far as their organic structure is concerned, consists entirely of inorganic compounds; and no organized body can serve for the nutrition of vegetables until it has been, by the process of decay, resolved into certain inorganic substances. These are carbonic acid, water and ammonia, which are well known to be the final products of putrefaction. But even when these are applied to vegetables, their growth will not proceed unless certain mineral substances are likewise furnished in small quantities, either by the soil or the water used to moisten it. Almost every plant, when burned, leaves ashes, which commonly contain silica, potassa and phosphate of lime; often, also, magnesia, soda, sulphates, and oxide of iron. These mineral bodies appear to be essential to the existence of the vegetable tissues; so that plants will not grow in soils destitute of them, however abundantly supplied with carbonic acid, ammonia and water. The carbon of plants is chiefly derived from carbonic acid, which is either absorbed from the atmosphere, and from rain water, by the leaves, or from the moisture and air in the soil, by the roots. Its carbon is retained and assimilated with the body of the plant, while its oxygen is given out in the gaseous form; this decomposition being always effected under the influence of light at ordinary temperatures. The hydrogen and oxygen of vegetables, which, when combined with carbon, constitute the ligneous, starchy, gummy, saccharine, oily and resinous matters of plants, are derived from water chiefly absorbed by the roots from the soil. The nitrogen of vegetables is derived chiefly, if not exclusively, from ammonia, which is supplied to them in rain, and in manures, and which remain in the soil till absorbed by the roots.

According to the celebrated "mineral theory" of agriculture advanced by Liebig, a soil is fertile or barren for any given plant according as it contains those mineral substances that enter into its composition. Thus, the "ashes of wheat-straw contain much silica and potassa, whilst the ashes of the seeds contain phosphate of magnesia. Hence, if a soil is deficient in any one of these, it will not yield wheat. On the other hand, a good crop of wheat will exhaust the soil of these substances, and it will not yield a second crop till they have been restored, either by manure or by the gradual action of the weather in disintegrating the subsoil. Hence the benefit derived from fallows and the rotation of crops.

"When, by an extraordinary supply of any one mineral ingredient, or of ammonia, a large crop has been obtained, it is not to be expected that a repetition of the same individual manure next year will produce the same effect. It must be remembered that the unusual crop has exhausted the soil probably of all the other mineral ingredients, and that they also must be restored before a second crop can be obtained.

"The salt most essential to the growth of the potato is the double phosphate of ammonia and magnesia; that chiefly required for hay is phosphate of lime; while for almost all plants potassa and ammonia are highly beneficial."

From these principles we "may deduce a few valuable conclusions in regard to the chemistry of agriculture. First, by examining the ashes of a thriving plant, we discover the mineral ingredients which must exist in a soil to render it fertile for that plant. Secondly, by examining a soil, we can say at once whether it is fertile in regard to any plants the ashes of which have been examined. Thirdly, when we know the defects of a soil, the deficient matters may be easily obtained and added to it, unmixed with such as are not required. Fourthly, the straw, leaves, etc., of any plant are the best manure for that plant, since every vegetable extracts from the soil such matters alone as are essential to it. This important principle has been amply verified by the success attending the use of wheat-straw, or its ashes, as manure for wheat, and of the clippings of vines as a manure for the vineyard. When these are used (in the proper quantity) no other manure is required. Fifthly, in the rotation of crops, those should be made to follow which require different materials; or a crop which extracts little or no mineral matter, such as peas, should come after one which exhausts the soil of its phosphates and potassa."

The experiments of Messrs. Lawes and Gilbert have forced upon them opinions differing from those of Baron Liebig on some important points in relation to his "mineral theory," which endeavors to prove that "the crops on a field diminish or increase in exact proportion to the diminution or increase of the mineral substances conveyed to it in manure." The results obtained by the English investigators appear to prove that it is impossible to get good crops by using mineral manures alone, and that nitrogenous manures (farm-yard manure, guano, ammoniacal salts, etc.) are fertilizing agents of the highest order.

Of the chemical manures now so much used, bone-dust is, perhaps, the most important, as it supplies the phosphates which have been extracted by successive crops of grass or grain, the whole of the bones of the cattle fed on these crops having been derived from the soil; its gelatin also yields ammonia by putrefaction. Guano acts as a source of ammonia, containing much oxalate and urate of ammonia, with some phosphates. Nightsoil and urine, especially the latter, are most valuable for the ammonia they yield, as well as for the phosphates and potassa, but are very much neglected in this country, although their importance is fully appreciated in Belgium, France, and China. Nitrate of soda is valued as a source of nitrogen.

All organic substances may be employed as manures; preference being, however, given to those abounding in nitrogen, and which readily decay when mixed with the soil.

The analysis of manures, soils, and the ashes of plants, for the purpose of ascertaining their composition and comparative value, is not easily performed by the inexperienced; but a rough approximation of their contents, sufficiently accurate for all practical purposes, may be generally made by any intelligent person with proper care and attention.

Artificial Manures.—1. (Anderson.) Sulphate of ammonia, common salt, and oil of vitriol, of each 10 parts; chloride of potassium, 15 parts; gypsum and sulphate of potassa, of each 17 parts; saltpeter, 20 parts; crude Epsom salts, 25 parts; sulphate of soda, 33 parts. For clover.

2. (Huxtable.) Crude potash, 28 lbs.; common salt, 1 cwt.; bone-dust and gypsum, of each 2 cwt.; wood-ashes, 15 bushels. For either grain, turnips, or grass.

3. (Johnstone.) Sulphate of soda (dry), 11 lbs.; wood-ashes, 28 lbs.; common salt, ½ cwt.; crude sulphate of ammonia, 1 cwt.; bone-dust, 7 bushels. As a substitute for guano.

4. (Fertilizing powder.) A mixture of very fine bone-dust, 18 parts; calcined gypsum and sulphate of ammonia, of each 1 part. The seed is ordered to be steeped in the "drainings" from a dunghill, and after being drained, but whilst still wet, to be sprinkled with the powder, and then dried.

MANUSCRIPTS, FADED — To Restore.

Faded manuscripts may be restored without the inconvenience of employing ammonia hydrosulphate, by using a moderately concentrated aqueous solution of gallotannic acid. The acid is applied with a camel's-hair brush, the excess washed off with water, and the manuscript dried in a warm current of air. The writing comes out clear and black.

MAPLE SUGAR — Without Maple Trees.

Though the secret I am about to reveal may seem very simple (when explained), I believe there are few who would discover it of their own accord. The value of the maple sugar crop is considerable, and there is ready sale for all that can be made. I was led by curiosity to boil down a little butternut sap one time with an equal quantity of maple sap, and the result was a sugar which I could not distinguish from pure maple. I experimented further and found that if a little common (cane) sugar was added to the sap of the butternut, it would do as well as an addition of maple sap. I found that the sap of birch and several other trees would also make, when a very little cane sugar was added, a sugar which in looks and taste exactly resembled maple.

MAPLE TREES — To Tap.

Do not tap the trees until they will run equally well on all sides, and then select the thriftiest part of the tree that is farthest from an old orifice. For a tree a foot in diameter put in one spout and no more, and never bore it but once in a season, but freshen them once at any time after a long freeze. Dry up the spouts as soon as possible after they are done running, to prevent decay. An auger from ⅜ in. to ⅝ is the best size, but none larger than ⅝ in. should be employed. Trees in open grounds discharge sweeter water and more of it than those in a forest.

MARBLE.

Marbles are merely purer and more compact varieties of limestone, which admit of being sawn into slabs, and are susceptible of a fine polish. White marble is employed for the preparation of carbonic acid and some of the salts of lime. It contains about 56 per cent. of lime. Sp. gr. 2.70 to 2.85.

To Clean Marble. — Marble is best cleaned with a little soap and water, to which some ox-gall may be added. Acids should be avoided. Oil and grease may be generally removed by spreading a paste made of soft soap, caustic potash lye and fuller's earth over the part, and allowing it to remain there for a few days, after which it must be washed off with clean water. Or, take 2 parts of common soda, 1 part of pumice stone, and 1 part of finely powdered chalk; sift it through a fine sieve, and mix it with water. Rub the marble well all over with the mixture; then wash with soap and water.

To Stain Marble. — Marble may be stained or dyed of various colors by applying colored solutions or tinctures to the stone, made sufficiently hot to make the liquid just simmer on the surface. The following are the substances usually employed for this purpose:

Blue: Tincture or solution of litmus, or an alkaline solution of indigo.

Brown: Tincture of logwood.

Crimson: A solution of alkanet root in oil of turpentine.

Flesh Color: Wax tinged with alkanet root, and applied to the marble hot enough to melt it freely.

Gold Color: A mixture of equal parts of white vitriol, sal ammoniac and verdigris, each in fine powder, and carefully applied.

Green: An alkaline solution or tincture of sap green, or wax strongly colored with verdigris; or the stone is first stained blue, and then the materials for yellow stain are applied.

Red: Tincture of dragon's blood, alkanet root, or cochineal.

Yellow: Tincture of gamboge, turmeric, or saffron; or wax colored with annotto. Success in the application of these colors requires considerable experience. By their skillful use, however, a very pleasing effect, both of color and grain, may be produced.

MARBLING — Of Books, etc.

The edges and covers of books are "marbled" by laying the color on them by means of a wooden trough containing mucilage, as follows: Provide a wooden trough, 2 inches deep; boil in a brass or copper pan any quantity of linseed and water until a thick mucilage is formed; strain this into the trough, and let it cool; then grind on a marble slab any of the following colors in table beer: For blue, Prussian blue, or indigo; red, rose-pink, vermilion, or drop lake; yellow, king's yellow, yellow ochre, etc.; white, flake white; black, ivory black, or burnt lampblack; brown, umber, burnt u., terra di sienna, burnt s.; black mixed with yellow or red also makes brown; green, blue and yellow mixed; purple, red and blue mixed. For each color provide two cups — one for the ground colors, the other to mix them with the ox-gall, which must be used to thin them at discretion. If too much gall is used the colors spread; when they keep their place on the surface of the trough, on being moved with a quill, they are fit for use. All things being in readiness, the prepared colors are successively sprinkled on the surface of the mucilage in the trough with a brush, and are waved or drawn about with a quill or stick according to taste. When the design is thus formed, the book, tied tightly between cutting boards of the same size, is lightly pressed with its edge on the surface of the liquid pattern, and then withdrawn and dried. The film of color in the trough may be as thin as possible, and if any remains after the marbling, it may be taken off by applying paper to it before you prepare for marbling again.

To diversify the effect, a little sweet oil is often mixed with the colors before sprinkling them on, by which means a light halo or circle appears round each spot. In like manner spirit of turpentine, sprinkled on the surface of the trough, produces white spots.

Sprinkling is performed by simply dipping a stiff-haired painter's brush into the color, and suddenly striking it against a small stick held in the left hand over the work. By this means the color is evenly scattered without producing "blurs" or "blots."

Paper, Pasteboard, etc., in sheets, are marbled and sprinkled in a similar manner to that above described, but in this case the trough must, of course, be larger.

MARMALADE.

Originally a conserve made of quinces and sugar; now commonly applied to the conserves of other fruit, more especially to those of oranges and lemons.

Marmalades are made either by pounding the pulped fruit in a mortar with an equal or a rather larger quantity of powdered white sugar, or by mixing them together by heat, passing them through a hair sieve whilst hot, and then putting them into pots or glasses. The fruit-pulps are obtained by rubbing the fruit through a fine hair sieve, either at once or after it has been softened by simmering it for a short time along with a little water. When heat is employed in mixing the ingredients, the evaporation should be continued until the marmalade "jellies" on cooling. The following recipes are to supplement those given under the head of Cookery:

Apricot Marmalade.—From equal parts of pulp and sugar.

Mixed Marmalade.—From plums, pears and apples, variously flavored to palate.

Orange Marmalade.—From oranges, by boiling the peels in syrup until soft, then pulping them through a sieve, adding as much white sugar, and boiling them with the former syrup and the juice of the fruit to a proper consistency.

Scotch Marmalade.—1. Orange juice, 1 quart; yellow peel of the fruit, grated; honey, 2 lbs.; boil to a proper consistency.

2\. Oranges, 3 lbs.; peel them as thinly as possible, then squeeze out the juice, boil it on the yellow peels for ½ of an hour, strain, add white sugar, 2 lbs., and boil to a proper consistency.

Tomato Marmalade.—Like apricot marmalade, adding a few slices of onion and a little parsley.

MATCHES.

The original "lucifers," or "light-bearing matches," invented in 1829, consisted of strips of pasteboard or flat splints of wood, tipped first with sulphur, and then with a mixture of sulphide of antimony and chlorate of potassa, and were ignited by drawing them briskly through folded glass-paper. They required a considerable effort to ignite them, and the composition was apt to be torn off by the violence of the friction. We need not describe the "chemical matches," "phosphorus bottles," and "prometheans," in use during the early part of the present century, as these are quite obsolete. The process for making ordinary phosphorus matches is as follows:

The wooden splints are cut by steam machinery from the very best quality of pine planks, perfectly dried at a temperature of 180° Fahr. In the manufacture double lengths are used, so that each splint may be coated with the igniting composition at both ends, and then cut asunder in the middle to form two matches. The ends of the double splints, having been slightly charred by contact with a red-hot plate, are coated with sulphur by dipping them to the requisite depth in the melted material. In some cases the ends are saturated with melted wax or paraffin instead of sulphur. The splints are then arranged in a frame between grooved boards in such a manner that the prepared ends project on each side of the frame. These projecting ends are then tipped with the phosphorus composition, which is spread to a uniform depth of about ⅛ inch on a smooth slab of stone, kept warm by means of steam beneath. When partially dry, the tipped splints are taken from the frames, cut through the middle, and placed in heaps ready for "boxing."

The different compositions for tipping the matches in use in different countries and factories all consist essentially of emulsions of phosphorus in a solution of glue or gum, with or without other matters for increasing the combustibility, for coloring, etc. In England the composition contains a considerable quantity of chlorate of potassa, which imparts a snapping and flaming quality to the matches tipped with it, and but little phosphorus, on account of the moisture of the climate. In Germany the proportion of phosphorus used is much larger, and niter, or some metallic peroxide, replaces chlorate of potassa. The German matches light quietly with a mild, lambent flame, and are injured quickly by damp. The following formulas have been selected:

1\. (English.) Fine glue, 2 parts, broken into small pieces, and soaked in water till quite soft, is added to water, 4 parts, and heated by means of a water bath until it is quite fluid, and at a temperature of 200° to 212° Fahr. The vessel is then removed from the fire, and phosphorus, 1½ to 2 parts, is gradually added, the mixture being agitated briskly and continually with a "stirrer" having wooden pegs or bristles projecting at its lower end. When a uniform emulsion is obtained, chlorate of potassa, 4 to 5 parts, powdered glass, 3 to 4 parts, and red lead, smalt, or other coloring matter, a sufficient quantity (all in a state of very fine powder) are added, one at a time, to prevent accidents, and the stirring continued until the mixture is comparatively cool.

According to Mr. G. Gore, the above proportions are those of the best quality of English composition. The matches tipped with it deflagrate with a snapping noise.

2. (German.) *a.* (Böttger.) Dissolve gum Arabic, 16 parts, in the least possible quantity of water, add of phosphorus (in powder), 9 parts, and mix by trituration; then add of nitre, 14 parts; vermilion or binoxide of manganese, 16 parts, and form the whole into a paste, as directed above; into this the matches are to be dipped, and then exposed to dry. As soon as the matches are quite dry, they are to be dipped into a very dilute copal varnish or lac varnish and again exposed to dry, by which means they are rendered waterproof, or at least less likely to suffer from exposure in damp weather.

b. (Böttger.) Glue, 6 parts, is soaked in a little cold water for 24 hours, after which it is liquefied by trituration in a heated mortar; phosphorus, 4 parts, is now added and rubbed down at a heat not exceeding 150° Fahrenheit; nitre (in fine powder), 10 parts, is next mixed in, and afterwards red ochre, 5 parts, and smalt, 2 parts, are further added, and the whole formed into a uniform paste, into which the matches are dipped, as before. Cheaper than the last.

c. (Diesel.) Phosphorus, 17 parts; glue, 21 parts; red lead, 24 parts; nitre, 38 parts. Proceed as above.

Obs. Matches tipped with the above (*a*, *b*, and *c*), inflame without detonation when rubbed against a rough surface, and are hence termed "noiseless matches" by the makers.

3. (Safety matches.) The latest improvement of note in the manufacture of matches consists in dividing the ingredients of the match-mixture into two separate compositions, one being placed on the ends of the splints as usual, and the other, which contains the phosphorus, being spread in a thin layer upon the end or lid of the box. The following are the compositions used by the patentee: *a.* (For the splints.) Chlorate of potassa, 6 parts; sulphuret of antimony, 2 to 3 parts; glue, 1 part. *b.* (For the friction surface.) Amorphous phosphorus, 10 parts; sulphuret of antimony or peroxide of manganese, 8 parts; glue, 3 to 6 parts. Spread thinly upon the surface, which has been previously made rough by a coating of glue and sand.

By thus dividing the composition the danger of fire arising from ignition of the matches by accidental friction is avoided, as neither the portion on the splint nor that on the box can be ignited by rubbing against an unprepared surface. Again, by using the innocuous red or amorphous phosphorus, the danger of poisoning is entirely prevented.

Cooper's Matches.—These are made by dipping strips of coarse linen or canvas into melted brimstone. For use, the brimstone on one of them is set on fire, and the match is then at once suspended in the cask and the bung loosely set in its place. After the lapse of 2 or 3 hours the match is removed and the cask filled with liquor. Some persons pour a gallon or two of the liquor into the cask before "matching" it. The object is to allay excessive fermentation.

MATTING—To Wash.

Matting should never be washed with anything but salt and water — a pint of salt to ½ pailful soft water, moderately warm. Dry quickly with a soft cloth. Twice during a season will probably be sufficient washing for a bed-room, but a room much used will require it somewhat oftener.

MATTRESSES—Care of.

A hair mattress very seldom receives the care it deserves. The maid who turns it once a day feels that she is doing her duty nobly. And then the mistress wonders that it doesn't wear evenly, and is surprised to find it worn in spots. It will always wear in spots unless the springs beneath it are covered. The iron either rusts or wears out the ticking invariably. Therefore, the springs should have a short cover of ticking, made to button at one end, so that it may be frequently taken off and washed, and that the springs may be dusted. An unbleached cotton cover on the mattress will preserve its freshness for a long time.

When spots and stains do make their appearance on the mattress, some warm water, made smooth by a little ammonia, and a rag, will usually remove them. The rag should be merely dampened, and when vigorous rubbing has removed the spot, a little clear water should be used to rinse the place and a dry cloth used to dry it.

Mattresses should be turned not only from side to side, but also from head to foot, frequently, to insure their wearing evenly and not developing the hills and hollows found in uncared-for couches. And, of course, it should be brushed with a whisk-broom each day and aired.

MEDALS—To Take Impressions of.

Melt a little isinglass-glue made with brandy and pour it thinly over the medal, so as to cover its whole surface; let it remain for a day or two, till it be thoroughly dry and hardened, and then, taking it off, it will be fine, clear and hard as a piece of glass, and will have a very elegant impression of the coin.

MILDEW.—To Extract from Linen.

Rub strong soap and salt on the mildewed spots; keep them moist and exposed to the sun; repeat several times. Use soap made with the lye from wood ashes.

MILK.

To Test Milk. — A cheap lactometer may be made by getting a glass bulb and stem, both hollow, and loading the bulb with shot until the instrument will float upright in pure milk. Mark on the stem the point to which it sinks—the surface point. Remove it from the milk and float it in pure water, marking the surface point as before, which will be considerably higher on the stem than the other mark. Now take a narrow slip of paper capable of being rolled lengthwise, and insert it in the stem of the instrument so that the figures on it will be visible through the glass. Lay off on this, in the direction of its length, a space equal to the distance between the two surface points, numbering the one 0 and the other 100. Subdivide this space into 10 or 20 proportional spaces, correspondingly numbered; roll the slip and insert it in the stem until the 0 is at the surface point of the milk, the 100 at the point of the water. Your lactometer is now complete. Float it in your milk can every morning, and the depth to which it sinks will register the percentage of dishonest water, if any, the milk contains.

To Preserve Milk. — Place the milk in a bottle and place the bottle in a pot of water over a slow fire. Let the bottle remain for half an hour after the water has begun to boil, and then cork it tightly.

To Deodorize Milk. — Sometimes, in the spring when cows are fed upon rutabagas, the milk has such a disagreeable taste and odor as to be unfit for butter-making. This can be obviated by putting a pinch of saltpeter, finely pulverized, into every gallon of cream.

MOSQUITOES.—To Destroy.

The inhabitant of a summer cottage, finding the insects very troublesome, traced them to their breeding-place, a rain-water pool in the neighborhood with a surface of 60 square feet. Finding that eggs were deposited, he sprinkled 1 oz. of kerosene over the surface of the pool. At the end of ten days it was covered with dead insects, of which 7,400 were counted. Most of these were gnats, but there were 371 female mosquitoes and many males. As the average number of eggs laid by a female mosquito is 300, the destruction of these 371 specimens prevented the development of 111,300 individuals of the next generation. Moreover, certain females flew away after touching the water, and undoubtedly died at some distance from the pool. The experiment proved so successful that it is likely to be repeated in districts where mosquitoes abound. The remedy has the double advantage of being simple and cheap. The propagation of insects could be arrested over 65,000 square feet of water surface by using a barrel of kerosene, and the cheaper oil is much preferable to the expensive for the purpose. It is suggested that if the application be made early in June, so as to head off the first generation, the numbers of the biting pests may be reduced to a minimum.

To Keep Out Mosquitoes. — If a bottle of the oil of pennyroyal is left uncorked in a room at night, not a mosquito, nor any other bloodsucker, will be found there in the morning. It is said that to burn a piece of gum camphor about the size of a walnut will drive out mosquitoes. It burns as readily as pitch, with a clear, bright flame, and apparently no odor.

A Cure for Mosquito Bites. — The best antidote is undoubtedly ammonia weakened with a little water or salt and water. Some people go so far as to press the poison out of the bite with some small metal instrument like the point of a watch-key, before applying the antidote. This prevents the painful swelling that sometimes occurs. As in other cases, "One man's meat is another man's poison," and the same remedy will not apply to all individuals. Some find camphor most efficacious and salt and water will not avail. Ammonia, however, seems to be generally successful as a neutralizer of the mosquito poison. Where there are large quantities of mosquitoes and no reason for their appearance is apparent, it is well to look about the premises for something which attracts them. An uncovered barrel of rain-water will bring them in hordes, and damp places and stagnant pools are spots where they delight to congregate.

MOTHS.

Furs and woolen goods may be preserved from the ravages of moths by putting them away in paper bags tightly closed. The articles should be well beaten and aired before putting away.

It is well to remember that the moth never destroys woolens; it is the worm. It is well to remember that camphor and all the other vile odors in the world will never protect fabrics in the least.

If a woman puts a garment away that has so much as one moth egg, a ton of camphor won't prevent that egg from hatching, if there's any hatch to it. The only way to preserve a garment from the ravages of the moth is to be absolutely sure in the first place that a moth has laid no eggs in it, and this is not easy to discover, because with the mother instinct it creeps into dark crevices, the more obscure the better, and its eggs are as small as the point of a pin. It coats these eggs or surrounds them with a covering, and you might beat and beat the garment and not in the slightest degree hurt the eggs. Now you can put that garment away in a camphor chest and heap a ton of camphor on top of it, yet if one of those eggs hatches a worm, that worm will start in to feed.

The only way to be sure that none of these eggs are put away in a garment is to keep the garment out under constant surveillance for two or three weeks before putting it away, and in that time any newly-hatched worm will develop into a size that can be readily seen. Once a garment is absolutely free of the egg or worm, it can then be tied up in a paper parcel, or anything else that will keep the living moth out, with perfect impunity, for a moth will never bore its way into anything.

To Kill Moths in Carpets.—Wring a coarse crash towel out of clear water, spread it smoothly on the carpet, iron it dry with a good hot iron, repeating the operation on all parts of the carpet suspected of being infected with moths. No need to press hard, and neither the pile nor color of the carpet will be injured, and the moths will be destroyed by the heat and steam.

MOULD—To Prevent.

A small quantity of carbolic acid added to paste, mucilage or ink will prevent mould. An ounce of the acid to a gallon of whitewash will keep cellars and dairies from the disagreeable odor which often taints milk and meat kept in such places.

MOUSE TRAP.

An ever-ready mouse trap which may be readily constructed at home has two frames to which a movable platform is pivoted. Above this platform is suspended a small stick, to the point of which is attached the bait that is to excite the appetite of the little rodent. The platform, being horizontal, is supported at one end and held in place by a book or box, but accessible to the mice. The bait is suspended above the loose end. As soon as the mouse has traversed the pivoted centre its weight is sufficient to rock the board, and the animal tumbles into the pail of water at that end. Its cries of distress before it drowns attract the other mice, and they come to see what is going on. They also tip the board and meet with a similar fate.

MOUTH WASH.

Powdered white Castile soap, 2 drams; alcohol, 3 oz.; honey, 1 oz.; essence or extract jasmine, 2 drams. Dissolve the soap in alcohol and add honey and extract.

MUCILAGE.

1. The best quality of mucilage in the market is made by dissolving clear glue in equal volumes of water and strong vinegar, and adding ¼ of an equal volume of alcohol, and a small quantity of a solution of alum in water. Some of the cheaper preparations offered for sale are merely boiled starch or flour, mixed with nitric acid to prevent their gelatinizing.

2. Dissolve 3 oz. of gum arabic in an earthenware vessel containing ½ pint of cold water. If stirred occasionally, the gum will be dissolved in 24 hours and ready for use.

3. Fine, clean glue, 1 lb.; gum arabic, 10 oz.; water, 1 quart; melt by heat in a glue kettle; when melted, add slowly 13 oz. strong nitric acid. Then bottle, adding a couple of cloves to each bottle to prevent moulding.

MUSTARD.

1. A recipe which results in a quality of mustard almost as delicious as the famous "Düsseldorf" is the following: To 150 grains of white mustard flour add as many grains of the black, and mix well and thoroughly with 1 pint of good Rhine wine and ½ pint of good wine vinegar, mixing them in an earthen pot. This mixture must be well covered and allowed to remain over night in a warm place, near a kitchen stove, for example.

On the following morning there must be added 250 grains of clear white sugar, 2½ grains powdered cinnamon, 2½ grains of powdered cloves, 5 grains of allspice, 1 grain cardamon, ½ grain ground nutmeg, and the peel of ½ lemon, cut fine. The mass must be constantly stirred while all these ingredients are added and enough wine vinegar is used to make it the proper thickness of mustard. When done it is filled into stone jars, covered with parchment. A delicious mustard is thus obtained.

2. Mustard (ground), 8½ lbs.; water, q. s. to form a stiff paste; in ½ hour add of common salt (rubbed very fine), 1 lb.; with vinegar, grape juice, lemon juice, or white wine, q. s. to reduce it to a proper consistency.

3. To the last add a little soluble cayenne pepper or essence of cayenne.

4. (Lenormand's). Best flour of mustard, 2 lbs.; fresh parsley, chervil, celery, and tarragon, of each ½ oz.; garlic, 1 clove; 12 salt anchovies (all well chopped); grind well together, add of salt, 1 oz.; grape juice or sugar q. s. to sweeten, with sufficient water to form the mass into a thinnish paste by trituration in a mortar. When put into pots, a red-hot poker is to be thrust into each, and a little vinegar afterward poured upon the surface.

5. (French.) From black mustard seed (gently dried until friable, then finely powdered), 1 lb.; salt, 2 oz.; tarragon vinegar, q. s. to mix. In a similar way the French prepare several other "mustards," by employing vinegars flavored with the respective substances, or walnut or mushroom catsup, or the liquors of the richer pickles.

6. (French.) Salt, 1½ lb.; scraped horse-radish, 1 lb.; garlic, 2 cloves; boiling vinegar, 2 gals.; macerate in a covered vessel for 24 hours, strain, and add of flour of mustard q. s.

7. (Patent.) Black ginger (bruised), 12 lbs.; common salt, 18 lbs.; water, 15 gals.; boil, strain, and add to each gallon flour of mustard, 5 lbs.

NAILS.

To Drive into Hard Timber.—Dip the points into lard, or rub with tallow.

To Keep Nails from Rusting.—Nails for garden uses or for training vines, where driven only part way and subjected to air and moisture, are liable to rust. After they have begun to oxidize it is almost impossible to stop them. They should be previously prepared for the position. To make them secure against rust, mix a pint of linseed oil with 2 oz. black lead, stirring until the whole is thoroughly incorporated; heat the nails red hot and steep them in the mixture. They should then be well drained and shaken up in an old nail bag until dry. The linseed oil and black lead cover them with a film of varnish which is impervious to wet. The above proportions will serve for a very large quantity. If the black lead and linseed oil are not easily obtained, heat the nails and throw them into any coarse grease. This latter process is not so effectual as the first, but will answer very well. The grease used should not contain a particle of salt.

ODORS — From Cooking.

A lump of bread about the size of a billiard ball, tied up in a linen bag and placed in the pot in which greens are boiling, will absorb the gases which oftentimes send such an unpleasant odor to the regions above. Or, put 1 or 2 red peppers or a few pieces of charcoal into a pot where ham, cabbage, etc., is boiling, and the house will not be filled with the odor.

OIL-CLOTH.

Oil-cloth for floors is made on stout hemp canvas, which is woven very wide so as to have no seams in it. This canvas is first stretched tight over a frame, then covered with thin glue, or size, and rubbed down with pumice. This is to fill in the spaces between the threads and make the whole very smooth. Then a coating of thick paint is spread over the surface and rubbed in with a trowel. When this is dry another thick coat is put on, and after that another, and then a coat of thin paint, laid on with a brush. All of these are of one color, and after they have been put on and dried, the pattern of the oil-cloth is printed on by means of wooden blocks. Oil-cloth for table covers is made of light cloth or canvas, two coats, or perhaps three, of common paint are laid on, and the design is printed in the same way that calico is printed.

Laying Oil-cloth.—In putting a fresh oil-cloth on a passageway or kitchen, or any much used space, it is a good plan to lay it on the old one. Raise the edges a little and wipe out the accumulated dust with a damp cloth, then let it fall again in place, and put the new one over it. The latter will wear half again as long, as the first cloth protects it from roughness on the floor beneath.

Washing Oil-cloth.—Kitchen oil-cloth does get shabby very often in a remarkably short time, and the manufacturer and the merchant who sold it get all the blame, whereas some of it should be shouldered by both mistress and maid. Tepid (not hot) water should be used in wiping up an oil-cloth, and soap only where there are grease spots. Wet only a small portion at a time, and as soon as the dust and dirt are removed, wipe perfectly dry. After the oil-cloth is cleaned, go over it with a flannel wet with linseed oil. Use plenty of strength rubbing in the oil. Once a year give the oil-cloth a good coat of varnish. With proper treatment a good oil-cloth lasts for years, and the colors keep bright even after constant use.

OIL PAINTINGS — To Clean.

Castile soap and water may be used without danger in cleaning oil paintings. Care must be taken not to wet the backs or let water through cracks. There are other methods of cleaning, but these should be employed only by experts. For dusting pictures, a silk handkerchief should be used.

To Restore Oil Paintings.—By lapse of time and physical and chemical changes, the paint loses in some degree its transparency and the picture fades, those colors containing the least oil changing the most. Pettenkofer has discovered that the vapor of alcohol will renew the qualities, and he restores old oil paintings by placing them over a tight box, in the bottom of which is a flannel cloth dampened with alcohol of 80 per cent. strength. The arrangement should be such that every part of the picture will be exposed to the alcoholic vapor.

OILS—Drying.

All the fixed oils have an attraction more or less powerful for oxygen, and, by exposure to air, they either become hard and resinous, or they only thicken slightly, and become sour and rancid. Those which exhibit the first property in a marked degree, as the oils of linseed, poppy, rape and walnut, are called "drying oils," and are used as vehicles for colors in painting. The others are frequently termed "glutinous" or "non-drying oils."

The resinifying or drying property of oils is greatly increased by boiling them, either alone or along with litharge, sugar of lead, or white vitriol, when the product forms the "boiled oil" or "drying oil" of commerce. The efficacy of the process, according to Liebig, depends on the elimination of substances which impede the oxidation of the oil. The following formulas are adapted for this purpose:

1. Linseed oil, 1 gal.; powdered litharge, ½ lb.; simmer, with frequent stirring, until a pellicle begins to form; remove the scum, and when it has become cold and has settled decant the clear portion. Dark colored; used by house-painters.

2. Linseed oil and water, of each 1 quart; white vitriol, in powder, 2 oz.; boil to dryness. Paler than the last.

3. Pale linseed or nut oil, 1 pint; litharge or dry sulphate of lead, in fine powder, 2 oz.; mix, agitate frequently for 10 days, then set the bottle in the sun or a warm place to settle, and decant the clear portion. Very pale.

4. Linseed oil, 100 gals.; calcined white vitriol (sulphate of zinc), in fine powder, 7 lbs.; mix in a clean copper boiler, heat the whole to 285° Fahr., and keep it at that temperature, with constant stirring, for at least 1 hour; then allow it to cool, in 24 hours decant the clear portion, and in 3 or 4 weeks more rack it for use. Used for varnishes.

5. (Liebig.) Sugar of lead, 1 lb., is dissolved in rain-water, ½ gal.; litharge, in fine powder, 1 lb., is then added, and the mixture is gently simmered until only a whitish sediment remains; levigated litharge, 1 lb., is next diffused through linseed oil, 2½ gals., and the mixture is gradually added to the lead solution, previously diluted with an equal bulk of water; the whole is now stirred together for some hours, with heat, and is, lastly, left to clear itself by exposure in a warm place. The lead solution which subsides from the oil may be used again for the same purpose, by dissolving in it another lb. of litharge, as before.

6. (Wilks.) Pale linseed oil, 236 gals.; pour oil of vitriol, 6 or 7 lbs., and stir the two together for 3 hours; then add a mixture of fuller's earth, 6 lbs., and hot lime, 14 lbs., and again stir for 3 hours; next put the whole into a copper, with an equal quantity of water, and boil for about 3 hours; lastly, withdraw the fire, and when the whole is cold, draw off the water, run the oil into any suitable vessel, and let it stand for a few weeks before using it. Patent.

7. Binoxide of manganese (in coarse powder, but not dusty), 1 part; nut or linseed oil, 10 parts; mix, and keep the whole gently heated and frequently stirred for 24 to 36 hours, or until the oil begins to turn reddish. Recommended for zinc paint, but is equally adapted for other purposes for which boiled oil is employed.

There is often a difficulty in obtaining the oils "bright" after boiling or heating them with the lead solutions; the best way, on the small scale, is either to filter them through coarse woolen filtering paper, or to expose the bottle for some time to the sun or in a warm place. On the large scale, the finer oils of this kind are often filtered through canton-flannel bags. The litharge and sulphate of lead used in the above processes may be again rendered available for the same purpose, by washing them in hot water, to remove adhering mucilage.

OILS—Empyreumatic.

The "empyreumatic oils" of the old pharmaceutical writers were oily fluids obtained by the dry distillation of various substances, animal, vegetable and mineral. But few of them are in use at the present day. Two or three have useful applications in the arts, and it is therefore necessary to briefly describe their preparation. When the ingredients are of a liquid or pasty nature, or become so when heated, they are usually mixed with about twice their weight of sand, powdered glass, or other like substance, to divide them, and thus expose them more effectually to the action of the fire. Care must also be taken to provide a well-cooled receiver, which must be furnished with a tube to carry off the non-condensable gases liberated at the same time as the oil. The products of the first distillation are generally purified by rectification, either alone or along with water. In general, they require to be preserved from the light and air.

Oil of Aloes.—1. From Socotrine or hepatic aloes distilled along with sand.

2. Olive oil, 1 lb.; hepatic aloes and myrrh, of each in powder, 2 oz.; olibanum, ½ oz.; distil in a sand bath, from a stoneware retort. Used as an external vermifuge for children; a portion is rubbed 2 or 3 times a day over the umbilical regions.

SOME ALTITUDES.

The famous tower of Utrecht is 464 feet.

Mount Pilatus, in the Alps, is 9,050 feet high.

Bunker Hill monument is 221 feet in height.

The Brooklyn bridge is 278 feet above the river.

The Holland dikes are from 10 to 40 feet in height.

The porcelain tower at Nankin was 248 feet high.

Mount Hecla, 5,000 feet, is the highest in Iceland.

Carthage is the highest town in Kansas, 5,002 feet.

Mount Shasta, the celebrated volcano of California, is 14,450 feet high.

The cross on the Duomo, in Florence, is 350 feet above the foundation.

Mauna Loa, in the Hawaiian islands, is 13,760 feet high; Mauna Kea, 13,953 feet; Mount Hualalai, 7,822.

Mount Sinai, the mountain from which the law of Moses is said to have been delivered, is 6,000 feet high.

The steeple of the cathedral at Freiburg, where is located the most famous organ in the world, is 387 feet high.

Worcester, in Wisconsin, at an elevation of 1,605 feet, is said to be the highest recorded altitude in that state.

California has 20 mountains each of which exceeds 10,000 feet, and quite a number are more than 12,000.

There are 412 mountain peaks in the United States or the territories each having a height greater than 10,000 feet.

The Simplon, under the shadow of which lay the once famous stage route from France to Italy, is 11,542 feet high.

New Springfield, said to be 1,553 feet above sea level, is declared by competent authorities to be the highest town in Missouri.—St. Louis Globe-Democrat.

government."

HON. JAMES A. MOUNT.

It is stated on the very best of authority—we have it from a very conservative, upright resident of South Bend—that Hon. James A. Mount, during his speech at that place, made a host of friends, and it is positively certain that he will run ahead of his ticket at the home of his competitor. His speech in the afternoon was so excellent, so clear and to the point, that those who heard it insisted that he should speak again in the evening, so that the thousands of men employed in the factories at that place could hear him. Although it was then four o'clock, a rousing meeting was the result. A torch-light procession followed, and Mr. Mount fairly outdid himself in the excellent speech he made. It will be remembered that Democratic newspapers poked fun at Mr. Mount, calling him the farmer candidate, and spoke very slightingly of him. They are not doing that just now. They have ascertained that though he is an out-and-out practical farmer—differing greatly in that particular from the egotistical Ridpath—yet he is one of the brightest men in the State, and on the stump is a host in himself. He is knocking Shively out of the race, and will be elected by an overwhelming majority.

First Voters.

The young man who on November 3

Oil of Birch.—From the inner bark of the birch, by heating it in an earthen pot with a hole in the bottom, to allow the oil to flow through into another jar sunk in the ground and luted to it. Thick, balsamic, fragrant. Used chiefly to dress Russia leather.

Oil of Tar.—By simple distillation from wood-tar. Reddish and strong-scented. By one or more rectifications it becomes colorless and limpid. It soon gets thick. Used in ringworm and several other skin diseases, made into an ointment with lard. Poisonous if swallowed in large doses.

Oil of Tobacco.—From tobacco, in coarse powder, gradually heated in a green-glass retort to dull redness, and kept at that temperature as long as any oil passes over; the oily portion is then separated from the water in the receiver, and kept for use. Highly narcotic and poisonous.

Oil of Wax.—From beeswax and sand distilled together; the product is rectified once or oftener. Reputed diuretic. *Dose*, 2 to 6 drops.

OILS—Fixed.

The fixed oils are compounds of carbon, hydrogen and oxygen (oxyhydro-carbons), obtained from the organic kingdom, and characterized by their insipidity, unctuosity, insolubility in water, and being lighter than that fluid. Olive oil, which is obtained from the vegetable kingdom, and spermaceti oil, which is obtained from the animal kingdom, may be taken as types of the sort.

Among the best known properties of the fixed oils are: The permanent stain they give to paper, which they render translucent; their non-volatility at the ordinary temperature of the atmosphere, or at that of boiling water, or, indeed, at any temperature insufficient for their decomposition; their constantly floating on the surface of water when added to it; and, lastly, their inability to mix with that fluid. Some of them, as palm oil and cocoanut oil, are solid at ordinary temperatures; but the majority are fluid, unless they have been considerably cooled, when they separate into two portions—the one solid, consisting chiefly of stearin, or some analogous substance, and the other liquid, consisting chiefly of olein or elain. Nearly all of them, when exposed to the air, absorb oxygen rapidly, and either gradually harden or become rancid and nauseous. From the first are selected the "drying oils" used by painters; the last are used as food, in cookery, and for machinery, lamps, etc. The whole of these oils, when heated to their boiling points (500° to 600° Fahr.), suffer decomposition, yielding various hydrocarbons; and when suddenly exposed to a red heat, they furnish a gaseous product (oil-gas), which was formerly employed for illumination. It is owing to this property of oil and liquid fats that candles and lamps give their light. The wick is a gas-producing apparatus in miniature. With the caustic alkalies and water the fixed oils unite to form soap. When some of these oils are absorbed by porous bodies, and thus expose a vastly increased surface to the air, they absorb oxygen with such rapidity as to generate a considerable degree of heat. Paper, tow, cotton, wool, straw, shavings, etc., slightly imbued with oil, and left in a heap, freely exposed to the air or sun, often spontaneously inflame. In this way many extensive fires have arisen. The above is more particularly the case with linseed, rape, nut and olive oil. The first, made into a paste with manganese, rapidly becomes hot, and ultimately inflames spontaneously.

The fixed oils, except where otherwise directed, are obtained from the bruised or ground fruit or seed, by means of powerful pressure, in screw or hydraulic presses, and are then either allowed to clarify themselves by subsidence or are filtered. Both methods are frequently applied to the same oil. In some cases the impurities are removed by ebullition with water, and subsequent separation of the pure oil. Heat is frequently employed to increase the liquidity of the oil, and thus lessen the difficulty of its expulsion from the mass. With this object the bruised mass, placed in bags, is commonly exposed to the heat of steam, and then pressed between heated plates of metal.

Another method is by boiling the bruised seed in water, and skimming off the oil as it rises to the surface. This is the plan adopted for castor oil in the West Indies.

In a few cases for medicinal purposes, the bruised mass is mixed with one-half its weight or an equal weight of alcohol or ether, and after 24 hours' digestion the whole is submitted to pressure, and the alcohol or ether removed by distillation at a gentle heat.

Purification.—Several methods are adopted for refining or purifying the fixed oils, among which are the following:

1. The oil is violently agitated along with 1½ to 2% of concentrated sulphuric acid, when it assumes a greenish color, and, after about a fortnight's repose, deposits much coloring matter, becomes paler, and burns with greater brilliancy, particularly if well washed with steam or hot water, and clarified by subsequent repose or by filtration. This answers well for most of the recently expressed vegetable oils. It also improves most of the fish oils.

2. A modification of the last method is to well mix the acid with the oil, then to blow

steam through the mixture for some time, and afterward to otherwise proceed as before.

3. Fish oil (whale, seal, etc.) is purified by—

a. Violently agitating it with boiling water or steam, by placing it in a deep vessel with perforated bottom, through which high-pressure steam is forced for some time; it is afterwards clarified by repose, and filtered through coarse charcoal.

b. The oil is violently agitated with a boiling hot and strong solution of oak bark, to remove albumen and gelatin, and next with high-pressure steam and hot water; it is, lastly, dried and filtered.

c. The oil, gently heated, is stirred for some time with about 1% of good chloride of lime, previously made into a milk by trituration with water; about 1½% of oil of vitriol, diluted with 20 times its weight of water, is then added, and the agitation renewed and maintained for at least 2 hours; it is, lastly, well washed with steam or hot water.

4. Almond, castor, linseed, nut, olive, rape and some other vegetable oils are readily bleached by either of the following processes:

a. Exposure in glass bottles to the sun's rays, on the leads or roofs of houses, or in any other suitable position, open to the southeast and south. This is the method employed by druggists and oilmen to whiten their castor and linseed oils. Fourteen to twenty-one days' exposure to the sun in clear weather during summer is usually sufficient for castor oil when contained in 2 to 4 quart pale green glass bottles (preferably the former), and covered with white gallipots inverted over them. The oil is filtered before exposing it to the light, as, if only in a slight degree opaque, it does not bleach well. Almond and olive oil are, when thus treated, apt to acquire a slight sulphurous smell; but this may be removed by filtration through a little animal charcoal, or, still better, by washing the oil with hot water.

b. Another method employed to decolor these oils is to heat them in a wooden, tinned or well-glazed earthen vessel along with some dry "filtering powder" (1 to 2 lbs. per gal.), with agitation for some time, and lastly, to filter them in the usual manner through an oil-bag. In this way the London perfumers prepare their "white almond oil" (oleum amygdalæ album), and their "white olive oil" (oleum olivæ album). Formerly, freshly burnt animal charcoal was used for this purpose, and is still so employed by some houses.

5. Mr. Bancroft refines oils for machinery and lubricating purposes generally, by agitating them with a lye of caustic soda of the sp. gr. 1.2. A sufficient quantity is known to have been added when, after repose, a portion begins to settle down clear at the bottom. About 4% to 8% is commonly required for lard oil and olive oil. After 24 hours' repose the clear supernatant oil is decanted from the soapy sediment, and filtered.

6. All oils and fats may be rendered perfectly colorless by the use of a little chromic acid; or what is the same, by a mixture of a solution of bichromate of potash and sufficient sulphuric, hydrochloric or nitric acid to seize on all the alkali, and thus liberate the chromic acid.

7. Palm-oil and cocoanut oil are generally refined and bleached by either chromic acid or chlorine, or by heat.

8. Effective methods of purifying fats and oils, especially for those intended for illumination, are as follows:

a. (For fish oils.) Each ton is boiled for ½ hour with caustic soda, ½ lb., previously made into a weak lye with water; or steam is blown through the mixture for a like period; oil of vitriol, ¾ lb., diluted with 6 times its weight of water, is next added, the whole again boiled for 15 minutes, and allowed to settle for an hour or longer, when the clear oil is run off from the water and sediment into the bleaching tubs; here solution of bichromate of potash, 4 lbs., in oil of vitriol, 2 lbs., previously diluted with water, q. s., together with a little nitric acid and some oxalic acid, are added, and after thorough admixture of the whole, by blowing steam through it, strong nitric acid, 1 lb., diluted with water, 1 quart, is poured in, and the boiling continued for ½ hour longer; a small quantity of naphtha or rectified spirit of turpentine is then mixed in, and the oil is finally well washed with hot water and left to settle.

b. (For palm oil.) The oil is melted by the heat of steam, and after it has settled and cooled down to about 130° Fahr., is carefully decanted from the water and sediment into the bleaching tubs; here a mixture of a saturated solution of bichromate of potash, 25 lbs., and oil of vitriol, 8 or 9 lbs., is added, and after thorough admixture, hydrochloric acid, 50 lbs., is poured in; the whole is then constantly stirred until it acquires a uniform greenish color, or is sufficiently decolored, a little more of the bleaching materials being added if the latter is not the case, after which it is allowed to repose for ½ hour to settle; it is next run into a wooden vat, where it is washed, etc., as before.

c. (For vegetable oils.) These are treated with a solution of chromic acid, or with a solution of bichromate of potash, or some mineral acid, as noticed at No. 6. For colza, linseed, mustard, nut and rape oil a little hydrochloric acid is added; but for almond, castor, olive oil and poppy oil no such addition (at least in excess) is required.

9. Rancid oils and fats are recovered by boiling them for about 15 minutes with a little water and calcined magnesia, or by filtering them through freshly burnt charcoal.

In reference to the above processes it may be useful to remark that chlorine, the common bleacher and deodorizer of other substances, cannot be well employed directly in the purification of oils, as certain chemical reactions occur when these substances are brought together, which increase the color instead of removing it, and are often otherwise injurious. The same remarks apply to the use of the "chlorides," which frequently fails in unskillful hands, and is, indeed, of questionable utility, except, perhaps, in the case of palm oil. Even charcoal exerts little of its usual energy on the oils, and whilst it removes or lessens their offensive odor, sometimes increases their color. The addition of 1% or 2% of very pure and recently rectified naphtha or oil of turpentine (camphine) to lamp oil is a real improvement, since it increases its combustibility and its illuminative power.

Oils for medical purposes, as castor oil, cod-liver oil, etc., must not be subjected to any process beyond mere clarification by subsidence, filtration through canton flannel or porous paper, or at the utmost, washing with warm water, as otherwise their active and valuable properties, if not wholly removed, will be considerably lessened.

The following are the *principal fixed oils of commerce:*

Castor Oil.—The oil prepared by heat, or by pressure, from the seed of *Ricinus communis*, the *Palma Christi* or Mexican oil bush.

The best castor oil is prepared by pressing the shelled and crushed fruit (seed) in hemp bags in a hydraulic press, and heating the oil thus obtained along with water in well tinned vessels, until the water boils and the albumen and gum separate as a scum; this is carefully removed, and the oil as soon as it has become cold is filtered through canton flannel and put into canisters. The commoner kinds are prepared by gently heating the crushed seeds, and pressing them whilst hot.

Cocoanut Oil.—By expression from the kernels of the cocoanut.

Cod-liver Oil.—The oil extracted from the liver of the *Gadus morrhua* (cod-fish) by a steam heat or water bath not exceeding 180° Fahr.

Cotton-seed Oil.—From the seeds of *Gossypium Barbadense.* Drying.

Croton Oil.—From the shelled seeds of *Croton tiglium* or Molucca grains. Imported chiefly from the East Indies. It is one of the most powerful cathartics known, and acts when either swallowed or merely placed in the mouth. Externally, it is a rubefacient and counter-irritant, often causing a crop of painful pustules, like tartar emetic. *Dose*, 1 to 2 drops, on sugar; in apoplexy, etc. It is poisonous in larger doses.

Lard Oil.—By separating the *oleine* of lard from the stearin by means of boiling alcohol. Only applicable where spirits are cheap. The product is, however, excellent. The crude oleic acid, or lard oil of commerce, is chiefly obtained as a secondary product in the manufacture of stearin. It is purified by agitation with sulphuric acid, and subsequently by steaming it, or washing it with hot water. Burns well in lamps if the wick tube is kept cool.

Linseed Oil.—1. From the seed of *Linum usitatissimum*, or common flax, bruised or crushed, and then ground and expressed without heat. Pale, insipid, viscous; does not keep so well as the next.

2. As the last, but employing a steam heat of about 200° Fahr. Amber-colored; less viscous than the last; congeals at 0°; soluble in 5 parts of boiling and 40 parts of cold alcohol. Both are drying and cathartic. *Dose*, 1 to 2 oz.; in piles, etc. Chiefly used in paints, varnishes, etc.

Neat's-foot Oil.—From neat's feet and tripe, by boiling them in water and skimming off the oil. Does not thicken by age. Used to soften leather, to clean fire-arms, and for other purposes.

Nut Oil.—From the kernels of *Corylus Avellana*, or hazel-nut tree. Pale, mild-tasting, drying; superior to linseed oil for paints and varnishes. It is commonly sold for oil of almonds and oil of ben, and is extensively employed to adulterate both. Walnut oil is also frequently sold for nut oil.

Oil of Nutmeg (Expressed).—The concrete oil is expressed from the seed of *Myristica officinalis*, or common nutmeg. The nutmegs are beaten to a paste, inclosed in a bag, exposed to the vapor of hot water, and then pressed between heated iron plates. Orange-colored, fragrant, spicy; butyraceous, or solid. It is a mixture of the fixed and volatile oils of the nutmeg. When discolored and hardened by age, it is called "Banda soap." When pure, it is soluble in 4 parts of boiling alcohol and in 2 parts of ether. Now chiefly employed for its odor and aromatic qualities.

Olive Oil.—The oil extracted from the fruit of *Olea europæa*, or common olive. Five different methods are employed to obtain the oil from the fruit:

1. (Virgin oil.) From olives, carefully garbled, either spontaneously or only by slight pressure, in the cold. That yielded by the pericarp of the fruit is the finest.

2. (Ordinary "fine oil.") This is obtained by either pressing the olives, previously crushed and mixed with boiling water, or by pressing, at a gentle heat, the olives from which the virgin oil has been obtained. The above processes furnish the finer salad oils of commerce. (The cake which is left is called "grignon.")

3. (Second quality.) By allowing the bruised fruit to ferment before pressing it. Yellow; darker than preceding; but mild and sweet-tasted. Much used for the table.

4. ("Gorgon.") By fermenting and boiling the pressed cake or marc in water, and skimming off the oil. Inferior.

5. (Oil of the infernal regions.) A very inferior quality of oil, which is skimmed off the surface of the water in the reservoirs into which the waste water which has been used in the above operations is received, and allowed to settle. The last two are chiefly used for lamps, and in soap-making, etc.

Olive oil is a nearly inodorous, pale greenish-yellow, unctuous fluid, with a purely oleaginous taste, peculiarly grateful to the palate of those who relish oil. It does not suffer active decomposition at a heat not exceeding 600° Fahr.; and when cooled to 36° it congeals into a granular solid mass. It is very slightly soluble in alcohol, but its solubility is increased by admixture with castor oil. It is soluble in $1\frac{1}{2}$ parts of ether. When pure it has little tendency to become rancid.

To Test Olive Oil.—When it is desired to ascertain whether the oil is pure or not, without precise reference to the nature of the oils used in adulteration, take equal quantities of olive oil known to be pure and the oil to be tested; place the samples in separate test tubes into which a good thermometer may also be inserted, and heat each separately to a high temperature. The pure oil will become somewhat paler during the heating, while the adulterant oils will give off an offensive odor.

Palm Oil.—From the fruit *Elais Guineensis*, and *E. melanococca*, the Guinea oil palms. Orange or red-colored; butyraceous or solid; smells of violets; unchanged by alkalies; bleached by sunlight, age, exposure, chlorine, chromic acid, and oil of vitriol; melts at $117\frac{1}{2}$° Fahr. Demulcent. Used to color and scent ointments, pomades, etc.; but chiefly to make soap and candles. From Africa.

Poppy Oil.—From the seeds of *Papaver somniferum*, or white poppy. Sweet; pale; dries and keeps well. Used for salads, paints and soaps; also (extensively) to adulterate almond oil, for the inferior qualities of which it is frequently sold. It does not freeze until cooled to 0° Fahr.

Rape Oil.—From the seed of *Brassica napus* (cole or rape), and from *Brassica campestris* (wild navew or rape). Glutinous; buttery at 25° Fahr. Dries slowly; makes soft soaps and good ointments, but bad plasters; smokes much in burning unless well refined.

Refined or pale rape oil is prepared from crude rape oil by agitating it with about 2% of oil of vitriol, previously diluted with about twice its weight of water, and, after 10 or 12 days' repose, decanting the clear oil, and filtering it through cotton flannel or felt. The quality is improved by washing it with hot water or steam before filtration. Used for lamps, blacking and machinery; also extensively employed to adulterate both almond and olive oil. It forms the common "sweet oil" of the oilmen and druggists.

Seal Oil.—From the hood seal, and harp seal, and other species of *Phocidae*. Pale seal oil is that which drains from the blubber before putrefaction commences, and forms about 60% of the whole quantity of oil obtained. It is very clear, free from smell, and, when recently prepared, not unpleasant in its taste. Refined seal oil is the last, washed and filtered. Ranks close after sperm oil. Brown or dark seal oil is that which subsequently drains from the putrid mass. It is very strong-scented and nauseous, and smokes in burning. Both are used for lamps and dressing leather.

Spermaceti Oil.—From the "head matter" of *Physeter macrocephalous*, or spermaceti whale. It is very limpid, smells little, and burns well, and has long been reputed the best oil for lamps and machinery, as it does not thicken by age or friction. It is frequently adulterated with refined seal oil.

Sunflower Oil.—From the seeds of *Helianthus annuus* and *H. perennis*. Clear, pale yellow, tasteless; thickens at 60° Fahr. Used for salads and lamps.

Walnut Oil.—From the kernels of the nuts of *Juglans regia*, or common walnut tree. Soon gets rank; dries well. Used in paints, and occasionally in plasters. When "cold drawn" and washed it is sometimes eaten with salad.

Oil of Wax.—From beeswax, by quick distillation in a closed vessel. Butyraceous. By rectification along with quicklime it yields a liquid oil.

Whale Oil.—From the blubber of the *Balaena mysticetus*, or the common or Greenland whale, by heat. Coarse, stinking. Southern whale oil is the best. Used for lamps, machinery, etc.

OILS — Medicated.

These are prepared by infusion or decoction. The bruised ingredients are either simply digested in 2 to 4 times their weight of olive oil for some days, or they are very gently boiled in it until they become dry and crisp, great care being taken that the heat toward the end of the process is not greater than that of boiling water. As soon as the process is complete, the oil is allowed to drain from the ingredients, which are then (if necessary) submitted to the action of the press. The product is commonly run through flannel or a hair sieve whilst still warm, after which it is allowed to repose for a week or ten days, when the clear portion is decanted from the dregs. The green or fresh plants are usually employed for this purpose, but, in many cases, the dried plants, reduced to powder, and digested for 6 or 8 hours in the oil, at the heat of hot water, with frequent agitation, yield a much more valuable product. They are nearly all employed as external applications only.

OILS — Mineral.

An important class of liquids, consisting solely of carbon and hydrogen — the elements of ordinary coal-gas, and obtained by the distillation of coal, lignite, petroleum and other bituminous substances. For the purposes of illumination, many of these oils are in most respects superior to the fixed or fat oils containing oxygen. They give a whiter and more brilliant light, and are produced at a much lower cost. The lamps in which they are burnt, when properly constructed, are less liable to get out of order than those adapted for the combustion of fat oils, and require less attention when in use. Experiments on the relative value of the ordinary illuminating agents prove that the mineral oils are cheaper than all other portable illuminating agents in common use, and that they give, while burning, the largest amount of light with the least development of heat, and the smallest production of carbonic acid. With the oils adapted for burning in lamps other oils are produced. Some are very volatile and highly inflammable, and the safety of the burning oils depends on their proper extraction. These volatile liquids, when isolated, are used in the arts as substitutes for spirits of turpentine, as solvents for various substances, and to increase the illuminating power of coal-gas. Others are of a greasy nature, and are too heavy to be used in lamps. These, however, are well adapted for lubricating fine machinery. When the more volatile ingredients are separated from the burning oils, the latter are perfectly safe. Most of the mineral burning oils now in use are, we believe, free from danger in this respect.

Petroleum Oil.—Most of the burning oils now in the market are derived from American petroleum. That obtained from natural petroleum is now manufactured solely in America. The native petroleums vary greatly in properties, and numerous methods of refining are employed by the manufacturers. The Canadian petroleum contains sulphuretted hydrogen, which imparts to it a very disagreeable smell, and is difficult of removal. Some make use of both acids and alkalies, others employ alkalies alone, and steam is applied at various stages of heat. Some of the oils produced are of excellent quality, but others are inferior, and do not ascend the wick in sufficient quantity to afford a constant light. See *Kerosene*.

OINTMENTS.

Ointment of Aconite.—Alcoholic extract of aconite, 1 part; lard, 2 parts; carefully triturated together. In neuralgia, etc.

Ointment of Aconitine.—1. Pure aconitine, 1 gr.; lard, 1 dram; mix by careful trituration.

2. Aconitine, 2 gr.; rectified spirit, 6 or 7 drops; triturate together, then add of lard, 1 dram, and mix well.

3. Aconitia (aconitine), 8 gr.; rectified spirit, ½ dram; dissolve, and add lard, 1 oz.; mix. Used as a topical benumber in neuralgic affections, rheumatic pains, etc. Its application generally occasions considerable tingling, and sometimes redness of the part to which it is applied, followed by temporary loss of sensation in the skin and the cessation of the pain. Owing to the intensely poisonous nature of aconitine, this ointment must be both prepared and used with great caution, and must never be applied to an abraded surface. It is seldom used, owing to its extreme costliness.

Ointment of Alum.—1. Alum, in very fine powder, 1 dram; lard, 1½ oz. In piles.

2. To the last add of powdered opium, 7 gr. In piles, when there is much pain.

Ointment of Belladonna.—1. Extract of belladonna (deadly nightshade), 1 dram; lard, 1 oz.; mix by trituration.

2. Fresh belladonna leaves (bruised), 1 part; lard, 2 parts; simmer together until the leaves become crisp, and, after digestion for a short time longer, drain with pressure.

3. Extract of belladonna, 1, rubbed with a few drops of water and mix with lard, 6½.

Used as a local anodyne in painful and indolent tumors, nervous irritations, etc.; also as an application to the neck of the uterus in cases of rigidity.

Ointment of Calomel.—Calomel, 1 dram; lard or simple ointment, 1 oz. Pre-eminently useful in skin diseases.

Ointment of Extract of Cantharides.—Alcoholic extract of cantharides, 6 gr.; oil of roses, ½ dram; beef marrow, 2 oz.; oil of lemon, 40 minims. To promote the growth of the hair.

Ointment of Chamomile.—Freshly powdered chamomile flowers, olive oil, and lard, in equal quantities. For the cure of itch.

Chilblain Ointment.—From made mustard (very thick), 2 parts; almond oil and glycerine, of each 1 part; triturated together. To be applied night and morning.

Ointment of Chloroform.—Chloroform, 1 dram; simple ointment, 1 oz. In neuralgic and rheumatic pains, etc. It must be kept in a stoppered, wide-mouthed phial.

Ointment of Cocculus Indicus.—Kernels of *cocculus indicus*, 1 part; beat them to a smooth paste in a mortar, first alone, and next with a little lard; then further add of lard, q. s., so that it may be equal to 5 times the weight of the kernels. Used to destroy pediculi, and in scald-head, etc.

Ointment of Croton Oil.—Croton oil, 15 to 30 drops; lard (softened by heat), 1 oz.; mix well. This is the usual and most useful strength to prepare the ointment. Rubefacient and counter-irritant; in rheumatism and various other diseases. When rubbed repeatedly on the skin it produces redness and a pustular eruption. It also often affects the bowels by absorption. The only advantage it possesses over other preparations of the class is the rapidity of its action.

Ointment of Glycerine.—Glycerine, 4 fl. oz.; oil of almonds, 8 fl. oz.; wax and spermaceti, of each ½ oz.

Eye Ointment.—1. Burnt alum, ½ dr.; powdered opium, 20 gr.; olive oil, 1 fl. dr.; spermaceti ointment, 2 dr. In inflammation of the eyelids, purulent ophthalmia, etc.

2. (W. Cooley.) Chloride of barium, 6 gr.; calomel, 10 gr.; simple ointment, 1 oz.; otto of roses, 1 or 2 drops. In scrofulous ophthalmia.

3. (Desault.) Nitric oxide of mercury, carbonate of zinc, acetate of lead, and dried alum, of each 1 dr.; corrosive sublimate, 10 gr.; rose ointment, 1 oz. In chronic ophthalmia, profuse discharges, etc.; in general, diluted.

Ointment of Hemlock.—Fresh hemlock leaves and lard, of each 1 lb.; boil them together (very gently) until the leaves become crisp, then strain through linen, with pressure. Used as a local anodyne in neuralgic and rheumatic pains, glandular enlargements, painful piles, etc., and as a dressing to painful and irritable ulcers, cancerous sores, etc.

Itch Ointment.—Several excellent formulæ for itch ointments will be found under the names of their leading ingredients. The following are additional:

1. Carbonate of potassa, ½ oz.; rose water, 1 fl. oz.; red sulphuret of mercury, 1 dr.; oil of bergamot, ½ fl. dr.; sublimed sulphur, and hog's lard, of each 11 oz.; mix them. (Bateman's "Cutaneous Diseases.") The nostrum vended under this name is made as follows: Carbonate of potash, 1 oz.; vermilion, 2 dr.; sulphur, 1 lb.; lard, 1½ lbs.; rose water, 3 fl. oz.; oil of bergamot, 1½ dr.

2. Chloride of lime, 1 dr.; rectified spirit, 2 fl. dr.; sweet oil, ½ fl. oz.; common salt and sulphur, of each 1 oz.; soft soap, 2 oz.; oil of lemon, 20 drops. Cheap, effectual and inoffensive.

Ointment of Ivy.—From the leaves of common ivy, by infusion, an ointment of lard. Used as an application to soft corns, in itch, and as a dressing to indolent ulcers and issues.

Ointment of Lard.—Prepared lard, 2 lbs.; melt, add of rose water, 3 fl. oz.; beat the two well together, then set the vessel aside, and when the whole is cold, separate the congealed fat. A simple emollient.

Ointment of Laurel.—1. Suet (softened by heat), 8 oz.; laurel oil (expressed oil of bay), 1 lb.; oil of turpentine, 1½ oz.

2. Fresh bay leaves and berries (bruised), of each 1 lb.; lard, 2 lbs.; as hemlock ointment. Highly esteemed on the continent as a stimulating friction, in bruises, strains, stiff joints, etc.; and in deafness.

3. From fresh bay leaves, 2 lbs.; bay berries, 1 lb.; neat's-foot oil, 5 pints; boil as last; to the strained oil add, of lard suet, 2 lbs.; true oil of bay, ¼ lb., and allow it to cool very slowly, in order that it may "grain" well. Sold for laurel ointment and common oil of bay.

Ointment of Lavender.—Lard, 2½ lbs.; lavender flowers, 10 lbs.; white wax, 8 oz. Melt the lard; digest with 2 lbs. of the flowers for 2 hours, and strain; repeat this with fresh flowers till all are used; melt the ointment and leave it at rest to cool; separate the moisture and dregs, and melt the ointment with the wax.

Mercurial Ointment.—1. Mercury, 1½; prepared lard, 1½; prepared suet, 1; rub together until metallic globules cease to be visible.

2. Mercury, 1 lb.; lard, 11½ oz.; suet, ½ oz.; rub the mercury with the suet and a little of the lard, until globules are no longer visible; then add the remaining lard, and triturate together.

3. Pure mercury and lard, of each 1 lb.; as before.

The mercurial ointment usually sold is made with a less quantity of mercury than that ordered by the colleges, and the color is brought up with finely ground blue black or wood char-

cent. This fraud may be detected by its inferior sp. gr., and by a portion being left undissolved when a little of the ointment is treated first with ether or oil of turpentine, to remove the fat, and then with dilute nitric acid, to remove the mercury.

Mercurial ointment is chiefly used to introduce mercury into the system when the stomach is too irritable to bear it; in syphilis, hepatic affections, hydrocephalus, etc. For this purpose ½ to 1 dram is commonly rubbed into the inside of one of the thighs until every particle of the ointment disappears. This operation is repeated night and morning until the desired effect is produced. This ointment has been employed to prevent the "pitting" in smallpox; and, diluted with 3 or 4 times its weight of lard, in several skin diseases, as a dressing for ulcers, to destroy pediculi, etc. Camphor is often added to this ointment to increase its activity.

Mercurial Ointment (Milder).—Stronger mercurial ointment, 1 lb.; lard, 2 lbs. In itch and several other cutaneous diseases, as a dressing to syphilitic ulcers, to destroy pediculi on the body, etc. Each dram contains 10 grains of mercury.

Ointment of Mustard.—1. Flour of mustard, ¾ oz.; water, 1 fl. oz.; mix, and add, of resin cerate, 2 oz.; oil of turpentine, ½ oz. Rubefacient and stimulant. As a friction in rheumatism, etc.

2. Flour of mustard, 3 oz.; oil of almonds, ½ fl. oz.; lemon juice, q. s. In neuralgia, toothache, etc.

Ointment for Piles.—1. Burnt alum and oxide of zinc, of each ½ dram; lard, 7 drams.

2. Morphia, 8 grains; melted spermaceti ointment, 1 oz.; triturate together until solution is complete, then add, of galls (in impalpable powder), 1½ dr.; essential oil of almonds (genuine crude), 12 to 15 drops, and stir until the mass concretes. In painful piles, prolapsus, etc. It is not only very effective, but does not soil the linen so much as most other ointments.

Simple Ointment.—1. Olive oil, 5½ fl. oz.; white wax, 2 oz.; melted together, and stirred whilst cooling.

2. Prepared lard, 4 lbs.; white wax, 1 lb.; as the last.

3. White wax, 2; prepared lard, 3; almond oil, 3; melt together, and stir till it becomes solid.

The above are mild emollients, useful in healthy ulcers, excoriations, etc., but chiefly as forming the basis for other ointments.

Ointment of Soap (Camphorated).—White soap (scraped), 1 lb.; water, ½ lb.; dissolve by heat; add of olive oil, 5 oz.; and when the mixture has partly cooled, further add of camphor, 1 oz., previously dissolved by heat in olive oil, 1 oz.; lastly, stir until the mass concretes. As an anodyne and stimulating friction in various local affections, as sprains, chilblains, rheumatism, etc.

Ointment of Tar.—1. Tar and suet, of each 1 lb.; melt them together, and press the mixture through a linen cloth.

2. Tar, 5 oz.; beeswax, 2 oz.; melt together, and stir the mixture briskly until it concretes.

3. Tar, ½ pint; yellow wax, 4 oz.; as the last.

Used as detergent applications in ringworm, scald-head, scabby eruptions, foul ulcers, etc. They should be, in general, at first diluted with half their weight of lard or oil.

Ointment of Turpentine.—1. Camphor, 1 dram; oil of turpentine, 1 to 2 fl. drams; dissolve, and add of resin cerate, 1 oz. As a stimulant and anodyne friction in nephritic and rheumatic pains, engorgements, etc.

2. Turpentine, 2 lbs.; simple ointment, 1 lb.; mix by a gentle heat. As a stimulant dressing.

3. Oil of turpentine, 16; camphor, 1; soft soap, 2; dissolve the camphor in the turpentine, add the soap, and rub till thoroughly mixed.

Ointment for Worms.—1. Aloes and ox-gall, of each 1 part; marshmallow ointment, 6 parts.

2. Aloes and oil of tansy, of each 1 part; dried ox-gall, 2 parts (both in fine powder); lard, 8 parts.

3. Aloes, 1 dram; dried ox-gall and petroleum, of each 1½ drams; lard, 1½ oz.

4. Powdered aloes, 2 drams; lard, 1 oz.

The above are purgative and vermifuge, applied as frictions to the abdomen. They are chiefly employed for children and delicate females.

ORANGES.—How to Choose.

The very sweetest orange and richest is the black or rusty-coated fruit. Pick out the dingiest oranges in the box and you will get the best. Another way to choose oranges is by weight. The heaviest is the best, because they have the thinnest skin and more weight of juice. Thick-skin oranges are apt to be dry; they either weigh less because of having so much skin or because of the poverty of the juice in those particular specimens. A slight freezing on the tree causes this condition in otherwise fine fruit. The "kid-glove" oranges are the two varieties of small fruit grown in Florida from stocks respectively brought from China and from Tangiers. They are called "Mandarin" and "Tangerine." They may be eaten without soiling a kid glove, because the skin is loose and the little "gores" or pockets of juice come apart very cleanly and without breaking.

All the above applies to Florida oranges. The Jamaica and Havana oranges are much paler yellow, and their juice is usually of more acid quality.

PAIN EXTRACTOR.

Spirits of ammonia, 1 oz.; laudanum, 1 oz.; oil of origanum, 1 oz.; mutton tallow, ½ lb.; combine the articles with the tallow when it is nearly cool.

PAINT AND PAINTING.

Paints.—The term "paints," in trade, is commonly applied to pigments ground with oil to a thick paste, ready to be "thinned down" with oil or turpentine to a consistence adapted for application with a brush.

Paints are prepared on the small scale by grinding the dry pigments with the oil by means of a stone and muller; on the large scale, they are ground in a color mill. There are several pigments, as king's yellow, Scheele's green, verdigris, white lead, etc., which from their poisonous character cannot be ground safely by hand, except in very small quantities at a time, and then only by the exercise of extreme caution.

In mixing, or thinning down paints for use, it may be useful to mention that for out-door work boiled oil is principally or wholly employed, unless it be for the decorative parts of houses, when a portion of turpentine and pale linseed oil is often added. For in-door work, linseed oil, turpentine, and a little "driers," are generally used in the same way. The smaller the proportion of oil employed for the purpose, the less will be the gloss and the greater the ultimate hardness of the coating. For "flatted white," etc., the color, being ground in oil, requires scarcely any further addition of that article, as the object is to leave it "dead" or dull. The best driers are ground litharge and ground sugar of lead; the first for dark and middle tints, and the last for light ones.

For outside painting avoid yellow colors, or shades in which yellow enters, as sun and weather affect yellow more disastrously than other colors.

To preserve mixed paints in pots from "skinning over" or drying up, they should be kept constantly covered with water, or what is better, with a thin film of linseed oil.

Brushes, when out of use, may be preserved in a similar manner to mixed paints. When dirty, or required for a paint of another color, they may be cleaned with a little oil of turpentine, which may be either preserved for the same purpose another time, or may be allowed to deposit its color and then used to thin down paints as usual. In no case, however, should it be thrown back into the cistern or pan with the pure "turps."

Why Paint Cracks.—Some lay the cracking of paint to absorption of the oil by wood, but this is not correct, for the same material spread upon iron, steel or glass, will crack just the same. Experience teaches that it may arise from three causes—poor material, boiled oil, and applying coats of paint with too little time for drying between them.

Boiled oil will appear to dry very rapidly, and the surface will become glazed over, but beneath this thin hard glaze the paint is only gummed. Where but one coat of paint is applied, there is little, if any, difficulty about cracking; but as there are generally from three to four coats, the paint does not become thoroughly dry on each, although it may appear to be so on the surface. The atmosphere will in time complete the drying, but, as a consequence, the coats dry unevenly and crack by the gradual contractions of the gummy portions beneath. To obviate the trouble, good pigments only should be used, and mixed with raw oil, and then plenty of time given for each separate coat to dry. The hardening may be advanced by the use of drier, but do not put in more than an ounce to the pound. But very little turpentine should be used. Too much drier will cause paint to contract rapidly and form fine checks, which will afterward increase in size.

Flexible Paints.—Take of good yellow soap (cut into slices), 2½ lbs.; boiling water, 1½ gall.; dissolve, and grind the solution whilst hot with good oil paint, 1¼ cwt. Used to paint canvas.

Heat-Proof Paints.—Steam pipes, steam chests, boiler fronts, smoke connections and iron chimneys are often so highly heated that the paint upon them burns, changes color, blisters and often flakes off. After a long protracted use, under varying circumstances, it has been found that a silica-graphite paint is well adapted to overcome these evils. Nothing but boiled linseed oil is required to thin the paint to the desired consistency for application, no dryer being necessary. This paint is applied in the usual manner with an ordinary brush. The color, of course, is black. But another paint, which admits of some variety in color, is mixed by using soapstone, in a state of fine powder, with a quick-drying varnish of great tenacity and hardness. This will give the painted object a seemingly enameled surface which is durable and not affected by heat, acid nor the action of the atmosphere. When applied to wood it prevents rotting, and it arrests disintegration when applied to stone. It is well known that the inside of an iron ship is much more severely affected by corrosion than the outside, and this paint has proven itself to be a most efficient protection from metallic corrosion.

Luminous Paint.—This useful paint may, it is said, be made by the following simple method: Take oyster shells and clean them with warm water; put them into the fire for half an hour; at the end of that time take them out and let them cool. When quite cool pound them fine and take away any gray parts, as they are of no use. Put the powder in a crucible in alternate layers with flour and sulphur. Put on the lid, and cement with sand made into a stiff paste with beer. When dry, put over the fire and bake for an hour. Wait until quite cold before opening the lid. The product ought to be white. You must separate all gray parts, as they are not luminous. Make a sifter in the following manner: Take a pot, put a piece of very fine muslin very loosely across it, tie around with a string, put the powder into the top, and rub about until only the coarse powder remains; open the pot and you will find a very small powder; mix it into a thin paint with gum water, as two thin applications are better than one thick one. This will give a paint that will remain luminous far into the night, provided it is exposed to light during the day.

Paint without Oil or Lead.—In a tub or barrel, which can be closely covered, slake stone lime in boiling water, and then pass 6 quarts of it through a fine sieve. Add to this 1 gallon of water and 1 quart of coarse salt. Boil the mixture and skim it until it is perfectly clear. To every 5 gallons of this add 1 lb. of copperas and 1 lb. of alum. Then slowly and gradually put in ½ lb. of potash and 4 quarts of sifted ashes or fine sand. Add any coloring that is desired.

Cheap Paint for Fences, etc.—Take a bushel of well-burnt lime, white and unslaked; 20 lbs. of Spanish whiting, 17 lbs. of rock salt, and 12 lbs. of brown sugar. Slake the lime, sift out any coarse lumps and mix it into a good whitewash with about 40 gallons of water; then add the other ingredients, stir the whole together thoroughly, and put on 2 or 3 coats with a common brush. This paint makes a coat that does not wash off, or easily rub off, and it looks well, while it will go far to preserve the wood. It is, therefore, especially adapted to the outside of buildings that are exposed to the weather. Three coats are needed on brick and two on wood. If you want to get a fine cream color, add 3 lbs. of yellow ochre to the above. If you prefer a brown color, add 4 lbs. of umber, 1 lb. of Indian red, and 1 lb. of lampblack. If you want a gray or stone color, add 4 lbs. of raw umber and 2 lbs. of lampblack.

Paint for Outbuildings.—Lime, 1 bushel, and water to make a whitewash; mineral paint 60 lbs.; sand dust, 30 lbs.; add oil till it makes a paste, and thin with sweet milk.

A Cheap Paint for Iron Fencing is made by mixing tar and yellow ochre. It will make a good green color, and is excellent for painting rough woodwork and iron.

Painters' Colic.—Make of tartaric acid a syrup similar to that of lemon syrup; add a sufficient quantity of water, and drink 2 or 3 glasses a day.

To Remove Dry Paint.—Make a saturated solution of caustic potash with water; apply to the paint with a swab; after a short time it will be easily removed. Hard putty is removed in the same manner.

To Remove Paint from Clothing.—Apply with a woolen cloth either benzine or spirits of turpentine. The turpentine may afterwards be got rid of by rubbing with a clean piece of cloth, which, if necessary, may be followed up with soap and water or spirits of wine.

To Clean Paint.—Scour with a soft brush, using warm soapsuds; wash off the soap immediately with old flannel dipped in clear water, and wipe dry with a linen or cotton cloth. The water must not be allowed to dry on the paint, as this will make it streaky.

To Remove Paint from Window-Glass.—Rub it well with hot, sharp vinegar.

To Get Rid of Paint Odor.—Place a vessel full of lighted charcoal in the middle of a newly-painted room, and throw on it 2 or 3 handfuls of juniper berries, shut the windows, the chimney and the door close; 24 hours afterwards the room may be opened, when it will be found that the sickly, unwholesome smell will be entirely gone. The smoke of the juniper berry possesses this advantage, that should anything be left in the room, such as tapestry, etc., none of it will be spoiled.

Another way to get rid of the smell of oil paint, let a pailful of water stand in the room newly painted.

Paintings.—*See Oil Paintings.*

PAPER.

The limits of this work preclude the introduction of a description of the manufacture of this well known and most useful article, which is now almost exclusively made by machinery of an elaborate and most ingenious description. We must, therefore, content ourselves with a short notice of a few of the preparations of the manufactured article.

To Test Paper.—The absolute strength is measured by its resistance to tearing. In machine-made paper the strength and stretching power vary according as the force acts lengthwise or across; in hand-made paper there is little difference. In the former the difference is in the proportion of 2 : 3, according to the direction of the tearing force. The stretching power acts inversely to the strength, i. e., is greater across than lengthwise.

In order to test the resistance of paper to the most varied mechanical wear, it is crumpled and kneaded between the hands. After such treatment a weak paper will be full of holes, a strong paper will assume a leathery texture. The test also gives a rough insight into the composition of a paper, much dust showing the presence of earthy impurities, while breaking up of paper shows overbleaching.

The thickness of paper is ascertained either by measuring the thickness of a certain number of sheets, or by taking that of a single sheet by means of a micrometer, where the paper is placed between two rules, one fixed and the other movable, acting as a pointer showing the thickness of the paper on a dial.

Over three per cent of ash shows the presence of clay, kaolin, heavy spar, gypsum, etc.

Microscopical investigation of paper aims at determining the kind and quality of paper. For this a magnifying power of 150 to 300 diameters suffices, when, by coloring the paper with a solution of iodine, a yellow coloration shows the presence of wood fiber, a brown coloration that of linen, cotton or flax, and no coloration that of cellulose.

The determination of the kind and quality of size may be made by boiling in distilled water and adding a concentrated solution of tannic acid, when a flocculent precipitate shows the presence of animal size; and by heating in absolute alcohol and adding distilled water, when a precipitate shows the presence of vegetable size.

Paper in Building.—A correspondent to *Carpentry and Building* says: "With reference to warm houses it is my opinion that we have nothing better or cheaper than paper, especially when it is afforded so cheaply as at present. Under these conditions, no one who builds should complain of a cold house. I used it on the outside of sheeting boards under the siding; also on the roof under the shingles, and under the floor. The first floor, which is used until the house is plastered, is laid with common dressed boards. On top of them is put the paper, and over the paper the floor proper is laid. My method of putting paper between studding is to cut the strips in the center, which leaves it just the right width by bending each edge at right angles. To secure a 'dead' air space, I put on lath next to the sheeting boards and put my paper back to this, holding it in place by lath nailed through the turned edges to the studding. The cold in our houses comes in by cracks in the floor and at the windows and doors. Sash, to work easily, must not work like a glove. In the west we use storm doors and storm windows—that is, double windows, with one light of glass hinged for ventilation. I frequently ask people why they try to make their houses air-tight elsewhere and leave such wind holes at the doors and windows. I advise putting the needless expense of brickwork or back-plastering in the cheaper and better material of paper and extra sash to the windows, to be removed in the springtime. Cut off all drafts of air between the upper and lower stories of the house, and, my word for it, the dwelling will be warm enough for comfort in the midst of a Dakota blizzard."

To Make Paper Fire-Proof.—Dip the paper in a solution of alum and throw over a line to dry. All kinds of paper, as well as textile fabrics, may be treated in this way. Try a slip of paper thus prepared in the flame of a candle, and, if not entirely fire-proof, repeat the operation. To render newspapers fire-proof, dip them into a solution of soluble glass of 25° Baumé; then neutralize the alkali by diluted muriatic acid of 10° Baumé, while hot, and dry by the atmosphere. The texture of the paper cannot then be destroyed by fire.

Copying Paper.—See p. 380.

Lithographic Paper.—Give the paper 3 coats of thin size, 1 coat good white starch, and 1 coat of a solution of gamboge in water; the whole to be applied cold, with a sponge, and each coat to be allowed to dry before the other is applied. The solutions should be freshly made.

Lithographic paper is written on with lithographic ink. The writing is transferred by simply moistening the back of the paper, placing it evenly on the stone, and then applying pressure; a reversed copy is obtained, which, when printed from, yields corrected copies resembling the original writing or drawing. In this way the necessity of executing the writing or drawing in a reversed direction is obviated.

Oiled Paper.—Brush sheets of paper over with "boiled oil," and suspend them on a line till dry. Water-proof. Extensively employed as a cheap substitute for bladder and gut skin to tie over pots and jars, and to wrap up paste blacking, ground white lead, etc.

Paper Parchment.—Plunge unsized paper for a few seconds into sulphuric acid diluted with half to a quarter its bulk of water (this solution being of the same temperature as the air), and afterwards wash with weak ammonia.

A tough substance, resembling animal parchment, and applicable to the same purposes. It is largely used for covering pots of pickles and preserves, and by the chemist for the intervening membrane in experiments in diffusion.

Protective Paper.—Various attempts have from time to time been made to prepare paper which might make the fraudulent alteration of checks and other documents difficult or impossible. These attempts have taken two different directions. The first and best known method consists in printing, in some delicate and easily destroyed color, a complicated pattern or even simple but close and delicate ruling, on the face of the paper. Any reagent which will remove the writing will, of course, destroy the pattern below, and so render the alteration evident. The obvious objection to this method is that it is possible for a skillful forger to replace the printed design before the completion of the alteration.

The other method consists in the introduction into the paper during its manufacture of some substance or mixture of substances which shall strike a characteristic color when chemical agents are applied to the ink.

One of the earliest attempts of this kind was that of Stephenson, who introduced ferrocyanide of potassium into the pulp. When any acid was applied to the writing, Prussian blue was formed with the aid of the iron of the ink. In another process iodide of potassium and starch were introduced into the paper, the application of chlorine then producing a blue stain (iodide of starch), while in a third the pulp was stained with the ingredients of common writing ink.

None of these methods gave, however, any very efficient protection against fraud, for in each case it was tolerably easy to restore the paper to its original condition. But another process which followed upon the others has proved more successful, and, when properly applied, gives a paper which is practically secure. This process was patented, and consists in the introduction into the pulp of ferrocyanide of manganese. When any acid is applied to the writing on this paper the blue stain of Prussian blue appears. This can, it is true, be removed by alkalies, but in that case the manganese is precipitated as the brown peroxide, an effect also produced by bleaching powder. This brown stain can be removed by sulphurous acid, but in that case Prussian blue appears simultaneously, so that the forger has merely a choice between a brown and a blue stain.

When such paper is printed with a delicate design in some fugitive ink (common writing ink would do best), the greatest attainable safety is obtained.

Ferrocyanide of manganese is easily formed by adding to the pulp pure crystallized chloride of manganese and rather more than an equal weight of ferrocyanide of potassium, both in solution.

Tracing Paper.—1. Open a quire of smooth, unsized white paper, and place it flat upon a table, then apply with a clean sash tool to the upper surface of the first sheet a coat of varnish made of equal parts of Canada balsam and oil of turpentine, and hang the prepared sheet across the line to dry; repeat the operation on fresh sheets until the proper quantity is finished. If not sufficiently transparent, a second coat of varnish may be applied as soon as the first has become quite dry.

2. Rub the paper with a mixture of equal parts of nut oil and oil of turpentine, and dry it immediately by rubbing it with wheaten flour; then hang it on a line for 24 hours to dry.

Both the above are used to copy drawings, writing, etc. If washed over with ox-gall and dried, they may be written on with ink or water colors. The first is the whitest and clearest, but the second is the toughest and most flexible.

To Make Paper Transparent.—Dampen any white paper with pure and fresh distilled benzine and it will become transparent, and tracings can be made upon it. As the benzine evaporates, the paper will become opaque again, but if the drawing is not complete dampen the part again until it is finished.

Varnished Paper.—Before proceeding to varnish paper, card-work, pasteboard, etc., it is necessary to give it two or three coats of size, to prevent the absorption of the varnish, and any injury to the color or design. The size may be made by dissolving a little isinglass in boiling water, or by boiling some clean parchment cuttings until they form a clear solution. This, after being strained through a piece of clean muslin, or, for very nice purposes, clarified with a little white of egg, is applied by means of a small clean brush called by painters a sash tool. A light, delicate touch must be adopted, especially for the first coat, lest the ink or colors be started or smothered. When the prepared surface is perfectly dry, it may be varnished in the usual manner.

Value of Waste Paper.—If every one knew the value of paper as fuel I believe it would be but a short time before there would be a demand for every scrap of paper. It makes a better fuel than cordwood, and is handier to start a fire of either hard or soft coal. The small scraps should be rolled up very tightly in bundles of 10 or 12 inches, and then rolled in old newspapers, two, three or more, as may be at hand, the ends to be twisted securely, so they will remain intact until placed in the stove or fireplace. Two or three such rolls of paper cordwood will burn steadily to prepare a meal or give warmth and comfort to the fireside. You have read of twisted hay for fuel used on the frontiers where fuel is scarce; twisted paper will double discount it. In the interest of clean streets, as well as economy, I hope this experiment will be adopted.

Packing Paper.—A packing paper impermeable to water may be made as follows: Take unsized paper and soak it with an aqueous solution of dextrine. When dry apply a layer of siccative oil paint.

PAPER-HANGING.

In choosing paper for a room, avoid that which has a variety of colors, or a large, showy figure, as no furniture can appear to advantage with such. Large-figured papering makes a small room look smaller, but, on the contrary, a paper covered with a small pattern makes a room look larger, and a striped paper, the stripes running from ceiling to floor, makes a low room look higher.

Those who do their own paper-hanging will find that if they follow the paper-hanger's example in cutting two rolls at a time into the desired lengths there will be no waste. After the first matching of figures at the beginning of the rolls no more matching is to be done. One has only to use a piece from each roll alternately. It is a good plan to cut up two rolls at a time and arrange the pieces alternately before pasting.

Cover the walls with a coating of good glue size, made of ½ lb. of glue in a gallon of water, or a coating of good paste, put on and allowed to dry before the paper is hung. Unless this is done the wall will absorb the paste so rapidly that, before drying, there will be too little paste on the surface to hold the paper. When the wall has been whitewashed it should first be scratched with a stiff brush, to remove every particle of loose lime from the surface, and then thoroughly swept down with a broom.

To Clean Paper-Hangings.—Put a clean, soft bag, or an old pillowcase over a new broom, and gently brush the dust from the paper; then take crusts of stale baker's bread, and wipe it down lightly, beginning at the top. If you rub it, the dirt will adhere to the paper. After thus brushing all around the upper part of the walls with the bread, begin just above where you left off, and go round again. Do thus until you have finished the paper. The dust and crumbs will fall together. Whenever a room is cleaned it is a good way, before the paint and windows are washed, to wipe the paper with a covered broom as above directed.

Damp Walls.—The following method is recommended to prevent the effect of damp walls on paper in rooms: Cover the damp part with a varnish formed of naphtha and shellac, in the proportion of ¼ lb. of the latter to a quart of the former. The smell of the mixture is unpleasant, but it wears off in a short time, and the wall is covered with a hard coating utterly impervious to damp, and to which the wall-paper can be attached in the usual way.

To Remove Stains from Wall-Paper.—The soiling caused by persons leaning their heads against a papered wall may be greatly lessened, if not obliterated, by laying a sheet of blotting paper upon the spot and passing over it a moderately warm flat-iron. A slight disfigurement of this kind may sometimes be removed by rubbing it lightly with a soft rag dipped in prepared chalk. Rubbing the spot gently with the soft edge of a thick slice of stale wheat bread will sometimes prove efficacious in such a case; the surface of the bread should be cut away as soon as it becomes soiled. Dust off the crumbs lightly with a soft cloth or brush.

PAPIER MACHÉ.

Pulped paper moulded into forms. It possesses great strength and lightness. It may be rendered partially waterproof by the addition of sulphate of iron, quicklime and glue or white of egg to the pulp; and incombustible by the addition of borax and phosphate of soda. The papier maché tea trays, waiters, snuff-boxes, etc., are prepared by pasting or glueing sheets of paper together, and then submitting them to powerful pressure, by which the composition acquires the hardness of board when dry. Such articles are afterward japanned, and are then perfectly waterproof.

PASTE—Adhesive.

Paste for Scrap Books.—Take ½ teaspoonful of starch, same of flour, pour on a little boiling water, let it stand a minute, add more water, stir and cook it until it is thick enough to starch a shirt bosom. It spreads smooth, sticks well, and will not mold or discolor paper. Starch alone will make a very good paste.

Paste for Printing Office.—Take 2 gallons of cold water, and 1 quart of wheat flour, rub out all the lumps, then add ¼ lb. of finely pulverized alum, and boil the mixture for 10 minutes, or until a thick consistency is reached. Now add 1 quart of hot water, and boil again until the paste becomes a pale brown color, and thick. The paste should be well stirred during both processes of cooking. Paste thus made will keep sweet for two weeks and prove very adhesive.

Paste to Fasten Cloth to Wood.—Take a plump pound of wheat flour, 1 tablespoonful of powdered resin, 1 tablespoonful of finely powdered alum, and rub the mixture in a suitable vessel, with water, to a uniform, smooth paste;

transfer this to a small kettle over a fire, and stir until the paste is perfectly homogeneous without lumps. As soon as the mass has become so stiff that the stirrer remains upright in it, transfer it to another vessel and cover it up so that no skin may form on its surface.

This paste is applied in a very thin layer to the surface of the table; the cloth, or leather, is then laid and pressed upon it, and smoothed with a roller. The ends are cut off after drying. If leather is to be fastened on, this must first be moistened with water. The paste is then applied, and the leather rubbed smooth with a cloth.

Acid-Proof Paste.—A paste formed by mixing powdered glass with a concentrated solution of silicate of soda makes an excellent acid-proof cement.

A Strong Paste.—A paste that will neither decay nor become mouldy. Mix good clean flour with cold water into a thick paste well blended together, then add boiling water, stirring well up until it is of a consistency that can be easily and smoothly spread with a brush; add to this a spoonful or two of brown sugar, a little corrosive sublimate, and about ½ dozen drops of oil of lavender, and you will have a paste that will hold with wonderful tenacity.

A Perpetual Paste is a paste that may be made by dissolving an ounce of alum in a quart of warm water. When cold, add as much flour as will make it the consistency of cream, then stir into it ½ teaspoonful of powdered resin, and 2 or 3 cloves. Boil it to a consistency of mush, stirring all the time. It will keep for 12 months, and when dry may be softened with warm water.

A Brilliant Paste.—A brilliant and adhesive paste, adapted to fancy articles, may be made by dissolving casein precipitated from milk by acetic acid and washed with pure water in a saturated solution of borax.

Paste for Papering Boxes.—Boil water and stir in batter of wheat or rye flour. Let it boil 1 minute, take off and strain through a colander. Add, while boiling, a little glue or powdered alum. Do plenty of stirring while the paste is cooling, and make of a consistency that will spread nicely.

Paper and Leather Paste.—Cover 4 parts, by weight, of glue, with 15 parts of cold water, and allow it to soak for several hours, then warm moderately till the solution is perfectly clear, and dilute with 60 parts of boiling water, intimately stirred in. Next prepare a solution of 30 parts of starch in 200 parts of cold water, so as to form a thin, homogeneous liquid, free from lumps, and pour the boiling glue solution into it with thorough stirring, and at the same time keep the mass boiling.

A Sugar Paste.—In order to prevent the gum from cracking, to 10 parts, by weight, of gum arabic and 3 parts of sugar, add water until the desired consistency is obtained. If a very strong paste is required, add a quantity of flour equal in weight to the gum, without boiling the mixture. The paste improves in strength when it begins to ferment.

Paste that will Adhere to any Substance.—Dissolve 720 gr. sugar of lead and 720 gr. alum, in water; then dissolve 2½ oz. gum arabic in 2 quarts warm water. Mix the gum water, when cold, with 1 lb. wheat flour, till of a pasty consistence; place the mixture in a dish on the fire, and pour into it the alum and sugar of lead. Shake well; take it off the fire when it shows signs of ebullition, and let it cool. If the paste is too thick, add gum water till in proper consistence.

Flour Paste.—One gill flour, 1 gill cold water, 2 gills boiling water. Pour the cold water slowly on the flour, stirring well; then stir in the boiling water, and let the paste boil until as thick as desired.

To Fasten Cloth on Wooden Surfaces.—Wheat flour, 2½ lbs.; resin (powdered), ½ oz.; alum, ½ oz.; water, sufficient. Rub together until a uniform paste is formed, transfer to a small kettle over a fire, heat and stir until the lumps are all dissolved and the paste becomes stiff; transfer to another vessel and cover up. This paste is applied in a thin layer to the surface of the wood to be covered; the cloth is then laid on and smoothed with a roller.

PASTE BLACKING.

Half pound ivory black, ½ lb. molasses, ½ oz. powdered alum, 1 dram turpentine, 1 oz. sulphuric acid, 2 oz. raw linseed oil. The ivory black and molasses must first be mixed together until thoroughly incorporated, then add the rest of the ingredients. It keeps best in a bladder.

PASTES.

Vitreous compounds made in imitation of the gems and precious stones. Like enamels, the artificial gems have for their basis a very fusible, highly transparent and brilliant, dense glass, which is known under the name of "frit," "paste," "strass," "flux," "fondant," or "Mayence base," and which, in its state of greatest excellence, constitutes the "artificial diamond."

Amethyst.—Paste or strass, 500 gr.; oxide of manganese, 8 gr.; oxide of cobalt, 24 gr.

Beryl.—Strass, 3,456 gr.; glass of antimony, 24 gr.; oxide of cobalt, 1½ gr.

Carbuncle.—See *Garnet.*

Chrysolite.—From strass, 7,000 gr.; pure calcined sesquioxide of iron ("crocus martis"), 65 gr.

Carnelian.—1. (Red.) From strass, 7,000 gr.; glass of antimony, 3,500 gr.; calcined peroxide of iron, 875 gr.; binoxide of manganese, 75 gr.

2. (White.) From strass, 7,000 gr.; calcined bones, 250 gr.; washed yellow ocher, 65 gr.

Diamond.—1. From rock crystal (purest), 1,000 gr.; borax, 500 gr.; carbonate of lead (pure), 3,200 gr.; oxide of manganese, 1/8 to 1 gr.; powder each separately, mix them together, fuse the mixture in a clean crucible, pour the melted mass into water, separate any reduced lead, and again powder and remelt the mass.

2. (Yellow diamond.) Strass, 500 gr.; glass of antimony, 10 gr.

Emerald.—1. From strass, 7,000 gr.; carbonate of copper, 55 gr.; glass of antimony, 7 gr.

2. Paste, 960 gr.; glass of antimony, 42 gr.; oxide of cobalt, 1½ gr.

Garnet.—1. Paste or strass, 1,200 gr.; glass of antimony, 580 gr.; purple of cassius and binoxide of manganese, of each 5 gr.

2. Paste, 513 gr.; glass of antimony, 265 gr.; purple of cassius and oxide of manganese, of each 2 gr.

3. (Vinegar garnet.) From paste, 7,000 gr.; glass of antimony, 3,450 gr.; calcined peroxide of iron, 58 gr.

Lapis Lazuli.—From paste, 7,000 gr.; calcined bone or bones, 570 gr.; oxides of cobalt and manganese, of each 24 gr. The golden veins are produced by painting them on the pieces with a mixture of gold powder, borax and gum water, and then gently heating them until the borax fuses.

Opal.—1. From strass, 960 gr.; calcined bones, 48 gr.

2. Paste, 1 oz.; horn silver, 10 gr.; calcined magnetic ore, 2 gr.; absorbent earth (calcined bones), 26 gr.

Ruby.—1. Paste, 15 parts; binoxide of manganese, 1 part.

2. Paste, 1 lb.; purple of cassius, 3 drams.

Sapphire.—From strass, 3,600 gr.; oxide of cobalt, 50 gr.; oxide of manganese, 11 gr.

Topaz.—From strass, 1,066 gr.; glass of antimony, 44 gr.; purple of cassius, 1 gr.

Turquoise.—From blue paste, 20 to 24 parts; calcined bones, 1 part.

It is absolutely necessary for the successful application of the preceding formulæ that the substances employed should be perfectly free from impurities, more particularly those of a mineral kind. The litharge, oxide of lead and carbonate of lead, above all things, must be entirely free from oxide of tin, as the smallest particle of that substance may impart a "milkiness" to the paste. All the ingredients must be separately reduced to powder, and, after being mixed, sifted through lawn. The fusion must be carefully conducted and continuous, and the melted mass should be allowed to cool very slowly, after having been left in the fire from 24 to 30 hours, at the least. Hessian crucibles are preferred for this purpose, and the heat of an ordinary pottery or porcelain kiln is sufficient in most cases; but a small wind-furnace, devoted exclusively to the purpose, is, in general, more convenient. It is found that the more tranquil, continuous and uniform the fusion, the denser and clearer is the paste, and the greater its refractive power and beauty.

The following method of obtaining artificial rubies and emeralds, first pointed out by Hoediger, is exceedingly simple and inexpensive, and deserves the serious attention of those interested in this ingenious art: Recently precipitated and well-washed hydrate of aluminum is moistened with a few drops of neutral chromate of potassium, and kneaded so that the mass assumes a tinge scarcely perceptible; it is then rolled up into small sticks, about the thickness of a finger, and slowly dried, taking the precaution to fill the fissures (if any) that form during desiccation with fresh hydrate of aluminum. When perfectly dry, and after having been submitted to a gentle heat, one end of these sticks is brought into the termination of the flame of an oxygen-hydrogen blowpipe, until a portion of the mass is fused into a small globule. After the lapse of a few minutes, several minute balls form, having a diameter of some millimeters, and of such intense hardness that quartz, glass, topaz and granite may be easily and perceptibly scratched with them. These, when cut and polished, appear, however, slightly opaque. By employing nitrate of nickel in lieu of chromate of potassium, green-colored globules, closely resembling the emerald, are obtained.

By the substitution of oxide of chromium for chromate of potassium, Mr. Cooley produced factitious gems of considerable hardness and beauty, though slightly opaque in some portion of the mass. The addition of a very little silica prevented, in a great measure, this tendency to opacity.

It may be observed that the beauty of pastes of factitious gems, and especially the brilliancy of mock diamonds, is greatly depending upon the cutting, setting-up and the skillful arrangement of the foil or tinsel behind them.

PEAS—Green, to Keep.

Pick and shell the peas and lay them on dishes or tins in a cool oven or before a bright fire. Do not heap them, and stir them frequently, so as to dry gradually. When they are hard, let them cool and pack them in stone jars. Cover them up closely, but, when wanted for use, take them out, soak them in cold water until plump. Then they are ready for boiling.

PICKLES—To Detect Copper in.

Take small pieces of the pickle and put them into a bottle in which is a little ammonia, diluted with half its quantity of water. Shake it all up well, and if there is any copper present the liquid will turn blue.

PICTURE FRAMES—To Clean.

Gilded frames can be cleaned by gently wiping them with a fine cotton cloth dipped in sweet oil. Be careful to rub very gently, as violent friction will be sure to scratch the gilding.

To Keep Flies Off.—Boil a few onions in a pint of water, and apply the liquid to the frames with a brush.

To Make Picture Nails Hold.—Sometimes a good deal of trouble is experienced in getting nails to hold in a plastered wall just where they should be to allow the pictures to hang at a given point, or exactly between two casings. If neither nail or screw can be driven to hold, make the hole by use of a gimlet larger than is required for the nail; then fill the hole with plaster of Paris wet with salt water, and insert a screw by turning it carefully in, then finish the job with a pocket knife blade, forcing in as much plaster as possible; but do the work rapidly, as the plaster will set quickly and hold firmly.

PILE OINTMENT.

Powdered nutgall, 2 drams; camphor, 1 dram; melted wax, 1 oz.; tincture of opium, 2 drams. Mix.

PLASTERS.

Plasters are external applications that possess sufficient consistency not to adhere to the fingers when cold, but which become soft and adhesive at the temperature of the human body.

In the preparation of plasters the heat of a water bath or of steam should alone be employed. On the large scale, well-cleaned and polished copper or tinned-copper pans, surrounded with iron jackets, supplied with high-pressure steam, are used for this purpose. The resins and gum resins that enter into their composition are previously purified by straining. After the ingredients are mixed, and the mass has acquired sufficient consistency by cooling, portions of it are taken into the hands, anointed with a little olive oil, and well pulled or worked until it becomes solid enough to admit of being formed into rolls.

Plasters are preserved by enveloping the rolls with paper, to exclude the air as much as possible, and by keeping them in a cool situation. A few, as those of belladonna and ammoniacum with mercury, are commonly placed in pots. When kept for any length of time, they are all more or less apt to become hard and brittle, and to lose their color. When this is the case, they should be remelted by a gentle heat, and sufficient oil added to the mass to restore it to a proper consistency.

The operation of spreading plasters for use requires skill and experience on the part of the operator. Various textures are employed for the purpose, of which linen or cotton cloth, or leather, are those most generally employed. Silk and satin are used for "court plaster." The shape and size must be regulated by the parts to which they are to be applied.

Plaster of Aconite.—Gently evaporate tincture of aconite to the consistency of a soft extract, then spread a very small portion over the surface of a common adhesive plaster, on either calico or leather. Mr. Curtis has strongly recommended this plaster in neuralgia. A little of the alcoholic extract may be employed instead of that obtained fresh from the tincture.

Ammoniacal Plaster.—Take of lead plaster, 1 oz.; white soap (almond form), ½ oz.; melt them together, and, when nearly cold, add of sal ammoniac (in fine powder), 1 dr. Stimulant and rubefacient. Its efficacy depends on the gradual extraction of free ammonia by the decomposition of the sal ammoniac, on which account it is proper to renew the application of it every 24 hours.

Arnica Plaster.—Alcoholic extract of arnica, 1½ oz.; resin plaster, 3 oz. Add the extract to the plaster, previously melted over a water bath, and mix it thoroughly.

Aromatic Plaster.—Strained frankincense, 3 oz.; beeswax, ½ oz.; melt them together, and when the mass has considerably cooled, add of powdered cinnamon, 6 drams; oils of allspice and lemon, of each 2 drams. Stimulant; applied over the stomach in dyspepsia, spasms, nausea, flatulence, etc. Camphor, 1 dram, is commonly added.

Plaster of Belladonna.—1. Soap plaster, 3 oz.; melt it by the heat of a water bath; add of extract of belladonna (deadly nightshade), 3 oz., and keep constantly stirring the mixture until it acquires a proper consistency.

2. Resin plaster, 3 oz.; extract of belladonna, 1½ oz.; as the last.

3. Resin plaster, 2 oz.; extract of belladonna, 1 oz.

4. Extract of belladonna, 3; resin plaster, 5; rectified spirit, 6. Rub the extract and spirit together in a mortar, and when the insoluble matter has subsided, decant the clear solution, remove the spirit by distillation or evaporation, and mix the alcoholic extract thus obtained with the resin plaster melted at the heat of a water bath, continuing the heat until with constant stirring the plaster has acquired a suitable consistency.

A powerful anodyne and anti-spasmodic; in neuralgia and rheumatic pains, and as an application to painful tumors. The plasters ordinarily sold are usually deficient in extract.

Corn Plaster.—1. Resin plaster, 5 parts; melt, stir in of sal ammoniac (in fine powder), 1 part, and at once spread it on linen or soft leather.

2. (Kennedy's.) Pure beeswax, 1 lb.; Venice turpentine, 3 oz.; verdigris (in fine powder), 1½ oz.; mixed by a gentle heat, and spread on cloth. It is cut into pieces and polished, and of these 4 dozen are put into each box.

3. (Le Forest.) Galbanum plaster, 2 oz.; melt by a very gentle heat; add sal ammoniac and saffron, of each ½ oz.; powdered camphor, 2 oz.; and, when nearly cold, stir in of liquor of ammonia, 2 oz. Applied, spread on leather, to the corn only, as it will blister the thinner skin surrounding its base.

4. Galbanum plaster, 1 oz.; pitch, ½ oz.; lead plaster, 2 drams; melt them together, and add verdigris and sal ammoniac (in fine powder), of each 1 dram.

Court Plaster.—See p. 281.

Mahy's Plaster.—Carbonate of lead (pure white lead), 1 lb.; olive oil, 32 fl. oz.; water, q. s. Boil them together, constantly stirring until perfectly incorporated; then add of yellow wax, 4 oz.; lead plaster, 1½ lb.; and when these are melted and the mass somewhat cooled, stir in of powdered orris root, 6 oz. A favorite application to inflamed and excoriated surfaces, bed sores, burns, etc.

Plaster of Mustard.—This is always an extemporaneous preparation. Flour of mustard is made into a stiff paste with lukewarm water, or with vinegar, and is then spread on a piece of calico or linen (folded two or three times); over the surface of the mustard is placed a piece of gauze or thin muslin, and the plaster is then applied to the part of the body it is intended to medicate. Its action is that of a powerful rubefacient and counter-irritant; but its application should not be continued long, unless in extreme cases. Its effects are often apparently wonderful. We have seen very severe cases of facial neuralgia, sore throat, painful joints, rheumatic pains, etc., relieved in a few minutes by means of a mustard plaster or "poultice."

Plaster of Soap.—1. To lead plaster, 3 lbs., melted by a slow heat, add of castile soap, sliced, ½ lb., resin, 1 oz., both (also) liquefied by heat, and, constantly stirring, evaporate to a proper consistency.

2. To litharge plaster, 4 oz., gum plaster, 2 oz., melted together, add of castile soap, in shavings, 1 oz., and boil a little.

3. To litharge plaster, 2½ lbs., melted over a gentle fire, add of castile soap, in powder, 4 oz., and heat them together (constantly stirring) until they combine.

4. Hard soap (in powder), 6; lead plaster, 36; resin (in powder), 1; to the lead plaster, previously melted, add the soap and the resin, first liquefied; then, constantly stirring, evaporate to a proper consistency.

Care must be taken to evaporate all the moisture from the above compounds, as, if any is left in the plaster, it turns out crumbly and does not keep well. Much heat discolors it. Soap plaster is emollient and resolvent, and is used to abrasions and excoriations, and as a dressing to soft corns, lymphatic tumors, etc.

Vermifuge Plaster.—From powdered aloes, 1 dram; oil of chamomile, 10 drops; croton oil, 2 drops; oil of turpentine, q. s.

PLASTER—To Fill Cracks in.

Use vinegar instead of water to mix your plaster of Paris. The resultant mass will be like putty, and will not "set" for 20 or 30 minutes, whereas, if you use water, the plaster will become hard almost immediately, before you have time to use it. Push it into the cracks and smooth it off nicely with a table knife.

PLATE.

This name is commonly given to gold and silver wrought into instruments or utensils for domestic use. The cleaning of plate is an important operation in a large establishment, as its durability, and much of its beauty, depend on this being properly done. The common practice of using mercurial plate powder is destructive to both of these, as mercury not only rapidly abrades the surface of silver, but renders it soft, and, in extreme cases, even brittle. The only powder that may be safely used for silver is prepared chalk, of the best quality. For gold, the form of red oxide of iron, known as "jeweler's rouge," is the most useful and appropriate.

Mr. Spon recommends the following: "Take an ounce of cream of tartar, common salt and alum, and boil in a gallon or more of water. After the plate is taken out and rubbed dry, it puts on a beautiful silvery whiteness. Powdered magnesia may be used dry for articles slightly tarnished, but if very dirty it must be used first wet and then dry."

Chamois leather, a plate-brush or very soft woolen rags should alone be used to apply them, and their application should be gentle and long continued, rather than the reverse. Dirty plate, after being cleaned with boiling water, may be restored by boiling it in water each quart of which contains a few grains of carbonate of soda and about an ounce of prepared chalk, calcined hartshorn, or cuttle-fish bone, in very fine powder. The ebullition sets up a gentle friction, which effects its purpose admirably. The boiled plate, after being dried, is best "finished off" with a piece of soft leather or woolen cloth which has been dipped into the cold mixture of chalk and water and then dried. The same method answers admirably with German silver, brass, pewter, and all the softer metals.

PLATING.

The act of covering copper and other metals with either silver or gold.

Plating is performed in various ways. Sometimes the silver is fused onto the surface of the copper by means of a solution of borax, and subsequent exposure in the "plating furnace;" and the compound ingot is then rolled to the requisite thinness between cylinders of polished steel. The common thickness of the silver plate before rolling is equal to about the 1-40th of that of the compound ingot. Sometimes the nobler metal is precipitated from its solution upon the copper by the action of chemical affinity, or more frequently by the agency of electro-chemical decomposition (electro-plating).

The metal employed for plating is a mixture of copper and brass, annealed or hardened, as the case may require. For electro-plated goods, "nickel silver" is now almost invariably employed.

PLOWS.—To Clean Rusty.

Take a quart of water and pour slowly into it ½ pint sulphuric acid. (The mixture will become quite warm from chemical action, and this is the reason why the acid should be poured slowly into water, rather than the water into the acid.) Wash the mould-board (or any other iron that is rusty) with this weak acid, and let it remain on the iron until it evaporates; then wash it once more. The object is to give time for the acid to dissolve the rust. Then wash with water and you will see where the worst rusty spots are. Apply some more acid, and rub those spots with a brick. The acid and scouring will remove most of the rust. Then wash the mould-board thoroughly with water, to remove all the acid, and rub it dry. Brush it over with petroleum or other oil, and let it be until spring. When you go to plowing, take a bottle of the acid water to the field, and apply it frequently to any spots of rust that may remain. The acid and the scouring of the earth will soon make it very bright and smooth.

POLISH.

To Polish Sundry Surfaces.—For ivory, prepared chalk, applied rapidly with chamois leather. For pearl, a paste of powdered rotten-stone and olive oil, thinned with oil of vitriol and applied with cork covered with velvet. For jewelry, spirits of wine and powdered French chalk. For marble, sand, then emery powder, and lastly putty powder. For horn, scrape with emery powder and water, finishing with jeweler's rouge.

Black Polish for Iron.—To obtain that beautiful deep black polish on iron or steel which is so much sought after, boil 1 part of sulphur in 10 parts of oil of turpentine, the product of which is a brown sulphuric oil of disagreeable smell. This should be put on the outside as lightly as possible, and heated over a spirit lamp till the required black polish is obtained.

A Brilliant Polish for Stoves.—Mix a teaspoonful of lye with the polish, and the use of this will give a brilliant and permanent luster to the stove.

Banana Polish for Russet Shoes.—One of the drawbacks to the wearing of russet shoes is the fact that they so easily take on a rusty look. An easy scheme for keeping them clean and bright is given by one whose own foot-gear testifies to the value of his plan. He says: "With a piece of nice ripe banana I can not only keep russet shoes clean, but can keep them polished as well. I simply take a piece of banana and grease the leather with it and then polish it with a cloth. In this way all the discolorations are removed and a polish is obtained."

French Polish Dressing for Leather.—Mix 2 pints best vinegar with 1 pint soft water; stir into it ¼ lb. of glue, broken up, ½ lb. logwood chips, ¼ oz. finely-powdered indigo, ¼ oz. of the best soft soap, ¼ oz. isinglass; put the mixture over the fire and let it boil 10 minutes or more;

then strain, bottle and cork. When cold, it is fit for use. Apply with a sponge.

Furniture Polish.—1. White wax, 3 parts; resin, 2 parts; true Venice turpentine, ½ pint; melt at a gentle heat. The warm mass, completely melted, is poured into a stone jar, agitated, and 6 parts of rectified oil of turpentine added thereto. After 24 hours the mass, having the consistency of soft butter, is ready for use. Before using the paste the furniture should be washed with soap and water, and then well dried.

2. Oil of turpentine, 1 pint; alkanet root, ½ oz.; digest until sufficiently colored, then add of beeswax (scraped small), 4 oz.; put the vessel into hot water, and stir until the mixture is complete, then put it into pots. If wanted pale, the alkanet root should be omitted.

3. (White.) White wax, 1 lb.; solution of potassa, ½ gallon; boil to a proper consistency.

French Polish Rubber.—Take a strip of thick woolen cloth that has been torn off so as to form a soft elastic edge, and roll it up so as to form a coil from 1 to 2 inches in diameter. The cloth must be prevented from unrolling by binding it securely with thread.

POP CORN.

To pop corn have a hot fire; put enough corn in popper to almost cover bottom one kernel deep, and shake over fire. It improves the flavor to continue shaking over the fire a little while after the grains are popped.

To Sugar Corn.—For 8 quarts of popped corn take 1 lb. of granulated sugar, 1 teacupful of water; boil until syrup "strings," or forms soft ball in cold water; pour over corn and stir with wooden ladle until syrup sugars. Vanilla or other flavoring may be added to syrup just before pouring over corn.

To Make Chocolate Corn.—Proceed same as for sugar corn, adding to syrup while cooking 4 oz. best chocolate. (One cup of fresh grated cocoanut may be substituted for the chocolate.)

To Make Corn Balls.—For 8 quarts of popped corn take 1 quart molasses and ½ cup sugar. Don't add water. Boil syrup until it hardens (not brittle) in water. The last thing, add ½ teaspoonful soda to improve color. Pour over corn, mix well, and make into balls. If no molasses be used, 2 cups of sugar, adding water, are requisite for above-named quantity of corn.

POTATOES.

Increasing the Potato Yield.—A remarkable series of experiments made by a French scientific agriculturist in the cultivation of potatoes has given astonishing results. In one instance he obtained a yield of not less than 42 tons of tubers per acre. He selected the best and soundest seed potatoes, ploughed the land very deeply and manured it heavily. He also steeped the potatoes for 24 hours in a solution made by dissolving 6 lbs. of saltpeter and 6 lbs. of sulphate of ammonia in 25 gallons of water; then he allowed them to drain and stand for 24 hours for their buds to swell before planting them.

To Destroy Potato Bugs.—The only sure remedy appears to be Paris green, which should be mixed with 5 or 6 times the quantity of meal, flour, ashes, or calcined plaster and lime.

Frozen Potatoes.—Potatoes that have been affected by frost should be laid in a perfectly dark place for some days after the thaw has commenced. If thawed in open day, they rot; but if in darkness, they do not rot, and they lose very little of their natural properties.

To Prevent Potato Rot.—Soon after hoeing the second time sow unbleached ashes over the field. Do this weekly 6 or 7 times, using 2 or 3 bushels to the acre.

Potatoes Preserved by Peat Charcoal.—When potatoes are slightly diseased, sprinkling peat charcoal among them instantly stops the rot, takes away the bad smell, and renders them sweet and wholesome food. Potatoes may be kept in this way two years, and when planted the third they will produce a good crop. The charcoal will also prevent the sound potatoes from being infected by the diseased ones. The charcoal may be mixed with other manures when the potatoes are removed.

To Keep Potatoes.—They should not be exposed to the sun and light more than is absolutely necessary after digging. Dig them when dry, and put them in a dark cellar. To keep potatoes intended for table use from sprouting until new potatoes grow, take boiling water, pour into a tub, turn in as many potatoes as the water will cover, then pour off all the water, handle the potatoes carefully, laying up in a dry place on boards, only one layer deep. You will thus have good potatoes all the year round, without the hard strings and watery ends caused by growing.

POULTICES.

External applications, generally extemporaneous, used to promote suppuration, allay pain and inflammation, resolve tumors, etc.

Poultices are generally prepared with substances capable of absorbing much water, and assuming a pulpy consistency, so as to admit of their application to any surface, however irregular. Their curative action principally depends upon the liquids with which they are moistened, and the heat retained by the mass. With this object they should never be heavy or very bulky, and should be frequently renewed, and lightly, but securely, bandaged on, to prevent displacement.

The addition of a little lard, olive oil, or, still better, glycerine, to a poultice, tends greatly to promote its emollient action, and to retard its hardening.

As the continued medication of the part with warmth and moisture, or with substances applied in the moist way, is the principal object to be attained in the application of poultices, a fold or two of lint or soft linen dipped in hot water, either simple or medicated, and covered with a thin sheet of rubber cloth, to prevent evaporation, may be often conveniently applied in their stead.

Poultice of Alum.—Alum (in powder), 1 dr.; white of 2 eggs; shake them together until they form a coagulum. Applied, between the folds of fine linen, to chilblains, sore nipples, inflamed eyes, etc.

Anodyne Poultice.—Poppy heads, 1 oz.; dried leaves of henbane, 2 oz.; water, 24 oz. Boil, strain, and add to the liquor 4 oz. of emollient seeds, to form a poultice.

Antiseptic Poultice.—Barley flour, 6 oz.; powdered Peruvian bark, 1 oz.; water, q. s. Boil, and, when cool enough, add camphor in powder, 1 dr.

Poultice of Belladonna.—Extract of belladonna, made in vacuo, 1 dr.; oatmeal, ¼ lb.; boiling water, q. s.

Bran Poultice.—Fine bran, with one-sixth of linseed meal, made into a poultice with boiling water.

Bread Poultice.—From crumbs of bread, soaked in hot water, slightly pressed, and then beaten up with a little lard, butter or oil. Emollient.

Linseed Poultice.—1. To boiling water, ½ pint, add, gradually, constantly stirring, of linseed meal, 4½ oz., or q. s. Emollient. Used to promote the suppuration or "ripening" of tumors. A little oil or lard should be added, and some smeared over the surface as well, to prevent its getting hard. For small "gatherings," as of the fingers, a little chewed bread and butter is an efficient and convenient substitute.

2. Linseed meal, 4; olive oil, ½; boiling water, 10; mix the linseed meal with the oil, add the water gradually, constantly stirring.

NOTE: Linseed meal prepared from the cake, from which the oil has been expressed, is less adapted for poultices than that prepared from the unpressed, whole seed.

Fig Poultice.—A dried fig, roasted or boiled (sometimes in milk), is frequently applied to gum boils, etc.

Mustard Poultice.—1. Linseed meal and powdered mustard, of each 2½ oz., or q. s.; boiling water, ½ pint; mix as before.

2. As the last, but substituting boiling vinegar for water. Used as a powerful counter-irritant, stimulant and rubefacient; in low fevers, apoplexy, coma, etc., where there is a determination of blood to the head; in deep-seated inflammatory pains, neuralgic pains, etc. It should not be left on long enough to raise a blister. See *Plasters.*

Onion Poultice.—Onions roasted and mashed.

Potato Poultice.—From the raw potato, scraped or grated fine. A popular application to fresh bruises, extravasations, burns, scalds, etc.

Roasted Apple Poultice.—The soft pulp of roasted apple, applied to inflamed eyes. Other ingredients are sometimes added.

Simple Poultice.—Powder for a cataplasm and boiling water, of each q. s. to form a poultice, the surface of which is to be smeared over with olive oil. Emollient. Bread poultice and linseed-meal poultice are now generally called by this name.

Turpentine Poultice.—Oil of turpentine, 2 drams; olive oil, 1 oz.; linseed meal, 1 oz.; oatmeal, 4 oz.; boiling water, q. s. To indolent ulcers, and, with more turpentine, to deep burns, scalds and chilblains.

POULTRY.

The following rules are observed on the large poultry farms, and will be found of value:

1. Feed at regular hours.
2. Clean the roosts daily.
3. Make new nests each week, and burn up the old ones.
4. Pour kerosene over the roosts once a week in summer, and once a month in winter.
5. Whitewash the interior four times a year.
6. Scatter air-slaked lime over the floor and dropping-boards each week.
7. Remove all the fowls that show signs of sickness at once to separate quarters.
8. Scald out the drinking-fountains once a month.
9. Fatten for marketing purposes all hens that have passed their third season on the farm.
10. Hatch the pullets, for fall laying, during the months of March, April and May.
11. Begin the incubators for broilers from October to March.

Hints about Feeding.—While it is essential to be careful not to overfeed, the extreme of underfeeding must be avoided. It isn't the gross amount of feed, but the mode in which it is distributed, that tells to the best advantage.

A variety of diet for fowls is a very important matter to be remembered by poultry-keepers, both on the score of economy and the best good of the fowls.

In winter season give a warm breakfast of scalded meal and mashed potatoes, seasoned with a little salt and pepper, which helps to keep the fowls in healthy condition. At noon a little wheat, or wheat and oats mixed; at night a little corn. Occasionally some butcher scraps boiled with their morning feed is very acceptable.

Feeding Young Chicks.—The chick comes from the egg full, nature having made preparations for its nourishment for at least 24 hours, by allowing it to absorb the contents of the yolk just previous to emerging from the egg. Consequently it should not be fed for 24 hours, and 36 will be no inconvenience.

The second day feed as early as possible; 5 o'clock is an excellent time to fix upon, and earlier if possible. The third day is not so urgent, and feeding need not begin until 8 o'clock. Give hard-boiled eggs, white and yolks mixed, finely crumbled; break finely all the egg shells and place within their reach. Give this as many times as they will eat it up clean during the day. After the third day vary their food as often as you may choose. Care should be taken that a little green food be one of the principal features, such as grass, onions, cabbage, or in fact most any wholesome green vegetable. Fine gravel and pounded bone should be kept before them constantly. The food should be supplied with a degree of neatness and care, as you will never succeed in filth. It is variety that keeps the chicks in health. Cracked corn, whole wheat and buckwheat may be fed as soon as they can eat it. Caution should be taken that their drinking water is fresh and free from dirt, and within their reach at all times. After the chicks are two weeks old, milk is one of the very best of foods.

Chicks raised in a properly constructed brooder, with nice, dry runs, will thrive better than those that run out, especially if supplied with a variety of food.

Dampness is fatal to chicks even when very slight; consequently the surroundings of the drinking vessels should be dry, as well as the floors.

Raising Young Ducks.—Ducklings are very easy to raise and are very profitable, and, if well cared for, are ready for market in ten weeks from the time they leave the shell. They must be kept perfectly dry and warm at first. They need no water, except to drink, and grow faster without it.

The best food for young ducks is stale bread and milk, with the infertile eggs boiled hard and chopped fine—about two eggs to the quart. When two or three weeks old they will eat anything in the shape of food, but have it reasonably clean. They require more green food than chicks—the tops of onions, turnips, or anything of like nature, will answer. Corn fodder cut fine is excellent.

Breeding ducks require one drake to five or six ducks. If the old ducks have a pond to swim in, and plenty of green food, their eggs will hatch a great deal better than hen's eggs. Ducks' eggs require more moisture than hens' eggs during the last week of incubation, as the lining membrane is very tough.

Raising Geese.—Goose eggs are extensively hatched in good incubators, and the goslings are raised with about the same treatment as young ducks, but they must have an abundance of grass to pasture on from the time they are able to run about until they are ready for market. They will live on grain through the winter, but will do much better if given hay with it.

Clover hay, cut short and steamed, with corn chop sprinkled through it, makes a splendid diet for geese. Small refuse potatoes chopped up are greedily relished. The shell and membrane of goose eggs are very tough, and should be moistened four or five times during the last week of incubation. Any one having plenty of grass land can do well raising geese. The feathers will pay for raising, leaving them, when dressed for market, clear profit. It is sometimes necessary to help goslings out of the shell, but it should never be done until the blood is all absorbed from the egg lining.

Raising and Feeding Turkeys.—Turkeys will do well with plenty of range, but if closely confined they are a failure. Sometimes young turkeys are indifferent about learning to eat and are often allowed to die from starvation through ignorance of the attendant. With those who show no inclination of helping themselves, place a piece of curd on the finger and make them taste it. When once they eat a little the trouble is all over, and they become very greedy. They are very tender at first, but, with proper care, after four weeks old, become strong and hardy. Feed well-peppered onions once or twice a week. Let them have whole wheat as soon as they will eat it. All grain food should be fed coarse. They must be kept warm and dry until they "shoot the red;" after that they will stand considerable exposure without injury. Feed regularly and at the same place and they will always come home at night.

Cooking Food for Poultry.—A little trouble in this respect will be amply repaid in the posi-

try yard. Every establishment where a hundred head of poultry are kept should have its lock-up food store-room, and if a stove can be put up its help is invaluable. House scraps can be regularly brought out from the kitchen to the food house by 8 A.M., and with boiling water hot meals of all sorts be mixed with scraps till it forms a crumbling mass. All food for ducklings is better given warm than cold; chicks also appreciate their milk and porridge with the chill off. Liver given raw is not palatable, but if put in boiling water over the stove for ten minutes, and chopped hot and thrown to the birds in pellets, it is greedily devoured. Grain baked in the oven dry and given to the fowls warm is very good in the winter time.

If the above diet is properly attended to the birds must lay. If not, watch for rats or egg-eating hens in the flock, or the need for a grab-lock on the poultry house door.

How to Run a Brooder.—Brooding and caring for small chickens is a part of the work not to be overlooked by the operators. You must remember that young chicks are as tender as little babies, and must not get chilled; for once they are chilled, the bowels become loose and they shortly die. This bowel trouble is often ascribed to the feed, but when the real cause is known, it comes from being in a brooder with the temperature too low. The temperature of the brooder should be 90 degrees, and for quite young chicks should be 95 degrees.

Remember that the hen broods at the same temperature that she hatches with. If the brooder is rather warm, the little chicks will spread out near the outer edge and even put their heads out, but if too cool they will all collect in the center of the brooder and pile up and become wet from the steam coming off the other chicks. As this always occurs at night, the operator is often sadly disappointed the next morning, to see what was a fine brood of chicks looking like so many drowned rats, and likely enough half of them dead.

Now then try a brood of chicks on *this* plan: Keep a brooder at 95 degrees for the first week; the second week at 90 degrees. Don't let the temperature get below these points. During the time mentioned the temperature should never get below 86 degrees. For winter chicks there is more in the temperature of the brooder than in the feed. Nine-tenths of the mortality is caused by chicks getting chilled in the brooder.

To Secure Early Laying.—Select pullets from 12 to 18 months old, house in warm quarters early in January, and avoid moving them about in various runs after they are mated. Supply them with plenty of litter, such as hay, chaff, leaves, fine cut straw, or in fact most anything that is clean and wholesome. Lay in a small load of fine gravel in the fall and place where all the fowls can supply themselves with false teeth.

To Make Hens Lay.—A good food for this purpose, fed each alternate day, is the following: To 3 gallons of boiling water add ½ oz. of common salt, a teaspoonful of cayenne pepper, and ¼ oz. of lard. Stir the mixture until the pepper has imparted considerable of its strength to the water. Meantime the salt will have dissolved and the lard melted. Then, while yet boiling, stir in meal made of oats and corn, ground together in equal parts, until a stiff mass is formed. Set away to cool down to a milk warmth. Before feeding, taste to see that you have neither an overdose of salt or pepper. In winter, on the days that the above mixture is omitted, give the hens fresh meat, chopped fine, and at all times plenty of pure water, grain, gravel and lime.

Leaves for the Floor.—When the leaves fall rake them and place them under cover. Secure a large pile of them, and use them in the poultry house. Leaves on the floor of the poultry house prevent draughts, and aid in retaining warmth, as well as serving as absorbents. The hens will scratch and work in them, thus assisting to promote warmth by exercise, and also keep in good laying condition. There should be enough leaves secured to keep the floor covered to the depth of 6 inches during the entire winter.

Cut Straw and Eggs.—An old farmer who secures eggs all through the winter, when asked for his secret, replied that he gave his hens plenty of cut straw. For a while there was much unbelief in the reply, as it was supposed that the farmer was feeding cut straw to his hens (according to his statement); but when the facts came out, it appeared that the cut straw was really the secret, but it was used 4 inches deep, on the floor of the poultry-house, in which millet seed and wheat were scattered, the hens thereby being provided with a warm place to work. The cut straw gave them a scratching bed, and it kept them in exercise, prevented disease and promoted the appetite. It will pay better, if the matter of profit from returns is considered, to use straw in the poultry-house than in the cow-stalls. Many cold poultry-houses can be rendered comfortable with straw, cut to 3-inch lengths, on the floor, and if the hens are warm and can exercise, the cost will be less and the number of eggs greater.

Chicken Cholera.—This disease is more to

be dreaded than roup, or any other disease that poultry is subject to, as it is of miasmatic origin, epidemic, and very contagious. Symptoms: The fowl has a dejected, sleepy and drooping appearance, and does not plume itself; it is very thirsty, has a slow, stalking gait, and gapes often. The comb and wattles lose their natural color, generally turning pale, but sometimes they are dark. There is diarrhœa with greenish discharge, or like sulphur and water; afterwards it becomes thin and frothy. Prostration comes on, the crop fills with mucus and wind, and at last food is not digested; breathing is heavy and fast, the eyes close, and in a few hours the fowl dies.

This fearful disease, when allowed to go unattended, will cause disaster, and "an ounce of prevention is worth a pound of cure." The preventive could not be more fully supplied than to have a bottle of "Combs' Chicken Cholera Cure" in your possession. One bottle is sufficient for 100 fowls, and if used judiciously will last from four to six months. It is guaranteed to effect a cure, even after the disease is apparent, is a splendid invigorative tonic, and especially adapted for poultry in all stages, from the newly hatched chick to the oldest males.

Roup.—An inflammation of the mucous membrane lining of the air-passages, which often makes its presence into the cleft palate, the mouth and the eyes. It is more destructive and harder to handle, when let run a while, than cholera. Its first symptoms are slightly catarrhal, affecting the appetite and health of the chick but very little, and in the second stage it becomes ulcerous or diphtherial roup, and is very nearly related to malignant diphtheria in the human family. It is caused from filth, bad food, cold and wet. The eyes water, the nostrils are closed, breathing becomes deep and difficult, together with cough and suffocation. Treatment: Pen up every fowl in large, dry, warm quarters, whitewash pens with carbolized lime, keep out all draughts of cold, damp air; feed hot bran, mashed potatoes and meat, and medicate the throat, mouth and nostrils with chloride of sodium or common salt, as follows: Take a bucketful of warm salt water, put a teacupful of salt to the amount of water; then, catching the fowl, examine the throat and nostrils, removing all cheesy matter and pressing all mucous matter out of the nostrils, and then, filling a pint cup for each affected fowl, hold it by the feet with head down, choke it until the mouth is wide open and then insert the head into the solution, comb down, so that the medicated water may enter the cleft in the palate and go out at each nostril and into the throat. Each should be separately treated, not all from the same water, but one cup will do for all. Kerosene injected into the nostrils is good, and camphorated sweet oil. But the best remedy, it is said, is the "hatchet," if this remedy fails. A great deal of this trouble may be avoided by keeping your poultry scrupulously clean.

Crop-Bound.—This complaint is frequent with fowls and chicks in confinement where no range is allowed, and in nearly every case the real cause is overfeeding of indigestible food. In most instances death is sure to follow, unless properly treated. It only requires about 24 hours for the symptoms to manifest themselves. The disease may be quickly relieved as follows: Open the crop on the side, lengthwise, cutting a slit sufficiently long to remove all the contents, using a sharp knife. After this is done, thoroughly cleanse with warm water; then close with several stitches, care being taken not to sew the skin of the bird to the sack of the crop. Close the crop first, using coarse white linen thread; also have knot come on the outside of crop, then take a few stitches in the skin. Place the fowl in dry, warm quarters; give no water the first 24 hours, and feed on soft food for 2 days; it will soon recover.

Coarse Grass and Crop-Bound.—From November until March is the season of the year when some of the hens may become crop-bound. It is due to the lack of green food, which tempts the hens to swallow bulky food of some kind as a substitute, the result being that they resort to the long, dried grass, which becomes packed in the crops and causes crop-bound.

A Sure Cure for Scurvy or Scaly Leg.—Wash the feet and the legs of the fowl well with castile soap. After drying, apply equal parts of mutton tallow and coal oil, and rub well. Two or three applications will usually cure the worst cases.

Caponizing.—Caponizing is castrating the male fowl. There are many advantages to be gained by this operation. The fowls grow larger, the meat richer, it costs less to fatten and they sell better. In fact, a capon ranks the same in poultry as the steer does among cattle. Caponizing has long ceased to be an experiment, and is recognized among practical poultrymen as an important factor in increasing the profit of the business.

PRICKLY HEAT—Cure for.

Mix a *large* portion of wheat bran with either cold or lukewarm water, and use it as a bath twice or thrice a day. Children who are covered with prickly heat in warm weather will be thus effectually relieved from that tormenting eruption. As soon as it begins to appear on the neck, face or arms, commence using the bran water on these parts repeatedly through the day, and it may probably spread no farther. If it does, the lime water bath will certainly cure it.

PUMPKINS — To Dry.

Take the ripe pumpkins; pare, cut into small pieces, stew soft, mash and strain through a colander, as if for making pies. Spread this pulp on plates in layers not quite an inch thick; dry it down in the stove oven, kept at so low a temperature as not to scorch it. In about a day it will become dry and crisp. The sheets thus made can be stored away in a dry place, and they are always ready for use for pies or sauce. Soak the pieces over night in a little milk, and they will return to a nice pulp as delicious as the fresh pumpkin. The quick drying after cooking prevents any portion from slightly souring, as is always the case when the uncooked pieces are dried; the flavor is much better preserved, and the after cooking is saved.

PUTTY.

This name is given to the following preparations (when used alone glazier's putty is generally indicated):

Glazier's Putty.—From whiting made into a stiff paste with drying oil. It is used to fix panes of glass in sashes, to fill holes and cracks in wood before painting it, etc.

French Putty.—Seven lbs. linseed oil and 4 lbs. brown umber are boiled for 2 hours, and 62 grammes wax stirred in. After removal from the fire 5½ lbs. fine chalk and 11 lbs. white lead are added and thoroughly incorporated; said to be very hard and permanent.

Putty for Plastering.—A very fine cement made of lime only. It is thus prepared: Dissolve in a small quantity of water, as 2 or 3 gals., an equal quantity of fresh lime, constantly mixing it with a stick until the lime be entirely slaked and the whole becomes of a suitable consistency, so that, when the stick is taken out of it, it will but just drop therefrom; this, being sifted or run through a hair sieve, to take out the gross parts of the lime, is fit for use. Putty differs from fine stuff, in the manner of preparing it, and in being used without hair.

Polisher's Putty.—A crude protoxide of tin, obtained by exposing metallic tin in a reverberatory furnace, and raking off the dross as it forms; this is afterwards calcined until it becomes whitish, and is then reduced to powder. Another method is to melt tin with rather more than an equal weight of lead, and then to rapidly raise the heat so as to render the mixed metal red hot, when the tin will be immediately flung out in the state of "putty" or "peroxide." The products of both these processes are very hard, and are used for polishing glass and japan work, and to color opaque white enamel.

To Soften Putty.—Take 1 lb. of pearlash and 3 lbs. of quicklime. After slaking the lime in water add the pearlash, and let the mixture be made of a consistency about the same as that of paint. When required for use apply it to both sides of the glass, and let it remain in contact with the putty for 12 hours; after which the putty will have become so softened that the glass may be removed from the frame without any difficulty.

To Remove Old Putty.—Many persons destroy their window sashes endeavoring to remove old putty. This may be obviated by applying a hot poker to the putty, which will then readily yield to the knife, and leave the sash clean.

QUILTS — Inexpensive.

Warm and inexpensive quilts are made of newspapers, with perforations every few inches, to permit ventilation. The papers are inclosed in chintz or cretonne.

PYROTECHNICS.

Colored Fires.—See p. 386.

Rockets.—The cases are made of stout cartridge paper, rolled on a mould and pasted, and then throttled a little below the mouth, like the neck of a phial. The diameter should be exactly equal to that of a leaden ball of the same weight, and the length should be equal to 5½ times the external diameter. Above the spindle there must be one interior diameter of composition driven solid. They are filled with the following mixtures, tightly driven in, and when intended for flight (sky-rockets) they are "garnished" and affixed to wooden or willow rods to direct their course:

The composition.—1. (Marsh.) *a.* For 2-oz. rockets. From niter, 54½ parts; sulphur, 18 parts; charcoal, 27½ parts; all in fine powder, and passed through lawn.

b. For 4-oz. rockets. From niter, 64 parts; sulphur, 16 parts; charcoal, 20 parts; as the last.

c. For ½-lb. to 1-lb. rockets. From niter, 62½ parts; sulphur, 15⅝ parts; charcoal, 21⅞ parts.

2. (Ruggieri.) *a.* For rockets of ½-inch diameter. From niter, 16 parts; charcoal, 7 parts; sulphur, 4 parts.

b. For ¾- to 1¼-inch rockets, use 1 part more of niter.

c. For 1½-inch rockets, use 2 parts more of niter.

d. By using 1 part less of charcoal and adding respectively 3, 4 and 5 parts of fine steel filings, the above are converted into "brilliant fires."

c. By the substitution of coarse cast-iron borings for filings, and a further omission of 2 parts of charcoal from each, the latter are converted into "Chinese fire."

Hand-rockets and ground-rockets are usually loaded with nothing but very fine meal gunpowder and iron or zinc filings or borings.

After sky-rockets and water-rockets are charged, a piece of clay is driven in, through which a hole is pierced, and the "head" or "garniture" filled with stars, and a little corn-powder is then applied.

Stars.—1. (Brilliant—Marsh.) Niter, 50¾ parts; sulphur and black antimony, of each 13 parts; reduce them to powder, make them into a stiff paste with isinglass, 1½ parts, dissolved in a mixture of vinegar, 8¾ parts; and spirit of wine, 13 parts; lastly, form this into small pieces and, whilst moist, roll them in meal gunpowder.

2. (White—Ruggieri.) Niter, 16 parts; sulphur, 7 parts; gunpowder, 4 parts; as the last.

3. (Golden rain.) a. (Ruggieri.) Niter and gunpowder, of each 16 parts; sulphur, 10 parts; charcoal, 4 parts; lampblack, 2 parts; mix, and pack it into small paper tubes.

b. (Ruggieri.) Niter, 16 parts; sulphur and gunpowder, of each 8 parts; charcoal and lampblack, of each 3 parts; as the last.

c. (Marsh.) Mealed gunpowder, 66¾ parts; sulphur, 11 parts; charcoal, 22½ parts; as before. Used for the "garniture" of rockets, etc.

RATS—To Destroy.

The following recipe for their destruction originated with Dr. Ure, and is highly recommended as the best known means of getting rid of these most obnoxious and destructive vermin: Melt hog's lard in a bottle plunged in water, heated to about 150° Fahr.; introduce into it ½ oz. phosphorus for every pound of lard, then add a pint of proof spirit, or whisky, cork the bottle firmly after its contents have been heated to 150°, taking it at the same time out of the water, and agitate smartly until the phosphorus becomes uniformly diffused, forming a milky-looking liquid. This liquid, being cooled, will afford a white compound of phosphorus and lard, from which the spirit spontaneously separates, and may be poured off to be used again for the same purpose, but not for drinking, for none of it enters into the combination, but it merely serves to comminute the phosphorus and diffuse it in very small particles through the lard. This compound, on being warmed very gently, may be poured out into a mixture of wheat flour and sugar, incorporated therewith, and then flavored with oil of rhodium, or not, at pleasure. The flavor may be varied with oil of aniseed, etc. This dough, being made into pellets, is to be laid into rat holes. By its luminousness in the dark it attracts their notice, and, being agreeable to their palates and noses, it is readily eaten, and proves certainly fatal.

Another Method.—Get a piece of lead pipe and use it as a funnel to introduce about 1½ oz. sulphide of potassium into any outside holes tenanted by rats. This must not be used in dwellings. To get rid of mice, use tartar emetic mingled with any favorite food. They will eat, sicken and take their leave.

RAIN-WATER—To Keep Sweet.

The best way to keep rain-water sweet in a cistern is to first collect it in a tank, and filter it into the cistern below the surface. This will remove the organic matters, and prevent fermentation. Care should also be taken to prevent surface drainage into it.

RAZOR.

How to Use a Razor and Strop.—In selecting a razor for use, adaptation to the beard is a very important consideration. For a heavy, coarse beard, a too thin-ground blade should not be used, as the edge will tremble, and the razor, however excellent, will prove unsatisfactory; on the other hand, a light, wiry beard and tender skin require a thin-ground blade, which will lie flat on the face.

To use a razor, let it lie flat on the face, and draw it with an easy diagonal motion against the beard. Do not scrape with the razor, or hold it almost at right angles to the face, as you will only spoil the edge, irritate the skin, and cause the best razor to fail. Persons who are not adepts are apt to complain that their razors do not shave well, and are liable to condemn a good one, when the fault lies not in the razor, but in the unskillful use of it.

It is important that the beard be thoroughly softened with hot water and soap, and the razor dipped in hot water before using, as this will add much to the comfort of shaving.

To strop a razor, always lay the blade flat, so that the back and edge both rest on the strop, drawing from heel to point with a firm, steady stroke, turning on the back. The best razor may be spoiled and rendered quite unfit for shaving by the use of an inferior strop.

The strop should be made of leather especially prepared to hold a sufficient quantity of cutting material, or dressing, wherein lies the sharpening quality of a good strop; too close grain leather will not retain the dressing, and is almost worthless for practical use. If a strop becomes hard or glazed, a few drops of oil, rubbed on the surface, will improve it, but if the leather is once cut or becomes uneven, it is rendered useless.

Use care in stropping a thin-ground razor, as such blades are highly tempered, and will break easily if roughly brought in contact with any hard substance. Always keep the razor bright; there is absolutely no excuse for a soiled or rusty razor.

Directions for Honing a Razor.—Either oil or shaving lather may be used on what is commonly called the "Italian rock" razor hone. Use one or the other exclusively. Good sperm or sweet oil is the best, but kerosene or any other non-drying oil will answer. The all-important consideration in honing a razor is to have the blade rest perfectly flat on the stone, so that both the edge and back rest on the surface. This is essential in order to secure a perfectly true and even bevel to the edge. Draw the blade "forward" *against* the edge, just as one would in cutting or shaving. The position of the blade should be somewhat diagonally across the stone, so that the heel is slightly in advance of the point. This sets the teeth at the proper angle for shaving. Turn the blade on the back at the end of each stroke. The edge may be tested by being drawn lightly with a steady hand across the moistened finger-nail, which tends to remove the feather edge and show when the edge is free from nicks, as such defects are readily detected in this manner.

After the blade has been honed sufficiently keen, it should be wiped and then carefully stropped, resting the blade flat as in honing, but drawing in the opposite direction, that is, *against* the back and from the edge. A few strokes on the dressing or prepared leather side of strop, and light finishing on the plain leather side, should be sufficient to give a very keen shaving edge to a good razor.

To Sharpen a Razor.—Place the razor for 30 minutes in a mixture of 20 parts water and 1 part muriatic or sulphuric acid. Wipe carefully and hone. The acid corrodes the surface of the blade uniformly, and thus takes the place of a whetstone.

Razor-strop Paste.—Wet the strop with a little sweet oil, and apply a little flour of emery evenly over the surface.

REFRIGERATOR HINTS.

Some provisions should not be put on ice. Every housekeeper ought to know that all meats, raw or cooked, lose in juiciness and tenderness by its action. For instance, a joint which was excellent when served hot will often become rough and tasteless if kept in the refrigerator 24 hours.

There is a simple treatment of boiled meat which keeps it palatable. If you wish to eat the meat when hot, after dinner plunge it again in boiling water or in the water in which it was cooked brought again to a boiling point, and there let it remain until cold. You will find that it will absorb enough moisture to keep it tender and juicy. Do not place it in the refrigerator warm.

Bologna sausage or any of the preparations in sausage skins will mould if put into the refrigerator or if shut up from the air.

Fish should not be brought in direct contact with ice, no matter what the general market practice may be. Salmon loses its delicate flavor almost completely if laid upon ice. In fact, no food should ever rest directly upon ice.

RENOVATING.

To Renovate an Old Coat.—First clean the coat of dirt and grease, then take 1 gal. of a strong decoction of logwood, made by boiling logwood chips in water. Strain this liquid, and when cool add 2 oz. of gum arabic in powder, which should be kept in well-stoppered bottles for use. Then go gently over the coat with a sponge wet in the above liquid, diluted to suit the color, and hang it in the shade to dry. Afterwards brush the nap smooth, and it will look as good as new. The liquid will suit all brown or dark colors, if properly diluted, of which it is easy to judge.

To Revive Faded Black Cloth.—Having cleaned it well, boil 2 or 3 oz. of logwood for ½ hour. Dip it in warm water and squeeze it dry, then put it into the copper kettle and boil ½ hour. Take it out and add a small piece of green copperas, and boil it another half hour. Hang it in the air for an hour or two, then rinse it in two or three cold waters, dry it, and let it be regularly brushed with a soft brush, over which one or two drops of oil of olives have been rubbed.

To Clean Men's Old Clothes.—Whip and brush thoroughly. Remove grease spots with ammonia, and with alcohol and water, equal parts, diminish the gloss of hard goods. Dealers in old clothes give the garments a new appearance by the use of tobacco.

How to Clean a Coat Collar.—Break a piece of soap tree bark about 2 inches square into small bits, and pour over it ½ pint of boiling water; let it stand an hour or two, then sponge the collar well with the liquor; a second sponging with clear water will clean it nicely. Both washing and rinsing water should be as warm as for flannel.

REMEDY for Dipsomania.

(Capt. Vine Hall's.) Sulphate of iron, 5 grs.; peppermint water, 11 drams; spirit of nutmeg,

1 dram. To be taken twice a day in doses of about a wineglassful or less, with or without water. This recipe is not only an inestimable boon to the victim of strong drink, but, properly "pushed," is capable of yielding a handsome income from its manufacture. This remedy is prepared by different persons under different titles, and sold at from $1 to $3 per bottle.

RIBBONS.—To Clean.

Take a clean cloth, moistened in benzine, and rub them off carefully. If not too dirty, this will clean them off nicely. Expose them to the air afterward to get rid of the odor.

To Smooth Ribbon.—Place a moderately hot flat-iron on the ironing-board, the ribbon under the iron, and pull it carefully through. If the ribbon is not pulled too fast, and the iron is the right warmth, this will be found to be a much better way than simply rubbing the iron over the ribbon.

To Clean Black Ribbon.—Take an old black kid glove, no matter how old, and boil it in a pint of water for a short time; then let it cool until the leather can be taken in the hand without burning; use the glove wet with the water to sponge off the ribbon. If the ribbon is very dirty, dip it into the water and draw it through the fingers a few times before sponging with the glove. After cleaning, lay a piece of paper over the ribbon and iron; paper is better than cloth. The ribbon will look like new.

To Wash Ribbons.—If dingy and greasy, rub the yolk of an egg upon them, or French chalk upon the wrong side, and let it dry; then lay it upon a clean cloth, and wash upon each side with a sponge, and press upon the wrong side. If very much soiled, use bran water, and add to the rinsing-water a little muriate of tin to set red; oil of vitriol for green, blue, maroon and bright yellow.

To Renew Ribbons or Silk.—Scrape several large potatoes and put a pint of cold water over them. When settled, pour it off; spread your ribbons (or silk) upon the table, wet with a sponge a small part, and iron with a flat just a little warmer than you can handle with your hands bare. If it is too hot it will injure the silk. To stiffen ribbons or old silk, take a lump of gum arabic about as large as a hickory nut, dissolve it in ½ pint water, and dip the silks or ribbons in it and iron immediately. If they are soiled they should be washed and dipped in a weak solution of alum water.

RIDING.

The following useful hints will be found instructive and interesting to all equestrians:

The legitimate gaits of horses are the walk, trot, canter and gallop. The walk is a gait of four distinct beats, each foot being planted in a regular order of succession. The trot has two distinct beats. The horse springs diagonally from one pair of feet to the other, while between the steps all the feet are in the air. The canter has three beats in regular order of succession, and the gallop has four beats in regular order of succession. A horse is "bit-wise" when, the bit being correctly fitted and properly adjusted, he obeys the lightest pressure upon either bar. He is "rein-wise" when he obeys the slightest pressure of the reins upon either side of the neck, the bit not being disturbed from its normal position. He is "leg-wise" when he obeys the lightest correctly combined action of the rider's legs.

The reins serve to prepare the horse to move, and to guide, support, and to halt him. Their action should be in harmony with that of the legs.

In riding the hand should be kept steady and ought not to move with the body. It should merely oscillate with the horse's head. At the same time it should be kept light, for the bit, if pressed constantly on the horse's mouth, destroys its sensibility and soon makes it hard. The hand is "light" when there is an almost imperceptible alternate feeling and easing of the hand in harmony with the motion of the horse, by which the delicacy of the mouth is preserved and the horse made to carry himself lightly. That hand is best which, by giving and taking properly and keeping constant touch of the bit, controls the horse with the least force.

The legs serve to assist, together with the reins, in controlling the horse. Closing the knees without pressure from the lower part of the leg tends to steady the horse in position. Carrying the lower legs slightly to the rear, closing them equally with slight pressure, prepares him to move; or, if moving, to keep him well up to the hand; closed with greater pressure behind the girth, they urge him forward. Carrying the right or left leg to the rear, closing it with pressure, causes the horse to move his haunches to the left or right. In fact, the lower legs govern the haunches.

The horse is made obedient and gentle and his good qualities best developed by patience, kindness and encouragement, and, above all, fearlessness. Punishment should be resorted to only when absolutely necessary. No punishment should be administered to a horse in anger. Under harsh treatment he will first become timid, then sullen, and at length violent and unmanageable. Every action of the rider should tend to induce full confidence, assuring the horse that no harm is intended and that nothing but kind treatment is to be expected.

The horse's balance and his lightness in hand depend largely on the proper carriage of his head and neck. A young horse will usually try to resist the bit, either by bending his neck to one side, or by setting his jaw against the bit, or by carrying his nose too high or too low. A horse, as a rule, champs the bit when he means to resist.

RING — To Remove.

When a ring happens to get tightly fixed on the finger, a piece of common twine should be well soaped, and then be wound round the finger as tight as can be borne. The twine should commence at the point of the finger, and be continued till the ring is reached; the end of the twine must then be forced through the ring with the head of a needle, or anything else that may be at hand. If the string is then unwound, the ring is almost sure to come off the finger with it. Or, soap the finger well, and slip the ring up while it is soapy, holding the finger up for a time first.

ROCKETS. See Pyrotechny.

ROSE-JAR — To Fill.

In England recipes for perfumes and balsams and things of that kind are handed down from generation to generation, and this recipe for making a rose-jar, given by an Englishwoman, may be of interest to American housewives. Gather the rose petals in the morning; let them stand in a cool place; toss them lightly for one hour to dry; then put them in layers, with salt sprinkled over each layer, in a large covered dish; a glass butter dish having a cover is a convenient receptacle. You can add to this for several mornings, till you have enough stock, for a pint to a quart, according to the size of the jar; stir every morning and let the whole stand for ten days. Then transfer it to a glass fruit jar, in the bottom of which you have placed 2 oz. of allspice, coarsely ground, and as much stick cinnamon, broken coarsely. This may now stand for six weeks, closely covered, when it is ready for the permanent jar, which may be as pretty as your ingenuity can devise or your means purchase. Have ready 1 oz. each of cloves, allspice, cinnamon and mace, all ground (not fine); 1 oz. of orris root, bruised and shredded; 1 oz. of lavender flowers and a small quantity of any other sweet-scented dried flowers or herbs. Mix together and put into the jar in alternate layers with the rose-stock, add a few drops of oil of rose, geranium or violet, and pour over the whole ½ pint of good cologne. This will last for years, though from time to time you may add a little lavender or orange flower water, or any nice perfume, and some seasons a few rose petals.

ROSES — To Keep.

Wrap them separately in wet tissue paper and keep it constantly wet. In this way flowers purchased the day before or early in the morning will be kept as bought until needed.

ROSE-WATER.

Preferable to the distilled for a perfume, or for culinary purposes. Attar of roses, 12 drops; rub it up with ½ oz. of white sugar and 2 drams carbonate magnesia, then add gradually 1 quart of water and 2 oz. of proof spirit, and filter through paper.

RUBBER — To Cement.

A cement which fastens equally well to rubber and to metal or wood is made by a solution of shellac in ammonia. Soak some pulverized gum shellac in 10 times its weight of strong ammonia. A slimy mass will be obtained, which in three or four weeks will become liquid without the use of hot water. This softens the rubber, and, after the volatilization of the ammonia, becomes hard and impermeable to gases and fluids.

RUBBER TYPE.

The matter or letters to be reproduced are first set up in ordinary metal type, which is then thoroughly oiled. A rim or guard about half an inch high should then be placed around the form, and with a camel's hair brush a thin cream of plaster of Paris is laid over it, to exclude all air bubbles. A thicker paste of plaster is then poured over the form, filling in the guard or rim up to its edge, and it is then set aside to harden. Alum water is often used to mix the plaster, making a harder mould, but it takes longer to set. When the mould has thoroughly stiffened, it is removed from the type and put in a dry, hot place to become well hardened. The mould is now fitted in a frame of suitable size, and a sheet of vulcanized rubber, about one-eighth of an inch in thickness, is adjusted upon it, and the whole is put in a screw clamp and heated slowly until the rubber becomes soft enough to be forced into the letter-spaces of the mould by tightening the screw. The rubber should be allowed to remain in the press at least 24 hours, and until it becomes quite cold. The sheet rubber used for this purpose is usually but slightly vulcanized, having had about three per cent. of sulphur kneaded into it with rollers while subjected to a very high temperature. After the impression has been made, therefore, it is necessary to add a greater proportion of sulphur to insure the required hardness in the type. This is done by immersing the rubber, which has been separated from the mould, in a mixture of 30 parts bi-sulphide of carbon and 1 part chloride of sulphur. This is exposed to a temperature of from 70 to 80 degrees until all the sulphide of carbon has volatilized, and is then immersed in a boiling alkaline solution — made by dissolving 8 oz. of caustic potash in 1 gal. of water — for a few minutes, and after a subsequent washing in clean, tepid water, is made quite ready for use.

RUST:

The Rusting of Iron.—Mr. Crum Brown explains in the following manner the chemical reactions which produce iron rust: When a drop of rain falls upon the smooth and polished surface of a piece of iron, the water changes color and a non-adherent brownish-red precipitate is formed. Water free from oxygen and carbonic acid does not produce any effect upon iron at ordinary temperatures. At high temperatures water or steam oxidizes iron rapidly to the state of ferric oxide, Fe_3O_4. This oxide forms an adherent coating, and the action ceases until the coating is removed. Gaseous oxygen at ordinary temperatures does not affect iron, but when heated its action is the same as that of steam. Carbonic oxide at ordinary temperatures does not act upon the iron, but at high temperatures it is reduced to carbonic acid, and the iron is oxidized. Water which contains oxygen alone produces no action upon iron. A piece of iron can be preserved indefinitely in lime water, if carbonic acid cannot be produced. Water charged with carbonic acid, and free from oxygen, dissolves iron into a bicarbonate, setting free the hydrogen. The presence of oxygen oxidizes this bicarbonate, and ferric oxide is precipitated. The carbonic acid set free can again act upon the metal, and an addition of oxygen will dissolve the bicarbonate thus formed.

To Keep Iron and Steel Goods from Rust.—Dissolve ½ oz. of camphor in 1 lb. of hog's lard; take off the scum; mix as much black lead as will give the mixture an iron color. Iron and steel goods, rubbed over with this mixture, and left with it on 24 hours, and then dried with a linen cloth, will keep clean for months. Valuable articles of cutlery should be wrapped in zinc foil, or be kept in boxes lined with zinc. This is at once an easy and most effective method.

Another Method.—The following is said to be a good application to prevent metals rusting: Melt 1 oz. of rosin in a gill of linseed oil, and while hot mix with it 2 quarts of kerosene oil. This can be kept ready to apply any time with a brush or rag to any tools or instruments required to lay by for a time, preventing any rust, and saving much vexation when the tool is to be used again.

To Take Out Rust.—By adding 2 parts cream of tartar to 1 part of oxalic acid, ground fine and kept dry in a bottle, you will find, by applying a little of the powder to rust stains while the article is wet, that the result is satisfactory. Wash out in clear warm water to prevent injury to the goods.

Another Method.—Soak in kerosene oil, and then rub dry.

To Remove Rust from Steel.—Brush the rusted steel with a paste composed of ¼ oz. cyanide potassium, ¼ oz. castile soap, 1 oz. whiting, and enough water to make a paste. Then wash the steel in a solution of ¼ oz. cyanide potassium in 2 oz. water.

To Keep Iron Pipes from Rusting.—The sections as made should be coated with coal tar and then filled with light wood shavings, and the latter set on fire. It is declared that the effect of this treatment will be to render the iron practically proof against rust for an indefinite period, rendering future painting unnecessary. In proof of this assertion the example is cited of a chimney of sheet iron that was erected seven years ago, and which, through being treated as described, is as bright and sound to-day as when erected, though it has never had a brushful of paint applied to it since. It is suggested that by strongly heating the iron after the tar is laid on the outside, the latter is literally burned into the metal, closing the pores and rendering it rust-proof in a far more complete manner than if the tar itself was first made hot and applied to cold iron, according to the usual practice. It is important, of course, that the iron should not be made too hot, or kept hot for too long a time, lest the tar should be burned off. Hence, the direction for the use of light shavings instead of any other means of heating.

To Preserve Polished Iron from Rust.—Apply with a bristle brush a mixture of 11 parts copal varnish and 9 parts spirits of turpentine to which has been added just sufficient sweet oil to give it a little greasiness. Protect against dust and ashes while drying.

SALT—Uses for.

Salt is excellent for cleaning the teeth. It hardens the gums and sweetens the breath.

If used persistently, salt will cure nasal catarrh. A weak brine should be made and snuffed up the nose, allowing it to run down the throat.

There is nothing better for the relief of tired or weak eyes than to bathe them with a strong solution of salt and water applied as hot as it can be borne.

Salt rubbed on the black spots on dishes will remove them, and salt placed over a fresh claret stain on the table linen will assist it to disappear when washed.

One of the most effective remedies known for a sick headache is to place a pinch of salt on the tongue and allow it to dissolve slowly. In about ten minutes it may be followed by a drink of water.

The colored Japanese straw mattings which are so generally used as floor coverings are best kept sweet and clean by washing them with a solution of salt and water after the weekly sweeping.

Salt enters into the composition of a sure cure for a felon. Take common rock salt, dry it thoroughly in the oven, pulverize it and mix with an equal amount of spirits of turpentine. Keep a rag saturated with this solution to the affected part for 24 hours, and the felon will disappear.

A fresh ink-stain on a carpet may be removed by immediately applying a layer of salt. The ink will be absorbed, and when the salt is black it should be removed and another layer applied, repeating the operation until all the ink is removed and the carpet returned to its former pleasing appearance.

SALVE — Grandmother's.

Put into a kettle 1 lb. of resin, ¼ pound of hard mutton tallow, half as much beeswax, and ½ oz. camphor gum. Let the mass dissolve and just come to a boil, stirring with a stick. Then pour in ½ of a pint of warm water, just the chill off, and stir carefully until you can get your hands around it. Pull like candy until quite white and brittle. Put a little grease on your hands to prevent sticking and keep them wet. Wet the table, roll out the salve and cut with a knife. Keep in a cool place.

SAND-PAPER.

The device for making sand-paper is simple and at hand to any one who has occasion to use the paper. A quantity of ordinary window glass is taken (that having a green color is said to be the best) and pounded fine, after which it is passed through one or more sieves of different degrees of fineness, to secure the glass for coarse or fine paper. Then any tough paper is covered evenly with glue, having about one-third more water than is generally employed for wood-work. The glass is sifted upon the paper, allowed a day or two in which to become fixed in the glue, when the refuse glass is shaken off, and the paper is fit for use.

SAUERKRAUT — To Make.

In the first place, let your "stand," holding from half a barrel to a barrel, be thoroughly scalded out; the cutter, the tub and the stamper also well scalded. Take off all the outer leaves of the cabbages, halve them, remove the heart and proceed with the cutting. Lay some clean leaves at the bottom of the stand, sprinkle with a handful of salt, fill in ½ bushel cut cabbage, stamp gently until the juice just makes its appearance, then add another handful of salt, and so on until the stand is full. Cover over with cabbage leaves, place on top a clean board fitting the space pretty well, and on top of that a stone weighing 12 or 15 lbs. Stand away in a cool place, and when hard freezing comes on remove to the cellar. It will be ready for use in from 4 to 6 weeks. The cabbage should be cut tolerably coarse. The Savoy variety makes the best article, but it is only half as productive as the Drumhead and Flat Dutch.

SCREW — To Move A Rusted.

Heat the top of the screw by applying the end of a red-hot poker for a minute or so; then apply the screwdriver at once.

SEALING-WAX.

1. (White.) Bleached shellac, 840 parts; Venice turpentine, 160 parts; plaster of Paris, 100 parts; magnesia, 15 parts; subnitrate of bismuth, 150 parts; carbonate of lead, 235 parts. Melt the turpentine in a capacious copper kettle over a charcoal fire, and gradually add the shellac. When a uniform melted mass has resulted, gradually add the solid ingredients, which must be in form of finest (bolted) powder, under constant stirring; then remove the kettle, keep stirring until the mass cools about of solidifying, and pour it out into forms.

2. (Yellow.) Shellac, 390 parts; Venice turpentine, 220 parts; resin, 160 parts; plaster of Paris, 50 parts; magnesia, 10 parts; chrome yellow, 80 parts. Proceed as directed under No. 1.

3. (Green.) Shellac, 360 parts; Venice turpentine, 260 parts; resin, 150 parts; magnesia, 20 parts; king's yellow (yellow litharge), 60 parts; mountain (Sanders') blue, 30 parts; oil of turpentine, 20 parts. Proceed as before, except that the coloring matters are first triturated to a fine paste with the oil of turpentine, and this paste added to the melted mass in small quantities at a time. Mountain blue is a copper color.

SEA-SICKNESS.

The most effectual preventive of sea-sickness appears to be the horizontal position. When there is much pain, after the stomach has been well cleared, a few drops of laudanum may be taken, or an opium plaster may be applied over the region of the stomach. Persons about to proceed to sea should put their stomach and bowels in proper order, by the use of mild aperients, and even an emetic, if required, when it will generally be found that a glass of warm water, to which 15 or 20 drops of laudanum, or, still better, 1 or 2 drops of creosote, have been added, will effectually prevent any disposition to sea-sickness, provided the bowels be attended to, and excess in eating and drinking be at the same time avoided. A spoonful of crushed ice in a wineglassful of cold water will often afford relief when all other means fail. Smoking at sea is very apt to induce sickness. M. F. Curie, in the *Comptes Rendus*, asserts that drawing in the breath as the vessel descends, and exhaling it as it ascends on the billows by preventing the movements of the diaphragm acting abnormally on the pneumatic nerves, prevents sea-sickness. On this Mr. Atkinson, at one of the meetings of the British Association, observed that if a person seated on board ship, holding a tumbler filled with water in his hand, makes an effort to prevent the water running over, at the same time allowing not merely his arm, but also his whole body, to participate in the movements, he will find that this has the effect of preventing the giddiness and nausea that the rolling and tossing of the vessel have a tendency to produce in inexperienced voyagers. If the person is suffering from sickness at the commencement of his experiment, as soon as he grasps the glass of liquid in his hand, and suffers his arm to take its course and go through the movements alluded to, he feels as if he were performing them of his own free will, and the nausea abates immediately, and very soon ceases entirely, and does not return so long as he suffers his arm and body to assume the postures into which they seem to be drawn. Should he, however, resist the free course of his hand, he instantly feels a thrill of pain of a peculiarly stunning kind shoot through his head, and experiences a sense of dizziness and returning nausea.

Dr. Dering, a Viennese physician, states that an ordinary dose of chloral hydrate is an unfailing remedy for sea-sickness. In various cases recorded by him it seems to have been of the greatest service, even during long sea voyages, insuring a good night's rest, arresting violent sickness when it has set in, and preventing its return.

SEWING-MACHINES—To Oil.

Sewing-machines should be re-oiled whenever they become gummy. Clean off the old oil with kerosene or benzine, and oil with a mixture of equal parts of paraffine oil and sperm oil. Use only the best.

SHAVING.

The following are Mr. Mechi's instructions for this, to many persons, troublesome operation: Never fail to well wash your beard with soap and cold water, and to rub it dry immediately before you apply the lather, of which the more you use the easier you will shave. Never use warm water, which makes a tender face. Place the razor (closed, of course) in your pocket, or under your arm, to warm it. The moment you leave your bed is the best time to shave. Always put your shaving-brush away with the lather on it. The razor (being only a very fine saw) should be moved in a sloping or sawing direction, holding it nearly flat to your face, care being taken to draw the skin as tight as possible with the left hand, so as to present an even surface and throw out the beard. The practice of pressing on the edge of a razor in stropping generally rounds it; the pressure should be directed to the back, which must never be raised from the strop. If you only once put away your razor without stropping or otherwise cleaning the edge, you must no longer expect to shave well, the soap and damp so soon rust the fine teeth or edge. A piece of plate leather should always be kept with the razors. See *Razor*.

Shaving Compound.—Half a pound of plain white soap, dissolved in a small quantity of alcohol, as little as can be used; add a tablespoonful of pulverized borax. Shave the soap and put it in a small tin basin or cup; place it on the fire in a dish of boiling water; when melted, add the alcohol, and remove from the fire; stir in oil of bergamot sufficient to perfume it.

SHAMPOO—Liquid.

Take bay rum, 2½ pints; water, ½ pint; glycerine, 1 oz.; tincture of cantharides, 2 drams; carbonate of ammonia, 2 drams; borax, ½ oz.; or take of New England rum, 1½ pints; bay rum, 1 pint; water, ½ pint; glycerine, 1 oz.; tincture of cantharides, 2 drams; ammonia carbonate, 2 drams; borax, ½ oz.; the salts to be dissolved in water and the other ingredients to be added gradually.

SHEEPSKINS—To Prepare for Mats.

Wash the fresh skin with a strong lather of hot water, allowed to stand until cold, and squeeze and rub the wool until it looks clean and white; then carefully rinse all the soap out of it. In 2 gallons of hot water, dissolve 1 lb. of salt and 1 lb. of alum, and soak the skin in it for 12 hours. Hang it up and let it drain thoroughly, then stretch it carefully on a board to dry. Stretch it several times while drying. Before quite dry, sprinkle over it, on the flesh side, 1 oz. each of finely pulverized alum and saltpeter. Rub it in well, then try the wool to see if it is firm on the skin. If not, let it remain a day or two, then rub over again with

stem. Fold the flesh sides together, hang in the shade 2 or 3 days, turning them over every day until quite dry; then scrape the flesh side with a blunt knife, and rub it with pumice or rotten stone.

SHOES.

To Soften and Make Waterproof.—Neat's-foot oil and castor oil, equal parts of each. Shake well. This may be applied and rubbed in with the hand. The neat's-foot oil penetrates the leather very easily, and keeps it soft, while the castor oil remains upon and near the surface, giving a glossiness, and resisting the entrance of water; and, if desired, enabling a coat of polish blacking to soon give a shine to the boots.

Another Method.—New boots and shoes, saturated with the following mixture and left to hang in a warm place for a week or 10 days, will not only be entirely waterproof, but the leather will also be soft and pliable: Melt in an earthen vessel, over a slow fire, ½ pint of linseed oil, 1 oz. of beeswax, ½ oz. of rosin, and 1 oz. of oil of turpentine.

The soles may be rendered waterproof by applying to them a coat of gum-copal varnish and repeating it until the pores of the leather are filled.

How to Dry Wet Kid Shoes.—First wipe off gently with a soft cloth all surface water and mud; then, while still wet, rub well with kerosene oil, using for the purpose the furred side of canton flannel. Set them aside till partially dry, when a second treatment with oil is advisable. They may then be deposited in a conveniently warm place where they will dry gradually and thoroughly. Before applying French kid dressing give them a final rubbing with the flannel, still slightly dampened with kerosene, and your boots will be soft and flexible as new kid and be very little affected by their bath in the rain.

French Shoe Dressing.—Vinegar, 1 pint; soft water, ¼ pint; glue (broken fine), 2 oz.; logwood chips, 4 oz.; powdered indigo, 1 dr.; bichromate potash, 2 drs.; gum tragacanth, 2 drs.; glycerine, 2 oz.

Polish for Kid Shoes.—Lampblack, 1 dr.; oil turpentine, 4 drs.; alcohol (methylic), 12 oz.; shellac, 1½ oz.; white turpentine, 5 drs.; sandarac, 2 drs. Digest in a close vessel at gentle heat and strain.

See also *Boots and Shoes.*

SILK.

Silks should not be folded in white paper, as the chloride of lime used in bleaching paper is apt to impair the color of the silk. White silk should always be kept in blue paper. Yellowish India paper is also good for keeping silks in.

To Take Stains out of Silk.—Mix together in a vial 2 oz. of essence of lemon and 1 oz. of oil of turpentine. Grease and other spots in silk must be rubbed gently with a linen rag dipped in the above composition. Paint may be removed from silk by rubbing first with spirits of turpentine and then with spirits of wine.

Wrinkled Silk.—Silk that has been wrinkled and tumbled will look like new if you sponge it on the surface with a weak solution of white glue or gum arabic, and iron it on the wrong side.

To Clean Silk—Parisian Method.—Brush thoroughly, wipe with a cloth, and then lay flat on a board or table. Sponge well with hot coffee thoroughly freed from sediment by being strained through muslin. The silk is sponged on the right side. Allow it to become partially dry and iron on the wrong side. The coffee removes all grease, restores the brilliancy of the silk, and does not give it a papery stiffness.

Wash Silks.—As silk is an animal fiber, like wool, it can not be treated in the same way as cotton, which may be subjected to water of all temperatures without injury. Silk should be washed as rapidly as possible. Examine the articles to be washed, and if there are any parts especially soiled clean them with a little benzine or gasoline, applied with a flannel cloth. Then prepare a soapsuds of lukewarm water and plunge the garments in it, moving them up and down, and rubbing them thoroughly in the suds. Rinse them into a water a little cooler, and so on until the final rinsing-water is perfectly cold. Wring them out as dry as possible with a machine. Lay them in sheets or other heavy cloths, and roll them as hard as you can in firm rolls. Put them away for an hour, and at the end of that time iron them on the wrong side.

To Make Silk Waterproof.—A ready method of rendering silk water-proof is to coat it with quick-drying linseed oil, but a more effective process owes its efficacy to the formation of an insoluble stearate of aluminum in the material. This is accomplished by passing the silk successively through a bath of aluminum sulphate, of soap and of water; then drying and calendering. For the first bath commercial alum cake dissolved in 10 times its weight of water is used. The soap bath is prepared by dissolving ordinary yellow soap in 30 times its weight of water, and this bath should be kept hot while the goods are passing through it. The three vessels should be alongside of each other, and special care should be taken to have the fabric thoroughly soaked in the first bath. For materials of white or light color a white soap should be used in the preparation of the soap solution.

To Wash Silk Underwear.—Use cool suds of fine Castile soap, rubbing very little by hand, and press dry in a cloth. Rinse twice, once in clear cold water, and again in water tinctured with cream of tartar, vinegar or alum. Dry quickly, first stretching in shape, and press under a heavy book, but do not iron. If the articles are black, add ammonia only to the rinsing-water.

To Renew Silk.—See *Ribbons.*

To Judge Silk.—Note the closeness and evenness of the rib in it, and hold it to the light to judge the better of this. That shows the texture. Then crush it in the hand and release it suddenly. If it springs out quickly and leaves no crease behind, it has verve, and the quality of the silk is denoted by the verve.

SILVER.

To Cleanse Silver.—Clean silver with hot water, followed by a solution of equal parts of ammonia and spirits of turpentine; and after this, if necessary, prepared chalk, whiting, magnesia or rouge.

It is claimed that water in which potatoes have been boiled exercises a remarkable cleaning influence upon silverware of all kinds, especially spoons that have become blackened by eggs. Even delicately chased and engraved articles can, it is said, be made bright by this method, even better than by the use of the ordinary polishing powder, which is apt to settle in the depressions, requiring particular care in its removal.

A formula for cleaning silver in use at a well-known Britannia factory is as follows: Half a pound of sal soda is dissolved in 3 quarts of boiling water, and the silver dipped in it. The silver is immediately washed in suds, and dried with canton flannel.

The proprietor of one of the oldest silver establishments in Philadelphia says that "house-keepers ruin their silver by washing it in soap-suds, as it makes it look like pewter."

Celebrated Recipe for Silver Wash.—One oz. of nitric acid, 1 10-cent piece, and 1 oz. of quicksilver. Put it in an open glass vessel and let it stand until dissolved; then add 1 pint of water, and it is ready for use. Make it into a powder by adding whiting, and it may be used on brass, copper, German silver, etc.

To Prevent Tarnishing.—Warm the articles and paint with a thin solution of collodion in alcohol. Use a wide, soft brush. Another way to keep articles of silverware bright is to place them in an air-tight case with a good-sized piece of camphor.

Silver-Plating Fluid.—Dissolve 1 oz. of nitrate of silver, in crystals, in 12 oz. of soft water; then dissolve in the water 2 oz. of cyanuret of potash; shake the whole together, and let it stand till it becomes clear. Have ready some half-ounce vials, and fill half full of Paris white, or fine whiting; and then fill up the bottles with the liquor, and it is ready for use. The whiting does not increase the coating power; it only helps to clean the articles, and save the silver fluid, by half filling the bottles.

SINKS—To Cleanse.

Greasy pipes and sinks may be purified by pouring down a pailful of boiling water in which 3 or 4 lbs. of washing soda have been dissolved.

SMELLING-SALTS—To Make.

One gill liquid ammonia, ½ dram each of English lavender and of rosemary, and 8 drops each of oil of bergamot and cloves. Mix all these ingredients together in a bottle and shake them thoroughly. Fill the vinaigrette, or any small bottle which has a good glass stopper, with small pieces of sponge, pour in as much of this liquid preparation as the sponge will absorb, and cork the bottle tightly.

SOAP.

Cheap Soap.—Cut 2 lbs. common brown soap into thin slices, to which add 1 oz. borax and 10 quarts water. Put the whole over the fire, and when the soap and borax are dissolved the soap is done. It requires but little time and trouble to make this soap, which is very valuable for washing dishes, cleaning paint, scrubbing floors, etc. It is, moreover, very healing to the hands. If less water is used, the soap will be harder.

Cheap Hard Soap.—1. Put 5 gallons water, 3 lbs. clean unslaked lime and 6 lbs. soda ash into a kettle; when it boils, strain it, and return it to the kettle; then add 12 lbs. clean grease. Let it boil slowly 3 hours, then put out the fire and let it get entirely cold. Remove the hard cake that will form without touching the hands to it; put this in a clean kettle, add 1 lb. borax, pounded fine, and let it melt, stirring it well together, and when hot pour it into moulds that have been previously well soaked in water. Set them in an airy place, not in the sunshine for the first day or two, as it would warp them out of shape; afterward dry perfectly, and then pack away in a dry place. The liquid remaining in the kettle is strong enough to make another lot by adding 6 lbs. grease, but the soap produced is not quite equal to the first.

2. One pound concentrated lye dissolved in 2 quarts soft water; pour into a large pitcher

To the Ladies of the M. E. Church.

There will be a called meeting of the ·adies' Social Society on Friday even- g, Sept. 25, in the lecture room. Im- ·rtant business. All are earnestly ·quested to be present. By order of e President.

Everybody Attend.

John H. Brubaker will address the ·cKinley and Hobart Club Friday ·ening at the club rooms. Every- ·dy come. JOE R. WILLIAMS, Sec.

Mrs. George J. Parrot is visiting rel- ·ives at Fort Wayne.

C. W. Murray, of Minneapolis, who ·as been the guest of his relatives, ·r. and Mrs. Daniel Jerrams, left to- ·ay for Delphos, Ohio. His wife and ·aughter will remain here for a short ·me.

The Jewish people of Evansville ·ere so incensed over Shively's re- ·arks at Peru referring to them, that ·ey held a meeting to take the mat- ·r under advisement. By this time ·ey have ascertained that he is guilty ·s charged in the original indictment.

THE MOUTH.

Many kinds of fish are provided wit teeth on their tongues.

The tortoise and the turtle are not pro vided with teeth, but can bite as well a though they were.

Many kinds of fish are not provide with tongues, or, at most, have these or gans in a rudimentary state.

The squirrel is provided with a pouch o each side of his mouth, in which he ca carry a considerable amount of nuts, co or other food.

According to the physiognomist, a pro jecting under lip is a bad sign, indicatin pigheaded obstinacy and dullness, if no actual stupidity.

The size of the tongue in the human rac bears no relation to the height. Th tongue of a woman 5 feet high is frequen ly longer than that of her husband, wh rejoices in 6 feet 2.

The siluroid fishes are provided wit rows of teeth on their upper and lowe jaws, on their tongues and even on th pharynx. Anything that the siluroi catches is not likely to get away.

The science of dentistry was introduc in the United States during the Revolu tionary war by Le Mair, a surgeon who a companied the French troops sent to th country to aid in the war against Englan

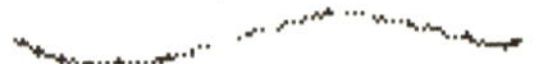

SCIENCE SCRAPS.

The physiologists say that the right side of the brain is of more importance to organic life than the left.

Microscopists are of the opinion that the best glasses ever made fail to reveal the smallest forms of animal and vegetable life.

In the ocean at a depth of 550 feet below the surface the sun has an illuminating power about equal to the light of the full moon.

Man is now scientifically defined as being composed of 44 pounds of carbon and nitrogen evenly diffused through 13 gallons of water.

Lyell, the geologist, says, "At a period comparatively recent all that portion of the United States south of the Black Hills was under from 500 to 900 feet of water."

Neptune is 2,746,000,000 miles from the sun and travels 11,200 miles an hour. Yet it takes 60,127 of our days for that planet to complete one revolution around the sun.

to cool. Melt 5 lbs. grease of any kind, have it milk warm and pour in the lye slowly, then stirring rapidly until it begins to thicken; add 1 or ½ oz. oil of sassafras. Pour into a box 1 foot square and cover it, leaving it in a warm place for 3 or 4 days. Cut into squares and it is ready for use.

White Hard Soap.—Seven pounds soda, 3 lbs. lime, 4 gallons water; boil together till dissolved. Let this stand to settle, then pour off as long as any remains clear, and add water to make 4 gallons. Boil this, adding 6 lbs. grease and 2 tablespoonfuls borax; boil till thick. Take up and put away to cool. When it is cold, cut the pieces rather larger than the size you want them, as it shrinks in drying.

Soft Soap.—Twelve pounds stone potash, 12 lbs. clean grease; put the potash in a piece of old carpet, and crack it with the back of an axe into pieces the size of an egg; put it in a large iron kettle with 1 gallon or more of water; when dissolved, add the grease, and when thoroughly melted, pour it in the soap-barrel, fill it with hot water and stir well, and for a day or two stir occasionally.

Concentrated Lye Soap.—Put 1 lb. concentrated lye into 1 gallon boiling water, let it stand 10 or 12 hours, then add another gallon of water and heat up to a boil, and add 4 lbs. clear melted grease; put in the grease slowly and stir briskly. Let it boil slowly for about half a day, then add 4 quarts hot water, in which has been dissolved 2 tablespoonfuls borax, 4 of soda, and 1 teacupful salt; cook an hour longer and it will probably be ready to set off. It is best, however, to test it first, which may be done by dipping a stick into it; if the substance drops off clear and hardens quickly, it is made. Pour the mass into some vessel large enough to have the soap cover the bottom about the thickness you would like the bars. The vessel should be wet when the soap is put in. When cool, cut into cakes the size you choose. This soap is very white and nice.

Erasive Soap.—Place on a hot stove 1 quart soft water; in this put 1 lb. bar soap finely cut up, 1 oz. borax, ½ oz. saltpeter, ½ oz. aqua ammonia, and boil until thoroughly mixed. This is one of the best materials in use for erasing grease, etc., or doing common washings.

Shaving Soap.—Use ½ pint soft water instead of a quart, and the other materials in quantity as in erasive soap. Cut into cakes of size to suit, when nearly cold.

Honey Soap.—White castile soap, 1½ lbs.; brown Windsor soap, ½ lb. Cut them into thin shavings and liquefy; then add 4 oz. honey, and keep it melted till most of the water is evaporated; then remove from the fire, and when cool enough, add any essential oil. According to Piesse, the honey soap usually sold consists of fine yellow soap, perfumed with oil of citronella.

Windsor Soap.—This is made with lard. In France they use lard with a portion of olive or bleached palm oil. It is made with 1 part olive oil to 9 parts tallow. But a great part of what is sold is only curd (tallow) soap, and scented with oil of carraway and bergamot. The brown is colored with burnt sugar, or umber.

Transparent Soap.—Slice 6 lbs. nice yellow bar-soap into shavings; put into a brass, tin or copper kettle, with alcohol, ½ gallon, heating gradually over a slow fire, stirring till all is dissolved; then add 1 oz. sassafras essence, and stir until all is mixed; now pour into pans about 1½ inches deep, and, when cold, cut into square bars the length or width of the pan, as desired.

Volatile Soap for Removing Paint, etc.—Four tablespoonfuls of spirits of hartshorn, 4 tablespoonfuls of alcohol, and a tablespoonful of salt. Shake the whole well together in a bottle, and apply with a sponge or brush.

To Save Soap.—Add ¼ oz. of borax to a pound of soap, melted in without boiling. This saves one-half of the cost of soap as well as of the labor of washing. This compound improves the whiteness of the fabrics, and leaves a soft and silky feeling to the hands, the usual caustic effect of soap being removed.

SOLDERING.

The union of metallic surfaces by means of a more fusible metal fused between them is called soldering. In all cases surfaces must be perfectly clean, and in absolute contact, and the air must be excluded, to prevent oxidation. For this last purpose the brazier and silversmith use powdered borax made into a paste with water; the coppersmith, powdered sal ammoniac; and the tinsmith, powdered resin. Tin-foil applied between the joints of fine brass-work, first wetted with a strong solution of sal ammoniac, makes an excellent juncture; care being taken to avoid too much heat.

Solders.—1. (For copper, iron and dark brass.) From copper and zinc, equal parts; melted together. For pale brass more zinc must be used.

2. (Fine solder.) From tin, 2 parts; lead, 1 part. Melts at 360° Fahr. Used to tin and solder copper, tin plates, etc.

3. (For German silver.) From German silver, 5 parts; zinc, 4 parts; melted together, run into thin flakes, and then powdered. Also as No. 7.

4. (Glazier's.) Fine lead, 3 parts; tin, 1 part. Melts at 500° Fahr.

5. (For gold.) Gold, 12 pennyweights; copper, 4 pennyweights; silver, 2 pennyweights.

6. (For lead and zinc.) Fine lead, 2 parts; tin, 1 part.

7. (For pewter, Britannia metal, etc.) Fine tin, 10 parts; lead, 6 parts; bismuth, 1 to 3 parts.

8. (For silver.) Fine brass, 6 parts; silver, 5 parts; zinc, 2 parts.

9. (For tin plate.) Fine tin, 2 parts; lead, 1 part. The addition of bismuth, 1 part, renders it fit for pewter.

SPLINT.

This is the common name given to an enlargement of the bone in horses which generally occurs below the knee, between the large and small splint bones, usually on the inside of the limb. It mostly results from fast driving or riding, or from the animal having been much worked while young, or made to unduly traverse hard roads. The splint is a frequent cause of lameness if it develops just under the knee, since it interferes with and circumscribes the free movement of the joint. It is very essential to have recourse to prompt measures directly this affection shows itself.

The treatment usually prescribed is the constant application to the part of cold water, if the splint is accompanied by much tenderness or inflammation. This may be accompanied by bandages soaked in cold water, taking care to renew the cold water as soon as it becomes warm. Mr. Finlay Dun advises the horse, where practicable, to stand for an hour several times a day up to the knees in a stream or pond of water. In addition he prescribes rest for ten days or a fortnight, and when the heat and tenderness have been subdued the application of a blister or of biniodide of mercury ointment, or the hot iron.

SPONGES — To Clean.

Without the greatest care, a sponge is apt to get slimy long before it is worn out. It may be made as good as new, in fact often better, by the following process: Take about 2 or 3 ozs. of carbonate of soda, or of potash; dissolve in 2½ pints of water; soak the sponge in it for 24 hours, then wash and rinse it in pure water. Then put it for some hours in a mixture, 1 glassful of muriatic acid to 3 pints of water. Finally, rinse in cold water and dry thoroughly. A sponge should always be dried, if possible, in the sun every time it has been used.

Another way to remove the gelatinous substance which frequently forms in sponges is to use a solution of permanganate of potash. To get rid of the brown stain caused by chemicals, soak the sponge in very dilute muriatic acid. To clean an old and dirty sponge, first soak it for several hours in a solution of permanganate of potash, then squeeze it, and put it into a weak solution of hydrochloric acid, about 1 part acid to 10 parts water.

SPONTANEOUS COMBUSTION.

Very often conflagrations occur for which no apparent cause can be assigned. These are almost invariably due to what is called spontaneous combustion. There is a remarkable tendency observable in tissues and cotton, when moistened with oil, to become heated when oxidation sets in, and sad results often follow when this is neglected. A wad of cotton used for rubbing a painting has been known to take fire when thrown through the air. The waste from vulcanized rubber, when thrown in a damp condition into a pile, takes fire spontaneously. Masses of coal stored in a yard have been known to take fire without a spark being applied, and one cannot be too careful in storing any substance in which oxidization is liable to take place.

Cotton-seed-oil will take fire even when mixed with twenty-five per cent. of petroleum oil; but ten per cent. of mineral oil mixed with animal or vegetable oil will go far to prevent combustion.

Olive oil is combustible, and, mixed with rags, hay or sawdust, will produce spontaneous combustion.

Coal-dust, flour-dust, starch (especially rye flour), are all explosive when with certain proportions of air.

New charcoal is highly explosive in its compressed state, also sawdust in a very fine state, when confined in a close chute, and water directed on it. Sawdust should never be used in oil shops or warehouses to collect drippings or leakages from casks.

Dry vegetable or animal oil inevitably takes fire, when saturating cotton waste, at 180° F. Spontaneous combustion occurs most quickly when the cotton is soaked with its own weight of oil. The addition of fifty per cent. of mineral oil (density .880) of great viscosity, and emitting no inflammable vapors, even in contact with an ignited body at any point below 338° F., is sufficient to prevent spontaneous combustion, and the addition of twenty per cent. of the same mineral oil doubles the time necessary to produce spontaneous combustion.

The following are also extremely dangerous:

Greasy rags from tallow and greasy bran bags.

Bituminous coal in large heaps, refuse heaps of pit coal, heated by wet, and especially when pyrites are present in the coal; the larger the heaps the more liable.

Timber dried by steam pipes or hot water, or hot air heating apparatus, owing to fine iron that being thrown off in close wood-casings, or boxings round the pipes, from the mere expansion and contraction of the pipes.

Patent dryers from leakages into sawdust, etc., oily waste of any kind, or waste cloths of silk or cotton, saturated with oil, varnish, turpentine.

SPOTS AND STAINS.

Oil and grease spots on boards, marble, etc., when recent, may be removed by covering them with a paste made of fuller's earth and hot water, and the next day, when the mixture has become perfectly dry, scouring it off with hot soap and water. For old spots, a mixture of fuller's earth and soft soap, or a paste made of fresh-slaked lime and pearlash, will be better, observing not to touch the last with the fingers.

Recent spots of oil, grease, or wax, on woolen cloth or silk, may be removed with a little clean oil of turpentine or benzol; or with a little fuller's earth or scraped French chalk, made into a paste with water, and allowed to dry on them. They may also be generally removed by means of a rather hot flat-iron and blotting-paper or spongy brown paper, more especially if the cloth or one of the pieces of paper be first slightly damped.

Old oil and grease spots require to be treated with ox-gall or yolk of egg, made into a paste with fuller's earth or soap.

Paint spots, when recent, generally yield to the last treatment. Old ones, however, are more obstinate, and require some fuller's earth and soft soap, made into a paste with either ox-gall or spirit of turpentine.

The *American Chemist* gives the following method for extracting grease spots from books or paper: Gently warm the greased or spotted part of the book or paper, and then press upon it pieces of blotting paper, one after another, so as to absorb as much of the grease as possible. Have ready some fine, clear essential oil of turpentine, heated almost to a boiling state;* warm the greased leaf a little, and then with a soft, clean brush, wet with the heated turpentine both sides of the spotted part. By repeating this application the grease will be extracted. Lastly, with another brush dipped in rectified spirits of wine, go over the place, and the grease will no longer appear, neither will the paper be discolored.

Fruit and wine stains, on linen, commonly yield easily to hot soap and water. If not, they must be treated as those below. See Silk.

Ink spots and recent iron mould, on washable fabrics, may be removed by dropping on the part a little melted tallow from a common candle, before washing the articles; or by the application of a little lemon juice, or of a little powdered cream of tartar made into a paste with hot water. Old ink spots and iron moulds will be found to yield almost immediately to a very little powdered oxalic acid, which must be well rubbed upon the spot previously moistened with boiling water, and kept hot over a basin filled with the same.

Boettger recommends the use of pyrophosphate of soda for the removal of ink stains from colored woven tissues, to be applied in the form of a concentrated solution. The recent ink stains are readily removed, but older stains require washing and rubbing with the solution for a long time.

Very frequently, when logwood has been used in manufacturing ink, a reddish stain still remains after the use of oxalic acid, as in the former directions. To remove it, procure a solution of the chloride of lime and apply it in the same manner as directed for the oxalic acid.

To remove ink stains from the fingers, moisten the spot and rub it gently with the head of a parlor-match, keeping the skin wet, and the stain will rapidly disappear.

To Remove Ink from Common Paper.—Shake well together 1 lb. chloride of lime in 4 quarts soft water; then let it stand for 24 hours, after which strain through a clean cotton cloth, and add 1 teaspoonful acetic acid to an ounce of chloride of lime water. Apply this to the blot and the ink will disappear. Absorb the fluid with a blotter.

Stains arising from alkalies and alkaline liquors, when the colors are not destroyed, give way before the application of a little lemon juice, whilst those arising from the weaker acids and acidulous liquids yield to the fumes of ammonia, or the application of a little spirit of hartshorn or sal volatile.

Stains of marking ink may be removed by soaking the part in a solution of chloride of lime, and afterwards rinsing it in a little solution of ammonia or of hyposulphite of soda; or they may be rubbed with the tincture of iodine and then rinsed as before.

Nitric Acid Stains.—The yellow stain left by nitric acid can be removed either from the skin or from brown or black woolen garments by moistening the spots for a while with permanganate of potash, and rinsing with water. A brownish stain of manganese remains, which may be removed from the skin by washing with aqueous solution of sulphurous acid. If the spots are old, they cannot be entirely removed.

Mildew Stains.—Use buttermilk.

* This operation ought to be very carefully accomplished, as the turpentine is a highly inflammable body.

Stains on the Hands.—Stains of acid fruit may be removed from the hands by washing in clean water, drying slightly and, while the hands are still moist, holding them around the flame of a match.

Stains on the hands may also be removed by rubbing with salt moistened with lemon juice. See *Ink Stains*, above.

Scorch Stains on white cloth may be removed by soaking the cloth in lukewarm water, squeezing lemon juice on it, sprinkling a little salt over it, and laying it in the hot sun to bleach.

To Remove Grass Stains.—Boiling water will remove the color. Pour boiling water through the stain, and it sets the green-coloring matter loose, rinsing it away. Grass stain, after washing with soap-suds, makes a dirt-colored mark, and remains an ugly blotch on children's white clothing.

To Remove Stains from Muslin.—If you have stained your muslin or gingham dress, or your white pants, with berries, before wetting with anything else, pour boiling water through the stains, and they will disappear. Before fruit juice dries it can often be removed by cold water, using a sponge and towel if necessary.

To Remove Kerosene Stains.—To drive it completely from any fabric, from paper or from wood, it must be heated high enough to form a vapor, when, if pure, it may be completely removed. Heat may be applied to the floor by using flat-irons sufficiently hot, first placing a piece of paper over the spot. It may be that after the oil is driven from the surface by heat, the stain will reappear; some of the oil remaining in the wood will be brought to the surface by capillary attraction. In such a case it will be necessary to repeat the operation as often as the stain appears.

To Remove Lime Spots.—Lime and acids do not really stain, but spot by the removal of color, and ammonia is the best remedy. A tablespoonful of ammonia in 1 gallon of water will often restore the color of carpets, even if destroyed by acid or alkali. If a ceiling has been whitewashed with the carpet down, and a few drops should fall, this will remove it.

Stains and Marks from Books.—A solution of oxalic acid, citric acid, or tartaric acid, is attended with the least risk, and may be applied without fear of damage. These acids, which take out writing ink, and do not touch the printing, can be used for restoring books where the margins have been written upon, without injuring the text.

To Remove Tar Stains.—Mix thoroughly soft soap and salt—say a tablespoonful of salt to a teacupful of soap—rub on the spots, and spread the cloth on the grass where the sun will shine on it. Let it lie 2 or 3 days, then wash. If the spots are wet occasionally while lying on the grass, it will hasten the bleaching.

To Remove Stains from Broadcloth.—Take an ounce of pipe clay, which has been ground fine, mix it with 12 drops of alcohol and the same quantity of spirits of turpentine. Whenever you wish to remove any stains from cloth, moisten a little of this mixture with alcohol and rub it on the spots. Let it remain till dry, then rub it off with a woolen cloth, and the spots will disappear.

To Remove Stains, Spots and Mildew from Furniture.—Take ½ pint of 95 per cent. alcohol, ¼ oz. each of pulverized resin and gum shellac, add ½ pint of linseed oil, shake well, and apply with a brush or sponge. Sweet oil will remove finger-marks from varnished furniture, and kerosene from oiled furniture.

To Take Smoke Stains from Walls.—An easy and sure way to remove smoke stains from common plain ceilings is to mix wood ashes with the whitewash just before applying. A pint of ashes to a small pail of whitewash is sufficient, but a little more or less will do no harm.

STAINING.—For Wood.

Antique Oak.—Walnut oil, mixed with the filling applied to red or white oak, produces the antique effect now so fashionable.

Mahogany.—Boil ½ oz. extract of logwood and 2 oz. fustic in 1 quart of water; brush the wood with this, then go over with a weak solution of potash.

Black Walnut.—1. Scald ½ lb. burnt umber in 1 pint of vinegar; strain and apply with a sponge, and when dry, rub hard; repeat the staining until sufficiently dark.

Walnut.—2. Asphaltum thinned with turpentine. A splendid imitation. It must be varnished.

Walnut.—3. Very thin sized shellac, 1 gal.; dry burnt umber, 1 lb.; rose pink, ½ lb.; Vandyke brown, burnt, ½ lb. Mix, let stand a day, and apply with a sponge.

Cherry.—Alcohol, 1 quart; ground turmeric, 3 oz.; raw gamboge, 1½ oz. Mix well, strain through fine muslin, apply two coats with a sponge, rub down well, and varnish.

Orange.—Put 1 oz. turmeric and 1 dram of gum tragacanth in 1 pint of alcohol; shake well, let it stand four days, then strain.

Black.—1. Drop a little sulphuric acid into a small quantity of water, brush over the wood and hold to the fire; it will turn a fine black, and take a good polish. 2. Take ½ gal. of vine-

gal. 1 oz. of bruised nut galls, of logwood chips and copperas each ¼ lb.—boil well; add ½ oz. of the tincture of sesquichloride of iron, formerly called the muriated tincture, and brush on hot. 3. Take ½ gal. of vinegar, ½ lb. of dry lampblack, and 3 lbs. of iron rust, sifted. Mix, and let stand for a week. Lay three coats of this on hot, and then rub with linseed oil, and you will have a fine deep black. 4. Add to the above stain 1 oz. of nut galls, ½ lb. of logwood chips, and ¼ lb. of copperas; lay on three coats, oil well, and you will have a black stain that will stand any kind of weather. 5. Take 1 lb. of logwood chips, ½ lb. of Brazil wood, and boil for an hour and a half in 1 gal. of water. Brush the wood several times with this decoction while hot. Make a decoction of nut galls by simmering gently, for three or four days, ¼ lb. of the galls in 2 quarts of water; give the wood three coats of this, and, while wet, lay on a solution of sulphate of iron (2 oz. to a quart), and, when dry, oil or varnish. 6. Dissolve 1 oz. extract of logwood in 1 quart of water; wash the wood with the solution. When dry wash with vinegar in which rusty iron has been steeped for several days.

Blue.—1. Dissolve copper filings in aquafortis, brush the wood with it, and then go over the work with a hot solution of pearlash (2 oz. to a pint of water) till it assumes a perfectly blue color. 2. Boil 1 lb. of indigo, 2 lbs. of woad, and 3 oz. of alum, in 1 gal. of water; brush well over until thoroughly stained.

Green.—Dissolve verdigris in vinegar, and brush over with the hot solution until of a proper color.

Purple.—Brush the work several times with the logwood decoction used for No. 5 black, and when perfectly dry, give a coat of pearlash solution—1 dram to a quart—taking care to lay it on evenly.

Red.—1. Boil 1 lb. of Brazil wood and 1 oz. of pearlash in 1 gal. of water, and while hot brush over the work until of a proper color. Dissolve 2 oz. of alum in a quart of water, and brush the solution over the work before it dries. 2. Take 1 gal. of the above stain, add 2 more oz. of pearlash; use hot, and brush often with the alum solution. 3. Two oz. potash and 2 oz. Brazil wood in 1 quart of water. Let stand in a warm place a few days, stirring occasionally; heat to a boiling point, and apply. Double the quantity of potash will give a brilliant rose color to the wood.

Yellow.—1. Brush over with the tincture of turmeric. 2. Warm the work and brush over with weak aquafortis, then hold to the fire. Varnish or oil as usual.

Golden Yellow.—Put ½ oz. powdered turmeric in 5 fl. oz. alcohol in a closely stoppered bottle. Let stand a week in a warm place, shake it occasionally, then strain off clear.

STABLES—To Deodorize.

Sawdust wetted with sulphuric acid, diluted with about 40 parts water, and distributed about the stable, is a good deodorizer. Keep the mixture in shallow earthenware vessels.

STAGGERS.

There are two varieties of the disease known under this name by which horses are affected, viz.: Stomach staggers, and grass or sleepy staggers. The first, which occasionally kills the horse in 12 or 18 hours after the attack, is generally induced by an overloaded stomach and improper food. The animal has perhaps partaken largely and rapidly, and after too long a fast, of something to which it is unaccustomed, such as clover or grass. These undergo decomposition within the stomach and intestines, and give rise to such an evolution of gas as either to set up inflammation of the stomach and intestines, or to lead to their rupture, in which latter case the result is, of course, fatal. The symptoms are a quick and feeble pulse, attempts at vomiting, a staggering gait, whilst frequently the animal sits on its haunches like a dog. Sleepy staggers, which is a more chronic manifestation of the disease, is most common during the summer and autumn months, and generally occurs among horses fed on tough and indigestible food. Both kinds of the disease require the same treatment.

Mr. Finlay Dun prescribes a brisk purge, consisting of 6 drams aloes in solution, with a dram of calomel and 2 oz. oil of turpentine; also the injection every hour of clysters, consisting of salt, soap, or tobacco smoke, the abdomen being at the same time diligently rubbed and fomented with water nearly boiling. To ward off stupor, he recommends the frequent administration of 2 or 3 drams carbonate of ammonia, with 1 or 2 oz. spirit of nitrous ether, or of strong whisky toddy, combined with plenty of ginger. To guard against a return of this attack, light and easily digestible food should be administered every 4 or 5 hours, and occasional mild purgatives should be given.

Horses are also subject to another form of staggers, called "mad staggers." This disease originates, however, in causes wholly dissimilar from those just stated, being the result of phrenitis or inflammation of the brain. The animal is frequently very furious and excited, and seems wholly unable to control itself, throwing itself madly about, and attempting to run down anybody that comes in its way; it is also frequently unable to keep on its legs, and when it falls, plunges and struggles violently. The treatment recommended is prompt and copious blood-letting, combined with active purges and enemas, with refrigerant lotions to the head.

STAMMERING.

Occasionally this depends on some organic affection, or slight malformation of the parts of the mouth or throat immediately connected with the utterance of vocal sounds; but, much more frequently, it is a habit resulting from carelessness, or acquired from example or imitation. When the latter is the case, it may be generally removed by perseveringly adopting the plan of never speaking without having the chest moderately filled with air, and then only slowly and deliberately.

STEAM-PIPES—Covering for.

A mixture of sawdust and common starch is recommended by the *Revue Industrielle*. It should be used in the form of a thick paste. A thickness of about four-fifths of an inch is as effective as the most costly non-conductors. For copper pipes a priming coat of potter's clay and water is first applied. Two parts wheat starch and 1 part rye starch in a diluted water solution has been found very effective.

To Thaw Out a Steam-Pipe.—A good way to thaw out a frozen steam-pipe is to take some old cloth, discarded clothes, waste, old carpet, or anything of that kind, and lay on the pipe to be thawed; then get some good hot water and pour it on. The cloth will hold the heat on the pipe, and thaw it out in 5 minutes. This holds good in any kind of a freeze, water-wheel or anything else.

STEEL—To Harden.

It is well known that glass acquires a remarkable toughness by being annealed in oil, and that a high degree of hardness is conferred upon metals by a similar process. It is said that engravers and watchmakers of Germany harden their tools in sealing wax. The tool is heated to whiteness and plunged into the wax, withdrawn after an instant and plunged in again, the process being repeated until the steel is too cold to enter the wax. The steel is said to become, after this process, almost as hard as the diamond, and, when touched with a little oil of turpentine, the tools are excellent for engraving and also for piercing the hardest metal.

Tempering Steel Tools.—Different tools need to be tempered differently, as different degrees of hardness are required for different purposes, and the degree of heat for each of these, with the corresponding color, will be found in the annexed table: Very pale straw color, 430 degrees, the temper required for lancets. A shade of darker yellow, 450 degrees—for razors and surgical instruments. Darker straw yellow, 470 degrees—for pen-knives. Still darker yellow, 490 degrees—chisels for cutting iron. A brown yellow, 500 degrees—axes and plane irons. Yellow, slightly tinged with purple, 520 degrees—table-knives and watch-springs.

To Clean Steel and Iron.—Make a paste of 1 oz. of soft soap and 2 oz. of emery; then rub the article for cleaning with wash-leather, and it will give a brilliant polish.

To Remove Rust from Steel.—This can be done by a free application of kerosene oil, allowing the oil to remain on until the rust is loosened and can be rubbed off.

To Distinguish Steel and Iron.—Apply a small quantity of aquafortis to the surface; if it turns black it is steel; if it remains clear or does not show any change in color it is iron. The slightest vein in iron or steel, where joined together, can be detected.

STONE—Artificial.

Artificial stone, or building cement, can be made in various ways, and several processes for its manufacture have been patented. The materials for this substance are obtained from beds of natural argillaceous marls and marly limestones, which contain certain proportions of lime, silica and alumina. These stones are first burned, then ground to powder in mills. This substance is mixed with water and sand in certain proportions and hardened, somewhat under pressure. What is known as imitation marble is made of burnt gypsum, to which is added lime and water. Hydraulic and other cements are also used to imitate stone in building. There have been patents granted on several processes for making artificial stone, but the mere mixture of lime or marls with water and sand cannot be patented.

How to Split Large Stones.—Kindle a fire on the upper surface of the stone, which, being expanded by the heat, splits. The hardest and largest stone may be split by this method, continuing the fire and increasing the heat in proportion to the size of the stone.

To Remove Grease from Stone.—Pour boiling hot water and strong soda over the spot, make a thin paste of fuller's earth with boiling water, lay it on the spot and let it remain all night; if the grease is not removed, repeat the process. It is sometimes taken out by rubbing the spot with a hard stone, using sand and very hot water with soap and soda.

STOVES—To Polish.

A mixture of turpentine and black varnish, if properly put on, will give a lasting polish.

To Mend Cracks in Stoves.—Take equal parts of wood ashes and common salt, and mix them to a proper consistency with water; with this fill the cracks.

To Clean Stovepipes.—A piece of zinc put on the live coals in the stove will clean out the stovepipe.

STUCCO.

This substance, much in use for walls, pillars, etc., is prepared by mixing plaster of Paris with a solution of gelatine or glue, instead of water. This, while stiffening more slowly, becomes much harder than with water alone. When the mass has been suitably applied and sufficiently hardened, the surface is moistened and rubbed down with pumice-stone until smooth. It is finally to be coated by means of a brush with a concentrated solution of gelatine, and, when perfectly dried, it may be polished with tripoli on a buffer.

SUN-DIALS.—To Make.

Upon a level, hard surface, describe with compasses a circle 8 or 10 inches in diameter. Drive a piece of heavy wire, 6 or 8 inches long, perpendicularly in the center, leaving it just high enough to allow the extreme end of the shadow to fall upon the circle about 9:30 or 10 o'clock. Mark this point and the point where the end of the shadow touches the circle in the afternoon. Draw a line from a point exactly half-way between the two to the center of the circle. This line will be the meridian line or noon-mark. The dial should be made either April 15, June 15, September 1, or December 24, as on these four days, and no other, the noon-mark or sun-dial will coincide with 12 o'clock.

SWEEPING.

New brooms sometimes give trouble by wearing the carpet with fine bits that break from the ends of the straws. This may be prevented by holding the broom for a few minutes, immersed nearly to the point where it is sewed, in boiling suds. The straws will not become brittle so soon with age if the broom is kept habitually moist. The handle of a broom should not be too thick, nor should it be painted or varnished. Never sweep in a sick-room; take up the dust by going over the carpet with a damp sponge.

SWIMMING.

Benjamin Franklin's Advice to Swimmers.—"The only obstacle to improvement in this necessary and life-preserving art is fear: and it is only by overcoming this timidity that you can expect to become a master of the following acquirements. It is very common for novices in the art of swimming to make use of cork or bladders to assist in keeping the body above water; some have utterly condemned the use of them; however, they may be of service for supporting the body while one is learning what is called the stroke, or that manner of drawing in and striking out the hands and feet that is necessary to produce progressive motion. But you will be no swimmer till you can place confidence in the power of the water to support you; I would, therefore, advise the acquiring that confidence in the first place; especially as I have known several who, by a little practice, necessary for that purpose, have insensibly acquired the stroke, taught, as it were, by nature. The practice I mean is this: choosing a place where the water deepens gradually, walk coolly into it till it is up to your breast; then turn round your face to the shore, and throw an egg into the water between you and the shore; it will sink to the bottom and be easily seen there if the water be clear. It must lie in the water so deep that you cannot reach it to take it up but by diving for it. To encourage yourself in order to do this, reflect that your progress will be from deep to shallow water, and that at any time you may, by bringing your legs under you, and standing on the bottom, raise your head far above the water; then plunge under it with your eyes open, which must be kept open on going under, as you cannot open the eyelids for the weight of water above you; throwing yourself toward the egg, and endeavoring by the action of your hands and feet against the water to get forward, till within reach of it. In this attempt you will find that the water buoys you up against your inclination; that it is not so easy to sink as you imagine, and that you cannot, but by active force, get down to the egg. Thus you feel the power of water to support you, and learn to confide in that power, while your endeavors to overcome it and reach the egg teach you the manner of acting on the water with your feet and hands, which action is afterwards used in swimming to support your head higher above the water, or to go forward through it.

"I would the more earnestly press you to the trial of this method, because I think I shall satisfy you that your body is lighter than water, and that you might float in it a long time with your mouth free for breathing, if you would put yourself into a proper posture, and would be still, and forbear struggling; yet, till you have obtained this experimental confidence in the water, I cannot depend upon your having the necessary presence of mind to recollect the posture, and the directions I gave you relating to it. The surprise may put all out of your mind.

"*Though the legs, arms and head of a* human body, being solid parts, are specifically somewhat heavier than fresh water, as the trunk, particularly the upper part, from its hollowness, is so much lighter than water, so the whole of the body, taken altogether, is too light to sink wholly under water, but some part will remain above until the lungs become filled with water, which happens when a person, in the fright, attempts breathing while the mouth and nostrils are under water.

"*The legs and arms are specifically lighter* than salt water, and will be supported by it, so that a human body cannot sink in salt water, though the lungs were filled as above, but from the greater specific gravity of the head. Therefore, a person throwing himself on his back in salt water, and extending his arms, may easily lie so as to keep his mouth and nostrils free for breathing; and, by a slight motion of his hand, may prevent turning, if he should perceive any tendency to it.

"*In fresh water, if a man throw himself on his back* near the surface, he cannot long continue in that situation, but by proper action of his hands on the water; if he use no such action, the legs and lower part of the body will gradually sink till he come into an upright position, in which he will continue suspended, the hollow of his breast keeping the head uppermost.

"*But if in this erect position* the head be kept erect above the shoulders, as when we stand on the ground, the immersion will, by the weight of that part of the head that is out of the water, reach above the mouth and nostrils, perhaps a little above the eyes, so that a man cannot long remain suspended in water with his head in that position.

"*The body continuing suspended* as before, and upright, if the head be leaned quite back, so that the face look upward, all the back part of the head being under water, and its weight consequently in a great measure supported by it, the face will remain above water quite free for breathing, will rise an inch higher every inspiration, and sink as much every expiration, but never so low as that the water may come over the mouth.

"*If, therefore, a person unacquainted with swimming* and falling accidentally into the water, could have presence of mind sufficient to avoid struggling and plunging, and to let the body take this natural position, he might continue long safe from drowning, till, perhaps, help should come; for, as to the clothes, their additional weight when immersed is very inconsiderable, the water supporting it; though when he comes out of the water, he will find them very heavy indeed. But I would not advise any one to depend on having this presence of mind on such an occasion, but learn fairly to swim, as I wish all men were taught to do in their youth.

"*I know by experience* that it is a great comfort to a swimmer, who has a considerable distance to go, to turn himself sometimes on his back, and to vary, in other respects, the means of procuring a progressive motion.

"When he is seized with the cramp in the leg, the method of driving it away is to give the parts affected a sudden, vigorous and violent shock; which he may do in the air as he swims on his back.

"During the great heats in summer, there is no danger in bathing, however warm we may be, in rivers which have been thoroughly warmed by the sun. But to throw one's self into cold spring water, when the body has been heated by exercise in the sun, is an imprudence which may prove fatal. I once knew an instance of four young men who, having worked at harvest in the heat of the day, with a view of refreshing themselves, plunged into a spring of cold water; two died upon the spot, a third the next morning, and the fourth recovered with great difficulty. A copious draught of cold water, in similar circumstances, is frequently attended with the same effect."

TALLOW.—To Clarify.

Dissolve 1 lb. of alum in 1 quart of water, and add to 100 lbs. of tallow in a jacket-kettle (that is a kettle set in a larger one, and the intervening space filled with water, to prevent the tallow from burning). After boiling ½ hour, skim, and add 1 lb. of salt, dissolved in ½ quart of water. Boil again and skim, and when clarified the tallow will be nearly the color of water.

To Harden Tallow.—Melt together 1 lb. of tallow and ¼ lb. of common rosin, and mould candles the usual way. This candle will be of superior lighting power, and as hard as a wax candle, in fact better than a tallow candle in all respects, except odor.

TANNING, Etc.

Green hides should first be thoroughly rubbed with salt, then put to soak in soft water from 9 to 12 days. Take from the water and scrape the flesh side as clean as you can with a blunt knife. The following liquor is used to remove hair or wool: Ten gallons cold soft water, 6 quarts slaked lime, and the same quantity of wood ashes. Soak until the hair or wool will pull off easily. As it is often desirable to keep the hair clean for other uses, the lime and wood ashes may be made into a paste and spread on the flesh side of the skin, which is rolled up and covered with water. After lying 10 days in this state the hair can be readily pulled out with the help of a knife. The skin should be then well scoured, soaked for 12 hours in soap-suds and thoroughly pounded before it is taken out to break it. Now, take equal parts of oil of vitriol and water and apply it to the flesh side of the skin by means of a cloth or sponge tied to a stick. When thoroughly wet, roll up the skin and let it lie for 20 minutes, then put it in a solution of sal-soda and water, 1 lb. of the soda to a bucket of water, letting it lie there for 2 hours, then wash in clean water. Now put into a tub and cover with a strong infusion of oak bark to which has been added about 2 lbs. of common salt and 1 lb. of alum for every 12 lbs. of skin. Turn the skin and stir the mixture, adding some fresh oak bark infusion daily. Calf skins will require from 20 days to a month in this liquid to become tanned, and horse hides some 2 months. If it is necessary to hasten the process, catechu may be used instead of oak bark, making a more astringent liquid. When the tanning process is about complete, take out the skins, and when nearly dry work over a beam to soften them, and rub with a piece of pumice stone.

Stretching and Curing Small Skins.—The market value of a skin is greatly affected by the care taken in removing it from the animal, and in drying it. The common way is to tack the skin to the barn-door and let it remain stretched until quite dry. The trapper in the woods, having no such convenience as the barn-door at hand, is obliged to resort to other methods. One plan is to dry the skin on a hoop. A skin to be dried in this manner must not be ripped down the belly, but it is cut from the lower jaw of the animal to just below its forelegs; the lips, eyes and ears being cut around, the skin is stripped off, leaving the fur side inward. The hoop consists of a branch of hickory or other elastic wood, an inch through at the butt. This is bent and pushed into the skin, which is drawn tight and fastened in place by notches in the bow, drawing the skin of the lip into these notches. A much neater way, and one generally preferred, is to use stretchers of thin wood. As these have to be carried by the trapper, they are made of light wood and very thin. They are three-sixteenths of an inch thick, 24 inches long, 6 inches wide at the larger end, and slightly tapering. They are rounded to a blunt point at the lower end, and the edges chamfered. The skin is drawn over the board and secured with tacks. Skins stretched by these methods should not be dried in the sun, nor by a fire, but in a cool place where they will be sheltered from the rain. No salt or other preservative is used upon skins intended for the market.

To Cure Rabbit Skins.—First lay the skin on a smooth board, placing the fur side under, and fasten the skin to the board with small tacks. Wash it over with a solution of salt; then dissolve 1½ oz. alum in ½ pint warm water, and with a sponge dipped in this solution, moisten the surface all over; repeat this every now and then for 3 days; when the skin is quite dry, take out the tacks, and, rolling it loosely the wrong way, the hair inside, draw it quickly backward and forward through a large smooth ring until it is quite soft; then roll it in the contrary way of the skin, and repeat the operation. Skins prepared thus are useful for many domestic purposes.

To Cure Sheep-Skins with the Wool on.—Take a spoonful of alum and two of saltpeter; pulverize and mix well together, then sprinkle the powder on the flesh side of the skin, and lay the two flesh sides together, leaving the wool outside. Then fold up the skin as tight as you can, and hang it in a dry place. In 2 or 3 days, or as soon as it is dry, take it down and scrape it with a blunt knife, till clean and supple. This completes the process, and makes you a most excellent saddle cover. If, when you kill your mutton, you treat the skins this way, you can get more for them from the saddler than you can get for the wool and skin separately disposed otherwise.

Other skins which you desire to cure with the fur or hair on, may be treated in the same way.

To Prepare Sheepskins for Mats.—See p. 448.

To Tan Small Skins.—When taken from the animal, let the skins be nailed in the shape of an oblong square on a board to dry, fur side down. Before taking them from the board, clean off all the fat or oily matter with a dull knife. Be careful not to cut the skins. When you wish to tan them, soak thoroughly in cold water until soft; then squeeze out the water, and take of soft water, 3 quarts, salt, ½ pint, and best oil of vitriol, 1 oz. Stir well with a stick, and put in the skins quickly and leave them in 30 minutes; then take them in your hand and squeeze (not wring) them out, and hang in the shade, fur side down, to dry. If you get the quantity of liquor proportioned to the skin, they will need no rubbing to make them soft; and, tanned in this way, the moths will never disturb them.

To Tan Skins with the Hair on.—Stretch the skin tightly and smoothly upon a board, hair side down, and tack it by the edges to its place. Scrape off the loose flesh and fat with a blunt knife, and work in chalk freely with plenty of hard rubbing. When the chalk begins to powder and fall off, remove the skin from the board, rub in plenty of powdered alum, wrap up closely, and keep it in a dry place for a few days. By this means it will be made pliable, and will retain the hair.

TAR, PITCH AND TURPENTINE.

Turpentine is an oily, resinous substance flowing from the pine and other cone-bearing trees. An excavation which has a capacity of about 2 pints is made in the trunk of the tree, and in this the exuded juice accumulates. It becomes stiff very soon on exposure to the air, and is taken from the tree, washed with warm water, then heated and purified by straining through straw filters. When this crude product is distilled with water the oil of turpentine is removed, and the residue left is the resin of commerce. The different cone-bearing trees furnish different grades and kinds of turpentine. Tar is obtained from pine-wood by the process of charring. The wood is placed in kilns or pits, or may be laid in mounds and covered closely with ashes. Fire is then applied and the wood slowly carbonized. The tar so formed trickles down into a gutter beneath the wood, and is conveyed thence by pipes into proper tanks. Pitch is the residuum obtained by boiling tar in an open iron pot, or in a still, until the volatile and liquid portion is driven off. It is soft and sticky when warm, but it becomes solid and brittle when cold. For use it is mixed with a small portion of oil to render it less brittle.

TARTAR—To Remove.

This preparation is used by dentists: Pure muriatic acid, 1 oz.; water, 1 oz.; honey, 2 oz.; mix thoroughly. Take a toothbrush, and wet it freely with this preparation, and briskly rub the black teeth, and in a moment's time they will be perfectly white; then immediately wash out the mouth well with water, that the acid may not act on the enamel of the teeth. This should be done only occasionally.

TATTOO-MARKS—To Remove.

Cover the mark with a plaster that will blister; after keeping the place open about a week with an ointment, dress it to get well. The tattoo-marks will disappear as the new skin grows.

TEA-KETTLE—To Clean.

Put into the tea-kettle a flat oyster-shell, and keep it constantly there. This will attract the stony particles in the water to itself, and prevent their forming upon the tea-kettle.

To Remove the Lime from Tea-kettles.—Put in your kettle ½ lb. of Spanish whiting, fill with water, and boil until the lime is removed.

THERMOMETER—To Test.

The common thermometer is usually inaccurate. To test the thermometer, bring water into the condition of active boiling, warm the thermometer gradually in the steam and then plunge it into the water. If it indicates a fixed temperature of 212 degrees, the instrument is a good one.

TIMBER.

Seasoning and Preserving.—For the purpose of seasoning, timber should be piled under shelter, where it may be kept dry, but not exposed to a strong current of air. At the same time there should be a free circulation of air about the timber, with which view slats or blocks of wood should be placed between the pieces that lie over each other, near enough to prevent the timber from bending.

In the sheds, the pieces of timber should be piled in this way, or in square piles, and classed according to age and kind. Each pile should be distinctly marked with the number and kind of pieces, and the age, or the date of receiving them.

The piles should be taken down and made over again at intervals, varying with the length of time which the timber has been cut.

The seasoning of timber requires from 2 to 4 years, according to its size.

Gradual drying and seasoning in this manner is considered the most favorable to the durability and strength of timber, but various methods have been proposed for hastening the process. For this purpose, steaming and boiling timber has been applied with success; kiln-drying is serviceable only for boards and pieces of small dimensions, and is apt to cause cracks, and to impair the strength of wood, unless performed very slowly.

Timber of large dimension is improved by immersion in water for some weeks, according to its size, after which it is less subject to warp and crack in seasoning.

Oak timber loses about one-fifth of its weight in seasoning, and about one-third of its weight in becoming dry.

Testing Soundness of Timber.—A good test is to bore into the tree as low down as possible with a long-handled inch-and-a-half or two-inch auger. The chips will show whether the tree is sound or not at the heart. When purchasing standing timber at a high price, this test is important.

TIRES—To Make Tight.

A correspondent writes to the *Southern Planter*: "Before putting on the tires I fill the fellies with linseed-oil. The tires will wear out, but will never be loose. The method of filling the fellies is as follows: I use a long cast-iron oil-heater; the oil is brought to a boiling heat; the wheel is placed on a stick so as to hang in the oil, each felloe an hour for a common-sized felloe. The timber should be dry, as green timber will not take oil. Be careful not to burn the timber by making the oil hotter than a boiling point. Timber filled with oil is not susceptible to water, and is much more durable."

TOOLS—To Grind.

Plane irons should be ground to a bevel of about 35 degrees; chisels and gouges to 30. Turning chisels may sometimes run to an angle of 45. Moulding tools, such as are used for ivory and for very hard wood, are made at from 50 to 60 degrees. Tools for working iron and steel are bevelled at an inclination to the edge of from 60 to 70 degrees, and for cutting gun and similar metal range from 80 to 90.

Mechanics claim and believe that by holding on the grindstone all edge tools, so that the action of the stone is at right angles with the plane of the edge, or, in plainer words, by holding the edge of the tools square across the stone, the direction of the fibers will be changed so as to present the ends instead of the side as a cutting edge. By grinding in this manner a finer and smoother edge is set, the tool is ground in less time, holds an edge a great deal longer, it is said, and is less liable to "nick out" and break.

Marking Metal, Tools, etc.—Mix well ½ oz. of nitric acid and 1 oz. of muriatic acid. Coat the place you wish to mark with melted beeswax; when cold, write plainly in the wax, clear to the metal, with any sharp-pointed instrument; then apply the acid with a feather, carefully filling each letter. Let it remain from 1 to 10 minutes according to appearance desired, then throw on water, which stops the process of cutting, and remove the wax.

To Prevent Handles Splitting.—To prevent handles (to be pounded upon) from splitting, where beauty is not sought, follow the shoemaker's plan, and put on the end, after sawing it off square, two round disks of sole leather. The two thicknesses of leather will prevent splitting, and if in the course of time they expand and overlap the wood of the handle, they are simply trimmed off all around. The leathers may be fastened with shoe-nails.

TOOTHACHE—Cure.

Compound tincture of benzoin is said to be one of the most certain and speedy cures for toothache; pour a few drops on cotton, and press at once into the diseased cavity, when the pain will almost instantly cease.

Toothache Tincture.—Mix tannin, 1 scruple; mastic, 3 grains; ether, 2 drams. Apply on cotton wool to the tooth, previously dried.

TOOTH POWDER.

1. Procure, at a druggist's, ½ oz. of powdered orris root, ½ oz. of prepared chalk, finely pulverized, and 2 or 3 small lumps of Dutch pink. Let them all be mixed in a mortar and pounded together. The Dutch pink is to impart a pale reddish color. Keep it in a close box.

2. Mix together, in a mortar, ½ oz. of red Peruvian bark, finely powdered, ¼ oz. of powdered myrrh, and ½ oz. of prepared chalk.

TREES—Wash for.

One ounce of copperas and 8 gallons of water. This is an effectual preventive against blight.

TRICOPHEROUS—For the Hair.

Castor oil, alcohol, 1 pint; tincture of cantharides, 1 oz.; oil of bergamot, ½ oz.; alkanet coloring, to color as wished. Mix and let it stand 48 hours, with occasional shaking, and then filter.

TURPENTINE—Virtues of.

After a housekeeper fully realizes the worth of turpentine in the household, she is never willing to be without a supply of it. It gives quick relief to burns, it is an excellent application for corns, it is good for rheumatism and sore throats, and it is the quickest remedy for convulsions or fits. Then it is a sure preventive against moths by just dropping a trifle in the bottom of drawers, chests and cupboards; it will render the garments secure from injury during the summer. It will keep ants and bugs from closets and store-rooms by putting a few drops in the corners and upon the shelves; it is sure destruction to bedbugs, and will effectually drive them away from their haunts if thoroughly applied to all the joints of the bedstead in the spring-cleaning time, and injures neither furniture nor clothing. A spoonful of it added to a pail of warm water is excellent for cleaning paint. A little in suds washing-days lightens laundry labor. See, also, *Tar, Pitch and Turpentine.*

UMBRELLAS.

A silk umbrella is much injured by being left open to dry. After coming in out of the rain let the umbrella down and stand it on the handle, that it may dry uniformly, the water dripping from the edges of the frame. If left open the silk becomes stretched and stiff, and is much more apt to split than if the folds are allowed to lie loose.

VARNISH.

Any liquid matter which, when applied to the surface of a solid body, becomes dry, and forms a hard, glossy coating, impervious to air and moisture.

Varnishes are commonly divided into two

classes—fat or oil varnishes and spirit varnishes. The fixed or volatile oils, or mixtures of them, are used as vehicles or solvents in the former, and concentrated alcohol in the latter. The sp. gr. of alcohol for the purpose of making varnishes should not be more than .8156 (=67 o. p.), and it should be preferably chosen of even greater strength. A little camphor is often dissolved in it, to increase its solvent power. The oil of turpentine, which is the essential oil chiefly employed for varnishes, should be pure and colorless. Pale drying linseed oil is the fixed oil generally used. Among the substances which are dissolved in the above menstrua are amber, animé, copal, elemi, lac, mastic and sandarach, to impart body and luster; benzoin, on account of its agreeable odor; annotta, gamboge, saffron, socotrine aloes and turmeric, to give a yellow color; dragon's blood and red sandal wood, to give a red tinge; asphaltum, to give a black color and body; and caoutchouc to impart toughness and elasticity.

In the preparation of spirit varnishes care should be taken to prevent the evaporation of the alcohol as much as possible, and also to preserve the portion that evaporates. On the large scale a common still may be advantageously employed, the head being furnished with a stuffing-box, to permit of the passage of a vertical rod, connected with a stirrer at one end and a working handle at the other. The gum and spirit being introduced, the head of the still closely fitted on and luted, and the connection made with a proper refrigerator, heat (preferably that of steam or a water bath) should be applied, and the spirit brought to a gentle boil, after which it should be partially withdrawn and agitation continued until the gum is dissolved. The spirit which has distilled over should be then added to the varnish, and after thorough admixture the whole should be run off, as rapidly as possible, through a silk-gauze sieve, into stone jars, which should be immediately corked down, and set aside to clarify. On the small scale, spirit varnishes are best made by maceration in closed bottles or tin cans, either in the cold or by the heat of a water bath. In order to prevent the agglutination of the resin, it is often advantageously mixed with clean siliceous sand or pounded glass, by which the surface is much increased, and the solvent power of the menstruum greatly promoted.

To insure the excellence of all varnishes, one of the most important points is the use of good drying oil. Linseed oil for this purpose should be very pale, perfectly limpid or transparent, scarcely odorous, and mellow and sweet to the taste. One hundred gallons of such an oil is put into an iron or copper boiler capable of holding fully 150 gallons, gradually heated to a gentle simmer, and kept near that point for about 2 hours to expel moisture; the scum is then carefully removed, and 14 lbs. finely pulverized scale litharge, 12 lbs. red lead and 8 lbs. powdered umber (all carefully dried and free from moisture), are gradually sprinkled in; the whole is then kept well stirred to prevent the driers sinking to the bottom, and the boiling is continued at a gentle heat for about 3 hours longer; the fire is next withdrawn, and, after 30 to 40 hours' repose, the scum is carefully removed, and the clear supernatant oil decanted from the "bottoms." The product forms the best boiled or drying oil of the varnish-maker.

In the preparation of oil varnishes, the gum is melted as rapidly as possible, without discoloring or burning it; and when completely fused, the oil, also heated to nearly the boiling point, is poured in, after which the mixture is boiled until it appears perfectly homogeneous and clear, like oil, when the heat is raised, the driers (if any are to be used) gradually and cautiously sprinkled in, and the boiling continued, with constant stirring, for 3 or 4 hours, or until a little, when cooled on a palette knife, feels strong and stringy between the fingers. The mixture is next allowed to cool considerably, but while still quite fluid, the turpentine, previously made moderately hot, is cautiously added and the whole thoroughly incorporated. The varnish is then run through a filter or sieve into stone jars, cans or other vessels, and set aside to clarify itself by subsidence. When no driers are used, the mixture of oil and gum is boiled until it runs perfectly clear, when it is removed from the fire, and, after it has cooled a little, the turpentine is added as before.

It is generally conceived that the more perfectly the gum is fused, or run, as it is called, the larger and stronger will be the product; and the longer the boiling of the gum and oil is continued, within moderation, the freer the resulting varnish will work and cover. An excess of heat renders the varnish stringy and injures its flowing qualities. For pale varnishes as little heat as possible should be employed throughout the whole process. Good body varnishes should contain 1½ lb.; carriage, wainscot and mahogany varnish, fully 1 lb.; and gold size and black japan, fully ½ lb. gum per gallon, besides the asphaltum in the latter. Spirit varnishes should contain about 2½ lbs. of gum per gallon. The use of too much driers is found to injure the brilliancy and transparency of the varnish. Copperas does not combine with varnish, but only hardens it. Sugar of lead, however, dissolves in it to a greater or less extent. Boiling oil of turpentine combines very readily with melted copal, and it is an improve-

mended as the common process, to use it either before or in conjunction with the oil, in the preparation of copal varnish that it is desired should be very white. Gums of difficult solubility are rendered more soluble by being exposed, in the state of powder, for some time to the air.

Varnishes, like wines, improve by age, and should always be kept as long as possible before use.

From the inflammable nature of the materials of which varnishes are composed, their manufacture should only be carried on in some detached building of little value and built of uninflammable materials. When a pot of varnish, gum or turpentine catches fire, it is most readily extinguished by closely covering it with a piece of stout woolen carpeting, which should be always kept at hand, ready for the purpose.

Amber Varnish.—1. Take of amber (clear and pale), 6 lbs.; fuse it; add of hot clarified linseed oil, 2 gallons; boil until it "strings well," then let it cool a little, and add of oil of turpentine, 4 gallons, or q. s. Nearly as pale as copal varnish; it soon becomes very hard, and is the most durable of the oil varnishes; but it requires some time before it is fit for polishing, unless the articles are "stoved." When required to dry and harden quicker, drying oil may be substituted for the linseed oil, or "driers" may be added during the boiling.

2. Amber, 4 oz.; pale boiled oil, 1 quart; proceed as last. Very hard.

Amber varnish is suited for all purposes where a very hard and durable oil varnish is required. The paler kind is superior to copal varnish, and is often mixed with the latter to increase its hardness and durability. The only objection to it is the difficulty of preparing it of a very pale color. It may, however, be easily bleached with some fresh-slaked lime.

Bessemer's Varnish.—This consists of a pale oil copal varnish, diluted with about 5 times its volume of oil of turpentine, the mixture being subsequently agitated with about 1-20th part of dry-slaked lime, and decanted after a few days' repose. Five parts of the product mixed with 4 parts bronze powder forms "Bessemer's gold paint."

Black Varnish.—1. (Black amber varnish.) From amber, 1 lb.; fuse; add of hot drying oil, ½ pint; powdered black resin, 3 oz.; asphaltum (Naples), 4 oz.; when properly incorporated and considerably cooled, add of oil of turpentine, 1 pint. This is the beautiful black varnish of the coachmakers.

2. (Ironwork black.) From asphaltum, 48 lbs.; fuse; add of boiled oil, 10 gallons; red lead and litharge, of each 7 lbs.; dried and powdered white copperas, 3 lbs.; boil for 2 hours, then add of dark gum amber (fused), 8 lbs.; hot linseed oil, 2 gallons; boil for 2 hours longer, or until a little of the mass, when cooled, may be rolled into pills; then withdraw the heat, and afterwards thin it down with oil of turpentine, 30 gallons. Used for the ironwork of carriages and other nice purposes.

3. (Black japan. Bituminous varnish.) From Naples asphaltum, 50 lbs.; dark gum anime, 8 lbs.; fuse; add of linseed oil, 12 gallons; boil as before, then add of dark gum amber, 10 lbs., previously fused and boiled with linseed oil, 2 gallons; next add of driers, q. s., and further proceed as ordered in No. 2. Excellent for either wood or metals.

4. From burnt amber, 8 oz.; true asphaltum, 4 oz.; boiled linseed oil, 1 gallon; grind the amber with a little of the oil; add it to the asphaltum, previously dissolved in a small quantity of the oil by heat; mix; add the remainder of the oil, boil, cool, and thin with a sufficient quantity of oil of turpentine. Flexible.

5. (Brunswick black.) To asphalt, 2 lbs., fused in an iron pot, add of hot boiled oil, 1 pint; mix well, remove the pot from the fire, and, when cooled a little, add of oil of turpentine, 2 quarts. Used to blacken and polish grates and ironwork. Some makers add driers.

Body Varnish.—1. From the finest African copal, 8 lbs.; drying oil, 2 gallons; oil of turpentine, 3½ gallons; proceed as for amber varnish. Very hard and durable.

Bookbinder's Varnish.—Take of pale gum sandarach, 3 oz.; rectified spirit, 1 pint; dissolve by cold digestion and frequent agitation. Used by binders to varnish morocco leather book-covers. A similar varnish is also prepared from very pale shellac and wood naphtha.

Carriage Varnish.—1. (Spirit.) Take of gum sandarach, 1¼ lb.; very pale shellac, ⅝ lb.; very pale transparent resin, ⅛ lb.; rectified spirit of .8221 (64 o. p.), 3 quarts; dissolve, and add of pure Canadian balsam, 1⅛ lb. Used for the internal parts of carriages, etc. Dries in 10 minutes or less.

2. (Oil. Best pale.) Take of pale African copal, 8 lbs.; fuse; add of clarified linseed oil, 2½ gallons; boil until very stringy, then add of dried copperas and litharge, of each ¼ lb.; again boil, thin with oil of turpentine, 5½ gallons; mix, while both are hot, with the following varnish, and immediately strain the mixture into a covered vessel: Gum anime, 8 lbs.; clarified linseed oil, 2½ gallons; dried sugar of lead and litharge, of each ¼ lb.; boil as before,

thin with oil of turpentine, 5½ gallons. Dries in 4 hours in summer and 6 in winter. Used for the wheels, springs and carriage part of coaches and other vehicles, and by house-painters, decorators, etc., who want a strong, quick-drying and durable varnish.

Chinese Varnish.—From mastic and sandarach, of each 2 oz.; rectified spirit (64 o. p.), 1 pint; dissolve. Dries in 5 minutes. Very tough and brilliant.

Copal Varnish.—1. (Oil.) From pale, hard copal, 2 lbs.; fuse, add of hot drying oil, 1 pint; boil as before directed, and thin with oil of turpentine, 3 pints, or q. s. Dries hard in 12 to 24 hours.

2. (Spirit.) From coarsely powdered copal and glass, of each 4 oz.; alcohol of 90% (64 o. p.), 1 pint; camphor, ½ oz.; heat the mixture, with frequent stirring, in a water bath, so that the bubbles may be counted as they rise until solution is complete, and, when cold, decant the clear portion.

3. (Turpentine.) To oil of turpentine, 1 pint, heated in a water bath, add, in small portions at a time, of powdered copal (prepared as above, 3 to 4 oz.; dissolve, etc., as before. Dries slowly, but is very pale and durable.

4. (Ripinton's copal varnish.) From pale African copal, 7 lbs.; pale drying oil, ½ gal.; oil of turpentine, 3 gals.; proceed as in No. 1. Dries in 20 to 60 minutes, and may be polished as soon as hard, particularly if stoved.

All copal varnishes, when properly made, are very hard and durable, though less so than that of amber; but they have the advantage over the latter of being paler.

Crystal Varnish.—From genuine pale Canada balsam and rectified turpentine, equal parts; Used for maps, prints, drawings and other articles of paper, and also to prepare tracing paper, and to transfer engravings.

Flexible Varnish.—From India rubber (cut small), 1½ oz.; chloroform, ether (washed), or bisulphuret of carbon, 1 pint; digest in the cold until solution is complete. Dries as soon as it is laid on. Gutta percha may be substituted for india rubber.

Furniture Varnish.—A solution of pure white wax, 1 part, in rectified oil of turpentine, 4 parts, frequently passes under this name.

Gilder's Varnish.—Pale gum-lac in grains, gamboge, dragon's blood and annotta, of each 12½ oz.; saffron, 3½ oz.; dissolve each resin separately in 5 pints of alcohol of 90%, and make two separate tinctures of the dragon's blood and annotta, with a like quantity of spirit; then mix the solutions in the proper proportions to produce the required shade. Used for gilded articles, etc.

Gun-barrel Varnish.—From shellac, 1½ oz.; dragon's blood, 3 dr.; rectified spirit, 1 quart. Applied after the barrels are "browned."

Italian Varnish.—Boil Scio turpentine until brittle; powder it, and dissolve this in oil of turpentine. Used for prints, etc.

Japan Varnish.—Pale amber or copal varnish. Used for japanning tin, papier maché, etc.

Lac Varnish.—1. Pale seed-lac (or shellac), 6 oz.; rectified spirit, 1 quart; dissolve.

2. Substitute lac bleached with chlorine for seed-lac. Both are very tough, hard and durable, but quite inflexible. Wood naphtha may be substituted for spirit. Used for pictures, metal, wood or leather, and particularly for toys.

Lac Varnish (Aqueous).—From pale shellac, 5 oz.; borax, 1 oz.; water, 1 pint; digest at nearly the boiling point until dissolved; then strain. Equal to the more costly spirit varnish for many purposes; it is an excellent vehicle for water colors, inks, etc.; when dry it is waterproof.

Lac Varnish (Colored).—1. Take of turmeric (ground), 1 lb.; rectified spirit, 2 gal.; macerate for a week, strain with expression, and add to the tincture, gamboge, 1½ oz.; pale shellac, ¾ lb.; gum sandarach, 3¼ lbs.; when dissolved, strain, and further add of good turpentine varnish, 1 quart. Gold-colored.

2. Seed-lac, 3 oz.; turmeric, 1 oz.; dragon's blood, ¼ oz.; rectified spirit, 1 pint; digest for a week, frequently shaking, then decant the clear portion. Deep gold-colored.

3. Spanish annotta, 3 lbs.; dragon's blood, 1 lb.; gum sandarach, 3¼ lbs.; rectified spirit, 2 gals.; turpentine varnish, 1 quart; as before. Red-colored.

4. Gamboge, 1 oz.; Cape aloes, 3 oz.; pale shellac, 1 lb.; rectified spirit, 2 gals.; as before. Pale brass-colored.

5. Seed-lac, dragon's blood, annotta and gamboge, of each ¼ lb.; gum sandarach, 2 oz.; saffron, 1 oz.; rectified spirit, 1 gal. Resembles the last.

Lacquers are used upon polished metals and wood, to impart to them the appearance of gold. Articles in brass, tin plate and pewter, or which are covered with tinfoil, are more especially so treated. As lacquers are required of different depths and shades of color, it is best to keep a concentrated solution of each of the coloring ingredients ready, so that it may be added, at any time, to produce any desired tint.

Mastic Varnish.—Take of pale and picked gum mastic, 5 lbs.; glass (pounded as small as barley, and well washed and dried), 3 lbs.; finest newly rectified oil of turpentine (lukewarm), 2 gals.; put them into a clean 4-gal. tin bottle or can; bung down securely, and keep rolling it backwards and forwards pretty smartly on a counter, or any other solid place, for at least 4 hours, when, if the gum is all dissolved, the varnish may be decanted, strained through muslin into another bottle, and allowed to settle; if the solution is still incomplete, the agitation must be continued for some time longer, or the gentle warmth applied as well. Very fine.

Oak Varnish.—1. Clear pale resin, 3½ lbs.; oil of turpentine, 1 gal.; dissolve.

2. To the last add of Canada balsam, 1 pint. Both are cheap and excellent common varnishes for wood or metal.

Oil Varnish.—The finer qualities are noticed under Amber, Body, Carriage, and Copal Varnish; the following produces the ordinary oil varnish of the trade: Take of good clear resin, 3 lbs.; drying oil, ½ gal.; melt, and thin with oil of turpentine, 2 quarts. A good and durable varnish for common work.

Spirit Varnish.—(Brown hard.)—a. From gum sandarach, 3 lbs.; pale seed-lac or shellac, 2 lbs.; rectified spirit (65 o. p.), 2 gals.; dissolve, and add of turpentine varnish, 1 quart; agitate well, strain (quickly) through gauze, and in a month decant the clear portion from the sediment. Very fine.

b. From seed-lac and yellow resin, of each 1½ lbs.; rectified spirit, 5 quarts; oil of turpentine, 1½ pint; dissolve.

2. (White hard.)—From gum sandarach (picked), 5 lbs.; camphor, 2 oz.; washed and dried coarsely-pounded glass, 3 lbs.; rectified spirit (65 o. p.), 7 quarts; proceed as in making mastic varnish; when strained, add of pure Canada balsam, 1 quart. Very pale, durable and brilliant.

3. (Soft brilliant.) From sandarach, 6 oz.; elemi (genuine), 4 oz.; anime, 1 oz.; camphor, ½ oz.; rectified spirit, 1 quart; as before.

4. (Scented.) To the preceding add some gum benzoin, balsam of Peru, balsam of Tolu, oil of lavender, or essence of musk or ambergris. The first two can only be employed for dark varnishes.

The above varnishes are chiefly applied to articles of the toilet, as work-boxes, card-cases, etc., but are also suitable for other articles, whether of paper, wood, linen or metal, that require a brilliant and quick-drying varnish. They dry almost as soon as applied, and are generally hard enough to polish in 24 hours. They are, however, much less durable, and more liable to crack, than oil varnishes.

Toy Varnish.—Similar to common spirit varnish, but using carefully rectified wood naphtha as the solvent.

Transfer Varnish.—From mastic (in tears) and sandarach, of each 4 oz.; rectified spirit, 1½ pints; dissolve, and add of pure Canada balsam, ½ pint. Used for transferring and fixing engravings or lithographs on wood, and for gilding, silvering, etc.

Wax Varnish.—1. Take of white wax (pure), 1 lb.; melt it with as gentle a heat as possible, add of warm rectified spirit, specific gravity .830 (60 o. p.), 1 pint; mix perfectly, and pour the liquid out upon a cold porphyry slab; next grind it with a muller to a perfectly smooth paste, adding more spirit as required; put the paste into a marble mortar, make an emulsion with water, 3½ pints, gradually added, and strain it through muslin. Used as a varnish for paintings; when dry, a hot iron is passed over it, or heat is otherwise evenly applied, so as to fuse it, and render it transparent, after which, when quite cold, it is polished with a clean linen cloth. The most protective of all varnishes.

2. Wax (pure), 5 oz.; oil of turpentine, 1 quart; dissolve. Used for furniture.

VARNISHING.

To give the highest degree of lustre to varnish after it is laid on, as well as to remove the marks of the brush, it undergoes the operation of polishing. This is performed by first rubbing it with very finely powdered pumice stone and water, and afterwards with an oiled rag and tripoli, until the required polish is produced. The surface is, last of all, cleaned with soft linen cloths, cleared of all greasiness with powdered starch, and then rubbed bright with the palm of the hand.

In varnishing great care must be taken that the surface is free from grease or smoke; as, unless this be the case, the best oil or turpentine varnish in the world will not dry or harden. Old articles are usually washed with soap and water, by the painters, before being varnished, to prevent any misadventure of the kind alluded to.

VEGETABLES—*To Keep.*

Dig a shallow trench in an elevated spot 4 feet wide and 6 inches deep, and long enough to hold all you want to put in it. Place 2 or 3 inches of oat-straw in the bottom of the trench. Then put in your roots or apples, piling them up 3 feet or so, and then cover with 6 inches of oat-straw. Then place upon the straw 15 inches of earth to keep the frost out. We say 15 inches because we mean it.

VELVET—To Raise the Nap.

Place a dampened towel over the face of a moderately hot flat-iron. Lay the piece of velvet on this immediately, and while the steam is passing through brush briskly in the direction that will raise the nap; a nail-brush will answer the purpose. I have found this method the most effectual of various ones tried.

VOLATILE SALTS—For Pungents.

Liquor ammonia, fort., 1 pint; oil lavender flowers, 1 dram; oil rosemary, fine, 1 dram; oil bergamot, ½ dram; oil peppermint, 10 minims. Mix thoroughly and fill pungents or keep in well-stoppered bottle. Another formula is: Sesqui-carbonate of ammonia, small pieces, 10 oz.; concentrated liquor ammonia, 5 oz. Put the sesqui-carbonate in a wide-mouthed jar with air-tight stopper, perfume the liquor ammonia to suit, and pour over the carbonate, close tightly the lid and place in a cool place, stir with a stiff spatula every other day for a week, and then keep it closed for 3 weeks, or until it becomes hard, when it is ready for use.

WASHING.

The following is a French way of washing clothes, and is very economical, and said to be very effective: Two lbs. of soap is reduced with a little water to pulp, which, having been slightly warmed, is cooled in 10 gallons of water, to which is added 1 teaspoonful of turpentine oil, and 2 teaspoonfuls of ammonia; then the mixture is agitated. The water is kept at a temperature which can be borne by the hand. In this solution the white clothes are put and left there for 2 hours before washing them with soap, taking care in the meantime to cover the tub. The solution may be warmed again and used once more, but it will be necessary to add ½ teaspoonful of ammonia. Once washed with soap, the clothes are put in hot water, and the blue is applied. This process, it is obvious, saves much time, much labor and fuel, while it gives to the clothes a whiteness much superior to that obtained by any other process, and the destructive use of the washboard is not necessary to clean the clothes from the impurities which they contain.

WASHING FLUID.

1. Take ½ lb. of sal soda, ¼ lb. of borax, dissolved in 1 gallon of hot water; let it settle; pour off in bottles. One gill of this mixture with a pint of soft soap, or ¼ bar of soap dissolved in hot water, is enough for a washing.

2. Put 1 lb. of saltpeter into a gallon of water and keep it in a corked jug; 2 tablespoonfuls for a pint of soap. Soak, wash and boil as usual. This bleaches the clothes beautifully without injuring the fabric.

3. An excellent washing fluid and one that will not injure the finest fabric is made of 1 bar of Russian soap cut up fine, 1 tablespoonful of kerosene oil, ½ cupful of washing soda and 1 gallon of water. The night before washday put your clothes to soak in warm water. In the morning boil the fluid 20 minutes, add whatever cold water is required for washing the clothes, put in the clothes and boil ½ hour; they are then ready to rinse and starch.

WATCHMAKER'S OIL.

Prepared by placing a clean strip or coil of lead in a small white-glass bottle filled with pure almond or olive oil, and exposing it to the sun's rays at a window for some time till a curdy matter ceases to be deposited, and the oil has become quite limpid and colorless. Used for fine work; does not become thick by age.

WATER.

To Tell Pure Water.—The color, odor, taste and purity of water can be ascertained as follows: Fill a large bottle made of colorless glass with water; look through the water at some black object. Pour out some of the water and leave the bottle half full; cork the bottle and place it for a few hours in a warm place; shake up the water, remove the cork, and critically smell the air contained in the bottle. If it has any smell, particularly if the odor is repulsive, the water should not be used for domestic purposes. By heating the water an odor is evolved that would not otherwise appear. Water fresh from the well is usually tasteless, even if it contains a large amount of putrescible organic matter. All water for domestic purposes should be perfectly tasteless, and remain so even after it has been warmed, since warming often develops a taste in water which is tasteless when cold.

To Purify Water.—Cistern water often becomes foul on account of a large amount of organic matter derived from the roof of the house. This matter undergoes rapid decay and multiplication when the temperature is warm. There are two ways to correct the evil: one is by filtering, which, unless done on some improved plan, is not perfect, and the second by the addition of hypermanganate of potassa, used in the proportion of about an ounce to each 50 gallons of water. A chemical change takes place, and the organic matter is oxidized, and the whole mass precipitated as a harmless sediment. The chemical reaction is marked by a purple coloring, and this color indicates the presence of organic matter. The hypermanganate should be added until this color disappears. This preparation of potash may be obtained at any drug store. As an aid in keeping water pure, frequent agitation is commended.

Another Method. — A little dissolved alum is effective in clearing muddy water. If thrown into a tub of soap-suds, the soap, curdled, and accompanied by the muddy particles, sinks to the bottom, leaving the water clear and pure. In times of scarcity of water this may be used a second time for washing clothes.

A few minnow fishes put into a well is one of the best means of keeping the water pure, so far as worms and insects are concerned.

To Test Water for Boilers. — Boiler-users who desire simple tests for the water they are using will find the following compilation of tests both useful and valuable:

Test for Hard or Soft Water. — Dissolve a small piece of good soap in alcohol. Let a few drops of the solution fall into a glass of the water. If it turns milky, it is hard water; if it remains clear, it is soft water.

Test for Earthy Matters or Alkali. — Take litmus-paper dipped in vinegar, and if on immersion the paper returns to its true shade, the water does not contain earthy matter or alkali. If a few drops of syrup be added to a water containing an earthy matter, it will turn green.

Test for Carbonic Acid. — Take equal parts of water and clear lime water. If combined or free carbonic acid is present, a precipitate is seen, to which if a few drops of muriatic acid be added, effervescence commences.

Test for Magnesia. — Boil the water to a twentieth part of its weight, and then drop a few grains of neutral carbonate of ammonia into a glass of it and a few drops of phosphate of soda. If magnesia is present, it will fall to the bottom.

Test for Iron. — Boil a little nut-gall and add to the water. If it turns grey or slate-black, iron is present. 2. Dissolve a little prussiate of potash, and, if iron is present, it will turn blue.

Test for Lime. — Into a glass of water put 2 drops of oxalic acid, and blow upon it. If it gets milky, lime is present.

Test for Acid. — Take a piece of litmus-paper. If it turns red, there must be acid. If it precipitates on adding lime water, it is carbonic acid. If a blue sugar paper is turned red, it is a mineral acid.

Test for Copper. — If present, it will turn bright polished steel a copper color. 2. A few drops of ammonia will turn it blue, if copper is present.

Test for Lead. — Take sulphuretted gas and water in equal quantity to be tested. If it contains lead, it will turn a blackish brown. Again: The same result will take place if sulphate of ammonia be used.

Test for Sulphur. — In a bottle of water add a little quicksilver, cork it for 6 hours, and if it looks dark on the top, and on shaking looks blackish, it proves the presence of sulphur.

WATER-PIPE — To Thaw.

Water-pipes usually freeze up where exposed, for inside the walls, where they cannot be reached, they are or should be packed to prevent freezing. To thaw out a frozen pipe, bundle a newspaper into a torch, light it, and pass it along the pipe slowly. The ice will yield to this much quicker than to hot water or wrappings of hot cloths, as is the common practice.

WATER-COLORS — To Use.

Always use clean water, a clean palette and brushes, and clean your brushes before putting them away.

The paper should be stretched before commencing to color your drawing. This is best done by soaking it in clean water for at least one hour. Then take off the superfluous water with a clean towel, used as blotting paper. Afterwards paste the paper down to your drawing-board by applying the paste, which should be strong, to a margin of your paper about one inch (for small and medium sizes) larger all round than the size of your subject. This allows you to cut your drawing out when completed.

Before beginning to color, allow the paste and damped paper to become quite dry; after which it will not wrinkle up when washes are applied.

In coloring large surfaces, incline your drawing and color downwards from left to right, and damp your paper beforehand.

Always allow one shade of color to dry before applying another over it.

Some useful tints, and mixed tints for skies are: Ultramarine; or ultramarine and Prussian blue. Clouds, ultramarine and light red. Dark clouds, Prussian blue, ivory black, carmine and light red. Evening effects, gamboge and vermilion and carmine. For sea water, Prussian blue or indigo, gamboge and light red. Running water, ivory black, Prussian blue and Vandyke brown; or indigo and light red and ultramarine.

Distant hills, or mountains, with verdure, ultramarine and light red, or Prussian blue, gamboge and yellow ochre. Hills or rocks without verdure, yellow ochre and light red.

For trees, in sunlight, gamboge, burnt sienna, and Prussian blue, or sepia and gamboge. For trees in shadow, Prussian blue, ivory black, Vandyke brown and burnt sienna, or indigo and sepia.

Grey for walls, rocks, and buildings — Prussian blue and ivory black, with sepia and lake or burnt sienna. Foregrounds, stones, walls, etc., yellow ochre, with gray as above. General rule for shadows: Brown and red should be prominent in foregrounds, and blues and grays in distances.

Warm colors should be laid over cold colors. Orange is the warmest color in nature.

In mixing all colors the proportion of each must be arranged according to the effect to be produced—a mixture of two colors producing many shades as one or the other color predominates.

WAX.

For Covering Fruits.—Resin, 1 lb.; lard, tallow and beeswax, each 1 oz. Melt and stir well together.

Wax for Grafting.—For cold weather, take resin, 4 lbs.; beeswax, 1 lb.; linseed oil, 1 lb. Melt all together and pour into cold water, and as soon as it is sufficiently cool to be handled, grease the hands a little and begin to work it by pulling out, doubling over, and pulling out again, etc. The more it is worked, the easier it will spread and the nicer it will be. For warm weather, add 1 lb. more of resin to the wax mixture above, and work otherwise the same.

To Take Out Wax.—Hold a very hot iron near, but not on, the spot till the wax melts; then scrape it off. Lay a clean blotting-paper over the place, and press it with a cooler iron till the wax has disappeared.

WELDING BY ELECTRICITY.

This process consists simply of passing through the metals to be welded a current of electricity of great power. The ends are forced together tightly before the current is passed, and the resistance to the passage of the electricity from one metal to the other creates heat sufficient to fuse it at the point of contact while the pressure makes the joint. The inventor of this process is Professor Thomson, of Lynn, Mass. Hitherto the process of welding has been successfully applied only to soft iron, steel and a few other metals. But by the new method, not only have cast-iron, brass, gun metal, bronze, German silver, zinc, tin, lead and many other metals been welded like to like, but it has been found in many cases very easy to unite unlike metals.

WELL—To Dig.

Dig down to a depth of 5 or 6 feet a hole 4 feet in diameter; brick it up, using water-lime mortar. Below this, dig your well in diameter a little less than the bricked top, and, as you go down, plaster the dirt or sand on the sides with water-lime mortar. A well dug and plastered in this way costs one-half the price of an ordinary well of the same depth and diameter, and is proof against all kinds of vermin, nor can any dirt wash down from the sides. There is no need of cleaning such a well, as there is no accumulation of filth in it. The bricking at the top is done to avoid injury from frost, as the plaster peels off where the ground behind it has frozen.

To Increase the Flow of Wells.—There is a simple way of increasing the flow of wells, devised some years ago by M. Donet, of Lyons, France. Ordinarily the mouths of wells are left open; hence, all along the water, from well to original source, there is an equilibrium of air pressure. M. Donet's plan is simply to close the well and pump out some of the air. This creates an excess of pressure to drive water into the well. The supply is thus increased temporarily, and at the same time the underground channels through which the water passes are enlarged by the stronger stream, and so the supply also becomes permanently augmented.

WELLS OR CHIMNEYS—To Examine.

To examine the bottom of a well, hold a mirror so as to reflect the sun's rays in the water in such a way that anything floating on the surface can be plainly seen. The smallest object on the bottom can also be distinguished if the contents of the well are not turbid. Objects dropped in wells 60 feet deep, and that contained 20 feet of water, have been found in this way. If the objects are very small, or you wish to make a minute examination of the bottom, you may use an opera glass. When the top of the well is not exposed to sunlight, you can place a mirror outside, even at some distance, so as to reflect the light over the top of the well, where a second mirror may be so placed as to reflect it downward. The above method is much better than using any artificial light, as the latter is weak compared with sunlight, and its glare prevents distinct vision. Employing two mirrors, one outside to reflect the solar rays into a room, and a smaller one in its path to reflect the rays in a dark cavity, is used by physicians for examining the cavities of the body. If you wish to examine a chimney, hold a piece of looking-glass at an angle of 45° in the hole in the chimney in which the stove-pipe is to go, or in the open fire-place. If you can see the sky, you can also see the whole interior of the chimney, and if there is any obstruction in the way it also will be visible.

WHEAT—To Prevent Rust in.

Several hours before sowing prepare a steep of 3 measures of powdered quicklime and 10 measures of cattle urine. Pour 2 quarts upon a peck of wheat, stirring until every kernel is white with it. By using this all kinds of rust will be avoided.

WHETSTONES.

Good sweet or olive oil is commonly used upon whetstones. In testing a stone, try water first; if it glazes, oil is required, and almost all stones, unless oiled, become glazed or burnished on the surface, so that they no longer abrade the metal. Most stones, after being oiled, give a finer edge than they do in a dry or merely wet state. The pores of the stone become in a measure filled up, and while the action is rendered continuous, its character is altered. A dry stone is very apt to give a wire edge to a tool, and, although this sometimes happens when oil is used, yet it does not occur nearly so often. Some stones, however, work better with water than with oil. Therefore the test should be made before the oil is used. If it cuts without glazing, oil need not be applied. Kerosene oil keeps the whetstone in better condition than any other liquid, and assists in the operation of sharpening. In fact, it is superior to any other liquid for the purpose.

WHITEWASHING.

When the spring comes there is always whitewashing, and often calcimining, to be done. In the city, where one can send for a professional worker, and put the whole business in his hands at a low price, the matter is easily attended to, but in the country districts this must be attended to by the housewife herself, or be done by the few unskillful hands in her employ, whose work will require her superintendence. The first thing to be done is to inspect the walls, and see if they will bear another coat over the one which has already been put on. If the wall has been whitewashed, and has begun to chip off, it must be scraped before another coat is put on, and this is quite a serious undertaking. It means the removal of the old coats that have been put on the wall. There are scrapers that come especially for this purpose. It is better to remove everything, furniture and all, out of the room to be scraped, as the fine dust of the old lime penetrates through everything. After the room has been thoroughly scraped the new whitewash can be applied, though it is best to fill in or mend any holes in the wall with plaster of Paris, wet with paste or water. It seems to us that the very best and sweetest whitewash is made by mixing ordinary slack lime in water, adding simply salt enough to make it cling to the wall and bluing enough to give it a pearl-white tint. Ordinary laundry bluing will not do for this purpose. What is known as Mason's bluing is the best to use.

It is an easy matter to apply whitewash, and a good whitewash brush does not cost over 75 cents. It may be found in any country store. A calciminer's brush is a more expensive article, and a satisfactory one may cost as much as $3. A calcimine wall which is to be recalcimined should be washed. It is impossible to apply calcimine to a wall that has been whitewashed. It would look streaked and queer. An ordinary rule for preparing calcimine calls for 10 lbs. of zinc-white, mixed to a thick cream with warm water, ½ lb. of dissolved glue, all stirred together. The calcimine must be applied while it is warm, adding a little hot water when it is too thick to spread easily. Old-fashioned calciminers always spread their calcimine on as painters usually spread their oil paint — evenly in one direction, row after row — and this is probably the easiest way for one who is not an expert.

It may be just as well for a beginner to use common whitening, which is less expensive than zinc-white, and which is applied in exactly the same way. For side walls 1 lb. of glue, instead of ½ lb., should be used. This is necessary to prevent the whitening rubbing off on the hands and clothes when they are brought in contact with it. The extra amount of glue will prevent all trouble for a year or two, but as there is nothing that will prevent old calcimine from rubbing off it is always best to paper or paint the sides of a room. When calcimine is applied to a fresh plastered wall it should be sized with glue, and a calcimined wall which is to be papered should be treated the same way.

A Good Whitewash.— Half a bushel of lime, slaked, boiling water; cover over to prevent evaporation; strain the liquor, add 1 peck of salt previously dissolved in warm water, 3 lbs. of boiled rice in paste form, 8 oz. of Spanish white, 1 lb. of glue, 5 gals. water. Heat before using.

Whitewash Said not to Rub or Wear off.— Make the whitewash in the ordinary manner, then place it over a fire and bring it to a boil; then stir into each gallon a tablespoonful of powdered alum, ½ pint of good flour paste, and ½ lb. of glue dissolved in water, while boiling.

WINDOWS — To Wash.

Never wash windows when the sun is shining upon them; otherwise they will be cloudy and streaky from drying before they are well polished off; and never wash the outside of the window first if you wish to save trouble. Dust the glass and sash and wash the window inside, using a little ammonia in the water, wipe with a cloth free from lint and polish off with soft paper. For the corners a small brush or pointed stick covered with one end of the cloth is useful. When you come to the glass outside the defects remaining will be more closely seen. Wipe the pane as soon as possible after washing and rinsing, and polish with either chamois or soft paper. In rinsing one may dash the water on the outside or use a large sponge. It is preferable to a cloth.

What to do when the Windows Stick.—When window frames have been newly painted they should not be shut down tight, as they are liable to stick, and panes of glass are often fractured in endeavoring to open them. A little bit of wood inserted between the frame and the sill leaves an aperture to dry the paint and can be removed in the course of a day or two. If, however, they should still prove obstinate, a piece of common soap rubbed smartly on the frame will generally ease them.

WOOD.

Shrinkage of Wood.—People generally have but little idea how greatly timber supposed to be seasoned will shrink. Some kinds of wood will shrink every time the surface is dressed off. Boards and planks that have been kept under shelter for years, when dressed out and employed as casing, or for making doors, will often shrink enough to form unsightly cracks at every joint. Lumber that has been sawed for several years even, should never be worked up into elegant articles before it has been kiln-dried or exposed, for at least two weeks, to the scorching sunshine and drying winds.

To Season and Prevent Warping.—Strip off the bark and bury the wood 1 foot deep in the spring, leaving in the ground for 6 months, and it will be thoroughly seasoned. The manzanita or mountain mahogany, in the Sierra Nevada, can be seasoned in no other way, it being one of the hardest and most brittle kinds of wood known.

To Prevent Wood from Cracking.—It is often desirable to keep small wooden articles, such as taps and faucets, from cracking by exposure to alternations of temperature and other causes. This is best prevented, says the *Artisan*, by putting the articles in melted paraffine and heating them at a temperature of 212° Fahr., until bubbles of air cease to escape from the wood. The whole is then allowed to cool to about 120° Fahr., when the articles are taken from the bath and cleaned from the adhering paraffine by rubbing with a dry, coarse piece of cloth.

Preparing Wood for Heat.—It is said that woodwork that is to be exposed to fire may be made almost incombustible by soaking in water in which a small quantity of alum and sulphate of copper have been dissolved. Six ounces of each is enough for a barrel of water.

How Wood is Preserved.—The great obstacle, hitherto, to the introduction on a large scale of any process for the preservation of wood has been the low price of lumber, which has apparently made it cheaper to renew wooden structures than to build them of treated lumber. Whether this is real economy is now being questioned, and experience is showing that the treated lumber is the cheaper in the long run. In the most approved method of rendering lumber water- and weather-proof, it is carefully measured and its cubic contents computed, after which it is placed in a seasoning cylinder. The doors of the cylinder are hermetically closed, and the timber is subjected to the influence of steam admitted directly to the cylinder, and of super-heated steam passed through pipes placed for that purpose in the cylinder. During the steaming process, the pores of the timber are opened, the fibers softened, the moisture and sap are evaporated, and the albumen is coagulated. The duration of the process depends upon the seasoning of the timber and the amount of oil to be injected; it is generally from 10 to 12 hours. When the steam is cut off, the vacuum pump is started, and the evaporated moisture and sap are withdrawn and discharged in condensed form. This takes about 6 hours, during which a vacuum of from 20 to 25 inches is produced in the cylinder. The next step in the process is the introduction of oil heated up to about 170 degrees into the cylinder. The quantity of oil that can be absorbed by each piece of timber is accurately computed beforehand, and part of it is drawn into the cylinder by vacuum, and the rest is pumped in with a pressure pump. The cylinders are tested to a pressure of 225 lbs. per square inch, and it generally requires from 150 to 160 lbs. of pressure to force 16 lbs. of oil into a cubic foot of the timber. The oil, being thoroughly heated, is readily absorbed by the open pores from which the sap and moisture have been withdrawn. While it penetrates to the heart of the wood, its heavy and tarry part will remain near the outside and form an air-tight coat around each piece. As soon as the charge is taken out of the cylinder, the change in temperature will cause the wood to contract, and the outer fibers on the sides of the stick will close themselves altogether and retain whatever oil has been absorbed. As the pure oil, formerly used, did not effectually protect timber from the ravages of the teredo and other marine borers, it is now mixed with "dead" oil. Dead oil is composed of naphthaline and carbolic acid, and pure oil is made by combining paraffine, creosote and wood acids.

Preservative Preparation for Wood.—Melt together in an iron pot 40 parts chalk, 50 parts resin, 4 parts linseed oil; to this add 1 part native oxide of copper, and afterward 1 part sulphuric acid. Apply with a brush, and when dry, this varnish will be as hard as stone.

To Dye Wood.—Light woods may be dyed by immersion. To make a crimson dye, boil 1 lb. of ground Brazil wood in 3 quarts of water; to this add ½ oz. of cochineal, and boil ½ hour; the wood should previously be washed with ½ oz. of saffron to 1 quart of water. This dye is used for pear-wood or sycamore. For purple satin finish, soak 1 lb. of logwood chips in 3 quarts of water, and boil well 1 hour; add pearl-ash, 4 oz., powdered indigo, 2 oz. To produce black, use copperas and nut galls, or 2 coats of black japan, afterwards varnish or polish, or use lampblack before laying on the japan. To produce a blue stain, put 1 lb. of oil of vitriol in a glass bottle, with 4 oz. of indigo; lay on the same as black. A fine green is produced by using 3 pints of the strongest vinegar, 4 oz. of best powdered verdigris (poison), ½ oz. of sap-green, and ½ oz. of indigo. To stain wood a bright yellow, use aloes; varnish or polish the whole. See also *Staining.*

WOOL.

To Wash Woolen Goods.—If the material is much soiled, a thorough brushing is the first step in the cleaning process. Some materials and shades will stand washing. Bran water is good for this purpose and can be prepared by putting the bran in a bag and boiling in clear water for 1 hour. After this it should be strained and the goods washed through it without any soap, then rinsed through clear water and hung up to partly dry without wringing, as such creases cannot be pressed out. A suds made of white castile soap and tepid water is well adapted to washing fabrics of delicate tints, no soap being used upon the goods, and carefully rinsing after the washing. To wash black material nothing is better than soap bark. Four ounces of the bark, which can be purchased at any druggist's, should be soaked in a pail of water over night. Strain it the next morning, and use the same as for ordinary washing, omitting the soap. It restores the color, and makes the goods look almost like new. It is also well to have some kept on hand in a bottle, and it is very useful in removing spots that so frequently appear upon the different garments.

WORCESTERSHIRE SAUCE.

Cider vinegar, 1 pint; sherry wine, ½ pint; allspice (ground), 1 dram; cloves (powdered), ½ dram; black pepper (powdered), ½ dram; ginger (powdered), ½ dram; cayenne, ½ dram; mustard (powdered), 1 oz.; salt, 1 oz.; shallots, 1 oz.; sugar, 4 oz.; tamarinds, 2 oz.; curry powder, ½ oz. Mix all the ingredients together, simmer over a slow fire for an hour, then add a little caramel to darken the color, if desired.

YEAST.—Potato.

Pare, boil and mash six potatoes; mix with them 3 tablespoonfuls of flour; pour on this a quart, boiling, of the water in which the potatoes have been cooked, and add ½ teacupful of sugar and a teaspoonful of salt. When cool, mix in a teacupful of home-made yeast or half as much brewer's yeast.

Patent Yeast.—Boil for ½ hour 2 oz. of best hops in 1 gallon of water; strain and cool till lukewarm; then add ½ lb. of sugar and a small handful of salt; beat up a pound of flour with some of the liquor, and mix all well together. Let the mixture stand 2 days, and then add 3 lbs. of potatoes, boiled and mashed; let stand again another day, stirring often. Then strain and bottle. This yeast will keep in a cool place 2 months.

Standard Time.

What is known as the "new standard time" was adopted by agreement by all the principal railroads of the United States at 12 o'clock, noon, on Nov. 18, 1883. The system divides the continent into five longitudinal belts, and fixes a meridian of time for each belt. These meridians are fifteen degrees of longitude, corresponding to one hour of time, apart. Eastern Maine, New Brunswick and Nova Scotia use the 60th meridian; the Canadas, New England, the Middle States, Virginia and the Carolinas use the 75th meridian, which is that of Philadelphia; the States of the Mississippi Valley, Alabama, Georgia and Florida, and westward, including Texas, Kansas, and the larger part of Nebraska and Dakota, use the 90th meridian, which is that of New Orleans. The Territories to the western border of Arizona and Montana go by the time of the 105th meridian, which is that of Denver; and the Pacific States employ the 120th meridian. The time divisions are known as intercolonial time, eastern time, central time, mountain time and Pacific time. A traveler passing from one time belt to another will find his watch an hour too fast or too slow, according to the direction in which he is going. All points in any time division using the time of the meridian must set their time-pieces faster or slower than the time indicated by the sun, according as their position is east or west of the line. This change of system reduced the time standards used by the railroads from fifty-three to five, a great convenience to the railroads and the traveling public. The suggestion leading to the adoption of this new system originated with Professor Abbe, of the Signal Bureau at Washington.

Etiquette... THE RULES OF GOOD SOCIETY

Never betray a confidence.

Do not give a present in hopes of a return.

Do not fail to return a friend's call in due time.

A compliment that is palpably insincere is no compliment at all.

Avoid awkwardness of attitude as well as awkwardness of speech.

Never question a child or a servant about the private affairs of others.

Gentlemen precede a lady in going up stairs, but follow in going down.

The man or woman who engrosses conversation is unpardonably selfish.

All irritability and gloom must be thrown off when one enters society.

Never fail to extend every kindly courtesy to an elderly person or an invalid.

When offered a seat in the street car, accept the same with audible thanks.

Never look at the superscription on a letter that you may be requested to mail.

Do not be quick to answer questions, in general company, that are put to others.

In walking with a lady through a crowd, precede her, in order to clear the way.

Never indicate an object by pointing at it. Move the head or wave the whole hand.

In walking on a public promenade, if you meet the same friends and acquaintances a number of times, it is only necessary to salute them once in passing.

When entrusted with a commission, do not fail to perform it. It is rude to "forget."

Avoid all exhibitions of excitement, anger or impatience when an accident happens.

On entering a room filled with people, do not fail to bow slightly to the general company.

It is rude to examine the cards in a card basket unless you have an invitation to that effect.

Avoid any familiarity with a new acquaintance. You never know when you may give offense.

If you accept favors and hospitalities, do not fail to return the same when the opportunity offers.

In conversation the face must be pleasant, wearing something that almost approaches to a smile.

Never allude to a present which you have given; do not even appear to see it if you are where it is.

Never fail to answer an invitation, either personally or by letter, within a week after its receipt.

No man or woman is well bred who is continually lolling, gesticulating or fidgeting in company.

When writing to ask a favor or to obtain information, do not fail to inclose postage stamp for reply.

If you cannot avoid passing between two persons who are talking, never fail to apologize for doing so.

You should not lend an article that you have borrowed without first obtaining permission from the owner.

Never play practical jokes. The results are frequently so serious as to entail life-long regret on the joker.

Never ridicule the lame, the halt or the blind. You never know when misfortune may be your own lot.

Do not appear to notice any defect, scar or peculiarity of any one. It is the height of rudeness to speak of them.

Remember, when you are prone to give in charity to the sick or the needy, that "he who gives quickly gives double."

Never speak of absent persons by their Christian names or their surnames; always refer to them as Mr. —— or Mrs. ——.

Always tell the truth. Veracity is the very foundation of character. Without it a man is a useless and unstable structure.

It is very awkward for one lady to rise and give another lady a seat in a street car, unless the lady standing be very old, or evidently ill and weak.

When an apology is offered, accept it, and do so with a good grace, not in a manner that implies you do not intend changing your opinion of the offense.

In conversing with a person, do not repeat the name frequently, as it implies one of two extremes, that of familiarity or haughtiness.

A good bit of advice is the saying, "Think twice before you speak once," as then only can you learn to always speak to the point.

Never enter a room noisily. Never enter the private bed-room of a friend without knocking. Never fail to close the door after you, and do not slam it.

Never seal a letter that is to be given to a friend for delivery. It looks as though you doubted his or her honor in refraining from examining the contents.

Never correct any slight inaccuracy in statement or fact. It is better to let it pass than to subject another to the mortification of being corrected in company.

Always adopt a pleasant mode of address. Whether you are speaking to inferiors or to your equals, it will alike give them a kindly and happy impression of you.

Do not quickly follow up a present by a return. It looks too much like payment. Never, however, fail to make an immediate acknowledgment of the receipt of a gift.

Never presume to attract the attention of an acquaintance by a touch, unless you are extremely intimate. Recognition by a simple and or spoken word is all that can be allowed.

The most contemptible meanness in the world is that of opening a private letter addressed to another. No one with the slightest self-respect would be guilty of such an act.

Long hair and a scrawling signature do not constitute a genius. Be careful, then, how you draw upon yourself the ridicule of being a shallow pretender by adopting either or both.

Sneezing, coughing and clearing the throat must be done quietly when it cannot possibly be avoided; but sniffing and expectorating must never be indulged in in decent society.

Do not make promises that you have no intention of fulfilling. A person who is ever ready with promises, which he fails to execute, is soon known as a very unreliable party.

It is extremely rude to look over the shoulder of one who is reading or writing. It is also rude to persist in reading aloud passages from your own book or paper to one who is also reading.

Temper has much more to do with good breeding than is generally supposed. The French are allowed to be the most polite people in the world when they are really only the most amiable.

Neither a gentleman nor a lady will boast of the conquests he or she has made. Such a course would have the effect of exciting the most profound contempt for the boasters in the breasts of all who heard them.

Punctuality is a most admirable quality. The man or woman who possesses it is a blessing to his or her friends. The one who lacks it is wanting in one of the first requisites of good-breeding.

The young of both sexes would find it an inestimable advantage through life to cultivate from the outset a clear intonation, a well-chosen phraseology, a logical habit of thought, and a correct accent.

A rich person should be careful how he gives to the poor, lest he hurt their pride, while a poor person can only give to those of greater wealth something which has cost only affection, time or talent.

We should not neglect very young people in our homes. If we wish our children to have polished manners, and to express themselves well, we must lead them to enter into the conversation that is going on.

When walking with a lady, it is etiquette to give her the wall, but if she have your arm it is quite unnecessary to be changing at every corner you come to. After one or two changes the habit becomes ridiculous.

The art of giving and receiving presents is not always an intuition. A generous person may unwittingly wound where he intends to please, while a really grateful person may, for want of tact, appear to depreciate the liberality of his friends.

If a person of greater age than yourself desire you to step into a carriage or through a door first, it is more polite to bow and obey than to decline. Compliance with and deference to the wishes of others is always the finest breeding.

If you present a book to a friend, do not write your name in it unless it be requested. By doing so you are taking for granted that your present will be accepted, and also that a specimen of your penmanship will give additional value to the gift.

Learn to make small sacrifices with a good grace; to accept small disappointments in a patient spirit. A little more of self-control, a little more allowance for the weaknesses of others, will oftentimes change the entire spirit of a household.

A well-educated person proclaims himself by his simple and terse language. Good and clear Saxon is much to be preferred to high-sounding phrases and long words. It is only the half educated who mistake verbosity for elegance.

In entering an exhibition or public room where ladies are present, gentlemen should always lift their hats. In France a gentleman lifts his hat on entering a public omnibus, but that is not necessary according to the American code of etiquette.

Married people are sometimes guilty of the vulgar habit of speaking of each other by the initial letter of their first name, or the wife of her husband as "Jones," omitting the "Mr." This denotes very ill breeding, and should be strenuously avoided.

We are not to be polite merely because we wish to please, but because we wish to consider the feelings and spare the time of others—because we wish to carry into daily practice the spirit of the precept, "Do unto others as you would have others do unto you."

To yawn in the presence of others, to put your feet on a chair, to stand with your back to the fire, to take the most comfortable seat in the room, to do anything in fact that displays selfishness and a lack of respect for those about you, is unequivocally vulgar and ill-bred.

Never employ "extravagance in conversation." Always employ the word that will express your precise meaning and no more. It is absurd to say it is "immensely jolly," or "disgustingly mean." Such expressions show neither wit nor wisdom, but mere flippancy.

It is a duty to always look pleased. It is likewise a duty to appear interested in a story that you may have heard a dozen times before; to smile on the most inveterate prosers; in short, to make such minor sacrifices of sincerity as one's good manners and good feelings may dictate.

It is in bad taste to undervalue a gift which you have yourself offered. If it is valueless, it is not good enough to give to your friend; and if you say you do not want it yourself, or that you would only throw it away if they did not take it, you are insulting the person whom you mean to benefit.

When in general conversation you cannot agree with the proposition advanced, it is best to observe silence, unless particularly asked for your opinion, in which case you will give it modestly, but decidedly. Never be betrayed into too much warmth in argument; if others remain unconvinced, drop the subject.

Never indulge in egotism in the drawing-room. The person who makes his family, his wealth, his affairs or his hobby the topic of conversation, is not only a bore, but a violator of good taste. We do not meet in society to display ourselves, but to give and take as much rational entertainment as our own accomplishments and those of others will afford.

A gift should always be valuable for something besides its price. It may have been brought by the giver from some famous place; it may have a valuable association with genius, or it may be unique in its workmanship. An author may offer his book or an artist his sketch, and any one may offer flowers, which are always a delicate and unexceptional gift.

Boasting is one of the most ill-bred habits a person can indulge in. Traveling is so universal a custom now that to mention the fact that you have been to Europe is to state nothing exceptional. Anybody with wealth, health and leisure can travel; but it is only those of real intelligence that derive any benefit from the art treasures of the Old World.

Never refuse a gift unless you have a very good reason for so doing. However poor the gift, you should show your appreciation of the kindness of heart which prompted it. All such deprecatory phrases as "I fear I rob you," or "I am really ashamed to take it," etc., are in bad taste, as they seem to imply that you think the giver cannot afford it.

Always look at the person who is conversing with you, and listen respectfully. In answering, try to express your thoughts in the best manner. A loose manner of expression injures ourselves much more than our hearers, since it is a habit which, once acquired, is not easily thrown off, and when we wish to express ourselves well it is not so easy to do so.

A good memory for names and faces, and a self-possessed manner, are necessary to every one who would make a good impression in society. Nothing is more delicately flattering to another than to find you can readily call his or her name, after a very slight acquaintance. The most popular of great men have gained their popularity principally through the possession of this faculty.

No lady of good breeding will sit sideways on her chair, or with her legs crossed or stretched apart, or hold her chin in her hands, or twist her watch-chain while she is talking; nor does a well-bred gentleman sit astride of his chair, or bite his nails, or nurse his leg. A man is always allowed more freedom than a woman, but both should be graceful and decorous in their deportment.

Shyness is very ungraceful and a positive injury to any one afflicted with it. It is only allowable in very young people. A person who blushes, stammers and fidgets in the presence of strangers will not create a very good impression upon their minds as to his personal worth and educational advantages. Shyness may be overcome by determined mixing in society. Nothing else will have an effect upon it.

A foreigner should always be addressed by his full name, as Monsieur de Montmorenci; never as Monsieur only. In speaking of him, give him his title, if he have one. For example, in speaking to a nobleman you would say, Monsieur le Marquis; in speaking of him in his absence, you would say, Monsieur le Marquis de Montmorenci. Converse with a foreigner in his own language. If you are not sufficiently at home in the language to do so, apologize to him, and beg permission to speak English.

No one can be polite who does not cultivate a "good memory." There is a class of absent-minded people who are to be dreaded on account of the mischief they are sure to create with their unlucky tongues. They always recall unlucky topics, speak of the dead as though they were living, talk of people in their hearing, and do a hundred and one things which, in slang parlance, is "treading on somebody's toes." Carelessness can be carried to such a pitch as to almost amount to a crime. Cultivate a good memory, therefore, if you wish to say pleasant things and to avoid disagreeable ones.

The Art of Conversation

The art of expressing one's thoughts in clear, simple, elegant English is one of the first to be attained by those who would mix in good society. You must talk, and talk fairly well, if you would not altogether fail of producing some kind of impression upon society. To have something to say, and to say it in the best possible manner, is to insure success and admiration. The first thing necessary for the attainment of this valuable accomplishment is a good education. An acquaintance with the current literature of the day is absolutely essential to a good talker. A perfect familiarity with the English language, its grammar, pronunciation, etc., is indispensable. Those who have to contend with a lack of early advantages in this respect can supply the deficiency by private study, and close observance wherever good English is spoken. Above all should they avoid associating with those who express themselves incorrectly or vulgarly.

Nothing is so infectious as a bad accent or incorrect form of speech.

All affectations of foreign accent, mannerisms, exaggerations and slang are detestable.

Equally to be avoided are inaccuracies of expression, hesitation, and undue use of French or other foreign words, and anything approaching to flippancy, coarseness, triviality or prevarication.

The voice should never be loud, no gesticulation should accompany the speech, and the features should be under strict control. Nothing is more ill-bred than a half-opened mouth, a vacant stare, a wandering eye or a smile ready to break into a laugh at any moment. Absolute suppression of emotion, whether of anger, laughter, mortification or disappointment, is one of the most certain marks of good-breeding.

Next to unexceptionable grammar, correct elocution and a frank, easy bearing, it is necessary to be genial. If you cannot be animated, sympathetic and cheerful, do not go into society. Dull and stupid people are but so many clogs to the machinery of social life.

The matter of conversation is as important as the manner. Tact and good feeling will, in people of sound sense, indicate the shoals and quicksands to be avoided in conversation, but for safety's sake it will be best to enumerate a few of these:

Complimentary speeches should be avoided, unless, indeed, so delicately put as to be scarcely discernible. Flattery is suggestive of snobbishness, particularly if it be paid to people of great wealth and high position. It induces disgust on the part of the receiver, and insincerity on that of the giver.

The habit of "fishing" for compliments is notably vulgar, and it is one in which a certain class of young people are very apt to indulge, especially among themselves in private. It indicates vanity in the angler and begets contempt on the part of the one who from interested motives nibbles gently at the bait.

All "slang" is vulgar. This fact cannot be too forcibly impressed upon the minds of the young people of this day, as the alarming prevalence of slangy conversational phrases is enough to cause our decorous fathers and mothers to turn in their graves.

Many of the daughters of our most wealthy and influential citizens have an idea that their position will excuse or gloss the vulgarity of a "cant" phrase now and then. Nothing was ever more erroneous. No position, however high, can redeem the vulgarity of this practice, and it is a grand mistake also to imagine slang to be a substitute for wit. We refer particularly to this habit among young ladies, as it is more reprehensible in them than in the opposite sex, although it indicates bad breeding on their part as well.

Scandal should be avoided above all things. It is a sin against morality as well as good taste.

Punning is a most objectionable habit in society. An inveterate punster is an intolerable bore, and unless a pun amounts to a positive witticism it should never be perpetrated in company.

Long arguments should be avoided in general company. They become tiresome to the hearers. Always endeavor to change the subject after it has continued a reasonable length of time.

Religion and politics are two subjects to be avoided in general conversation. People usually have strong prejudices on both these points, and it is a rule of good-breeding to respect the prejudices of those about you.

Never interrupt the speech of another. This is an unpardonable sin against good-breeding.

A good listener is more to be desired than a fine conversationalist. In order to be a good listener you must appear to be interested, answer appropriately, briefly and to the point, and give your companion generally the impression that you are in sympathy with and highly entertained by what he is saying.

Avoid pedantic displays of learning.

All topics specially interesting to gentlemen, such as the farm and business matters generally, should be excluded in general society.

The expression of immature opinions is always in bad taste. Persons, young or old, should not attempt to criticise books or art unless positively certain that their knowledge of the subject is sufficient to justify the criticism.

Be very careful of introducing long-winded anecdotes into the conversation. Nothing is more awkward than to find an array of bored faces when one is not more than half through a long story.

Repartee should be indulged in only moderately. Otherwise it may degenerate into flippancy, a habit much to be condemned in a certain class of young persons who think themselves unusually clever, or, as our American word goes, "smart."

In using titles, such as "General," "Doctor," etc., you must always append the surname if you are a stranger or any other than a most intimate friend. For example, you should say, "What did you observe, Doctor Gray?" not "What did you observe, Doctor?" Names should be used as little as possible, and never familiarly. Few solecisms give greater offense than a liberty taken with a name.

In addressing a person of title in England, "My Lord" and "My Lady" are seldom used except by servants. The Prince of Wales may be addressed as "Sir," and the Queen as "Madame." A Frenchman, however, whatever his rank, is addressed as "Monsieur," and a Frenchwoman, whether duchess or dressmaker, as "Madame." It would be as ill-bred to omit to say Monsieur, Mein Herr and Signor, in France, Germany and Italy, respectively, as it would to say, Sir, Ma'am and Miss, as the servants do in this country.

The great secret of talking well is to adapt your conversation to your company as skillfully as may be.

People take more interest in their own affairs than in anything else which you can name. A wise host or hostess will then lead a mother to talk of her children, an author of his book, an artist of his picture, etc. Having furnished the topic, you have but to listen and acquire a reputation for being amiable, agreeable, intelligent and well-bred.

If you would not be unpopular, do not always be witty, no matter what your natural abilities may be in that line. People do not like to be always outshone.

Do not too officiously supply a word or phrase if a speaker hesitate for a moment; he will think of the one he wants or supply another in good time.

Never correct a fault in pronunciation or in facts, in company or in private, if you wish to retain a friend.

Avoid such colloquialisms as "says I," "you know," and other senseless repetitions that might be mentioned. Never speak of a person as "a party," nor refer to absent persons as "he" or "she." Give the name of the lady or gentleman referred to.

In telling a joke, do not laugh yourself before the point is reached. If the joke is original, do not laugh at all.

In a *tete-a-tete* conversation it is ill-bred to drop the voice to a whisper.

Egotism is always in bad taste. Allow others the privilege of proclaiming your merits.

Never speak of personal or private matters in general company.

Avoid as much as possible beginning a conversation with stale commonplaces, such as "It is a fine day," "The weather is charming," etc.

Do not speak slightingly of the city or neighborhood in which you may be visiting. By offending the prejudices of those about you, you render yourself extremely disagreeable.

Avoid all excitability and dogmatism in conversation. Nothing is more annoying than to converse with an arrogant, loud-speaking person.

Always yield the point in conversation if you find the argument is likely to become violent.

Avoid lavishing praise on the members of your own family. It is almost as bad as praising yourself.

It is exceedingly bad taste to parade the fact that you have traveled in foreign countries, or that you are acquainted with distinguished or wealthy people, that you have been to college, or that your family is distinguished for gentility and blue blood.

In speaking of husband or wife, do not use the surname alone. To say "I was telling Brown," is extremely vulgar. Always prefix the Mr.

Always endeavour to contribute your quota to the general conversation. It is as much your duty to entertain as to be entertained. Bashfulness is as much to be avoided as too much assurance.

Never ask questions of a personal nature, such as what a certain article cost, or why so-and-so did not go to the opera. They are decidedly impertinent.

Look at the person with whom you are conversing, but do not stare.

Avoid loud laughter in society.

If you carry on the thread of a conversation after the entrance of a visitor, you should always recapitulate what has been said before his or her arrival.

Remember that "an excellent thing in woman is a voice low, but sweet," and cultivate a distinct but subdued tone.

Emerson says: "You cannot have one well-bred man without a whole society of such." Elsewhere he says: "It makes no difference, in looking back five years, how we have dined or dressed; but it counts much whether we have had good companions in that time — almost as much as what we have been doing."

Table Etiquette

Sit yourself in an upright position — not too close nor yet too far.

Take your napkin, partially unfold it and lay it across your lap. It is not the correct thing to fasten it to your button-hole or spread it over your breast.

Do not trifle with your knife or fork, or drum on the table, or fidget in any way, while waiting to be served.

Keep your hands quietly in your lap, your mind composed and pleasantly fixed upon the conversation. Let all your movements be easy and deliberate. Undue haste indicates a nervous lack of ease.

Should grace be said, you will give the most reverent attention in respectful silence during the ceremony.

Exhibit no impatience to be served. During the intervals between the courses is your opportunity for displaying your conversational abilities to those sitting near you. Pleasant chat and witty remarks compose the best possible sauce to a good dinner.

Eat slowly; it will contribute to your good health as well as your good manners. Thorough mastication of your food is necessary to digestion. An ordinary meal should occupy from thirty minutes to an hour.

You may not desire the soup, which is usually the first course, but you should not refuse to take it. You can eat as much or as little as you please, but you would look awkward sitting with nothing before you while the others are eating.

When eating soup, take it from the side of the spoon, and avoid making any noise in so doing.

Should you be asked by the host what part of the fowl you prefer, always have a choice, and mention promptly which you prefer. Nothing is more annoying than to have to serve two or three people who have no preferences and will take "anything."

Never place waste matter on the table-cloth. The side of your plate, or side dishes that have contained sauces or vegetables, will answer as a receptacle for bones, potato skins, etc.

You will use your fork to convey all your food to your mouth, except it may be certain sauces that would be more conveniently eaten with a spoon. For instance, you should not attempt to eat peas with a fork. If you are not provided with a spoon, ask for one.

The knife is used only for cutting meat and other articles of food, for spreading butter on bread, etc.

Here is a summary of blunders to avoid:

Do not eat fast.

Do not make noise with mouth or throat.

Do not fill the mouth too full.

Do not open the mouth in masticating.

Do not leave the table with food in your mouth.

Be careful to avoid soiling the cloth.

Never carry anything like food with you from the table.

Never apologize to the waiters for making them trouble. It is their business to serve you. It is proper, however, to treat them with courtesy, and say, "No, I thank you," or "If you please," in answer to their inquiries.

Do not introduce disgusting or unpleasant topics of conversation.

Do not pick your teeth or put your finger in your mouth at the table.

Do not come to table in your shirt-sleeves, or with soiled hands or tousled hair.

Do not cut your bread; break it.

Do not refuse to take the last piece of bread or cake; it looks as though you imagined there might be no more.

Do not express a preference for any part of a dish unless asked to do so.

HOW TO CARVE.

We propose to give here a few rules upon the practice of carving, which may be of benefit to the tyro, and help him to acquire that ease and dexterity which is so conducive to peace and comfort around the family board:

In carving a sirloin of beef, the upper cuts should be made lengthwise of the beef, while the under cuts are crosswise — the under cuts being also much thicker than the upper cuts. As there is much difference of opinion as to which is the choicest piece, it is best for the carver to ask his guests which cut they prefer.

Rib roasts, rolled, and a round of beef are always cut in very thin horizontal slices, across the whole surface of the meat. It is essential, though, that these slices be quite thin.

The leg, the loin, the shoulder and the saddle are the four pieces of mutton usually brought to the table to be carved. First as to the leg: This must be placed on the table with the knuckle to the left hand. Then cut into the side farthest from you toward the bone, beginning thin slices from the right and thick slices toward the knuckle. Always divide the little bunch of fat near the thick end among your guests, as it is a great delicacy.

A saddle of mutton is often ordered for a small dinner party. It is cut in very thin slices, close to the back-bone, and then downward.

Place a "shoulder" with the knuckle toward the right hand, the blade bone toward the left. Place your fork firmly in the middle of the edge farthest from you, and cut dexterously from the edge to the bone. This causes the meat to fly open; when you can cut slices on each side of the opening, until there is no more to cut, when the meat should be turned over and slices cut from the under side. Another method of carving this joint is to cut slices lengthwise from the end to the knuckle.

The loin of mutton, which is a piece intended specially for family use, should be carved either through the joints, or may be cut lengthwise in a parallel line with the joints.

A fillet of veal is, in shape and appearance, very similar to a round of beef, and is carved in the same way by cutting horizontal slices over the whole surface of the meat. The slices, however, should not be nearly so thin as beef. A fillet of veal is cut from the leg, the bone is removed by the butcher, and the pocket thus made is filled with dressing, which is taken out and helped with a spoon by the carver.

A breast of veal may be either roasted or stewed. If used as a roasting-piece, you will have the butcher make an opening or hole in it for the reception of the dressing. In carving it, the ribs may be separated from the brisket and sent round.

A fore-quarter of lamb consists of shoulder, breast and ribs. The knife must be first placed upon the shoulder, drawn through horizontally, and the joint removed and placed upon another dish. The ribs can then be separated, and the breast sliced and sent around.

A calf's head, which is by some considered a delicacy, must be cut down the center in thin slices on each side. A small piece of the palate, of the sweetbread, and of the meat around the eye, must be put on each plate and sent around.

In carving a haunch of venison, make a cut

across the knuckle, m
ing straight incision

There are three
a ham. The most
cut it like a leg of m
dle, and cutting o
over, begin at the
slanting direction,
thick end. The sl
and delicate as poss
companiment to fow

Tongue must alw
slices. Make the fi
tip, where a slice
himself. The tip is c
some people.

In carving a chic
This is easily done
the joint. Then sl
the merry-thought a
should always be he
the liver wing being
is better to always
white meat to be se

Pigeon, snipe and
piece sent to each g
small, you send a wh

Goose and turke
slices of the breast
legs are removed.
the best meat, after

Boiled rabbits are
the legs, then take
sharp-pointed knife
three or four pieces
the choice help, sep
ter. The shoulder
back, and the legs
a delicate bit.

For cutting fish
vided. Salmon and
cut in slices down t
and then in slices ne
piece of each should

Mackerel divides
the fish-knife bene
half from head to ta
help to a quarter.

Cut cod crosswis
ward, and send a sm
plate as well.

Large flat fish,
Dory, etc., are first
head to tail, then e
The fin, being cons
should be helped to

Small fish, like sm
whole to each guest

George Washington's Rules of Conduct

Let your discourse with men of business be short and comprehensive.

In visiting the sick do not presently play the physician.

In the presence of others sing not to yourself with a humming noise, nor drum with your fingers or feet.

Read no letters, books or papers in company.

Come not near the book or writings of any one so as to read them, unless desired.

Let your countenance be pleasant, but in serious matters somewhat grave.

Show not yourself glad at the misfortune of another, even though he were your enemy.

Strive not with your superiors in argument, but always submit your judgment to others with modesty.

When a man does all he can, though it succeeds not well, blame not him that did it.

Mock not, nor jest at anything of importance; break no jests that are sharp-biting, and if you deliver anything witty and pleasant, abstain from laughing thereat yourself.

Use no reproachful language against any one, neither curse nor revile.

Associate yourself with men of good quality, if you esteem your own reputation.

Be not immodest in urging your friend to discover a secret.

Speak not of doleful things in time of mirth, nor at the table.

Break not a jest where none take pleasure in mirth.

Laugh not loud, nor at all without occasion.

Treat with men at fit times about business.

Whisper not in the company of others.

Make no comparisons, and if any of the company be commended for any brave act, commend not another for the same.

Be not curious to know the affairs of others, neither approach to those that speak in private.

Undertake not what you cannot perform, but be careful to keep your promise.

Be not tedious in discourse.

Speak not evil of the absent, for it is unjust.

Let your recreations be manful, not sinful.

Etiquette of the Street

A lady will bow first if she meets a gentleman acquaintance on the street.

A lady will not stop on the street to converse with a gentleman. If he wishes to chat with her, he will turn and walk by her side until he has finished his conversation, then raise his hat and leave her.

It is not etiquette for a lady to take the arm of a gentleman on the street in the day-time, unless he be a lover or a husband, and even then it is seldom done in America.

In England it is permissible for a lady to accept the arm of even an ordinary acquaintance on the street. In foreign cities it is not comme il faut for ladies to appear on the street at all without a gentleman.

A gentleman escorting two ladies may offer each an arm, but a lady should never under any circumstances walk between two gentlemen, holding an arm of each.

On meeting friends or acquaintances on the street or in public places, you should be careful not to call their names so loudly as to attract the attention of those around.

Never call across the street, and never carry on a conversation in a public vehicle unless you are seated side by side.

Gentlemen should never stare at ladies on the street.

In walking with a lady a gentleman should take charge of any small parcel, book, etc., with which she may be burdened.

Never recognize a gentleman unless you are perfectly sure of his identity. Nothing is more awkward than a mistake of this kind.

A well-bred man must entertain no respect for the brim of his hat. True politeness demands that the hat be removed entirely from the head. Merely to nod or to touch the brim of your hat is a lack of courtesy. The body should not be bent at all in bowing.

A gentleman will always give a lady the inside of the walk on the street.

Ladies should avoid walking rapidly on the street, as it is ungraceful.

A gentleman walking with a lady should accommodate his step to hers. It looks exceedingly awkward to see a gentleman two or three paces ahead of a lady with whom he is supposed to be walking.

Staring at people, expectorating, looking back on the street, calling in a loud voice, laughing, etc., are very bad manners on the street.

A gentleman attending a lady will hold the door open for her to pass. He will also perform the same service for any lady passing in or out unattended.

A gentleman may assist a lady from an omnibus, or over a bad crossing, without the formality of an introduction. Having performed the service, he will bow and retire.

No gentleman will smoke when standing or walking with a lady on the street.

A quiet and unobtrusive demeanor upon the street is the sign of a true lady, who goes about her own affairs in a business-like way, and has always a pleasant nod and smile for friends and acquaintances.

Hints on Traveling

Consider what route you are taking when you are contemplating a journey, and decide definitely upon it. Go to the ticket office of the road and procure a time-table, where you will find the hour for leaving, together with names of stations on the road, etc.

When you intend taking a sleeping-berth, secure your ticket for same a day or two before you intend starting, so as to obtain a desirable location. A lower berth in the center of the car is always the most comfortable, as you escape the jar of the wheels and drafts from the opening door.

Take as little baggage as possible, and see that your trunks are strong and securely fastened. A good, stout leather strap is a safeguard against bursting locks.

In checking your baggage, look to the checks yourself, to make sure the numbers correspond. Having once received your check, you need not concern yourself further about your baggage. The company is responsible for its safe delivery.

It is a wise precaution to have your name and address carefully written upon any small article of baggage, such as satchel, umbrella, duster, etc., so that in case you leave them in the car the railway employes may know where to send them.

An overcoat or package lying upon a seat is an indication that the seat is taken and the owner has only left temporarily. It would therefore be rude in you to remove the articles and occupy the seat.

A courteous gentleman will also relinquish his place to two ladies, or a gentleman and lady who are together, and seek other accommodations. Such a sacrifice always receives its reward in grateful admiration of his character.

It is only courteous for a gentleman, seeing a lady looking for a seat, to offer the one beside him, as she scarcely likes to seat herself beside him without such invitation, although she will, of course, if there are no entirely vacant seats, do so in preference to standing.

Ladies traveling alone, when addressed in a courteous manner by gentlemen, should reply politely to the remark; and in long journeys it is even allowable to enter into conversation without the formality of an introduction. But a true lady will always know how to keep the conversation from bordering on familiarity, and by a quiet dignity and sudden hauteur will effectually check any attempt at presumption on the part of her strange acquaintance.

Always consult the comfort of others when traveling. You should not open either door or window in a railway coach without first ascertaining if it will be agreeable to those near enough to be affected by it. Ladies, in particular, should remember that they have not chartered the whole coach, but only paid for a small fraction of it, and be careful not to monopolize the dressing-room for two or three hours at a stretch, while half a dozen or more are waiting outside to arrange their toilets.

Genteel travelers will always carry their own toilet articles, and not depend on the public brush and comb.

A lady will avoid over-dressing in traveling; Silks and velvets, laces and jewelry are terribly out of place on a railroad train. The appointments of the traveler may be as elegant as you please, but they should be distinguished by exceeding plainness and quietness of tone. Some ladies have an idea that any old thing is good enough to travel in, and so look exceedingly shabby on the train.

The Secrets of Success

While it is impossible, in a world made up of widely differing individuals, to formulate a set of rules by which each could be shown the surest and swiftest way to social success in life, still it is possible to call attention to certain qualities of mind and character whose possession has come to be universally looked upon as essential to those who may aspire to struggle into the front rank of the world's workers. As a matter of fact, it would be as difficult to define the common expression, "success in life," as it would be to lay down a royal road which leads to it. Given a hundred definitions, from as many men, each treating the subject from his own standpoint, and no two of them would be found alike; and the opinion of each of these, as time passed along with its inevitable ups and downs, would be found to vary considerably. Flushed with recent success, the speculator to-day would see in the possession of millions and in the control of vast interests the only proper goal for a man of his great genius; ruined a few days later by unexpected reverses, and he sees in some conservative enterprise the fittest sphere of his future usefulness. Perhaps, then, without attempting the impossible, in a definition of success in life which will fit all, it will do to look upon it as the accomplishment of the laudable life-purpose of a man of natural abilities. In the smoke and din of battle, it was the genius of Napoleon which enabled him to see where one or two bold and rapid movements would secure the advantage; but it was his decision of character which enabled him to profit to the full by the discovery. To be decisive on important occasions, one must keep cool. The Duke of Wellington's calmness never forsook him, even in the most trying emergencies. At sea, one terrible night, the captain of the vessel rushed to the Duke, who was preparing for bed, and announced that the vessel would soon sink. "Then I shall not take off my boots," the imperturbable hero of Waterloo responded as he paused in his preparations for sleep. There is need for this coolness of manner and decision of action in all lines of business. The surgeon, brought face to face with a sudden complication in the case beneath his knife; the lawyer, surprised by the springing of the trap which his wily opponent had prepared for him; the merchant, apprised of a turn in his enterprises that threatens immediate disaster — all are called upon to exercise this quality, and in thousands of cases the dullest man in a company has obtained the prize simply because he grasped it while others were revolving in their minds what they had better do in order to secure it.

NEVER DESPAIR.

Columbus was the son of a weaver, and a weaver himself. Oliver Cromwell was the son of a brewer. Howard, an apprentice to a grocer. Benjamin Franklin, a journeyman printer. Claude Lorraine was bred up a pastry cook. Molière was the son of a tapestry-maker. Cervantes served as a common soldier. Homer was a beggar. Demosthenes was the son of a cutler. Terence was a slave. Daniel De Foe was a hosier, and the son of a butcher. Whitfield, son of an inn-keeper. Sir Cloudesley Shovel, rear-admiral of England, was an apprentice to a shoemaker, and afterwards a cabin boy. Bishop Prideaux worked in the kitchen at Exeter College, Oxford. Cardinal Wolsey was the son of a butcher. Ferguson was a shepherd. William Hogarth was but an apprentice to an engraver of pewter pots. Dr. Mountain was the son of a beggar. Virgil, son of a porter; Horace, of a shop-keeper.

TALENT AND TACT.

To excel others is a proof of talent; to know when to conceal superiority is the fruit of tact. Further comparison of these qualities is thus set forth by a recent English writer:

Talent is something, but tact is everything. Talent is power — tact is skill; talent is weight — tact is momentum; talent knows what to do — tact knows how to do it; talent makes a man respectable — tact will make a man respected; talent is wealth — tact is ready money. For all practical purposes of life, tact carries it against talent — ten to one. Talent makes the world wonder that it gets on no faster — tact excites astonishment that it gets on so fast; and the secret is that it has no weight to carry; it makes no false steps — it hits the right nail on the head — it loses no time — it takes all hints — and by keeping its eye on the weather-cock, is ready to take advantage of every wind that blows. It has the air of commonplace and all the force and power of genius. It can change sides with hey-presto movement and be at all points of the compass, while talent is ponderously and learnedly shifting a single point. Talent calculates clearly, reasons logically, makes out a case clear as daylight, utters its oracles with all the weight of justice and reason. Tact refutes without contradicting, puzzles the profound with profundity, and without wit outwits the wise. Setting them together on a race for popularity, pen in hand, and tact will distance talent by half the course. Talent brings to market that which is wanted; tact produces that which is wished for. Talent instructs; tact enlightens. Talent leads where no man follows; tact follows where humor leads. Talent is pleased that it ought to have succeeded; tact is delighted that it has succeeded. Talent toils for posterity, which may never repay it; tact throws away no pains, but catches the drift of the passing hour. Talent builds for eternity, tact on short lease, and gets good interest. Talent is certainly a very fine thing to talk about, a very good thing to be proud of, a very glorious eminence to look down from; but tact is useful, portable, applicable, always marketable; it is the talent of talent, the availableness of resources, the applicability of power, the eye of discrimination, the right hand of intellect.

Religions and Creeds

THE WORLD'S RELIGIOUS BELIEFS

Deism is the term for natural as opposed to revealed religion.

Marabouts are religious devotees held in great reverence by the Berbers.

Some writers insist that absolute atheism has never existed in a reasoning mind.

The adherents of *Zoroastrianism*, the ancient faith of Persia, are called Parsees.

The shamrock is said to have been used by St. Patrick as a symbol of the Trinity.

Giaour is a term applied by the Turks to all who do not believe in Mohammedanism.

What are called the *monastic vows* are three in number—poverty, chastity and obedience.

The *canonical books* are those books of Holy Scripture accepted as genuine by the Christian churches.

The ascetics were ancient Christians who sought a higher and more spiritual life by means of severe penances.

Sir Isaac Newton said: "I find more sure marks of authenticity in the Bible than in any profane history whatever."

A stricter definition of *nihilism* is that system of philosophy which totally rejects religion and substitutes nothing for it.

Freethinker was the name applied from one to two centuries ago to those deists who favored natural as against revealed religion.

The *Stoics* taught that God is the soul of the world, and that man's supreme good is to live in the perfect harmony of the universe.

The *Gnostics* were an early speculative school, with principles based on oriental philosophy, combined with certain tenets of Christianity.

The belief in and worship of one personal God is called monotheism. Judaism, Christianity and Mohammedanism are all monotheistic.

Dervishes are Mohammedan devotees. They are divided into two sections—the Mevlevins, or dancing, and the Nakshbendies, or howling dervishes.

The chamber or vault beneath a church, generally under the altar, where the dead, and particularly ecclesiastics, were formerly entombed, is called a *crypt*.

The *Apple of Sodom* is a fruit mentioned by Strabo, Josephus, and others, as growing on the shores of the Dead Sea. It was tempting to the eye, but if tasted filled the mouth with bitter ashes. It is supposed to have been an oak-gall, or the fruit of the solanum.

Antichrist is a name which occurs only in the epistles of St. John, and is identified by different writers with more or less probability with false Christs and other enemies of Christianity.

The *Angelus Bell* is, in Catholic churches, a bell rung at morning, noon and sunset, to invite the faithful to recite the Angelic Salutation. It gives name to a famous picture by Millet.

The great writers and teachers who succeeded the Apostles from the second to the sixth centuries are called the *Fathers of the Church*. They included St. Athanasius, St. Augustine, etc.

Many of the South Sea islanders believe that paradise can be inherited only by persons of perfect physical frame. Where this belief prevails a man will die rather than submit to amputation.

An assembly of the clergy of cathedral churches, usually held in the chapter-house, is called a *chapter*. The Parliaments of England were held in the chapter-house of Westminster Abbey from 1377 to 1547.

The five points of *Calvinism* as set forth by John Calvin of Picardy are: (1) Predestination and reprobation; (2) original sin; (3) particular redemption; (4) irresistible grace; (5) the perseverance of the saints.

The primary meaning of *chapel* was a chest containing relics or their shrine. Now it is a place of worship subordinate to a cathedral or large church, or connected with a castle, university or other institution.

Though often treated as a proper name by the translators, *Belial* is really an abstract term meaning "that which is without use or profit," hence "wickedness." "Sons of Belial" is one of the commonest forms in use.

The staff, terminating in a cross, carried before archbishops, is known as the crosier; it was used as early as 800 A.D. The crosier of an archbishop differs from that of a bishop in having a cross instead of a crook on the top.

Canonization is the act by the Pope of declaring a deceased person to be a saint. The deceased's name is then put in the canon or litany of the saints, and a day dedicated to his honor. Canonization cannot take place within fifty years of the death of the person to be canonized.

The *Cartesian doctrines*, founded on the principle "I think, therefore I am," were first promulgated by René Descartes of Touraine in 1637. He held that thought proceeded from the soul, so that man was not entirely material, and that the soul must be from some being not material—i. e., God.

In the Roman Catholic Church, the reception of the tonsure, a bare circle on the crown of the head, precedes admission into orders, and is administered by the bishop. The Greek priests also bear the tonsure. The earliest ecclesiastical precept on the tonsure occurs in a canon of the Council of Toledo (633 A.D.).

There are three religious systems in China: That of Yu, restored by Kong-fou-tse (Confucius); the State religion, in which the emperor acts as the priest and intermediary; and the third is Buddhism. There are, however, Moslems, Christians, and a few Jews, in China.

The name of *Buddhists* (*i.e.*, "the enlightened.") is applied to the followers of Gautama Siddhartha, the Sakya Muni, generally called Buddha, a prince of Central India. Founded about 500 B.C., Buddhism is the chief religion in India beyond the Ganges, China, Japan and Ceylon.

The *Swedenborgians*, or "The New Jerusalem Church," are the followers of Dr. Emanuel Swedenborg (1688-1772). They hold peculiar views respecting salvation, inspiration, and the Trinity. In regard to the Trinity, they believe it to be centred in the person of Jesus Christ.

The purgatory of the Islamites is called Al Araf, and it is supposed to be located half way between hell and paradise. Mohammed is believed by the whole sect of Islam to be the only person who has ever gone to paradise without being forced to go through a preparatory course at Al Araf.

Among early versions of the Scriptures is one known as the *Breeches Bible*, printed in 1577 by Whittingham, Gilby, and Sampson. So called because Gen. iii. 7 runs thus: "The eyes of them bothe were opened . . . and they sewed figge-leaves together and made themselves breeches." It is also called the "Geneva Bible."

Dies Irae (day of wrath) are the opening words of a Latin hymn which describes the judgment of the world. Ascribed to various authors, among others to Pope Gregory the Great (590) and St. Bernard, but more generally to Tommaso da Celano (fifteenth century); c. 1385 adopted into the Roman Catholic Church liturgy.

The *Zendavesta* is said to have been written by Zoroaster in letters of gold on twelve thousand skins of parchment, and to have been deposited by Darius Hystaspes in the Castle of Persepolis, about B.C. 500. "Zend" is the language and "avesta" = text. The compound word means the sacred books of Zoroaster in the Zend tongue.

Gehenna is the place of everlasting torment. Strictly speaking, it means the Valley of Hinnom (*Ge Hinnom*) where sacrifices to Moloch were offered, and where refuse of all sorts was subsequently cast, for the consumption of which fires were kept constantly burning.

Kulturkampf is the term applied to the ecclesiastical controversy with the Church of Rome in Germany, arising from an effort of the State to vindicate its right to interfere in the affairs of all religious societies. The contest began in 1872 with the expulsion of the Jesuits, and ended with Prince Bismarck's concessions in revisions of the politico-ecclesiastical legislation in 1886 and 1887.

Taoism is the name given to a religious system in China founded by Lao-Tsze, who was born B. C. 604. It has degenerated into a sort of polytheism. Its priests, who are looked on as magicians and astrologers, are consulted about the sites of houses, burial grounds, fortunate days, and other responses of the fortune-teller's character.

The Methodist Episcopal Church in the United States holds a general conference once in four years, which is the highest legislative body in that church. The Wesleyan Methodists also hold an annual conference in Great Britain, at which the business of the body is transacted and arrangements for the circuits made for the year.

The religion of the followers of Mohammed (570-632) is embodied in the *Koran*. It includes belief in one God, in angels, in good and evil spirits, in a general resurrection and judgment, with future rewards and punishments, in predestination and in a paradise where the faithful spend their time in the society of beautiful women (houris).

Ultramontane, meaning "beyond the mountains," originally referred to the Alps—namely, in relation to France. Later it had reference to the party in the Church of Rome which assigns the greatest weight to the papal prerogative. Italians of course use the word in a converse geographical sense for people beyond the Alps, and so in the north of Europe.

American pioneers were God-fearing and Bible-loving. They staked out town lots in twenty-two Bethels, ten Jordans, nine Jerichos, fourteen Bethlehems, twenty-two Goshens, twenty-one Shilohs, eleven Carmels, eighteen Tabors and Mount Tabors, twenty-two Zions and Mount Zions, twenty-six Edens, thirty Lebanons, twenty-six Hebrons and thirty-six Sharons.

Secularism is the name given to the principles advocated (about 1846) by George Jacob Holyoake, a native of Birmingham. The central idea of Secularism is freedom of thought and freedom of action without injury to others. It is the religion of the present life only, and its standard of morals is utilitarian. Mr. G. J. Holyoake was succeeded in the leadership of English Secularists by Mr. Charles Bradlaugh, who died in 1891.

The *secular clergy* are the clergy generally who live in private houses. Nearly all archbishops, bishops, deans, canons and parochial clergymen are seculars, in contradistinction to the regulars, who, having vowed obedience, chastity and poverty, live in some religious house, dead to the world and the "civil law" by their "entrance into religion." Called "regulars" because they live under the *regula* or rule of some religious house.

Hades, in the religion of ancient Greece, was the name applied to the kingdom of the underworld, the abode of the departed spirits or shades. Hades and Pluto are also personal names for its king. It is the Greek word by which the Septuagint translates the Hebrew *sheol*, the abode of the dead, in which sense it occurs frequently in the New Testament.

The devotional term litany applies to a form of prayer in which the same thing is repeated several times at no long intervals. Hence in Latin the word is always used in the plural, *litaniæ*. The common formula, *Kyrie eleison, Christe eleison, Kyrie eleison*—"Lord, have mercy upon us—Christ, have mercy upon us—Lord, have mercy upon us"—is the simplest ("lesser") litany.

In the ceremony of the greater excommunication by the Catholic Church, since the eighth century, after reading the sentence a bell is rung, the book closed, and a candle extinguished; and from that moment the person excommunicated is excluded from the communion of the faithful, from public worship and the sacraments. Hence comes the expression, "bell, book and candle."

Camp-meetings are gatherings of devout persons, held mostly in thinly populated districts and continued for several days at a time. It was in connection with Methodism in America that such meetings became especially prominent. The introduction of the protracted camp-meetings into England in 1798 by Lorenzo Dow led to the separation of the Primitive Methodists from the Wesleyans.

Humanitarians is a name assigned to anti-Trinitarians, who regard Christ as a mere man, and refuse to ascribe to him any supernatural character, whether of origin or of nature. The name Humanitarian is also sometimes applied to the disciples of St. Simon, and in general to those who look to the perfectibility of human nature as a great moral and social dogma; also to those who object to severe measures, such as capital punishment, etc.

The *Temple Society* is a body of German Christians who wait for the second coming of Christ. They separated from the Church in Württemberg and formed a separate sect, and many of them settled in Palestine in 1868, where they now have colonies at Haifa, Jaffa, Sarona and near Jerusalem. They are distinguished for industry, enterprise and success. There may be about five thousand in all of the community, of whom about fifteen hundred are in Palestine.

The *Septuagint* is the Greek translation of the Old Testament, made from the Massoretic text at Alexandria. Tradition says that it was executed in the reign of Ptolemy Philadelphus (284-47 B. C.), by seventy-two translators in 72 days; but critics hold that it is the work of different times. The Septuagint was the official Bible of the Hellenistic Jews until after the destruction of the Temple, and it became the official Bible of the Catholic Church. Most of the Old Testament quotations in the New Testament are taken from the Septuagint.

The word *bull* is derived from the Latin *bulla*, "bubble of water," and then "a round ball of any kind." In the middle ages it came to signify the capsule of the seal appended to letters from emperors or popes, next it was used for the seal itself, and lastly for the document to which the seal was appended. Its use is now commonly restricted to papal documents issued with certain indispensable formalities.

The *Douay Bible* is a translation made by the professors connected with the College of Douay, founded in 1568 by Dr. William Allen for the education of English boys designed for the Roman Catholic priesthood. These students were to be sent into England as itinerant preachers, with the view of creating a reactionary feeling and upsetting the Reformed Church. Dr. Allen himself worked on the translation.

The title of *Beelzebub* was given to the form of Baal worshipped by the Philistines at Ekron. As the heathen deities were all regarded as demons by the Jews, the name Beelzebub became, in course of time, commonly applied to the chief of evil spirits, and in this sense it is employed in the Gospels. The more correct reading of the word is *Beelzebul*, variously explained as "lord of the dwelling," "lord of the dunghill."

The *Grail*, or "The Holy Grail," was a mysterious chalice made of a single emerald, which was stated to possess the power of preserving chastity and prolonging life. It is said to have been the cup from which Christ drank at the last supper, and in which Joseph of Arimathea caught the last drops of blood as Christ was taken down from the cross. In 1170

Chrétien of Troyes sang of the search by knights for this miraculous cup, which was a favorite subject in the middle ages.

THE *Veda* is the sacred canon of the Brahmins. It is divided into four collections: (1) the Rig-veda, or lore of praise (hymns); (2) the Sama-veda, or lore of tunes (chants); (3) the Yajur-veda, or lore of prayer, and (4) the Atharva-veda, or lore of the Atharvans. Each collection is divided into three parts: (1) The sacred texts (Mantra); (2) the ritual (Brahmana); (3) the philosophical portion (Upanishads). The hymns of the Rig-veda are supposed to have been collected about 1000 B.C.

The Targums are paraphrastic translations of the Hebrew Scriptures into Aramaic, the only tongue generally known to the Jews in post-exilic times. No single Targum covers the whole of the Old Testament, but in one and another there are versions of all the books, except Ezra and Nehemiah. The Targums, long oral, were committed to writing in Christian times. The Onkelos Targum and the Targum ascribed to Jonathan ben Uzziel, the principal of the eighty disciples of Hillel, are the most famous.

Among the great monastic orders *Benedictines* is the general name given to the followers of St. Benedict (480-543), whose rule bound the monk to permanent abode in the monastery, chastity, renunciation of private property, daily and public solemnization of the divine office, a life of frugality and labor, and filial obedience to the abbot. The order has produced many literary works, but has taken little interest in politics. Though at one time very powerful, the membership to-day does not exceed eight hundred.

THE *Tabernacle* was the portable tent in which the Ark of the Covenant was conveyed, and as such the sanctuary of Israel. It seems to have been superseded by a more permanent building at Shiloh before David's time. In Roman Catholic churches the name is given to the receptacle in which the consecrated elements of the Eucharist are retained. It is commonly a small structure of marble, metal or wood, placed over the high altar and appropriated exclusively to the reservation of the Eucharist, no other object whatever being allowed to be kept in it.

THE word *cabbala*, which literally means "tradition," in itself might be used for any Jewish doctrine not explicitly contained in the Hebrew Bible since the text assumed its present form. The moral and ritual precepts of the Talmud are all ascribed to a tradition that can be traced step by step. But in its technical sense the cabbala signifies a secret system of theology, metaphysics and magic prevalent among the Jews. The cabbalists taught a pantheistic doctrine which came to them from the later and degenerate philosophies of Greece.

THE *Shakers* are a religious sect the official title of which is "The United Society of Believers in Christ's Second Appearing." They are an offshoot of the Quakers founded by Ann Lee, of Manchester, England, who with eight of her disciples came to America in 1774. Here the Shakers have founded eighteen societies, distributed over seven States. They practise celibacy and community of goods, and are firm believers in the doctrine of spiritualism. The wild, violent motions from which they obtained their name have given place to a regular dance to the singing of a hymn.

A SYNAGOGUE is a Jewish place of worship. The origin of this institution is probably to be traced to the period of the Babylonian captivity, although tradition finds it in the patriarchal times. When, through Ezra's instrumentality, the ancient order of things was restored in Judea, synagogues were established in all the towns for the benefit of those who could not take part oftener than three times a year in the worship of the temple at Jerusalem, and a special ritual of readings and prayers was instituted. From the time of the Maccabees we find them even in all the villages.

HOSPITALLERS, in the Roman Catholic Church, are charitable brotherhoods, founded for the care of the poor and of the sick in hospitals. They follow for the most part the rule of St. Augustine, and add to the ordinary vows of poverty, chastity and obedience that of self-dedication to the particular work of their order. The Knights of St. John of Jerusalem and the Teutonic Knights were both originally hospitallers. The Knights Hospitallers of the Holy Spirit were founded at Montpellier in 1195 by Guy of Montpellier, and the hospitallers of Our Lady of Christian Charity at Paris in the end of the thirteenth century by Guy de Joinville. And numerous similar orders have been established since then.

THE Society of Friends, or Quakers, was founded in 1624 by George Fox, a shoemaker, of Drayton, in Leicestershire. They believe in the main fundamental principles of what is called "Orthodox Christianity," but they express their religious creed in the very words of the New Testament Scripture, and each member has the liberty of interpreting the words. Their main specialty is the belief of "The Light of Christ in man," and hence they entertain a broader view of the Spirit's influence than other Christians. In morals, propriety of conduct, good order and philanthropy, the Quakers are a pattern society.

THE Tunkers, by corruption *Dunkards* (but by themselves called "the Brethren"), is a religious sect found chiefly in Pennsylvania, Maryland, Virginia, Ohio, Indiana, Illinois, Iowa, Missouri, Nebraska and Kansas. Altogether they number nearly one hundred thousand, and are almost confined to the United States, although small bodies exist in Denmark and Sweden. Yet the sect had its birth in Germany, being indeed a child of the Pietist movement of the seventeenth century; but between 1719 and 1729 all the members, harassed and persecuted at home, had, on Penn's old invitation, removed to Pennsylvania and settled about Germantown and Philadelphia, from whence they gradually spread southward and westward. In their creed the Brethren are thoroughly evangelical.

THE term *Apocrypha* (a Greek word meaning "hidden," "secret"), seems, when applied to religious books or writings, to have been used (1) for such as were suitable, not for the mass of believers, but for the initiated only; works containing the esoteric or recondite teaching of the faith or sect; (2) works the date, origin and authorship of which were unknown or doubtful; (3) works which claimed to be what they were not, were spurious or pseudepigraphic. When the Apocrypha is spoken of, the Apocrypha of the Old Testament is generally meant. Another large group may be called the apocryphal books of the New Testament.

THE *Vulgate* is the authorized translation of the Scriptures into Latin in use in the Roman Catholic Church. Before the end of the fourth century the *Vetus*, or old Latin version, called also the *Itala* (because in use in Italy), had become exceedingly corrupt, and in 382 Jerome, at the request of Pope Damasus, undertook to revise and correct this version. The Gospels were completed in 384, and the whole New Testament soon after; and this revision of the old version is the present text of the Vulgate New Testament. The official edition of the authentic Vulgate text in use in the Roman Catholic Church is that published by Clement VIII. in 1592.

The *Trappists* are a religious order founded in 1140 in Normandy by Rotrou, Comte de Perche. It was reformed by Abbé de Rancé in 1636. It is a reformed Benedictine order. The female order, called Trappistines, was instituted 1822. When driven out of France in 1791 the Trappists went to Switzerland and built the monastery called *Val-Sainte*, which was suppressed in 1811. Fifty-nine monks of La Trappe migrated from England to France in 1817 and settled in La Loire Inférieure. In 1822 the Trappists had sixteen houses in France. Their chief monastery was burnt to the ground in August, 1871. They have several houses in the United States.

UNDER the name of *breviary*, Roman Catholics understand the book which contains all the ordinary and daily services of their church except (*a*) those connected with the celebration of the Eucharist, which are contained in the *Missal*, and (*b*) those for special occasions, such as baptisms, marriages, ordinations, funerals, etc., which are contained in the *Ritual* or *Pontifical*, according as they fall within the sphere of ordinary priests or bishops. In the Established Church of England, therefore, the breviary would be exactly represented by a prayer-book containing, after the preface, tables, etc., the morning and evening prayer, litany, Athanasian creed, collects, psalter and all the lessons for every day in the year, with the addition of a complete set of hymns for the different occasions.

THEOSOPHY is a name often applied to the systems of the speculative mystics of the mediæval and later times, as Eckhart, Böhme, Schelling and others. The term is now applied to the tenets of the Theosophical Society, founded at New York (1875) by Colonel Olcott and Madame Blavatsky (d. 1891), an American Russian. The search after divine knowledge, the investigation of the powers of man and of the hitherto unexplained laws of nature, the study of Eastern philosophy, and the establishment of a universal brotherhood, are some of the objects which it sets before itself. The most striking tenet of theosophy to outsiders is that which asserts that man is possessed of hitherto undeveloped powers over nature, in which respect it has affinities with mediæval Rosicrucianism and modern Spiritualism.

AMONG the Jews the *Talmud* is a book held in high veneration, containing the *Mishna*, or oral law, and the *Gemara*, or commentary on the Mishna. There are two forms or editions of the Talmud: (1) The Palestinian (commonly called the Jerusalem Talmud), completed about the middle of the fifth century, and (2) the Babylonian Talmud, completed towards the end of the sixth century. The latter is the larger and more valuable of the two. The Talmud is divided into *Halakha*, or legal part, and *Hagada*, or legendary part. The Halakha still rules Jewish life, especially in regard to dietary laws, marriages and festivals, and is the authoritative text-book of all rabbinic tribunals.

THE *Flagellants* were fanatics who appeared at sundry times in Europe, and marched about in procession along the streets and public roads to appease the wrath of God. They marched two and two, singing dolorous hymns, mingled with groans, and every now and then stopped to whip each other with scourges to "atone for the sins of the people." They first appeared in the eleventh century under St. Peter Damian; again in 1260, when Rainier, a Dominican, formed them into a sect; again in 1348, when Germany was attacked with the pestilence called the Black Death; again in 1574, when Henry III. of France joined the sect.

The natives of Botocudos, one of the hottest regions of the earth, believe that heaven will be a land of cool streams and shady groves entirely cleared of all underbrush and cacti. All desert-dwellers, it is said, die expecting to awake in a wooded land supplied bountifully with cold water. Natives of the frozen north have paradise pictured as a land of warm sunshine, with glowing fires overhung with pots of boiling whale's blubber, and easeful couches of fur scattered here and there. The Caroline islanders, who are passionately fond of liquor, but who are in mortal dread of breaking their necks by falling from one of the millions of cliffs with which their islands abound, believe that paradise will be a land as level as the floor, where one can get drunk and not be in constant dread of cracking his cervical vertebra.

The Society of Jesus, or *Jesuits*, was founded by Ignatius Loyola and confirmed by Paul III. in 1540. It was monarchical in its constitution and secular, while all other Catholic societies are more or less democratic and regular. The head of the society is called the General, or *Præpositus Generalis*, and holds his office for life. This General has absolute command over the whole society, and from his decisions there is no appeal. The four objects of the society are: (1) The education of youth; (2) the education of others by preaching, etc.; (3) the defense of the Catholic faith against all heretics and unbelievers, and (4) the propagation of the Catholic faith among the heathen. The Jesuits wear no monastic garb, but dress like any other of the "secular clergy," and live in no religious house, but in private dwellings.

Candlemas is an ecclesiastical festival observed on 2d February in honor of the Purification of the Virgin Mary, when she presented the infant Jesus in the temple. The great feast of expiation and purification (*Februa*) in ancient Rome was held on the 15th of February. Its institution as a Christian festival took place in the reign of Emperor Justinian in 541 or 542. A principal part of the celebration is a procession of lighted candles—hence the name.

The societies formed to distribute the Holy Scriptures are called Bible societies. The following are the names of the chief societies, their nationality, date of foundation, and approximate total issue of copies (in whole or in part) of the Bible: England, British and Foreign, 1804 (due to the initiative of a Welsh clergyman), translated into some three hundred different languages), 100,000,000; Scotland, National, 1861 (from union of older societies, as the Edinburgh, 1809), 6,000,000; Ireland, Hibernian, 1806, 5,000,000; United States, 1816, 40,000,000; France, two societies, 1818 and 1833; Germany, Prussian, 1814; Switzerland, Basle, 1804; Russian, 1826, suppressed, but revived 1831; Sweden, 1808; Norway, 1816; Netherlands, 1815.

The Kaaba, or "Cube," was taken possession of by Cosroi about 450, and was rebuilt in 1630 by the Sultan Mustapha. The word means "the square house," and it designates a stone building in the great mosque at Mecca. Next the silver door is the famous Black Stone, "dropped from Paradise." It was originally white, but the sin of the world has turned it black. In pilgrimages the devotee walks round the Kaaba seven times, and each time he passes the stone either kisses it or lays his hand thereon. According to Arabian legend, Adam, after his expulsion from the garden, worshiped Allah on this spot. A tent was then sent down from heaven, but Seth substituted a hut for the tent. After the flood Abraham and Ishmael rebuilt the Kaaba.

By *Infallibility* is meant entire exemption from liability to error when the Pope speaks *ex cathedra*. The dogma of papal infallibility was promulgated by the Vatican Council in 1870. As adopted by the Council it is thus defined: "We teach and define that it is a dogma divinely revealed, that the Roman pontiff, when he speaks *ex cathedra*, that is, when in discharge of the office of pastor and doctor of all Christians, by virtue of his supreme authority, he defines a doctrine regarding faith and morals to be held by the universal Church, by the divine assistance promised him in blessed Peter is possessed of that infallibility with which the Divine Redeemer willed that his Church should be endowed for defining doctrines regarding faith or morals; and that, therefore, such definitions of the Roman pontiffs are irreformable of themselves and not by consent of the Church."

The Waldenses, or Vaudois, is a sect inhabiting the valleys of the Cottian Alps, in Northern Italy. It was founded by Peter Waldo (1170), a rich merchant of Lyons, who sold his goods and gave the money to the poor, and went forth as a preacher of the doctrine of Christ from a translation of the New Testament made into Provençal. The preaching of the Waldenses led to collision with the ecclesiastical authorities, and they were formally condemned by the Lateran Council of 1215. Persecution increased, and the Waldenses, originally an esoteric society within the church, withdrew altogether from its ministrations, and appointed ministers of their own, election taking the place of ordination. By the end of the thirteenth century they were found in France, Italy, Spain and Germany; but their numbers were greatly reduced, and their limits circumscribed, by persecution on the one hand, and the general turn of Protestantism at the Reformation on the other. They have, at present, about forty churches, with four thousand members.

To Obtain Standard Time

At places named below, add to or substract from local or sun time the figures given. The standards, or divisions, are indicated as follows: E., Eastern; C., Central; M., Mountain. Addition is indicated by a; subtraction by s. To find local time from standard time reverse the operation:

Albany, N. Y.	E., s.. 5
Austin, Texas	C., a..31
Baltimore, Md.	E., a.. 6
Bismarck, N. D.	C., a..43
Boston, Mass.	E., s..16
Buffalo, N. Y.	E., a..16
Burlington, Ia.	C., a.. 4
Cairo, Ill.	C., s.. 3
Charleston, S. C.	E., a..20
Chicago, Ill.	C., s..10
Cincinnati, O.	C., s..22
Cleveland, O.	C., s..33
Columbus, O.	C., s..28
Columbia, S. C.	E., a..24
Dayton, O.	C., s..23
Denver, Col.	M., a.. 0
Des Moines, Ia.	C., a..14
Detroit, Mich.	C., s..28
Dubuque, Ia.	C., a.. 3
Duluth, Minn.	C., a.. 8
Erie, Pa.	C., s..40
Evansville, Ind.	C., s..10
Ft. Gibson, Cher. N.	C., a..21
Ft. Wayne, Ind.	C., s..19
Galena, Ill.	C., a.. 2
Galveston, Tex.	C., a..19
Grand Haven, Mich.	C., s..15
Harrisburg, Pa.	E., a.. 7
Houston, Tex.	C., a..21
Huntsville, Ala.	C., s..13
Indianapolis, Ind.	C., s..15
Jackson, Miss.	C., a.. 1
Jacksonville, Fla.	C., s..33
Janesville, Wis.	C., s.. 4
Jefferson City, Mo.	C., a.. 9
Kansas City, Mo.	C., a..18
Keokuk, Ia.	C., a.. 6
Knoxville, Tenn.	C., s..24
La Crosse, Wis.	C., a.. 5
Lawrence, Kas.	C., a..21
Lexington, Ky.	C., s..22
Little Rock, Ark.	C., a.. 9
Louisville, Ky.	C., s..18
Lynchburg, Va.	E., a..17
Memphis, Tenn.	C., a.. 0
Milwaukee, Wis.	C., s.. 8
Mobile, Ala.	C., s.. 8
Montgomery, Ala.	C., s..15
Nashville, Tenn.	C., s..13
New Haven, Conn.	E., s.. 8
New Orleans, La.	C., a.. 0
New York, N. Y.	E., s.. 4
Norfolk, Va.	E., a.. 5
Ogdensburg, N. Y.	E., a.. 2
Omaha, Neb.	C., a..24
Pensacola, Fla.	C., s..11
Philadelphia, Pa.	E., s.. 1
Pittsburg, Pa.	E., a..20
Portland, Me.	E., s..19
Providence, R. I.	E., s..14
Quincy, Ill.	C., a.. 6
Raleigh, N. C.	E., a..15
Richmond, Va.	E., a..10
Rock Island, Ill.	C., a.. 2
Rochester, N. Y.	E., a..11
Santa Fe, N. M.	M., a.. 4
Savannah, Ga.	C., s..36
Shreveport, La.	C., a..15
Springfield, Ill.	C., s.. 2
St. Joseph, Mo.	C., a..19
St. Louis, Mo.	C., a.. 1
St. Paul, Minn.	C., a..12
Superior City, Wis.	C., a.. 8
Syracuse, N. Y.	E., a.. 4
Toledo, O.	C., s..26
Trenton, N. J.	E., s.. 1
Utica, N. Y.	E., a.. 1
Washington, D. C.	E., a.. 8
Wheeling, W. Va.	E., a..23
Wilmington, Del.	E., a.. 2
Wilmington, N. C.	E., a..12
Yankton, S. D.	C., a..30

ALPHABETICAL INDEX

www.ingramcontent.com/pod-product-compliance
Lightning Source LLC
Chambersburg PA
CBHW022129020426
42334CB00015B/817

9783742827364